NO POSTAGE
NECESSARY
IF MAILED
IN THE
UNITED STATES

BUSINESS REPLY MAIL
FIRST-CLASS MAIL PERMIT NO. 4764 TRENTON, NJ

POSTAGE WILL BE PAID BY ADDRESSEE

REGIONAL COLLEGES CONSORTIUM
THOMSON PETERSON'S
PRINCETON PIKE CORPORATE CENTER
2000 LENOX DRIVE
P.O. BOX 67005
LAWRENCEVILLE, NJ 08648-9901

▲ Fold here to return (do not detach) ▲

Please tape closed to mail
▼

PETERSON'S COLLEGES IN THE WEST

2005

THOMSON
PETERSON'S™

Australia • Canada • Mexico • Singapore • Spain • United Kingdom • United States

THOMSON

PETERSON'S

About Thomson Peterson's

Thomson Peterson's (www.petersons.com) is a leading provider of education information and advice, with books and online resources focusing on education search, test preparation, and financial aid. Its Web site offers searchable databases and interactive tools for contacting educational institutions, online practice tests and instruction, and planning tools for securing financial aid. Thomson Peterson's serves 110 million education consumers annually.

For more information, contact Thomson Peterson's, 2000 Lenox Drive, Lawrenceville, NJ 08648; 800-338-3282; or find us on the World Wide Web at www.petersons.com/about.

Editor: Fern A. Oram; Production Editor: Linda Seghers; Copy Editors: Brett Bollmann, Jim Colbert, Michele N. Firestone, Michael Haines, Sally Ross, Jill C. Schwartz, Pam Sullivan, Valerie Bolus Vaughan; Research Project Manager: Daniel Margolin; Research Associates: Mary Meyer-Penniston, Jared A. Stein, Amy L. Weber; Programmer: Phyllis Johnson; Manufacturing Manager: Judy Coleman; Composition Manager: Linda M. Williams; Client Relations Representatives: Mimi Kaufman, Lois Regina Milton, Mary Ann Murphy, Jim Swinarski, Eric Wallace.

ISSN 1525-3813
ISBN 0-7689-1387-X

Printed in the United States of America

10 9 8 7 6 5 4 3 2 1 06 05 04

Eighteenth Edition

CONTENTS

A Note from the Peterson's Editors

Welcome to the world of college decision making. This guide can be an invaluable tool as you think about college and where to apply. You are probably considering at least one college that is relatively near your home. It may surprise you to learn that the majority of all students go to college within a 300-mile radius of where they live. Because of that factor, we publish this series of college guides that focuses on the colleges in each of six regions of the country so that students can easily compare the colleges in their own area. (Two-year public and proprietary colleges are not included because their admission patterns are significantly different from other colleges.)

For advice and guidance in the college search and selection process, just turn the page. "Surviving Standardized Tests" describes the most frequently used test and lists test dates for 2004–05. Of course, part of the college selections process involves visiting the schools themselves and "The Whys and Whats of College Visits" is just the planner you need to make those trips well worth your while. Next, "Applying 101" provides advice on how best to approach the application phase of the process. If you've got questions about transferring, "Successful Transfer" has got the answers you need. "Who's Paying for This? Financial Aid Basics" and the "Financial Aid Programs for Schools in the West" articles provide you with the essential information on how to meet your educational expenses. "Searching for Four-Year Colleges Online" gives you all the tips you'll need to integrate the Web into your college search. Lastly, you'll want to read through the "How to Use This Guide" and learn how to use all the information presented in this volume.

Following these articles are the **Profiles of Colleges** sections. The college profiles are easy to read and should give you a good sense of whether a college meets your basic needs and should be considered further. This consistently formatted collection of data can provide a reference balance to the individual mailings you are likely to receive from colleges. The profiles appear in geographical order by state.

In a number of the profiles (those marked with a U.S. map icon), you will find helpful information about social life, academic life, campus visits, and interviews. These **Special Messages to Students** are written in each case by a college admissions office staff member. You will find valuable insights into what each writer considers special about his or her institution (both socially and academically), what is expected of you during your interview at that college, and how important the interview is there. You will also be alerted to outstanding attractions on campus or nearby so you can plan a productive visit. In many cases travel information (nearest commercial airport and nearest interstate highway) is included that will be of help on your campus visit.

And if you still thirst for even more information, look for the two-page narrative descriptions appearing in the **In-Depth Descriptions of Colleges** sections of the book. These descriptions are written by admissions deans and provide great detail about each college. They are edited to provide a consistent format across entries for your ease of comparison.

The **Indexes** at the back of the book ("Majors and Degrees," "Athletic Programs and Scholarships," and "ROTC Programs") enable you to pinpoint colleges listed in the profiles according to their specific offerings. Additionally, there is an "Alphabetical Listing of Colleges and Universities" to enable you to quickly find a school that you may have already determined meets your criteria.

We hope you will find this information helpful. Try to remember that admission directors are as interested in you and the possibility of your attending their college as you are in the possibility of applying. They spend most of their time reaching out to students, explaining their colleges' programs and policies, and easing the application process whenever they can. If you think of them as people who like students and if you can picture them taking the time to carefully provide the information in this book for you, it might help to lessen any anxiety you are feeling right now about applying.

Our advice is to relax, enjoy high school, and do as well as you can in your courses. Give yourself enough time during the early stages of your search to think about what kind of person you are and what you want to become so you can choose colleges for the right reasons. Read all college materials with an open mind, and visit as many campuses as you can. Plan ahead so you do not rush through your applications. If you can keep yourself in balance during this process, it need not become the panic period you may have seen some friends go through. We urge you to contact admission staff members at any college in which you are interested. They are all willing to help you. In fact, the admission people whose names you will find in this book hope to hear from you. We at Peterson's wish you success and happiness wherever you enroll.

The College Admissions Process

Surviving Standardized Tests

WHAT ARE STANDARDIZED TESTS?

Colleges and universities in the United States use tests to help evaluate applicants' readiness for admission or to place them in appropriate courses. The tests that are most frequently used by colleges are the ACT Assessment of American College Testing, Inc., and the College Board's SAT. In addition, the Educational Testing Service (ETS) offers the TOEFL test, which evaluates the English-language proficiency of nonnative speakers. The tests are offered at designated testing centers located at high schools and colleges throughout the United States and U.S. territories and at testing centers in various countries throughout the world. The ACT Assessment test and the SAT tests are each taken by more than a million students each year. The TOEFL test is taken by more than 700,000 students each year.

Upon request, special accommodations for students with documented visual, hearing, physical, or learning disabilities are available. Examples of special accommodations include tests in Braille or large print and such aids as a reader, recorder, magnifying glass, or sign language interpreter. Additional testing time may be allowed in some instances. Contact the appropriate testing program or your guidance counselor for details on how to request special accommodations.

College Board SAT Program

Currently, the SAT Program consists of the SAT I Reasoning Test and the SAT II Subject Tests. The SAT I is a 3-hour test made up of seven sections, primarily multiple-choice, that measures verbal and mathematical abilities. The three verbal sections test vocabulary, verbal reasoning, and critical reading skills. Emphasis is placed on reading passages, which are 400–850 words in length. Some reading passages are paired; the second opposes, supports, or in some way complements the point of view expressed in the first. The three mathematics sections test a student's ability to solve problems involving arithmetic, algebra, and geometry. They include questions that require students to produce their own responses, in addition to questions that students can choose from four or five answer choices. Calculators may be used on the SAT I mathematics sections. Beginning in the spring of 2005, the SAT will be a 3-hour and 35-minute test that focuses on college success skills of writing, critical reading, and mathematics. The new writing component will measure grammar and usage and include a short, student-written essay.

The SAT II Subject Tests are 1-hour tests, primarily multiple-choice, in specific subjects that measure students' knowledge of these subjects and their ability to apply that knowledge. Some colleges may require or recommend these tests for placement, or even admission. The Subject Tests measure a student's academic achievement in high school and may indicate readiness for certain college programs. Tests offered include Writing, Literature, U.S. History, World History, Mathematics Level IC, Mathematics Level IIC, Biology E/M (Ecological/Molecular), Chemistry, Physics, French, German, Modern Hebrew, Italian, Latin, and Spanish, as well as Foreign Language Tests with Listening in Chinese, French, German, Japanese, Korean, Spanish, and English Language Proficiency (ELPT). The Mathematics Level IC and IIC tests require the use of a scientific calculator.

SAT scores are automatically sent to each student who has taken the test. On average, they are mailed about three weeks after the test. Students may request that the scores be reported to their high schools or to the colleges to which they are applying.

DON'T FORGET TO . . .

- Take the SAT or ACT Assessment before application deadlines.
- Note that test registration deadlines precede test dates by about six weeks.
- Register to take the TOEFL test if English is not your native language and you are planning on studying at a North American college.
- Practice your test-taking skills with **Peterson's Ultimate SAT Tool Kit, Peterson's Ultimate ACT Tool Kit,** and **Peterson's TOEFL Success** (all available with software).
- Contact the College Board or American College Testing, Inc., in advance if you need special accommodations when taking tests.

ACT Assessment Program

The ACT Assessment Program is a comprehensive data collection, processing, and reporting service designed to assist in educational and career planning. The ACT Assessment instrument consists of four academic tests, taken under timed conditions, and a Student Profile Section and Interest Inventory, completed when students register for the ACT Assessment.

The academic tests cover four areas—English, mathematics, reading, and science reasoning. The ACT Assessment consists of 215 multiple-choice questions and takes approximately 3 hours and 30 minutes to complete with breaks (testing time is actually 2 hours and 55 minutes). They are designed to assess the student's educational development and readiness to handle college-level work. The minimum standard score is 1, the maximum is 36, and the national average is 21. Students should note that beginning in February 2005, an optional writing test will be offered.

The Student Profile Section requests information about each student's admission and enrollment plans, academic and out-of-class high school achievements and aspirations, and high school course work. The student is also asked to supply biographical data and self-reported high school grades in the four subject-matter areas covered by the academic tests.

The ACT Assessment has a number of career planning services, including the ACT Assessment Interest Inventory, which is designed to measure six major dimensions of student interests–business contact, business operations, technical, science, arts, and social service. Results are used to compare the student's interests with those of college-bound students who later majored in each of a wide variety of areas. Inventory results are also used to help students compare their work-activity preferences with work activities that characterize twenty-three "job families."

Because the information resulting from the ACT Assessment Program is used in a variety of educational settings, American College Testing, Inc., prepares three reports for each student: the Student Report, the High School Report, and the College Report. The Student Report normally is sent to the student's high school, except after the June test date, when it is sent directly to the student's home address. The College Report is sent to the colleges the student designates.

Early in the school year, American College Testing, Inc., sends registration packets to high schools across the country that contain all the information a student needs to

2004–05 ACT ASSESSMENT AND SAT TEST DATES

ACT Assessment

September 25, 2004*
October 23, 2004
December 11, 2004
February 12, 2005**
April 9, 2005
June 11, 2005

All test dates fall on a Saturday. Tests are also given on the Sundays following the Saturday test dates for students who cannot take the test on Saturday because of religious reasons. The basic ACT Assessment registration fee for 2003–04 was $26 ($29 in Florida and $42 outside of the U.S.).

*The September test is available only in Arizona, California, Florida, Georgia, Illinois, Indiana, Maryland, Nevada, North Carolina, Pennsylvania, South Carolina, Texas, and Washington.

**The February test date is not available in New York.

SAT

October 9, 2004 (SAT I and SAT II)
November 6, 2004 (SAT I, SAT II, and Language Tests with Listening, including ELPT*)
December 4, 2004 (SAT I and SAT II)
January 22, 2005 (SAT I, SAT II, and ELPT)
March 12, 2005 (SAT I only)** NEW SAT
May 7, 2005 (SAT I and SAT II) NEW SAT
June 4, 2005 (SAT I and SAT II) NEW SAT

For the 2003–04 academic year, the basic fee for the SAT I Reasoning Test was $28.50, which included the $16 basic registration and reporting fee. The basic fee for the SAT II Subject Tests was $16 for the Writing Test, $13 for the Language Tests with Listening, and $8 each for all other Subject Tests. Students can take up to three SAT II Subject Tests on a single date, and a $16 basic registration and reporting fee should be added for each test date. Tests are also given on the Sundays following the Saturday test dates for students who cannot take the test on Saturday because of religious reasons. Fee waivers are available to juniors and seniors who cannot afford test fees.

*Language Tests with Listening (including the English Language Proficiency Test, or ELPT) are only offered on November 6; the ELPT is offered on November 6 and January 22 at some test centers. See the Registration Bulletin for details.

**The March 12 test date is only available in the U.S. and its territories.

register for the ACT Assessment. High school guidance offices also receive a supply of *Preparing for the ACT Assessment*, a booklet that contains a complete practice test, an answer key, and general information about preparing for the test.

Test of English as a Foreign Language (TOEFL)

The TOEFL test is used by various organizations, such as colleges and universities, to determine English proficiency. The test is mainly offered in a computer-based format (TOEFL CBT), although the paper-based test is still offered in some areas. Eventually, the TOEFL will be completely computer-based.

The TOEFL tests students in the areas of listening, structure, reading comprehension, and writing. Score requirements are set by individual institutions. For more information on TOEFL, and to obtain a copy of the Information Bulletin, contact the Educational Testing Service.

Peterson's *TOEFL CBT Success* can help you prepare for the exam. The CD version of the book includes a TOEFL practice test and adaptive English skill building exercise. An online CBT test can also be taken for a small fee at petersons.com.

Contact your secondary school counselor for full information about the SAT and ACT Assessment programs and the TOEFL test.

The Whys and Whats of College Visits

Dawn B. Sova, Ph.D.

The campus visit should not be a passive activity for you and your parents, and you will have to take the initiative and use all of your senses to gather information beyond that provided in the official tour. You will see many important indicators during your visit that will tell you more about the true character of a college and its students than the tour guide will reveal. Know what to look for and how to assess the importance of such indicators.

WHAT SHOULD YOU ASK AND WHAT SHOULD YOU LOOK FOR?

Your first stop on a campus visit is the visitor center or admissions office, where you will probably have to wait to meet with a counselor. Colleges usually plan to greet visitors later than the appointed time in order to give them the opportunity to review some of the campus information that is liberally scattered throughout the visitor waiting room. Take advantage of the time to become even more familiar with the college by arriving 15 to 30 minutes before your appointment to observe the behavior of staff members and to browse through the yearbooks and student newspapers that will be available.

If you prepare in advance, you will have already reviewed the college catalog and map of the campus. These materials familiarize you with the academic offerings and the physical layout of the campus, but the true character of the college and its students emerges in other ways.

Begin your investigation with the visitor center staff members. As a student's first official contact with the college, they should make every effort to welcome prospective students and to project a friendly image.

- How do they treat you and other prospective students who are waiting? Are they friendly and willing to speak with you, or do they try their hardest to avoid eye contact and conversation?
- Are they friendly with each other and with students who enter the office, or are they curt and unwilling to help?
- Does the waiting room have a friendly feeling or is it cold and sterile?

If the visitor center staff members seem indifferent to *prospective* students, there is little reason to believe that they will be warm and welcoming to current students. View such behavior as a warning to watch very carefully the interaction of others with you during the tour. An indifferent or unfriendly reception in the admissions office may be simply the first of many signs that attending this college will not be a pleasant experience.

Look through several yearbooks and see the types of activities that are actually photographed, as opposed to the activities that colleges promise in their promotional literature. Some questions are impossible to answer if the college is very large, but for small and moderately sized colleges the yearbook is a good indicator of campus activity.

- Has the number of clubs and organizations increased or decreased in the past five years?
- Do the same students appear repeatedly in activities?
- Do sororities and fraternities dominate campus activities?
- Are participants limited to one sex or one ethnic group or are the participants diverse?
- Are all activities limited to the campus, or are students involved in activities in the community?

Use what you observe in the yearbooks as a means of forming a more complete understanding of the college, but don't base your entire impression on just one facet. If time permits, look through several copies of the school newspaper, which should reflect the major concerns and interests of the students. The paper is also a good way to learn about the campus social life.

- Does the paper contain a mix of national and local news?
- What products or services are advertised?
- How assertive are the editorials?
- With what topics are the columnists concerned?
- Are movies and concerts that meet your tastes advertised or reviewed?
- What types of ads appear in the classified section?

The newspaper should be a public forum for students, and, as such, should reflect the character of the campus and of the student body. A paper that deals only with seemingly safe and well-edited topics on the editorial page and in regular feature columns might indicate administrative censorship. A lack of ads for restaurants might indicate either a lack of good places to eat or that area restaurants do not welcome student business. A limited mention of movies, concerts, or other entertainment might reveal a severely limited campus social life. Even if ads and reviews are included, you can also learn a lot about how such activities reflect your tastes.

You will have only a limited amount of time to ask questions during your initial meeting with the admissions counselor, for very few schools include a formal interview in the initial campus visit or tour. Instead, this brief meeting is often just a nicety that allows the admissions office to begin a file for the student and to record some initial impressions. Save your questions for the tour guide and for campus members that you meet along the way.

HOW CAN YOU ASSESS THE TRUE CHARACTER OF A COLLEGE AND ITS STUDENTS?

Colleges do not train their tour guides to deceive prospective students, but they do caution guides to avoid unflattering topics and campus sites. Does this mean that you are condemned to see only a sugarcoated version of life on a particular college campus? Not at all, especially not if you are observant.

Most organized campus visits include such campus facilities as dormitories, dining halls, libraries, student activity and recreation centers, and the health and student services centers. Some may only be pointed out, while you will walk through others. Either way, you will find that many signs of the true character of the college emerge if you keep your eyes open.

Bulletin boards in dormitories and student centers contain a wealth of information about campus activities, student concerns, and campus groups. Read the posters, notices, and messages to learn what *really* interests students. Unlike ads in the school newspaper, posters put up by students advertise both on- and off-campus events, so they will give you an idea of what is also available in the surrounding community.

Review the notices, which may cover either campuswide events or events that concern only small groups of students. The catalog may not mention a performance group, but an individual dormitory with its own small theater may offer regular productions. Poetry readings, jam sessions, writers' groups, and other activities may be announced and shows diversity of student interests.

Even the brief bulletin board messages offering objects for sale and noting objects that people want to purchase reveal a lot about a campus. Are most of the items computer related? Or do the messages specify compact discs, audio equipment, or musical instruments? Are offers to barter goods or services posted? Don't ignore the "ride wanted" messages. Students who want to share rides home during a break may specify widely diverse geographical locations. If so, then you know that the student body is not limited to only the immediate area or one locale. Other messages can also enhance your knowledge of the true character of the campus and its students.

As you walk through various buildings, examine their condition carefully.

- Is the paint peeling, and do the exteriors look worn?
- Are the exteriors and interiors of the building clean?
- Is the equipment in the classrooms up-to-date or outdated?

Pay particular attention to the dormitories, especially to factors that might affect your safety. Observe the appearance of the structure, and ask about the security measures in and around the dormitories.

- Are the dormitories noisy or quiet?
- Do they seem crowded?
- How good is the lighting around each dormitory?
- Are the dormitories spread throughout the campus or are they clustered in one main area?
- Who has access to the dormitories in addition to students?
- How secure are the means by which students enter and leave the dormitory?

While you are on the subject of dormitory safety, you should also ask about campus safety. Don't expect that the guide will rattle off a list of crimes that have been committed in the past year. To obtain that information, access the recent year of issues of *The Chronicle of Higher Education* and locate its yearly report on campus crime. Also ask the guide about safety measures that the campus police take and those that students have initiated.

- Can students request escorts to their residences late at night?
- Do campus shuttle buses run at frequent intervals all night?
- Are "blue-light" telephones liberally placed throughout the campus for students to use to call for help?
- Do the campus police patrol the campus regularly?

If the guide does not answer your questions satisfactorily, wait until after the tour to contact the campus police or traffic office for answers.

Campus tours usually just point out the health services center without taking the time to walk through. Even if you don't see the inside of the building, you should take a close look at the location of the health services center and ask the guide questions about services.

- How far is the health center from the dormitories?
- Is a doctor always on call?
- Does the campus transport sick students from their dormitories or must they walk?
- What are the operating hours of the health center?
- Does the health center refer students to a nearby hospital?

If the guide can't answer your questions, visit the health center later and ask someone there.

Most campus tours take pride in showing students their activities centers, which may contain snack bars, game rooms, workout facilities, and other means of entertainment. Should you scrutinize this building as carefully as the rest? Of course. Outdated and poorly maintained activity equipment contributes to your total impression of the college. You should also ask about the hours, availability, and cost (no, the activities are usually *not* free) of using the bowling alleys, pool tables, air hockey tables, and other items.

As you walk through campus with the tour, also look carefully at the appearance of the students who pass. The way in which both men and women groom themselves, the way they dress, and even their physical bearing communicate a lot more than any guidebook can. If everyone seems to conform to the same look, you might feel that you would be uncomfortable at the college, however nonconformist that look might be. On the other hand, you might not feel comfortable on a campus that stresses diversity of dress and behavior, and your observations now can save you discomfort later.

- Does every student seem to wear a sorority or fraternity t-shirt or jacket?
- Is everyone of your sex sporting the latest fad haircut?
- Do all of the men or the women seem to be wearing expensive name-brand clothes?
- Do most of the students seem to be working hard to look outrageous in regard to clothing, hair color, and body art?
- Would you feel uncomfortable in a room full of these students?

Is appearance important to you? If it is, then you should consider very seriously if you answer *yes* to any of the above questions. You don't have to be the same as everyone else on campus, but standing out too rigorously may make you unhappy.

As you observe the physical appearance of the students, also listen to their conversations as you pass them? What are they talking about? How are they speaking? Are their voices and accents all the same, or do you hear diversity in their speech? Are you offended by their language? Think how you will feel if surrounded by the same speech habits and patterns for four years.

WHERE SHOULD YOU VISIT ON YOUR OWN?

Your campus visit is not over when the tour ends because you will probably have many questions yet to be answered and many places to still be seen. Where you go depends upon the extent to which the organized tour covers the campus. Your tour should take you to view residential halls, health and student services centers, the gymnasium or field house, dining halls, the library, and recreational centers. If any of the facilities on this list have been omitted, visit them on your own and ask questions of the students and staff members you meet. In addition, you should step off campus and gain an impression of the surrounding community. You will probably become bored with life on campus and spend at least some time off campus. Make certain that you know what the surrounding area is like.

The campus tour leaves little time to ask impromptu questions of current students, but you can do so after the tour. Eat lunch in one of the dining halls. Most will allow visitors to pay cash to experience a typical student meal. Food may not be important to you now while you are living at home and can simply take anything you want from the refrigerator at any time, but it will be when you are away at college with only a meal ticket to feed you.

- How clean is the dining hall? Consider serving tables, floors, and seating.
- What is the quality of the food?
- How big are the portions?
- How much variety do students have at each meal?
- How healthy are the food choices?

While you are eating, try to strike up a conversation with students and tell them that you are considering attending their college. Their reactions and advice can be eye-opening. Ask them questions about the academic atmosphere and the professors.

- Are the classes large or small?
- Do the majority of the professors only lecture or are tutorials and seminars common?
- Is the emphasis of the faculty career-oriented or abstract?
- Are the teaching methods innovative and stimulating or boring and dull?
- Is the academic atmosphere pressured, lax, or somewhere in between?
- Which are the strong majors? The weak majors?
- Is the emphasis on grades or social life or a mix of both at the college?

- How hard do students have to work to receive high grades?

Current students can also give you the inside line on the true nature of the college social life. You may gain some idea through looking in the yearbook, in the newspaper, and on the bulletin boards, but students will reveal the true highs and lows of campus life. Ask them about drug use, partying, dating rituals, drinking, and anything else that may affect your life as a student.

- Which are the most popular club activities?
- What do students do on weekends? Do most go home?
- How frequently do concerts occur on campus? Which groups have recently performed?
- How can you become involved in specific activities (name them)?
- How strictly are campus rules enforced and how severe are penalties?
- What counseling services are available?
- Are academic tutoring services available?
- Do they feel that the faculty really cares about students, especially freshmen?

You will receive the most valuable information from current students, but you will only be able to speak with them after the tour is over. And you might have to risk rejection as you try to initiate conversations with students who might not want to reveal how they feel about the campus. Still, the value of this information is worth the chance.

If you have the time, you should also visit the library to see just how accessible research materials are and to observe the physical layout. The catalog usually specifies the days and hours of operation, as well as the number of volumes contained in the library and the number of periodicals to which it subscribes. A library also requires accessibility, good lighting, an adequate number of study carrels, and lounge areas for students. Many colleges have created 24-hour study lounges for students who find the residence halls too noisy for studying, although most colleges claim that they designate areas of the residences as "quiet study" areas. You may not be interested in any of this information, but when you are a student you will have to make frequent use of the campus library so you should know what is available. You should at least ask how extensive their holdings are in your proposed major area. If they have virtually nothing, you will have to spend a lot of time ordering items via interlibrary loan or making copies, which can become expensive. The ready answer of students that they will obtain their information from the Internet is unpleasantly countered by professors who demand journal articles with documentation.

Make a point of at least driving through the community surrounding the college, because you will be spending time there shopping, dining, working in a part-time job, or attending events. Even the largest and best-stocked campus will not meet all of your social and personal needs. If you can spare the time, stop in several stores to see if they welcome college students.

- Is the surrounding community suburban, urban, or rural?
- Does the community offer stores of interest, such as bookstores, craft shops, and boutiques?
- Do the businesses employ college students?
- Does the community have a movie or stage theater?
- Are there several types of interesting restaurants?
- Do there seem to be any clubs that court a college clientele?
- Is the center of activity easy to walk to, or do you need a car or other transportation?

You might feel that a day is not enough to answer all of your questions, but even answering some questions will provide you with a stronger basis for choosing a college. Many students visit a college campus several times before making their decision, as you also should. Keep in mind that for the rest of your life you will be associated with the college that you attend. You will spend four years of your life at this college. The effort of spending several days to obtain the information to make your decision is worthwhile.

Dawn B. Sova, Ph.D., is a former newspaper reporter and columnist, as well as the author of more than eight books and numerous magazine articles. She teaches creative and research writing, as well as scientific and technical writing, newswriting, and journalism.

Applying 101

The words "applying yourself" have several important meanings in the college application process. One meaning refers to the fact that you need to keep focused during this important time in your life, keep your priorities straight, and know the dates that your applications are due so you can apply on time. The phrase might also refer to the person who is really responsible for your application--you.

You are the only person who should compile your college application. You need to take ownership of this process. The intervention of others should be for advisement only. The guidance counselor is not responsible for completing your applications, and your parents shouldn't be typing them. College applications must be completed in addition to your normal workload at school, college visits, and SAT, ACT Assessment, or possibly, TOEFL testing.

THE APPLICATION

The application is your way of introducing yourself to a college admissions office. As with any introduction, you should try to make a good first impression. The first thing you should do in presenting your application is to find out what the college or university needs from you. Read the application carefully to find out the application fee and deadline, required standardized tests, number of essays, interview requirements, and anything else you can do or submit to help improve your chances for acceptance.

Completing college applications yourself helps you learn more about the schools to which you are applying. The information a college asks for in its application can tell you much about the school. State university applications often tell you how they are going to view their applicants. Usually, they select students based on GPAs and test scores. Colleges that request an interview, ask you to respond to a few open-ended questions, or require an essay are interested in a more personal approach to the application process and may be looking for different types of students than those sought by a state school.

In addition to submitting the actual application, there are several other items that are commonly required. You will be responsible for ensuring that your standardized test scores and your high school transcript arrive at the colleges to which you apply. Most colleges will ask that you submit teacher recommendations as well. Select teachers who know you and your abilities well and allow them plenty of time to complete the recommendations. When all portions of the application have been completed and sent in, whether electronically or by mail, make sure you follow up with the college to ensure their receipt.

FOLLOW THESE TIPS WHEN FILLING OUT YOUR APPLICATION

- **Follow the directions to the letter.** You don't want to be in a position to ask an admissions officer for exceptions due to your inattentiveness.
- **Make a photocopy** of the application and work through a rough draft before you actually fill out the application copy to be submitted.
- **Proofread all parts of your application,** including your essay. Again, the final product indicates to the admissions staff how meticulous and careful you are in your work.
- **Submit your application as early as possible,** provided all of the pieces are available. If there is a problem with your application, this will allow you to work through it with the admissions staff in plenty of time. If you wait until the last minute, it not only takes away that cushion but also reflects poorly on your sense of priorities.

THE APPLICATION ESSAY

Some colleges may request one essay or a combination of essays and short-answer topics to learn more about who you are and how well you can communicate your thoughts. Common essay topics cover such simple themes as writing about yourself and your experiences or why you want to attend that particular school. Other colleges will ask that you show your imaginative or creative side by writing about a favorite author, for instance, or commenting on a hypothetical situation. In such cases, they will be looking at your thought processes and your level of creativity.

Whereas the other portions of your application—your transcript, test scores, and involvement in extracurricular activities—are a reflection of what you've accomplished up to this point, your application essay is an opportunity to present yourself in the here and now. The essay shows your originality and verbal skills and is very important. Test scores and grades may represent your academic results, but your essay shows how you approach a topic or problem and express your opinion.

Admissions officers, particularly those at small or mid-size colleges, use the essay to determine how you, as a student, will fit into life at that college. The essay, therefore, is a critical component of the application process. Here are some tips for writing a winning essay:

- Colleges are looking for an honest representation of who you are and what you think. Make sure that the tone of the essay reflects enthusiasm, maturity, creativity, the ability to communicate, talent, and your leadership skills.
- Be sure you set aside enough time to write the essay, revise it, and revise it *again.* Running the "spell check" feature on your computer will only detect a fraction of the errors you probably made on your first pass at writing it. Take a break and then come back to it and reread it. You will probably notice other style, content, and grammar problems—and ways that you can improve the essay overall.
- Always answer the question that is being asked, making sure that you are specific, clear, and true to your personality.
- Enlist the help of reviewers who know you well—friends, parents, teachers—since they are likely to be the most honest and will keep you on track in the presentation of your true self.

THE PERSONAL INTERVIEW

Although it is relatively rare that a personal interview is required, many colleges recommend that you take this opportunity for a face-to-face discussion with a member of the admissions staff. Read through the application materials to determine whether or not a college places great emphasis on the interview. If they strongly recommend that you have one, it may work against you to forego it.

In contrast to a group interview and some alumni interviews, which are intended to provide information about a college, the personal interview is viewed both as an information session and as further evaluation of your skills and strengths. You will meet with a member of the admissions staff who will be assessing your personal qualities, high school preparation, and your capacity to contribute to undergraduate life at the institution. On average, these meetings last about 45 minutes—a relatively short amount of time in which to gather information and leave the desired impression—so here are some suggestions on how to make the most of it.

Scheduling Your Visit. Generally, students choose to visit campuses in the summer or fall of their senior year. Both times have their advantages. A summer visit, when the campus is not in session, generally allows for a less hectic visit and interview. Visiting in the fall, on the other hand, provides the opportunity to see what campus life is like in full swing. If you choose the fall, consider arranging an overnight trip so that you can stay in one of the college dormitories. At the very least, you should make your way around campus to take part in classes, athletic events, and social activities. Always make an appointment and avoid scheduling more than two college interviews on any given day. Multiple interviews in a single day hinder your chances of making a good impression, and your impressions of the colleges will blur into each other as you hurriedly make your way from place to place.

Preparation. Know the basics about the college before going for your interview. Read the college viewbook or catalog in addition to this guide. You will be better prepared to ask questions that are not answered in the literature and that will give you a better understanding of what the college has to offer. You should also spend some time thinking about your strengths and weaknesses and, in particular, what you are looking for in a college education. You will find that as you get a few interviews under your belt, they will get easier. You might consider starting with a college that is not a top contender on your list, where the stakes are not as high.

Asking Questions. Inevitably, your interviewer will ask you, "Do you have any questions?" Not having one may suggest that you're unprepared or, even worse, not interested. When you do ask questions, make sure that they are ones that matter to you and that have a bearing on your decision about whether or not to attend. The questions that you ask will give the interviewer some insight into your personality and priorities. Avoid asking questions that can be answered in the college literature—again, a sign of unpreparedness. Although the interviewer will undoubtedly pose questions to you, the interview should not be viewed merely as a question-and-answer session. If a conversation evolves out of a particular question, so much the better. Your interviewer can learn a great deal about you from how you sustain a conversation. Similarly, you will be able to learn a great deal about the college in a conversational format.

Separate the Interview from the Interviewer. Many students base their feelings about a college solely on their impressions of the interviewer. Try not to characterize a college based only on your personal reaction, however, since your impressions can be skewed by whether you and your interviewer hit it off. Pay lots of attention to everything else that you see, hear, and learn about a college. Once on campus, you may never see your interviewer again.

In the end, remember to relax and be yourself. Don't drink jitters-producing caffeinated beverages prior to the interview, and suppress nervous fidgets like leg-wagging, finger-drumming, or bracelet-jangling. Your interviewer will expect you to be somewhat nervous, which will relieve some of the pressure. Consider this an opportunity to put forth your best effort and to enhance everything that the college knows about you up to this point.

THE FINAL DECISION

Once you have received your acceptance letters, it is time to go back and look at the whole picture. Provided you received more than one acceptance, you are now in a position to compare your options. The best way to do this is to compare your original list of important college-ranking criteria with what you've discovered about each college along the way. In addition, you and your family will need to factor in the financial aid component. You will need to look beyond these cost issues and the quantifiable pros and cons of each college, however, and know that you have a good feeling about your final choice. Before sending off your acceptance letter, you need to feel confident that the college will feel like home for the next four years. Once the choice is made, the only hard part will be waiting for an entire summer before heading off to college!

Successful Transfer

Adrienne Aaron Rulnick

Transfer students need and deserve detailed and accurate information but often lack direction as to where it can be obtained. Few general college guides offer information about transfer deadlines and required minimum grade point averages for transfer admission. College catalogs are not always clear about the specific requirements and procedures for transfer students who may be confused about whether they need to present high school records, SAT I or ACT Assessment scores, or a guidance counselor's recommendation, particularly if they have been out of high school for several years. Transfer advisers are not available to those enrolled at a baccalaureate institution; at community and junior colleges, the transfer advising function may be performed by a designated transfer counselor or by a variety of college advisers who are less clearly identified.

The challenge for transfer students is to determine what they need to know in order to make good, informed decisions and identify the individuals and resources that can provide that information. An organized research process is very much at the heart of a successful transfer.

HOW TO BEGIN

Perhaps the most important first step in this process is one of self-analysis. Adopting a consumer approach is appropriate—higher education is a formidable purchase, no matter how it is financed. The reputation of the college from which you obtain your degree may open doors to future jobs and careers; friendships and contacts you make at college can provide a significant network for lifelong social and professional relationships. The environment of a transfer school may be the perfect opportunity for you to test out urban living or the joys of country life, explore a different area of the country, experience college residential living for the first time, or move out of the family nest into your first apartment. Like any major purchase in your life, there are costs and benefits to be weighed. Trade-offs include cost, distance, rigor of academic work, extra time in school required by a cooperative education program, and specific requirements, such as foreign language competence at a liberal arts institution or courses in religion at an institution with a denominational affiliation.

USE EXPERIENCE AS A GUIDE

The wise consumer reflects on his or her own experience with a product (i.e., your initial college or colleges) and then seeks out people who have firsthand experience with the new product being considered. Talk to friends and family members who have attended the colleges you are considering; ask college faculty members you know to tell you about the colleges they attended and how they view these schools. Talk to people engaged in the careers you are considering: what are their impressions of the best programs and schools in their field? Make sure you sample a variety of opinions, but beware of dated experiences. An engineering department considered top-notch when Uncle Joe attended college twenty years ago might be very different today!

THE NITTY-GRITTY

Once your list is reduced to a manageable number of schools, usually fewer than ten, it is important to identify academic requirements, requisite grade point averages for admission, and deadline dates. Most schools admit for both the fall and spring semesters; those on a trimester system may have winter and summer admissions as well. Some schools have rolling admission policies and will process applications as they are received; others, particularly the more selective colleges, have firm deadlines because their admission process involves a committee review, and decisions are made on a competitive basis. It is helpful to know how many transfer students are typically accepted for the semester you wish to begin, whether the minimum grade point average is indicative of the actual average of accepted students (this can vary widely), and whether the major you are seeking has special prerequisites and admission procedures. For example, fine arts programs admission procedures usually require portfolios or auditions. For engineering, computer science, and some business majors, there are specific requirements in mathematics that must be met before a student is considered for admission. Many specialized health-care programs, including nursing, may only admit once a year. Some schools have different standards for sophomore and junior transfers or for in-state and out-of-state students.

Other criteria that you should identify include whether college housing and financial aid are available for transfer students. Some colleges have special transfer scholarships that require separate applications and references, while others simply award aid based on applications that indicate a high grade point average or membership in a nationally recognized junior and community college honor society, such as Phi Theta Kappa. There are also scholarships for transfer students who demonstrate accomplishment in specified academic and performance areas; the latter may be based on talent competitions or accomplishment evidenced in a portfolio or audition.

NONTRADITIONAL STUDENTS

For the nontraditional student, usually defined as anyone beyond the traditional college age of 18 to 23, there may be additional aspects to investigate. Some colleges award credit based on demonstrated life experience; many colleges grant credit for qualifying scores on the CLEP exams or for participation in the DANTES program. Experience in industry may yield college credit as well. If you are ready and able to pursue further college work but are not in a position to attend regular classes at a senior college, there are a variety of distance learning options at fully accredited colleges. Other colleges provide specialized support services for nontraditional students and may allow students the opportunity to attend part-time if they have family and work responsibilities. In some cases, usually at large universities, there may be married student housing or family housing available. More and more schools have established daycare facilities, although the waiting lists are often very long.

APPLYING

Once you have identified the schools that meet the needs you have established as priorities, it is time to begin the application process. Make sure you observe all the indicated deadlines: it never hurts to have everything in early, as there are consequences, such as closed-out majors and the loss of housing and financial aid, if you submit your application late. Make appointments with faculty members and others who are providing references; make sure they understand what is required of them and when and where their references must be sent. It is your responsibility to follow through to make sure all of your credentials are received, including transcripts from all colleges previously attended, even if you only took one summer course or attended for less than a semester. If you have not yet had the opportunity to visit the schools to which you are applying, now is the time to do so. Arrange interviews wherever possible, and make sure to include a tour of the campus and visits to the department and career offices to gain a picture of the facilities and future opportunities. If you have questions about financial aid, schedule an appointment in the financial aid office, and make sure you are aware of all the deadlines and requirements and any scholarship opportunities for which you are eligible.

MAKING YOUR CHOICE

Congratulations! You have been accepted at the colleges of your choice. Now what? Carefully review the acceptance of your previous college credit and how it has been applied. You are entitled to know how many transfer credits you have received and your expected date of graduation. Compare financial aid packages and housing options. The best choice should emerge from this review process. Then, send a note to the schools you will not be attending. Acknowledge your acceptance, but indicate that you have chosen to attend elsewhere. Carefully read everything you have received from the college of your choice. Return required deposits within the deadline, reserve time to attend transfer orientation, arrange to have your final transcript sent from the college you currently attend, and review the financial picture. This is the time to finalize college loan applications and make sure you are in a position to meet all the costs entailed at this college. Don't forget to include the costs of travel and housing.

You've done it! While many transfer students reflect on how much work was involved in the transfer admission process, those who took the time to follow all of the steps outlined above report a sense of satisfaction with their choices and increased confidence in themselves. We wish you an equally rewarding experience.

Adrienne Aaron Rulnick is a Transfer Counselor at Berkshire Community College.

Who's Paying for This? Financial Aid Basics

A college education can be expensive—costing more than $100,000 for four years at some of the higher priced private colleges and universities. Even at the lower cost state colleges and universities, the cost of a four-year education can approach $50,000. Determining how you and your family will come up with the necessary funds to pay for your education requires planning, perseverance, and learning as much as you can about the options that are available to you.

Paying for college should not be looked on as a four-year financial commitment. For most families, paying the total cost of a student's college education out of current savings is usually not realistic. For families that have planned ahead and have financial savings established for higher education, the burden is a lot easier. But for most, meeting the cost of college requires the pooling of current income and assets and investing in longer-term loan options. These family resources, together with possible financial assistance from the state, federal, and institutional resources enable millions of students each year to attend the institution of their choice.

HOW NEED-BASED FINANCIAL AID IS AWARDED

When you apply for aid, your family's financial situation is analyzed using a government-approved formula called the Federal Methodology. This formula looks at five items:

1. Demographic information of the family.
2. Income of the parents.
3. Assets of the parents.
4. Income of the student.
5. Assets of the student.

This analysis determines the amount you and your family are expected to contribute toward your college expenses, called your Expected Family Contribution or EFC. If the EFC is equal to or more than the cost at a particular college, then you do not demonstrate financial need. However, even if you don't have financial need, you may still qualify for aid, as there are grants, scholarships, and loan programs that are not need-based.

If the cost of your education is greater than your EFC, then you do demonstrate financial need and qualify for assistance. The amount of your financial need that can be met varies from school to school. Some are able to meet your full need, while others can only cover a certain percentage of need. Here's the formula:

Cost of Attendance
– Expected Family Contribution

= Financial Need

The EFC remains constant, but your need will vary according to the costs of attendance at a particular college. In general, the higher the tuition and fees at a particular college, the higher the cost of attendance will be. Expenses for books and supplies, room and board, and other miscellaneous costs are included in the overall cost of attendance. It is important to remember that you do not have to be "needy" to qualify for financial aid. Many middle and upper-middle income families qualify for need-based financial aid.

SOURCES OF FINANCIAL AID

The largest single source of aid is the federal government, which awards almost $84 billion to more than 8.9 million students each year.

The next largest source of financial aid is found in the college and university community. Institutions award an estimated $20 billion to students each year. Most of this aid is awarded to students who have a demonstrated need based on the Federal Methodology. Some institutions use a different formula, the Institutional Methodology, to award their own funds in conjunction with other forms of aid. Institutional aid may be either need-based or non-need based. Aid that is not based on need is usually awarded for a student's academic performance (merit awards), specific talents or abilities, or to attract the type of students a college seeks to enroll.

Another source of financial aid is from state government, awarding more than $5.6 billion per year. All states offer grant and/or scholarship aid, most of which is need-based. However, more and more states are offering substantial merit-based aid programs. Most state programs award aid only to students attending college in their home state.

Other sources of financial aid include:

- Private agencies
- Foundations
- Corporations
- Clubs
- Fraternal and service organizations
- Civic associations
- Unions
- Religious groups that award grants, scholarships, and low-interest loans
- Employers that provide tuition reimbursement benefits for employees and their children

More information about these different sources of aid is available from high school guidance offices, public libraries, college financial aid offices, directly from the sponsoring organizations and on the Web at www.finaid.org.

APPLYING FOR FINANCIAL AID

Every student must complete the Free Application for Federal Student Aid (FAFSA) to be considered for financial aid. The FAFSA is available from your high school guidance office, many public libraries, colleges in your area, or directly from the U.S. Department of Education.

Students also can apply for federal student aid over the Internet using the interactive FAFSA on the Web. FAFSA on the Web can be accessed at http:www.fafsa.ed.gov. Both the student and at least one parent must apply for a federal pin number at http://www.pin.ed.gov. The pin number serves as your electronic signature when applying for aid on the Web.

To award their own funds, some colleges require an additional application, the Financial Aid PROFILE® form. The PROFILE asks supplemental questions that some colleges and awarding agencies feel provide a more accurate assessment of the family's ability to pay for college. It is up to the college to decide whether it will use only the FAFSA or both the FAFSA and the PROFILE. PROFILE applications are available from the high school guidance office and on the Web. Both the paper application and the Web site list those colleges and programs that require the PROFILE application.

If Every College You're Applying to for Fall 2005 Requires Just the FAFSA

. . . then it's pretty simple: Complete the FAFSA after January 1, 2005, being certain to send it in before any college-imposed deadlines. (You are not permitted to send in the 2005-06 FAFSA before January 1, 2005.) Most college FAFSA application deadlines are in February or early March. It is easier if you have all your financial records for the previous year available, but if that is not possible, you are strongly encouraged to use estimated figures.

After you send in your FAFSA, either with the paper application or electronically, you'll receive a Student Aid Report (SAR) that includes all of the information you reported and shows your EFC. If you provided an e-mail address, the SAR is sent to you electronically; otherwise, you will receive a paper copy in the mail. Be sure to review the SAR, checking to see if the information you reported is accurate. If you used estimated numbers to complete the FAFSA, you may have to resubmit the SAR with any corrections to the data. The college(s) you have designated on the FAFSA will receive the information you reported and will use that data to make their decision. In many instances, the colleges you've applied to will ask you to send copies of your and your parents' federal income tax returns for 2004, plus any other documents needed to verify the information you reported.

If a College Requires the PROFILE

Step 1: Register for the Financial Aid PROFILE in the fall of your senior year in high school.

Registering for the Financial Aid PROFILE begins the financial aid process. You can register by calling the College Scholarship Service at 1-800-778-6888 and providing basic demographic information, a list of colleges to which you are applying, and your credit card number to pay for the service. You can also apply for the PROFILE online at http://profileonline.collegeboard.com/index.jsp. Registration packets with a list of the colleges that require the PROFILE are available in most high school guidance offices. There is a fee for using the Financial Aid PROFILE application ($23 for the first college and $18 for each additional college). You must pay for the service by credit card when you register. If you do not have a credit card, you will be billed.

Step 2: Fill out your customized Financial Aid PROFILE.

A few weeks after you register, you'll receive in the mail a customized financial aid application that you can use to apply for institutional aid at the colleges you've designated, as well as from some private scholarship programs, like the National Merit Scholarship. (Note: If you've waited until winter and a college's financial aid application deadline is approaching, you can get overnight delivery by paying an extra fee.) The PROFILE contains all the questions necessary to calculate your "institutional" EFC, plus any additional questions that the colleges and organizations you've designated require you to answer. Your individualized packet will also contain a customized cover letter instructing you what to do and informing you about deadlines and requirements for the colleges and programs you designated when you registered for the PROFILE, codes that indicate which colleges wanted which additional questions, and supplemental forms (if any of the colleges to which you are applying require them—e.g. the Business/Farm Supplement for students whose parents own a business or farm or the Divorced/Separated Parents' Statement).

Make sure you submit your PROFILE by the earliest deadline listed. Two to four weeks after you do so, you will receive an acknowledgment and a report estimating your "institutional" EFC based on the data elements you provided on your PROFILE. Remember, this is a different formula from the federal system that uses the FAFSA.

FINANCIAL AID PROGRAMS

There are three types of financial aid:

1. Gift-aid—Scholarships and grants are funds that do not have to be repaid.
2. Loans—Loans must be repaid, usually after graduation; the amount you have to pay back is the total you've borrowed plus any accrued interest. This is considered a source of self-help aid.
3. Student employment—Student employment is a job arranged for you by the financial aid office. This is another source of self-help aid.

The federal government has two major grant programs—the Federal Pell Grant and the Federal Supplemental Educational Opportunity Grant. These grants are targeted to low-to-moderate income families with significant financial need. The federal government also sponsors a student employment program called Federal Work-Study, which offers jobs both on and off campus; and several loan programs, including those for students and for parents of undergraduate students.

There are two types of student loan programs, subsidized and unsubsidized. The Subsidized Stafford Loan and the Federal Perkins Loan are need-based, government-subsidized loans. Students who borrow through these programs do not have to pay interest on the loan until after they graduate or leave school. The Unsubsidized Stafford Loan and the Parent Loan Programs are not based on need, and borrowers are responsible for the interest while the student is in school. There are different methods on how these loans are administered. Once you choose your college, the financial aid office will guide you through this process.

After you've submitted your financial aid application and you've been accepted for admission, each college will send you a letter describing your financial aid award. Most award letters show estimated college costs, how much you and your family are expected to contribute, and the amount and types of aid you have been awarded. Most students are awarded aid from a combination of sources and programs. Hence, your award is often called a financial aid "package."

IF YOU DON'T QUALIFY FOR NEED-BASED AID

If you are not eligible for need-based aid, you can still find ways to lessen the burden on your parents.

Here are some suggestions:

- Search for merit scholarships. You can start at the initial stages of your application process. College merit awards are becoming increasingly important as more and more colleges award these grants to students they especially want to attract. As a result, applying to a college at which your qualifications put you at the top of the entering class may give you a larger merit award. Another source of aid to look for is private scholarships that are given for special skills and talents. Additional information can be found at petersons.com and at www.finaid.org.
- Seek employment during the summer and the academic year. The student employment office at your college can help you locate a school-year job. Many colleges and local businesses have vacancies remaining after they have hired students who are receiving Federal Work-Study financial aid.
- Borrow through the Unsubsidized Stafford Loan programs. These are open to all students. The terms and conditions are similar to the subsidized loans. The biggest difference is that the borrower is responsible for the interest while still in college, although most lenders permit students to delay paying the interest right away and add the accrued interest to the total amount owed. You must file the FAFSA to be considered.
- After you've secured what you can through scholarships, working, and borrowing, your parents will be expected to meet their share of the college bill (the Expected Family Contribution). Many colleges offer monthly payment plans that spread the cost over the academic year. If the monthly payments are too high, parents can borrow through the Federal Parent Loan for Undergraduate Students (PLUS program), through one of the many private education loan programs available, or through home equity loans and lines of credit. Families seeking assistance in financing college expenses should inquire at the financial aid office about what programs are available at the college. Some families seek the advice of professional financial advisers and tax consultants.

HOW IS YOUR FAMILY CONTRIBUTION CALCULATED?

The chart on the next page makes the following assumptions:

- two parent family where age of older parent is 45
- lower income families will file the 1040A or 1040EZ tax form
- student income is less than $2300
- there are no student assets
- there is only one family member in college

All figures are estimates and may vary when the complete FAFSA or PROFILE application is submitted.

Approximate Expected Family Contribution

	INCOME BEFORE TAXES								
ASSETS	$20,000	30,000	40,000	50,000	60,000	70,000	80,000	90,000	100,000
$ 20,000									
FAMILY SIZE 3	$ 0	870	2,450	4,350	7,000	9,800	12,600	15,500	18,000
4	0	80	1,670	3,350	5,600	8,300	11,000	14,000	17,100
5	0	0	930	2,500	4,500	7,000	9,700	12,600	15,600
6	0	0	100	1,700	3,350	5,500	8,100	11,000	14,000
$ 30,000									
FAMILY SIZE 3	$ 0	870	2,450	4,350	7,000	9,800	12,600	15,500	18,000
4	0	80	1,670	3,350	5,600	8,300	11,000	14,000	17,100
5	0	0	930	2,500	4,500	7,000	9,700	12,600	15,600
6	0	0	100	1,700	3,350	5,500	8,100	11,000	14,000
$ 40,000									
FAMILY SIZE 3	$ 0	870	2,450	4,350	7,000	9,800	12,600	15,500	18,000
4	0	80	1,670	3,350	5,600	8,300	11,000	14,000	17,100
5	0	0	930	2,500	4,500	7,000	9,700	12,600	15,600
6	0	0	100	1,700	3,350	5,500	8,100	11,000	14,000
$ 50,000									
FAMILY SIZE 3	$ 0	870	2,450	4,350	7,500	10,300	13,000	16,000	19,000
4	0	80	1,670	3,350	6,000	8,800	11,500	14,400	17,500
5	0	0	930	2,500	4,700	7,400	10,100	13,000	16,100
6	0	0	100	1,700	3,600	5,900	8,500	11,400	14,500
$ 60,000									
FAMILY SIZE 3	$ 0	870	2,450	5,100	8,050	10,800	13,600	16,500	19,600
4	0	80	1,670	3,950	6,550	9,300	12,200	15,000	18,100
5	0	0	930	3,000	5,300	7,900	10,800	13,600	16,700
6	0	0	100	2,150	4,000	6,300	9,100	12,000	15,000
$ 80,000									
FAMILY SIZE 3	$ 0	870	2,450	6,000	9,200	12,000	14,800	17,600	20,700
4	0	80	1,670	4,700	7,600	10,500	13,200	16,100	19,200
5	0	0	930	3,700	6,100	9,000	11,800	14,700	17,800
6	0	0	100	2,700	4,700	7,400	10,200	13,100	16,200
$ 100,000									
FAMILY SIZE 3	$ 0	870	2,450	7,000	10,300	13,000	15,900	18,800	21,850
4	0	80	1,670	5,600	8,700	11,500	14,300	17,200	20,300
5	0	0	930	4,400	7,100	10,200	12,900	15,800	18,900
6	0	0	100	3,300	5,500	8,500	11,300	14,200	17,300
$ 120,000									
FAMILY SIZE 3	$ 0	870	2,450	8,100	11,400	14,200	17,000	19,900	23,000
4	0	80	1,670	6,600	9,800	12,600	15,500	18,400	21,500
5	0	0	930	5,300	8,200	11,300	14,100	17,000	20,000
6	0	0	100	4,000	6,500	9,700	12,500	15,300	18,400
$ 140,000									
FAMILY SIZE 3	$ 0	870	2,450	9,300	12,600	15,400	18,200	21,000	24,100
4	0	80	1,670	7,600	11,000	13,900	16,700	19,500	22,600
5	0	0	930	6,100	9,500	12,500	15,200	18,100	21,200
6	0	0	100	4,700	7,600	10,800	13,600	16,500	19,600

Financial Aid Programs for Schools in the West

Each state government has established one or more state-administered financial aid programs for qualified students. The state programs may be restricted to legal residents of the state, or they also may be available to out-of-state students who are attending public or private colleges or universities within the state. In addition, other qualifications may apply.

The programs are described below in alphabetical order by state, along with information about how to determine eligibility and how to apply. The information refers to awards for 2003–04, unless otherwise stated. Students should write to the address given for each program to request that award details for 2004–05 be sent to them as soon as they are available.

ALASKA

A.W. "Winn" Brindle Memorial Education Loans. Renewable loan for study of approved curriculum in fisheries, seafood processing, food technology or related fields for Alaska residents. Must maintain good standing at institution. Eligible for up to 50% forgiveness if recipient returns to Alaska for employment in fisheries-related field. *Academic Fields/Career Goals:* Agribusiness; Animal/Veterinary Sciences; Biology; Food Science/Nutrition; Natural Resources. *Award:* Forgivable loan for use in freshman, sophomore, junior, senior, or graduate year; renewable. *Eligibility Requirements:* Applicant must be enrolled or expecting to enroll full-time at a two-year, four-year, or technical institution or university and resident of Alaska. Available to U.S. citizens. *Application Requirements:* Application, essay. *Deadline:* May 15. **Contact:** Lori Stedman, Administrative Assistant, Special Programs, Alaska Commission on Postsecondary Education, 3030 Vintage Boulevard, Juneau, AK 99801-7100. *Phone:* 907-465-6741. *Fax:* 907-465-5316. *Web site:* www.state.ak.us/acpe/.

Alaska Commission on Postsecondary Education Teacher Education Loan. Renewable loans for graduates of an Alaskan high school pursuing teaching careers in rural elementary and secondary schools in Alaska. Must be nominated by rural school district. Eligible for 100% forgiveness if loan recipient teaches in rural Alaska upon graduation. Several awards of up to $7500 each. Must maintain good standing at institution. *Academic Fields/Career Goals:* Education. *Award:* Forgivable loan for use in freshman, sophomore, junior, or senior year; renewable. *Award amount:* up to $7500. *Number of awards:* varies. *Eligibility Requirements:* Applicant must be enrolled or expecting to enroll full-time at a four-year institution or university. Available to U.S. citizens. *Application Requirements:* Application, transcript. *Deadline:* July 1. **Contact:** Lori Stedman, Administrative Assistant, Special Programs, Alaska Commission on Postsecondary Education, 3030 Vintage Boulevard, Juneau, AK 99801-7100. *Phone:* 907-465-6741. *Fax:* 907-465-5316. *Web site:* www.state.ak.us/acpe/.

Western Undergraduate Exchange (WUE) Program. Program allowing Alaska residents to enroll at two-or four-year institutions in participating states at a reduced tuition level, which is the in-state tuition plus a percentage of that amount. To be used for full-time undergraduate studies. See Web site at http://www.state.ak.us/acpe for further information, a list of eligible institutions, and deadlines. *Award:* Grant for use in freshman, sophomore, junior, or senior year; renewable. *Award amount:* varies. *Number of awards:* varies. *Eligibility Requirements:* Applicant must be enrolled or expecting to enroll full-time at a two-year or four-year institution or university; resident of Alaska and studying in Arizona, Colorado, Hawaii, Idaho, Montana, Nevada, New Mexico, North Dakota, Oregon, South Dakota, Utah, or Washington. Available to U.S. citizens. *Application Requirements: Deadline:* varies. **Contact:** Program Office, Alaska Commission on Postsecondary Education. *Phone:* 800-441-2962. *Web site:* www.state.ak.us/acpe/.

ARIZONA

Arizona Private Postsecondary Education Student Financial Assistance Program. Provides grants to financially needy Arizona Community College graduates to attend a private postsecondary baccalaureate degree-granting institution.*Award:* Forgivable loan for use in junior or senior year; renewable. *Award amount:* $750–$1500. *Number of awards:* varies. *Eligibility Requirements:* Applicant must be enrolled or expecting to enroll full-time at a four-year institution or university; resident of Arizona and studying in Arizona. Available to U.S. citizens. *Application Requirements:* Financial need analysis, transcript, promissory note. *Deadline:* continuous. **Contact:** Danny Lee, PFAP Program Manager, Arizona Commission for Postsecondary Education, 2020 North Central Avenue, Suite 550, Phoenix, AZ 85004-4503. *E-mail:* dan_lee@azhighered.org. *Phone:* 602-258-2435 Ext. 103. *Fax:* 602-258-2483. *Web site:* www.azhighered.org.

Leveraging Educational Assistance Partnership. LEAP provides grants to financially needy students who enroll in and attend postsecondary education or training in Arizona schools. LEAP Program was formerly known as the State Student Incentive Grant or SSIG Program. *Award:* Grant for use in freshman, sophomore, junior, senior, or graduate year; not renewable. *Award amount:* $100–$2500. *Number of awards:* varies. *Eligibility Requirements:* Applicant must be enrolled or expecting to enroll full or part-time at a two-year, four-year, or technical institution or university; resident of Arizona and studying in Arizona. Available to U.S. citizens.*Application Requirements:* Financial need analysis. *Deadline:* continuous. **Contact:** Mila A. Zaporteza, Business Manager/LEAP Financial Aid Manager, Arizona Commission for Postsecondary Education, 2020 North Central Avenue, Suite 550, Phoenix, AZ 85004-4503. *E-mail:* mila@azhighered.org. *Phone:* 602-258-2435 Ext. 102. *Fax:* 602-258-2483. *Web site:* www.azhighered.org.

CALIFORNIA

Assumption Programs of Loans for Education. The APLE is a competitive teacher loan assumption program designed to encourage outstanding students and out-of-state teachers to become California teachers within subject areas where a teacher shortage has been identified or in schools meeting specific criteria identified annually. Participants may receive up to $19,000 towards outstanding student loans. *Award:* Forgivable loan for use in junior, senior, or graduate year; renewable. *Award amount:* $11,000–$19,000. *Number of awards:* up to 7700. *Eligibility Requirements:* Applicant must be enrolled or expecting to enroll full or part-time at a four-year institution or university; resident of California and studying in California. Available to U.S. citizens. *Application Requirements:* Application, references. *Deadline:* June 30. **Contact:** California Student Aid Commission, PO Box 419027, Rancho Cordova, CA 95741-9027. *E-mail:* custsvcs@csac.ca.gov. *Phone:* 916-526-7590. *Fax:* 916-526-8002. *Web site:* www.csac.ca.gov.

Cal Grant C. Award for California residents who are enrolled in a short-term vocational training program. Program must lead to a recognized degree or certificate. Course length must be a minimum of 4 months and no longer than 24 months. Students must be attending an approved California institution and show financial need. *Award:* Grant for use in freshman, sophomore, junior, or senior year; renewable. *Award amount:* $576–$3168. *Number of awards:* up to 7761. *Eligibility Requirements:* Applicant must be enrolled or expecting to enroll full or part-time at a two-year or technical institution; resident of California and studying in California. Available to U.S. citizens. *Application Requirements:* Application, financial need analysis, GPA verification. *Deadline:* March 2. **Contact:** California Student Aid Commission, PO Box 419027, Rancho Cordova, CA 95741-9027. *E-mail:* custsvs@csac.ca.gov. *Phone:* 916-526-7590. *Fax:* 916-526-8002. *Web site:* www.csac.ca.gov.

Child Development Teacher and Supervisor Grant Program. Award is for those students pursuing an approved course of study leading to a Child Development Permit issued by the California Commission on Teacher Credentialing. In exchange for each year funding is received, recipients agree to provide one year of service in a licensed childcare center. *Award:* Grant for use in freshman, sophomore, junior, or senior year; renewable. *Award amount:* $1000–$2000. *Number of awards:* up to 300. *Eligibility Requirements:* Applicant must be enrolled or expecting to enroll full or part-time at a two-year, four-year, or technical institution or university; resident of California and studying in California. Available to U.S. citizens. *Application Requirements:* Application, financial need analysis, references, FAFSA. *Deadline:* June 1. **Contact:** California Student Aid Commission, PO Box 419027, Rancho Cordova, CA 95741-9027. *E-mail:* custsvcs@csac.ca.gov. *Phone:* 916-526-7590. *Fax:* 916-526-8002. *Web site:* www.csac.ca.gov.

Competitive Cal Grant A. Award for California residents who are not recent high school graduates attending an approved college or university within the state. Must show financial need and meet minimum 3.0 GPA requirement. *Award:* Grant for use in freshman, sophomore, junior, or senior year; renewable. *Award amount:* $2046–$9708. *Number of awards:* up to 22,500. *Eligibility Requirements:* Applicant must be enrolled or expecting to enroll full or part-time at a two-year, four-year, or technical institution or university; resident of California and studying in California. Applicant must have 3.0 GPA or higher. Available to U.S. citizens. *Application Requirements:* Application, financial need analysis, GPA verification. *Deadline:* March 2. **Contact:** California Student Aid Commission, PO Box 419027, Rancho Cordova, CA 95741-9027. *E-mail:* custsvcs@csac.ca.gov. *Phone:* 916-526-7590. *Fax:* 916-526-8002. *Web site:* www.csac.ca.gov.

Competitive Cal Grant B. Award is for California residents who are not recent high school graduates attending an approved college or university within the state. Must show financial need and meet the minimum 2.0 GPA requirement. *Award:* Grant for use in freshman, sophomore, or junior year; renewable. *Award amount:* $700–$11,259. *Number of awards:* up to 22,500. *Eligibility Requirements:* Applicant must be enrolled or expecting to enroll full or part-time at a two-year, four-year, or technical institution or university; resident of California and studying in California. Available to U.S. citizens. *Application Requirements:* Application, financial need analysis, GPA verification. *Deadline:* March 2. **Contact:** California Student Aid Commission, PO Box 419027, Rancho Cordova, CA 95741-9027. *E-mail:* custsvcs@csac.ca.gov. *Phone:* 916-526-7590. *Fax:* 916-526-8002. *Web site:* www.csac.ca.gov.

Cooperative Agencies Resources for Education Program. Renewable award available to California resident attending a two-year California community college. Must have no more than 70 degree-applicable units, currently receive CALWORKS/TANF, and have at least one child under 14 years of age. Must be in EOPS, single head of household, and 18 or older. Contact local college EOPS-CARE office. *Award:* Grant for use in freshman or sophomore year; renewable. *Number of awards:* 11,000. *Eligibility Requirements:* Applicant must be age 18; enrolled or expecting to enroll full-time at a two-year institution; single; resident of California and studying in California. Available to U.S. citizens. *Application Requirements:* Application, financial need analysis, test scores, transcript. *Deadline:* continuous. **Contact:** Local Community College EOPS/CARE Program, California Community Colleges, 1102 Q Street, Sacramento, CA 95814-6511. *Web site:* www.cccco.edu.

Entitlement Cal Grant A. Award is for California residents who are recent high school graduates attending an approved college or university within the state. Must show financial need and meet the minimum 3.0 GPA requirement. *Award:* Grant for use in freshman, sophomore, junior, or senior year; renewable. *Award amount:* $2046–$9708. *Number of awards:* varies. *Eligibility Requirements:* Applicant must be enrolled or expecting to enroll full or part-time at a two-year, four-year, or technical institution or university; resident of California and studying in California. Applicant must have 3.0 GPA or higher. Available to U.S. citizens. *Application Requirements:* Application, financial need analysis, GPA verification. *Deadline:* March 2. **Contact:** California Student Aid Commission, PO Box 419027, Rancho Cordova, CA 95741-9027. *E-mail:* custsvcs@csac.ca.gov. *Phone:* 916-526-7590. *Fax:* 916-526-8002. *Web site:* www.csac.ca.gov.

Entitlement Cal Grant B. Award for California residents who are high school graduates attending an approved college or university within the state. Must show financial need and meet the minimum 2.0 GPA requirement. *Award:* Grant for use in freshman, sophomore, junior, or senior year; renewable. *Award amount:* $700–$11,259. *Number of awards:* varies. *Eligibility Requirements:* Applicant must be enrolled or expecting to enroll full or part-time at a two-year, four-year, or technical institution or university; resident of California and studying in California. Available to U.S. citizens. *Application Requirements:* Application, financial need analysis. *Deadline:* March 2. **Contact:** California Student Aid Commission, PO Box 419027, Rancho Cordova, CA 95741-9027. *E-mail:* custsvcs@csac.ca.gov. *Phone:* 916-526-7590. *Fax:* 916-526-8002. *Web site:* www.csac.ca.gov.

Law Enforcement Personnel Development Scholarship. The Law Enforcement Personnel Dependents Scholarship Program provides college grants to needy dependents of California law enforcement officers, officers and employees of the Department of Corrections and Department of Youth Authority, and firefighters killed or disabled in the line of duty. *Award:* Grant for use in freshman, sophomore, junior, or senior year; renewable. *Award amount:* \$100–\$11,259. *Number of awards:* varies. *Eligibility Requirements:* Applicant must be enrolled or expecting to enroll full or part-time at a two-year, four-year, or technical institution or university; resident of California and studying in California. Applicant or parent of applicant must have employment or volunteer experience in police/firefighting. Available to U.S. citizens. *Application Requirements:* Application, financial need analysis. *Deadline:* continuous. **Contact:** California Student Aid Commission, PO Box 419027, Rancho Cordova, CA 95741-9027. *E-mail:* custsvcs@csac.ca.gov. *Phone:* 916-526-7590. *Fax:* 916-526-8002. *Web site:* www.csac.ca.gov.

COLORADO

Colorado Leveraging Educational Assistance Partnership (CLEAP) and SLEAP. Renewable awards for Colorado residents who are attending Colorado state-supported postsecondary institutions at the undergraduate level. Must document financial need. Contact colleges for complete information and deadlines. *Award:* Grant for use in freshman, sophomore, junior, or senior year; not renewable. *Award amount:* \$50–\$900. *Number of awards:* 5000. *Eligibility Requirements:* Applicant must be enrolled or expecting to enroll full or part-time at a two-year, four-year, or technical institution or university; resident of Colorado and studying in Colorado. Available to U.S. citizens. *Application Requirements:* Application, financial need analysis. *Deadline:* varies. **Contact:** Financial Aid Office at college/institution, Colorado Commission on Higher Education, 1380 Lawrence Street, Suite 1200, Denver, CO 80204-2059. *Web site:* www.state.co.us/cche.

Colorado Student Grant. Assists Colorado residents attending eligible public, private, or vocational institutions within the state. Application deadlines vary by institution. Renewable award for undergraduates. Contact the financial aid office at the college/institution for more information and an application. *Award:* Grant for use in freshman, sophomore, junior, or senior year; renewable. *Award amount:* \$500–\$5000. *Number of awards:* varies. *Eligibility Requirements:* Applicant must be enrolled or expecting to enroll full or part-time at a two-year, four-year, or technical institution or university; resident of Colorado and studying in Colorado.*Application Requirements:* Application, financial need analysis. *Deadline:* varies. **Contact:** Financial Aid Office at college/institution, Colorado Commission on Higher Education, 1380 Lawrence Street, Suite 1200, Denver, CO 80204-2059. *Web site:* www.state.co.us/cche.

Colorado Undergraduate Merit Scholarships. Renewable awards for students attending Colorado state-supported institutions at the undergraduate level. Must demonstrate superior scholarship or talent. Contact college financial aid office for complete information and deadlines. *Award:* Scholarship for use in freshman, sophomore, junior, or senior year; renewable. *Award amount:* \$1230. *Number of awards:* 10,823. *Eligibility Requirements:* Applicant must be enrolled or expecting to enroll full or part-time at a two-year, four-year, or technical institution or university; resident of Colorado and studying in Colorado. Applicant must have 3.0 GPA or higher. *Application Requirements:* Application, test scores, transcript. *Deadline:* varies. **Contact:** Financial Aid Office at college/institution, Colorado Commission on Higher Education, 1380 Lawrence Street, Suite 1200, Denver, CO 80204-2059. *Web site:* www.state.co.us/cche.

Department of Military Affairs Colorado National Guard State Tuition Assistance Program. Applicant must be member of Colorado National Guard for six months. Applicant must maintain 2.0 GPA during Tuition Assistance Program. Please refer to Web site http://www.coloradoguard.com. *Award:* Forgivable loan for use in freshman, sophomore, junior, or senior year; renewable. *Award amount:* varies. *Number of awards:* varies. *Eligibility Requirements:* Applicant must be enrolled or expecting to enroll full or part-time at a two-year, four-year, or technical institution or university; resident of Colorado and studying in Colorado. Available to U.S. citizens. Applicant or parent must meet one or more of the following requirements: Air Force National Guard or Army National Guard experience; retired from active duty; disabled or killed as a result of military service; prisoner of war; or missing in action. *Application Requirements:* Application, financial need analysis. *Deadline:* varies. **Contact:** Refer to Web site, Department of Military Affairs. *Web site:* www.coloradoguard.com.

Governor's Opportunity Scholarship. Scholarship available for the most needy first-time freshmen whose parents' adjusted gross income is less than \$26,000. Must be U.S. citizen or permanent legal resident. Work-study is part of the program.*Award:* Scholarship for use in freshman, sophomore, junior, or senior year; renewable. *Award amount:* \$5665. *Number of awards:* up to 1052. *Eligibility Requirements:* Applicant must be high school student; planning to enroll or expecting to enroll full-time at a two-year, four-year, or technical institution or university; resident of Colorado and studying in Colorado. Available to U.S. citizens. *Application Requirements:* Application, financial need analysis, test scores, transcript. *Deadline:* continuous. **Contact:** Financial Aid Office at college/institution, Colorado Commission on Higher Education, 1380 Lawrence Street, Suite 1200, Denver, CO 80204-2059. *Web site:* www.state.co.us/cche.

Western Undergraduate Exchange Program. Residents of Alaska, Arizona, Colorado, Hawaii, Idaho, Montana, Nevada, New Mexico, North Dakota, Oregon, South Dakota, Utah, Washington and Wyoming can enroll in designated two- and four-year undergraduate programs at public institutions in participating states at reduced tuition level (resident tuition plus half). Contact Western Interstate Commission for Higher Education for list and deadlines. *Award:* Scholarship for use in freshman, sophomore, junior, or senior year; renewable. *Eligibility Requirements:* Applicant must be enrolled or expecting to enroll full or part-time at a two-year or four-year institution; resident of Alaska, Arizona, Colorado, Hawaii, Idaho, Montana, Nevada, New Mexico, North Dakota, Oregon, South Dakota, Utah, Washington, or Wyoming and studying in Alaska, Colorado, Hawaii, Idaho, Montana, Nevada, New Mexico, North Dakota, Oregon, South Dakota, Utah, or Wyoming. Available to U.S. citizens. *Application Requirements:* Application. **Contact:** Ms. Sandy Jackson, Program Coordinator, Western Interstate Commission for Higher Education, PO Box 9752, Boulder, CO 80301-9752. *E-mail:* info-sep@wiche.edu. *Phone:* 303-541-0214. *Fax:* 303-541-0291. *Web site:* www.wiche.edu/sep.

HAWAII

Hawaii State Student Incentive Grant. Grants are given to residents of Hawaii who are enrolled in a participating Hawaiian state school. Funds are for undergraduate tuition only. Applicants must submit a financial need analysis. *Award:* Grant for use in freshman, sophomore, junior, or senior year; renewable. *Award amount:* varies. *Number of awards:* varies. *Eligibility Requirements:* Applicant must be enrolled or expecting to enroll full or part-time at a two-year, four-year, or technical institution or university; resident of Hawaii and studying in Hawaii. Available to U.S. citizens. *Application Requirements:* Financial need analysis. *Deadline:* varies. **Contact:** Jo Ann Yoshida, Financial Aid Specialist, Hawaii State Postsecondary Education Commission, University of Hawaii, Honolulu, HI 96822. *E-mail:* iha@hawaii.edu. *Phone:* 808-956-6066.

Kumu Kahua Theater/UHM Theater Department Playwriting Contest, Hawaii Prize. Contest for residents and non-residents of Hawaii. Contestants will be judged on full-length plays dealing with some aspect of the Hawaii experience or plays set in Hawaii. Submissions should be a minimum of 50 pages in standard form. Write for details. *Award:* Prize for use in freshman, sophomore, junior, senior, graduate, or postgraduate years; not renewable. *Award amount:* $500. *Number of awards:* 1. *Eligibility Requirements:* Applicant must be enrolled or expecting to enroll at an institution or university and must have an interest in writing. Available to U.S. and non-U.S. citizens. *Application Requirements:* Applicant must enter a contest, 3 copies of manuscript. *Deadline:* January 2. **Contact:** Kumu Kahua Playwriting Contest, Kumu Kahua Theatre, 46 Merchant Street, Honolulu, HI 96813. *E-mail:* info@kumukahua.com.

Kumu Kahua Theater/UHM Theater Department Playwriting Contest, Pacific Rim Prize. Contest for residents and non-residents of Hawaii. Play must be set in or deal with the Pacific Islands, the Pacific Rim, or the Pacific/Asian-American experience. Restricted to full-length plays of a minimum of 50 pages in standard form. Write for details. *Award:* Prize for use in freshman, sophomore, junior, senior, graduate, or postgraduate years; not renewable. *Award amount:* $400. *Number of awards:* 1. *Eligibility Requirements:* Applicant must be enrolled or expecting to enroll at an institution or university and must have an interest in writing. Available to U.S. and non-U.S. citizens. *Application Requirements:* Applicant must enter a contest, 3 copies of manuscript. *Deadline:* January 2. **Contact:** Kuma Kahua Playwriting Contest, Kumu Kahua Theatre, 46 Merchant Street, Honolulu, HI 96813. *E-mail:* info@kumukahua.com.

Kumu Kahua Theater/UHM Theater Department Playwriting Contest, Resident Prize. Contest for residents in Hawaii. Play may be any length on any topic. Write for details. *Award:* Prize for use in freshman, sophomore, junior, senior, graduate, or postgraduate years; not renewable. *Award amount:* $200. *Number of awards:* 1. *Eligibility Requirements:* Applicant must be enrolled or expecting to enroll at an institution or university; resident of Hawaii and must have an interest in writing. Available to U.S. citizens. *Application Requirements:* Applicant must enter a contest, 3 copies of manuscript. *Deadline:* January 2. **Contact:** Kuma Kahua Playwriting Contest, Kumu Kahua Theatre, 46 Merchant Street, Honolulu, HI 96813. *E-mail:* info@kumukahua.com.

IDAHO

Education Incentive Loan Forgiveness Contract-Idaho. Renewable award assists Idaho residents enrolling in teacher education or nursing programs within state. Must rank in top 15% of high school graduating class, have a 3.0 GPA or above, and agree to work in Idaho for two years. Deadlines vary. Contact financial aid office at institution of choice. *Academic Fields/Career Goals:* Education; Nursing. *Award:* Forgivable loan for use in freshman, sophomore, junior, or senior year; renewable. *Award amount:* varies. *Number of awards:* 13–45. *Eligibility Requirements:* Applicant must be enrolled or expecting to enroll full-time at a two-year or four-year institution or university; resident of Idaho and studying in Idaho. Applicant must have 3.0 GPA or higher. Available to U.S. citizens. *Application Requirements:* Application, test scores, transcript. *Deadline:* varies. **Contact:** Financial Aid Office, Idaho State Board of Education. *Web site:* www.idahoboardofed.org.

Idaho Minority and "At Risk" Student Scholarship. Renewable award for Idaho residents who are disabled or members of a minority group and have financial need. Must attend one of eight postsecondary institutions in the state for undergraduate study. Deadlines vary by institution. Must be a U.S. citizen and be a graduate of an Idaho high school. Contact college financial aid office. *Award:* Scholarship for use in freshman, sophomore, junior, or senior year; renewable. *Award amount:* $3000. *Number of awards:* 35–40. *Eligibility Requirements:* Applicant must be American Indian/Alaska Native, Black (non-Hispanic), or Hispanic; enrolled or expecting to enroll full-time at a two-year, four-year, or technical institution or university; resident of Idaho and studying in Idaho. Applicant must be hearing impaired, physically disabled, or visually impaired. Available to U.S. citizens. *Application Requirements:* Application, financial need analysis, transcript. *Deadline:* varies. **Contact:** Financial Aid Office, Idaho State Board of Education. *Web site:* www.idahoboardofed.org.

Idaho Promise Category A Scholarship Program. Renewable award available to Idaho residents who are graduating high school seniors. Must attend an approved Idaho institute of higher education full-time. Based on class rank (must be verified by school official), GPA, and ACT scores. Professional-technical student applicants must take COMPASS. *Award:* Scholarship for use in freshman, sophomore, junior, or senior year; renewable. *Award amount:* $3000. *Number of awards:* 25–30. *Eligibility Requirements:* Applicant must be high school student; planning to enroll or expecting to enroll full-time at a two-year, four-year, or technical institution or university; resident of Idaho and studying in Idaho. Applicant must have 3.5 GPA or higher. Available to U.S. citizens. *Application Requirements:* Application, test scores. *Deadline:* December 15. **Contact:** Lynn Humphrey, Manager, Student Aid Programs, Idaho State Board of Education, PO Box 83720, Boise, ID 83720-0037. *E-mail:* lhumphre@osbe.state.id.us. *Phone:* 208-334-2270. *Fax:* 208-334-2632. *Web site:* www.idahoboardofed.org.

Idaho Promise Category B Scholarship Program. Available to Idaho residents entering college for the first time prior to the age of 22. Must have completed high school or its equivalent in Idaho and have a minimum GPA of 3.0 or an ACT score of 20 or higher. Scholarship limited to two years or 4 semesters. *Award:* Scholarship for use in freshman or sophomore year; renewable. *Award amount:* $500. *Number of awards:* varies. *Eligibility Requirements:* Applicant must be age 21 or under; enrolled or expecting to enroll full-time at a two-year, four-year, or technical institution or university; resident of Idaho and studying in Idaho. Applicant must have 3.0 GPA or higher. Available to U.S. citizens. *Application Requirements:* Application, transcript. *Deadline:* continuous. **Contact:** Lynn Humphrey, Manager, Student Aid Programs, Idaho State Board of Education, PO Box 83720, Boise, ID 83720-0037. *Phone:* 208-334-2270. *Fax:* 208-334-2632. *Web site:* www.idahoboardofed.org.

Leveraging Educational Assistance State Partnership Program (LEAP). One-time award assists students attending participating

Idaho trade schools, colleges, and universities majoring in any field except theology or divinity. Must be U.S. citizen or permanent resident, and show financial need. Application deadlines vary by institution. *Award:* Grant for use in freshman, sophomore, junior, senior, or graduate year; not renewable. *Award amount:* $400–$5000. *Number of awards:* varies. *Eligibility Requirements:* Applicant must be enrolled or expecting to enroll full or part-time at a two-year, four-year, or technical institution or university; resident of Idaho and studying in Idaho. Available to U.S. citizens. *Application Requirements:* Application, financial need analysis, self-addressed stamped envelope. *Deadline:* continuous. **Contact:** Lynn Humphrey, Manager, Student Aid Programs, Idaho State Board of Education, PO Box 83720, Boise, ID 83720-0037. *Phone:* 208-334-2270. *Fax:* 208-334-2632. *Web site:* www.idahoboardofed.org.

MONTANA

Indian Student Fee Waiver. Fee waiver awarded by the Montana University System to undergraduate and graduate students meeting the criteria. Amount varies depending upon the tuition and registration fee at each participating college. Students must provide documentation of one-fourth Indian blood or more; must be a resident of Montana for at least one year prior to enrolling in school and must demonstrate financial need. Full-or part-time study qualifies. Complete and submit the FAFSA by March 1 and a Montana Indian Fee Waiver application form. Contact the financial aid office at the college of attendance to determine eligibility. *Award:* Scholarship for use in freshman, sophomore, junior, senior, or graduate year; renewable. *Award amount:* $2000. *Number of awards:* 600. *Eligibility Requirements:* Applicant must be American Indian/Alaska Native; enrolled or expecting to enroll full or part-time at a two-year or four-year institution or university; resident of Montana and studying in Montana. Available to U.S. citizens. *Application Requirements:* Application, financial need analysis, FAFSA. *Deadline:* March 1. **Contact:** Sally Speer, Grants and Scholarship Coordinator, Montana Guaranteed Student Loan Program, Office of Commissioner of Higher Education, 2500 Broadway, PO Box 203101, Helena, MT 59620-3101. *E-mail:* sspeer@mgslp.state.mt.us. *Phone:* 406-444-0638. *Fax:* 406-444-1869. *Web site:* www.mgslp.state.mt.us.

Life Member Montana Federation of Garden Clubs Scholarship. Applicant must be at least a sophomore, majoring in conservation, horticulture, park or forestry, floriculture, greenhouse management, land management, or related subjects. Must be in need of assistance. Must have a potential for a successful future. Must be ranked in upper half of class or have a minimum 2.8 GPA. Must be a Montana resident and all study must be done in Montana. Deadline: May 1. *Academic Fields/Career Goals:* Biology; Earth Science; Horticulture/Floriculture; Landscape Architecture. *Award:* Scholarship for use in sophomore, junior, or senior year; not renewable. *Award amount:* $1000. *Number of awards:* 1. *Eligibility Requirements:* Applicant must be enrolled or expecting to enroll full-time at a four-year institution or university; resident of Montana and studying in Montana. Available to U.S. citizens.*Application Requirements:* Autobiography, financial need analysis, photo, references, transcript. *Deadline:* May 1. **Contact:** Elizabeth Kehmeier, Life Members Scholarship Chairman, Montana Federation of Garden Clubs, 214 Wyant Lane, Hamilton, MT 59840. *E-mail:* elizabethhammt@aol.com. *Phone:* 406-363-5693.

Montana Higher Education Opportunity Grant. This grant is awarded based on need to undergraduate students attending either part-time or full-time who are residents of Montana and attending participating Montana schools. Awards are limited to the most needy students. A specific major or program of study is not required. This grant does not need to be repaid, and students may apply each year. Apply by filing a Free Application for Federal Student Aid by March 1 and contacting the financial aid office at the admitting college. *Award:* Grant for use in freshman, sophomore, junior, or senior year; not renewable. *Award amount:* $400–$600. *Number of awards:* up to 800. *Eligibility Requirements:* Applicant must be enrolled or expecting to enroll full or part-time at a two-year or four-year institution or university; resident of Montana and studying in Montana. Available to U.S. citizens. *Application Requirements:* Financial need analysis, FAFSA. *Deadline:* March 1. **Contact:** Sally Speer, Grants and Scholarship Coordinator, Montana Guaranteed Student Loan Program, Office of Commissioner of Higher Education, 2500 Broadway, PO Box 203101, Helena, MT 59620-3101. *E-mail:* sspeer@mgslp.state.mt.us. *Phone:* 406-444-0638. *Fax:* 406-444-1869. *Web site:* www.mgslp.state.mt.us.

Montana Tuition Assistance Program-Baker Grant. Need-based grant for Montana residents attending participating Montana schools who have earned at least $2,575 during the previous calendar year. Must be enrolled full time. Grant does not need to be repaid. Award covers the first undergraduate degree or certificate. Apply by filing a Free Application for Federal Student Aid by March 1 and contacting the financial aid office at the admitting college. *Award:* Grant for use in freshman, sophomore, junior, or senior year; not renewable. *Award amount:* $100–$1000. *Number of awards:* varies. *Eligibility Requirements:* Applicant must be enrolled or expecting to enroll full-time at a two-year or four-year institution or university; resident of Montana and studying in Montana. Available to U.S. citizens.*Application Requirements:* Financial need analysis, FAFSA. *Deadline:* March 1. **Contact:** Sally Speer, Grants and Scholarship Coordinator, Montana Guaranteed Student Loan Program, Office of Commissioner of Higher Education, 2500 Broadway, PO Box 203101, Helena, MT 59620-3101. *E-mail:* sspeer@mgslp.state.mt.us. *Phone:* 406-444-0638. *Fax:* 406-444-1869. *Web site:* www.mgslp.state.mt.us.

Montana University System Honor Scholarship. Scholarship provides a four-year renewable fee waiver of tuition and registration and is awarded to graduating high school seniors from accredited high schools in Montana. 300-400 scholarships are awarded each year averaging $2,000-$3,000 per recipient. The value of the award varies, depending on the tuition and registration fee at each participating Montana university or college. Must have a minimum 3.5 GPA, meet all college preparatory requirements, and be enrolled in an accredited high school for at least three years prior to graduation. Awarded to highest-ranking student in class attending a participating school. Contact high school counselor to apply. Deadline: January 31. *Award:* Scholarship for use in freshman, sophomore, junior, or senior year; renewable. *Award amount:* $2000–$3000. *Number of awards:* 300–400. *Eligibility Requirements:* Applicant must be high school student; planning to enroll or expecting to enroll full or part-time at a two-year or four-year institution or university; resident of Montana and studying in Montana. Applicant must have 3.5 GPA or higher. Available to U.S. citizens. *Application Requirements:* Application, transcript. *Deadline:* January 31. **Contact:** high school counselor, Montana Guaranteed Student Loan Program, Office of Commissioner of Higher Education. *Web site:* www.mgslp.state.mt.us.

NEVADA

Nevada Student Incentive Grant. Award available to Nevada residents for use at an accredited Nevada college or university. Must show financial need. Any field of study eligible. High school students may not apply. One-time award of up to $5000. Contact financial aid office at local college. *Award:* Grant for use in freshman, sophomore, junior, or senior year; not renewable. *Award amount:* $100–$5000. *Number of awards:* 400–800. *Eligibility Requirements:* Applicant must be enrolled or expecting to enroll full or part-time at a two-year, four-year, or technical institution or university; resident of Nevada and studying in Nevada. Available to U.S. citizens. *Application Requirements:* Application, financial need analysis. *Deadline:* continuous. **Contact:** Financial Aid Office at local college, Nevada Department of Education, 700 East 5th Street, Carson City, NV 89701.

NEW MEXICO

Allied Health Student Loan Program-New Mexico. Renewable loans for New Mexico residents enrolled in an undergraduate allied health program. Loans can be forgiven through service in a medically underserved area or can be repaid. Penalties apply for failure to provide service. May borrow up to $12,000 per year for four years. *Academic Fields/Career Goals:* Dental Health/Services; Health and Medical Sciences; Nursing; Social Sciences; Therapy/Rehabilitation. *Award:* Forgivable loan for use in freshman, sophomore, junior, or senior year; renewable. *Award amount:* up to $12,000. *Number of awards:* 1–40. *Eligibility Requirements:* Applicant must be enrolled or expecting to enroll full or part-time at a two-year or four-year institution or university; resident of New Mexico and studying in New Mexico. Available to U.S. citizens. *Application Requirements:* Application, financial need analysis, transcript, FAFSA. *Deadline:* July 1. **Contact:** Maria Barele, Financial Specialist, New Mexico Commission on Higher Education, PO Box 15910, Santa Fe, NM 87506-5910. *Phone:* 505-827-4026. *Fax:* 505-827-7392. *Web site:* www.nmche.org.

Children of Deceased Veterans Scholarship-New Mexico. Award for New Mexico residents who are children of veterans killed or disabled as a result of service, prisoner of war, or veterans missing-in-action. Must be between ages 16 to 26. For use at New Mexico schools for undergraduate study. Submit parent's death certificate and DD form 214. *Award:* Scholarship for use in freshman, sophomore, junior, or senior year; renewable. *Award amount:* $250–$600. *Eligibility Requirements:* Applicant must be age 16-26; enrolled or expecting to enroll full or part-time at an institution or university; resident of New Mexico and studying in New Mexico. Applicant or parent must meet one or more of the following requirements: general military experience; retired from active duty; disabled or killed as a result of military service; prisoner of war; or missing in action.*Application Requirements:* Application, transcript. *Deadline:* continuous. **Contact:** Alan Martinez, Manager of State Benefits, New Mexico Veterans' Service Commission, PO Box 2324, Sante Fe, NM 87504. *Phone:* 505-827-6300. *Fax:* 505-827-6372. *Web site:* www.state.nm.us/veterans.

Legislative Endowment Scholarships. Awards for undergraduate students with substantial financial need who are attending public postsecondary institutions in New Mexico. Preference given to returning adult students at two-year and four-year institutions and students transferring from two-year to four-year institutions. Deadline set by each institution. Must be resident of New Mexico. Contact financial aid office of any New Mexico public postsecondary institution to apply. *Award:* Scholarship for use in freshman, sophomore, junior, or senior year; not renewable. *Award amount:* $1000–$2500. *Eligibility Requirements:* Applicant must be enrolled or expecting to enroll full or part-time at a two-year or four-year institution or university; resident of New Mexico and studying in New Mexico. Available to U.S. citizens.*Application Requirements:* Application, financial need analysis, FAFSA. **Contact:** Maria Barele, Financial Specialist, New Mexico Commission on Higher Education, PO Box 15910, Santa Fe, NM 87506-5910. *Phone:* 505-827-7383. *Fax:* 505-827-7392. *Web site:* www.nmche.org.

Lottery Success Scholarships. Awards equal to 100% of tuition at New Mexico public postsecondary institution. Must have New Mexico high school degree and be enrolled at New Mexico public college or university in first regular semester following high school graduation. Must obtain 2.5 GPA during this semester. May be eligible for up to eight consecutive semesters of support. Deadlines vary by institution. Apply through financial aid office of any New Mexico public postsecondary institution. *Award:* Scholarship for use in freshman, sophomore, junior, or senior year; renewable. *Eligibility Requirements:* Applicant must be enrolled or expecting to enroll full-time at a two-year or four-year institution; resident of New Mexico and studying in New Mexico. Applicant must have 2.5 GPA or higher. Available to U.S. citizens. *Application Requirements:* Application. **Contact:** Maria Barele, Financial Specialist, New Mexico Commission on Higher Education, PO Box 15910, Santa Fe, NM 87506-5910. *Phone:* 505-827-4026. *Fax:* 505-827-7392. *Web site:* www.nmche.org.

New Mexico Competitive Scholarship. Scholarship available to encourage out-of-state students who have demonstrated high academic achievement to enroll in public institutions of higher education in New Mexico. One-time award for undergraduate students. Deadlines set by each institution. Contact financial aid office of any New Mexico public postsecondary institution to apply. *Award:* Scholarship for use in freshman, sophomore, junior, or senior year; not renewable. *Award amount:* $100. *Eligibility Requirements:* Applicant must be enrolled or expecting to enroll full or part-time at a two-year or four-year institution or university and studying in New Mexico. Applicant must have 3.0 GPA or higher. Available to U.S. citizens. *Application Requirements:* Application, essay, references, test scores. **Contact:** Maria Barele, Financial Specialist, New Mexico Commission on Higher Education, PO Box 15910, Santa Fe, NM 87506-5910. *Phone:* 505-827-4026. *Fax:* 505-827-7392. *Web site:* www.nmche.org.

New Mexico Scholars' Program. Several scholarships to encourage New Mexico high school graduates to enroll in college at a public or selected private nonprofit postsecondary institution in New Mexico before their 22nd birthday. Selected private colleges are College of Santa Fe, St. John's College in Santa Fe, and College of the Southwest. Must have graduated in top 5% of their class or obtained an ACT score of 25 or SAT score of 1140. One-time scholarship for tuition, books, and fees. Contact financial aid office at college to apply. *Award:* Scholarship for use in freshman, sophomore, junior, or senior year; not renewable. *Eligibility Requirements:* Applicant must be age 22 or under; enrolled or expecting to enroll full or part-time at a two-year or four-year institution; resident of New Mexico and studying in New Mexico. Available to U.S. citizens. *Application Requirements:* Application, financial need analysis, test scores, FAFSA. **Contact:** Maria Barele, Financial Specialist, New Mexico Commission on Higher Education, PO Box 15910, Santa Fe, NM 87506-5910. *Phone:* 505-827-4026. *Fax:* 505-827-7392. *Web site:* www.nmche.org.

New Mexico Student Incentive Grant. Several grants available for resident undergraduate students attending public and selected private nonprofit institutions in New Mexico. Must demonstrate financial need. To apply contact financial aid office at any public or private nonprofit postsecondary institution in New Mexico.*Award:* Grant for use in freshman, sophomore, junior, or senior year; not renewable. *Award amount:* $200–$2500. *Eligibility Requirements:* Applicant must be enrolled or expecting to enroll at a two-year or four-year institution or university; resident of New Mexico and studying in New Mexico. Available to U.S. citizens. *Application Requirements:* Application, financial need analysis, FAFSA. **Contact:** Maria Barele, Financial Specialist, New Mexico Commission on Higher Education, PO Box 15910, Santa Fe, NM 87506-5910. *Phone:* 505-827-4026. *Fax:* 505-827-7392. *Web site:* www.nmche.org.

New Mexico Vietnam Veterans' Scholarship. Renewable award for Vietnam veterans who are New Mexico residents attending state-sponsored schools. Must have been awarded the Vietnam Campaign medal. Submit DD214. Must include discharge papers. *Award:* Scholarship for use in freshman, sophomore, junior, or senior year; renewable. *Award amount:* up to $1554. *Eligibility Requirements:* Applicant must be enrolled or expecting to enroll at an institution or university; resident of New Mexico and studying in New Mexico. Available to U.S. citizens. Applicant must have general military experience. *Application Requirements:* Application. *Deadline:* continuous. **Contact:** Alan Martinez, Manager State Benefits, New Mexico Veterans' Service Commission, PO Box 2324, Sante Fe, NM 87504. *Phone:* 505-827-6300. *Fax:* 505-827-6372. *Web site:* www.state.nm.us/veterans.

Nursing Student Loan-For-Service Program. Award for New Mexico residents accepted or enrolled in nursing program at New Mexico public postsecondary institution. Must practice as nurse in designated health professional shortage area in New Mexico. Award dependent upon financial need but may not exceed $12,000. Deadline: July 1. *Academic Fields/Career Goals:* Nursing. *Award:* Forgivable loan for use in freshman, sophomore, junior, or senior year; not renewable. *Award amount:* up to $12,000. *Eligibility Requirements:* Applicant must be enrolled or expecting to enroll full or part-time at a two-year or four-year institution; resident of New Mexico and studying in New Mexico. Available to U.S. citizens. *Application Requirements:* Application, financial need analysis, FAFSA. *Deadline:* July 1. **Contact:** Maria Barele, Financial Specialist, New Mexico Commission on Higher Education, PO Box 15910, Santa Fe, NM 87506-5910. *Phone:* 505-827-4026. *Fax:* 505-827-7392. *Web site:* www.nmche.org.

3% Scholarship Program. Award equal to tuition and required fees for New Mexico residents who are undergraduate students attending public postsecondary institutions in New Mexico. Contact financial aid office of any public postsecondary institution in New Mexico for deadline. *Award:* Scholarship for use in freshman, sophomore, junior, senior, or graduate year; not renewable. *Eligibility Requirements:* Applicant must be enrolled or expecting to enroll full or part-time at a two-year or four-year institution or university; resident of New Mexico and studying in New Mexico. Available to U.S. citizens. *Application Requirements:* Application. **Contact:** Maria Barele, Financial Specialist, New Mexico Commission on Higher Education, PO Box 15910, Santa Fe, NM 87506-5910. *Phone:* 505-827-4026. *Fax:* 505-827-7392. *Web site:* www.nmche.org.

Vietnam Veterans' Scholarship Program. Award for New Mexico residents who are Vietnam veterans enrolled in undergraduate or master's-level course work at public or selected private New Mexico postsecondary institutions. Award may include tuition, required fees, and book allowance. Contact financial aid office of any public or eligible private New Mexico postsecondary institution for deadline.*Award:* Scholarship for use in freshman, sophomore, junior, senior, or graduate year; not renewable. *Eligibility Requirements:* Applicant must be enrolled or expecting to enroll full or part-time at a two-year or four-year institution; resident of New Mexico and studying in New Mexico. Available to U.S. citizens. Applicant must have general military experience. *Application Requirements:* Application, certification by the NM Veteran's commission. **Contact:** Maria Barele, Financial Specialist, New Mexico Commission on Higher Education, PO Box 15910, Santa Fe, NM 87506-5910. *Phone:* 505-827-4026. *Fax:* 505-827-7392. *Web site:* www.nmche.org.

OREGON

American Ex-Prisoner of War Scholarships: Peter Connacher Memorial Scholarship. Renewable award for American prisoners-of-war and their descendants. Written proof of prisoner-of-war status and discharge papers from the U.S. Armed Forces must accompany application. Statement of relationship between applicant and former prisoner-of-war is required. See Web site at http://www.osac.state.or.us for details. *Award:* Scholarship for use in freshman, sophomore, junior, or senior year; renewable. *Award amount:* $1150. *Number of awards:* 4. *Eligibility Requirements:* Applicant must be enrolled or expecting to enroll at a two-year or four-year institution and resident of Oregon. Available to U.S. citizens. Applicant or parent must meet one or more of the following requirements: general military experience; retired from active duty; disabled or killed as a result of military service; prisoner of war; or missing in action. *Application Requirements:* Application, essay, financial need analysis, transcript. *Deadline:* March 1. **Contact:** Director of Grant Programs, Oregon Student Assistance Commission, 1500 Valley River Drive, Suite 100, Eugene, OR 97401-7020. *E-mail:* awardinfo@mercury.osac.state.or.us. *Phone:* 800-452-8807 Ext. 7395. *Web site:* www.osac.state.or.us.

Children, Adult, and Family Services Scholarship. One-time award for graduating high school seniors, GED recipients, and college students currently or formerly in foster care or an Independent Living Program (ILP) financially supported through the Oregon State Office for Services to Children and Families. Must attend an Oregon public college. Visit Web site for more details (http://www.osac.state.or.us). Award varies between $500-$5000. *Award:* Scholarship for use in freshman, sophomore, junior, senior, or graduate year; not renewable. *Award amount:* $500–$5000. *Number of awards:* varies. *Eligibility Requirements:* Applicant must be enrolled or expecting to enroll at a two-year or four-year institution; resident of Oregon and studying in Oregon. Available to U.S. citizens. *Application Requirements:* Application, essay, financial need analysis, references, transcript, activity chart. *Deadline:* March 1. **Contact:** Director of Grant Programs, Oregon Student Assistance Commission, 1500 Valley River Drive, Suite 100, Eugene, OR 97401-7020. *E-mail:* awardinfo@mercury.osac.state.or.us. *Phone:* 800-452-8807 Ext. 7395. *Web site:* www.osac.state.or.us.

Dorothy Campbell Memorial Scholarship. Renewable award for female Oregon high school senior with a minimum 2.75 GPA. Must submit essay describing strong, continuing interest in golf and the contribution that sport has made to applicant's development. *Award:* Scholarship for use in freshman, sophomore, junior, or senior year; renewable. *Award amount:* $1500. *Number of awards:*

2. *Eligibility Requirements:* Applicant must be high school student; planning to enroll or expecting to enroll at a four-year institution; female; resident of Oregon; studying in Oregon and must have an interest in golf. Available to U.S. citizens. *Application Requirements:* Application, essay, financial need analysis, test scores, transcript, activity chart. *Deadline:* March 1. **Contact:** Director of Grant Programs, Oregon Student Assistance Commission, 1500 Valley River Drive, Suite 100, Eugene, OR 97401-7020. *E-mail:* awardinfo@mercury.osac.state.or.us. *Phone:* 800-452-8807 Ext. 7395. *Web site:* www.osac.state.or.us.

Glenn Jackson Scholars Scholarships (OCF). Award for graduating high school seniors who are dependents of employees or retirees of Oregon Department of Transportation or Parks and Recreation Department. Employees must have worked in their department at least three years. Award for maximum twelve undergraduate quarters or six quarters at a two-year institution. Must be U.S. citizen or permanent resident. Visit Web site (http://www.osac.state.or.us) for more details. *Award:* Scholarship for use in freshman, sophomore, junior, or senior year; renewable. *Award amount:* $2500. *Number of awards:* 2. *Eligibility Requirements:* Applicant must be high school student; planning to enroll or expecting to enroll at a four-year institution and resident of Oregon. Applicant or parent of applicant must be affiliated with Oregon Department of Transportation Parks and Recreation. Applicant or parent of applicant must have employment or volunteer experience in designated career field. Available to U.S. citizens. *Application Requirements:* Application, essay, financial need analysis, references, transcript, activity chart. *Deadline:* March 1. **Contact:** Director of Grant Programs, Oregon Student Assistance Commission, 1500 Valley River Drive, Suite 100, Eugene, OR 97401-7020. *E-mail:* awardinfo@mercury.osac.state.or.us. *Phone:* 800-452-8807 Ext. 7395. *Web site:* www.osac.state.or.us.

Lawrence R. Foster Memorial Scholarship. One-time award to students enrolled or planning to enroll in a public health degree program. First preference given to those working in the public health field and those pursuing a graduate degree in public health. Undergraduates entering junior or senior year health programs may apply if seeking a public health career, and not private practice. Prefer applicants from diverse cultures. Must provide 3 references. Additional essay required. Must be resident of Oregon. *Academic Fields/Career Goals:* Health and Medical Sciences. *Award:* Scholarship for use in junior, senior, graduate, or postgraduate years; not renewable. *Award amount:* $4167. *Number of awards:* 6. *Eligibility Requirements:* Applicant must be enrolled or expecting to enroll at a four-year institution and resident of Oregon. Available to U.S. citizens. *Application Requirements:* Application, essay, financial need analysis, references, transcript, activity chart. *Deadline:* March 1. **Contact:** Director of Grant Programs, Oregon Student Assistance Commission, 1500 Valley River Drive, Suite 100, Eugene, OR 97401-7020. *E-mail:* awardinfo@mercury.osac.state.or.us. *Phone:* 800-452-8807 Ext. 7395. *Web site:* www.osac.state.or.us.

Oregon Occupational Safety and Health Division Workers Memorial Scholarship. Available to Oregon residents who are the dependents or spouses of an Oregon worker who was killed or permanently disabled on the job. Submit essay of 500 words or less titled "How has the injury or death of your parent or spouse affected or influenced your decision to further your education?" See Web site for more details. (http://www.osac.state.or.us)*Award:* Scholarship for use in freshman, sophomore, junior, senior, or graduate year; not renewable. *Award amount:* $4786. *Number of awards:* 1. *Eligibility Requirements:* Applicant must be enrolled or expecting to enroll at a two-year or four-year institution and resident of Oregon. Applicant or parent of applicant must have employment or volunteer experience in designated career field. Available to U.S. citizens. *Application Requirements:* Application, essay, financial need analysis, test scores, transcript, workers compensation claim number. *Deadline:* March 1. **Contact:** Director of Grant Programs, Oregon Student Assistance Commission, 1500 Valley River Drive, Suite 100, Eugene, OR 97401-7020. *E-mail:* awardinfo@mercury.osac.state.or.us. *Phone:* 800-452-8807 Ext. 7395. *Web site:* www.osac.state.or.us.

Oregon Scholarship Fund Community College Student Award. Scholarship open to Oregon residents enrolled or planning to enroll in Oregon community college programs. May apply for one additional year. *Award:* Scholarship for use in freshman or sophomore year; not renewable. *Award amount:* $500. *Number of awards:* varies. *Eligibility Requirements:* Applicant must be enrolled or expecting to enroll at a two-year institution; resident of Oregon and studying in Oregon. Available to U.S. citizens. *Application Requirements:* Application, essay, financial need analysis, transcript, activity chart. *Deadline:* March 1. **Contact:** Director of Grant Programs, Oregon Student Assistance Commission, 1500 Valley River Drive, Suite 100, Eugene, OR 97401-7020. *E-mail:* awardinfo@mercury.osac.state.or.us. *Phone:* 800-452-8807 Ext. 7395. *Web site:* www.osac.state.or.us.

Oregon Scholarship Fund Transfer Student Award. Award open to Oregon residents who are currently enrolled in their second year at a community college and are planning to transfer to a four-year college in Oregon. Prior recipients may apply for one additional year. *Award:* Scholarship for use in junior or senior year; not renewable. *Award amount:* $500. *Number of awards:* varies. *Eligibility Requirements:* Applicant must be enrolled or expecting to enroll at a four-year institution; resident of Oregon and studying in Oregon. Available to U.S. citizens.*Application Requirements:* Application, essay, financial need analysis, transcript, activity chart. *Deadline:* March 1. **Contact:** Director of Grant Programs, Oregon Student Assistance Commission, 1500 Valley River Drive, Suite 100, Eugene, OR 97401-7020. *E-mail:* awardinfo@mercury.osac.state.or.us. *Phone:* 800-452-8807 Ext. 7395. *Web site:* www.osac.state.or.us.

Oregon Student Assistance Commission Employee and Dependent Scholarship. One-time award for current permanent employee of the Oregon Student Assistance Commission or legally dependent children of employee. Also available to dependent children of an employee who retires, is permanently disabled, or deceased directly from employment at OSAC. Dependent must enroll full time. Employee may enroll part time. *Award:* Scholarship for use in freshman, sophomore, junior, or senior year; not renewable. *Award amount:* $500. *Number of awards:* 7. *Eligibility Requirements:* Applicant must be enrolled or expecting to enroll full or part-time at an institution or university and resident of Oregon. *Application Requirements:* Application, essay, financial need analysis, transcript. *Deadline:* March 1. **Contact:** Director of Grant Programs, Oregon Student Assistance Commission, 1500 Valley River Drive, Suite 100, Eugene, OR 97401-7020. *E-mail:* awardinfo@mercury.osac.state.or.us. *Phone:* 800-452-8807 Ext. 7395. *Web site:* www.osac.state.or.us.

Oregon Trucking Association Scholarship. One scholarship available to a child of an Oregon Trucking Association member, or child of employee of member. Applicants must be Oregon residents who are graduating high school seniors from an Oregon high school. One-time award. *Award:* Scholarship for use in freshman year; not renewable. *Award amount:* $750. *Number of awards:* 4. *Eligibility Requirements:* Applicant must be high school student; planning to enroll or expecting to enroll at a four-year institution and resident of Oregon. Applicant or parent of applicant must have employment or volunteer experience in designated career field. Available to U.S. citizens. *Application Requirements:* Application, essay, financial need analysis, references, transcript, activity chart. *Deadline:* March 1. **Contact:** Director of Grant Programs, Oregon Student Assistance Commission, 1500 Valley River Drive, Suite 100, Eugene, OR 97401-7020. *E-mail:* awardinfo@mercury.osac.state.or.us. *Phone:* 800-452-8807 Ext. 7395. *Web site:* www.osac.state.or.us.

Oregon Veterans' Education Aid. To be eligible, veteran must have served in U.S. armed forces 90 days and been discharged under honorable conditions; U.S. citizen and Oregon resident; Korean War veteran or received campaign or expeditionary medal or ribbon awarded by U.S. armed forces for services after June 30, 1958. Full-time students receive $50/month, part-time students receive $35/month.*Award:* Grant for use in freshman, sophomore, junior, senior, graduate, or postgraduate years; renewable. *Award amount:* varies. *Number of awards:* varies. *Eligibility Requirements:* Applicant must be enrolled or expecting to enroll full or part-time at a two-year, four-year, or technical institution or university; resident of Oregon and studying in Oregon. Available to U.S. citizens. Applicant must have general military experience. *Application Requirements:* Application, certified copy of DD Form 214. *Deadline:* continuous. **Contact:** Ruth Sherman, Educational Aid Coordinator, Oregon Department of Veterans' Affairs, 700 Summer Street, NE, Salem, OR 97301-1289. *E-mail:* shermar@odva.state.or.us. *Phone:* 503-373-2085. *Fax:* 503-373-2392. *Web site:* www.odva.state.or.us.

UTAH

Leveraging Educational Assistance Partnership (LEAP). Available to students with substantial financial need for use at participating Utah schools. Contact Financial Aid Office of specific school for application requirements and deadlines. Must be Utah resident. *Award:* Grant for use in freshman, sophomore, junior, or senior year; renewable. *Award amount:* up to $2500. *Number of awards:* up to 3000. *Eligibility Requirements:* Applicant must be enrolled or expecting to enroll full or part-time at a two-year, four-year, or technical institution or university; resident of Utah and studying in Utah. Available to U.S. citizens. *Application Requirements:* Application, financial need analysis. *Deadline:* continuous. **Contact:** Financial Aid Office, Utah State Board of Regents. *Web site:* www.uheaa.org.

T.H. Bell Teaching Incentive Loan-Utah. Renewable awards for Utah residents who are high school seniors and wish to pursue teaching careers. Award pays for tuition and fees at a Utah institution. Must agree to teach in a Utah public school or pay back loan through monthly installments. Must be a U.S. citizen. *Academic Fields/Career Goals:* Education; Special Education. *Award:* Forgivable loan for use in freshman, sophomore, junior, or senior year; renewable. *Award amount:* varies. *Number of awards:* 25. *Eligibility Requirements:* Applicant must be high school student; planning to enroll or expecting to enroll full-time at a two-year or four-year institution or university; resident of Utah and studying in Utah. Available to U.S. citizens. *Application Requirements:* Application, essay, test scores, transcript. *Deadline:* March 29. **Contact:** Diane DeMan, Executive Secretary, Utah State Office of Education, 250 East 500 South, Salt Lake City, UT 84111. *Phone:* 801-538-7741. *Fax:* 801-538-7973. *Web site:* www.usoe.k12.ut.us/cert/scholarships/scholars.htm.

Utah Centennial Opportunity Program for Education. Renewable awards for undergraduate college student in Utah institution. Must be a Utah resident. Contact financial aid office at participating institutions for more information. *Award:* Scholarship for use in freshman, sophomore, junior, or senior year; renewable. *Award amount:* $300–$5000. *Number of awards:* varies. *Eligibility Requirements:* Applicant must be enrolled or expecting to enroll at a two-year or four-year institution; resident of Utah and studying in Utah. Available to U.S. citizens. *Application Requirements:* Application. *Deadline:* varies. **Contact:** Lynda Reid, Administrative Officer, Utah State Board of Regents, 60 South 400 West, The Board of Regents Building, The Gateway, Salt Lake City, UT 84101-1284. *Phone:* 801-321-7207. *Fax:* 801-321-7299. *Web site:* www.uheaa.org.

Utah Educationally Disadvantaged Program. Renewable award for residents of Utah who are disadvantaged and attending an eligible institution in Utah. Must demonstrate need and satisfactory progress. Contact financial aid office of participating institution. *Award:* Scholarship for use in freshman, sophomore, junior, or senior year; renewable. *Award amount:* varies. *Number of awards:* varies. *Eligibility Requirements:* Applicant must be enrolled or expecting to enroll at a two-year or four-year institution; resident of Utah and studying in Utah. Applicant must be hearing impaired, learning disabled, physically disabled, or visually impaired.*Application Requirements:* Application. *Deadline:* continuous. **Contact:** Lynda Reid, Administrative Officer, Utah State Board of Regents, 60 South 400 West, The Board of Regents Building, The Gateway, Salt Lake City, UT 84101-1284. *Phone:* 801-321-7207. *Fax:* 801-321-7299. *Web site:* www.uheaa.org.

Utah Tuition Waiver. Renewable awards ranging from partial to full tuition waivers at eligible Utah institutions. A limited number of waivers are available for nonresidents. Deadlines vary by institutions. Contact Financial Aid Office. *Award:* Scholarship for use in freshman, sophomore, junior, senior, or graduate year; renewable. *Award amount:* varies. *Number of awards:* varies. *Eligibility Requirements:* Applicant must be enrolled or expecting to enroll full or part-time at a two-year or four-year institution and studying in Utah. Available to U.S. and non-U.S. citizens. *Application Requirements:* Application, financial need analysis, interview. *Deadline:* varies. **Contact:** Lynda Reid, Administrative Officer, Utah State Board of Regents, 60 South 400 West, The Board of Regents Building, The Gateway, Salt Lake City, UT 84101-1284. *Phone:* 801-321-7207. *Fax:* 801-321-7299. *Web site:* www.uheaa.org.

WASHINGTON

American Indian Endowed Scholarship. Awarded to financially needy undergraduate and graduate students with close social and cultural ties to a Native-American community. Must be Washington resident, enrolled full time at Washington School. Deadline is May 15. *Award:* Scholarship for use in freshman, sophomore, junior, senior, or graduate year; renewable. *Award amount:* $1000–$2000. *Number of awards:* up to 15. *Eligibility Requirements:* Applicant must be American Indian/Alaska Native; enrolled or expecting to enroll full-time at a two-year, four-year, or technical institution or university; resident of Washington and studying in Washington. Available to U.S. citizens. *Application Requirements:* Application, financial need analysis. *Deadline:* May 15. **Contact:** Ann Lee,

Washington Higher Education Coordinating Board, 917 Lakeridge Way SW, PO Box 43430, Olympia, WA 98504-3430. *E-mail:* annl@hecb.wa.gov. *Phone:* 360-755-7843. *Fax:* 360-753-7808. *Web site:* www.hecb.wa.gov.

Educational Opportunity Grant. Annual grants of $2500 to encourage financially needy, placebound students to complete bachelor's degree. Must be unable to continue education due to family or work commitments, health concerns, financial needs, or similar. Must be Washington residents, live in one of 13 designated counties, and have completed two years of college. Grant only used at eligible four-year colleges in Washington. Applications accepted beginning in April and following months until funds are depleted. *Award:* Grant for use in junior or senior year; not renewable. *Award amount:* $2500. *Number of awards:* varies. *Eligibility Requirements:* Applicant must be enrolled or expecting to enroll at a four-year institution or university; resident of Washington and studying in Washington. Available to U.S. citizens. *Application Requirements:* Application, financial need analysis. *Deadline:* varies. **Contact:** Betty Gebhardt, Washington Higher Education Coordinating Board, 917 Lakeridge Way SW, PO Box 43430, Olympia, WA 98504-3430. *E-mail:* bettyg@hecb.wa.gov. *Phone:* 360-753-7852. *Fax:* 360-753-7808. *Web site:* www.hecb.wa.gov.

State Need Grant. Grants for undergraduate students with significant financial need. Must be Washington resident and attend school in Washington. Must have family income equal or less than 55% of state median. *Award:* Grant for use in freshman, sophomore, junior, or senior year; not renewable. *Award amount:* $1900–$4300. *Number of awards:* varies. *Eligibility Requirements:* Applicant must be enrolled or expecting to enroll full or part-time at a two-year, four-year, or technical institution or university; resident of Washington and studying in Washington. Available to U.S. citizens. *Application Requirements:* Application, financial need analysis. *Deadline:* continuous. **Contact:** Colleen Scovill, Washington Higher Education Coordinating Board, 917 Lakeridge Way SW, PO Box 43430, Olympia, WA 98504-3430. *E-mail:* colleens@hecb.wa.gov. *Phone:* 360-753-7850. *Fax:* 360-753-7808. *Web site:* www.hecb.wa.gov.

Washington Award for Vocational Excellence. Tuition-only award for those completing a vocational education program as graduating seniors or community/technical college students who have completed first year of a two-year program. The scholarship is for 6 quarters or 4 semesters. Three are awarded in each of 49 legislative districts in the state. Must be a Washington State resident attending a postsecondary institution in Washington State. *Award:* Grant for use in freshman, sophomore, junior, or senior year; renewable. *Award amount:* $4284–$9498. *Number of awards:* 147. *Eligibility Requirements:* Applicant must be enrolled or expecting to enroll full or part-time at a two-year, four-year, or technical institution or university; resident of Washington and studying in Washington. Available to U.S. and non-U.S. citizens. *Application Requirements:* Application, essay, references. *Deadline:* March 1. **Contact:** Lee Williams, Program Administrator, Washington State Workforce Training and Education Coordinating Board, 128 Tenth Avenue SW, PO Box 43105, Olympia, WA 98504-3105. *E-mail:* lwilliams@wtb.wa.gov. *Phone:* 360-586-3321. *Fax:* 360-586-5862. *Web site:* www.wtb.wa.gov/wave-abt.html.

Washington Award for Vocational Excellence (WAVE). Award to honor three vocational students from each of the state's 49 legislative districts. Grants for up to two years of undergraduate resident tuition. Must be enrolled in Washington high school, skills center, or technical college at time of application. Complete 360 hours in single vocational program in high school or one year at technical college. Contact principal or guidance counselor for more information. *Award:* Grant for use in freshman, sophomore, junior, or senior year; renewable. *Award amount:* varies. *Number of awards:* varies. *Eligibility Requirements:* Applicant must be enrolled or expecting to enroll full-time at a two-year, four-year, or technical institution or university; resident of Washington and studying in Washington. Available to U.S. citizens. *Application Requirements: Deadline:* continuous. **Contact:** Ann Lee, Program Manager, Washington Higher Education Coordinating Board, 917 Lakeridge Way, SW, PO Box 43430, Olympia, WA 98504-3430. *E-mail:* annl@hecb.wa.gov. *Phone:* 360-753-7843. *Fax:* 360-753-7808. *Web site:* www.hecb.wa.gov.

Washington National Guard Scholarship Program. A state funded retention incentive/loan program for both Washington Army and Air Guard members meeting all eligibility requirements. The loans are forgiven if the soldier/airman completes their service requirements. Failure to meet/complete service obligations incurs the requirement to repay the loan plus 8% interest. Minimum 2.5 GPA required. Deadline is April 30. *Award:* Forgivable loan for use in freshman, sophomore, junior, or senior year; not renewable. *Award amount:* $200–$4000. *Number of awards:* varies. *Eligibility Requirements:* Applicant must be enrolled or expecting to enroll full or part-time at a two-year, four-year, or technical institution or university and resident of Washington. Applicant must have 2.5 GPA or higher. Available to U.S. and non-U.S. citizens. Applicant must have served in the Air Force National Guard or Army National Guard. *Application Requirements:* Application, transcript, enlistment/extension documents. *Deadline:* April 30. **Contact:** Mark M. Rhoden, Educational Services Officer, Washington National Guard, Building 15, Camp Murray, Tacoma, WA 98430-5073. *E-mail:* mark.rhoden@wa.ngb.army.mil. *Phone:* 253-512-8899. *Fax:* 253-512-8936. *Web site:* www.washingtonguard.com/education/education.htm.

Washington Promise Scholarship. College scholarships to low- and middle-income students in high school. Must either rank in top 15 percent of senior class or score a combined 1200 on SAT or 27 on ACT on first attempt. Family income cannot exceed 135% of state median family income. Must be Washington resident, attend a Washington school. School must identify applicants. Contact principal or guidance counselor for more information. *Award:* Scholarship for use in freshman or sophomore year; renewable. *Award amount:* up to $1000. *Number of awards:* varies. *Eligibility Requirements:* Applicant must be high school student; planning to enroll or expecting to enroll full or part-time at a two-year, four-year, or technical institution or university; resident of Washington and studying in Washington. Available to U.S. citizens. *Application Requirements:* Financial need analysis. *Deadline:* continuous. **Contact:** John Klacik, Washington Higher Education Coordinating Board, 917 Lakeridge Way SW, PO Box 43430, Olympia, WA 98504-3430. *E-mail:* johnk@hecb.wa.gov. *Phone:* 360-753-7851. *Fax:* 360-753-7808. *Web site:* www.hecb.wa.gov.

Washington Scholars Program. Awarded to three high school students from each of the 49 state legislative districts. Must be Washington resident and enroll in college or university in Washington. Scholarships equal up to four years of full-time resident undergraduate tuition and fees. Contact principal or guidance counselor for more information. *Award:* Grant for use in freshman, sophomore, junior, or senior year; renewable. *Award amount:* varies. *Number of awards:* varies. *Eligibility Requirements:* Applicant must be high school student; planning to enroll or expecting to enroll full-time at a four-year institution or university; resident of Washington and studying in Washington. Available to U.S. citizens. *Application Requirements: Deadline:* continuous. **Contact:** Ann Lee, Program Manager, Washington Higher Education Coordinating Board, 917 Lakeridge Way SW, PO Box 43430, Olympia, WA 98504-3430. *E-mail:* annl@hecb.wa.gov. *Phone:* 360-753-7843. *Fax:* 360-753-7808. *Web site:* www.hecb.wa.gov.

WYOMING

Douvas Memorial Scholarship. Available to Wyoming residents who are first-generation Americans. Must be between 18-22 years old. Must be used at any Wyoming public institution of higher education for study in freshman year. *Award:* Scholarship for use in freshman year; not renewable. *Award amount:* $500. *Number of awards:* 1. *Eligibility Requirements:* Applicant must be age 18-22; enrolled or expecting to enroll at a two-year or four-year institution or university; resident of Wyoming and studying in Wyoming. Available to U.S. citizens. *Application Requirements:* Application. *Deadline:* April 18. **Contact:** Gerry Maas, Director, Health and Safety, Wyoming Department of Education, 2300 Capitol Avenue, Hathaway Building, 2nd Floor, Cheyenne, WY 82002-0050. *E-mail:* gmaas@educ.state.wy.us. *Phone:* 307-777-6282. *Fax:* 307-777-6234.

Superior Student in Education Scholarship-Wyoming. Available to Wyoming high school graduates who have demonstrated high academic achievement and plan to teach in Wyoming public schools. Award is for tuition at Wyoming institutions. Must maintain 3.0 GPA. *Academic Fields/Career Goals:* Education. *Award:* Scholarship for use in freshman, sophomore, junior, or senior year; renewable. *Award amount:* varies. *Number of awards:* 16–80. *Eligibility Requirements:* Applicant must be enrolled or expecting to enroll full-time at a two-year or four-year institution or university; resident of Wyoming and studying in Wyoming. Applicant must have 3.0 GPA or higher. Available to U.S. citizens. *Application Requirements:* Application, references, test scores, transcript. *Deadline:* October 31. **Contact:** Joel Anne Berrigan, Assistant Director, Scholarships, State of Wyoming, administered by University of Wyoming, Student Financial Aid, Department 3335, 1000 East University Avenue, Laramie, WY 82071-3335. *E-mail:* finaid@uwyo.edu. *Phone:* 307-766-2117. *Fax:* 307-766-3800. *Web site:* www.uwyo.edu/scholarships.

Vietnam Veterans Award/Wyoming. Available to Wyoming residents who served in the armed forces between August 5, 1964, and May 7, 1975, and received a Vietnam service medal. Award is free tuition at the University of Wyoming or a state (WY) community college. *Award:* Scholarship for use in freshman, sophomore, junior, or senior year; renewable. *Award amount:* varies. *Number of awards:* varies. *Eligibility Requirements:* Applicant must be enrolled or expecting to enroll full or part-time at a two-year or four-year institution or university; resident of Wyoming and studying in Wyoming. Available to U.S. citizens. Applicant must have general military experience. *Application Requirements:* Application. *Deadline:* continuous. **Contact:** Joel Anne Berrigan, Assistant Director, Scholarships, State of Wyoming, administered by University of Wyoming, Student Financial Aid, Department 3335, 1000 East University Avenue, Laramie, WY 82071-3335. *E-mail:* finaid@uwyo.edu. *Phone:* 307-766-2117. *Fax:* 307-766-3800. *Web site:* www.uwyo.edu/scholarships.

Searching for Four-Year Colleges Online

The Internet can be a great tool for gathering information about four-year colleges and universities. There are many worthwhile sites that are ready to help guide you through the various aspects of the selection process, including Peterson's Undergraduate Channel at www.petersons.com/ugchannel.

HOW PETERSON'S UNDERGRADUATE CHANNEL CAN HELP

Choosing a college involves a serious commitment of time and resources. Therefore, it is important to have the most up-to-date information about prospective schools at your fingertips. That is why Peterson's Undergraduate Channel is a great place to start your college search and selection process.

Find a College

Peterson's Undergraduate Channel is a comprehensive information resource that will help you make sense of the college admissions process. Peterson's Undergraduate Channel offers visitors enhanced search criteria and an easily navigable interface. The Channel is organized into various sections that make finding a program easy and fun. You can search for colleges based on name or location for starters, or do a detailed search on the following criteria:

- *Location*
- *Major*
- *Tuition*
- *Size*
- *Student/faculty ratio*
- *Average GPA*
- *Type of college*
- *Sports*
- *Religion*

Once you have found the school of your choice, simply click on it to get information about the institution, including majors, off-campus programs, costs, faculty, admission requirements, location, academic programs, academic facilities, athletics, student life, financial aid, student government, and application information and contacts.

E-mail the School

If, after looking at the information provided on Peterson's Undergraduate Channel, you still have questions, you can send an e-mail directly to the admissions department of the school. Just click on the "E-mail the School" button and send your message. In most instances, if you keep your questions short and to the point, you will receive an answer in no time at all.

School Web Site

For institutions that have provided information about their Web sites, simply click on the "School Web Site" button and you will be taken directly to that institution's Web page. Once you arrive at the school's Web site, look around and get a feel for the place. Often, schools offer virtual tours of the campus, complete with photos and commentary. If you have specific questions about the school, a visit to a school's Web site will often yield an answer.

Detailed Description

If the schools you are interested in have provided Peterson's with an **In-Depth Description,** you can do a keyword search on that description. Here, schools are given the opportunity to communicate unique features of their programs to prospective students.

Microsite

Several educational institutions provide students access to microsites, where more information about the types of resources and services offered can be found. In addition, students can take campus tours, apply for admissions, and explore academic majors.

Apply

The Apply link gives you the ability to directly apply to the school online.

Add to My List

The My List feature is designed to help you with your college planning. Here you can save the list of schools you're interested in, which you can then revisit at any time, access all the features of the site, and be reminded of important dates. You'll also be notified when new features are added to the site.

Get Recruited

Here's your chance to stop looking for colleges and let them find you with CollegesWantYou℠ (www.collegeswantyou.com), the new approach to the search and selection process. Unlike other college search and selection tools, CollegesWantYou℠ allows you to enter information on your preferences, test scores, and extracurricular activities into the online form, and before you know it, colleges that meet your specifications will be in touch with you. Registration is free, and all you need to do is complete a short profile indicating your preferences and then sit back and wait as colleges contact you directly!

Write Admissions Essays

This year, 500,000 college applicants will write 500,000 different admissions essays. Half will be rejected by their first-choice school, while only an 11 eleven percent will gain admission to the nation's most selective colleges. With acceptance rates at all-time lows, setting yourself apart requires more than just blockbuster SAT scores and impeccable transcripts--it requires the perfect application essay. Named "the world's premier application essay editing service" by the New York Times Learning Network and "one of the best essay services on the Internet" by the *Washington Post*, EssayEdge (www.essayedge.com) has helped more applicants write successful personal statements than any other company in the world. Learn more about EssayEdge and how it can give you an edge over hundreds of applicants with comparable academic credentials.

Practice for Your Test

At Peterson's, we understand that the college admissions process can be very stressful. With the stakes so high and the competition getting tighter every year, it's easy to feel like the process is out of your control. Fortunately, preparing for college admissions tests like the SAT, ACT, and PSAT helps you exert some control over the options you will have available to you. You can visit Peterson's Test Prep Channel (www.petersonstestprep.com) to learn more about how Peterson's can help you maximize your scores—and your options.

USE THE TOOLS TO YOUR ADVANTAGE

Choosing a college is an involved and complicated process. The tools available to you on www.petersons.com/ugchannel can help you to be more productive in this process. So, what are you waiting for? Fire up your computer; your future alma mater may be just a click away!

How to Use This Guide

This article provides an outline of the profile format, describing the items covered. All college information presented was supplied to Peterson's by the colleges themselves. Any item that does not apply to a particular college or for which no information was supplied is omitted from that college's profile. Colleges that were unable to supply usable data in time for publication are listed by name and, if available, address.

PROFILES OF COLLEGES IN THE WEST

This section presents pertinent factual and statistical data for each college in a standard format for easy comparison.

General Information

The first paragraph gives a brief introduction to the college, covering the following elements.

Type of student body: The categories are *men's* (100 percent of the student body), *primarily men's*, *women's* (100 percent of the student body), *primarily women's*, and *coed*. A college may also be designated as coordinate with another institution, indicating that there are separate colleges or campuses for men and women, but facilities, courses, and institutional governance are shared.

Institutional control: A *public* college receives its funding wholly or primarily from the federal, state, and/or local government. The term *private* indicates an independent, nonprofit institution, that is, one whose funding comes primarily from private sources and tuition. This category includes independent, religious colleges, which may also specify a particular religious denomination or church affiliation. Profit-making institutions are designated as *proprietary*.

Institutional type: A *two-year college* awards associate degrees and/or offers the first two years of a bachelor's degree program. A *primarily two-year college* awards bachelor's degrees, but the vast majority of students are enrolled in two-year programs. A *four-year college* awards bachelor's degrees and may also award associate degrees, but it does not offer graduate (postbachelor's) degree programs. A *five-year college* offers a five-year bachelor's program in a professional field such as architecture or pharmacy but does not award graduate degrees. An *upper-level institution* awards bachelor's degrees, but entering students must have at least two years of previous college-level credit; it may also offer graduate degree programs. A *comprehensive institution* awards bachelor's degrees and may also award associate degrees; graduate degree programs are offered primarily at the master's, specialist's, or professional level, although one or two doctoral programs may also be offered. A *university* offers four years of undergraduate work plus graduate degrees through the doctorate in more than two academic and/or professional fields.

Founding date: This is the year the college came into existence or was chartered, reflecting the period during which it has existed as an educational institution, regardless of subsequent mergers or other organizational changes.

Degree levels: An *associate* degree program may consist of either a college-transfer program, equivalent to the first two years of a bachelor's degree, or a one- to three-year terminal program that provides training for a specific occupation. A *bachelor's* degree program represents a three- to five-year liberal arts, science, professional, or preprofessional program. A *master's* degree is the first graduate degree in the liberal arts and sciences and certain professional fields and usually requires one to two years of full-time study. A *doctoral* degree is the highest degree awarded in research-oriented academic disciplines and usually requires from three to six years of full-time graduate study; the *first professional* degrees in such fields as law and medicine are also at the doctoral level. For colleges that award degrees in one field only, such as art or music, the field of specialization is indicated.

Campus setting: This indicates the size of the campus in acres or hectares and its location.

Academic Information

This paragraph contains information on the following items.

Faculty: The number of full-time and part-time faculty members as of fall 2003 is given, followed by the percentage of the full-time faculty members who hold doctoral, first professional, or terminal degrees and the student-faculty ratio. (Not all colleges calculate the student-faculty ratio in the same way; Peterson's prints the ratio as provided by the college.)

Library holdings: The numbers of books, serials, and audiovisual materials in the college's collections are listed.

Special programs: *Academic remediation for entering students* consists of instructional courses designed for students deficient in the general competencies necessary for a regular postsecondary curriculum and educational setting. *Services for LD students* include special help for learning-disabled students with resolvable difficulties, such as dyslexia. *Honors programs* are any special programs for very able students offering the opportunity for educational enrichment, independent study, acceleration, or some combination of these. *Cooperative (co-op) education programs* are formal arrangements with off-campus employers allowing students to combine work and study in order to gain degree-related experience, usually extending the time required to complete a degree. *Study abroad* is an arrangement by which a student completes part of the academic program studying in another country. A college may operate a campus abroad or it may have a cooperative agreement with other U.S. institutions or institutions in other countries. *Advanced placement* gives credit toward a degree awarded for acceptable scores on College Board Advanced Placement tests. *Accelerated degree programs* allow students to earn a bachelor's degree in three academic years. *Freshmen honors college* is a separate academic program for talented freshmen. *Tutorials* allow undergraduates to arrange for special in-depth academic assignments (not for remediation) working with faculty members one-on-one or in small groups. *English as a second language (ESL)* is a course of study designed specifically for students whose native language is not English. *Double major* consists of a program of study in which a student concurrently completes the requirements of two majors. *Independent study* consists of academic work, usually undertaken outside the regular classroom structure, chosen or designed by the student with the departmental approval and instructor supervision. *Distance learning* consists of credit courses that can be accessed off campus via cable television, the Internet, satellite, videotapes, correspondence courses, or other media. *Self-designed major* is a program of study based on individual interests, designed by the student with the assistance of an adviser. *Summer session for credit* includes summer courses through which students may make up degree work or accelerate their program. *Part-time degree programs* offer students the ability to earn a degree through part-time enrollment in regular session (daytime) classes or evening, weekend, or summer classes. *External degree programs* are programs of study in which students earn credits toward a degree through a combination of independent study, college courses, proficiency examinations, and personal experience. External degree programs require minimal or no classroom attendance. *Adult/continuing education programs* are courses offered for nontraditional students who are currently working or are returning to formal education. *Internships* are any short-term, supervised work experience usually related to a student's major field, for which the student earns academic credit. The work can be full- or part-time, on or off campus, paid or unpaid. *Off-campus study* is a formal arrangement with one or more domestic institutions under which students may take courses at the other institution(s) for credit.

Most popular majors: The most popular field or fields of study at the college, in terms of the number of undergraduate degrees conferred in 2003, are listed.

Student Body Statistics

Enrollment: The total number of students, undergraduates, and freshmen (or entering students for an upper-level institution) enrolled in degree programs as of fall 2003 are given.

With reference to the undergraduate enrollment for fall 2003, the percentages of women and men and the number of states and countries from which students hail are listed. The following percentages are also provided: in-state students, international students, and the percentage of last year's graduating class who went on to graduate and professional schools.

Expenses

Costs are given, as indicated in the heading of this paragraph in each profile, in one of three ways according to the most up-to-date figures available from each college: (1) actual expenses for the 2003-04 academic year; (2) estimated expenses for 2003-04; or (3) actual expenses for 2002-03.

Annual expenses may be expressed as a comprehensive fee (includes full-time tuition, mandatory fees, and college room and board) or as separate figures for full-time tuition, fees, room and board, and/or room only. For public institutions where tuition differs according to residence, separate figures are given for area and/or state residents and for nonresidents. Part-time tuition and fees are expressed in terms of a per-unit rate (per credit, per semester hour, etc.) as specified by the college.

The tuition structure at some institutions is complex in that freshmen and sophomores may be charged a different rate from that for juniors and seniors, a professional or vocational division may have a different fee structure from the liberal arts division of the same institution, or part-time tuition may be prorated on a sliding scale according to the number of credit hours taken. In all of these cases, the average figures are given along with an explanation of the basis for the variable rate. For colleges that report that room and board costs vary according to the type of accommodation and meal plan, the average costs are given. The phrase *no college housing* indicates that the college does not own or operate any housing facilities for its undergraduate students.

Financial Aid

This paragraph contains information on the following items.

Forms of financial aid: The categories of college-administered aid available to undergraduates are listed. College-administered means that the college itself determines the recipient and amount of each award. The types of aid covered are non-need scholarships, need-based scholarships, athletic grants, and part-time jobs.

Financial aid: This item pertains to undergraduates who enrolled full-time in a four-year college in 2002 or 2003. The figures given are the dollar amount of the average financial aid package, including scholarships, grants, loans, and part-time jobs, received by such undergraduates.

Financial aid application deadline: This deadline may be given as a specific date, as continuous processing up to a specific date or until all available aid has been awarded, or as a priority date rather than a strict deadline, meaning that students are encouraged to apply by that date in order to have the best chance of obtaining aid.

Freshman Admission

The supporting data that a student must submit when applying for freshman admission are grouped into three categories: required for all, recommended, and required for some. They may include an essay, a high school transcript, high school course requirements (e.g., three years of math), letters of recommendation, an interview on campus or with local alumni, standardized test scores, and, for certain types of schools or programs, special requirements such as a musical audition or an art portfolio.

The most commonly required standardized tests are the ACT Assessment and the College Board's SAT I and SAT II Subject Tests. TOEFL (Test of English as a Foreign Language) is for international students whose native language is not English.

The application deadline for admission is given as either a specific date or *rolling*. Rolling means that applications are processed as they are received, and qualified students are accepted as long as there are openings. The application deadline for out-of-state students is indicated if it differs from the date for state residents. *Early decision* and *early action* deadlines are also given when applicable. Early decision is a program whereby students may apply early, are notified of acceptance or rejection well in advance of the usual notification date, and agree to accept an offer of admission, the assumption being that only one early application has been made. Early action is the same as early decision except that applicants are not obligated to accept an offer of admission.

Transfer Admission

This paragraph gives the application requirements and application deadline for a student applying for admission as a transfer from another institution. In addition to the requirements for freshman applicants listed above, requirements for transfers may also include a college transcript and a minimum college grade point average (expressed as a number on a scale of 0 to 4.0, where 4.0 equals A, 3.0 equals B, etc.). The name of the person to contact for additional transfer information is also given if it is different from the person listed in **For Further Information**.

Transfer Associate Degree Program Admission

This paragraph may be substituted for the **Freshman Admission** paragraph for two-year colleges that offer a college transfer program. The categories and requirements are listed in the same way as in the **Freshman Admission** paragraph.

Terminal Associate Degree Program Admission

This paragraph may also be substituted for the **Freshman Admission** paragraph for two-year colleges. It contains the requirements for admission to a terminal program that provides specific occupational training. The format for this paragraph also follows that of the **Freshman Admission**.

Entrance Difficulty

This paragraph contains the college's own assessment of its *entrance difficulty level*, including notation of an *open admission policy* where applicable. Open admission means that virtually all applicants are accepted without regard to standardized test scores, grade average, or class rank. A college may indicate that open admission is limited to a certain category of applicants, such as state residents, or does not apply to certain selective programs, often those in the health professions.

The five levels of entrance difficulty are: *most difficult*, *very difficult*, *moderately difficult*, *minimally difficult*, and *noncompetitive*.

The final item in this paragraph is the percentage of applicants accepted for the fall 2003 freshman (or entering) class.

For Further Information

The name, title, and mailing address of the person to contact for more information on application and admission procedures are given at the end of the profile. A telephone number, fax number, e-mail address, and Web site are also included in this paragraph for profiles that do not contain this information in the paragraph on interviews and campus visits.

SPECIAL MESSAGE TO STUDENTS

In addition, a number of college admissions office staff members, as part of a major information-dissemination effort, have supplemented the basic profile with special descriptive information on four topics of particular interest to students. This section appears only for those colleges that submitted supplementary information and covers the following:

Social Life: This paragraph conveys a feeling for life on campus by addressing such questions as: What are the most popular activities? Are there active fraternities and sororities? What is the role of student government? Do most students live on campus or commute? Does the college have a religious orientation?

Academic Highlights: This paragraph describes some of the special features and characteristics of the college's academic program, such as special degree programs and opportunities for study abroad or internships.

Interviews and Campus Visits: Colleges that conduct on-campus admission interviews describe the importance of an interview in their admission process and what they try to learn about a student through the interview. For those colleges that do not interview applicants individually, there is information on how a student interested in the college can visit the campus to meet administrators, faculty members, and currently enrolled students as well as on what the prospective applicant should try to accomplish through such a visit. This paragraph may also include a list of the most noteworthy places or things to see during a campus visit and the location, telephone number (including toll-free numbers if available), and business hours of the office to contact for information about appointments and campus visits. Also included, when available, is travel information, specifically the nearest commercial airport and the nearest interstate highway, with the appropriate exit.

IN-DEPTH DESCRIPTIONS OF COLLEGES IN THE WEST

Two-page narrative descriptions appear in this section, providing an inside look at colleges and universities, shifting the focus to a variety of other factors, some of them intangible, that should also be considered. The descriptions presented in this section provide a wealth of statistics that are crucial components in the college decision-making equation—components such as tuition, financial aid, and major fields of study. Prepared exclusively by college officials, the descriptions are designed to help give students a better sense of the individuality of each institution, in terms that include campus environment, student activities, and lifestyle. Such quality-of-life intangibles can be the deciding factors in the college selection process. The absence from this section of any college or university does not constitute an editorial decision on the part of Peterson's. In essence, this section is an open forum for colleges and universities, on a voluntary basis, to communicate their particular message to prospective college students. The colleges included have pad a fee to Peterson's to provide this information. The descriptions are edited to provide a consistent format across entries for your ease of comparison and are presented alphabetically by the official name of the institution.

PROFILES AND IN-DEPTH DESCRIPTIONS OF OTHER COLLEGES TO CONSIDER

Do you know that schools sometimes target specific areas of the country for student recruitment, even if those states are not part of a specific region? In this section, you'll find profiles and **In-Depth Descriptions** of schools outside the region of this guide looking to recruit students like you. The format of both the profiles and the **In-Depth Descriptions** in this section matches the format in the previous sections.

INDEXES

Majors and Degrees

This index lists hundreds of undergraduate major fields of study that are currently offered most widely. The majors appear in alphabetical order, each followed by an alphabetical list of the colleges that report offering a program in that field and the degree levels (*A* for associate, *B* for bachelor's) available. The majors represented here are based on the National Center for Education Statistics (NCES) 2000 Classification of Instructional Programs (CIP). The CIP is a taxonomic coding scheme that contains titles and descriptions of instructional programs, primarily at the postsecondary level. CIP was originally developed to facilitate NCES's collection and reporting of postsecondary degree completions, by major field of study, using standard classifications that capture the majority of program activity. The CIP is now the accepted federal government statistical standard for classifying instructional programs. However, although the term "major" is used in this guide, some colleges may use other terms, such as "concentration," "program of study," or "field."

Athletic Programs and Scholarships

This index lists the colleges that report offering intercollegiate athletic programs, listed alphabetically. An *M* or *W* following the college name indicates that the sport is offered for men or women, respectively. An *s* in parentheses following an *M* or *W* indicates that athletic scholarships (or grants-in-aid) are offered by the college for men or women, respectively, in that sport.

ROTC Programs

This index lists the colleges that report offering Reserve Officers' Training Corps programs in one or more branches of the armed services, as indicated by letter codes following the college name: *A* for Army, *N* for Navy, and *AF* for Air Force. A *c* in parentheses following the branch letter code indicates that the program is offered through a cooperative arrangement on another college's campus.

Alphabetical Listing of Colleges and Universities

This index gives the page locations of various entries for all the colleges and universities in this book. The page numbers for the college profiles are printed in regular type, those for profiles with **Special Messages** in *italic* type, and those for **In-Depth Descriptions** in **boldface** type. When there is more than one number in **boldface** type, it indicates that the institution has more than one **In-Depth Description**.

DATA COLLECTION PROCEDURES

The data contained in the College Profiles and Indexes were researched between fall 2003 and spring 2004 through *Thomson Peterson's Annual Survey of Undergraduate Institutions*. Questionnaires were sent to the more than 2,000 colleges and universities that met the outlined inclusion criteria. All data included in this edition have been submitted by officials (usually admissions and financial aid officers, registrars, or institutional research personnel) at the colleges. In addition, many of the institutions that submitted data were contacted directly by the Thomson Peterson's research staff to verify unusual figures, resolve discrepancies, or obtain additional data. All usable information received in time for publication has been included. The omission of any particular item from an index or profile listing signifies that the information is either not applicable to that institution or not available. Because of Thomson Peterson's comprehensive editorial review and because all material comes directly from college officials, we believe that the information presented in this guide is accurate. You should check with a specific college or university at the time of application to verify such figures as tuition and fees, which may have changed since the publication of this volume.

CRITERIA FOR INCLUSION IN THIS BOOK

The term "four-year college" is the commonly used designation for institutions that grant the baccalaureate degree. Four years is the expected amount of time required to earn this degree, although some bachelor's degree programs may be completed in three years, others require five years, and part-time programs may take considerably longer. Upper-level institutions offer only the junior and senior years and accept only students with two years of college-level credit. Therefore, "four-year college" is a conventional term that accurately describes most of the institutions included in this guide, but should not be taken literally in all cases.

To be included in this guide, an institution must have full accreditation or be a candidate for accreditation (preaccreditation) status by an institutional or specialized accrediting body recognized by the U.S. Department of Education or the Council for Higher Education Accreditation (CHEA). Institutional accrediting bodies, which review each institution as a whole, include the six regional associations of schools and colleges (Middle States, New England, North Central, Northwest, Southern, and Western), each of which is responsible for a specified portion of the United States and its territories. Other institutional accrediting bodies are national in scope and accredit specific kinds of institutions (e.g., Bible colleges, independent colleges, and rabbinical and Talmudic schools). Program registration by the New York State Board of Regents is considered to be the equivalent of institutional accreditation, since the board requires that all programs offered by an institution meet its standards before recognition is granted. A Canadian institution must be chartered and authorized to grant degrees by the provincial government, affiliated with a chartered institution, or accredited by a recognized U.S. accrediting body. This guide also includes institutions outside the United States that are accredited by these U.S. accrediting bodies. There are recognized specialized or professional accrediting bodies in more than forty different fields, each of which is authorized to accredit institutions or specific programs in its particular field. For specialized institutions that offer programs in one field only, we designate this to be the equivalent of institutional accreditation. A full explanation of the accrediting process and complete information on recognized, institutional (regional and national) and specialized accrediting bodies can be found online at www.chea.org or at www.ed.gov/admins/finaid/accred/index.html.

Profiles of Colleges in the West

Map of the West

This map provides a general perspective on the West and shows the major metropolitan areas and capital of each state.

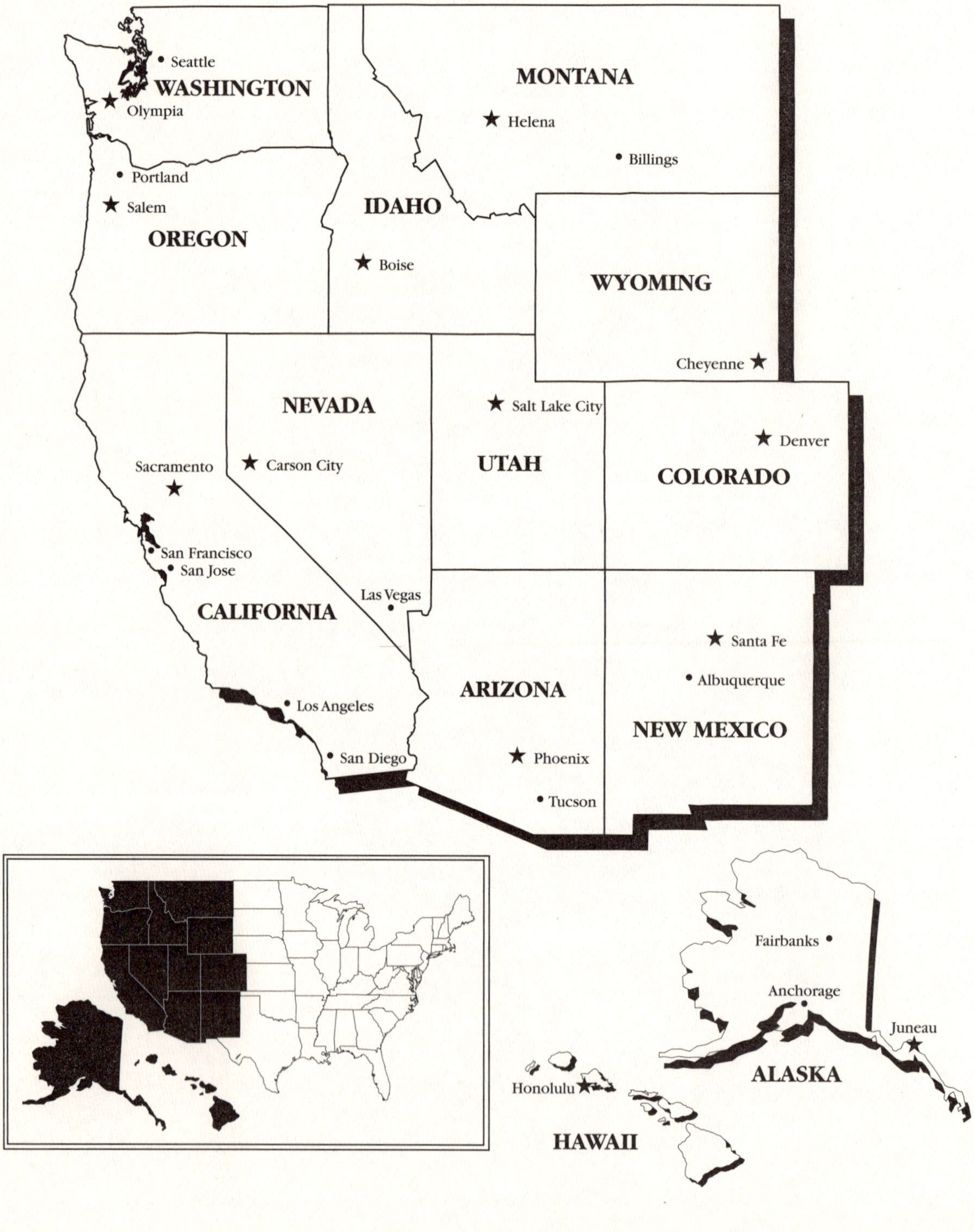

Alaska

ALASKA BIBLE COLLEGE

Glennallen, Alaska

ABC is a coed, private, nondenominational, four-year college, founded in 1966, offering degrees at the associate and bachelor's levels. It has an 80-acre campus in Glennallen.

Academic Information The faculty has 5 members (40% full-time), 20% with terminal degrees. The student-faculty ratio is 15:1. The library holds 27,911 titles, 130 serial subscriptions, and 252 audiovisual materials. Special programs include academic remediation, advanced placement credit, double majors, self-designed majors, part-time degree programs (daytime), and internships.
Student Body Statistics The student body is made up of 56 undergraduates (7 freshmen). 39 percent are women and 61 percent are men. Students come from 20 states and territories. 32 percent are from Alaska.
Expenses for 2004–05 *Application fee:* $35. *Comprehensive fee:* $9800 includes full-time tuition ($5450) and college room and board ($4350). Room and board charges vary according to board plan and housing facility. *Part-time tuition:* $240 per credit.
Financial Aid Forms of aid include need-based and non-need-based scholarships and part-time jobs. The application deadline for financial aid is July 5 with a priority deadline of May 31.
Freshman Admission ABC requires an essay, a high school transcript, a minimum 2.0 high school GPA, 2 recommendations, an interview, SAT I or ACT scores, and TOEFL scores for international students. The application deadline for regular admission is July 1.
Transfer Admission The application deadline for admission is July 1.
Entrance Difficulty ABC assesses its entrance difficulty level as minimally difficult. For the fall 2003 freshman class, 100 percent of the applicants were accepted.

For Further Information Contact Ms. Jackie Colwell, Admissions Officer, Alaska Bible College, Box 289, 200 College Road, Glennallen, AK 99588-0289. *Telephone:* 907-822-3201 or 800-478-7884 (toll-free). *Fax:* 907-822-5027. *E-mail:* info@akbible.edu. *Web site:* http://www.akbible.edu/.

ALASKA PACIFIC UNIVERSITY

Anchorage, Alaska

Alaska Pacific is a coed, private, comprehensive institution, founded in 1959, offering degrees at the associate, bachelor's, and master's levels. It has a 170-acre campus in Anchorage.

Academic Information The faculty has 85 members (36% full-time), 35% with terminal degrees. The undergraduate student-faculty ratio is 9:1. The library holds 676,745 titles and 3,842 serial subscriptions. Special programs include academic remediation, services for learning-disabled students, study abroad, advanced placement credit, accelerated degree programs, double majors, independent study, distance learning, self-designed majors, summer session for credit, part-time degree programs (daytime, evenings, weekends, summer), adult/continuing education programs, and internships. The most frequently chosen baccalaureate fields are business/marketing, education, protective services/public administration.
Student Body Statistics The student body totals 673, of whom 478 are undergraduates (27 freshmen). 67 percent are women and 33 percent are men. Students come from 34 states and territories. 74 percent are from Alaska. 0.5 percent are international students.
Expenses for 2003–04 *Application fee:* $25. *Comprehensive fee:* $21,828 includes full-time tuition ($16,218), mandatory fees ($110), and college room and board ($5500). *College room only:* $3000. Full-time tuition and fees vary according to class time, location, and program. Room and board charges vary according to board plan and housing facility. *Part-time tuition:* $675 per semester hour. *Part-time mandatory fees:* $55 per term. Part-time tuition and fees vary according to class time, location, and program.
Financial Aid Forms of aid include need-based and non-need-based scholarships, athletic grants, and part-time jobs. The average aided 2003–04 undergraduate received an aid package worth an estimated $10,113. The priority application deadline for financial aid is April 15.
Freshman Admission Alaska Pacific requires an essay, a high school transcript, a minimum 2.5 high school GPA, 2 recommendations, SAT I or ACT scores, and TOEFL scores for international students. An interview is required for some. The application deadline for regular admission is February 1 and for early decision it is January 1.
Transfer Admission The application deadline for admission is February 1.
Entrance Difficulty Alaska Pacific assesses its entrance difficulty level as moderately difficult. For the fall 2003 freshman class, 91 percent of the applicants were accepted.

For Further Information Contact Mr. Michael Worner, Co-Director of Admissions, Alaska Pacific University, Anchorage, AK 99508. *Telephone:* 907-564-8248 or 800-252-7528 (toll-free). *Fax:* 907-564-8317. *E-mail:* admissions@alaskapacific.edu. *Web site:* http://www.alaskapacific.edu/.

See page 158 for a narrative description.

CHARTER COLLEGE

Anchorage, Alaska

For Information Write to Charter College, Anchorage, AK 99508-4140.

SHELDON JACKSON COLLEGE

Sitka, Alaska

Sheldon Jackson is a coed, private, four-year college, founded in 1878, affiliated with the Presbyterian Church (U.S.A.), offering degrees at the associate and bachelor's levels. It has a 320-acre campus in Sitka.

Academic Information The faculty has 38 members (53% full-time), 34% with terminal degrees. The student-faculty ratio is 6:1. The library holds 46,000 titles and 150 serial subscriptions. Special programs include academic remediation, services for learning-disabled students, advanced placement credit, double majors, independent study, self-designed majors, part-time degree programs (daytime, evenings), and internships.
Student Body Statistics The student body is made up of 221 undergraduates (34 freshmen). 64 percent are women and 36 percent are men. Students come from 25 states and territories. 49 percent are from Alaska.
Expenses for 2004–05 *Comprehensive fee:* $18,500 includes full-time tuition ($10,600), mandatory fees ($600), and college room and board ($7300). *College room only:* $3700. Room and board charges vary according to board plan and housing facility. *Part-time tuition:* varies with course load, degree level.
Financial Aid Forms of aid include need-based and non-need-based scholarships and part-time jobs. The average aided 2003–04 undergraduate received an aid package worth an estimated $11,974. The application deadline for financial aid is March 1.
Freshman Admission Sheldon Jackson requires a high school transcript and TOEFL scores for international students. An essay and a minimum 2.0 high school GPA are recommended. The application deadline for regular admission is rolling.
Transfer Admission The application deadline for admission is rolling.
Entrance Difficulty Sheldon Jackson has an open admission policy.

For Further Information Contact Mr. Michael Santarosa, Director of Admissions, Sheldon Jackson College, 801 Lincoln Street, Sitka, AK 99835. *Telephone:* 907-747-5208 or 800-478-4556 (toll-free). *Fax:* 907-747-6366. *E-mail:* admissions@sj-alaska.edu. *Web site:* http://www.sj-alaska.edu/.

UNIVERSITY OF ALASKA ANCHORAGE

Anchorage, Alaska

UAA is a coed, public, comprehensive unit of University of Alaska System, founded in 1954, offering degrees at the associate, bachelor's, and master's levels. It has a 428-acre campus in Anchorage.

Academic Information The faculty has 1,318 members (40% full-time), 25% with terminal degrees. The undergraduate student-faculty ratio is 18:1. The library holds 894,080 titles, 3,833 serial subscriptions, and 9,006 audiovisual materials. Special programs include academic remediation, services for learning-disabled students, an honors program, cooperative (work-study) education, study abroad, advanced placement credit, ESL programs, double majors, independent study, self-designed majors, summer session for credit, part-time degree programs (daytime, evenings, weekends, summer), adult/continuing education programs, internships, and arrangement for off-campus study with members of the National Student Exchange, Western Interstate Commission for Higher Education, Western Undergraduate Exchange. The most frequently chosen baccalaureate fields are business/marketing, education, social sciences and history.
Student Body Statistics The student body totals 16,607, of whom 15,810 are undergraduates (1,379 freshmen). 62 percent are women and 38 percent are men. Students come from 50 states and territories and 41 other countries. 95 percent are from Alaska. 2.5 percent are international students.
Expenses for 2003–04 *Application fee:* $40. *State resident tuition:* $2304 full-time. *Nonresident tuition:* $6800 full-time. *Mandatory fees:* $352 full-time. *College room and board:* $6830. *College room only:* $3730.
Financial Aid Forms of aid include need-based and non-need-based scholarships, athletic grants, and part-time jobs. The application deadline for financial aid is August 1 with a priority deadline of April 1.
Freshman Admission UAA requires a minimum 2.0 high school GPA, SAT I or ACT scores, and TOEFL scores for international students. A high school transcript is required for some. The application deadline for regular admission is August 1.
Entrance Difficulty UAA assesses its entrance difficulty level as noncompetitive; minimally difficult for transfers; minimally difficult for bachelor's degree programs. For the fall 2003 freshman class, 76 percent of the applicants were accepted.

For Further Information Contact Ms. Cecile Mitchell, Director of Enrollment Services, University of Alaska Anchorage, 3211 Providence Drive, Anchorage, AK 99508-8046. *Telephone:* 907-786-1558. *Fax:* 907-786-4888. *E-mail:* enroll@uaa.alaska.edu. *Web site:* http://www.uaa.alaska.edu/.

UNIVERSITY OF ALASKA FAIRBANKS

Fairbanks, Alaska

UAF is a coed, public unit of University of Alaska System, founded in 1917, offering degrees at the associate, bachelor's, master's, and doctoral levels. It has a 2,250-acre campus in Fairbanks.

Academic Information The faculty has 311 members (98% full-time). The undergraduate student-faculty ratio is 19:1. The library holds 608,575 titles, 2,754 serial subscriptions, and 664,448 audiovisual materials. Special programs include academic remediation, services for learning-disabled students, an honors program, cooperative (work-study) education, study abroad, advanced placement credit, accelerated degree programs, double majors, independent study, distance learning, self-designed majors, summer session for credit, part-time degree programs (daytime, evenings, weekends, summer), internships, and arrangement for off-campus study with National Student Exchange. The most frequently chosen baccalaureate fields are biological/life sciences, business/marketing, protective services/public administration.
Student Body Statistics The student body totals 8,724, of whom 7,708 are undergraduates (1,021 freshmen). 59 percent are women and 41 percent are men. Students come from 56 states and territories and 27 other countries. 86 percent are from Alaska. 1.9 percent are international students.
Expenses for 2004–05 *Application fee:* $35. *State resident tuition:* $3165 full-time, $105.50 per credit part-time. *Nonresident tuition:* $10,195 full-time, $336.50 per credit part-time. *Mandatory fees:* $1000 full-time. Full-time tuition and fees vary according to course level and course load. Part-time tuition varies according to course level and course load. *College room and board:* $5130. *College room only:* $2690. Room and board charges vary according to board plan and housing facility.
Financial Aid Forms of aid include need-based and non-need-based scholarships, athletic grants, and part-time jobs. The average aided 2003–04 undergraduate received an aid package worth an estimated $9137. The priority application deadline for financial aid is July 1.
Freshman Admission UAF requires a high school transcript, a minimum 2.0 high school GPA, SAT I or ACT scores, and TOEFL scores for international students. The application deadline for regular admission is August 1.
Transfer Admission The application deadline for admission is August 1.
Entrance Difficulty UAF assesses its entrance difficulty level as minimally difficult. For the fall 2003 freshman class, 84 percent of the applicants were accepted.

For Further Information Contact Ms. Nancy Dix, Director, Admissions, University of Alaska Fairbanks, PO Box 757480, Fairbanks, AK 99775-7480. *Telephone:* 907-474-7500 or 800-478-1823 (toll-free). *Fax:* 907-474-5379. *E-mail:* fyapply@uaf.edu. *Web site:* http://www.uaf.edu/.

See page 192 for a narrative description.

UNIVERSITY OF ALASKA SOUTHEAST

Juneau, Alaska

UAS is a coed, public, comprehensive unit of University of Alaska System, founded in 1972, offering degrees at the associate, bachelor's, and master's levels. It has a 198-acre campus in Juneau.

Academic Information The faculty has 240 members (40% full-time), 20% with terminal degrees. The undergraduate student-faculty ratio is 12:1. The library holds 112,500 titles, 537 serial subscriptions, and 2,763 audiovisual materials. Special programs include academic remediation, services for learning-disabled students, cooperative (work-study) education, study abroad, advanced placement credit, independent study, distance learning, self-designed majors, summer session for credit, part-time degree programs (daytime, evenings, weekends, summer), adult/continuing education programs, internships, and arrangement for off-campus study with National Student Exchange. The most frequently chosen baccalaureate fields are business/marketing, education, liberal arts/general studies.
Student Body Statistics The student body totals 3,268, of whom 3,126 are undergraduates (145 freshmen). 62 percent are women and 38 percent are men. Students come from 39 states and territories and 6 other countries. 86 percent are from Alaska.
Expenses for 2004–05 *Application fee:* $40. *State resident tuition:* $3360 full-time, $112 per credit hour part-time. *Nonresident tuition:* $10,290 full-time, $343 per credit hour part-time. *Mandatory fees:* $423 full-time. *College room and board:* $5320. *College room only:* $3350.
Financial Aid Forms of aid include need-based and non-need-based scholarships and part-time jobs. The average aided 2003–04 undergraduate received an aid package worth an estimated $6417. The priority application deadline for financial aid is June 1.
Freshman Admission UAS requires a high school transcript, a minimum 2.0 high school GPA, SAT I or ACT scores, and TOEFL scores for international students. An essay is required for some. The application deadline for regular admission is rolling.
Transfer Admission The application deadline for admission is rolling.
Entrance Difficulty UAS has an open admission policy.

For Further Information Contact Mr. Bill Stenberg, Director of Admissions, University of Alaska Southeast, 11120 Glacier Highway, Juneau, AK 99801-8625. *Telephone:* 907-465-6239 or 877-465-4827 (toll-free). *Fax:* 907-465-6365. *E-mail:* info.uas@uas.alaska.edu. *Web site:* http://www.uas.alaska.edu/.

See page 194 for a narrative description.

Arizona

AIBT INTERNATIONAL INSTITUTE OF THE AMERICAS

See International Institute of the Americas

AL COLLINS GRAPHIC DESIGN SCHOOL

See Collins College: A School of Design and Technology

AMERICAN INDIAN COLLEGE OF THE ASSEMBLIES OF GOD, INC.

Phoenix, Arizona

American Indian College of the Assemblies of God, Inc. is a coed, private, four-year college, founded in 1957, affiliated with the Assemblies of God, offering degrees at the associate and bachelor's levels. It has a 10-acre campus in Phoenix.

Academic Information The faculty has 20 members (25% full-time), 10% with terminal degrees. The student-faculty ratio is 8:1. The library holds 19,899 titles and 120 serial subscriptions. Special programs include academic remediation, double majors, independent study, distance learning, and internships. The most frequently chosen baccalaureate field is education.

Student Body Statistics The student body is made up of 73 undergraduates (8 freshmen). 48 percent are women and 52 percent are men. Students come from 10 states and territories. 71 percent are from Arizona. 1.4 percent are international students.

Expenses for 2004–05 *Application fee:* $0. *Comprehensive fee:* $9275 includes full-time tuition ($4800), mandatory fees ($625), and college room and board ($3850). Full-time tuition and fees vary according to course load. *Part-time tuition:* $160 per credit hour. Part-time tuition varies according to course load.

Financial Aid Forms of aid include need-based and non-need-based scholarships and part-time jobs. The priority application deadline for financial aid is April 1.

Freshman Admission American Indian College of the Assemblies of God, Inc. requires an essay, a high school transcript, 1 recommendation, SAT I or ACT scores, and TOEFL scores for international students. The application deadline for regular admission is August 15.

Transfer Admission The application deadline for admission is August 15.

Entrance Difficulty American Indian College of the Assemblies of God, Inc. assesses its entrance difficulty level as minimally difficult. For the fall 2003 freshman class, 44 percent of the applicants were accepted.

For Further Information Contact Rev. Steve Clindaniel, Admissions Director, American Indian College of the Assemblies of God, Inc., 10020 North 15th Avenue, Phoenix, AZ 85021. *Telephone:* 602-944-3335 Ext. 235 or 800-933-3828 (toll-free). *Fax:* 602-943-8299. *E-mail:* aicadm@aicag.edu. *Web site:* http://www.aicag.edu/.

ARGOSY UNIVERSITY/PHOENIX

Phoenix, Arizona

Argosy University/Phoenix is a coed, proprietary, upper-level unit of Argosy University, founded in 1997, offering degrees at the bachelor's, master's, and doctoral levels. It has a 1-acre campus in Phoenix.

Academic Information The faculty has 26 members (62% full-time), 100% with terminal degrees. The undergraduate student-faculty ratio is 13:1. The most frequently chosen baccalaureate field is psychology.

Student Body Statistics The student body totals 372, of whom 14 are undergraduates. 86 percent are women and 14 percent are men. Students come from 50 states and territories and 5 other countries. 20 percent are from Arizona.

Expenses for 2003–04 *Tuition:* $12,960 full-time, $360 per credit hour part-time. *Mandatory fees:* $25 full-time.

Financial Aid Forms of aid include need-based and non-need-based scholarships and part-time jobs. The average aided 2003–04 undergraduate received an aid package worth an estimated $4213. The application deadline for financial aid is continuous.

For Further Information Contact Mr. Andy Hughes, Director of Admissions, Argosy University/Phoenix, 2301 West Dunlap Avenue, Suite 211, Phoenix, AZ 85021. *Telephone:* 602-216-2600 Ext. 277 or 866-216-2777 (toll-free). *Fax:* 602-216-2601. *E-mail:* ahughes@argosyu.edu. *Web site:* http://www.argosyu.edu/.

ARIZONA STATE UNIVERSITY

Tempe, Arizona

ASU Main is a coed, public unit of Arizona State University, founded in 1885, offering degrees at the bachelor's, master's, doctoral, and first professional levels and post-master's and postbachelor's certificates. It has an 814-acre campus in Tempe near Phoenix.

Academic Information The faculty has 1,844 members (93% full-time), 82% with terminal degrees. The undergraduate student-faculty ratio is 23:1. The library holds 2 million titles, 28,159 serial subscriptions, and 1 million audiovisual materials. Special programs include academic remediation, services for learning-disabled students, an honors program, cooperative (work-study) education, study abroad, advanced placement credit, accelerated degree programs, double majors, independent study, distance learning, summer session for credit, part-time degree programs (daytime, evenings, summer), adult/continuing education programs, internships, and arrangement for off-campus study with University of Arizona, Northern Arizona University. The most frequently chosen baccalaureate fields are business/marketing, communications/communication technologies, interdisciplinary studies.

Student Body Statistics The student body totals 48,901, of whom 38,627 are undergraduates (7,126 freshmen). 52 percent are women and 48 percent are men. Students come from 53 states and territories and 108 other countries. 77 percent are from Arizona. 3.1 percent are international students.

Expenses for 2003–04 *State resident tuition:* $3508 full-time, $183 per credit part-time. *Nonresident tuition:* $12,028 full-time, $501 per credit part-time. *Mandatory fees:* $87 full-time. Full-time tuition and fees vary according to program. Part-time tuition varies according to program. *College room and board:* $6453. *College room only:* $4101. Room and board charges vary according to board plan and housing facility.

Financial Aid Forms of aid include need-based and non-need-based scholarships, athletic grants, and part-time jobs. The average aided 2002–03 undergraduate received an aid package worth $7225. The priority application deadline for financial aid is March 1.

Freshman Admission ASU Main requires a high school transcript, a minimum 3.0 high school GPA, SAT I or ACT scores, and TOEFL scores for international students. The application deadline for regular admission is rolling and for early action it is November 1.

Transfer Admission The application deadline for admission is rolling.

Entrance Difficulty ASU Main assesses its entrance difficulty level as moderately difficult; very difficult for engineering, computer science, business programs. For the fall 2003 freshman class, 88 percent of the applicants were accepted.

For Further Information Contact Mr. Timothy J. Desch, Director of Undergraduate Admissions, Arizona State University, Box 870112, Tempe, AZ 85287-0112. *Telephone:* 480-965-7788. *Fax:* 480-965-3610. *E-mail:* ugradinq@asu.edu. *Web site:* http://www.asu.edu/.

ARIZONA STATE UNIVERSITY EAST

Mesa, Arizona

ASU East is a coed, public, comprehensive unit of Arizona State University, founded in 1995, offering degrees at the bachelor's and master's levels. It has a 600-acre campus in Mesa near Phoenix.

Academic Information The faculty has 99 members (89% full-time), 100% with terminal degrees. The undergraduate student-faculty ratio is 22:1. The library holds 4 million titles, 206 serial subscriptions, and 105 audiovisual materials. Special programs include services for learning-disabled students, an honors program, study abroad, advanced placement credit, accelerated degree programs, double majors, independent study, distance learning, self-designed majors, summer session for credit, part-time degree programs (daytime, evenings, weekends, summer), and internships. The most frequently chosen baccalaureate fields are business/marketing, education, engineering/engineering technologies.
Student Body Statistics The student body totals 3,551, of whom 2,862 are undergraduates (137 freshmen). 48 percent are women and 52 percent are men. Students come from 43 states and territories. 90 percent are from Arizona. 1.9 percent are international students.
Expenses for 2003–04 *Application fee:* $50. *State resident tuition:* $3508 full-time, $183 per semester hour part-time. *Nonresident tuition:* $12,028 full-time, $501 per semester hour part-time. *Mandatory fees:* $36 full-time. Full-time tuition and fees vary according to degree level and location. Part-time tuition varies according to course load, degree level, and location. *College room and board:* $4770. *College room only:* $2610. Room and board charges vary according to board plan and housing facility.
Financial Aid Forms of aid include need-based and non-need-based scholarships, athletic grants, and part-time jobs. The average aided 2002–03 undergraduate received an aid package worth $6963. The priority application deadline for financial aid is March 1.
Freshman Admission ASU East requires a high school transcript and TOEFL scores for international students. A minimum 3.0 high school GPA and SAT I or ACT scores are recommended. An essay and an interview are required for some. The application deadline for regular admission is rolling and for early action it is November 1.
Transfer Admission The application deadline for admission is rolling.
Entrance Difficulty ASU East assesses its entrance difficulty level as moderately difficult. For the fall 2003 freshman class, 79 percent of the applicants were accepted.

For Further Information Contact Stacie Dana, Student Recruitment/ Retention Specialist, Arizona State University East, 7001 East Williams Field Road #350, Mesa, AZ 85212. *Telephone:* 480-727-1041. *Fax:* 480-727-1008. *E-mail:* asueast@asu.edu. *Web site:* http://www.east.asu.edu/.

ARIZONA STATE UNIVERSITY WEST

Phoenix, Arizona

ASU West is a coed, public, comprehensive unit of Arizona State University, founded in 1984, offering degrees at the bachelor's and master's levels and postbachelor's certificates. It has a 300-acre campus in Phoenix.

Academic Information The faculty has 335 members (56% full-time), 64% with terminal degrees. The undergraduate student-faculty ratio is 20:1. The library holds 334,625 titles, 3,318 serial subscriptions, and 26,369 audiovisual materials. Special programs include services for learning-disabled students, an honors program, double majors, independent study, distance learning, self-designed majors, summer session for credit, part-time degree programs (daytime, evenings), adult/continuing education programs, and internships. The most frequently chosen baccalaureate fields are business/marketing, education, psychology.
Student Body Statistics The student body totals 7,105, of whom 5,751 are undergraduates (357 freshmen). 68 percent are women and 32 percent are men. Students come from 29 states and territories and 23 other countries. 98 percent are from Arizona. 1 percent are international students.
Expenses for 2003–04 *State resident tuition:* $3508 full-time, $183 per credit hour part-time. *Nonresident tuition:* $12,028 full-time, $501 per credit hour part-time. *Mandatory fees:* $87 full-time, $19 per term part-time. Part-time tuition and fees vary according to course load. *College room only:* $4101.
Financial Aid Forms of aid include need-based and non-need-based scholarships and part-time jobs. The average aided 2002–03 undergraduate received an aid package worth $6911. The priority application deadline for financial aid is March 1.
Freshman Admission ASU West requires a high school transcript, SAT I or ACT scores, and TOEFL scores for international students. A minimum 3.0 high school GPA is recommended. The application deadline for regular admission is rolling.
Transfer Admission The application deadline for admission is rolling.
Entrance Difficulty ASU West assesses its entrance difficulty level as moderately difficult. For the fall 2003 freshman class, 62 percent of the applicants were accepted.

For Further Information Contact Ms. Deborah Moore, Program Coordinator, Arizona State University West, PO Box 37100, 4701 West Thunderbird Road, Phoenix, AZ 85069-7100. *Telephone:* 602-543-8134. *Fax:* 602-543-8312. *Web site:* http://www.west.asu.edu/.

THE ART CENTER DESIGN COLLEGE

Tucson, Arizona

For Information Write to The Art Center Design College, Tucson, AZ 85716-2505.

THE ART INSTITUTE OF PHOENIX

Phoenix, Arizona

AIPX is a coed, proprietary, four-year college of The Art Institutes, founded in 1995, offering degrees at the associate and bachelor's levels. It has a 3-acre campus in Phoenix.

Academic Information The faculty has 80 members (39% full-time). The student-faculty ratio is 20:1. The library holds 11,000 titles, 120 serial subscriptions, and 2,850 audiovisual materials. Special programs include academic remediation, services for learning-disabled students, an honors program, cooperative (work-study) education, advanced placement credit, independent study, distance learning, and internships. The most frequently chosen baccalaureate fields are communications/communication technologies, computer/information sciences, visual/performing arts.
Student Body Statistics The student body is made up of 1,216 undergraduates (388 freshmen). 39 percent are women and 61 percent are men. Students come from 32 states and territories. 60 percent are from Arizona. 0.1 percent are international students.
Expenses for 2004–05 *Application fee:* $50. *One-time mandatory fee:* $100. *Tuition:* $16,320 full-time, $325 per credit part-time.
Financial Aid Forms of aid include need-based scholarships and part-time jobs. The application deadline for financial aid is continuous.
Freshman Admission AIPX requires an essay, a high school transcript, an interview, and TOEFL scores for international students. A minimum 2.0 high school GPA, SAT I or ACT scores, and ACT ASSET are recommended. The application deadline for regular admission is rolling.
Transfer Admission The application deadline for admission is rolling.
Entrance Difficulty AIPX assesses its entrance difficulty level as minimally difficult.

For Further Information Contact Mr. Jerry Driskill, Director of Admissions, The Art Institute of Phoenix, 2233 West Dunlap Avenue, Phoenix, AZ 85021-2859. *Telephone:* 602-678-4300 Ext. 102 or 800-474-2479 (toll-free). *Fax:* 602-216-0439. *E-mail:* infoaipx@aii.edu. *Web site:* http://www.aipx.artinstitutes.edu/.

See page 160 for a narrative description.

CHAPARRAL COLLEGE

Tucson, Arizona

Chaparral College is a coed, proprietary, primarily two-year college, founded in 1972, offering degrees at the associate and bachelor's levels (bachelor's degree in business administration only). It is located in Tucson near Phoenix.

Academic Information The faculty has 38 members (37% full-time), 58% with terminal degrees. The student-faculty ratio is 20:1. The library holds 6,000 titles, 65 serial subscriptions, and 500 audiovisual materials. Special programs include academic remediation, summer session for credit, and internships. The most frequently chosen baccalaureate fields are business/marketing, computer/information sciences.
Student Body Statistics The student body is made up of 400 undergraduates. Students come from 1 state or territory and 3 other countries.
Financial Aid Forms of aid include need-based scholarships. The application deadline for financial aid is continuous.
Freshman Admission Chaparral College requires a high school transcript, an interview, TOEFL scores for international students, and CPAt. Recommendations and entrance test are required for some. The application deadline for regular admission is rolling.
Transfer Admission The application deadline for admission is rolling.
Entrance Difficulty Chaparral College has an open admission policy.

For Further Information Contact Ms. Becki Rossini, Director of Admissions, Chaparral College, 4585 East Speedway No. 204, Tucson, AZ 85712. *Telephone:* 520-327-6866. *Fax:* 520-325-0108. *E-mail:* admissions@chap-col.edu. *Web site:* http://www.chap-col.edu/.

COLLEGE OF THE HUMANITIES AND SCIENCES

Tempe, Arizona

For Information Write to College of the Humanities and Sciences, Tempe, AZ 85282.

COLLINS COLLEGE: A SCHOOL OF DESIGN AND TECHNOLOGY

Tempe, Arizona

Collins College: A School of Design and Technology is a coed, proprietary, four-year college of Career Education Corporation, founded in 1978, offering degrees at the associate and bachelor's levels. It has a 3-acre campus in Tempe near Phoenix.

Expenses for 2003–04 tuition varies by program.

For Further Information Contact Collins College: A School of Design and Technology, 1140 South Priest, Tempe, AZ 85281. *Telephone:* 480-966-3000 or 800-876-7070 (toll-free out-of-state). *Fax:* 480-966-2599. *E-mail:* info@collinscollege.edu. *Web site:* http://www.collinscollege.edu/.

DEVRY UNIVERSITY

Mesa, Arizona

For Information Write to DeVry University, Mesa, AZ 85210-2011.

DEVRY UNIVERSITY

Phoenix, Arizona

DeVry is a coed, proprietary, comprehensive unit of DeVry University, founded in 1967, offering degrees at the associate, bachelor's, and master's levels and postbachelor's certificates. It has an 18-acre campus in Phoenix.

Academic Information The faculty has 101 members (72% full-time). The undergraduate student-faculty ratio is 24:1. The library holds 22,500 titles, 7,230 serial subscriptions, and 11 audiovisual materials. Special programs include academic remediation, services for learning-disabled students, cooperative (work-study) education, advanced placement credit, accelerated degree programs, distance learning, summer session for credit, part-time degree programs (daytime, evenings, weekends, summer), and adult/continuing education programs.
Student Body Statistics The student body totals 2,282, of whom 2,079 are undergraduates (416 freshmen). 24 percent are women and 76 percent are men. Students come from 41 states and territories and 4 other countries. 71 percent are from Arizona. 0.7 percent are international students.
Expenses for 2003–04 *Application fee:* $50. *Tuition:* $9990 full-time, $355 per credit hour part-time. *Mandatory fees:* $165 full-time. Full-time tuition and fees vary according to course load. Part-time tuition varies according to course load.
Financial Aid Forms of aid include need-based and non-need-based scholarships. The average aided 2002–03 undergraduate received an aid package worth $9288. The application deadline for financial aid is continuous.
Freshman Admission DeVry requires a high school transcript, an interview, and TOEFL scores for international students. SAT I, ACT or CPT is recommended. The application deadline for regular admission is rolling.
Transfer Admission The application deadline for admission is rolling.
Entrance Difficulty DeVry assesses its entrance difficulty level as minimally difficult; moderately difficult for electronics engineering technology program.

For Further Information Contact Mr. Jerry Driskill, Director of Admissions, DeVry University, 2149 West Dunlap Avenue, Phoenix, AZ 85021-2995. *Telephone:* 602-870-9201 or 800-528-0250 (toll-free). *Fax:* 602-331-1494. *E-mail:* admissions@phx.devry.edu. *Web site:* http://www.devry.edu/.

EDUCATION AMERICA, TEMPE CAMPUS

See Remington College–Tempe Campus

EMBRY-RIDDLE AERONAUTICAL UNIVERSITY

Prescott, Arizona

Embry-Riddle is a coed, primarily men's, private, comprehensive institution, founded in 1978, offering degrees at the bachelor's and master's levels in aviation/aerospace. It has a 547-acre campus in Prescott.

Academic Information The faculty has 113 members (79% full-time), 50% with terminal degrees. The undergraduate student-faculty ratio is 15:1. The library holds 28,264 titles, 629 serial subscriptions, and 2,518 audiovisual materials. Special programs include academic remediation, services for learning-disabled students, cooperative (work-study) education, study abroad, advanced placement credit, ESL programs, double majors, independent study, distance learning, summer session for credit, part-time degree programs, adult/continuing education programs, and internships. The most frequently chosen baccalaureate fields are engineering/engineering technologies, interdisciplinary studies, trade and industry.
Student Body Statistics The student body totals 1,669, of whom 1,631 are undergraduates (304 freshmen). 16 percent are women and 84 percent

Embry-Riddle Aeronautical University (continued)

are men. Students come from 52 states and territories and 31 other countries. 23 percent are from Arizona. 2 percent are international students. 5 percent of the 2003 graduating class went on to graduate and professional schools.
Expenses for 2004–05 *Application fee:* $30. *Comprehensive fee:* $28,386 includes full-time tuition ($21,530), mandatory fees ($650), and college room and board ($6206). *College room only:* $3370. Full-time tuition and fees vary according to course load and program. Room and board charges vary according to board plan, housing facility, and location. *Part-time tuition:* $900 per credit hour. Part-time tuition varies according to course load and program.
Financial Aid Forms of aid include need-based and non-need-based scholarships, athletic grants, and part-time jobs. The average aided 2003–04 undergraduate received an aid package worth an estimated $12,420. The application deadline for financial aid is June 30 with a priority deadline of April 15.
Freshman Admission Embry-Riddle requires a high school transcript, a minimum 2.0 high school GPA, SAT I or ACT scores, and TOEFL scores for international students. An essay, recommendations, and an interview are recommended. A minimum 3.0 high school GPA and medical examination for flight students are required for some. The application deadline for regular admission is March 1 and for early decision it is December 1.
Transfer Admission The application deadline for admission is July 1.
Entrance Difficulty Embry-Riddle assesses its entrance difficulty level as moderately difficult. For the fall 2003 freshman class, 80 percent of the applicants were accepted.

For Further Information Contact Mr. Bill Thompson, Director of Admissions, Embry-Riddle Aeronautical University, 3700 Willow Creek Road, Prescott, AZ 86301-3720. *Telephone:* 928-777-6692 or 800-888-3728 (toll-free). *Fax:* 928-777-6606. *E-mail:* pradmit@erau.edu. *Web site:* http://www.embryriddle.edu/.

See page 170 for a narrative description.

GRAND CANYON UNIVERSITY

Phoenix, Arizona

Grand Canyon University is a coed, private, Southern Baptist, comprehensive institution, founded in 1949, offering degrees at the bachelor's and master's levels. It has a 90-acre campus in Phoenix.

Academic Information The faculty has 274 members (35% full-time), 22% with terminal degrees. The undergraduate student-faculty ratio is 16:1. The library holds 75,905 titles, 1,174 serial subscriptions, and 404 audiovisual materials. Special programs include academic remediation, an honors program, cooperative (work-study) education, study abroad, advanced placement credit, accelerated degree programs, Freshman Honors College, ESL programs, double majors, independent study, distance learning, summer session for credit, part-time degree programs, adult/continuing education programs, internships, and arrangement for off-campus study with Coalition for Christian Colleges and Universities. The most frequently chosen baccalaureate fields are business/marketing, education, health professions and related sciences.
Student Body Statistics The student body totals 4,113, of whom 1,609 are undergraduates (371 freshmen). 64 percent are women and 36 percent are men. Students come from 40 states and territories and 14 other countries. 81 percent are from Arizona. 2.5 percent are international students.
Expenses for 2003–04 *Application fee:* $50. *Comprehensive fee:* $21,630 includes full-time tuition ($14,500) and college room and board ($7130). Full-time tuition varies according to course load. Room and board charges vary according to board plan and housing facility. *Part-time tuition:* varies with course load.
Financial Aid Forms of aid include need-based and non-need-based scholarships, athletic grants, and part-time jobs. The application deadline for financial aid is continuous.
Freshman Admission Grand Canyon University requires a high school transcript, a minimum 3.0 high school GPA, SAT I or ACT scores, and TOEFL scores for international students. An essay, 3 recommendations, and an interview are required for some. The application deadline for regular admission is rolling.
Transfer Admission The application deadline for admission is rolling.
Entrance Difficulty Grand Canyon University assesses its entrance difficulty level as moderately difficult. For the fall 2003 freshman class, 69 percent of the applicants were accepted.

For Further Information Contact Mrs. April Chapman, Director of Admissions, Grand Canyon University, 3300 West Camelback Road, PO Box 11097, Phoenix, AZ 86017-3030. *Telephone:* 602-589-2855 Ext. 2811 or 800-800-9776 (toll-free in-state). *Fax:* 602-589-2580. *E-mail:* admissions@gcu.edu. *Web site:* http://www.gcu.edu/.

See page 176 for a narrative description.

HIGH-TECH INSTITUTE

Phoenix, Arizona

High-Tech Institute is a coed, proprietary, primarily two-year college, offering degrees at the associate and bachelor's levels. It has a 4-acre campus in Phoenix.

Academic Information The faculty has 60 members (92% full-time), 2% with terminal degrees. The student-faculty ratio is 27:1.
Student Body Statistics The student body is made up of 1,544 undergraduates (768 freshmen). 28 percent are women and 72 percent are men.
Expenses for 2003–04 *Tuition:* $12,351 full-time. *Mandatory fees:* $461 full-time.
Financial Aid Forms of aid include need-based scholarships and part-time jobs. The application deadline for financial aid is continuous.
Freshman Admission High-Tech Institute requires a high school transcript. The application deadline for regular admission is rolling.
Transfer Admission The application deadline for admission is rolling.
Entrance Difficulty High-Tech Institute has an open admission policy.

For Further Information Contact Mr. Glen Husband, Vice President of Admissions, High-Tech Institute, 1515 East Indian School Road, Phoenix, AZ 85014-4901. *Telephone:* 602-279-9700. *Fax:* 602-279-2999. *Web site:* http://www.hightechschools.com/.

INTERNATIONAL BAPTIST COLLEGE

Tempe, Arizona

For Information Write to International Baptist College, Tempe, AZ 85282.

INTERNATIONAL IMPORT-EXPORT INSTITUTE

Phoenix, Arizona

For Information Write to International Import-Export Institute, Phoenix, AZ 85029.

INTERNATIONAL INSTITUTE OF THE AMERICAS

Mesa, Arizona

For Information Write to International Institute of the Americas, Mesa, AZ 85204-4448.

INTERNATIONAL INSTITUTE OF THE AMERICAS

Phoenix, Arizona

For Information Write to International Institute of the Americas, Phoenix, AZ 85033-3196.

INTERNATIONAL INSTITUTE OF THE AMERICAS

Phoenix, Arizona

International Institute of the Americas is a coed, private, primarily two-year college, founded in 1979, offering degrees at the associate and bachelor's levels.

Academic Information The faculty has 130 members (40% full-time), 33% with terminal degrees. The student-faculty ratio is 17:1. The library holds 1,974 titles, 1,750 serial subscriptions, and 120 audiovisual materials. Special programs include cooperative (work-study) education, accelerated degree programs, distance learning, summer session for credit, adult/continuing education programs, and internships.
Student Body Statistics The student body is made up of 1,386 undergraduates. Students come from 7 states and territories. 98 percent are from Arizona.
Expenses for 2003–04 *Tuition:* $8500 full-time, $283 per credit part-time. *Mandatory fees:* $350 full-time. Full-time tuition and fees vary according to program.
Freshman Admission International Institute of the Americas requires an interview and TOEFL scores for international students. The application deadline for regular admission is rolling.
Entrance Difficulty International Institute of the Americas has an open admission policy.

For Further Information Contact John Pechota, Admissions Director, International Institute of the Americas, 6049 North 43 Avenue, Phoenix, AZ 85019. *Telephone:* 800-793-2428 or 800-793-2428 (toll-free). *Fax:* 602-973-2572. *E-mail:* info@aibt.edu. *Web site:* http://www.aibtonline.com/.

INTERNATIONAL INSTITUTE OF THE AMERICAS

Tucson, Arizona

For Information Write to International Institute of the Americas, Tucson, AZ 85711-5444.

ITT TECHNICAL INSTITUTE

Phoenix, Arizona

ITT Technical Institute is a coed, proprietary, primarily two-year college of ITT Educational Services, Inc., founded in 1972, offering degrees at the associate and bachelor's levels. It has a 2-acre campus in Phoenix.

Expenses for 2003–04 *Application fee:* $100. *Tuition:* $347 per credit hour part-time.

For Further Information Contact Mr. Gene McWhorter, Director of Recruitment, ITT Technical Institute, 4837 East McDowell Road, Phoenix, AZ 85008. *Telephone:* 602-252-2331 or 800-879-4881 (toll-free). *Fax:* 602-267-8727. *Web site:* http://www.itt-tech.edu/.

ITT TECHNICAL INSTITUTE

Tempe, Arizona

For Information Write to ITT Technical Institute, Tempe, AZ 85282.

ITT TECHNICAL INSTITUTE

Tucson, Arizona

ITT Tech is a coed, proprietary, primarily two-year college of ITT Educational Services, Inc., founded in 1984, offering degrees at the associate and bachelor's levels. It has a 3-acre campus in Tucson.

Student Body Statistics The student body is made up of 375 undergraduates.
Financial Aid Forms of aid include need-based scholarships and part-time jobs. The application deadline for financial aid is continuous.
Freshman Admission ITT Tech requires a high school transcript, an interview, TOEFL scores for international students, and Wonderlic aptitude test. Recommendations are recommended. The application deadline for regular admission is rolling.
Transfer Admission The application deadline for admission is rolling.
Entrance Difficulty ITT Tech assesses its entrance difficulty level as minimally difficult.

For Further Information Contact Ms. Linda Lemken, Director of Recruitment, ITT Technical Institute, 1455 West River Road, Tucson, AZ 85704. *Telephone:* 520-408-7488 or 800-870-9730 (toll-free). *Fax:* 520-292-9899. *Web site:* http://www.itt-tech.edu/.

METROPOLITAN COLLEGE OF COURT REPORTING

Phoenix, Arizona

For Information Write to Metropolitan College of Court Reporting, Phoenix, AZ 85040.

MIDWESTERN UNIVERSITY, GLENDALE CAMPUS

Glendale, Arizona

Midwestern University, Glendale Campus is a coed, private, upper-level institution, founded in 1996, offering degrees at the bachelor's, master's, and doctoral levels and postbachelor's certificates.

Expenses for 2003–04 *Tuition:* $14,440 full-time. *Mandatory fees:* $250 full-time.

For Further Information Contact Mr. James Walter, Director of Admissions, Midwestern University, Glendale Campus, 19555 North 59th Avenue, Glendale, AZ 85308. *Telephone:* 623-572-3340, 888-247-9277 (toll-free in-state), or 888-247-9271 (toll-free out-of-state). *Fax:* 623-572-3229. *E-mail:* admissionaz@arizona.midwestern.edu. *Web site:* http://www.midwestern.edu/.

NORTHCENTRAL UNIVERSITY

Prescott, Arizona

Northcentral University is a coed, proprietary, comprehensive institution, offering degrees at the bachelor's, master's, and doctoral levels (offers only distance learning programs).

Academic Information The faculty has 103 members (9% full-time), 82% with terminal degrees. The undergraduate student-faculty ratio is 1:1. Special programs include advanced placement credit, accelerated degree programs, distance learning, summer session for credit, part-time degree

Northcentral University (continued)

programs, and external degree programs. The most frequently chosen baccalaureate fields are business/marketing, computer/information sciences.
Student Body Statistics The student body totals 1,101, of whom 132 are undergraduates (4 freshmen). 44 percent are women and 56 percent are men. Students come from 51 states and territories. 7 percent are from Arizona.
Expenses for 2003–04 *Application fee:* $100. *Tuition:* $335 per credit part-time.
Freshman Admission Northcentral University requires an essay, a high school transcript, and TOEFL scores for international students. The application deadline for regular admission is rolling.
Transfer Admission The application deadline for admission is rolling.
Entrance Difficulty Northcentral University assesses its entrance difficulty level as minimally difficult.

For Further Information Contact Ms. Poppy Keegan, Admissions Counselor, Northcentral University, 505 West Whipple Street, Prescott, AZ 86301. *Telephone:* 888-327-2877 Ext. 8072 or 888-327-2877 (toll-free). *Fax:* 928-541-7817. *E-mail:* info@ncu.edu. *Web site:* http://www.ncu.edu/.

NORTHERN ARIZONA UNIVERSITY

Flagstaff, Arizona

NAU is a coed, public unit of Arizona University System, founded in 1899, offering degrees at the bachelor's, master's, doctoral, and first professional levels and post-master's and postbachelor's certificates. It has a 730-acre campus in Flagstaff.

Academic Information The faculty has 1,142 members (62% full-time), 61% with terminal degrees. The undergraduate student-faculty ratio is 17:1. The library holds 633,417 titles, 2,595 serial subscriptions, and 31,746 audiovisual materials. Special programs include services for learning-disabled students, an honors program, cooperative (work-study) education, study abroad, advanced placement credit, accelerated degree programs, Freshman Honors College, ESL programs, double majors, independent study, distance learning, summer session for credit, part-time degree programs (daytime, evenings, summer), internships, and arrangement for off-campus study with National Student Exchange. The most frequently chosen baccalaureate fields are business/marketing, education, liberal arts/general studies.
Student Body Statistics The student body totals 18,824, of whom 13,015 are undergraduates. 60 percent are women and 40 percent are men. Students come from 50 states and territories and 66 other countries. 85 percent are from Arizona. 1.8 percent are international students. 51 percent of the 2003 graduating class went on to graduate and professional schools.
Expenses for 2003–04 *Application fee:* $25. *State resident tuition:* $3508 full-time, $183 per credit part-time. *Nonresident tuition:* $12,028 full-time, $501 per credit part-time. *Mandatory fees:* $120 full-time, $22 per term part-time. Full-time tuition and fees vary according to program. Part-time tuition and fees vary according to course load and program. *College room and board:* $5374. *College room only:* $2708. Room and board charges vary according to board plan and housing facility.
Financial Aid Forms of aid include need-based and non-need-based scholarships, athletic grants, and part-time jobs. The average aided 2003–04 undergraduate received an aid package worth an estimated $7898. The priority application deadline for financial aid is February 14.
Freshman Admission NAU requires a high school transcript and TOEFL scores for international students. A minimum 3.0 high school GPA is recommended. An essay, recommendations, an interview, SAT I scores, ACT scores, and SAT I or ACT scores are required for some. The application deadline for regular admission is August 1.
Transfer Admission The application deadline for admission is rolling.
Entrance Difficulty NAU assesses its entrance difficulty level as moderately difficult.

For Further Information Contact Janet Heinrichs, Assistant Director, Northern Arizona University, PO Box 4084, Flagstaff, AZ 86011. *Telephone:* 928-523-8483 or 888-MORE-NAU (toll-free). *Fax:* 928-523-6023. *E-mail:* undergraduate.admissions@nau.edu. *Web site:* http://www.nau.edu/.

See page 184 for a narrative description.

PRESCOTT COLLEGE

Prescott, Arizona

Prescott College is a coed, private, comprehensive institution, founded in 1966, offering degrees at the bachelor's and master's levels.

Academic Information The faculty has 63 members (98% full-time), 54% with terminal degrees. The undergraduate student-faculty ratio is 12:1. The library holds 23,293 titles, 262 serial subscriptions, and 1,364 audiovisual materials. Special programs include services for learning-disabled students, advanced placement credit, double majors, independent study, self-designed majors, summer session for credit, external degree programs, adult/continuing education programs, internships, and arrangement for off-campus study with Four Corners School of Outdoor Education, Grand Canyon Field Institute. The most frequently chosen baccalaureate fields are education, natural resources/environmental science, psychology.
Student Body Statistics The student body totals 995, of whom 778 are undergraduates (31 freshmen). 59 percent are women and 41 percent are men. Students come from 44 states and territories and 1 other country. 13 percent are from Arizona. 0.7 percent are international students.
Expenses for 2003–04 *Application fee:* $25. *Tuition:* $14,970 full-time, $453 per credit hour part-time. *Mandatory fees:* $1652 full-time. Full-time tuition and fees vary according to course load and program. Part-time tuition varies according to course load and program.
Financial Aid Forms of aid include need-based scholarships and part-time jobs. The average aided 2002–03 undergraduate received an aid package worth $4560. The application deadline for financial aid is continuous.
Freshman Admission Prescott College requires an essay, a high school transcript, 2 recommendations, and TOEFL scores for international students. An interview is required for some. The application deadline for regular admission is February 1.
Transfer Admission The application deadline for admission is February 1.
Entrance Difficulty Prescott College assesses its entrance difficulty level as moderately difficult. For the fall 2003 freshman class, 86 percent of the applicants were accepted.

For Further Information Contact Ms. Shari Sterling, Director of Admissions, Prescott College, 220 Grove Avenue, Prescott, AZ 86301. *Telephone:* 928-778-2090 Ext. 2101 or 877-350-2100 (toll-free). *Fax:* 928-776-5242. *E-mail:* admissions@prescott.edu. *Web site:* http://www.prescott.edu/.

REMINGTON COLLEGE–TEMPE CAMPUS

Tempe, Arizona

For Information Write to Remington College–Tempe Campus, Tempe, AZ 85284.

SOUTHWESTERN COLLEGE

Phoenix, Arizona

SWC is a coed, private, Conservative Baptist, four-year college, founded in 1960, offering degrees at the associate and bachelor's levels. It has a 19-acre campus in Phoenix.

Academic Information The faculty has 33 members (27% full-time), 100% with terminal degrees. The student-faculty ratio is 17:1. The library holds 32,000 titles, 293 serial subscriptions, and 2,567 audiovisual materials. Special programs include academic remediation, advanced placement credit, accelerated degree programs, summer session for credit, adult/continuing education programs, and internships. The most frequently chosen baccalaureate fields are education, philosophy, religion, and theology, psychology.
Student Body Statistics The student body is made up of 267 undergraduates (29 freshmen). 52 percent are women and 48 percent are men. Students come from 19 states and territories and 3 other countries. 84 percent are from Arizona. 1.1 percent are international students.
Expenses for 2004–05 *Application fee:* $25. *Comprehensive fee:* $15,240 includes full-time tuition ($10,600), mandatory fees ($440), and college room and board ($4200). *College room only:* $3200. Full-time tuition and fees vary according to course load and program. Room and board charges vary according to housing facility. *Part-time tuition:* $442 per credit hour. *Part-time mandatory fees:* $220 per term. Part-time tuition and fees vary according to course load and program.
Financial Aid Forms of aid include need-based and non-need-based scholarships and part-time jobs. The average aided 2003–04 undergraduate received an aid package worth an estimated $5500. The priority application deadline for financial aid is March 15.
Freshman Admission SWC requires an essay, a high school transcript, a minimum 2.0 high school GPA, 1 recommendation, SAT I and SAT II or ACT scores, and TOEFL scores for international students. The application deadline for regular admission is August 1.
Transfer Admission The application deadline for admission is August 1.
Entrance Difficulty SWC assesses its entrance difficulty level as minimally difficult. For the fall 2003 freshman class, 61 percent of the applicants were accepted.

For Further Information Contact Lambur Cruz, Admissions/Financial Aid Counselor, Southwestern College, 2625 East Cactus Road, Administration Building, Phoenix, AZ 85015. *Telephone:* 602-992-6101 Ext. 114 or 800-247-2697 (toll-free). *Fax:* 602-404-2159. *E-mail:* admissions@swcaz.edu. *Web site:* http://www.swcaz.edu/.

TOHONO O'ODHAM COMMUNITY COLLEGE

Sells, Arizona

For Information Write to Tohono O'odham Community College, Sells, AZ 85634.

UNIVERSITY OF ADVANCING TECHNOLOGY

Tempe, Arizona

UAT is a coed, proprietary, comprehensive institution, founded in 1983, offering degrees at the associate, bachelor's, and master's levels.

Academic Information The faculty has 50 members (82% full-time). The undergraduate student-faculty ratio is 15:1. Special programs include accelerated degree programs and distance learning.
Student Body Statistics The student body totals 760, of whom 744 are undergraduates (170 freshmen). 7 percent are women and 93 percent are men. 1.5 percent are international students.
Expenses for 2003–04 *Application fee:* $0. *Comprehensive fee:* $21,400 includes full-time tuition ($13,600) and college room and board ($7800). *College room only:* $4200.
Financial Aid Forms of aid include need-based and non-need-based scholarships and part-time jobs. The application deadline for financial aid is continuous.
Freshman Admission UAT requires a high school transcript, an interview, SAT I or ACT scores, and TOEFL scores for international students. An essay is recommended. A minimum 2.5 high school GPA and Wonderlic aptitude test are required for some. The application deadline for regular admission is rolling.

For Further Information Contact Mr. Dominic Pistillo, President, University of Advancing Technology, 2625 West Baseline Road, Tempe, AZ 85283-1042. *Telephone:* 602-383-8228, 602-383-8228 (toll-free in-state), or 800-658-5744 (toll-free out-of-state). *Fax:* 602-383-8222. *E-mail:* admissions@uact.edu. *Web site:* http://www.uat.edu/.

See page 190 for a narrative description.

THE UNIVERSITY OF ARIZONA

Tucson, Arizona

UA is a coed, public unit of Arizona Board of Regents, founded in 1885, offering degrees at the bachelor's, master's, doctoral, and first professional levels and postbachelor's certificates. It has a 362-acre campus in Tucson.

Academic Information The faculty has 1,362 members. The undergraduate student-faculty ratio is 20:1. The library holds 4 million titles, 23,790 serial subscriptions, and 51,136 audiovisual materials. Special programs include services for learning-disabled students, an honors program, study abroad, advanced placement credit, Freshman Honors College, ESL programs, double majors, independent study, distance learning, summer session for credit, part-time degree programs (daytime, evenings, summer), adult/continuing education programs, and internships. The most frequently chosen baccalaureate fields are business/marketing, communications/communication technologies, social sciences and history.
Student Body Statistics The student body totals 37,083, of whom 28,482 are undergraduates (5,958 freshmen). 53 percent are women and 47 percent are men. Students come from 56 states and territories and 135 other countries. 72 percent are from Arizona. 3.4 percent are international students.
Expenses for 2003–04 *Application fee:* $0. *State resident tuition:* $3508 full-time, $197 per unit part-time. *Nonresident tuition:* $12,278 full-time, $526 per unit part-time. *Mandatory fees:* $95 full-time. Full-time tuition and fees vary according to course load and program. Part-time tuition varies according to course load. *College room and board:* $6810. *College room only:* $3570. Room and board charges vary according to board plan and housing facility.
Financial Aid Forms of aid include need-based and non-need-based scholarships and part-time jobs. The average aided 2002–03 undergraduate received an aid package worth $9993. The priority application deadline for financial aid is March 1.
Freshman Admission UA requires a high school transcript, SAT I or ACT scores, and TOEFL scores for international students. A minimum 3.0 high school GPA, recommendations, and an interview are required for some. The application deadline for regular admission is April 1.
Transfer Admission The application deadline for admission is June 1.
Entrance Difficulty UA assesses its entrance difficulty level as moderately difficult; very difficult for architecture, engineering, allied health, pharmacy, nursing, business, public administration, education programs. For the fall 2003 freshman class, 85 percent of the applicants were accepted.

For Further Information Contact Ms. Lori Goldman, Director of Admissions, The University of Arizona, PO Box 210011, Tucson, AZ 85721-0040. *Telephone:* 520-621-3237. *Fax:* 520-621-9799. *E-mail:* appinfo@arizona.edu. *Web site:* http://www.arizona.edu/.

UNIVERSITY OF PHOENIX ONLINE CAMPUS

Phoenix, Arizona

UOP is a coed, proprietary, comprehensive institution, founded in 1989, offering degrees at the associate, bachelor's, master's, and

University of Phoenix Online Campus (continued)

doctoral levels and post-master's and postbachelor's certificates (courses conducted at 121 campuses and learning centers in 25 states).

Academic Information The faculty has 4,363 members, 23% with terminal degrees. The undergraduate student-faculty ratio is 12:1. The library holds 27 million titles and 11,648 serial subscriptions. Special programs include advanced placement credit, accelerated degree programs, independent study, distance learning, external degree programs, and adult/continuing education programs. The most frequently chosen baccalaureate fields are business/marketing, computer/information sciences, health professions and related sciences.

Student Body Statistics The student body totals 45,827, of whom 27,799 are undergraduates (1,671 freshmen). 64 percent are women and 36 percent are men. 9.4 percent are international students.

Expenses for 2003–04 *Tuition:* $12,660 full-time, $422 per credit part-time.

Financial Aid Forms of aid include need-based and non-need-based scholarships. The average aided 2002–03 undergraduate received an aid package worth $1301. The application deadline for financial aid is continuous.

Freshman Admission UOP requires 1 recommendation and 2 years of work experience, 23 years of age. A high school transcript is required for some. The application deadline for regular admission is rolling.

Transfer Admission The application deadline for admission is rolling.

Entrance Difficulty UOP has an open admission policy.

For Further Information Contact Ms. Beth Barilla, Director of Admissions, University of Phoenix Online Campus, 4615 East Elwood Street, Mail Stop AA-K101, Phoenix, AZ 85040-1958. *Telephone:* 480-557-1712, 800-776-4867 (toll-free in-state), or 800-228-7240 (toll-free out-of-state). *E-mail:* beth.barilla@apollogrp.edu. *Web site:* http://www.uoponline.com/.

UNIVERSITY OF PHOENIX–PHOENIX CAMPUS

Phoenix, Arizona

UOP is a coed, proprietary, comprehensive institution, founded in 1976, offering degrees at the associate, bachelor's, master's, and doctoral levels and post-master's and postbachelor's certificates (courses conducted at 121 campuses and learning centers in 25 states).

Academic Information The faculty has 2,256 members (2% full-time), 25% with terminal degrees. The undergraduate student-faculty ratio is 9:1. The library holds 27 million titles and 11,648 serial subscriptions. Special programs include advanced placement credit, accelerated degree programs, independent study, distance learning, external degree programs, and adult/continuing education programs. The most frequently chosen baccalaureate fields are business/marketing, computer/information sciences, health professions and related sciences.

Student Body Statistics The student body totals 4,766, of whom 3,071 are undergraduates (112 freshmen). 58 percent are women and 42 percent are men. 5.3 percent are international students.

Expenses for 2003–04 *Application fee:* $85. *Tuition:* $8760 full-time, $292 per credit part-time.

Financial Aid Forms of aid include need-based and non-need-based scholarships. The average aided 2002–03 undergraduate received an aid package worth $1437. The application deadline for financial aid is continuous.

Freshman Admission UOP requires 1 recommendation, 2 years of work experience, 23 years of age, and TOEFL scores for international students. A high school transcript is required for some. The application deadline for regular admission is rolling.

Transfer Admission The application deadline for admission is rolling.

Entrance Difficulty UOP has an open admission policy.

For Further Information Contact Ms. Beth Barilla, Director of Admissions, University of Phoenix–Phoenix Campus, 4615 East Elwood Street, Mail Stop AA-K101, Phoenix, AZ 85040-1958. *Telephone:* 480-557-1712, 800-776-4867 (toll-free in-state), or 800-228-7240 (toll-free out-of-state). *Fax:* 480-894-1758. *E-mail:* beth.barilla@phoenix.edu. *Web site:* http://www.phoenix.edu/.

UNIVERSITY OF PHOENIX–SOUTHERN ARIZONA CAMPUS

Tucson, Arizona

University of Phoenix–Southern Arizona Campus is a coed, proprietary, comprehensive institution, founded in 1979, offering degrees at the associate, bachelor's, master's, and doctoral levels and post-master's and postbachelor's certificates (courses conducted at 121 campuses and learning centers in 25 states).

Academic Information The faculty has 650 members (1% full-time), 27% with terminal degrees. The undergraduate student-faculty ratio is 8:1. The library holds 27 million titles and 11,648 serial subscriptions. Special programs include advanced placement credit, accelerated degree programs, independent study, distance learning, external degree programs, and adult/continuing education programs. The most frequently chosen baccalaureate fields are business/marketing, computer/information sciences, health professions and related sciences.

Student Body Statistics The student body totals 1,683, of whom 1,107 are undergraduates (46 freshmen). 61 percent are women and 39 percent are men. 16.2 percent are international students.

Expenses for 2003–04 *Application fee:* $85. *Tuition:* $8490 full-time, $283 per credit part-time.

Financial Aid The application deadline for financial aid is continuous.

Freshman Admission University of Phoenix–Southern Arizona Campus requires 1 recommendation, 2 years of work experience, 23 years of age, and TOEFL scores for international students. A high school transcript is required for some. The application deadline for regular admission is rolling.

Transfer Admission The application deadline for admission is rolling.

Entrance Difficulty University of Phoenix–Southern Arizona Campus has an open admission policy.

For Further Information Contact Ms. Beth Barilla, Director of Admissions, University of Phoenix–Southern Arizona Campus, 4615 East Elwood Street, Mail Stop AA-K101, Phoenix, AZ 85040-1958. *Telephone:* 480-557-1712 or 800-228-7240 (toll-free). *Fax:* 480-594-1756. *E-mail:* beth.barilla@phoenix.edu. *Web site:* http://www.phoenix.edu/.

WESTERN INTERNATIONAL UNIVERSITY

Phoenix, Arizona

WIU is a coed, proprietary, comprehensive institution, founded in 1978, offering degrees at the associate, bachelor's, and master's levels. It has a 4-acre campus in Phoenix.

Expenses for 2003–04 *Application fee:* $85. *Tuition:* $9180 full-time.

For Further Information Contact Ms. Jo Arney, Director of Student Services, Western International University, 9215 North Black Canyon Highway, Phoenix, AZ 85021. *Telephone:* 602-943-2311 Ext. 139. *Web site:* http://www.wintu.edu/.

California

ACADEMY OF ART UNIVERSITY

San Francisco, California

Academy of Art University is a coed, proprietary, comprehensive institution, founded in 1929, offering degrees at the associate, bachelor's, and master's levels in art. It has a 3-acre campus in San Francisco.

Academic Information The faculty has 725 members (17% full-time), 93% with terminal degrees. The undergraduate student-faculty ratio is 15:1. The library holds 35,000 titles, 300 serial subscriptions, and 115,000 audiovisual materials. Special programs include academic remediation, ESL programs, independent study, summer session for credit, part-time degree programs, adult/continuing education programs, and internships. The most frequently chosen baccalaureate field is visual/performing arts.
Student Body Statistics The student body totals 6,702, of whom 5,693 are undergraduates (1,397 freshmen). 47 percent are women and 53 percent are men. Students come from 53 states and territories and 52 other countries. 61 percent are from California. 13 percent of the 2003 graduating class went on to graduate and professional schools.
Expenses for 2004–05 *Application fee:* $100. *Comprehensive fee:* $25,200 includes full-time tuition ($13,200) and college room and board ($12,000). *College room only:* $8400. Full-time tuition varies according to course load. Room and board charges vary according to housing facility. *Part-time tuition:* $550 per unit. *Part-time mandatory fees:* $30 per term. Part-time tuition and fees vary according to course load.
Financial Aid Forms of aid include need-based scholarships and part-time jobs. The average aided 2002–03 undergraduate received an aid package worth $6217. The priority application deadline for financial aid is March 2.
Freshman Admission Academy of Art University requires a high school transcript. A minimum 2.0 high school GPA, an interview, and a portfolio are recommended. The application deadline for regular admission is rolling.
Transfer Admission The application deadline for admission is rolling.
Entrance Difficulty Academy of Art University has an open admission policy. It assesses its entrance difficulty as minimally difficult for transfers.

For Further Information Contact Mr. John Meurer, Vice President-Admissions, Academy of Art University, 79 New Montgomery Street, San Francisco, CA 94105. *Telephone:* 415-263-5518 Ext. 5518 or 800-544-ARTS (toll-free). *Fax:* 415-263-4130. *E-mail:* info@academyart.edu. *Web site:* http://www.academyart.edu/.

See page 156 for a narrative description.

ALLIANT INTERNATIONAL UNIVERSITY

San Diego, California

Alliant International University is a coed, private unit of Alliant International University, founded in 1952, offering degrees at the bachelor's, master's, and doctoral levels and postbachelor's certificates. It has a 60-acre campus in San Diego.

Academic Information The faculty has 589 members (27% full-time), 98% with terminal degrees. The undergraduate student-faculty ratio is 15:1. The library holds 142,303 titles, 15,150 serial subscriptions, and 1,658 audiovisual materials. Special programs include academic remediation, services for learning-disabled students, an honors program, study abroad, advanced placement credit, ESL programs, independent study, summer session for credit, part-time degree programs (daytime, evenings), adult/continuing education programs, and internships. The most frequently chosen baccalaureate fields are business/marketing, psychology, social sciences and history.
Student Body Statistics The student body totals 3,508, of whom 420 are undergraduates (71 freshmen). 55 percent are women and 45 percent are men. Students come from 16 states and territories and 78 other countries. 84 percent are from California. 32.4 percent are international students. 14 percent of the 2003 graduating class went on to graduate and professional schools.
Expenses for 2004–05 *Application fee:* $40. *Comprehensive fee:* $26,790 includes full-time tuition ($18,990), mandatory fees ($370), and college room and board ($7430). Full-time tuition and fees vary according to course load. Room and board charges vary according to board plan and housing facility. *Part-time tuition:* $695 per unit. Part-time tuition varies according to course load.
Financial Aid Forms of aid include need-based and non-need-based scholarships, athletic grants, and part-time jobs. The average aided 2002–03 undergraduate received an aid package worth $21,250. The priority application deadline for financial aid is March 2.
Freshman Admission Alliant International University requires a high school transcript, a minimum 2.0 high school GPA, and TOEFL scores for international students. A minimum 3.0 high school GPA is recommended. The application deadline for regular admission is rolling.
Entrance Difficulty Alliant International University assesses its entrance difficulty level as moderately difficult. For the fall 2003 freshman class, 60 percent of the applicants were accepted.

For Further Information Contact Mr. Hernan Bucheli, System Director of Enrollment Management, Alliant International University, 10455 Pomerado Road, San Diego, CA 92131-1799. *Telephone:* 858-635-4777 or 866-825-5426 (toll-free). *Fax:* 858-635-4739. *E-mail:* admissions@alliant.edu. *Web site:* http://www.alliant.edu/.

AMERICAN ACADEMY OF DRAMATIC ARTS/HOLLYWOOD

Hollywood, California

AADA/Hollywood is a coed, private, two-year college, founded in 1974, offering degrees at the associate level in theater arts. It has a 4-acre campus in Hollywood near Los Angeles.

Academic Information The faculty has 28 members, 29% with terminal degrees. The student-faculty ratio is 15:1. The library holds 7,700 titles, 24 serial subscriptions, and 320 audiovisual materials.
Student Body Statistics The student body is made up of 177 undergraduates (45 freshmen). 58 percent are women and 42 percent are men. Students come from 21 states and territories and 3 other countries. 60 percent are from California. 8.5 percent are international students.
Expenses for 2004–05 *Application fee:* $50. *Tuition:* $14,900 full-time. *Mandatory fees:* $450 full-time.
Financial Aid Forms of aid include need-based scholarships and part-time jobs. The application deadline for financial aid is continuous.
Freshman Admission AADA/Hollywood requires an essay, a high school transcript, 2 recommendations, an interview, and audition. A minimum 2.0 high school GPA is recommended. The application deadline for regular admission is rolling.
Transfer Admission The application deadline for admission is rolling.
Entrance Difficulty AADA/Hollywood assesses its entrance difficulty level as moderately difficult. For the fall 2003 freshman class, 35 percent of the applicants were accepted.

For Further Information Contact Mr. Dan Justin, Director of Admissions, American Academy of Dramatic Arts/Hollywood, 1336 North LaBrea Avenue, Hollywood, CA 90028. *Telephone:* 800-222-2867 Ext. 103 or 800-222-2867 (toll-free). *Fax:* 323-464-1250. *E-mail:* admissions-ca@aada.org. *Web site:* http://www.aada.org/.

THE AMERICAN COLLEGE

See American InterContinental University

AMERICAN INTERCONTINENTAL UNIVERSITY

Los Angeles, California

AMLA is a coed, proprietary, comprehensive institution, founded in 1982, offering degrees at the associate, bachelor's, and master's levels.

Academic Information The faculty has 133 members (18% full-time), 29% with terminal degrees. The undergraduate student-faculty ratio is 24:1. The library holds 20,000 titles and 228 serial subscriptions. Special programs include academic remediation, study abroad, accelerated degree programs, double majors, distance learning, summer session for credit, part-time degree programs (daytime, evenings, summer), and internships. The most frequently chosen baccalaureate fields are business/marketing, computer/information sciences, visual/performing arts.

Student Body Statistics The student body totals 1,405, of whom 1,304 are undergraduates. 44 percent are women and 56 percent are men. Students come from 50 states and territories and 21 other countries. 73 percent are from California. 2.4 percent are international students. 10 percent of the 2003 graduating class went on to graduate and professional schools.

Financial Aid Forms of aid include need-based and non-need-based scholarships and part-time jobs. The application deadline for financial aid is continuous.

Freshman Admission AMLA requires an essay, a high school transcript, an interview, and TOEFL scores for international students. The application deadline for regular admission is rolling.

Transfer Admission The application deadline for admission is rolling.

Entrance Difficulty AMLA has an open admission policy.

For Further Information Contact Amadou Tall, Vice President-Marketing and Admissions, American InterContinental University, 12655 West Jefferson Boulevard, Los Angeles, CA 90066. *Telephone:* 310-302-2000 or 800-333-2652 (toll-free out-of-state). *Fax:* 310-302-2001. *Web site:* http://www.aiuniv.edu/.

ANTIOCH UNIVERSITY LOS ANGELES

Culver City, California

Antioch Los Angeles is a coed, private, upper-level unit of Antioch University, founded in 1972, offering degrees at the bachelor's and master's levels and post-master's and postbachelor's certificates. It has a 1-acre campus in Culver City near Los Angeles.

Academic Information The faculty has 172 members (12% full-time), 52% with terminal degrees. The undergraduate student-faculty ratio is 14:1. Special programs include academic remediation, services for learning-disabled students, cooperative (work-study) education, advanced placement credit, accelerated degree programs, double majors, independent study, distance learning, self-designed majors, summer session for credit, part-time degree programs (daytime, evenings, weekends, summer), external degree programs, adult/continuing education programs, and internships.

Student Body Statistics The student body totals 650, of whom 188 are undergraduates. 75 percent are women and 25 percent are men. Students come from 1 state or territory.

Expenses for 2003–04 *Application fee:* $60. *Tuition:* $15,995 full-time, $405 per unit part-time. *Mandatory fees:* $65 full-time. Full-time tuition and fees vary according to course load and program. Part-time tuition varies according to course load and program.

Transfer Admission Antioch Los Angeles requires a college transcript. Standardized test scores are required for some. The application deadline for admission is August 1.

Entrance Difficulty Antioch Los Angeles assesses its entrance difficulty level as moderately difficult. For the fall 2003 entering class, 88 percent of the applicants were accepted.

For Further Information Contact Ms. Kathie Rawding, Director of Admissions and Financial Aid, Antioch University Los Angeles, 400 Corporate Pointe, Culver City, CA 90230. *Telephone:* 310-578-1080 Ext. 217 or 800-7ANTIOCH (toll-free). *Fax:* 310-822-4824. *E-mail:* admissions@antiochla.edu. *Web site:* http://www.antiochla.edu/.

ANTIOCH UNIVERSITY SANTA BARBARA

Santa Barbara, California

Antioch University Santa Barbara is a coed, private, upper-level unit of Antioch University, founded in 1977, offering degrees at the bachelor's and master's levels. It is located in Santa Barbara near Los Angeles.

Academic Information The faculty has 62 members (19% full-time). The undergraduate student-faculty ratio is 15:1. Special programs include academic remediation, accelerated degree programs, independent study, self-designed majors, summer session for credit, part-time degree programs, adult/continuing education programs, and internships. The most frequently chosen baccalaureate field is liberal arts/general studies.

Student Body Statistics The student body totals 289, of whom 103 are undergraduates. 75 percent are women and 25 percent are men. 1.9 percent are international students. 30 percent of the 2003 graduating class went on to graduate and professional schools.

Expenses for 2003–04 *Application fee:* $60. *Tuition:* $11,985 full-time, $395 per unit part-time. *Mandatory fees:* $48 full-time. Full-time tuition and fees vary according to degree level. Part-time tuition varies according to course load and degree level.

Financial Aid Forms of aid include need-based scholarships and part-time jobs. The application deadline for financial aid is continuous.

Transfer Admission Antioch University Santa Barbara requires a college transcript and a minimum 2.0 college GPA. The application deadline for admission is rolling.

Entrance Difficulty Antioch University Santa Barbara assesses its entrance difficulty level as minimally difficult.

For Further Information Contact Mr. Richard Grisel, Director of Admissions, Antioch University Santa Barbara, 801 Garden Street, Santa Barbara, CA 93101-1580. *Telephone:* 805-962-8179 Ext. 113. *Fax:* 805-962-4786. *E-mail:* admissions@antiochsb.edu. *Web site:* http://www.antiochsb.edu/.

ARGOSY UNIVERSITY/ORANGE COUNTY

Orange, California

Argosy University/Orange County is a coed, proprietary, upper-level institution, offering degrees at the bachelor's, master's, and doctoral levels. It is located in Orange near Los Angeles and San Diego.

Academic Information The faculty has 81 members (14% full-time), 90% with terminal degrees. The undergraduate student-faculty ratio is 22:1. The library holds 1,200 titles and 50 serial subscriptions. Special programs include academic remediation, services for learning-disabled students, distance learning, and part-time degree programs (daytime, evenings, weekends, summer).

Student Body Statistics The student body totals 646, of whom 81 are undergraduates. 59 percent are women and 41 percent are men.

Expenses for 2003–04 *Application fee:* $50. *Tuition:* $360 per credit hour part-time. *Mandatory fees:* $25 per year part-time. Part-time tuition and fees vary according to degree level and location.

Financial Aid Forms of aid include need-based and non-need-based scholarships and part-time jobs. The average aided 2003–04 undergraduate received an aid package worth an estimated $3586.

Entrance Difficulty Argosy University/Orange County assesses its entrance difficulty level as moderately difficult.

For Further Information Contact Mark Betz, Director, Admissions, Argosy University/Orange County, 3745 West Chapman Avenue, Suite 100, Orange, CA 92868. *Telephone:* 714-940-0025 Ext. 4815 or 800-716-9598 Ext. 4819 (toll-free). *Fax:* 714-940-0767. *E-mail:* auocadmissions@argosyu.edu. *Web site:* http://www.argosyu.edu/.

ARGOSY UNIVERSITY/SAN FRANCISCO BAY AREA

Point Richmond, California

Argosy University/San Francisco Bay Area is a coed, proprietary, upper-level institution, founded in 1998, offering degrees at the bachelor's, master's, and doctoral levels. It is located in Point Richmond near Oakland and San Francisco.

Academic Information The faculty has 11 members (9% full-time), 100% with terminal degrees. The undergraduate student-faculty ratio is 10:1.
Student Body Statistics The student body is made up of 45 undergraduates. 56 percent are women and 44 percent are men. Students come from 1 state or territory and 2 other countries. 4.4 percent are international students. 50 percent of the 2003 graduating class went on to graduate and professional schools.
Expenses for 2003–04 *Tuition:* $360 per credit hour part-time.
Financial Aid Forms of aid include need-based and non-need-based scholarships and part-time jobs. The average aided 2003–04 undergraduate received an aid package worth an estimated $2973. The application deadline for financial aid is continuous.

For Further Information Contact Argosy University/San Francisco Bay Area, 999 Canal Boulevard, Suite A, Point Richmond, CA 94804. *Telephone:* 510-215-0277, 866-215-2777 Ext. 205 (toll-free in-state), or 866-215-2777 (toll-free out-of-state). *Fax:* 510-215-0299. *E-mail:* jstofan@argosyu.edu. *Web site:* http://www.argosyu.edu/.

ART CENTER COLLEGE OF DESIGN

Pasadena, California

Art Center is a coed, private, comprehensive institution, founded in 1930, offering degrees at the bachelor's and master's levels. It has a 175-acre campus in Pasadena near Los Angeles.

Academic Information The faculty has 407 members (16% full-time). The undergraduate student-faculty ratio is 12:1. The library holds 77,000 titles, 400 serial subscriptions, and 7,000 audiovisual materials. Special programs include advanced placement credit, accelerated degree programs, independent study, summer session for credit, adult/continuing education programs, and internships. The most frequently chosen baccalaureate field is visual/performing arts.
Student Body Statistics The student body totals 1,533, of whom 1,412 are undergraduates (43 freshmen). 42 percent are women and 58 percent are men. Students come from 36 states and territories and 32 other countries. 79 percent are from California. 15.6 percent are international students.
Expenses for 2004–05 *Application fee:* $45. *Tuition:* $23,450 full-time.
Financial Aid Forms of aid include need-based scholarships and part-time jobs. The average aided 2003–04 undergraduate received an aid package worth an estimated $21,214. The priority application deadline for financial aid is March 1.
Freshman Admission Art Center requires an essay, a high school transcript, a portfolio, and TOEFL scores for international students. A minimum 3.0 high school GPA and an interview are recommended. SAT I or ACT scores are required for some. The application deadline for regular admission is rolling.
Transfer Admission The application deadline for admission is rolling.
Entrance Difficulty Art Center assesses its entrance difficulty level as very difficult. For the fall 2003 freshman class, 72 percent of the applicants were accepted.

For Further Information Contact Ms. Kit Baron, Vice President of Admissions, Art Center College of Design, 1700 Lida Street, Pasadena, CA 91103-1999. *Telephone:* 626-396-2373. *Fax:* 626-795-0578. *E-mail:* admissions@artcenter.edu. *Web site:* http://www.artcenter.edu/.

THE ART INSTITUTE OF CALIFORNIA–LOS ANGELES

Santa Monica, California

For Information Write to The Art Institute of California–Los Angeles, Santa Monica, CA 90405-3035.

THE ART INSTITUTE OF CALIFORNIA–ORANGE COUNTY

Santa Ana, California

For Information Write to The Art Institute of California–Orange County, Santa Ana, CA 92704-9888.

THE ART INSTITUTE OF CALIFORNIA–SAN DIEGO

San Diego, California

The Art Institute of California–San Diego is a coed, proprietary, four-year college of The Art Institutes/Argosy, founded in 1981, offering degrees at the associate and bachelor's levels.

Academic Information The faculty has 91 members. The student-faculty ratio is 22:1. The library holds 1,100 titles and 17 serial subscriptions. Special programs include services for learning-disabled students, cooperative (work-study) education, double majors, summer session for credit, and internships. The most frequently chosen baccalaureate fields are communications/communication technologies, visual/performing arts.
Student Body Statistics The student body is made up of 1,329 undergraduates. 42 percent are women and 58 percent are men. Students come from 23 states and territories. 80 percent are from California. 3.9 percent are international students.
Expenses for 2004–05 *Application fee:* $50. *Tuition:* $17,472 full-time, $364 per credit part-time. *Mandatory fees:* $595 full-time. Full-time tuition and fees vary according to program. *College room only:* $8580.
Financial Aid Forms of aid include need-based and non-need-based scholarships and part-time jobs. The application deadline for financial aid is continuous.
Freshman Admission The Art Institute of California–San Diego requires an essay, a high school transcript, an interview, and TOEFL scores for international students. The application deadline for regular admission is rolling.
Transfer Admission The application deadline for admission is rolling.
Entrance Difficulty The Art Institute of California–San Diego assesses its entrance difficulty level as minimally difficult.

For Further Information Contact Ms. Sandy Park, Director of Admissions, The Art Institute of California–San Diego, 7650 Mission Valley Road, San Diego, CA 92108. *Telephone:* 858-598-1399 Ext. 1208 or 800-591-2422 Ext. 3117 (toll-free in-state). *Fax:* 619-291-3206. *E-mail:* info@aii.edu. *Web site:* http://www.aica.artinstitutes.edu/.

THE ART INSTITUTE OF CALIFORNIA–SAN FRANCISCO

San Francisco, California

The Art Institute of California–San Francisco is a coed, proprietary, four-year college of Education Management Corporation, founded in 1939, offering degrees at the associate and bachelor's levels in fashion.

Academic Information The faculty has 66 members (8% full-time). The student-faculty ratio is 16:1. Special programs include accelerated degree programs, distance learning, summer session for credit, part-time degree programs (daytime, evenings, summer), and internships.
Student Body Statistics The student body is made up of 918 undergraduates.
Expenses for 2003–04 *Application fee:* $50. *Tuition:* $17,472 full-time, $364 per credit hour part-time. *Mandatory fees:* $150 full-time.
Financial Aid Forms of aid include need-based and non-need-based scholarships and part-time jobs. The priority application deadline for financial aid is March 2.
Freshman Admission The Art Institute of California–San Francisco requires an essay, a high school transcript, and TOEFL scores for international students. A minimum 2.0 high school GPA, 2 recommendations, and an interview are recommended. The application deadline for regular admission is rolling.
Transfer Admission The application deadline for admission is rolling.
Entrance Difficulty The Art Institute of California–San Francisco assesses its entrance difficulty level as moderately difficult; minimally difficult for transfers.

For Further Information Contact Daniel Cardenas, Admissions Department, The Art Institute of California–San Francisco, 1170 Market Street, San Francisco, CA 94102-4908. *Telephone:* 415-865-0198 or 888-493-3261 (toll-free). *Fax:* 415-863-6344. *E-mail:* aisfadm@aii.edu. *Web site:* http://www.aicasf.artinstitutes.edu/.

ART INSTITUTE OF SOUTHERN CALIFORNIA

See Laguna College of Art & Design

ART INSTITUTES INTERNATIONAL AT SAN FRANCISCO

See The Art Institute of California–San Francisco

AZUSA PACIFIC UNIVERSITY

Azusa, California

APU is a coed, private, nondenominational, comprehensive institution, founded in 1899, offering degrees at the bachelor's, master's, doctoral, and first professional levels. It has a 60-acre campus in Azusa near Los Angeles.

Academic Information The faculty has 920 members (29% full-time). The undergraduate student-faculty ratio is 12:1. The library holds 176,679 titles, 14,000 serial subscriptions, and 6,004 audiovisual materials. Special programs include academic remediation, services for learning-disabled students, an honors program, cooperative (work-study) education, study abroad, advanced placement credit, accelerated degree programs, Freshman Honors College, ESL programs, double majors, distance learning, summer session for credit, part-time degree programs (daytime), adult/continuing education programs, internships, and arrangement for off-campus study. The most frequently chosen baccalaureate fields are business/marketing, health professions and related sciences, liberal arts/general studies.
Student Body Statistics The student body totals 8,191, of whom 4,373 are undergraduates (912 freshmen). 64 percent are women and 36 percent are men. Students come from 44 states and territories and 52 other countries. 81 percent are from California. 1.8 percent are international students.
Expenses for 2003–04 *Application fee:* $45. *Comprehensive fee:* $24,720 includes full-time tuition ($18,790), mandatory fees ($234), and college room and board ($5696). *College room only:* $3150. Room and board charges vary according to board plan, housing facility, and student level. *Part-time tuition:* $750 per credit hour. Part-time tuition varies according to course load.
Financial Aid Forms of aid include need-based and non-need-based scholarships, athletic grants, and part-time jobs. The average aided 2002–03 undergraduate received an aid package worth $12,616. The application deadline for financial aid is July 1 with a priority deadline of March 2.
Freshman Admission APU requires an essay, a high school transcript, a minimum 2.5 high school GPA, 2 recommendations, SAT I or ACT scores, and TOEFL scores for international students. An interview is required for some. The application deadline for regular admission is June 1 and for early action it is December 1.
Transfer Admission The application deadline for admission is June 1.
Entrance Difficulty APU assesses its entrance difficulty level as moderately difficult. For the fall 2003 freshman class, 83 percent of the applicants were accepted.

SPECIAL MESSAGE TO STUDENTS

Social Life Students participate in many social activities, including Christian outreach groups, community service organizations, music ensembles, theatrical performances, campus publications, student government, and intramural sports. Specific opportunities include University Choir, the Oxford Study Abroad Program, Multi-Ethnic Student Alliance, overseas missions, the Alpha Chi Honor Society, and powder puff football. Azusa Pacific University (APU) sponsors fourteen teams, including football, in a dominant, nationally ranked athletic program and is a member of the National Association of Intercollegiate Athletics (NAIA).

Academic Highlights Azusa Pacific University recommends more students for credentials in education, business, behavioral sciences, nursing, and the liberal arts than almost any other private university in California. Recognized in the top twenty-five of *U.S. News & World Report's* America's Best Colleges, Western Universities-Master's classification, securing twenty-second place for the third consecutive year, APU's academics have received national acclaim. With more than forty dynamic fields of undergraduate study and preprofessional programs to choose from, APU has an academically well-rounded student body. In addition, APU sponsors programs that increase international awareness, cultural understanding, and critical-thinking skills, such as the intensive global-learning and inner-city terms. Many state-of-the-art facilities also provide environments that are conducive to the twenty-first-century learner. These contemporary buildings include the $14-million Richard and Vivian Felix Event Center, the $5-million Wilden Hall of Business and Management, the $8-million Hugh and Hazel Darling Library, and the new Duke Academic Center and Technology Library.

Interviews and Campus Visits APU provides students with a solid comprehensive education, introduces them to the Christian faith, initiates lifelong learning, and prepares them to enter the world as disciples and scholars. An admissions interview is strongly recommended, and preview days enable prospective students to experience campus life firsthand—visiting classes, meeting with faculty members, and interacting with current students. APU is located 26 miles northeast of Los Angeles, the fastest-growing metropolitan area in the United States. For information about appointments and campus visits, students should contact the Office of Undergraduate Admissions at 800-TALK-APU (toll-free), Monday through Thursday, 8:30 a.m. to 5 p.m., and Friday, 8:30 a.m. to 4:30 p.m. The nearest commercial airport is Ontario International.

For Further Information Write to Undergraduate Admissions, Azusa Pacific University, 901 East Alosta Avenue, P.O. Box 7000, Azusa, CA 91702-7000. *Web site:* http://www.apu.edu.

BETHANY COLLEGE OF THE ASSEMBLIES OF GOD

Scotts Valley, California

Bethany College is a coed, private, Assemblies of God, comprehensive institution, founded in 1919, offering degrees at the associate, bachelor's, and master's levels. It has a 40-acre campus in Scotts Valley near San Francisco and San Jose.

Expenses for 2003–04 *Application fee:* $35. *Comprehensive fee:* $17,960 includes full-time tuition ($11,940), mandatory fees ($640), and college room and board ($5380). *College room only:* $2520. *Part-time tuition:* $500 per unit. *Part-time mandatory fees:* $90 per term.

For Further Information Contact Ms. Pam Smallwood, Director of Admissions, Bethany College of the Assemblies of God, 800 Bethany Drive, Scotts Valley, CA 95066-2820. *Telephone:* 831-438-3800 Ext. 1400 or 800-843-9410 (toll-free). *Fax:* 831-438-4517. *E-mail:* info@bethany.edu. *Web site:* http://www.bethany.edu/.

BETHESDA CHRISTIAN UNIVERSITY

Anaheim, California

Bethesda Christian University is a coed, private, comprehensive institution, founded in 1978, affiliated with the Full Gospel World Mission, offering degrees at the bachelor's, master's, and first professional levels. It is located in Anaheim near Los Angeles.

Academic Information The faculty has 25 members (24% full-time), 80% with terminal degrees. The undergraduate student-faculty ratio is 15:1. The library holds 27,763 titles, 99 serial subscriptions, and 3,042 audiovisual materials. Special programs include study abroad, accelerated degree programs, ESL programs, double majors, independent study, summer session for credit, part-time degree programs (daytime, evenings, summer), adult/continuing education programs, and internships. The most frequently chosen baccalaureate fields are education, visual/performing arts.
Student Body Statistics The student body totals 206, of whom 164 are undergraduates (32 freshmen). 54 percent are women and 46 percent are men. Students come from 3 states and territories and 3 other countries. 100 percent are from California. 70.1 percent are international students. 55 percent of the 2003 graduating class went on to graduate and professional schools.
Expenses for 2004–05 *Application fee:* $35. *Tuition:* $6000 full-time, $200 per credit part-time. *Mandatory fees:* $120 full-time, $60 per term part-time.
Financial Aid Forms of aid include need-based and non-need-based scholarships. The average aided 2002–03 undergraduate received an aid package worth $4557. The application deadline for financial aid is continuous.
Freshman Admission Bethesda Christian University requires an essay, a high school transcript, a minimum 2.0 high school GPA, 2 recommendations, an interview, and 2 photographs. TOEFL scores for international students are recommended. The application deadline for regular admission is August 11.
Entrance Difficulty Bethesda Christian University has an open admission policy. It assesses its entrance difficulty as moderately difficult for music programs.

For Further Information Contact Mr. Samuel C. Jung, Director of Admission, Bethesda Christian University, 730 North Euclid Street, Anaheim, CA 92801. *Telephone:* 714-517-1945. *Fax:* 714-517-1948. *E-mail:* admission@bcu.edu. *Web site:* http://www.bcu.edu/.

BIOLA UNIVERSITY

La Mirada, California

Biola is a coed, private, interdenominational university, founded in 1908, offering degrees at the bachelor's, master's, doctoral, and first professional levels. It has a 95-acre campus in La Mirada near Los Angeles.

Academic Information The faculty has 404 members (45% full-time), 62% with terminal degrees. The undergraduate student-faculty ratio is 18:1. The library holds 270,456 titles, 13,123 serial subscriptions, and 12,482 audiovisual materials. Special programs include academic remediation, services for learning-disabled students, an honors program, cooperative (work-study) education, study abroad, advanced placement credit, accelerated degree programs, Freshman Honors College, ESL programs, double majors, independent study, summer session for credit, part-time degree programs, adult/continuing education programs, internships, and arrangement for off-campus study with Coalition for Christian Colleges and Universities, University of Southern California, California State University, Long Beach, University of California, Los Angeles.
Student Body Statistics The student body totals 4,666, of whom 3,232 are undergraduates (814 freshmen). 63 percent are women and 37 percent are men. Students come from 47 states and territories and 40 other countries. 71 percent are from California. 3.5 percent are international students.
Expenses for 2003–04 *Application fee:* $45. *Comprehensive fee:* $25,531 includes full-time tuition ($19,564) and college room and board ($5967). *College room only:* $3207. Full-time tuition varies according to program. Room and board charges vary according to board plan and housing facility. *Part-time tuition:* varies with course load, program.
Financial Aid Forms of aid include need-based and non-need-based scholarships and part-time jobs. The average aided 2003–04 undergraduate received an aid package worth an estimated $15,434. The priority application deadline for financial aid is March 2.
Freshman Admission Biola requires an essay, a high school transcript, 2 recommendations, an interview, SAT I or ACT scores, and TOEFL scores for international students. A minimum 3.0 high school GPA is recommended. The application deadline for regular admission is March 1 and for early action it is December 1.
Transfer Admission The application deadline for admission is March 1.
Entrance Difficulty Biola assesses its entrance difficulty level as moderately difficult. For the fall 2003 freshman class, 78 percent of the applicants were accepted.

For Further Information Contact Mr. Greg Vaughan, Director of Enrollment Management, Biola University, 13800 Biola Avenue, La Mirada, CA 90639. *Telephone:* 562-903-4752 or 800-652-4652 (toll-free). *Fax:* 562-903-4709. *E-mail:* admissions@biola.edu. *Web site:* http://www.biola.edu/.

BROOKS INSTITUTE OF PHOTOGRAPHY

Santa Barbara, California

Brooks Institute is a coed, proprietary, comprehensive institution, founded in 1945, offering degrees at the bachelor's and master's levels in photography. It has a 25-acre campus in Santa Barbara.

Expenses for 2003–04 *Application fee:* $35. *Tuition:* $19,650 full-time. *Mandatory fees:* $600 full-time.

For Further Information Contact Ms. Inge B. Kautzmann, Director of Admissions, Brooks Institute of Photography, 801 Alston Road, Santa Barbara, CA 93108. *Telephone:* 805-966-3888 Ext. 4601 or 888-304-3456 (toll-free out-of-state). *Fax:* 805-564-1475. *E-mail:* admissions@brooks.edu. *Web site:* http://www.brooks.edu/.

CALIFORNIA BAPTIST UNIVERSITY

Riverside, California

Cal Baptist is a coed, private, Southern Baptist, comprehensive institution, founded in 1950, offering degrees at the bachelor's and master's levels. It has an 82-acre campus in Riverside near Los Angeles.

Academic Information The faculty has 162 members (51% full-time), 52% with terminal degrees. The undergraduate student-faculty ratio is 16:1. The library holds 97,615 titles, 38 serial subscriptions, and 4,271 audiovisual materials. Special programs include study abroad, advanced placement credit, accelerated degree programs, double majors, independent study, summer session for credit, part-time degree programs (daytime, evenings, weekends, summer), adult/continuing education programs, internships, and arrangement for off-campus study with Council for Christian Colleges and Universities.

Student Body Statistics The student body totals 2,359, of whom 1,753 are undergraduates (221 freshmen). 66 percent are women and 34 percent are men. Students come from 30 states and territories and 14 other countries. 92 percent are from California.

Expenses for 2004–05 *Application fee:* $45. *Comprehensive fee:* $22,250 includes full-time tuition ($14,950), mandatory fees ($990), and college room and board ($6310). *College room only:* $2640. Full-time tuition and fees vary according to course load and program. Room and board charges vary according to board plan and housing facility. *Part-time tuition:* $575 per semester hour. Part-time tuition varies according to course load and program.

Financial Aid Forms of aid include need-based and non-need-based scholarships, athletic grants, and part-time jobs. The average aided 2003–04 undergraduate received an aid package worth an estimated $10,700. The priority application deadline for financial aid is March 2.

Freshman Admission Cal Baptist requires an essay, a high school transcript, a minimum 2.5 high school GPA, 2 recommendations, SAT I or ACT scores, and TOEFL scores for international students. An interview is recommended. The application deadline for regular admission is rolling and for early action it is December 12.

Entrance Difficulty Cal Baptist assesses its entrance difficulty level as minimally difficult. For the fall 2003 freshman class, 84 percent of the applicants were accepted.

For Further Information Contact Mr. Allen Johnson, Director, Undergraduate Admissions, California Baptist University, 8432 Magnolia Avenue, Riverside, CA 92504-3297. *Telephone:* 909-343-5037 or 877-228-8866 (toll-free). *Fax:* 909-343-4525. *E-mail:* admissions@calbaptist.edu. *Web site:* http://www.calbaptist.edu/.

CALIFORNIA CHRISTIAN COLLEGE

Fresno, California

California Christian College is a coed, private, four-year college, offering degrees at the associate and bachelor's levels. It has a 5-acre campus in Fresno near Fresno.

Academic Information The faculty has 18 members (39% full-time), 89% with terminal degrees. The student-faculty ratio is 8:1. The library holds 13,154 titles, 7 serial subscriptions, and 430 audiovisual materials. Special programs include academic remediation, cooperative (work-study) education, accelerated degree programs, independent study, summer session for credit, and part-time degree programs (daytime, evenings, summer). The most frequently chosen baccalaureate field is philosophy, religion, and theology.

Student Body Statistics The student body is made up of 52 undergraduates (5 freshmen). 31 percent are women and 69 percent are men. Students come from 4 states and territories and 2 other countries. 96 percent are from California. 3.8 percent are international students. 17 percent of the 2003 graduating class went on to graduate and professional schools.

Expenses for 2003–04 *Application fee:* $40. *Comprehensive fee:* $8900 includes full-time tuition ($5040), mandatory fees ($660), and college room and board ($3200). Full-time tuition and fees vary according to course load. *Part-time tuition:* $210 per unit. *Part-time mandatory fees:* $55 per term. Part-time tuition and fees vary according to course load.

Financial Aid Forms of aid include need-based scholarships and part-time jobs. The average aided 2003–04 undergraduate received an aid package worth an estimated $8730. The priority application deadline for financial aid is March 2.

Freshman Admission California Christian College requires an essay, a high school transcript, a minimum 2.0 high school GPA, 3 recommendations, statement of faith, moral/ethical statement, TOEFL scores for international students, and standardized Bible content tests. An interview and SAT I or ACT scores are recommended. The application deadline for regular admission is rolling.

Transfer Admission The application deadline for admission is rolling.

Entrance Difficulty California Christian College has an open admission policy.

For Further Information Contact Mr. Brian Henderer, Director of Admissions, California Christian College, 4881 East University Avenue, Fresno, CA 93703. *Telephone:* 559-251-4215 Ext. 5571. *Fax:* 559-251-4231. *E-mail:* cccfresno@aol.com. *Web site:* http://www.calchristiancollege.org/.

CALIFORNIA COLLEGE FOR HEALTH SCIENCES

National City, California

California College is a coed, proprietary, comprehensive institution, founded in 1978, offering degrees at the associate, bachelor's, and master's levels (offers primarily external degree programs). It has a 2-acre campus in National City near San Diego.

Expenses for 2003–04 *Application fee:* $50. *Tuition:* $13,975 full-time.

For Further Information Contact Ms. Loreli L. Relova, Student Services Manager, California College for Health Sciences, 2423 Hoover Avenue, National City, CA 91950. *Telephone:* 619-477-4800 Ext. 313 or 800-221-7374 (toll-free out-of-state). *Fax:* 619-477-4360. *E-mail:* admissions@cchs.edu. *Web site:* http://www.cchs.edu/.

CALIFORNIA COLLEGE OF THE ARTS

San Francisco, California

CCAC is a coed, private, comprehensive institution, founded in 1907, offering degrees at the bachelor's and master's levels in art. It has a 4-acre campus in San Francisco.

Academic Information The faculty has 337 members (10% full-time), 63% with terminal degrees. The undergraduate student-faculty ratio is 9:1. The library holds 39,000 titles, 340 serial subscriptions, and 520 audiovisual materials. Special programs include academic remediation, services for learning-disabled students, study abroad, advanced placement credit, double majors, independent study, self-designed majors, summer session for credit, internships, and arrangement for off-campus study with Mills College, Holy Names College, AICAD Mobility Program, University of San Francisco. The most frequently chosen baccalaureate fields are architecture, trade and industry, visual/performing arts.

Student Body Statistics The student body totals 1,492, of whom 1,303 are undergraduates (164 freshmen). 60 percent are women and 40 percent are men. Students come from 39 states and territories and 21 other countries. 73 percent are from California. 6 percent are international students.

Expenses for 2003–04 *Application fee:* $50. *Comprehensive fee:* $31,280 includes full-time tuition ($22,970), mandatory fees ($280), and college room and board ($8030). *College room only:* $5800. Full-time tuition and fees vary according to course load. Room and board charges vary according to housing facility. *Part-time tuition:* varies with course load.

Financial Aid Forms of aid include need-based and non-need-based scholarships and part-time jobs. The average aided 2003–04 undergraduate received an aid package worth an estimated $18,896. The priority application deadline for financial aid is March 1.

Freshman Admission CCAC requires an essay, a high school transcript, a minimum 2.0 high school GPA, 2 recommendations, a portfolio, and TOEFL scores for international students. SAT I or ACT scores are recommended. An interview is required for some. The application deadline for regular admission is February 15.
Transfer Admission The application deadline for admission is rolling.
Entrance Difficulty CCAC assesses its entrance difficulty level as moderately difficult. For the fall 2003 freshman class, 79 percent of the applicants were accepted.

For Further Information Contact Ms. Molly Ryan, Director of Admissions, California College of the Arts, 1111 Eighth Street at 16th and Wisconsin, San Francisco, CA 94107. *Telephone:* 415-703-9523 Ext. 9535 or 800-447-1ART (toll-free). *Fax:* 415-703-9539. *E-mail:* enroll@ccac-art.edu. *Web site:* http://www.cca.edu/.

CALIFORNIA INSTITUTE OF INTEGRAL STUDIES

San Francisco, California

For Information Write to California Institute of Integral Studies, San Francisco, CA 94103.

CALIFORNIA INSTITUTE OF TECHNOLOGY

Pasadena, California

Caltech is a coed, private university, founded in 1891, offering degrees at the bachelor's, master's, and doctoral levels. It has a 124-acre campus in Pasadena near Los Angeles.

Academic Information The faculty has 324 members (90% full-time), 94% with terminal degrees. The undergraduate student-faculty ratio is 3:1. The library holds 3 million titles and 3,500 serial subscriptions. Special programs include services for learning-disabled students, study abroad, ESL programs, double majors, independent study, self-designed majors, internships, and arrangement for off-campus study with Occidental College, Scripps College, Art Center College of Design. The most frequently chosen baccalaureate fields are engineering/engineering technologies, mathematics, physical sciences.
Student Body Statistics The student body totals 2,172, of whom 891 are undergraduates (191 freshmen). 33 percent are women and 67 percent are men. Students come from 46 states and territories and 28 other countries. 41 percent are from California. 7.5 percent are international students.
Expenses for 2004–05 *Application fee:* $50. *Comprehensive fee:* $33,564 includes full-time tuition ($25,335), mandatory fees ($216), and college room and board ($8013).
Financial Aid Forms of aid include need-based and non-need-based scholarships and part-time jobs. The average aided 2003–04 undergraduate received an aid package worth an estimated $26,230. The priority application deadline for financial aid is January 15.
Freshman Admission Caltech requires an essay, a high school transcript, 2 recommendations, SAT I or ACT scores, SAT II: Writing Test scores, and SAT II Subject Test in Math Level II C and either physics, chemistry, or biology. TOEFL scores for international students are recommended. The application deadline for regular admission is January 1 and for early action it is November 1.
Transfer Admission The application deadline for admission is March 1.
Entrance Difficulty Caltech assesses its entrance difficulty level as most difficult. For the fall 2003 freshman class, 17 percent of the applicants were accepted.

For Further Information Contact Mr. Daniel T. Langdale, Director of Admissions, California Institute of Technology, 1200 East California Boulevard, Pasadena, CA 91125-0001. *Telephone:* 626-395-6341. *Fax:* 626-683-3026. *E-mail:* ugadmissions@caltech.edu. *Web site:* http://www.caltech.edu/.

CALIFORNIA INSTITUTE OF THE ARTS

Valencia, California

Cal Arts is a coed, private, comprehensive institution, founded in 1961, offering degrees at the bachelor's and master's levels and postbachelor's certificates. It has a 60-acre campus in Valencia near Los Angeles.

Academic Information The faculty has 270 members (50% full-time). The undergraduate student-faculty ratio is 7:1. The library holds 95,973 titles, 613 serial subscriptions, and 20,611 audiovisual materials. Special programs include services for learning-disabled students, study abroad, advanced placement credit, independent study, self-designed majors, and internships. The most frequently chosen baccalaureate field is visual/performing arts.
Student Body Statistics The student body totals 1,222, of whom 753 are undergraduates (130 freshmen). 43 percent are women and 57 percent are men. Students come from 51 states and territories and 40 other countries. 45 percent are from California. 8.4 percent are international students.
Expenses for 2003–04 *Application fee:* $60. *Comprehensive fee:* $31,805 includes full-time tuition ($23,920), mandatory fees ($765), and college room and board ($7120). *College room only:* $3700. Room and board charges vary according to board plan, housing facility, and location.
Financial Aid Forms of aid include need-based and non-need-based scholarships and part-time jobs. The average aided 2003–04 undergraduate received an aid package worth an estimated $20,922. The priority application deadline for financial aid is March 2.
Freshman Admission Cal Arts requires an essay, a high school transcript, 2 recommendations, portfolio or audition, and TOEFL scores for international students. An interview is required for some. The application deadline for regular admission is January 5.
Transfer Admission The application deadline for admission is rolling.
Entrance Difficulty Cal Arts assesses its entrance difficulty level as very difficult. For the fall 2003 freshman class, 36 percent of the applicants were accepted.

For Further Information Contact Ms. Carol Kim, Director of Enrollment Services, California Institute of the Arts, 24700 McBean Parkway, Valencia, CA 91355. *Telephone:* 661-255-1050 or 800-545-2787 (toll-free). *Fax:* 661-253-7710. *E-mail:* admiss@calarts.edu. *Web site:* http://www.calarts.edu/.

CALIFORNIA LUTHERAN UNIVERSITY

Thousand Oaks, California

CLU is a coed, private, Lutheran, comprehensive institution, founded in 1959, offering degrees at the bachelor's, master's, and doctoral levels and post-master's and postbachelor's certificates. It has a 290-acre campus in Thousand Oaks near Los Angeles.

Academic Information The faculty has 249 members (49% full-time). The undergraduate student-faculty ratio is 15:1. The library holds 139,476 titles, 10,600 serial subscriptions, and 1,457 audiovisual materials. Special programs include an honors program, cooperative (work-study) education, study abroad, advanced placement credit, accelerated degree programs, double majors, independent study, self-designed majors, summer session for credit, part-time degree programs (daytime, evenings, weekends, summer), adult/continuing education programs, internships, and arrangement for off-campus study with Wagner College, American University (Washington Semester). The most frequently chosen baccalaureate fields are business/marketing, communications/communication technologies, liberal arts/general studies.
Student Body Statistics The student body totals 2,920, of whom 1,920 are undergraduates (336 freshmen). 56 percent are women and 44 percent are men. Students come from 36 states and territories and 20 other countries. 79 percent are from California. 2.1 percent are international students. 33 percent of the 2003 graduating class went on to graduate and professional schools.
Expenses for 2003–04 *Application fee:* $45. *Comprehensive fee:* $27,600 includes full-time tuition ($20,200), mandatory fees ($200), and college

California Lutheran University (continued)
room and board ($7200). *College room only:* $3550. Room and board charges vary according to board plan. *Part-time tuition:* $665 per unit. *Part-time mandatory fees:* $200 per year.
Financial Aid Forms of aid include need-based and non-need-based scholarships and part-time jobs. The average aided 2002–03 undergraduate received an aid package worth $16,800. The priority application deadline for financial aid is March 1.
Freshman Admission CLU requires an essay, a high school transcript, a minimum 2.8 high school GPA, 1 recommendation, SAT I or ACT scores, and TOEFL scores for international students. A minimum 3.0 high school GPA and an interview are recommended. The application deadline for regular admission is June 1 and for early action it is November 15.
Transfer Admission The application deadline for admission is June 1.
Entrance Difficulty CLU assesses its entrance difficulty level as moderately difficult. For the fall 2003 freshman class, 77 percent of the applicants were accepted.

For Further Information Contact Mr. Darryl Calkins, Dean of Undergraduate Enrollment, California Lutheran University, Office of Admission, #1350, Thousand Oaks, CA 91360. *Telephone:* 805-493-3135 or 877-258-3678 (toll-free). *Fax:* 805-493-3114. *E-mail:* cluadm@clunet.edu. *Web site:* http://www.clunet.edu/.

CALIFORNIA MARITIME ACADEMY

Vallejo, California

Cal Maritime is a coed, primarily men's, public, four-year college of California State University System, founded in 1929, offering degrees at the bachelor's level. It has a 64-acre campus in Vallejo near San Francisco.

Academic Information The student-faculty ratio is 17:1. The library holds 28,377 titles, 273 serial subscriptions, and 241 audiovisual materials. Special programs include academic remediation, advanced placement credit, distance learning, summer session for credit, and internships. The most frequently chosen baccalaureate fields are business/marketing, engineering/engineering technologies.
Student Body Statistics The student body is made up of 670 undergraduates. 19 percent are women and 81 percent are men. Students come from 18 states and territories and 16 other countries. 87 percent are from California. 1 percent of the 2003 graduating class went on to graduate and professional schools.
Expenses for 2003–04 *Application fee:* $55. *State resident tuition:* $0 full-time. *Nonresident tuition:* $8460 full-time. *Mandatory fees:* $2396 full-time. Full-time tuition and fees vary according to program and student level. *College room and board:* $6750. *College room only:* $3130. Room and board charges vary according to board plan and housing facility.
Financial Aid Forms of aid include need-based and non-need-based scholarships and part-time jobs. The average aided 2003–04 undergraduate received an aid package worth an estimated $15,329. The priority application deadline for financial aid is March 3.
Freshman Admission Cal Maritime requires a high school transcript, a minimum 2.0 high school GPA, a health form, SAT I or ACT scores, and TOEFL scores for international students. The application deadline for regular admission is April 1.
Transfer Admission The application deadline for admission is April 1.
Entrance Difficulty Cal Maritime assesses its entrance difficulty level as moderately difficult. For the fall 2003 freshman class, 61 percent of the applicants were accepted.

For Further Information Contact Mr. Chris Krzak, Enrollment Services Director, California Maritime Academy, PO Box 1392, Vallejo, CA 94590-0644. *Telephone:* 707-654-1331 or 800-561-1945 (toll-free). *Fax:* 707-654-1336. *E-mail:* admission@csum.edu. *Web site:* http://www.csum.edu/.

CALIFORNIA NATIONAL UNIVERSITY FOR ADVANCED STUDIES

Northridge, California

California National University for Advanced Studies is a coed, proprietary, comprehensive institution, founded in 1993, offering degrees at the bachelor's and master's levels and postbachelor's certificates.

Expenses for 2003–04 *Application fee:* $50. *Tuition:* $4230 full-time, $235 per semester hour part-time. *Mandatory fees:* $175 full-time. Part-time tuition varies according to degree level and program.

For Further Information Contact Ms. Stephanie M. Smith, Registrar, California National University for Advanced Studies, California National University Admissions, 8550 Balboa Boulevard, Suite 210, Northridge, CA 91325. *Telephone:* 818-830-2411, 800-744-2822 (toll-free in-state), or 800-782-2422 (toll-free out-of-state). *Fax:* 818-830-2418. *E-mail:* cnuadms@mail.cnuas.edu. *Web site:* http://www.cnuas.edu/.

CALIFORNIA POLYTECHNIC STATE UNIVERSITY, SAN LUIS OBISPO

San Luis Obispo, California

Cal Poly State University is a coed, public, comprehensive unit of California State University System, founded in 1901, offering degrees at the bachelor's and master's levels. It has a 6,000-acre campus in San Luis Obispo.

Academic Information The faculty has 1,268 members (62% full-time), 49% with terminal degrees. The undergraduate student-faculty ratio is 19:1. The library holds 763,651 titles, 5,529 serial subscriptions, and 5,204 audiovisual materials. Special programs include academic remediation, services for learning-disabled students, an honors program, cooperative (work-study) education, study abroad, advanced placement credit, ESL programs, double majors, independent study, distance learning, summer session for credit, part-time degree programs, external degree programs, internships, and arrangement for off-campus study with other units of the California State University System. The most frequently chosen baccalaureate fields are agriculture, business/marketing, engineering/engineering technologies.
Student Body Statistics The student body totals 18,303, of whom 17,257 are undergraduates (2,828 freshmen). 44 percent are women and 56 percent are men. Students come from 48 states and territories and 41 other countries. 94 percent are from California. 0.9 percent are international students. 15 percent of the 2003 graduating class went on to graduate and professional schools.
Expenses for 2004–05 *Application fee:* $55. *State resident tuition:* $0 full-time. *Nonresident tuition:* $6768 full-time, $188 per unit part-time. *Mandatory fees:* $3459 full-time. Full-time tuition and fees vary according to course load. Part-time tuition varies according to course load. *College room and board:* $7479. *College room only:* $4221. Room and board charges vary according to board plan.
Financial Aid Forms of aid include need-based and non-need-based scholarships and part-time jobs. The average aided 2003–04 undergraduate received an aid package worth an estimated $6998. The application deadline for financial aid is June 30 with a priority deadline of March 2.
Freshman Admission Cal Poly State University requires a high school transcript, SAT I or ACT scores, and TOEFL scores for international students. The application deadline for regular admission is November 30 and for early decision it is October 31.
Transfer Admission The application deadline for admission is November 30.
Entrance Difficulty Cal Poly State University assesses its entrance difficulty level as moderately difficult; most difficult for business, electronic

engineering, electrical engineering, aeronautical engineering, architecture, architectural engineering programs. For the fall 2003 freshman class, 38 percent of the applicants were accepted.

For Further Information Contact Mr. James Maraviglia, Director of Admissions and Evaluations, California Polytechnic State University, San Luis Obispo, San Luis Obispo, CA 93407. *Telephone:* 805-756-2311. *Fax:* 805-756-5400. *E-mail:* admprosp@calpoly.edu. *Web site:* http://www.calpoly.edu/.

CALIFORNIA SCHOOL OF PROFESSIONAL PSYCHOLOGY

See Alliant International University

CALIFORNIA STATE POLYTECHNIC UNIVERSITY, POMONA

Pomona, California

Cal Poly Pomona is a coed, public, comprehensive unit of California State University System, founded in 1938, offering degrees at the bachelor's and master's levels. It has a 1,400-acre campus in Pomona near Los Angeles.

Academic Information The faculty has 1,224 members (55% full-time), 40% with terminal degrees. The undergraduate student-faculty ratio is 21:1. The library holds 465,018 titles, 6,017 serial subscriptions, and 13,260 audiovisual materials. Special programs include academic remediation, services for learning-disabled students, cooperative (work-study) education, study abroad, advanced placement credit, ESL programs, double majors, summer session for credit, part-time degree programs, adult/continuing education programs, internships, and arrangement for off-campus study with other units of the California State University System, Desert Studies Consortium, Southern California Ocean Studies Consortium. The most frequently chosen baccalaureate fields are business/marketing, computer/information sciences, engineering/engineering technologies.
Student Body Statistics The student body totals 19,804, of whom 17,650 are undergraduates (2,284 freshmen). 43 percent are women and 57 percent are men. Students come from 52 states and territories and 116 other countries. 98 percent are from California. 4.5 percent are international students.
Expenses for 2004–05 *Application fee:* $55. *Area resident tuition:* $0 full-time. *State resident tuition:* $0 full-time. *Nonresident tuition:* $8460 full-time, $188 per unit part-time. *Mandatory fees:* $2046 full-time, $682 per term part-time. *College room and board:* $6747. Room and board charges vary according to board plan and housing facility.
Financial Aid Forms of aid include need-based and non-need-based scholarships, athletic grants, and part-time jobs. The average aided 2003–04 undergraduate received an aid package worth an estimated $8258. The application deadline for financial aid is continuous.
Freshman Admission Cal Poly Pomona requires a high school transcript, a minimum 2.0 high school GPA, SAT I or ACT scores, and TOEFL scores for international students. The application deadline for regular admission is April 1.
Transfer Admission The application deadline for admission is May 1.
Entrance Difficulty Cal Poly Pomona assesses its entrance difficulty level as moderately difficult; minimally difficult for exceptional admit, Equal Opportunity Programs. For the fall 2003 freshman class, 30 percent of the applicants were accepted.

For Further Information Contact Dr. George R. Bradshaw, Director, Admissions and Outreach, California State Polytechnic University, Pomona, Pomona, CA 91768. *Telephone:* 909-869-3427. *Fax:* 909-869-4529. *E-mail:* cppadmit@csupomona.edu. *Web site:* http://www.csupomona.edu/.

CALIFORNIA STATE UNIVERSITY, BAKERSFIELD

Bakersfield, California

CSUB is a coed, public, comprehensive unit of California State University System, founded in 1970, offering degrees at the bachelor's and master's levels. It has a 575-acre campus in Bakersfield.

Academic Information The faculty has 515 members (64% full-time), 47% with terminal degrees. The undergraduate student-faculty ratio is 17:1. The library holds 354,016 titles and 2,260 serial subscriptions. Special programs include academic remediation, services for learning-disabled students, an honors program, cooperative (work-study) education, study abroad, advanced placement credit, accelerated degree programs, Freshman Honors College, ESL programs, double majors, independent study, distance learning, self-designed majors, summer session for credit, part-time degree programs (daytime, evenings, weekends, summer), external degree programs, adult/continuing education programs, internships, and arrangement for off-campus study with National Student Exchange.
Student Body Statistics The student body totals 7,924, of whom 5,882 are undergraduates. Students come from 16 states and territories and 48 other countries. 3 percent are from California. 1.8 percent are international students.
Expenses for 2003–04 *Application fee:* $55. *State resident tuition:* $0 full-time. *Nonresident tuition:* $5640 full-time. *Mandatory fees:* $2427 full-time. *College room and board:* $4900. Room and board charges vary according to board plan.
Financial Aid Forms of aid include need-based and non-need-based scholarships, athletic grants, and part-time jobs. The average aided 2002–03 undergraduate received an aid package worth $6150. The priority application deadline for financial aid is March 2.
Freshman Admission CSUB requires a high school transcript, SAT I or ACT scores, and TOEFL scores for international students. SAT II: Subject Test scores are recommended. The application deadline for regular admission is September 23.
Transfer Admission The application deadline for admission is September 23.
Entrance Difficulty CSUB assesses its entrance difficulty level as moderately difficult; very difficult for out-of-state applicants. For the fall 2003 freshman class, 63 percent of the applicants were accepted.

For Further Information Contact Dr. Homer S. Montalvo, Associate Dean of Admissions and Records, California State University, Bakersfield, 9001 Stockdale Highway, Balersfield, CA 93311-1099. *Telephone:* 805-664-2160 or 800-788-2782 (toll-free in-state). *Fax:* 661-664-3188. *E-mail:* admissions@csub.edu. *Web site:* http://www.csubak.edu/.

CALIFORNIA STATE UNIVERSITY, CHICO

Chico, California

CSU, Chico is a coed, public, comprehensive unit of California State University System, founded in 1887, offering degrees at the bachelor's and master's levels and post-master's and postbachelor's certificates. It has a 119-acre campus in Chico.

Academic Information The faculty has 883 members (60% full-time), 65% with terminal degrees. The undergraduate student-faculty ratio is 20:1. The library holds 942,322 titles, 24,244 serial subscriptions, and 23,608 audiovisual materials. Special programs include academic remediation, services for learning-disabled students, an honors program, cooperative (work-study) education, study abroad, advanced placement credit, ESL programs, double majors, independent study, distance learning, self-designed majors, summer session for credit, part-time degree programs (daytime, evenings), external degree programs, adult/continuing education programs, internships, and arrangement for off-campus study with other units of the California State University System, National Student Exchange. The most frequently chosen baccalaureate fields are business/marketing, liberal arts/general studies, social sciences and history.
Student Body Statistics The student body totals 15,516, of whom 13,903 are undergraduates (2,001 freshmen). 54 percent are women and 46

California State University, Chico (continued)

percent are men. Students come from 39 states and territories and 50 other countries. 99 percent are from California. 2.4 percent are international students. 30 percent of the 2003 graduating class went on to graduate and professional schools.

Expenses for 2003–04 *Application fee:* $55. *State resident tuition:* $0 full-time. *Nonresident tuition:* $10,506 full-time, $282 per unit part-time. *Mandatory fees:* $2796 full-time. Part-time tuition varies according to course load. *College room and board:* $7245. *College room only:* $4910. Room and board charges vary according to board plan and housing facility.

Financial Aid Forms of aid include need-based and non-need-based scholarships and part-time jobs. The priority application deadline for financial aid is March 2.

Freshman Admission CSU, Chico requires a high school transcript, GPA of 10th and 11th grade college prep courses only, SAT I or ACT scores, and TOEFL scores for international students. The application deadline for regular admission is November 30.

Transfer Admission The application deadline for admission is November 30.

Entrance Difficulty CSU, Chico assesses its entrance difficulty level as moderately difficult; very difficult for out-of-state applicants. For the fall 2003 freshman class, 73 percent of the applicants were accepted.

For Further Information Contact Dr. John F. Swiney, Director of Admissions, California State University, Chico, 400 West First Street, Chico, CA 95929-0722. *Telephone:* 530-898-4879 or 800-542-4426 (toll-free). *Fax:* 530-898-6456. *E-mail:* info@csuchico.edu. *Web site:* http://www.csuchico.edu/.

CALIFORNIA STATE UNIVERSITY, DOMINGUEZ HILLS

Carson, California

CSU Dominguez Hills is a coed, public, comprehensive unit of California State University System, founded in 1960, offering degrees at the bachelor's and master's levels. It has a 350-acre campus in Carson near Los Angeles.

Academic Information The faculty has 762 members (42% full-time), 48% with terminal degrees. The undergraduate student-faculty ratio is 20:1. The library holds 440,181 titles. Special programs include academic remediation, an honors program, cooperative (work-study) education, study abroad, advanced placement credit, ESL programs, self-designed majors, summer session for credit, part-time degree programs, external degree programs, adult/continuing education programs, internships, and arrangement for off-campus study with other institutions of the California State University System, National Student Exchange. The most frequently chosen baccalaureate fields are business/marketing, health professions and related sciences, liberal arts/general studies.

Student Body Statistics The student body totals 13,248, of whom 8,134 are undergraduates (693 freshmen). 69 percent are women and 31 percent are men. Students come from 29 states and territories and 42 other countries. 98 percent are from California. 1.7 percent are international students.

Expenses for 2004–05 *Application fee:* $55. *State resident tuition:* $0 full-time. *Nonresident tuition:* $8460 full-time, $282 per unit part-time. *Mandatory fees:* $2478 full-time, $216 per term part-time. Part-time tuition and fees vary according to course load. *College room only:* $5022. Room charges vary according to housing facility.

Financial Aid Forms of aid include need-based and non-need-based scholarships, athletic grants, and part-time jobs. The average aided 2002–03 undergraduate received an aid package worth $7910. The application deadline for financial aid is April 15 with a priority deadline of March 2.

Freshman Admission CSU Dominguez Hills requires a high school transcript and TOEFL scores for international students. SAT I or ACT scores are required for some. The application deadline for regular admission is rolling.

Transfer Admission The application deadline for admission is rolling.

Entrance Difficulty CSU Dominguez Hills assesses its entrance difficulty level as moderately difficult. For the fall 2003 freshman class, 47 percent of the applicants were accepted.

For Further Information Contact Mr. James Woods, Director of Admissions, California State University, Dominguez Hills, 1000 East Victoria Street, Carson, CA 90747-0001. *Telephone:* 310-243-3600. *Web site:* http://www.csudh.edu/.

CALIFORNIA STATE UNIVERSITY, FRESNO

Fresno, California

Fresno State is a coed, public, comprehensive unit of California State University System, founded in 1911, offering degrees at the bachelor's, master's, and doctoral levels. It has a 1,410-acre campus in Fresno.

Academic Information The faculty has 1,234 members (55% full-time). The undergraduate student-faculty ratio is 18:1. The library holds 977,198 titles, 2,500 serial subscriptions, and 71,482 audiovisual materials. Special programs include academic remediation, services for learning-disabled students, an honors program, cooperative (work-study) education, study abroad, advanced placement credit, accelerated degree programs, Freshman Honors College, ESL programs, double majors, independent study, distance learning, self-designed majors, summer session for credit, part-time degree programs (daytime, evenings, summer), adult/continuing education programs, internships, and arrangement for off-campus study with other units of the California State University System. The most frequently chosen baccalaureate fields are education, health professions and related sciences, social sciences and history.

Student Body Statistics The student body totals 22,348, of whom 18,574 are undergraduates (2,590 freshmen). 58 percent are women and 42 percent are men. Students come from 50 states and territories and 74 other countries. 99 percent are from California. 2.7 percent are international students.

Expenses for 2004–05 *Application fee:* $55. *State resident tuition:* $0 full-time. *Nonresident tuition:* $10,874 full-time, $282 per unit part-time. *Mandatory fees:* $2414 full-time, $778 per term part-time. *College room and board:* $7073. Room and board charges vary according to board plan.

Financial Aid Forms of aid include need-based and non-need-based scholarships, athletic grants, and part-time jobs. The average aided 2003–04 undergraduate received an aid package worth an estimated $8026. The priority application deadline for financial aid is March 1.

Freshman Admission Fresno State requires a high school transcript, SAT I or ACT scores, and TOEFL scores for international students. The application deadline for regular admission is July 28.

Transfer Admission The application deadline for admission is February 1.

Entrance Difficulty Fresno State assesses its entrance difficulty level as moderately difficult; very difficult for physical therapy, athletic training programs. For the fall 2003 freshman class, 70 percent of the applicants were accepted.

For Further Information Contact Ms. Vivian Franco, Director, California State University, Fresno, 5150 North Maple Avenue, M/S JA 57, Fresno, CA 93740-8026. *Telephone:* 559-278-2261. *Fax:* 559-278-4812. *E-mail:* donna_mills@csufresno.edu. *Web site:* http://www.csufresno.edu/.

CALIFORNIA STATE UNIVERSITY, FULLERTON

Fullerton, California

Cal State Fullerton is a coed, public, comprehensive unit of California State University System, founded in 1957, offering degrees at the bachelor's and master's levels. It has a 225-acre campus in Fullerton near Los Angeles.

Academic Information The faculty has 1,940 members (41% full-time). The undergraduate student-faculty ratio is 21:1. The library holds 743,945 titles, 7,454 serial subscriptions, and 19,620 audiovisual materials. Special

programs include academic remediation, services for learning-disabled students, an honors program, cooperative (work-study) education, study abroad, advanced placement credit, ESL programs, double majors, independent study, distance learning, self-designed majors, summer session for credit, part-time degree programs (daytime, evenings, summer), adult/continuing education programs, internships, and arrangement for off-campus study with other institutions of the California State University System. The most frequently chosen baccalaureate fields are business/marketing, communications/communication technologies, social sciences and history.
Student Body Statistics The student body totals 32,592, of whom 26,896 are undergraduates (3,271 freshmen). 60 percent are women and 40 percent are men. Students come from 43 states and territories and 73 other countries. 99 percent are from California. 3.5 percent are international students.
Expenses for 2003–04 *Application fee:* $55. *State resident tuition:* $0 full-time. *Nonresident tuition:* $8460 full-time, $282 per unit part-time. *Mandatory fees:* $2516 full-time, $829 per term part-time. Full-time tuition and fees vary according to course load. Part-time tuition and fees vary according to course load. *College room only:* $4127.
Financial Aid Forms of aid include need-based and non-need-based scholarships, athletic grants, and part-time jobs. The average aided 2003–04 undergraduate received an aid package worth an estimated $6916. The priority application deadline for financial aid is March 2.
Freshman Admission Cal State Fullerton requires a high school transcript, a minimum 2.0 high school GPA, SAT I or ACT scores, and TOEFL scores for international students. The application deadline for regular admission is November 30.
Transfer Admission The application deadline for admission is rolling.
Entrance Difficulty Cal State Fullerton assesses its entrance difficulty level as moderately difficult. For the fall 2003 freshman class, 66 percent of the applicants were accepted.

For Further Information Contact Ms. Nancy J. Dority, Admissions Director, California State University, Fullerton, Office of Admissions and Records, PO Box 6900, 800 North State College Boulevard, Fullerton, CA 92834-6900. *Telephone:* 714-278-2300. *Web site:* http://www.fullerton.edu/.

CALIFORNIA STATE UNIVERSITY, HAYWARD

Hayward, California

Cal State, Hayward is a coed, public, comprehensive unit of California State University System, founded in 1957, offering degrees at the bachelor's and master's levels and postbachelor's certificates. It has a 343-acre campus in Hayward near San Francisco.

Academic Information The faculty has 741 members (45% full-time), 90% with terminal degrees. The undergraduate student-faculty ratio is 21:1. The library holds 908,577 titles, 2,210 serial subscriptions, and 28,416 audiovisual materials. Special programs include academic remediation, services for learning-disabled students, an honors program, cooperative (work-study) education, study abroad, advanced placement credit, accelerated degree programs, ESL programs, double majors, independent study, distance learning, self-designed majors, summer session for credit, part-time degree programs (daytime, evenings, weekends, summer), adult/continuing education programs, internships, and arrangement for off-campus study with Regional Association of East Bay Colleges and Universities, National Student Exchange. The most frequently chosen baccalaureate fields are business/marketing, liberal arts/general studies, social sciences and history.
Student Body Statistics The student body totals 13,455, of whom 9,380 are undergraduates (682 freshmen). 63 percent are women and 37 percent are men. Students come from 50 states and territories and 86 other countries. 5.5 percent are international students.
Expenses for 2004–05 *Application fee:* $55. *State resident tuition:* $0 full-time. *Nonresident tuition:* $8460 full-time, $188 per unit part-time. *Mandatory fees:* $2418 full-time, $520 per term part-time. *College room only:* $3705.
Financial Aid Forms of aid include need-based and non-need-based scholarships and part-time jobs. The average aided 2003–04 undergraduate received an aid package worth an estimated $7251. The priority application deadline for financial aid is March 2.
Freshman Admission Cal State, Hayward requires a high school transcript and TOEFL scores for international students. SAT I or ACT scores are required for some. The application deadline for regular admission is September 7.
Transfer Admission The application deadline for admission is September 7.
Entrance Difficulty Cal State, Hayward assesses its entrance difficulty level as moderately difficult. For the fall 2003 freshman class, 47 percent of the applicants were accepted.

For Further Information Contact Ms. Susan Lakis, Associate Director of Admissions, California State University, Hayward, 25800 Carlos Bee Boulevard, Hayward, CA 94542-3035. *Telephone:* 510-885-7576. *Fax:* 510-885-3816. *E-mail:* adminfo@csuhayward.edu. *Web site:* http://www.csuhayward.edu/.

CALIFORNIA STATE UNIVERSITY, LONG BEACH

Long Beach, California

CSULB is a coed, public, comprehensive unit of California State University System, founded in 1949, offering degrees at the bachelor's and master's levels and postbachelor's certificates. It has a 320-acre campus in Long Beach near Los Angeles.

Academic Information The faculty has 2,080 members (52% full-time), 55% with terminal degrees. The undergraduate student-faculty ratio is 20:1. The library holds 1 million titles, 3,965 serial subscriptions, and 26,679 audiovisual materials. Special programs include academic remediation, services for learning-disabled students, an honors program, study abroad, advanced placement credit, accelerated degree programs, ESL programs, double majors, independent study, distance learning, self-designed majors, summer session for credit, part-time degree programs (daytime, evenings, summer), adult/continuing education programs, internships, and arrangement for off-campus study with other institutions of the California State University System. The most frequently chosen baccalaureate fields are business/marketing, liberal arts/general studies, visual/performing arts.
Student Body Statistics The student body totals 34,715, of whom 28,067 are undergraduates (3,516 freshmen). 60 percent are women and 40 percent are men. Students come from 45 states and territories and 89 other countries. 99 percent are from California. 5.1 percent are international students.
Expenses for 2004–05 *Application fee:* $55. *State resident tuition:* $0 full-time. *Nonresident tuition:* $8460 full-time, $282 per unit part-time. *Mandatory fees:* $2362 full-time, $752 per term part-time. Full-time tuition and fees vary according to program. Part-time tuition and fees vary according to course load and program. *College room and board:* $5800. Room and board charges vary according to board plan.
Financial Aid Forms of aid include need-based and non-need-based scholarships, athletic grants, and part-time jobs. The average aided 2003–04 undergraduate received an aid package worth an estimated $7635. The priority application deadline for financial aid is March 2.
Freshman Admission CSULB requires a high school transcript, SAT I or ACT scores, and TOEFL scores for international students. A minimum 2.0 high school GPA and minimum GPA of 2.4 for nonresidents are required for some. The application deadline for regular admission is November 30.
Transfer Admission The application deadline for admission is November 30.

California State University, Long Beach (continued)

Entrance Difficulty CSULB assesses its entrance difficulty level as moderately difficult. For the fall 2003 freshman class, 49 percent of the applicants were accepted.

For Further Information Contact Mr. Thomas Enders, Director of Enrollment Services, California State University, Long Beach, Brotman Hall, 1250 Bellflower Boulevard, Long Beach, CA 90840. *Telephone:* 562-985-4641. *Web site:* http://www.csulb.edu/.

CALIFORNIA STATE UNIVERSITY, LOS ANGELES

Los Angeles, California

Cal State LA is a coed, public, comprehensive unit of California State University System, founded in 1947, offering degrees at the bachelor's, master's, and doctoral levels. It has a 173-acre campus in Los Angeles.

Academic Information The faculty has 1,062 members (58% full-time). The undergraduate student-faculty ratio is 21:1. The library holds 2 million titles, 2,724 serial subscriptions, and 1,163 audiovisual materials. Special programs include academic remediation, services for learning-disabled students, an honors program, cooperative (work-study) education, study abroad, advanced placement credit, accelerated degree programs, ESL programs, self-designed majors, summer session for credit, part-time degree programs, adult/continuing education programs, internships, and arrangement for off-campus study with other units of the California State University System. The most frequently chosen baccalaureate fields are business/marketing, home economics/vocational home economics, protective services/public administration.

Student Body Statistics The student body totals 20,637, of whom 14,421 are undergraduates. 62 percent are women and 38 percent are men. 96 percent are from California. 4.8 percent are international students.

Expenses for 2003–04 *Application fee:* $55. *State resident tuition:* $0 full-time. *Nonresident tuition:* $9208 full-time, $188 per unit part-time. *Mandatory fees:* $2440 full-time, $527 per term part-time. *College room only:* $3338.

Financial Aid Forms of aid include need-based and non-need-based scholarships and part-time jobs. The average aided 2003–04 undergraduate received an aid package worth an estimated $7416. The priority application deadline for financial aid is March 2.

Freshman Admission Cal State LA requires a high school transcript, SAT I or ACT scores, and TOEFL scores for international students. The application deadline for regular admission is June 15.

Transfer Admission The application deadline for admission is June 15.

Entrance Difficulty Cal State LA assesses its entrance difficulty level as moderately difficult; minimally difficult for transfers. For the fall 2003 freshman class, 54 percent of the applicants were accepted.

For Further Information Contact Mr. Vince Lopez, Assistant Director of Outreach and Recruitment, California State University, Los Angeles, 5151 State University Drive, Los Angeles, CA 90032-8530. *Telephone:* 323-343-3940. *Fax:* 323-343-2670. *E-mail:* admission@calstatela.edu. *Web site:* http://www.calstatela.edu/.

CALIFORNIA STATE UNIVERSITY, MONTEREY BAY

Seaside, California

For Information Write to California State University, Monterey Bay, Seaside, CA 93955-8001.

CALIFORNIA STATE UNIVERSITY, NORTHRIDGE

Northridge, California

CSUN is a coed, public, comprehensive unit of California State University System, founded in 1958, offering degrees at the bachelor's and master's levels. It has a 353-acre campus in Northridge near Los Angeles.

Expenses for 2003–04 *Application fee:* $55. *State resident tuition:* $0 full-time. *Nonresident tuition:* $9024 full-time. *Mandatory fees:* $2444 full-time. *College room and board:* $6400.

For Further Information Contact Ms. Mary Baxton, Associate Director of Admissions and Records, California State University, Northridge, 18111 Nordhoff Street, Northridge, CA 91330-8207. *Telephone:* 818-677-3700. *Fax:* 818-677-3766. *E-mail:* admissions.records@csun.edu. *Web site:* http://www.csun.edu/.

CALIFORNIA STATE UNIVERSITY, SACRAMENTO

Sacramento, California

CSUS is a coed, public, comprehensive unit of California State University System, founded in 1947, offering degrees at the bachelor's, master's, and doctoral levels. It has a 300-acre campus in Sacramento.

Academic Information The faculty has 1,587 members (56% full-time), 56% with terminal degrees. The undergraduate student-faculty ratio is 21:1. The library holds 967,418 titles, 4,071 serial subscriptions, and 135,074 audiovisual materials. Special programs include academic remediation, services for learning-disabled students, cooperative (work-study) education, study abroad, advanced placement credit, accelerated degree programs, ESL programs, double majors, independent study, distance learning, self-designed majors, summer session for credit, part-time degree programs (daytime, evenings, weekends, summer), external degree programs, internships, and arrangement for off-campus study with other units of the California State University System. The most frequently chosen baccalaureate fields are business/marketing, protective services/public administration, social sciences and history.

Student Body Statistics The student body totals 28,375, of whom 22,562 are undergraduates (2,446 freshmen). 58 percent are women and 42 percent are men. Students come from 36 states and territories and 47 other countries. 99 percent are from California. 1.8 percent are international students.

Expenses for 2003–04 *Application fee:* $55. *State resident tuition:* $0 full-time. *Nonresident tuition:* $8927 full-time, $282 per unit part-time. *Mandatory fees:* $2513 full-time, $827.50 per term part-time. *College room and board:* $6523. Room and board charges vary according to board plan.

Financial Aid Forms of aid include need-based and non-need-based scholarships and part-time jobs. The average aided 2002–03 undergraduate received an aid package worth $7779. The priority application deadline for financial aid is March 2.

Freshman Admission CSUS requires a high school transcript, a minimum 2.0 high school GPA, and TOEFL scores for international students. SAT I or ACT scores are required for some. The application deadline for regular admission is November 30 and for early action it is the same.

Entrance Difficulty CSUS assesses its entrance difficulty level as moderately difficult; very difficult for out-of-state applicants. For the fall 2003 freshman class, 52 percent of the applicants were accepted.

For Further Information Contact Mr. Emiliano Diaz, Director of University Outreach Services, California State University, Sacramento, 6000 J Street, Lassen Hall, Sacramento, CA 95819-6048. *Telephone:* 916-278-7362. *Fax:* 916-278-5603. *E-mail:* admissions@csus.edu. *Web site:* http://www.csus.edu/.

CALIFORNIA STATE UNIVERSITY, SAN BERNARDINO

San Bernardino, California

CSUSB is a coed, public, comprehensive unit of California State University System, founded in 1965, offering degrees at the bachelor's and master's levels. It has a 430-acre campus in San Bernardino near Los Angeles.

Academic Information The faculty has 981 members (51% full-time). The undergraduate student-faculty ratio is 21:1. The library holds 731,259 titles, 2,028 serial subscriptions, and 15,252 audiovisual materials. Special programs include academic remediation, services for learning-disabled students, an honors program, cooperative (work-study) education, study abroad, advanced placement credit, double majors, independent study, distance learning, self-designed majors, summer session for credit, part-time degree programs (daytime, evenings, weekends, summer), adult/continuing education programs, internships, and arrangement for off-campus study with National Student Exchange. The most frequently chosen baccalaureate fields are business/marketing, liberal arts/general studies, social sciences and history.
Student Body Statistics The student body totals 16,927, of whom 12,119 are undergraduates (1,383 freshmen). 65 percent are women and 35 percent are men. 99 percent are from California. 3 percent are international students.
Expenses for 2003–04 *Application fee:* $55. *State resident tuition:* $0 full-time. *Nonresident tuition:* $6768 full-time, $188 per credit part-time. *Mandatory fees:* $1932 full-time, $404 per term part-time. Part-time tuition and fees vary according to course load. *College room and board:* $5383. *College room only:* $4205. Room and board charges vary according to board plan and housing facility.
Financial Aid Forms of aid include need-based and non-need-based scholarships and part-time jobs. The priority application deadline for financial aid is March 2.
Freshman Admission CSUSB requires a high school transcript, a minimum 2.0 high school GPA, and TOEFL scores for international students. SAT I or ACT scores are required for some. The application deadline for regular admission is rolling.
Transfer Admission The application deadline for admission is rolling.
Entrance Difficulty CSUSB assesses its entrance difficulty level as moderately difficult. For the fall 2003 freshman class, 61 percent of the applicants were accepted.

For Further Information Contact Ms. Cynthia Shum, Admissions Counselor, California State University, San Bernardino, 5500 University Parkway, University Hall, Room 107, San Bernardino, CA 92407-2397. *Telephone:* 909-880-5200 or 909-880-5188 (toll-free). *Fax:* 909-880-7034. *E-mail:* moreinfo@mail.csusb.edu. *Web site:* http://www.csusb.edu/.

CALIFORNIA STATE UNIVERSITY, SAN MARCOS

San Marcos, California

CSU San Marcos is a coed, public, comprehensive unit of California State University System, founded in 1990, offering degrees at the bachelor's and master's levels. It has a 304-acre campus in San Marcos near San Diego.

Academic Information The faculty has 408 members (49% full-time), 63% with terminal degrees. The undergraduate student-faculty ratio is 19:1. The library holds 179,439 titles, 2,984 serial subscriptions, and 7,576 audiovisual materials. Special programs include academic remediation, services for learning-disabled students, study abroad, advanced placement credit, ESL programs, double majors, independent study, distance learning, self-designed majors, summer session for credit, part-time degree programs, adult/continuing education programs, internships, and arrangement for off-campus study with San Diego State University, Palomar College, Mira Costa College. The most frequently chosen baccalaureate fields are business/marketing, liberal arts/general studies, social sciences and history.
Student Body Statistics The student body totals 7,723, of whom 6,407 are undergraduates (890 freshmen). 60 percent are women and 40 percent are men. 99 percent are from California. 2.6 percent are international students.
Expenses for 2003–04 *Application fee:* $55. *State resident tuition:* $0 full-time. *Nonresident tuition:* $6768 full-time, $282 per credit hour part-time. *Mandatory fees:* $2414 full-time. Part-time tuition varies according to course load. *College room only:* $7470. Room charges vary according to housing facility.
Financial Aid Forms of aid include need-based and non-need-based scholarships, athletic grants, and part-time jobs. The average aided 2002–03 undergraduate received an aid package worth $6068. The priority application deadline for financial aid is March 2.
Freshman Admission CSU San Marcos requires a high school transcript, a minimum 3.0 high school GPA, SAT I or ACT scores, and TOEFL scores for international students. The application deadline for regular admission is November 30.
Transfer Admission The application deadline for admission is November 30.
Entrance Difficulty CSU San Marcos assesses its entrance difficulty level as moderately difficult. For the fall 2003 freshman class, 73 percent of the applicants were accepted.

For Further Information Contact Ms. Cherine Heckman, Director of Admissions, California State University, San Marcos, 333 South Twin Oaks Valley Road, San Marcos, CA 92096-0001. *Telephone:* 760-750-4848. *Fax:* 760-750-3248. *E-mail:* apply@csusm.edu. *Web site:* http://www.csusm.edu/.

CALIFORNIA STATE UNIVERSITY, STANISLAUS

Turlock, California

CSU, Stanislaus is a coed, public, comprehensive unit of California State University System, founded in 1957, offering degrees at the bachelor's and master's levels. It has a 220-acre campus in Turlock.

Academic Information The faculty has 495 members (57% full-time), 57% with terminal degrees. The library holds 347,674 titles, 1,924 serial subscriptions, and 4,676 audiovisual materials. Special programs include academic remediation, services for learning-disabled students, an honors program, cooperative (work-study) education, study abroad, advanced placement credit, accelerated degree programs, ESL programs, double majors, independent study, distance learning, self-designed majors, summer session for credit, part-time degree programs (daytime, evenings, summer), external degree programs, adult/continuing education programs, internships, and arrangement for off-campus study with other units of the California State University System. The most frequently chosen baccalaureate fields are business/marketing, liberal arts/general studies, social sciences and history.
Student Body Statistics The student body totals 8,072, of whom 6,154 are undergraduates (670 freshmen). 66 percent are women and 34 percent are men. Students come from 25 states and territories and 71 other countries. 99 percent are from California. 1.5 percent are international students.
Expenses for 2003–04 *Application fee:* $55. *State resident tuition:* $0 full-time. *Nonresident tuition:* $8460 full-time, $282 per unit part-time. *Mandatory fees:* $2503 full-time, $691 per term part-time. *College room and board:* $7242. *College room only:* $4322. Room and board charges vary according to board plan and housing facility.
Financial Aid Forms of aid include need-based and non-need-based scholarships, athletic grants, and part-time jobs. The average aided 2003–04 undergraduate received an aid package worth an estimated $7472. The priority application deadline for financial aid is March 2.
Freshman Admission CSU, Stanislaus requires a high school transcript, SAT I or ACT scores, and TOEFL scores for international students. A minimum 3.0 high school GPA is recommended. The application deadline for regular admission is May 1 and for early decision it is November 30.

California State University, Stanislaus (continued)

Transfer Admission The application deadline for admission is May 31.
Entrance Difficulty CSU, Stanislaus assesses its entrance difficulty level as moderately difficult. For the fall 2003 freshman class, 64 percent of the applicants were accepted.

For Further Information Contact Mrs. Lisa Bernardo, Director of Admissions and Records, California State University, Stanislaus, Enrollment Services, 801 West Monte Vista Avenue, Mary Stuart Rogers Gateway Center, Room 120, Turlock, CA 95382. *Telephone:* 209-667-3070 or 800-300-7420 (toll-free in-state). *Fax:* 209-667-3788. *E-mail:* outreach_help_desk@stan.csustan.edu. *Web site:* http://www.csustan.edu/.

CHAPMAN UNIVERSITY

Orange, California

Chapman is a coed, private, comprehensive institution, founded in 1861, affiliated with the Christian Church (Disciples of Christ), offering degrees at the bachelor's, master's, and first professional levels and postbachelor's certificates. It has a 45-acre campus in Orange near Los Angeles.

Academic Information The faculty has 518 members (45% full-time). The undergraduate student-faculty ratio is 16:1. The library holds 188,682 titles, 1,777 serial subscriptions, and 6,334 audiovisual materials. Special programs include academic remediation, services for learning-disabled students, an honors program, cooperative (work-study) education, study abroad, advanced placement credit, accelerated degree programs, ESL programs, double majors, independent study, summer session for credit, part-time degree programs (daytime, evenings, summer), adult/continuing education programs, and internships. The most frequently chosen baccalaureate fields are business/marketing, communications/communication technologies, visual/performing arts.
Student Body Statistics The student body totals 5,138, of whom 3,443 are undergraduates (850 freshmen). 57 percent are women and 43 percent are men. Students come from 40 states and territories and 45 other countries. 74 percent are from California. 2.8 percent are international students.
Expenses for 2004–05 *Application fee:* $50. *Comprehensive fee:* $35,232 includes full-time tuition ($25,500), mandatory fees ($650), and college room and board ($9082). Room and board charges vary according to board plan and housing facility. *Part-time tuition:* $795 per credit. Part-time tuition varies according to course load.
Financial Aid Forms of aid include need-based and non-need-based scholarships and part-time jobs. The average aided 2002–03 undergraduate received an aid package worth $18,066. The priority application deadline for financial aid is March 2.
Freshman Admission Chapman requires an essay, a high school transcript, a minimum 2.75 high school GPA, 1 recommendation, SAT I or ACT scores, and TOEFL scores for international students. A minimum 3.5 high school GPA, an interview, SAT II: Subject Test scores, SAT II: Writing Test scores, are recommended. The application deadline for regular admission is January 31 and for early action it is November 30.
Transfer Admission The application deadline for admission is March 15.
Entrance Difficulty Chapman assesses its entrance difficulty level as moderately difficult. For the fall 2003 freshman class, 62 percent of the applicants were accepted.

For Further Information Contact Mr. Michael O. Drummy, Associate Dean for Enrollment Services and Chief Admission Officer, Chapman University, One University Drive, Orange, CA 92866. *Telephone:* 714-997-6711 or 888-CUAPPLY (toll-free). *Fax:* 714-997-6713. *E-mail:* admit@chapman.edu. *Web site:* http://www.chapman.edu/.

See page 164 for a narrative description.

CHARLES R. DREW UNIVERSITY OF MEDICINE AND SCIENCE

Los Angeles, California

For Information Write to Charles R. Drew University of Medicine and Science, Los Angeles, CA 90059.

CHRISTIAN HERITAGE COLLEGE

El Cajon, California

Christian Heritage is a coed, private, nondenominational, four-year college, founded in 1970, offering degrees at the bachelor's level and postbachelor's certificates. It has a 55-acre campus in El Cajon near San Diego.

Academic Information The faculty has 71 members (48% full-time), 24% with terminal degrees. The student-faculty ratio is 14:1. The library holds 71,000 titles, 6,250 serial subscriptions, and 3,784 audiovisual materials. Special programs include academic remediation, study abroad, advanced placement credit, ESL programs, double majors, independent study, self-designed majors, summer session for credit, part-time degree programs (daytime, evenings, summer), adult/continuing education programs, and internships. The most frequently chosen baccalaureate fields are home economics/vocational home economics, interdisciplinary studies, philosophy, religion, and theology.
Student Body Statistics The student body totals 554, of whom 524 are undergraduates (90 freshmen). 62 percent are women and 38 percent are men. Students come from 25 states and territories and 6 other countries. 87 percent are from California. 1.8 percent are international students. 36 percent of the 2003 graduating class went on to graduate and professional schools.
Expenses for 2003–04 *Application fee:* $25. *Comprehensive fee:* $19,990 includes full-time tuition ($14,000) and college room and board ($5990). Full-time tuition varies according to class time, course load, and program. Room and board charges vary according to housing facility. *Part-time tuition:* $470 per credit. Part-time tuition varies according to class time, course load, and program.
Financial Aid Forms of aid include need-based and non-need-based scholarships, athletic grants, and part-time jobs. The average aided 2002–03 undergraduate received an aid package worth $12,802. The priority application deadline for financial aid is March 2.
Freshman Admission Christian Heritage requires an essay, a high school transcript, 2 recommendations, SAT I or ACT scores, and TOEFL scores for international students. A minimum 2.75 high school GPA and an interview are recommended. The application deadline for regular admission is September 1.
Transfer Admission The application deadline for admission is September 1.
Entrance Difficulty Christian Heritage assesses its entrance difficulty level as moderately difficult. For the fall 2003 freshman class, 71 percent of the applicants were accepted.

For Further Information Contact Ms. Misty Blount, Director of Admissions, Christian Heritage College, 2100 Greenfield Drive, El Cajon, CA 92019-1157. *Telephone:* 619-588-7747 or 800-676-2242 (toll-free). *Fax:* 619-440-0209. *E-mail:* chcadm@christianheritage.edu. *Web site:* http://www.christianheritage.edu/.

CLAREMONT MCKENNA COLLEGE

Claremont, California

CMC is a coed, private, four-year college of The Claremont Colleges Consortium, founded in 1946, offering degrees at the bachelor's level. It has a 50-acre campus in Claremont near Los Angeles.

Academic Information The faculty has 159 members (89% full-time), 82% with terminal degrees. The student-faculty ratio is 7:1. The library holds 2 million titles, 6,028 serial subscriptions, and 606 audiovisual materials. Special programs include services for learning-disabled students, an honors program, study abroad, advanced placement credit, accelerated degree programs, double majors, independent study, self-designed majors, internships, and arrangement for off-campus study with 5 members of The Claremont Colleges, Haverford College, Colby College, Spelman College, Morehouse College. The most frequently chosen baccalaureate fields are interdisciplinary studies, psychology, social sciences and history.

Student Body Statistics The student body is made up of 1,050 undergraduates (284 freshmen). 45 percent are women and 55 percent are men. Students come from 45 states and territories and 21 other countries. 49 percent are from California. 25 percent of the 2003 graduating class went on to graduate and professional schools.

Expenses for 2003–04 *Application fee:* $50. *Comprehensive fee:* $36,880 includes full-time tuition ($27,500), mandatory fees ($200), and college room and board ($9180). *College room only:* $4590. Room and board charges vary according to board plan and housing facility.

Financial Aid Forms of aid include need-based and non-need-based scholarships and part-time jobs. The average aided 2002–03 undergraduate received an aid package worth $23,920. The application deadline for financial aid is February 1.

Freshman Admission CMC requires an essay, a high school transcript, a minimum 3.0 high school GPA, 3 recommendations, SAT I or ACT scores, and TOEFL scores for international students. An interview and SAT II: Subject Test scores are recommended. The application deadline for regular admission is January 2; for early decision plan 1 it is November 15; and for early decision plan 2 it is January 2.

Transfer Admission The application deadline for admission is April 1.

Entrance Difficulty CMC assesses its entrance difficulty level as very difficult; most difficult for transfers. For the fall 2003 freshman class, 29 percent of the applicants were accepted.

SPECIAL MESSAGE TO STUDENTS

Social Life Claremont McKenna College (CMC) students take full advantage of the social life offered both on their own 1,000-student campus and within the five-college consortium, where numerous concerts, parties, dance performances, and lectures take place nightly. With a total undergraduate population of nearly 5,000 students, the Claremont Colleges offer a vast number of intellectual, social, and athletic opportunities for CMC students. After class is over for the day, there are nearly 200 student clubs and organizations, twenty competitive varsity sports, and strong community service programs which students all participate in during their four years at the College.

Academic Highlights CMC infuses a pragmatic, application-based philosophy into a traditional liberal arts curriculum. Students are pushed to define and redefine their ideas through constant investigation of the world around them. Each year more than 200 students participate in interships, gaining practical experience in such fields as politics, government, law, and business. In addition, nine nationally recognized research institutes allow students and faculty members the opportunity to conduct collaborative research at a level often found only at top graduate schools and universities. About half of all students spend either a semester or a year in one of the College's 100 study-abroad programs offered throughout Africa, Asia, Europe, the Middle East, and Central and South America.

Interviews and Campus Visits CMC recommends, though does not require, personal interviews for high school seniors. Students are interviewed by admissions officers or senior interviewers. Alumni interviewers are available in select cities outside of southern California. Prospective students should read the College's publications, prepare questions, relax, and be themselves during the interview. Visitors to CMC should see the Athenaeum, an elegant dining facility designed to bring students, faculty members, and guest speakers together to exchange ideas. For more information about appointments and campus visits, students should contact the Office of Admission and Financial Aid at 909-621-8088, Monday through Friday, 8 a.m. to 5 p.m. or e-mail the office at the address listed below. The nearest commercial airport is Ontario International.

For Further Information Write to Mr. Richard C. Vos, Dean of Admission and Financial Aid, Claremont McKenna College, 890 Columbia Avenue, Claremont, CA 91711-6425. *E-mail:* admission@claremontmckenna.edu. *Web site:* http://www.claremontmckenna.edu.

See page 166 for a narrative description.

CLEVELAND CHIROPRACTIC COLLEGE-LOS ANGELES CAMPUS

Los Angeles, California

Cleveland Chiropractic College-Los Angeles Campus is a coed, private, upper-level institution, founded in 1911, offering degrees at the associate, bachelor's, and first professional levels.

Academic Information The most frequently chosen baccalaureate field is biological/life sciences.

Student Body Statistics The student body totals 507, of whom 113 are undergraduates. 43 percent are women and 57 percent are men. 4.4 percent are international students.

Expenses for 2003–04 *Tuition:* $4752 full-time, $198 per credit part-time. *Mandatory fees:* $200 full-time, $200 per year part-time.

For Further Information Contact Ms. Melissa Denton, Director of MultiCampus Admissions, Cleveland Chiropractic College-Los Angeles Campus, 590 North Vermont Avenue, Los Angeles, CA 90004-2196. *Telephone:* 323-906-2031 or 800-446-CCLA (toll-free). *Fax:* 323-906-2094. *E-mail:* la.admissions@cleveland.edu. *Web site:* http://www.clevelandchiropractic.edu/.

COGSWELL POLYTECHNICAL COLLEGE

Sunnyvale, California

Cogswell College is a coed, primarily men's, private, four-year college of Foundation for Educational Achievement, San Diego, founded in 1887, offering degrees at the bachelor's level. It has a 2-acre campus in Sunnyvale near San Francisco and San Jose.

Academic Information The faculty has 48 members (29% full-time), 31% with terminal degrees. The student-faculty ratio is 15:1. The library holds 11,257 titles, 102 serial subscriptions, and 359 audiovisual materials. Special programs include advanced placement credit, distance learning, summer session for credit, part-time degree programs (daytime, evenings, summer), external degree programs, adult/continuing education programs, and internships.

Student Body Statistics The student body is made up of 376 undergraduates (25 freshmen). 14 percent are women and 86 percent are men. Students come from 20 states and territories and 5 other countries. 89 percent are from California. 1.3 percent are international students. 2 percent of the 2003 graduating class went on to graduate and professional schools.

Expenses for 2003–04 *Application fee:* $50. *Tuition:* $10,880 full-time, $470 per credit part-time. *Mandatory fees:* $40 full-time, $10 per term part-time. Full-time tuition and fees vary according to course load. Part-time tuition and fees vary according to course load. *College room only:* $6300.

Financial Aid Forms of aid include need-based and non-need-based scholarships and part-time jobs. The average aided 2002–03 undergraduate received an aid package worth $5960. The application deadline for financial aid is continuous.

Freshman Admission Cogswell College requires an essay, a high school transcript, a minimum 2.5 high school GPA, and TOEFL scores for international students. SAT I and SAT II or ACT scores are recommended. Recommendations, an interview, and a portfolio are required for some. The application deadline for regular admission is June 1.

Transfer Admission The application deadline for admission is June 1.

Cogswell Polytechnical College (continued)

Entrance Difficulty Cogswell College assesses its entrance difficulty level as moderately difficult. For the fall 2003 freshman class, 90 percent of the applicants were accepted.

For Further Information Contact Mr. Matt Clemons, Enrollment Manager, Cogswell Polytechnical College, 1175 Bordeaux Drive, Sunnyvale, CA 94089. *Telephone:* 408-541-0100 Ext. 107 or 800-264-7955 (toll-free). *Fax:* 408-747-0764. *E-mail:* info@cogswell.edu. *Web site:* http://www.cogswell.edu/.

THE COLBURN SCHOOL OF PERFORMING ARTS

Los Angeles, California

The Colburn School of Performing Arts is a coed, private, four-year college, founded in 1980, offering degrees at the bachelor's level and postbachelor's certificates. It is located in Los Angeles near Los Angeles.

Academic Information The faculty has 9 members (22% full-time), 22% with terminal degrees.
Student Body Statistics The student body totals 16, of whom 7 are undergraduates (7 freshmen). 57 percent are women and 43 percent are men. Students come from 3 states and territories and 1 other country. 57 percent are from California. 14.3 percent are international students.
Expenses for 2004–05 *Application fee:* $100. *Comprehensive fee:* $500 includes full-time tuition ($0), mandatory fees ($500), and college room and board ($0).
Freshman Admission The Colburn School of Performing Arts requires an essay, a high school transcript, 2 recommendations, and an interview. SAT I or ACT scores are recommended. The application deadline for regular admission is January 2.
Transfer Admission The application deadline for admission is January 2.
Entrance Difficulty For the fall 2003 freshman class, 90 percent of the applicants were accepted.

For Further Information Contact Ms. Kathleen Tesar, Director of Student Affairs/Admissions, The Colburn School of Performing Arts, CA. *Telephone:* 213-687-8500. *Fax:* 213-621-2110. *E-mail:* ktesar@colburnschool.edu. *Web site:* http://www.colburnschool.edu/.

COLEMAN COLLEGE

San Marcos, California

Coleman College is a coed, private, two-year college, founded in 1967, offering degrees at the associate level.

Student Body Statistics The student body is made up of 203 undergraduates (138 freshmen). 27 percent are women and 73 percent are men.

For Further Information Contact Mr. James Warner, Senior Admissions Officer, Coleman College, 1284 West San Marcos Boulevard, San Marcos, CA 92069. *Telephone:* 760-747-3990. *Fax:* 760-752-9808. *Web site:* http://www.coleman.edu/.

COLEMAN COLLEGE

La Mesa, California

Coleman College is a coed, private, comprehensive institution, founded in 1963, offering degrees at the associate, bachelor's, and master's levels. It has a 3-acre campus in La Mesa near San Diego.

Academic Information The faculty has 93 members (67% full-time). The library holds 66,800 titles and 69 serial subscriptions. Special programs include services for learning-disabled students, accelerated degree programs, summer session for credit, and part-time degree programs (daytime, evenings). The most frequently chosen baccalaureate field is computer/information sciences.
Student Body Statistics The student body totals 740, of whom 704 are undergraduates (395 freshmen). 26 percent are women and 74 percent are men. Students come from 19 states and territories. 99 percent are from California. 1.4 percent are international students.
Expenses for 2004–05 *Application fee:* $100. *Tuition:* $15,960 full-time, $220 per unit part-time. *Mandatory fees:* $100 full-time.
Financial Aid Forms of aid include need-based and non-need-based scholarships and part-time jobs. The application deadline for financial aid is continuous.
Freshman Admission Coleman College requires a high school transcript, an interview, and TOEFL scores for international students. The application deadline for regular admission is August 1.
Transfer Admission The application deadline for admission is rolling.
Entrance Difficulty Coleman College assesses its entrance difficulty level as moderately difficult.

For Further Information Contact Ms. Debbie Coleman, Director of Admissions, Coleman College, 7380 Parkway Drive, La Mesa, CA 91942-1500. *Telephone:* 619-465-3990 Ext. 101. *Fax:* 619-463-0162. *E-mail:* admissions@coleman.edu. *Web site:* http://www.coleman.edu/.

COLLEGE OF NOTRE DAME

See Notre Dame de Namur University

COLUMBIA COLLEGE HOLLYWOOD

Tarzana, California

CCH is a coed, private, four-year college, founded in 1952, offering degrees at the associate and bachelor's levels. It has a 1-acre campus in Tarzana.

Academic Information The faculty has 27 full-time members. The student-faculty ratio is 5:1. The library holds 5,500 titles, 23 serial subscriptions, and 220 audiovisual materials. Special programs include accelerated degree programs, summer session for credit, part-time degree programs (daytime, weekends, summer), and adult/continuing education programs. The most frequently chosen baccalaureate field is communications/communication technologies.
Student Body Statistics The student body is made up of 150 undergraduates (60 freshmen). 31 percent are women and 69 percent are men. 50 percent are from California. 10 percent are international students. 5 percent of the 2003 graduating class went on to graduate and professional schools.
Expenses for 2003–04 *Application fee:* $50. *Tuition:* $11,400 full-time, $4000 per term part-time. *Mandatory fees:* $225 full-time. Full-time tuition and fees vary according to course level, course load, and program.
Financial Aid Forms of aid include need-based scholarships and part-time jobs. The average aided 2003–04 undergraduate received an aid package worth an estimated $3827. The application deadline for financial aid is continuous.
Freshman Admission CCH requires an essay, a high school transcript, a minimum 2.0 high school GPA, 2 recommendations, an interview, and TOEFL scores for international students. SAT I scores are recommended. The application deadline for regular admission is rolling.
Entrance Difficulty CCH assesses its entrance difficulty level as minimally difficult; moderately difficult for cinema program. For the fall 2003 freshman class, 77 percent of the applicants were accepted.

For Further Information Contact Mr. Adam McDaniel, Admissions and Marketing Coordinator, Columbia College Hollywood, 18618 Oxnard Street, Tarzana, CA 91356. *Telephone:* 818-345-8414 Ext. 203 or 800-785-0585 Ext. 105 (toll-free in-state). *Fax:* 818-345-9053. *E-mail:* admissions@columbiacollege.edu. *Web site:* http://www.columbiacollege.edu/.

CONCORDIA UNIVERSITY

Irvine, California

Concordia at Irvine is a coed, private, comprehensive unit of The Ten-campus Concordia University System, founded in 1972, affiliated with the Lutheran Church–Missouri Synod, offering degrees at the associate, bachelor's, and master's levels and postbachelor's certificates (associate's degree for international students only). It has a 70-acre campus in Irvine near Los Angeles.

Academic Information The faculty has 168 members (44% full-time), 42% with terminal degrees. The undergraduate student-faculty ratio is 15:1. The library holds 94,250 titles, 377 serial subscriptions, and 2,079 audiovisual materials. Special programs include an honors program, advanced placement credit, accelerated degree programs, ESL programs, double majors, independent study, self-designed majors, summer session for credit, part-time degree programs (daytime, evenings, summer), adult/continuing education programs, and internships. The most frequently chosen baccalaureate fields are business/marketing, liberal arts/general studies, social sciences and history.
Student Body Statistics The student body totals 1,747, of whom 1,337 are undergraduates (261 freshmen). 65 percent are women and 35 percent are men. Students come from 36 states and territories and 7 other countries. 85 percent are from California. 1.7 percent are international students. 33 percent of the 2003 graduating class went on to graduate and professional schools.
Expenses for 2004–05 *Application fee:* $40. *Comprehensive fee:* $25,470 includes full-time tuition ($18,800) and college room and board ($6670). *College room only:* $4000. Room and board charges vary according to board plan. *Part-time tuition:* $565 per unit.
Financial Aid Forms of aid include need-based and non-need-based scholarships, athletic grants, and part-time jobs. The average aided 2003–04 undergraduate received an aid package worth an estimated $13,979. The application deadline for financial aid is April 1 with a priority deadline of March 2.
Freshman Admission Concordia at Irvine requires a high school transcript, 2 recommendations, SAT I or ACT scores, and TOEFL scores for international students. A minimum 2.8 high school GPA and an interview are recommended. The application deadline for regular admission is rolling.
Transfer Admission The application deadline for admission is rolling.
Entrance Difficulty Concordia at Irvine assesses its entrance difficulty level as moderately difficult. For the fall 2003 freshman class, 27 percent of the applicants were accepted.

For Further Information Contact Ms. Lori McDonald, Executive Director of Enrollment Services, Concordia University, 1530 Concordia West, Irvine, CA 92612-3299. *Telephone:* 949-854-8002 Ext. 1419 or 800-229-1200 (toll-free). *Fax:* 949-854-6894. *E-mail:* admission@cui.edu. *Web site:* http://www.cui.edu/.

CRESTMONT COLLEGE

Rancho Palos Verdes, California

Crestmont College is a coed, private, primarily two-year college, founded in 1878, offering degrees at the associate and bachelor's levels in ministries. It has a 44-acre campus in Rancho Palos Verdes near Los Angeles.

Academic Information The faculty has 63 members (51% full-time), 62% with terminal degrees. The student-faculty ratio is 5:1. The library holds 35,700 titles and 125 serial subscriptions. Special programs include academic remediation, cooperative (work-study) education, accelerated degree programs, ESL programs, independent study, distance learning, self-designed majors, external degree programs, internships, and arrangement for off-campus study.
Student Body Statistics The student body is made up of 213 undergraduates (4 freshmen). 56 percent are women and 44 percent are men. Students come from 14 states and territories and 1 other country. 51 percent are from California. 2.3 percent are international students.
Expenses for 2004–05 *Application fee:* $15. *Comprehensive fee:* $10,600 includes full-time tuition ($1500), mandatory fees ($850), and college room and board ($8250). *Part-time tuition:* $100 per quarter hour. *Part-time mandatory fees:* $850 per year.
Freshman Admission Crestmont College requires an essay, a high school transcript, recommendations, and an interview. The application deadline for regular admission is June 1.
Entrance Difficulty Crestmont College assesses its entrance difficulty level as noncompetitive. For the fall 2003 freshman class, 65 percent of the applicants were accepted.

For Further Information Contact Maj. Donna Jackson, Director of Records and Admissions, Crestmont College, 30840 Hawthorne Boulevard, Rancho Palos Verdes, CA 90275. *Telephone:* 310-544-6440 or 310-544-6440 (toll-free in-state). *Fax:* 310-265-6520. *Web site:* http://www.crestmontcollege.edu/.

DEEP SPRINGS COLLEGE

Deep Springs, California

Deep Springs College is a men's, private, two-year college, founded in 1917, offering degrees at the associate level. It has a 3,000-acre campus in Deep Springs.

For Further Information Contact Dr. L. Jackson Newell, President, Deep Springs College, HC 72, Box 45001, Dyer, NV 89010-9803. *Telephone:* 760-872-2000. *E-mail:* apcom@deepsprings.edu. *Web site:* http://www.deepsprings.edu/.

DESIGN INSTITUTE OF SAN DIEGO

San Diego, California

Design Institute of San Diego is a coed, proprietary, four-year college, founded in 1977, offering degrees at the bachelor's level in interior design.

Academic Information The faculty has 50 members. The library holds 5,000 titles and 90 serial subscriptions. Special programs include study abroad, part-time degree programs, and internships.
Student Body Statistics The student body is made up of 450 undergraduates. Students come from 10 states and territories and 15 other countries.
Expenses for 2004–05 *Application fee:* $25. *Tuition:* $11,800 full-time.
Financial Aid Forms of aid include need-based scholarships and part-time jobs. The application deadline for financial aid is continuous.
Freshman Admission Design Institute of San Diego requires a high school transcript, a minimum 2.0 high school GPA, and TOEFL scores for international students. An interview is recommended. The application deadline for regular admission is rolling.
Transfer Admission The application deadline for admission is rolling.
Entrance Difficulty Design Institute of San Diego assesses its entrance difficulty level as noncompetitive.

For Further Information Contact Ms. Paula Parrish, Director of Admissions, Design Institute of San Diego, 8555 Commerce Avenue, San Diego, CA 92121. *Telephone:* 858-566-1200 or 800-619-4337 (toll-free). *Fax:* 858-566-2711. *E-mail:* admissions@disd.edu. *Web site:* http://www.disd.edu/.

DEVRY UNIVERSITY

Irvine, California

For Information Write to DeVry University, Irvine, CA 92612-1682.

DEVRY UNIVERSITY

San Diego, California

For Information Write to DeVry University, San Diego, CA 92108-1633.

DEVRY UNIVERSITY

San Francisco, California

For Information Write to DeVry University, San Francisco, CA 94105-2472.

DEVRY UNIVERSITY

Elk Grove, California

For Information Write to DeVry University, Elk Grove, CA 95758.

DEVRY UNIVERSITY

Fremont, California

DeVry is a coed, proprietary, comprehensive unit of DeVry University, founded in 1998, offering degrees at the associate, bachelor's, and master's levels and postbachelor's certificates. It has a 17-acre campus in Fremont near San Francisco.

Academic Information The undergraduate student-faculty ratio is 29:1. The library holds 40,000 titles, 3,060 serial subscriptions, and 2,000 audiovisual materials. Special programs include academic remediation, services for learning-disabled students, cooperative (work-study) education, advanced placement credit, accelerated degree programs, distance learning, summer session for credit, part-time degree programs (daytime, evenings, weekends, summer), and adult/continuing education programs. The most frequently chosen baccalaureate fields are business/marketing, computer/information sciences, engineering/engineering technologies.
Student Body Statistics The student body totals 1,762, of whom 1,654 are undergraduates (348 freshmen). 23 percent are women and 77 percent are men. Students come from 25 states and territories and 9 other countries. 97 percent are from California. 2 percent are international students.
Expenses for 2003–04 *Application fee:* $50. *Tuition:* $11,100 full-time, $395 per credit hour part-time. *Mandatory fees:* $165 full-time. Full-time tuition and fees vary according to course load. Part-time tuition varies according to course load.
Financial Aid Forms of aid include need-based and non-need-based scholarships and part-time jobs. The average aided 2002–03 undergraduate received an aid package worth $10,351. The application deadline for financial aid is continuous.
Freshman Admission DeVry requires a high school transcript, an interview, and TOEFL scores for international students. SAT I, ACT or CPT is recommended. The application deadline for regular admission is rolling.
Transfer Admission The application deadline for admission is rolling.
Entrance Difficulty DeVry assesses its entrance difficulty level as minimally difficult; moderately difficult for electronics engineering technology program.

For Further Information Contact Mr. Bruce Williams, New Student Coordinator, DeVry University, 6600 Dumbarton Circle, Fremont, CA 94555-3615. *Telephone:* 510-574-1111 or 888-201-9941 (toll-free). *Fax:* 510-742-0868. *Web site:* http://www.devry.edu/.

DEVRY UNIVERSITY

Long Beach, California

DeVry is a coed, proprietary, comprehensive unit of DeVry University, founded in 1984, offering degrees at the associate, bachelor's, and master's levels and postbachelor's certificates. It has a 23-acre campus in Long Beach near Los Angeles.

Academic Information The library holds 15,500 titles, 85 serial subscriptions, and 2,000 audiovisual materials. Special programs include academic remediation, services for learning-disabled students, cooperative (work-study) education, advanced placement credit, accelerated degree programs, distance learning, summer session for credit, part-time degree programs (daytime, evenings, weekends, summer), and adult/continuing education programs. The most frequently chosen baccalaureate fields are business/marketing, computer/information sciences, engineering/engineering technologies.
Student Body Statistics The student body totals 2,186, of whom 1,928 are undergraduates (484 freshmen). 26 percent are women and 74 percent are men. Students come from 23 states and territories and 11 other countries. 98 percent are from California. 1.7 percent are international students.
Expenses for 2003–04 *Application fee:* $50. *Tuition:* $10,590 full-time, $370 per credit hour part-time. *Mandatory fees:* $165 full-time. Full-time tuition and fees vary according to course load. Part-time tuition varies according to course load.
Financial Aid Forms of aid include need-based and non-need-based scholarships and part-time jobs. The average aided 2003–04 undergraduate received an aid package worth an estimated $10,063. The application deadline for financial aid is continuous.
Freshman Admission DeVry requires a high school transcript, an interview, and TOEFL scores for international students. SAT I, ACT or CPT is recommended. The application deadline for regular admission is rolling.
Transfer Admission The application deadline for admission is rolling.
Entrance Difficulty DeVry assesses its entrance difficulty level as minimally difficult; moderately difficult for electronics engineering technology program.

For Further Information Contact Ms. Lisa Flores, New Student Coordinator, DeVry University, 3880 Kilroy Airport Way, Long Beach, CA 90806-2449. *Telephone:* 562-427-0861 or 800-597-0444 (toll-free). *Fax:* 562-997-5371. *E-mail:* cblas@socal.devry.edu. *Web site:* http://www.devry.edu/.

DEVRY UNIVERSITY

Pomona, California

DeVry is a coed, proprietary, comprehensive unit of DeVry University, founded in 1983, offering degrees at the associate, bachelor's, and master's levels and postbachelor's certificates. It has a 15-acre campus in Pomona near Los Angeles.

Academic Information The library holds 17,000 titles, 77 serial subscriptions, and 1,234 audiovisual materials. Special programs include academic remediation, services for learning-disabled students, cooperative (work-study) education, advanced placement credit, accelerated degree programs, distance learning, summer session for credit, part-time degree programs (daytime, evenings, weekends, summer), and adult/continuing education programs. The most frequently chosen baccalaureate fields are business/marketing, computer/information sciences, engineering/engineering technologies.
Student Body Statistics The student body totals 2,565, of whom 2,376 are undergraduates (504 freshmen). 25 percent are women and 75 percent are men. Students come from 25 states and territories and 19 other countries. 98 percent are from California. 2.5 percent are international students.
Expenses for 2003–04 *Application fee:* $50. *Tuition:* $10,590 full-time, $370 per credit hour part-time. *Mandatory fees:* $165 full-time. Full-time tuition and fees vary according to course load. Part-time tuition varies according to course load.

Financial Aid Forms of aid include need-based and non-need-based scholarships and part-time jobs. The average aided 2002–03 undergraduate received an aid package worth $9829. The application deadline for financial aid is continuous.
Freshman Admission DeVry requires a high school transcript, an interview, and TOEFL scores for international students. SAT I, ACT or CPT is recommended. The application deadline for regular admission is rolling.
Transfer Admission The application deadline for admission is rolling.
Entrance Difficulty DeVry assesses its entrance difficulty level as minimally difficult; moderately difficult for electronics engineering technology program.

For Further Information Contact Ms. Melanie Guerra, New Student Coordinator, DeVry University, 901 Corporate Center Drive, University Center, Pomona, CA 91768-2642. *Telephone:* 909-622-8866 or 800-882-7536 (toll-free). *Fax:* 909-868-4165. *Web site:* http://www.devry.edu/.

DEVRY UNIVERSITY

West Hills, California

DeVry University is a coed, proprietary, comprehensive unit of DeVry University, founded in 1999, offering degrees at the associate, bachelor's, and master's levels and postbachelor's certificates. It has a 20-acre campus in West Hills.

Academic Information The undergraduate student-faculty ratio is 15:1. The library holds 16,177 titles, 130 serial subscriptions, and 597 audiovisual materials. Special programs include academic remediation, services for learning-disabled students, cooperative (work-study) education, advanced placement credit, accelerated degree programs, distance learning, summer session for credit, part-time degree programs (daytime, evenings, weekends, summer), and adult/continuing education programs. The most frequently chosen baccalaureate fields are business/marketing, computer/information sciences, engineering/engineering technologies.
Student Body Statistics The student body totals 1,278, of whom 1,168 are undergraduates (259 freshmen). 26 percent are women and 74 percent are men. Students come from 10 states and territories and 13 other countries. 97 percent are from California. 3 percent are international students.
Expenses for 2003–04 *Application fee:* $50. *Tuition:* $10,590 full-time, $370 per credit hour part-time. *Mandatory fees:* $165 full-time. Full-time tuition and fees vary according to course load. Part-time tuition varies according to course load.
Financial Aid Forms of aid include need-based and non-need-based scholarships and part-time jobs. The average aided 2002–03 undergraduate received an aid package worth $9557. The application deadline for financial aid is continuous.
Freshman Admission DeVry University requires a high school transcript, an interview, and TOEFL scores for international students. SAT I, ACT or CPT is recommended. The application deadline for regular admission is rolling.
Transfer Admission The application deadline for admission is rolling.
Entrance Difficulty DeVry University assesses its entrance difficulty level as minimally difficult; moderately difficult for electronics engineering technology program.

For Further Information Contact Ms. Denise Barba, Acting Director of Admissions, DeVry University, 22801 Roscoe Boulevard, West Hills, CA 91304-3200. *Telephone:* 818-932-3001 or 888-610-0800 (toll-free). *Fax:* 909-868-4165. *E-mail:* admissions@devry.edu. *Web site:* http://www.devry.edu/.

DOMINICAN SCHOOL OF PHILOSOPHY AND THEOLOGY

Berkeley, California

DSPT is a coed, private, Roman Catholic, upper-level institution, founded in 1932, offering degrees at the bachelor's, master's, and first professional levels in philosophy. It is located in Berkeley near San Francisco.

Expenses for 2003–04 *Application fee:* $30. *Tuition:* $9456 full-time, $394 per credit part-time. *Mandatory fees:* $50 full-time, $50 per year part-time. Full-time tuition and fees vary according to program. Part-time tuition and fees vary according to program. *College room only:* $7081. Room charges vary according to housing facility.

For Further Information Contact Ms. Susan McGinnis Hardie, Director of Admissions, Dominican School of Philosophy and Theology, 2401 Ridge Road, Berkeley, CA 94709-1295. *Telephone:* 510-883-2073. *Fax:* 510-849-1372. *E-mail:* admissions@dspt.edu. *Web site:* http://www.dspt.edu/.

DOMINICAN UNIVERSITY OF CALIFORNIA

San Rafael, California

Dominican is a coed, private, comprehensive institution, founded in 1890, affiliated with the Roman Catholic Church, offering degrees at the bachelor's and master's levels and postbachelor's certificates. It has an 80-acre campus in San Rafael near San Francisco.

Academic Information The faculty has 228 members (30% full-time), 45% with terminal degrees. The undergraduate student-faculty ratio is 10:1. The library holds 94,800 titles, 400 serial subscriptions, and 775 audiovisual materials. Special programs include academic remediation, services for learning-disabled students, an honors program, study abroad, advanced placement credit, ESL programs, double majors, independent study, self-designed majors, summer session for credit, part-time degree programs (daytime, evenings, weekends, summer), adult/continuing education programs, internships, and arrangement for off-campus study with University of California, Berkeley, Aquinas College, St. Thomas Aquinas College, Barry University. The most frequently chosen baccalaureate fields are health professions and related sciences, liberal arts/general studies, psychology.
Student Body Statistics The student body totals 1,742, of whom 1,124 are undergraduates (245 freshmen). 75 percent are women and 25 percent are men. Students come from 19 states and territories and 21 other countries. 94 percent are from California. 3.9 percent are international students.
Expenses for 2003–04 *Application fee:* $40. *Comprehensive fee:* $32,070 includes full-time tuition ($22,250), mandatory fees ($400), and college room and board ($9420). Full-time tuition and fees vary according to class time, degree level, location, and program. Room and board charges vary according to board plan. *Part-time tuition:* $927 per unit. *Part-time mandatory fees:* $200 per term. Part-time tuition and fees vary according to class time, degree level, location, and program.
Financial Aid Forms of aid include need-based and non-need-based scholarships, athletic grants, and part-time jobs. The average aided 2003–04 undergraduate received an aid package worth an estimated $19,762. The priority application deadline for financial aid is March 2.
Freshman Admission Dominican requires an essay, a high school transcript, a minimum 2.5 high school GPA, 1 recommendation, SAT I or ACT scores, and TOEFL scores for international students. SAT II: Subject Test scores are recommended. An interview is required for some. The application deadline for regular admission is August 1.
Transfer Admission The application deadline for admission is rolling.

Dominican University of California (continued)

Entrance Difficulty Dominican assesses its entrance difficulty level as moderately difficult; noncompetitive for evening, weekend programs. For the fall 2003 freshman class, 55 percent of the applicants were accepted.

For Further Information Contact Mr. Art Criss, Director of Undergraduate Admissions, Dominican University of California, 50 Acacia Avenue, San Rafael, CA 94901-2298. *Telephone:* 415-257-1376/458-3754 or 888-323-6763 (toll-free). *Fax:* 415-385-3214. *E-mail:* enroll@dominican.edu. *Web site:* http://www.dominican.edu/.

DON BOSCO COLLEGE OF SCIENCE AND TECHNOLOGY

Rosemead, California

For Information Write to Don Bosco College of Science and Technology, Rosemead, CA 91770-4299.

D-Q UNIVERSITY

Davis, California

For Information Write to D-Q University, Davis, CA 95617-0409.

EDUCATION AMERICA UNIVERSITY

See Remington College–San Diego Campus

EMMANUEL BIBLE COLLEGE

Pasadena, California

For Information Write to Emmanuel Bible College, Pasadena, CA 91104.

FOUNDATION COLLEGE

San Diego, California

Foundation College is a coed, private, two-year college, offering degrees at the associate level.

Academic Information The faculty has 13 members (77% full-time).
Expenses for 2004–05 *Tuition:* $260 per credit part-time.
Financial Aid Forms of aid include part-time jobs. The application deadline for financial aid is continuous.
Freshman Admission The application deadline for regular admission is rolling.
Transfer Admission The application deadline for admission is rolling.
Entrance Difficulty Foundation College assesses its entrance difficulty level as minimally difficult.

For Further Information Contact Peggy Aplin, Admissions Manager, Foundation College, 5353 Mission Center Road, Suite 100, San Diego, CA 92108-1306. *Telephone:* 619-683-3273 Ext. 105 or 888-707-3273 (toll-free). *Fax:* 619-683-3224. *E-mail:* jdurb@foundationcollege.com. *Web site:* http://www.foundationcollege.org/.

FRESNO PACIFIC UNIVERSITY

Fresno, California

Fresno Pacific is a coed, private, comprehensive institution, founded in 1944, affiliated with the Mennonite Brethren Church, offering degrees at the associate, bachelor's, and master's levels. It has a 42-acre campus in Fresno.

Academic Information The faculty has 92 members (83% full-time). The undergraduate student-faculty ratio is 16:1. The library holds 158,000 titles, 3,064 serial subscriptions, and 9,400 audiovisual materials. Special programs include services for learning-disabled students, cooperative (work-study) education, study abroad, advanced placement credit, accelerated degree programs, ESL programs, double majors, independent study, distance learning, self-designed majors, summer session for credit, part-time degree programs (daytime, evenings, weekends, summer), adult/continuing education programs, internships, and arrangement for off-campus study with California State University, Fresno; Mennonite Brethren Biblical Seminary; San Joaquin College of Law. The most frequently chosen baccalaureate fields are business/marketing, education, philosophy, religion, and theology.
Student Body Statistics The student body totals 2,243, of whom 1,380 are undergraduates (191 freshmen). 61 percent are women and 39 percent are men. Students come from 20 states and territories and 14 other countries. 97 percent are from California. 2.7 percent are international students.
Expenses for 2003–04 *Application fee:* $40. *Comprehensive fee:* $22,462 includes full-time tuition ($17,370), mandatory fees ($222), and college room and board ($4870). *College room only:* $2130. Full-time tuition and fees vary according to program. Room and board charges vary according to board plan and housing facility. *Part-time tuition:* $615 per unit. *Part-time mandatory fees:* $72 per term. Part-time tuition and fees vary according to program.
Financial Aid Forms of aid include need-based and non-need-based scholarships and part-time jobs. The average aided 2003–04 undergraduate received an aid package worth an estimated $13,688. The priority application deadline for financial aid is March 2.
Freshman Admission Fresno Pacific requires an essay, a high school transcript, 1 recommendation, SAT I or ACT scores, and TOEFL scores for international students. A minimum 3.10 high school GPA is recommended. The application deadline for regular admission is rolling.
Transfer Admission The application deadline for admission is rolling.
Entrance Difficulty Fresno Pacific assesses its entrance difficulty level as moderately difficult. For the fall 2003 freshman class, 62 percent of the applicants were accepted.

For Further Information Contact Ms. Suzana Dobric, Associate Director of Undergraduate Admissions, Fresno Pacific University, 1717 South Chestnut Avenue, Fresno, CA 93702-4709. *Telephone:* 559-453-2231 or 800-660-6089 (toll-free in-state). *Fax:* 559-453-2007. *E-mail:* ugadmis@fresno.edu. *Web site:* http://www.fresno.edu/.

GOLDEN GATE UNIVERSITY

San Francisco, California

Golden Gate is a coed, private university, founded in 1853, offering degrees at the associate, bachelor's, master's, doctoral, and first professional levels.

Academic Information The faculty has 662 members (5% full-time), 19% with terminal degrees. The undergraduate student-faculty ratio is 14:1. The library holds 79,204 titles and 3,335 serial subscriptions. Special programs include academic remediation, cooperative (work-study) education, advanced placement credit, accelerated degree programs, ESL programs, distance learning, summer session for credit, part-time degree programs (daytime, evenings, weekends, summer), adult/continuing education programs, internships, and arrangement for off-campus study with The San Francisco Consortium. The most frequently chosen baccalaureate fields are business/marketing, computer/information sciences, protective services/public administration.
Student Body Statistics The student body totals 4,299, of whom 686 are undergraduates (2 freshmen). 53 percent are women and 47 percent are men. 95 percent are from California. 11.7 percent are international students.
Expenses for 2003–04 *Application fee:* $55. *Tuition:* $9984 full-time, $1248 per course part-time. Full-time tuition varies according to course load, degree level, and program. Part-time tuition varies according to course load and program.

Financial Aid Forms of aid include need-based and non-need-based scholarships and part-time jobs. The average aided 2003–04 undergraduate received an aid package worth an estimated $2931. The application deadline for financial aid is continuous.
Freshman Admission Golden Gate requires a high school transcript, a minimum 2.0 high school GPA, and TOEFL scores for international students. An essay and a minimum 3.0 high school GPA are recommended. A minimum 3.2 high school GPA and an interview are required for some. The application deadline for regular admission is June 1.
Transfer Admission The application deadline for admission is June 1.
Entrance Difficulty Golden Gate assesses its entrance difficulty level as moderately difficult; minimally difficult for transfers. For the fall 2003 freshman class, 100 percent of the applicants were accepted.

For Further Information Contact Ms. Cherron Hoppes, Director of Admission, Golden Gate University, 536 Mission Street, San Francisco, CA 94105-2968. *Telephone:* 415-442-7800 or 800-448-4968 (toll-free). *Fax:* 415-442-7807. *E-mail:* info@ggu.edu. *Web site:* http://www.ggu.edu/.

HARVEY MUDD COLLEGE

Claremont, California

Harvey Mudd is a coed, private, four-year college of The Claremont Colleges Consortium, founded in 1955, offering degrees at the bachelor's and master's levels. It has a 33-acre campus in Claremont near Los Angeles.

Academic Information The faculty has 91 members (91% full-time), 99% with terminal degrees. The undergraduate student-faculty ratio is 9:1. The library holds 1 million titles, 4,321 serial subscriptions, and 606 audiovisual materials. Special programs include services for learning-disabled students, study abroad, advanced placement credit, double majors, self-designed majors, internships, and arrangement for off-campus study with other members of The Claremont Colleges, Swarthmore College, Rensselaer Polytechnic Institute. The most frequently chosen baccalaureate fields are computer/information sciences, engineering/engineering technologies, mathematics.
Student Body Statistics The student body is made up of 704 undergraduates (191 freshmen). 32 percent are women and 68 percent are men. Students come from 47 states and territories and 14 other countries. 43 percent are from California. 3 percent are international students. 42 percent of the 2003 graduating class went on to graduate and professional schools.
Expenses for 2004–05 *Application fee:* $50. *Comprehensive fee:* $38,080 includes full-time tuition ($28,012), mandatory fees ($648), and college room and board ($9420). *College room only:* $4790. Room and board charges vary according to board plan.
Financial Aid Forms of aid include need-based and non-need-based scholarships and part-time jobs. The average aided 2003–04 undergraduate received an aid package worth an estimated $22,740. The application deadline for financial aid is February 1.
Freshman Admission Harvey Mudd requires an essay, a high school transcript, 3 recommendations, SAT I scores, SAT II: Writing Test scores, and SAT II Subject Test in Math 2C, third SAT II Subject Test (Math 1C is not accepted). An interview and TOEFL scores for international students are recommended. The application deadline for regular admission is January 15 and for early decision it is November 15.
Transfer Admission The application deadline for admission is April 1.
Entrance Difficulty Harvey Mudd assesses its entrance difficulty level as most difficult. For the fall 2003 freshman class, 40 percent of the applicants were accepted.

For Further Information Contact Mr. Deren Finks, Vice President and Dean of Admissions and Financial Aid, Harvey Mudd College, 301 East 12th Street, Claremont, CA 91711. *Telephone:* 909-621-8011. *Fax:* 909-607-7046. *E-mail:* admission@hmc.edu. *Web site:* http://www.hmc.edu/.

HEALD COLLEGE-CONCORD

Concord, California

Heald College is a coed, private, two-year college, founded in 1863, offering degrees at the associate level. It has a 5-acre campus in Concord near San Francisco.

For Further Information Contact Heald College-Concord, 5130 Commercial Circle, Concord, CA 94520. *Telephone:* 925-288-5800 or 800-755-3550 (toll-free in-state). *Fax:* 925-288-5896. *E-mail:* info@heald.edu. *Web site:* http://www.heald.edu/.

HEALD COLLEGE-FRESNO

Fresno, California

Heald College-Fresno is a coed, private, two-year college, founded in 1863, offering degrees at the associate level. It has a 3-acre campus in Fresno.

For Further Information Contact Heald College-Fresno, 255 West Bullard Avenue, Fresno, CA 93704-1706. *Telephone:* 559-438-4222 or 800-755-3550 (toll-free in-state). *E-mail:* info@heald.edu. *Web site:* http://www.heald.edu/.

HEALD COLLEGE-HAYWARD

Hayward, California

Heald College-Hayward is a coed, private, two-year college, founded in 1863, offering degrees at the associate level. It is located in Hayward near San Francisco.

For Further Information Contact Heald College-Hayward, 25500 Industrial Boulevard, Hayward, CA 94545. *Telephone:* 510-783-2100 or 800-755-3550 (toll-free in-state). *Fax:* 510-783-3287. *E-mail:* info@heald.edu. *Web site:* http://www.heald.edu/.

HEALD COLLEGE-RANCHO CORDOVA

Rancho Cordova, California

Heald College-Rancho Cordova is a coed, private, two-year college, founded in 1863, offering degrees at the associate level. It has a 1-acre campus in Rancho Cordova near Sacramento.

For Further Information Contact Heald College-Rancho Cordova, 2910 Prospect Park Drive, Rancho Cordova, CA 95670-6005. *Telephone:* 916-638-1616 or 800-755-3550 (toll-free in-state). *Fax:* 916-853-8282. *E-mail:* info@heald.edu. *Web site:* http://www.heald.edu/.

HEALD COLLEGE-ROSEVILLE

Roseville, California

Heald College-Roseville is a coed, private, two-year college, founded in 1863, offering degrees at the associate level. It has a 5-acre campus in Roseville.

For Further Information Contact Heald College-Roseville, 7 Sierra Gate Plaza, Roseville, CA 95678. *Telephone:* 916-789-8600 or 800-755-3550 (toll-free in-state). *E-mail:* info@heald.edu. *Web site:* http://www.heald.edu/.

HEALD COLLEGE-SALINAS

Salinas, California

Heald is a coed, private, two-year college, founded in 1863, offering degrees at the associate level. It is located in Salinas near San Jose.

For Further Information Contact Heald College-Salinas, 1450 North Main Street, Salinas, CA 93906. *Telephone:* 831-443-1700 or 800-755-3550 (toll-free in-state). *Fax:* 831-443-1050. *E-mail:* info@heald.edu. *Web site:* http://www.heald.edu/.

HEALD COLLEGE-SAN FRANCISCO

San Francisco, California

Heald College-San Francisco is a coed, private, two-year college, founded in 1863, offering degrees at the associate level.

For Further Information Contact Heald College-San Francisco, 350 Mission Street, San Francisco, CA 94105. *Telephone:* 415-808-3000 or 800-755-3550 (toll-free in-state). *Fax:* 415-808-3003. *E-mail:* info@heald.edu. *Web site:* http://www.heald.edu/.

HEALD COLLEGE-SAN JOSE

Milpitas, California

Heald College-San Jose is a coed, private, two-year college, founded in 1863, offering degrees at the associate level. It has a 5-acre campus in Milpitas near San Jose.

For Further Information Contact Heald College-San Jose, 341 Great Mall Parkway, Milpitas, CA 95035. *Telephone:* 408-934-4900 or 800-755-3550 (toll-free in-state). *Fax:* 408-934-7777. *E-mail:* info@heald.edu. *Web site:* http://www.heald.edu/.

HEALD COLLEGE-STOCKTON

Stockton, California

Heald College-Stockton is a coed, private, two-year college, founded in 1863, offering degrees at the associate level.

For Further Information Contact Heald College-Stockton, 1605 East March Lane, Stockton, CA 95210. *Telephone:* 209-473-5200 or 800-755-3550 (toll-free in-state). *Fax:* 209-477-2739. *E-mail:* info@heald.edu. *Web site:* http://www.heald.edu/.

HOLY NAMES UNIVERSITY

Oakland, California

HNC is a coed, primarily women's, private, Roman Catholic, comprehensive institution, founded in 1868, offering degrees at the bachelor's and master's levels and postbachelor's certificates. It has a 60-acre campus in Oakland near San Francisco.

Academic Information The faculty has 127 members (24% full-time), 55% with terminal degrees. The undergraduate student-faculty ratio is 12:1. The library holds 116,031 titles, 200 serial subscriptions, and 4,378 audiovisual materials. Special programs include academic remediation, services for learning-disabled students, an honors program, study abroad, advanced placement credit, accelerated degree programs, ESL programs, double majors, independent study, distance learning, self-designed majors, summer session for credit, part-time degree programs (evenings, weekends), adult/continuing education programs, internships, and arrangement for off-campus study. The most frequently chosen baccalaureate fields are business/marketing, health professions and related sciences, psychology.

Student Body Statistics The student body totals 943, of whom 593 are undergraduates (58 freshmen). 78 percent are women and 22 percent are men. Students come from 15 states and territories and 11 other countries. 96 percent are from California. 2.7 percent are international students.

Expenses for 2004–05 *Application fee:* $35. *Comprehensive fee:* $28,780 includes full-time tuition ($20,770), mandatory fees ($210), and college room and board ($7800). *College room only:* $4000. Full-time tuition and fees vary according to course load. Room and board charges vary according to board plan. *Part-time tuition:* $690 per unit. *Part-time mandatory fees:* $105 per term.

Financial Aid Forms of aid include need-based and non-need-based scholarships, athletic grants, and part-time jobs. The average aided 2003–04 undergraduate received an aid package worth an estimated $22,883. The priority application deadline for financial aid is March 2.

Freshman Admission HNC requires an essay, a high school transcript, 1 recommendation, SAT I or ACT scores, and TOEFL scores for international students. An interview is required for some. The application deadline for regular admission is August 1.

Transfer Admission The application deadline for admission is August 1.

Entrance Difficulty HNC assesses its entrance difficulty level as moderately difficult. For the fall 2003 freshman class, 62 percent of the applicants were accepted.

For Further Information Contact Mr. Jeffrey D. Miller, Vice President for Enrollment Management, Holy Names University, 3200 Mountain Boulevard, Oakland, CA 94619. *Telephone:* 510-436-1351 or 800-430-1321 (toll-free). *Fax:* 510-436-1325. *E-mail:* admissions@admin.hnc.edu. *Web site:* http://www.hnu.edu/.

HOPE INTERNATIONAL UNIVERSITY

Fullerton, California

Hope International University is a coed, private, comprehensive institution, founded in 1928, affiliated with the Christian Churches and Churches of Christ, offering degrees at the associate, bachelor's, and master's levels. It has a 16-acre campus in Fullerton near Los Angeles.

Expenses for 2003–04 *Application fee:* $20. *Comprehensive fee:* $21,074 includes full-time tuition ($14,900), mandatory fees ($300), and college room and board ($5874). *College room only:* $3098.

For Further Information Contact Ms. Midge Madden, Office Manager, Hope International University, 2500 East Nutwood Avenue, Fullerton, CA 92831-3138. *Telephone:* 714-879-3901 Ext. 2215 or 800-762-1294 (toll-free). *Fax:* 714-526-0231. *E-mail:* mfmadden@hiu.edu. *Web site:* http://www.hiu.edu/.

HSI LAI UNIVERSITY

See University of the West

HUMBOLDT STATE UNIVERSITY

Arcata, California

Humboldt is a coed, public, comprehensive unit of California State University System, founded in 1913, offering degrees at the bachelor's and master's levels. It has a 161-acre campus in Arcata.

Academic Information The faculty has 489 members (59% full-time), 56% with terminal degrees. The undergraduate student-faculty ratio is 19:1. The library holds 585,386 titles, 2,629 serial subscriptions, and 4,947 audiovisual materials. Special programs include academic remediation, services for learning-disabled students, an honors program, cooperative (work-study) education, study abroad, advanced placement credit, ESL programs, double majors, independent study, distance learning, self-designed majors, summer session for credit, part-time degree programs (daytime, summer), adult/continuing education programs, internships, and arrangement for off-campus study with members of the National Student Exchange, California State University System. The most frequently chosen

baccalaureate fields are interdisciplinary studies, natural resources/environmental science, social sciences and history.
Student Body Statistics The student body totals 7,725, of whom 6,682 are undergraduates (861 freshmen). 55 percent are women and 45 percent are men. Students come from 50 states and territories and 24 other countries. 97 percent are from California.
Expenses for 2003–04 *Application fee:* $55. *State resident tuition:* $0 full-time. *Nonresident tuition:* $6768 full-time, $282 per unit part-time. *Mandatory fees:* $2539 full-time. *College room and board:* $6861. *College room only:* $3595. Room and board charges vary according to board plan and housing facility.
Financial Aid Forms of aid include need-based and non-need-based scholarships and part-time jobs. The average aided 2003–04 undergraduate received an aid package worth an estimated $8050. The priority application deadline for financial aid is March 2.
Freshman Admission Humboldt requires a high school transcript, a minimum 2.0 high school GPA, and TOEFL scores for international students. SAT I or ACT scores are required for some. The application deadline for regular admission is rolling.
Transfer Admission The application deadline for admission is November 30.
Entrance Difficulty Humboldt assesses its entrance difficulty level as moderately difficult; very difficult for out-of-state applicants. For the fall 2003 freshman class, 67 percent of the applicants were accepted.

For Further Information Contact Ms. Rebecca Kalal, Assistant Director of Admissions, Humboldt State University, 1 Harpst Street, Arcata, CA 95521-8299. *Telephone:* 707-826-6220. *Fax:* 707-826-6194. *E-mail:* hsuinfo@humboldt.edu. *Web site:* http://www.humboldt.edu/.

HUMPHREYS COLLEGE

Stockton, California

For Information Write to Humphreys College, Stockton, CA 95207-3896.

INSTITUTE OF COMPUTER TECHNOLOGY

Los Angeles, California

ICT College is a coed, proprietary, four-year college, founded in 1981, offering degrees at the associate and bachelor's levels.

For Further Information Contact Mr. Randy Taylor, Director of Admissions, Institute of Computer Technology, 3200 Wilshire Boulevard 4th Floor, Los Angeles, CA 90010. *Telephone:* 213-381-3333 or 800-57 GO ICT (toll-free in-state). *Fax:* 213-383-9369. *Web site:* http://www.ictcollege.edu/.

INTERIOR DESIGNERS INSTITUTE

Newport Beach, California

For Information Write to Interior Designers Institute, Newport Beach, CA 92660.

INTERNATIONAL TECHNOLOGICAL UNIVERSITY

Santa Clara, California

International Technological University is a coed, private, upper-level institution, offering degrees at the bachelor's and master's levels and postbachelor's certificates.

Expenses for 2003–04 *Tuition:* $8250 full-time, $275 per semester hour part-time. *Mandatory fees:* $500 full-time, $75 per term part-time.

For Further Information Contact Chun Mou Peng, Director of Operations, International Technological University, 1650 Warbunton Avenue, Santa Clara, CA 95050. *Telephone:* 408-556-9027. *Fax:* 408-556-9016. *E-mail:* chunmou@itu.edu. *Web site:* http://www.itu.edu/.

ITT TECHNICAL INSTITUTE

Anaheim, California

ITT Tech is a coed, proprietary, primarily two-year college of ITT Educational Services, Inc., founded in 1982, offering degrees at the associate and bachelor's levels. It has a 5-acre campus in Anaheim near Los Angeles.

Student Body Statistics The student body is made up of 642 undergraduates.
Expenses for 2003–04 *Application fee:* $100. Total Program Cost varies depending on course of study. Consult school catalog.
Financial Aid Forms of aid include need-based scholarships and part-time jobs. The application deadline for financial aid is continuous.
Freshman Admission ITT Tech requires a high school transcript, an interview, TOEFL scores for international students, and Wonderlic aptitude test. Recommendations are recommended. The application deadline for regular admission is rolling.
Transfer Admission The application deadline for admission is rolling.
Entrance Difficulty ITT Tech assesses its entrance difficulty level as minimally difficult.

For Further Information Contact Mr. Albert A. Naranjo, Director of Recruitment, ITT Technical Institute, 525 North Muller Avenue, Anaheim, CA 92801. *Telephone:* 714-535-3700. *Fax:* 714-535-1802. *Web site:* http://www.itt-tech.edu/.

ITT TECHNICAL INSTITUTE

Lathrop, California

ITT Technical Institute is a coed, proprietary, primarily two-year college of ITT Educational Services, offering degrees at the associate and bachelor's levels.

Expenses for 2003–04 *Application fee:* $100. *Tuition:* $347 per credit hour part-time.

For Further Information Contact Mr. Donald Fraser, Director of Recruitment, ITT Technical Institute, 16916 South Harlan Road, Lathrop, CA 95330. *Telephone:* 209-858-0077 or 800-346-1786 (toll-free in-state). *Fax:* 209-858-0277. *Web site:* http://www.itt-tech.edu/.

ITT TECHNICAL INSTITUTE

Oxnard, California

ITT Tech is a coed, proprietary, primarily two-year college of ITT Educational Services, Inc., founded in 1993, offering degrees at the associate and bachelor's levels. It is located in Oxnard near Los Angeles.

Expenses for 2003–04 *Application fee:* $100. *Tuition:* $347 per credit hour part-time.

For Further Information Contact Mr. Dean K. Dunbar, Director of Recruitment, ITT Technical Institute, 2051 Solar Drive, Building B, Oxnard, CA 93036. *Telephone:* 805-988-0143 Ext. 112 or 800-530-1582 (toll-free in-state). *Fax:* 805-988-1813. *Web site:* http://www.itt-tech.edu/.

ITT TECHNICAL INSTITUTE

Rancho Cordova, California

ITT Tech is a coed, proprietary, primarily two-year college of ITT Educational Services, Inc., founded in 1954, offering degrees at the associate and bachelor's levels. It has a 5-acre campus in Rancho Cordova.

Student Body Statistics The student body is made up of 518 undergraduates.
Financial Aid Forms of aid include need-based scholarships and part-time jobs. The application deadline for financial aid is continuous.
Freshman Admission ITT Tech requires a high school transcript, an interview, TOEFL scores for international students, and Wonderlic aptitude test. Recommendations are recommended. The application deadline for regular admission is rolling.
Transfer Admission The application deadline for admission is rolling.
Entrance Difficulty ITT Tech assesses its entrance difficulty level as minimally difficult.

For Further Information Contact Mr. Robert Menszer, Director of Recruitment, ITT Technical Institute, 10863 Gold Center Drive, Rancho Cordova, CA 95670. *Telephone:* 916-851-3900 or 800-488-8466 (toll-free). *Fax:* 916-851-9225. *Web site:* http://www.itt-tech.edu/.

ITT TECHNICAL INSTITUTE

San Bernardino, California

ITT Tech is a coed, proprietary, primarily two-year college of ITT Educational Services, Inc., founded in 1987, offering degrees at the associate and bachelor's levels. It is located in San Bernardino near Los Angeles.

Student Body Statistics The student body is made up of 920 undergraduates.
Expenses for 2003–04 *Application fee:* $100. Total Program Cost varies depending on course of study. Consult school catalog.
Financial Aid Forms of aid include need-based scholarships and part-time jobs. The application deadline for financial aid is continuous.
Freshman Admission ITT Tech requires a high school transcript, an interview, TOEFL scores for international students, and Wonderlic aptitude test. Recommendations are recommended. The application deadline for regular admission is rolling.
Transfer Admission The application deadline for admission is rolling.
Entrance Difficulty ITT Tech assesses its entrance difficulty level as minimally difficult.

For Further Information Contact Ms. Maria Alamat, Director of Recruitment, ITT Technical Institute, 630 East Brier Drive, Suite 150, San Bernardino, CA 92408. *Telephone:* 909-889-3800 Ext. 20 or 800-888-3801 (toll-free in-state). *Fax:* 909-888-6970. *Web site:* http://www.itt-tech.edu/.

ITT TECHNICAL INSTITUTE

San Diego, California

ITT Tech is a coed, proprietary, primarily two-year college of ITT Educational Services, Inc., founded in 1981, offering degrees at the associate and bachelor's levels.

Student Body Statistics The student body is made up of 990 undergraduates.
Expenses for 2003–04 *Application fee:* $100. Total Program Cost varies depending on course of study. Consult school catalog.
Financial Aid Forms of aid include need-based scholarships and part-time jobs. The application deadline for financial aid is continuous.
Freshman Admission ITT Tech requires a high school transcript, an interview, and Wonderlic aptitude test. Recommendations are recommended. The application deadline for regular admission is rolling.
Transfer Admission The application deadline for admission is rolling.
Entrance Difficulty ITT Tech assesses its entrance difficulty level as minimally difficult.

For Further Information Contact Ms. Sheryl Schulgen, Director of Recruitment, ITT Technical Institute, 9680 Granite Ridge Drive, San Diego, CA 92123. *Telephone:* 858-571-8500 or 800-883-0380 (toll-free in-state). *Fax:* 858-571-1277. *Web site:* http://www.itt-tech.edu/.

ITT TECHNICAL INSTITUTE

Sylmar, California

ITT Tech is a coed, proprietary, primarily two-year college of ITT Educational Services, Inc., founded in 1982, offering degrees at the associate and bachelor's levels. It is located in Sylmar near Los Angeles.

Student Body Statistics The student body is made up of 755 undergraduates.
Expenses for 2003–04 *Application fee:* $100. Total Program Cost varies depending on course of study. Consult school catalog.
Financial Aid Forms of aid include need-based scholarships and part-time jobs. The application deadline for financial aid is continuous.
Freshman Admission ITT Tech requires a high school transcript, an interview, and Wonderlic aptitude test. Recommendations are recommended. The application deadline for regular admission is rolling.
Transfer Admission The application deadline for admission is rolling.
Entrance Difficulty ITT Tech assesses its entrance difficulty level as minimally difficult.

For Further Information Contact Mr. Dominick Miciotta, Director of Recruitment, ITT Technical Institute, 12669 Encinitas Avenue, Sylmar, CA 91342. *Telephone:* 818-364-5151 or 800-363-2086 (toll-free in-state). *Fax:* 818-364-5150. *Web site:* http://www.itt-tech.edu/.

ITT TECHNICAL INSTITUTE

Torrance, California

ITT Tech is a coed, proprietary, primarily two-year college of ITT Educational Services, Inc., founded in 1987, offering degrees at the associate and bachelor's levels. It is located in Torrance near Los Angeles.

Student Body Statistics The student body is made up of 708 undergraduates.
Expenses for 2003–04 *Application fee:* $100. Total Program Cost varies depending on course of study. Consult school catalog.
Financial Aid Forms of aid include need-based scholarships and part-time jobs. The application deadline for financial aid is continuous.
Freshman Admission ITT Tech requires a high school transcript, an interview, TOEFL scores for international students, and Wonderlic aptitude test. Recommendations are recommended. The application deadline for regular admission is rolling.
Transfer Admission The application deadline for admission is rolling.
Entrance Difficulty ITT Tech assesses its entrance difficulty level as minimally difficult.

For Further Information Contact Mr. Freddie Polk, Director of Recruitment, ITT Technical Institute, 20050 South Vermont Avenue, Torrance, CA 90502. *Telephone:* 310-380-1555. *Fax:* 310-380-1557. *Web site:* http://www.itt-tech.edu/.

ITT TECHNICAL INSTITUTE

West Covina, California

ITT Tech is a coed, proprietary, primarily two-year college of ITT Educational Services, Inc., founded in 1982, offering degrees at the associate and bachelor's levels. It has a 4-acre campus in West Covina near Los Angeles.

Student Body Statistics The student body is made up of 816 undergraduates.
Expenses for 2003–04 *Application fee:* $100. Total Program Cost varies depending on course of study. Consult school catalog.
Financial Aid Forms of aid include need-based scholarships and part-time jobs. The application deadline for financial aid is continuous.
Freshman Admission ITT Tech requires a high school transcript, an interview, TOEFL scores for international students, and Wonderlic aptitude test. Recommendations are recommended. The application deadline for regular admission is rolling.
Transfer Admission The application deadline for admission is rolling.
Entrance Difficulty ITT Tech assesses its entrance difficulty level as minimally difficult.

For Further Information Contact Mr. Michael Snyder, Director of Recruitment, ITT Technical Institute, 1530 West Cameron Avenue, West Covina, CA 91790. *Telephone:* 626-960-8681 or 800-414-6522 (toll-free in-state). *Fax:* 626-337-5271. *Web site:* http://www.itt-tech.edu/.

JOHN F. KENNEDY UNIVERSITY

Pleasant Hill, California

JFKU is a coed, private, comprehensive institution, founded in 1964, offering degrees at the bachelor's, master's, doctoral, and first professional levels and postbachelor's certificates. It has a 5-acre campus in Pleasant Hill near San Francisco.

Academic Information The faculty has 715 members (5% full-time), 67% with terminal degrees. The undergraduate student-faculty ratio is 12:1. The library holds 91,170 titles, 811 serial subscriptions, and 1,854 audiovisual materials. Special programs include services for learning-disabled students, advanced placement credit, independent study, self-designed majors, summer session for credit, part-time degree programs, adult/continuing education programs, and arrangement for off-campus study with University of California, Berkeley, California State University, Hayward, Contra Costa College, Laney College. The most frequently chosen baccalaureate fields are business/marketing, liberal arts/general studies, psychology.
Student Body Statistics The student body totals 1,606, of whom 237 are undergraduates. 77 percent are women and 23 percent are men.
Expenses for 2003–04 *Application fee:* $50. *Tuition:* $13,920 full-time, $290 per quarter hour part-time. *Mandatory fees:* $27 full-time, $9 per term part-time. Full-time tuition and fees vary according to course load and program. Part-time tuition and fees vary according to course load and program.
Financial Aid Forms of aid include need-based scholarships. The average aided 2002–03 undergraduate received an aid package worth $7000. The priority application deadline for financial aid is March 2.
Freshman Admission JFKU requires TOEFL scores for international students.
Transfer Admission The application deadline for admission is rolling.
Entrance Difficulty JFKU has an open admission policy.

For Further Information Contact Ms. Ellena Bloedorn, Director of Admissions and Records, John F. Kennedy University, 100 Ellinwood Way, Pleasant Hill, CA 94523-4817. *Telephone:* 925-969-3330 or 800-696-JFKU (toll-free). *Fax:* 925-969-3328. *E-mail:* skierce@jfku.edu. *Web site:* http://www.jfku.edu/.

THE KING'S COLLEGE AND SEMINARY

Van Nuys, California

For Information Write to The King's College and Seminary, Van Nuys, CA 91405-8040.

LAGUNA COLLEGE OF ART & DESIGN

Laguna Beach, California

Laguna College of Art & Design is a coed, private, four-year college, founded in 1962, offering degrees at the bachelor's level in art. It has a 9-acre campus in Laguna Beach near Los Angeles.

Academic Information The faculty has 72 members (14% full-time). The student-faculty ratio is 10:1. The library holds 16,000 titles, 100 serial subscriptions, and 8 audiovisual materials. Special programs include academic remediation, advanced placement credit, ESL programs, independent study, summer session for credit, part-time degree programs (daytime, evenings, weekends), adult/continuing education programs, internships, and arrangement for off-campus study with Art College Exchange, Association of Independent Colleges of Art and Design. The most frequently chosen baccalaureate field is visual/performing arts.
Student Body Statistics The student body is made up of 310 undergraduates (70 freshmen). 47 percent are women and 53 percent are men. Students come from 32 states and territories. 58 percent are from California. 6.5 percent are international students.
Expenses for 2004–05 *Application fee:* $45. *Tuition:* $16,500 full-time, $688 per unit part-time.
Financial Aid Forms of aid include need-based and non-need-based scholarships and part-time jobs. The average aided 2003–04 undergraduate received an aid package worth an estimated $8000. The application deadline for financial aid is continuous.
Freshman Admission Laguna College of Art & Design requires an essay, a high school transcript, a minimum 3.0 high school GPA, 1 recommendation, an interview, a portfolio, SAT I or ACT scores, and TOEFL scores for international students. A minimum 3.5 high school GPA is recommended. The application deadline for regular admission is February 2.
Transfer Admission The application deadline for admission is March 2.
Entrance Difficulty Laguna College of Art & Design assesses its entrance difficulty level as very difficult. For the fall 2003 freshman class, 88 percent of the applicants were accepted.

For Further Information Contact Mr. Anthony Padilla, Vice President of Enrollment, Laguna College of Art & Design, 2222 Laguna Canyon Road, Laguna Beach, CA 92651-1136. *Telephone:* 949-376-6000 Ext. 232 or 800-255-0762 (toll-free). *Fax:* 949-376-6009. *E-mail:* admissions@lagunacollege.edu. *Web site:* http://www.lagunacollege.edu/.

LA SIERRA UNIVERSITY

Riverside, California

La Sierra is a coed, private, Seventh-day Adventist, comprehensive institution, founded in 1922, offering degrees at the bachelor's, master's, and doctoral levels and post-master's and postbachelor's certificates. It has a 630-acre campus in Riverside near Los Angeles.

Expenses for 2003–04 *Application fee:* $30. *Comprehensive fee:* $21,300 includes full-time tuition ($16,272), mandatory fees ($468), and college room and board ($4560). *College room only:* $2700.

For Further Information Contact Dr. Tom Smith, Director of Admissions, La Sierra University, 4700 Pierce Street, Riverside, CA 92515-8247. *Telephone:* 909-785-2176 or 800-874-5587 (toll-free). *Fax:* 909-785-2477. *E-mail:* ivy@lasierra.edu. *Web site:* http://www.lasierra.edu/.

LEE COLLEGE AT THE UNIVERSITY OF JUDAISM

See University of Judaism

LIFE PACIFIC COLLEGE

San Dimas, California

LIFE is a coed, private, four-year college, founded in 1923, affiliated with the International Church of the Foursquare Gospel, offering degrees at the associate and bachelor's levels in biblical studies. It has a 9-acre campus in San Dimas near Los Angeles.

Academic Information The faculty has 36 members (47% full-time), 28% with terminal degrees. The student-faculty ratio is 24:1. The library holds 38,084 titles, 244 serial subscriptions, and 1,104 audiovisual materials. Special programs include services for learning-disabled students, cooperative (work-study) education, advanced placement credit, independent study, distance learning, summer session for credit, part-time degree programs (daytime, evenings, summer), external degree programs, adult/continuing education programs, and internships. The most frequently chosen baccalaureate field is philosophy, religion, and theology.
Student Body Statistics The student body is made up of 446 undergraduates (51 freshmen). 49 percent are women and 51 percent are men. Students come from 32 states and territories and 2 other countries. 59 percent are from California. 0.4 percent are international students. 15 percent of the 2003 graduating class went on to graduate and professional schools.
Expenses for 2003–04 *Application fee:* $35. *Comprehensive fee:* $11,300 includes full-time tuition ($7050), mandatory fees ($250), and college room and board ($4000). *Part-time tuition:* $235 per credit hour. Part-time tuition varies according to course load.
Financial Aid Forms of aid include need-based and non-need-based scholarships and part-time jobs. The average aided 2002–03 undergraduate received an aid package worth $5890. The priority application deadline for financial aid is July 1.
Freshman Admission LIFE requires an essay, a high school transcript, a minimum 2.0 high school GPA, 3 recommendations, Christian testimony, SAT I or ACT scores, and TOEFL scores for international students. SAT II: Writing Test scores are recommended. The application deadline for regular admission is July 1.
Transfer Admission The application deadline for admission is July 1.
Entrance Difficulty LIFE assesses its entrance difficulty level as moderately difficult. For the fall 2003 freshman class, 97 percent of the applicants were accepted.

For Further Information Contact Mrs. Linda Hibdon, Admissions Director, Life Pacific College, 1100 Covina Boulevard, San Dimas, CA 91773-3298. *Telephone:* 909-599-5433 Ext. 314 or 877-886-5433 (toll-free). *Fax:* 909-706-3070. *E-mail:* adm@lifepacific.edu. *Web site:* http://www.lifepacific.edu/.

LINCOLN UNIVERSITY

Oakland, California

Lincoln is a coed, private, comprehensive institution, founded in 1919, offering degrees at the bachelor's and master's levels. It has a 2-acre campus in Oakland.

Expenses for 2003–04 *Application fee:* $50. *Tuition:* $6840 full-time. *Mandatory fees:* $255 full-time.

For Further Information Contact Ms. Vivian Xu, Admissions Officer, Lincoln University, 401 15th Street, Oakland, CA 94612-2801. *Telephone:* 510-628-8010. *Fax:* 510-628-8012. *Web site:* http://www.lincolnuca.edu/.

LOMA LINDA UNIVERSITY

Loma Linda, California

LLU is a coed, private, Seventh-day Adventist, upper-level institution, founded in 1905, offering degrees at the associate, bachelor's, master's, doctoral, and first professional levels and postbachelor's certificates in health sciences (associate degree and nursing students may enter at the sophomore level). It is located in Loma Linda near Los Angeles.

Academic Information The faculty has 202 members (72% full-time), 41% with terminal degrees. The undergraduate student-faculty ratio is 5:1. The library holds 322,657 titles and 1,394 serial subscriptions. Special programs include ESL programs, independent study, distance learning, internships, and arrangement for off-campus study. The most frequently chosen baccalaureate field is health professions and related sciences.
Student Body Statistics The student body totals 3,574, of whom 978 are undergraduates. 75 percent are women and 25 percent are men. Students come from 29 states and territories and 28 other countries. 77 percent are from California. 5.9 percent are international students.
Expenses for 2003–04 *Application fee:* $60. *Tuition:* $21,805 full-time. *College room only:* $2780.
Financial Aid Forms of aid include need-based scholarships and part-time jobs. The average aided 2002–03 undergraduate received an aid package worth $16,862. The priority application deadline for financial aid is March 2.
Entrance Difficulty For the fall 2003 entering class, 33 percent of the applicants were accepted.

For Further Information Contact Loma Linda University, Loma Linda, CA 92350. *Telephone:* 909-558-1000. *Fax:* 909-558-4577. *Web site:* http://www.llu.edu/.

LOYOLA MARYMOUNT UNIVERSITY

Los Angeles, California

LMU is a coed, private, Roman Catholic, comprehensive institution, founded in 1911, offering degrees at the bachelor's, master's, and first professional levels and postbachelor's certificates. It has a 128-acre campus in Los Angeles.

Academic Information The faculty has 865 members (48% full-time). The undergraduate student-faculty ratio is 13:1. The library holds 484,273 titles, 36,650 serial subscriptions, and 40,158 audiovisual materials. Special programs include services for learning-disabled students, an honors program, cooperative (work-study) education, study abroad, advanced placement credit, accelerated degree programs, double majors, independent study, self-designed majors, summer session for credit, part-time degree programs (daytime, evenings, summer), adult/continuing education programs, and internships. The most frequently chosen baccalaureate fields are business/marketing, biological/life sciences, visual/performing arts.
Student Body Statistics The student body totals 8,880, of whom 5,699 are undergraduates (1,335 freshmen). 60 percent are women and 40 percent are men. Students come from 51 states and territories and 52 other countries. 77 percent are from California. 1.9 percent are international students.
Expenses for 2003–04 *Application fee:* $50. *Comprehensive fee:* $32,194 includes full-time tuition ($23,504), mandatory fees ($430), and college room and board ($8260). *College room only:* $6010. Room and board charges vary according to board plan and housing facility. *Part-time tuition:* $979 per unit. Part-time tuition varies according to course load.
Financial Aid Forms of aid include need-based and non-need-based scholarships, athletic grants, and part-time jobs. The average aided 2003–04 undergraduate received an aid package worth an estimated $18,095. The priority application deadline for financial aid is February 15.
Freshman Admission LMU requires an essay, a high school transcript, 1 recommendation, SAT I or ACT scores, and TOEFL scores for international students. An interview is recommended. The application deadline for regular admission is February 1.
Transfer Admission The application deadline for admission is June 1.
Entrance Difficulty LMU assesses its entrance difficulty level as very difficult. For the fall 2003 freshman class, 58 percent of the applicants were accepted.

For Further Information Contact Mr. Matthew X. Fissinger, Director of Admissions, Loyola Marymount University, 1 LMU Drive Suite 100, Los Angeles, CA 90045-8350. *Telephone:* 310-338-2750 or 800-LMU-INFO (toll-free). *Fax:* 310-338-2797. *E-mail:* admissions@lmu.edu. *Web site:* http://www.lmu.edu/.

MARYMOUNT COLLEGE, PALOS VERDES, CALIFORNIA

Rancho Palos Verdes, California

For Information Write to Marymount College, Palos Verdes, California, Rancho Palos Verdes, CA 90275-6299.

THE MASTER'S COLLEGE AND SEMINARY

Santa Clarita, California

Master's is a coed, private, nondenominational, comprehensive institution, founded in 1927, offering degrees at the bachelor's, master's, doctoral, and first professional levels and first professional certificates. It has a 110-acre campus in Santa Clarita near Los Angeles.

Academic Information The faculty has 140 members (49% full-time), 51% with terminal degrees. The undergraduate student-faculty ratio is 14:1. The library holds 211,895 titles, 1,288 serial subscriptions, and 7,001 audiovisual materials. Special programs include academic remediation, services for learning-disabled students, cooperative (work-study) education, study abroad, advanced placement credit, accelerated degree programs, double majors, independent study, summer session for credit, part-time degree programs (daytime, evenings, weekends), external degree programs, adult/continuing education programs, and internships. The most frequently chosen baccalaureate fields are business/marketing, education, philosophy, religion, and theology.
Student Body Statistics The student body totals 1,426, of whom 1,132 are undergraduates (209 freshmen). 51 percent are women and 49 percent are men. Students come from 42 states and territories and 24 other countries. 67 percent are from California. 2.9 percent are international students.
Expenses for 2003–04 *Application fee:* $40. *Comprehensive fee:* $23,250 includes full-time tuition ($17,000), mandatory fees ($200), and college room and board ($6050). *College room only:* $3370. Full-time tuition and fees vary according to course load, degree level, and program. Room and board charges vary according to board plan. *Part-time tuition:* $710 per credit hour. Part-time tuition varies according to course load, degree level, and program.
Financial Aid Forms of aid include need-based and non-need-based scholarships, athletic grants, and part-time jobs. The average aided 2003–04 undergraduate received an aid package worth an estimated $14,157. The priority application deadline for financial aid is March 2.
Freshman Admission Master's requires an essay, a high school transcript, a minimum 2.50 high school GPA, 2 recommendations, an interview, SAT I or ACT scores, and TOEFL scores for international students. The application deadline for for early action it is November 17.
Transfer Admission The application deadline for admission is March 6.
Entrance Difficulty Master's assesses its entrance difficulty level as moderately difficult. For the fall 2003 freshman class, 54 percent of the applicants were accepted.

For Further Information Contact Mr. Yaphet Peterson, Director of Enrollment, The Master's College and Seminary, Santa Clarita, CA 91321. *Telephone:* 661-259-3540 Ext. 3365 or 800-568-6248 (toll-free). *Fax:* 661-288-1037. *E-mail:* enrollment@masters.edu. *Web site:* http://www.masters.edu/.

MENLO COLLEGE

Atherton, California

Menlo is a coed, private, four-year college, founded in 1927, offering degrees at the bachelor's level. It has a 45-acre campus in Atherton near San Francisco.

Academic Information The faculty has 58 members (43% full-time), 40% with terminal degrees. The student-faculty ratio is 17:1. The library holds 55,000 titles, 172 serial subscriptions, and 600 audiovisual materials. Special programs include academic remediation, services for learning-disabled students, an honors program, study abroad, advanced placement credit, accelerated degree programs, double majors, independent study, self-designed majors, summer session for credit, part-time degree programs (daytime, evenings, summer), adult/continuing education programs, and internships.
Student Body Statistics The student body is made up of 660 undergraduates (172 freshmen). 37 percent are women and 63 percent are men. Students come from 24 states and territories and 34 other countries. 82 percent are from California. 12 percent are international students.
Expenses for 2003–04 *Application fee:* $40. *Comprehensive fee:* $30,860 includes full-time tuition ($21,630), mandatory fees ($150), and college room and board ($9080). Full-time tuition and fees vary according to program. Room and board charges vary according to housing facility. *Part-time tuition:* $901 per unit. *Part-time mandatory fees:* $50 per term. Part-time tuition and fees vary according to course load and program.
Financial Aid Forms of aid include need-based and non-need-based scholarships and part-time jobs. The average aided 2003–04 undergraduate received an aid package worth an estimated $19,717. The priority application deadline for financial aid is March 2.
Freshman Admission Menlo requires an essay, a high school transcript, 1 recommendation, SAT I or ACT scores, and TOEFL scores for international students. A minimum 3.0 high school GPA and an interview are recommended. The application deadline for regular admission is rolling; for early decision it is February 1; and for early action it is December 1.
Transfer Admission The application deadline for admission is rolling.
Entrance Difficulty Menlo assesses its entrance difficulty level as moderately difficult. For the fall 2003 freshman class, 56 percent of the applicants were accepted.

For Further Information Contact Dr. Greg Smith, Dean of Admission and Financial Aid, Menlo College, 1000 El Camino Real, Atherton, CA 94027. *Telephone:* 650-543-3910 or 800-556-3656 (toll-free). *Fax:* 650-617-2395. *E-mail:* admissions@menlo.edu. *Web site:* http://www.menlo.edu/.

MILLS COLLEGE

Oakland, California

Mills is a women's, private, comprehensive institution, founded in 1852, offering degrees at the bachelor's, master's, and doctoral levels and postbachelor's certificates. It has a 135-acre campus in Oakland near San Francisco.

Academic Information The faculty has 159 members (60% full-time), 70% with terminal degrees. The undergraduate student-faculty ratio is 10:1. The library holds 189,814 titles, 2,029 serial subscriptions, and 6,046 audiovisual materials. Special programs include services for learning-disabled students, advanced placement credit, double majors, independent study, self-designed majors, part-time degree programs, adult/continuing education programs, internships, and arrangement for off-campus study with University of California, Berkeley, California State University, Hayward, Sonoma State University, 9 other California colleges, American University, Agnes Scott College, Barnard College, Fisk University, Hollins College, Howard University, Manhattanville College, Mount Holyoke College, Simmons College, Spelman College, Swarthmore College, Wellesley College, Wheaton College. The most frequently chosen baccalaureate fields are area/ethnic studies, social sciences and history, visual/performing arts.
Student Body Statistics The student body totals 1,210, of whom 735 are undergraduates (115 freshmen). Students come from 35 states and territories and 6 other countries. 76 percent are from California. 3.8 percent are international students.
Expenses for 2003–04 *Application fee:* $40. *Comprehensive fee:* $33,371 includes full-time tuition ($23,000), mandatory fees ($1441), and college room and board ($8930). Room and board charges vary according to board plan and housing facility. *Part-time tuition:* $3835 per course. Part-time tuition varies according to course load.
Financial Aid Forms of aid include need-based and non-need-based scholarships and part-time jobs. The average aided 2003–04 undergraduate received an aid package worth an estimated $20,190. The priority application deadline for financial aid is February 15.

Mills College (continued)

Freshman Admission Mills requires a high school transcript, 3 recommendations, essay or graded paper, SAT I or ACT scores, and TOEFL scores for international students. An interview and SAT II: Subject Test scores are recommended. The application deadline for regular admission is March 1 and for early action it is November 15.
Transfer Admission The application deadline for admission is April 1.
Entrance Difficulty Mills assesses its entrance difficulty level as moderately difficult. For the fall 2003 freshman class, 73 percent of the applicants were accepted.

For Further Information Contact Myrt Whitcomb, Dean of Admission, Mills College, 5000 MacArthur Boulevard, Oakland, CA 94613-1301. *Telephone:* 510-430-2135 or 800-87-MILLS (toll-free). *Fax:* 510-430-3314. *E-mail:* admission@mills.edu. *Web site:* http://www.mills.edu/.

MOUNT ST. MARY'S COLLEGE

Los Angeles, California

Mount St. Mary's is a coed, primarily women's, private, Roman Catholic, comprehensive institution, founded in 1925, offering degrees at the associate, bachelor's, and master's levels and postbachelor's certificates. It has a 71-acre campus in Los Angeles.

Academic Information The faculty has 268 members (27% full-time), 29% with terminal degrees. The undergraduate student-faculty ratio is 17:1. The library holds 140,000 titles and 750 serial subscriptions. Special programs include academic remediation, services for learning-disabled students, an honors program, study abroad, advanced placement credit, accelerated degree programs, Freshman Honors College, ESL programs, double majors, independent study, self-designed majors, summer session for credit, part-time degree programs, adult/continuing education programs, internships, and arrangement for off-campus study with University of Southern California, University of California, Los Angeles, Sisters of Saint Joseph College Consortium. The most frequently chosen baccalaureate fields are health professions and related sciences, business/marketing, social sciences and history.
Student Body Statistics The student body totals 2,127, of whom 1,719 are undergraduates (374 freshmen). 95 percent are women and 5 percent are men. Students come from 23 states and territories. 97 percent are from California. 0.1 percent are international students. 30 percent of the 2003 graduating class went on to graduate and professional schools.
Expenses for 2003–04 *Application fee:* $40. *Comprehensive fee:* $28,980 includes full-time tuition ($19,722), mandatory fees ($1034), and college room and board ($8224). *Part-time tuition:* $750 per unit. *Part-time mandatory fees:* $365 per term.
Financial Aid Forms of aid include need-based and non-need-based scholarships and part-time jobs. The application deadline for financial aid is May 15 with a priority deadline of March 2.
Freshman Admission Mount St. Mary's requires an essay, a high school transcript, a minimum 2.0 high school GPA, 1 recommendation, SAT I or ACT scores, and TOEFL scores for international students. A minimum 3.0 high school GPA, an interview, and SAT I scores are recommended. The application deadline for regular admission is February 15 and for early action it is December 1.
Transfer Admission The application deadline for admission is March 15.
Entrance Difficulty Mount St. Mary's assesses its entrance difficulty level as moderately difficult; minimally difficult for associate degree programs. For the fall 2003 freshman class, 86 percent of the applicants were accepted.

For Further Information Contact Mr. Dean Kilgour, Director of Admissions, Mount St. Mary's College, 12001 Chalon Road, Los Angeles, CA 90049-1599. *Telephone:* 310-954-4252 or 800-999-9893 (toll-free). *E-mail:* admissions@msmc.la.edu. *Web site:* http://www.msmc.la.edu/.

MT. SIERRA COLLEGE

Monrovia, California

Mt. Sierra College is a coed, proprietary, four-year college, founded in 1990, offering degrees at the bachelor's level. It has a 5-acre campus in Monrovia.

Academic Information The faculty has 50 members (44% full-time), 14% with terminal degrees. The student-faculty ratio is 15:1. The library holds 6,000 titles, 5,000 serial subscriptions, and 100 audiovisual materials. Special programs include accelerated degree programs, independent study, distance learning, summer session for credit, adult/continuing education programs, and internships. The most frequently chosen baccalaureate fields are computer/information sciences, visual/performing arts.
Student Body Statistics The student body is made up of 1,100 undergraduates (279 freshmen). 30 percent are women and 70 percent are men. Students come from 7 states and territories. 95 percent are from California. 5 percent of the 2003 graduating class went on to graduate and professional schools.
Expenses for 2004–05 *Application fee:* $95. *Tuition:* $16,200 full-time.
Financial Aid The application deadline for financial aid is continuous.
Freshman Admission Mt. Sierra College requires an essay, a high school transcript, an interview, and TOEFL scores for international students.
Transfer Admission The application deadline for admission is October 8.
Entrance Difficulty Mt. Sierra College has an open admission policy.

For Further Information Contact Mr. Al Desrosiors, Director of Admissions, Mt. Sierra College, 101 East Huntington Drive, Monrovia, CA 91016. *Telephone:* 626-873-2100 Ext. 213 or 888-828-8800. (toll-free). *Fax:* 626-359-5528. *Web site:* http://www.mtsierra.edu/.

MUSICIANS INSTITUTE

Hollywood, California

Musicians Institute is a coed, proprietary, four-year college, founded in 1976, offering degrees at the associate and bachelor's levels in music.

Student Body Statistics The student body is made up of 650 undergraduates.
Expenses for 2003–04 *Application fee:* $100. *Tuition:* $13,200 full-time, $220 per unit part-time. *Mandatory fees:* $400 full-time, $100 per term part-time.
Financial Aid Forms of aid include need-based scholarships and part-time jobs. The average aided 2002–03 undergraduate received an aid package worth $6100. The application deadline for financial aid is continuous.
Freshman Admission Musicians Institute requires TOEFL scores for international students. The application deadline for regular admission is rolling.
Entrance Difficulty Musicians Institute assesses its entrance difficulty level as minimally difficult.

For Further Information Contact Mr. Steve Lunn, Admissions Representative, Musicians Institute, 1655 North McCadden Place, Hollywood, CA 90028. *Telephone:* 323-462-1384 Ext. 156 or 800-255-PLAY (toll-free). *Fax:* 323-462-6978. *Web site:* http://www.mi.edu/.

THE NATIONAL HISPANIC UNIVERSITY

San Jose, California

NHU is a coed, private, four-year college, founded in 1981, offering degrees at the associate and bachelor's levels and postbachelor's certificates. It has a 1-acre campus in San Jose.

Expenses for 2003–04 *Application fee:* $50. *Tuition:* $3360 full-time, $140 per credit hour part-time. *Mandatory fees:* $200 full-time, $100 per term part-time.

For Further Information Contact The National Hispanic University, 14271 Story Road, San Jose, CA 95127-3823. *Telephone:* 408-254-6900. *Web site:* http://www.nhu.edu/.

NATIONAL UNIVERSITY

La Jolla, California

National University is a coed, private, comprehensive institution, founded in 1971, offering degrees at the associate, bachelor's, and master's levels and postbachelor's certificates.

Academic Information The faculty has 2,357 members (8% full-time), 7% with terminal degrees. The undergraduate student-faculty ratio is 17:1. The library holds 226,049 titles, 2,794 serial subscriptions, and 5,539 audiovisual materials. Special programs include services for learning-disabled students, advanced placement credit, accelerated degree programs, ESL programs, double majors, independent study, distance learning, summer session for credit, part-time degree programs (daytime, evenings, summer), adult/continuing education programs, internships, and arrangement for off-campus study with Servicemembers Opportunity Colleges. The most frequently chosen baccalaureate fields are business/marketing, computer/information sciences, interdisciplinary studies.
Student Body Statistics The student body totals 17,064, of whom 4,031 are undergraduates (60 freshmen). 57 percent are women and 43 percent are men. 1.4 percent are international students.
Expenses for 2003–04 *Application fee:* $60. *Tuition:* $8550 full-time, $950 per course part-time.
Financial Aid Forms of aid include need-based and non-need-based scholarships. The application deadline for financial aid is continuous.
Freshman Admission National University requires a high school transcript, an interview, and TOEFL scores for international students. An essay is required for some. The application deadline for regular admission is rolling.
Transfer Admission The application deadline for admission is rolling.
Entrance Difficulty National University has an open admission policy.

For Further Information Contact Ms. Nancy Rohland-Heinrich, Associate Dean, UCNU, National University, 11255 North Torrey Pines Road, La Jolla, CA 92037. *Telephone:* 858-642-8000 or 800-628-8648 (toll-free). *Fax:* 858-642-8710. *E-mail:* jwilson@nu.edu. *Web site:* http://www.nu.edu/.

NEW COLLEGE OF CALIFORNIA

San Francisco, California

New College is a coed, private, comprehensive institution, founded in 1971, offering degrees at the bachelor's and master's levels and postbachelor's certificates.

Academic Information The faculty has 90 members (44% full-time). The undergraduate student-faculty ratio is 15:1. The library holds 24,000 titles and 50 serial subscriptions. Special programs include academic remediation, cooperative (work-study) education, study abroad, advanced placement credit, accelerated degree programs, ESL programs, self-designed majors, part-time degree programs (daytime, evenings, weekends, summer), and internships. The most frequently chosen baccalaureate field is liberal arts/general studies.
Student Body Statistics The student body totals 1,133, of whom 618 are undergraduates (300 freshmen). 49 percent are women and 51 percent are men. 0.5 percent are international students. 22 percent of the 2003 graduating class went on to graduate and professional schools.
Expenses for 2004–05 *Application fee:* $50. *Tuition:* $12,023 full-time, $484 per unit part-time. *Mandatory fees:* $200 full-time, $100 per term part-time.
Financial Aid Forms of aid include part-time jobs.
Freshman Admission New College requires an essay, a high school transcript, and TOEFL scores for international students. An interview is recommended. 2 recommendations are required for some. The application deadline for regular admission is rolling.
Transfer Admission The application deadline for admission is rolling.
Entrance Difficulty New College has an open admission policy.

For Further Information Contact Ms. Sarah Starpoli, Admissions Inquiry Office, New College of California, 777 Valencia Street, San Francisco, CA 94110. *Telephone:* 415-437-3460 or 888-437-3460 (toll-free). *Fax:* 415-865-2636. *E-mail:* admissions@newcollege.edu. *Web site:* http://www.newcollege.edu/.

NEWSCHOOL OF ARCHITECTURE & DESIGN

San Diego, California

Newschool of Architecture & Design is a coed, primarily men's, proprietary, comprehensive institution, founded in 1980, offering degrees at the associate, bachelor's, master's, and first professional levels. It has a 1-acre campus in San Diego.

Expenses for 2003–04 *Tuition:* $18,675 full-time. *Mandatory fees:* $195 full-time.

For Further Information Contact Ms. Lexi Rogers, Director of Admissions, Newschool of Architecture & Design, 1249 F Street, San Diego, CA 92101-6634. *Telephone:* 619-235-4100 Ext. 104. *E-mail:* admissions@newschoolarch.edu. *Web site:* http://www.newschoolarch.edu/.

NORTHWESTERN POLYTECHNIC UNIVERSITY

Fremont, California

NPU is a coed, private, comprehensive institution, founded in 1984, offering degrees at the bachelor's, master's, and doctoral levels. It has a 2-acre campus in Fremont near San Francisco and San Jose.

Academic Information The faculty has 60 members (15% full-time), 45% with terminal degrees. The undergraduate student-faculty ratio is 10:1. The library holds 12,000 titles, 200 serial subscriptions, and 200 audiovisual materials. Special programs include advanced placement credit, ESL programs, summer session for credit, part-time degree programs (evenings, weekends, summer), adult/continuing education programs, and internships. The most frequently chosen baccalaureate fields are computer/information sciences, engineering/engineering technologies.
Student Body Statistics The student body totals 413, of whom 150 are undergraduates (15 freshmen). 35 percent are women and 65 percent are men. Students come from 20 states and territories and 13 other countries. 95 percent are from California. 40 percent of the 2003 graduating class went on to graduate and professional schools.
Expenses for 2004–05 *Application fee:* $50. *Tuition:* $6000 full-time, $250 per unit part-time. *Mandatory fees:* $340 full-time, $170 per term part-time. *College room only:* $2800.
Freshman Admission NPU requires a high school transcript and a minimum 2.0 high school GPA. An interview and TOEFL scores for international students are recommended. An essay is required for some. The application deadline for regular admission is August 12.
Transfer Admission The application deadline for admission is August 12.
Entrance Difficulty For the fall 2003 freshman class, 100 percent of the applicants were accepted.

For Further Information Contact Ms. Alice Ye, Admission Officer, Northwestern Polytechnic University, 117 Fourier Avenue, Fremont, CA 94539. *Telephone:* 510-657-0256. *Fax:* 510-657-8975. *E-mail:* admission@npu.edu. *Web site:* http://www.npu.edu/.

NOTRE DAME DE NAMUR UNIVERSITY

Belmont, California

Notre Dame de Namur University is a coed, private, Roman Catholic, comprehensive institution, founded in 1851, offering degrees at the bachelor's and master's levels. It has an 80-acre campus in Belmont near San Francisco.

Academic Information The faculty has 189 members (30% full-time), 52% with terminal degrees. The undergraduate student-faculty ratio is 13:1. The library holds 726 serial subscriptions and 8,314 audiovisual materials. Special programs include academic remediation, services for learning-disabled students, cooperative (work-study) education, study abroad, advanced placement credit, accelerated degree programs, ESL programs, double majors, independent study, summer session for credit, part-time degree programs (daytime, evenings, summer), adult/continuing education programs, internships, and arrangement for off-campus study with Trinity College (DC), Emmanuel College (MA).

Student Body Statistics The student body totals 1,798, of whom 988 are undergraduates (191 freshmen). 68 percent are women and 32 percent are men. Students come from 24 states and territories and 17 other countries. 90 percent are from California. 4.4 percent are international students. 11 percent of the 2003 graduating class went on to graduate and professional schools.

Expenses for 2004–05 *Application fee:* $40. *Comprehensive fee:* $31,150 includes full-time tuition ($21,350), mandatory fees ($150), and college room and board ($9650). Room and board charges vary according to board plan and housing facility. *Part-time tuition:* $510 per unit. *Part-time mandatory fees:* $15 per term.

Financial Aid Forms of aid include need-based and non-need-based scholarships and part-time jobs. The priority application deadline for financial aid is March 2.

Freshman Admission Notre Dame de Namur University requires an essay, a high school transcript, 1 recommendation, SAT I or ACT scores, and TOEFL scores for international students. An interview is required for some. The application deadline for regular admission is rolling.

Transfer Admission The application deadline for admission is rolling.

Entrance Difficulty Notre Dame de Namur University assesses its entrance difficulty level as moderately difficult; minimally difficult for transfers. For the fall 2003 freshman class, 89 percent of the applicants were accepted.

SPECIAL MESSAGE TO STUDENTS

Social Life Notre Dame de Namur University (NDNU) requires freshmen and sophomores to live on campus. Housing is assured for all undergraduates who submit housing applications by May 1. Popular campus activities range from the student newspaper and the Hawaiian Club to musical and theatrical productions as well as NAIA sports (including men's and women's soccer, basketball, cross-country, and golf; and women's volleyball and softball) and men's lacrosse.

Academic Highlights NDNU's distinguished, caring faculty members challenge students to strengthen communication and analytical abilities through classes that average 15 people. Fine computer facilities, research laboratories, and a renowned art gallery are examples of NDNU's commitment to providing top-quality educational resources. Most NDNU students fulfill internships at such places as CNN, the American Red Cross, Enterprise, and TheatreWorks. Graduate school placement is also impressive, including a 90 percent entry rate for NDNU students applying to medical school.

Interviews and Campus Visits Interviews are usually not required, but applicants are encouraged to see for themselves the scenic, wooded campus and its proximity to the recreational, cultural, and business opportunities of San Francisco and Silicon Valley. For a campus tour and individual meeting with an NDNU admission counselor—or maybe even to arrange meeting professors and sitting in on a class—interested students should use the address below or call 650-508-3600 or 800-263-0545 (toll-free). The nearest commercial airport is San Francisco International.

For Further Information Write to the Office of Admission, Notre Dame de Namur University, 1500 Ralston Avenue, Belmont, CA 94002. *E-mail:* admiss@ndnu.edu. *Web site:* http://www.ndnu.edu.

OCCIDENTAL COLLEGE

Los Angeles, California

OXY is a coed, private, comprehensive institution, founded in 1887, offering degrees at the bachelor's and master's levels. It has a 120-acre campus in Los Angeles.

Academic Information The faculty has 206 members (66% full-time). The undergraduate student-faculty ratio is 11:1. The library holds 481,822 titles and 1,135 serial subscriptions. Special programs include services for learning-disabled students, an honors program, study abroad, advanced placement credit, accelerated degree programs, double majors, independent study, self-designed majors, summer session for credit, internships, and arrangement for off-campus study with California Institute of Technology, Art Center College of Design, Morehouse College, Spelman College. The most frequently chosen baccalaureate fields are business/marketing, social sciences and history, visual/performing arts.

Student Body Statistics The student body totals 1,858, of whom 1,840 are undergraduates (441 freshmen). 58 percent are women and 42 percent are men. Students come from 45 states and territories and 24 other countries. 68 percent are from California. 4.1 percent are international students. 30 percent of the 2003 graduating class went on to graduate and professional schools.

Expenses for 2003–04 *Application fee:* $50. *Comprehensive fee:* $36,126 includes full-time tuition ($27,734), mandatory fees ($572), and college room and board ($7820). *College room only:* $4300. Room and board charges vary according to board plan and housing facility. *Part-time tuition:* $1156 per credit. *Part-time mandatory fees:* $179 per term.

Financial Aid Forms of aid include need-based and non-need-based scholarships and part-time jobs. The average aided 2003–04 undergraduate received an aid package worth an estimated $28,003. The priority application deadline for financial aid is February 1.

Freshman Admission OXY requires an essay, a high school transcript, 2 recommendations, SAT I or ACT scores, and TOEFL scores for international students. An interview, SAT II: Subject Test scores, and SAT II: Writing Test scores are recommended. The application deadline for regular admission is January 10 and for early decision it is November 15.

Transfer Admission The application deadline for admission is March 15.

Entrance Difficulty OXY assesses its entrance difficulty level as very difficult. For the fall 2003 freshman class, 44 percent of the applicants were accepted.

For Further Information Contact Mr. Vince Cuseo, Director of Admission, Occidental College, 1600 Campus Road M-18, Los Angeles, CA 90041. *Telephone:* 323-259-2700 or 800-825-5262 (toll-free). *Fax:* 323-341-4875. *E-mail:* admission@oxy.edu. *Web site:* http://www.oxy.edu/.

OTIS COLLEGE OF ART AND DESIGN

Los Angeles, California

Otis is a coed, private, comprehensive institution, founded in 1918, offering degrees at the bachelor's and master's levels in art and design. It has a 5-acre campus in Los Angeles.

Academic Information The faculty has 214 members (18% full-time), 41% with terminal degrees. The undergraduate student-faculty ratio is 11:1. The library holds 42,000 titles, 150 serial subscriptions, and 2,500 audiovisual materials. Special programs include academic remediation, an honors program, cooperative (work-study) education, study abroad, advanced placement credit, Freshman Honors College, ESL programs, independent study, summer session for credit, adult/continuing education programs, internships, and arrangement for off-campus study with The Consortium of East Coast Art Schools. The most frequently chosen baccalaureate field is visual/performing arts.

Student Body Statistics The student body totals 1,066, of whom 1,023 are undergraduates (162 freshmen). 65 percent are women and 35 percent are men. 74 percent are from California. 11.6 percent are international students. 5 percent of the 2003 graduating class went on to graduate and professional schools.

Expenses for 2003–04 *Application fee:* $50. *Tuition:* $22,820 full-time, $761 per credit part-time. *Mandatory fees:* $600 full-time.

Financial Aid Forms of aid include need-based and non-need-based scholarships and part-time jobs. The average aided 2002–03 undergraduate received an aid package worth $12,774. The priority application deadline for financial aid is February 15.

Freshman Admission Otis requires an essay, a high school transcript, a minimum 2.5 high school GPA, a portfolio, SAT I or ACT scores, and TOEFL scores for international students. 1 recommendation and an interview are recommended. The application deadline for regular admission is rolling.

Transfer Admission The application deadline for admission is rolling.

Entrance Difficulty Otis assesses its entrance difficulty level as moderately difficult; very difficult for transfer students in toy design, digital media programs. For the fall 2003 freshman class, 63 percent of the applicants were accepted.

For Further Information Contact Mr. Marc D. Meredith, Dean of Admissions, Otis College of Art and Design, 9045 Lincoln Boulevard, Los Angeles, CA 90045-9785. *Telephone:* 310-665-6820 or 800-527-OTIS (toll-free). *Fax:* 310-665-6821. *E-mail:* admissions@otis.edu. *Web site:* http://www.otis.edu/.

PACIFIC OAKS COLLEGE

Pasadena, California

PO is a coed, primarily women's, private, upper-level institution, founded in 1945, offering degrees at the bachelor's and master's levels and post-master's and postbachelor's certificates. It has a 2-acre campus in Pasadena near Los Angeles.

Academic Information The faculty has 68 members (43% full-time). The undergraduate student-faculty ratio is 9:1. The library holds 18,451 titles, 106 serial subscriptions, and 161 audiovisual materials. Special programs include independent study, distance learning, summer session for credit, part-time degree programs (evenings, weekends, summer), adult/continuing education programs, internships, and arrangement for off-campus study with Pacific Oaks Northern California, Pacific Oakes College Northwest. The most frequently chosen baccalaureate field is home economics/vocational home economics.

Student Body Statistics The student body totals 909, of whom 210 are undergraduates (37 in entering class). 92 percent are women and 8 percent are men. Students come from 34 states and territories. 81 percent are from California.

Expenses for 2004–05 *Application fee:* $55. *Tuition:* $18,900 full-time, $630 per unit part-time. *Mandatory fees:* $60 full-time, $30 per term part-time. Full-time tuition and fees vary according to program. Part-time tuition and fees vary according to program.

Financial Aid Forms of aid include need-based scholarships and part-time jobs. The average aided 2002–03 undergraduate received an aid package worth $4750. The application deadline for financial aid is continuous.

Transfer Admission PO requires a college transcript. Standardized test scores are required for some. The application deadline for admission is June 1.

Entrance Difficulty PO assesses its entrance difficulty level as noncompetitive for transfers.

For Further Information Contact Ms. Teresa Cook, Director of Admissions, Pacific Oaks College, 5 Westmoreland Place, Pasadena, CA 91103. *Telephone:* 626-397-4945 or 800-684-0900 (toll-free). *Fax:* 626-685-2531. *E-mail:* admissions@pacificoaks.edu. *Web site:* http://www.pacificoaks.edu/.

PACIFIC STATES UNIVERSITY

Los Angeles, California

PSU is a coed, private, comprehensive institution, founded in 1928, offering degrees at the bachelor's and master's levels. It has a 1-acre campus in Los Angeles.

Academic Information The faculty has 16 members (25% full-time), 62% with terminal degrees. The undergraduate student-faculty ratio is 20:1. The library holds 15,000 titles and 108 serial subscriptions. Special programs include study abroad, accelerated degree programs, ESL programs, independent study, self-designed majors, summer session for credit, and adult/continuing education programs. The most frequently chosen baccalaureate fields are business/marketing, computer/information sciences.

Student Body Statistics The student body totals 129, of whom 38 are undergraduates (27 freshmen). 32 percent are women and 68 percent are men. 90 percent are from California. 20 percent of the 2003 graduating class went on to graduate and professional schools.

Expenses for 2003–04 *Application fee:* $100. *Tuition:* $8400 full-time. *Mandatory fees:* $480 full-time.

Freshman Admission PSU requires an essay, a high school transcript, a minimum 2.5 high school GPA, and TOEFL scores for international students. The application deadline for regular admission is September 21.

Transfer Admission The application deadline for admission is October 27.

Entrance Difficulty PSU has an open admission policy.

For Further Information Contact Ms. Marina Miller, Assistant Director of Admissions, Pacific States University, 1516 South Western Avenue, Los Angeles, CA 90006. *Telephone:* 323-731-2383 or 888-200-0383 (toll-free). *Fax:* 323-731-7276. *E-mail:* admission@psuca.edu. *Web site:* http://www.psuca.edu/.

PACIFIC UNION COLLEGE

Angwin, California

PUC is a coed, private, Seventh-day Adventist, comprehensive institution, founded in 1882, offering degrees at the associate, bachelor's, and master's levels. It has a 200-acre campus in Angwin near San Francisco.

Academic Information The faculty has 104 members (79% full-time), 55% with terminal degrees. The undergraduate student-faculty ratio is 14:1. The library holds 165,321 titles, 839 serial subscriptions, and 55,502 audiovisual materials. Special programs include academic remediation, services for learning-disabled students, an honors program, cooperative (work-study) education, study abroad, advanced placement credit, accelerated degree programs, Freshman Honors College, ESL programs, double majors, independent study, distance learning, self-designed majors, summer session for credit, part-time degree programs (daytime, summer), adult/continuing education programs, internships, and arrangement for off-campus study. The most frequently chosen baccalaureate fields are business/marketing, health professions and related sciences, trade and industry.

Student Body Statistics The student body totals 1,502, of whom 1,494 are undergraduates (282 freshmen). 54 percent are women and 46 percent are men. Students come from 18 states and territories and 20 other countries. 91 percent are from California. 7.8 percent are international students.

Expenses for 2003–04 *Application fee:* $30. *One-time mandatory fee:* $30. *Comprehensive fee:* $22,257 includes full-time tuition ($17,235), mandatory fees ($120), and college room and board ($4902). *College room only:* $2952. *Part-time tuition:* $492 per credit. *Part-time mandatory fees:* $40 per term.

Financial Aid Forms of aid include need-based and non-need-based scholarships and part-time jobs. The average aided 2003–04 undergraduate received an aid package worth an estimated $10,958. The priority application deadline for financial aid is March 2.

Freshman Admission PUC requires a high school transcript, a minimum 2.3 high school GPA, 3 recommendations, SAT I and SAT II or ACT scores, and TOEFL scores for international students. The application deadline for regular admission is rolling.

Pacific Union College (continued)

Transfer Admission The application deadline for admission is rolling.
Entrance Difficulty PUC assesses its entrance difficulty level as moderately difficult. For the fall 2003 freshman class, 35 percent of the applicants were accepted.

For Further Information Contact Mr. Sean Kootsey, Director of Enrollment Services, Pacific Union College, Enrollment Services, One Angwin Avenue, Angwin, CA 94508. *Telephone:* 707-965-6425 or 800-862-7080 (toll-free). *Fax:* 707-965-6432. *E-mail:* enroll@puc.edu. *Web site:* http://www.puc.edu/.

PATTEN UNIVERSITY

Oakland, California

Patten is a coed, private, interdenominational, comprehensive institution, founded in 1944, offering degrees at the associate, bachelor's, and master's levels and postbachelor's certificates. It has a 5-acre campus in Oakland near San Francisco.

Expenses for 2003–04 *Application fee:* $30. *Comprehensive fee:* $15,640 includes full-time tuition ($9840) and college room and board ($5800).

For Further Information Contact Ms. Inez Bailey, Director of Admissions, Patten University, 2433 Coolidge Avenue, Oakland, CA 94601. *Telephone:* 510-261-8500 Ext. 765. *Fax:* 510-534-4344. *Web site:* http://www.patten.edu/.

PEPPERDINE UNIVERSITY

Malibu, California

Pepperdine is a coed, private university, founded in 1937, affiliated with the Church of Christ, offering degrees at the bachelor's, master's, doctoral, and first professional levels. It has an 830-acre campus in Malibu near Los Angeles.

Academic Information The faculty has 332 members (58% full-time). The undergraduate student-faculty ratio is 12:1. The library holds 315,078 titles, 3,182 serial subscriptions, and 5,044 audiovisual materials. Special programs include an honors program, study abroad, advanced placement credit, accelerated degree programs, double majors, independent study, self-designed majors, summer session for credit, part-time degree programs (daytime, evenings), and internships. The most frequently chosen baccalaureate fields are business/marketing, communications/communication technologies, social sciences and history.
Student Body Statistics The student body totals 8,021, of whom 3,098 are undergraduates (615 freshmen). 56 percent are women and 44 percent are men. Students come from 51 states and territories and 70 other countries. 52 percent are from California. 6 percent are international students. 63 percent of the 2003 graduating class went on to graduate and professional schools.
Expenses for 2004–05 *Application fee:* $55. *Comprehensive fee:* $37,360 includes full-time tuition ($28,630), mandatory fees ($90), and college room and board ($8640). Room and board charges vary according to board plan and housing facility. *Part-time tuition:* $890 per unit.
Financial Aid Forms of aid include need-based and non-need-based scholarships, athletic grants, and part-time jobs. The average aided 2003–04 undergraduate received an aid package worth an estimated $22,611. The priority application deadline for financial aid is February 15.
Freshman Admission Pepperdine requires an essay, a high school transcript, 2 recommendations, SAT I or ACT scores, and TOEFL scores for international students. An interview is recommended. The application deadline for regular admission is January 15 and for early action it is November 15.
Transfer Admission The application deadline for admission is January 15.
Entrance Difficulty Pepperdine assesses its entrance difficulty level as very difficult. For the fall 2003 freshman class, 23 percent of the applicants were accepted.

For Further Information Contact Mr. Paul A. Long, Dean of Admission and Enrollment Management, Pepperdine University, 24255 Pacific Coast Highway, Malibu, CA 90263-4392. *Telephone:* 310-506-4392. *Fax:* 310-506-4861. *E-mail:* admission-seaver@pepperdine.edu. *Web site:* http://www.pepperdine.edu/.

PITZER COLLEGE

Claremont, California

Pitzer is a coed, private, four-year college of The Claremont Colleges Consortium, founded in 1963, offering degrees at the bachelor's level. It has a 35-acre campus in Claremont near Los Angeles.

Academic Information The faculty has 91 members (78% full-time), 93% with terminal degrees. The student-faculty ratio is 11:1. The library holds 2 million titles, 6,000 serial subscriptions, and 606 audiovisual materials. Special programs include services for learning-disabled students, an honors program, cooperative (work-study) education, study abroad, advanced placement credit, ESL programs, double majors, independent study, self-designed majors, part-time degree programs (daytime, evenings), adult/continuing education programs, internships, and arrangement for off-campus study with The Claremont Colleges, Colby College, Haverford College, Spelman College, Morehouse College. The most frequently chosen baccalaureate fields are psychology, English, social sciences and history.
Student Body Statistics The student body is made up of 942 undergraduates (230 freshmen). 60 percent are women and 40 percent are men. Students come from 44 states and territories and 11 other countries. 53 percent are from California. 3 percent are international students.
Expenses for 2003–04 *Application fee:* $50. *Comprehensive fee:* $37,590 includes full-time tuition ($26,640), mandatory fees ($3154), and college room and board ($7796). *College room only:* $4880. Full-time tuition and fees vary according to course load. Room and board charges vary according to board plan. *Part-time tuition:* $3330 per course. Part-time tuition varies according to course load.
Financial Aid Forms of aid include need-based and non-need-based scholarships and part-time jobs. The average aided 2003–04 undergraduate received an aid package worth an estimated $27,950. The application deadline for financial aid is February 1.
Freshman Admission Pitzer requires an essay, a high school transcript, 3 recommendations, and TOEFL scores for international students. An interview is recommended. SAT I or ACT scores are required for some. The application deadline for regular admission is January 15 and for early action it is December 1.
Transfer Admission The application deadline for admission is April 15.
Entrance Difficulty Pitzer assesses its entrance difficulty level as moderately difficult. For the fall 2003 freshman class, 50 percent of the applicants were accepted.

For Further Information Contact Dr. Arnaldo Rodriguez, Vice President for Admission and Financial Aid, Pitzer College, 1050 North Mills Avenue, Claremont, CA 91711-6101. *Telephone:* 909-621-8129 or 800-748-9371 (toll-free). *Fax:* 909-621-8770. *E-mail:* admission@pitzer.edu. *Web site:* http://www.pitzer.edu/.

PLATT COLLEGE

Newport Beach, California

Platt College is a coed, private, primarily two-year college, founded in 1985, offering degrees at the associate and bachelor's levels.

Academic Information The faculty has 24 members (33% full-time). The student-faculty ratio is 16:1. The library holds 1,100 titles, 15 serial subscriptions, and 100 audiovisual materials. Special programs include accelerated degree programs, summer session for credit, and adult/continuing education programs. The most frequently chosen baccalaureate field is visual/performing arts.

Student Body Statistics The student body is made up of 270 undergraduates. 33 percent are women and 67 percent are men. Students come from 12 states and territories and 5 other countries.
Expenses for 2003–04 *Application fee:* $75. *Tuition:* $24,000 full-time. Full-time tuition varies according to program.
Freshman Admission Platt College requires an essay, a high school transcript, an interview, and CPAt. The application deadline for regular admission is rolling.
Entrance Difficulty Platt College assesses its entrance difficulty level as moderately difficult. For the fall 2003 freshman class, 80 percent of the applicants were accepted.

For Further Information Contact Ms. Lisa Rhodes, President, Platt College, 3901 MacArthur Boulevard, Suite 101, Newport Beach, CA 92660. *Telephone:* 949-833-2300 Ext. 222 or 888-866-6697 Ext. 230 (toll-free out-of-state). *Fax:* 949-833-0269. *E-mail:* lrhodes@plattcollege.edu. *Web site:* http://www.plattcollege.edu/.

PLATT COLLEGE

Ontario, California

Platt College is a coed, private, two-year college, offering degrees at the associate level.

Expenses for 2003–04 *Application fee:* $75. *Tuition:* $24,000 full-time.

For Further Information Contact Ms. Jennifer Abandonato, Director of Admissions, Platt College, 3700 Inland Empire Boulevard, Ontario, CA 91764. *Telephone:* 909-941-9410 or 888-866-6697 (toll-free). *Fax:* 909-989-8974. *Web site:* http://www.plattcollege.edu/.

PLATT COLLEGE SAN DIEGO

San Diego, California

Platt College is a coed, proprietary, primarily two-year college, founded in 1879, offering degrees at the associate and bachelor's levels. It is located in San Diego near San Diego.

Academic Information The faculty has 21 members (33% full-time), 5% with terminal degrees. The student-faculty ratio is 20:1.
Student Body Statistics The student body is made up of 335 undergraduates (109 freshmen). 27 percent are women and 73 percent are men. Students come from 4 states and territories and 2 other countries. 95 percent are from California. 90 percent of the 2003 graduating class went on to four-year colleges.
Expenses for 2003–04 *Application fee:* $75. *Tuition:* $13,952 full-time. *Mandatory fees:* $75 full-time. Full-time tuition and fees vary according to program.
Freshman Admission Platt College requires a high school transcript and an interview.

For Further Information Contact Carly Westerfield, Coordinator, Platt College San Diego, 6250 El Cajon Boulevard, San Diego, CA 92115-3919. *Telephone:* 619-265-0107 or 800-255-0613 (toll-free). *Fax:* 619-265-8655. *E-mail:* info@platt.edu. *Web site:* http://www.platt.edu/.

POINT LOMA NAZARENE UNIVERSITY

San Diego, California

PLNU is a coed, private, Nazarene, comprehensive institution, founded in 1902, offering degrees at the bachelor's and master's levels. It has an 88-acre campus in San Diego.

Academic Information The faculty has 272 members (50% full-time), 42% with terminal degrees. The undergraduate student-faculty ratio is 16:1. The library holds 146,016 titles, 836 serial subscriptions, and 18,685 audiovisual materials. Special programs include academic remediation, services for learning-disabled students, study abroad, advanced placement credit, double majors, summer session for credit, part-time degree programs (daytime, evenings, weekends, summer), internships, and arrangement for off-campus study with American University, Coalition for Christian Colleges and Universities. The most frequently chosen baccalaureate fields are business/marketing, liberal arts/general studies, psychology.
Student Body Statistics The student body totals 3,170, of whom 2,375 are undergraduates (555 freshmen). 59 percent are women and 41 percent are men. Students come from 42 states and territories and 17 other countries. 78 percent are from California. 1.1 percent are international students.
Expenses for 2003–04 *Application fee:* $45. *Comprehensive fee:* $24,880 includes full-time tuition ($18,000), mandatory fees ($500), and college room and board ($6380). Full-time tuition and fees vary according to course load. Room and board charges vary according to board plan. *Part-time tuition:* $750 per unit. *Part-time mandatory fees:* $20 per unit. Part-time tuition and fees vary according to course load.
Financial Aid Forms of aid include need-based and non-need-based scholarships and part-time jobs. The average aided 2002–03 undergraduate received an aid package worth $12,676. The priority application deadline for financial aid is March 2.
Freshman Admission PLNU requires an essay, a high school transcript, a minimum 2.8 high school GPA, 2 recommendations, SAT I or ACT scores, and TOEFL scores for international students. SAT I scores are recommended. An interview is required for some. The application deadline for regular admission is March 1 and for early action it is December 1.
Transfer Admission The application deadline for admission is rolling.
Entrance Difficulty PLNU assesses its entrance difficulty level as moderately difficult. For the fall 2003 freshman class, 64 percent of the applicants were accepted.

For Further Information Contact Mr. Scott Shoemaker, Dean of Enrollment, Point Loma Nazarene University, 3900 Lomaland Drive, San Diego, CA 92106. *Telephone:* 619-849-2273 or 800-733-7770 (toll-free). *Fax:* 619-849-2601. *E-mail:* admissions@ptloma.edu. *Web site:* http://www.ptloma.edu/.

POMONA COLLEGE

Claremont, California

Pomona is a coed, private, four-year college of The Claremont Colleges Consortium, founded in 1887, offering degrees at the bachelor's level. It has a 140-acre campus in Claremont near Los Angeles.

Academic Information The faculty has 212 members (75% full-time), 85% with terminal degrees. The student-faculty ratio is 8:1. The library holds 2 million titles, 5,968 serial subscriptions, and 16,524 audiovisual materials. Special programs include study abroad, advanced placement credit, double majors, independent study, self-designed majors, internships, and arrangement for off-campus study with other members of The Claremont Colleges, Swarthmore College, Colby College, Smith College, Spelman College. The most frequently chosen baccalaureate fields are interdisciplinary studies, English, social sciences and history.
Student Body Statistics The student body is made up of 1,555 undergraduates (399 freshmen). 51 percent are women and 49 percent are men. Students come from 48 states and territories and 18 other countries. 35 percent are from California. 2 percent are international students. 33 percent of the 2003 graduating class went on to graduate and professional schools.
Expenses for 2003–04 *Application fee:* $60. *Comprehensive fee:* $37,130 includes full-time tuition ($26,890), mandatory fees ($260), and college room and board ($9980). Room and board charges vary according to board plan. *Part-time tuition:* $4485 per course.
Financial Aid Forms of aid include need-based scholarships and part-time jobs. The average aided 2002–03 undergraduate received an aid package worth $25,700. The application deadline for financial aid is February 1.
Freshman Admission Pomona requires an essay, a high school transcript, 2 recommendations, SAT I and SAT II or ACT scores, TOEFL scores for international students, and 3 SAT II Subject Tests (including SAT II: Writing Test). A minimum 3.0 high school GPA, an interview, and portfolio or tapes for art and performing arts programs are recommended.

Pomona College (continued)

The application deadline for regular admission is January 2; for early decision plan 1 it is November 15; and for early decision plan 2 it is December 28.

Transfer Admission The application deadline for admission is March 15.

Entrance Difficulty Pomona assesses its entrance difficulty level as most difficult. For the fall 2003 freshman class, 21 percent of the applicants were accepted.

For Further Information Contact Mr. Bruce Poch, Vice President and Dean of Admissions, Pomona College, 333 North College Way, Claremont, CA 91711. *Telephone:* 909-621-8134. *Fax:* 909-621-8952. *E-mail:* admissions@pomona.edu. *Web site:* http://www.pomona.edu/.

PROFESSIONAL GOLFERS CAREER COLLEGE

Temecula, California

Professional Golfers Career College is a coed, primarily men's, private, two-year college, offering degrees at the associate level.

Expenses for 2004–05 *Tuition:* $4790 full-time. *Mandatory fees:* $120 full-time. *College room only:* $5000.

For Further Information Contact Ms. Sandi Somerville, Director of Admissions, Professional Golfers Career College, PO Box 892319, Temecula, CA 92589. *Telephone:* 909-693-2963 Ext. 17 or 800-877-4380 (toll-free out-of-state). *Fax:* 909-693-2863. *Web site:* http://www.progolfed.com/.

QUEEN OF THE HOLY ROSARY COLLEGE

Mission San Jose, California

Queen of the Holy Rosary College is a coed, primarily women's, private, Roman Catholic, two-year college, founded in 1930, offering degrees at the associate level in religious studies. It has a 37-acre campus in Mission San Jose near San Jose.

Expenses for 2003–04 *Application fee:* $15. *One-time mandatory fee:* $15. *Tuition:* $2500 full-time, $100 per credit part-time. *Mandatory fees:* $30 full-time.

For Further Information Contact Sr. Mary Paul Mehegan, Dean of the College, Queen of the Holy Rosary College, 43326 Mission Boulevard, PO Box 3908, Mission San Jose, CA 94539. *Telephone:* 510-657-2468 Ext. 322. *Fax:* 510-657-1734. *Web site:* http://www.msjdominicans.org/college.html.

REMINGTON COLLEGE–SAN DIEGO CAMPUS

San Diego, California

For Information Write to Remington College–San Diego Campus, San Diego, CA 92108.

SAINT MARY'S COLLEGE OF CALIFORNIA

Moraga, California

Saint Mary's is a coed, private, Roman Catholic, comprehensive institution, founded in 1863, offering degrees at the bachelor's, master's, and doctoral levels. It has a 420-acre campus in Moraga near San Francisco.

Academic Information The faculty has 524 members (40% full-time). The undergraduate student-faculty ratio is 12:1. The library holds 207,076 titles, 1,070 serial subscriptions, and 6,296 audiovisual materials. Special programs include an honors program, study abroad, advanced placement credit, double majors, independent study, self-designed majors, part-time degree programs (daytime, evenings, weekends), external degree programs, adult/continuing education programs, internships, and arrangement for off-campus study with members of the January Interim Program. The most frequently chosen baccalaureate fields are business/marketing, communications/communication technologies, psychology.

Student Body Statistics The student body totals 4,486, of whom 3,337 are undergraduates (562 freshmen). 60 percent are women and 40 percent are men. Students come from 26 states and territories and 21 other countries. 83 percent are from California. 3 percent are international students. 18 percent of the 2003 graduating class went on to graduate and professional schools.

Expenses for 2003–04 *Application fee:* $45. *Comprehensive fee:* $32,850 includes full-time tuition ($23,640), mandatory fees ($135), and college room and board ($9075). *College room only:* $5065. Full-time tuition and fees vary according to program. Room and board charges vary according to board plan and housing facility. *Part-time tuition:* $2750 per course.

Financial Aid Forms of aid include need-based and non-need-based scholarships, athletic grants, and part-time jobs. The average aided 2003–04 undergraduate received an aid package worth an estimated $20,460. The application deadline for financial aid is March 2.

Freshman Admission Saint Mary's requires an essay, a high school transcript, a minimum 2.0 high school GPA, 1 recommendation, SAT I or ACT scores, and TOEFL scores for international students. A minimum 3.0 high school GPA is recommended. A minimum 3.0 high school GPA and an interview are required for some. The application deadline for regular admission is February 1 and for early action it is November 30.

Transfer Admission The application deadline for admission is July 1.

Entrance Difficulty Saint Mary's assesses its entrance difficulty level as moderately difficult. For the fall 2003 freshman class, 82 percent of the applicants were accepted.

For Further Information Contact Ms. Dorothy Jones, Dean of Admissions, Saint Mary's College of California, PO Box 4800, Moraga, CA 94556-4800. *Telephone:* 925-631-4224 or 800-800-4SMC (toll-free). *Fax:* 925-376-7193. *E-mail:* smcadmit@stmarys-ca.edu. *Web site:* http://www.stmarys-ca.edu/.

SALVATION ARMY COLLEGE FOR OFFICER TRAINING

See Crestmont College

SAMUEL MERRITT COLLEGE

Oakland, California

Samuel Merritt College is a coed, primarily women's, private, comprehensive institution, founded in 1909, offering degrees at the bachelor's, master's, doctoral, and first professional levels (bachelor's degree offered jointly with Saint Mary's College of California). It has a 1-acre campus in Oakland near San Francisco.

Academic Information The faculty has 120 members (48% full-time), 39% with terminal degrees. The undergraduate student-faculty ratio is 11:1. The library holds 11,000 titles, 540 serial subscriptions, and 900 audiovisual materials. Special programs include academic remediation, services for learning-disabled students, study abroad, advanced placement credit, double majors, independent study, distance learning, summer session for credit, internships, and arrangement for off-campus study with Saint Mary's College of California. The most frequently chosen baccalaureate field is health professions and related sciences.

Student Body Statistics The student body totals 896, of whom 285 are undergraduates (15 freshmen). 93 percent are women and 7 percent are men. Students come from 1 state or territory. 2 percent of the 2003 graduating class went on to graduate and professional schools.

Expenses for 2003–04 *Application fee:* $35. *Comprehensive fee:* $30,669 includes full-time tuition ($21,790), mandatory fees ($50), and college room and board ($8829). *College room only:* $5661. *Part-time tuition:* $911 per unit.
Financial Aid Forms of aid include need-based scholarships and part-time jobs. The priority application deadline for financial aid is March 2.
Freshman Admission Samuel Merritt College requires an essay, a high school transcript, a minimum 2.5 high school GPA, 1 recommendation, SAT I or ACT scores, and TOEFL scores for international students. An interview is required for some. The application deadline for regular admission is March 1.
Transfer Admission The application deadline for admission is March 1.
Entrance Difficulty Samuel Merritt College assesses its entrance difficulty level as moderately difficult. For the fall 2003 freshman class, 63 percent of the applicants were accepted.

For Further Information Contact Ms. Anne Seed, Director of Admissions, Samuel Merritt College, 570 Hawthorne Avenue, Oakland, CA 94609. *Telephone:* 510-869-6610 or 800-607-MERRITT (toll-free). *Fax:* 510-869-6525. *E-mail:* admission@samuelmerritt.edu. *Web site:* http://www.samuelmerritt.edu/.

SAN DIEGO STATE UNIVERSITY

San Diego, California

SDSU is a coed, public unit of California State University System, founded in 1897, offering degrees at the bachelor's, master's, and doctoral levels and post-master's and postbachelor's certificates. It has a 300-acre campus in San Diego.

Academic Information The faculty has 1,684 members (60% full-time), 47% with terminal degrees. The undergraduate student-faculty ratio is 19:1. The library holds 1 million titles, 8,245 serial subscriptions, and 12,616 audiovisual materials. Special programs include academic remediation, services for learning-disabled students, an honors program, study abroad, advanced placement credit, ESL programs, double majors, independent study, distance learning, self-designed majors, summer session for credit, part-time degree programs (daytime, evenings, summer), internships, and arrangement for off-campus study with other units of the California State University System. The most frequently chosen baccalaureate fields are business/marketing, protective services/public administration, social sciences and history.
Student Body Statistics The student body totals 33,676, of whom 27,345 are undergraduates (3,730 freshmen). 58 percent are women and 42 percent are men. Students come from 50 states and territories and 125 other countries. 93 percent are from California. 2.9 percent are international students.
Expenses for 2003–04 *Application fee:* $55. *State resident tuition:* $0 full-time. *Nonresident tuition:* $8460 full-time, $282 per unit part-time. *Mandatory fees:* $2488 full-time, $815 per term part-time. *College room and board:* $8787. *College room only:* $5096.
Financial Aid Forms of aid include need-based and non-need-based scholarships, athletic grants, and part-time jobs. The average aided 2003–04 undergraduate received an aid package worth an estimated $8500. The application deadline for financial aid is continuous.
Freshman Admission SDSU requires a high school transcript, a minimum 2.0 high school GPA, 2.5 GPA for non-California residents, SAT I or ACT scores, and TOEFL scores for international students. The application deadline for regular admission is November 30.
Transfer Admission The application deadline for admission is November 30.
Entrance Difficulty SDSU assesses its entrance difficulty level as moderately difficult. For the fall 2003 freshman class, 50 percent of the applicants were accepted.

For Further Information Contact Ms. Beverly Arata, Director of Admissions, San Diego State University, 5500 Campanile Drive, San Diego, CA 92182-7455. *Telephone:* 619-594-7800. *Fax:* 619-594-1250. *E-mail:* admissions@sdsu.edu. *Web site:* http://www.sdsu.edu/.

SAN FRANCISCO ART INSTITUTE

San Francisco, California

SFAI is a coed, private, comprehensive institution, founded in 1871, offering degrees at the bachelor's and master's levels and postbachelor's certificates in art. It has a 3-acre campus in San Francisco.

Academic Information The faculty has 115 members (30% full-time). The undergraduate student-faculty ratio is 6:1. The library holds 35,500 titles, 210 serial subscriptions, and 121,000 audiovisual materials. Special programs include academic remediation, services for learning-disabled students, study abroad, advanced placement credit, accelerated degree programs, ESL programs, double majors, independent study, summer session for credit, part-time degree programs (daytime, evenings, weekends, summer), external degree programs, adult/continuing education programs, internships, and arrangement for off-campus study with Association of Independent Colleges of Art and Design. The most frequently chosen baccalaureate field is visual/performing arts.
Student Body Statistics The student body totals 655, of whom 407 are undergraduates (39 freshmen). 53 percent are women and 47 percent are men. Students come from 24 states and territories and 18 other countries. 67 percent are from California. 6.4 percent are international students.
Expenses for 2004–05 *Application fee:* $50. *Comprehensive fee:* $33,690 includes full-time tuition ($24,240) and college room and board ($9450). *Part-time tuition:* $1010 per unit. Part-time tuition varies according to course load.
Financial Aid Forms of aid include need-based and non-need-based scholarships and part-time jobs. The application deadline for financial aid is continuous.
Freshman Admission SFAI requires an essay, a high school transcript, a portfolio, SAT I or ACT scores, and TOEFL scores for international students. An interview is recommended. The application deadline for regular admission is August 27.
Transfer Admission The application deadline for admission is rolling.
Entrance Difficulty SFAI assesses its entrance difficulty level as moderately difficult. For the fall 2003 freshman class, 83 percent of the applicants were accepted.

For Further Information Contact Mark Takiguchi, Director of Admissions, San Francisco Art Institute, 800 Chestnut Street, San Francisco, CA 94133. *Telephone:* 415-749-4580 or 800-345-SFAI (toll-free). *E-mail:* admissions@sfai.edu. *Web site:* http://www.sfai.edu/.

SAN FRANCISCO CONSERVATORY OF MUSIC

San Francisco, California

SFCM is a coed, private, comprehensive institution, founded in 1917, offering degrees at the bachelor's and master's levels. It has a 2-acre campus in San Francisco.

Expenses for 2003–04 *Application fee:* $70. *Tuition:* $23,500 full-time. *Mandatory fees:* $280 full-time.

For Further Information Contact Ms. Susan Dean, Director of Admissions, San Francisco Conservatory of Music, 1201 Ortega Street, San Francisco, CA 94122-4411. *Telephone:* 415-759-3431. *Fax:* 415-759-3499. *E-mail:* admit@sfcm.edu. *Web site:* http://www.sfcm.edu/.

SAN FRANCISCO STATE UNIVERSITY

San Francisco, California

SF State is a coed, public, comprehensive unit of California State University System, founded in 1899, offering degrees at the bachelor's, master's, and doctoral levels and postbachelor's certificates. It has a 90-acre campus in San Francisco.

San Francisco State University (continued)

Academic Information The faculty has 1,646 members (54% full-time), 50% with terminal degrees. The undergraduate student-faculty ratio is 18:1. The library holds 780,230 titles, 5,679 serial subscriptions, and 72,245 audiovisual materials. Special programs include academic remediation, services for learning-disabled students, an honors program, cooperative (work-study) education, study abroad, advanced placement credit, accelerated degree programs, ESL programs, double majors, independent study, distance learning, self-designed majors, summer session for credit, part-time degree programs (daytime, evenings, weekends, summer), adult/continuing education programs, internships, and arrangement for off-campus study with The San Francisco Consortium, 18 other institutions of the California State University System. The most frequently chosen baccalaureate fields are business/marketing, social sciences and history, visual/performing arts.
Student Body Statistics The student body totals 29,686, of whom 21,892 are undergraduates (2,499 freshmen). 59 percent are women and 41 percent are men. Students come from 48 states and territories and 113 other countries. 99 percent are from California. 6.1 percent are international students.
Expenses for 2003–04 *Application fee:* $55. *State resident tuition:* $0 full-time. *Nonresident tuition:* $8460 full-time, $282 per unit part-time. *Mandatory fees:* $2498 full-time. *College room and board:* $8090. *College room only:* $5030. Room and board charges vary according to board plan and housing facility.
Financial Aid Forms of aid include need-based scholarships, athletic grants, and part-time jobs. The average aided 2002–03 undergraduate received an aid package worth $8638. The priority application deadline for financial aid is March 3.
Freshman Admission SF State requires a high school transcript and TOEFL scores for international students. SAT I or ACT scores are required for some. The application deadline for regular admission is rolling.
Entrance Difficulty SF State assesses its entrance difficulty level as moderately difficult; very difficult for out-of-state applicants. For the fall 2003 freshman class, 64 percent of the applicants were accepted.

For Further Information Contact Ms. Patricia Wade, Admissions Officer, San Francisco State University, 1600 Holloway Avenue, San Francisco, CA 94132. *Telephone:* 415-338-6191. *Fax:* 415-338-7196. *E-mail:* ugadmit@sfsu.edu. *Web site:* http://www.sfsu.edu/.

SAN JOAQUIN VALLEY COLLEGE

Visalia, California

SJVC is a coed, private, two-year college, founded in 1977, offering degrees at the associate level.

Expenses for 2004–05 *Tuition:* $10,440 full-time. *Mandatory fees:* $100 full-time.

For Further Information Contact Mr. Joseph Holt, Director of Marketing and Admissions, San Joaquin Valley College, 8400 West Mineral King Avenue, Visalia, CA 93291. *Telephone:* 559-651-2500. *Web site:* http://www.sjvc.com/.

SAN JOSE CHRISTIAN COLLEGE

See William Jessup University

SAN JOSE STATE UNIVERSITY

San Jose, California

SJSU is a coed, public, comprehensive unit of California State University System, founded in 1857, offering degrees at the bachelor's and master's levels. It has a 104-acre campus in San Jose.

Academic Information The faculty has 1,685 members (46% full-time). The undergraduate student-faculty ratio is 18:1. The library holds 1 million titles, 2,504 serial subscriptions, and 37,146 audiovisual materials. Special programs include academic remediation, services for learning-disabled students, an honors program, cooperative (work-study) education, study abroad, advanced placement credit, accelerated degree programs, ESL programs, double majors, independent study, distance learning, self-designed majors, summer session for credit, part-time degree programs (daytime, evenings, summer), adult/continuing education programs, internships, and arrangement for off-campus study with other institutions of the California State University System. The most frequently chosen baccalaureate fields are business/marketing, computer/information sciences, engineering/engineering technologies.
Student Body Statistics The student body totals 28,932, of whom 21,396 are undergraduates (1,978 freshmen). 51 percent are women and 49 percent are men. Students come from 38 states and territories. 17 percent are from California. 0.1 percent are international students.
Expenses for 2003–04 *Application fee:* $55. *State resident tuition:* $0 full-time. *Nonresident tuition:* $6768 full-time, $282 per unit part-time. *Mandatory fees:* $2,562 full-time, $897.20 per term part-time. Part-time tuition and fees vary according to course load. *College room and board:* $8465. Room and board charges vary according to board plan and housing facility.
Financial Aid Forms of aid include need-based and non-need-based scholarships, athletic grants, and part-time jobs. The average aided 2002–03 undergraduate received an aid package worth $6439. The priority application deadline for financial aid is March 2.
Freshman Admission SJSU requires a high school transcript and TOEFL scores for international students. SAT I or ACT scores are required for some. The application deadline for regular admission is November 30.
Transfer Admission The application deadline for admission is rolling.
Entrance Difficulty SJSU assesses its entrance difficulty level as moderately difficult; very difficult for out-of-state applicants. For the fall 2003 freshman class, 52 percent of the applicants were accepted.

For Further Information Contact Mr. John Loera, Director of Admissions, San Jose State University, One Washington Square, San Jose, CA 95192-0001. *Telephone:* 408-283-7500. *Fax:* 408-924-2050. *E-mail:* contact@sjsu.edu. *Web site:* http://www.sjsu.edu/.

SANTA CLARA UNIVERSITY

Santa Clara, California

Santa Clara is a coed, private, Roman Catholic (Jesuit) university, founded in 1851, offering degrees at the bachelor's, master's, doctoral, and first professional levels and post-master's, first professional, and postbachelor's certificates. It has a 104-acre campus in Santa Clara near San Francisco and San Jose.

Academic Information The faculty has 695 members (60% full-time), 77% with terminal degrees. The undergraduate student-faculty ratio is 12:1. The library holds 639,691 titles, 11,952 serial subscriptions, and 12,622 audiovisual materials. Special programs include an honors program, cooperative (work-study) education, study abroad, advanced placement credit, double majors, independent study, self-designed majors, summer session for credit, and internships. The most frequently chosen baccalaureate fields are business/marketing, engineering/engineering technologies, social sciences and history.
Student Body Statistics The student body totals 7,794, of whom 4,298 are undergraduates (897 freshmen). 55 percent are women and 45 percent are men. Students come from 35 states and territories and 12 other countries. 66 percent are from California. 2.9 percent are international students. 20.4 percent of the 2003 graduating class went on to graduate and professional schools.
Expenses for 2003–04 *Application fee:* $55. *Comprehensive fee:* $34,701 includes full-time tuition ($25,365) and college room and board ($9336). Room and board charges vary according to housing facility. *Part-time tuition:* varies with course load.
Financial Aid Forms of aid include need-based and non-need-based scholarships, athletic grants, and part-time jobs. The average aided 2003–04 undergraduate received an aid package worth an estimated $18,400. The priority application deadline for financial aid is February 1.
Freshman Admission Santa Clara requires an essay, a high school transcript, 1 recommendation, SAT I or ACT scores, and TOEFL scores

for international students. An interview is recommended. The application deadline for regular admission is January 15 and for early action it is November 15.
Transfer Admission The application deadline for admission is May 15.
Entrance Difficulty Santa Clara assesses its entrance difficulty level as moderately difficult; very difficult for transfer students in business programs. For the fall 2003 freshman class, 66 percent of the applicants were accepted.

For Further Information Contact Ms. Sandra Hayes, Dean of Undergraduate Admissions, Santa Clara University, 500 El Camino Real, Santa Clara, CA 95053. *Telephone:* 408-554-4700. *Fax:* 408-554-5255. *E-mail:* ugadmissions@scu.edu. *Web site:* http://www.scu.edu/.

SCRIPPS COLLEGE

Claremont, California

Scripps is a women's, private, four-year college of The Claremont Colleges Consortium, founded in 1926, offering degrees at the bachelor's level and postbachelor's certificates. It has a 30-acre campus in Claremont near Los Angeles.

Academic Information The faculty has 89 members (69% full-time), 88% with terminal degrees. The student-faculty ratio is 11:1. The library holds 998,823 titles, 5,733 serial subscriptions, and 4,361 audiovisual materials. Special programs include an honors program, study abroad, advanced placement credit, accelerated degree programs, double majors, independent study, self-designed majors, part-time degree programs (daytime, evenings), internships, and arrangement for off-campus study with 5 members of The Claremont Colleges, Colby College, Haverford College, Spelman College, California Institute of Technology, American University (Washington Semester), Drew University, George Washington University. The most frequently chosen baccalaureate fields are social sciences and history, area/ethnic studies, visual/performing arts.
Student Body Statistics The student body totals 834, of whom 819 are undergraduates (210 freshmen). Students come from 45 states and territories. 44 percent are from California. 1.7 percent are international students. 36 percent of the 2003 graduating class went on to graduate and professional schools.
Expenses for 2003–04 *Application fee:* $50. *Comprehensive fee:* $35,700 includes full-time tuition ($26,964), mandatory fees ($136), and college room and board ($8600). *College room only:* $4600. Full-time tuition and fees vary according to program. Room and board charges vary according to board plan. *Part-time tuition:* $3,371 per course. Part-time tuition varies according to program.
Financial Aid Forms of aid include need-based and non-need-based scholarships and part-time jobs. The average aided 2002–03 undergraduate received an aid package worth $23,861. The priority application deadline for financial aid is February 1.
Freshman Admission Scripps requires an essay, a high school transcript, 3 recommendations, a graded writing sample, SAT I or ACT scores, and TOEFL scores for international students. A minimum 3.0 high school GPA and an interview are recommended. The application deadline for regular admission is February 1; for early decision plan 1 it is November 1; and for early decision plan 2 it is January 1.
Transfer Admission The application deadline for admission is April 1.
Entrance Difficulty Scripps assesses its entrance difficulty level as very difficult. For the fall 2003 freshman class, 54 percent of the applicants were accepted.

For Further Information Contact Ms. Patricia F. Goldsmith, Dean of Admission and Financial Aid, Scripps College, 1030 Columbia Avenue, Claremont, CA 91711-3948. *Telephone:* 909-621-8149 or 800-770-1333 (toll-free). *Fax:* 909-607-7508. *E-mail:* admission@scrippscollege.edu. *Web site:* http://www.scrippscollege.edu/.

SHASTA BIBLE COLLEGE

Redding, California

Shasta Bible College is a coed, private, nondenominational, comprehensive institution, founded in 1971, offering degrees at the associate, bachelor's, and master's levels. It has a 25-acre campus in Redding.

Academic Information The faculty has 28 members (21% full-time), 82% with terminal degrees. The undergraduate student-faculty ratio is 11:1. The library holds 30,321 titles and 103 serial subscriptions. Special programs include academic remediation, double majors, independent study, distance learning, part-time degree programs, and adult/continuing education programs. The most frequently chosen baccalaureate fields are education, philosophy, religion, and theology.
Student Body Statistics The student body totals 178, of whom 84 are undergraduates (43 freshmen). 36 percent are women and 64 percent are men. Students come from 5 states and territories and 1 other country. 97 percent are from California. 3.6 percent are international students.
Expenses for 2004–05 *Application fee:* $35. *Tuition:* $6000 full-time, $200 per unit part-time. *Mandatory fees:* $300 full-time, $300 per year part-time. *College room only:* $1575.
Financial Aid Forms of aid include need-based and non-need-based scholarships and part-time jobs. The average aided 2003–04 undergraduate received an aid package worth an estimated $4019. The application deadline for financial aid is continuous.
Freshman Admission Shasta Bible College requires an essay, a high school transcript, 4 recommendations, and TOEFL scores for international students.
Entrance Difficulty Shasta Bible College has an open admission policy.

For Further Information Contact Mr. Mark A. Mueller, Registrar, Shasta Bible College, 2951 Goodwater Avenue, Redding, CA 96002. *Telephone:* 530-221-4275 Ext. 205, 800-800-45BC (toll-free in-state), or 800-800-6929 (toll-free out-of-state). *Fax:* 530-221-6929. *E-mail:* ggunn@shasta.edu. *Web site:* http://www.shasta.edu/.

SILICON VALLEY COLLEGE

Emeryville, California

Silicon Valley College is a coed, proprietary, primarily two-year college, founded in 2001, offering degrees at the associate and bachelor's levels.

For Further Information Contact Ms. Marianne Dulay, Admissions Representative, Silicon Valley College, 1400 65th Street, Suite 200, Emeryville, CA 94608. *Telephone:* 510-601-0133 Ext. 14 or 800-750-5627 (toll-free in-state). *Fax:* 510-601-0793. *E-mail:* mdulay@svcollege.com. *Web site:* http://www.siliconvalley.edu/.

SILICON VALLEY COLLEGE

Fremont, California

Silicon Valley College is a coed, proprietary, primarily two-year college, founded in 1989, offering degrees at the associate and bachelor's levels.

Expenses for 2003–04 *Application fee:* $125. *Tuition:* $9450 full-time. *Mandatory fees:* $625 full-time. Full-time tuition and fees vary according to program.

For Further Information Contact Mr. Anton Croos, Admissions Director, Silicon Valley College, 41350 Christy Street, Fremont, CA 94538. *Telephone:* 510-623-9966 Ext. 212 or 800-750-5627 (toll-free in-state). *Fax:* 510-623-9822. *E-mail:* acroos@svcollege.com. *Web site:* http://www.siliconvalley.edu/.

SILICON VALLEY COLLEGE

San Jose, California

Silicon Valley College is a coed, proprietary, primarily two-year college, founded in 1999, offering degrees at the associate and bachelor's levels.

Expenses for 2003–04 *Application fee:* $125. *Tuition:* $9450 full-time. *Mandatory fees:* $625 full-time. Full-time tuition and fees vary according to program.

For Further Information Contact Ms. Patricia Fraser, Admissions Director, Silicon Valley College, 6201 San Ignacio Avenue, San Jose, CA 95119. *Telephone:* 408-360-0840 Ext. 247 or 800-750-5627 (toll-free in-state). *Fax:* 408-360-0840. *E-mail:* pfraser@svcollege.com. *Web site:* http://www.siliconvalley.edu/.

SILICON VALLEY COLLEGE

Walnut Creek, California

Silicon Valley College is a coed, proprietary, primarily two-year college, founded in 1997, offering degrees at the associate and bachelor's levels. It is located in Walnut Creek near San Francisco.

Academic Information The faculty has 17 members (71% full-time), 18% with terminal degrees. The library holds 1,000 titles and 50 audiovisual materials. Special programs include cooperative (work-study) education and accelerated degree programs.
Student Body Statistics The student body is made up of 472 undergraduates. Students come from 4 states and territories. 0.4 percent are international students.
Expenses for 2004–05 *Application fee:* $125. *Tuition:* $12,000 full-time. Full-time tuition varies according to degree level.
Freshman Admission Silicon Valley College requires a high school transcript, an interview, entrance exam, and CPAt. An essay is required for some.
Transfer Admission A college transcript is required for some.

For Further Information Contact Mr. Mark Millen, Admissions Director, Silicon Valley College, 2800 Mitchell Drive, Walnut Creek, CA 94598. *Telephone:* 925-280-0235 Ext. 37 or 800-750-5627 (toll-free in-state). *E-mail:* mmillen@svcollege.com. *Web site:* http://www.siliconvalley.edu/.

SILICON VALLEY UNIVERSITY

San Jose, California

For Information Write to Silicon Valley University, San Jose, CA 95134.

SIMPSON COLLEGE AND GRADUATE SCHOOL

Redding, California

Simpson is a coed, private, comprehensive institution, founded in 1921, affiliated with The Christian and Missionary Alliance, offering degrees at the associate, bachelor's, and master's levels. It has a 92-acre campus in Redding.

Academic Information The faculty has 80 members (52% full-time). The undergraduate student-faculty ratio is 17:1. The library holds 62,237 titles, 327 serial subscriptions, and 2,021 audiovisual materials. Special programs include services for learning-disabled students, an honors program, study abroad, advanced placement credit, accelerated degree programs, double majors, independent study, distance learning, self-designed majors, summer session for credit, part-time degree programs (daytime, evenings, summer), adult/continuing education programs, internships, and arrangement for off-campus study with Coalition for Christian Colleges and Universities. The most frequently chosen baccalaureate fields are business/marketing, liberal arts/general studies, psychology.
Student Body Statistics The student body totals 1,175, of whom 964 are undergraduates (154 freshmen). 63 percent are women and 37 percent are men. Students come from 24 states and territories. 86 percent are from California. 0.5 percent are international students.
Expenses for 2003–04 *Application fee:* $20. *Comprehensive fee:* $20,500 includes full-time tuition ($14,760) and college room and board ($5740). Room and board charges vary according to board plan. *Part-time tuition:* $620 per credit hour.
Financial Aid Forms of aid include need-based and non-need-based scholarships and part-time jobs. The average aided 2003–04 undergraduate received an aid package worth an estimated $12,507. The priority application deadline for financial aid is March 2.
Freshman Admission Simpson requires an essay, a high school transcript, a minimum 2.0 high school GPA, 2 recommendations, Christian commitment, SAT I or ACT scores, and TOEFL scores for international students. An interview is required for some. The application deadline for regular admission is rolling.
Transfer Admission The application deadline for admission is rolling.
Entrance Difficulty Simpson assesses its entrance difficulty level as moderately difficult. For the fall 2003 freshman class, 95 percent of the applicants were accepted.

For Further Information Contact Mrs. Beth Spencer, Director of Enrollment Support, Simpson College and Graduate School, 2211 College View Drive, Redding, CA 96003. *Telephone:* 530-226-4606 Ext. 2609 or 800-598-2493 (toll-free). *Fax:* 530-226-4861. *E-mail:* admissions@simpsonca.edu. *Web site:* http://www.simpsonca.edu/.

SOKA UNIVERSITY OF AMERICA

Aliso Viejo, California

For Information Write to Soka University of America, Aliso Viejo, CA 92656.

SONOMA STATE UNIVERSITY

Rohnert Park, California

SSU is a coed, public, comprehensive unit of California State University System, founded in 1960, offering degrees at the bachelor's and master's levels. It has a 280-acre campus in Rohnert Park near San Francisco.

Academic Information The faculty has 590 members (42% full-time), 61% with terminal degrees. The undergraduate student-faculty ratio is 22:1. The library holds 602,415 titles, 21,040 serial subscriptions, and 27,799 audiovisual materials. Special programs include academic remediation, services for learning-disabled students, an honors program, cooperative (work-study) education, study abroad, advanced placement credit, accelerated degree programs, ESL programs, double majors, independent study, distance learning, self-designed majors, summer session for credit, part-time degree programs (daytime, evenings), adult/continuing education programs, internships, and arrangement for off-campus study with other units of the California State University System, National Student Exchange, Mills College. The most frequently chosen baccalaureate fields are business/marketing, psychology, social sciences and history.
Student Body Statistics The student body totals 8,371, of whom 6,996 are undergraduates (1,303 freshmen). 63 percent are women and 37 percent are men. Students come from 39 states and territories and 36 other countries. 98 percent are from California. 1 percent are international students.
Expenses for 2003–04 *Application fee:* $55. *State resident tuition:* $0 full-time. *Nonresident tuition:* $8460 full-time. *Mandatory fees:* $3010 full-time. *College room and board:* $7411. *College room only:* $4645. Room and board charges vary according to board plan and housing facility.
Financial Aid Forms of aid include need-based and non-need-based scholarships, athletic grants, and part-time jobs. The average aided

2003–04 undergraduate received an aid package worth an estimated $6838. The priority application deadline for financial aid is January 31.
Freshman Admission SSU requires a high school transcript, SAT I or ACT scores, and TOEFL scores for international students. The application deadline for regular admission is December 31.
Transfer Admission The application deadline for admission is January 31.
Entrance Difficulty SSU assesses its entrance difficulty level as moderately difficult; very difficult for out-of-state applicants. For the fall 2003 freshman class, 84 percent of the applicants were accepted.

For Further Information Contact Mr. Gustavo Flores, Interim Director of Admissions, Sonoma State University, 1801 East Cotati Avenue, Rohnert Park, CA 94928. *Telephone:* 707-664-2846. *Fax:* 707-664-2060. *E-mail:* csumentor@sonoma.edu. *Web site:* http://www.sonoma.edu/.

SOUTHERN CALIFORNIA BIBLE COLLEGE & SEMINARY

El Cajon, California

For Information Write to Southern California Bible College & Seminary, El Cajon, CA 92019.

SOUTHERN CALIFORNIA COLLEGE

See Vanguard University of Southern California

SOUTHERN CALIFORNIA INSTITUTE OF ARCHITECTURE

Los Angeles, California

SCI-Arc is a coed, private, comprehensive institution, founded in 1972, offering degrees at the bachelor's, master's, and first professional levels in architecture.

Academic Information The faculty has 80 members. The undergraduate student-faculty ratio is 15:1. The library holds 10,000 titles and 70 serial subscriptions. Special programs include academic remediation, cooperative (work-study) education, study abroad, advanced placement credit, ESL programs, summer session for credit, and internships.
Student Body Statistics The student body totals 447, of whom 183 are undergraduates (5 freshmen). 27 percent are women and 73 percent are men. Students come from 35 states and territories and 17 other countries. 12 percent are international students. 12 percent of the 2003 graduating class went on to graduate and professional schools.
Expenses for 2004–05 *Application fee:* $60. *Tuition:* $18,376 full-time. *Mandatory fees:* $70 full-time.
Financial Aid Forms of aid include need-based scholarships and part-time jobs. The average aided 2003–04 undergraduate received an aid package worth an estimated $9500. The priority application deadline for financial aid is March 2.
Freshman Admission SCI-Arc requires an essay, a high school transcript, a minimum 2.0 high school GPA, 3 recommendations, a portfolio, SAT I or ACT scores, and TOEFL scores for international students. An interview is recommended. The application deadline for regular admission is February 1.
Transfer Admission The application deadline for admission is rolling.
Entrance Difficulty SCI-Arc assesses its entrance difficulty level as moderately difficult.

For Further Information Contact Ms. Wenona Colinco, Director of Admissions, Southern California Institute of Architecture, Freight Yard, 960 East 3rd Street, Los Angeles, CA 90013. *Telephone:* 213-613-2200 Ext. 321 or 800-774-7242 (toll-free). *Fax:* 213-613-2260. *E-mail:* admissions@sciarc.edu. *Web site:* http://www.sciarc.edu/.

SOUTHERN CALIFORNIA INSTITUTE OF TECHNOLOGY

Anaheim, California

Southern California Institute of Technology is a proprietary, primarily two-year college, offering degrees at the associate, bachelor's, and master's levels.

For Further Information Contact Ms. Flor Rojas, Director of Admissions, Southern California Institute of Technology, 1900 West Crescent Avenue, Building B, Anaheim, CA 92801. *Telephone:* 714-520-5552. *Web site:* http://www.scitcollege.com/.

STANFORD UNIVERSITY

Stanford, California

Stanford is a coed, private university, founded in 1891, offering degrees at the bachelor's, master's, doctoral, and first professional levels. It has an 8,180-acre campus in Stanford near San Francisco.

Academic Information The faculty has 1,749 members (98% full-time), 99% with terminal degrees. The undergraduate student-faculty ratio is 7:1. The library holds 8 million titles, 50,056 serial subscriptions, and 1 million audiovisual materials. Special programs include services for learning-disabled students, an honors program, study abroad, advanced placement credit, double majors, independent study, self-designed majors, summer session for credit, internships, and arrangement for off-campus study with Howard University; Hopkins Marine Station; Spelman College; Morehouse College, Dartmouth College. The most frequently chosen baccalaureate fields are engineering/engineering technologies, interdisciplinary studies, social sciences and history.
Student Body Statistics The student body totals 17,823, of whom 7,054 are undergraduates (1,640 freshmen). 50 percent are women and 50 percent are men. Students come from 52 states and territories and 62 other countries. 52 percent are from California. 5.8 percent are international students. 30 percent of the 2003 graduating class went on to graduate and professional schools.
Expenses for 2004–05 *Application fee:* $75. *Comprehensive fee:* $39,347 includes full-time tuition ($29,847) and college room and board ($9500). *College room only:* $5012. Room and board charges vary according to board plan.
Financial Aid Forms of aid include need-based scholarships, athletic grants, and part-time jobs. The average aided 2002–03 undergraduate received an aid package worth $25,634. The priority application deadline for financial aid is February 1.
Freshman Admission Stanford requires an essay, a high school transcript, 2 recommendations, and SAT I or ACT scores. SAT II: Subject Test scores, SAT II: Writing Test scores, and TOEFL scores for international students are recommended. The application deadline for regular admission is December 15 and for early action it is November 1.
Transfer Admission The application deadline for admission is March 15.
Entrance Difficulty Stanford assesses its entrance difficulty level as most difficult. For the fall 2003 freshman class, 13 percent of the applicants were accepted.

For Further Information Contact Ms. Robin G. Mamlet, Dean of Undergraduate Admissions and Financial Aid, Stanford University, Old Union 232, 520 Lasuen Mall, Stanford, CA 94305. *Telephone:* 650-723-2091. *Fax:* 650-723-6050. *E-mail:* admission@stanford.edu. *Web site:* http://www.stanford.edu/.

THOMAS AQUINAS COLLEGE

Santa Paula, California

TAC is a coed, private, Roman Catholic, four-year college, founded in 1971, offering degrees at the bachelor's level. It has a 170-acre campus in Santa Paula near Los Angeles.

Thomas Aquinas College (continued)

Academic Information The faculty has 33 members (91% full-time), 73% with terminal degrees. The student-faculty ratio is 11:1. The library holds 51,000 titles, 80 serial subscriptions, and 2,200 audiovisual materials. The most frequently chosen baccalaureate field is liberal arts/general studies.

Student Body Statistics The student body is made up of 332 undergraduates (101 freshmen). 54 percent are women and 46 percent are men. Students come from 42 states and territories and 7 other countries. 47 percent are from California. 7.8 percent are international students.

Expenses for 2003–04 *Application fee:* $0. *Comprehensive fee:* $22,000 includes full-time tuition ($16,800) and college room and board ($5200).

Financial Aid Forms of aid include need-based scholarships and part-time jobs. The average aided 2003–04 undergraduate received an aid package worth an estimated $14,936. The application deadline for financial aid is continuous.

Freshman Admission TAC requires an essay, a high school transcript, 3 recommendations, SAT I or ACT scores, and TOEFL scores for international students. A minimum 2.0 high school GPA is recommended. An interview is required for some. The application deadline for regular admission is rolling.

Entrance Difficulty TAC assesses its entrance difficulty level as very difficult. For the fall 2003 freshman class, 78 percent of the applicants were accepted.

For Further Information Contact Mr. Thomas J. Susanka Jr., Director of Admissions, Thomas Aquinas College, 10000 North Ojai Road, Santa Paula, CA 93060-9980. *Telephone:* 805-525-4417 Ext. 361 or 800-634-9797 (toll-free). *Fax:* 805-525-9342. *E-mail:* admissions@thomasaquinas.edu. *Web site:* http://www.thomasaquinas.edu/.

TOURO UNIVERSITY INTERNATIONAL

Cypress, California

Touro University International is a coed, private university, offering degrees at the bachelor's, master's, and doctoral levels and postbachelor's certificates (offers only online degree programs).

Academic Information The faculty has 89 members (69% full-time), 98% with terminal degrees. The undergraduate student-faculty ratio is 18:1. The library holds 18,352 titles and 12,000 serial subscriptions. Special programs include distance learning, summer session for credit, part-time degree programs (daytime, evenings, weekends, summer), adult/continuing education programs, and arrangement for off-campus study. The most frequently chosen baccalaureate fields are business/marketing, computer/information sciences, health professions and related sciences.

Student Body Statistics The student body is made up of 1,748 undergraduates (112 freshmen). 33 percent are women and 67 percent are men. Students come from 50 states and territories and 15 other countries. 10 percent are from California. 5 percent of the 2003 graduating class went on to graduate and professional schools.

Expenses for 2004–05 *Application fee:* $75. *Tuition:* $7200 full-time, $225 per credit part-time.

Freshman Admission Touro University International requires a high school transcript, a minimum 3.0 high school GPA, and TOEFL scores for international students. An interview is recommended. An essay is required for some. The application deadline for regular admission is rolling.

Entrance Difficulty Touro University International has an open admission policy.

For Further Information Contact Wei Ren, Registrar, Touro University International, 5336 Plaza Drive, 3rd Floor, Cypress, CA 90630. *Telephone:* 714-816-0366. *Fax:* 714-827-7407. *E-mail:* registration@tourou.edu. *Web site:* http://www.tourou.edu/.

TRINITY LIFE BIBLE COLLEGE

Sacramento, California

For Information Write to Trinity Life Bible College, Sacramento, CA 95842.

UNITED STATES INTERNATIONAL UNIVERSITY

See Alliant International University

UNIVERSITY OF CALIFORNIA, BERKELEY

Berkeley, California

Cal is a coed, public unit of University of California System, founded in 1868, offering degrees at the bachelor's, master's, doctoral, and first professional levels. It has a 1,232-acre campus in Berkeley near San Francisco.

Academic Information The faculty has 1,889 members (78% full-time), 95% with terminal degrees. The undergraduate student-faculty ratio is 16:1. The library holds 14 million titles, 181,071 serial subscriptions, and 100,560 audiovisual materials. Special programs include services for learning-disabled students, an honors program, study abroad, advanced placement credit, accelerated degree programs, ESL programs, double majors, independent study, distance learning, self-designed majors, summer session for credit, adult/continuing education programs, internships, and arrangement for off-campus study with Holy Names College, Mills College, Dominican College, John F. Kennedy University, San Francisco State University, Sonoma State University, California State University, Hayward. The most frequently chosen baccalaureate fields are engineering/engineering technologies, biological/life sciences, social sciences and history.

Student Body Statistics The student body totals 33,076, of whom 23,206 are undergraduates (3,653 freshmen). 54 percent are women and 46 percent are men. Students come from 53 states and territories and 100 other countries. 89 percent are from California. 3 percent are international students.

Expenses for 2003–04 *Application fee:* $40. *State resident tuition:* $0 full-time. *Nonresident tuition:* $14,210 full-time. *Mandatory fees:* $5250 full-time. Full-time tuition and fees vary according to program. *College room and board:* $11,212. Room and board charges vary according to board plan and housing facility.

Financial Aid Forms of aid include need-based and non-need-based scholarships, athletic grants, and part-time jobs. The average aided 2003–04 undergraduate received an aid package worth an estimated $13,481. The application deadline for financial aid is March 2 with a priority deadline of March 2.

Freshman Admission Cal requires an essay, a high school transcript, SAT I or ACT scores, SAT II: Subject Test scores, SAT II: Writing Test scores, and TOEFL scores for international students. The application deadline for regular admission is November 30.

Transfer Admission The application deadline for admission is November 30.

Entrance Difficulty Cal assesses its entrance difficulty level as very difficult; most difficult for out-of-state applicants; most difficult for some engineering programs. For the fall 2003 freshman class, 24 percent of the applicants were accepted.

For Further Information Contact Ms. Pamela Burnett, Director of Undergraduate Admission and Relations with Schools, University of California, Berkeley, Berkeley, CA 94720. *Telephone:* 510-642-2316. *Fax:* 510-642-7333. *E-mail:* ouars@uclink.berkeley.edu. *Web site:* http://www.berkeley.edu/.

UNIVERSITY OF CALIFORNIA, DAVIS

Davis, California

UC Davis is a coed, public unit of University of California System, founded in 1905, offering degrees at the bachelor's, master's, doctoral, and first professional levels and postbachelor's certificates. It has a 5,993-acre campus in Davis near San Francisco.

Academic Information The faculty has 1,950 members (83% full-time), 98% with terminal degrees. The undergraduate student-faculty ratio is 20:1. The library holds 3 million titles and 45,665 serial subscriptions.

Special programs include academic remediation, services for learning-disabled students, an honors program, study abroad, advanced placement credit, Freshman Honors College, ESL programs, double majors, independent study, self-designed majors, summer session for credit, part-time degree programs, adult/continuing education programs, and internships. The most frequently chosen baccalaureate fields are biological/life sciences, engineering/engineering technologies, social sciences and history.
Student Body Statistics The student body totals 30,229, of whom 23,472 are undergraduates (4,786 freshmen). 56 percent are women and 44 percent are men. Students come from 49 states and territories and 113 other countries. 96 percent are from California. 1.8 percent are international students. 38 percent of the 2003 graduating class went on to graduate and professional schools.
Expenses for 2003–04 *Application fee:* $40. *State resident tuition:* $0 full-time. *Nonresident tuition:* $14,210 full-time. *Mandatory fees:* $5853 full-time. *College room and board:* $9,143. Room and board charges vary according to board plan.
Financial Aid Forms of aid include need-based and non-need-based scholarships and part-time jobs. The average aided 2003–04 undergraduate received an aid package worth an estimated $9864. The priority application deadline for financial aid is March 2.
Freshman Admission UC Davis requires an essay, a high school transcript, SAT I and SAT II or ACT scores, SAT II: Writing Test scores, and TOEFL scores for international students. The application deadline for regular admission is November 30.
Transfer Admission The application deadline for admission is November 30.
Entrance Difficulty UC Davis assesses its entrance difficulty level as very difficult. For the fall 2003 freshman class, 60 percent of the applicants were accepted.

For Further Information Contact Dr. Gary Tudor, Director of Undergraduate Admissions, University of California, Davis, Undergraduate Admission and Outreach Services, 175 Mrak Hall, Davis, CA 95616. *Telephone:* 530-752-2971. *Fax:* 530-752-1280. *E-mail:* thinkucd@ucdavis.edu. *Web site:* http://www.ucdavis.edu/.

UNIVERSITY OF CALIFORNIA, IRVINE

Irvine, California

UCI is a coed, public unit of University of California System, founded in 1965, offering degrees at the bachelor's, master's, doctoral, and first professional levels and postbachelor's certificates. It has a 1,477-acre campus in Irvine near Los Angeles.

Academic Information The faculty has 1,194 members (71% full-time), 98% with terminal degrees. The undergraduate student-faculty ratio is 18:1. The library holds 3 million titles, 28,416 serial subscriptions, and 101,335 audiovisual materials. Special programs include academic remediation, services for learning-disabled students, an honors program, cooperative (work-study) education, study abroad, advanced placement credit, ESL programs, double majors, independent study, summer session for credit, adult/continuing education programs, internships, and arrangement for off-campus study with other campuses of University of California System. The most frequently chosen baccalaureate fields are biological/life sciences, psychology, social sciences and history.
Student Body Statistics The student body totals 24,874, of whom 19,967 are undergraduates (4,043 freshmen). 50 percent are women and 50 percent are men. Students come from 45 states and territories and 38 other countries. 98 percent are from California. 2.6 percent are international students.
Expenses for 2003–04 *Application fee:* $40. *State resident tuition:* $0 full-time. *Nonresident tuition:* $14,210 full-time. *Mandatory fees:* $6165 full-time. *College room and board:* $8055. Room and board charges vary according to board plan and housing facility.
Financial Aid Forms of aid include need-based and non-need-based scholarships, athletic grants, and part-time jobs. The average aided 2003–04 undergraduate received an aid package worth an estimated $10,882. The priority application deadline for financial aid is March 2.
Freshman Admission UCI requires an essay, a high school transcript, a minimum 2.0 high school GPA, SAT I and SAT II or ACT scores, SAT II: Writing Test scores, and TOEFL scores for international students. The application deadline for regular admission is November 30.
Transfer Admission The application deadline for admission is November 30.
Entrance Difficulty UCI assesses its entrance difficulty level as moderately difficult; most difficult for out-of-state applicants. For the fall 2003 freshman class, 54 percent of the applicants were accepted.

For Further Information Contact Marguerit Bonous-Hammarth, Director of Admissions and Relations with Schools, University of California, Irvine, 204 Administration, Irvine, CA 92697-1075. *Telephone:* 949-824-6703. *Web site:* http://www.uci.edu/.

UNIVERSITY OF CALIFORNIA, LOS ANGELES

Los Angeles, California

UCLA is a coed, public unit of University of California System, founded in 1919, offering degrees at the bachelor's, master's, doctoral, and first professional levels. It has a 419-acre campus in Los Angeles.

Academic Information The faculty has 2,462 members (76% full-time), 98% with terminal degrees. The undergraduate student-faculty ratio is 18:1. The library holds 8 million titles, 94,801 serial subscriptions, and 5 million audiovisual materials. Special programs include academic remediation, services for learning-disabled students, an honors program, study abroad, advanced placement credit, Freshman Honors College, ESL programs, double majors, independent study, distance learning, self-designed majors, summer session for credit, adult/continuing education programs, internships, and arrangement for off-campus study with University of Southern California. The most frequently chosen baccalaureate fields are psychology, biological/life sciences, social sciences and history.
Student Body Statistics The student body totals 38,598, of whom 25,715 are undergraduates (4,268 freshmen). 56 percent are women and 44 percent are men. Students come from 49 states and territories and 66 other countries. 96 percent are from California. 3.4 percent are international students.
Expenses for 2003–04 *Application fee:* $40. *State resident tuition:* $0 full-time. *Nonresident tuition:* $14,210 full-time. *Mandatory fees:* $5820 full-time. *College room and board:* $10,452. Room and board charges vary according to board plan and housing facility.
Financial Aid Forms of aid include need-based and non-need-based scholarships, athletic grants, and part-time jobs. The average aided 2003–04 undergraduate received an aid package worth an estimated $12,122. The priority application deadline for financial aid is March 2.
Freshman Admission UCLA requires an essay, a high school transcript, SAT I or ACT scores, SAT II: Subject Test scores, SAT II: Writing Test scores, TOEFL scores for international students, and SAT II Subject Test in math, third SAT II Subject Test. The application deadline for regular admission is November 30.
Transfer Admission The application deadline for admission is November 30.
Entrance Difficulty UCLA assesses its entrance difficulty level as very difficult. For the fall 2003 freshman class, 24 percent of the applicants were accepted.

For Further Information Contact Mr. Vu T. Tran, Director of Undergraduate Admissions, University of California, Los Angeles, 405 Hilgard Avenue, Box 951436, Los Angeles, CA 90095-1436. *Telephone:* 310-825-3101. *E-mail:* ugadm@saonet.ucla.edu. *Web site:* http://www.ucla.edu/.

UNIVERSITY OF CALIFORNIA, RIVERSIDE

Riverside, California

UCR is a coed, public unit of University of California System, founded in 1954, offering degrees at the bachelor's, master's, and doctoral levels. It has a 1,200-acre campus in Riverside near Los Angeles.

University of California, Riverside (continued)

Academic Information The faculty has 816 members (81% full-time), 98% with terminal degrees. The undergraduate student-faculty ratio is 19:1. The library holds 2 million titles, 21,323 serial subscriptions, and 141,663 audiovisual materials. Special programs include academic remediation, services for learning-disabled students, an honors program, cooperative (work-study) education, study abroad, advanced placement credit, accelerated degree programs, Freshman Honors College, ESL programs, double majors, independent study, distance learning, self-designed majors, summer session for credit, part-time degree programs (daytime, evenings, summer), adult/continuing education programs, internships, and arrangement for off-campus study with University of California, Santa Barbara, University of California, Davis, University of California, Los Angeles. The most frequently chosen baccalaureate fields are business/marketing, biological/life sciences, social sciences and history.
Student Body Statistics The student body totals 17,302, of whom 15,282 are undergraduates (3,889 freshmen). 54 percent are women and 46 percent are men. Students come from 40 states and territories and 21 other countries. 99 percent are from California. 1.7 percent are international students. 35 percent of the 2003 graduating class went on to graduate and professional schools.
Expenses for 2003–04 *Application fee:* $40. *State resident tuition:* $0 full-time. *Nonresident tuition:* $13,731 full-time. *Mandatory fees:* $5950 full-time. *College room and board:* $9350. Room and board charges vary according to board plan and housing facility.
Financial Aid Forms of aid include need-based and non-need-based scholarships, athletic grants, and part-time jobs. The average aided 2003–04 undergraduate received an aid package worth an estimated $10,439. The priority application deadline for financial aid is March 2.
Freshman Admission UCR requires an essay, a high school transcript, a minimum 2.82 high school GPA, SAT I or ACT scores, SAT II: Subject Test scores, SAT II: Writing Test scores, and TOEFL scores for international students. The application deadline for regular admission is November 30.
Transfer Admission The application deadline for admission is November 30.
Entrance Difficulty UCR assesses its entrance difficulty level as very difficult. For the fall 2003 freshman class, 79 percent of the applicants were accepted.

For Further Information Contact LaRae Lundgren, Director of Undergraduate Admission, University of California, Riverside, 1138 Hinderaker Hall, 900 University Avenue, Riverside, CA 92521. *Telephone:* 909-787-3411. *Fax:* 909-787-6344. *E-mail:* discover@pop.ucr.edu. *Web site:* http://www.ucr.edu/.

UNIVERSITY OF CALIFORNIA, SAN DIEGO

La Jolla, California

UCSD is a coed, public unit of University of California System, founded in 1959, offering degrees at the bachelor's, master's, doctoral, and first professional levels. It has a 1,976-acre campus in La Jolla near San Diego.

Academic Information The faculty has 1,092 members (84% full-time), 98% with terminal degrees. The undergraduate student-faculty ratio is 19:1. The library holds 3 million titles, 19,517 serial subscriptions, and 381,099 audiovisual materials. Special programs include services for learning-disabled students, an honors program, cooperative (work-study) education, study abroad, advanced placement credit, accelerated degree programs, Freshman Honors College, ESL programs, double majors, independent study, self-designed majors, summer session for credit, internships, and arrangement for off-campus study with Dartmouth College, Spelman College, Morehouse College. The most frequently chosen baccalaureate fields are biological/life sciences, engineering/engineering technologies, social sciences and history.
Student Body Statistics The student body totals 24,707, of whom 19,872 are undergraduates (3,799 freshmen). 52 percent are women and 48 percent are men. 97 percent are from California. 3.2 percent are international students. 35 percent of the 2003 graduating class went on to graduate and professional schools.
Expenses for 2003–04 *Application fee:* $40. *One-time mandatory fee:* $597. *State resident tuition:* $0 full-time. *Nonresident tuition:* $13,730 full-time. *Mandatory fees:* $5507 full-time. Full-time tuition and fees vary according to location. *College room and board:* $8620. Room and board charges vary according to board plan and location.
Financial Aid Forms of aid include need-based and non-need-based scholarships and part-time jobs. The average aided 2003–04 undergraduate received an aid package worth an estimated $12,420. The priority application deadline for financial aid is March 2.
Freshman Admission UCSD requires an essay, a high school transcript, a minimum 2.8 high school GPA, SAT I or ACT scores, TOEFL scores for international students, and 3 SAT II Subject Tests (including SAT II: Writing Test). A minimum 3.4 high school GPA is required for some. The application deadline for regular admission is November 30.
Transfer Admission The application deadline for admission is November 30.
Entrance Difficulty UCSD assesses its entrance difficulty level as very difficult; most difficult for out-of-state applicants. For the fall 2003 freshman class, 42 percent of the applicants were accepted.

For Further Information Contact Mr. Nathan Evans, Associate Director of Admissions and Relations with Schools, University of California, San Diego, 9500 Gilman Drive, 0021, La Jolla, CA 92093-0021. *Telephone:* 858-534-4831. *E-mail:* admissionsinfo@ucsd.edu. *Web site:* http://www.ucsd.edu/.

UNIVERSITY OF CALIFORNIA, SANTA BARBARA

Santa Barbara, California

UCSB is a coed, public unit of University of California System, founded in 1909, offering degrees at the bachelor's, master's, and doctoral levels and first professional certificates. It has a 989-acre campus in Santa Barbara.

Academic Information The faculty has 1,036 members (83% full-time). The undergraduate student-faculty ratio is 19:1. The library holds 3 million titles, 18,898 serial subscriptions, and 103,495 audiovisual materials. Special programs include services for learning-disabled students, an honors program, cooperative (work-study) education, study abroad, advanced placement credit, accelerated degree programs, ESL programs, double majors, independent study, distance learning, self-designed majors, summer session for credit, internships, and arrangement for off-campus study with other campuses of the University of California System. The most frequently chosen baccalaureate fields are business/marketing, interdisciplinary studies, social sciences and history.
Student Body Statistics The student body totals 20,847, of whom 17,844 are undergraduates (3,993 freshmen). 55 percent are women and 45 percent are men. Students come from 51 states and territories and 110 other countries. 95 percent are from California. 1.4 percent are international students. 24 percent of the 2003 graduating class went on to graduate and professional schools.
Expenses for 2003–04 *Application fee:* $40. *State resident tuition:* $0 full-time. *Nonresident tuition:* $13,731 full-time. *Mandatory fees:* $5639 full-time. *College room and board:* $9236. *College room only:* $6849.
Financial Aid Forms of aid include need-based and non-need-based scholarships, athletic grants, and part-time jobs. The average aided 2003–04 undergraduate received an aid package worth an estimated $11,068. The priority application deadline for financial aid is March 2.
Freshman Admission UCSB requires an essay, a high school transcript, SAT I or ACT scores, SAT II: Subject Test scores, SAT II: Writing Test scores, and TOEFL scores for international students. An interview is required for some. The application deadline for regular admission is November 30.
Transfer Admission The application deadline for admission is November 30.

Entrance Difficulty UCSB assesses its entrance difficulty level as very difficult. For the fall 2003 freshman class, 50 percent of the applicants were accepted.

For Further Information Contact Ms. Christine Van Gieson, Director of Admissions/Outreach Services, University of California, Santa Barbara, 1234 Cheadle Hall, Santa Barbara, CA 93106-2014. *Telephone:* 805-893-2485. *Fax:* 805-893-2676. *E-mail:* appinfo@sa.ucsb.edu. *Web site:* http://www.ucsb.edu/.

UNIVERSITY OF CALIFORNIA, SANTA CRUZ

Santa Cruz, California

UCSC is a coed, public unit of University of California System, founded in 1965, offering degrees at the bachelor's, master's, and doctoral levels and postbachelor's certificates. It has a 2,000-acre campus in Santa Cruz near San Francisco and San Jose.

Academic Information The faculty has 717 members (72% full-time), 98% with terminal degrees. The undergraduate student-faculty ratio is 19:1. The library holds 1 million titles, 9,190 serial subscriptions, and 43,785 audiovisual materials. Special programs include academic remediation, services for learning-disabled students, an honors program, cooperative (work-study) education, study abroad, advanced placement credit, Freshman Honors College, ESL programs, double majors, independent study, self-designed majors, summer session for credit, part-time degree programs, adult/continuing education programs, internships, and arrangement for off-campus study with other campuses of the University of California System, University of New Hampshire, University of New Mexico. The most frequently chosen baccalaureate fields are social sciences and history, psychology, visual/performing arts.
Student Body Statistics The student body totals 14,997, of whom 13,660 are undergraduates (3,434 freshmen). 55 percent are women and 45 percent are men. 95 percent are from California. 0.9 percent are international students.
Expenses for 2003–04 *Application fee:* $40. *State resident tuition:* $0 full-time. *Nonresident tuition:* $18,109 full-time. *Mandatory fees:* $4629 full-time. *College room and board:* $10,314. Room and board charges vary according to board plan and housing facility.
Financial Aid Forms of aid include need-based and non-need-based scholarships and part-time jobs. The priority application deadline for financial aid is March 2.
Freshman Admission UCSC requires an essay, a high school transcript, SAT I and SAT II or ACT scores, TOEFL scores for international students, and SAT I or ACT composite score and three SAT II subject tests required including SAT II Writing, Math Level 1 or 2, and one test from each of the following areas: english literature, foreign language, science or social studies. The application deadline for regular admission is November 30.
Transfer Admission The application deadline for admission is November 30.
Entrance Difficulty UCSC assesses its entrance difficulty level as very difficult. For the fall 2003 freshman class, 80 percent of the applicants were accepted.

For Further Information Contact Mr. Kevin M. Browne, Executive Director of Admissions and University Registrar, University of California, Santa Cruz, Admissions Office, Cook House, Santa Cruz, CA 95064. *Telephone:* 831-459-5779. *Fax:* 831-459-4452. *E-mail:* admissions@ucsc.edu. *Web site:* http://www.ucsc.edu/.

UNIVERSITY OF JUDAISM

Bel Air, California

UJ is a coed, private, Jewish, comprehensive institution, founded in 1947, offering degrees at the bachelor's and master's levels. It has a 28-acre campus in Bel Air near Los Angeles.

Academic Information The faculty has 91 members (21% full-time), 42% with terminal degrees. The undergraduate student-faculty ratio is 7:1. The library holds 105,000 titles and 400 serial subscriptions. Special programs include academic remediation, services for learning-disabled students, an honors program, study abroad, advanced placement credit, accelerated degree programs, independent study, self-designed majors, part-time degree programs, adult/continuing education programs, internships, and arrangement for off-campus study with Mount Saint Mary's College, Cedars-Sinai Medical Center, University of California, Los Angeles.
Student Body Statistics The student body totals 287, of whom 142 are undergraduates. Students come from 22 states and territories and 4 other countries. 69 percent are from California. 5.6 percent are international students. 85 percent of the 2003 graduating class went on to graduate and professional schools.
Expenses for 2004–05 *Application fee:* $35. *Comprehensive fee:* $27,830 includes full-time tuition ($17,500), mandatory fees ($750), and college room and board ($9580). *College room only:* $4970. *Part-time tuition:* $730 per credit.
Financial Aid Forms of aid include need-based and non-need-based scholarships and part-time jobs. The average aided 2003–04 undergraduate received an aid package worth an estimated $19,214. The priority application deadline for financial aid is March 2.
Freshman Admission UJ requires an essay, a high school transcript, 2 recommendations, SAT I or ACT scores, and TOEFL scores for international students. A minimum 3.2 high school GPA and an interview are recommended. An interview is required for some. The application deadline for regular admission is January 31 and for early decision it is November 15.
Transfer Admission The application deadline for admission is April 15.
Entrance Difficulty UJ assesses its entrance difficulty level as moderately difficult; very difficult for President's Scholars Program. For the fall 2003 freshman class, 79 percent of the applicants were accepted.

For Further Information Contact Ms. Shoshana Kapnek, Assistant Director of Undergraduate Admissions, University of Judaism, 15600 Mulholland Drive, Bel Air, CA 90077. *Telephone:* 310-476-9777 Ext. 241 or 888-853-6763 (toll-free). *Fax:* 310-471-3657. *E-mail:* admissions@uj.edu. *Web site:* http://www.uj.edu/.

UNIVERSITY OF LA VERNE

La Verne, California

ULV is a coed, private university, founded in 1891, offering degrees at the associate, bachelor's, master's, doctoral, and first professional levels and post-master's and postbachelor's certificates (also offers continuing education program with significant enrollment not reflected in profile). It has a 26-acre campus in La Verne near Los Angeles.

Academic Information The faculty has 263 members (40% full-time), 40% with terminal degrees. The undergraduate student-faculty ratio is 9:1. The library holds 215,000 titles and 4,500 serial subscriptions. Special programs include academic remediation, services for learning-disabled students, an honors program, study abroad, advanced placement credit, accelerated degree programs, Freshman Honors College, ESL programs, double majors, independent study, distance learning, self-designed majors, summer session for credit, part-time degree programs (daytime, evenings, weekends, summer), external degree programs, adult/continuing education programs, internships, and arrangement for off-campus study with Elizabethtown College, Juniata College, McPherson College, Bridgewater College, Manchester College. The most frequently chosen baccalaureate fields are business/marketing, liberal arts/general studies, social sciences and history.
Student Body Statistics The student body totals 3,604, of whom 1,396 are undergraduates (290 freshmen). 63 percent are women and 37 percent are men. Students come from 13 states and territories and 9 other countries. 95 percent are from California. 0.7 percent are international students.

University of La Verne (continued)

Expenses for 2004–05 *Application fee:* $50. *One-time mandatory fee:* $110. *Comprehensive fee:* $30,010 includes full-time tuition ($21,500) and college room and board ($8510). *College room only:* $4150. Full-time tuition varies according to course load, degree level, location, and program. Room and board charges vary according to board plan, housing facility, and location. *Part-time tuition:* varies with course load, degree level, location, program.
Financial Aid Forms of aid include need-based and non-need-based scholarships and part-time jobs. The average aided 2003–04 undergraduate received an aid package worth an estimated $24,188. The priority application deadline for financial aid is March 2.
Freshman Admission ULV requires an essay, a high school transcript, 2 recommendations, SAT I or ACT scores, and TOEFL scores for international students. An interview is recommended. The application deadline for regular admission is February 1.
Transfer Admission The application deadline for admission is April 1.
Entrance Difficulty ULV assesses its entrance difficulty level as moderately difficult. For the fall 2003 freshman class, 56 percent of the applicants were accepted.

SPECIAL MESSAGE TO STUDENTS

Social Life University of La Verne (ULV) students participate in activities such as intercollegiate and intramural sports; fraternities and sororities; cultural, political, or religious clubs; student government; campus publications; and theater. Three residence halls house a culturally and ethnically diverse student body.

Academic Highlights The University comprises the College of Arts and Sciences, School of Education, School of Business and Global Studies, School of Organizational Management, School of Continuing Education, and the College of Law. ULV offers bachelor's, master's, and doctoral degrees. Students are encouraged to take advantage of the study-abroad program to expand and enhance their lives. The University of La Verne campus in Greece is one of the most popular study-abroad locations.

Interviews and Campus Visits Students and their families are encouraged to visit the University. Located in Miller Hall, the Office of Undergraduate Admissions is open from 8 a.m. to 5 p.m., Monday through Friday. For more information about campus visits, students should call the Office of Undergraduate Admissions at 909-392-2800 or 800-876-4858 (toll-free). The nearest commercial airport is Ontario International.

For Further Information Write to the Office of Undergraduate Admissions, University of La Verne, 1950 3rd Street, La Verne, CA 91750. *E-mail:* admissions@ulv.edu. *Web site:* http://www.ulv.edu.

UNIVERSITY OF PHOENIX–NORTHERN CALIFORNIA CAMPUS

Pleasanton, California

University of Phoenix–Northern California Campus is a coed, proprietary, comprehensive institution, offering degrees at the associate, bachelor's, master's, and doctoral levels and post-master's and postbachelor's certificates (courses conducted at 121 campuses and learning centers in 25 states).

Academic Information The faculty has 1,424 members, 23% with terminal degrees. The undergraduate student-faculty ratio is 8:1. The library holds 27 million titles and 11,648 serial subscriptions. Special programs include advanced placement credit, accelerated degree programs, independent study, distance learning, external degree programs, and adult/continuing education programs. The most frequently chosen baccalaureate fields are business/marketing, computer/information sciences, health professions and related sciences.
Student Body Statistics The student body totals 4,765, of whom 3,731 are undergraduates (123 freshmen). 60 percent are women and 40 percent are men. 12.1 percent are international students.
Expenses for 2003–04 *Application fee:* $85. *Tuition:* $12,150 full-time, $405 per credit part-time.
Financial Aid Forms of aid include need-based and non-need-based scholarships. The average aided 2002–03 undergraduate received an aid package worth $1311. The application deadline for financial aid is continuous.
Freshman Admission University of Phoenix–Northern California Campus requires 1 recommendation, 2 years of work experience, 23 years of age, and TOEFL scores for international students. A high school transcript is required for some. The application deadline for regular admission is rolling.
Transfer Admission The application deadline for admission is rolling.
Entrance Difficulty University of Phoenix–Northern California Campus has an open admission policy.

For Further Information Contact Ms. Beth Barilla, Director of Admissions, University of Phoenix–Northern California Campus, 4615 East Elwood Street, Mail Stop AA-K101, Phoenix, AZ 85040-1958. *Telephone:* 480-557-1712 or 877-4-STUDENT (toll-free). *Fax:* 480-594-1758. *E-mail:* beth.barilla@phoenix.edu. *Web site:* http://www.phoenix.edu/.

UNIVERSITY OF PHOENIX–SACRAMENTO CAMPUS

Sacramento, California

University of Phoenix–Sacramento Campus is a coed, proprietary, comprehensive institution, founded in 1993, offering degrees at the associate, bachelor's, master's, and doctoral levels and post-master's and postbachelor's certificates (courses conducted at 121 campuses and learning centers in 25 states).

Academic Information The faculty has 608 members (1% full-time), 18% with terminal degrees. The undergraduate student-faculty ratio is 8:1. The library holds 27 million titles and 11,648 serial subscriptions. Special programs include advanced placement credit, accelerated degree programs, independent study, distance learning, external degree programs, and adult/continuing education programs. The most frequently chosen baccalaureate fields are business/marketing, computer/information sciences, health professions and related sciences.
Student Body Statistics The student body totals 2,192, of whom 1,730 are undergraduates (45 freshmen). 62 percent are women and 38 percent are men. 15 percent are international students.
Expenses for 2003–04 *Application fee:* $85. *Tuition:* $12,540 full-time, $418 per credit part-time.
Financial Aid Forms of aid include need-based and non-need-based scholarships. The average aided 2002–03 undergraduate received an aid package worth $1413. The application deadline for financial aid is continuous.
Freshman Admission University of Phoenix–Sacramento Campus requires 1 recommendation, 2 years of work experience, 23 years of age, and TOEFL scores for international students. A high school transcript is required for some. The application deadline for regular admission is rolling.
Transfer Admission The application deadline for admission is rolling.
Entrance Difficulty University of Phoenix–Sacramento Campus has an open admission policy.

For Further Information Contact Ms. Beth Barilla, Director of Admissions, University of Phoenix–Sacramento Campus, 4615 East Elwood Street, Mail Stop AA-K101, Phoenix, AZ 85040-1958. *Telephone:* 480-557-1712 or 800-266-2107 (toll-free). *Fax:* 480-594-1758. *E-mail:* beth.barilla@phoenix.edu. *Web site:* http://www.phoenix.edu/.

UNIVERSITY OF PHOENIX–SAN DIEGO CAMPUS

San Diego, California

University of Phoenix–San Diego Campus is a coed, proprietary, comprehensive institution, founded in 1988, offering degrees at the associate, bachelor's, master's, and doctoral levels and post-master's and postbachelor's certificates (courses conducted at 121 campuses and learning centers in 25 states).

Academic Information The faculty has 956 members (0.8% full-time), 28% with terminal degrees. The undergraduate student-faculty ratio is 9:1. The library holds 27 million titles and 11,648 serial subscriptions. Special programs include advanced placement credit, accelerated degree programs, independent study, distance learning, external degree programs, and adult/continuing education programs. The most frequently chosen baccalaureate fields are business/marketing, computer/information sciences, health professions and related sciences.

Student Body Statistics The student body totals 2,453, of whom 1,829 are undergraduates (44 freshmen). 56 percent are women and 44 percent are men. 10.8 percent are international students.

Expenses for 2003–04 *Application fee:* $85. *Tuition:* $11,760 full-time, $392 per credit part-time.

Financial Aid Forms of aid include need-based and non-need-based scholarships. The average aided 2002–03 undergraduate received an aid package worth $1229. The application deadline for financial aid is continuous.

Freshman Admission University of Phoenix–San Diego Campus requires 1 recommendation, 2 years of work experience, 23 years of age, and TOEFL scores for international students. A high school transcript is required for some. The application deadline for regular admission is rolling.

Transfer Admission The application deadline for admission is rolling.

Entrance Difficulty University of Phoenix–San Diego Campus has an open admission policy.

For Further Information Contact Ms. Beth Barilla, Director of Admissions, University of Phoenix–San Diego Campus, 4615 East Elwood Street, Mail Stop AA-K101, Phoenix, AZ 85040-1958. *Telephone:* 480-557-1712 or 888-UOP-INFO (toll-free). *Fax:* 480-594-1758. *E-mail:* beth.barilla@phoenix.edu. *Web site:* http://www.phoenix.edu/.

UNIVERSITY OF PHOENIX–SOUTHERN CALIFORNIA CAMPUS

Fountain Valley, California

University of Phoenix–Southern California Campus is a coed, proprietary, comprehensive institution, founded in 1980, offering degrees at the associate, bachelor's, master's, and doctoral levels and post-master's and postbachelor's certificates (courses conducted at 121 campuses and learning centers in 25 states).

Academic Information The faculty has 2,890 members, 28% with terminal degrees. The undergraduate student-faculty ratio is 11:1. The library holds 27 million titles and 11,648 serial subscriptions. Special programs include advanced placement credit, accelerated degree programs, independent study, distance learning, external degree programs, and adult/continuing education programs. The most frequently chosen baccalaureate fields are business/marketing, computer/information sciences, health professions and related sciences.

Student Body Statistics The student body totals 7,757, of whom 6,269 are undergraduates (205 freshmen). 59 percent are women and 41 percent are men. 8.8 percent are international students.

Expenses for 2003–04 *Application fee:* $85. *Tuition:* $12,660 full-time, $422 per credit part-time.

Financial Aid Forms of aid include need-based scholarships. The average aided 2002–03 undergraduate received an aid package worth $1346. The application deadline for financial aid is continuous.

Freshman Admission University of Phoenix–Southern California Campus requires 1 recommendation, 2 years of work experience, 23 years of age, and TOEFL scores for international students. A high school transcript is required for some. The application deadline for regular admission is rolling.

Transfer Admission The application deadline for admission is rolling.

Entrance Difficulty University of Phoenix–Southern California Campus has an open admission policy.

For Further Information Contact Ms. Beth Barilla, Director of Admissions, University of Phoenix–Southern California Campus, 4615 East Elwood Street, Mail Stop AA-K101, Phoenix, AZ 85040-1958. *Telephone:* 480-557-1712 or 800-228-7240 (toll-free). *E-mail:* beth.barilla@phoenix.edu. *Web site:* http://www.phoenix.edu/.

UNIVERSITY OF REDLANDS

Redlands, California

Redlands is a coed, private, comprehensive institution, founded in 1907, offering degrees at the bachelor's and master's levels and post-master's and postbachelor's certificates. It has a 140-acre campus in Redlands near Los Angeles.

Academic Information The faculty has 275 members (57% full-time), 64% with terminal degrees. The undergraduate student-faculty ratio is 12:1. The library holds 251,053 titles, 7,786 serial subscriptions, and 9,151 audiovisual materials. Special programs include academic remediation, services for learning-disabled students, an honors program, study abroad, advanced placement credit, Freshman Honors College, double majors, independent study, self-designed majors, adult/continuing education programs, internships, and arrangement for off-campus study with members of the Association for Innovation in Higher Education, American University. The most frequently chosen baccalaureate fields are liberal arts/general studies, business/marketing, social sciences and history.

Student Body Statistics The student body totals 2,311, of whom 2,223 are undergraduates (574 freshmen). 59 percent are women and 41 percent are men. Students come from 42 states and territories and 10 other countries. 73 percent are from California. 0.9 percent are international students.

Expenses for 2003–04 *Application fee:* $40. *Comprehensive fee:* $32,574 includes full-time tuition ($23,796), mandatory fees ($300), and college room and board ($8478). Room and board charges vary according to board plan and housing facility. *Part-time tuition:* $744 per credit. *Part-time mandatory fees:* $150 per term. Part-time tuition and fees vary according to course load.

Financial Aid Forms of aid include need-based and non-need-based scholarships and part-time jobs. The average aided 2003–04 undergraduate received an aid package worth an estimated $23,120. The priority application deadline for financial aid is February 15.

Freshman Admission Redlands requires an essay, a high school transcript, 2 recommendations, SAT I or ACT scores, and TOEFL scores for international students. An interview is recommended. The application deadline for regular admission is December 15.

Transfer Admission The application deadline for admission is March 1.

Entrance Difficulty Redlands assesses its entrance difficulty level as moderately difficult. For the fall 2003 freshman class, 71 percent of the applicants were accepted.

For Further Information Contact Mr. Paul Driscoll, Dean of Admissions, University of Redlands, PO Box 3080, Redlands, CA 92373-0999. *Telephone:* 909-335-4074 or 800-455-5064 (toll-free). *Fax:* 909-335-4089. *E-mail:* admissions@redlands.edu. *Web site:* http://www.redlands.edu/.

UNIVERSITY OF SAN DIEGO

San Diego, California

USD is a coed, private, Roman Catholic university, founded in 1949, offering degrees at the bachelor's, master's, doctoral, and first professional levels and post-master's, first professional, and postbachelor's certificates. It has a 180-acre campus in San Diego.

Academic Information The faculty has 683 members (51% full-time), 77% with terminal degrees. The undergraduate student-faculty ratio is 14:1. The library holds 500,000 titles, 4,986 serial subscriptions, and 8,103 audiovisual materials. Special programs include services for learning-disabled students, an honors program, study abroad, advanced placement

University of San Diego (continued)

credit, double majors, independent study, summer session for credit, part-time degree programs (daytime, evenings, summer), and internships. The most frequently chosen baccalaureate fields are business/marketing, communications/communication technologies, social sciences and history.
Student Body Statistics The student body totals 7,262, of whom 4,803 are undergraduates (1,064 freshmen). 62 percent are women and 38 percent are men. Students come from 50 states and territories and 63 other countries. 62 percent are from California. 2.4 percent are international students. 40 percent of the 2003 graduating class went on to graduate and professional schools.
Expenses for 2003–04 *Application fee:* $55. *Comprehensive fee:* $33,148 includes full-time tuition ($23,410), mandatory fees ($108), and college room and board ($9630). *College room only:* $6970. Room and board charges vary according to board plan and housing facility. *Part-time tuition:* $810 per unit. Part-time tuition varies according to course load.
Financial Aid Forms of aid include need-based and non-need-based scholarships, athletic grants, and part-time jobs. The average aided 2002–03 undergraduate received an aid package worth $21,804. The priority application deadline for financial aid is February 20.
Freshman Admission USD requires an essay, a high school transcript, 1 recommendation, SAT I or ACT scores, and TOEFL scores for international students. SAT II: Writing Test scores are recommended. The application deadline for regular admission is January 5 and for early action it is November 15.
Transfer Admission The application deadline for admission is March 1.
Entrance Difficulty USD assesses its entrance difficulty level as very difficult; moderately difficult for transfers. For the fall 2003 freshman class, 51 percent of the applicants were accepted.

For Further Information Contact Mr. Stephen Pultz, Director of Admission, University of San Diego, 5998 Alcala Park, San Diego, CA 92110. *Telephone:* 619-260-4506 or 800-248-4873 (toll-free). *Fax:* 619-260-6836. *E-mail:* admissions@sandiego.edu. *Web site:* http://www.sandiego.edu/.

UNIVERSITY OF SAN FRANCISCO

San Francisco, California

USF is a coed, private, Roman Catholic (Jesuit) university, founded in 1855, offering degrees at the bachelor's, master's, doctoral, and first professional levels and post-master's certificates. It has a 55-acre campus in San Francisco near in San Francisco.

Academic Information The faculty has 767 members (45% full-time), 87% with terminal degrees. The undergraduate student-faculty ratio is 14:1. The library holds 1 million titles, 5,560 serial subscriptions, and 4,591 audiovisual materials. Special programs include academic remediation, services for learning-disabled students, an honors program, cooperative (work-study) education, study abroad, advanced placement credit, ESL programs, double majors, distance learning, self-designed majors, summer session for credit, part-time degree programs (daytime, evenings, weekends, summer), external degree programs, adult/continuing education programs, internships, and arrangement for off-campus study with Fordham University, American University, Jackson State University. The most frequently chosen baccalaureate fields are business/marketing, computer/information sciences, social sciences and history.
Student Body Statistics The student body totals 8,159, of whom 4,718 are undergraduates (918 freshmen). 65 percent are women and 35 percent are men. Students come from 51 states and territories and 70 other countries. 78 percent are from California. 7.6 percent are international students. 42 percent of the 2003 graduating class went on to graduate and professional schools.
Expenses for 2004–05 *Application fee:* $55. *Comprehensive fee:* $34,700 includes full-time tuition ($24,800), mandatory fees ($120), and college room and board ($9780). *College room only:* $6180. Full-time tuition and fees vary according to program. Room and board charges vary according to board plan. *Part-time tuition:* $886 per credit. *Part-time mandatory fees:* $120 per year.
Financial Aid Forms of aid include need-based and non-need-based scholarships, athletic grants, and part-time jobs. The average aided 2003–04 undergraduate received an aid package worth an estimated $19,440. The priority application deadline for financial aid is February 15.
Freshman Admission USF requires an essay, a high school transcript, a minimum 2.8 high school GPA, 1 recommendation, SAT I or ACT scores, and TOEFL scores for international students. A minimum 3.0 high school GPA is recommended. An interview is required for some. The application deadline for regular admission is February 1 and for early action it is November 15.
Transfer Admission The application deadline for admission is rolling.
Entrance Difficulty USF assesses its entrance difficulty level as moderately difficult. For the fall 2003 freshman class, 82 percent of the applicants were accepted.

For Further Information Contact Mr. Tom Matos, Director, University of San Francisco, 2130 Fulton Street, San Francisco, CA 94117-1080. *Telephone:* 415-422-6563 or 800-CALL USF (toll-free out-of-state). *Fax:* 415-422-2217. *E-mail:* admissions@usfca.edu. *Web site:* http://www.usfca.edu/.

UNIVERSITY OF SARASOTA, CALIFORNIA CAMPUS

See Argosy University/Orange County

UNIVERSITY OF SOUTHERN CALIFORNIA

Los Angeles, California

USC is a coed, private university, founded in 1880, offering degrees at the bachelor's, master's, doctoral, and first professional levels and post-master's, first professional, and postbachelor's certificates. It has a 155-acre campus in Los Angeles.

Academic Information The faculty has 2,341 members (62% full-time). The undergraduate student-faculty ratio is 10:1. The library holds 4 million titles, 28,561 serial subscriptions, and 3 million audiovisual materials. Special programs include services for learning-disabled students, an honors program, cooperative (work-study) education, study abroad, advanced placement credit, accelerated degree programs, Freshman Honors College, ESL programs, double majors, independent study, self-designed majors, summer session for credit, part-time degree programs (daytime, evenings, weekends), internships, and arrangement for off-campus study with Hebrew Union College–Jewish Institute of Religion, Howard University, American University. The most frequently chosen baccalaureate fields are business/marketing, social sciences and history, visual/performing arts.
Student Body Statistics The student body totals 31,606, of whom 16,381 are undergraduates (2,976 freshmen). 50 percent are women and 50 percent are men. Students come from 52 states and territories and 148 other countries. 67 percent are from California. 8.1 percent are international students.
Expenses for 2003–04 *Application fee:* $65. *Comprehensive fee:* $37,324 includes full-time tuition ($28,184), mandatory fees ($508), and college room and board ($8632). *College room only:* $4750. Room and board charges vary according to board plan and housing facility. *Part-time tuition:* $949 per credit hour. *Part-time mandatory fees:* $508 per term. Part-time tuition and fees vary according to course load.
Financial Aid Forms of aid include need-based and non-need-based scholarships, athletic grants, and part-time jobs. The average aided 2002–03 undergraduate received an aid package worth $25,521. The priority application deadline for financial aid is January 20.
Freshman Admission USC requires an essay, a high school transcript, SAT I or ACT scores, and TOEFL scores for international students. Recommendations and an interview are recommended. Recommendations and SAT II: Subject Test scores are required for some. The application deadline for regular admission is January 10.
Transfer Admission The application deadline for admission is March 1.

Entrance Difficulty USC assesses its entrance difficulty level as most difficult. For the fall 2003 freshman class, 30 percent of the applicants were accepted.

For Further Information Contact Ms. Laurel Baker-Tew, Director of Admission, University of Southern California, University Park Campus, Los Angeles, CA 90089. *Telephone:* 213-740-1111. *Fax:* 213-740-6364. *E-mail:* admitusc@usc.edu. *Web site:* http://www.usc.edu/.

UNIVERSITY OF THE PACIFIC

Stockton, California

UOP is a coed, private university, founded in 1851, offering degrees at the bachelor's, master's, doctoral, and first professional levels. It has a 175-acre campus in Stockton near Sacramento.

Academic Information The faculty has 627 members (62% full-time), 87% with terminal degrees. The undergraduate student-faculty ratio is 13:1. The library holds 268,365 titles, 1,361 serial subscriptions, and 10,110 audiovisual materials. Special programs include academic remediation, services for learning-disabled students, an honors program, cooperative (work-study) education, study abroad, advanced placement credit, accelerated degree programs, ESL programs, double majors, independent study, self-designed majors, summer session for credit, part-time degree programs, adult/continuing education programs, and internships. The most frequently chosen baccalaureate fields are biological/life sciences, business/marketing, social sciences and history.
Student Body Statistics The student body totals 6,121, of whom 3,357 are undergraduates (818 freshmen). 58 percent are women and 42 percent are men. Students come from 41 states and territories and 16 other countries. 87 percent are from California. 2.6 percent are international students.
Expenses for 2003–04 *Application fee:* $50. *Comprehensive fee:* $31,090 includes full-time tuition ($23,180), mandatory fees ($420), and college room and board ($7490). *College room only:* $3736. Room and board charges vary according to board plan and housing facility. *Part-time tuition:* varies with course load.
Financial Aid Forms of aid include need-based and non-need-based scholarships, athletic grants, and part-time jobs. The average aided 2003–04 undergraduate received an aid package worth an estimated $22,096. The priority application deadline for financial aid is February 15.
Freshman Admission UOP requires an essay, a high school transcript, a minimum 2.5 high school GPA, 1 recommendation, SAT I or ACT scores, and TOEFL scores for international students. A minimum 3.0 high school GPA and an interview are recommended. Audition for music program is required for some. The application deadline for regular admission is January 15 and for early action it is December 1.
Transfer Admission The application deadline for admission is June 1.
Entrance Difficulty UOP assesses its entrance difficulty level as moderately difficult. For the fall 2003 freshman class, 70 percent of the applicants were accepted.

For Further Information Contact Mr. Marc McGee, Director of Admissions, University of the Pacific, 3601 Pacific Avenue, Stockton, CA 95211. *Telephone:* 209-946-2211 or 800-959-2867 (toll-free). *Fax:* 209-946-2413. *E-mail:* admissions@pacific.edu. *Web site:* http://www.pacific.edu/.

See page 196 for a narrative description.

UNIVERSITY OF THE WEST

Rosemead, California

University of the West is a coed, private, comprehensive institution, founded in 1991, offering degrees at the bachelor's, master's, doctoral, and first professional levels and post-master's certificates.

Expenses for 2004–05 *Application fee:* $50. *Comprehensive fee:* $11,750 includes full-time tuition ($6750), mandatory fees ($200), and college room and board ($4800). *Part-time tuition:* $200 per unit.
Financial Aid Forms of aid include need-based and non-need-based scholarships and part-time jobs. The application deadline for financial aid is continuous.
Freshman Admission TOEFL scores for international students are recommended. The application deadline for regular admission is August 15 and for nonresidents it is July 31.

For Further Information Contact Ms. Grace Hsiao, Registrar and Admissions Officer, University of the West, 1409 North Walnut Grove Avenue, Rosemead, CA 91770. *Telephone:* 626-571-8811 Ext. 120. *Fax:* 626-571-1413. *Web site:* http://www.hlu.edu/.

UNIVERSITY OF WEST LOS ANGELES

Inglewood, California

UWLA is a coed, private, upper-level institution, founded in 1966, offering degrees at the bachelor's and first professional levels and postbachelor's certificates in law. It has a 2-acre campus in Inglewood near Los Angeles.

Academic Information The faculty has 21 members (5% full-time), 95% with terminal degrees. The undergraduate student-faculty ratio is 10:1. The library holds 33,000 titles and 250 serial subscriptions. Special programs include academic remediation, independent study, part-time degree programs (evenings), adult/continuing education programs, and internships. The most frequently chosen baccalaureate field is law/legal studies.
Student Body Statistics The student body totals 330, of whom 71 are undergraduates. 75 percent are women and 25 percent are men. Students come from 1 state or territory. 10 percent of the 2003 graduating class went on to graduate and professional schools.
Expenses for 2003–04 *Application fee:* $55. *Tuition:* $7650 full-time, $255 per unit part-time. *Mandatory fees:* $360 full-time, $120 per term part-time.
Financial Aid Forms of aid include need-based and non-need-based scholarships. The average aided 2003–04 undergraduate received an aid package worth an estimated $9797. The application deadline for financial aid is continuous.
Transfer Admission UWLA requires a college transcript and a minimum 2.0 college GPA. Standardized test scores are required for some. The application deadline for admission is rolling.
Entrance Difficulty UWLA assesses its entrance difficulty level as minimally difficult.

For Further Information Contact Ms. Yvonne Alwag, Admissions Counselor, University of West Los Angeles, School of Paralegal Studies, 1155 West Arbor Vitae Street, Inglewood, CA 90301-2902. *Telephone:* 310-342-5287. *Fax:* 310-342-5296. *E-mail:* aalwag@uwla.edu. *Web site:* http://www.uwla.edu/.

VANGUARD UNIVERSITY OF SOUTHERN CALIFORNIA

Costa Mesa, California

VU is a coed, private, comprehensive institution, founded in 1920, affiliated with the Assemblies of God, offering degrees at the bachelor's and master's levels. It has a 38-acre campus in Costa Mesa near Los Angeles.

Academic Information The faculty has 164 members (46% full-time), 51% with terminal degrees. The undergraduate student-faculty ratio is 16:1. The library holds 144,952 titles, 1,066 serial subscriptions, and 4,668 audiovisual materials. Special programs include services for learning-disabled students, study abroad, advanced placement credit, accelerated degree programs, double majors, independent study, summer session for credit, part-time degree programs (evenings, weekends, summer), external degree programs, adult/continuing education programs, internships, and arrangement for off-campus study with Council for Christian Colleges and Universities. The most frequently chosen baccalaureate fields are business/marketing, philosophy, religion, and theology, psychology.

Vanguard University of Southern California (continued)

Student Body Statistics The student body totals 1,673, of whom 1,340 are undergraduates (347 freshmen). 64 percent are women and 36 percent are men. Students come from 40 states and territories and 10 other countries. 79 percent are from California. 1.1 percent are international students.

Expenses for 2003–04 *Application fee:* $45. *Comprehensive fee:* $21,868 includes full-time tuition ($15,928), mandatory fees ($430), and college room and board ($5510). *College room only:* $3060. Room and board charges vary according to board plan and housing facility. *Part-time tuition:* $664 per credit hour.

Financial Aid Forms of aid include need-based and non-need-based scholarships, athletic grants, and part-time jobs. The average aided 2003–04 undergraduate received an aid package worth an estimated $9700. The application deadline for financial aid is March 2.

Freshman Admission VU requires an essay, a high school transcript, a minimum 2.8 high school GPA, 1 recommendation, SAT I or ACT scores, and TOEFL scores for international students. An interview is required for some. The application deadline for regular admission is December 1.

Transfer Admission The application deadline for admission is December 1.

Entrance Difficulty VU assesses its entrance difficulty level as moderately difficult. For the fall 2003 freshman class, 80 percent of the applicants were accepted.

For Further Information Contact Ms. Jessica Mireles, Associate Vice President of Enrollment Management, Vanguard University of Southern California, 55 Fair Drive, Costa Mesa, CA 92626. *Telephone:* 714-556-3610 Ext. 327 or 800-722-6279 (toll-free). *Fax:* 714-966-5471. *E-mail:* admissions@vanguard.edu. *Web site:* http://www.vanguard.edu/.

WESTMONT COLLEGE

Santa Barbara, California

Westmont is a coed, private, nondenominational, four-year college, founded in 1937, offering degrees at the bachelor's level and postbachelor's certificates. It has a 133-acre campus in Santa Barbara near Los Angeles.

Academic Information The faculty has 139 members (60% full-time). The student-faculty ratio is 13:1. The library holds 165,512 titles, 3,211 serial subscriptions, and 8,032 audiovisual materials. Special programs include services for learning-disabled students, an honors program, cooperative (work-study) education, study abroad, advanced placement credit, accelerated degree programs, double majors, independent study, self-designed majors, summer session for credit, internships, and arrangement for off-campus study with 13 members of the Christian College Consortium, 90 members of the Christian Colleges and Universities, American University (Washington Semester). The most frequently chosen baccalaureate fields are communications/communication technologies, English, social sciences and history.

Student Body Statistics The student body is made up of 1,343 undergraduates (355 freshmen). 65 percent are women and 35 percent are men. Students come from 41 states and territories. 66 percent are from California. 0.8 percent are international students. 69 percent of the 2003 graduating class went on to graduate and professional schools.

Expenses for 2003–04 *Application fee:* $50. *Comprehensive fee:* $33,280 includes full-time tuition ($24,224), mandatory fees ($666), and college room and board ($8390). *College room only:* $4888. Room and board charges vary according to board plan.

Financial Aid Forms of aid include need-based and non-need-based scholarships, athletic grants, and part-time jobs. The average aided 2003–04 undergraduate received an aid package worth an estimated $16,571. The priority application deadline for financial aid is March 1.

Freshman Admission Westmont requires an essay, a high school transcript, 3 recommendations, SAT I or ACT scores, and TOEFL scores for international students. A minimum 3.0 high school GPA, an interview, and SAT II: Writing Test scores are recommended. An interview is required for some. The application deadline for regular admission is February 15 and for early action it is December 1.

Transfer Admission The application deadline for admission is March 15.

Entrance Difficulty Westmont assesses its entrance difficulty level as moderately difficult. For the fall 2003 freshman class, 85 percent of the applicants were accepted.

For Further Information Contact Mrs. Joyce Luy, Director of Admissions, Westmont College, 955 La Paz Road, Santa Barbara, CA 93108. *Telephone:* 805-565-6200 Ext. 6005 or 800-777-9011 (toll-free). *Fax:* 805-565-6234. *E-mail:* admissions@westmont.edu. *Web site:* http://www.westmont.edu/.

WESTWOOD COLLEGE–ANAHEIM

Anaheim, California

Westwood College–Anaheim is a coed, proprietary, primarily two-year college, offering degrees at the associate and bachelor's levels. It is located in Anaheim near Los Angeles.

Academic Information The faculty has 52 members. The most frequently chosen baccalaureate field is visual/performing arts.

Student Body Statistics The student body is made up of 674 undergraduates (278 freshmen). 23 percent are women and 77 percent are men. 0.1 percent are international students.

Financial Aid Forms of aid include need-based scholarships and part-time jobs. The application deadline for financial aid is continuous.

Freshman Admission Westwood College–Anaheim requires an interview and HS diploma or GED and passing scores on SAT/ACT or Accuplacer test.

Entrance Difficulty For the fall 2003 freshman class, 37 percent of the applicants were accepted.

For Further Information Contact Mr. Paul Sallenbach, Director of Admissions, Westwood College–Anaheim, 2461 West La Palma Avenue, Anaheim, CA 92801-2610. *Telephone:* 714-226-9990 or 877-650-6050 (toll-free in-state). *Fax:* 714-826-7398. *E-mail:* info@westwood.edu. *Web site:* http://www.westwood.edu/.

WESTWOOD COLLEGE–INLAND EMPIRE

Upland, California

Westwood College–Inland Empire is a coed, proprietary, primarily two-year college, offering degrees at the associate and bachelor's levels. It is located in Upland near Los Angeles.

Academic Information The faculty has 41 members.

Student Body Statistics The student body is made up of 803 undergraduates (801 freshmen). 27 percent are women and 73 percent are men.

Financial Aid Forms of aid include need-based scholarships and part-time jobs. The application deadline for financial aid is continuous.

Freshman Admission Westwood College–Inland Empire requires an interview and H.S. diploma or GED, pass entrance exam (or provide acceptable SAT/ACT scores).

For Further Information Contact Mr. Lyle Seavers, Director of Admissions, Westwood College–Inland Empire, 20 West 7th Street, Upland, CA 91786-7148. *Telephone:* 909-931-7550 or 866-288-9488 (toll-free in-state). *Fax:* 909-931-9195. *E-mail:* info@westwood.edu. *Web site:* http://www.westwood.edu/.

WESTWOOD COLLEGE–LOS ANGELES

Los Angeles, California

Westwood College–Los Angeles is a coed, proprietary, primarily two-year college, offering degrees at the associate and bachelor's levels. It is located in Los Angeles near Los Angeles.

Academic Information The faculty has 52 members.

Student Body Statistics The student body is made up of 679 undergraduates (341 freshmen). 26 percent are women and 74 percent are men.
Financial Aid Forms of aid include need-based scholarships and part-time jobs. The application deadline for financial aid is continuous.
Freshman Admission Westwood College–Los Angeles requires an interview and HS diploma/GED and passing scores on ACT/SAT or Accuplacer.

For Further Information Contact Mr. Ron Milman, Director of Admissions, Westwood College–Los Angeles, 3460 Wilshire Boulevard, Suite 700, Los Angeles, CA 90010-2210. *Telephone:* 213-739-9999 or 877-377-4600 (toll-free in-state). *Fax:* 213-382-2468. *E-mail:* info@westwood.edu. *Web site:* http://www.westwood.edu/.

WESTWOOD COLLEGE–LONG BEACH

Long Beach, California

Westwood College–Long Beach is a coed, proprietary, primarily two-year college, founded in 2002, offering degrees at the associate and bachelor's levels. It has a 1-acre campus in Long Beach near Los Angeles.

Academic Information The faculty has 19 members (11% full-time), 11% with terminal degrees. The student-faculty ratio is 15:1.
Student Body Statistics The student body is made up of 154 undergraduates. 31 percent are women and 69 percent are men. Students come from 4 states and territories. 98 percent are from California.
Expenses for 2004–05 *Application fee:* $100. *Tuition:* $18,645 full-time. *Mandatory fees:* $2726 full-time. Full-time tuition and fees vary according to course load and program. *Part-time tuition:* varies with course load, program.
Financial Aid Forms of aid include need-based scholarships and part-time jobs. The application deadline for financial aid is continuous.
Freshman Admission Westwood College–Long Beach requires a high school transcript, an interview, and ACCUPLACER. SAT I or ACT scores are recommended.
Transfer Admission The application deadline for admission is October 4.
Entrance Difficulty For the fall 2003 freshman class, 62 percent of the applicants were accepted.

For Further Information Contact Mr. Craig McVey, Director of Admissions, Westwood College–Long Beach, 3901 Via Oro Avenue, Suite 103, Long Beach, CA 90810. *Telephone:* 310-522-2088 Ext. 100 or 888-403-3308 (toll-free). *Fax:* 310-522-2098. *E-mail:* cmcvey@westwood.edu. *Web site:* http://www.westwood.edu/.

WHITTIER COLLEGE

Whittier, California

Whittier is a coed, private, comprehensive institution, founded in 1887, offering degrees at the bachelor's, master's, and first professional levels. It has a 95-acre campus in Whittier near Los Angeles.

Expenses for 2003–04 *Application fee:* $35. *Comprehensive fee:* $31,080 includes full-time tuition ($23,192), mandatory fees ($300), and college room and board ($7588). *College room only:* $4162.

For Further Information Contact Ms. Urmi Kar, Dean of Enrollment, Whittier College, PO Box 634, Whittier, CA 90608-0634. *Telephone:* 562-907-4238. *Fax:* 562-907-4870. *E-mail:* admission@whittier.edu. *Web site:* http://www.whittier.edu/.

WILLIAM JESSUP UNIVERSITY

Rocklin, California

William Jessup University is a coed, private, nondenominational, four-year college, founded in 1939, offering degrees at the associate and bachelor's levels. It has a 156-acre campus in Rocklin near Sacramento.

Academic Information The faculty has 69 members (22% full-time), 32% with terminal degrees. The student-faculty ratio is 15:1. The library holds 31,689 titles and 157 serial subscriptions. Special programs include academic remediation, cooperative (work-study) education, advanced placement credit, accelerated degree programs, double majors, summer session for credit, part-time degree programs (daytime, evenings), and internships. The most frequently chosen baccalaureate fields are philosophy, religion, and theology, education, protective services/public administration.
Student Body Statistics The student body is made up of 358 undergraduates (28 freshmen). 45 percent are women and 55 percent are men. Students come from 9 states and territories. 94 percent are from California. 5 percent are international students.
Expenses for 2004–05 *Application fee:* $35. *Comprehensive fee:* $20,244 includes full-time tuition ($13,590), mandatory fees ($796), and college room and board ($5858). *Part-time tuition:* $566 per semester hour.
Financial Aid Forms of aid include need-based and non-need-based scholarships, athletic grants, and part-time jobs. The priority application deadline for financial aid is June 1.
Freshman Admission William Jessup University requires an essay, a high school transcript, a minimum 2.0 high school GPA, 1 recommendation, letter of introduction, minimum SAT score of 830 or ACT score of 17, SAT I or ACT scores, and TOEFL scores for international students. The application deadline for regular admission is August 1.
Transfer Admission The application deadline for admission is August 1.
Entrance Difficulty William Jessup University assesses its entrance difficulty level as noncompetitive. For the fall 2003 freshman class, 58 percent of the applicants were accepted.

For Further Information Contact Mr. Rob Jones, Director of Admissions, William Jessup University, 333 Sunset Boulevard, Rocklin, CA 95765. *Telephone:* 916-577-1800 or 800-355-7522 (toll-free). *Fax:* 916-624-1722. *E-mail:* admissions@jessup.edu. *Web site:* http://www.jessup.edu/.

WOODBURY UNIVERSITY

Burbank, California

Woodbury is a coed, private, comprehensive institution, founded in 1884, offering degrees at the bachelor's and master's levels. It has a 22-acre campus in Burbank near Los Angeles.

Academic Information The faculty has 206 members (20% full-time), 44% with terminal degrees. The undergraduate student-faculty ratio is 18:1. The library holds 63,079 titles, 4,014 serial subscriptions, and 16,420 audiovisual materials. Special programs include academic remediation, services for learning-disabled students, study abroad, advanced placement credit, accelerated degree programs, double majors, independent study, summer session for credit, part-time degree programs (daytime, evenings, weekends, summer), adult/continuing education programs, and internships. The most frequently chosen baccalaureate fields are architecture, business/marketing, computer/information sciences.
Student Body Statistics The student body totals 1,404, of whom 1,189 are undergraduates (118 freshmen). 56 percent are women and 44 percent are men. 7.4 percent are international students.
Expenses for 2003–04 *Application fee:* $30. *Comprehensive fee:* $27,493 includes full-time tuition ($20,070), mandatory fees ($240), and college room and board ($7183). *College room only:* $4298. Full-time tuition and fees vary according to program. Room and board charges vary according to board plan and housing facility. *Part-time tuition:* varies with class time, program.

Woodbury University (continued)

Financial Aid Forms of aid include need-based and non-need-based scholarships and part-time jobs. The average aided 2003–04 undergraduate received an aid package worth an estimated $15,369. The application deadline for financial aid is continuous.
Freshman Admission Woodbury requires a high school transcript, a minimum 2.0 high school GPA, SAT I or ACT scores, and TOEFL scores for international students. An essay, a minimum 3.0 high school GPA, 2 recommendations, and an interview are recommended. A portfolio is required for some. The application deadline for regular admission is rolling.
Transfer Admission The application deadline for admission is rolling.
Entrance Difficulty Woodbury assesses its entrance difficulty level as moderately difficult. For the fall 2003 freshman class, 79 percent of the applicants were accepted.

For Further Information Contact Mr. Don St. Clair, Vice President of Enrollment Management and University Marketing, Woodbury University, 7500 Glenoaks Boulevard, Burbank, CA 91510-7846. *Telephone:* 818-767-0888 or 800-784-WOOD (toll-free). *Fax:* 818-767-7520. *E-mail:* info@woodbury.edu. *Web site:* http://www.woodbury.edu/.

YESHIVA OHR ELCHONON CHABAD/WEST COAST TALMUDICAL SEMINARY

Los Angeles, California

For Information Write to Yeshiva Ohr Elchonon Chabad/West Coast Talmudical Seminary, Los Angeles, CA 90046-7660.

Colorado

ADAMS STATE COLLEGE

Alamosa, Colorado

ASC is a coed, public, comprehensive unit of State Colleges in Colorado, founded in 1921, offering degrees at the associate, bachelor's, and master's levels. It has a 90-acre campus in Alamosa.

Academic Information The faculty has 198 members (47% full-time), 41% with terminal degrees. The undergraduate student-faculty ratio is 15:1. The library holds 472,594 titles, 1,646 serial subscriptions, and 1,954 audiovisual materials. Special programs include academic remediation, services for learning-disabled students, advanced placement credit, accelerated degree programs, double majors, independent study, distance learning, self-designed majors, summer session for credit, part-time degree programs (daytime, evenings, weekends, summer), adult/continuing education programs, internships, and arrangement for off-campus study with members of the Consortium of State Colleges in Colorado. The most frequently chosen baccalaureate fields are business/marketing, education, parks and recreation.
Student Body Statistics The student body totals 8,370, of whom 2,423 are undergraduates (461 freshmen). 58 percent are women and 42 percent are men. Students come from 46 states and territories and 5 other countries. 81 percent are from Colorado. 0.3 percent are international students. 21 percent of the 2003 graduating class went on to graduate and professional schools.
Expenses for 2003–04 *Application fee:* $25. *State resident tuition:* $1798 full-time. *Nonresident tuition:* $7428 full-time. *Mandatory fees:* $694 full-time. Full-time tuition and fees vary according to course load and reciprocity agreements. *College room and board:* $5730. *College room only:* $2880. Room and board charges vary according to board plan and housing facility.
Financial Aid Forms of aid include need-based and non-need-based scholarships, athletic grants, and part-time jobs. The average aided 2002–03 undergraduate received an aid package worth $4586. The application deadline for financial aid is continuous.
Freshman Admission ASC requires a high school transcript, a minimum 2.0 high school GPA, SAT I or ACT scores, and TOEFL scores for international students. An essay, recommendations, and an interview are required for some. The application deadline for regular admission is August 1.
Transfer Admission The application deadline for admission is August 1.
Entrance Difficulty ASC assesses its entrance difficulty level as moderately difficult. For the fall 2003 freshman class, 75 percent of the applicants were accepted.

For Further Information Contact Mr. Matt Gallegas, Director of Admissions, Adams State College, 208 Edgemont Boulevard, Alamosa, CO 81102. *Telephone:* 719-587-7712 or 800-824-6494 (toll-free). *Fax:* 719-587-7522. *E-mail:* ascadmit@adams.edu. *Web site:* http://www.adams.edu/.

THE ART INSTITUTE OF COLORADO

Denver, Colorado

The Art Institute of Colorado is a coed, proprietary, four-year college of Education Management Corporation, founded in 1952, offering degrees at the associate and bachelor's levels.

Academic Information The faculty has 135 members (47% full-time), 13% with terminal degrees. The student-faculty ratio is 20:1. The library holds 13,100 titles and 200 serial subscriptions. Special programs include academic remediation, services for learning-disabled students, study abroad, advanced placement credit, independent study, distance learning, part-time degree programs (daytime, evenings, weekends, summer), external degree programs, adult/continuing education programs, and internships.
Student Body Statistics The student body is made up of 2,226 undergraduates (674 freshmen). 46 percent are women and 54 percent are men. Students come from 49 states and territories and 22 other countries. 50 percent are from Colorado.
Expenses for 2003–04 *Application fee:* $50. *Comprehensive fee:* $24,512 includes full-time tuition ($18,752) and college room and board ($5760). Full-time tuition varies according to course load. *Part-time tuition:* $330 per credit. Part-time tuition varies according to course load.
Financial Aid Forms of aid include need-based and non-need-based scholarships and part-time jobs. The application deadline for financial aid is continuous.
Freshman Admission The Art Institute of Colorado requires an essay, a high school transcript, an interview, and TOEFL scores for international students. The application deadline for regular admission is rolling.
Transfer Admission The application deadline for admission is rolling.
Entrance Difficulty The Art Institute of Colorado assesses its entrance difficulty level as minimally difficult.

For Further Information Contact Ms. Barbara Browning, Vice President and Director of Admissions, The Art Institute of Colorado, 1200 Lincoln Street, Denver, CO 80203. *Telephone:* 303-837-0825 Ext. 4729 or 800-275-2420 (toll-free). *Fax:* 303-860-8520. *E-mail:* aicinfo@aii.edu. *Web site:* http://www.aic.artinstitutes.edu/.

ASPEN UNIVERSITY

Denver, Colorado

For Information Write to Aspen University, Denver, CO 80246.

BOULDER COLLEGE OF MASSAGE THERAPY

Boulder, Colorado

For Information Write to Boulder College of Massage Therapy, Boulder, CO 80301.

CAMBRIDGE COLLEGE

Aurora, Colorado

For Information Write to Cambridge College, Aurora, CO 80014.

COLLEGEAMERICA–FORT COLLINS

Fort Collins, Colorado

CollegeAmerica–Fort Collins is a coed, proprietary, primarily two-year college, founded in 1962, offering degrees at the associate and bachelor's levels.

Academic Information The faculty has 33 members (33% full-time). The student-faculty ratio is 22:1. The library holds 12 serial subscriptions and 30 audiovisual materials. Special programs include independent study and internships.
Student Body Statistics The student body is made up of 232 undergraduates. Students come from 3 states and territories.
Expenses for 2004–05 *Application fee:* $0. *Comprehensive fee:* $14,325. *Part-time tuition:* $275 per credit. *Tuition:* $275 per credit part-time.
Freshman Admission CollegeAmerica–Fort Collins requires an essay, a high school transcript, and an interview. A minimum 2.0 high school GPA is recommended. Recommendations are required for some.
Entrance Difficulty CollegeAmerica–Fort Collins has an open admission policy.

For Further Information Contact Ms. Anna DiTorrice-Mull, Director of Admissions, CollegeAmerica–Fort Collins, 4601 South Mason Street, Fort Collins, CO 80525. *Telephone:* 970-223-6060 Ext. 8002 or 800-97-SKILLS (toll-free in-state). *Fax:* 970-225-6059. *E-mail:* anna@collegeamerica.edu. *Web site:* http://www.collegeamerica.edu/.

COLORADO CHRISTIAN UNIVERSITY

Lakewood, Colorado

CCU is a coed, private, interdenominational, comprehensive institution, founded in 1914, offering degrees at the associate, bachelor's, and master's levels. It has a 26-acre campus in Lakewood near Denver.

Academic Information The faculty has 334 members (12% full-time), 33% with terminal degrees. The undergraduate student-faculty ratio is 21:1. The library holds 71,565 titles, 1,192 serial subscriptions, and 4,200 audiovisual materials. Special programs include academic remediation, services for learning-disabled students, an honors program, cooperative (work-study) education, study abroad, advanced placement credit, accelerated degree programs, double majors, independent study, distance learning, self-designed majors, summer session for credit, part-time degree programs (daytime, evenings, weekends, summer), adult/continuing education programs, internships, and arrangement for off-campus study with Colorado Institute of Art, Metropolitan State College, University of Colorado at Denver, Red Rocks Community College. The most frequently chosen baccalaureate fields are business/marketing, liberal arts/general studies, psychology.
Student Body Statistics The student body totals 1,583, of whom 1,462 are undergraduates (265 freshmen). 60 percent are women and 40 percent are men. Students come from 45 states and territories and 9 other countries. 59 percent are from Colorado. 0.6 percent are international students.
Expenses for 2004–05 *Application fee:* $40. *Comprehensive fee:* $21,182 includes full-time tuition ($15,040), mandatory fees ($100), and college room and board ($6042). *College room only:* $3452. Full-time tuition and fees vary according to degree level, location, and program. Room and board charges vary according to board plan and housing facility. *Part-time tuition:* $615 per semester hour. Part-time tuition varies according to degree level, location, and program.
Financial Aid Forms of aid include need-based and non-need-based scholarships, athletic grants, and part-time jobs. The average aided 2003–04 undergraduate received an aid package worth an estimated $8771. The priority application deadline for financial aid is March 15.
Freshman Admission CCU requires an essay, a high school transcript, 2 recommendations, SAT I or ACT scores, and TOEFL scores for international students. A minimum 2.8 high school GPA, 3 recommendations, and an interview are required for some. The application deadline for regular admission is August 1.
Entrance Difficulty CCU assesses its entrance difficulty level as moderately difficult. For the fall 2003 freshman class, 76 percent of the applicants were accepted.

For Further Information Contact Mr. Rodney Stanford, Director of Undergraduate Admission, Colorado Christian University, 180 South Garrison Street, Lakewood, CO 80226. *Telephone:* 303-202-0100 or 800-44-FAITH (toll-free). *Fax:* 303-963-3201. *E-mail:* admission@ccu.edu. *Web site:* http://www.ccu.edu/.

THE COLORADO COLLEGE

Colorado Springs, Colorado

CC is a coed, private, comprehensive institution, founded in 1874, offering degrees at the bachelor's and master's levels (master's degree in education only). It has a 90-acre campus in Colorado Springs near Denver.

Academic Information The faculty has 211 members (79% full-time). The undergraduate student-faculty ratio is 9:1. The library holds 535,657 titles, 1,313 serial subscriptions, and 21,419 audiovisual materials. Special programs include services for learning-disabled students, study abroad, advanced placement credit, ESL programs, double majors, independent study, self-designed majors, summer session for credit, internships, and arrangement for off-campus study with American University, Associated Colleges of the Midwest Programs. The most frequently chosen baccalaureate fields are biological/life sciences, English, social sciences and history.
Student Body Statistics The student body totals 1,968, of whom 1,941 are undergraduates (524 freshmen). 54 percent are women and 46 percent are men. Students come from 52 states and territories and 26 other countries. 30 percent are from Colorado. 1.9 percent are international students. 6.69 percent of the 2003 graduating class went on to graduate and professional schools.
Expenses for 2003–04 *Application fee:* $50. *Comprehensive fee:* $34,475 includes full-time tuition ($27,270), mandatory fees ($365), and college room and board ($6840). *College room only:* $3664. Room and board charges vary according to board plan. *Part-time tuition:* $852.19 per credit hour.
Financial Aid Forms of aid include need-based and non-need-based scholarships, athletic grants, and part-time jobs. The average aided 2003–04 undergraduate received an aid package worth an estimated $23,278. The priority application deadline for financial aid is February 15.
Freshman Admission CC requires an essay, a high school transcript, 3 recommendations, SAT I or ACT scores, and TOEFL scores for international students. An interview is recommended. The application deadline for regular admission is January 15 and for early action it is November 15.
Transfer Admission The application deadline for admission is March 1.

The Colorado College (continued)

Entrance Difficulty CC assesses its entrance difficulty level as very difficult. For the fall 2003 freshman class, 56 percent of the applicants were accepted.

For Further Information Contact Mr. Mark Hatch, Dean of Admission and Financial Aid, The Colorado College, 900 Block North Cascade, West, Colorado Springs, CO 80903-3294. *Telephone:* 719-389-6344 or 800-542-7214 (toll-free). *Fax:* 719-389-6816. *E-mail:* admission@coloradocollege.edu. *Web site:* http://www.coloradocollege.edu/.

COLORADO SCHOOL OF MINES

Golden, Colorado

CSM is a coed, public university, founded in 1874, offering degrees at the bachelor's, master's, and doctoral levels. It has a 373-acre campus in Golden near Denver.

Academic Information The faculty has 282 members (67% full-time), 78% with terminal degrees. The undergraduate student-faculty ratio is 15:1. The library holds 150,000 titles, 4,883 serial subscriptions, and 20 audiovisual materials. Special programs include academic remediation, services for learning-disabled students, an honors program, cooperative (work-study) education, study abroad, advanced placement credit, accelerated degree programs, ESL programs, double majors, independent study, summer session for credit, and internships. The most frequently chosen baccalaureate fields are engineering/engineering technologies, mathematics, physical sciences.
Student Body Statistics The student body totals 3,398, of whom 2,664 are undergraduates (668 freshmen). 23 percent are women and 77 percent are men. Students come from 51 states and territories and 62 other countries. 79 percent are from Colorado. 3.6 percent are international students. 15 percent of the 2003 graduating class went on to graduate and professional schools.
Expenses for 2004–05 *Application fee:* $45. *State resident tuition:* $5700 full-time. *Nonresident tuition:* $19,030 full-time. *Mandatory fees:* $733 full-time. *College room and board:* $6100. *College room only:* $3200. Room and board charges vary according to board plan and housing facility.
Financial Aid Forms of aid include need-based and non-need-based scholarships, athletic grants, and part-time jobs. The average aided 2003–04 undergraduate received an aid package worth an estimated $13,100. The priority application deadline for financial aid is March 1.
Freshman Admission CSM requires a high school transcript, SAT I or ACT scores, and TOEFL scores for international students. Rank in upper one-third of high school class is recommended. An essay, recommendations, and an interview are required for some. The application deadline for regular admission is June 1.
Transfer Admission The application deadline for admission is June 1.
Entrance Difficulty CSM assesses its entrance difficulty level as very difficult. For the fall 2003 freshman class, 79 percent of the applicants were accepted.

For Further Information Contact Ms. Tricia Douthit, Associate Director of Admissions, Colorado School of Mines, Student Center, 1600 Maple Street, Golden, CO 80401. *Telephone:* 303-273-3227 or 800-446-9488 Ext. 3220 (toll-free out-of-state). *Fax:* 303-273-3509. *E-mail:* admit@mines.edu. *Web site:* http://www.mines.edu/.

COLORADO STATE UNIVERSITY

Fort Collins, Colorado

Colorado State is a coed, public unit of Colorado State University System, founded in 1870, offering degrees at the bachelor's, master's, doctoral, and first professional levels. It has a 666-acre campus in Fort Collins near Denver.

Academic Information The faculty has 901 members (96% full-time), 99% with terminal degrees. The undergraduate student-faculty ratio is 17:1. The library holds 2 million titles, 20,712 serial subscriptions, and 31,850 audiovisual materials. Special programs include services for learning-disabled students, an honors program, cooperative (work-study) education, study abroad, advanced placement credit, accelerated degree programs, ESL programs, double majors, independent study, distance learning, self-designed majors, summer session for credit, part-time degree programs, adult/continuing education programs, internships, and arrangement for off-campus study with Aims Community College. The most frequently chosen baccalaureate fields are business/marketing, engineering/engineering technologies, social sciences and history.
Student Body Statistics The student body totals 26,870, of whom 21,689 are undergraduates (3,802 freshmen). 51 percent are women and 49 percent are men. 81 percent are from Colorado. 1.2 percent are international students.
Expenses for 2003–04 *Application fee:* $50. *State resident tuition:* $2908 full-time, $162 per credit part-time. *Nonresident tuition:* $13,380 full-time, $743 per credit part-time. *Mandatory fees:* $836 full-time, $51 per credit part-time. *College room and board:* $6045. Room and board charges vary according to board plan and housing facility.
Financial Aid Forms of aid include need-based and non-need-based scholarships, athletic grants, and part-time jobs. The average aided 2002–03 undergraduate received an aid package worth $7948. The priority application deadline for financial aid is March 1.
Freshman Admission Colorado State requires a high school transcript, SAT I or ACT scores, and TOEFL scores for international students. An essay and recommendations are recommended. The application deadline for regular admission is July 1.
Transfer Admission The application deadline for admission is July 1.
Entrance Difficulty Colorado State assesses its entrance difficulty level as moderately difficult; most difficult for engineering, technical journalism, business, landscape architecture, art, computer and science programs. For the fall 2003 freshman class, 79 percent of the applicants were accepted.

For Further Information Contact Ms. Mary Ontiveros, Director of Admissions, Colorado State University, Spruce Hall, Fort Collins, CO 80523-0015. *Telephone:* 970-491-6909. *Fax:* 970-491-7799. *E-mail:* admissions@vines.colostate.edu. *Web site:* http://www.colostate.edu/.

COLORADO STATE UNIVERSITY-PUEBLO

Pueblo, Colorado

Colorado State University-Pueblo is a coed, public, comprehensive unit of Colorado State University System, founded in 1933, offering degrees at the bachelor's and master's levels. It has a 275-acre campus in Pueblo near Colorado Springs.

Academic Information The faculty has 293 members (51% full-time), 43% with terminal degrees. The undergraduate student-faculty ratio is 17:1. The library holds 270,761 titles, 1,327 serial subscriptions, and 16,862 audiovisual materials. Special programs include services for learning-disabled students, an honors program, cooperative (work-study) education, study abroad, advanced placement credit, accelerated degree programs, ESL programs, double majors, independent study, distance learning, summer session for credit, part-time degree programs (daytime, evenings, weekends), external degree programs, adult/continuing education programs, internships, and arrangement for off-campus study with Adams State College, Colorado State University, University of Colorado at Denver.
Student Body Statistics The student body totals 6,299, of whom 6,078 are undergraduates (637 freshmen). 60 percent are women and 40 percent are men. Students come from 44 states and territories and 37 other countries. 92 percent are from Colorado. 3.3 percent are international students.
Expenses for 2003–04 *Application fee:* $25. *State resident tuition:* $2289 full-time, $104.03 per credit part-time. *Nonresident tuition:* $12,279 full-time, $558.14 per credit part-time. *Mandatory fees:* $641 full-time, $27.67 per credit part-time. Full-time tuition and fees vary according to reciprocity agreements. Part-time tuition and fees vary according to reciprocity agreements. *College room and board:* $5742. *College room only:* $2794. Room and board charges vary according to board plan and housing facility.
Financial Aid Forms of aid include need-based and non-need-based scholarships, athletic grants, and part-time jobs. The average aided

2003–04 undergraduate received an aid package worth an estimated $6601. The priority application deadline for financial aid is March 1.
Freshman Admission Colorado State University-Pueblo requires a high school transcript, a minimum 2.0 high school GPA, SAT I or ACT scores, and TOEFL scores for international students. An essay and recommendations are required for some. The application deadline for regular admission is August 1.
Transfer Admission The application deadline for admission is August 1.
Entrance Difficulty Colorado State University-Pueblo assesses its entrance difficulty level as moderately difficult; minimally difficult for transfers; very difficult for nursing program. For the fall 2003 freshman class, 95 percent of the applicants were accepted.

For Further Information Contact Jennifer Jensen, Director of Admissions and Records (Interim), Colorado State University-Pueblo, 2200 Bonforte Boulevard, Pueblo, CO 81001. *Telephone:* 719-549-2461 or 877-872-9653 (toll-free). *Fax:* 719-549-2419. *E-mail:* info@uscolo.edu. *Web site:* http://www.colostate-pueblo.edu/.

COLORADO TECHNICAL UNIVERSITY

Colorado Springs, Colorado

Colorado Tech is a coed, proprietary, comprehensive unit of Whitman Education Group, founded in 1965, offering degrees at the associate, bachelor's, master's, and doctoral levels and postbachelor's certificates. It has a 14-acre campus in Colorado Springs near Denver.

Expenses for 2003–04 *Application fee:* $50. *One-time mandatory fee:* $100. *Tuition:* $9225 full-time, $205 per quarter hour part-time. *Mandatory fees:* $213 full-time, $10 per credit part-time, $6 per term part-time. Full-time tuition and fees vary according to course load. Part-time tuition and fees vary according to course load.

For Further Information Contact Mr. Ron Begora, Director of Admissions, Colorado Technical University, 4435 North Chestnut Street, Colorado Springs, CO 80907-3896. *Telephone:* 719-598-0200. *Fax:* 719-598-3740. *E-mail:* rbegora@coloradotech.edu. *Web site:* http://www.coloradotech.edu/.

COLORADO TECHNICAL UNIVERSITY DENVER CAMPUS

Greenwood Village, Colorado

Colorado Tech is a coed, proprietary, comprehensive unit of Whitman Education Group, founded in 1965, offering degrees at the associate, bachelor's, and master's levels and postbachelor's certificates. It has a 1-acre campus in Greenwood Village near Denver.

Expenses for 2003–04 *Application fee:* $50. *One-time mandatory fee:* $100. *Tuition:* $9225 full-time, $205 per quarter hour part-time. *Mandatory fees:* $213 full-time, $10 per credit part-time, $6 per term part-time. Full-time tuition and fees vary according to course load. Part-time tuition and fees vary according to course load.

For Further Information Contact Ms. Suzanne Hyman, Director of Admissions, Colorado Technical University Denver Campus, 5775 DTC Boulevard, Suite 100, Greenwood Village, CO 80111. *Telephone:* 303-694-6600. *Fax:* 303-694-6673. *E-mail:* ctudenver@coloradotech.edu. *Web site:* http://www.coloradotech.edu/.

DENVER INSTITUTE OF TECHNOLOGY

See Westwood College–Denver North

DENVER TECHNICAL COLLEGE AT COLORADO SPRINGS

See DeVry University

DEVRY UNIVERSITY

Broomfield, Colorado

DeVry is a coed, proprietary, comprehensive unit of DeVry University, founded in 2001, offering degrees at the associate and bachelor's levels.

Expenses for 2003–04 *Tuition:* $10,590 full-time, $370 per credit hour part-time. *Mandatory fees:* $165 full-time. Full-time tuition and fees vary according to course load. Part-time tuition varies according to course load.

For Further Information Contact DeVry University, 12202 Airport Way, Suite 190, Broomfield, CO 80021-2588. *Telephone:* 303-329-3340. *Fax:* 303-469-9224. *Web site:* http://www.devry.edu/.

DEVRY UNIVERSITY

Colorado Springs, Colorado

DeVry is a coed, proprietary, comprehensive unit of DeVry University, founded in 2001, offering degrees at the associate, bachelor's, and master's levels and postbachelor's certificates. It has a 9-acre campus in Colorado Springs.

Academic Information The faculty has 50 members (22% full-time). Special programs include academic remediation, services for learning-disabled students, cooperative (work-study) education, advanced placement credit, accelerated degree programs, distance learning, summer session for credit, part-time degree programs (daytime, evenings, weekends, summer), and adult/continuing education programs. The most frequently chosen baccalaureate field is computer/information sciences.
Student Body Statistics The student body totals 335, of whom 301 are undergraduates (83 freshmen). 28 percent are women and 72 percent are men. Students come from 12 states and territories and 1 other country. 94 percent are from Colorado. 0.3 percent are international students.
Expenses for 2003–04 *Application fee:* $50. *Tuition:* $10,590 full-time, $370 per credit hour part-time. *Mandatory fees:* $165 full-time. Full-time tuition and fees vary according to course load. Part-time tuition varies according to course load.
Financial Aid Forms of aid include need-based and non-need-based scholarships and part-time jobs. The average aided 2003–04 undergraduate received an aid package worth an estimated $8534. The application deadline for financial aid is continuous.
Freshman Admission DeVry requires a high school transcript, an interview, and TOEFL scores for international students. SAT I, ACT or CPT is recommended. The application deadline for regular admission is rolling.
Transfer Admission The application deadline for admission is rolling.
Entrance Difficulty DeVry assesses its entrance difficulty level as minimally difficult; moderately difficult for electronics engineering technology.

For Further Information Contact Mr. Rick Rodman, Director of Admissions, DeVry University, 225 South Union Boulevard, Colorado Springs, CO 80910-3124. *Telephone:* 719-632-5566. *Fax:* 719-632-1909. *E-mail:* admitcs@cs.devry.edu. *Web site:* http://www.devry.edu/.

DEVRY UNIVERSITY

Westminster, Colorado

DeVry University is a coed, proprietary, four-year college, founded in 1945, offering degrees at the associate and bachelor's levels and postbachelor's certificates. It has a 3-acre campus in Westminster near Denver.

DeVry University (continued)

Academic Information The library holds 500,000 titles and 27 serial subscriptions. Special programs include academic remediation, cooperative (work-study) education, double majors, summer session for credit, adult/continuing education programs, and internships.
Student Body Statistics The student body is made up of 673 undergraduates (255 freshmen). 26 percent are women and 74 percent are men. 98 percent are from Colorado. 0.9 percent are international students.
Expenses for 2003–04 *Application fee:* $50. *Tuition:* $5295 per term part-time.
Financial Aid Forms of aid include need-based and non-need-based scholarships and part-time jobs. The average aided 2002–03 undergraduate received an aid package worth $7172. The application deadline for financial aid is continuous.
Freshman Admission DeVry University requires a high school transcript and TOEFL scores for international students. SAT I, ACT or CPT is recommended. An essay and an interview are required for some. The application deadline for regular admission is rolling.
Entrance Difficulty DeVry University has an open admission policy.

For Further Information Contact Mr. Rick Modman, Director of Admissions, DeVry University, 1870 West 122nd Avenue, Westminster, CO 80234-2010. *Telephone:* 719-632-3000 Ext. 8133 or 888-212-1857 (toll-free). *Fax:* 303-280-7606. *E-mail:* denver-admissions@den.devry.edu. *Web site:* http://www.devry.edu/.

EDUCATION AMERICA, COLORADO SPRINGS CAMPUS

See Remington College–Colorado Springs Campus

EDUCATION AMERICA, DENVER CAMPUS

See Remington College–Denver Campus

FORT LEWIS COLLEGE

Durango, Colorado

Fort Lewis is a coed, public, four-year college, founded in 1911, offering degrees at the associate and bachelor's levels. It has a 350-acre campus in Durango.

Academic Information The faculty has 243 members (72% full-time), 58% with terminal degrees. The student-faculty ratio is 19:1. The library holds 184,860 titles, 5,800 serial subscriptions, and 4,334 audiovisual materials. Special programs include academic remediation, services for learning-disabled students, an honors program, cooperative (work-study) education, study abroad, advanced placement credit, accelerated degree programs, ESL programs, double majors, independent study, distance learning, self-designed majors, summer session for credit, part-time degree programs (daytime, evenings, summer), adult/continuing education programs, internships, and arrangement for off-campus study with National Student Exchange. The most frequently chosen baccalaureate fields are business/marketing, English, social sciences and history.
Student Body Statistics The student body is made up of 4,182 undergraduates (923 freshmen). 48 percent are women and 52 percent are men. Students come from 49 states and territories and 15 other countries. 68 percent are from Colorado. 1.2 percent are international students. 20 percent of the 2003 graduating class went on to graduate and professional schools.
Expenses for 2003–04 *Application fee:* $30. *State resident tuition:* $2020 full-time. *Nonresident tuition:* $10,560 full-time. *Mandatory fees:* $768 full-time. Full-time tuition and fees vary according to reciprocity agreements. *College room and board:* $5564. *College room only:* $3014. Room and board charges vary according to board plan and housing facility.
Financial Aid Forms of aid include need-based and non-need-based scholarships, athletic grants, and part-time jobs. The average aided 2002–03 undergraduate received an aid package worth $7318. The application deadline for financial aid is continuous.
Freshman Admission Fort Lewis requires a high school transcript, a minimum 2.0 high school GPA, SAT I or ACT scores, and TOEFL scores for international students. An essay, recommendations, and an interview are recommended. The application deadline for regular admission is August 1.
Transfer Admission The application deadline for admission is July 15.
Entrance Difficulty Fort Lewis assesses its entrance difficulty level as moderately difficult. For the fall 2003 freshman class, 78 percent of the applicants were accepted.

For Further Information Contact Ms. Gretchen Foster, Director of Admissions, Fort Lewis College, 1000 Rim Drive, Durango, CO 81301. *Telephone:* 970-247-7184. *Fax:* 970-247-7179. *E-mail:* admission@fortlewis.edu. *Web site:* http://www.fortlewis.edu/.

INTERNATIONAL UNIVERSITY

See Jones International University

ITT TECHNICAL INSTITUTE

Thornton, Colorado

ITT Tech is a coed, proprietary, primarily two-year college of ITT Educational Services, Inc., founded in 1984, offering degrees at the associate and bachelor's levels. It has a 2-acre campus in Thornton near Denver.

Student Body Statistics The student body is made up of 491 undergraduates.
Expenses for 2003–04 *Application fee:* $100. Total Program Cost varies depending on course of study. Consult school catalog.
Financial Aid Forms of aid include need-based scholarships and part-time jobs. The application deadline for financial aid is continuous.
Freshman Admission ITT Tech requires a high school transcript, an interview, TOEFL scores for international students, and Wonderlic aptitude test. Recommendations are recommended. The application deadline for regular admission is rolling.
Transfer Admission The application deadline for admission is rolling.
Entrance Difficulty ITT Tech assesses its entrance difficulty level as minimally difficult.

For Further Information Contact Niki Donahue, Director of Recruitment, ITT Technical Institute, 500 East 84th Avenue, Suite B12, Thornton, CO 80229. *Telephone:* 303-288-4488 or 800-395-4488 (toll-free). *Fax:* 303-288-8166. *Web site:* http://www.itt-tech.edu/.

JOHNSON & WALES UNIVERSITY

Denver, Colorado

Johnson & Wales University is a coed, private, four-year college, founded in 1993, offering degrees at the associate and bachelor's levels in culinary arts.

Academic Information The faculty has 70 members (59% full-time). The library holds 14,000 titles, 150 serial subscriptions, and 660 audiovisual materials. Special programs include services for learning-disabled students, cooperative (work-study) education, summer session for credit, part-time degree programs (daytime, evenings), adult/continuing education programs, and internships.
Student Body Statistics The student body is made up of 1,328 undergraduates. 46 percent are women and 54 percent are men. Students come from 44 states and territories and 13 other countries. 58 percent are from Colorado. 1.3 percent are international students.
Expenses for 2004–05 *Application fee:* $0. *Comprehensive fee:* $28,107 includes full-time tuition ($19,182), mandatory fees ($810), and college room and board ($8115). Full-time tuition and fees vary according to course load, location, and program. Room and board charges vary according to housing facility and location. *Part-time tuition:* $355 per quarter hour. Part-time tuition varies according to course load, location, and program.

Financial Aid Forms of aid include need-based and non-need-based scholarships and part-time jobs. The average aided 2003–04 undergraduate received an aid package worth an estimated $12,343. The application deadline for financial aid is continuous.
Freshman Admission Johnson & Wales University requires a high school transcript and TOEFL scores for international students. A minimum 2.0 high school GPA and SAT I or ACT scores are recommended. A minimum 3.0 high school GPA, an interview, and SAT I or ACT scores are required for some. The application deadline for regular admission is rolling.
Transfer Admission The application deadline for admission is rolling.
Entrance Difficulty Johnson & Wales University assesses its entrance difficulty level as minimally difficult. For the fall 2003 freshman class, 88 percent of the applicants were accepted.

For Further Information Contact Mr. Dave McKlveen, Director of Admissions, Johnson & Wales University, 7150 Montview Boulevard, Denver, CO 80220. *Telephone:* 303-256-9300 or 877-598-3368 (toll-free). *Fax:* 303-256-9333. *E-mail:* admissions@jwu.edu. *Web site:* http://www.jwu.edu/.

JONES INTERNATIONAL UNIVERSITY

Englewood, Colorado

JIU is a coed, proprietary, comprehensive institution, founded in 1995, offering degrees at the bachelor's and master's levels in business communications (offers only online degree programs).

Academic Information The faculty has 93 members (6% full-time), 67% with terminal degrees. The undergraduate student-faculty ratio is 12:1. Special programs include academic remediation, advanced placement credit, accelerated degree programs, double majors, independent study, distance learning, self-designed majors, summer session for credit, part-time degree programs (daytime, evenings, weekends, summer), external degree programs, and adult/continuing education programs.
Student Body Statistics The student body totals 1,053, of whom 312 are undergraduates. 48 percent are women and 52 percent are men. Students come from 45 states and territories. 10 percent are from Colorado.
Expenses for 2003–04 *Application fee:* $100. *Comprehensive fee:* $9520 includes full-time tuition ($7680), mandatory fees ($480), and college room and board ($1360). Full-time tuition and fees vary according to degree level. *Part-time tuition:* $835 per course.
Financial Aid Forms of aid include need-based scholarships. The application deadline for financial aid is continuous.
Freshman Admission JIU requires an essay, a high school transcript, a minimum 2.5 high school GPA, 3 recommendations, and TOEFL scores for international students. The application deadline for regular admission is rolling.
Entrance Difficulty JIU has an open admission policy.

For Further Information Contact Ms. Candice Morrissey, Associate Director of Admissions, Jones International University, 9697 East Mineral Avenue, Englewood, CO 80112. *Telephone:* 303-784-8247 or 800-811-5663 (toll-free). *Fax:* 303-799-0966. *E-mail:* admissions@international.edu. *Web site:* http://www.jonesinternational.edu/.

MESA STATE COLLEGE

Grand Junction, Colorado

Mesa State is a coed, public, comprehensive unit of State Colleges in Colorado, founded in 1925, offering degrees at the associate, bachelor's, and master's levels. It has a 42-acre campus in Grand Junction.

Expenses for 2003–04 *Application fee:* $30. *State resident tuition:* $1856 full-time. *Nonresident tuition:* $7508 full-time. *Mandatory fees:* $660 full-time. *College room and board:* $6266. *College room only:* $3106.

For Further Information Contact Ms. Tyre Bush, Director of Admission, Mesa State College, 1100 North Avenue, Grand Junction, CO 81501. *Telephone:* 970-248-1875 or 800-982-MESA (toll-free). *Fax:* 970-248-1973. *E-mail:* admissions@mesastate.edu. *Web site:* http://www.mesastate.edu/.

METROPOLITAN STATE COLLEGE OF DENVER

Denver, Colorado

The Met is a coed, public, four-year college, founded in 1963, offering degrees at the bachelor's level. It has a 175-acre campus in Denver.

Academic Information The faculty has 1,000 members (39% full-time), 35% with terminal degrees. The student-faculty ratio is 23:1. The library holds 607,971 titles, 2,380 serial subscriptions, and 16,309 audiovisual materials. Special programs include services for learning-disabled students, an honors program, cooperative (work-study) education, study abroad, advanced placement credit, accelerated degree programs, double majors, independent study, distance learning, self-designed majors, summer session for credit, part-time degree programs (daytime, evenings, weekends, summer), external degree programs, adult/continuing education programs, internships, and arrangement for off-campus study with 3 members of the Consortium of State Colleges in Colorado, University of Colorado at Denver, Community College of Denver. The most frequently chosen baccalaureate fields are business/marketing, protective services/public administration, social sciences and history.
Student Body Statistics The student body is made up of 20,261 undergraduates (2,330 freshmen). 56 percent are women and 44 percent are men. Students come from 40 states and territories and 58 other countries. 98 percent are from Colorado. 1.1 percent are international students. 23.5 percent of the 2003 graduating class went on to graduate and professional schools.
Expenses for 2003–04 *Application fee:* $25. *One-time mandatory fee:* $1025. *State resident tuition:* $2130 full-time, $89 per credit part-time. *Nonresident tuition:* $8737 full-time, $364 per credit part-time. *Mandatory fees:* $538 full-time, $35 per credit part-time. Full-time tuition and fees vary according to course load and location. Part-time tuition and fees vary according to course load and location.
Financial Aid Forms of aid include need-based and non-need-based scholarships, athletic grants, and part-time jobs. The average aided 2003–04 undergraduate received an aid package worth an estimated $7481. The application deadline for financial aid is continuous.
Freshman Admission The Met requires a high school transcript and TOEFL scores for international students. A minimum 2.0 high school GPA is recommended. An essay, recommendations, and SAT I or ACT scores are required for some. The application deadline for regular admission is August 12.
Transfer Admission The application deadline for admission is rolling.
Entrance Difficulty The Met assesses its entrance difficulty level as minimally difficult; noncompetitive for students 20 or over. For the fall 2003 freshman class, 79 percent of the applicants were accepted.

For Further Information Contact Ms. Miriam Tapia, Associate Director, Metropolitan State College of Denver, PO Box 173362, Campus Box 16, Denver, CO 80217-3362. *Telephone:* 303-556-3058. *Fax:* 303-556-6345. *Web site:* http://www.mscd.edu/.

NAROPA UNIVERSITY

Boulder, Colorado

Naropa is a coed, private, comprehensive institution, founded in 1974, offering degrees at the bachelor's, master's, and first professional levels and post-master's and postbachelor's certificates. It has a 12-acre campus in Boulder near Denver.

Naropa University (continued)

Academic Information The faculty has 288 members (16% full-time), 43% with terminal degrees. The undergraduate student-faculty ratio is 12:1. The library holds 30,500 titles, 155 serial subscriptions, and 12,000 audiovisual materials. Special programs include services for learning-disabled students, cooperative (work-study) education, study abroad, advanced placement credit, double majors, independent study, distance learning, self-designed majors, summer session for credit, part-time degree programs (daytime), adult/continuing education programs, and internships. The most frequently chosen baccalaureate fields are English, psychology, visual/performing arts.
Student Body Statistics The student body totals 1,234, of whom 507 are undergraduates (39 freshmen). 61 percent are women and 39 percent are men. Students come from 44 states and territories and 15 other countries. 27 percent are from Colorado. 4 percent are international students.
Expenses for 2003–04 *Application fee:* $35. *Comprehensive fee:* $22,072 includes full-time tuition ($15,204), mandatory fees ($560), and college room and board ($6308). *College room only:* $4826. Full-time tuition and fees vary according to course load. Room and board charges vary according to board plan. *Part-time tuition:* $543 per semester hour. *Part-time mandatory fees:* $280 per term. Part-time tuition and fees vary according to course load.
Financial Aid Forms of aid include need-based scholarships and part-time jobs. The average aided 2003–04 undergraduate received an aid package worth an estimated $16,759. The priority application deadline for financial aid is March 1.
Freshman Admission Naropa requires an essay, a high school transcript, 2 recommendations, an interview, and TOEFL scores for international students. SAT I or ACT scores are recommended. The application deadline for regular admission is January 15.
Transfer Admission The application deadline for admission is rolling.
Entrance Difficulty Naropa assesses its entrance difficulty level as moderately difficult. For the fall 2003 freshman class, 95 percent of the applicants were accepted.

For Further Information Contact Ms. Sally Forester, Admissions Counselor, Naropa University, 2130 Arapahoe Avenue, Boulder, CO 80302. *Telephone:* 303-546-3572 or 800-772-0410 (toll-free out-of-state). *Fax:* 303-546-3583. *E-mail:* admissions@naropa.edu. *Web site:* http://www.naropa.edu/.

NATIONAL AMERICAN UNIVERSITY

Colorado Springs, Colorado

NAU is a coed, proprietary, four-year college, founded in 1941, offering degrees at the associate, bachelor's, and master's levels. It has a 1-acre campus in Colorado Springs near Denver.

Academic Information The faculty has 37 members (27% full-time). The undergraduate student-faculty ratio is 15:1. The library holds 15,000 titles and 100 serial subscriptions. Special programs include academic remediation, accelerated degree programs, ESL programs, independent study, distance learning, summer session for credit, part-time degree programs (daytime, evenings, weekends, summer), external degree programs, adult/continuing education programs, internships, and arrangement for off-campus study. The most frequently chosen baccalaureate fields are business/marketing, computer/information sciences.
Student Body Statistics The student body is made up of 230 undergraduates. Students come from 25 states and territories.
Expenses for 2004–05 *Application fee:* $25. *Tuition:* $10,575 full-time. *Mandatory fees:* $200 full-time.
Financial Aid Forms of aid include need-based and non-need-based scholarships and part-time jobs. The priority application deadline for financial aid is March 1.
Freshman Admission NAU requires a high school transcript, an interview, and TOEFL scores for international students. The application deadline for regular admission is September 1.
Transfer Admission The application deadline for admission is rolling.
Entrance Difficulty NAU has an open admission policy.

For Further Information Contact Mr. John West, Director of Admissions, National American University, 5125 North Academy Boulevard, Colorado Springs, CO 80918. *Telephone:* 719-277-0588. *Fax:* 719-277-0589. *E-mail:* jwest@national.edu. *Web site:* http://www.national.edu/.

NATIONAL AMERICAN UNIVERSITY

Denver, Colorado

NAU, Denver is a coed, proprietary, four-year college, founded in 1974, offering degrees at the associate, bachelor's, and master's levels.

Academic Information The faculty has 35 members. The undergraduate student-faculty ratio is 10:1. The library holds 400 titles and 33 serial subscriptions. Special programs include academic remediation, advanced placement credit, accelerated degree programs, ESL programs, double majors, independent study, distance learning, summer session for credit, part-time degree programs (daytime, evenings, weekends, summer), adult/continuing education programs, and internships.
Student Body Statistics The student body totals 350.
Expenses for 2004–05 *Application fee:* $25. *Tuition:* $8208 full-time. Full-time tuition varies according to course load, location, and program. *Part-time tuition:* varies with course load, location, program.
Financial Aid Forms of aid include need-based and non-need-based scholarships and part-time jobs. The application deadline for financial aid is continuous.
Freshman Admission NAU, Denver requires a high school transcript and TOEFL scores for international students. SAT I or ACT scores are recommended. The application deadline for regular admission is rolling.
Transfer Admission The application deadline for admission is rolling.
Entrance Difficulty NAU, Denver has an open admission policy.

For Further Information Contact Ms. Karen Walker, Director of Admissions, National American University, 1325 South Colorado Blvd, Suite 100, Denver, CO 80222. *Telephone:* 303-758-6700. *Fax:* 303-758-6810. *Web site:* http://www.national.edu/.

NAZARENE BIBLE COLLEGE

Colorado Springs, Colorado

NBC is a coed, private, four-year college, founded in 1967, affiliated with the Church of the Nazarene, offering degrees at the associate and bachelor's levels in religious studies. It has a 64-acre campus in Colorado Springs near Denver.

Expenses for 2003–04 *Application fee:* $20. *Tuition:* $6624 full-time, $207 per semester hour part-time. *Mandatory fees:* $300 full-time, $10 per term part-time.

For Further Information Contact Dr. David Phillips, Director of Admissions/Public Relations, Nazarene Bible College, 1111 Academy Park Loop, Colorado Springs, CO 80910-3704. *Telephone:* 719-884-5031 or 800-873-3873 (toll-free). *Fax:* 719-884-5199. *Web site:* http://www.nbc.edu/.

PLATT COLLEGE

Aurora, Colorado

For Information Write to Platt College, Aurora, CO 80014-3141.

REGIS UNIVERSITY

Denver, Colorado

Regis University is a coed, private, Roman Catholic (Jesuit), comprehensive institution, founded in 1877, offering degrees at the bachelor's and master's levels. It has a 90-acre campus in Denver.

Academic Information The faculty has 1,225 members (14% full-time). The undergraduate student-faculty ratio is 14:1. The library holds 430,514 titles, 7,850 serial subscriptions, and 104,887 audiovisual materials. Special programs include academic remediation, services for learning-disabled students, an honors program, cooperative (work-study) education, study abroad, advanced placement credit, accelerated degree programs, Freshman Honors College, double majors, independent study, self-designed majors, summer session for credit, part-time degree programs (daytime, evenings, weekends, summer), external degree programs, adult/continuing education programs, internships, and arrangement for off-campus study with other Jesuit colleges and universities.

Student Body Statistics The student body is made up of 1,268 undergraduates (381 freshmen). 56 percent are women and 44 percent are men. Students come from 40 states and territories and 11 other countries. 57 percent are from Colorado. 15 percent of the 2003 graduating class went on to graduate and professional schools.

Expenses for 2003–04 *Application fee:* $40. *Comprehensive fee:* $28,500 includes full-time tuition ($20,700), mandatory fees ($200), and college room and board ($7600). *College room only:* $4300.

Financial Aid Forms of aid include need-based and non-need-based scholarships, athletic grants, and part-time jobs. The average aided 2003–04 undergraduate received an aid package worth an estimated $20,738. The priority application deadline for financial aid is March 5.

Freshman Admission Regis University requires an essay, a high school transcript, a minimum 2.5 high school GPA, 1 recommendation, SAT I or ACT scores, and TOEFL scores for international students. SAT II: Subject Test scores are recommended. 2 recommendations and an interview are required for some. The application deadline for regular admission is rolling.

Transfer Admission The application deadline for admission is August 1.

Entrance Difficulty Regis University assesses its entrance difficulty level as moderately difficult. For the fall 2003 freshman class, 83 percent of the applicants were accepted.

For Further Information Contact Mr. Vic Davolt, Director of Admissions, Regis University, 3333 Regis Boulevard, Denver, CO 80221-1099. *Telephone:* 303-458-4905 or 800-388-2366 Ext. 4900 (toll-free). *Fax:* 303-964-5534. *E-mail:* regisadm@regis.edu. *Web site:* http://www.regis.edu/.

See page 186 for a narrative description.

REMINGTON COLLEGE–COLORADO SPRINGS CAMPUS

Colorado Springs, Colorado

Remington College–Colorado Springs Campus is a coed, proprietary, four-year college, offering degrees at the associate and bachelor's levels. It has a 3-acre campus in Colorado Springs.

Academic Information The faculty has 30 members (23% full-time), 10% with terminal degrees. The student-faculty ratio is 17:1. The most frequently chosen baccalaureate field is protective services/public administration.

Student Body Statistics The student body is made up of 282 undergraduates (71 freshmen). 51 percent are women and 49 percent are men.

Expenses for 2004–05 *Tuition:* $15,240 full-time.

Entrance Difficulty Remington College–Colorado Springs Campus assesses its entrance difficulty level as noncompetitive. For the fall 2003 freshman class, 100 percent of the applicants were accepted.

For Further Information Contact Mr. Shibu Thomas, Campus Vice-President, Remington College–Colorado Springs Campus, 6050 Erin Park Drive, #250, Colorado Springs, CO 80918. *Telephone:* 769-532-1234 Ext. 202. *Fax:* 719-264-1234. *Web site:* http://www.remingtoncollege.edu/.

REMINGTON COLLEGE–DENVER CAMPUS

Lakewood, Colorado

For Information Write to Remington College–Denver Campus, Lakewood, CO 80215-0090.

REVANS UNIVERSITY–THE UNIVERSITY OF ACTION LEARNING

Boulder, Colorado

For Information Write to Revans University–The University of Action Learning, Boulder, CO 80301.

ROCKY MOUNTAIN COLLEGE OF ART & DESIGN

Lakewood, Colorado

Rocky Mountain College of Art & Design is a coed, proprietary, four-year college, founded in 1963, offering degrees at the bachelor's level in art and design. It has a 23-acre campus in Lakewood.

Academic Information The faculty has 57 members (32% full-time), 88% with terminal degrees. The student-faculty ratio is 12:1. The library holds 6,287 titles and 65 serial subscriptions. Special programs include academic remediation, cooperative (work-study) education, study abroad, advanced placement credit, accelerated degree programs, double majors, independent study, summer session for credit, part-time degree programs (daytime, summer), and internships. The most frequently chosen baccalaureate field is visual/performing arts.

Student Body Statistics The student body is made up of 503 undergraduates (54 freshmen). 55 percent are women and 45 percent are men. Students come from 36 states and territories and 4 other countries. 76 percent are from Colorado. 1.1 percent are international students. 5 percent of the 2003 graduating class went on to graduate and professional schools.

Expenses for 2003–04 *Application fee:* $50. *Tuition:* $14,184 full-time, $591 per credit part-time. *Mandatory fees:* $90 full-time, $15 per term part-time. *College room only:* $3840. Room charges vary according to housing facility.

Financial Aid Forms of aid include need-based and non-need-based scholarships and part-time jobs. The average aided 2002–03 undergraduate received an aid package worth $5260. The priority application deadline for financial aid is April 1.

Freshman Admission Rocky Mountain College of Art & Design requires a minimum 2.0 high school GPA and a portfolio. TOEFL scores for international students are recommended. The application deadline for regular admission is rolling.

Transfer Admission The application deadline for admission is rolling.

Rocky Mountain College of Art & Design (continued)

Entrance Difficulty Rocky Mountain College of Art & Design assesses its entrance difficulty level as moderately difficult. For the fall 2003 freshman class, 92 percent of the applicants were accepted.

For Further Information Contact Ms. Sandy Sprock, Director of Admissions, Rocky Mountain College of Art & Design, 1600 Pierce Street, Lakewood, CO 80214. *Telephone:* 303-753-6046 or 800-888-ARTS (toll-free). *Fax:* 303-759-4970. *E-mail:* admit@rmcad.edu. *Web site:* http://www.rmcad.edu/.

TEIKYO LORETTO HEIGHTS UNIVERSITY

Denver, Colorado

For Information Write to Teikyo Loretto Heights University, Denver, CO 80236-2711.

UNITED STATES AIR FORCE ACADEMY

Colorado Springs, Colorado

USAFA is a coed, primarily men's, public, four-year college, founded in 1954, offering degrees at the bachelor's level. It has an 18,000-acre campus in Colorado Springs near Denver.

Academic Information The faculty has 531 members (100% full-time), 57% with terminal degrees. The student-faculty ratio is 8:1. The library holds 445,379 titles, 1,693 serial subscriptions, and 4,458 audiovisual materials. Special programs include academic remediation, study abroad, advanced placement credit, ESL programs, double majors, independent study, self-designed majors, summer session for credit, internships, and arrangement for off-campus study with other United States service academies. The most frequently chosen baccalaureate fields are business/marketing, engineering/engineering technologies, social sciences and history.

Student Body Statistics The student body is made up of 4,157 undergraduates (1,214 freshmen). 17 percent are women and 83 percent are men. Students come from 54 states and territories and 21 other countries. 5 percent are from Colorado. 1.1 percent are international students. 6.5 percent of the 2003 graduating class went on to graduate and professional schools.

Expenses for 2004–05 *Application fee:* $0. Tuition, room and board, and medical and dental care are provided by the U.S. government. Each cadet receives a salary from which to pay for uniforms, supplies, and personal expenses. Entering freshmen are required to deposit $2500 to defray the initial cost of uniforms and equipment.

Freshman Admission USAFA requires an essay, a high school transcript, a minimum 2.0 high school GPA, an interview, authorized nomination, SAT I or ACT scores, and TOEFL scores for international students. SAT I or ACT scores are recommended. The application deadline for regular admission is January 31.

Transfer Admission The application deadline for admission is January 31.

Entrance Difficulty USAFA assesses its entrance difficulty level as most difficult. For the fall 2003 freshman class, 12 percent of the applicants were accepted.

For Further Information Contact Mr. Rolland Stoneman, Associate Director of Admissions/Selections, United States Air Force Academy, HQ USAFA/RR 2304 Cadet Drive, Suite 200, USAF Academy, CO 80840-5025. *Telephone:* 719-333-2520 or 800-443-9266 (toll-free). *Fax:* 719-333-3012. *E-mail:* rr_webmail@usafa.af.mil. *Web site:* http://www.usafa.edu/.

UNIVERSITY OF ACTION LEARNING AT BOULDER

See Revans University–The University of Action Learning

UNIVERSITY OF COLORADO AT BOULDER

Boulder, Colorado

CU-Boulder is a coed, public unit of University of Colorado System, founded in 1876, offering degrees at the bachelor's, master's, doctoral, and first professional levels. It has a 600-acre campus in Boulder near Denver.

Academic Information The faculty has 1,737 members (68% full-time), 73% with terminal degrees. The undergraduate student-faculty ratio is 17:1. The library holds 2 million titles, 25,607 serial subscriptions, and 63,314 audiovisual materials. Special programs include services for learning-disabled students, an honors program, cooperative (work-study) education, study abroad, advanced placement credit, accelerated degree programs, Freshman Honors College, ESL programs, double majors, independent study, distance learning, self-designed majors, summer session for credit, part-time degree programs (daytime, evenings, summer), adult/continuing education programs, internships, and arrangement for off-campus study with other units of the University of Colorado System. The most frequently chosen baccalaureate fields are business/marketing, communications/communication technologies, social sciences and history.

Student Body Statistics The student body totals 32,041, of whom 26,186 are undergraduates (5,630 freshmen). 47 percent are women and 53 percent are men. Students come from 53 states and territories and 100 other countries. 67 percent are from Colorado. 1.3 percent are international students.

Expenses for 2003–04 *Application fee:* $50. *State resident tuition:* $3192 full-time. *Nonresident tuition:* $19,508 full-time. *Mandatory fees:* $828 full-time. Full-time tuition and fees vary according to program. *College room and board:* $6754. Room and board charges vary according to board plan, housing facility, and location.

Financial Aid Forms of aid include need-based and non-need-based scholarships, athletic grants, and part-time jobs. The average aided 2003–04 undergraduate received an aid package worth an estimated $9962. The priority application deadline for financial aid is April 1.

Freshman Admission CU-Boulder requires a high school transcript, a minimum 2.0 high school GPA, SAT I or ACT scores, and TOEFL scores for international students. An essay, a minimum 3.0 high school GPA, and recommendations are recommended. Audition for music program is required for some. The application deadline for regular admission is January 15.

Transfer Admission The application deadline for admission is April 1.

Entrance Difficulty CU-Boulder assesses its entrance difficulty level as moderately difficult; very difficult for engineering programs. For the fall 2003 freshman class, 80 percent of the applicants were accepted.

For Further Information Contact Mr. Kevin MacLennan, Associate Director, University of Colorado at Boulder, 552 UCB, Boulder, CO 80309-0030. *Telephone:* 303-492-6301. *Fax:* 303-492-7115. *Web site:* http://www.colorado.edu/.

UNIVERSITY OF COLORADO AT COLORADO SPRINGS

Colorado Springs, Colorado

CU-Colorado Springs is a coed, public, comprehensive institution, founded in 1965, offering degrees at the bachelor's, master's, and doctoral levels. It has a 400-acre campus in Colorado Springs near Denver.

Academic Information The faculty has 423 members (65% full-time), 73% with terminal degrees. The undergraduate student-faculty ratio is 17:1. The library holds 391,638 titles, 2,201 serial subscriptions, and 5,229 audiovisual materials. Special programs include services for learning-disabled students, cooperative (work-study) education, advanced placement credit, accelerated degree programs, double majors, independent study, distance learning, summer session for credit, part-time degree programs (daytime, evenings, weekends, summer), and internships. The most frequently chosen baccalaureate fields are business/marketing, psychology, social sciences and history.

Student Body Statistics The student body totals 7,620, of whom 5,875 are undergraduates (690 freshmen). 62 percent are women and 38 percent are men. Students come from 44 states and territories and 26 other countries. 93 percent are from Colorado. 0.4 percent are international students.
Expenses for 2003–04 *Application fee:* $45. *State resident tuition:* $4378 full-time, $150 per credit hour part-time. *Nonresident tuition:* $19,210 full-time, $768 per credit hour part-time. *Mandatory fees:* $778 full-time, $389 per term part-time. Full-time tuition and fees vary according to program and student level. Part-time tuition and fees vary according to program and student level. *College room and board:* $6729. Room and board charges vary according to board plan and housing facility.
Financial Aid Forms of aid include need-based and non-need-based scholarships and part-time jobs. The average aided 2003–04 undergraduate received an aid package worth an estimated $6859. The priority application deadline for financial aid is April 1.
Freshman Admission CU-Colorado Springs requires a high school transcript, SAT I or ACT scores, and TOEFL scores for international students. The application deadline for regular admission is July 1.
Transfer Admission The application deadline for admission is July 1.
Entrance Difficulty CU-Colorado Springs assesses its entrance difficulty level as moderately difficult; very difficult for business, engineering, nursing programs. For the fall 2003 freshman class, 74 percent of the applicants were accepted.

For Further Information Contact Mr. James Tidwell, Assistant Admissions Director, University of Colorado at Colorado Springs, PO Box 7150, Colorado Springs, CO 80918. *Telephone:* 719-262-3375 or 800-990-8227 Ext. 3383 (toll-free). *Fax:* 719-262-3116. *E-mail:* admrec@uccs.edu. *Web site:* http://www.uccs.edu/.

UNIVERSITY OF COLORADO AT DENVER

Denver, Colorado

UCD is a coed, public unit of University of Colorado System, founded in 1912, offering degrees at the bachelor's, master's, and doctoral levels. It has a 171-acre campus in Denver.

Academic Information The faculty has 916 members (50% full-time). The undergraduate student-faculty ratio is 14:1. The library holds 588,582 titles, 4,364 serial subscriptions, and 15,720 audiovisual materials. Special programs include services for learning-disabled students, an honors program, cooperative (work-study) education, study abroad, advanced placement credit, accelerated degree programs, ESL programs, double majors, independent study, distance learning, self-designed majors, summer session for credit, part-time degree programs (daytime, evenings, weekends, summer), adult/continuing education programs, internships, and arrangement for off-campus study with Metropolitan State College, Community College of Denver. The most frequently chosen baccalaureate fields are business/marketing, engineering/engineering technologies, library science.
Student Body Statistics The student body totals 15,596, of whom 8,903 are undergraduates (645 freshmen). 57 percent are women and 43 percent are men. Students come from 51 states and territories and 117 other countries. 6.9 percent are international students. 9 percent of the 2003 graduating class went on to graduate and professional schools.
Expenses for 2003–04 *Application fee:* $40. *State resident tuition:* $3028 full-time, $161 per semester hour part-time. *Nonresident tuition:* $14,656 full-time, $880 per semester hour part-time. *Mandatory fees:* $523 full-time, $249 per year part-time. Full-time tuition and fees vary according to program and student level. Part-time tuition and fees vary according to program and student level.
Financial Aid Forms of aid include need-based and non-need-based scholarships and part-time jobs. The average aided 2002–03 undergraduate received an aid package worth $6586. The priority application deadline for financial aid is April 1.
Freshman Admission UCD requires a high school transcript, a minimum 2.5 high school GPA, SAT I or ACT scores, and TOEFL scores for international students. The application deadline for regular admission is July 22.
Transfer Admission The application deadline for admission is July 22.
Entrance Difficulty UCD assesses its entrance difficulty level as moderately difficult; very difficult for engineering, business programs. For the fall 2003 freshman class, 70 percent of the applicants were accepted.

For Further Information Contact Ms. Barbara Edwards, Director of Admissions, University of Colorado at Denver, PO Box 173364, Campus Box 167, Denver, CO 80217. *Telephone:* 303-556-3287. *Fax:* 303-556-4838. *Web site:* http://www.cudenver.edu/.

UNIVERSITY OF COLORADO HEALTH SCIENCES CENTER

Denver, Colorado

UCHSC is a coed, public, upper-level unit of University of Colorado System, founded in 1883, offering degrees at the bachelor's, master's, doctoral, and first professional levels and post-master's and first professional certificates. It has a 40-acre campus in Denver.

Academic Information The faculty has 2,573 members. The library holds 250,000 titles and 1,650 serial subscriptions. Special programs include advanced placement credit, distance learning, summer session for credit, adult/continuing education programs, and internships. The most frequently chosen baccalaureate field is health professions and related sciences.
Student Body Statistics The student body totals 2,567, of whom 320 are undergraduates. 92 percent are women and 8 percent are men. 97 percent are from Colorado.
Expenses for 2003–04 *Application fee:* $40. *State resident tuition:* $5730 full-time. *Nonresident tuition:* $20,010 full-time. *Mandatory fees:* $380 full-time.
Financial Aid Forms of aid include need-based and non-need-based scholarships and part-time jobs. The average aided 2003–04 undergraduate received an aid package worth an estimated $12,452. The application deadline for financial aid is continuous.
Transfer Admission UCHSC requires a college transcript and a minimum 2.5 college GPA. The application deadline for admission is October 1.
Entrance Difficulty UCHSC assesses its entrance difficulty level as moderately difficult.

For Further Information Contact Dr. Lynn Mason, Director of Admissions, University of Colorado Health Sciences Center, A-054, 4200 East 9th Avenue, Denver, CO 80262. *Telephone:* 303-315-7676. *Fax:* 303-315-3358. *Web site:* http://www.uchsc.edu/.

UNIVERSITY OF DENVER

Denver, Colorado

DU is a coed, private university, founded in 1864, offering degrees at the bachelor's, master's, doctoral, and first professional levels. It has a 125-acre campus in Denver.

Academic Information The faculty has 972 members (45% full-time). The undergraduate student-faculty ratio is 9:1. The library holds 1 million titles, 6,283 serial subscriptions, and 6,293 audiovisual materials. Special programs include services for learning-disabled students, an honors program, cooperative (work-study) education, study abroad, advanced placement credit, accelerated degree programs, Freshman Honors College, ESL programs, double majors, independent study, self-designed majors, summer session for credit, part-time degree programs (daytime, evenings, weekends, summer), adult/continuing education programs, and internships. The most frequently chosen baccalaureate fields are business/marketing, communications/communication technologies, social sciences and history.
Student Body Statistics The student body totals 9,521, of whom 4,456 are undergraduates (1,031 freshmen). 56 percent are women and 44 percent are men. Students come from 52 states and territories and 54 other countries. 50 percent are from Colorado. 4.2 percent are international students. 24 percent of the 2003 graduating class went on to graduate and professional schools.

University of Denver (continued)

Expenses for 2004–05 *Application fee:* $50. *Comprehensive fee:* $34,973 includes full-time tuition ($25,956), mandatory fees ($654), and college room and board ($8363). *College room only:* $5093. *Part-time tuition:* $721 per quarter hour.
Financial Aid Forms of aid include need-based and non-need-based scholarships, athletic grants, and part-time jobs. The average aided 2002–03 undergraduate received an aid package worth $17,271. The priority application deadline for financial aid is February 15.
Freshman Admission DU requires an essay, a high school transcript, 2 recommendations, and SAT I or ACT scores. A minimum 2.7 high school GPA, an interview, and TOEFL scores for international students are recommended. A minimum 2.0 high school GPA is required for some. The application deadline for regular admission is January 15 and for early action it is November 15.
Transfer Admission The application deadline for admission is February 15.
Entrance Difficulty DU assesses its entrance difficulty level as moderately difficult. For the fall 2003 freshman class, 79 percent of the applicants were accepted.

For Further Information Contact Cezar Mesquita, Director of Admission Counselors, University of Denver, University Park, Denver, CO 80208. *Telephone:* 303-871-3383 or 800-525-9495 (toll-free out-of-state). *Fax:* 303-871-3301. *E-mail:* admission@du.edu. *Web site:* http://www.du.edu/.

UNIVERSITY OF NORTHERN COLORADO

Greeley, Colorado

UNC is a coed, public university, founded in 1890, offering degrees at the bachelor's, master's, and doctoral levels. It has a 240-acre campus in Greeley near Denver.

Academic Information The faculty has 547 members (76% full-time), 69% with terminal degrees. The undergraduate student-faculty ratio is 21:1. The library holds 1 million titles, 3,621 serial subscriptions, and 44,843 audiovisual materials. Special programs include academic remediation, services for learning-disabled students, an honors program, cooperative (work-study) education, study abroad, advanced placement credit, ESL programs, double majors, independent study, distance learning, self-designed majors, summer session for credit, part-time degree programs (daytime, evenings, weekends, summer), external degree programs, adult/continuing education programs, internships, and arrangement for off-campus study with National Student Exchange. The most frequently chosen baccalaureate fields are business/marketing, communications/communication technologies, social sciences and history.
Student Body Statistics The student body totals 13,204, of whom 10,664 are undergraduates (2,140 freshmen). 62 percent are women and 38 percent are men. Students come from 48 states and territories. 90 percent are from Colorado. 0.4 percent are international students. 11.6 percent of the 2003 graduating class went on to graduate and professional schools.
Expenses for 2003–04 *Application fee:* $30. *State resident tuition:* $2520 full-time, $140 per credit hour part-time. *Nonresident tuition:* $11,646 full-time, $647 per credit hour part-time. *Mandatory fees:* $685 full-time, $35 per credit hour part-time. *College room and board:* $5782. *College room only:* $2704. Room and board charges vary according to board plan and housing facility.
Financial Aid Forms of aid include need-based and non-need-based scholarships, athletic grants, and part-time jobs. The average aided 2002–03 undergraduate received an aid package worth $7557. The priority application deadline for financial aid is March 1.
Freshman Admission UNC requires a high school transcript, a minimum 2.9 high school GPA, SAT I or ACT scores, and TOEFL scores for international students. An interview is required for some. The application deadline for regular admission is August 1.
Transfer Admission The application deadline for admission is rolling.
Entrance Difficulty UNC assesses its entrance difficulty level as moderately difficult. For the fall 2003 freshman class, 71 percent of the applicants were accepted.

For Further Information Contact Mr. Gary O. Gullickson, Director of Admissions, University of Northern Colorado, Campus Box 10, Carter Hall 3006, Greeley, CO 80639. *Telephone:* 970-351-2881 or 888-700-4UNC (toll-free in-state). *Fax:* 970-351-2984. *E-mail:* unc@mail.unco.edu. *Web site:* http://www.unco.edu/.

UNIVERSITY OF PHOENIX–COLORADO CAMPUS

Lone Tree, Colorado

University of Phoenix–Colorado Campus is a coed, proprietary, comprehensive institution, offering degrees at the associate, bachelor's, master's, and doctoral levels and post-master's and postbachelor's certificates (courses conducted at 121 campuses and learning centers in 25 states).

Academic Information The faculty has 827 members (0.7% full-time), 29% with terminal degrees. The undergraduate student-faculty ratio is 10:1. The library holds 27 million titles and 1,648 serial subscriptions. Special programs include advanced placement credit, accelerated degree programs, independent study, distance learning, external degree programs, and adult/continuing education programs. The most frequently chosen baccalaureate fields are business/marketing, computer/information sciences, health professions and related sciences.
Student Body Statistics The student body totals 2,905, of whom 1,781 are undergraduates (88 freshmen). 53 percent are women and 47 percent are men. 2.7 percent are international students.
Expenses for 2003–04 *Application fee:* $100. *Tuition:* $8610 full-time, $287 per credit part-time.
Financial Aid Forms of aid include need-based scholarships. The average aided 2002–03 undergraduate received an aid package worth $1400. The application deadline for financial aid is continuous.
Freshman Admission University of Phoenix–Colorado Campus requires 1 recommendation, 2 years of work experience, 23 years of age, and TOEFL scores for international students. A high school transcript is required for some. The application deadline for regular admission is rolling.
Transfer Admission The application deadline for admission is rolling.
Entrance Difficulty University of Phoenix–Colorado Campus has an open admission policy.

For Further Information Contact Ms. Beth Barilla, Director of Admissions, University of Phoenix–Colorado Campus, 4615 East Elwood Street, Mail Stop AA-K101, Phoenix, AZ 85040-1958. *Telephone:* 480-557-1712 or 800-228-7240 (toll-free). *Fax:* 480-594-1758. *E-mail:* beth.barilla@phoenix.edu. *Web site:* http://www.phoenix.edu/.

UNIVERSITY OF PHOENIX–SOUTHERN COLORADO CAMPUS

Colorado Springs, Colorado

University of Phoenix–Southern Colorado Campus is a coed, proprietary, comprehensive institution, founded in 1999, offering degrees at the associate, bachelor's, master's, and doctoral levels and post-master's and postbachelor's certificates (courses conducted at 121 campuses and learning centers in 25 states).

Academic Information The faculty has 232 members (1% full-time), 20% with terminal degrees. The undergraduate student-faculty ratio is 7:1. The library holds 27 million titles and 11,648 serial subscriptions. Special programs include advanced placement credit, accelerated degree programs, independent study, distance learning, external degree programs, and adult/continuing education programs. The most frequently chosen baccalaureate fields are business/marketing, computer/information sciences, health professions and related sciences.

Student Body Statistics The student body totals 624, of whom 461 are undergraduates (20 freshmen). 51 percent are women and 49 percent are men. 15.6 percent are international students.
Expenses for 2003–04 *Application fee:* $85. *Tuition:* $8610 full-time, $287 per credit part-time.
Financial Aid Forms of aid include need-based and non-need-based scholarships. The average aided 2002–03 undergraduate received an aid package worth $1563. The application deadline for financial aid is continuous.
Freshman Admission University of Phoenix–Southern Colorado Campus requires 1 recommendation, 2 years of work experience, 23 years of age, and TOEFL scores for international students. A high school transcript is required for some. The application deadline for regular admission is rolling.
Transfer Admission The application deadline for admission is rolling.
Entrance Difficulty University of Phoenix–Southern Colorado Campus has an open admission policy.

For Further Information Contact Ms. Beth Barilla, Director of Admissions, University of Phoenix–Southern Colorado Campus, 4615 East Elwood Street, Mail Stop AA-K101, Phoenix, AZ 85040-1958. *Telephone:* 480-557-1712 or 800-228-7240 (toll-free). *Fax:* 480-894-1758. *E-mail:* beth.barilla@phoenix.edu. *Web site:* http://www.phoenix.edu/.

UNIVERSITY OF SOUTHERN COLORADO

See Colorado State University-Pueblo

WESTERN STATE COLLEGE OF COLORADO

Gunnison, Colorado

Western State College is a coed, public, four-year college, founded in 1901, offering degrees at the bachelor's level. It has a 381-acre campus in Gunnison.

Academic Information The faculty has 120 members (83% full-time), 68% with terminal degrees. The student-faculty ratio is 21:1. The library holds 158,698 titles, 719 serial subscriptions, and 1,539 audiovisual materials. Special programs include services for learning-disabled students, an honors program, cooperative (work-study) education, study abroad, advanced placement credit, accelerated degree programs, double majors, self-designed majors, summer session for credit, part-time degree programs (summer), adult/continuing education programs, internships, and arrangement for off-campus study with State Colleges of Colorado, National Student Exchange. The most frequently chosen baccalaureate fields are business/marketing, parks and recreation, social sciences and history.
Student Body Statistics The student body is made up of 2,385 undergraduates (634 freshmen). 41 percent are women and 59 percent are men. Students come from 50 states and territories. 72 percent are from Colorado. 12 percent of the 2003 graduating class went on to graduate and professional schools.
Expenses for 2003–04 *Application fee:* $40. *State resident tuition:* $1783 full-time, $89.15 per credit hour part-time. *Nonresident tuition:* $8965 full-time, $448.25 per credit hour part-time. *Mandatory fees:* $781 full-time, $33.35 per credit hour part-time. Full-time tuition and fees vary according to course load. Part-time tuition and fees vary according to course load. *College room and board:* $5680. *College room only:* $3524. Room and board charges vary according to board plan and housing facility.
Financial Aid Forms of aid include need-based and non-need-based scholarships, athletic grants, and part-time jobs. The average aided 2003–04 undergraduate received an aid package worth an estimated $8800. The priority application deadline for financial aid is April 1.
Freshman Admission Western State College requires a high school transcript, SAT I or ACT scores, and TOEFL scores for international students. A minimum 2.5 high school GPA is recommended. An essay, 2 recommendations, and an interview are required for some. The application deadline for regular admission is August 1.
Entrance Difficulty Western State College assesses its entrance difficulty level as moderately difficult. For the fall 2003 freshman class, 79 percent of the applicants were accepted.

For Further Information Contact Mr. Timothy L. Albers, Director of Admissions, Western State College of Colorado, Western State College of Colorado, 6 Admission Office, 600 North Adams, Gunnison, CO 81231. *Telephone:* 970-943-2119 or 800-876-5309 (toll-free). *Fax:* 970-943-2212. *E-mail:* discover@western.edu. *Web site:* http://www.western.edu/.

WESTWOOD COLLEGE–DENVER SOUTH

Denver, Colorado

Westwood College–Denver South is a coed, proprietary, primarily two-year college, offering degrees at the associate and bachelor's levels. It is located in Denver near Denver, CO.

Academic Information The faculty has 38 members. The most frequently chosen baccalaureate fields are computer/information sciences, visual/performing arts.
Student Body Statistics The student body is made up of 429 undergraduates (47 freshmen). 31 percent are women and 69 percent are men.
Financial Aid Forms of aid include need-based scholarships and part-time jobs. The application deadline for financial aid is continuous.
Freshman Admission Westwood College–Denver South requires an interview and HS diploma or GED and entrance exam (SAT/ACT or Accuplacer).
Entrance Difficulty For the fall 2003 freshman class, 58 percent of the applicants were accepted.

For Further Information Contact Mr. Ron DeJong, Director of Admissions, Westwood College–Denver South, 3150 South Sheridan Boulevard, Denver, CO 80227-5548. *Telephone:* 303-934-2790. *Fax:* 303-934-2583. *E-mail:* info@westwood.edu. *Web site:* http://www.westwood.edu/.

WESTWOOD COLLEGE–DENVER NORTH

Denver, Colorado

Westwood is a coed, proprietary, primarily two-year college, founded in 1953, offering degrees at the associate and bachelor's levels. It has an 11-acre campus in Denver.

Academic Information The faculty has 101 members (41% full-time), 4% with terminal degrees. The student-faculty ratio is 16:1. The library holds 2,500 titles, 160 serial subscriptions, and 40 audiovisual materials. Special programs include academic remediation, services for learning-disabled students, advanced placement credit, accelerated degree programs, independent study, distance learning, summer session for credit, part-time degree programs (evenings, summer), and internships. The most frequently chosen baccalaureate fields are computer/information sciences, business/marketing, visual/performing arts.
Student Body Statistics The student body is made up of 1,368 undergraduates (254 freshmen). 29 percent are women and 71 percent are men. Students come from 31 states and territories and 3 other countries. 88 percent are from Colorado. 0.2 percent are international students.
Expenses for 2004–05 *Application fee:* $100. *Tuition:* $18,645 full-time, $2654 per term part-time. *Mandatory fees:* $950 full-time, $404 per credit part-time. Full-time tuition and fees vary according to course load and program. Part-time tuition and fees vary according to course load and program.
Financial Aid Forms of aid include need-based and non-need-based scholarships and part-time jobs. The application deadline for financial aid is continuous.
Freshman Admission Westwood requires a high school transcript. An interview, SAT I and SAT II or ACT scores, and SAT II: Writing Test scores are recommended. ACCUPLACER is required for some. The application deadline for regular admission is rolling.
Transfer Admission The application deadline for admission is rolling.

Westwood College–Denver North (continued)

Entrance Difficulty Westwood assesses its entrance difficulty level as moderately difficult. For the fall 2003 freshman class, 48 percent of the applicants were accepted.

For Further Information Contact Ms. Nicole Blaschko, New Student Coordinator, Westwood College–Denver North, 7350 North Broadway, Denver, CO 80221-3653. *Telephone:* 303-650-5050 Ext. 100 or 800-992-5050 (toll-free). *Fax:* 303-426-0702. *Web site:* http://www.westwood.edu/.

YESHIVA TORAS CHAIM TALMUDICAL SEMINARY

Denver, Colorado

For Information Write to Yeshiva Toras Chaim Talmudical Seminary, Denver, CO 80204-1415.

Hawaii

ARGOSY UNIVERSITY/HONOLULU

Honolulu, Hawaii

For Information Write to Argosy University/Honolulu, Honolulu, HI 96813.

BRIGHAM YOUNG UNIVERSITY–HAWAII

Laie, Hawaii

BYU-Hawaii is a coed, private, Latter-day Saints, four-year college, founded in 1955, offering degrees at the associate and bachelor's levels and postbachelor's certificates. It has a 60-acre campus in Laie near Honolulu.

Academic Information The faculty has 208 members (59% full-time), 37% with terminal degrees. The student-faculty ratio is 16:1. The library holds 321,400 titles, 11,325 serial subscriptions, and 7,000 audiovisual materials. Special programs include academic remediation, services for learning-disabled students, an honors program, cooperative (work-study) education, advanced placement credit, accelerated degree programs, Freshman Honors College, ESL programs, double majors, summer session for credit, part-time degree programs (daytime, evenings, summer), adult/continuing education programs, internships, and arrangement for off-campus study. The most frequently chosen baccalaureate fields are business/marketing, computer/information sciences, education.
Student Body Statistics The student body is made up of 2,703 undergraduates (262 freshmen). 54 percent are women and 46 percent are men. Students come from 44 states and territories and 68 other countries. 63 percent are from Hawaii. 47 percent are international students.
Expenses for 2003–04 *Application fee:* $25. *Comprehensive fee:* $7240 includes full-time tuition ($2580) and college room and board ($4660). *College room only:* $2000. Full-time tuition varies according to program. Room and board charges vary according to board plan and housing facility. *Part-time tuition:* $175 per credit. Part-time tuition varies according to program.
Financial Aid Forms of aid include need-based and non-need-based scholarships, athletic grants, and part-time jobs. The average aided 2002–03 undergraduate received an aid package worth $2850. The priority application deadline for financial aid is April 30.
Freshman Admission BYU-Hawaii requires an essay, a high school transcript, a minimum 3.0 high school GPA, resume of activities, ecclesiastical endorsement, SAT I or ACT scores, and TOEFL scores for international students. ACT scores are recommended. Recommendations are required for some. The application deadline for regular admission is February 15.
Transfer Admission The application deadline for admission is March 15.
Entrance Difficulty BYU-Hawaii assesses its entrance difficulty level as moderately difficult. For the fall 2003 freshman class, 29 percent of the applicants were accepted.

For Further Information Contact Mr. Jeffrey N. Bunker, Dean for Admissions and Records, Brigham Young University–Hawaii, 55-220 Kulanui Street, BYUH 1973, Laie, Oahu, HI 96762. *Telephone:* 808-293-3731. *Fax:* 808-293-3741. *E-mail:* admissions@byuh.edu. *Web site:* http://www.byuh.edu/.

CHAMINADE UNIVERSITY OF HONOLULU

Honolulu, Hawaii

Chaminade University is a coed, private, Roman Catholic, comprehensive institution, founded in 1955, offering degrees at the associate, bachelor's, and master's levels and postbachelor's certificates. It has a 62-acre campus in Honolulu.

Academic Information The faculty has 182 members (42% full-time), 40% with terminal degrees. The undergraduate student-faculty ratio is 14:1. The library holds 78,000 titles, 6,730 serial subscriptions, and 566 audiovisual materials. Special programs include academic remediation, advanced placement credit, accelerated degree programs, double majors, independent study, distance learning, self-designed majors, summer session for credit, part-time degree programs (daytime, evenings, weekends, summer), adult/continuing education programs, internships, and arrangement for off-campus study with University of Hawaii at Manoa, Brigham Young University, Hawaii Pacific University. The most frequently chosen baccalaureate fields are protective services/public administration, psychology, social sciences and history.
Student Body Statistics The student body totals 1,742, of whom 1,063 are undergraduates (254 freshmen). 68 percent are women and 32 percent are men. Students come from 41 states and territories and 11 other countries. 57 percent are from Hawaii. 2.5 percent are international students.
Expenses for 2003–04 *Application fee:* $50. *Comprehensive fee:* $21,430 includes full-time tuition ($13,380), mandatory fees ($120), and college room and board ($7930). *College room only:* $4150.
Financial Aid Forms of aid include need-based and non-need-based scholarships, athletic grants, and part-time jobs. The average aided 2003–04 undergraduate received an aid package worth an estimated $12,201. The priority application deadline for financial aid is March 1.
Freshman Admission Chaminade University requires a high school transcript, SAT I or ACT scores, and TOEFL scores for international students. A minimum 2.0 high school GPA is recommended. An interview is required for some. The application deadline for regular admission is rolling.
Transfer Admission The application deadline for admission is rolling.
Entrance Difficulty Chaminade University assesses its entrance difficulty level as moderately difficult. For the fall 2003 freshman class, 96 percent of the applicants were accepted.

For Further Information Contact Ao' Lani Lorenzo, Admissions Counselor, Chaminade University of Honolulu, 3140 Waialae Avenue, Honolulu, HI 96816-1578. *Telephone:* 808-735-4735 or 800-735-3733 (toll-free out-of-state). *Fax:* 808-739-4647. *E-mail:* admissions@chaminade.edu. *Web site:* http://www.chaminade.edu/.

See page 162 for a narrative description.

EDUCATION AMERICA, HONOLULU CAMPUS

See Remington College–Honolulu Campus

HAWAII BUSINESS COLLEGE

Honolulu, Hawaii

Hawaii Business College is a coed, private, two-year college, founded in 1973, offering degrees at the associate level.

For Further Information Contact Ms. Michell Basilio, Director of Admissions, Hawaii Business College, 33 South King Street, Fourth Floor, Honolulu, HI 96813. *Telephone:* 808-524-4014. *Fax:* 808-524-0284. *E-mail:* admin@hbc.edu. *Web site:* http://www.hbc.edu/.

HAWAI'I PACIFIC UNIVERSITY

Honolulu, Hawaii

HPU is a coed, private, comprehensive institution, founded in 1965, offering degrees at the associate, bachelor's, and master's levels and post-master's and postbachelor's certificates. It has a 140-acre campus in Honolulu.

Academic Information The faculty has 582 members (39% full-time), 48% with terminal degrees. The undergraduate student-faculty ratio is 18:1. The library holds 160,000 titles, 12,000 serial subscriptions, and 8,695 audiovisual materials. Special programs include academic remediation, services for learning-disabled students, an honors program, cooperative (work-study) education, study abroad, advanced placement credit, accelerated degree programs, Freshman Honors College, ESL programs, double majors, independent study, distance learning, self-designed majors, summer session for credit, part-time degree programs (daytime, evenings, weekends, summer), adult/continuing education programs, and internships. The most frequently chosen baccalaureate fields are business/marketing, health professions and related sciences, protective services/public administration.
Student Body Statistics The student body totals 7,900, of whom 6,735 are undergraduates (590 freshmen). 56 percent are women and 44 percent are men. Students come from 52 states and territories and 85 other countries. 73 percent are from Hawaii. 14.8 percent are international students. 56 percent of the 2003 graduating class went on to graduate and professional schools.
Expenses for 2003–04 *Application fee:* $50. *Comprehensive fee:* $19,138 includes full-time tuition ($10,368) and college room and board ($8770). Full-time tuition varies according to program and student level. Room and board charges vary according to housing facility. *Part-time tuition:* $200 per credit. Part-time tuition varies according to course load.
Financial Aid Forms of aid include need-based and non-need-based scholarships, athletic grants, and part-time jobs. The average aided 2002–03 undergraduate received an aid package worth $10,392. The priority application deadline for financial aid is March 1.
Freshman Admission HPU requires a high school transcript, a minimum 2.5 high school GPA, and SAT I or ACT scores. An essay, 2 recommendations, and TOEFL scores for international students are recommended. An interview is required for some. The application deadline for regular admission is rolling.
Transfer Admission The application deadline for admission is rolling.
Entrance Difficulty HPU assesses its entrance difficulty level as moderately difficult. For the fall 2003 freshman class, 81 percent of the applicants were accepted.

SPECIAL MESSAGE TO STUDENTS

Social Life Student life at Hawai'i Pacific University (HPU) is designed to meet students' needs at both the commuter campus in downtown Honolulu and windward Hawai'i Loa campus. Student government and a variety of clubs and organizations—representing student interest in preprofessional, service, cultural, and sports activities—offer opportunities for leadership development. Students participate in an array of intramural sports, including aerobics, basketball, tennis, and volleyball. With its culturally diverse student body and faculty, HPU is rich in exciting and stimulating experiences, both in and out of the classroom.

Academic Highlights Career Services is central to the philosophy at HPU. The Cooperative Education and Internship Program offers students in most majors the option of paid work experience and up to 12 semester hours of credit for that work. International programs are offered in the context of Hawai'i's multicultural society and also provide opportunities to study abroad. The marine science program involves extensive fieldwork aboard the University's 42-foot research vessel *Kaholo*. Four summer sessions are available during which a student may earn credit equivalent to a regular academic semester.

Interviews and Campus Visits HPU believes a visit to the campus by prospective students and their parents to be of great value. The University encourages students to make arrangements for a full campus tour. Admissions coordinators are available to review academic and cocurricular programs and to answer any questions. A visit can be arranged by phone, e-mail, or fax or via regular mail to suit the convenience of students and parents. Visitors to HPU should visit both the downtown campus and the windward Hawai'i Loa campus. The two are located 8 miles apart and are connected by a free intercampus shuttle. At the downtown campus, visitors should see Meader Library, the Learning Assistance Center, the Frear Center, and the Career Services Center. On the windward campus, visitors should see the Atherton Learning Center and the residence halls. For information about appointments and campus visits, prospective students should call the Office of Admissions at 808-544-0238 or 866–CALL–HPU (toll-free), Monday through Friday, 8 a.m. to 5 p.m. The fax number is 808-544-1136. The office is located at 1164 Bishop Street, Suite 200, on campus. The nearest commercial airport is Honolulu International.

For Further Information Write to the Office of Admissions, Hawai'i Pacific University, 1164 Bishop Street, Suite 200, Honolulu, HI 96813. *E-mail:* admissions@hpu.edu/jump. *Web site:* http://www.hpu.edu/jump.

See page 178 for a narrative description.

HAWAII TOKAI INTERNATIONAL COLLEGE

Honolulu, Hawaii

HTIC is a coed, private, two-year college of Tokai University Educational System (Japan), founded in 1992, offering degrees at the associate level.

Academic Information The faculty has 21 members (33% full-time), 19% with terminal degrees. The student-faculty ratio is 12:1. The library holds 7,000 titles, 100 serial subscriptions, and 500 audiovisual materials. Special programs include ESL programs and summer session for credit.
Student Body Statistics The student body is made up of 50 undergraduates (6 freshmen). 62 percent are women and 38 percent are men. Students come from 1 state or territory and 3 other countries. 88 percent of the 2003 graduating class went on to four-year colleges.
Expenses for 2003–04 *Application fee:* $50. *Comprehensive fee:* $10,775 includes full-time tuition ($8700), mandatory fees ($75), and college room and board ($2000). *College room only:* $1000. Room and board charges vary according to board plan. *Part-time tuition:* $375 per credit. *Part-time mandatory fees:* $25 per term. Part-time tuition and fees vary according to course load.
Financial Aid Forms of aid include need-based scholarships. The priority application deadline for financial aid is April 1.
Freshman Admission HTIC requires an essay, a high school transcript, an interview, and TOEFL scores for international students. The application deadline for regular admission is September 1.
Entrance Difficulty HTIC assesses its entrance difficulty level as noncompetitive. For the fall 2003 freshman class, 100 percent of the applicants were accepted.

For Further Information Contact Ms. Terry Lee McCandliss, Admissions Officer, Hawaii Tokai International College, 2241 Kapiolani Boulevard, Honolulu, HI 96826. *Telephone:* 808-983-4154. *Fax:* 808-983-4107. *E-mail:* htic@tokai.edu. *Web site:* http://www.tokai.edu/.

HEALD COLLEGE-HONOLULU

Honolulu, Hawaii

Heald College-Honolulu is a coed, private, two-year college, founded in 1863, offering degrees at the associate level.

For Further Information Contact Heald College-Honolulu, 1500 Kapiolani Boulevard, Suite 201, Honolulu, HI 96814. *Telephone:* 808-955-1500 or 800-755-3550 (toll-free in-state). *Fax:* 808-955-6964. *E-mail:* info@heald.edu. *Web site:* http://www.heald.edu/.

INTERNATIONAL COLLEGE AND GRADUATE SCHOOL

Honolulu, Hawaii

International College and Graduate School is a coed, private, interdenominational, upper-level institution, founded in 1967, offering degrees at the bachelor's, master's, and first professional levels in theology.

Academic Information The faculty has 39 members (8% full-time). The undergraduate student-faculty ratio is 12:1. The library holds 20,000 titles, 65 serial subscriptions, and 703 audiovisual materials. Special programs include study abroad, advanced placement credit, independent study, summer session for credit, part-time degree programs (daytime, evenings, summer), adult/continuing education programs, and internships.
Student Body Statistics The student body totals 64, of whom 26 are undergraduates (7 in entering class). 19 percent are women and 81 percent are men. Students come from 1 state or territory and 4 other countries. 42.3 percent are international students.
Financial Aid Forms of aid include need-based and non-need-based scholarships. The average aided 2003–04 undergraduate received an aid package worth an estimated $3500. The application deadline for financial aid is June 1.
Transfer Admission International College and Graduate School requires a college transcript and a minimum 2.5 college GPA. The application deadline for admission is rolling.
Entrance Difficulty International College and Graduate School has an open admission policy. It assesses its entrance difficulty as minimally difficult for transfers.

For Further Information Contact Mr. Jon Rawlings, Director of Admissions, International College and Graduate School, 20 Dowsett Avenue, Honolulu, HI 96817. *Telephone:* 808-595-4247 Ext. 108. *Fax:* 808-595-4779. *E-mail:* icgs@hawaii.rr.com. *Web site:* http://www.icgshawaii.org/.

REMINGTON COLLEGE–HONOLULU CAMPUS

Honolulu, Hawaii

For Information Write to Remington College–Honolulu Campus, Honolulu, HI 96813.

TRANSPACIFIC HAWAII COLLEGE

Honolulu, Hawaii

For Information Write to TransPacific Hawaii College, Honolulu, HI 96821-1884.

UNIVERSITY OF HAWAII AT HILO

Hilo, Hawaii

UH Hilo is a coed, public, comprehensive unit of University of Hawaii System, founded in 1970, offering degrees at the bachelor's and master's levels. It has a 115-acre campus in Hilo.

Academic Information The faculty has 264 members (65% full-time), 58% with terminal degrees. The undergraduate student-faculty ratio is 14:1. The library holds 250,000 titles and 2,500 serial subscriptions. Special programs include services for learning-disabled students, an honors program, study abroad, advanced placement credit, ESL programs, double majors, independent study, distance learning, self-designed majors, summer session for credit, part-time degree programs (daytime, evenings, summer), internships, and arrangement for off-campus study with members of the National Student Exchange.
Student Body Statistics The student body totals 3,300, of whom 3,214 are undergraduates. Students come from 48 states and territories and 40 other countries. 79 percent are from Hawaii. 10.3 percent are international students.
Expenses for 2004–05 *Application fee:* $40. *State resident tuition:* $2424 full-time, $101 per credit hour part-time. *Nonresident tuition:* $7992 full-time, $333 per credit hour part-time. *Mandatory fees:* $114 full-time, $32 per term part-time. Full-time tuition and fees vary according to course level and student level. Part-time tuition and fees vary according to course level and student level. *College room and board:* $5081. *College room only:* $2360. Room and board charges vary according to board plan and housing facility.
Financial Aid Forms of aid include need-based and non-need-based scholarships, athletic grants, and part-time jobs. The priority application deadline for financial aid is March 1.
Freshman Admission UH Hilo requires a high school transcript and SAT I or ACT scores. A minimum 3.0 high school GPA and TOEFL scores for international students are recommended. Recommendations are required for some. The application deadline for regular admission is July 1.
Transfer Admission The application deadline for admission is July 1.
Entrance Difficulty UH Hilo assesses its entrance difficulty level as moderately difficult. For the fall 2003 freshman class, 66 percent of the applicants were accepted.

For Further Information Contact Mr. James Cromwell, UH Student Services Specialist III/Director of Admissions, University of Hawaii at Hilo, 200 West Kawili Street, Hilo, HI 96720-4091. *Telephone:* 808-974-7414, 808-974-7414 (toll-free in-state), or 800-897-4456 (toll-free out-of-state). *Fax:* 808-933-0861. *E-mail:* uhhao@hawaii.edu. *Web site:* http://www.uhh.hawaii.edu/.

UNIVERSITY OF HAWAII AT MANOA

Honolulu, Hawaii

UHM is a coed, public university, founded in 1907, offering degrees at the bachelor's, master's, doctoral, and first professional levels and postbachelor's certificates. It has a 300-acre campus in Honolulu.

Academic Information The faculty has 1,215 members (93% full-time), 81% with terminal degrees. The undergraduate student-faculty ratio is 13:1. The library holds 3 million titles, 27,328 serial subscriptions, and 53,383 audiovisual materials. Special programs include services for learning-disabled students, an honors program, cooperative (work-study) education, study abroad, advanced placement credit, accelerated degree programs, ESL programs, double majors, independent study, distance learning, self-designed majors, summer session for credit, part-time degree programs (daytime, evenings, summer), adult/continuing education programs, internships, and arrangement for off-campus study with members of the National Student Exchange. The most frequently chosen baccalaureate fields are business/marketing, education, social sciences and history.
Student Body Statistics The student body totals 19,863, of whom 13,755 are undergraduates (1,996 freshmen). 56 percent are women and 44 percent are men. 84 percent are from Hawaii. 5.1 percent are international students.

Expenses for 2003–04 *Application fee:* $40. *Area resident tuition:* $138 per credit part-time. *State resident tuition:* $3408 full-time, $138 per credit part-time. *Nonresident tuition:* $9888 full-time, $408 per credit part-time. *Mandatory fees:* $153 full-time, $68.80 per credit part-time. Full-time tuition and fees vary according to class time, course load, and program. Part-time tuition and fees vary according to class time, course load, and program. *College room and board:* $5675. *College room only:* $3314. Room and board charges vary according to board plan and housing facility.
Financial Aid Forms of aid include need-based and non-need-based scholarships, athletic grants, and part-time jobs. The average aided 2002–03 undergraduate received an aid package worth $6092. The priority application deadline for financial aid is March 1.
Freshman Admission UHM requires a high school transcript, a minimum 2.8 high school GPA, minimum SAT I score of 510 for verbal and math sections, SAT I or ACT scores, and TOEFL scores for international students. The application deadline for regular admission is May 1.
Transfer Admission The application deadline for admission is May 1.
Entrance Difficulty UHM assesses its entrance difficulty level as moderately difficult. For the fall 2003 freshman class, 59 percent of the applicants were accepted.

For Further Information Contact Ms. Janice Heu, Interim Director of Admissions and Records, University of Hawaii at Manoa, 2600 Campus Road, Room 001, Honolulu, HI 96822. *Telephone:* 808-956-8975 or 800-823-9771 (toll-free). *Fax:* 808-956-4148. *E-mail:* ar-info@hawaii.edu. *Web site:* http://www.uhm.hawaii.edu/.

UNIVERSITY OF HAWAII–WEST OAHU

Pearl City, Hawaii

UH-West Oahu is a coed, public, upper-level unit of University of Hawaii System, founded in 1976, offering degrees at the bachelor's level. It is located in Pearl City near Honolulu.

Expenses for 2003–04 *Application fee:* $25. *State resident tuition:* $2112 full-time, $88 per credit part-time. *Nonresident tuition:* $7248 full-time, $302 per credit part-time. *Mandatory fees:* $10 full-time, $5 per term part-time.

For Further Information Contact Jean M. Osumi, Dean of Student Services, University of Hawaii–West Oahu, 96-043 Ala Ike, Pearl City, HI 96782. *Telephone:* 808-453-4700. *Fax:* 805-453-6076. *E-mail:* jeano@uhwo.hawaii.edu.

UNIVERSITY OF PHOENIX–HAWAII CAMPUS

Honolulu, Hawaii

University of Phoenix–Hawaii Campus is a coed, proprietary, comprehensive institution, offering degrees at the associate, bachelor's, master's, and doctoral levels and post-master's and postbachelor's certificates (courses conducted at 121 campuses and learning centers in 25 states).

Academic Information The faculty has 292 members (2% full-time), 26% with terminal degrees. The undergraduate student-faculty ratio is 10:1. The library holds 27 million titles and 11,648 serial subscriptions. Special programs include advanced placement credit, accelerated degree programs, independent study, distance learning, external degree programs, and adult/continuing education programs. The most frequently chosen baccalaureate fields are business/marketing, health professions and related sciences.
Student Body Statistics The student body totals 1,273, of whom 816 are undergraduates (22 freshmen). 63 percent are women and 37 percent are men. 7 percent are international students.
Expenses for 2003–04 *Application fee:* $100. *Tuition:* $11,070 full-time, $369 per credit part-time.
Financial Aid Forms of aid include need-based scholarships. The average aided 2002–03 undergraduate received an aid package worth $1402. The application deadline for financial aid is continuous.
Freshman Admission University of Phoenix–Hawaii Campus requires 1 recommendation, 2 years of work experience, 23 years of age, and TOEFL scores for international students. A high school transcript is required for some. The application deadline for regular admission is rolling.
Transfer Admission The application deadline for admission is rolling.
Entrance Difficulty University of Phoenix–Hawaii Campus has an open admission policy.

For Further Information Contact Ms. Beth Barilla, Director of Admissions, University of Phoenix–Hawaii Campus, 4615 East Elwood Street, Mail Stop AA-K101, Phoenix, AZ 85040-1958. *Telephone:* 480-317-6000 or 800-228-7240 (toll-free out-of-state). *Fax:* 480-594-1758. *E-mail:* beth.barilla@phoenix.edu. *Web site:* http://www.phoenix.edu/.

Idaho

ALBERTSON COLLEGE OF IDAHO

Caldwell, Idaho

Albertson is a coed, private, comprehensive institution, founded in 1891, offering degrees at the bachelor's and master's levels. It has a 50-acre campus in Caldwell.

Academic Information The faculty has 69 members (83% full-time), 88% with terminal degrees. The undergraduate student-faculty ratio is 13:1. The library holds 183,308 titles and 703 serial subscriptions. Special programs include services for learning-disabled students, an honors program, study abroad, advanced placement credit, ESL programs, double majors, independent study, self-designed majors, part-time degree programs (daytime), internships, and arrangement for off-campus study with Northwest Nazarene University.
Student Body Statistics The student body totals 830, of whom 821 are undergraduates (182 freshmen). 54 percent are women and 46 percent are men. Students come from 21 states and territories. 75 percent are from Idaho. 1.4 percent are international students. 22 percent of the 2003 graduating class went on to graduate and professional schools.
Expenses for 2003–04 *Application fee:* $50. *Comprehensive fee:* $19,450 includes full-time tuition ($13,900), mandatory fees ($500), and college room and board ($5050). *College room only:* $2450. Room and board charges vary according to board plan and housing facility. *Part-time tuition:* $580 per credit. *Part-time mandatory fees:* $600 per term. Part-time tuition and fees vary according to course load.
Financial Aid Forms of aid include need-based and non-need-based scholarships, athletic grants, and part-time jobs. The average aided 2003–04 undergraduate received an aid package worth an estimated $14,738. The priority application deadline for financial aid is February 15.
Freshman Admission Albertson requires an essay, a high school transcript, 1 recommendation, SAT I or ACT scores, and TOEFL scores for international students. An interview is recommended. The application deadline for regular admission is June 1 and for early action it is November 15.
Transfer Admission The application deadline for admission is August 1.
Entrance Difficulty Albertson assesses its entrance difficulty level as moderately difficult. For the fall 2003 freshman class, 79 percent of the applicants were accepted.

For Further Information Contact Ms. Brandie Holly, Associate Dean of Admission, Albertson College of Idaho, 2112 Cleveland Boulevard, Caldwell, ID 83605-4494. *Telephone:* 208-459-5305 or 800-224-3246 (toll-free). *Fax:* 208-459-5757. *E-mail:* admission@albertson.edu. *Web site:* http://www.albertson.edu/.

BOISE BIBLE COLLEGE

Boise, Idaho

BBC is a coed, private, nondenominational, four-year college, founded in 1945, offering degrees at the associate and bachelor's levels in Christian ministries. It has a 17-acre campus in Boise.

Expenses for 2003–04 *Application fee:* $25. *Comprehensive fee:* $10,288 includes full-time tuition ($6000), mandatory fees ($88), and college room and board ($4200).

For Further Information Contact Mr. Ross Knudsen, Director of Admissions, Boise Bible College, 8695 Marigold Street, Boise, ID 83704. *Telephone:* 208-376-7731 or 800-893-7755 (toll-free). *Fax:* 208-376-7743. *E-mail:* boibible@micron.net. *Web site:* http://www.boisebible.edu/.

BOISE STATE UNIVERSITY

Boise, Idaho

Boise State is a coed, public, comprehensive unit of Idaho System of Higher Education, founded in 1932, offering degrees at the associate, bachelor's, master's, and doctoral levels. It has a 130-acre campus in Boise.

Academic Information The faculty has 1,015 members (61% full-time), 68% with terminal degrees. The undergraduate student-faculty ratio is 21:1. The library holds 505,618 titles and 4,797 serial subscriptions. Special programs include academic remediation, services for learning-disabled students, an honors program, cooperative (work-study) education, study abroad, advanced placement credit, Freshman Honors College, ESL programs, double majors, independent study, distance learning, self-designed majors, summer session for credit, part-time degree programs (daytime, evenings, weekends, summer), adult/continuing education programs, internships, and arrangement for off-campus study with National Student Exchange. The most frequently chosen baccalaureate fields are business/marketing, education, social sciences and history.
Student Body Statistics The student body totals 18,332, of whom 16,551 are undergraduates (2,137 freshmen). 54 percent are women and 46 percent are men. Students come from 43 states and territories and 47 other countries. 93 percent are from Idaho. 1.1 percent are international students. 40 percent of the 2003 graduating class went on to graduate and professional schools.
Expenses for 2003–04 *Application fee:* $30. *State resident tuition:* $3251 full-time, $162 per credit part-time. *Nonresident tuition:* $9971 full-time, $162 per credit part-time. Part-time tuition varies according to course load. *College room and board:* $4426. Room and board charges vary according to board plan and housing facility.
Financial Aid Forms of aid include need-based and non-need-based scholarships, athletic grants, and part-time jobs. The average aided 2003–04 undergraduate received an aid package worth an estimated $6978. The application deadline for financial aid is June 1 with a priority deadline of February 15.
Freshman Admission Boise State requires TOEFL scores for international students. A high school transcript, a minimum 2.0 high school GPA, and SAT I or ACT scores are required for some. The application deadline for regular admission is July 14.
Transfer Admission The application deadline for admission is July 14.
Entrance Difficulty Boise State assesses its entrance difficulty level as minimally difficult; moderately difficult for transfers; moderately difficult for nursing program. For the fall 2003 freshman class, 92 percent of the applicants were accepted.

For Further Information Contact Ms. Barbara Fortin, Dean of Admissions, Boise State University, Enrollment Services, 1910 University Drive, Boise, ID 83725. *Telephone:* 208-426-1177, 800-632-6586 (toll-free in-state), or 800-824-7017 (toll-free out-of-state). *E-mail:* bsuinfo@boisestate.edu. *Web site:* http://www.boisestate.edu/.

BRIGHAM YOUNG UNIVERSITY –IDAHO

Rexburg, Idaho

BYU-Idaho is a coed, private, two-year college, founded in 1888, affiliated with The Church of Jesus Christ of Latter-day Saints, offering degrees at the associate level. It has a 255-acre campus in Rexburg.

Expenses for 2003–04 *Application fee:* $30. *Comprehensive fee:* $5950 includes full-time tuition ($2554) and college room and board ($3396). *College room only:* $2998.

For Further Information Contact Mr. Steven Davis, Assistant Director of Admissions, Brigham Young University –Idaho, 120 Kimball, Rexburg, ID 83460-1615. *Telephone:* 208-496-1026. *Fax:* 208-356-1220. *E-mail:* harrisk@ricks.edu. *Web site:* http://www.byui.edu/.

IDAHO STATE UNIVERSITY

Pocatello, Idaho

ISU is a coed, public university, founded in 1901, offering degrees at the associate, bachelor's, master's, doctoral, and first professional levels and post-master's, first professional, and postbachelor's certificates. It has a 972-acre campus in Pocatello.

Academic Information The faculty has 615 members (89% full-time), 54% with terminal degrees. The undergraduate student-faculty ratio is 17:1. The library holds 682,954 titles, 3,800 serial subscriptions, and 701 audiovisual materials. Special programs include academic remediation, services for learning-disabled students, an honors program, study abroad, advanced placement credit, ESL programs, double majors, independent study, distance learning, self-designed majors, summer session for credit, part-time degree programs (daytime, evenings, summer), external degree programs, adult/continuing education programs, internships, and arrangement for off-campus study with University of Idaho, National Student Exchange. The most frequently chosen baccalaureate fields are business/marketing, education, health professions and related sciences.
Student Body Statistics The student body totals 13,621, of whom 11,451 are undergraduates (1,971 freshmen). 55 percent are women and 45 percent are men. Students come from 46 states and territories and 62 other countries. 95 percent are from Idaho. 1.4 percent are international students.
Expenses for 2003–04 *Application fee:* $35. *State resident tuition:* $0 full-time, $172 per credit hour part-time. *Nonresident tuition:* $6600 full-time, $267 per credit hour part-time. *Mandatory fees:* $3448 full-time. Full-time tuition and fees vary according to reciprocity agreements. Part-time tuition varies according to reciprocity agreements. *College room and board:* $4680. *College room only:* $1980. Room and board charges vary according to board plan and housing facility.
Financial Aid Forms of aid include need-based and non-need-based scholarships, athletic grants, and part-time jobs. The application deadline for financial aid is continuous.
Freshman Admission ISU requires a high school transcript, a minimum 2.0 high school GPA, SAT I or ACT scores, and TOEFL scores for international students. The application deadline for regular admission is August 1.
Transfer Admission The application deadline for admission is August 1.
Entrance Difficulty ISU assesses its entrance difficulty level as minimally difficult; noncompetitive for applicants over 21 with GED. For the fall 2003 freshman class, 74 percent of the applicants were accepted.

For Further Information Contact Mr. Nathan Peterson, Associate Director of Recruitment, Idaho State University, Campus Box 8270, Pocatello, ID 83209. *Telephone:* 208-282-2477. *Fax:* 208-282-4231. *E-mail:* info@isu.edu. *Web site:* http://www.isu.edu/.

ITT TECHNICAL INSTITUTE

Boise, Idaho

ITT Tech is a coed, proprietary, primarily two-year college of ITT Educational Services, Inc., founded in 1906, offering degrees at the associate and bachelor's levels. It has a 1-acre campus in Boise.

Student Body Statistics The student body is made up of 389 undergraduates.
Expenses for 2003–04 *Application fee:* $100. Total Program Cost varies depending on course of study. Consult school catalog.
Financial Aid Forms of aid include need-based scholarships and part-time jobs. The application deadline for financial aid is continuous.
Freshman Admission ITT Tech requires a high school transcript, an interview, TOEFL scores for international students, and Wonderlic aptitude test. Recommendations are recommended. The application deadline for regular admission is rolling.
Transfer Admission The application deadline for admission is rolling.
Entrance Difficulty ITT Tech assesses its entrance difficulty level as minimally difficult.

For Further Information Contact Terry G. Lowder, Director of Recruitment, ITT Technical Institute, 12302 West Explorer Drive, Boise, ID 83713. *Telephone:* 208-322-8844 or 800-666-4888 (toll-free in-state). *Fax:* 208-322-0173. *Web site:* http://www.itt-tech.edu/.

LEWIS-CLARK STATE COLLEGE

Lewiston, Idaho

LCSC is a coed, public, four-year college, founded in 1893, offering degrees at the associate and bachelor's levels. It has a 44-acre campus in Lewiston.

Academic Information The faculty has 186 members (73% full-time), 49% with terminal degrees. The student-faculty ratio is 17:1. The library holds 139,499 titles, 1,612 serial subscriptions, and 6,957 audiovisual materials. Special programs include academic remediation, services for learning-disabled students, cooperative (work-study) education, study abroad, advanced placement credit, accelerated degree programs, ESL programs, double majors, independent study, distance learning, self-designed majors, summer session for credit, part-time degree programs (daytime, evenings, weekends, summer), external degree programs, adult/continuing education programs, internships, and arrangement for off-campus study. The most frequently chosen baccalaureate fields are business/marketing, health professions and related sciences, protective services/public administration.
Student Body Statistics The student body is made up of 3,471 undergraduates (514 freshmen). 61 percent are women and 39 percent are men. Students come from 20 states and territories and 30 other countries. 87 percent are from Idaho. 2.8 percent are international students.
Expenses for 2003–04 *Application fee:* $35. *State resident tuition:* $0 full-time. *Nonresident tuition:* $5998 full-time. *Mandatory fees:* $3126 full-time, $153 per credit part-time. Full-time tuition and fees vary according to course load and reciprocity agreements. *College room and board:* $4336. *College room only:* $1880. Room and board charges vary according to board plan and housing facility.
Financial Aid Forms of aid include need-based and non-need-based scholarships, athletic grants, and part-time jobs. The average aided 2002–03 undergraduate received an aid package worth $5239. The priority application deadline for financial aid is March 1.
Freshman Admission LCSC requires a high school transcript, a minimum 2.0 high school GPA, and TOEFL scores for international students. An interview, SAT I or ACT scores, and ACT COMPASS are required for some. The application deadline for regular admission is rolling.
Transfer Admission The application deadline for admission is rolling.
Entrance Difficulty LCSC assesses its entrance difficulty level as minimally difficult; moderately difficult for nursing program, international students. For the fall 2003 freshman class, 64 percent of the applicants were accepted.

For Further Information Contact Ms. Tracy Waffle, Admissions Supervisor, Lewis-Clark State College, 500 8th Avenue, Lewiston, ID 83501. *Telephone:* 208-792-2210 or 800-933-LCSC Ext. 2210 (toll-free). *Fax:* 208-792-2876. *E-mail:* admissions@lcsc.edu. *Web site:* http://www.lcsc.edu/.

NEW SAINT ANDREWS COLLEGE

Moscow, Idaho

For Information Write to New Saint Andrews College, Moscow, ID 83843.

NORTHWEST NAZARENE UNIVERSITY

Nampa, Idaho

Northwest Nazarene University is a coed, private, comprehensive institution, founded in 1913, affiliated with the Church of the Nazarene, offering degrees at the bachelor's and master's levels. It has an 85-acre campus in Nampa.

Academic Information The faculty has 98 members (98% full-time), 62% with terminal degrees. The undergraduate student-faculty ratio is 13:1. The library holds 100,966 titles and 821 serial subscriptions. Special programs include academic remediation, services for learning-disabled students, an honors program, cooperative (work-study) education, study abroad, advanced placement credit, accelerated degree programs, Freshman Honors College, independent study, self-designed majors, summer session for credit, part-time degree programs (daytime, evenings, summer), internships, and arrangement for off-campus study with Albertson College of Idaho. The most frequently chosen baccalaureate fields are business/marketing, education, protective services/public administration.
Student Body Statistics The student body totals 1,565, of whom 1,156 are undergraduates (283 freshmen). 56 percent are women and 44 percent are men. Students come from 22 states and territories. 44 percent are from Idaho. 0.4 percent are international students.
Expenses for 2004–05 *Application fee:* $25. *Comprehensive fee:* $21,200 includes full-time tuition ($15,980), mandatory fees ($590), and college room and board ($4630). Room and board charges vary according to board plan and student level. *Part-time tuition:* $693 per credit. *Part-time mandatory fees:* $70 per term. Part-time tuition and fees vary according to course load.
Financial Aid Forms of aid include need-based and non-need-based scholarships, athletic grants, and part-time jobs. The average aided 2003–04 undergraduate received an aid package worth an estimated $12,598. The priority application deadline for financial aid is March 1.
Freshman Admission Northwest Nazarene University requires an essay, a high school transcript, a minimum 2.5 high school GPA, 2 recommendations, ACT scores, and TOEFL scores for international students. An interview is required for some. The application deadline for regular admission is August 8 and for early action it is December 1.
Transfer Admission The application deadline for admission is August 8.
Entrance Difficulty Northwest Nazarene University assesses its entrance difficulty level as moderately difficult. For the fall 2003 freshman class, 70 percent of the applicants were accepted.

For Further Information Contact Ms. Dianna Gibney, Director of Admissions, Northwest Nazarene University, 623 Holly Street, Admissions Welcome Center, Nampa, ID 83686. *Telephone:* 208-467-8000 or 877-NNU-4YOU (toll-free). *Fax:* 208-467-8645. *E-mail:* admissions@nnu.edu. *Web site:* http://www.nnu.edu/.

UNIVERSITY OF IDAHO

Moscow, Idaho

Idaho is a coed, public university, founded in 1889, offering degrees at the bachelor's, master's, doctoral, and first professional levels and post-master's certificates. It has a 1,450-acre campus in Moscow.

Academic Information The faculty has 585 members (93% full-time), 79% with terminal degrees. The undergraduate student-faculty ratio is 20:1. The library holds 1 million titles, 14,230 serial subscriptions, and 8,717 audiovisual materials. Special programs include academic remediation, services for learning-disabled students, an honors program, cooperative (work-study) education, study abroad, advanced placement credit, accelerated degree programs, double majors, independent study, distance learning, self-designed majors, summer session for credit, part-

University of Idaho (continued)
time degree programs (daytime, evenings, summer), adult/continuing education programs, internships, and arrangement for off-campus study with National Student Exchange. The most frequently chosen baccalaureate fields are business/marketing, education, engineering/engineering technologies.
Student Body Statistics The student body totals 12,894, of whom 9,607 are undergraduates (1,650 freshmen). 45 percent are women and 55 percent are men. 78 percent are from Idaho. 2.4 percent are international students.
Expenses for 2003–04 *Application fee:* $40. *State resident tuition:* $0 full-time. *Nonresident tuition:* $7392 full-time, $167 per credit part-time. *Mandatory fees:* $3348 full-time. Full-time tuition and fees vary according to degree level and program. Part-time tuition varies according to course load, degree level, and program. *College room and board:* $4868. Room and board charges vary according to board plan and housing facility.
Financial Aid Forms of aid include need-based and non-need-based scholarships, athletic grants, and part-time jobs. The average aided 2002–03 undergraduate received an aid package worth $8951. The priority application deadline for financial aid is February 15.
Freshman Admission Idaho requires a high school transcript, a minimum 2.2 high school GPA, SAT I or ACT scores, and TOEFL scores for international students. SAT I scores are recommended. An essay is required for some. The application deadline for regular admission is August 1.
Transfer Admission The application deadline for admission is rolling.
Entrance Difficulty Idaho assesses its entrance difficulty level as moderately difficult. For the fall 2003 freshman class, 81 percent of the applicants were accepted.

For Further Information Contact Mr. Dan Davenport, Director of Admissions, University of Idaho, PO Box 444264, Moscow, ID 83844-4264. *Telephone:* 208-885-6326 or 888-884-3246 (toll-free out-of-state). *Fax:* 208-885-9119. *E-mail:* admappl@uidaho.edu. *Web site:* http://www.uidaho.edu/.

UNIVERSITY OF PHOENIX–IDAHO CAMPUS

Meridian, Idaho

University of Phoenix–Idaho Campus is a coed, proprietary, comprehensive institution, offering degrees at the associate, bachelor's, master's, and doctoral levels and post-master's and postbachelor's certificates (courses conducted at 121 campuses and learning centers in 25 states).

Academic Information The faculty has 26 members (4% full-time), 27% with terminal degrees. The undergraduate student-faculty ratio is 7:1. The library holds 27 million titles and 11,648 serial subscriptions. Special programs include advanced placement credit, accelerated degree programs, independent study, distance learning, external degree programs, and adult/continuing education programs. The most frequently chosen baccalaureate field is business/marketing.
Student Body Statistics The student body is made up of 376 undergraduates. 51.9 percent are international students.
Expenses for 2003–04 *Application fee:* $100. *Tuition:* $9000 full-time, $300 per credit part-time.
Financial Aid Forms of aid include need-based and non-need-based scholarships. The average aided 2002–03 undergraduate received an aid package worth $1162. The application deadline for financial aid is continuous.
Freshman Admission University of Phoenix–Idaho Campus requires 1 recommendation, 2 years of work experience, 23 years of age, and TOEFL scores for international students.
Entrance Difficulty University of Phoenix–Idaho Campus has an open admission policy.

For Further Information Contact Ms. Beth Barilla, Director of Admissions, University of Phoenix–Idaho Campus, 4615 East Elwood Street, Mail Stop AA-K101, Phoenix, AZ 85040-1958. *Telephone:* 480-557-1712 or 800-228-7240 (toll-free). *Fax:* 480-574-1758. *E-mail:* beth.barilla@phoenix.edu. *Web site:* http://www.phoenix.edu/.

Montana

BLACKFEET COMMUNITY COLLEGE

Browning, Montana

Blackfeet Community College is a coed, private, two-year college, founded in 1974, offering degrees at the associate level. It has a 5-acre campus in Browning.

Academic Information The faculty has 63 members (43% full-time), 2% with terminal degrees. The student-faculty ratio is 12:1. The library holds 10,000 titles and 175 serial subscriptions. Special programs include academic remediation, part-time degree programs (daytime, evenings, weekends), adult/continuing education programs, and arrangement for off-campus study with members of the American Indian Higher Education Consortium.
Student Body Statistics The student body is made up of 503 undergraduates (137 freshmen). 64 percent are women and 36 percent are men. Students come from 2 states and territories.
Expenses for 2004–05 *Application fee:* $20. *Tuition:* $1650 full-time. *Mandatory fees:* $350 full-time, $80 per term part-time, $175 per term part-time. Full-time tuition and fees vary according to course load. Part-time feesvary according to course load.
Financial Aid Forms of aid include need-based scholarships and part-time jobs. The application deadline for financial aid is June 30 with a priority deadline of March 1.
Freshman Admission Blackfeet Community College requires a high school transcript and application, immunization with 2nd MMR, certificate of Indian blood. The application deadline for regular admission is August 29.
Transfer Admission The application deadline for admission is rolling.
Entrance Difficulty Blackfeet Community College has an open admission policy.

For Further Information Contact Ms. Deana M. McNabb, Registrar and Admissions Officer, Blackfeet Community College, PO Box 819, Browning, MT 59417. *Telephone:* 406-338-5421 Ext. 243 or 800-549-7457 (toll-free). *Fax:* 406-338-3272. *E-mail:* helen_morris@bfcc.org. *Web site:* http://www.bfcc.org/.

CARROLL COLLEGE

Helena, Montana

Carroll is a coed, private, Roman Catholic, four-year college, founded in 1909, offering degrees at the associate and bachelor's levels. It has a 64-acre campus in Helena.

Academic Information The faculty has 126 members (63% full-time), 45% with terminal degrees. The student-faculty ratio is 13:1. The library holds 89,003 titles, 2,721 serial subscriptions, and 3,890 audiovisual materials. Special programs include an honors program, cooperative (work-study) education, study abroad, advanced placement credit, accelerated degree programs, Freshman Honors College, ESL programs, double majors, independent study, self-designed majors, summer session for credit, part-time degree programs (daytime, evenings, summer), adult/continuing education programs, and internships. The most frequently chosen baccalaureate fields are education, biological/life sciences, social sciences and history.

Student Body Statistics The student body is made up of 1,411 undergraduates (310 freshmen). 58 percent are women and 42 percent are men. Students come from 27 states and territories and 8 other countries. 65 percent are from Montana. 0.9 percent are international students. 22 percent of the 2003 graduating class went on to graduate and professional schools.
Expenses for 2003–04 *Application fee:* $35. *Comprehensive fee:* $20,476 includes full-time tuition ($14,466), mandatory fees ($200), and college room and board ($5810). *College room only:* $2720. Room and board charges vary according to board plan, housing facility, and student level. *Part-time tuition:* $483 per semester hour.
Financial Aid Forms of aid include need-based and non-need-based scholarships, athletic grants, and part-time jobs. The average aided 2003–04 undergraduate received an aid package worth an estimated $13,799. The application deadline for financial aid is continuous.
Freshman Admission Carroll requires an essay, a high school transcript, a minimum 2.0 high school GPA, 1 recommendation, SAT I or ACT scores, and TOEFL scores for international students. A minimum 3.0 high school GPA and an interview are recommended. An interview, SAT II: Subject Test scores, and SAT II: Writing Test scores are required for some. The application deadline for regular admission is June 1.
Transfer Admission The application deadline for admission is June 1.
Entrance Difficulty Carroll assesses its entrance difficulty level as moderately difficult; very difficult for biology, nursing, math, communication studies programs, 3-2 programs in engineering. For the fall 2003 freshman class, 83 percent of the applicants were accepted.

For Further Information Contact Ms. Candace A. Cain, Director of Admission, Carroll College, 1601 North Benton Avenue, Helena, MT 59625-0002. *Telephone:* 406-447-4384 or 800-992-3648 (toll-free). *Fax:* 406-447-4533. *E-mail:* enroll@carroll.edu. *Web site:* http://www.carroll.edu/.

CHIEF DULL KNIFE COLLEGE

Lame Deer, Montana

For Information Write to Chief Dull Knife College, Lame Deer, MT 59043-0098.

DULL KNIFE MEMORIAL COLLEGE

See Chief Dull Knife College

FORT PECK COMMUNITY COLLEGE

Poplar, Montana

For Information Write to Fort Peck Community College, Poplar, MT 59255-0398.

LITTLE BIG HORN COLLEGE

Crow Agency, Montana

Little Big Horn College is a coed, private, two-year college, founded in 1980, offering degrees at the associate level. It has a 5-acre campus in Crow Agency.

For Further Information Contact Ms. Ann Bullis, Dean of Student Services, Little Big Horn College, Box 370, Crow Agency, MT 59022-0370. *Telephone:* 406-638-3116. *Web site:* http://www.lbhc.cc.mt.us/.

MONTANA STATE UNIVERSITY–BILLINGS

Billings, Montana

MSU-Billings is a coed, public, comprehensive unit of Montana University System, founded in 1927, offering degrees at the associate, bachelor's, and master's levels and post-master's and postbachelor's certificates. It has a 92-acre campus in Billings.

Academic Information The faculty has 244 members (64% full-time). The undergraduate student-faculty ratio is 20:1. The library holds 488,004 titles, 3,276 serial subscriptions, and 2,125 audiovisual materials. Special programs include academic remediation, services for learning-disabled students, an honors program, cooperative (work-study) education, study abroad, advanced placement credit, accelerated degree programs, ESL programs, double majors, independent study, distance learning, summer session for credit, part-time degree programs (daytime, evenings, summer), external degree programs, adult/continuing education programs, internships, and arrangement for off-campus study. The most frequently chosen baccalaureate fields are business/marketing, education, interdisciplinary studies.
Student Body Statistics The student body totals 4,670, of whom 4,139 are undergraduates (845 freshmen). 63 percent are women and 37 percent are men. Students come from 33 states and territories and 19 other countries. 93 percent are from Montana. 0.6 percent are international students. 8 percent of the 2003 graduating class went on to graduate and professional schools.
Expenses for 2003–04 *Application fee:* $30. *State resident tuition:* $4180 full-time, $116 per credit hour part-time. *Nonresident tuition:* $11,540 full-time, $321 per credit hour part-time. Full-time tuition varies according to course level, course load, degree level, location, reciprocity agreements, and student level. Part-time tuition varies according to course level, course load, degree level, location, reciprocity agreements, and student level. *College room and board:* $4430. Room and board charges vary according to board plan and housing facility.
Financial Aid Forms of aid include need-based and non-need-based scholarships, athletic grants, and part-time jobs. The average aided 2002–03 undergraduate received an aid package worth $7109. The priority application deadline for financial aid is March 1.
Freshman Admission MSU-Billings requires a high school transcript, a minimum 2.5 high school GPA, SAT I or ACT scores, and TOEFL scores for international students. The application deadline for regular admission is July 1.
Transfer Admission The application deadline for admission is rolling.
Entrance Difficulty MSU-Billings assesses its entrance difficulty level as moderately difficult. For the fall 2003 freshman class, 96 percent of the applicants were accepted.

For Further Information Contact Ms. Shelly Andersen, Associate Director of Admissions, Montana State University–Billings, 1500 University Drive, Billings, MT 59101. *Telephone:* 406-657-2158 or 800-565-6782 (toll-free). *Fax:* 406-657-2302. *E-mail:* keverett@msubillings.edu. *Web site:* http://www.msubillings.edu/.

MONTANA STATE UNIVERSITY–BOZEMAN

Bozeman, Montana

MSU-Bozeman is a coed, public unit of Montana University System, founded in 1893, offering degrees at the bachelor's, master's, and doctoral levels and post-master's certificates. It has a 1,170-acre campus in Bozeman.

Academic Information The faculty has 808 members (67% full-time), 67% with terminal degrees. The undergraduate student-faculty ratio is 17:1. The library holds 574,634 titles, 6,643 serial subscriptions, and 4,822 audiovisual materials. Special programs include academic remediation, services for learning-disabled students, an honors program, study abroad, advanced placement credit, ESL programs, double majors, independent study, distance learning, self-designed majors, summer session for credit, part-time degree programs (daytime, evenings, summer), adult/continuing education programs, internships, and arrangement for off-campus study

Montana State University–Bozeman (continued)

with members of the National Student Exchange. The most frequently chosen baccalaureate fields are business/marketing, education, engineering/engineering technologies.

Student Body Statistics The student body totals 12,135, of whom 10,750 are undergraduates (2,149 freshmen). 46 percent are women and 54 percent are men. Students come from 50 states and territories and 60 other countries. 71 percent are from Montana. 1.1 percent are international students.

Expenses for 2003–04 *Application fee:* $30. *State resident tuition:* $4145 full-time. *Nonresident tuition:* $12,707 full-time. Full-time tuition varies according to course load. *College room and board:* $5370. Room and board charges vary according to board plan and housing facility.

Financial Aid Forms of aid include need-based and non-need-based scholarships, athletic grants, and part-time jobs. The average aided 2002–03 undergraduate received an aid package worth $6919. The priority application deadline for financial aid is March 1.

Freshman Admission MSU-Bozeman requires a high school transcript, a minimum 2.5 high school GPA, SAT I or ACT scores, and TOEFL scores for international students. The application deadline for regular admission is rolling.

Transfer Admission The application deadline for admission is rolling.

Entrance Difficulty MSU-Bozeman assesses its entrance difficulty level as moderately difficult. For the fall 2003 freshman class, 81 percent of the applicants were accepted.

For Further Information Contact Ms. Ronda Russell, Director of New Student Services, Montana State University–Bozeman, PO Box 172190, Bozeman, MT 59717-2190. *Telephone:* 406-994-2601 or 888-MSU-CATS (toll-free). *Fax:* 406-994-1923. *E-mail:* admissions@montana.edu. *Web site:* http://www.montana.edu/.

MONTANA STATE UNIVERSITY–NORTHERN

Havre, Montana

MSU-Northern is a coed, public, comprehensive unit of Montana University System, founded in 1929, offering degrees at the associate, bachelor's, and master's levels. It has a 105-acre campus in Havre.

Expenses for 2003–04 *Application fee:* $30. *State resident tuition:* $4100 full-time. *Nonresident tuition:* $11,220 full-time. *College room and board:* $5600.

For Further Information Contact Ms. Rosalie Spinler, Director of Admissions, Montana State University–Northern, PO Box 7751, Havre, MT 59501-7751. *Telephone:* 406-265-3704 or 800-662-6132 (toll-free in-state). *Fax:* 406-265-3777. *E-mail:* msunadmit@nmc1.nmclites.edu. *Web site:* http://www.msun.edu/.

MONTANA TECH OF THE UNIVERSITY OF MONTANA

Butte, Montana

Montana Tech is a coed, public, comprehensive unit of Montana University System, founded in 1895, offering degrees at the associate, bachelor's, and master's levels and postbachelor's certificates. It has a 56-acre campus in Butte.

Academic Information The faculty has 156 members (71% full-time), 35% with terminal degrees. The undergraduate student-faculty ratio is 16:1. The library holds 161,187 titles, 495 serial subscriptions, and 38 audiovisual materials. Special programs include academic remediation, services for learning-disabled students, cooperative (work-study) education, advanced placement credit, double majors, independent study, distance learning, self-designed majors, summer session for credit, part-time degree programs (daytime, evenings, summer), adult/continuing education programs, and internships. The most frequently chosen baccalaureate fields are business/marketing, engineering/engineering technologies, health professions and related sciences.

Student Body Statistics The student body totals 2,232, of whom 2,142 are undergraduates (410 freshmen). 46 percent are women and 54 percent are men. Students come from 34 states and territories and 13 other countries. 89 percent are from Montana. 14 percent of the 2003 graduating class went on to graduate and professional schools.

Expenses for 2003–04 *Application fee:* $30. *State resident tuition:* $3350 full-time, $175 per credit part-time. *Nonresident tuition:* $8060 full-time, $500 per credit part-time. *Mandatory fees:* $1000 full-time, $36 per credit part-time, $482. Full-time tuition and fees vary according to course level, course load, degree level, and reciprocity agreements. Part-time tuition and fees vary according to course level, course load, degree level, location, and reciprocity agreements. *College room and board:* $4980. *College room only:* $2120. Room and board charges vary according to board plan and housing facility.

Financial Aid Forms of aid include need-based and non-need-based scholarships, athletic grants, and part-time jobs. The average aided 2003–04 undergraduate received an aid package worth an estimated $7000. The priority application deadline for financial aid is March 1.

Freshman Admission Montana Tech requires a high school transcript, a minimum 2.5 high school GPA, proof of immunization, SAT I or ACT scores, and TOEFL scores for international students. The application deadline for regular admission is rolling.

Transfer Admission The application deadline for admission is rolling.

Entrance Difficulty Montana Tech has an open admission policy for students attending the College of Technology.

For Further Information Contact Mr. Tony Campeau, Associate Director of Admissions, Montana Tech of The University of Montana, 1300 West Park Street, Butte, MT 59701-8997. *Telephone:* 406-496-4178 Ext. 4614 or 800-445-TECH Ext. 1 (toll-free). *Fax:* 406-496-4170. *E-mail:* admissions@mtech.edu. *Web site:* http://www.mtech.edu/.

ROCKY MOUNTAIN COLLEGE

Billings, Montana

Rocky is a coed, private, interdenominational, four-year college, founded in 1878, offering degrees at the associate, bachelor's, and master's levels. It has a 60-acre campus in Billings.

Academic Information The faculty has 104 members (46% full-time), 44% with terminal degrees. The undergraduate student-faculty ratio is 13:1. The library holds 67,877 titles, 364 serial subscriptions, and 782 audiovisual materials. Special programs include academic remediation, services for learning-disabled students, an honors program, cooperative (work-study) education, study abroad, advanced placement credit, accelerated degree programs, ESL programs, double majors, independent study, distance learning, self-designed majors, summer session for credit, part-time degree programs (daytime, evenings, summer), adult/continuing education programs, and internships. The most frequently chosen baccalaureate fields are business/marketing, education, health professions and related sciences.

Student Body Statistics The student body totals 938, of whom 919 are undergraduates (233 freshmen). 56 percent are women and 44 percent are men. Students come from 39 states and territories and 23 other countries. 72 percent are from Montana. 6.5 percent are international students. 13 percent of the 2003 graduating class went on to graduate and professional schools.

Expenses for 2003–04 *Application fee:* $25. *Comprehensive fee:* $19,015 includes full-time tuition ($13,950), mandatory fees ($165), and college room and board ($4900). *College room only:* $2112. Full-time tuition and fees vary according to course load and program. Room and board charges vary according to board plan and housing facility. *Part-time tuition:* $582 per credit. *Part-time mandatory fees:* $35 per term. Part-time tuition and fees vary according to course load and program.

Financial Aid Forms of aid include need-based and non-need-based scholarships, athletic grants, and part-time jobs. The average aided 2003–04 undergraduate received an aid package worth an estimated $13,276. The priority application deadline for financial aid is April 1.

Freshman Admission Rocky requires a high school transcript, a minimum 2.5 high school GPA, SAT I or ACT scores, and TOEFL scores for international students. 2 recommendations and ACT scores are recommended. An essay and an interview are required for some. The application deadline for regular admission is rolling.
Transfer Admission The application deadline for admission is rolling.
Entrance Difficulty Rocky assesses its entrance difficulty level as moderately difficult. For the fall 2003 freshman class, 85 percent of the applicants were accepted.

For Further Information Contact Ms. LynAnn Henderson, Director of Admissions, Rocky Mountain College, 1511 Poly Drive, Billings, MT 59102. *Telephone:* 406-657-1026 or 800-877-6259 (toll-free). *Fax:* 406-259-9751. *E-mail:* admissions@rocky.edu. *Web site:* http://www.rocky.edu/.

SALISH KOOTENAI COLLEGE

Pablo, Montana

Salish Kootenai College is a coed, private, primarily two-year college, founded in 1977, offering degrees at the associate and bachelor's levels. It has a 4-acre campus in Pablo.

For Further Information Contact Ms. Jackie Moran, Admissions Officer, Salish Kootenai College, PO 117, Highway 93, Pablo, MT 59855. *Telephone:* 406-275-4866. *Fax:* 406-275-4810. *E-mail:* jackie_moran@skc.edu. *Web site:* http://www.skc.edu/.

STONE CHILD COLLEGE

Box Elder, Montana

For Information Write to Stone Child College, Box Elder, MT 59521.

UNIVERSITY OF GREAT FALLS

Great Falls, Montana

UGF is a coed, private, Roman Catholic, comprehensive institution, founded in 1932, offering degrees at the associate, bachelor's, and master's levels. It has a 40-acre campus in Great Falls.

Academic Information The faculty has 108 members (33% full-time), 29% with terminal degrees. The undergraduate student-faculty ratio is 8:1. The library holds 101,110 titles, 549 serial subscriptions, and 4,069 audiovisual materials. Special programs include academic remediation, services for learning-disabled students, cooperative (work-study) education, advanced placement credit, double majors, independent study, distance learning, summer session for credit, part-time degree programs (daytime, evenings, weekends, summer), external degree programs, adult/continuing education programs, and internships. The most frequently chosen baccalaureate fields are business/marketing, education, psychology.
Student Body Statistics The student body totals 801, of whom 682 are undergraduates (84 freshmen). 71 percent are women and 29 percent are men. Students come from 27 states and territories and 3 other countries. 89 percent are from Montana. 1.4 percent are international students. 19 percent of the 2003 graduating class went on to graduate and professional schools.
Expenses for 2003–04 *Application fee:* $35. *Comprehensive fee:* $17,040 includes full-time tuition ($11,500), mandatory fees ($440), and college room and board ($5100). *College room only:* $2100. Full-time tuition and fees vary according to course load, degree level, and reciprocity agreements. Room and board charges vary according to board plan and housing facility. *Part-time tuition:* $365 per credit. *Part-time mandatory fees:* $10 per credit, $50 per term. Part-time tuition and fees vary according to course load, degree level, and reciprocity agreements.
Financial Aid Forms of aid include need-based and non-need-based scholarships and part-time jobs. The average aided 2003–04 undergraduate received an aid package worth an estimated $9312. The application deadline for financial aid is continuous.
Freshman Admission UGF requires a high school transcript and TOEFL scores for international students. An interview, SAT I scores, ACT scores, SAT I or ACT scores, and SAT I and SAT II or ACT scores are recommended. The application deadline for regular admission is August 1.
Transfer Admission The application deadline for admission is August 1.
Entrance Difficulty UGF has an open admission policy.

For Further Information Contact Ms. Sarah Harris, Director of Admissions, University of Great Falls, 1301 20th Street South, Great Falls, MT 59405. *Telephone:* 406-791-5200 Ext. 5203 or 800-856-9544 (toll-free). *Fax:* 406-791-5209. *E-mail:* enroll@ugf.edu. *Web site:* http://www.ugf.edu/.

THE UNIVERSITY OF MONTANA–MISSOULA

Missoula, Montana

U of M is a coed, public unit of Montana University System, founded in 1893, offering degrees at the associate, bachelor's, master's, doctoral, and first professional levels and post-master's certificates. It has a 220-acre campus in Missoula.

Academic Information The faculty has 658 members (76% full-time), 69% with terminal degrees. The undergraduate student-faculty ratio is 21:1. The library holds 570,287 titles, 6,248 serial subscriptions, and 118,190 audiovisual materials. Special programs include academic remediation, services for learning-disabled students, an honors program, cooperative (work-study) education, study abroad, advanced placement credit, Freshman Honors College, ESL programs, double majors, independent study, distance learning, summer session for credit, part-time degree programs, adult/continuing education programs, internships, and arrangement for off-campus study with members of the National Student Exchange. The most frequently chosen baccalaureate fields are business/marketing, natural resources/environmental science, social sciences and history.
Student Body Statistics The student body totals 13,352, of whom 11,343 are undergraduates (2,286 freshmen). 53 percent are women and 47 percent are men. Students come from 52 states and territories and 61 other countries. 74 percent are from Montana. 1.7 percent are international students. 28 percent of the 2003 graduating class went on to graduate and professional schools.
Expenses for 2004–05 *Application fee:* $30. *State resident tuition:* $3221 full-time, $141 per credit part-time. *Nonresident tuition:* $11,212 full-time, $485 per credit part-time. *Mandatory fees:* $1156 full-time, $37 per credit part-time. Full-time tuition and fees vary according to student level. Part-time tuition and fees vary according to course load. *College room and board:* $5432. *College room only:* $2448. Room and board charges vary according to board plan and housing facility.
Financial Aid Forms of aid include need-based and non-need-based scholarships, athletic grants, and part-time jobs. The average aided 2002–03 undergraduate received an aid package worth $8034. The priority application deadline for financial aid is March 1.
Freshman Admission U of M requires a high school transcript, a minimum 2.5 high school GPA, SAT I or ACT scores, and TOEFL scores for international students. ACT ASSET or ACT COMPASS is required for some. The application deadline for regular admission is March 1.
Transfer Admission The application deadline for admission is rolling.
Entrance Difficulty U of M assesses its entrance difficulty level as moderately difficult; most difficult for Davidson Honors College. For the fall 2003 freshman class, 93 percent of the applicants were accepted.

For Further Information Contact Dr. Frank L. Matule, Executive Director, Enrollment Services, The University of Montana–Missoula, Missoula, MT 59812-0002. *Telephone:* 406-243-2362 or 800-462-8636 (toll-free). *Fax:* 406-243-5711. *E-mail:* admiss@selway.umt.edu. *Web site:* http://www.umt.edu/.

THE UNIVERSITY OF MONTANA–WESTERN

Dillon, Montana

The University of Montana–Western is a coed, public, four-year college of Montana University System, founded in 1893, offering degrees at the associate and bachelor's levels. It has a 36-acre campus in Dillon.

Academic Information The faculty has 69 members (70% full-time), 57% with terminal degrees. The student-faculty ratio is 19:1. The library holds 90,431 titles, 7,127 serial subscriptions, and 3,718 audiovisual materials. Special programs include academic remediation, services for learning-disabled students, an honors program, cooperative (work-study) education, advanced placement credit, accelerated degree programs, double majors, independent study, distance learning, self-designed majors, summer session for credit, part-time degree programs (daytime, evenings, weekends, summer), adult/continuing education programs, and internships. The most frequently chosen baccalaureate fields are business/marketing, education, social sciences and history.
Student Body Statistics The student body is made up of 1,160 undergraduates (171 freshmen). 60 percent are women and 40 percent are men. Students come from 12 states and territories and 2 other countries. 85 percent are from Montana. 0.3 percent are international students.
Expenses for 2004–05 *Application fee:* $30. *State resident tuition:* $3030 full-time, $131 per credit part-time. *Nonresident tuition:* $10,860 full-time, $458 per credit part-time. *Mandatory fees:* $750 full-time, $114 per credit part-time, $370 per term part-time. Full-time tuition and fees vary according to course load and student level. Part-time tuition and fees vary according to course load and student level. *College room and board:* $4600. *College room only:* $1800. Room and board charges vary according to board plan and housing facility.
Financial Aid Forms of aid include need-based and non-need-based scholarships, athletic grants, and part-time jobs. The average aided 2003–04 undergraduate received an aid package worth an estimated $4991. The priority application deadline for financial aid is March 1.
Freshman Admission The University of Montana–Western requires a high school transcript, a minimum 2.5 high school GPA, SAT I or ACT scores, and TOEFL scores for international students. The application deadline for regular admission is July 1.
Transfer Admission The application deadline for admission is July 1.
Entrance Difficulty The University of Montana–Western assesses its entrance difficulty level as minimally difficult. For the fall 2003 freshman class, 100 percent of the applicants were accepted.

For Further Information Contact Ms. Arlene Williams, Director of Admissions, The University of Montana–Western, 710 South Atlantic, Dillon, MT 59725. *Telephone:* 406-683-7331 or 866-869-6668 (toll-free). *Fax:* 406-683-7493. *E-mail:* admissions@umwestern.edu. *Web site:* http://www.umwestern.edu/.

WESTERN MONTANA COLLEGE

See The University of Montana–Western

Nevada

THE ART INSTITUTE OF LAS VEGAS

Henderson, Nevada

The Art Institute of Las Vegas is a coed, proprietary, primarily two-year college, founded in 2002, offering degrees at the associate and bachelor's levels.

Academic Information The faculty has 45 members (24% full-time). The student-faculty ratio is 21:1. The most frequently chosen baccalaureate fields are computer/information sciences, visual/performing arts.
Student Body Statistics The student body is made up of 678 undergraduates (172 freshmen). 50 percent are women and 50 percent are men.
Expenses for 2004–05 *Tuition:* $16,464 full-time, $343 per credit part-time.

For Further Information Contact Suzanne Noel, Director of Admissions, The Art Institute of Las Vegas, 2350 Corporate Circle Drive, Henderson, NV 89074. *Telephone:* 702-369-9944 Ext. 8459. *Fax:* 702-992-8558. *Web site:* http://www.ailv.artinstitutes.edu/.

DEVRY UNIVERSITY

Henderson, Nevada

DeVry University is a coed, proprietary, comprehensive unit of DeVry University, offering degrees at the bachelor's and master's levels and postbachelor's certificates.

Freshman Admission The application deadline for regular admission is rolling.

For Further Information Contact DeVry University, 2490 Paseo Verde Parkway, Henderson, NV 89074-7120. *Telephone:* 866-78DEVRY (toll-free). *Fax:* 702-407-2950. *E-mail:* admissions@devry.edu. *Web site:* http://www.devry.edu/.

GREAT BASIN COLLEGE

Elko, Nevada

GBC is a coed, public, primarily two-year college of University and Community College System of Nevada, founded in 1967, offering degrees at the associate and bachelor's levels and first professional certificates. It has a 45-acre campus in Elko.

Academic Information The faculty has 225 members (24% full-time). The student-faculty ratio is 12:1. The library holds 27,521 titles and 250 serial subscriptions. Special programs include academic remediation, services for learning-disabled students, cooperative (work-study) education, ESL programs, independent study, distance learning, summer session for credit, part-time degree programs (daytime, evenings, weekends, summer), external degree programs, and adult/continuing education programs. The most frequently chosen baccalaureate fields are business/marketing, education.
Student Body Statistics The student body is made up of 2,731 undergraduates.
Expenses for 2004–05 *Application fee:* $5. *Area resident tuition:* $49.40 per credit part-time. Part-time tuition varies according to course load.
Financial Aid Forms of aid include need-based scholarships and part-time jobs. The priority application deadline for financial aid is May 20.
Freshman Admission GBC requires a high school transcript. SAT I or ACT scores are recommended. The application deadline for regular admission is rolling.
Transfer Admission The application deadline for admission is rolling.
Entrance Difficulty GBC has an open admission policy except for nursing program. It assesses its entrance difficulty as moderately difficult for nursing program.

For Further Information Contact Ms. Julie Byrnes, Director of Enrollment Management, Great Basin College, 1500 College Parkway, Elko, NV 89801-3348. *Telephone:* 775-753-2271. *Fax:* 775-753-2102. *E-mail:* stdsvc@gbcnv.edu.

ITT TECHNICAL INSTITUTE

Henderson, Nevada

ITT Technical Institute is a coed, proprietary, primarily two-year college of ITT Educational Services, Inc., offering degrees at the associate and bachelor's levels.

Student Body Statistics The student body is made up of 536 undergraduates.
Expenses for 2003–04 *Application fee:* $100. Total Program Cost varies depending on course of study. Consult school catalog.
Financial Aid Forms of aid include need-based scholarships and part-time jobs. The application deadline for financial aid is continuous.
Freshman Admission ITT Technical Institute requires a high school transcript, an interview, and Wonderlic aptitude test. Recommendations are recommended. The application deadline for regular admission is rolling.
Transfer Admission The application deadline for admission is rolling.
Entrance Difficulty ITT Technical Institute assesses its entrance difficulty level as minimally difficult.

For Further Information Contact Ms. Sandra Turkington, Director of Recruitment, ITT Technical Institute, 168 North Gibson Road, Henderson, NV 89014. *Telephone:* 702-558-5404 or 800-488-8459 (toll-free in-state). *Fax:* 702-558-5412. *Web site:* http://www.itt-tech.edu/.

MORRISON UNIVERSITY

Reno, Nevada

Morrison University is a coed, proprietary, comprehensive institution, founded in 1902, offering degrees at the associate, bachelor's, and master's levels. It has a 2-acre campus in Reno.

Academic Information The faculty has 25 members (60% full-time). The library holds 6,000 titles and 20 serial subscriptions. Special programs include academic remediation, accelerated degree programs, ESL programs, summer session for credit, part-time degree programs (daytime, evenings, summer), adult/continuing education programs, and internships.
Student Body Statistics The student body totals 130, of whom 110 are undergraduates. 68 percent are women and 32 percent are men. Students come from 8 states and territories and 5 other countries. 2 percent of the 2003 graduating class went on to graduate and professional schools.
Expenses for 2003–04 *Application fee:* $25. *Tuition:* $12,000 full-time, $200 per credit part-time.
Financial Aid Forms of aid include need-based and non-need-based scholarships. The application deadline for financial aid is continuous.
Freshman Admission Morrison University requires a high school transcript and an interview. CPAt of 160 for paralegal program is recommended. An essay is required for some.
Entrance Difficulty Morrison University has an open admission policy.

For Further Information Contact Dr. Richard Carl Farmer, President, Morrison University, 10315 Professional Circle, Reno, NV 89521. *Telephone:* 775-850-0700 Ext. 115 or 800-369-6144 (toll-free). *Fax:* 775-850-0711. *Web site:* http://www.morrison.northface.edu/.

NEVADA STATE COLLEGE AT HENDERSON

Henderson, Nevada

Nevada State College at Henderson is a coed, public, four-year college of Nevada System of Higher Education, founded in 2002, offering degrees at the bachelor's level. It has a 520-acre campus in Henderson near Las Vegas.

Academic Information The faculty has 88 members (17% full-time), 32% with terminal degrees. The student-faculty ratio is 9:1.
Student Body Statistics The student body is made up of 535 undergraduates (89 freshmen). 72 percent are women and 28 percent are men. Students come from 8 states and territories. 91 percent are from Nevada.
Expenses for 2004–05 *Application fee:* $30. *State resident tuition:* $2200 full-time, $74 per credit part-time. *Nonresident tuition:* $6676 full-time, $74 per credit part-time. *Mandatory fees:* $2200 full-time.
Freshman Admission Nevada State College at Henderson requires a high school transcript and a minimum 2.0 high school GPA. SAT I or ACT scores are recommended. The application deadline for regular admission is August 20.
Transfer Admission The application deadline for admission is August 20.
Entrance Difficulty For the fall 2003 freshman class, 58 percent of the applicants were accepted.

For Further Information Contact Kathy Gonzales, Assistant Registrar, Nevada State College at Henderson, 1125 Nevada State Drive, Henderson, NV 89107. *Telephone:* 702-992-2000. *Fax:* 702-992-2226. *E-mail:* students@nsc.nevada.edu. *Web site:* http://www.nsc.nevada.edu/.

SIERRA NEVADA COLLEGE

Incline Village, Nevada

SNC is a coed, private, comprehensive institution, founded in 1969, offering degrees at the bachelor's level and postbachelor's certificates. It has a 20-acre campus in Incline Village near Reno.

Academic Information The faculty has 75 members (25% full-time). The student-faculty ratio is 8:1. The library holds 18,500 titles and 175 serial subscriptions. Special programs include academic remediation, services for learning-disabled students, an honors program, cooperative (work-study) education, study abroad, advanced placement credit, accelerated degree programs, double majors, independent study, summer session for credit, part-time degree programs (daytime, evenings), adult/continuing education programs, and internships. The most frequently chosen baccalaureate fields are business/marketing, interdisciplinary studies, visual/performing arts.
Student Body Statistics The student body totals 492, of whom 302 are undergraduates (67 freshmen). 51 percent are women and 49 percent are men. Students come from 32 states and territories and 5 other countries. 29 percent are from Nevada. 3 percent are international students.
Expenses for 2004–05 *Application fee:* $0. *Comprehensive fee:* $27,100 includes full-time tuition ($19,500), mandatory fees ($150), and college room and board ($7450). Full-time tuition and fees vary according to course load, location, and program. Room and board charges vary according to gender and housing facility. *Part-time tuition:* $850 per hour. *Part-time mandatory fees:* $75 per term. Part-time tuition and fees vary according to course load, location, and program.
Financial Aid Forms of aid include need-based and non-need-based scholarships, athletic grants, and part-time jobs. The average aided 2002–03 undergraduate received an aid package worth $14,000. The priority application deadline for financial aid is June 1.
Freshman Admission SNC requires an essay, a high school transcript, a minimum 2.0 high school GPA, SAT I and SAT II or ACT scores, and TOEFL scores for international students. An interview is recommended. Recommendations and school report form for high school seniors are required for some. The application deadline for regular admission is rolling.
Transfer Admission The application deadline for admission is rolling.
Entrance Difficulty SNC assesses its entrance difficulty level as moderately difficult. For the fall 2003 freshman class, 68 percent of the applicants were accepted.

For Further Information Contact Mr. Brett Schraeder, Dean of Enrollment, Sierra Nevada College, 999 Tahoe Boulevard, David Hall II, Incline Village, NV 89451. *Telephone:* 775-831-7799 Ext. 4047 or 775-831-1314 (toll-free in-state). *Fax:* 775-831-1347. *E-mail:* admissions@sierranevada.edu. *Web site:* http://www.sierranevada.edu/.

UNIVERSITY OF NEVADA, LAS VEGAS

Las Vegas, Nevada

UNLV is a coed, public unit of University and Community College System of Nevada, founded in 1957, offering degrees at the bachelor's, master's, doctoral, and first professional levels and post-master's and postbachelor's certificates. It has a 335-acre campus in Las Vegas.

Academic Information The faculty has 1,435 members (54% full-time). The undergraduate student-faculty ratio is 20:1. The library holds 1 million titles, 9,536 serial subscriptions, and 120,128 audiovisual materials.

University of Nevada, Las Vegas (continued)

Special programs include academic remediation, services for learning-disabled students, an honors program, cooperative (work-study) education, study abroad, advanced placement credit, ESL programs, double majors, independent study, distance learning, self-designed majors, summer session for credit, part-time degree programs (daytime, evenings, weekends, summer), adult/continuing education programs, internships, and arrangement for off-campus study with National Student Exchange, Western Interstate Commission for Higher Education, Western Undergraduate Exchange. The most frequently chosen baccalaureate fields are business/marketing, communications/communication technologies, education.

Student Body Statistics The student body totals 25,749, of whom 20,680 are undergraduates (2,976 freshmen). 56 percent are women and 44 percent are men. Students come from 51 states and territories and 84 other countries. 78 percent are from Nevada. 3.9 percent are international students. 9 percent of the 2003 graduating class went on to graduate and professional schools.

Expenses for 2004–05 *Application fee:* $60. *State resident tuition:* $2850 full-time, $95 per credit hour part-time. *Nonresident tuition:* $11,524 full-time, $95 per credit hour part-time. *Mandatory fees:* $156 full-time. Full-time tuition and fees vary according to course load. Part-time tuition varies according to course load. *College room and board:* $8258. *College room only:* $5200. Room and board charges vary according to board plan.

Financial Aid Forms of aid include need-based and non-need-based scholarships, athletic grants, and part-time jobs. The average aided 2003–04 undergraduate received an aid package worth an estimated $6911. The priority application deadline for financial aid is February 1.

Freshman Admission UNLV requires a high school transcript, a minimum 2.5 high school GPA, and TOEFL scores for international students. SAT I or ACT scores are recommended. 2 recommendations and SAT I or ACT scores are required for some. The application deadline for regular admission is April 2.

Transfer Admission The application deadline for admission is May 1.

Entrance Difficulty UNLV assesses its entrance difficulty level as moderately difficult. For the fall 2003 freshman class, 80 percent of the applicants were accepted.

For Further Information Contact Ms. Kristi Rodriguez, Assistant Director for Undergraduate Recruitment, University of Nevada, Las Vegas, 4505 Maryland Parkway, Box 451021, Las Vegas, NV 89154-1021. *Telephone:* 702-895-4627. *Fax:* 702-774-8008. *E-mail:* gounlv@ccmail.nevada.edu. *Web site:* http://www.unlv.edu/.

UNIVERSITY OF NEVADA, RENO

Reno, Nevada

Nevada is a coed, public unit of University and Community College System of Nevada, founded in 1874, offering degrees at the bachelor's, master's, doctoral, and first professional levels and post-master's, first professional, and postbachelor's certificates. It has a 200-acre campus in Reno.

Academic Information The faculty has 1,134 members (60% full-time), 65% with terminal degrees. The undergraduate student-faculty ratio is 15:1. The library holds 1 million titles, 18,656 serial subscriptions, and 460,751 audiovisual materials. Special programs include academic remediation, services for learning-disabled students, an honors program, study abroad, advanced placement credit, ESL programs, double majors, independent study, distance learning, summer session for credit, part-time degree programs (daytime, evenings, summer), adult/continuing education programs, internships, and arrangement for off-campus study with National Student Exchange. The most frequently chosen baccalaureate fields are business/marketing, education, engineering/engineering technologies.

Student Body Statistics The student body totals 15,534, of whom 12,118 are undergraduates (2,097 freshmen). 55 percent are women and 45 percent are men. Students come from 54 states and territories and 73 other countries. 82 percent are from Nevada. 2.7 percent are international students.

Expenses for 2004–05 *Application fee:* $40. *State resident tuition:* $91 per credit part-time. *Nonresident tuition:* $191 per credit part-time.

Financial Aid Forms of aid include need-based and non-need-based scholarships, athletic grants, and part-time jobs. The average aided 2002–03 undergraduate received an aid package worth $7003. The priority application deadline for financial aid is February 1.

Freshman Admission Nevada requires a high school transcript, a minimum 2.5 high school GPA, and TOEFL scores for international students. SAT I or ACT scores are recommended. The application deadline for regular admission is rolling and for early action it is November 15.

Transfer Admission The application deadline for admission is rolling.

Entrance Difficulty Nevada assesses its entrance difficulty level as moderately difficult. For the fall 2003 freshman class, 88 percent of the applicants were accepted.

For Further Information Contact Dr. Melissa N. Choroszy, Associate Dean of Records and Enrollment Services, University of Nevada, Reno, Mail Stop 120, Reno, NV 89557. *Telephone:* 775-784-6865 or 866-263-8232 (toll-free). *Fax:* 775-784-4283. *E-mail:* asknevada@unr.edu. *Web site:* http://www.unr.edu/.

UNIVERSITY OF PHOENIX–NEVADA CAMPUS

Las Vegas, Nevada

University of Phoenix–Nevada Campus is a coed, proprietary, comprehensive institution, founded in 1994, offering degrees at the associate, bachelor's, master's, and doctoral levels and post-master's and postbachelor's certificates (courses conducted at 121 campuses and learning centers in 25 states).

Academic Information The faculty has 495 members (0.8% full-time), 24% with terminal degrees. The undergraduate student-faculty ratio is 9:1. The library holds 27 million titles and 11,648 serial subscriptions. Special programs include advanced placement credit, accelerated degree programs, independent study, distance learning, external degree programs, and adult/continuing education programs. The most frequently chosen baccalaureate fields are business/marketing, computer/information sciences, protective services/public administration.

Student Body Statistics The student body totals 3,170, of whom 2,152 are undergraduates (119 freshmen). 57 percent are women and 43 percent are men. 9.5 percent are international students.

Expenses for 2003–04 *Application fee:* $85. *Tuition:* $8910 full-time, $297 per credit part-time.

Financial Aid Forms of aid include need-based and non-need-based scholarships. The average aided 2002–03 undergraduate received an aid package worth $1406. The application deadline for financial aid is continuous.

Freshman Admission University of Phoenix–Nevada Campus requires 1 recommendation, 2 years of work experience, 23 years of age, and TOEFL scores for international students. A high school transcript is required for some. The application deadline for regular admission is rolling.

Transfer Admission The application deadline for admission is rolling.

Entrance Difficulty University of Phoenix–Nevada Campus has an open admission policy.

For Further Information Contact Ms. Beth Barilla, Director of Admissions, University of Phoenix–Nevada Campus, 4615 East Elwood Street, Mail Stop AA-K101, Phoenix, AZ 85040-1958. *Telephone:* 480-557-1712 or 800-228-7240 (toll-free). *Fax:* 480-594-1758. *E-mail:* beth.barilla@phoenix.edu. *Web site:* http://www.phoenix.edu/.

New Mexico

COLLEGE OF SANTA FE

Santa Fe, New Mexico

CSF is a coed, private, comprehensive institution, founded in 1947, offering degrees at the associate, bachelor's, and master's levels. It has a 100-acre campus in Santa Fe near Albuquerque.

Academic Information The faculty has 251 members (28% full-time). The undergraduate student-faculty ratio is 9:1. The library holds 128,982 titles, 421 serial subscriptions, and 10,082 audiovisual materials. Special programs include academic remediation, services for learning-disabled students, study abroad, advanced placement credit, accelerated degree programs, double majors, independent study, self-designed majors, summer session for credit, part-time degree programs (daytime, evenings, weekends, summer), adult/continuing education programs, internships, and arrangement for off-campus study with Great Lakes Colleges Association, New York City Arts Program. The most frequently chosen baccalaureate fields are business/marketing, computer/information sciences, visual/performing arts.

Student Body Statistics The student body totals 1,761, of whom 1,389 are undergraduates (163 freshmen). 60 percent are women and 40 percent are men. Students come from 45 states and territories and 5 other countries. 18 percent are from New Mexico. 0.4 percent are international students. 31 percent of the 2003 graduating class went on to graduate and professional schools.

Expenses for 2003–04 *Application fee:* $35. *Comprehensive fee:* $25,293 includes full-time tuition ($18,980), mandatory fees ($525), and college room and board ($5788). *College room only:* $2724. Room and board charges vary according to board plan and housing facility. *Part-time tuition:* $632 per credit hour. *Part-time mandatory fees:* $5 per credit hour.

Financial Aid Forms of aid include need-based and non-need-based scholarships, athletic grants, and part-time jobs. The average aided 2003–04 undergraduate received an aid package worth an estimated $18,190. The priority application deadline for financial aid is March 15.

Freshman Admission CSF requires an essay, a high school transcript, 2 recommendations, an interview, portfolio or audition for visual and performing arts programs, SAT I or ACT scores, and TOEFL scores for international students. A minimum 3.0 high school GPA is recommended. The application deadline for regular admission is rolling and for early decision it is November 15.

Transfer Admission The application deadline for admission is rolling.

Entrance Difficulty CSF assesses its entrance difficulty level as moderately difficult; very difficult for performing arts, moving image arts, creative writing. For the fall 2003 freshman class, 81 percent of the applicants were accepted.

For Further Information Contact Mr. Dale H. Reinhart, Director of Admissions and Enrollment Management, College of Santa Fe, 1600 Saint Michael's Drive, Santa Fe, NM 87505-7634. *Telephone:* 505-473-6133 or 800-456-2673 (toll-free). *Fax:* 505-473-6129. *E-mail:* admissions@csf.edu. *Web site:* http://www.csf.edu/.

COLLEGE OF THE SOUTHWEST

Hobbs, New Mexico

CSW is a coed, private, comprehensive institution, founded in 1962, offering degrees at the bachelor's and master's levels. It has a 162-acre campus in Hobbs.

Academic Information The faculty has 108 members (24% full-time), 17% with terminal degrees. The undergraduate student-faculty ratio is 12:1. The library holds 73,876 titles, 302 serial subscriptions, and 1,538 audiovisual materials. Special programs include advanced placement credit, accelerated degree programs, distance learning, summer session for credit, part-time degree programs (daytime, evenings, summer), external degree programs, adult/continuing education programs, and internships. The most frequently chosen baccalaureate fields are business/marketing, education, psychology.

Student Body Statistics The student body totals 894, of whom 696 are undergraduates (64 freshmen). 66 percent are women and 34 percent are men. Students come from 11 states and territories and 6 other countries. 79 percent are from New Mexico. 2.3 percent are international students.

Expenses for 2004–05 *Application fee:* $25. *Comprehensive fee:* $13,015 includes full-time tuition ($8000), mandatory fees ($415), and college room and board ($4600). Full-time tuition and fees vary according to course load. Room and board charges vary according to housing facility. *Part-time tuition:* $250 per semester hour. *Part-time mandatory fees:* $150 per term. Part-time tuition and fees vary according to course load.

Financial Aid Forms of aid include need-based and non-need-based scholarships, athletic grants, and part-time jobs. The average aided 2003–04 undergraduate received an aid package worth an estimated $3562. The priority application deadline for financial aid is April 1.

Freshman Admission CSW requires a high school transcript, medical history, SAT I or ACT scores, and TOEFL scores for international students. The application deadline for regular admission is rolling.

Transfer Admission The application deadline for admission is rolling.

Entrance Difficulty CSW assesses its entrance difficulty level as moderately difficult; noncompetitive for transfers. For the fall 2003 freshman class, 16 percent of the applicants were accepted.

For Further Information Contact Ms. Karen Workentin, Director of Admissions, College of the Southwest, 6610 Lovington Highway, Hobbs, NM 88240. *Telephone:* 505-392-6563 or 800-530-4400 (toll-free). *Fax:* 505-392-6006. *Web site:* http://www.csw.edu/.

CROWNPOINT INSTITUTE OF TECHNOLOGY

Crownpoint, New Mexico

For Information Write to Crownpoint Institute of Technology, Crownpoint, NM 87313.

EASTERN NEW MEXICO UNIVERSITY

Portales, New Mexico

ENMU is a coed, public, comprehensive unit of Eastern New Mexico University System, founded in 1934, offering degrees at the associate, bachelor's, and master's levels. It has a 240-acre campus in Portales.

Academic Information The faculty has 199 members (71% full-time), 62% with terminal degrees. The undergraduate student-faculty ratio is 17:1. The library holds 240,163 titles, 1,903 serial subscriptions, and 24,005 audiovisual materials. Special programs include academic remediation, services for learning-disabled students, an honors program, cooperative (work-study) education, study abroad, advanced placement credit, accelerated degree programs, ESL programs, double majors, distance learning, self-designed majors, summer session for credit, part-time degree programs (daytime, evenings, summer), external degree programs, adult/continuing education programs, and internships. The most frequently chosen baccalaureate fields are education, business/marketing, social sciences and history.

Student Body Statistics The student body totals 3,706, of whom 3,015 are undergraduates (558 freshmen). 58 percent are women and 42 percent are men. Students come from 42 states and territories. 83 percent are from New Mexico. 0.4 percent are international students.

Expenses for 2003–04 *Application fee:* $0. *State resident tuition:* $1776 full-time, $103 per credit hour part-time. *Nonresident tuition:* $7332 full-time, $334.50 per credit hour part-time. *Mandatory fees:* $696 full-time, $29 per credit hour part-time. *College room and board:* $4290. *College room only:* $1990. Room and board charges vary according to board plan and housing facility.

Financial Aid Forms of aid include need-based and non-need-based scholarships and part-time jobs. The priority application deadline for financial aid is March 1.

Eastern New Mexico University (continued)

Freshman Admission ENMU requires a high school transcript, a minimum 2.0 high school GPA, SAT I or ACT scores, and TOEFL scores for international students. The application deadline for regular admission is rolling.
Transfer Admission The application deadline for admission is rolling.
Entrance Difficulty ENMU assesses its entrance difficulty level as minimally difficult. For the fall 2003 freshman class, 74 percent of the applicants were accepted.

For Further Information Contact Ms. Phyllis Seefeld, Interim Director, Eastern New Mexico University, Station #7 ENMU, Portales, NM 88130. *Telephone:* 505-562-2178 or 800-367-3668 (toll-free). *Fax:* 505-562-2118. *E-mail:* phyllis.seefeld@enmu.edu. *Web site:* http://www.enmu.edu/.

INSTITUTE OF AMERICAN INDIAN ARTS

Santa Fe, New Mexico

For Information Write to Institute of American Indian Arts, Santa Fe, NM 87508.

INTERNATIONAL INSTITUTE OF THE AMERICAS

Albuquerque, New Mexico

International Institute of the Americas is a coed, private, primarily two-year college, offering degrees at the associate and bachelor's levels. It has a 1-acre campus in Albuquerque.

Academic Information The faculty has 9 members (56% full-time), 22% with terminal degrees. The student-faculty ratio is 10:1.
Student Body Statistics The student body is made up of 163 undergraduates (19 freshmen). 85 percent are women and 15 percent are men.
Expenses for 2004–05 *Tuition:* $9000 full-time. *Mandatory fees:* $350 full-time.
Entrance Difficulty For the fall 2003 freshman class, 60 percent of the applicants were accepted.

For Further Information Contact Mr. Scott Yelton, Campus Director, International Institute of the Americas, 4201 Central Avenue NW, Suite J, Albuquerque, NM 87105-1649. *Telephone:* 505-880-2877 or 888-660-2428 (toll-free). *Fax:* 505-352-0199. *Web site:* http://www.aibtonline.com/.

ITT TECHNICAL INSTITUTE

Albuquerque, New Mexico

ITT Tech is a coed, proprietary, primarily two-year college of ITT Educational Services, Inc., founded in 1989, offering degrees at the associate and bachelor's levels.

Student Body Statistics The student body is made up of 487 undergraduates.
Expenses for 2003–04 *Application fee:* $100. Total Program Cost varies depending on course of study. Consult school catalog.
Financial Aid Forms of aid include need-based scholarships and part-time jobs. The application deadline for financial aid is continuous.
Freshman Admission ITT Tech requires a high school transcript, an interview, and Wonderlic aptitude test. Recommendations are recommended. The application deadline for regular admission is rolling.
Transfer Admission The application deadline for admission is rolling.
Entrance Difficulty ITT Tech assesses its entrance difficulty level as minimally difficult.

For Further Information Contact Mr. John Crooks, Director of Recruitment, ITT Technical Institute, 5100 Masthead Street NE, Albuquerque, NM 87109. *Telephone:* 505-828-1114 or 800-636-1114 (toll-free in-state). *Fax:* 505-828-1849. *Web site:* http://www.itt-tech.edu/.

METROPOLITAN COLLEGE OF COURT REPORTING

Albuquerque, New Mexico

Metropolitan College of Court Reporting is a coed, proprietary, four-year college, founded in 1980.

Expenses for 2003–04 *Tuition:* $6534 full-time.

For Further Information Contact Metropolitan College of Court Reporting, 8100 Mountain Road NE, Suite 200, Albuquerque, NM 87110-4129. *Telephone:* 505-888-3400. *Fax:* 505-254-3738. *Web site:* http://www.metropolitancollege.edu/.

NATIONAL AMERICAN UNIVERSITY

Albuquerque, New Mexico

National American University is a coed, proprietary, four-year college, founded in 1941, offering degrees at the associate, bachelor's, and master's levels. It has a 5-acre campus in Albuquerque.

Academic Information The faculty has 56 members, 9% with terminal degrees. The undergraduate student-faculty ratio is 12:1. Special programs include cooperative (work-study) education, accelerated degree programs, double majors, independent study, distance learning, summer session for credit, part-time degree programs (daytime, evenings, summer), external degree programs, adult/continuing education programs, internships, and arrangement for off-campus study. The most frequently chosen baccalaureate fields are business/marketing, computer/information sciences.
Student Body Statistics The student body is made up of 625 undergraduates. 49 percent are women and 51 percent are men. Students come from 1 state or territory and 2 other countries.
Expenses for 2004–05 *Application fee:* $25. *Tuition:* $225 per credit hour part-time.
Financial Aid Forms of aid include need-based and non-need-based scholarships and part-time jobs. The application deadline for financial aid is continuous.
Freshman Admission National American University requires a high school transcript and TOEFL scores for international students. The application deadline for regular admission is rolling.
Transfer Admission The application deadline for admission is rolling.
Entrance Difficulty National American University has an open admission policy.

For Further Information Contact Ms. Kim Hauser, Executive Admissions Representative, National American University, 4775 Indian School, NE, Albuquerque, NM 87110. *Telephone:* 505-265-7517 or 800-843-8892 (toll-free). *Fax:* 505-265-7542. *Web site:* http://www.national.edu/.

NATIONAL COLLEGE OF MIDWIFERY

Taos, New Mexico

National College of Midwifery is a women's, private, comprehensive institution, founded in 1989, offering degrees at the associate, bachelor's, master's, and doctoral levels.

Academic Information The faculty has 31 members (100% full-time), 87% with terminal degrees. The undergraduate student-faculty ratio is 2:1.

Student Body Statistics The student body totals 59, of whom 57 are undergraduates (30 freshmen).
Expenses for 2003–04 *One-time mandatory fee:* $3000. *Tuition:* $6000 full-time, $3000 per year part-time. *Mandatory fees:* $150 full-time.
Entrance Difficulty For the fall 2003 freshman class, 100 percent of the applicants were accepted.

For Further Information Contact Ms. Beth Enson, Registrar, National College of Midwifery, 209 State Road 240, Taos, NM 87571. *Telephone:* 505-758-8914. *Fax:* 505-758-0302. *Web site:* http://www.midwiferycollege.org/.

NEW MEXICO HIGHLANDS UNIVERSITY

Las Vegas, New Mexico

Highlands is a coed, public, comprehensive institution, founded in 1893, offering degrees at the associate, bachelor's, and master's levels. It has a 120-acre campus in Las Vegas.

Academic Information The faculty has 241 members (48% full-time), 42% with terminal degrees. The undergraduate student-faculty ratio is 16:1. The library holds 429,533 titles, 850 serial subscriptions, and 807 audiovisual materials. Special programs include academic remediation, services for learning-disabled students, an honors program, cooperative (work-study) education, advanced placement credit, accelerated degree programs, double majors, independent study, distance learning, summer session for credit, part-time degree programs, internships, and arrangement for off-campus study with San Juan Community College, Santa Fe Community College, Northern New Mexico Community College. The most frequently chosen baccalaureate fields are education, business/marketing, health professions and related sciences.
Student Body Statistics The student body totals 3,960, of whom 2,103 are undergraduates (255 freshmen). 59 percent are women and 41 percent are men. Students come from 15 states and territories and 4 other countries. 94 percent are from New Mexico. 0.7 percent are international students.
Expenses for 2003–04 *Application fee:* $15. *State resident tuition:* $2184 full-time, $91 per hour part-time. *Nonresident tuition:* $9096 full-time, $379 per hour part-time. *Mandatory fees:* $45 full-time. *College room and board:* $4085. *College room only:* $1973.
Financial Aid Forms of aid include need-based and non-need-based scholarships, athletic grants, and part-time jobs. The average aided 2002–03 undergraduate received an aid package worth $3830. The priority application deadline for financial aid is March 1.
Freshman Admission Highlands requires a high school transcript, a minimum 2.0 high school GPA, ACT scores, and TOEFL scores for international students. 2 recommendations, an interview, are required for some. The application deadline for regular admission is rolling.
Transfer Admission The application deadline for admission is rolling.
Entrance Difficulty Highlands assesses its entrance difficulty level as minimally difficult. For the fall 2003 freshman class, 100 percent of the applicants were accepted.

For Further Information Contact Ms. Betsy Yost, Interim Dean of Students, New Mexico Highlands University, Box 9000, Las Vegas, NM 87701. *Telephone:* 505-454-3424 or 800-338-6648 (toll-free). *Fax:* 505-454-3311. *E-mail:* admission@venus.nmnu.edu. *Web site:* http://www.nmhu.edu/.

NEW MEXICO INSTITUTE OF MINING AND TECHNOLOGY

Socorro, New Mexico

New Mexico Tech is a coed, public university, founded in 1889, offering degrees at the associate, bachelor's, master's, and doctoral levels. It has a 320-acre campus in Socorro near Albuquerque.

Academic Information The faculty has 148 members (82% full-time), 84% with terminal degrees. The undergraduate student-faculty ratio is 12:1. The library holds 318,429 titles, 833 serial subscriptions, and 2,410 audiovisual materials. Special programs include services for learning-disabled students, cooperative (work-study) education, advanced placement credit, accelerated degree programs, double majors, independent study, distance learning, self-designed majors, summer session for credit, part-time degree programs (daytime), and internships. The most frequently chosen baccalaureate fields are engineering/engineering technologies, computer/information sciences, physical sciences.
Student Body Statistics The student body totals 1,798, of whom 1,365 are undergraduates (285 freshmen). 32 percent are women and 68 percent are men. Students come from 52 states and territories and 14 other countries. 84 percent are from New Mexico. 2.8 percent are international students.
Expenses for 2003–04 *Application fee:* $15. *State resident tuition:* $2156 full-time, $89.82 per credit hour part-time. *Nonresident tuition:* $8677 full-time, $361.54 per credit hour part-time. *Mandatory fees:* $924 full-time, $26.92 per credit hour part-time, $107.32 per term part-time. Part-time tuition and fees vary according to course load. *College room and board:* $4200. *College room only:* $1850. Room and board charges vary according to board plan and housing facility.
Financial Aid Forms of aid include need-based and non-need-based scholarships and part-time jobs. The average aided 2003–04 undergraduate received an aid package worth an estimated $7641. The priority application deadline for financial aid is June 1.
Freshman Admission New Mexico Tech requires a high school transcript, a minimum 2.5 high school GPA, SAT I or ACT scores, and TOEFL scores for international students. An interview is recommended. 2 recommendations are required for some. The application deadline for regular admission is August 1.
Transfer Admission The application deadline for admission is August 1.
Entrance Difficulty New Mexico Tech assesses its entrance difficulty level as moderately difficult. For the fall 2003 freshman class, 98 percent of the applicants were accepted.

For Further Information Contact Mr. Mike Kloeppel, Director of Admissions, New Mexico Institute of Mining and Technology, 801 Leroy Place, Socorro, NM 87801. *Telephone:* 505-835-5424 or 800-428-TECH (toll-free). *Fax:* 505-835-5989. *E-mail:* admission@admin.nmt.edu. *Web site:* http://www.nmt.edu/.

NEW MEXICO STATE UNIVERSITY

Las Cruces, New Mexico

NMSU is a coed, public unit of New Mexico State University System, founded in 1888, offering degrees at the associate, bachelor's, master's, and doctoral levels and post-master's certificates. It has a 900-acre campus in Las Cruces near El Paso.

Academic Information The faculty has 977 members (71% full-time), 69% with terminal degrees. The undergraduate student-faculty ratio is 19:1. The library holds 3 million titles, 6,747 serial subscriptions, and 1,066 audiovisual materials. Special programs include academic remediation, services for learning-disabled students, an honors program, cooperative (work-study) education, study abroad, advanced placement credit, accelerated degree programs, double majors, independent study, distance learning, self-designed majors, summer session for credit, part-time degree programs (daytime, evenings, weekends, summer), adult/continuing education programs, internships, and arrangement for off-campus study with members of the National Student Exchange, other units of the New Mexico State University System. The most frequently chosen baccalaureate fields are business/marketing, education, engineering/engineering technologies.
Student Body Statistics The student body totals 16,174, of whom 12,797 are undergraduates (2,067 freshmen). 55 percent are women and 45 percent are men. Students come from 53 states and territories and 42 other countries. 83 percent are from New Mexico. 0.9 percent are international students.
Expenses for 2003–04 *Application fee:* $15. *State resident tuition:* $2418 full-time, $140.50 per credit part-time. *Nonresident tuition:* $10,296 full-time, $468.75 per credit part-time. *Mandatory fees:* $954 full-time. *College room and board:* $4560. *College room only:* $2440. Room and board charges vary according to board plan and gender.

New Mexico State University (continued)

Financial Aid Forms of aid include need-based and non-need-based scholarships, athletic grants, and part-time jobs. The average aided 2003–04 undergraduate received an aid package worth an estimated $8292. The priority application deadline for financial aid is March 1.

Freshman Admission NMSU requires a high school transcript, a minimum 2.0 high school GPA, SAT I or ACT scores, and TOEFL scores for international students. The application deadline for regular admission is August 19.

Transfer Admission The application deadline for admission is August 14.

Entrance Difficulty NMSU assesses its entrance difficulty level as moderately difficult. For the fall 2003 freshman class, 84 percent of the applicants were accepted.

For Further Information Contact Ms. Angela Mora-Riley, Director of Admissions, New Mexico State University, Box 30001, MSC, Las Cruces, NM 88003-8001. *Telephone:* 505-646-3121 or 800-662-6678 (toll-free). *Fax:* 505-646-6330. *E-mail:* admssions@nmsu.edu. *Web site:* http://www.nmsu.edu/.

ST. JOHN'S COLLEGE

Santa Fe, New Mexico

St. John's is a coed, private, comprehensive institution, founded in 1964, offering degrees at the bachelor's and master's levels. It has a 250-acre campus in Santa Fe.

Academic Information The faculty has 70 members (97% full-time), 79% with terminal degrees. The undergraduate student-faculty ratio is 8:1. The library holds 65,000 titles and 140 serial subscriptions. Special programs include summer session for credit and arrangement for off-campus study with St. John's College (MD). The most frequently chosen baccalaureate field is liberal arts/general studies.

Student Body Statistics The student body totals 535, of whom 434 are undergraduates (138 freshmen). 46 percent are women and 54 percent are men. Students come from 56 states and territories and 8 other countries. 12 percent are from New Mexico. 1.8 percent are international students. 75 percent of the 2003 graduating class went on to graduate and professional schools.

Expenses for 2003–04 *Application fee:* $0. *Comprehensive fee:* $36,360 includes full-time tuition ($28,840), mandatory fees ($200), and college room and board ($7320). *College room only:* $4164. Room and board charges vary according to board plan and housing facility.

Financial Aid Forms of aid include need-based and non-need-based scholarships and part-time jobs. The average aided 2002–03 undergraduate received an aid package worth $19,898. The priority application deadline for financial aid is February 15.

Freshman Admission St. John's requires an essay, a high school transcript, 2 recommendations, and TOEFL scores for international students. 3 recommendations and an interview are recommended. An interview and SAT I or ACT scores are required for some. The application deadline for regular admission is rolling.

Transfer Admission The application deadline for admission is rolling.

Entrance Difficulty St. John's assesses its entrance difficulty level as very difficult. For the fall 2003 freshman class, 81 percent of the applicants were accepted.

SPECIAL MESSAGE TO STUDENTS

Social Life St John's College offers popular student activities including search and rescue, skiing, backpacking, fencing, karate, dancing, community service, drama, student government, newspaper, and intramural sports. Santa Fe is a sophisticated, multicultural, historic, and artistic community, offering great coffee shops, bookstores, cinema, and performing arts. At 7000 feet, the campus is nestled in the Rocky Mountains, where the air is fresh and clear, and the sun always shines.

Academic Highlights Reading and discussing the Great Books—seminal works in philosophy, literature, political theory, history, mathematics, science, economics, theology, music—from Homer to Freud, Euclid to Einstein—studying in a curriculum common to all, creates a cohesive intellectual community. Small seminar-style classes, led by tutors, generate an active, conversational mode of learning, requiring students to make sense of important ideas for themselves. The atmosphere is cooperative and intellectual, and the workload is demanding. Student progress is monitored through oral evaluations and largely based on daily participation in class as well as written papers. There are no midterm or final examinations.

Interviews and Campus Visits The application process is partially self-selective, and the interview and campus visit are ways to demonstrate knowledge of and interest in the Great Books Program. Both are strongly encouraged due to the College's uncommon program and methods of learning. Interviews are normally conducted on campus and are offered to interested juniors and seniors throughout the year. The campus visits are comprehensive, lasting 24 hours, and incorporate observing several classes, conversing informally with faculty members and students, sleeping in student housing, eating in the dining hall, and interviewing with an admissions counselor. For more information, prospective students should call the Office of Admission at 800-331-5232 (toll-free). The nearest commercial airport is Albuquerque International.

For Further Information Write to Mr. Larry Clendenin, Director of Admissions, St. John's College, 1160 Camino Cruz Blanca, Santa Fe, NM 87505. *E-mail:* admissions@sjcsf.edu. *Web site:* http://www.stjohnscollege.edu.

UNIVERSITY OF NEW MEXICO

Albuquerque, New Mexico

UNM is a coed, public university, founded in 1889, offering degrees at the associate, bachelor's, master's, doctoral, and first professional levels and post-master's certificates. It has an 875-acre campus in Albuquerque near Albuquerque.

Academic Information The faculty has 1,372 members (64% full-time), 72% with terminal degrees. The undergraduate student-faculty ratio is 16:1. The library holds 2 million titles, 339,266 serial subscriptions, and 2 million audiovisual materials. Special programs include academic remediation, services for learning-disabled students, an honors program, cooperative (work-study) education, study abroad, advanced placement credit, accelerated degree programs, ESL programs, double majors, independent study, distance learning, self-designed majors, summer session for credit, part-time degree programs (daytime, evenings, weekends, summer), adult/continuing education programs, internships, and arrangement for off-campus study with National Student Exchange, Western Undergraduate Exchange, Western Interstate Commission for Higher Education. The most frequently chosen baccalaureate fields are business/marketing, education, social sciences and history.

Student Body Statistics The student body totals 25,686, of whom 17,932 are undergraduates (3,004 freshmen). 57 percent are women and 43 percent are men. Students come from 51 states and territories and 90 other countries. 81 percent are from New Mexico. 0.7 percent are international students.

Expenses for 2003–04 *Application fee:* $20. *State resident tuition:* $3313 full-time. *Nonresident tuition:* $11,954 full-time. *College room and board:* $5910. *College room only:* $3410. Room and board charges vary according to board plan and housing facility.

Financial Aid Forms of aid include need-based and non-need-based scholarships, athletic grants, and part-time jobs. The priority application deadline for financial aid is March 1.

Freshman Admission UNM requires a high school transcript, a minimum 2.25 high school GPA, SAT I or ACT scores, and TOEFL scores for international students. An essay, recommendations, SAT II: Subject Test scores, and SAT II: Writing Test scores are required for some. The application deadline for regular admission is June 15.

Entrance Difficulty UNM assesses its entrance difficulty level as moderately difficult. For the fall 2003 freshman class, 75 percent of the applicants were accepted.

For Further Information Contact Ms. Robin Ryan, Associate Director of Admissions, University of New Mexico, Student Service Center Room 140, MSC063720, 1 University of New Mexico, Albuquerque, NM 87131-0001. *Telephone:* 505-277-2446 or 800-CALLUNM (toll-free in-state). *Fax:* 505-277-6686. *E-mail:* apply@unm.edu. *Web site:* http://www.unm.edu/.

UNIVERSITY OF NEW MEXICO–GALLUP

Gallup, New Mexico

UNM-Gallup is a coed, public, primarily two-year college of New Mexico Commission on Higher Education, founded in 1968, offering degrees at the associate and bachelor's levels. It has an 80-acre campus in Gallup.

Expenses for 2003–04 *Application fee:* $15. *State resident tuition:* $1032 full-time, $43 per credit hour part-time. *Nonresident tuition:* $2436 full-time, $87 per credit hour part-time.

For Further Information Contact Ms. Pearl A. Morris, Admissions Representative, University of New Mexico–Gallup, 200 College Road, Gallup, NM 87301-5603. *Telephone:* 505-863-7576. *Fax:* 505-863-7610. *E-mail:* pmorris@gallup.unm.edu. *Web site:* http://www.gallup.unm.edu/.

UNIVERSITY OF PHOENIX–NEW MEXICO CAMPUS

Albuquerque, New Mexico

University of Phoenix–New Mexico Campus is a coed, proprietary, comprehensive institution, offering degrees at the associate, bachelor's, master's, and doctoral levels and post-master's and postbachelor's certificates (courses conducted at 121 campuses and learning centers in 25 states).

Academic Information The faculty has 507 members, 25% with terminal degrees. The undergraduate student-faculty ratio is 11:1. The library holds 27 million titles and 11,648 serial subscriptions. Special programs include advanced placement credit, accelerated degree programs, independent study, distance learning, external degree programs, and adult/continuing education programs. The most frequently chosen baccalaureate fields are business/marketing, computer/information sciences, health professions and related sciences.
Student Body Statistics The student body totals 3,584, of whom 2,767 are undergraduates (156 freshmen). 59 percent are women and 41 percent are men. 11.5 percent are international students.
Expenses for 2003–04 *Application fee:* $85. *Tuition:* $8550 full-time, $285 per credit part-time.
Financial Aid Forms of aid include need-based and non-need-based scholarships. The average aided 2002–03 undergraduate received an aid package worth $1375. The application deadline for financial aid is continuous.
Freshman Admission University of Phoenix–New Mexico Campus requires 1 recommendation, 2 years of work experience, 23 years of age, and TOEFL scores for international students. A high school transcript is required for some. The application deadline for regular admission is rolling.
Transfer Admission The application deadline for admission is rolling.
Entrance Difficulty University of Phoenix–New Mexico Campus has an open admission policy.

For Further Information Contact Ms. Beth Barilla, Director of Admissions, University of Phoenix–New Mexico Campus, 4615 East Elwood Street, Mail Stop AA-K101, Phoenix, AZ 85040-1958. *Telephone:* 480-557-1712 or 800-228-7240 (toll-free). *Fax:* 480-594-1758. *E-mail:* beth.barilla@phoenix.edu. *Web site:* http://www.phoenix.edu/.

WESTERN NEW MEXICO UNIVERSITY

Silver City, New Mexico

WNMU is a coed, public, comprehensive institution, founded in 1893, offering degrees at the associate, bachelor's, and master's levels. It has an 83-acre campus in Silver City.

Expenses for 2003–04 *Application fee:* $10. *State resident tuition:* $2371 full-time. *Nonresident tuition:* $8923 full-time. *Mandatory fees:* $80 full-time. *College room and board:* $4280. *College room only:* $1550.

For Further Information Contact Mr. Michael Alecksen, Director of Admissions, Western New Mexico University, College Avenue, Silver City, NM 88062-0680. *Telephone:* 505-538-6106 or 800-872-WNMU (toll-free in-state). *Fax:* 505-538-6155. *Web site:* http://www.wnmu.edu/.

Oregon

THE ART INSTITUTE OF PORTLAND

Portland, Oregon

AIPD is a coed, proprietary, four-year college of Education Management Corporation, founded in 1963, offering degrees at the associate and bachelor's levels. It has a 1-acre campus in Portland.

Academic Information The faculty has 118 members (25% full-time), 28% with terminal degrees. The student-faculty ratio is 19:1. The library holds 19,831 titles, 200 serial subscriptions, and 400 audiovisual materials. Special programs include academic remediation, services for learning-disabled students, study abroad, advanced placement credit, independent study, summer session for credit, part-time degree programs (daytime, evenings, weekends, summer), and internships. The most frequently chosen baccalaureate fields are computer/information sciences, visual/performing arts.
Student Body Statistics The student body is made up of 1,327 undergraduates (137 freshmen). 54 percent are women and 46 percent are men. 2 percent are international students. 2 percent of the 2003 graduating class went on to graduate and professional schools.
Expenses for 2003–04 *Application fee:* $50. *Comprehensive fee:* $23,445 includes full-time tuition ($15,750) and college room and board ($7695). Full-time tuition varies according to student level. *Part-time tuition:* $350 per credit. Part-time tuition varies according to student level.
Financial Aid Forms of aid include need-based and non-need-based scholarships and part-time jobs. The average aided 2003–04 undergraduate received an aid package worth an estimated $4765. The application deadline for financial aid is continuous.
Freshman Admission AIPD requires an essay, a high school transcript, an interview, and TOEFL scores for international students. Recommendations are recommended. The application deadline for regular admission is rolling.
Transfer Admission The application deadline for admission is rolling.
Entrance Difficulty AIPD assesses its entrance difficulty level as minimally difficult.

For Further Information Contact Ms. Lori Murray, Director of Admissions, The Art Institute of Portland, 1122 NW Davis Street, Portland, OR 97209-2911. *Telephone:* 503-228-6528 Ext. 4794 or 888-228-6528 (toll-free). *Fax:* 503-227-1945. *E-mail:* aipdadm@aii.edu. *Web site:* http://www.aipd.artinstitutes.edu/.

BASSIST COLLEGE

See The Art Institute of Portland

CASCADE COLLEGE

Portland, Oregon

Cascade is a coed, private, four-year college, founded in 1994, affiliated with the Church of Christ, offering degrees at the bachelor's level. It has a 13-acre campus in Portland.

Academic Information The faculty has 33 members (39% full-time), 30% with terminal degrees. The student-faculty ratio is 14:1. The library holds 28,050 titles and 104 serial subscriptions. Special programs include academic remediation, services for learning-disabled students, study abroad, advanced placement credit, accelerated degree programs, double majors, independent study, summer session for credit, part-time degree programs (daytime, evenings, summer), internships, and arrangement for off-campus study with Mt. Hood Community College. The most frequently chosen baccalaureate fields are business/marketing, liberal arts/general studies, philosophy, religion, and theology.
Student Body Statistics The student body is made up of 280 undergraduates (74 freshmen). 51 percent are women and 49 percent are men. Students come from 20 states and territories and 6 other countries. 36 percent are from Oregon. 2.2 percent are international students. 8 percent of the 2003 graduating class went on to graduate and professional schools.
Expenses for 2004–05 *Application fee:* $25. *Comprehensive fee:* $16,990 includes full-time tuition ($10,790), mandatory fees ($400), and college room and board ($5800). Full-time tuition and fees vary according to course load.
Financial Aid Forms of aid include need-based and non-need-based scholarships, athletic grants, and part-time jobs. The average aided 2003–04 undergraduate received an aid package worth an estimated $10,972. The application deadline for financial aid is July 31 with a priority deadline of March 1.
Freshman Admission Cascade requires a high school transcript, SAT I or ACT scores, and TOEFL scores for international students. An essay and 1 recommendation are recommended. The application deadline for regular admission is rolling.
Transfer Admission The application deadline for admission is rolling.
Entrance Difficulty Cascade has an open admission policy.

For Further Information Contact Mr. Clint La Rue, Director of Admissions, Cascade College, 9101 East Burnside, Portland, OR 97216-1515. *Telephone:* 503-257-1202 or 800-550-7678 (toll-free). *E-mail:* admissions@cascade.edu. *Web site:* http://www.cascade.edu/.

CONCORDIA UNIVERSITY

Portland, Oregon

Concordia Portland is a coed, private, comprehensive unit of Concordia University System, founded in 1905, affiliated with the Lutheran Church–Missouri Synod, offering degrees at the associate, bachelor's, and master's levels and postbachelor's certificates. It has a 13-acre campus in Portland.

Academic Information The faculty has 103 members (41% full-time), 48% with terminal degrees. The undergraduate student-faculty ratio is 18:1. The library holds 61,000 titles, 374 serial subscriptions, and 9,178 audiovisual materials. Special programs include academic remediation, study abroad, advanced placement credit, accelerated degree programs, ESL programs, double majors, self-designed majors, summer session for credit, part-time degree programs (evenings, weekends, summer), adult/continuing education programs, internships, and arrangement for off-campus study with Oregon Independent Colleges Association, Concordia University System. The most frequently chosen baccalaureate fields are business/marketing, education, health professions and related sciences.
Student Body Statistics The student body totals 1,274, of whom 905 are undergraduates (128 freshmen). 62 percent are women and 38 percent are men. Students come from 24 states and territories. 1.8 percent are international students.
Expenses for 2003–04 *Application fee:* $20. *Comprehensive fee:* $22,540 includes full-time tuition ($17,400), mandatory fees ($90), and college room and board ($5050). Full-time tuition and fees vary according to program. Room and board charges vary according to housing facility. *Part-time tuition:* $535 per credit. *Part-time mandatory fees:* $20 per term. Part-time tuition and fees vary according to course load and program.
Financial Aid Forms of aid include need-based and non-need-based scholarships, athletic grants, and part-time jobs. The average aided 2003–04 undergraduate received an aid package worth an estimated $13,500. The application deadline for financial aid is continuous.
Freshman Admission Concordia Portland requires an essay, a high school transcript, a minimum 2.5 high school GPA, 1 recommendation, SAT I or ACT scores, and TOEFL scores for international students. An interview is recommended. An interview is required for some. The application deadline for regular admission is rolling.
Transfer Admission The application deadline for admission is rolling.
Entrance Difficulty Concordia Portland assesses its entrance difficulty level as moderately difficult; minimally difficult for transfers. For the fall 2003 freshman class, 72 percent of the applicants were accepted.

For Further Information Contact Bobi L. Swan, Dean of Admission, Concordia University, 2811 Northeast Holman, Portland, OR 97211-6099. *Telephone:* 503-493-6526 or 800-321-9371 (toll-free). *Fax:* 503-280-8531. *E-mail:* admissions@portland.edu. *Web site:* http://www.cu-portland.edu/.

DEVRY UNIVERSITY

Portland, Oregon

DeVry University is a coed, proprietary, comprehensive unit of DeVry University.

Student Body Statistics The student body is made up of 4 undergraduates (3 freshmen). 50 percent are women and 50 percent are men.
Freshman Admission SAT I, ACT or CPT is recommended. The application deadline for regular admission is rolling.

For Further Information Contact DeVry University, 9755 SW Barnes Road, Suite 150, Portland, OR 97225-6651. *Telephone:* 503-296-7468. *Web site:* http://www.devry.edu/.

EASTERN OREGON UNIVERSITY

La Grande, Oregon

Eastern is a coed, public, comprehensive unit of Oregon University System, founded in 1929, offering degrees at the bachelor's and master's levels. It has a 121-acre campus in La Grande.

Academic Information The faculty has 114 members (82% full-time). The undergraduate student-faculty ratio is 15:1. The library holds 329,942 titles, 998 serial subscriptions, and 35,556 audiovisual materials. Special programs include services for learning-disabled students, an honors program, cooperative (work-study) education, study abroad, advanced placement credit, ESL programs, double majors, independent study, distance learning, self-designed majors, summer session for credit, part-time degree programs, external degree programs, adult/continuing education programs, internships, and arrangement for off-campus study with National Student Exchange.
Student Body Statistics The student body totals 3,287, of whom 3,041 are undergraduates (339 freshmen). 58 percent are women and 42 percent are men. Students come from 42 states and territories and 25 other countries. 70 percent are from Oregon. 2.1 percent are international students.
Expenses for 2004–05 *Application fee:* $50. *State resident tuition:* $4257 full-time, $95 per credit hour part-time. *Nonresident tuition:* $4257 full-time. *Mandatory fees:* $1260 full-time. Full-time tuition and fees vary according to course load. Part-time tuition varies according to course load. *College room and board:* $6100. *College room only:* $3250. Room and board charges vary according to board plan and housing facility.
Financial Aid Forms of aid include need-based and non-need-based scholarships and part-time jobs. The average aided 2003–04 undergraduate received an aid package worth an estimated $9461. The priority application deadline for financial aid is March 1.

Freshman Admission Eastern requires a high school transcript, a minimum 3.0 high school GPA, SAT I or ACT scores, and TOEFL scores for international students. An essay and 2 recommendations are required for some. The application deadline for regular admission is September 24 and for early action it is December 1.
Entrance Difficulty Eastern assesses its entrance difficulty level as moderately difficult; minimally difficult for transfers. For the fall 2003 freshman class, 99 percent of the applicants were accepted.

For Further Information Contact Ms. Sherri Edvalson, Director, Admissions, Eastern Oregon University, One University Boulevard, La Grande, OR 97850. *Telephone:* 541-962-3393, 800-452-8639 (toll-free in-state), or 800-452-3393 (toll-free out-of-state). *Fax:* 541-962-3418. *E-mail:* admissions@eou.edu. *Web site:* http://www.eou.edu/.

EUGENE BIBLE COLLEGE

Eugene, Oregon

EBC is a coed, private, four-year college, founded in 1925, affiliated with the Open Bible Standard Churches, offering degrees at the bachelor's level in Christian ministries. It has a 40-acre campus in Eugene.

Academic Information The faculty has 25 members (48% full-time), 28% with terminal degrees. The student-faculty ratio is 14:1. The library holds 34,000 titles, 260 serial subscriptions, and 350 audiovisual materials. Special programs include academic remediation, advanced placement credit, double majors, independent study, distance learning, summer session for credit, part-time degree programs (daytime), and internships. The most frequently chosen baccalaureate fields are philosophy, religion, and theology, interdisciplinary studies, psychology.
Student Body Statistics The student body is made up of 163 undergraduates (67 freshmen). 56 percent are women and 44 percent are men. Students come from 18 states and territories and 4 other countries. 51 percent are from Oregon. 1.8 percent are international students. 12 percent of the 2003 graduating class went on to graduate and professional schools.
Expenses for 2003–04 *Application fee:* $30. *Comprehensive fee:* $11,586 includes full-time tuition ($6855), mandatory fees ($651), and college room and board ($4080). Room and board charges vary according to housing facility. *Part-time tuition:* $195 per credit. *Part-time mandatory fees:* $138 per term. Part-time tuition and fees vary according to class time and course load.
Financial Aid Forms of aid include need-based and non-need-based scholarships and part-time jobs. The average aided 2003–04 undergraduate received an aid package worth an estimated $6300. The application deadline for financial aid is September 1 with a priority deadline of March 1.
Freshman Admission EBC requires an essay, a high school transcript, a minimum 2.0 high school GPA, 2 recommendations, SAT I or ACT scores, and TOEFL scores for international students. The application deadline for regular admission is September 1.
Transfer Admission The application deadline for admission is September 1.
Entrance Difficulty EBC assesses its entrance difficulty level as minimally difficult. For the fall 2003 freshman class, 73 percent of the applicants were accepted.

For Further Information Contact Mr. Trent Combs, Director of Admissions, Eugene Bible College, 2155 Bailey Hill Road, Eugene, OR 97405. *Telephone:* 541-485-1780 Ext. 135 or 800-322-2638 (toll-free). *Fax:* 541-343-5801. *E-mail:* admissions@ebc.edu. *Web site:* http://www.ebc.edu/.

GEORGE FOX UNIVERSITY

Newberg, Oregon

George Fox is a coed, private, Friends university, founded in 1891, offering degrees at the bachelor's, master's, doctoral, and first professional levels. It has a 73-acre campus in Newberg near Portland.

Academic Information The faculty has 361 members (37% full-time), 29% with terminal degrees. The undergraduate student-faculty ratio is 15:1. The library holds 123,734 titles, 1,323 serial subscriptions, and 2,687 audiovisual materials. Special programs include academic remediation, services for learning-disabled students, an honors program, cooperative (work-study) education, study abroad, advanced placement credit, accelerated degree programs, ESL programs, double majors, independent study, distance learning, self-designed majors, part-time degree programs (evenings, weekends), external degree programs, adult/continuing education programs, internships, and arrangement for off-campus study with members of the Christian College Consortium, Coalition for Christian Colleges and Universities, Oregon Independent Colleges Association. The most frequently chosen baccalaureate fields are business/marketing, education, interdisciplinary studies.
Student Body Statistics The student body totals 3,022, of whom 1,717 are undergraduates (337 freshmen). 59 percent are women and 41 percent are men. Students come from 25 states and territories and 16 other countries. 64 percent are from Oregon. 2.9 percent are international students. 18 percent of the 2003 graduating class went on to graduate and professional schools.
Expenses for 2003–04 *Application fee:* $40. *Comprehensive fee:* $26,110 includes full-time tuition ($19,500), mandatory fees ($310), and college room and board ($6300). *College room only:* $3500. Full-time tuition and fees vary according to program. Room and board charges vary according to housing facility and location. *Part-time tuition:* $600 per semester hour. Part-time tuition varies according to course load.
Financial Aid Forms of aid include need-based and non-need-based scholarships and part-time jobs. The average aided 2003–04 undergraduate received an aid package worth an estimated $14,902. The priority application deadline for financial aid is February 1.
Freshman Admission George Fox requires an essay, a high school transcript, 2 recommendations, and SAT I or ACT scores. An interview and TOEFL scores for international students are recommended. An interview is required for some. The application deadline for regular admission is June 1.
Transfer Admission The application deadline for admission is April 1.
Entrance Difficulty George Fox assesses its entrance difficulty level as moderately difficult. For the fall 2003 freshman class, 93 percent of the applicants were accepted.

SPECIAL MESSAGE TO STUDENTS

Social Life Student organizations at George Fox provide opportunities for the development of leadership qualities and interpersonal relationships. They are designed to supplement classroom work with practical experience and to provide wholesome and profitable recreation. Many activities are available, including campus government, athletics, music, drama, publications, social and religious organizations, and various special interest groups.

Academic Highlights In order to enrich the intercultural and international awareness of the campus community, George Fox University offers the Juniors Abroad program, a transportation-subsidized overseas course of approximately three weeks, to qualified juniors. To enhance the learning and research of students, the University developed Computers Across the Curriculum, which provides every new freshman a computer that is his or hers to keep after graduation.

Interviews and Campus Visits Students interested in enrolling at George Fox are encouraged to visit the campus, preferably while classes are in session. A visit provides an opportunity to observe classes, see the campus facilities, and talk with current students and professors. Visits should be arranged five days in advance through the admissions office. Bounded on three sides by a residential area, the George Fox campus borders Hess Creek, a natural setting

George Fox University (continued)

that is being preserved with its tall trees, ferns, and wildflowers. The spacious century-old campus has been developed in recent years and features an academic quadrangle. For information about appointments and campus visits, prospective students should call the Undergraduate Admissions Office at 800-765-4369 (toll-free), Monday through Friday, 8 a.m. to 5 p.m. The office is located in the Edward F. Stevens Center. The nearest commercial airport is Portland International.

For Further Information Write to Undergraduate Admissions, George Fox University, 414 North Meridian, Newberg, OR 97132-2697.

See page 174 for a narrative description.

HEALD COLLEGE-PORTLAND

Portland, Oregon

Heald College-Portland is a coed, private, two-year college, founded in 1863, offering degrees at the associate level.

For Further Information Contact Heald College-Portland, 625 Southwest Broadway, Suite 200, Portland, OR 97205. *Telephone:* 503-229-0492 or 800-755-3550 (toll-free in-state). *Fax:* 503-229-0498. *E-mail:* info@heald.edu. *Web site:* http://www.heald.edu/.

ITT TECHNICAL INSTITUTE

Portland, Oregon

ITT Tech is a coed, proprietary, primarily two-year college of ITT Educational Services, Inc., founded in 1971, offering degrees at the associate and bachelor's levels. It has a 4-acre campus in Portland.

Student Body Statistics The student body is made up of 525 undergraduates.
Expenses for 2003–04 *Application fee:* $100. Total Program Cost varies depending on course of study. Consult school catalog.
Financial Aid Forms of aid include need-based scholarships and part-time jobs. The application deadline for financial aid is continuous.
Freshman Admission ITT Tech requires a high school transcript, an interview, TOEFL scores for international students, and Wonderlic aptitude test. Recommendations are recommended. The application deadline for regular admission is rolling.
Transfer Admission The application deadline for admission is rolling.
Entrance Difficulty ITT Tech assesses its entrance difficulty level as minimally difficult.

For Further Information Contact Mr. Ed Yakimchick, Director of Recruitment, ITT Technical Institute, 6035 Northeast 78th Court, Portland, OR 97218. *Telephone:* 503-255-6500 or 800-234-5488 (toll-free). *Fax:* 503-255-8381. *Web site:* http://www.itt-tech.edu/.

LEWIS & CLARK COLLEGE

Portland, Oregon

L & C is a coed, private, comprehensive institution, founded in 1867, offering degrees at the bachelor's, master's, and first professional levels and first professional certificates. It has a 137-acre campus in Portland.

Academic Information The faculty has 331 members (59% full-time), 77% with terminal degrees. The undergraduate student-faculty ratio is 12:1. The library holds 227,609 titles, 7,477 serial subscriptions, and 11,586 audiovisual materials. Special programs include services for learning-disabled students, an honors program, study abroad, advanced placement credit, accelerated degree programs, ESL programs, double majors, independent study, self-designed majors, summer session for credit, part-time degree programs (daytime, summer), internships, and arrangement for off-campus study with Oregon Independent Colleges Association. The most frequently chosen baccalaureate fields are foreign language/literature, psychology, social sciences and history.
Student Body Statistics The student body totals 3,071, of whom 1,792 are undergraduates (493 freshmen). 61 percent are women and 39 percent are men. Students come from 51 states and territories and 40 other countries. 20 percent are from Oregon. 4.7 percent are international students. 19 percent of the 2003 graduating class went on to graduate and professional schools.
Expenses for 2003–04 *Application fee:* $50. *Comprehensive fee:* $31,700 includes full-time tuition ($23,886), mandatory fees ($784), and college room and board ($7030). *College room only:* $3710. Room and board charges vary according to board plan and housing facility.
Financial Aid Forms of aid include need-based and non-need-based scholarships and part-time jobs. The average aided 2003–04 undergraduate received an aid package worth an estimated $18,654. The priority application deadline for financial aid is March 1.
Freshman Admission L & C requires an essay, a high school transcript, a minimum 2.0 high school GPA, 2 recommendations, TOEFL scores for international students, and SAT I, ACT, or academic portfolio. A minimum 3.0 high school GPA and an interview are recommended. 4 recommendations and portfolio applicants must submit samples of graded work are required for some. The application deadline for regular admission is February 1 and for early action it is December 1.
Entrance Difficulty L & C assesses its entrance difficulty level as very difficult. For the fall 2003 freshman class, 68 percent of the applicants were accepted.

For Further Information Contact Mr. Michael Sexton, Dean of Admissions, Lewis & Clark College, 0615 SW Palatine Hill Road, Portland, OR 97219-7899. *Telephone:* 503-768-7040 or 800-444-4111 (toll-free). *Fax:* 503-768-7055. *E-mail:* admissions@lclark.edu. *Web site:* http://www.lclark.edu/.

See page 180 for a narrative description.

LINFIELD COLLEGE

McMinnville, Oregon

Linfield is a coed, private, American Baptist Churches in the USA, four-year college, founded in 1849, offering degrees at the bachelor's level. It has a 193-acre campus in McMinnville near Portland.

Academic Information The faculty has 164 members (63% full-time), 68% with terminal degrees. The student-faculty ratio is 13:1. The library holds 163,744 titles, 1,296 serial subscriptions, and 19,549 audiovisual materials. Special programs include services for learning-disabled students, an honors program, cooperative (work-study) education, study abroad, advanced placement credit, accelerated degree programs, ESL programs, double majors, independent study, distance learning, self-designed majors, summer session for credit, part-time degree programs (daytime, summer), external degree programs, adult/continuing education programs, internships, and arrangement for off-campus study with American Baptist Colleges and Universities. The most frequently chosen baccalaureate fields are business/marketing, education, parks and recreation.
Student Body Statistics The student body is made up of 1,659 undergraduates (453 freshmen). 55 percent are women and 45 percent are men. Students come from 30 states and territories and 19 other countries. 55 percent are from Oregon. 2.1 percent are international students. 20 percent of the 2003 graduating class went on to graduate and professional schools.
Expenses for 2003–04 *Application fee:* $40. *Comprehensive fee:* $27,090 includes full-time tuition ($20,770), mandatory fees ($200), and college room and board ($6120). *College room only:* $3200. Room and board charges vary according to board plan and housing facility. *Part-time tuition:* $650 per credit. *Part-time mandatory fees:* $60 per term. Part-time tuition and fees vary according to course load.
Financial Aid Forms of aid include need-based and non-need-based scholarships and part-time jobs. The average aided 2003–04 undergraduate received an aid package worth an estimated $16,638. The priority application deadline for financial aid is February 1.
Freshman Admission Linfield requires an essay, a high school transcript, 1 recommendation, SAT I or ACT scores, and TOEFL scores

for international students. An interview is recommended. The application deadline for regular admission is February 15 and for early action it is November 15.
Transfer Admission The application deadline for admission is April 15.
Entrance Difficulty Linfield assesses its entrance difficulty level as moderately difficult. For the fall 2003 freshman class, 78 percent of the applicants were accepted.

SPECIAL MESSAGE TO STUDENTS

Social Life As a residential college, Linfield emphasizes on-campus activities. Linfield's student government sponsors programs and entertainment each weekend, charters almost forty student-interest clubs, publishes a weekly newspaper, operates an FCC-licensed radio station, and coordinates a popular intramural agenda. With the college located near Portland and the coast, students have off-campus options as well.

Academic Highlights Linfield has made a commitment to provide students with an international experience while enrolled. The environment for students encourages exploration and unity in an increasingly global society. The College offers semester options in Austria, China, Costa Rica, England, France, Ireland, Japan, Korea, Mexico, and Norway. In addition, there are numerous travel-study programs available during January term. The student-faculty ratio is 12:1. The professors are accessible, provide help outside the classroom, and challenge students to excel and grow. Research and internships are generated through professors and advisers, as well as through the career and counseling center. Linfield's new 56,000-square-foot library combines traditional print collections and wireless electronic technology to provide access to the Web and Web-based databases. Linfield is technologically up-to-date with Internet access, e-mail, voice mail, and cable television in each residence hall room.

Interviews and Campus Visits Students are encouraged to visit campus during the academic year. Overnight stays, appointments to meet with faculty members and coaches, and visits to classes can be arranged in advance. Current students guide tours twice a day, Monday through Saturday. Lunch is provided for students. Student-guided tours are available during the summer, but meals and housing are not provided. For information about appointments and campus visits, students should call the Office of Admission at 800-640-2287, Monday through Friday, 7:30 a.m. to 5:30 p.m. The office is located in the Michelbook House on campus. The nearest commercial airport is Portland International; the nearest highway is Highway 99W.

For Further Information Write to Office of Admission, Linfield College, 900 South Baker Street, McMinnville, OR 97128. *E-mail:* admission@linfield.edu. *Web site:* http://www.linfield.edu.

See page 182 for a narrative description.

MARYLHURST UNIVERSITY

Marylhurst, Oregon

Marylhurst University is a coed, private, Roman Catholic, comprehensive institution, founded in 1893, offering degrees at the bachelor's and master's levels and postbachelor's certificates. It has a 73-acre campus in Marylhurst near Portland.

Academic Information The faculty has 184 members (17% full-time), 33% with terminal degrees. The undergraduate student-faculty ratio is 7:1. The library holds 1,449 audiovisual materials. Special programs include services for learning-disabled students, advanced placement credit, accelerated degree programs, ESL programs, double majors, independent study, distance learning, self-designed majors, summer session for credit, part-time degree programs (daytime, evenings, weekends, summer), adult/continuing education programs, internships, and arrangement for off-campus study with members of the Oregon Independent Colleges Association. The most frequently chosen baccalaureate fields are business/marketing, communications/communication technologies, visual/performing arts.
Student Body Statistics The student body totals 1,212, of whom 804 are undergraduates (11 freshmen). 75 percent are women and 25 percent are men. Students come from 9 states and territories and 22 other countries. 88 percent are from Oregon. 3.6 percent are international students.
Expenses for 2004–05 *Application fee:* $20. *Tuition:* $13,185 full-time, $293 per credit hour part-time. *Mandatory fees:* $270 full-time, $6 per credit hour part-time. Full-time tuition and fees vary according to course load. Part-time tuition and fees vary according to course load.
Financial Aid Forms of aid include need-based scholarships and part-time jobs. The average aided 2003–04 undergraduate received an aid package worth an estimated $12,933. The application deadline for financial aid is continuous.
Freshman Admission Marylhurst University requires a high school transcript. TOEFL scores for international students are recommended. The application deadline for regular admission is rolling.
Transfer Admission The application deadline for admission is rolling.
Entrance Difficulty Marylhurst University has an open admission policy except for some programs. It assesses its entrance difficulty as minimally difficult for some majors.

For Further Information Contact Mr. John French, Academic Advising Specialist, Marylhurst University, 17600 Pacific Highway (Hwy 43), PO Box 261, Marylhurst, OR 97036. *Telephone:* 503-636-8141 Ext. 4430 or 800-634-9982 (toll-free). *Fax:* 503-635-6585. *E-mail:* admissions@marylhurst.edu. *Web site:* http://www.marylhurst.edu/.

MOUNT ANGEL SEMINARY

Saint Benedict, Oregon

For Information Write to Mount Angel Seminary, Saint Benedict, OR 97373.

MULTNOMAH BIBLE COLLEGE AND BIBLICAL SEMINARY

Portland, Oregon

Multnomah is a coed, private, interdenominational, comprehensive institution, founded in 1936, offering degrees at the bachelor's, master's, and first professional levels and postbachelor's certificates in religious studies. It has a 22-acre campus in Portland.

Academic Information The faculty has 51 members (47% full-time), 35% with terminal degrees. The undergraduate student-faculty ratio is 16:1. The library holds 73,591 titles, 369 serial subscriptions, and 11,693 audiovisual materials. Special programs include academic remediation, services for learning-disabled students, advanced placement credit, double majors, summer session for credit, part-time degree programs (daytime, summer), adult/continuing education programs, and internships. The most frequently chosen baccalaureate field is philosophy, religion, and theology.
Student Body Statistics The student body totals 785, of whom 564 are undergraduates (85 freshmen). 45 percent are women and 55 percent are men. Students come from 34 states and territories. 45 percent are from Oregon. 0.4 percent are international students.
Expenses for 2003–04 *Application fee:* $40. *Comprehensive fee:* $15,310 includes full-time tuition ($10,560) and college room and board ($4750). Room and board charges vary according to board plan and housing facility. *Part-time tuition:* $440 per semester hour. Part-time tuition varies according to course load.
Financial Aid Forms of aid include need-based and non-need-based scholarships and part-time jobs. The average aided 2002–03 undergraduate received an aid package worth $7328. The priority application deadline for financial aid is March 1.
Freshman Admission Multnomah requires an essay, a high school transcript, a minimum 2.5 high school GPA, 4 recommendations, SAT I or ACT scores, and TOEFL scores for international students. The application deadline for regular admission is July 15.
Transfer Admission The application deadline for admission is July 15.

Multnomah Bible College and Biblical Seminary (continued)

Entrance Difficulty Multnomah assesses its entrance difficulty level as moderately difficult. For the fall 2003 freshman class, 80 percent of the applicants were accepted.

For Further Information Contact Ms. Nancy Gerecz, Admissions Assistant, Multnomah Bible College and Biblical Seminary, 8435 Northeast Glisan Street, Portland, OR 97220-5898. *Telephone:* 503-255-0332 Ext. 371 or 800-275-4672 (toll-free). *Fax:* 503-254-1268. *E-mail:* admiss@multnomah.edu. *Web site:* http://www.multnomah.edu/.

NORTHWEST CHRISTIAN COLLEGE

Eugene, Oregon

NCC is a coed, private, Christian, comprehensive institution, founded in 1895, offering degrees at the associate, bachelor's, and master's levels and postbachelor's certificates. It has an 8-acre campus in Eugene near Portland.

Academic Information The faculty has 56 members (41% full-time), 41% with terminal degrees. The undergraduate student-faculty ratio is 13:1. The library holds 62,220 titles, 261 serial subscriptions, and 8,677 audiovisual materials. Special programs include academic remediation, services for learning-disabled students, cooperative (work-study) education, study abroad, advanced placement credit, accelerated degree programs, ESL programs, double majors, independent study, distance learning, summer session for credit, part-time degree programs (daytime, evenings), adult/continuing education programs, internships, and arrangement for off-campus study with University of Oregon, Lane Community College. The most frequently chosen baccalaureate fields are business/marketing, education, psychology.
Student Body Statistics The student body totals 491, of whom 392 are undergraduates (53 freshmen). 59 percent are women and 41 percent are men. Students come from 14 states and territories and 2 other countries. 89 percent are from Oregon. 0.8 percent are international students.
Expenses for 2003–04 *Application fee:* $25. *Comprehensive fee:* $21,710 includes full-time tuition ($16,200) and college room and board ($5510). *College room only:* $2300. Full-time tuition varies according to course load and program. Room and board charges vary according to board plan and housing facility. *Part-time tuition:* $360 per credit. Part-time tuition varies according to course load.
Financial Aid Forms of aid include need-based and non-need-based scholarships, athletic grants, and part-time jobs. The average aided 2003–04 undergraduate received an aid package worth an estimated $13,790. The application deadline for financial aid is continuous.
Freshman Admission NCC requires an essay, a high school transcript, a minimum 2.5 high school GPA, 2 recommendations, SAT I or ACT scores, and TOEFL scores for international students. An interview is recommended. SAT II: Subject Test scores are required for some. The application deadline for regular admission is rolling.
Transfer Admission The application deadline for admission is rolling.
Entrance Difficulty NCC assesses its entrance difficulty level as moderately difficult. For the fall 2003 freshman class, 65 percent of the applicants were accepted.

For Further Information Contact Ms. Cheryl Brelsford, Interim Director of Admissions, Northwest Christian College, 828 East 11th Avenue, Eugene, OR 97401-3745. *Telephone:* 541-684-7210 or 877-463-6622 (toll-free). *Fax:* 541-684-7317. *E-mail:* admissions@nwcc.edu. *Web site:* http://www.nwcc.edu/.

OREGON COLLEGE OF ART & CRAFT

Portland, Oregon

OCAC is a coed, private, four-year college, founded in 1907, offering degrees at the bachelor's level and postbachelor's certificates in art. It has an 11-acre campus in Portland.

Academic Information The faculty has 18 members (44% full-time), 89% with terminal degrees. The student-faculty ratio is 8:1. The library holds 6,500 titles, 90 serial subscriptions, and 24,000 audiovisual materials. Special programs include advanced placement credit, double majors, independent study, part-time degree programs (daytime), adult/continuing education programs, internships, and arrangement for off-campus study. The most frequently chosen baccalaureate field is visual/performing arts.
Student Body Statistics The student body totals 129, of whom 120 are undergraduates (15 freshmen). 73 percent are women and 28 percent are men. Students come from 21 states and territories and 2 other countries. 62 percent are from Oregon. 2.7 percent are international students.
Expenses for 2004–05 *Application fee:* $35. *Tuition:* $14,800 full-time, $1935 per course part-time. *Mandatory fees:* $1050 full-time. Part-time tuition varies according to course load.
Financial Aid Forms of aid include need-based and non-need-based scholarships and part-time jobs. The average aided 2002–03 undergraduate received an aid package worth $12,100. The priority application deadline for financial aid is March 1.
Freshman Admission OCAC requires an essay, a high school transcript, a minimum 2.5 high school GPA, 2 recommendations, an interview, and a portfolio. The application deadline for regular admission is rolling.
Transfer Admission The application deadline for admission is rolling.
Entrance Difficulty OCAC assesses its entrance difficulty level as minimally difficult.

For Further Information Contact Mr. Barry Beach, Director of Admissions, Oregon College of Art & Craft, 8245 Southwest Barnes Road, Portland, OR 97225. *Telephone:* 503-297-5544 or 800-390-0632 (toll-free). *Fax:* 503-297-9651. *E-mail:* admissions@ocac.edu. *Web site:* http://www.ocac.edu/.

OREGON HEALTH & SCIENCE UNIVERSITY

Portland, Oregon

For Information Write to Oregon Health & Science University, Portland, OR 97239-3098.

OREGON INSTITUTE OF TECHNOLOGY

Klamath Falls, Oregon

OIT is a coed, public, four-year college of Oregon University System, founded in 1947, offering degrees at the associate and bachelor's levels. It has a 173-acre campus in Klamath Falls.

Academic Information The faculty has 130 members (88% full-time). The student-faculty ratio is 15:1. The library holds 90,389 titles, 1,764 serial subscriptions, and 1,905 audiovisual materials. Special programs include academic remediation, services for learning-disabled students, cooperative (work-study) education, study abroad, advanced placement credit, ESL programs, double majors, distance learning, summer session for credit, part-time degree programs (daytime, evenings, summer), adult/continuing education programs, internships, and arrangement for off-campus study with Portland State University. The most frequently chosen baccalaureate fields are engineering/engineering technologies, health professions and related sciences, protective services/public administration.
Student Body Statistics The student body totals 3,236, of whom 3,235 are undergraduates (354 freshmen). 46 percent are women and 54 percent are men. Students come from 35 states and territories and 10 other countries. 1 percent are international students.
Expenses for 2003–04 *Application fee:* $50. *State resident tuition:* $3348 full-time, $93 per credit part-time. *Nonresident tuition:* $12,528 full-time, $93 per credit part-time. *Mandatory fees:* $1095 full-time. Full-time tuition and fees vary according to course load. *College room and board:* $6135. Room and board charges vary according to board plan.
Financial Aid Forms of aid include need-based and non-need-based scholarships, athletic grants, and part-time jobs. The average aided 2002–03 undergraduate received an aid package worth $5791. The priority application deadline for financial aid is March 1.

Freshman Admission OIT requires a high school transcript, a minimum 2.5 high school GPA, SAT I or ACT scores, and TOEFL scores for international students. Recommendations are required for some. The application deadline for regular admission is June 1.
Transfer Admission The application deadline for admission is June 1.
Entrance Difficulty OIT assesses its entrance difficulty level as moderately difficult. For the fall 2003 freshman class, 54 percent of the applicants were accepted.

For Further Information Contact Mr. Palmer Muntz, Director of Admissions, Oregon Institute of Technology, 3201 Campus Drive, Klamath Falls, OR 97601. *Telephone:* 541-885-1150, 800-422-2017 (toll-free in-state), or 800-343-6653 (toll-free out-of-state). *Fax:* 541-885-1115. *E-mail:* oit@oit.edu. *Web site:* http://www.oit.edu/.

OREGON STATE UNIVERSITY

Corvallis, Oregon

OSU is a coed, public unit of Oregon University System, founded in 1868, offering degrees at the bachelor's, master's, doctoral, and first professional levels. It has a 422-acre campus in Corvallis near Portland.

Academic Information The faculty has 789 members (80% full-time), 64% with terminal degrees. The undergraduate student-faculty ratio is 21:1. The library holds 689,119 titles, 12,254 serial subscriptions, and 6,225 audiovisual materials. Special programs include academic remediation, services for learning-disabled students, an honors program, cooperative (work-study) education, study abroad, advanced placement credit, Freshman Honors College, ESL programs, double majors, distance learning, self-designed majors, summer session for credit, part-time degree programs, internships, and arrangement for off-campus study with members of the National Student Exchange, members of the Western Interstate Commission for Higher Education. The most frequently chosen baccalaureate fields are business/marketing, engineering/engineering technologies, home economics/vocational home economics.
Student Body Statistics The student body totals 18,979, of whom 15,599 are undergraduates (2,949 freshmen). 47 percent are women and 53 percent are men. Students come from 50 states and territories and 91 other countries. 89 percent are from Oregon. 1.6 percent are international students.
Expenses for 2003–04 *Application fee:* $50. *State resident tuition:* $3642 full-time, $97 per credit part-time. *Nonresident tuition:* $16,398 full-time, $451 per credit part-time. *Mandatory fees:* $1227 full-time. Part-time tuition varies according to course load. *College room and board:* $6336. Room and board charges vary according to board plan and housing facility.
Financial Aid Forms of aid include need-based and non-need-based scholarships and part-time jobs. The application deadline for financial aid is May 1.
Freshman Admission OSU requires a high school transcript, a minimum 3.0 high school GPA, SAT I or ACT scores, and TOEFL scores for international students. SAT II: Subject Test scores are required for some. The application deadline for regular admission is March 1.
Transfer Admission The application deadline for admission is May 1.
Entrance Difficulty OSU assesses its entrance difficulty level as moderately difficult. For the fall 2003 freshman class, 88 percent of the applicants were accepted.

For Further Information Contact Ms. Michele Sandlin, Director of Admissions, Oregon State University, Corvallis, OR 97331. *Telephone:* 541-737-4411 or 800-291-4192 (toll-free in-state). *Fax:* 541-737-6157. *E-mail:* osuadmit@orst.edu. *Web site:* http://oregonstate.edu/.

PACIFIC NORTHWEST COLLEGE OF ART

Portland, Oregon

PNCA is a coed, private, four-year college, founded in 1909, offering degrees at the bachelor's level in art. It has a 2-acre campus in Portland.

Academic Information The faculty has 53 members (26% full-time), 47% with terminal degrees. The student-faculty ratio is 12:1. The library holds 12,716 titles, 65 serial subscriptions, and 62,300 audiovisual materials. Special programs include services for learning-disabled students, cooperative (work-study) education, study abroad, advanced placement credit, independent study, self-designed majors, summer session for credit, part-time degree programs (daytime, evenings, summer), adult/continuing education programs, internships, and arrangement for off-campus study with Reed College, Oregon Independent Colleges Association, Association of Independent Colleges of Art and Design. The most frequently chosen baccalaureate field is visual/performing arts.
Student Body Statistics The student body is made up of 308 undergraduates (30 freshmen). 53 percent are women and 47 percent are men. Students come from 20 states and territories and 4 other countries. 80 percent are from Oregon. 1.3 percent are international students.
Expenses for 2003–04 *Application fee:* $35. *Tuition:* $14,270 full-time, $615 per semester hour part-time. *Mandatory fees:* $530 full-time, $157 per term part-time. Part-time tuition and fees vary according to course load.
Financial Aid Forms of aid include need-based and non-need-based scholarships and part-time jobs. The priority application deadline for financial aid is March 11.
Freshman Admission PNCA requires an essay, a high school transcript, a minimum 2.5 high school GPA, 1 recommendation, portfolio of artwork, and TOEFL scores for international students. An interview is recommended.
Entrance Difficulty PNCA assesses its entrance difficulty level as moderately difficult. For the fall 2003 freshman class, 91 percent of the applicants were accepted.

For Further Information Contact Ms. Rebecca Haas, Director of Admissions, Pacific Northwest College of Art, 1241 NW Johnson Street, Portland, OR 97209. *Telephone:* 503-821-8972. *Fax:* 503-821-8972. *E-mail:* admissions@pnca.edu. *Web site:* http://www.pnca.edu/.

PACIFIC UNIVERSITY

Forest Grove, Oregon

Pacific is a coed, private, comprehensive institution, founded in 1849, offering degrees at the bachelor's, master's, doctoral, and first professional levels. It has a 55-acre campus in Forest Grove near Portland.

Academic Information The faculty has 140 members (60% full-time), 62% with terminal degrees. The undergraduate student-faculty ratio is 11:1. The library holds 244,691 titles, 1,180 serial subscriptions, and 5,715 audiovisual materials. Special programs include services for learning-disabled students, an honors program, study abroad, advanced placement credit, accelerated degree programs, ESL programs, double majors, independent study, summer session for credit, internships, and arrangement for off-campus study with United Church of Christ related colleges and universities. The most frequently chosen baccalaureate fields are business/marketing, education, parks and recreation.
Student Body Statistics The student body totals 2,420, of whom 1,203 are undergraduates (303 freshmen). 61 percent are women and 39 percent are men. Students come from 35 states and territories and 6 other countries. 53 percent are from Oregon. 0.4 percent are international students. 40 percent of the 2003 graduating class went on to graduate and professional schools.
Expenses for 2003–04 *Application fee:* $30. *Comprehensive fee:* $25,430 includes full-time tuition ($19,330), mandatory fees ($560), and college room and board ($5540). *College room only:* $2680. Room and board charges vary according to board plan and housing facility. *Part-time tuition:* varies with course load.
Financial Aid Forms of aid include need-based and non-need-based scholarships and part-time jobs. The average aided 2003–04 undergraduate received an aid package worth an estimated $17,369. The priority application deadline for financial aid is February 15.
Freshman Admission Pacific requires an essay, a high school transcript, a minimum 3.0 high school GPA, 1 recommendation, SAT I or ACT scores, and TOEFL scores for international students. An interview is recommended. The application deadline for regular admission is August 15.

Pacific University (continued)

Transfer Admission The application deadline for admission is August 15.

Entrance Difficulty Pacific assesses its entrance difficulty level as moderately difficult. For the fall 2003 freshman class, 84 percent of the applicants were accepted.

For Further Information Contact Mr. Ian Symmonds, Executive Director of Admissions, Pacific University, 2043 College Way, Forest Grove, OR 97116-1797. *Telephone:* 503-352-2218 or 877-722-8648 (toll-free). *Fax:* 503-352-2975. *E-mail:* admissions@pacificu.edu. *Web site:* http://www.pacificu.edu/.

PIONEER PACIFIC COLLEGE

Wilsonville, Oregon

Pioneer Pacific College is a coed, proprietary, primarily two-year college, founded in 1981, offering degrees at the associate and bachelor's levels. It is located in Wilsonville near Portland.

Academic Information The faculty has 74 members (50% full-time), 11% with terminal degrees. The student-faculty ratio is 15:1. The library holds 2,500 titles. Special programs include accelerated degree programs.

Student Body Statistics The student body is made up of 760 undergraduates (316 freshmen). 73 percent are women and 28 percent are men. Students come from 2 states and territories and 1 other country. 94 percent are from Oregon.

Expenses for 2004–05 *Application fee:* $50. *One-time mandatory fee:* $150. *Tuition:* $7200 full-time, $160 per credit hour part-time. *Mandatory fees:* $150 full-time.

Financial Aid Forms of aid include need-based scholarships. The application deadline for financial aid is continuous.

Freshman Admission Pioneer Pacific College requires a high school transcript, an interview, TOEFL scores for international students, and CPAt. The application deadline for regular admission is rolling.

Entrance Difficulty Pioneer Pacific College has an open admission policy.

For Further Information Contact Ms. Mary Harris, Director of Admissions, Pioneer Pacific College, 27501 Southwest Parkway Avenue, Wilsonville, OR 97070. *Telephone:* 503-682-3903 or 866-772-4636 (toll-free in-state). *Fax:* 503-682-1514. *E-mail:* inquiries@pioneerpacific.edu. *Web site:* http://www.pioneerpacific.edu/.

PORTLAND STATE UNIVERSITY

Portland, Oregon

PSU is a coed, public unit of Oregon University System, founded in 1946, offering degrees at the bachelor's, master's, and doctoral levels and postbachelor's certificates. It has a 49-acre campus in Portland.

Academic Information The faculty has 1,138 members (57% full-time). The undergraduate student-faculty ratio is 20:1. The library holds 2 million titles, 8,698 serial subscriptions, and 91,912 audiovisual materials. Special programs include academic remediation, services for learning-disabled students, an honors program, cooperative (work-study) education, study abroad, advanced placement credit, accelerated degree programs, ESL programs, double majors, independent study, distance learning, self-designed majors, summer session for credit, part-time degree programs (daytime, evenings, weekends, summer), adult/continuing education programs, internships, and arrangement for off-campus study with other members of the Oregon University System. The most frequently chosen baccalaureate fields are business/marketing, liberal arts/general studies, social sciences and history.

Student Body Statistics The student body totals 23,117, of whom 16,906 are undergraduates (1,538 freshmen). 54 percent are women and 46 percent are men. Students come from 47 states and territories and 67 other countries. 87 percent are from Oregon. 3.4 percent are international students.

Expenses for 2003–04 *Application fee:* $50. *State resident tuition:* $3240 full-time, $107 per credit part-time. *Nonresident tuition:* $12,636 full-time, $107 per credit part-time. *Mandatory fees:* $1038 full-time, $17 per credit part-time, $35 per term part-time. Part-time tuition and fees vary according to course load. *College room and board:* $8175. *College room only:* $6075. Room and board charges vary according to board plan and housing facility.

Financial Aid Forms of aid include need-based and non-need-based scholarships and part-time jobs. The average aided 2002–03 undergraduate received an aid package worth $7712. The application deadline for financial aid is continuous.

Freshman Admission PSU requires a high school transcript, a minimum 3.0 high school GPA, SAT I or ACT scores, and TOEFL scores for international students. The application deadline for regular admission is rolling.

Transfer Admission The application deadline for admission is rolling.

Entrance Difficulty PSU assesses its entrance difficulty level as minimally difficult. For the fall 2003 freshman class, 85 percent of the applicants were accepted.

For Further Information Contact Ms. Agnes A. Hoffman, Director of Admissions and Records, Portland State University, PO Box 751, Portland, OR 97207-0751. *Telephone:* 503-725-3511 or 800-547-8887 (toll-free). *Fax:* 503-725-5525. *E-mail:* admissions@pdx.edu. *Web site:* http://www.pdx.edu/.

REED COLLEGE

Portland, Oregon

Reed is a coed, private, comprehensive institution, founded in 1908, offering degrees at the bachelor's and master's levels. It has a 98-acre campus in Portland.

Academic Information The faculty has 133 members (90% full-time), 86% with terminal degrees. The undergraduate student-faculty ratio is 10:1. The library holds 5 million titles, 2,300 serial subscriptions, and 16,596 audiovisual materials. Special programs include services for learning-disabled students, study abroad, advanced placement credit, accelerated degree programs, double majors, independent study, part-time degree programs (daytime), and arrangement for off-campus study with Oregon Independent Colleges Association. The most frequently chosen baccalaureate fields are English, biological/life sciences, social sciences and history.

Student Body Statistics The student body totals 1,340, of whom 1,312 are undergraduates (301 freshmen). 54 percent are women and 46 percent are men. Students come from 49 states and territories and 38 other countries. 18 percent are from Oregon. 3.3 percent are international students.

Expenses for 2003–04 *Application fee:* $40. *Comprehensive fee:* $36,950 includes full-time tuition ($29,000), mandatory fees ($200), and college room and board ($7750). *College room only:* $4020. Full-time tuition and fees vary according to degree level. Room and board charges vary according to board plan and housing facility. *Part-time tuition:* $4900 per course. Part-time tuition varies according to course load and degree level.

Financial Aid Forms of aid include need-based scholarships and part-time jobs. The average aided 2003–04 undergraduate received an aid package worth an estimated $24,309. The application deadline for financial aid is February 1 with a priority deadline of January 15.

Freshman Admission Reed requires an essay, a high school transcript, 2 recommendations, SAT I or ACT scores, and TOEFL scores for international students. A minimum 3.0 high school GPA, an interview, SAT II: Subject Test scores, and SAT II: Writing Test scores are recommended. The application deadline for regular admission is January 15; for early decision plan 1 it is November 15; and for early decision plan 2 it is January 2.

Transfer Admission The application deadline for admission is March 1.

Entrance Difficulty Reed assesses its entrance difficulty level as most difficult. For the fall 2003 freshman class, 46 percent of the applicants were accepted.

For Further Information Contact Mr. Paul Marthers, Dean of Admission, Reed College, 3203 Southeast Woodstock Boulevard, Portland, OR 97202-8199. *Telephone:* 503-777-7511 or 800-547-4750 (toll-free out-of-state). *Fax:* 503-777-7553. *E-mail:* admission@reed.edu. *Web site:* http://www.reed.edu/.

SOUTHERN OREGON UNIVERSITY

Ashland, Oregon

Southern Oregon is a coed, public, comprehensive unit of Oregon University System, founded in 1926, offering degrees at the bachelor's and master's levels and postbachelor's certificates. It has a 175-acre campus in Ashland.

Academic Information The faculty has 337 members (56% full-time). The undergraduate student-faculty ratio is 19:1. The library holds 272,319 titles, 2,040 serial subscriptions, and 20,241 audiovisual materials. Special programs include academic remediation, services for learning-disabled students, an honors program, cooperative (work-study) education, study abroad, advanced placement credit, accelerated degree programs, Freshman Honors College, ESL programs, double majors, independent study, distance learning, self-designed majors, summer session for credit, part-time degree programs, adult/continuing education programs, internships, and arrangement for off-campus study with National Student Exchange, other members of the Oregon University System. The most frequently chosen baccalaureate fields are business/marketing, communications/communication technologies, social sciences and history.
Student Body Statistics The student body totals 5,506, of whom 4,964 are undergraduates (968 freshmen). 55 percent are women and 45 percent are men. Students come from 45 states and territories and 33 other countries. 80 percent are from Oregon. 2 percent are international students.
Expenses for 2003–04 *Application fee:* $50. *State resident tuition:* $3138 full-time. *Nonresident tuition:* $11,808 full-time. *Mandatory fees:* $1015 full-time. Full-time tuition and fees vary according to course load, location, and reciprocity agreements. *College room and board:* $6039. Room and board charges vary according to board plan and housing facility.
Financial Aid Forms of aid include need-based and non-need-based scholarships, athletic grants, and part-time jobs. The average aided 2002–03 undergraduate received an aid package worth $5118. The priority application deadline for financial aid is March 1.
Freshman Admission Southern Oregon requires a high school transcript, 2.75 high school GPA or minimum SAT score of 1010, SAT I or ACT scores, and TOEFL scores for international students. SAT II: Subject Test scores are required for some. The application deadline for regular admission is rolling.
Transfer Admission The application deadline for admission is rolling.
Entrance Difficulty Southern Oregon assesses its entrance difficulty level as moderately difficult. For the fall 2003 freshman class, 90 percent of the applicants were accepted.

For Further Information Contact Ms. Mara A. Affre, Director of Admissions, Southern Oregon University, 1250 Siskiyou Boulevard, Ashland, OR 97520. *Telephone:* 541-552-6411 or 800-482-7672 (toll-free in-state). *Fax:* 541-552-6614. *E-mail:* admissions@sou.edu. *Web site:* http://www.sou.edu/.

UNIVERSITY OF OREGON

Eugene, Oregon

UO is a coed, public unit of Oregon University System, founded in 1872, offering degrees at the bachelor's, master's, doctoral, and first professional levels. It has a 295-acre campus in Eugene.

Academic Information The faculty has 1,131 members (70% full-time), 94% with terminal degrees. The undergraduate student-faculty ratio is 19:1. The library holds 2 million titles, 17,840 serial subscriptions, and 1 million audiovisual materials. Special programs include academic remediation, services for learning-disabled students, an honors program, study abroad, advanced placement credit, accelerated degree programs, Freshman Honors College, ESL programs, double majors, independent study, distance learning, self-designed majors, summer session for credit, part-time degree programs, adult/continuing education programs, internships, and arrangement for off-campus study with National Student Exchange. The most frequently chosen baccalaureate fields are business/marketing, communications/communication technologies, social sciences and history.
Student Body Statistics The student body totals 19,992, of whom 15,983 are undergraduates (2,865 freshmen). 53 percent are women and 47 percent are men. Students come from 54 states and territories and 86 other countries. 76 percent are from Oregon. 4.7 percent are international students. 20 percent of the 2003 graduating class went on to graduate and professional schools.
Expenses for 2003–04 *Application fee:* $50. *State resident tuition:* $3543 full-time, $92 per credit hour part-time. *Nonresident tuition:* $14,979 full-time, $393 per credit hour part-time. *Mandatory fees:* $1371 full-time, $305. Part-time tuition and fees vary according to course load. *College room and board:* $6981. Room and board charges vary according to board plan and housing facility.
Financial Aid Forms of aid include need-based and non-need-based scholarships, athletic grants, and part-time jobs. The average aided 2003–04 undergraduate received an aid package worth an estimated $8054. The priority application deadline for financial aid is March 1.
Freshman Admission UO requires a high school transcript, a minimum 3.25 high school GPA, SAT I or ACT scores, and TOEFL scores for international students. An essay and 2 recommendations are required for some. The application deadline for regular admission is January 15.
Transfer Admission The application deadline for admission is May 15.
Entrance Difficulty UO assesses its entrance difficulty level as moderately difficult; very difficult for architecture, Honors College programs. For the fall 2003 freshman class, 84 percent of the applicants were accepted.

For Further Information Contact Ms. Martha Pitts, Assistant Vice President for Enrollment Services and Director of Admissions, University of Oregon, Eugene, OR 97403. *Telephone:* 541-346-3201 or 800-232-3825 (toll-free in-state). *Fax:* 541-346-5815. *E-mail:* uoadmit@uoregon.edu. *Web site:* http://www.uoregon.edu/.

UNIVERSITY OF PHOENIX–OREGON CAMPUS

Portland, Oregon

University of Phoenix–Oregon Campus is a coed, proprietary, comprehensive institution, founded in 1976, offering degrees at the associate, bachelor's, master's, and doctoral levels and post-master's and postbachelor's certificates (courses conducted at 121 campuses and learning centers in 25 states).

Academic Information The faculty has 355 members (1% full-time), 18% with terminal degrees. The undergraduate student-faculty ratio is 7:1. The library holds 27 million titles and 11,648 serial subscriptions. Special programs include advanced placement credit, accelerated degree programs, independent study, distance learning, external degree programs, and adult/continuing education programs. The most frequently chosen baccalaureate fields are business/marketing, computer/information sciences, protective services/public administration.
Student Body Statistics The student body totals 1,514, of whom 1,241 are undergraduates (30 freshmen). 44 percent are women and 56 percent are men. 2.5 percent are international students.
Expenses for 2003–04 *Application fee:* $85. *Tuition:* $9540 full-time, $318 per credit part-time.
Financial Aid Forms of aid include need-based and non-need-based scholarships. The average aided 2002–03 undergraduate received an aid package worth $1243. The application deadline for financial aid is continuous.
Freshman Admission University of Phoenix–Oregon Campus requires 1 recommendation, 2 years of work experience, 23 years of age, and TOEFL

University of Phoenix–Oregon Campus (continued)

scores for international students. A high school transcript is required for some. The application deadline for regular admission is rolling.
Transfer Admission The application deadline for admission is rolling.
Entrance Difficulty University of Phoenix–Oregon Campus has an open admission policy.

For Further Information Contact Ms. Beth Barilla, Director of Admissions, University of Phoenix–Oregon Campus, 4615 East Elwood Street, Mail Stop AA-K101, Phoenix, AZ 85040-1958. *Telephone:* 480-557-1712 or 800-228-7240 (toll-free). *Fax:* 480-594-1758. *E-mail:* beth.barilla@phoenix.edu. *Web site:* http://www.phoenix.edu/.

UNIVERSITY OF PORTLAND

Portland, Oregon

U of P is a coed, private, Roman Catholic, comprehensive institution, founded in 1901, offering degrees at the bachelor's and master's levels and post-master's certificates. It has a 125-acre campus in Portland.

Academic Information The faculty has 275 members (64% full-time). The undergraduate student-faculty ratio is 13:1. The library holds 350,000 titles, 1,400 serial subscriptions, and 11,044 audiovisual materials. Special programs include services for learning-disabled students, an honors program, study abroad, advanced placement credit, double majors, independent study, summer session for credit, part-time degree programs, adult/continuing education programs, internships, and arrangement for off-campus study. The most frequently chosen baccalaureate fields are business/marketing, engineering/engineering technologies, health professions and related sciences.
Student Body Statistics The student body totals 3,263, of whom 2,739 are undergraduates (674 freshmen). 60 percent are women and 40 percent are men. Students come from 42 states and territories and 19 other countries. 44 percent are from Oregon. 2.1 percent are international students.
Expenses for 2003–04 *Application fee:* $45. *Comprehensive fee:* $28,810 includes full-time tuition ($21,800), mandatory fees ($340), and college room and board ($6670). Full-time tuition and fees vary according to program. Room and board charges vary according to board plan and housing facility. *Part-time tuition:* $690 per credit hour. Part-time tuition varies according to program.
Financial Aid Forms of aid include need-based and non-need-based scholarships, athletic grants, and part-time jobs. The average aided 2003–04 undergraduate received an aid package worth an estimated $19,304. The priority application deadline for financial aid is March 1.
Freshman Admission U of P requires an essay, a high school transcript, 1 recommendation, SAT I or ACT scores, and TOEFL scores for international students. The application deadline for regular admission is June 1.
Transfer Admission The application deadline for admission is June 1.
Entrance Difficulty U of P assesses its entrance difficulty level as moderately difficult; very difficult for business, computer, engineering programs. For the fall 2003 freshman class, 72 percent of the applicants were accepted.

For Further Information Contact Mr. James C. Lyons, Dean of Admissions, University of Portland, 5000 North Willamette Boulevard, Portland, OR 97203. *Telephone:* 503-943-7147 or 888-627-5601 (toll-free out-of-state). *Fax:* 503-943-7315. *E-mail:* admissio@up.edu. *Web site:* http://www.up.edu/.

WARNER PACIFIC COLLEGE

Portland, Oregon

Warner Pacific is a coed, private, comprehensive institution, founded in 1937, affiliated with the Church of God, offering degrees at the associate, bachelor's, and master's levels and postbachelor's certificates. It has a 15-acre campus in Portland.

Academic Information The faculty has 35 members (100% full-time). The undergraduate student-faculty ratio is 14:1. The library holds 54,000 titles and 400 serial subscriptions. Special programs include academic remediation, services for learning-disabled students, an honors program, cooperative (work-study) education, study abroad, advanced placement credit, double majors, independent study, self-designed majors, summer session for credit, part-time degree programs (evenings), adult/continuing education programs, internships, and arrangement for off-campus study with Mt. Hood Community College, Concordia College (OR), Oregon Independent Colleges Association.
Student Body Statistics The student body totals 510, of whom 504 are undergraduates (68 freshmen). 61 percent are women and 39 percent are men. Students come from 20 states and territories. 75 percent are from Oregon. 0.6 percent are international students.
Expenses for 2003–04 *Application fee:* $25. *Comprehensive fee:* $21,900 includes full-time tuition ($16,510), mandatory fees ($400), and college room and board ($4990). Room and board charges vary according to board plan and housing facility. *Part-time tuition:* $365 per credit. Part-time tuition varies according to course load.
Financial Aid Forms of aid include need-based and non-need-based scholarships, athletic grants, and part-time jobs. The average aided 2002–03 undergraduate received an aid package worth $16,830. The application deadline for financial aid is continuous.
Freshman Admission Warner Pacific requires an essay, a high school transcript, a minimum 2.5 high school GPA, SAT I or ACT scores, and TOEFL scores for international students. A minimum 3.0 high school GPA, an interview, SAT II: Subject Test scores, and SAT II: Writing Test scores are recommended. 1 recommendation and an interview are required for some. The application deadline for regular admission is rolling.
Transfer Admission The application deadline for admission is rolling.
Entrance Difficulty Warner Pacific assesses its entrance difficulty level as moderately difficult. For the fall 2003 freshman class, 44 percent of the applicants were accepted.

For Further Information Contact Dr. Jack P. Powell, Dean of Enrollment Management, Warner Pacific College, 2219 Southeast 68th Avenue, Portland, OR 97215. *Telephone:* 503-517-1020, 800-582-7885 (toll-free in-state), or 800-804-1510 (toll-free out-of-state). *Fax:* 503-517-1352. *E-mail:* admiss@warnerpacific.edu. *Web site:* http://www.warnerpacific.edu/.

WESTERN BAPTIST COLLEGE

Salem, Oregon

Western is a coed, private, four-year college, founded in 1935, offering degrees at the associate and bachelor's levels. It has a 107-acre campus in Salem near Portland.

Academic Information The faculty has 66 members (52% full-time), 29% with terminal degrees. The student-faculty ratio is 15:1. The library holds 85,000 titles, 600 serial subscriptions, and 4,500 audiovisual materials. Special programs include services for learning-disabled students, an honors program, study abroad, advanced placement credit, accelerated degree programs, Freshman Honors College, double majors, independent study, distance learning, summer session for credit, adult/continuing education programs, internships, and arrangement for off-campus study with Oregon Independent Colleges Association, Council of Christian Colleges and Universities. The most frequently chosen baccalaureate fields are business/marketing, education, home economics/vocational home economics.
Student Body Statistics The student body is made up of 737 undergraduates (167 freshmen). 59 percent are women and 41 percent are men. Students come from 30 states and territories and 5 other countries. 69 percent are from Oregon. 0.7 percent are international students.
Expenses for 2004–05 *Application fee:* $35. *One-time mandatory fee:* $200. *Comprehensive fee:* $23,100 includes full-time tuition ($16,825), mandatory fees ($210), and college room and board ($6065). Room and board charges vary according to board plan. *Part-time tuition:* $700 per credit. *Part-time mandatory fees:* $30 per term. Part-time tuition and fees vary according to course load.
Financial Aid Forms of aid include need-based and non-need-based scholarships, athletic grants, and part-time jobs. The average aided

2003–04 undergraduate received an aid package worth an estimated $12,689. The priority application deadline for financial aid is February 15.
Freshman Admission Western requires an essay, a high school transcript, a minimum 2.5 high school GPA, 3 recommendations, SAT I or ACT scores, and TOEFL scores for international students. The application deadline for regular admission is August 1.
Transfer Admission The application deadline for admission is August 1.
Entrance Difficulty Western assesses its entrance difficulty level as moderately difficult. For the fall 2003 freshman class, 84 percent of the applicants were accepted.

For Further Information Contact Mr. Marty Ziesemer, Director of Admissions, Western Baptist College, 5000 Deer Park Drive, SE, Salem, OR 97301-9392. *Telephone:* 503-375-7115 or 800-845-3005 (toll-free out-of-state). *Fax:* 503-585-4316. *E-mail:* admissions@wbc.edu. *Web site:* http://www.wbc.edu/.

WESTERN OREGON UNIVERSITY

Monmouth, Oregon

Western Oregon University is a coed, public, comprehensive unit of Oregon University System, founded in 1856, offering degrees at the associate, bachelor's, and master's levels and postbachelor's certificates. It has a 157-acre campus in Monmouth near Portland.

Academic Information The faculty has 323 members (56% full-time), 60% with terminal degrees. The undergraduate student-faculty ratio is 21:1. The library holds 157,186 titles, 3,680 serial subscriptions, and 3,169 audiovisual materials. Special programs include academic remediation, services for learning-disabled students, an honors program, study abroad, advanced placement credit, Freshman Honors College, ESL programs, double majors, independent study, distance learning, self-designed majors, summer session for credit, part-time degree programs, adult/continuing education programs, internships, and arrangement for off-campus study with other members of the Oregon University System. The most frequently chosen baccalaureate fields are business/marketing, interdisciplinary studies, protective services/public administration.
Student Body Statistics The student body totals 5,032, of whom 4,470 are undergraduates (926 freshmen). 59 percent are women and 41 percent are men. Students come from 23 states and territories and 19 other countries. 91 percent are from Oregon. 1.5 percent are international students. 6 percent of the 2003 graduating class went on to graduate and professional schools.
Expenses for 2003–04 *Application fee:* $50. *State resident tuition:* $3240 full-time, $90 per credit part-time. *Nonresident tuition:* $11,505 full-time, $320 per credit part-time. *Mandatory fees:* $1065 full-time. *College room and board:* $5976. Room and board charges vary according to board plan and housing facility.
Financial Aid Forms of aid include need-based and non-need-based scholarships, athletic grants, and part-time jobs. The average aided 2003–04 undergraduate received an aid package worth an estimated $6447. The priority application deadline for financial aid is March 1.
Freshman Admission Western Oregon University requires a high school transcript, a minimum 2.75 high school GPA, SAT I or ACT scores, and TOEFL scores for international students. SAT I and SAT II or ACT scores and SAT II: Subject Test scores are recommended. The application deadline for regular admission is rolling.
Transfer Admission The application deadline for admission is rolling.
Entrance Difficulty Western Oregon University assesses its entrance difficulty level as moderately difficult. For the fall 2003 freshman class, 94 percent of the applicants were accepted.

For Further Information Contact Mr. Rob Kvidt, Director of Admissions, Western Oregon University, 345 North Monmouth Avenue, Monmouth, OR 97361. *Telephone:* 503-838-8211 or 877-877-1593 (toll-free). *Fax:* 503-838-8067. *E-mail:* wolfgram@wou.edu. *Web site:* http://www.wou.edu/.

WILLAMETTE UNIVERSITY

Salem, Oregon

Willamette is a coed, private, United Methodist, comprehensive institution, founded in 1842, offering degrees at the bachelor's, master's, and first professional levels and first professional and postbachelor's certificates. It has a 72-acre campus in Salem near Portland.

Academic Information The faculty has 269 members (69% full-time), 77% with terminal degrees. The undergraduate student-faculty ratio is 11:1. The library holds 317,000 titles, 1,400 serial subscriptions, and 8,800 audiovisual materials. Special programs include services for learning-disabled students, cooperative (work-study) education, study abroad, advanced placement credit, accelerated degree programs, double majors, independent study, self-designed majors, part-time degree programs, internships, and arrangement for off-campus study with American University, Urban Life Center (Chicago). The most frequently chosen baccalaureate fields are English, foreign language/literature, social sciences and history.
Student Body Statistics The student body totals 2,590, of whom 1,945 are undergraduates (541 freshmen). 55 percent are women and 45 percent are men. Students come from 36 states and territories and 12 other countries. 41 percent are from Oregon. 0.7 percent are international students. 25 percent of the 2003 graduating class went on to graduate and professional schools.
Expenses for 2003–04 *Application fee:* $50. *Comprehensive fee:* $32,062 includes full-time tuition ($25,300), mandatory fees ($162), and college room and board ($6600). Full-time tuition and fees vary according to course load. Room and board charges vary according to board plan and housing facility. *Part-time tuition:* $3162 per course. Part-time tuition varies according to course load.
Financial Aid Forms of aid include need-based and non-need-based scholarships and part-time jobs. The average aided 2003–04 undergraduate received an aid package worth an estimated $21,027. The priority application deadline for financial aid is February 1.
Freshman Admission Willamette requires an essay, a high school transcript, a minimum 2.0 high school GPA, 1 recommendation, SAT I or ACT scores, and TOEFL scores for international students. An interview is recommended. An interview is required for some. The application deadline for regular admission is February 1 and for early action it is December 1.
Transfer Admission The application deadline for admission is February 1.
Entrance Difficulty Willamette assesses its entrance difficulty level as very difficult. For the fall 2003 freshman class, 74 percent of the applicants were accepted.

For Further Information Contact Dr. Robin Brown, Vice President for Enrollment, Willamette University, 900 State Street, Salem, OR 97301-3931. *Telephone:* 503-370-6303 or 877-542-2787 (toll-free). *Fax:* 503-375-5363. *E-mail:* libarts@willamette.edu. *Web site:* http://www.willamette.edu/.

Utah

BRIGHAM YOUNG UNIVERSITY

Provo, Utah

BYU is a coed, private unit of Church Education System (CES) of The Church of Jesus Christ of Latter-day Saints, founded in 1875, affiliated with The Church of Jesus Christ of Latter-day Saints, offering degrees at the bachelor's, master's, doctoral, and first professional levels. It has a 557-acre campus in Provo near Salt Lake City.

Academic Information The faculty has 1,741 members (73% full-time). The undergraduate student-faculty ratio is 21:1. The library holds 3 million titles, 619,493 serial subscriptions, and 56,353 audiovisual materials. Special programs include academic remediation, services for learning-

Brigham Young University (continued)

disabled students, an honors program, cooperative (work-study) education, study abroad, advanced placement credit, accelerated degree programs, Freshman Honors College, ESL programs, double majors, independent study, distance learning, summer session for credit, part-time degree programs (daytime, evenings, summer), external degree programs, adult/continuing education programs, internships, and arrangement for off-campus study. The most frequently chosen baccalaureate fields are business/marketing, education, social sciences and history.

Student Body Statistics The student body totals 33,008, of whom 29,932 are undergraduates (5,331 freshmen). 49 percent are women and 51 percent are men. Students come from 54 states and territories and 119 other countries. 28 percent are from Utah. 3.3 percent are international students.

Expenses for 2003–04 *Application fee:* $25. *Comprehensive fee:* $8504 includes full-time tuition ($3150) and college room and board ($5354). Full-time tuition varies according to reciprocity agreements. Room and board charges vary according to board plan and housing facility. *Part-time tuition:* $161 per credit hour. Part-time tuition varies according to course load and reciprocity agreements.

Financial Aid Forms of aid include need-based and non-need-based scholarships, athletic grants, and part-time jobs. The average aided 2003–04 undergraduate received an aid package worth an estimated $4215. The application deadline for financial aid is continuous.

Freshman Admission BYU requires an essay, a high school transcript, 1 recommendation, an interview, ACT scores, and TOEFL scores for international students. The application deadline for regular admission is February 15.

Transfer Admission The application deadline for admission is March 15.

Entrance Difficulty BYU assesses its entrance difficulty level as moderately difficult. For the fall 2003 freshman class, 78 percent of the applicants were accepted.

For Further Information Contact Mr. Tom Gourley, Dean of Admissions and Records, Brigham Young University, A-153 Abraham Smoot Building, Provo, UT 84602. *Telephone:* 801-422-2507. *Fax:* 801-422-0005. *E-mail:* admissions@byu.edu. *Web site:* http://www.byu.edu/.

DIXIE STATE COLLEGE OF UTAH

St. George, Utah

Dixie State College of Utah is a coed, public, primarily two-year college of Utah System of Higher Education, founded in 1911, offering degrees at the associate and bachelor's levels. It has a 60-acre campus in St. George.

Expenses for 2004–05 *Application fee:* $25. *State resident tuition:* $1524 full-time, $64 per credit part-time. *Nonresident tuition:* $6672 full-time, $278 per credit part-time. *Mandatory fees:* $362 full-time. Full-time tuition and fees vary according to course level. Part-time tuition varies according to course level and course load. *College room and board:* $2380.

For Further Information Contact Ms. Darla Rollins, Admissions Coordinator, Dixie State College of Utah, 225 South 700 East Street, St. George, UT 84770-3876. *Telephone:* 435-652-7704 or 888-GO2DIXIE (toll-free). *Fax:* 435-656-4005. *E-mail:* admissions@dixie.edu. *Web site:* http://www.dixie.edu/.

ITT TECHNICAL INSTITUTE

Murray, Utah

ITT Tech is a coed, proprietary, primarily two-year college of ITT Educational Services, Inc., founded in 1984, offering degrees at the associate and bachelor's levels. It has a 3-acre campus in Murray near Salt Lake City.

Student Body Statistics The student body is made up of 494 undergraduates.

Expenses for 2003–04 *Application fee:* $100. Total Program Cost varies depending on course of study. Consult school catalog.

Financial Aid Forms of aid include need-based scholarships and part-time jobs. The application deadline for financial aid is continuous.

Freshman Admission ITT Tech requires a high school transcript, an interview, TOEFL scores for international students, and Wonderlic aptitude test. Recommendations are recommended. The application deadline for regular admission is rolling.

Transfer Admission The application deadline for admission is rolling.

Entrance Difficulty ITT Tech assesses its entrance difficulty level as minimally difficult.

For Further Information Contact Ms. JoAnn Meron, Director of Recruitment, ITT Technical Institute, 920 West LeVoy Drive, Murray, UT 84123. *Telephone:* 801-263-3313 or 800-365-2136 (toll-free). *Fax:* 801-263-3497. *Web site:* http://www.itt-tech.edu/.

LDS BUSINESS COLLEGE

Salt Lake City, Utah

LDS Business is a coed, private, two-year college of Latter-day Saints Church Educational System, founded in 1886, affiliated with The Church of Jesus Christ of Latter-day Saints, offering degrees at the associate level.

Academic Information The faculty has 95 members (15% full-time), 3% with terminal degrees. The student-faculty ratio is 20:1. The library holds 24,000 titles, 130 serial subscriptions, and 300 audiovisual materials. Special programs include academic remediation, cooperative (work-study) education, advanced placement credit, summer session for credit, part-time degree programs (daytime, evenings, weekends, summer), adult/continuing education programs, and internships.

Student Body Statistics The student body is made up of 1,282 undergraduates (467 freshmen). 61 percent are women and 39 percent are men. Students come from 40 states and territories and 45 other countries. 47 percent are from Utah. 22.3 percent are international students.

Expenses for 2004–05 *Application fee:* $25. *Tuition:* $2400 full-time, $100 per credit hour part-time. Full-time tuition varies according to course load. Part-time tuition varies according to course load. *College room only:* $2236.

Financial Aid Forms of aid include need-based scholarships. The application deadline for financial aid is continuous.

Freshman Admission LDS Business requires a high school transcript, an interview, and TOEFL scores for international students. ACT scores are recommended. The application deadline for regular admission is rolling.

Transfer Admission The application deadline for admission is rolling.

Entrance Difficulty LDS Business has an open admission policy.

For Further Information Contact Mr. Matt D. Tittle, Assistant Dean of Students, LDS Business College, 411 East South Temple, Salt Lake City, UT 84111-1392. *Telephone:* 801-524-8144 or 800-999-5767 (toll-free). *Fax:* 801-524-1900. *E-mail:* admissions@ldsbc.edu. *Web site:* http://www.ldsbc.edu/.

NORTHFACE UNIVERSITY

Salt Lake City, Utah

Northface University is a coed, proprietary, comprehensive institution, founded in 2002, offering degrees at the bachelor's and master's levels.

Academic Information The faculty has 17 members. The undergraduate student-faculty ratio is 11:1. The most frequently chosen baccalaureate field is computer/information sciences.

Student Body Statistics The student body is made up of 100 undergraduates. 2 percent are international students.

Expenses for 2003–04 *Application fee:* $125. *One-time mandatory fee:* $75. *Comprehensive fee:* $32,445 includes full-time tuition ($25,700), mandatory fees ($1120), and college room and board ($5625). *Tuition:* $59,500 per degree program.

Freshman Admission Northface University requires TOEFL scores for international students.

Entrance Difficulty For the fall 2003 freshman class, 25 percent of the applicants were accepted.

For Further Information Contact Mr. Jamie Wyse, Senior Vice President, Strategic Development, Northface University, 2755 East Cottonwood Parkway, Suite 600, Salt Lake City, UT 84121. *Telephone:* 801-438-1107. *Fax:* 801-438-1111. *Web site:* http://www.northface.edu/.

SOUTHERN UTAH UNIVERSITY

Cedar City, Utah

SUU is a coed, public, comprehensive unit of Utah System of Higher Education, founded in 1897, offering degrees at the associate, bachelor's, and master's levels. It has a 113-acre campus in Cedar City.

Academic Information The faculty has 252 members (83% full-time), 58% with terminal degrees. The undergraduate student-faculty ratio is 22:1. The library holds 180,424 titles, 6,165 serial subscriptions, and 13,352 audiovisual materials. Special programs include academic remediation, services for learning-disabled students, an honors program, cooperative (work-study) education, advanced placement credit, ESL programs, double majors, independent study, distance learning, summer session for credit, part-time degree programs, adult/continuing education programs, and internships. The most frequently chosen baccalaureate fields are business/marketing, communications/communication technologies, education.
Student Body Statistics The student body totals 6,048, of whom 5,840 are undergraduates (725 freshmen). 55 percent are women and 45 percent are men. Students come from 40 states and territories and 14 other countries. 85 percent are from Utah. 1 percent are international students.
Expenses for 2003–04 *Application fee:* $25. *State resident tuition:* $2332 full-time, $117 per credit hour part-time. *Nonresident tuition:* $7696 full-time, $385 per credit hour part-time. *Mandatory fees:* $462 full-time. Part-time tuition varies according to course load. *College room and board:* $5400. *College room only:* $2400. Room and board charges vary according to board plan and housing facility.
Financial Aid Forms of aid include need-based and non-need-based scholarships, athletic grants, and part-time jobs. The average aided 2002–03 undergraduate received an aid package worth $3418. The application deadline for financial aid is continuous.
Freshman Admission SUU requires a high school transcript, a minimum 2.0 high school GPA, SAT I or ACT scores, and TOEFL scores for international students. ACT scores are recommended.
Transfer Admission The application deadline for admission is rolling.
Entrance Difficulty SUU assesses its entrance difficulty level as moderately difficult. For the fall 2003 freshman class, 78 percent of the applicants were accepted.

For Further Information Contact Mr. Dale S. Orton, Director of Admissions, Southern Utah University, 351 West Center Street, Cedar City, UT 84720. *Telephone:* 801-586-7740. *Fax:* 435-865-8223. *E-mail:* adminfo@suu.edu. *Web site:* http://www.suu.edu/.

STEVENS-HENAGER COLLEGE

Ogden, Utah

Stevens-Henager College is a coed, proprietary, primarily two-year college of CollegeAmerica, Inc., founded in 1891, offering degrees at the associate and bachelor's levels. It has a 1-acre campus in Ogden near Salt Lake City.

For Further Information Contact Ms. Wynn Hurtado, Director of Admissions, Stevens-Henager College, PO Box 9428, Ogden, UT 84409. *Telephone:* 801-394-7791 or 800-371-7791 (toll-free). *Fax:* 801-393-1745. *Web site:* http://www.stevenshenager.edu/.

UNIVERSITY OF PHOENIX–UTAH CAMPUS

Salt Lake City, Utah

University of Phoenix–Utah Campus is a coed, proprietary, comprehensive institution, founded in 1984, offering degrees at the associate, bachelor's, master's, and doctoral levels and post-master's and postbachelor's certificates (courses conducted at 121 campuses and learning centers in 25 states).

Academic Information The faculty has 629 members (1% full-time), 26% with terminal degrees. The undergraduate student-faculty ratio is 8:1. The library holds 27 million titles and 11,648 serial subscriptions. Special programs include advanced placement credit, accelerated degree programs, independent study, distance learning, external degree programs, and adult/continuing education programs. The most frequently chosen baccalaureate fields are business/marketing, computer/information sciences, health professions and related sciences.
Student Body Statistics The student body totals 2,001, of whom 1,432 are undergraduates (45 freshmen). 41 percent are women and 59 percent are men. 2.4 percent are international students.
Expenses for 2003–04 *Application fee:* $85. *Tuition:* $9120 full-time, $304 per credit part-time.
Financial Aid Forms of aid include need-based and non-need-based scholarships. The average aided 2002–03 undergraduate received an aid package worth $1492. The application deadline for financial aid is continuous.
Freshman Admission University of Phoenix–Utah Campus requires 1 recommendation, 2 years of work experience, 23 years of age, and TOEFL scores for international students. A high school transcript is required for some. The application deadline for regular admission is rolling.
Transfer Admission The application deadline for admission is rolling.
Entrance Difficulty University of Phoenix–Utah Campus has an open admission policy.

For Further Information Contact Ms. Beth Barilla, Director of Admissions, University of Phoenix–Utah Campus, 4615 East Elwood Street, Mail Stop AA-K101, Phoenix, AZ 85040-1958. *Telephone:* 480-557-1712 or 800-224-2844 (toll-free). *Fax:* 480-594-1758. *E-mail:* beth.barilla@phoenix.edu. *Web site:* http://www.phoenix.edu/.

UNIVERSITY OF UTAH

Salt Lake City, Utah

U of U is a coed, public unit of Utah System of Higher Education, founded in 1850, offering degrees at the bachelor's, master's, doctoral, and first professional levels and post-master's and postbachelor's certificates. It has a 1,500-acre campus in Salt Lake City.

Academic Information The faculty has 1,246 members (89% full-time), 85% with terminal degrees. The undergraduate student-faculty ratio is 16:1. The library holds 3 million titles, 33,517 serial subscriptions, and 62,356 audiovisual materials. Special programs include academic remediation, services for learning-disabled students, an honors program, cooperative (work-study) education, study abroad, advanced placement credit, accelerated degree programs, ESL programs, double majors, independent study, distance learning, self-designed majors, summer session for credit, part-time degree programs (daytime, evenings, weekends, summer), adult/continuing education programs, internships, and arrangement for off-campus study with members of the National Student Exchange. The most frequently chosen baccalaureate fields are business/marketing, communications/communication technologies, social sciences and history.
Student Body Statistics The student body totals 28,437, of whom 22,421 are undergraduates (2,653 freshmen). 45 percent are women and 55 percent are men. Students come from 55 states and territories and 106 other countries. 93 percent are from Utah. 2.6 percent are international students.
Expenses for 2003–04 *Application fee:* $35. *State resident tuition:* $3058 full-time, $85.90 per credit part-time. *Nonresident tuition:* $10,704 full-time, $295.36 per credit part-time. *Mandatory fees:* $589 full-time, $294.50 per term part-time. Full-time tuition and fees vary according to course level, course load, degree level, and program. Part-time tuition and fees vary

University of Utah (continued)

according to course level, course load, degree level, and program. *College room and board:* $5036. *College room only:* $2472. Room and board charges vary according to board plan and housing facility.

Financial Aid Forms of aid include need-based and non-need-based scholarships, athletic grants, and part-time jobs. The average aided 2003–04 undergraduate received an aid package worth an estimated $7286. The priority application deadline for financial aid is March 15.

Freshman Admission U of U requires a high school transcript, a minimum 2.0 high school GPA, SAT I or ACT scores, and TOEFL scores for international students. A minimum 3.0 high school GPA and ACT scores are recommended. The application deadline for regular admission is April 1.

Transfer Admission The application deadline for admission is April 1.

Entrance Difficulty U of U assesses its entrance difficulty level as moderately difficult. For the fall 2003 freshman class, 86 percent of the applicants were accepted.

For Further Information Contact Ms. Suzanne Espinoza, Director of High School Services, University of Utah, 250 South Student Services Building, 201 South, 460 E Room 205, Salt Lake City, UT 84112. *Telephone:* 801-581-7281 or 800-444-8638 (toll-free). *Fax:* 801-585-7864. *E-mail:* admissions@sa.utah.edu. *Web site:* http://www.utah.edu/.

UTAH COLLEGE OF MIDWIFERY

Orem, Utah

Utah College of Midwifery is a women's, private, comprehensive institution, founded in 1980, offering degrees at the bachelor's and master's levels.

Academic Information The faculty has 8 members, 88% with terminal degrees. The undergraduate student-faculty ratio is 1:1.

Student Body Statistics The student body totals 73, of whom 66 are undergraduates.

Expenses for 2004–05 *Tuition:* $115 per credit part-time. *Mandatory fees:* $100 per year part-time.

Entrance Difficulty For the fall 2003 freshman class, 100 percent of the applicants were accepted.

For Further Information Contact Ms. Jodie Fisher, President, Utah College of Midwifery, 282 North State Street, Orem, UT 84057. *Telephone:* 801-764-9068 or 888-489-1238 (toll-free). *Fax:* 801-434-8704. *Web site:* http://www.midwifery.edu/.

UTAH STATE UNIVERSITY

Logan, Utah

USU is a coed, public unit of Utah System of Higher Education, founded in 1888, offering degrees at the associate, bachelor's, master's, and doctoral levels. It has a 456-acre campus in Logan.

Academic Information The faculty has 737 members (96% full-time), 82% with terminal degrees. The undergraduate student-faculty ratio is 19:1. The library holds 1 million titles, 13,971 serial subscriptions, and 17,008 audiovisual materials. Special programs include academic remediation, services for learning-disabled students, an honors program, cooperative (work-study) education, study abroad, advanced placement credit, accelerated degree programs, Freshman Honors College, ESL programs, double majors, independent study, distance learning, self-designed majors, summer session for credit, part-time degree programs (daytime, evenings, summer), adult/continuing education programs, internships, and arrangement for off-campus study with Weber State University. The most frequently chosen baccalaureate fields are business/marketing, education, home economics/vocational home economics.

Student Body Statistics The student body totals 16,460, of whom 13,958 are undergraduates (2,548 freshmen). 49 percent are women and 51 percent are men. Students come from 52 states and territories and 49 other countries. 71 percent are from Utah. 2.6 percent are international students. 23 percent of the 2003 graduating class went on to graduate and professional schools.

Expenses for 2003–04 *Application fee:* $35. *State resident tuition:* $2615 full-time. *Nonresident tuition:* $8420 full-time. *Mandatory fees:* $526 full-time. Full-time tuition and fees vary according to course load and student level. *College room and board:* $3930. *College room only:* $1550. Room and board charges vary according to board plan and housing facility.

Financial Aid Forms of aid include need-based and non-need-based scholarships, athletic grants, and part-time jobs. The average aided 2002–03 undergraduate received an aid package worth $5000. The application deadline for financial aid is continuous.

Freshman Admission USU requires a high school transcript, SAT I or ACT scores, and TOEFL scores for international students. A minimum 2.75 high school GPA and ACT scores are recommended. The application deadline for regular admission is rolling.

Transfer Admission The application deadline for admission is rolling.

Entrance Difficulty USU assesses its entrance difficulty level as moderately difficult. For the fall 2003 freshman class, 94 percent of the applicants were accepted.

For Further Information Contact Dr. Eric Olsen, Director, Recruitment and Enrollment Services, Utah State University, 0160 Old Main Hill, Logan, UT 84322-0160. *Telephone:* 435-797-1129 or 800-488-8108 (toll-free). *Fax:* 435-797-3708. *E-mail:* admit@cc.usu.edu. *Web site:* http://www.usu.edu/.

UTAH VALLEY STATE COLLEGE

Orem, Utah

UVSC is a coed, public, primarily two-year college of Utah System of Higher Education, founded in 1941, offering degrees at the associate and bachelor's levels. It has a 200-acre campus in Orem near Salt Lake City.

Academic Information The faculty has 972 members (38% full-time), 17% with terminal degrees. The student-faculty ratio is 19:1. The library holds 173,000 titles, 6,000 serial subscriptions, and 9,000 audiovisual materials. Special programs include academic remediation, services for learning-disabled students, an honors program, cooperative (work-study) education, study abroad, advanced placement credit, accelerated degree programs, ESL programs, independent study, distance learning, self-designed majors, summer session for credit, part-time degree programs (daytime, evenings, weekends, summer), internships, and arrangement for off-campus study. The most frequently chosen baccalaureate fields are business/marketing, education, psychology.

Student Body Statistics The student body is made up of 23,803 undergraduates (2,629 freshmen). 42 percent are women and 58 percent are men. Students come from 50 states and territories and 99 other countries. 89 percent are from Utah. 2.3 percent are international students.

Expenses for 2004–05 *Application fee:* $30. *State resident tuition:* $2788 full-time. *Nonresident tuition:* $8718 full-time. Full-time tuition varies according to course level.

Financial Aid Forms of aid include need-based scholarships and part-time jobs. The priority application deadline for financial aid is June 1.

Freshman Admission UVSC requires TOEFL scores for international students and SAT I, ACT, or in-house tests. A high school transcript is recommended. The application deadline for regular admission is rolling.

Transfer Admission The application deadline for admission is rolling.

Entrance Difficulty UVSC has an open admission policy.

For Further Information Contact Mrs. Liz Childs, Director of Admissions, Utah Valley State College, 800 West University Parkway, Orem, UT 84058-5999. *Telephone:* 801-863-8460. *Fax:* 801-225-4677. *E-mail:* info@uvsc.edu. *Web site:* http://www.uvsc.edu/.

WEBER STATE UNIVERSITY

Ogden, Utah

Weber State is a coed, public, comprehensive unit of Utah System of Higher Education, founded in 1889, offering degrees at the associate, bachelor's, and master's levels and postbachelor's certificates. It has a 526-acre campus in Ogden near Salt Lake City.

Academic Information The faculty has 802 members (57% full-time), 53% with terminal degrees. The undergraduate student-faculty ratio is 22:1. The library holds 686,681 titles, 2,331 serial subscriptions, and 17,499 audiovisual materials. Special programs include academic remediation, services for learning-disabled students, an honors program, cooperative (work-study) education, study abroad, advanced placement credit, accelerated degree programs, Freshman Honors College, ESL programs, double majors, independent study, distance learning, self-designed majors, summer session for credit, part-time degree programs (daytime, evenings, summer), external degree programs, adult/continuing education programs, internships, and arrangement for off-campus study with Utah State University, Southern Utah University, Dixie College, Utah Valley State College, Salt Lake Community College. The most frequently chosen baccalaureate fields are business/marketing, education, health professions and related sciences.
Student Body Statistics The student body totals 18,821, of whom 18,452 are undergraduates (2,878 freshmen). 51 percent are women and 49 percent are men. Students come from 50 states and territories and 39 other countries. 93 percent are from Utah. 0.9 percent are international students. 46 percent of the 2003 graduating class went on to graduate and professional schools.
Expenses for 2003–04 *Application fee:* $30. *State resident tuition:* $2632 full-time. *Nonresident tuition:* $7958 full-time. *Mandatory fees:* $502 full-time. *College room and board:* $5313. *College room only:* $2223. Room and board charges vary according to board plan and housing facility.
Financial Aid Forms of aid include need-based scholarships, athletic grants, and part-time jobs. The priority application deadline for financial aid is March 1.
Freshman Admission Weber State requires a high school transcript and SAT I or ACT scores. TOEFL scores for international students are recommended. The application deadline for regular admission is August 22.
Transfer Admission The application deadline for admission is rolling.
Entrance Difficulty Weber State has an open admission policy.

For Further Information Contact John Allred, Admissions Advisor, Weber State University, 1137 University Circle, 3750 Harrison Boulevard, Ogden, UT 84408-1137. *Telephone:* 801-626-6046, 800-634-6568 (toll-free in-state), or 800-848-7770 (toll-free out-of-state). *Fax:* 801-626-6744. *E-mail:* admissions@weber.edu. *Web site:* http://weber.edu/.

WESTERN GOVERNORS UNIVERSITY

Salt Lake City, Utah

Western Governors University is a coed, private, comprehensive institution, founded in 1998, offering degrees at the associate, bachelor's, and master's levels and post-master's and postbachelor's certificates.

Expenses for 2003–04 *Application fee:* $100. *Tuition:* $4780 full-time. *Mandatory fees:* $50 full-time.

For Further Information Contact Ms. Wendy Gregory, Admissions Manager, Western Governors University, 2040 East Murray Holladay Road, Suite 106, Salt Lake City, UT 84117. *Telephone:* 801-274-3280 Ext. 315 or 877-435-7948 (toll-free). *Fax:* 801-274-3305. *E-mail:* info@wgu.edu. *Web site:* http://www.wgu.edu/.

WESTMINSTER COLLEGE

Salt Lake City, Utah

Westminster College is a coed, private, comprehensive institution, founded in 1875, offering degrees at the bachelor's and master's levels and postbachelor's certificates. It has a 27-acre campus in Salt Lake City.

Academic Information The faculty has 253 members (47% full-time), 52% with terminal degrees. The undergraduate student-faculty ratio is 11:1. The library holds 119,212 titles, 437 serial subscriptions, and 6,165 audiovisual materials. Special programs include academic remediation, services for learning-disabled students, an honors program, cooperative (work-study) education, advanced placement credit, accelerated degree programs, ESL programs, independent study, self-designed majors, summer session for credit, part-time degree programs (daytime, evenings, weekends, summer), and internships. The most frequently chosen baccalaureate fields are business/marketing, education, health professions and related sciences.
Student Body Statistics The student body totals 2,498, of whom 2,017 are undergraduates (374 freshmen). 58 percent are women and 42 percent are men. Students come from 34 states and territories and 28 other countries. 92 percent are from Utah. 1.9 percent are international students. 38 percent of the 2003 graduating class went on to graduate and professional schools.
Expenses for 2003–04 *Application fee:* $30. *Comprehensive fee:* $22,294 includes full-time tuition ($16,704), mandatory fees ($290), and college room and board ($5300). Full-time tuition and fees vary according to course load. Room and board charges vary according to board plan. *Part-time tuition:* $696. *Part-time mandatory fees:* $50 per term.
Financial Aid Forms of aid include need-based and non-need-based scholarships and part-time jobs. The average aided 2003–04 undergraduate received an aid package worth an estimated $14,130. The priority application deadline for financial aid is April 15.
Freshman Admission Westminster College requires a high school transcript, a minimum 2.5 high school GPA, SAT I or ACT scores, and TOEFL scores for international students. An essay, a minimum 3.0 high school GPA, 1 recommendation, and an interview are recommended. The application deadline for regular admission is rolling.
Transfer Admission The application deadline for admission is rolling.
Entrance Difficulty Westminster College assesses its entrance difficulty level as moderately difficult. For the fall 2003 freshman class, 82 percent of the applicants were accepted.

For Further Information Contact Ms. Mary Hyland, Director of Admissions, Westminster College, 1840 South 1300 East, Salt Lake City, UT 84105-3697. *Telephone:* 801-832-2200 or 800-748-4753 (toll-free). *Fax:* 801-832-3101. *E-mail:* admispub@westminstercollege.edu. *Web site:* http://www.westminstercollege.edu/.

Washington

ANTIOCH UNIVERSITY SEATTLE

Seattle, Washington

Antioch University Seattle is a coed, private, upper-level unit of Antioch University, founded in 1975, offering degrees at the bachelor's, master's, and doctoral levels. It is located in Seattle near Seattle.

Academic Information The faculty has 19 members (42% full-time), 58% with terminal degrees. The undergraduate student-faculty ratio is 10:1. The library holds 4,750 titles and 85 serial subscriptions. Special programs include academic remediation, study abroad, advanced placement credit, accelerated degree programs, self-designed majors, summer session for credit, part-time degree programs (daytime, evenings, weekends, summer), external degree programs, and adult/continuing education programs. The most frequently chosen baccalaureate field is liberal arts/general studies.

Antioch University Seattle (continued)

Student Body Statistics The student body totals 950, of whom 209 are undergraduates. Students come from 3 states and territories and 2 other countries. 99 percent are from Washington. 1 percent are international students.

Expenses for 2004–05 *Application fee:* $50. *Tuition:* $18,480 full-time, $385 per credit part-time. *Mandatory fees:* $180 full-time, $25 per term part-time. Full-time tuition and fees vary according to course load. Part-time tuition and fees vary according to course load and program.

Financial Aid Forms of aid include need-based scholarships and part-time jobs. The average aided 2002–03 undergraduate received an aid package worth $6681. The priority application deadline for financial aid is April 15.

Transfer Admission Antioch University Seattle requires a minimum 2.0 college GPA and a college transcript. The application deadline for admission is September 15.

Entrance Difficulty Antioch University Seattle assesses its entrance difficulty level as noncompetitive.

For Further Information Contact Ms. Vickie Lopez, Admissions Associate, Antioch University Seattle, 2326 Sixth Avenue, Seattle, WA 98121-1814. *Telephone:* 206-441-5352 Ext. 5200. *E-mail:* admissions@antiochsea.edu. *Web site:* http://www.antiochsea.edu/.

ARGOSY UNIVERSITY/SEATTLE

Seattle, Washington

Argosy University/Seattle is a coed, proprietary, upper-level institution, founded in 1995, offering degrees at the bachelor's, master's, and doctoral levels. It is located in Seattle near Seattle.

Academic Information The faculty has 5 members (20% full-time), 100% with terminal degrees. The most frequently chosen baccalaureate field is psychology.

Student Body Statistics The student body totals 168, of whom 23 are undergraduates. 87 percent are women and 13 percent are men. Students come from 23 states and territories. 96 percent are from Washington. 83 percent of the 2003 graduating class went on to graduate and professional schools.

Expenses for 2003–04 *Tuition:* $360 per credit hour part-time. *Mandatory fees:* $30 per term part-time. Part-time tuition and fees vary according to course load.

Financial Aid Forms of aid include need-based and non-need-based scholarships and part-time jobs. The average aided 2003–04 undergraduate received an aid package worth an estimated $4734. The application deadline for financial aid is continuous.

Transfer Admission Argosy University/Seattle requires a college transcript and a minimum 2.0 college GPA. Standardized test scores are required for some.

Entrance Difficulty For the fall 2003 entering class, 100 percent of the applicants were accepted.

For Further Information Contact Ms. Heather Simpson, Director of Admissions, Argosy University/Seattle, 1019 Eighth Avenue North, Seattle, WA 98109. *Telephone:* 206-283-4500 Ext. 206 or 866-283-2777 (toll-free out-of-state). *Fax:* 206-283-5777. *E-mail:* seattleadmissions@argosyu.edu. *Web site:* http://www.argosyu.edu/.

THE ART INSTITUTE OF SEATTLE

Seattle, Washington

AIS is a coed, proprietary, primarily two-year college of Art Institutes International, founded in 1982, offering degrees at the associate and bachelor's levels.

Academic Information The faculty has 172 members (48% full-time), 12% with terminal degrees. The student-faculty ratio is 19:1. The library holds 17,164 titles, 303 serial subscriptions, and 5,416 audiovisual materials. Special programs include academic remediation, services for learning-disabled students, an honors program, summer session for credit, part-time degree programs (daytime, evenings, weekends, summer), adult/continuing education programs, internships, and arrangement for off-campus study with other members of The Art Institutes International, City University.

Student Body Statistics The student body is made up of 2,520 undergraduates (446 freshmen). 48 percent are women and 52 percent are men. Students come from 49 states and territories and 21 other countries. 81 percent are from Washington. 6.4 percent are international students.

Expenses for 2004–05 *Application fee:* $50. *Tuition:* $15,750 full-time, $350 per credit part-time. *College room only:* $8355.

Financial Aid Forms of aid include need-based scholarships and part-time jobs. The application deadline for financial aid is continuous.

Freshman Admission AIS requires an essay, a high school transcript, an interview, and TOEFL scores for international students. 3 recommendations and SAT I or ACT scores are recommended. The application deadline for regular admission is rolling.

Entrance Difficulty AIS assesses its entrance difficulty level as moderately difficult. For the fall 2003 freshman class, 77 percent of the applicants were accepted.

For Further Information Contact Ms. Laine Morgan, Director of Admissions, The Art Institute of Seattle, 2323 Elliott Avenue, Seattle, WA 98121-1622. *Telephone:* 800-275-2471 or 800-275-2471 (toll-free). *Fax:* 206-269-0275. *E-mail:* adm@ais.edu. *Web site:* http://www.ais.artinstitutes.edu/.

BASTYR UNIVERSITY

Kenmore, Washington

Bastyr is a coed, private, upper-level institution, founded in 1978, offering degrees at the bachelor's, master's, and first professional levels and post-master's, first professional, and postbachelor's certificates in health sciences. It has a 50-acre campus in Kenmore near Seattle.

Academic Information The faculty has 130 members (38% full-time), 100% with terminal degrees. The undergraduate student-faculty ratio is 15:1. The library holds 12,000 titles, 250 serial subscriptions, and 4,800 audiovisual materials. Special programs include cooperative (work-study) education, double majors, independent study, summer session for credit, part-time degree programs (daytime, summer), and internships.

Student Body Statistics The student body totals 1,005, of whom 224 are undergraduates (124 in entering class). 81 percent are women and 19 percent are men. Students come from 20 states and territories and 5 other countries. 5.6 percent are international students.

Expenses for 2003–04 *Application fee:* $60. *Tuition:* $11,600 full-time, $252 per credit part-time. *Mandatory fees:* $918 full-time. Full-time tuition and fees vary according to course load and program. Part-time tuition varies according to course load and program. *College room only:* $4420. Room charges vary according to housing facility.

Financial Aid Forms of aid include need-based and non-need-based scholarships and part-time jobs. The average aided 2003–04 undergraduate received an aid package worth an estimated $15,650. The priority application deadline for financial aid is May 1.

Transfer Admission Bastyr requires a college transcript and a minimum 2.25 college GPA. Standardized test scores are required for some. The application deadline for admission is March 15.

Entrance Difficulty For the fall 2003 entering class, 82 percent of the applicants were accepted.

For Further Information Contact Mr. Richard Dent, Director of Student Enrollment, Bastyr University, 14500 Juanita Drive NE, Kenmore, WA 98028-4966. *Telephone:* 425-602-3080. *Fax:* 425-602-3090. *E-mail:* admiss@bastyr.edu. *Web site:* http://www.bastyr.edu/.

CENTRAL WASHINGTON UNIVERSITY

Ellensburg, Washington

CWU is a coed, public, comprehensive institution, founded in 1891, offering degrees at the bachelor's and master's levels and postbachelor's certificates. It has a 380-acre campus in Ellensburg.

Academic Information The faculty has 494 members (68% full-time), 71% with terminal degrees. The undergraduate student-faculty ratio is 23:1. The library holds 434,424 titles, 1,469 serial subscriptions, and 9,230 audiovisual materials. Special programs include academic remediation, services for learning-disabled students, an honors program, cooperative (work-study) education, study abroad, advanced placement credit, ESL programs, double majors, independent study, distance learning, self-designed majors, summer session for credit, part-time degree programs (daytime, evenings, summer), adult/continuing education programs, internships, and arrangement for off-campus study with National Student Exchange. The most frequently chosen baccalaureate fields are business/marketing, education, social sciences and history.
Student Body Statistics The student body totals 9,903, of whom 9,296 are undergraduates (1,336 freshmen). 52 percent are women and 48 percent are men. Students come from 29 states and territories and 40 other countries. 98 percent are from Washington. 1 percent are international students.
Expenses for 2003–04 *Application fee:* $35. *State resident tuition:* $3654 full-time, $121.80 per credit part-time. *Nonresident tuition:* $11,430 full-time, $381 per credit part-time. *Mandatory fees:* $369 full-time. Full-time tuition and fees vary according to location. Part-time tuition varies according to course load and location. *College room and board:* $5745. *College room only:* $3000. Room and board charges vary according to board plan and housing facility.
Financial Aid Forms of aid include need-based and non-need-based scholarships, athletic grants, and part-time jobs. The average aided 2002–03 undergraduate received an aid package worth $4567. The priority application deadline for financial aid is March 1.
Freshman Admission CWU requires a high school transcript, a minimum 2.0 high school GPA, SAT I or ACT scores, and TOEFL scores for international students. An essay, recommendations, and an interview are required for some. The application deadline for regular admission is May 1.
Transfer Admission The application deadline for admission is rolling.
Entrance Difficulty CWU assesses its entrance difficulty level as moderately difficult; very difficult for Douglas Honors College. For the fall 2003 freshman class, 84 percent of the applicants were accepted.

For Further Information Contact Mr. Mike Reilly, Director of Admissions, Central Washington University, 400 East University Way, Ellensburg, WA 98926-7463. *Telephone:* 509-963-1211 or 866-298-4968 (toll-free). *Fax:* 509-963-3022. *E-mail:* cwuadmis@cwu.edu. *Web site:* http://www.cwu.edu/.

CITY UNIVERSITY

Bellevue, Washington

City U is a coed, private, comprehensive institution, founded in 1973, offering degrees at the associate, bachelor's, and master's levels and postbachelor's certificates. It is located in Bellevue near Seattle.

Academic Information The faculty has 1,095 members (5% full-time), 98% with terminal degrees. The undergraduate student-faculty ratio is 18:1. The library holds 32,329 titles, 1,518 serial subscriptions, and 5,184 audiovisual materials. Special programs include services for learning-disabled students, an honors program, advanced placement credit, accelerated degree programs, ESL programs, double majors, independent study, distance learning, summer session for credit, part-time degree programs (daytime, evenings, weekends, summer), external degree programs, adult/continuing education programs, and internships. The most frequently chosen baccalaureate fields are business/marketing, computer/information sciences, liberal arts/general studies.
Student Body Statistics The student body totals 7,124, of whom 2,877 are undergraduates. 45 percent are women and 55 percent are men. Students come from 47 states and territories and 33 other countries. 65 percent are from Washington. 4.7 percent are international students.
Expenses for 2003–04 *Application fee:* $80. *Tuition:* $7960 full-time, $199 per credit hour part-time. *Mandatory fees:* $100 full-time.
Financial Aid Forms of aid include need-based and non-need-based scholarships. The average aided 2002–03 undergraduate received an aid package worth $4690. The application deadline for financial aid is continuous.
Freshman Admission City U requires TOEFL scores for international students. A high school transcript is recommended. The application deadline for regular admission is rolling.
Transfer Admission The application deadline for admission is rolling.
Entrance Difficulty City U has an open admission policy.

For Further Information Contact Mr. Kent Gibson, Executive Vice President, Admissions and Administration, City University, 11900 NE First Street, Bellevue, WA 98005. *Telephone:* 800-426-5596 Ext. 4661 or 888-42-CITYU (toll-free). *Fax:* 425-709-7699. *E-mail:* info@cityu.edu. *Web site:* http://www.cityu.edu/.

CORNISH COLLEGE OF THE ARTS

Seattle, Washington

Cornish is a coed, private, four-year college, founded in 1914, offering degrees at the bachelor's level. It has a 4-acre campus in Seattle.

Academic Information The faculty has 135 members (39% full-time), 35% with terminal degrees. The student-faculty ratio is 12:1. The library holds 12,000 titles and 3,000 serial subscriptions. Special programs include academic remediation, services for learning-disabled students, study abroad, advanced placement credit, independent study, summer session for credit, and internships. The most frequently chosen baccalaureate field is visual/performing arts.
Student Body Statistics The student body is made up of 696 undergraduates (128 freshmen). 64 percent are women and 36 percent are men. Students come from 27 states and territories and 14 other countries. 60 percent are from Washington. 3.4 percent are international students. 5 percent of the 2003 graduating class went on to graduate and professional schools.
Expenses for 2003–04 *Application fee:* $35. *Tuition:* $18,300 full-time, $775 per credit part-time. *Mandatory fees:* $300 full-time. Part-time tuition varies according to program.
Financial Aid Forms of aid include need-based and non-need-based scholarships and part-time jobs. The priority application deadline for financial aid is February 15.
Freshman Admission Cornish requires an essay, a high school transcript, a minimum 2.0 high school GPA, portfolio or audition, and TOEFL scores for international students. 2 recommendations, an interview, and SAT I or ACT scores are recommended. 2 recommendations are required for some. The application deadline for regular admission is August 15.
Transfer Admission The application deadline for admission is August 15.
Entrance Difficulty Cornish assesses its entrance difficulty level as moderately difficult. For the fall 2003 freshman class, 81 percent of the applicants were accepted.

For Further Information Contact Ms. Sharron Starling, Associate Director of Admissions, Cornish College of the Arts, 1000 Lenora Street, Seattle, WA 98121. *Telephone:* 206-726-5018 or 800-726-ARTS (toll-free). *Fax:* 206-720-1011. *E-mail:* admissions@cornish.edu. *Web site:* http://www.cornish.edu/.

CROWN COLLEGE

Tacoma, Washington

Crown College is a coed, proprietary, primarily two-year college, founded in 1969, offering degrees at the associate and bachelor's levels (bachelor's degree in public administration only). It is located in Tacoma near Seattle.

Academic Information The faculty has 23 members (30% full-time). The student-faculty ratio is 20:1. The library holds 9,500 titles, 37 serial subscriptions, and 70 audiovisual materials. Special programs include academic remediation, an honors program, cooperative (work-study) education, study abroad, double majors, distance learning, internships, and arrangement for off-campus study. The most frequently chosen baccalaureate field is protective services/public administration.

Crown College (continued)

Student Body Statistics The student body is made up of 316 undergraduates. Students come from 39 states and territories and 1 other country.

Financial Aid Forms of aid include need-based scholarships and part-time jobs.

Freshman Admission Crown College requires a high school transcript and an interview. An essay is required for some.

Entrance Difficulty For the fall 2003 freshman class, 95 percent of the applicants were accepted.

For Further Information Contact Ms. Sheila Millineaux, Admissions Director, Crown College, 8739 South Hosmer, Tacoma, WA 98444. *Telephone:* 253-531-3123, 800-755-9525 (toll-free in-state), or 888-689-3688 (toll-free out-of-state). *Fax:* 253-531-3521. *E-mail:* admissions@crowncollege.edu. *Web site:* http://www.crowncollege.edu/.

DEVRY UNIVERSITY

Bellevue, Washington

For Information Write to DeVry University, Bellevue, WA 98004-5519.

DEVRY UNIVERSITY

Federal Way, Washington

DeVry is a coed, proprietary, comprehensive unit of DeVry University, founded in 2001, offering degrees at the associate and bachelor's levels and postbachelor's certificates. It has a 12-acre campus in Federal Way.

Academic Information The library holds 6,021 titles, 6,807 serial subscriptions, and 61 audiovisual materials. Special programs include academic remediation, services for learning-disabled students, cooperative (work-study) education, advanced placement credit, accelerated degree programs, distance learning, summer session for credit, part-time degree programs (daytime, evenings, weekends, summer), and adult/continuing education programs.

Student Body Statistics The student body totals 1,124, of whom 1,076 are undergraduates (351 freshmen). 25 percent are women and 75 percent are men. 0.5 percent are international students.

Expenses for 2003–04 *Application fee:* $50. *Tuition:* $11,100 full-time, $395 per credit hour part-time. *Mandatory fees:* $165 full-time. Full-time tuition and fees vary according to course load. Part-time tuition varies according to course load.

Financial Aid Forms of aid include need-based and non-need-based scholarships and part-time jobs. The average aided 2002–03 undergraduate received an aid package worth $7190. The application deadline for financial aid is continuous.

Freshman Admission DeVry requires a high school transcript, an interview, and TOEFL scores for international students. SAT I, ACT or CPT is recommended. The application deadline for regular admission is rolling.

Entrance Difficulty DeVry assesses its entrance difficulty level as minimally difficult; moderately difficult for electronics engineering technology.

For Further Information Contact Ms. Latanya Kibby, Assistant New Student Coordinator, DeVry University, 3600 South 344th Way, Federal Way, WA 98001-9558. *Telephone:* 253-943-2800 or 877-923-3879 (toll-free). *Fax:* 253-943-3291. *E-mail:* admissions@sea.devry.edu. *Web site:* http://www.devry.edu/.

EASTERN WASHINGTON UNIVERSITY

Cheney, Washington

Eastern is a coed, public, comprehensive institution, founded in 1882, offering degrees at the bachelor's, master's, and doctoral levels. It has a 335-acre campus in Cheney.

Academic Information The faculty has 505 members (73% full-time), 72% with terminal degrees. The undergraduate student-faculty ratio is 23:1. The library holds 852,186 titles, 6,429 serial subscriptions, and 31,832 audiovisual materials. Special programs include services for learning-disabled students, an honors program, cooperative (work-study) education, study abroad, advanced placement credit, ESL programs, double majors, independent study, distance learning, self-designed majors, summer session for credit, part-time degree programs (daytime, evenings, weekends, summer), internships, and arrangement for off-campus study with Intercollegiate Center for Nursing.

Student Body Statistics The student body totals 10,337, of whom 9,067 are undergraduates (1,393 freshmen). 58 percent are women and 42 percent are men. 91 percent are from Washington. 1.4 percent are international students.

Expenses for 2003–04 *Application fee:* $35. *State resident tuition:* $3582 full-time, $119 per credit part-time. *Nonresident tuition:* $12,438 full-time, $415 per credit part-time. *Mandatory fees:* $230 full-time. Part-time tuition varies according to course load. *College room and board:* $5200. Room and board charges vary according to board plan and housing facility.

Financial Aid Forms of aid include need-based and non-need-based scholarships, athletic grants, and part-time jobs. The average aided 2002–03 undergraduate received an aid package worth $15,444. The priority application deadline for financial aid is February 15.

Freshman Admission Eastern requires a high school transcript, a minimum 2.0 high school GPA, SAT I or ACT scores, and TOEFL scores for international students. A minimum 3.0 high school GPA is recommended. An essay, recommendations, and an interview are required for some. The application deadline for regular admission is rolling.

Transfer Admission The application deadline for admission is rolling.

Entrance Difficulty Eastern assesses its entrance difficulty level as moderately difficult. For the fall 2003 freshman class, 81 percent of the applicants were accepted.

SPECIAL MESSAGE TO STUDENTS

Social Life Four seasons of world-class outdoor recreational activities at some of America's finest locations for mountain, snow, and river sports are a short drive from campus. Epic, Eastern's Outdoor Program, makes participation easy. Students enjoy workouts in the Body Shop, social events, Division I athletic events, intramural competition, or an evening in Spokane.

Academic Highlights Eastern focuses on preparing students for careers. The low student-faculty ratio means small classes and close interactions between faculty members and students. A commitment to internships and career exploration helps students identify their interests, select a major, attain real-world work experience, and participate in professional development long before they graduate. The proximity of Spokane, one of Washington's largest cities and a regional hub for commerce and health care, provides opportunities for work and clinical experiences for students.

Interviews and Campus Visits Visiting opportunities range from a self-guided walking tour or student-led daily tours to special-interest visits that include interviews with faculty members or overnight Eagle Previews for a real on-campus experience. Weekend and holiday visits can be arranged. For more information about campus visits, students should call the Office of Admissions at 509-359-2397. The nearest commercial airport is Spokane International.

For Further Information Write to the Office of Admissions, 101 Sutton Hall, Eastern Washington University, Cheney, WA 99004. *E-mail:* admissions@mail.ewu.edu. *Web site:* http://www.ewu.edu.

See page 168 for a narrative description.

THE EVERGREEN STATE COLLEGE

Olympia, Washington

Evergreen is a coed, public, comprehensive institution, founded in 1967, offering degrees at the bachelor's and master's levels. It has a 1,000-acre campus in Olympia near Seattle.

Academic Information The faculty has 219 members (72% full-time), 74% with terminal degrees. The undergraduate student-faculty ratio is 21:1. The library holds 473,386 titles, 7,682 serial subscriptions, and 90,396 audiovisual materials. Special programs include services for learning-disabled students, cooperative (work-study) education, study abroad, advanced placement credit, accelerated degree programs, double majors, independent study, distance learning, self-designed majors, summer session for credit, part-time degree programs (evenings, weekends, summer), internships, and arrangement for off-campus study with University of Washington. The most frequently chosen baccalaureate field is liberal arts/general studies.

Student Body Statistics The student body totals 4,380, of whom 4,103 are undergraduates (460 freshmen). 56 percent are women and 44 percent are men. Students come from 54 states and territories and 15 other countries. 77 percent are from Washington. 0.2 percent are international students. 17 percent of the 2003 graduating class went on to graduate and professional schools.

Expenses for 2003–04 *Application fee:* $36. *State resident tuition:* $3651 full-time, $121.70 per quarter hour part-time. *Nonresident tuition:* $13,332 full-time, $444.40 per quarter hour part-time. *Mandatory fees:* $153 full-time, $1 per credit hour part-time, $39 per term part-time. Full-time tuition and fees vary according to course load and degree level. Part-time tuition and fees vary according to course load and degree level. *College room and board:* $5772. *College room only:* $3582. Room and board charges vary according to board plan and housing facility.

Financial Aid Forms of aid include need-based and non-need-based scholarships and part-time jobs. The average aided 2002–03 undergraduate received an aid package worth $10,006. The priority application deadline for financial aid is March 15.

Freshman Admission Evergreen requires a high school transcript, a minimum 2.0 high school GPA, SAT I or ACT scores, and TOEFL scores for international students. An essay is recommended. An interview is required for some. The application deadline for regular admission is March 1.

Transfer Admission The application deadline for admission is March 1.

Entrance Difficulty Evergreen assesses its entrance difficulty level as moderately difficult. For the fall 2003 freshman class, 93 percent of the applicants were accepted.

For Further Information Contact Mr. Doug P. Scrima, Director of Admissions, The Evergreen State College, 2700 Evergreen Parkway NW, Olympia, WA 98505. *Telephone:* 360-867-6170. *Fax:* 360-867-6576. *E-mail:* admissions@evergreen.edu. *Web site:* http://www.evergreen.edu/.

See page 172 for a narrative description.

GONZAGA UNIVERSITY

Spokane, Washington

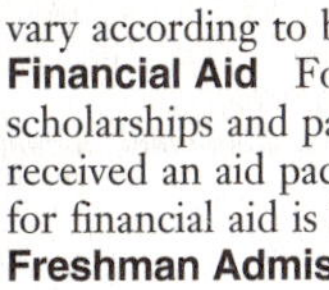

Gonzaga is a coed, private, Roman Catholic, comprehensive institution, founded in 1887, offering degrees at the bachelor's, master's, doctoral, and first professional levels and post-master's certificates. It has a 94-acre campus in Spokane.

Academic Information The faculty has 532 members (57% full-time). The undergraduate student-faculty ratio is 12:1. The library holds 228,622 titles, 1,435 serial subscriptions, and 2,617 audiovisual materials. Special programs include services for learning-disabled students, an honors program, study abroad, advanced placement credit, ESL programs, double majors, independent study, distance learning, self-designed majors, summer session for credit, part-time degree programs (daytime, evenings, weekends, summer), adult/continuing education programs, internships, and arrangement for off-campus study with American University. The most frequently chosen baccalaureate fields are business/marketing, engineering/engineering technologies, social sciences and history.

Student Body Statistics The student body totals 5,778, of whom 3,981 are undergraduates (908 freshmen). 55 percent are women and 45 percent are men. Students come from 44 states and territories and 33 other countries. 52 percent are from Washington. 1.3 percent are international students.

Expenses for 2003–04 *Application fee:* $40. *Comprehensive fee:* $26,695 includes full-time tuition ($20,510), mandatory fees ($225), and college room and board ($5960). *College room only:* $3110. Room and board charges vary according to board plan and housing facility. *Part-time tuition:* $595 per credit. *Part-time mandatory fees:* $25 per term.

Financial Aid Forms of aid include need-based and non-need-based scholarships, athletic grants, and part-time jobs. The average aided 2002–03 undergraduate received an aid package worth $13,271. The priority application deadline for financial aid is February 1.

Freshman Admission Gonzaga requires an essay, a high school transcript, a minimum 3.0 high school GPA, 1 recommendation, SAT I or ACT scores, and TOEFL scores for international students. An interview is recommended. The application deadline for regular admission is February 1 and for early action it is November 15.

Transfer Admission The application deadline for admission is July 1.

Entrance Difficulty Gonzaga assesses its entrance difficulty level as moderately difficult. For the fall 2003 freshman class, 77 percent of the applicants were accepted.

SPECIAL MESSAGE TO STUDENTS

Social Life Because personal growth is as important as intellectual development, Gonzaga University (GU) places great emphasis on student life outside of class. As a residential community, 98 percent of freshmen and 43 percent of the total student body live on campus in GU's sixteen residence halls and seven apartment complexes. Residence halls range in size from 35 people in a single-sex hall to 361 in Gonzaga's largest coed hall. In addition, students are encouraged to participate in more than 100 different clubs and organizations, including NCAA Division I athletics, intramural sports, a nationally ranked debate team, a nationally recognized mock trials team, and a variety of service clubs. As a testament to its students' commitment to service, Gonzaga provides the greatest number of service hours in the entire city of Spokane.

Academic Highlights All undergraduates complete Gonzaga's core curriculum emphasizing a comprehensive liberal arts and sciences education. GU offers more than seventy-five areas of study in arts and sciences, business (accounting and business administration with various concentrations), education (physical, special, teacher certification, and sport management), engineering (civil, computer, electrical, general, and mechanical majors and a joint M.B.A. program), and professional studies (exercise science, general studies, and nursing). GU offers qualified students the opportunity to study abroad through programs in Australia, British West Indies, China, Costa Rica, England, France, Ireland, Italy, Japan, Mexico, and Spain.

Interviews and Campus Visits All interested students are encouraged to visit the campus through Gonzaga's Visit Office. Personalized schedules include a financial aid session, an interview with an admissions counselor, and a campus tour through the Foley library, the Martin Centre athletic facility (with its new state-of-the-art student fitness center), the Jundt Art Center and Museum, and many other facilities. Students may also sit in on classes, meet with professors, and stay overnight in a residence hall on a space-available basis. For appointments, students should call the Office of Admission at 800-322-2584 Ext. 6531 (toll-free), Monday through Friday, 8 a.m. to 4:30 p.m. (Pacific time), at least two weeks prior to visiting. The office is located in the Administration Building, 502 East Boone Avenue, on the campus. The nearest commercial airport, Spokane International, is about 15 minutes from the campus.

For Further Information Write to Julie McCulloh, Dean of Admission, Gonzaga University, 502 East Boone Avenue, Spokane, WA 99258-0102. *E-mail:* admissions@gonzaga.edu.

HENRY COGSWELL COLLEGE

Everett, Washington

Cogswell College is a coed, private, four-year college, founded in 1979, offering degrees at the bachelor's level. It has a 1-acre campus in Everett near Seattle.

Academic Information The faculty has 31 members (26% full-time), 32% with terminal degrees. The student-faculty ratio is 12:1. The library holds 9,423 titles, 60 serial subscriptions, and 53 audiovisual materials. Special programs include academic remediation, cooperative (work-study) education, advanced placement credit, accelerated degree programs, double majors, independent study, summer session for credit, part-time degree programs (daytime, evenings, weekends, summer), and adult/continuing education programs. The most frequently chosen baccalaureate fields are engineering/engineering technologies, business/marketing, visual/performing arts.
Student Body Statistics The student body is made up of 230 undergraduates (27 freshmen). 25 percent are women and 75 percent are men. Students come from 3 states and territories. 2.6 percent are international students. 10 percent of the 2003 graduating class went on to graduate and professional schools.
Expenses for 2004–05 *Application fee:* $50. *One-time mandatory fee:* $75. *Tuition:* $15,840 full-time, $660 per credit part-time. Full-time tuition varies according to course load.
Financial Aid Forms of aid include need-based and non-need-based scholarships and part-time jobs. The average aided 2003–04 undergraduate received an aid package worth an estimated $5584. The application deadline for financial aid is continuous.
Freshman Admission Cogswell College requires an essay, a high school transcript, SAT I or ACT scores, and TOEFL scores for international students. An interview and SAT I scores are recommended. 3 recommendations and a portfolio are required for some. The application deadline for regular admission is rolling.
Transfer Admission The application deadline for admission is rolling.
Entrance Difficulty Cogswell College assesses its entrance difficulty level as noncompetitive; minimally difficult for first-time freshman day students. For the fall 2003 freshman class, 83 percent of the applicants were accepted.

For Further Information Contact Mr. Paul Wells, Director of Admissions, Henry Cogswell College, 3002 Colby Avenue, Everett, WA 98201. *Telephone:* 425-258-3351 Ext. 116 or 866-411-HCC1 (toll-free). *Fax:* 425-257-0405. *E-mail:* information@henrycogswell.edu. *Web site:* http://www.henrycogswell.edu/.

HERITAGE COLLEGE

Toppenish, Washington

For Information Write to Heritage College, Toppenish, WA 98948-9599.

ITT TECHNICAL INSTITUTE

Bothell, Washington

ITT Tech is a coed, proprietary, primarily two-year college of ITT Educational Services, Inc., founded in 1993, offering degrees at the associate and bachelor's levels.

Student Body Statistics The student body is made up of 263 undergraduates.
Expenses for 2003–04 *Application fee:* $100. Total Program Cost varies depending on course of study. Consult school catalog.
Financial Aid Forms of aid include need-based scholarships and part-time jobs. The application deadline for financial aid is continuous.
Freshman Admission ITT Tech requires a high school transcript, an interview, and Wonderlic aptitude test. Recommendations are recommended. The application deadline for regular admission is rolling.
Transfer Admission The application deadline for admission is rolling.
Entrance Difficulty ITT Tech assesses its entrance difficulty level as minimally difficult.

For Further Information Contact Mr. Jon L. Scherrer, Director of Recruitment, ITT Technical Institute, 2525 223rd Street SE, Bothell, WA 98021. *Telephone:* 425-485-0303 or 800-272-3791 (toll-free in-state). *Fax:* 425-485-3438. *Web site:* http://www.itt-tech.edu/.

ITT TECHNICAL INSTITUTE

Seattle, Washington

ITT Tech is a coed, proprietary, primarily two-year college of ITT Educational Services, Inc., founded in 1932, offering degrees at the associate and bachelor's levels.

Student Body Statistics The student body is made up of 422 undergraduates.
Expenses for 2003–04 *Application fee:* $100. Total Program Cost varies depending on course of study. Consult school catalog.
Financial Aid Forms of aid include need-based scholarships and part-time jobs. The application deadline for financial aid is continuous.
Freshman Admission ITT Tech requires a high school transcript, an interview, TOEFL scores for international students, and Wonderlic aptitude test. Recommendations are recommended. The application deadline for regular admission is rolling.
Transfer Admission The application deadline for admission is rolling.
Entrance Difficulty ITT Tech assesses its entrance difficulty level as minimally difficult.

For Further Information Contact Mr. Rocco Liace, Director of Recruitment, ITT Technical Institute, 12720 Gateway Drive, Suite 100, Seattle, WA 98168. *Telephone:* 206-244-3300 or 800-422-2029 (toll-free). *Fax:* 206-246-7635. *Web site:* http://www.itt-tech.edu/.

ITT TECHNICAL INSTITUTE

Spokane, Washington

ITT Tech is a coed, proprietary, primarily two-year college of ITT Educational Services, Inc., founded in 1985, offering degrees at the associate and bachelor's levels. It has a 3-acre campus in Spokane.

Student Body Statistics The student body is made up of 455 undergraduates.
Expenses for 2003–04 *Application fee:* $100. Total Program Cost varies depending on course of study. Consult school catalog.
Financial Aid Forms of aid include need-based scholarships and part-time jobs. The application deadline for financial aid is continuous.
Freshman Admission ITT Tech requires a high school transcript, an interview, TOEFL scores for international students, and Wonderlic aptitude test. Recommendations are recommended. The application deadline for regular admission is rolling.
Transfer Admission The application deadline for admission is rolling.
Entrance Difficulty ITT Tech assesses its entrance difficulty level as minimally difficult.

For Further Information Contact Mr. Gregory L. Alexander, Director of Recruitment, ITT Technical Institute, North 1050 Argonne Road, Spokane, WA 99212. *Telephone:* 509-926-2900 or 800-777-8324 (toll-free). *Fax:* 509-926-2908. *Web site:* http://www.itt-tech.edu/.

NORTHWEST COLLEGE

Kirkland, Washington

NC is a coed, private, comprehensive institution, founded in 1934, affiliated with the Assemblies of God, offering degrees at the associate, bachelor's, and master's levels. It has a 56-acre campus in Kirkland near Seattle.

Academic Information The faculty has 80 members (62% full-time), 38% with terminal degrees. The undergraduate student-faculty ratio is

15:1. The library holds 159,115 titles, 814 serial subscriptions, and 16,887 audiovisual materials. Special programs include academic remediation, cooperative (work-study) education, study abroad, advanced placement credit, accelerated degree programs, ESL programs, double majors, independent study, self-designed majors, summer session for credit, part-time degree programs, adult/continuing education programs, and internships. The most frequently chosen baccalaureate fields are biological/life sciences, education, philosophy, religion, and theology.
Student Body Statistics The student body totals 1,161, of whom 1,080 are undergraduates (174 freshmen). 62 percent are women and 38 percent are men. Students come from 28 states and territories and 13 other countries. 82 percent are from Washington. 1.6 percent are international students.
Expenses for 2004–05 *Application fee:* $30. *Comprehensive fee:* $21,210 includes full-time tuition ($14,200), mandatory fees ($560), and college room and board ($6450). *Part-time tuition:* $595 per credit. Part-time tuition varies according to course load.
Financial Aid Forms of aid include need-based and non-need-based scholarships, athletic grants, and part-time jobs. The average aided 2003–04 undergraduate received an aid package worth an estimated $10,592. The priority application deadline for financial aid is March 1.
Freshman Admission NC requires an essay, a high school transcript, a minimum 2.3 high school GPA, 2 recommendations, SAT I or ACT scores, and TOEFL scores for international students. An interview is required for some. The application deadline for regular admission is August 1 and for early action it is November 15.
Transfer Admission The application deadline for admission is August 1.
Entrance Difficulty NC assesses its entrance difficulty level as moderately difficult. For the fall 2003 freshman class, 90 percent of the applicants were accepted.

For Further Information Contact Ms. Rose-Mary K. Smith, Director of Admissions, Northwest College, PO Box 579, Kirkland, WA 98083-0579. *Telephone:* 425-889-5209 or 800-669-3781 (toll-free). *Fax:* 425-889-5224. *E-mail:* admissions@ncag.edu. *Web site:* http://www.nwcollege.edu/.

NORTHWEST COLLEGE OF ART

Poulsbo, Washington

NCA is a coed, proprietary, four-year college, founded in 1982, offering degrees at the bachelor's level in art. It has a 26-acre campus in Poulsbo near Seattle.

Academic Information Special programs include double majors, summer session for credit, and internships.
Student Body Statistics The student body is made up of 134 undergraduates.
Expenses for 2004–05 *Application fee:* $50. *Tuition:* $13,500 full-time, $585 per credit part-time. *Mandatory fees:* $100 full-time. Part-time tuition varies according to course load.
Financial Aid Forms of aid include need-based and non-need-based scholarships. The application deadline for financial aid is May 1.
Freshman Admission NCA requires an essay, a high school transcript, a minimum 2.0 high school GPA, 3 recommendations, an interview, a portfolio, and TOEFL scores for international students. The application deadline for regular admission is June 1.
Transfer Admission The application deadline for admission is June 1.
Entrance Difficulty NCA assesses its entrance difficulty level as moderately difficult.

For Further Information Contact Mr. Craig Freeman, President, Northwest College of Art, 16464 State Highway 305, Poulsbo, WA 98370. *Telephone:* 360-779-9993 or 800-769-ARTS (toll-free). *Fax:* 360-779-9933. *E-mail:* kperigard@nca.edu. *Web site:* http://www.nca.edu/.

NORTHWEST SCHOOL OF WOODEN BOATBUILDING

Port Townsend, Washington

For Information Write to Northwest School of Wooden Boatbuilding, Port Townsend, WA 98368.

PACIFIC LUTHERAN UNIVERSITY

Tacoma, Washington

PLU is a coed, private, comprehensive institution, founded in 1890, affiliated with the Evangelical Lutheran Church in America, offering degrees at the bachelor's and master's levels and post-master's and postbachelor's certificates. It has a 126-acre campus in Tacoma near Seattle.

Academic Information The faculty has 304 members (77% full-time), 74% with terminal degrees. The undergraduate student-faculty ratio is 13:1. The library holds 367,628 titles, 1,949 serial subscriptions, and 13,965 audiovisual materials. Special programs include services for learning-disabled students, an honors program, cooperative (work-study) education, study abroad, advanced placement credit, accelerated degree programs, ESL programs, double majors, independent study, self-designed majors, summer session for credit, part-time degree programs (daytime, summer), adult/continuing education programs, and internships. The most frequently chosen baccalaureate fields are business/marketing, education, social sciences and history.
Student Body Statistics The student body totals 3,462, of whom 3,185 are undergraduates (694 freshmen). 63 percent are women and 37 percent are men. Students come from 42 states and territories and 23 other countries. 74 percent are from Washington. 5 percent are international students. 13 percent of the 2003 graduating class went on to graduate and professional schools.
Expenses for 2003–04 *Application fee:* $35. *Comprehensive fee:* $25,715 includes full-time tuition ($19,610) and college room and board ($6105). *College room only:* $3000. Full-time tuition varies according to course load. Room and board charges vary according to board plan and housing facility. *Part-time tuition:* $612 per semester hour. Part-time tuition varies according to course load.
Financial Aid Forms of aid include need-based and non-need-based scholarships and part-time jobs. The average aided 2003–04 undergraduate received an aid package worth an estimated $17,229. The priority application deadline for financial aid is March 1.
Freshman Admission PLU requires an essay, a high school transcript, a minimum 2.5 high school GPA, 1 recommendation, SAT I or ACT scores, and TOEFL scores for international students. An interview is required for some. The application deadline for regular admission is rolling.
Transfer Admission The application deadline for admission is rolling.
Entrance Difficulty PLU assesses its entrance difficulty level as moderately difficult. For the fall 2003 freshman class, 80 percent of the applicants were accepted.

For Further Information Contact Dr. Laura Majovski, Vice President for Admissions and Student Life, Pacific Lutheran University, Tacoma, WA 98447. *Telephone:* 253-535-7151 or 800-274-6758 (toll-free). *Fax:* 253-536-5136. *E-mail:* admissions@plu.edu. *Web site:* http://www.plu.edu/.

PUGET SOUND CHRISTIAN COLLEGE

Mountlake Terrace, Washington

For Information Write to Puget Sound Christian College, Mountlake Terrace, WA 98043.

SAINT MARTIN'S COLLEGE

Lacey, Washington

St. Martin's is a coed, private, Roman Catholic, comprehensive institution, founded in 1895, offering degrees at the bachelor's and master's levels. It has a 300-acre campus in Lacey near Tacoma.

Academic Information The faculty has 72 members (79% full-time), 74% with terminal degrees. The undergraduate student-faculty ratio is 14:1. The library holds 84,220 titles, 852 serial subscriptions, and 1,239 audiovisual materials. Special programs include academic remediation, services for learning-disabled students, cooperative (work-study) education, study abroad, advanced placement credit, accelerated degree programs, ESL programs, double majors, independent study, summer session for credit, part-time degree programs (daytime, evenings, weekends, summer), adult/continuing education programs, internships, and arrangement for off-campus study with American University. The most frequently chosen baccalaureate fields are business/marketing, psychology, social sciences and history.
Student Body Statistics The student body totals 1,489, of whom 1,246 are undergraduates (145 freshmen). 56 percent are women and 44 percent are men. Students come from 19 states and territories and 13 other countries. 93 percent are from Washington. 4.3 percent are international students. 8 percent of the 2003 graduating class went on to graduate and professional schools.
Expenses for 2004–05 *Application fee:* $35. *One-time mandatory fee:* $130. *Comprehensive fee:* $24,670 includes full-time tuition ($18,660), mandatory fees ($290), and college room and board ($5720). *College room only:* $2420. *Part-time tuition:* $622 per credit. *Part-time mandatory fees:* $130 per term. Part-time tuition and fees vary according to course load.
Financial Aid Forms of aid include need-based and non-need-based scholarships and part-time jobs. The average aided 2003–04 undergraduate received an aid package worth an estimated $14,451. The priority application deadline for financial aid is March 1.
Freshman Admission St. Martin's requires an essay, a high school transcript, a minimum 2.5 high school GPA, 1 recommendation, SAT I or ACT scores, and TOEFL scores for international students. An interview is required for some.
Transfer Admission The application deadline for admission is August 1.
Entrance Difficulty St. Martin's assesses its entrance difficulty level as moderately difficult. For the fall 2003 freshman class, 76 percent of the applicants were accepted.

For Further Information Contact Mr. Todd Abbott, Director of Admission, Saint Martin's College, 5300 Pacific Avenue, SE, Lacey, WA 98503. *Telephone:* 360-438-4485 or 800-368-8803 (toll-free). *Fax:* 360-412-6189. *E-mail:* admissions@stmartin.edu. *Web site:* http://www.stmartin.edu/.

SEATTLE PACIFIC UNIVERSITY

Seattle, Washington

SPU is a coed, private, Free Methodist, comprehensive institution, founded in 1891, offering degrees at the bachelor's, master's, and doctoral levels and post-master's certificates. It has a 35-acre campus in Seattle.

Academic Information The faculty has 283 members (60% full-time). The undergraduate student-faculty ratio is 15:1. The library holds 169,527 titles, 1,336 serial subscriptions, and 3,002 audiovisual materials. Special programs include academic remediation, services for learning-disabled students, an honors program, cooperative (work-study) education, study abroad, advanced placement credit, ESL programs, double majors, independent study, distance learning, self-designed majors, summer session for credit, part-time degree programs (daytime, evenings, weekends, summer), external degree programs, adult/continuing education programs, internships, and arrangement for off-campus study with 13 members of the Coalition for Christian Colleges and Universities. The most frequently chosen baccalaureate fields are business/marketing, health professions and related sciences, social sciences and history.
Student Body Statistics The student body totals 3,728, of whom 2,859 are undergraduates (683 freshmen). 67 percent are women and 33 percent are men. Students come from 39 states and territories and 34 other countries. 63 percent are from Washington. 1 percent are international students. 12 percent of the 2003 graduating class went on to graduate and professional schools.
Expenses for 2003–04 *Application fee:* $45. *Comprehensive fee:* $26,175 includes full-time tuition ($18,822), mandatory fees ($336), and college room and board ($7017). *College room only:* $3762. Room and board charges vary according to board plan and housing facility. *Part-time tuition:* $523 per credit. Part-time tuition varies according to course load.
Financial Aid Forms of aid include need-based and non-need-based scholarships, athletic grants, and part-time jobs. The average aided 2002–03 undergraduate received an aid package worth $16,249. The priority application deadline for financial aid is April 1.
Freshman Admission SPU requires an essay, a high school transcript, a minimum 2.5 high school GPA, 2 recommendations, SAT I or ACT scores, and TOEFL scores for international students. SAT I scores are recommended. The application deadline for regular admission is June 1 and for early action it is December 1.
Transfer Admission The application deadline for admission is August 1.
Entrance Difficulty SPU assesses its entrance difficulty level as moderately difficult. For the fall 2003 freshman class, 92 percent of the applicants were accepted.

For Further Information Contact Mrs. Jennifer Feddern Kenney, Director of Admissions, Seattle Pacific University, 3307 Third Avenue West, Seattle, WA 98119-1997. *Telephone:* 206-281-2517 or 800-366-3344 (toll-free). *Fax:* 206-281-2544. *E-mail:* admissions@spu.edu. *Web site:* http://www.spu.edu/.

SEATTLE UNIVERSITY

Seattle, Washington

Seattle U is a coed, private, Roman Catholic, comprehensive institution, founded in 1891, offering degrees at the bachelor's, master's, doctoral, and first professional levels and post-master's and postbachelor's certificates. It has a 46-acre campus in Seattle.

Academic Information The faculty has 522 members (66% full-time), 77% with terminal degrees. The undergraduate student-faculty ratio is 14:1. The library holds 141,478 titles, 2,701 serial subscriptions, and 5,649 audiovisual materials. Special programs include services for learning-disabled students, an honors program, study abroad, advanced placement credit, accelerated degree programs, Freshman Honors College, ESL programs, double majors, independent study, self-designed majors, summer session for credit, part-time degree programs, adult/continuing education programs, internships, and arrangement for off-campus study with Photographic Center Northwest. The most frequently chosen baccalaureate fields are business/marketing, health professions and related sciences, social sciences and history.
Student Body Statistics The student body totals 6,659, of whom 3,765 are undergraduates (665 freshmen). 62 percent are women and 38 percent are men. Students come from 49 states and territories and 75 other countries. 65 percent are from Washington. 9.9 percent are international students.
Expenses for 2003–04 *Application fee:* $45. *Comprehensive fee:* $26,928 includes full-time tuition ($20,070) and college room and board ($6858). *College room only:* $4473. Full-time tuition varies according to course load. Room and board charges vary according to board plan. *Part-time tuition:* $446 per credit hour. Part-time tuition varies according to course load.
Financial Aid Forms of aid include need-based and non-need-based scholarships, athletic grants, and part-time jobs. The average aided 2003–04 undergraduate received an aid package worth an estimated $19,380. The priority application deadline for financial aid is February 1.
Freshman Admission Seattle U requires an essay, a high school transcript, a minimum 2.5 high school GPA, 2 recommendations, SAT I or ACT scores, and TOEFL scores for international students. The application deadline for regular admission is July 1.
Transfer Admission The application deadline for admission is August 1.

Entrance Difficulty Seattle U assesses its entrance difficulty level as moderately difficult; very difficult for upper-level nursing, engineering, diagnostic ultrasound, honors programs. For the fall 2003 freshman class, 78 percent of the applicants were accepted.

SPECIAL MESSAGE TO STUDENTS

Social Life Opportunities for involvement outside of class are extensive, varied, and as diverse as the students who attend Seattle University. The school is within walking distance of the major cultural and athletic facilities of one of America's finest cities. Therefore, most campus activities focus upon taking advantage of this major metropolis and on promoting student community and cohesiveness. There are more than eighty-five clubs, which include Hui o'Nani (the Hawaiian Student Organization), Earth Action Coalition, the National Society of Black Engineers, Forensics, and the Hiyu Coulee Hiking Club. There are twelve NCAA Division II athletic teams (men's and women's basketball, soccer, swimming, cross-country and track, and women's softball and volleyball) as well as a variety of intramural and club sports, such as tennis, cycling, skiing, and ice hockey. Service and leadership are central to Seattle University. Campus ministry plays a major role in student life as reflected by the Peace and Social Justice Center, involvement in Habitat for Humanity, and the student-run "Street Feed." Seattle University has the only Calcutta Club on any campus in the nation, and annually students travel to India to perform volunteer work. Approximately 1,600 of Seattle University's 3,765 undergraduates live on campus in three residence halls and in campus garden apartments.

Academic Highlights Seattle University is the only classically urban institute in the Northwest—accordingly, a firm academic foundation is established on campus, and the city is used as an extension of the classroom. Internship and part-time employment opportunities abound for students in all majors. Seattle University is noted as a fine liberal arts institution as well as for incorporating three professional schools, which produce leaders respected throughout the Puget Sound region. Major corporate, industrial, government, and health-care leaders assist students as professional mentors as well as actively serving on specific business, nursing, and science and engineering advisory boards. The University is distinctive for the significant percentage of women teaching in fields such as business, the sciences, and engineering; the prevalence of writing requirements throughout the curriculum; and its strong emphasis on students acquiring experience working on academic projects as teams.

Within the past fifteen years, academic facilities have been enhanced by $157 million in renovations and new construction.

Interviews and Campus Visit Seattle University is a short ride from Seatac International Airport, and its location at the juncture of Broadway and Madison Street is convenient to Interstates 5 and 90. Visitors find themselves within walking distance of major museums, the symphony, theater district, the Pike Place Market, the International District, historic Pioneer Square, and eclectic Capitol Hill. Interviews are strongly encouraged though not required. Appointments are typically available 9 a.m. to 5 p.m., Monday and Tuesday, and 9 a.m. to 4 p.m., Wednesday through Friday, with interviews available 9 a.m to 1 p.m. many Saturdays. Campus tours are offered several times a day during the week and during the Saturdays the Admissions Office is open. During the week, admissions visits can be combined with appointments with financial aid and athletics, and students may also visit classes. Students should call 206-296-2000 or 800-426-7123 (toll-free) two weeks in advance to schedule an appointment to allow the best possible service.

For Further Information Write to Mr. Michael K. McKeon, Dean, Admissions Office, Seattle University, 900 Broadway, Seattle, WA 98122-4340. *E-mail:* admissions@seattleu.edu. *Web site:* http://www.seattleu.edu.

See page 188 for a narrative description.

TRINITY LUTHERAN COLLEGE

Issaquah, Washington

Trinity Lutheran College is a coed, private, Lutheran, four-year college, founded in 1944, offering degrees at the associate and bachelor's levels and postbachelor's certificates in religious studies. It has a 46-acre campus in Issaquah near Seattle.

Expenses for 2003–04 *Application fee:* $30. *Comprehensive fee:* $15,990 includes full-time tuition ($10,170), mandatory fees ($200), and college room and board ($5620).

For Further Information Contact Ms. Sigrid Olsen, Director of Admission, Trinity Lutheran College, 4221 228th Avenue, SE, Issaquah, WA 98029-9299. *Telephone:* 425-961-5516 or 800-843-5659 (toll-free). *Fax:* 425-392-0404. *E-mail:* admission@tlc.edu. *Web site:* http://www.tlc.edu/.

UNIVERSITY OF PHOENIX–SPOKANE CAMPUS

Spokane, Washington

For Information Write to University of Phoenix–Spokane Campus, Spokane, WA 99201.

UNIVERSITY OF PHOENIX–WASHINGTON CAMPUS

Seattle, Washington

University of Phoenix–Washington Campus is a coed, proprietary, comprehensive institution, founded in 1997, offering degrees at the associate, bachelor's, master's, and doctoral levels and post-master's and postbachelor's certificates (courses conducted at 121 campuses and learning centers in 25 states).

Academic Information The faculty has 232 members (2% full-time), 22% with terminal degrees. The undergraduate student-faculty ratio is 8:1. The library holds 27 million titles and 11,648 serial subscriptions. Special programs include advanced placement credit, accelerated degree programs, independent study, distance learning, external degree programs, and adult/continuing education programs. The most frequently chosen baccalaureate fields are business/marketing, computer/information sciences, protective services/public administration.
Student Body Statistics The student body totals 1,401, of whom 1,012 are undergraduates (33 freshmen). 57 percent are women and 43 percent are men. 2.2 percent are international students.
Expenses for 2003–04 *Application fee:* $100. *Tuition:* $9900 full-time, $330 per credit part-time.
Financial Aid Forms of aid include need-based and non-need-based scholarships. The average aided 2002–03 undergraduate received an aid package worth $1285. The application deadline for financial aid is continuous.
Freshman Admission University of Phoenix–Washington Campus requires a minimum 1 high school GPA, 2 years of work experience, 23 years of age, and TOEFL scores for international students. A high school transcript is required for some. The application deadline for regular admission is rolling.
Transfer Admission The application deadline for admission is rolling.
Entrance Difficulty University of Phoenix–Washington Campus has an open admission policy.

For Further Information Contact Ms. Beth Barilla, Director of Admissions, University of Phoenix–Washington Campus, 4615 East Elwood Street, Mail Stop AA-K101, Phoenix, AZ 85040-1958. *Telephone:* 480-557-1712 or 800-228-7240 (toll-free). *Fax:* 480-894-1758. *E-mail:* beth.barilla@pheonix.edu. *Web site:* http://www.phoenix.edu/.

UNIVERSITY OF PUGET SOUND

Tacoma, Washington

Puget Sound is a coed, private, comprehensive institution, founded in 1888, offering degrees at the bachelor's, master's, and first professional levels and post-master's certificates. It has a 97-acre campus in Tacoma near Seattle.

Academic Information The faculty has 259 members (83% full-time), 77% with terminal degrees. The undergraduate student-faculty ratio is 11:1. The library holds 343,787 titles, 5,609 serial subscriptions, and 17,328 audiovisual materials. Special programs include an honors program, cooperative (work-study) education, study abroad, advanced placement credit, double majors, independent study, self-designed majors, summer session for credit, part-time degree programs, and internships. The most frequently chosen baccalaureate fields are business/marketing, biological/life sciences, social sciences and history.
Student Body Statistics The student body totals 2,760, of whom 2,516 are undergraduates (641 freshmen). 59 percent are women and 41 percent are men. Students come from 46 states and territories and 14 other countries. 29 percent are from Washington. 0.9 percent are international students. 34 percent of the 2003 graduating class went on to graduate and professional schools.
Expenses for 2003–04 *Application fee:* $40. *Comprehensive fee:* $31,760 includes full-time tuition ($25,190), mandatory fees ($170), and college room and board ($6400). *College room only:* $3500. Room and board charges vary according to board plan and housing facility.
Financial Aid Forms of aid include need-based and non-need-based scholarships and part-time jobs. The average aided 2003–04 undergraduate received an aid package worth an estimated $19,217. The application deadline for financial aid is February 1.
Freshman Admission Puget Sound requires an essay, a high school transcript, 2 recommendations, SAT I or ACT scores, and TOEFL scores for international students. A minimum 3.0 high school GPA and an interview are recommended. The application deadline for regular admission is May 1; for early decision plan 1 it is November 15; and for early decision plan 2 it is December 15.
Transfer Admission The application deadline for admission is July 1.
Entrance Difficulty Puget Sound assesses its entrance difficulty level as very difficult. For the fall 2003 freshman class, 71 percent of the applicants were accepted.

For Further Information Contact Dr. George H. Mills Jr., Vice President for Enrollment, University of Puget Sound, 1500 North Warner Street, Tacoma, WA 98416-1062. *Telephone:* 253-879-3211 or 800-396-7191 (toll-free). *Fax:* 253-879-3993. *E-mail:* admission@ups.edu. *Web site:* http://www.ups.edu/.

UNIVERSITY OF WASHINGTON

Seattle, Washington

UW is a coed, public university, founded in 1861, offering degrees at the bachelor's, master's, doctoral, and first professional levels. It has a 703-acre campus in Seattle.

Academic Information The faculty has 3,383 members (82% full-time), 93% with terminal degrees. The undergraduate student-faculty ratio is 11:1. The library holds 6 million titles, 50,245 serial subscriptions, and 1 million audiovisual materials. Special programs include academic remediation, services for learning-disabled students, an honors program, cooperative (work-study) education, study abroad, advanced placement credit, accelerated degree programs, ESL programs, double majors, independent study, distance learning, self-designed majors, summer session for credit, part-time degree programs, external degree programs, adult/continuing education programs, and internships. The most frequently chosen baccalaureate fields are business/marketing, biological/life sciences, social sciences and history.
Student Body Statistics The student body totals 39,246, of whom 28,362 are undergraduates (4,771 freshmen). 52 percent are women and 48 percent are men. Students come from 52 states and territories and 59 other countries. 87 percent are from Washington. 3.3 percent are international students.
Expenses for 2003–04 *Application fee:* $37. *State resident tuition:* $4968 full-time. *Nonresident tuition:* $16,124 full-time. *College room and board:* $6726.
Financial Aid Forms of aid include need-based and non-need-based scholarships, athletic grants, and part-time jobs. The average aided 2002–03 undergraduate received an aid package worth $10,043. The priority application deadline for financial aid is February 28.
Freshman Admission UW requires an essay, a high school transcript, a minimum 2.0 high school GPA, SAT I or ACT scores, and TOEFL scores for international students. The application deadline for regular admission is January 15.
Transfer Admission The application deadline for admission is February 15.
Entrance Difficulty UW assesses its entrance difficulty level as moderately difficult; very difficult for out-of-state applicants; very difficult for transfers. For the fall 2003 freshman class, 68 percent of the applicants were accepted.

For Further Information Contact Mr. Wilbur W. Washburn, IV, Assistant Vice President for Enrollment Services, University of Washington, Box 355852, Seattle, WA 98195-5852. *Telephone:* 206-543-9686. *Web site:* http://www.washington.edu/.

WALLA WALLA COLLEGE

College Place, Washington

WWC is a coed, private, Seventh-day Adventist, comprehensive institution, founded in 1892, offering degrees at the associate, bachelor's, and master's levels. It has a 77-acre campus in College Place.

Academic Information The faculty has 201 members (60% full-time), 43% with terminal degrees. The undergraduate student-faculty ratio is 13:1. The library holds 128,747 titles, 1,317 serial subscriptions, and 3,483 audiovisual materials. Special programs include academic remediation, services for learning-disabled students, an honors program, cooperative (work-study) education, study abroad, advanced placement credit, Freshman Honors College, ESL programs, double majors, independent study, summer session for credit, part-time degree programs (daytime, evenings, summer), and internships. The most frequently chosen baccalaureate fields are business/marketing, engineering/engineering technologies, health professions and related sciences.
Student Body Statistics The student body totals 1,917, of whom 1,667 are undergraduates (326 freshmen). 48 percent are women and 52 percent are men. Students come from 45 states and territories. 39 percent are from Washington. 0.2 percent are international students.
Expenses for 2003–04 *Application fee:* $30. *Comprehensive fee:* $20,880 includes full-time tuition ($16,860), mandatory fees ($165), and college room and board ($3855). *College room only:* $2280. Full-time tuition and fees vary according to course load, degree level, and location. Room and board charges vary according to housing facility and location. *Part-time tuition:* $442 per credit.
Financial Aid Forms of aid include need-based and non-need-based scholarships and part-time jobs. The average aided 2002–03 undergraduate received an aid package worth $14,161. The application deadline for financial aid is continuous.
Freshman Admission WWC requires a high school transcript, a minimum 2.0 high school GPA, 3 recommendations, SAT I or ACT scores, and TOEFL scores for international students. ACT scores are recommended. The application deadline for regular admission is rolling.
Transfer Admission The application deadline for admission is rolling.
Entrance Difficulty WWC assesses its entrance difficulty level as moderately difficult. For the fall 2003 freshman class, 55 percent of the applicants were accepted.

For Further Information Contact Mr. Dallas Weis, Director of Admissions, Walla Walla College, 204 South College Avenue, College Place, WA 99324. *Telephone:* 509-527-2327 or 800-541-8900 (toll-free). *Fax:* 509-527-2397. *E-mail:* info@wwc.edu. *Web site:* http://www.wwc.edu/.

WASHINGTON STATE UNIVERSITY

Pullman, Washington

WSU is a coed, public university, founded in 1890, offering degrees at the bachelor's, master's, doctoral, and first professional levels and postbachelor's certificates. It has a 620-acre campus in Pullman.

Academic Information The faculty has 1,289 members (83% full-time), 82% with terminal degrees. The undergraduate student-faculty ratio is 18:1. The library holds 2 million titles, 31,237 serial subscriptions, and 316,707 audiovisual materials. Special programs include academic remediation, services for learning-disabled students, an honors program, cooperative (work-study) education, study abroad, advanced placement credit, ESL programs, double majors, distance learning, summer session for credit, part-time degree programs (daytime, summer), external degree programs, adult/continuing education programs, internships, and arrangement for off-campus study with University of Idaho. The most frequently chosen baccalaureate fields are business/marketing, communications/communication technologies, social sciences and history.
Student Body Statistics The student body totals 22,712, of whom 18,746 are undergraduates (3,043 freshmen). 53 percent are women and 47 percent are men. Students come from 55 states and territories and 77 other countries. 98 percent are from Washington. 3.4 percent are international students.
Expenses for 2003–04 *Application fee:* $37. *State resident tuition:* $4435 full-time. *Nonresident tuition:* $12,537 full-time. *Mandatory fees:* $775 full-time. *College room and board:* $6054. *College room only:* $3010. Room and board charges vary according to board plan and housing facility.
Financial Aid Forms of aid include need-based and non-need-based scholarships, athletic grants, and part-time jobs. The average aided 2002–03 undergraduate received an aid package worth $11,511. The priority application deadline for financial aid is March 1.
Freshman Admission WSU requires an essay, a high school transcript, a minimum 2.0 high school GPA, SAT I or ACT scores, and TOEFL scores for international students. 3 recommendations are required for some.
Entrance Difficulty WSU assesses its entrance difficulty level as moderately difficult. For the fall 2003 freshman class, 78 percent of the applicants were accepted.

For Further Information Contact Ms. Wendy Peterson, Director of Admissions, Washington State University, Lighty 370, Pullman, WA 99164-1067. *Telephone:* 509-335-5586 or 888-468-6978 (toll-free). *Fax:* 509-335-7468. *E-mail:* admiss2@wsu.edu. *Web site:* http://www.wsu.edu/.

WESTERN WASHINGTON UNIVERSITY

Bellingham, Washington

Western is a coed, public, comprehensive institution, founded in 1893, offering degrees at the bachelor's and master's levels and postbachelor's certificates. It has a 223-acre campus in Bellingham near Seattle and Vancouver.

Academic Information The faculty has 618 members (73% full-time), 74% with terminal degrees. The undergraduate student-faculty ratio is 20:1. The library holds 1 million titles, 4,834 serial subscriptions, and 26,095 audiovisual materials. Special programs include services for learning-disabled students, an honors program, cooperative (work-study) education, study abroad, advanced placement credit, accelerated degree programs, ESL programs, double majors, independent study, distance learning, self-designed majors, summer session for credit, adult/continuing education programs, internships, and arrangement for off-campus study with National Student Exchange, International Student Exchange Program. The most frequently chosen baccalaureate fields are business/marketing, engineering/engineering technologies, social sciences and history.
Student Body Statistics The student body totals 13,845, of whom 12,477 are undergraduates (2,214 freshmen). 57 percent are women and 43 percent are men. Students come from 47 states and territories and 35 other countries. 93 percent are from Washington. 0.4 percent are international students. 14 percent of the 2003 graduating class went on to graduate and professional schools.
Expenses for 2003–04 *Application fee:* $37. *State resident tuition:* $3639 full-time, $121 per credit part-time. *Nonresident tuition:* $12,411 full-time, $414 per credit part-time. *Mandatory fees:* $543 full-time, $181 per year part-time. Full-time tuition and fees vary according to location. Part-time tuition and fees vary according to location. *College room and board:* $5945. *College room only:* $3902. Room and board charges vary according to board plan and housing facility.
Financial Aid Forms of aid include need-based and non-need-based scholarships, athletic grants, and part-time jobs. The average aided 2003–04 undergraduate received an aid package worth an estimated $8258. The priority application deadline for financial aid is February 15.
Freshman Admission Western requires a high school transcript, a minimum 2.5 high school GPA, SAT I or ACT scores, and TOEFL scores for international students. An essay is recommended. The application deadline for regular admission is March 1.
Transfer Admission The application deadline for admission is April 1.
Entrance Difficulty Western assesses its entrance difficulty level as moderately difficult. For the fall 2003 freshman class, 76 percent of the applicants were accepted.

For Further Information Contact Ms. Karen Copetas, Director of Admissions, Western Washington University, 516 High Street, Bellingham, WA 98225-9009. *Telephone:* 360-650-3440. *Fax:* 360-650-7369. *E-mail:* admit@wwu.edu. *Web site:* http://www.wwu.edu/.

WHITMAN COLLEGE

Walla Walla, Washington

Whitman is a coed, private, four-year college, founded in 1859, offering degrees at the bachelor's level. It has a 117-acre campus in Walla Walla.

Academic Information The faculty has 185 members (63% full-time), 82% with terminal degrees. The student-faculty ratio is 10:1. The library holds 350,699 titles, 2,175 serial subscriptions, and 4,500 audiovisual materials. Special programs include services for learning-disabled students, an honors program, study abroad, advanced placement credit, double majors, independent study, self-designed majors, internships, and arrangement for off-campus study with American University, Associated Colleges of the Midwest, Great Lakes Colleges Association, Columbia University. The most frequently chosen baccalaureate fields are biological/life sciences, psychology, social sciences and history.
Student Body Statistics The student body is made up of 1,454 undergraduates (362 freshmen). 56 percent are women and 44 percent are men. Students come from 27 states and territories and 24 other countries. 49 percent are from Washington. 2.5 percent are international students.
Expenses for 2003–04 *Application fee:* $45. *Comprehensive fee:* $32,526 includes full-time tuition ($25,400), mandatory fees ($226), and college room and board ($6900). *College room only:* $3170. Room and board charges vary according to board plan and housing facility.
Financial Aid Forms of aid include need-based and non-need-based scholarships and part-time jobs. The average aided 2003–04 undergraduate received an aid package worth an estimated $17,750. The priority application deadline for financial aid is November 15.
Freshman Admission Whitman requires an essay, a high school transcript, 1 recommendation, SAT I or ACT scores, and TOEFL scores for international students. An interview and SAT II: Writing Test scores are recommended. The application deadline for regular admission is January 15; for early decision plan 1 it is November 15; and for early decision plan 2 it is January 1.
Transfer Admission The application deadline for admission is January 15.
Entrance Difficulty Whitman assesses its entrance difficulty level as very difficult. For the fall 2003 freshman class, 56 percent of the applicants were accepted.

For Further Information Contact Mr. Tony Cabasco, Acting Dean of Admission and Financial Aid, Whitman College, 345 Boyer Avenue, Walla Walla, WA 99362-2083. *Telephone:* 509-527-5176 or 877-462-9448 (toll-free). *Fax:* 509-527-4967. *E-mail:* admission@whitman.edu. *Web site:* http://www.whitman.edu/.

WHITWORTH COLLEGE

Spokane, Washington

Whitworth is a coed, private, Presbyterian, comprehensive institution, founded in 1890, offering degrees at the bachelor's and master's levels. It has a 200-acre campus in Spokane.

Academic Information The undergraduate student-faculty ratio is 13:1. The library holds 17,982 titles and 773 serial subscriptions. Special programs include services for learning-disabled students, cooperative (work-study) education, study abroad, advanced placement credit, ESL programs, double majors, independent study, self-designed majors, summer session for credit, part-time degree programs, adult/continuing education programs, internships, and arrangement for off-campus study with 3 members of the Intercollegiate Center for Nursing, 2 members of the Intercollegiate Language Study Consortium.
Student Body Statistics The student body totals 2,298, of whom 2,071 are undergraduates. 59 percent are women and 41 percent are men. Students come from 31 states and territories and 25 other countries. 62 percent are from Washington. 2.8 percent are international students. 20 percent of the 2003 graduating class went on to graduate and professional schools.
Expenses for 2003–04 *Application fee:* $0. *Comprehensive fee:* $26,428 includes full-time tuition ($19,810), mandatory fees ($268), and college room and board ($6350). Room and board charges vary according to board plan and housing facility. *Part-time tuition:* varies with class time.
Financial Aid Forms of aid include need-based and non-need-based scholarships and part-time jobs. The average aided 2003–04 undergraduate received an aid package worth an estimated $17,443. The priority application deadline for financial aid is March 1.
Freshman Admission Whitworth requires an essay, a high school transcript, recommendations, SAT I or ACT scores, and TOEFL scores for international students. An interview is required for some. The application deadline for regular admission is March 1 and for early action it is November 30.
Transfer Admission The application deadline for admission is August 1.
Entrance Difficulty Whitworth assesses its entrance difficulty level as very difficult; moderately difficult for transfers. For the fall 2003 freshman class, 75 percent of the applicants were accepted.

For Further Information Contact Ms. Marianne Hansen, Director of Admission, Whitworth College, 300 West, Hawthorne Road, Spokane, WA 99251. *Telephone:* 509-777-4348 or 800-533-4668 (toll-free out-of-state). *Fax:* 509-777-3758. *E-mail:* admission@whitworth.edu. *Web site:* http://www.whitworth.edu/.

See page 200 for a narrative description.

Wyoming

UNIVERSITY OF WYOMING

Laramie, Wyoming

UW is a coed, public university, founded in 1886, offering degrees at the bachelor's, master's, doctoral, and first professional levels and post-master's certificates. It has a 785-acre campus in Laramie.

Academic Information The faculty has 655 members (95% full-time), 86% with terminal degrees. The undergraduate student-faculty ratio is 16:1. The library holds 1 million titles, 13,256 serial subscriptions, and 4,161 audiovisual materials. Special programs include services for learning-disabled students, an honors program, study abroad, advanced placement credit, accelerated degree programs, double majors, independent study, distance learning, self-designed majors, summer session for credit, part-time degree programs (daytime, evenings, summer), external degree programs, internships, and arrangement for off-campus study. The most frequently chosen baccalaureate fields are business/marketing, education, engineering/engineering technologies.
Student Body Statistics The student body totals 13,130, of whom 9,385 are undergraduates (1,416 freshmen). 53 percent are women and 47 percent are men. Students come from 52 states and territories and 48 other countries. 73 percent are from Wyoming. 1 percent are international students.
Expenses for 2003–04 *Application fee:* $30. *State resident tuition:* $2520 full-time, $84 per credit hour part-time. *Nonresident tuition:* $8370 full-time, $279 per credit hour part-time. *Mandatory fees:* $570 full-time, $134 per term part-time. Full-time tuition and fees vary according to course load, program, and reciprocity agreements. Part-time tuition and fees vary according to course load, program, and reciprocity agreements. *College room and board:* $5546. *College room only:* $2372. Room and board charges vary according to board plan and housing facility.
Financial Aid Forms of aid include need-based and non-need-based scholarships, athletic grants, and part-time jobs. The average aided 2002–03 undergraduate received an aid package worth $8944. The priority application deadline for financial aid is February 1.
Freshman Admission UW requires a high school transcript, a minimum 2.75 high school GPA, and TOEFL scores for international students. An interview is recommended. A minimum 3.0 high school GPA and SAT I or ACT scores are required for some. The application deadline for regular admission is August 10.
Transfer Admission The application deadline for admission is August 10.
Entrance Difficulty UW assesses its entrance difficulty level as moderately difficult. For the fall 2003 freshman class, 95 percent of the applicants were accepted.

SPECIAL MESSAGE TO STUDENTS

Social Life The University of Wyoming (UW), offers more than 190 campus clubs and organizations to give students the opportunity to get involved. Students may join a fraternity or sorority, run for a student government office, or participate in an honor or professional society. Whether it is writing for a campus publication, voicing political views, or getting involved in student religious organizations, opportunities as diverse as its student body abound on UW's campus. Featured musical performances and concerts, plays, comedians, and other fun events are highlights of the campus every year. Students also enjoy nearly sixty different intramural and club sports and all the outdoor adventure the Rocky Mountains can supply.

Academic Highlights UW students enjoy small class sizes that average 24 students and individual attention from professors that reflect UW's low student-faculty ratio of 16:1. Overall, 87 percent of UW courses are taught by professors, not graduate assistants. This outstanding academic environment allows for relationships to develop between students and their professors in all six colleges: Agriculture, Arts and Sciences, Business, Education, Engineering, and Health Sciences. At UW, academic excellence is evident. UW proudly claimed a Rhodes scholar and a Goldwater scholar for 2003. Senior agriculture students routinely score in the top quartile nationwide against all other seniors completing the ACT-comprehensive exams. The College of Arts and Sciences, UW's largest, offers more than 50 percent of all majors, including a self-designed major. (A student who designed her own major was chosen last year as one of *USA Today*'s All-USA College Academic Team.) The debate team won two national championships, and the theater and dance students performed at Kennedy Center in Washington, D.C., in a national competition. Senior business students consistently score in the top 10 percent against all other business students completing the Major Field Achievement Test in Business. The NEA ranked UW's College of Education as one of the top seven teacher-preparation programs in the nation. Senior engineering students consistently score higher on their national examinations, Fundamentals of Engineering Exam, and their engineering honor society was recently voted as the most outstanding chapter in the nation. The College of Health Sciences also boasts nearly 100 percent job placement within six months after graduation. Also, the UW honors program has been cited as one of the best in the nation for its innovative courses, award-winning faculty, and lively and supportive atmosphere.

Interviews and Campus Visits Seeing is believing! UW strongly encourages prospective students to visit the campus. It is the easiest way to determine if UW is the right choice. UW campus visits, with advance notice, include a tour with a current student, individual meetings with professors/department staff members, and a visit with an admissions representative as well as opportunities to speak with representatives from financial aid, residence life, varsity sports, and the honors program. To schedule a visit, prospective students can call 307-766-5160 or 800-DIAL-WYO (toll-free). The nearest commercial airport is Laramie Regional.

For Further Information Write to the Admissions Office, University of Wyoming, Department 3435, 1000 East University Avenue, Laramie, WY 82071-3435. *E-mail:* why-wyo@uwyo.edu.

See page 198 for a narrative description.

In-Depth Descriptions of Colleges in the West

ACADEMY OF ART UNIVERSITY

SAN FRANCISCO, CALIFORNIA

The University

In 1929, Academy of Art University founder Richard S. Stephens, who was the advertising creative director of *Sunset* magazine, acted on his belief that "aspiring artists and designers, given proper instruction, hard work, and dedication, can learn the skills needed to become successful professionals." His new school of advertising art consisted of 46 students meeting in one room on San Francisco's Kearny Street. The instructors, who were professional artists, brought real-world problems, situations, solutions, and practical experience to the students. Thus was born the school's philosophy by the founder: Hire today's best practicing professionals to teach the art and design professionals of tomorrow. At that time, advertising consisted primarily of illustrations, photos, and copy. Consequently, it became necessary to teach beginning students the fundamentals of drawing, painting, color, light, and photography as well as layout and typography.

When Richard A. Stephens succeeded his father as president in 1951, the Foundations Department was added, ensuring all students comprehended the basic principles of traditional art and design. Illustration soon expanded to include fine arts (drawing, painting, sculpture, and printmaking), and advertising design spawned the Graphic Design Department. Fashion (design, textiles, and merchandising) and Interior Design Departments were also added. In 1966, the Academy officially became a college, and in a decade, the Master of Fine Arts degree was offered. Five more buildings were purchased, and by 1992, there were more than 2,500 students. The leadership of the Academy was then turned over to the third generation, Elisa Stephens, granddaughter of the school's founder. She quickly determined that the school's small Computer Arts Department had enormous potential to prepare students for multimedia careers when allied with such companies as Silicon Graphics, Pixar, Adobe, and Walt Disney Productions. It is now the fastest-growing department at the Academy.

Today, Academy of Art University is the largest private art and design school in the nation and has an enrollment of more than 7,000 students from nearly every country in the world. More than one third of the student body is made up of international students. The Academy has more than twenty facilities that house classrooms, studios, galleries, and dormitories. The students, who are admitted through an open enrollment policy, aspire to earn either an A.A., a B.F.A., or a certificate in one of twelve design majors. The school maintains a fleet of buses to connect the different points of the campus, all of which are located within the city limits of San Francisco, one of the world's most vibrant and beautiful cities. The faculty, which is 80 percent part-time and made up of working art and design professionals, is recruited from all across the nation and is drawn to the creative and intellectual center that is the Bay Area. Extensive senior-year internship programs allow students to gain valuable experience and develop strong portfolios in their chosen field before graduation.

Academy of Art University offers an M.F.A. program in architecture.

Location

The city of San Francisco is one of the great cultural centers of the world; a melting pot of diversity, ethnicity, and creativity that has spawned major museums and galleries, world-class opera and theaters, dance companies, film production and recording studios, technological innovation, performing artists ranging from classical to popular music, and numerous other cultural opportunities. The city's status as a tourist mecca located on the Pacific Rim ensures that one encounters people from all corners of the world. The climate is moderate and offers kaleidoscopic blends of sunshine and fog nine months of the year. The Northpoint campus is located at world-famous Pier 39; one can view Alcatraz Island from classroom windows. Four other buildings are two blocks from historic Union Square in the commercial heart of the city. Three other buildings are located near the Financial District. The city offers myriad locations for field trips and studio visits. World-renowned artists display their creations in the Academy's four nonprofit art galleries, which are open to the public. The University is an urban institution that both draws upon and contributes to the cultural wealth of the community in which it resides.

Majors and Degrees

The University offers A.A. and B.F.A. degrees and certificates in the following majors: advertising (account planning, art direction, copywriting, and television commercials), animation/visual effects (storyboard art, background painting/layout design, game design, visual development, 3-D modeling, character development, and VFX/compositing), computer arts/new media (computer graphics, new media, Web design, and digital imaging), fashion (fashion design, fashion illustration, knitwear, merchandising, and textiles), fine art (ceramics, metal arts, painting/drawing, printmaking, and sculpture), graphic design (corporate and brand identity, Web site design, motion graphics, multimedia, package design, print and collateral), illustration (cartooning, children's books, editorial, feature film animation, and 2-D animation), industrial design (product, transportation, furniture, and toy design), interior architecture and design (commercial, residential, and furniture design), motion pictures and television (acting, advertising/director–camera, cinematography, directing, editing, producing, production design, screenwriting, and special effects), and photography (advertising, documentary, digital photography, fashion, fine art, photo illustration, and photojournalism).

Academic Programs

A total of 132 credit units are required to earn a Bachelor of Fine Arts degree, consisting of 18 units of foundations courses, 60 units in the major, 12 units of art electives, and 42 units of liberal arts/art history courses. First-year students must complete six foundations courses before the end of the year. Fundamental courses are related specifically to students' majors in preparation to begin intense focus courses in his or her field by the sophomore year. All major courses of study are structured so the student builds upon skills learned the previous semester and advances to the next level of technical or creative proficiency. Some related major courses may be taken concurrently. Each course is worth 3 credits. Liberal arts courses teach practical applications for forging a professional career in art and design. International students who come from countries where English is not the primary language may take additional ESL classes, as determined by English language proficiency testing. Students are advised to meet with departmental directors at least once during the academic year to have their progress assessed. Portfolios are reviewed before the junior year to determine whether or not a student has progressed sufficiently to continue study at the Academy.

Academic Facilities

The Academy's facilities reflect its commitment to training students for careers in art and design; not only do students have access to some of the most advanced facilities in the nation, but the Academy continually invests in new equipment to ensure that it remains on the cutting edge of technology. By learning on industry-standard equipment, students gain valuable professional techniques that make them highly employable.

The Academy's eight-story Digital Arts Center offers students from the Computer Arts, Animation/Visual Effects, Motion Pictures and Television, Advertising, and Fashion Departments access to an incredible array of technology. The center has more than 800 computer workstations, including approximately 100 Silicon Graphics workstations, 300 Adobe Premier workstations, and more than 200 autoCAD workstations. Students also have the use of fourteen Avid digital editing suites, seven multitrack sound editing studios, one dedicated blue screen studio, and various other video equipment, including Bosch Telecine equipment.

The Photography Department occupies its own building and shares half of another Academy building with the fine arts, painting, and printmaking departments. Photography students can utilize a wide range of equipment, including full-length shooting studios; Hasselblad, Mamyia, Canon, and Sinar cameras; Broncolor, Norman, and Speedotron strobe systems; seven black-and-white darkrooms; a color lab facility with fifteen single-print stations; and the latest technology, including eight MAC G4 computers, for digital imaging and output. In addition, the Academy's modern, professional studio is one of the largest of any photography school in the nation and is ideal for shooting automobiles, motorcycles, and large sets.

The Academy's Fine Art Sculpture Center is a 58,000-square-foot facility that houses state-of-the-art studios for figure, ceramic, neon/illumination, bronze, metal fabrication, and mold-making sculpture. Students also have use of an off-site bronze-casting facility. When students graduate from the Academy, they have the opportunity to exhibit in one of four nonprofit galleries in the heart of downtown San Francisco's premier gallery district. These street-level facilities are an excellent way for students to promote and sell their work and to gain networking experience.

The Library houses more than 30,000 books and magazines, as well as 375 CD-ROM titles, 150,000 slides, and 2,000 videos. Computers with Internet access are available to students as well as an online catalog, color scanners, and color and black-and-white copiers. Workshops and electronic study guides are also available. The Academy Resource Center offers all students free learning support services that include study hall, tutoring, mentoring, midpoint review and study skills workshops, a writing lab, a state-of-the-art multimedia language lab, an English for Art Program, and a Conversation Partner Program.

Costs

Tuition is $550 per credit unit for undergraduates. Full-time students carry either 12 or 15 units per semester. There is a nonrefundable $140 registration fee—$100 is applicable toward tuition. Lab fees run from $25 to $400 per semester, depending on the class. Tuition and fees are subject to change at any time. Art supplies can run from $250 to $500 per semester, depending on the major. The Academy has most of the expensive technical equipment available for students to borrow or use in a lab.

The Academy of Art University operates more than ten campus housing facilities within the city. Several housing options are offered, and costs vary from $6600 to $10,000 per academic year (fall and spring semesters). For further information, students may contact the Academy Housing Office directly at 415-263-7727 or via e-mail at housing@academyart.edu.

Financial Aid

The Academy offers financial aid packages consisting of grants, loans, and work-study to eligible students with a demonstrated need. Low-interest loans are available to all eligible students, regardless of need. As financial aid programs, procedures, and eligibility requirements change frequently, applicants should contact the Financial Aid Office for current requirements at the address or phone number listed below.

Faculty

The Academy averages nearly 500 faculty members each semester, most of whom are full-time art and design professionals and part-time teachers. The student-teacher ratio for undergraduate classes averages 15:1.

Student Government

Although there is no formal student government, each department has between 2 and 3 student representatives who meet with the president as needed throughout the semester to discuss any student issues.

Admission Requirements

Applicants for the B.F.A. program must have a high school diploma or GED equivalent. There is no portfolio requirement for the A.A. and B.F.A. programs. International students take a written and speech test to determine which ESL classes may have to be completed. Most ESL classes can be taken in conjunction with art and design classes. All foundations classes offer specialized ESL sections with instructors trained for language assistance. The application fee is $100 for undergraduates. A $500 tuition deposit applies to international applicants.

Application and Information

Students may apply to enter the Academy at the beginning of the spring, fall, or summer semesters. Information in this profile is subject to change. Students should contact the Academy of Art University for current information or visit its Web site, which is listed below.

For further information and a catalog, students may contact:

Prospective Student Services
Academy of Art University
79 New Montgomery Street
San Francisco, California 94105
Telephone: 415-274-2222
800-544-ARTS (2787) (toll-free)
Fax: 415-263-4130
World Wide Web: http://academyart.edu

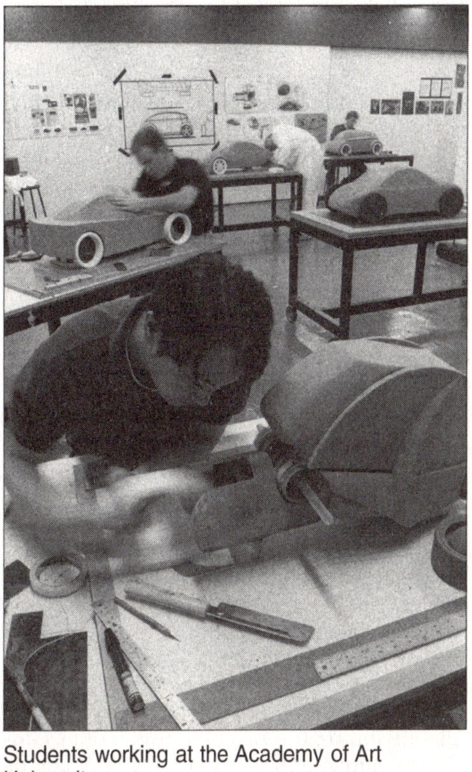

Students working at the Academy of Art University.

ALASKA PACIFIC UNIVERSITY

ANCHORAGE, ALASKA

The University

Alaska Pacific University (APU) believes that how a student learns is as important as what a student learns. Alaska Pacific University employs an active model of learning that transcends the traditional classroom and the conventional format of lecture and examination. APU students—through projects, self-directed study, collaborative study, internships, research, field study, and study abroad—are prepared for leadership and self-direction in their careers, professions, or graduate school. All undergraduate students are involved in internships and project-based learning from the first year forward, a process that culminates in each student's senior project. Upon graduation, every APU student has not only learned, but also has demonstrated the ability to apply what has been learned in the real world.

APU's 284 undergraduate students currently represent thirty-four states and three countries. Minority students make up a growing portion of APU's undergraduate enrollment, which is strengthened by close working relationships between native Alaskan communities and the University. Small classes; lively interaction among students, faculty members, and staff members; and personal academic advising are special benefits of the Alaska Pacific experience. There are 102 men and 182 women currently enrolled in undergraduate programs at APU. APU is proud of its 10:1 student-faculty ratio, and that 99 percent of classes consist of less than 20 students. Class size is kept deliberately small to maintain Alaska Pacific's commitment to individualized learning and the freedom necessary for its students to create an expressive and meaningful relationship with their academic interests.

All freshmen are required to live on campus during their first year. APU's residence halls are centrally located, offering breathtaking views of the Chugach mountains and convenient access to the dining facility, sports center, and classes. The residence halls offer 1-, 2-, and 3-bedroom suites, while upperclassmen and graduate students have the opportunity to live in alternative housing on campus.

Alaska Pacific University has a world-class Nordic ski team that trains in Alaska and competes in national and international events. The Nordic ski team has a summer Nordic ski facility on Eagle Glacier, where the American Olympic Team trains, along with other world-class skiers. Downhill skiers and snowboarders take advantage of two major ski resorts, each within an hour's drive of the campus, offering some of the most challenging, exciting, and varied ski conditions in the world.

Alaska Pacific students are encouraged to take a high degree of initiative in organizing and participating in campus activities. Extracurricular activities range from intramural club sports such as ice-skating, snowshoe softball, volleyball, Nordic skiing, and basketball to participation in the various student government–sponsored activities such as the student newspaper and yearbook. APU offers a wide variety of programs for all ability levels, including the use of a new indoor climbing wall, kayaking, ice climbing, and weekend camping and hiking trips. Students are also encouraged to take advantage of the extensive collection of recreational equipment offered through the Moseley Sports Center, including, but not limited to, backpacks, tents, sleeping bags, kayaks, canoes, skis, and snowshoes.

Graduate programs include the Master of Arts in Teaching (M.A.T., K–8), Master of Business Administration (M.B.A.), M.B.A. in telecommunications management, M.B.A. in global financial management, Master of Arts, Master of Science in Counseling Psychology, and the Master of Science in Environmental Science.

Location

Alaska Pacific University is located on a 170-acre campus in suburban Anchorage. It is unquestionably one of the most beautiful campuses in the United States. Expansive lawns, woods, and University Lake frame nearly 3 miles of campus trails that lead bikers, hikers, in-line skaters, skiers, and runners into an extensive regional trail system that stretches from the ocean waters of Cook Inlet throughout the city and into the mountains to the east. The campus is a world unto itself, with no through roads or traffic; it has an atmosphere appropriate to the dynamic, student-centered, personal style of education for which APU is known.

Anchorage is an outdoor enthusiast's dream. In spring and summer, opportunities for fishing, hiking, mountain climbing, biking, sea kayaking, and camping abound. Winter sports activities include downhill and cross-country skiing, hockey, broomball, and sled-dog racing.

Anchorage's resident population has a strong interest in arts and entertainment. Cultural facilities and organizations in the Anchorage community include the Anchorage Museum of History and Art, the Alaskan Center for the Performing Arts, the Anchorage Symphony Orchestra, the Anchorage Concert Association, and the Anchorage Opera. APU's Grant Hall Theatre is the scene of a variety of student-sponsored and local productions, concerts, and lectures. With a population of 263,000, Anchorage offers a multitude of malls, cafés, clubs, and restaurants.

Majors and Degrees

Alaska Pacific University offers the Bachelor of Arts degree with majors in business administration, counseling and psychological studies, education (with K–8 certification), environmental science, environmental policy and planning, liberal studies, marine biology, and outdoor studies.

Academic Programs

Alaska Pacific University's undergraduate curriculum is designed to integrate a comprehensive background in the liberal arts and in-depth study in their major, a chosen career discipline. APU structures its classes around its active, hands-on learning philosophy. The curriculum emphasizes personal growth through student-centered, experiential education using Alaska, the Arctic, the Pacific Rim, and study abroad as active laboratories for learning.

APU focuses on developing student leadership skills for active service to society by encouraging openness to positive change, innovation, and individual initiative. Central to the philosophy of education at APU is the block-and-session academic calendar. In addition to two traditional sessions, three times per year students may take a block class—a one-month intensive course allowing students to focus entirely on a specific subject. Block courses enable students and faculty members to travel together to different parts of Alaska and the world and also to pursue internships and self-directed studies. Block courses regularly travel to such locations as rural Alaska, Russia, England, Italy, Costa Rica, Mexico, and the Pacific Rim.

Academic Facilities

The Consortium Library serves University students and faculty members. It is operated through an agreement between APU and the University of Alaska, Anchorage. Centrally located, the library contains more than 384,000 bound volumes, including original government documents, sheet music, nonprint media, and a special Alaskana collection. The Academic Support Center located in Atwood Center has forty-two computers no more than 1½ years old and offers Internet access and e-mail accounts for all APU students. The Atwood Center also contains an excellent climbing wall, exercise room, ski team facilities, bookstore, art center, and photo lab along with the cafeteria and two residence halls; Grant Hall houses the community theater, coffee shop, art gallery, numerous faculty offices, and classrooms; the Carr-Gottstein Building features seminar and conference rooms, lecture halls, a computer lab, and an art exhibition area.

Costs

Undergraduate tuition for 2003–04 was $17,200 for all students. Room and board charges were $6000 per year. The year's activity fees for full-time students were $110, and books and miscellaneous supplies were estimated at $1000. Incoming freshmen are guaranteed no tuition increases for up to five years; transfer students receive the same guarantee, prorated.

Financial Aid

The primary purpose of student financial assistance at Alaska Pacific University is to provide financial resources to students who would otherwise be unable to pursue their educational goals. Most assistance is available on the basis of demonstrated need, although some funds are specifically allocated for the recognition of academic excellence and special talents. While the primary responsibility for financing their education rests with the student and his or her family, APU supplements their efforts with aid in the form of grants, loans, work opportunities, and scholarships. In order to be considered for assistance, students are required to submit the Free Application for Federal Student Aid (FAFSA). APU's federal school code is #001061. Funds are also available for international students.

Faculty

Alaska Pacific University is a teaching university, not a research university. Members of the full-time faculty are selected for their teaching abilities and are encouraged to involve their students in their research and professional activities. Sixty-six percent hold terminal degrees in their fields, and many are in demand as consultants in areas such as international business, environmental quality, telecommunications, and multicultural education. The University's faculty-student ratio of 1:10 allows frequent and meaningful faculty-student interaction, resulting in a learning environment of the highest quality.

Student Government

The Associated Students of Alaska Pacific University (ASAPU) is the student-elected governance responsible for campus leadership. ASAPU initiates and sponsors many student activities, including student orientation events, student banquets, sports events, cultural activities, special awards, and student assemblies. All campus clubs and organizations work through ASAPU for formal recognition and funding. Student representatives sit on most major University committees and task forces.

Admission Requirements

In admitting students, Alaska Pacific University considers grade point average, SAT or ACT scores, essays, letters of recommendation, and extracurricular activities. In general, APU recognizes that some students may flourish for the first time within APU's distinctive approach to education. APU welcomes diversity, uniqueness, and personal integrity. To apply, a candidate for freshman admission must submit an application for admission, two letters of recommendation, a personal essay, official high school transcripts, SAT or ACT scores, and a $25 application fee. Transfer applicants must submit an application for admission, transcripts from all colleges or universities they have attended, a personal essay, and a $25 application fee. International students must meet all of the above requirements, as well as submit evidence of financial support and obtain a minimum of 550 on the pen-and-paper TOEFL or 213 on the computerized version.

Application and Information

Applications for fall should be received by February 1. Thereafter, admission decisions are made on a rolling basis; however, competition for a space in each class intensifies following each application deadline.

All inquiries and application material should be directed to:

Office of Admission
Alaska Pacific University
4101 University Drive
Anchorage, Alaska 99508-4672
Telephone: 907-564-8248
800-252-7528 (toll-free)
E-mail: admissions@alaskapacific.edu
World Wide Web: http://www.alaskapacific.edu

Students gathered at the entrance to APU's campus.

THE ART INSTITUTE OF PHOENIX

PHOENIX, ARIZONA

The Art Institute of Phoenix

The Institute

The Art Institute of Phoenix was established in 1995 as a private postsecondary school and is accredited by the Accrediting Council for Independent Colleges and Schools (ACICS). The mission of the Art Institute of Phoenix is to accomplish its vision by providing employers with high-quality, skilled graduates prepared by an experienced faculty using market-driven curricula.

At the Art Institute of Phoenix, students learn how to use program-specific technology to bring their creative career goals to life. When they graduate, they have the specialized skills and competencies employers seek.

As of fall 2003, there were 1,216 students attending the school seeking Bachelor of Arts (B.A.) and Associate of Applied Science (A.A.S.) degrees or diplomas. There are 747 men and 469 women enrolled, of whom 1,045 are full-time and 171 are part-time students. The average class size is 20 students, and the faculty-student ratio is 1:20.

The Art Institute of Phoenix was recognized by the Arizona Private School Association as the "2001–2002 Outstanding School of the Year."

Location

The Art Institute of Phoenix is located in one of the fastest-growing metropolitan areas of the country. Located in the middle of the state of Arizona and in the heart of the beautiful Sonoran Desert, Phoenix is the gateway to cool pine forests, the red rock towers of Sedona, and nature's greatest wonder, the Grand Canyon. The nation's fifth-largest city, Phoenix offers sun-filled days and nightlife that ranges from top comedy and music clubs to such cultural icons as the Phoenix Art Museum and the Phoenix Symphony Orchestra. Professional sports teams include the Diamondbacks, Suns, Arizona Cardinals, and Coyotes.

Majors and Degrees

The Art Institute of Phoenix offers programs in four areas: animation, culinary arts, design, and media arts. The specific degree programs and specializations within those programs include an A.A.S. in culinary arts and a B.A. in advertising, digital media production, fashion marketing, game art and design, graphic design, interior design, media arts and animation, multimedia and Web design, and visual effects and motion graphics. Diplomas can be earned in baking and pastry and in the art of cooking. These programs are offered on a year-round basis, enabling students to work continually toward their degrees. The faculty members, many of whom are working professionals, strengthen students' skills and cultivate their talents through well-designed curricula.

Each program of study has its own technology needs. The media arts and animation program relies heavily on PC-platform computers and software used to produce 3-D animation, 2-D ink-and-paint, digital paint, and compositing effects. Game art and design students use much of the same equipment as the media arts and animation students, but with additional tools that allow game prototyping and simulations. Graphic design students have access to Macintosh and PC platforms to produce camera-ready and final copies of design projects. Interior design students work with PC-based computers and high-quality software to produce their design plans and renderings. Multimedia and Web design students concentrate on designing and producing interactive disks that may be educational, commercial, or entertaining in nature. Digital media production students use program-specific technologies to create, develop, and deliver content, combining traditional production techniques with digital tools as they prepare for a career where creativity and technology come face to face with the future.

The visual effects and motion graphics program offers students the opportunity to acquire skills in a specialization that focuses on communication arts for film, television, and the Web. By combining graphic design, filmmaking, animation, and sound, graduates of the program are qualified to create attention-grabbing visuals that inform and entertain.

Academic Programs

Programs range from 27 to 186 credit hours. Nine programs lead to the Bachelor of Arts degree. In the digital media production program, students learn to combine traditional production techniques with the latest digital tools to shoot, edit, refine sound, and develop special effects. In game art and design, the curriculum includes modeling (creating a character or object), scene and set design, motion capture, animation, texture mapping, and more; students become skilled in drawing, visualizing, and using color. In the graphic design program, students learn to package communication and commerce as art in order to enhance a company's image or to sell ideas, products, and services by coupling graphic design with advertising copy and concepts. Interior design students gain a strong foundation in the basics, including drawing, perspective, proportion, and color, and they use computer-aided drawing (CAD) to help plan residential and commercial spaces. As computer animators in the media arts and animation program, students work in 3-D to create characters with the subtleties and realistic motion of everyday life, learning to artfully blend creative vision with technology. Multimedia system and Web page design, video, animation, and scripting are just some of the key elements covered in the multimedia and Web design program's curriculum. Students in the visual effects and motion graphics program learn to deal with the interrelated fields of design, layering, and movement of digital elements and imagery to enhance or tell a visual story. Three culinary arts programs are offered. Both the art of cooking program and the baking and pastry program lead to a diploma; the culinary arts program culminates with an A.A.S. degree. The programs begin with the basics, from knife skills and kitchen procedures to nutrition, speed and timing, and presentation. Building on those basics, students progress to more advanced areas, such as baking and pastry, garde-manger (cold kitchen), international and American cuisine, à la carte, and dining room operations.

Academic Facilities

The Art Institute of Phoenix is located in a four-story building in the northwest corner of Phoenix, and the students can enjoy scenic mountain views from many of its large picture windows. With the sun streaming into the classrooms and computer laboratories, student creativity flows easily. Classroom and computer laboratory facilities are clean and well maintained, with a full-time technology manager located on-site. The culinary arts kitchens are spacious and filled with commercial equipment that students will work with in the real world. Digital media production students have a full television studio and control room at their command, along with editing suites to complete their work.

The Art Institute of Phoenix provides Internet access to its students throughout the school. Students can also avail themselves of multiple computer labs, a Learning Resource Center, student supply store, Career Services Center, and student lounge. Students can join student organizations and clubs and make friends with classmates who are also refining their creative talents.

Costs

Tuition is $340 per credit hour. School-sponsored housing costs are in addition to tuition. Through a special arrangement with select apartment complexes close to the school, the Art Institute of Phoenix can offer students the opportunity to live in furnished apartments with rent that includes the utilities. Students share these apartments with others studying at the Art Institute of Phoenix, and they are located just 1 mile from the school.

Financial Aid

Financial assistance is available for those who qualify. The Art Institute of Phoenix participates in federal, state, and other financial aid programs. Financial aid is divided into three general categories: gift aid, loans, and work-study. Gift aid includes grants, scholarships, and other benefits that do not have to be repaid. Loans need to be repaid, but repayment can usually be delayed until several months after the student leaves school. The Art Institute of Phoenix participates in the Federal Work-Study Program and also assists students in finding part-time jobs in the community.

Faculty

The Art Institute of Phoenix offers personal attention from knowledgeable, professional instructors. Many of the faculty members are working professionals who bring practical knowledge and real-world experience to the classroom. The Art Institute of Phoenix faculty members are available for student appointments and to discuss academic issues. They offer tutoring to those students in need of extra help.

Student Government

The President's Club is a school organization that promotes the philosophy of "students helping students." Those students selected assist new students with adjusting to life in Phoenix and at the Art Institute of Phoenix, as well as to school activities. Criteria for selection are a GPA of 3.0 or greater at the Art Institute of Phoenix, good attendance, completion of at least one full quarter, a desire to assist other students, responsible behavior, and being in good academic standing at the Art Institute of Phoenix.

Admission Requirements

An Assistant Director of Admissions is usually one of the first people prospective students speak with at the Art Institute of Phoenix. This person meets with students to talk about their future goals and assists them in navigating the admissions process. The Admissions Office sets up an appointment for a tour. For admission to the Art Institute of Phoenix, students are evaluated on the basis of previous education, background, and a demonstrated interest in one of the programs. Portfolios are encouraged but not required.

As part of the application process, applicants are required to independently conceive and write an essay of approximately 150 words stating how their education at the Art Institute of Phoenix will help them to attain their career goals. Successful admission into the Art Institute of Phoenix and a satisfactory program start is dependent on the level of accomplishment exhibited in the essay, all grade point averages as evidenced through transcript evaluation, an evaluation of GED scores, a review of the results of any nationally based exams (preferred but not required) such as the SAT I or ACT, and a personal interview with an Assistant Director of Admissions.

The Art Institute of Phoenix programs are technical in nature; therefore, international students are required to demonstrate proficiency in the English language and satisfy all admissions requirements and procedures. The English-language requirement is met when an applicant has submitted proof of a score of 480 or better on the TOEFL or has completed level 108 at an ESL Language Center or a recognized equivalent.

Application and Information

To arrange an interview or obtain more information, prospective students should contact:

The Art Institute of Phoenix
2233 West Dunlap Avenue
Phoenix, Arizona 85021
Telephone: 602-678-4300
800-474-2479 (toll-free)
World Wide Web: http://www.aipx.edu

The Art Institute of Phoenix.

CHAMINADE UNIVERSITY OF HONOLULU

HONOLULU, HAWAII

The University

Chaminade University of Honolulu, a private, coeducational institution, was established in 1955 by the Society of Mary (Marianists). Named after Father William Joseph Chaminade, a French Catholic priest who ministered to his people during the late eighteenth and early nineteenth centuries and who founded the Society in 1817, the University today continues the Marianist mission of educating leaders through faith and reason. To achieve this mission, Chaminade forms a community encompassing people from diverse cultural origins, both traditional and nontraditional, who hold a variety of religious beliefs. The University encourages learning through cooperation, self-discipline, caring, and mutual respect while offering individualized attention that promotes personal and intellectual growth. A major goal of the University is to educate and train students for leadership both within Chaminade and in communities beyond the campus. The University advocates a personal concern for social justice, ethics, responsibility, and service to the community and exerts institutional leadership by promoting Chaminade's ideals outside the University community.

At any one time, 2,600 to 2,800 students are enrolled in a range of daytime and evening classes. Of this number, approximately 1,100 are full-time undergraduates, 1,200 are part-time undergraduates enrolled in the evening program, and 500 are graduate students. Nearly 60 percent of the full-time undergraduates are from Hawaii, 24 percent are from the mainland, 13 percent are from U.S. trust territories, and 3 percent are from other countries. Thirty-four states and thirty-one countries are represented in the student body.

Clubs and associations offer all Chaminade students a chance to pursue interests and extend their activities beyond the classroom. Student publications include the *Aulama,* a literary and art magazine; the *Silverword,* the monthly student newspaper; and *Ahinahina,* the Chaminade yearbook. Chaminade also sponsors chapters of Delta Epsilon Sigma, the national scholastic honor society for students at colleges and universities with a Catholic tradition; Phi Alpha Theta, the history national honor society; Delta Mu Delta, a national honor society in business administration; Sigma Tau Delta, the national English honor society; Pi Sigma Alpha, a national honor society in political science, and Alpha Phi Sigma, a national honor society for criminal justice.

Intercollegiate athletic teams are currently sponsored in men's basketball and water polo, women's softball and volleyball, and men's and women's cross-country and tennis. Intramural competitive and noncompetitive sports and recreation programs are open to all students, faculty and staff members, and alumni.

Chaminade University of Honolulu is accredited by the Accrediting Commission for Senior Colleges and Universities of the Western Association of Schools and Colleges. The University also has two sister universities on the mainland: the University of Dayton in Dayton, Ohio, and St. Mary's University in San Antonio, Texas.

Chaminade offers graduate degrees in business administration (M.B.A.), counseling psychology (M.S.C.P.), criminal justice administration (M.S.C.J.A.), education (M.Ed.), pastoral leadership (M.A.P.L.), and public administration (M.P.A.).

Location

Honolulu, a multicultural community, is enriched by a great diversity of ethnic activities and traditions. Chaminade is located on a hillside with a spectacular view sweeping across Waikiki to downtown Honolulu, from Diamond Head to the blue Pacific Ocean. This idyllic site is only minutes from the city, cultural activities, and the beach. The University also operates ten off-campus sites, primarily at military installations on the island of Oahu.

Majors and Degrees

The University offers twenty-one major programs of study at the undergraduate level as well as two associate degree programs. The Bachelor of Arts (B.A.) degree is offered in biology, chemistry, communication, English, historical and political studies, humanities, international studies, management, philosophy, psychology, religious studies, and social studies; the Bachelor of Fine Arts (B.F.A.) degree is offered in interior design; and the Bachelor of Science (B.S.) degree is offered in accounting, behavioral sciences, biology, computer information systems, criminal justice, early childhood education, elementary education, environmental studies, and forensic science. The Associate in Arts (A.A.) degree is offered in management; the Associate in Science (A.S.) degree is offered in computer science and criminal justice.

Preprofessional programs are offered in law, health sciences, nursing, and engineering.

Students may elect to pursue a minor program in most major programs as well as in anthropology, history, physics, political science, sociology, and studio art.

Academic Programs

The core curriculum at Chaminade is in liberal arts. The University is committed to a broad liberal education for its students and believes that such an education provides a basis for long-term personal growth, a foundation for a career that may encounter job changes, and a background that allows students to rise to leadership positions in their chosen fields and communities. Through undergraduate programs based on the liberal arts tradition, Chaminade seeks to heighten cultural awareness. Coupled with understanding diverse methods of inquiry and participation in Chaminade's multicultural interdependent community, cultural awareness prepares all students for lifelong learning—about themselves, each other, and the world in which they live.

Undergraduate study is structured into four parts: practice in basic skills, liberal arts course work that provides a general education, intensive study in a chosen field of concentration (the major), and elective courses outside the major field to complement general and specialized knowledge. All baccalaureate degrees require a minimum of 124 credit hours of course work with a minimum of 45 hours in upper-division courses. Within these guidelines, the student selects a program of study appropriate to personal needs and interests. All appropriate courses at Chaminade require writing assignments from students. Upper-division courses in most fields train students to write in the style and format appropriate to the discipline.

In all fields of study at Chaminade, students are encouraged to apply their academic experience to on-the-job practice for academic credit. Faculty members may ask students to work with a specific organization, or students may develop internship possibilities on their own. Interns usually have at least junior-level standing, but in special cases sophomores are considered. Depending on the organization with which they work, students may or may not receive a salary for their internship experience.

The First Year Experience Seminar supports students in their transition from high school to college. The program provides an orientation to University functions and resources. This course also helps freshmen adjust to the University, gain a better understanding of the learning process and develop critical-thinking skills and provides a support group for students by examining problems that are common to the freshman experience.

Chaminade cooperates with two major programs that enable students to receive college credit prior to admission. These two programs, Advanced Placement and College-Level Examination Program, are sponsored by the College Board.

Off-Campus Programs

In 1990, Chaminade University and its sister universities signed an agreement through which any student at any of the three universities can enroll for their junior year at any of the other campuses. Full credit is given by Chaminade for approved courses taken at either university. Chaminade also encourages students to pursue part of their undergraduate education in another country.

Academic Facilities

Located in Henry Hall, Sullivan Library occupies three floors and houses a collection of approximately 74,000 volumes and 874 periodicals. Special collections include the Oceania Collection, the Catholic Authors Collection, the Julius J. Nodel Judaica Collection, and the David L. Carlson Japan Collection. Services offered include reference consultation, computerized information retrieval, and instruction in library use. Also in Henry Hall, the Computer Center provides students and faculty members with a variety of microcomputers, software programs, and reference materials for instruction, word processing, and programming. The multipurpose Audio Visual Media Resource Center provides instructional media technology support to all divisions of the University, student activities, special programs, and other events. The center is also a resource for films, slides, records, and videotapes.

Costs

Full-time undergraduate tuition for 2004–05 is $6925 per semester. Part-time undergraduate tuition is $462 per semester hour. Housing costs per semester range from $1468 to $2508, depending upon accommodations. Meal plans range from $1400 to $1960 per semester, depending upon the plan chosen. Various other fees for independent/individualized directed studies, parking, labs, and studios are also charged. The tuition charged by Chaminade University does not cover the total cost of instruction for each student. Gifts and grants are used to balance the difference. Tuition and fees must be paid at or prior to the time of registration.

Financial Aid

Those with a high school GPA between 3.5 and 4.0 are eligible for a $6000 yearly scholarship; between 3.0 and 3.49, a $5000 yearly scholarship; between 2.5 and 2.99, a $4500 yearly grant; and between 2.25 to 2.49, a $3000 yearly Father Chaminade Grant. The Hawaii Grant for new full-time day session students from Hawaii is $1500 per semester. Scholarships and grants, available to regular full-time undergraduate students, are renewable for four years and are awarded without regard to financial need. Students may obtain only one of the Chaminade scholarships or grants. When a first member of a family pays full-time day undergraduate tuition, additional members who are concurrently enrolled in the day undergraduate program may receive a tuition discount of 20 percent.

Faculty

The University is dedicated to teaching and to building the leadership skills of its students, and its major strengths lie in its relatively small size and its talented faculty. Classes are small, allowing faculty members to provide a significant amount of individual and small-group attention. Classes are taught by professors or professionals in their fields, not graduate students.

Student Government

The Chaminade University Student Association is the official representative of the student body. Each full-time student of Chaminade becomes a member upon payment of fees. Membership is open to all students at all instructional sites. The Senate, chaired by the student body president and composed of elected representatives, focuses on improving the quality of undergraduate student life and represents the needs, interests, and concerns of its constituents.

The Dean of Students, through the Assistant Dean of Students, initiates all disciplinary action. The committee is composed of administrators, faculty and staff members, and students. Chaminade does not condone activities on campus that violate state or federal regulations, including illegal possession of drugs or the illegal consumption of alcoholic beverages. Students found to be in violation of these regulations are subject to immediate disciplinary action.

Admission Requirements

Applications for admission are reviewed for specific majors or, when applicable, for "undecided" status. Chaminade considers several factors when assessing students' preparation for a selected area of study: grades throughout high school, selection of courses in preparation for college, scores from either the SAT I or ACT, and an essay that provides information about the applicant's character and record of leadership and service.

Application and Information

Chaminade University has a rolling admission process. As soon as all required information is received by the Admission Office, the application is reviewed by an application committee. Students are notified of the committee's decision usually within three to four weeks. Applications are accepted throughout the year. A $50 fee is payable upon application. Web site applications are also available for a $25 fee. All students desiring housing must file an application along with a $300 deposit applicable to the total cost per semester. Space and placement are not guaranteed without this deposit. A housing damage deposit of $100 is also required. Evidence of health insurance coverage from a U.S. insurer is required of all dormitory residents and international students.

To ensure full consideration for scholarships or grants, students are urged to complete the appropriate application by April 1. Award notices are mailed by April 30. For more information and application materials, students should contact:

Admission Office
Chaminade University
3140 Waialae Avenue
Honolulu, Hawaii 96816

Telephone: 808-735-4735
800-735-3733 (toll-free)
Fax: 808-739-4647
E-mail: admissions@chaminade.edu
World Wide Web: http://www.chaminade.edu

CHAPMAN UNIVERSITY

ORANGE, CALIFORNIA

The University

During its 142-year history, Chapman has evolved from a small, traditional liberal arts college that was founded in 1861 by members of the First Christian Church (Disciples of Christ) into a midsize comprehensive liberal arts and sciences university that is distinguished for its nationally recognized programs in film and television production, business and economics, music, education, communication arts, and the natural and applied sciences. The mission of Chapman University is to provide personalized education of distinction that leads to inquiring, ethical, and productive lives as global citizens.

Chapman's parklike, ivy-covered, and tree-lined campus features a blending of fully refurbished historic structures with the newest in state-of-the-art Internet- and satellite-connected learning environments. Five residence halls and six on-campus apartment buildings are conveniently located on the edge of the campus. Also recently completed have been a five-story parking structure, the 100,000-square-foot School of Law facility, and Liberty Plaza, which features a large section of the Berlin Wall.

Chapman University's academic structure includes the Wilkinson College of Letters and Sciences, the Argyros School of Business and Economics, the School of Communication Arts, the School of Education, the School of Film and Television, the School of Music, and the School of Law. Programs of distinction include the A. Gary Anderson Center for Economic Research, which is internationally recognized for econometric forecasting; the nationally recognized School of Film and Television; and the ABA-accredited School of Law. Other nationally accredited programs include the School of Business and Economics, which is accredited by AACSB International–The Association to Advance Collegiate Schools of Business; the IFT-accredited program in food science and nutrition; the NASM-accredited School of Music; and the APTA-accredited graduate program in physical therapy. Chapman was also recently recognized by the Templeton Foundation as one of only 100 colleges nationally to be designated as a Templeton Foundation "Character-Building College."

In addition to approximately 4,800 undergraduate, graduate, and professional school students enrolled on the campus in Orange, Chapman also enrolls more than 5,000 undergraduate and graduate students annually through its Chapman University College and network of thirty University College centers that are located in California and Washington.

The University is electric, involving, and outdoor-oriented. In addition to taking advantage of the obvious benefits associated with the southern California climate, Chapman students enjoy a dynamic student activities program. Although predominantly from California, Chapman students come from forty different states; in addition, approximately 10 percent of its students come from thirty-four other countries. Over the past five years, Chapman students have been named Truman Scholars, Coro Fellows, *USA Today* All-USA College Academic Team members, NCAA All-Americans, and NCAA academic all-Americans. Chapman's long and distinguished heritage in intercollegiate sports includes five NCAA national championships in baseball, tennis, and softball. Chapman competes as an independent in the NCAA Division III level and fields teams in baseball, basketball (m/w), crew (m/w), cross-country (m/w), football, golf, lacrosse, soccer (m/w), softball, swimming (w), tennis (m/w), track and field (w), volleyball (w), and water polo (m/w). Approximately 20 percent of Chapman's student body participates in intercollegiate athletics, and last year, 4 student-athletes were honored as all-Americans and 14 as academic all-Americans.

More than seventy clubs and organizations are available, many with commitments to a wide range of community service efforts. Chapman's Greek system includes five nationally chartered fraternities and sororities. A comprehensive intramural sports program involves a myriad of sports activities for all campus community members throughout the school year. On-campus intercollegiate athletic events, music, art, and theater productions provide students with numerous ongoing extracurricular activity options. Chapman's proximity to area recreational and cultural opportunities allows Chapman students to enjoy the essence of what makes Orange County's south coast area an enviable environment in which to live and learn.

Prominent Chapman alumni include the Honorable Loretta Sanchez ('88), member of Congress; the Honorable David Bonior ('85), member of Congress and current House Minority Whip; television and film producer John Copeland ('73); UCLA head basketball coach Steve Lavin ('88); former San Diego Padre stars Tim Flannery ('80) and Randy Jones ('72); current U.S. ambassador to Spain/philanthropist George L. Argyros ('65), and star of Broadway's *Showboat*, Michael Bell ('68).

Location

Orange County, California, was recently rated by *Places Rated Almanac* as "the #1 place to live in North America," citing superior climate, cultural, recreational, educational, and career-entree opportunities. Los Angeles is 35 miles to the north, and San Diego is 80 miles to the south. Nearby entertainment venues include Disneyland, Knott's Berry Farm, the Orange County Performing Arts Center, major-league baseball, and hockey. Pristine West Coast beaches are less than 10 miles from the campus, and seasonal snow skiing is 90 minutes away. The average year-round temperature on campus is 71 degrees Fahrenheit, and the air is normally smog-free, due to a daily prevailing sea breeze from nearby southwest-facing beaches.

Majors and Degrees

Chapman awards the Bachelor of Arts degree in the fields of art, biology, chemistry, communications, dance, economics, English and comparative literature, film and television, French, health science, history, international studies, liberal studies (elementary education), movement and exercise science, music, peace studies, philosophy, political science, psychology, religion, social science, sociology, Spanish, and theater. The Bachelor of Fine Arts degree is conferred in art, dance, film and television, and theater. The Bachelor of Science degree is offered in accounting, applied mathematics, biology, business administration, chemistry, computer information systems, computer science, environmental science, food science and nutrition, health science, movement and exercise science, and natural science. The Bachelor of Music degree is granted in composition, conducting, music education (vocal and instrumental), music performance (vocal and instrumental), and music therapy.

Preprofessional or prevocational programs are offered in dentistry, law, medicine, physical therapy, social service, teaching, theology, and veterinary medicine.

Academic Programs

The requirements for graduation are commensurate with the liberal arts philosophy of education maintained by Chapman. The program of studies is designed to ensure a breadth of subject matter selection in the liberal arts as well as depth of preparation in the student's major field. The minimum graduation requirements include successful completion (C average) of 124 semester credits, of which 36 must be earned in the upper division. Competence in reading, written communication, oral communication, computation, and library usage is required of all students. Chapman's general education sequence provides a broad introduction to the humanities, social sciences, and natural sciences. Students select general education classes with the guidance of their faculty adviser. A maximum of 32 credits may be gained through Advanced Placement (AP), College-Level Examination Program (CLEP), and departmental examinations.

Chapman's academic year operates on a 4-1-4 modified semester system. January is reserved for an optional Interterm, allowing a period for experimental, short-term course work or individual study.

Ample opportunities are available for alternative learning experiences. Internships and cooperative education programs are recommended. Students may also undertake in-depth individual study or research in their major field in conjunction with a faculty member.

Academic Facilities

The 90,000-square-foot Argyros Forum includes the primary campus dining area, conference and classroom facilities, and associated student offices. Bertea Hall is home to the School of Music. Memorial Auditorium seats 1,000 and is listed on the National Register of Historic Places. The Hutton Sports Center includes a 3,000-seat arena, a 5,000-seat outdoor stadium, four championship tennis courts, and training and fitness facilities for the campus and the surrounding community. Currently under construction, the Leatherby Libraries will feature five school-specific libraries in one five-story facility. Newly completed Beckman Hall for business and information technology houses the Argyros School of Business and Economics, including its endowed centers: the A. Gary Anderson Center for Economic Research, the Ralph W. Leatherby Center for Entrepreneurship and Business Ethics, and the Walter Schmid Center for International Business. The School of Communication Arts includes the Guggenheim Art Gallery and the 250-seat repertory-style Waltmar Theatre. The Hashinger Science Center features laboratories for nuclear science, radiation, crystallography, genetics, food science, and physical therapy.

Costs

For the 2003–04 academic year, full-time tuition and fees (including accident and sickness fee, health center fee, and associated student membership fee) were $24,590. Annual room and board averaged $8528. Books were estimated at $700 per year.

Financial Aid

More than 85 percent of Chapman students benefit from some form of financial aid or scholarship assistance. Need-based financial awards include a combination of grants, scholarships, loans, and work-study jobs. Awards are renewable, assuming that students complete the annual application process on time. The family contribution component of an award stays mostly the same annually if the family's financial circumstances remain the same. By using a combination of Chapman's internal resources and federal and state funding, an individual financial aid package can be tailored to meet the student's financial need. Merit and talent scholarship awards, regardless of financial need, round out the types of financial assistance that Chapman offers. Chapman offers an Early Aid Estimator service that gives students an up-front picture of what their prospective aid/scholarship eligibility is, rather than waiting for the postadmission, official aid-awarding period. Students asking for information about Chapman automatically receive the Early Estimator form, along with instructions for completion and submission.

Faculty

The University's faculty is composed of 222 full-time and 288 part-time members, more than 80 percent of whom hold doctoral or other terminal degrees. Their primary commitment is to undergraduate teaching, although most are also actively involved in scholarly research and publication. Many faculty members teach both undergraduate and graduate courses. Teaching assistants or graduate assistants are not used for the instruction of undergraduate classes. Chapman's favorable student-faculty ratio of 16:1 allows extensive interaction between the faculty members and students.

Student Government

Chapman has an associated student government that actively participates in the administration of the University.

Admission Requirements

Admission to Chapman is selective. In 2003, admission was offered to 60 percent of the applicant pool. The University is interested in admitting students whose prior records indicate that they will be successful in a competitive collegiate environment. Freshman applicants are considered for admission based primarily on the nature and sequence of their high school course work, the grade point average achieved, and their results on either the SAT I or ACT examination. Transfer candidates are considered for admission on the basis of their course work and cumulative grade point average earned at other regionally accredited post-secondary institutions.

Application and Information

When applying, candidates are strongly encouraged to visit the campus and meet with a member of the admission staff. Arrangements for an interview and a tour of the campus can be made through the Office of Admission at either of the phone numbers listed below. Freshman applicants can choose between a nonbinding November 30 early action application deadline or the January 31 regular application deadline. Transfer applicants must apply before the March 15 transfer deadline. Prospective freshmen who apply after the January 31 deadline are considered on a space-available basis.

For further information, students should contact:

Michael O. Drummy
Assistant Vice President and Chief Admission Officer
Chapman University
One University Drive
Orange, California 92866
Telephone: 714-997-6711
888-CUAPPLY (toll-free)
Fax: 714-997-6713
E-mail: admit@chapman.edu

CLAREMONT McKENNA COLLEGE

CLAREMONT, CALIFORNIA

The College

Founded in 1946 as the third undergraduate college within the Claremont Consortium, Claremont McKenna College (CMC) occupies a unique place in American higher education. By infusing pragmatic sensibilities into an otherwise traditional liberal arts curriculum, CMC is committed to educating future leaders in business, the professions, and public affairs. Economics, government, and international relations are the most popular among twenty-three majors offered at CMC. The College is especially appropriate for students seeking to pursue careers in law, politics, government, international relations, business, management, and finance.

Claremont McKenna College is one of seven institutions—five undergraduate colleges and two graduate schools—that constitute the Claremont Colleges. The others are Harvey Mudd College, Pitzer College, Pomona College, Scripps College, the Claremont Graduate University, and the Keck Graduate Institute of Applied Life Sciences.

The current undergraduate enrollment at CMC is 1,050 (580 men and 470 women). Fifty-three percent of the student body are out-of-state residents and 5 percent are international. Forty-eight states and thirty countries are represented on campus. Thirty-one percent of the students at CMC are members of ethnic minority groups.

Because 96 percent of CMC students live on campus in coed residence halls and apartments, campus life is vibrant and active. Dorms provide the foundation for social life at CMC; the student-run government often plans field trips, movie nights, barbecues, dinners, and socials for each dorm or apartment group. Intramural athletic teams are typically formed by each residence hall.

One of the more distinctive features on campus is the Athenaeum, a facility that serves as a social, cultural, and academic center. Faculty members often arrange to meet their classes at the Athenaeum for lunch, dinner, and coffee hours. The Athenaeum program features guest speakers on a variety of topics four nights a week throughout the academic year. Other special resources at CMC include a center for religious activities, a bookstore that carries more than 40,000 titles, a professionally staffed counseling and medical center, the Office of Black Student Affairs, the Chicano/Latino Student Affairs Center, and an international center.

Claremont supports a wide variety of cultural events—concerts, plays, lectures, conferences, art exhibits, and films—and the Claremont Colleges cooperate to provide organized extracurricular activities. Although each campus is autonomous, many activities include students from several of the colleges. There are intercollegiate athletics programs, a four-college chorus, a five-college theater program, a five-college weekly newspaper, a five-college orchestra, and a five-college debate team. Five-college parties are also scheduled throughout the year.

Claremont McKenna College, Harvey Mudd College, and Scripps College are associated in a joint program of intercollegiate athletics, physical education, and recreation. Facilities include a football field, a track, a gymnasium (housing two gym floors, a squash court, a Nautilus and weight room, a fitness center, a boxing ring, offices, and locker rooms), a baseball field, a soccer field, a lacrosse field, three swimming pools, eight tennis courts, volleyball courts, intramural fields, and a climbing wall. The sports teams compete in the Southern California Intercollegiate Athletic Conference (SCIAC). The men's teams, known as the Stags, compete in baseball, basketball, cross-country, football, golf, soccer, swimming/diving, tennis, track, volleyball, and water polo. Women's teams, known as the Athenas, compete in basketball, cross-country, lacrosse, soccer, softball, swimming/diving, tennis, track, volleyball, and water polo. The Claremont-Mudd-Scripps intercollegiate athletics program is consistently at the top of the SCIAC All-Sports Championship race.

Location

Claremont McKenna College is in Claremont, California, a suburban community of 34,000 people about 35 miles east of downtown Los Angeles. It is a pleasant town with tree-lined streets and well-tended homes. Other educational resources in Claremont are the School of Theology, the Rancho Santa Ana Botanical Garden, the Blaisdell Institute for Advanced Study in World Cultures and Religions, and the Institute for Antiquity and Christianity.

"The Village," home to attractive restaurants, art galleries, and shops, is only a 10-minute walk from the College. All of the cultural, educational, social, and entertainment centers of greater Los Angeles are nearby, including major art museums, a ranking symphony orchestra, abundant theater productions, and a variety of professional sports teams. Mount Baldy is close by for skiing and hiking, and Pacific Ocean beaches and the Mojave Desert are each only an hour away. The weather throughout the academic year is usually warm, dry, and sunny.

Majors and Degrees

Claremont McKenna College grants the Bachelor of Arts degree in applied biology; biology; chemistry; economics; economics-accounting; the environment, economics, and politics; environmental science; French; German; government; history; international relations; Korean; literature; management-engineering; mathematics; neuroscience; philosophy; philosophy, politics, and economics; physics; psychology; religious studies; science and management; and Spanish.

In addition to these CMC-based majors, cooperative programs with the other Claremont Colleges allow students to major in American studies, art, Asian studies, black studies, Chicano studies, classics, film studies, music, and theater. Sequences, a series of courses related to a subject and selected from different disciplines, are offered in the areas of Asian-American studies, computer science, ethics, leadership, legal studies, and women's studies. Almost half of CMC students opt to pursue dual and double majors and/or to create individualized majors.

Academic Programs

Students must satisfactorily complete thirty-two semester courses, including general education and major requirements, in order to graduate. General education requirements include one course in mathematics, one course in English composition and analysis, two courses in the natural sciences, two courses in the humanities, three courses in the social sciences, and a senior thesis. In addition, students must complete three semesters of a foreign language and a Questions of Civilization course.

Depending on the department, credit or advanced placement, or both, may be granted for college courses taken while in high school. Also, CMC may grant credit for scores of 4 or 5 on Advanced Placement (AP) examinations and for scores of 6 or 7 on higher level International Baccalaureate (I.B.) examinations.

CMC sponsors a joint science program with two other Claremont Colleges, Pitzer and Scripps. The Keck Science Center houses modern laboratories for teaching and research, and a large biological field station is located adjacent to the campus. Virtually all students in the joint science program do independent research, and reports on many student-faculty projects have been published in professional journals.

By intercollegiate agreement, CMC students may take courses not offered at Claremont McKenna at any of the Claremont Colleges. Up to one third of a student's courses may be taken at the other Claremont Colleges.

CMC operates on a semester calendar, beginning the first week in September and ending in mid-May.

Off-Campus Programs

Nearly 50 percent of CMC students elect to study off campus for a semester or a full year. Students may choose from almost 100 programs in thirty-eight countries; CMC's own Washington, D.C., Semester Program; college exchanges with Colby College, Haverford College, Instituto Tecnologico de Mexico, Morehouse College, McGill University (Canada), and Spelman College; and the Semester in Environmental Science at the Marine Biological Laboratory in Woods Hole, Massachusetts.

Academic Facilities

The Claremont Colleges pool their funds to support impressive central resources: libraries with more than 2 million volumes, a center for religious activities, medical and counseling centers, a 2,600-seat concert hall, a 700-seat theater, an Office of Black Student Affairs, and a Chicano/Latino Student Affairs Center.

Eleven research institutes within Claremont McKenna enrich the curriculum, attract distinguished scholars to the College, and give outstanding students research and internship experience and the opportunity to work closely with faculty scholars. The institutes are The Lowe Institute of Political Economy; The Reed Institute for Decision Science; The Keck Center for International and Strategic Studies; The Roberts Environmental Center; The Rose Institute of State and Local Government; The Salvatori Center for the Study of Individual Freedom in the Modern World; The Henry Kravis Leadership Institute; The Gould Center for Humanistic Studies; The Berger Institute on Work, Family, and Children; The Institute for Financial Economics; and The Center for the Study of the Holocaust, Genocide, and Human Rights.

Costs

Tuition for 2003–04 was $27,500. Room and board was $9180. Expenses for 2003–04, including tuition, fees, room and board, and personal expenses, totaled approximately $36,680. Travel expenses vary.

Financial Aid

Financial aid is awarded in the form of grants (nonrepayable gift aid), student loans, and part-time employment. Grants range from $1000 to $31,000 per year and average $25,780; loans for entering freshmen average $3000 per year. The total amount of aid a student is awarded is based on need.

The College offers approximately thirty McKenna Achievement Awards to members of each entering freshman class. These awards are valued at $5000 each and are renewable for each of the four years, provided the student earns at least a B average. To be considered for one of these awards, a student usually must rank among the top 5 percent in his or her high school class and earn a score of more than 690 on both the mathematical and verbal portions of the SAT I. Candidates must also have excellent school recommendations and strong extracurricular involvement, including leadership, and must have filed a completed application by December 20.

Faculty

CMC's faculty members are teacher-scholars who are dedicated to teaching undergraduates and to making contributions to their disciplines. Except in fields in which the doctorate is not the terminal degree, all tenured faculty members have doctorates. The student-faculty ratio is 8:1, and the average class size is 19.

Student Government

Officers of the Associated Students of Claremont McKenna College are elected each spring and serve a one-year term. Each residence hall is self-governing, and students sit on virtually all faculty, trustee, and staff committees. CMC has a history of active and responsible participation in student government.

Admission Requirements

College admission standards place CMC in the "highly selective" category. Eighty-three percent of the 2003 freshmen were in the top tenth of their high school graduating class; 94 percent were in the top fifth. The middle 50 percent of the class had SAT I math and verbal scores ranging from 660 to 740. CMC strives to enroll a class that is academically strong but also places a strong emphasis on extracurricular involvement, community participation, and leadership potential. Admission to CMC is need blind.

Early decision and deferred entrance are options. Students are strongly encouraged to visit the campus.

Applicants are expected to furnish transcripts of all academic work in high school and college; a recommendation from a guidance counselor, principal, or headmaster; recommendations from 2 academic course teachers; two essays; and scores on either the SAT I or ACT. Students whose first language is not English are strongly encouraged to take the Test of English as a Foreign Language (TOEFL).

Application and Information

Application materials must be received by November 15 or January 2 from applicants seeking early decision, November 15 for midyear entrance, and January 2 for those seeking entrance in the fall. CMC accepts only the Common Application and asks applicants to also complete a supplement to the Common Application.

Further information is available from:

Richard C. Vos, Vice President and
Dean of Admission and Financial Aid
Claremont McKenna College
890 Columbia Avenue
Claremont, California 91711-6425
Telephone: 909-621-8088
E-mail: admission@claremontmckenna.edu
World Wide Web: http://www.claremontmckenna.edu

View of the Claremont McKenna College campus, with the San Gabriel Mountain Range in the background.

EASTERN WASHINGTON UNIVERSITY

CHENEY, WASHINGTON

The University

Established in 1882 as the Benjamin P. Cheney Academy, Eastern Washington University (EWU) has grown from a premier teachers' college into a comprehensive state university providing an excellent student-centered learning environment; professionally accomplished faculty members who are strongly committed to student learning; high-quality, integrated, interdependent academic programs; and exceptional student support services, resources, and facilities. The University retains the charm and personality of its founding on the parklike campus in Cheney. It also exhibits the distinctive marks of the modern comprehensive university in its newer facilities and the expansion of higher educational opportunities into downtown Spokane. Eastern is fully accredited by the Northwest Association of Schools and Colleges and by numerous professional accreditation agencies in specific disciplines. In addition to the undergraduate degrees that are listed, Eastern offers master's degrees in the arts and sciences, business administration, creative writing, education, nursing, public administration, social work, and urban and regional planning. Eastern also offers a doctorate in physical therapy.

Eastern's 9,500 students come from more than forty states and twenty-four countries. Nonwhite students make up 12 percent of the student body, and international students make up 2 percent. About 58 percent of Eastern's students are women. Educational and support services are available through the American Indian Studies, Chicano Education, and African American Education Programs; the English Language Institute; and the Academic Support Center. Seven residence halls can accommodate 2,086 students on campus. Additional housing is available for married students and students with children. Fraternity and sorority housing, as well as off-campus housing within walking distance in Cheney, affords a variety of housing options. All residence halls are smoke free. Students and the University community enjoy one of the Northwest's premier sports and recreation centers. The PHASE complex includes a 5,500-seat pavilion, an indoor aquatics center, a field house with indoor track and tennis, and the main PHASE building, which houses indoor courts for basketball, volleyball, and racquetball; dance studios; a fitness center; and a large, multisurfaced rock for climbing practice. These facilities, totaling 100,000 square feet, and Woodward Field are the venues for the NCAA Division I Eagles, who compete in the Big Sky Conference.

Location

The University's main campus is located in Cheney, a comfortable and compact city of 9,000, where students may find a variety of services, facilities, and shopping while enjoying the pleasant, secure feel of a small town. Spokane, one of the state's largest cities and a regional hub for manufacturing, business, transportation, and health services for more than 400,000 residents, is just 17 miles away and offers a full range of social, cultural, recreational, and consumer opportunities. The Inland Northwest region offers virtually unlimited scenic and recreational attractions in a four-season climate. More than seventy-five lakes lie within 50 miles of the campus, and the mountains and many rivers are easily accessible. Other outdoor activities include excellent skiing within a short drive in nearly every direction. The University sits amid fascinating geological and geographic diversity, with the arid high country to the west, the rich Palouse farming area to the south, and the fir-covered mountains climbing from Spokane into Idaho and Montana. The Spokane International Airport, rail and bus service, and interstate access serve the region.

Majors and Degrees

Electrical engineering is soon to become the newest degree program, pending final approval. EWU is responding to the needs of the state as defined by the Washington Council of the American Electronics Association. The following majors are available: anthropology; art; biology (including biochemistry/biotechnology, predental, premedicine, and preveterinarian); business administration (including accounting, economics, finance, general management, human resource management, international business, management information systems, marketing, operations management, and pre-M.B.A.); chemistry and biochemistry; communication disorders; communication studies (including interpersonal, organizational, public communication, and public relations); computer science (including computer information systems and multimedia programming and development); counseling, developmental, and educational psychology; criminal justice; dental hygiene; earth science; economics; education (including elementary and secondary options); electronic media, film, and theater; engineering technology and multimedia design (including computer engineering technology, construction design, electronics, graphic communications, manufacturing, and mechanical engineering technology); English (including creative writing, literary studies, and technical communication); environmental science; geography; geology (including environmental); government (including prelaw); health services administration; history; humanities; interdisciplinary studies; international affairs; journalism (including computer science, news editorial, public relations, and technology); mathematics (including computer science, economics, and statistics); military science; modern languages and literature (including French, German, and Spanish); music (including instrumental performance, liberal arts, music composition, piano performance, and vocal performance); natural science; nursing; occupational therapy; physical education, health, and recreation (including athletic training, coaching, community health education, exercise science, health, health and fitness/elementary or secondary education, health education, health promotion and wellness, outdoor recreation, recreation management, and therapeutic recreation); physics; psychology; social work; sociology; theater; and urban and regional planning.

Academic Programs

Eastern's mission is to prepare broadly educated, technologically proficient, and highly productive citizens to attain meaningful careers, to enjoy enriched lives, and to contribute to a culturally diverse society. Graduates must have well-developed skills in critical thinking and the ability to express themselves in oral, written, and quantitative forms of communication. The liberal arts core curriculum extends throughout the student's four-year program and includes both breadth and depth requirements as well as writing instruction and assessment in all areas of the curriculum. Small classes, a student-faculty ratio of 24:1, and facilities like the Writers' Center offer the student the resources to meet high expectations. Eastern's unique core curriculum and liberal arts goals were designed as a direct response to input from Eastern alumni, employers, and students. Minors are available in many areas of study, and teacher certification requirements and specific endorsements are available in conjunction with academic disciplines. The prestigious University Honors Program offers motivated students the opportunity to challenge their limits through special honors courses that are part of the core curriculum. University and departmental honor societies continue to provide these opportunities in the major fields. Career preparation is a focus during each student's entire program. Internships and career exploration opportunities for freshmen and sophomores assist in early career and major selection, enhanced employment skills, and locating professional internships as upper-division students.

Off-Campus Programs

Study-abroad opportunities are available for Eastern students as well as for students from other campuses. Programs are available in more than twenty-five countries. In addition, internships are available for students in the Inland Northwest, across the United States, and internationally. These programs provide countless training and research opportunities for graduate and undergraduate students.

Academic Facilities

Eastern's campus includes more than 300 acres in Cheney. The University also maintains classroom, office, and laboratory/clinic facilities in downtown Spokane and shares facilities at the Riverpoint Higher Education Center, also in downtown Spokane. The University libraries include the Kennedy Library on the Cheney campus, with more than 800,000 items, online catalogs, and computer search capabilities covering Eastern as well as other Washington State libraries. Eastern and Washington State University jointly support a downtown library facility. Student computer labs, including a multimedia lab, are located throughout campus. The Pence Union Building houses the main computer lab, with Macintosh and IBM-compatible systems, on-site assistance, DEC mainframe access with faculty sponsorship, and Internet access. The residence halls are wired for both voice and data communications. Additional facilities for learning and teaching include the planetarium, the Robert Reid Laboratory School (an elementary school directly on campus that includes observation facilities), a speech and hearing clinic, and the Turnbull Laboratory for Ecological Studies.

Costs

Annual undergraduate tuition and fees for 2003–04 were $3812 for Washington State residents and $12,668 for nonresidents. Students participating in the Western Undergraduate Exchange Program paid $5373 for tuition. Typical on-campus room and board cost about $5470.

Financial Aid

The Financial Aid and Scholarship Office assists students in identifying the most appropriate sources of funding for their college education. Students who are admitted to the University may apply for federal, state, and University funds by using the Free Application for Federal Student Aid and by applying before the priority deadline of February 15. Although most financial aid is based on need, a number of scholarships are available for students who meet competitive academic criteria. Academic scholarships also reward outstanding performance by continuing students at Eastern. A reduction of the nonresident tuition is available to qualified students from Idaho, Montana, Nevada, New Mexico, North Dakota, Oregon, South Dakota, Utah, and Wyoming through the Western Undergraduate Exchange Program. Applicants interested in need-based financial aid and academic scholarships should contact the Financial Aid and Scholarship Office, 102 Sutton Hall, Eastern Washington University, Cheney, Washington, 99004.

Faculty

More than 600 faculty members provide highly personalized instruction to undergraduates at Eastern. Faculty members are committed to keeping class sizes small and to helping students graduate in a timely manner. Eastern's faculty members are teachers and take pride in innovative curricula, in maintaining close relationships with the community and with professionals outside of the University for the benefit of their students, and in their research, which brings new information and methods into the classroom.

Student Government

All students are members of the Associated Students of Eastern Washington University. A president, executive officers, and a 12-member council are elected annually. The 12 council members represent the students' interest in every facet of student life at Eastern. The student government is responsible for budgeting and managing student fees collected from all students. These funds are used for the operation of the student union, the Pence Union Building, athletic and intramural programs, and the more than seventy-five clubs and organizations that provide opportunities for involvement of students both on campus and in the community.

Admission Requirements

Freshman applicants are admitted based on their high school GPA and test scores on the SAT I or ACT. Applicants also must meet the following core requirements in high school (having extra core classes is highly encouraged): English, 4; math, 3 (algebra I and II and geometry); social science, 3; science, 2 (including 1 lab science); foreign language, 2 (same language); and fine arts (or elective from above subject areas), 1. Transfer students with fewer than 40 transferable credits must meet the high school core and admissions index requirements and have a 2.0 cumulative GPA. Transfer students with more than 40 transferable credits must have a cumulative GPA of 2.0 and completed a minimum of precollege-level English and intermediate algebra with a 2.0 or better. Students who do not meet the academic criteria for admission may be considered on the basis of additional evidence of potential presented to the Office of Admissions. Many majors require considerably higher grade point averages for entry into the major field. Transfer students should consult the University catalog or contact the department for specific program requirements.

Application and Information

All freshman applicants should submit an application, complete high school (and any college) transcripts, and SAT I or ACT scores to the Office of Admissions. Decisions for fall freshmen are made on December 1 and on a rolling basis thereafter. Transfer students should submit an application, an official high school transcript, and official transcripts from all colleges and universities attended. A nonrefundable application fee of $35 is required of all applicants. A campus visit or participation in an overnight on-campus program is the best way to learn more about Eastern. Students should contact the Office of Admissions to find out more about these and other programs designed to provide an opportunity to explore Eastern Washington University. For additional information, students should contact:

Office of Admissions
101 Sutton Hall
Eastern Washington University
Cheney, Washington 99004
Telephone: 509-359-2397
Fax: 509-359-6692
E-mail: admissions@mail.ewu.edu
World Wide Web: http://www.ewu.edu

The state-of-the-art John F. Kennedy Library has 50 different databases available, 500 study carrels, wireless laptops that may be checked out, and more.

EMBRY-RIDDLE AERONAUTICAL UNIVERSITY

PRESCOTT, ARIZONA

The University

Students at Embry-Riddle Aeronautical University–Arizona (Embry-Riddle/AZ) receive a comprehensive, technical, and applied education geared toward designing the next generation of aviation and aerospace vehicles and the systems that support them. Embry-Riddle's reputation is based upon its leadership role in aviation education as well as its commitment to a strong academic preparation and learning environment. Embry-Riddle is a private, independent four-year university and is accredited by the Commission on Colleges of the Southern Association of Colleges and Schools.

The campus team takes pride in providing Embry-Riddle/AZ students with a unique combination of features not readily found on other campuses. A sense of belonging exists, with the total focus on undergraduate education. Students share a love of aviation and a special motivation to succeed and become experts in their field. There is a close-knit residential atmosphere; nearly 850 students live in fourteen on-campus residence halls, which offer both suites and apartments. Housing priority is given to freshmen and sophomores. Most students take advantage of on-campus dining facilities and a variety of meal-plan options. The coed (17 percent women) student population of 1,700 undergraduates comes from fifty states and territories and thirty-two other countries. Seven percent of the students are international.

The students' pride in their campus experience is reflected in the enthusiasm and diversity of activities available. There are more than fifty student clubs and organizations, five professional associations, three fraternities and two sororities, three sports clubs, and thirty-five intramural sports. The NAIA men's soccer and wrestling teams, the NAIA women's soccer and volleyball teams, and the intercollegiate flight team compete with regional and national universities. The student precision flight team has consistently ranked among the top in the country in the SAFECON competitions, sponsored by the National Intercollegiate Flying Association (NIFA).

The extended Embry-Riddle family consists of more than 20,000 students and 38,000 alumni. The Embry-Riddle Daytona Beach, Florida, campus, with 4,500 undergraduate and 300 graduate students, offers additional resources. At Extended Campus Centers around the U.S. and the world, 9,000 undergraduate and 5,000 graduate students find Embry-Riddle's programs geared toward the needs of adult and part-time learners. Guided by its worldwide network of alumni, Embry-Riddle's reputation has grown steadily throughout the aviation, aerospace, and business communities. Embry-Riddle's placement rate for residential campus students one year after graduation is 91 percent. Since its inception in 1926, the flight-related school has added engineering and related majors, as well as six master's degree programs, to become the world-renowned university it is today.

Location

Just like its people, the University's location is warm and friendly. Prescott, a mile-high city on the Colorado Plateau, a beautiful geologic region, is home to the world's largest stand of ponderosa pine trees. The campus is about 100 miles northwest of Phoenix, 260 miles southeast of Las Vegas, and 375 miles east of Los Angeles. Prescott's climate reflects seasonable weather, with daytime averages of 80 degrees in the summer and 45 degrees in the winter. The local mountains exhibit the spirit of the rugged West, with students enjoying snow skiing, hiking, and tours of the Grand Canyon.

Known as a vacation getaway, Prescott offers shopping, entertainment, health, and recreational options and a friendly small-town atmosphere. For a flavor of city lights, Phoenix is a 2-hour drive away. The campus is situated on 557 acres, but campus life is centered within a 1-mile walking radius. Most of the eighty-four individual buildings are interconnected by walkways and indoor and outdoor lounging areas, making it easy to bump into friends and faculty members. The campus Flight Training Center is located nearby at the Prescott Municipal Airport.

Majors and Degrees

The B.S. in aeronautical science (professional pilot program) emphasizes multiengine training and prepares students for a career as an airline, military, or corporate pilot. The first two years include courses leading to FAA certification as an instrument-rated commercial pilot. The last two years stress professional-level courses in aircraft systems and flight methodology. Training in the late-model fleet is combined with the use of simulators, including two Level A Boeing 727 motion simulators. The program is accredited by the Council on Aviation Accreditation (CAA).

Aerospace engineering centers on the design of aircraft and spacecraft; electrical engineering focuses on circuits, communication and control systems, and electronic/avionics materials and devices. Embry-Riddle is consistently rated as one of the country's best engineering schools by *U.S. News & World Report*'s "America's Best Colleges." In the B.S. in computer science program, studies consist of graphics, simulation, computer architecture, database management, operating systems, software engineering, artificial intelligence, and applications to the aviation industry. The B.S. programs in aerospace engineering, electrical engineering, and computer engineering are approved by the Accreditation Board for Engineering and Technology (ABET).

The B.S. in science, technology, and globalization (STG) is an interdisciplinary program for the global work environment. The program is based primarily on humanities and social sciences in conjunction with the hard sciences and technology. STG students specialize in one of two significant areas for the aviation and aerospace industries: global aviation ecology and global management.

The B.S. in applied meteorology, new in 2004, provides a practical understanding of the physics and dynamics of the atmosphere and prepares the graduate for a range of meterologist positions in government or industry. Students use state-of-the-art Weather Center and computer-equipped classrooms to understand and forecast complex atmospheric phenomena ranging from severe thunderstorms and tornadoes, cyclones, fronts, and jet streams to the global climate and how it is changing.

The B.S. degree in aviation business administration prepares the student for managerial and business-related positions within the constantly evolving aviation and aerospace industries.

The B.S. in space physics, new to Embry-Riddle in 2003, consists of four areas of concentration: astrophysics, particle physics and cosmology, advanced propulsion systems, and remote sensing.

The B.S. in aerospace studies is an interdisciplinary program that draws upon a strong core of general education and advanced-level courses in a variety of areas to enhance communication, critical thinking, and technical skills; students also choose three minor areas of study.

Academic Programs

The undergraduate academic preparation provides a strong foundation for all students, whether or not they choose a career in aviation. Each major is a combination of general education, specialized aviation focus, and applied technology. The general education component consists of courses in communication skills, social sciences/humanities, mathematics, computer science, and physical science.

Along with their major, students may opt to select a minor from the following fields: Asian studies, aviation safety, aviation weather, computer applications, computer science, environmental studies, humanities, mathematics, psychology, security studies, and technology, policy, and management. Army and Air Force Reserve Officer Training Corps (ROTC) courses are also available to all Embry-Riddle students and may lead to a position as a commissioned officer. Entering high school students with selected ROTC scholarships receive additional subsidies from Embry-Riddle.

Through participation in internships and cooperative education (co-op) arrangements, students in all fields of study gain valuable work experience with companies such as Continental Airlines, Delta Air Lines, Federal Aviation Administration (FAA), Honeywell, Gulfstream Aerospace Corporation, Lockheed Martin, NASA, Northwest Airlines, the Naval Air Systems Command, and Raytheon.

The academic year is divided into two semesters of fifteen weeks each. The average course load is 12–18 semester hours of credit. Two summer terms of approximately seven weeks each allow for additional enrollment. Many support programs exist to encourage students' development. The Student Success Center offers the college success course, orientation programs, academic advisement and counseling, and tutoring and supplemental instruction. In the Career Placement and Co-Op Services Office, students find assistance through job fairs, resume preparation and referral, the job bank and interviews, and the careers library.

Academic Facilities

Tucked into the rolling hillsides, the campus blends nature with the layout of the eighty-four buildings. Landmarks include the King Science and Technology Center; Davis Learning Center, with its auditorium and classrooms; the Bookstore; and the Visitor Center. Students and faculty members stroll down the many pathways and past outdoor lounging areas. The center of campus focuses on student life and services such as the library, cafeteria, the radio station and student government offices, student activities and financial aid offices, and the post office. The recreational and athletic facilities on campus include two gymnasiums, an athletic field, a weight room, an aerobic room, tennis courts, racquetball courts, a pool, sand volleyball courts, and several running trails.

Most of the classrooms, laboratories, and faculty offices are situated between the middle of campus and the hillside residence halls. These buildings house specialized labs, including the Airway Science Lab, Robertson Aviation Safety Center, Physics Lab, Engineering Graphics Lab, Aerospace Engineering Wind Tunnel, Aerospace Engineering Structures, and Aerospace Engineering Materials Lab.

Halfway up the sloping hillside stands the 22,000-square-foot King Engineering and Technology Center, which opened in 1995. The center's computer science classroom, the Computer-Aided Engineering Lab, and the UNIX Lab provide students with the latest in computer technologies. This center also houses the Linear Lab, Senior Design Lab, Electronics Power Lab, Honeywell Control and System Integration Lab, and Communications Lab. Here, too, the distance learning classroom connects Embry-Riddle/AZ students to faculty members and students at other Embry-Riddle sites as well as to worldwide teleconferencing facilities. The campus computer network links all student rooms, an e-mail system, library resources, engineering research labs, and distance learning facilities. The Embry-Riddle libraries are known for their outstanding aviation collections, which can be utilized by either visiting the facility or accessing the World Wide Web.

The University is currently building its new Academic Complex I, planned to house 46,000 square feet of classrooms, conference rooms, and offices.

Two miles from campus, the Embry-Riddle Flight Training Center occupies several buildings at the Prescott Municipal Airport. Embry-Riddle owns and maintains about fifty aircraft at Prescott. Currently, the Prescott fleet includes 2 Cessna 150s (flight team), 30 Cessna 172s, 4 Aerobatic Beechcraft Bonanza E33Cs, 2 Cessna 340s, and 8 Piper Seminole PA-44s. Cockpit procedural trainers include 3 PA-44 CPTs and 2 C-172 CPTs. Flight training devices include 1 Frasca PA-44 (FTD) with 220-degree visual, 2 Frasca C-172 FTD with 220-degree visual display, 3 Frasca 141 single-engine trainers, 1 Frasca 142 multi-engine trainer, 2 AST-300 multi-engine trainers, and 1 Boeing 727 full-motion simulator.

Costs

The 2003–04 academic year tuition for all programs is $10,350 per semester. Flight fees are charged in addition to tuition. On-campus housing accommodations range from $1570 to $1790 per semester, depending upon the accommodations; meal-plan options are an approximate $386 to $1284 per semester in addition to these charges. Students also need to include costs for books, transportation, and personal expenses. Since the tuition is similar for all students, in many instances these costs are lower than out-of-state tuition for state universities and are in the lower tier of costs for all national private universities.

Financial Aid

Students and their families find many sources of aid available to assist with paying the costs of a private university; more than 81 percent of students receive financial assistance. Embry-Riddle participates in all national and state assistance programs. The completion of the Department of Education's Free Application for Federal Student Aid (FAFSA) forms assures students consideration for these funds. In addition, Embry-Riddle/AZ provides assistance in the form of on-campus jobs, academic scholarships, veterans' educational benefits, and ROTC incentives.

Faculty

Easy access to faculty members is another strength of Embry-Riddle/AZ. Faculty members, not graduate students, teach classes. The average class size is 23, with an overall student-faculty ratio of 17:1. Faculty members keep regular office hours and consider it their most important role to enhance the individual learning of each student. As academic advisers, faculty members help in course selection and career guidance. Faculty members bring both teaching and industry backgrounds to the classroom; most have extensive practical experience in their field along with outstanding academic credentials. The faculty participates with members of Advisory Boards, consisting of experts from their field, to continually update the curriculum and technology.

Student Government

The Student Government Association (SGA) has an extremely important role. It provides many student activities, including service and community organizations, Activities Planning Board, *Horizons* newspaper, and representation and funding for clubs and committees. Also, the SGA is the key communication link to the University administration, and the council president serves as a member of the University Board of Trustees.

Admission Requirements

Each student receives individual consideration for admission based upon a variety of factors and circumstances. Completion of the Embry-Riddle/AZ Application for Admission begins this process; official transcripts and score reports for either the SAT I or ACT should also be submitted. Notification takes place throughout the year.

Application and Information

A virtual tour of Embry-Riddle/AZ is available on the World Wide Web (see address below). For additional information, including information on campus visits, and application forms, students may contact:

Embry-Riddle Admissions
3700 Willow Creek Road
Prescott, Arizona 86301

Telephone: 928-777-6600
800-888-ERAU (toll-free)
E-mail: dbadmit@erau.edu
World Wide Web: http://www.embryriddle.edu

THE EVERGREEN STATE COLLEGE

OLYMPIA, WASHINGTON

The College

"Unique," "innovative," and "challenging" are all words that have been used to describe the curriculum offered by the Evergreen State College, a public liberal arts and sciences college offering undergraduate and graduate studies. Established in 1971 to provide innovation in higher education, Evergreen is one of the smallest and newest four-year public institutions in the state of Washington. Since its beginning, Evergreen has designed and refined a format for higher education that has been recognized nationally and internationally as remarkable and exciting. Evergreen seeks qualified students who demonstrate a spirit of inquiry and a willingness to participate in their educational process within a collaborative framework. The College desires students who also express an interest in campus or community involvement, a respect and tolerance for individual differences, and a willingness to experiment with innovative modes of teaching and learning.

An education at Evergreen emphasizes interdisciplinary studies and collaborative learning. Instruction relies heavily on seminars—small discussion groups that involve students and faculty members in active participation. A state-supported college that offers the advantages of a small private liberal arts college, Evergreen is fully accredited by the Northwest Association of Schools and Colleges.

Graduate programs in public administration, environmental studies, and teaching are available.

Nearly 4,100 undergraduates from almost every state in the Union are enrolled at Evergreen; 43 percent are men, 57 percent are women, and 18 percent are members of minority groups. The average age of the student body is 25. About 1,000 students live on campus in apartment-style units. Accommodations include single and double studios as well as one- to six-bedroom apartments. Housing is within walking distance of classrooms and other campus facilities. Campus life is centered in academic programs, the residence halls, student clubs, and special-interest groups. On-campus activities include dances, plays, films, distinguished visiting speakers, concerts, and a variety of recreational activities. Notable among campus activities and services are those sponsored by the First Peoples Community, a network of minority student groups that offers peer support, guest speakers, and campus ethnic festivals.

Evergreen's women's and men's intercollegiate teams compete in the National Association of Intercollegiate Athletics (NAIA) in basketball, cross-country, and soccer. Intercollegiate volleyball is offered for women only. Numerous intramural sports are also available. The Campus Recreation Center is equipped with an eleven-lane swimming pool, a separate diving well, a sun deck, five racquetball/handball courts, a gymnasium, a wellness center, a challenge course, rock-climbing practice walls, two multipurpose rooms for dance and the martial arts, and exercise/weight-training rooms/classes with the latest in weight training equipment.

Location

The College is just outside Washington's capital city of Olympia in the midst of 1,000 acres of woods, with a 3,300-foot waterfront on Puget Sound. The campus is heavily forested with alder, maple, cedar, and Douglas firs and has trails for walking, jogging, and bicycling. The beachfront provides a delightful place for strolling, sunbathing, or marine research.

Olympia is a seaport community of about 81,760 located at the southernmost tip of Puget Sound. The Pacific Ocean is about an hour's drive to the west. The rain forests and mountains of the Olympic Peninsula lie to the north, and the Cascade mountain range is 2 hours east. Seattle, 60 miles north of the campus by freeway, offers all the cultural and recreational activities typically found in a large city, while Portland, Oregon, is a 2-hour drive south.

Majors and Degrees

Students are able to design undergraduate academic concentrations in anthropology, art, biology, chemistry, communications, community studies, computer science, creative writing, cultural studies, ecology, economics, energy studies, environmental studies, ethnic studies, film and video, history, humanities, journalism, languages (French, Japanese, Russian, Spanish), literature, management, marine studies, mathematics, Native American studies, performing arts, physics, prelaw, premedicine, psychology, public administration, social sciences, sociology, theater, and zoology.

Academic Programs

Evergreen provides innovative academic programs that enable students to enroll each quarter in a single comprehensive program rather than in several separate courses. These coordinated programs bring a group of students and faculty members into extended contact, allowing them to work intensively in ways that encourage intellectual growth and friendship. The study of one topic at a time from a variety of perspectives provides students an excellent opportunity to combine the elements of an undergraduate education into a meaningful, cohesive whole.

The curriculum is founded on (1) collaborative, interdisciplinary teaching and learning; (2) small classes and close personal interaction of students and faculty members; (3) studies and group projects that encourage the understanding of theory as well as the development of practical applications; (4) narrative evaluations of the student's academic achievement; and (5) areas of concentration designed jointly by students and faculty members.

Studies at Evergreen are interdisciplinary. Students master one or more major fields of study by drawing knowledge from several different academic disciplines to develop an understanding of the relationships between the arts, the humanities, and the natural and social sciences. The academic program is based on the conviction that coordinated interdisciplinary study produces better conceptualizers, analysts, and problem-solvers and ultimately better citizens. A student's academic progress is assessed through narrative evaluations written by faculty members that describe in detail each student's academic activities, objectives, area of concentration, and degree of success in the attempted program. Narrative evaluations provide a comprehensive and insightful analysis of every student's work.

Each bachelor's degree requires the completion of 180 quarter credit hours. The academic calendar consists of three 10-week quarters and a summer session.

Off-Campus Programs

Evergreen offers an extensive internship program for advanced students. Placements are sponsored by faculty members and may be located anywhere in the world, although most are located in the Pacific Northwest. An international student exchange program exists with Miyazaki and Kobe Universities in Japan. Each year, Evergreen offers coordinated programs that enable students to spend a portion of the year overseas. Other study-abroad arrangements can also be made.

Academic Facilities

As one of the state's newest four-year colleges, Evergreen offers undergraduates some of the most modern academic facilities in the Pacific Northwest. The regional accreditation team that reviewed Evergreen described its scientific and artistic plant as "superior to that which can be found in any institution of which we have knowledge." Some of the resources available include a library containing 300,000 books, 15,000 reference volumes, 2,000 periodical subscriptions, and 4,000 items of media loan equipment. The science laboratory buildings house a lab supply store, a number of teaching and research laboratories, an advanced microscopy laboratory, and several instrument laboratories that feature spectrophotometers, chromatographs, ultracentrifuges, scintillation counters, and other equipment necessary for advanced work in the sciences. The computer applications lab is a facility designed to provide students in the laboratory science curriculum with language instruction, experiment and instrument interfacing, high-resolution color graphics, simulations, complex calculations, scientific software development, local networking, linear and digital electronics, and microprocessor applications.

The art facility includes ceramics, painting, and drawing studios; areas for weaving, batik, jewelry, drawing, and design; and a large high-ceilinged area for sculpture, casting, welding, glassblowing, lapidary work, spray painting, shop, and sheet-metal work. The communications laboratory building is a comprehensive instructional, performance, and production facility for audio and video communications, including dance, film, music, speech, theater, and two-dimensional design. This state-of-the-art facility also includes equipment for the performance of electronic music and for conventional filmmaking and previewing.

All Evergreen students have free access to computer facilities. The computer center's resources include microcomputer laboratories, clusters of microcomputers, 280 computer workstations, and minicomputers. Other on-campus computer facilities include NOVA minicomputers, micro-Plato workstations, plotters and graphic terminals, a hybrid analog/digital system, and additional scientific data acquisition devices. An extensive computer science teaching lab provides microcomputing resources and overhead display projection systems. The graphics imaging lab provides facilities for graphics and imaging projects.

Costs

Annual undergraduate tuition for the 2003–04 academic year was $3651 for Washington State residents and $13,329 for nonresidents. Evergreen is no longer a participant in the Western Undergraduate Exchange program. The estimated cost of books and supplies is $780. The cost of room and board is $5772, and personal living expenses are estimated at $2058.

Financial Aid

Evergreen's goal is to provide sufficient financial aid to make it possible for all qualified students to attend. Awards from Evergreen's aid programs, which are based on financial need, are designed to supplement the contribution of the student and his or her family. Once a student's level of financial need has been determined, his or her application is reviewed to evaluate eligibility for all programs. A financial aid package, which may combine a grant, scholarship, loan, and work opportunity, is then offered to meet the student's needs as closely as possible. Financial aid applications received by the processor by February 15 will have priority.

A variety of scholarships funded by the College's Foundation and private donors are available. Most of these scholarships are awarded on the basis of merit, high academic achievement, community service, and artistic or musical talent. For more information about these scholarships, students should write to the Office of the Associate Vice President of Enrollment Management or call 360-867-6310.

Faculty

Evergreen has a dedicated faculty committed to teaching. Seventy-three percent of faculty members hold the Ph.D. or other terminal degree; 49 percent are women, and 24 percent are members of minority groups. The favorable faculty-student ratio of 1:25 ensures close interaction between students and faculty members. Faculty members teach in one full-time program at a time, enabling them to have direct contact with a small group of students. Students work in small seminar groups from their freshman through their senior year and engage with academic content in unique ways. Faculty members strive to foster the environment of a learning community where common goals can include working across cultural and personal differences, engaging with difficult intellectual ideas through discussion, and making the abstract real and applicable to true-life situations. At Evergreen, students spend an average of 12–16 hours a week in the classroom, in direct contact with faculty members.

Student Government

Students at Evergreen have chosen to actively serve on a variety of campuswide committees and task forces rather than participate in a more traditional student government. With direct access to governance policies and resolutions, all Evergreen students are encouraged to become involved with campus issues. Students also directly administer the funds collected from the student services and activities fees, which are used to support a wide variety of student organizations.

Admission Requirements

First-year students are admitted on the basis of their high school GPA and test scores (SAT I or ACT). Essays and letters of recommendation are not required. First-year students are required to have completed the following college-preparatory program in high school: 4 years of English courses designed to develop college-level reading and writing proficiencies (composition, creative writing, and literature); 3 years of mathematics selected from algebra, geometry, trigonometry, advanced algebra, and higher-level courses; 3 years of social studies; 2 years of science, including 1 year of laboratory science (biology, chemistry, or physics); 2 years of the same foreign language; and 1 year in the visual/performing arts or in any of the aforementioned areas.

Students with at least 40 transferable credits are considered under transfer admission criteria. Transfer students are admitted on the basis of their cumulative college GPA, good standing at the last institution attended, and satisfactory completion of a variety of courses in the liberal arts and sciences.

Because Evergreen seeks to achieve a diverse student body, special consideration is given to applicants who are Vietnam-era veterans, adults 25 years of age and older, and students whose parents do not have a baccalaureate degree. In addition, special recognition is given to applicants who have 90 quarter credits of transferable work, an Associate in Arts degree from a Washington community college, or an Associate in Technical Arts degree from a Washington community college with which Evergreen has negotiated an "Upside Down" degree program.

Application and Information

Applications for fall entrance are accepted from September 1 to March 1; applicants are notified by April 1. Applications for winter entrance are accepted from April 1 to October 1; applicants are notified by November 1. Applications for spring entrance are accepted from June 1 to December 1; applicants are notified by January 1. Applications received after the deadline are considered on a space-available basis.

For more information about Evergreen, students should contact:

Office of Admissions
The Evergreen State College
Olympia, Washington 98505
Telephone: 360-867-6170
E-mail: admissions@evergreen.edu
World Wide Web: http://www.evergreen.edu

GEORGE FOX UNIVERSITY

NEWBERG, OREGON

The University

George Fox University was founded in 1891 by the Society of Friends (Quakers) with the purpose of providing students a challenging academic atmosphere within a community of Christian faith. Today, George Fox maintains the same mission and has grown to an enrollment of 2,700 students.

Students find George Fox to be a place where spiritual growth and intellectual challenge take place in a friendly, caring environment. This tradition of integration of faith and learning has been recognized by the Templeton Foundation, which named George Fox University to its honor roll of character-building colleges.

Seventy-five percent of George Fox students live in campus residence halls, suites, and apartments. Opportunities for extracurricular involvement are available in music, drama, journalism, student government, radio, clubs, and athletics. George Fox is a member of the NCAA Division III and competes in six men's sports (baseball, basketball, cross-country, soccer, tennis, and track) and seven women's sports (basketball, cross-country, soccer, softball, tennis, track, and volleyball). Intramural sports are also played.

Regular chapel services bring the campus community together in worship. Students have the opportunity to put their faith into action on volunteer mission trips and during community outreach activities.

In addition to its undergraduate degrees, George Fox confers the Master of Business Administration, Master of Education, Doctor of Education, Master of Arts in Teaching, and Doctor of Psychology degrees and eight graduate degrees through George Fox Evangelical Seminary.

Location

George Fox University is located in Newberg, a residential community of 18,000 people. The 75-acre tree-shaded campus is a 30-minute drive from the major metropolitan environment of Portland. The University is situated in the beautiful Pacific Northwest, with scenic Mt. Hood and the rugged Pacific coastline within short driving distances.

Tilikum Retreat Center, set on a 90-acre lake and just 10 minutes away, provides students a change of pace from the classroom. Students enjoy hiking, canoeing, and fishing at the camp. Tilikum has an extensive summer day camp program that employs many University students.

Majors and Degrees

George Fox confers the Bachelor of Arts and Bachelor of Science degrees. The following undergraduate majors are available: accounting, art, biblical studies, biology, business and economics, chemistry, Christian educational ministries, cognitive science, communication arts, communication/video production, computer and information science, electrical engineering, elementary education, family and consumer science, fashion merchandising, foods and nutrition in business, history, interdisciplinary studies, interior design, international studies, mathematics, mechanical engineering, music, philosophy, physical education, political science, religion, social work, sociology, and writing/literature.

Academic Programs

The academic year at George Fox University is divided into two semesters of fifteen weeks. In addition to the two semesters, the University sponsors a three-week May Term. For graduation, students are required to earn 126 credit hours, including 54 general education and 42 upper-division credits.

Students may reduce the number of required courses and add flexibility to their undergraduate years with credit earned through Advanced Placement, International Baccalaureate (IB), the College-Level Examination Program, and credit by examination. All traditional undergraduates are given a personal computer to use and keep upon graduation.

George Fox demonstrates its commitment to freshmen by providing a Freshman Seminar Program to assist students as they integrate themselves into the academic and social life of the University community.

Off-Campus Programs

The importance of international study is shown through a variety of programs. Each year during May Term, George Fox sponsors a number of three-week study tours led by University faculty members. Transportation costs are subsidized by the University. These international learning experiences are designed for students completing their junior year. Through the Coalition for Christian Colleges and Universities, students are also given the opportunity to study for a semester in China, Costa Rica, England, Kenya, Russia, the Middle East, and Washington, D.C.

Membership in the Christian College Consortium enables George Fox University students to attend for a semester one of twelve colleges located throughout the United States.

Academic Facilities

The new Edward F. Stevens Center provides 40,000 square feet of office and classroom space. All student service-oriented offices are now housed under one roof that provides greater efficiency and access for students. The building has been selected as part of the "Ten Shades of Green" by Portland General Electric for its use of recycled materials and minimal environmental impact.

The three-story Murdock Learning Resource Center houses more than 175,000 books and periodicals. Its features include rare book collections, study carrels, computer and audiovisual laboratories, a recording studio, and a darkroom.

The Edwards/Holman Science Center is home to the University's science programs. The 36,000-square-foot building provides classrooms, offices, and laboratories for biology, chemistry, premedicine, mathematics, computer science, and engineering programs.

The William and Mary Bauman Auditorium seats 1,150 people in a facility that is among the finest in the Northwest. Rotating art exhibits appear in the adjoining Lindgren Art Gallery.

Costs

Tuition for the 2003–04 year was $19,500. Room and board were $6300. Fees cost $310. Books are estimated to cost $600 per year.

Financial Aid

George Fox maintains that every qualified student should be able to attend the university of his or her choice without letting limited finances stand in the way. To this end, federal, state, and institutional need-based funds are available, as are merit awards. About 87 percent of all students receive financial aid.

Faculty

The faculty at George Fox University fosters an atmosphere of discussion and independent thinking in the classroom. Faculty members have found a healthy balance between teaching and research by devoting a majority of their time to educating students. The University employs 120 full-time and 112 part-time faculty members. Seventy percent of the full-time faculty members hold earned doctoral degrees. Faculty members are personally committed Christians who are involved in the lives of their students. The student-faculty ratio is 15:1.

Student Government

The Associated Student Community of George Fox University serves as a unifying force and voice for the campus student community and plays a significant role in organizing cultural, social, and recreational activities.

Admission Requirements

Students admitted to George Fox University must show academic ability, high moral character, and social concern. These qualities are evaluated by consideration of each applicant's academic record, test scores, recommendations, interview reports, and participation in extracurricular activities. The priority application deadline is February 1. In order to provide a solid foundation for college-level work, it is recommended that the applicant present the equivalent of 16 academic units from an approved high school. The following units are suggested: English, 4; social studies, 2; science, 2; mathematics, 2; foreign language, 2; and health and physical education, 1.

Application and Information

For additional information, students should contact:

Office of Undergraduate Admission
George Fox University
Newberg, Oregon 97132-2697
Telephone: 800-765-4369 Ext. 2240 (toll-free)
E-mail: admissions@georgefox.edu
World Wide Web: http://www.georgefox.edu

GRAND CANYON UNIVERSITY

PHOENIX, ARIZONA

The University

Grand Canyon University is Arizona's only private, Christian, liberal arts university. The purposeful integration of faith and learning has made Grand Canyon the distinguished university it is today. Since the University's founding in 1949, professors at Grand Canyon have believed in a rare holistic approach to education wherein the mind, the body, and the spirit are seen as essential partners in the learning experience. With approximately 4,000 students, Grand Canyon University is committed to providing students with individual attention from faculty members and administrators. Grand Canyon offers more than sixty programs of study that all have their foundation in a core of liberal arts courses.

As a member of both the Council of Christian Colleges and Universities and the Council of Independent Colleges, Grand Canyon University belongs to an elite group. Less than 3 percent of all colleges and universities in the United States are Christ-centered, providing a value-added educational environment that synthesizes faith, learning, and life. At Grand Canyon, students seeking to learn and grow within a Christian value system find a sense of community, a demanding academic curriculum, and countless opportunities for community leadership and service both on and off campus. Grand Canyon University is open to students from all faith perspectives.

A degree from Grand Canyon University represents a well-rounded education. The Grand Canyon curriculum is challenging and radiates from a strong core of liberal arts and sciences. The University provides both traditional and innovative programs that enable students to think critically and creatively, solve problems through open-minded analysis, and communicate effectively. Academic habits acquired at Grand Canyon University stay with Grand Canyon graduates, enabling them to live flexible lives, to be open to new career opportunities, and to develop confidence in their ability to learn and adapt.

Grand Canyon University offers graduate degrees that include the Master of Arts in Education, Master of Arts in Teaching, Master of Education, Master of Science in executive fire service leadership, Master of Business Administration, Master of Science in leadership, and Master of Science in Nursing.

Location

Grand Canyon University is located just minutes from central Phoenix, Arizona's state capital and sixth-largest city in the United States. Phoenix is the nerve center of the Southwest, one of the fastest-growing regions in the nation. The greater Phoenix metropolitan area, known as the Valley of the Sun for its more than 300 days of sunshine each year, offers numerous educational, social, cultural, and recreational activities that enhance university life. Phoenix is a major-league city in many ways. The city is one of only eleven in the nation to be home to four major-league sports teams—the Phoenix Suns, Arizona Cardinals, Phoenix Coyotes, and Arizona Diamondbacks. The valley also provides opportunities for hiking, camping, cycling, golf, water sports, and virtually any other activity all year long. Also within a 2-hour drive of the Grand Canyon campus is some of the best snow skiing in the Western United States. Grand Canyon University students flourish in the school's southwestern environment. Surrounded by rugged mountains, lush valleys, and the arid beauty of the Sonoran Desert, Grand Canyon students feel a part of the larger human experience. Grand Canyon University and the Grand Canyon State are wonderful places in which to learn.

Majors and Degrees

Grand Canyon University awards bachelor's degrees in more than sixty areas of study. Specific degrees awarded are the Bachelor of Arts, Bachelor of Business Administration, Bachelor of Liberal Studies, Bachelor of Music, Bachelor of Science, and Bachelor of Science in Nursing.

Specific study areas include accounting, allied health, applied management, applied music, art education, athletic training, biochemistry, biology (environmental/general/human/secondary teaching), business administration, chemistry (general/secondary teaching), Christian leadership, Christian studies, communications (with emphasis in broadcasting/journalism/photojournalism/public relations), corporate fitness and wellness, elementary education, English literature, English teaching for secondary teachers, graphic design, history, international studies, justice studies, marketing, mathematics (engineering/general/secondary teaching), organizational sociology, piano performance, political science, predentistry, premedicine, pre–occupational therapy, pre–optometry, pre–osteopathic medicine, prepharmacy, pre–physical therapy, pre–physician assistant studies, prepodiatry, pre–sports health care, pre–veterinary medicine, psychology, public safety administration, recreation, science for elementary teachers, secondary education, sociology, special education (emotional handicaps and learning disabilities), speech teaching for secondary teachers, speech/theater, studio art, teaching English as a second language, theater/drama, and vocal performance.

Academic Programs

Grand Canyon University is accredited by the Higher Learning Commission of the North Central Association of Colleges and Schools (30 North LaSalle Street, Suite 2400, Chicago, Illinois 60602-2504; telephone: 800-621-7440, toll-free). Grand Canyon Bachelor of Business Administration and Master of Business Administration degree programs are additionally accredited by the Association of Collegiate Business Schools and Programs. The work of Grand Canyon students seeking certification as elementary, secondary, and special education teachers, or for the renewal of teaching certificates, is approved by the Arizona State Department of Education. Over the past ten years, 94 percent of Grand Canyon University College of Education graduates have been placed in teaching positions. Grand Canyon University Samaritan College of Nursing is accredited by both the National League for Nursing Accrediting Commission and the Arizona State Board of Nursing for the Bachelor of Science in Nursing degree. Over the past five years, 94 percent of nursing program graduates have passed the state board exams on their first attempt.

Graduates of Grand Canyon University's College of Science benefit from Grand Canyon's relationship with the Kirksville College of Osteopathic Medicine. Kirksville's southwest center, Arizona School of Health Sciences, reserves a large number of admission slots in each of its programs exclusively for qualified Grand Canyon students. These programs include physical therapy, occupational therapy, and physician assistant studies. Grand Canyon graduates are also in demand at a national level, with approximately 150 reserved admission slots in health-care programs across the country.

Off-campus internships are an important educational experience available to Grand Canyon students. Classroom sessions are more relevant when subject matter is seen in the light of the work environment. Students from all disciplines hone their skills through off-campus clinical and intern programs. Some internships result in permanent positions after graduation, an invaluable benefit.

While exploring a major field of study in depth at Grand Canyon, students are exposed to a wide range of experiences both on and off campus. This diversity is a key element of Grand Canyon's vision of educating students for successful careers and lives. Students benefit from Grand Canyon's blend of characteristics for a high-quality Christian education—small classes, accessible faculty members, a challenging curriculum, and hands-on learning experiences.

Academic Facilities

Grand Canyon University consists of thirty-six buildings on a 90-acre campus. The campus features the Fleming Library, which houses a collection of more than 166,000 volumes, 700 periodicals, newspapers, microfilm, and audiovisual materials. Fleming Library is a member of the CCLC network and as a designated depository receives a variety of government documents. Library holdings are expanded by CD-ROM databases, computerized database searches, and interlibrary loans. Computers housed in the library have Internet access to assist students.

The majority of classes are held in the Fleming Classroom Building, with additional classes held in the Weidenaar Classroom Building, Wallace Building, Williams Building, Tell Science Building, and Samaritan College of Nursing. Ethington Memorial Theatre sets the perfect stage for drama and other productions, with more than 300 seats. The C. J. and Thema Smith Arts Complex houses the A. P. Tell Gallery and other tailored creative spaces. The Tell Science Building and Samaritan College of Nursing are both equipped with state-of-the-art laboratory, computer, multimedia, and clinical learning spaces.

Grand Canyon University features two microcomputer laboratories utilizing IBM-compatible personal computers and a separate Macintosh computer laboratory.

Costs

In 2003–04, tuition and fees were $14,500 (24 to 36 hours), and room and board were $7130.

Financial Aid

Grand Canyon University has made a commitment to its students by keeping costs down year after year and focusing its dollars on what benefits students directly. The result of this effort yields an educational experience that offers high value and quality for the investment students make. The Office of Financial Aid and the Business Office at Grand Canyon University are committed to working with students and their families. They can help explain various options and ensure that every available resource is utilized to meet individual financial needs. More than 79 percent of Grand Canyon students receive some form of financial assistance to help meet the cost of their education. In addition to federal and state financial aid, Grand Canyon University has academic and other specific-criteria scholarships and aid available. Students wishing to apply for financial aid must be accepted for admission and complete the Free Application for Federal Student Aid (FAFSA) and have it on file in the Office of Financial Aid.

Faculty

Faculty members are drawn to Grand Canyon University due to a love of teaching. Rather than concentrating mainly on research and publication, Grand Canyon faculty members focus on assisting students to acquire knowledge and attain higher standards that help them reach their potential as people and as scholars. More than three quarters of Grand Canyon faculty members have earned doctoral or terminal degrees from some of the nation's most prestigious universities, and many are considered experts in their field. Beyond their academic qualifications, Grand Canyon faculty members are good friends. They help students become involved in the community and guide them through further explorations of their faith.

Student Government

Grand Canyon University understands that student involvement is essential in the university experience. Grand Canyon's Campus Leadership Council (CLC) is student-led and staff-supported. CLC is responsible for developing student leaders and programs that provide opportunities for contribution to the Grand Canyon campus and surrounding community. The election of Student Body President is held in the spring semester of each year. CLC positions for Chief of Staff, Director of Organizations, Director of Intramurals, Chief Financial Officer, Director of Marketing, and Director of Student Activities are determined through an application and interview process.

Admission Requirements

For admission to Grand Canyon University, students should submit an application for admission with a $50 nonrefundable application fee to the Grand Canyon University Office of Admission. Freshmen must submit their official high school transcript and/or GED scores plus have their ACT or SAT I scores submitted to Grand Canyon University. Transfer students must have their transcripts forwarded to Grand Canyon University. Both freshman and transfer students must bring a health history, with proof of immunization for mumps, measles, and rubella, to put on file.

Application and Information

Grand Canyon operates on a rolling admission system. Applicants generally receive an admission decision within ten days after all required documents are on file in the Office of Admission. It is to the student's advantage to apply as early as possible. Applications for financial aid and housing cannot be completely processed and transcripts are not evaluated until the admission application is complete.

For further information and application materials, students should contact:

Office of Admission
Grand Canyon University
3300 West Camelback Road
Phoenix, Arizona 85017
Telephone: 602-589-2855
800-800-9776 (toll-free)
E-mail: admissions@gcu.edu
World Wide Web: http://www.gcu.edu

Students in front of Fleming Library at Grand Canyon University in Phoenix, Arizona, experience the integration of faith in their learning process while surrounded by the beauty of the Southwest.

HAWAI'I PACIFIC UNIVERSITY

HONOLULU, HAWAI'I

The University

Hawai'i Pacific University (HPU) is an independent, coeducational, career-oriented comprehensive university with a foundation in the liberal arts. Undergraduate and graduate degrees are offered in more than fifty areas. Hawai'i Pacific prides itself on maintaining strong academic programs, small class sizes, individual attention to students, an outstanding faculty, and a student population as diverse as the United Nations. HPU is accredited by the Western Association of Schools and Colleges and the National League for Nursing Accrediting Commission.

HPU is the largest private university in Hawai'i, with more than 8,000 students from every state in the union and more than 100 countries. The diversity of the student body stimulates learning about other cultures firsthand, both in and out of the classroom. There is no majority population at HPU. Students are encouraged to examine the values, customs, traditions, and principles of others to gain a clearer understanding of their own perspectives. HPU students develop friendships with students from throughout the United States and the world, important connections for success in the global economy of the twenty-first century.

In addition to the undergraduate programs, HPU offers several graduate programs: the M.B.A. (with ten concentrations), the Master of Science in Information Systems (M.S.I.S.), the Master of Science in Nursing (M.S.N.), and the Master of Arts (M.A.) in communications, diplomacy and military studies, global leadership, human resource management, organizational change, and teaching English as a second language.

HPU has NCAA Division II intercollegiate sports. Men's athletic programs include baseball, basketball, cheerleading, cross-country, and tennis. Women's athletics include cheerleading, cross-country, softball, tennis, and volleyball.

The housing office at HPU offers many services and options for students. Residence halls with cafeteria service are available on the windward Hawai'i Loa campus, while off-campus apartments are available in the Honolulu and Waikiki areas for those seeking more independent living arrangements.

Location

With two campuses linked by shuttle, Hawai'i Pacific combines the excitement of an urban, downtown campus with the serenity of the windward Hawai'i Loa residential campus, which is set in the lush foothills of the Ko'olau mountains. The main campus is located in downtown Honolulu, the business and financial center of the Pacific. Eight miles away, situated on 135 acres in Kaneohe, the windward Hawai'i Loa campus is the site of the School of Nursing, the marine science program, and a variety of other course offerings. Students may take classes on whichever campus is most convenient. The Hawai'i Loa campus is home to recreational facilities such as a soccer field, tennis courts, a softball field, a student center, and an exercise room. The beautiful weather, for which Hawai'i is famous, allows for unlimited recreation opportunities year-round. The emphasis on a career-related curriculum keeps students focused on their academic goals. The economy in Hawai'i makes cooperative education and internship opportunities hard to beat. Students desiring to expand their horizons in preparation for the changing global economy find Hawai'i an exciting learning laboratory where East meets West. The many opportunities available at HPU provide for a healthy combination of school, work, and fun.

Majors and Degrees

Hawai'i Pacific University offers programs that lead to the degrees of Bachelor of Arts (B.A.), Bachelor of Science in Business Administration (B.S.B.A.), Bachelor of Science in Computer Science (B.S.C.S.), Bachelor of Science in environmental science, Bachelor of Science in marine science, Bachelor of Science in Nursing (B.S.N.), Bachelor of Science in premedical studies, and Bachelor of Social Work (B.S.W.).

Undergraduate majors include the B.A. in advertising, anthropology, applied sociology, communication (concentrations in speech and visual communication), East-West classical studies, economics, engineering (a 3-2 program), English, environmental studies, history, human resource development, human services, international relations, international studies (concentrations in American, Asian, comparative, European, and Pacific studies), justice administration, political science, psychology, social sciences, and teaching English as a second language. The School of Business programs include the B.S. in accounting, advertising, business economics, computer information systems, corporate communication, entrepreneurial studies, finance, human resource management, international business, management, marketing, public administration, and travel industry management. The B.S. is also available in applied mathematics, biology, computer science, diplomacy and military studies, environmental science, marine biology, nursing, oceanography, and premedical studies. The Bachelor of Social Work is also available. Dual degrees, double majors, and minors are also offered.

Academic Programs

The baccalaureate student must complete at least 124 semester hours of credit. Forty-five of these credits provide the student with a strong foundation in the liberal arts, with the remaining credits composed of appropriate upper-division classes in the student's major and related areas. The academic year operates on a modified 4-1-4 semester system, featuring a five-week winter intersession. The University also offers extensive summer sessions. A student can earn up to 15 semester hours of credit during the summer. By attending these supplemental sessions, a student may complete the baccalaureate degree program in three years. A five-year B.S.B.A./M.B.A. program is also available.

Off-Campus Programs

Hawai'i Pacific's academic and cocurricular programs are intertwined with the world of work. The University offers a comprehensive cooperative education/internship program through the Career Services Center, in which a student may enroll throughout his or her course of study. This program enables students to gain significant experience in a career-related position as well as earn academic credit and a salary. At the upper-division level, the position is generally an internship with a leading Honolulu firm. Recent internship employers have included Aloha Airlines; Bank of Hawai'i; the city and county of Honolulu; the state of Hawai'i; Hilton Hawaiian Village Hotel; IBM; KGMB-TV and Radio; Merrill Lynch; New York Life; Ogilvy & Mather; PricewaterhouseCoopers; Sears, Roebuck and Company; Sheraton; Starr Siegle Communications; and U.S. agencies and departments. The staff at the Career Services Center continues to work with students after graduation, from resume writing to job interview preparation.

Academic Facilities

The downtown campus comprises six buildings in the center of Honolulu's business district. HPU's newest facility is the Frear Center, which houses state-of-the-art classrooms, a communication lab, a robotics lab, and a graduate M.S.I.S. high-tech classroom. Hawai'i Pacific's Meader Library provides a large collection of circulating books, special reference resources, newspapers from around the world, and periodicals. A number of special collections are housed with extensive business collections and a separate career development section. Meader Library has a tutoring center that provides free tutoring in all core subjects, a graduate reading room, and ample study space. A computerized search system allows students access to information from libraries throughout the nation. The Learning Assistance Center is the home of language labs and an audiotape and audiovisual library as well as the multimedia lab with the latest in interactive computer and CD-ROM technology. The recently expanded computer lab has more than 420 IBM-compatible PCs.

On the suburban and residential windward Hawai'i Loa campus, academic life revolves around the Amos N. Starr and Juliette Montague Cooke Academic Center (AC). The AC houses faculty and staff member offices, classrooms, a theater, an art gallery, and the Atherton Learning Resources Center, which includes a library with extensive collections in the areas of Asian studies, marine science, and nursing. The Boyd MacNaughton Pacific Resource Room houses the Hawaiiana and Pacific special collections. The Academic Computer Center provides access to IBM computers.

Costs

For the 2003–04 academic year, tuition was $10,368 (for most majors), and books, supplies, and health insurance cost approximately $1865. For students who live in residence halls, room and board were $6610. Off-campus apartments, operated by Cadmus Properties Corporation, rented for between $2700 and $2900 per semester. There was an additional $500 refundable security deposit required for residence halls and off-campus apartments. Tuition for marine science majors was $12,320, and tuition for junior- or senior-year nursing majors was $14,840.

Financial Aid

The University provides financial aid for qualified students through institutional, state, and federal aid programs. Approximately 40 percent of the University's undergraduate students receive financial aid. Among the forms of aid available are Federal Perkins Loans, Federal Stafford Student Loans, Guaranteed Parental Loans, Federal Pell Grants, and Federal Supplemental Educational Opportunity Grants. To apply for aid, students must submit the Free Application for Federal Student Aid (FAFSA). The FAFSA may be submitted at any time, but the priority deadline is March 1.

Faculty

Hawai'i Pacific's dedicated professors put a priority on teaching. At HPU, teaching assistants are not found in the classroom, only qualified professors. Students receive the personal attention they need to excel. The student-faculty ratio is 18:1, and class size averages 25 students. Students get to know their professors as colleagues and mentors. HPU faculty members are actively involved in their academic fields and bring this experience to the classroom. Many of them are renowned leaders in their particular disciplines and come to HPU from leadership positions in business and industry. The University has 225 full-time and 220 part-time faculty members. Eighty percent have earned Ph.D.'s or terminal degrees in their fields. Hawai'i Pacific has a staff of professional academic advisers whose primary responsibility is to assist students with academic programs and help them choose the right courses in the right sequence to meet their individual goals. Students meet with an adviser prior to every semester's registration.

Student Government

All registered students are members of the Associated Students of Hawai'i Pacific University (ASHPU), which is headed by elected officers and class representatives. ASHPU supervises more than eighty clubs, organizations, and activities, including a literary magazine; a national award–winning student newspaper; a pep band; an international vocal ensemble; preprofessional, cultural, and social organizations; service societies; dances; luaus; and cheerleading.

Admission Requirements

Hawai'i Pacific seeks students who are motivated and show academic promise. The admissions office requires that applicants complete and forward the admission application and their high school transcripts. Transfer students should also submit college transcripts. SAT and/or ACT scores should be submitted if these scores are not posted in the transcripts. First-time freshmen are expected to have a minimum GPA of 2.5 (on a 4.0 scale) in college-preparatory courses. Students with less than a 2.5 may be considered for admission but should also submit three letters of recommendation and a short essay on educational and personal objectives. HPU recommends that students complete 4 years of English, 2 years of math and social studies, and at least 1 year of history and science. Transfer students with 24 or more postsecondary credits are required to have a GPA of 2.0 or above. For students with less than 24 credits, a combination of college and high school GPA is used.

The Marine Science and Environmental Science Programs require a high school GPA of 3.0 or above and 3 years of science, including biology, chemistry, and physics, as well as mathematics through precalculus (trigonometry). Transfer students must demonstrate ability in science and math at the college level. Students not meeting the above criteria are encouraged to enroll at HPU without declaring a major to demonstrate the ability to do college-level work in science and math.

Application and Information

Candidates are notified of admission decisions on a rolling basis, usually within two weeks of receipt of application materials. Early entrance and deferred entrance are available.

For further information and for application materials, students should contact:

Office of Admissions
Hawai'i Pacific University
1164 Bishop Street, Suite 200
Honolulu, Hawai'i 96813
Telephone: 808-544-0238
866-CALL-HPU (toll-free in U.S. and Canada)
Fax: 808-544-1136
E-mail: admissions@hpu.edu
World Wide Web: http://www.hpu.edu/four

Students on the HPU downtown campus.

LEWIS & CLARK COLLEGE

PORTLAND, OREGON

The College

Founded in 1867 in a small town south of Portland, Lewis & Clark College moved to its present location in Portland's southwest hills in 1942. The 137-acre campus is situated in a wooded residential area 6 miles from the center of the city and overlooks the lush Willamette Valley and Mount Hood in the distance. The student body is known for its geographic diversity. In fall 2003, of the 1,792 undergraduates, 18 percent were from Oregon and 82 percent came from forty-nine other states and forty-six countries. Approximately 63 percent live in housing on campus, most of which is coed (91 percent). Residence halls allow for interaction among students, and the units are governed through student representation and hall councils. There are no fraternities or sororities. The College offers numerous cocurricular activities, including athletics and cultural events such as lectures, symposia, art exhibits, theater productions, concerts, recitals, and dance performances. Currently, there are eighteen NCAA Division III teams, eight club teams, and eight to ten intramural sports. Athletic facilities include three basketball courts, a competition-size swimming pool, a weight-training room, a stadium, a baseball/softball complex, and six tennis courts, three of which are covered by an airdome. The renowned College Outdoors Program offers backpacking, rafting, skiing, and sea kayaking in Oregon's nearby wilderness areas.

Location

Portland has long been known for its livability and its excellent transportation service. Public buses and a free College shuttle run from the Lewis & Clark campus to the center of Portland. The metropolitan area (population 1.8 million) is bisected by the Willamette River. Mount Hood, offering year-round skiing, is 50 miles away, and Oregon's rugged coastline lies 90 miles to the west. The city has 10,447 acres of parks, 33 music associations, 35 theater and dance companies, more than 90 galleries and museums, and more than 1,000 restaurants. Professional sports teams compete in baseball, hockey, indoor soccer, and NBA basketball.

Majors and Degrees

Lewis & Clark offers programs leading to the Bachelor of Arts degree. Academic majors include art, biochemistry, biology, chemistry, communications, computer science and mathematics, East Asian studies, economics, English, environmental studies, foreign languages, French, German, Hispanic studies, history, international affairs, mathematics, music, philosophy, physics, political science, psychology, religious studies, sociology/anthropology, and theater. Students may also design a major or pursue a double major and numerous minors. Preprofessional programs are available in dentistry, education, law, and medicine.

Dual-degree (3-2 and 4-2) programs in engineering are offered in cooperation with Columbia University, Washington University (St. Louis), the University of Southern California, and the Oregon Graduate Institute.

Academic Programs

The liberal arts curriculum offers sufficient structure to ensure depth and breadth of study, but it also incorporates a high degree of freedom in order to promote creative and critical thinking. In the four-year plan of study, approximately one third of a student's time is devoted to general education, one third to a major program, and one third to elective courses. Students are also encouraged to participate in departmental honors programs, undergraduate research, independent study, and internships.

The academic calendar consists of two 15-week semesters. A normal load is four 4-semester-hour academic courses, plus one or more activity courses. By graduation a student is expected to have earned at least 128 semester hours—equivalent, roughly, to eight different classes a year. The fall semester begins early in September and ends before Christmas, and the spring semester begins in mid-January and ends in early May. There are also a limited number of courses offered during two summer sessions.

The community of scholars at Lewis & Clark College is dedicated to personal and academic excellence. Joining the Lewis & Clark community obligates each member to observe the principles of mutual respect, academic integrity, civil discourse, and responsible decision making.

Off-Campus Programs

Lewis & Clark offers nationally recognized international and off-campus study opportunities that have been in existence for more than forty years. Twenty-four to twenty-seven different overseas study programs and two domestic programs are available annually. Usually, 20 to 24 students, plus a faculty leader, participate in each program. More than 60 percent of the College's graduates have taken advantage of these outstanding programs, often satisfying General Education or major requirements at the same time.

Overseas study may have either a general-culture focus or a specialized academic focus. On general-culture programs, students become immersed in the everyday life of the host country by living with local families, traveling, studying in classes and seminars, and working on independent projects. Programs with a more specific academic focus may include studying German language and literature in Munich; perfecting language skills in France, Ecuador, Russia, Japan, or China; or studying literature in England. Sites for overseas study programs from 2004 through 2007 are Australia, Chile, China, Dominican Republic, Ecuador, England, France, Germany, India, Italy, Japan, Kenya/Tanzania, Micronesia, New Zealand, Russia, Scotland, and Senegal. Domestic programs are available in New York or Washington, D.C., for those interested in economics, political science, theater, or art. All programs, both overseas and domestic, are for credit and are similar in cost to full-time, on-campus study for the same period. Students with financial aid or scholarships can apply their assistance to the expenses of these programs.

Academic Facilities

The Aubrey R. Watzek Library (open 24 hours per day during the week when school is in session) houses approximately 280,000 volumes, 1,300 periodical subscriptions, 456,000 microforms, and 13,000 units of audiovisual materials. Its mission is to provide a solid core of materials designed to support the curriculum and the research needs of the Lewis & Clark community. The library offers individualized reference assistance in the use of both print and electronic resources. The library's Web site provides access to its catalog as well as to a full range of electronic databases and links to useful Internet resources. The library is a member of Summit, a consortium of twenty-six academic libraries that have a unified catalog that enables students to request and receive materials from member libraries within two days.

Music department facilities include Evans Auditorium, a 410-seat recital hall equipped with an orchestra pit and stage elevator; an extensive record, CD, and tape collection; twenty-two practice rooms; forty-three pianos, including several 6-foot and 7-foot concert grands and a 9-foot Steinway concert grand; two harpsichords; a Baroque organ; an electronic music studio with CD production capability; Zimbabwe marimbas; and an Indonesian gamelan orchestra. The 600-seat chapel houses an 85-rank Casavant organ. A $20-million construction project resulted in a new art building that is equipped with expanded studios for ceramics, sculpture, painting and drawing, calligraphy, design, and printmaking. The department also has a library of 50,000 art history slides. The arts center contains two gallery spaces as well. A three-story humanities center also opened its doors in 1996.

The natural sciences are housed in the Biology/Psychology, BoDine, and Olin Buildings, which are well equipped with modern instrumentation to support the College's emphasis on collaborative student-faculty research. These buildings contain numerous research laboratories and equipment, used by students in classes or research projects, in addition to teaching labs and classrooms. Among the notable facilities are a laboratory for the study of human-computer interactions, a scanning electron microscope, a modern greenhouse, an astronomical observatory with several telescopes, a molecular modeling laboratory equipped with high-speed computers, a laboratory for the study of parallel computing, a laboratory for studying the biomechanics of animal locomotion, and an astrophysics laboratory that is equipped to remotely operate and acquire data from a specialized telescope at Kitts Peak, Arizona. All labs are computerized for acquiring and analyzing data and are networked to allow sharing and acquisition of data remotely. Ecological investigations and studies of the environmental impacts of human activity can be conducted both on the College's heavily wooded campus and at the nearby Tryon Creek State Park.

Computer facilities include several computer laboratories in academic buildings that are for student use. More than 130 Macintosh, IBM, and compatible computers are available for student use, along with peripherals such as color scanners, color printers, digital cameras, and digital video editing. All residence halls have direct Internet access. Parts of the campus also have wireless network capability.

Costs

Tuition and fees for 2002–03 were $23,730. The room and board charge was $6630 for fourteen meals per week; other meal plans are also available. The estimate for books and personal expenses is $1800.

Financial Aid

In 2002–03, 70 percent of the College's students received some form of financial assistance. Institutional, state, and federal resources, including Federal Pell Grants, Federal Supplemental Educational Opportunity Grants, Federal Perkins Loans, and Federal Work-Study awards, may be part of an aid award. Other options include low-interest Federal Stafford Student Loans and opportunities to work on and off campus. To receive priority consideration for financial aid, students must meet appropriate deadlines for admission and should submit the Free Application for Federal Student Aid (FAFSA) by March 1. Merit-based awards are offered to exceptional students who are selected as Neely Scholars (up to ten full-tuition scholarships), Trustee Scholars (up to fifteen half-tuition scholarships per year), and more than a hundred Dean's Scholars ($4000–$8000 scholarships per year). In addition, nearly thirty $5000 Leadership and Service Awards are made annually. Students designated as National Merit Finalists with Lewis & Clark officially named as their first choice receive up to $2000.

Faculty

The 167-member faculty, which is committed to undergraduate teaching and advising, is also active in research, writing, and publishing. Involving students in the research process is of high priority. Ninety-eight percent of the full-time faculty members hold a Ph.D. or the highest advanced degree in their discipline. The student-faculty ratio is approximately 12:1. The average class size is 19, with an average size of 24 for first-year-level courses and 16 for upper-division courses.

Student Government

The Associated Students of Lewis & Clark (ASLC) has a decentralized structure that encourages cocurricular participation by students and places a high priority on participation with faculty and staff in the process of enriching the academic environment. ASLC consists of an Executive Council, governing boards, and appointed students who serve on faculty constitutional, standing, and special committees. The 24 members of the Student Academic Affairs Board (SAAB) are appointed on a departmental basis to solicit, evaluate, and support undergraduate and faculty research, instruction, curriculum, and program enhancement. One quarter of the total ASLC budget of more than $330,000 is used by SAAB in support of undergraduate research grants and speakers.

Admission Requirements

Lewis & Clark College seeks first-year and transfer applicants who are committed to academic excellence and personal growth. Admission is competitive. Applications are carefully reviewed and examined for degree of academic preparation, ability to express ideas in essay form, participation in activities, citizenship and community service, and support given by the school through recommendations. Interviews and campus visits are encouraged but are not required. Recommended high school preparation includes 4 years of English, 4 years of history or social science, 3 to 4 years of mathematics, 3 years of laboratory science, 2 to 3 years of foreign language, and 1 year of fine arts. The SAT I or ACT is required, unless the student is applying via the Portfolio Path.

Application and Information

First-year applicants should submit the Lewis & Clark or Common Application; a personal essay; an official academic transcript, including senior grades from the first marking period; one recommendation from a counselor; and at least one reference from an academic teacher. Lewis & Clark's application form can be found online at the College's Web site (address below). The application fee is waived if the applicant uses the College's online option or the online Common Application. Application deadlines are December 1 for early action (notification by January 15) and February 1 for regular admission (notification by April 1). The optional Portfolio Path Admissions Program provides an opportunity for applicants who have shown exceptional academic initiative to demonstrate the full extent of their pursuits by presenting a portfolio of their academic work. Under this plan, SAT I or ACT scores are optional. For more information about Lewis & Clark College or to arrange a visit, students should contact:

Office of Admissions
Lewis & Clark College
0615 Southwest Palatine Hill Road
Portland, Oregon 97219-7899

Telephone: 503-768-7040
800-444-4111 (toll-free)
Fax: 503-768-7055
E-mail: admissions@lclark.edu
World Wide Web: http://www.lclark.edu

LINFIELD COLLEGE

MCMINNVILLE, OREGON

The College

Linfield College (1858) is an independent, coeducational, residential, comprehensive liberal arts college dedicated to providing an educational environment conducive to learning and participation. There are 1,600 full-time students on the McMinnville campus. These students come primarily from the thirteen Western states (twenty-eight states overall) but also from twenty-four countries. Members of minority groups make up 11 percent of the student body, and 4 percent of students are international. Most students are between 18 and 22. Linfield is primarily residential, with one residence hall for men, three for women, and eleven that are coeducational, each accommodating between 10 and 100 residents. There are also four fraternity houses. Each hall establishes its own calendar of social, educational, and recreational events throughout the year. Students who reside on campus eat their meals in the College dining hall. Houses and apartments are available for upper-division students. Social clubs, professional organizations, sororities (one local: Sigma Kappa Phi, and three national: Alpha Phi, Phi Sigma Sigma, and Zeta Tau Alpha) and fraternities (one local: Delta Psi Delta, and three national: Kappa Sigma, Pi Kappa Alpha, and Theta Chi), service clubs, and almost forty other organizations play an important role in the daily life of a Linfield student. Linfield's winning athletics tradition fosters participation at all levels of competition. Women compete in intercollegiate basketball, cross-country, golf, lacrosse, soccer, softball, swimming, tennis, track and field, and volleyball. Men compete in intercollegiate baseball, basketball, cross-country, football, golf, soccer, swimming, tennis, and track and field. Water polo, Ultimate Frisbee, and men's lacrosse are club sports. Linfield also has an extensive and active year-round intramural program.

Linfield hosts the Oregon Nobel Laureate Symposium. (There are only five such symposiums worldwide.) At each symposium, several Nobel laureates come to share their backgrounds and expertise within the context of a basic theme.

The Linfield–Good Samaritan School of Nursing, an academic unit of the College at its Portland campus, prepares students for the B.S.N. or a degree in health science. This campus, at the Good Samaritan Hospital and Medical Center, has residence facilities, food service options, and a residence life program. The Portland campus median age is 24.

Location

Located in McMinnville, 36 miles southwest of Portland, Linfield College is a leader in the cultural, educational, and recreational events of the fast-growing community of 27,000. The seat of county government, McMinnville provides Linfield faculty and students with many opportunities to participate in community service activities. Cinemas, a community theater, bowling alleys, coffeehouses, and a wide variety of restaurants welcome Linfield students. Shopping is within walking distance. The central Oregon coast is an hour to the west, and the outdoor activity areas of the Oregon Cascade mountains, including year-round skiing at Mt. Hood, are 2 hours to the east. Salem, the state capital of Oregon, is 23 miles to the southeast, and Eugene is 80 miles south. Rainfall in western Oregon averages 42 inches annually, and the winter temperature averages 41°F.

Majors and Degrees

The Bachelor of Arts degree is awarded in art, communication, creative writing, English, French, German, history, music, philosophy, political science, religious studies, sociology, Spanish, and theater arts. The Bachelor of Arts or Bachelor of Science degree is offered in accounting, anthropology, applied physics, athletic training, biology, business, chemistry, computing science, economics, elementary education, environmental studies, exercise science, finance, general science, health education, international business, mathematics, medical technology, physical education, physics, and psychology. The College has programs to prepare students for advanced study in dentistry, law, and medicine. The education department offers a strong program of teacher certification at the secondary and elementary levels. A 3-2 engineering program is available with Oregon State University, Washington State University, and the University of Southern California.

Academic Programs

The academic year is divided into two 15-week semesters (fall and spring) and an optional four-week winter term in January. (There is a $103 per-credit fee for January Term classes.) The January Term offers regular departmental courses and cultural-epochs study. Academic courses are assigned 1–5 semester credit hours each; 125 credits are required for a B.A. or a B.S. degree. Students divide their time equally among required general education courses, a major area of study, and elective subjects. The Linfield Curriculum courses, selected to provide a solid foundation in the liberal arts, require students to take 6 semester hours in at least two courses in each of the five areas of inquiry. These areas of inquiry are as follows: the Vital Past; Ultimate Questions; Individual, Systems, and Societies; the Natural World; and Images and Arts. In addition, students are required to take a writing-intensive course, a course addressing global diversity, and a course dealing with American pluralism. Major requirements differ from department to department. Individually designed majors are available with faculty approval. Students majoring in a foreign language spend an academic year in a country in which the language being studied is the native tongue. Language majors have recently studied in such cities as Avignon, Guadalajara, Nantes, Munich, Quebec, and Valencia. The Advanced Placement (AP) Program of the College Board is recognized, and up to 5 semester hours of credit are granted for a score of 4 or 5 on an AP test. AP examinations do not satisfy general education requirements. The College recognizes the International Baccalaureate (IB) Diploma and awards up to 30 semester hours of credit for higher-level courses on a course-by-course basis. Total credit awarded by AP or IB may not exceed 30 semester hours.

The College offers an intensive course in English as a second language. It is designed to help international students whose native language is other than English to achieve competence in academic and social English skills, so that they can work effectively in their undergraduate classes at Linfield.

Off-Campus Programs

Off-campus educational experiences include the Semester Abroad Program, involving four months of study in San José, Costa Rica; Paris, France; Vienna, Austria; Yokohama, Japan; Cuernavaca, Mexico; Oslo, Norway; Hong Kong, China; Seoul, South Korea; Galway, Ireland; or Nottingham, England. Sophomores, juniors, and seniors are encouraged to participate, and approximately 20 students are selected for each country each year. The program is designed to serve students who have successfully completed one year of study at Linfield in the appropriate language and who will return to the campus to share their international experiences with the College community. Transportation for the first round trip is included in the cost of tuition, and most of these study programs cost the same as a semester on campus. January Term study-abroad programs for four weeks are also offered. Recent offerings included the Emergence of Modern Ghana (West Africa); Mainland Southeast Asia History (Cambodia, Vietnam, and China); American Expatriate Writers in Europe: The Lost Generation Tour (nine European cities); and Australia: From Colony to Asian Power.

Academic Facilities

Murdock Hall houses the biology and chemistry departments and up-to-date laboratories and equipment. Laboratory and research space is provided for general and advanced chemistry and biology, organic chemistry, biochemistry, microbiology, bacteriology, immunology, ecology, botany, physiology, embryology, and gross and microscopic anatomy. Taylor Hall houses the economics department, a computer center, a resource library, a seminar room, and classrooms. The physics and mathematics departments are housed in Graf Hall. There are approximately 200 IBM and Macintosh computers on campus available for student use. Services on the network that students can use include the two UNIX hosts (available for programming, e-mail, and other communication services), a connection to the Internet, file servers, and both laser and dot-matrix printers. Linfield students benefit from a communications and technology network, including phone service, voice mail, e-mail, and Internet connections in each residence hall room.

The Health and Physical Education/Recreation Complex houses three gymnasiums; weight rooms; fitness laboratories with a hydrostatic weighing tank, a metabolic and pulmonary measuring system, and an electrocardiovascular exercise ECG system; an eight-lane, 25-yard-long indoor pool; handball and racquetball courts; classrooms; offices; and a 28,000-square-foot field house.

Since 2000, there have been many exciting changes at Linfield. The College has opened six new apartment buildings as well as the James F. Miller Fine Arts Complex. In July of 2003, Linfield opened its new library and theater and communication arts facility. The new library covers 56,000 square feet and combines traditional collections of books and journals with the new and changing digital and electronic technology to provide access to the Web and Web-based designs. There is seating for up to 500 students and 35 computer work stations as well as wireless access to the campus network, the Internet, and the World Wide Web for student who bring their own laptops or check out those available at the library. The new studio theater has an audience seating capacity of up to 140, more than double the former facility. It includes space for set construction and design as well as faculty offices. Other facilities include art galleries and studios, a 250-watt FM radio station, an experimental psychology laboratory, dance and music studios, a preschool, and a 425-seat auditorium that houses a three-manual, 48-rank Casavant pipe organ.

Costs

For 2003–04, tuition and fees were $20,770 per two-semester year. Board was $2920, and a double room was $3200.

Financial Aid

Eligibility for most of Linfield's assistance programs is based on need as determined by a federally approved needs analysis processor. The only form required for need-based programs is the Free Application for Federal Student Aid (FAFSA). Linfield participates in the Federal Perkins and Federal Stafford Student Loan programs, Federal Supplemental Educational Opportunity Grants, Federal Work-Study, and other forms of financial assistance on the basis of demonstrated need.

The College awards a number of scholarships to full-time students based on scholastic achievement, independent of financial need. These academic scholarships vary from 20 to 75 percent of tuition. To be considered, students must have a minimum GPA of 3.4. A number of other criteria are used when determining scholarships. Linfield sponsors special scholarships for National Merit finalists. The minimum award is 50 percent of tuition. Awards can range to full tuition, depending on financial need, provided the student has indicated that Linfield is his or her first-choice college. The College also sponsors the annual Academic Competitive Scholarship Program in early spring each year. Participation is limited to high school seniors who meet particular academic requirements. Each academic department offers prizes ranging from $10,000 to $16,000, divided over the student's four years at Linfield, provided the student maintains a grade point average of at least 3.0. Scholarships of varying amounts are awarded to entering students who are particularly talented in music performance. Amounts range from $1500 to $2500 annually. Interested students are required to audition either in person or by cassette tape by February 15. Financial assistance for non–U.S. citizens is limited to partial tuition scholarships and the opportunity to work part-time on campus. Other scholarships are available for students who demonstrate outstanding leadership and community service.

Faculty

There are 137 full-time faculty members, who are committed to undergraduate teaching and scholarship. Ninety-eight percent have doctoral or other terminal degrees within their field. The faculty-student ratio is 1:12. Faculty members serve as academic advisers. There are no teaching assistants.

Student Government

Students have a significant voice in establishing and changing College policies and regulations. The Student Senate, chosen through campus elections, is the focus of student opinion and debate. Students are represented on most College governing councils and committees, with faculty members and trustees, and are encouraged to express and implement their ideas on academic or extracurricular matters.

Admission Requirements

Admission to Linfield College is selective. Admission is granted to students who are likely to grow and succeed in a personal and challenging liberal arts environment. Each applicant is judged on individual merit. A faculty admission committee evaluates candidates in a number of areas that commonly indicate academic potential. These include high school performance, a writing sample, recommendations from teachers and counselors, and precollege standardized test results (ACT or SAT I). The committee also considers the depth and quality of an applicant's involvement in community and school activities. It reviews all applications as a group, selecting those students who show the greatest likelihood of benefitting from and contributing to the Linfield community. Linfield is a member of the Common Application Association.

International students whose education has been in a language other than English must submit certified English translations of their academic work. Proficiency in English is required, as demonstrated by an official TOEFL score report, including a Test of Written English (TWE) score. Admitted international students must show evidence of financial responsibility and submit a $2000 deposit.

Early action applicants must apply by November 15, and notification is made by January 15. The priority application deadline for regular admission is February 15, with notification made on or before April 1.

Application and Information

Interviews are not required, but students are encouraged to visit. Appointments should be made in advance. The Office of Admission is open Monday through Friday, 7:30 a.m. to 5:30 p.m. and on Saturdays during the school year from 9 a.m. to 2 p.m. The Linfield Web site provides students with information on student life, academic programs, and athletics. Students may also complete their application for admission online or ask for additional information. Interested students are encouraged to contact:

Director of Admission
Linfield College
McMinnville, Oregon 97128

Telephone: 503-883-2213
800-640-2287 (toll-free)
Fax: 503-883-2472
E-mail: admission@linfield.edu
World Wide Web: http://www.linfield.edu

NORTHERN ARIZONA UNIVERSITY

FLAGSTAFF, ARIZONA

The University

Northern Arizona University (NAU) is a fully accredited, state-supported, four-year institution with approximately 13,390 full-time students on its main campus. Since 1899, the University has made a major commitment to undergraduate education, and its goal has been to preserve a friendly campus atmosphere and close student-faculty relationships through classroom teaching of the highest quality and faculty guidance for each student.

The University is composed of the Colleges of Arts and Science, Business Administration, Education, Engineering and Technology, Fine and Performing Arts, Health Professions, and Social and Behavioral Sciences and the Schools of Communication, Forestry, and Hotel and Restaurant Management. Undergraduate, master's, and doctoral degrees are offered in more than 150 major areas and in a number of interdisciplinary and preprofessional curricula. A graduate degree is available in physical therapy.

Ten advisement centers assist the University in realizing its strong commitment to one-on-one advising, and regular office hours are maintained by faculty members. The new Gateway Student Success Center offers academic advising services and career exploration assistance for all students who are undecided in terms of a degree program. An average class size of 29 is another example of the institution's attention to high-quality education.

Nonacademic facilities include seven buildings listed on the National Register of Historic Places. In addition, there are three student unions, a student health center, an Olympic-size swimming and diving complex, a 16,230-seat multiuse wooden dome, and a multipurpose recreational facility.

As a residential campus, NAU provides an atmosphere of friendship and community. Fifty percent of the undergraduate students live in the sixteen residence halls and 346 family housing apartments located on the campus. Of the 11,487 full-time undergraduates enrolled in the 2003 fall semester, 4,432 were men and 6,648 were women.

Northern Arizona University is an Equal Opportunity/Affirmative Action institution.

Location

Northern Arizona University's 730-acre mountain campus is located in Flagstaff, which is a community with 58,000 residents. Flagstaff is located at an elevation of 7,000 feet, just south of the 12,600-foot-high San Francisco Peaks, a major winter-sports center. The University is at the junction of Interstate Highways 40 (U.S. 66) and 17, less than a 3-hour drive from Phoenix and about a 5-hour drive from Tucson, Arizona; Albuquerque, New Mexico; and Las Vegas, Nevada. The city is served by Amtrak, Greyhound buses, and a commercial airline. The campus is surrounded by scenic beauty and natural wonders, such as the Grand Canyon and a student favorite, Oak Creek Canyon. The varied northern land of mountains, gorges, forests, and lakes provides the University with natural classrooms and laboratories for research as well as recreation.

Majors and Degrees

Northern Arizona University offers baccalaureate degrees in approximately ninety major areas, embracing most of the recognized fields in the arts and sciences and a number of interdisciplinary majors. NAU also offers a number of special programs, including arts management, criminal justice, dental hygiene, forestry, hotel and restaurant management, and parks and recreation management.

Academic Programs

A four-year baccalaureate degree program at Northern Arizona University requires the successful completion of 120 semester hours of course work, including 35 hours of liberal studies courses. The liberal studies program consists of foundation studies and studies in various disciplines designed to assist students in cultivating their abilities to recognize significant problems and to define, analyze, and defend solutions in a variety of contexts. Major-field requirements vary from 35 to 73 semester hours. Students may combine a major field with one or more 18-hour minors, take two majors or an extended major of 63 to 65 hours in a field of their interest, or select the merged major programs.

NAU has a long-established honors program designed to challenge the talented student. This leads to graduation with honors, and honor students may elect to take the special degree of Bachelor of Arts: Honors. The program provides special courses and seminars and offers superior students opportunities for independent study and research.

A three-year bachelor's degree program is available in forty-six majors. The program offers intellectual and academic challenges for well-prepared and motivated students, allowing them to take the fast track to graduation and graduate programs.

Off-Campus Programs

NAU actively cooperates in the work and research programs of several major scientific institutions that are located close to its campus. These include the Lowell Observatory; the U.S. Naval Observatory's Flagstaff station; various facilities of the U.S. Geological Survey, including its space-oriented Astrogeology Center; the U.S. Forest Service Rocky Mountain and Range Experiment station; and the Museum of Northern Arizona and its multidisciplinary Colton Research Center. The specialized libraries, laboratories, and other facilities of these institutions are available to qualified students at the University. NAU sponsors a marine biology camp in Mexico on the Gulf of California, as well as scientific field trips to many of the distinctive natural areas of northern Arizona, including an annual geological study tour through the nearby Grand Canyon.

The Northern Arizona University Centers in London, England; Tübingen, Germany; Granada, Spain; Montpellier, France; and Shanghai and Beijing, China, offer students an opportunity for exciting enrichment programs for one or two semesters in Europe or Asia. Students may also study for one semester in Cuernavaca, Mexico. Through field trips, students explore the history, literature, and culture of these regions. All students except freshmen may enroll.

Through the National Student Exchange program, NAU students have an opportunity to broaden their educational horizons by attending a college or university in another state for one semester or one year while paying tuition and fees at NAU. There are more than 150 participating institutions nationwide from which students may choose.

Academic Facilities

NAU's facilities for education and research are extensive. The University library contains more than 1.6 million volumes, approximately 6,253 current periodical titles, a media center, and a number of special research collections of original documents relating to the history, economy, and culture of Arizona and the Southwest. The facility now has an online public access catalog and a book capacity of 2 million volumes.

Well-equipped general and specialized laboratories serve students in the basic sciences and health professions. Specially designed studios, workrooms, theaters, auditoriums, and an art gallery are available to students in the creative arts. Closed-circuit television hookups, student-paced audiovisual systems, language laboratories, an observatory, and a major computer center are used regularly by students for both learning and research. The Bilby Research Center augments NAU's research facilities.

NAU makes extensive use of the spectacular Colorado Plateau country surrounding its campus as a natural laboratory for anthropology, biology, ecology, geology, geophysics, paleontology, and other sciences. Prehistoric Indian ruins and the living cultures of the Navajo, Hopi, and many other Indian peoples of the Southwest provide rich resources for students of archaeology, ethnology, and linguistics. The University also maintains a 4,000-acre research forest for forestry students. The area's 7,000-foot elevation and unusually clear, dry air have made it a major center for astronomy and the atmospheric sciences.

Costs

For 2003–04, the charges for an academic year of two semesters for an in-state student were tuition and fees, $3594, and average board and room, $5374. Books and supplies averaged $750. The total cost for Arizona residents was $9718 per academic year. The out-of-state tuition and fees were $12,114, for an academic-year cost of $18,238. This does not include travel or personal expenses, which vary for each student. All costs are subject to change by the Arizona Board of Regents.

Financial Aid

Northern Arizona University maintains an extensive program of financial assistance to aid students in pursuing their educational goals. The amount of financial aid awarded to a student is based upon the student's need level, as computed from the Free Application for Federal Student Aid (FAFSA). However, some scholarships are awarded on the basis of a student's demonstration of academic excellence and/or participation in various University activities.

In the 2003–04 academic year, more than $120 million was available for loans, scholarships, grants, veterans' benefits, and work-study programs. About 60 percent of the students at NAU received some form of financial aid.

Along with grants, loans, and scholarships, on- and off-campus employment is available to help students meet financial obligations. More than 4,500 NAU students are currently employed in a wide variety of jobs on the campus.

Faculty

NAU's faculty is made up of outstanding and dedicated professionals. More than 85 percent of the 698 full-time and 630 part-time faculty members hold doctoral degrees. Many are nationally distinguished scientists and scholars. The student-faculty ratio is 17:1, with more than 80 percent of the classes taught by faculty members rather than graduate assistants.

Student Government

Each student who enters NAU is a member of the Associated Students of Northern Arizona University (ASNAU), which represents the students' interests in all matters that affect them.

Besides ASNAU, other student governing groups are the Associated Women Students, Association of University Residence Halls, Panhellenic Council, and Inter-Fraternity Council. About 50 percent of the students belong to one or more of the 192 student groups and organizations.

Admission Requirements

Applicants for admission must complete both general aptitude and basic competence requirements. Conditional admission for non-Arizona residents is granted on a space-available basis. Participation in some form of assistance program may be required for those admitted conditionally.

For unconditional admission, the general aptitude requirements for new freshmen are any one of the following: a cumulative GPA of 3.0 or better (on a 4.0 scale), a class rank in the upper quarter, a minimum ACT composite score of 22 (24 for non-Arizona residents), or a minimum combined SAT I score of 1040 (1100 for nonresidents). For conditional admission, the requirements are a cumulative GPA between 2.5 and 2.99 or a class rank at least in the upper half with test scores below the previously stated minimums. The GPA to meet the general aptitude requirement for admission is calculated using only the sixteen required core courses. Transfer students with fewer than 12 transferable academic semester credits must meet the same standards as new freshmen. If 12 or more semester credits have been earned, then the cumulative GPA must be at least 2.0 for unconditional or conditional admission for Arizona residents. Non-Arizona residents must have a cumulative GPA of at least 2.5 for unconditional admission or between 2.0 and 2.49 for conditional admission.

Basic competency requirements must be met by all freshmen and transfer students, either through high school course work and/or transferable higher education courses. Generally, one 3-hour college course equals one year of high school study. Core course requirements include 4 years of English, 4 years of mathematics, 3 years of laboratory science, 2 years of social science, 2 years of foreign language, and 1 year of fine art. There are specific course requirements within these areas, and some requirements may be met by achieving minimum scores on standardized tests. Students should contact the Admissions Office for more information.

March 1 is the priority deadline for the summer and fall semesters; December 1 is for the spring semester. Applications and supporting documents received after these dates are processed on a space-available basis.

Application and Information

The NAU information booklet, which includes an application for admission and information about financial aid, housing, and academic programs, may be obtained by contacting:

Admissions Office
Northern Arizona University
Box 4084
Flagstaff, Arizona 86011-4084
Telephone: 888-667-3628 (toll-free)
E-mail: undergraduate.admissions@nau.edu

A friendly residential campus and the four-season climate of Flagstaff, Arizona, attract about 12,000 undergraduate students each year to Northern Arizona University.

REGIS UNIVERSITY

DENVER, COLORADO

The University

In its 126th year, Regis University is the Rocky Mountain region's only Jesuit university and is well-known for innovation and educational leadership. Continuing a 450-year tradition of academic excellence, Regis is one of twenty-eight Jesuit colleges and universities located in the United States.

U.S. News & World Report named Regis University a "Top School" among colleges and universities in the western United States, marking the ninth consecutive year Regis has been in the publication's top tier. The University was also recognized as one of the top 100 universities and colleges for leadership in the field of student character development in *The Templeton Guide: Colleges That Encourage Character Development*. Regis University is ranked by *U.S. News & World Report* as the second-best university in the western United States for the highest proportion of classes with 20 students or fewer.

The University has an American Rhodes Scholar, 2 *USA Today* College All-Academic Team selectees (in 1993 and 2000), the top female collegiate athlete in NCAA Division II for 1998–99, 5 Fulbright professors, 2 Fuld Fellows, and a wealth of other national recognition of outstanding academic excellence. More than 90 percent of Regis's full-time faculty members have a Ph.D.

However, Regis University was not always Regis. The school was started in 1877 in Las Vegas, New Mexico, by a group of exiled Italian Jesuits. It was known as Las Vegas College. In 1884, a second venture, known as Sacred Heart College, was started at Morrison, Colorado.

In 1887, Las Vegas College and Sacred Heart College moved to North Denver, where the joint operation became known as the College of the Sacred Heart. The college was renamed Regis in 1921, in honor of St. John Francis Regis, an eighteenth-century Jesuit missionary and saint who was revered for his exemplary work with poor people in the mountains of France.

On July 1, 1991, Regis College became Regis University, with three constituent schools: Regis College, the School for Professional Studies, and the School for Health Care Professions. Regis College is the traditional residential school, with nearly 1,200 students, primarily in the 18- to 23-year-old range. The School for Professional Studies focuses on undergraduate and graduate adult higher education. The School for Health Care Professions educates men and women to be leaders who are committed to excellence within the health-care professions.

Regis College primarily serves traditional-aged, mostly residential undergraduate students. The college offers a full range of programs in the liberal arts, sciences, business, and education. Students may choose from twenty-four structured areas of study or design their own programs through the interdisciplinary and flexible major plans. A low student-faculty ratio permits small classes and learning formats that encourage critical thinking, thoughtful discussion, and well-developed communication skills. In the college, students receive highly personalized attention from more than 83 skilled professors and dedicated scholars.

Athletic opportunities are offered on all levels: recreational, intramural, and intercollegiate. Regis University is a member of NCAA Division II and the Rocky Mountain Athletic Conference and competes in twelve intercollegiate sports as well as a variety of intramural and club sport programs.

In addition to the undergraduate degree programs listed below, Regis offers a Master of Arts degree in education (learning and teaching).

Location

Regis University is located near the base of the Rocky Mountains in a residential suburban neighborhood of northwest Denver, just north of I-70 and 25 minutes from Denver International Airport. Within 15 minutes of the campus is one of the most exciting international downtowns in the world. Thirty minutes west of the campus are the snow-capped peaks of the Rocky Mountains. Denver is one of America's fastest-growing metropolitan regions, with an abundance of cultural and recreational opportunities; it is one of only a few American cities with seven professional sports franchises. Denver has low humidity, and the sun shines about 300 days a year. The metropolitan area averages only 15 inches of precipitation a year, about the same as Los Angeles. Midwinter temperatures of 60 degrees are common. Colorado ski country is nearby; the campus is just 2 hours from Breckenridge, Vail, and Winter Park.

Majors and Degrees

Undergraduate degree offerings include the Bachelor of Arts (B.A.), Bachelor of Science (B.S.), Bachelor of Arts and Science, Classical Bachelor of Arts, and Bachelor of Science in Nursing (B.S.N.), as well as special majors.

Business programs include accounting (major and minor); accounting/M.B.A. (major); business administration, with concentrations in finance, international business, management, management information systems, and marketing (major and minor); economics (major and minor); flexible major; and political economy (major and minor).

Programs in humanities include communication (major and minor), English (major and minor), fine arts: visual arts (major and minor), flexible major, French (major and minor), German (minor), Hispanic studies (minor), literature (minor), Spanish (major and minor), women's studies (major and minor), and writing (minor).

The University offers natural sciences and mathematics programs in biochemistry (major and minor), biology (B.A. and B.S., major and minor), chemistry (major and minor), computer science (major and minor), environmental studies/human ecology (major and minor), flexible major, kinesiology (minor), mathematics (major and minor), neuroscience (major and minor), and physics (minor).

Programs in philosophy and religious studies include Catholic studies (minor), Christian leadership (minor), flexible major, philosophy (major and minor), and religious studies (major and minor).

Social sciences programs include criminal justice (major and minor), education (minor), elementary education (minor), flexible major, history (major and minor), peace and justice studies (minor), physical education (minor), physical education: coaching/recreation (minor), political science (major and minor), psychology (major and minor), secondary education (minor), and sociology (major and minor).

Preprofessional programs are offered in dentistry, law, medicine, and physical therapy. A dual-degree engineering program is also offered.

Academic Programs

Regis is part of a 450-year-old Jesuit tradition that provides a values-centered liberal arts education and is known for service to others. The Core Curriculum, designed to prepare students for life as well as a career, requires students to reflect on the purpose of human existence, to understand the roots of modern culture, to embrace philosophical and religious perspectives, and to think critically. These courses enrich perceptions, challenge assumptions, and broaden visions.

A total of 128 semester hours is required for a bachelor's degree. Regis chooses a select group of students for its honors program each year and offers a schedule of undergraduate courses in the summer session. The University's Center for Service Learning actively involves students in community service projects. Internships and study abroad are offered as well. Other academic programs include the writing program, teacher licensure, the Commitment Program, Air Force Reserve Officer Training Corps, Air Force University Scholarship Program, and the Army Reserve Officer Training Corps (military science).

Academic Facilities

Regis is committed to providing state-of-the-art facilities. The University offers students 24-hour access to personal computers, online service, and research tools in common lab facilities. In addition, labs are located in the three coeducational residence halls, in the town houses, and in specific departments. All students are offered full access to an e-mail account on the Internet.

The University has two libraries, housing more than 280,000 volumes, 2,100 periodical subscriptions, 150,000 microforms, and a 90,000-slide art history collection. Its CARL online catalog is a comprehensive index to the collections and provides 10,000 databases, document delivery options, and full-text online journals. The main library, which includes media services, provides network ports at every place that a student studies for ease of access to the Internet and the Regis database.

The Coors Life Direction Center houses the Office of Career Services and Personal Counseling as well as the Fitness Program and the Health Center.

Four modern residence halls—O'Connell, DeSmet, West, and the new townhouse complex—are fully staffed and offer computer labs, free cable TV, local phone service and voice mail, free laundry facilities, lounges, vending machines, and two phone and data lines in each room. More than 80 percent of freshmen live on campus.

Costs

Undergraduate tuition at Regis College for the 2003–04 academic year is $20,700. Room and board for the academic year cost $7600.

Financial Aid

In an effort to keep its high-quality Jesuit education affordable, Regis is committed to helping as many students as possible by continuing to increase scholarships and University grant funds. The student financial aid program invests more than $14 million in undergraduates. More than 90 percent of full-time Regis College students receive some financial assistance. Scholarships and grants are awarded on the basis of need, academic achievement, and leadership. The University participates in all federal and Colorado-supported programs. The Free Application for Federal Student Aid (FAFSA) or Renewal Application must be filed.

Faculty

Regis College has 83 full-time faculty members; 92 percent hold terminal degrees. Ten percent of the faculty members are Jesuit priests, and Regis has no graduate students/teaching assistants on its staff. The college has a 15:1 student-faculty ratio. Some professional staff members and Jesuit priests live and teach on Regis's campus. These committed adults are available for both academic and personal direction for Regis students. In addition, each undergraduate has an individual faculty adviser, who assists students in their academic choices.

Student Government

The Student Government at Regis is led by the Executive Board. The board is supported by the Senate, which comprises class representatives. The student leaders serve on University committees, plan entertainment, help determine student policy, and oversee more than thirty student organizations.

Admission Requirements

Regis College actively recruits students for equal opportunity and nondiscriminatory consideration of eligibility. In 2003, the average ACT composite score for incoming freshmen was 23, and the average SAT combined score was 1108. Admission is determined by a student's high school record, including grades, test scores, personal ability, and leadership qualities.

Requirements for freshman admission include high school graduation or its equivalent and evidence of college-level competency, as shown in high school courses, grades, ACT or SAT I test scores, a personal essay, and recommendations. Freshmen should present a minimum of 15 academic units. Successful candidates must have a satisfactory high school or college record in order to be admitted.

Application and Information

Completed applications for admission should be submitted to the Director of Admissions. Applications may be submitted any time after the beginning of the year. The Office of Admissions usually notifies each applicant regarding the decision within four weeks after the completed application and supporting documents have been received by the Office of Admissions. All requests for information or application forms should be addressed to:

Director of Admissions
Regis College Office of Admissions, A-12
Regis University
3333 Regis Boulevard
Denver, Colorado 80221-1099
Telephone: 303-458-4900
800-388-2366 Ext. 4900 (toll-free)
Fax: 303-964-5534
E-mail: regisadm@regis.edu
World Wide Web: http://www.regis.edu

The Regis University campus is located in a pleasant residential neighborhood with beautiful Rocky Mountain views, just a few minutes from downtown Denver.

SEATTLE UNIVERSITY
SEATTLE, WASHINGTON

The University

Seattle University (SU) provides an ideal environment for motivated students interested in self-reliance, awareness of different cultures, social justice, and the fulfillment that comes from making a difference. Its location in the center of one of the nation's most diverse and progressive cities attracts a varied student body, faculty, and staff. Its urban setting promotes the development of leadership skills and independence and provides a variety of opportunities for students to apply what they learn through internships, clinical experiences, and volunteer work. It is an environment that allows students to "connect the mind to what matters."

As a Jesuit institution, Seattle University is part of a network of twenty-eight colleges and universities and forty-six high schools noted for academic strength across the United States. Academic offerings are designed to provide leadership opportunities, develop global awareness, and enable graduates to serve society through a demanding liberal arts and sciences foundation. In the Jesuit educational tradition, students are taught how to think, not what to think. Professional undergraduate offerings include highly respected Schools of Business, Nursing, and Science and Engineering and career-oriented liberal arts programs such as communications, creative writing, criminal justice, and journalism. The University's Schools of Education, Law, and Theology and Ministry offer graduate-level opportunities.

Seattle University is noted for its focus on the individual through small, faculty-taught classes and excellent service. The result is mirrored by graduates who lead fulfilling and economically successful lives. SU leads the Pacific Northwest in producing Truman and Wilson scholars.

The fall quarter has a freshman class of 665, and 45 percent are from outside Washington State. The 3,765 undergraduate students represent forty-six states and seventy-six nations. Approximately 10 percent are international students. The ethnic breakdown for the fall 2003 freshman class was 56 percent white, 20 percent Asian American, and 18 percent African American, Latino, and American Indian.

The residential campus has undergone $157 million in recent improvements. Although it is in the center of Seattle, the campus has been designated by Washington State as an Official Backyard Sanctuary for its distinctive landscaping and environmentally conscious practices.

There is a wide variety of on-campus housing that accommodates 1,596 students, including a new apartment complex, and 85 percent of freshmen live on campus. There is a two-year on-campus residence requirement.

Seattle University has more than eighty-five extracurricular clubs and organizations and has five varsity teams for men (basketball, cross-country, soccer, swimming, and track) and seven for women (basketball, cross-country, soccer, softball, swimming, track, and volleyball). SU is in NCAA Division II. The student life program includes sixty extracurricular clubs and organizations, including the Hawaiian Club, Associated Students of African Descent, Hiyu Coulee Hiking Club, Beta Alpha Psi (national accounting honorary), and other professional honoraries and clubs.

The Connolly Athletic Center serves as the major facility for varsity and intramural athletics and recreation. It features two swimming pools, two full-size gymnasiums, and locker room saunas. A 6-acre complex provides fields for outdoor sports.

Seattle University receives the highest professional accreditation from the Accreditation Board for Engineering and Technology, Inc.; AACSB International–The Association to Advance Collegiate Schools of Business; the American Bar Association; the American Chemical Society; the Association of Theological Schools; the Commission on Accreditation of Allied Health Education Programs; the National Council for Accreditation of Teacher Education; the Commission on Collegiate Nursing Education; the Council on Social Work Education; and the Northwest Association of Schools and Colleges.

Location

Seattle University is located on First Hill in a port city of unsurpassed natural beauty. As the Pacific Northwest's largest city (and the fourteenth-largest metropolitan area in the U.S.), Seattle is a scenic and cultural center in a setting that includes breathtaking mountain views of the Cascades to the east and the Olympics to the west; skiing is within 60 minutes of campus. In addition to being situated along Puget Sound, Seattle also contains Lakes Union and Washington; both provide a wide variety of recreational opportunities. Seattle's residents love the outdoors, and areas for hiking, backpacking, and climbing are minutes from campus. Biking is also popular and special trails for cycling and running are located throughout the city.

Seattle's sights and sounds, rich ethnic diversity, celebrated restaurants, first–run entertainment, major-league athletics, theater, opera, and ballet are within walking distance and enhance campus life.

Majors and Degrees

Seattle University offers the following undergraduate degrees: Bachelor of Arts, Bachelor of Science, Bachelor of Science in nursing, Bachelor of Social Work, Bachelor of Criminal Justice, Bachelor of Public Affairs, and the Bachelor of Arts in business administration.

The University offers programs in six major academic units. The Albers School of Business and Economics awards degrees in accounting, business economics, e-commerce, finance, general business, international business, management, and marketing. The College of Arts and Sciences grants degrees in art, Asian studies, communication studies, criminal justice, drama, ecological studies, economics, English, fine arts, foreign languages, history, humanities, international studies, journalism, liberal studies, philosophy, political science, psychology, public affairs, social work, sociology, and theology and religious studies. The College of Nursing offers a Bachelor of Science in Nursing degree. The College of Science and Engineering offers degree programs in biochemistry, biology, chemistry, civil engineering, computer engineering, computer science, diagnostic ultrasound, electrical engineering, environmental engineering, general science, mechanical engineering, mathematics, medical technology, and physics. Preprofessional programs include dentistry, law, medicine, optometry, and veterinary medicine.

Academic Programs

The Core Curriculum is known for its strength and has several distinguishing characteristics in keeping with the Jesuit tradition: it provides an integrated freshman year; it gives order and sequence to student learning; it provides experience in the methods and content of the range of liberal arts, sciences, philosophy, and theology; it calls for active learning in all classes for practice in writing and thinking, and for an awareness of values; and it fosters a global perspective and a sense of social and personal responsibility.

Seattle University offers two honors program options for students seeking the greatest possible challenge. The University Honors Program is a small, select two-year-long learning community. It is humanities focused, and its fully integrated curriculum examines the most significant texts and ideas of Western culture. The Core Honors Program involves seminar sections of nine required courses in English, history, philosophy, social science, and theology/religious studies. This option is particularly suited to students in profession-oriented majors where participation in University Honors is less feasible due to specific major requirements and scheduling conflicts.

SU operates on a quarter calendar. The fall quarter begins in mid-September; the winter quarter in early January; the spring quarter in late March; and the summer quarter in mid-June. Undergraduates typically take 15 hours each during the fall, winter, and spring quarters.

Off-Campus Programs

SU offers international study programs—one for French in France, one for Latin American studies in Mexico, and two reciprocal exchange programs with the University of Graz in Austria and Sophia University in Japan. These are open to all students in all majors and emphasize appreciation of the language and culture. This is accomplished through the total immersion concept. Other programs include Campus Ministry missions in Nicaragua and Belize and Albers School of Business and Economics tours in Mexico, Italy, Hong Kong, and Vietnam. Seattle University maintains the only Calcutta Club in which students volunteer annually on behalf of Mother Teresa's ministry. Additional study-abroad programs in other nations, in conjunction with other colleges' overseas programs, are also offered. Arrangements are made through SU's Study Abroad Office.

Academic Facilities

The University is located on 45 acres in the First Hill neighborhood in the center of Seattle. There are twenty-eight buildings recently enhanced by $157 million in additions, renovations, and new construction.

Costs

In 2003–04, tuition was $20,070; room and meals were $6858. The estimate for books, fees, and personal expenses is an additional $2982. Travel costs varies among students. Costs are subject to change.

Financial Aid

Seattle University awarded $5.4 million in its own financial aid to fall 2003 freshmen, including 196 scholarships ranging from $6000 to $27,378. Sixty-nine percent of freshmen received University aid. Students are required to apply for financial aid by February 1 as awards are made early each spring for the following fall quarter. Applications that are received after this deadline will be evaluated in order received for any remaining aid. Students must submit the Free Application for Federal Student Aid (FAFSA) and be accepted for admission to be considered for financial assistance. There are also a number of scholarships for freshmen that are awarded on the basis of academic achievement, extracurricular involvement, and community service. Similar transfer scholarships are determined primarily on the basis of course selection and cumulative grade point average.

Faculty

There are 522 faculty members; 88 percent of full-time faculty members possess doctoral or terminal degrees. Like the University, the mission of faculty members who choose Seattle University is teaching. Most classes average 20; the faculty-student ratio is 1:14. All classes are taught by faculty members. The involvement of faculty members extends beyond the classroom. Faculty members are available to provide extra assistance, to help students with their research, and to assist in the arranging of internships. Faculty advisers provide guidance, direction, and encouragement throughout the year. New students are assigned faculty advisers according to major prior to registration.

Student Government

All undergraduates belong to the Associated Students of Seattle University (ASSU). This is the central student organization on campus. ASSU is organized around an elected president, an executive vice president, and an activities vice president. In addition, a 12-member representative council oversees every facet of the student body and is responsible for policymaking. Its primary responsibility is to provide a diverse activities program to meet the needs of SU's diverse student body. In addition, ASSU communicates student needs to the administration and faculty. ASSU oversees eighty-five clubs and organizations.

Admission Requirements

Freshman applicants are required to have a college-preparatory program, including 4 years of English, 3 years of social studies/history, 3 years of mathematics, 2 years of laboratory science, and 2 years of a foreign language. ACT or SAT scores, two recommendations, and an essay are also required. The middle 50 percent of freshman GPAs are between 3.3 and 3.8 on a 4.0 scale. The average score on the ACT is between 21 and 27, and the average SAT I scores are between 510 and 626 (verbal) and 510 and 620 (math). Seattle University accepts the Common Application, the Uniform Application, Peterson's Universal Application, the Catholic College Admissions Association Application, and its own admission application.

Essays or personal statements are required for admission and are carefully considered during application review.

College credit is awarded to those who have successfully completed Advanced Placement or International Baccalaureate examinations. Minimum scores can be obtained by contacting the Office of the Registrar.

Application and Information

Applications can be obtained by contacting the Admissions Office. Secondary school students who have completed at least six semesters are encouraged to apply by January of their senior year. Transfer students must submit official transcripts from all postsecondary institutions attended, regardless of whether course work was completed. For fall admission, freshmen should complete the process by February 1 to receive consideration for scholarships and other Seattle University financial aid; the recommended financial aid/admissions deadline for transfers is March 1. Please note that applications will usually be accepted after these dates but funds for financial aid may no longer be available. Campus visits can be scheduled Monday through Friday and most Saturdays. Guests can attend a class, meet with a faculty adviser, participate in a campus tour, and speak individually with representatives from admissions and financial aid.

For additional information students should contact:

Michael K. McKeon, Dean
Admissions Office
Seattle University
900 Broadway
Seattle, Washington 98122-4340
Telephone: 206-296-2000
800-426-7123 (toll-free)
E-mail: admissions@seattleu.edu
World Wide Web: http://www.seattleu.edu

UNIVERSITY OF ADVANCING TECHNOLOGY

TEMPE, ARIZONA

The University

The University of Advancing Technology (UAT) is a prestigious private university with a dynamic and innovative campus culture. UAT offers unique bachelor's and master's computer technical degrees. Programs include digital animation, digital video production, Web design, game design, computer programming, database programming, game programming, Internet development and administration, network engineering, network security, e-commerce marketing, technology management, and Web site production.

UAT was founded in 1983 and has grown from a small computer manufacturer and corporate training center to today's modern University, located in the Phoenix metropolitan area. The school has close ties to industry through technology forums, a corporate training program, and an industry advisory board. These industry leaders provide input into the curriculum and insight into computer technologies needed in the workforce. This constant two-way communication between UAT and industry means that the University is on the leading edge of technology education and careers.

Classes are small, and students attend a full-time accelerated program in three 15-week semesters each year. Bachelor's degree programs are completed in fewer than three years and associate degrees in sixteen months. There are three regular start dates in January, May, and August/September and three early-entry start dates in March, July, and November.

Programs utilize a cutting-edge educational model called *Year-Round Balanced Learning*. Students are expected to attend lectures, participate in hands-on computer labs, and work on projects emphasizing teamwork and individual study. There is a focus on teaching and collaboration with emphasis placed on problem-solving skills. The Balanced Learning teaching method employs lecture, instructor or self-directed tutorial teaching, group recollection, and student teachback models.

UAT students graduate with not only expertise in today's latest technologies, but also with the framework and foundation needed to continue to be a leader as technology changes in the future. To provide the hands-on skills necessary to succeed today and also immerse students in theory and background so they may grow with technology, Balanced Learning uses a unique three-tiered approach of educational delivery. First, conceptual foundations give students an understanding of the intellectual and systemic underpinnings of their technology discipline. Then skills development trains them in the latest technologies, from software packages and applications to networking hardware, communication, and writing within the discipline. Finally, synthesis has the students utilize the conceptual foundations and their skills as they create and produce complete, complex projects representative of their discipline. Past works have included the creation of a Governor's Award-winning Web site for an Arizona nonprofit organization; completed game mods, for titles like Battlefield 1942 and Starcraft, that have received interest from studios and design companies; and development of new software and database applications.

The UAT campus is designed to enhance Balanced Learning techniques as well as to develop the creative skills needed in the new technologies. There are drawing and art studios, digital media production studios, computer classrooms, computer commons, a technology laboratory to explore the latest in hardware and software, and an output lab with a variety of plotters and printers. The computer commons can be viewed through the UAT Web Cam at http://www.uat.edu.

The student body is composed of students from all fifty states and twenty countries. They are a variety of ages, ranging from recent high school graduates to individuals working on their second career. Students live off campus in surrounding neighborhoods accessible by public transportation or bicycle as well as automobile. The University is close to major freeways and an international airport located in the Phoenix metropolitan area.

Higher education is all about opportunities for growth, self-expression, and interaction. Students at the University of Advancing Technology have a wide range of choices for academic, personal, and professional growth both inside and outside the classroom. They are a part of a rich learning environment where students and faculty have a passion for learning and playing with computers, while relentlessly pursuing technology.

Students are surrounded by the technology they come to study. They gather at Cuban Pete's for cappuccino or to watch UATv. Students play computer games at the Computer Gaming Center or work on projects in the New Technologies Lab. Students are encouraged to join local computer user groups or campus-based clubs and/or the national student Siggraph Chapter. There are organized trips to regional conferences, including Siggraph, E3, and other large industry trade shows. UAT plays a key role in facilitating communication between technology professionals and students.

The University hosts several technology forums annually to bring industry experts on campus for presentations and conversation with UAT students. The campus environment promotes awareness and involvement in the latest computer applications in modern industry. UAT students work with a community of passionate professionals and peers, and they have access to tutors and lab monitors to help them master the wide variety of software they are exposed to in the curriculum.

The Center for Learning Research (CLR) is under the auspices of the Graduate College. The CLR centralizes and supports research and development efforts by faculty members and students as well as select industry groups. The CLR is intended as a catalyst between technology in industry and higher education. It also is the mechanism through which more theoretical questions about educational processes can be explored. The Balanced Learning teaching method was developed by a team of faculty members within the CLR, where their research into learning methods continues.

A Master of Science in technology degree program is offered, with a thesis option or a capstone project option.

Location

Arizona is a land of incredible beauty, contrast, and opportunity. The Grand Canyon, as well as snow-covered mountains and forest streams, is a short drive from the exquisite Sonoran Desert surrounding metropolitan Phoenix.

The Phoenix metropolitan area, which includes Tempe, is a cosmopolitan Southwestern center nestled in a beautiful desert valley. There are more than 3 million people who live, work, and play in this modern financial and commercial hub. The weather is dry, the temperature is mild, and there are more than 300 days of sunshine a year.

The University is strategically located near the center of the Valley of the Sun, as the area is known. Students are minutes from the airport, Arizona State University, shops, restaurants and nightclubs, sports arenas, theaters, concert halls, and many culturally diverse activities. The school is within easy reach of Old Mexico, with its culture and beautiful beaches; Los Angeles and Disneyland; Las Vegas; and San Diego and Sea World. It's a short flight to skiing in Vail, Aspen, and Utah.

There are year-round outdoor activities, such as hiking, camping, horseback riding, snow skiing, hunting, tennis, and golf. Numerous lakes offer boating, swimming, fishing, and water skiing.

Majors and Degrees

UAT offers Associate of Arts and Bachelor's of Arts degrees in digital animation, digital art and design, digital video production, game design, and Web design.

Associate of Science and Bachelor's of Sciences degrees are offered in entrepreneurship, game programming, network administration and architecture, network security administration and architecture, software and database development, system administration and architecture, technology management, and Web programming.

UAT-Online offers today's most sought-after technology degrees in a success-oriented, proven, and totally online format. Accredited academic associate degrees are available in such exciting fields as digital animation, game design, and network defense (with a bachelor's in game programming and a master's in technology coming). Classes are highly interactive and faculty members are responsive, and these factors build upon each other progressively, with technology courses up front. Students take one course every five weeks and utilize the software currently used by industry—plus students complete portfolio-quality work as part of the program.

Academic Programs

The Bachelor of Arts in multimedia is a 120-week program that requires a minimum of 120 semester credits, 84 area-of-concentration credits, 40 300- and 400-level credits, and 36 general-studies credits. The Associate of Arts in multimedia is a sixty-week program that requires a minimum of 60 semester credits, 45 area-of-concentration credits, and 15 general-studies credits. The Bachelor of Science in software engineering is a 120-week program that requires a minimum of 120 semester credits, 84 area-of-concentration credits, 40 300-and 400-level credits, and 36 general-studies credits. The Associate of Science in software engineering is a sixty-week program that requires a minimum of 60 semester credits, 45 area-of-concentration credits, and 15 general-studies credits. The Bachelor of Science in technology commerce is a 120-week program that requires a minimum of 120 semester credits, 84 area-of-concentration credits, 40 300- and 400-level credits, and 36 general-studies credits. The Associate of Science in technology commerce is a sixty-week program that requires a minimum of 60 semester credits, 45 area-of-concentration credits, and 15 general-studies credits.

Academic Facilities

The UAT campus was completed in 1998. The entire facility is designed for networked workstations connected by fiber-optic cable throughout the facility. There are a digital media theater, projection systems in the classrooms, a video and digital effects production studio, artists' studios, electronic classrooms, a technology laboratory, and a large computer commons area that looks out on the desert mountain landscape.

Costs

There is a processing fee, upon enrollment, of $100 for U.S. residents and $250 for non-U.S. residents. For 2004–05, tuition is $6800 per full time semester (12 or more credits).

Financial Aid

The professionals in the UAT Financial Aid Department work closely with each student to develop specific programs for obtaining funding for his or her education. The University of Advancing Technology is approved for the training of veterans, and the University was among the first in the country to participate in the Direct Student Loan Program. For information about scholarships awarded through the University, students should contact the Admissions Department. Financial aid and scholarship applications are available online at http://www.uat.edu.

Faculty

There are approximately 50 full-time faculty members. Technical instructors have experience in industry and often utilize real-world examples in their classes. Faculty members are committed to helping students achieve their educational goals.

Student Government

There is no formal student government. Student feedback is achieved through meetings, surveys, focus groups, a volunteer student mentor program, and other campus community-based informal groups.

Admission Requirements

University of Advancing Technology programs are open to all persons who have a high school diploma or hold the educational equivalent and display a serious intent toward their education. Applicants under the age of 18 must have a legal guardian sign all admission agreements and a financial responsibility statement.

Prospective students must provide evidence of the required SAT I or ACT scores, proof of a cumulative high school grade point average of 2.5 or better, the required GED composite score, or a college credential from an accredited institution. An ACT minimum score of 21 meets the minimal requirement for admission. An SAT I minimum score of 500 in the verbal and 520 in the math or a combined minimum score of 1020 meets the minimal requirement for admission. A college credential at the associate or bachelor's level meets the requirement for admission in place of a cumulative high school GPA of 2.5 or GED average scores. A personality profile that is used only for retention studies may be administered.

In addition to the standard admission requirements, non-U.S. citizens applying for admission to the University of Advancing Technology must provide proof of English proficiency if English is not the native language in one of the following ways: the Test of English as a Foreign Language (TOEFL) with a score of 500 or higher (Test of Written English must be included), successful completion of Level 108 from an ESL Center, completion of the ASPECT English Language Proficiency Level 5, or attendance for at least one year at a regionally accredited U.S. college or university and completion of English 101 and 102 (or equivalent) with grades of C or better. International students are not required to provide ACT or SAT I scores if they are high school graduates in their country of origin.

Transcripts must be submitted with an English translation and be evaluated for educational credentials (must show U.S. high school equivalent) by the Educational Credential Evaluators, Inc., P.O. Box 17499, Milwaukee, Wisconsin 53217-0499, U.S.A.

Application and Information

Applications are accepted throughout the year, and students may choose one of six start dates. Students may request an application from the address below.

UAT Admissions
2625 West Baseline Road
Tempe, Arizona 85283
Telephone: 602-383-8228
800-658-5744 (toll-free)
E-mail: admission@uat.edu
World Wide Web: http://www.uat.edu

UNIVERSITY OF ALASKA FAIRBANKS

FAIRBANKS, ALASKA

1917–1997 80 YEARS University of Alaska Fairbanks

The University

Founded in 1917, the University provides education, research, and service in the "last frontier." The Fairbanks campus, one of three in the statewide system of higher education, is the primary administrative and research center and has branches in Bethel, Dillingham, Kotzebue, and Nome, along with Rural Centers throughout the state.

The total University of Alaska Fairbanks (UAF) enrollment in fall 2002 was 9,390. Eighty-five percent of the students have Alaskan residency, although nearly half of the students graduated from high schools in forty-nine states and thirty-eight other countries. The nine residence halls on campus are renovated and are capable of lodging 1,322 students. The Student Apartment Complex has sixty furnished two-bedroom units reserved for sophomore and upperclass students. The Eileen Panigeo MacLean House, housing for rural students, holds 22 students. The University also manages 153 furnished apartments for students with families.

The large campus contains a core of academic buildings and residences, as well as miles of ski trails, two lakes, and an arboretum. Most of the University's research institutes, including the noted Geophysical Institute and the new International Arctic Research Center, are clustered on the West Ridge. The University's Agricultural Experiment Station farm is on campus, as are a Cooperative Fish and Wildlife Research Unit and various state and federal agencies and laboratories. The University awards graduate degrees in many of the same areas as the undergraduate studies, often in conjunction with one of its research institutes. A natural science facility, housing chemistry, physics, geology, and earth sciences, was completed in 1995.

Intercollegiate athletics include men's and women's basketball, cross-country running and skiing, and riflery and a women's volleyball team. The University sponsors an outstanding men's intercollegiate ice hockey team, which plays at the 4,665-seat Carlson Center. The UAF hockey team is a member of the Central Collegiate Hockey Association (CCHA). The Student Recreation Complex houses a variety of sports and physical activities facilities, including multipurpose areas for basketball, volleyball, badminton, tennis, calisthenics, dance, gymnastics, judo, and karate; a rifle and pistol range; courts for handball, racquetball, and squash; an elevated 200-meter, three-lane jogging track; a swimming pool; weight-training and modern fitness equipment areas; an ice arena for recreational skating and hockey; a special aerobics area; and a three-story climbing wall. The cheery and roomy student union, the William Ransom Wood Center, is the focus of various out-of-class activities for students and faculty members. The center houses meeting and exhibit rooms, lounges and television areas, the student government offices, campus information, a pub, a bowling alley, a games room, a cafeteria, a snack bar, an espresso bar, and a photography darkroom.

Location

The campus of the University of Alaska Fairbanks is situated on a ridge overlooking the valley of the Tanana River and the city of Fairbanks. Serving a population of more than 85,000 within the 7,561-square-mile North Star Borough, Fairbanks is a major trade center for outlying villages in Interior Alaska. The city is connected with the rest of the state and the lower forty-eight states by air and highway. Municipal bus service is available between downtown Fairbanks, the surrounding area, and the campus. Shuttle bus service is available around the UAF campus at no cost.

Fairbanks offers the sophistication of larger cities through such luxuries as first-run movies and fine restaurants while maintaining the atmosphere of smaller, more personal towns. Denali National Park and other vast wilderness areas are close at hand, and Anchorage is 350 miles south via the Parks Highway. Members of the Fairbanks community and the University join together in the University-Fairbanks Symphony Orchestra and in many other musical and theatrical enterprises.

Majors and Degrees

The University of Alaska Fairbanks awards certificates, A.A. and A.A.S. degrees, and B.A., B.S., B.T., B.B.A., B.Ed., B.M., and B.F.A. degrees in accounting, airframe studies, Alaska Native studies, anthropology, applied accounting, applied business, applied physics, apprenticeship technology, art, arts and sciences, aviation maintenance technology, aviation technology, biochemistry, biological sciences, business administration, chemistry, civil engineering, communication, community health, computer science, culinary arts, dental assistant studies, drafting technology, early childhood, earth science, economics, electrical engineering, elementary education, emergency medical services, emergency services, English, Eskimo, fisheries, foreign languages, general science, geography (environmental studies), geological engineering, geology, ground vehicle maintenance technology, health-care reimbursement, health technology, history, human services, Japanese studies, journalism, justice, linguistics, maintenance technology, mathematics, mechanical engineering, medical assistant studies, microcomputer support specialist studies, mining engineering, molecular biology, music, Native language education, natural resources management (including forestry), Northern studies, office management and technology, paralegal studies, petroleum engineering, philosophy, phlebotomy, physics, political science, powerplant studies, process technology, psychology, renewable resources, rural development, rural human services, Russian studies, social work, sociology, statistics, technology, theater, tribal management, and wildlife biology. Preprofessional advising is available in dentistry, law, library science, medicine, physical therapy, and veterinary medicine.

Academic Programs

The academic year is divided into two semesters; registration is in early April for the fall semester and in November for the spring semester. Preregistration is available for returning students. In addition, there are three-week, six-week, and twelve-week summer sessions. UAF offers an early orientation for new students in the fall and spring semesters. The University is organized into three colleges and five professional schools: the College of Liberal Arts; the College of Science, Engineering and Mathematics; the College of Rural Alaska; and the Schools of Agricultural and Land Resources Management, Education, Fisheries and Ocean Sciences, Management, and Mineral Engineering. A minimum of 120 semester credits must be completed for the four-year baccalaureate degree programs.

Students who receive scores of 3 or higher on the College Board's Advanced Placement tests may be awarded advanced-placement credit by the University. Currently enrolled students may challenge courses for credit by successfully completing College-Level Examination Program examinations or by completing locally prepared examinations. Requests for advanced-placement credit and credit by examination are coordinated through the Office of Admissions.

The honors program is designed for highly motivated undergraduate students who wish to acquire a superior understanding of the natural and social sciences, the arts, and the humanities. Prospective honors students need a minimum ACT composite score of 28 or a combined SAT I score of approximately 1270 with a minimum 3.6 high school GPA.

Off-Campus Programs

The University maintains exchange programs with McGill University in Canada and with universities in Australia, Denmark, Ecuador, England, Finland, Japan, Mexico, Norway, Russia, and Taiwan. The University also participates in the Northwest Interinstitutional Council for Study Abroad, providing students with an opportunity to enroll in liberal arts programs in Austria, England, France, Greece, Italy, and Spain. UAF is also a member of the National Student Exchange, participating with 177 colleges and universities throughout the United States and in U.S. territories and at five locations in Canada.

Academic Facilities

The Fine Arts Complex features a 480-seat theater, a 1,072-seat concert hall, FM public radio (KUAC) and educational-television (PBS) studios, an art gallery, and the Elmer E. Rasmuson Library. The library collection contains more than 1.75 million volumes, including the prestigious Alaska and Polar Regions Collection. Electronic catalogs provide access to collections in 11,000 libraries nationwide.

Students have free use of the University's academic computing facilities (Aurora), which are accessible from Windows and Macintosh computer labs and by remote access. Various schools and colleges have their own special-purpose computer labs.

The University Museum attracts more than 100,000 visitors a year to Interior Alaska and is located on the UAF campus. The museum collects, preserves, and exhibits materials from Alaska and the North.

Costs

In 2003–04, tuition and fees were $1705 per semester for full-time (12 credits) students. Nonresident students paid an additional $2292 for 12 credits of tuition each semester. Residents of Alaska, the Yukon Territory, British Columbia, and the Northwest Territories are exempt from the nonresident tuition fee. Students must live in Alaska for twelve months to qualify as residents. The approximate cost per semester for books and supplies is $500 and for personal items and recreation, $450. A double-occupancy residence hall room on campus costs $1255 per semester. Meals, which all residence hall occupants are required to purchase, cost approximately $1220 per semester. (These costs are subject to change.) Married student housing on campus is also available.

Financial Aid

A large portion of financial aid is derived from the Alaska Supplemental Education Loan Program, which is available to all students attending UAF, regardless of residency. Three kinds of aid are available: grants and scholarships (which need not be repaid), loans, and part-time employment. Students seeking financial assistance for the fall term should submit applications by March 15. Inquiries should be addressed to the Financial Aid Office, University of Alaska Fairbanks, P.O. Box 756560, Fairbanks, Alaska 99775-6560.

The Chancellor's Scholarship, a one-year tuition waiver, is available to entering freshmen with a minimum 3.0 GPA and 1150 SAT I combined score or 25 ACT composite score. To apply, students should submit an application for admission, a high school transcript, a tuition waiver application, and test scores for review. the deadline for scholarships is February 15. National Merit Finalists qualify for a four-year tuition waiver plus a $10,000 scholarship.

Faculty

Sixty-six percent of the 784 faculty members hold doctoral degrees, and many are actively engaged in research. In keeping with University policy, faculty members provide academic counseling for students. The combination of a student-faculty ratio of 12:1 and easy access to instructors for help outside of class produces a maximum educational benefit for students.

Student Government

The Associated Students of the University of Alaska Fairbanks (ASUAF) protects students' rights through its various governmental functions and also offers educational, social, recreational, and service activities. The school newspaper, *Sun Star*, is published weekly with the sponsorship of ASUAF, which also supports KSUA, the campus radio station; the international cinema and weekly movie series; and dances, concerts, and other entertainment. ASUAF publishes the results of its faculty evaluations and sends several student lobbyists to the Alaska state legislature in Juneau each spring. A student member sits on the Board of Regents of the University.

Admission Requirements

For admission to a baccalaureate program, applicants must be high school graduates with a cumulative grade point average of at least 2.0 and have earned a GPA of at least 2.5 in a high school core curriculum of 16 credits. Transfer students must also have a minimum grade point average of 2.0 in all previous college work. Applicants for a major in a scientific or technical field may be required to present a higher grade point average and to have completed specific background courses before being accepted into the major department. All entering freshmen are required to submit the results of either an ACT or SAT I examination prior to registration for placement in English and math courses.

Application and Information

The application deadlines are August 1 for the fall semester (April 1 for nonresident freshmen) and December 1 for the spring semester. Applications are processed after the deadlines only as long as space is available. Applicants are notified of the admission decision as soon as all application material has been received. Only accepted students are allowed to apply for campus housing. Students desiring campus housing should apply for admission as early as possible prior to the start of the semester to increase their chances of obtaining residence hall accommodations.

For further information, applicants should contact:

Office of Admissions
University of Alaska Fairbanks
P.O. Box 757480
Fairbanks, Alaska 99775-7480
Telephone: 907-474-7500
800-478-1UAF (toll-free)
World Wide Web: http://www.uaf.edu

The Plaza outside the classroom buildings at the University of Alaska Fairbanks. The flags represent the fifty states of the United States.

UNIVERSITY OF ALASKA SOUTHEAST

JUNEAU, KETCHIKAN, AND SITKA, ALASKA

The University

The University of Alaska Southeast (UAS) is a growing university with the main campus located in Juneau, Alaska's capital city, and branch campuses located in Ketchikan and Sitka. UAS is part of the University of Alaska system of higher education.

Enrollment at the main campus is about 700 full-time and 1,900 part-time students. About 60 percent of students are women and 40 percent are men. About 20 percent of the students are Alaska Natives, Asian, African American, and Hispanic. UAS offers a rich cultural environment plus varied activities and special events at both indoor and outdoor locations. Students may take part in intramural sports such as basketball, softball, and volleyball. Other activities include rock climbing, dances, swimming and local racquet club use in Juneau, and a variety of special-interest clubs.

More than a million people visit Juneau each year to enjoy its abundant forests and beautiful waterways. Ample opportunities exist for activities such as rock and ice climbing, kayaking, canoeing, camping, fishing, hiking, snowboarding, scuba diving, and skiing. Few areas in the world offer Juneau's world-class wilderness access combined with its big city amenities, such as shopping and restaurants.

Master's degrees include a Master of Arts in Teaching, with an emphasis in elementary education, early childhood education, or secondary education; a Master of Education with an emphasis in early childhood education, reading education, or educational technology; a Master of Business Administration; and a Master of Public Administration.

Professional development programs include post-baccalaureate endorsements in early childhood education, educational technology, reading, or special education; and post-baccalaureate credentials in early childhood or elementary education.

Location

Juneau is small by "Lower 48" standards, but with a population of 32,000 it is the third-largest city in the state and the largest in Southeast Alaska. Located along the shores of the Inside Passage, Juneau is surrounded by the world's largest expanse of an ancient temperate rainforest. The rainforest provides a surprisingly mild climate. The January mean temperature is 26 degrees. During the summer months, the normal high temperature is in the upper 60s. The area around the UAS campus averages 56 inches of annual precipitation.

Juneau is accessible by plane and ferry but not by road. Jet service from Seattle and Anchorage is offered daily. The state runs a year-round ferry service between Bellingham, Washington, and Southeast Alaskan cities. Those who bring cars must use the barge service from Seattle or the Alaska Marine Highway System. The ferries provide a spectacular cruise through the breathtakingly beautiful Inside Passage.

Majors and Degrees

One of the many advantages to the University's small campus is the ability of faculty and staff members to work with individual students to meet their educational goals. UAS offers a Bachelor of Arts in elementary education, with a special education endorsement; a Bachelor of Arts in English; a Bachelor of Arts in social science with an emphasis in anthropology, economics, government/political science, history, psychology, or sociology; a Bachelor of Business Administration with an emphasis in accounting, general business, management, or marketing; a Bachelor of Liberal Arts with an emphasis in art, communications, general studies, government, human communication, or mathematics; a Bachelor of Science in biology with an emphasis in general biology or marine biology; a Bachelor of Science in environmental science; and a Bachelor of Science in information systems with an emphasis in e-commerce, networking, or programming.

UAS also offers an Associate of Arts degree and Associate of Applied Science degrees in apprenticeship technology, business administration, computer information office systems, construction technology, early childhood education, environmental technology, health information management, paralegal studies, power technology–automotive, or power technology–diesel. In addition, certificate programs are available in subjects such as accounting technician studies, automotive technology, computer information and office systems, early childhood education, environmental technology, health information management coding specialist studies, law enforcement, outdoor skills and leadership, residential building science, or small business management.

Academic Programs

UAS operates on the semester system. Fall semester begins in early September and spring semester begins in mid-January. The summer semester begins in May with courses offered through June and July.

A minimum of 120 semester credits is required to complete a baccalaureate degree program, a minimum of 60 semester credits to complete an associate degree program, and a minimum of 30 semester credits to complete a certificate program.

For all programs, students must maintain a minimum 2.0 GPA; in some core program areas, the minimum GPA requirement is higher.

Advanced placement credit is given to high school students who achieve scores of 3 or higher on the College Board's Advanced Placement tests. Scores above 620 on the SAT verbal or 30 on the ACT English qualify new students for advanced UAS class placement.

Students who are currently enrolled may challenge courses for credit through either the College-Level Examination Program (CLEP) or University challenge examinations. Requests by students for Advanced Placement credit and credit by examination are coordinated through the Office of Records and Registration.

Academic Facilities

The main campus is located 11 miles from downtown Juneau, between the shores of Auke Lake and Auke Bay. The campus faces the Mendenhall Glacier and is often referred to as the most beautiful place in Juneau. Located across from the spectacular Auke Bay, the Student Activity Center houses a climbing wall, the Outdoor Recreation Center, a big-screen TV, a movie screen with a surround-sound system, exercise facilities, and a student lounge with computers, pool tables, and other games. The Technical Education Center is located in downtown Juneau, on the waterfront. It serves as the base for the vocational/technical programs such as auto, construction, power, and welding.

The Egan Library contains more than 420,000 volumes. This award-winning facility offers seating for more than 200 users, the most current computer technology for access to information, and extended hours for student study. The Learning Center and Media Services are also housed in the Egan library, as is a representative collection of southeastern Alaskan Native art.

The campus operates on a state-of-the-art wireless network that students may access with the addition of a wireless Internet card. The card allows students access to the network, Internet, and e-mail from virtually anywhere on the campus.

Costs

For purposes of tuition costs, a resident is any person who has been physically present in Alaska for one year and who declares their intention to remain in Alaska indefinitely. In most instances, students may establish residency in Alaska after one year. Others exempt from nonresident fees are residents of British Columbia, Yukon, Northwest and Nunavut Territories, military personnel stationed in Alaska and their dependents, and residents of several foreign sister cities. UAS also participates in the Western Undergraduate Exchange (WUE) program for all degree programs. Students from the fourteen member states are eligible for WUE tuition rates.

For 2004–05, in-state full-time tuition, which is 12 or more credit hours, costs from $1188 to $1485 a semester. Lower division 100- and 200-level courses are $99 per credit hour; upper division 300- and 400-level courses are $112 per credit hour. Full-time nonresident students can expect to pay between $4116 and $5145 a semester, depending on the level of classes. Western Undergraduate Exchange students can expect to pay between $1782 and $2227 a semester, depending on the level of classes. In addition, all students must pay a mandatory $3 per-credit-hour (not to exceed $45) student government fee, a $5 per-credit-hour (not to exceed $60) technology fee, a $4 newspaper fee, and a $100 student-activity fee each semester.

Campus housing is available in Juneau. Freshman housing at Banfield Hall is $1675 per semester per person. Residents of Banfield Hall are required to have a roommate and purchase the meal plan at an additional cost of $985 per semester. Banfield Hall is reserved for freshmen, but on-campus housing, including apartment-style housing, is available to all students. Apartment-style housing with private rooms is available at a cost of $1840 per person per semester and family housing is available at a cost of $4400 per semester.

Financial Aid

UAS participates in the Federal Pell Grant, Federal Supplemental Educational Opportunity Grant, Federal Stafford Student Loan, and Federal Work-Study programs in addition to state student loan, family loan, and grant programs. Most aid is awarded on the basis of financial need. Some scholarships, however, are based on academic potential and performance. The deadline for merit-based UAS scholarships is early February. To apply for need-based programs, students should request a packet from the financial aid office.

Faculty

Classes are taught by highly qualified and experienced faculty members. Classes vary in size but are typically much smaller than at larger institutions; the average class size is approximately 15 students. The size of UAS contributes to a high degree of personal interaction between students and faculty members. In addition to their primary teaching responsibilities, some faculty members also serve as advisers for undergraduate students as well as on advisory committees for graduate students.

Student Government

The student government plays an important role in the development of UAS policies and activities. Students serve on a number of important committees and participate in lobbying the state legislature on behalf of students' interests.

Admission Requirements

Students are qualified for admission as an undergraduate if they are a high school graduate with a minimum high school GPA of 2.0 and can supply all the required documentation. Successful completion of the GED test is accepted as an equivalency of high school graduation. Official transcripts from all regionally accredited colleges and universities are also required if applicable. ACT and/or SAT I test scores are also required.

Admission is on a rolling basis; applications are processed in the order they are received. Applicants generally receive an initial response within two weeks of receipt of the completed application packet.

Application and Information

To apply, students must complete an application form and send it with the required $40 application processing fee to the Office of Admissions on the campus of intended enrollment. Students can mail or fax applications or apply online. Official high school transcripts showing graduation or a GED credential are required of applicants seeking bachelor degees, as are official transcripts from all regionally accredited colleges and universities attended, if applicable.

For further information, application forms, or any other materials, prospective applicants can use the inquiry form on the UAS Website or contact:

Admissions Office
University of Alaska Southeast
11120 Glacier Highway
Juneau, Alaska 99801
Telephone: 907-465-6350
877-465-4827 (toll-free)
Fax: 907-465-6365
E-mail: admissions@uas.alaska.edu
World Wide Web: http://www.uas.alaska.edu

Environmental science students at UAS have measured the face of the LeConte Glacier near Petersburg.

UNIVERSITY OF THE PACIFIC

STOCKTON, CALIFORNIA

The University

The University of the Pacific was established in 1851 as California's first chartered institution of higher education. The University's classic college environment combined with modern facilities provides students with the best of both worlds. An independent university known for the diversity of its academic programs and outstanding teaching faculty, Pacific has also acquired a reputation for educational innovation, as demonstrated by the development of its cooperative engineering program and its three-year professional programs in pharmacy and dentistry. The University, which draws its 3,100 undergraduate students from more than forty states and fifty countries, is located in a residential area of Stockton, and the architecture and landscaping of the 175-acre main campus provide an Ivy League type of setting.

The University of the Pacific is a residential university, offering on-campus housing in twelve residence halls, six fraternities, four sororities, and four apartment complexes (including a married student apartment complex). Approximately 62 percent of the undergraduate students live in these facilities. Excellent support services are available to Pacific students to enhance their academic and personal development; these are offered through the Career and Internship Center, the Health Center, and the Counseling Center. Extracurricular activities include plays, concerts, speakers, and movies in one of four theater/auditoriums on campus; excellent athletic programs at the intercollegiate, intramural, and physical education levels; broadcasting (on KUOP-FM), journalism, and forensics; professional organizations and honor societies; and more than seventy special interest clubs. The McCaffrey Center (student union) houses a grocery store, a bookstore, a movie theater, a games area, two additional dining areas, and the Associated Students of the University of the Pacific (ASUOP) offices. Recreation and athletic facilities include three gyms; playing fields; tennis, volleyball, basketball, and racquetball courts; a 28,000-seat stadium; the 6,000-seat Spanos Center; an Olympic-size swimming pool; and a student fitness center.

The University's School of Dentistry is located in San Francisco, and Pacific's McGeorge School of Law is in Sacramento. Professional and graduate programs on the Stockton campus include the Doctor of Pharmacy (Pharm.D.) degree; master's and doctoral programs in a variety of areas in education; Master of Arts programs in communication, music therapy, psychology, and sport sciences; Master of Business Administration; Master of Science programs in biological sciences, chemistry, pharmaceutical sciences, and speech-language pathology; and Doctor of Philosophy programs in chemistry and pharmaceutical sciences. A Doctor of Physical Therapy program is also available.

Location

Stockton (population 250,000) is California's largest inland port. Situated between San Francisco and the Sierra Nevada, the area provides unlimited cultural and recreational opportunities within a short drive, including entertainment in San Francisco; skiing, camping, and backpacking in the Sierra Nevada; and waterskiing and boating in the California Delta area. Stockton is served by Amtrak, bus lines, and three major freeways. Sacramento and Oakland International Airports are both within an hour drive from campus. The climate during the school year is pleasantly warm, with the rainy season generally restricted to the period between December and March. Summer temperatures are in the 80- and 90-degree ranges. Stockton has a diverse ethnic and economic background, offering opportunities for cultural enrichment and community service.

Majors and Degrees

The University of the Pacific offers the undergraduate degrees of Bachelor of Arts, Bachelor of Arts in Liberal Studies, Bachelor of Fine Arts, Bachelor of Music, Bachelor of Science, and Bachelor of Science in Engineering. Major areas are accounting, art, arts and entertainment management, athletic training, biochemistry, biological sciences, business administration, chemistry, chemistry-biology, classics, communication, computer science, dental hygiene, economics, education, engineering (bio, civil, computer, electrical, management, and mechanical), engineering physics, English, entrepreneurship, finance, French, geology, geophysics, German, global economic relations, graphic design, history, international environmental policy, international management, international relations, international studies, Japanese, liberal studies, marketing, mathematics, music (composition, education, history, management, performance, and therapy), philosophy, physical sciences, physics, political science, psychology, religious studies, social science, sociology, Spanish, speech-language pathology, sport management, sports medicine, studio art, and theater arts. For a complete listing of majors, prospective students should visit the University's Web site at http://www.pacific.edu/majors.

Special programs include a five-year bachelor's/M.B.A. option; a six-year bachelor's/J.D. option; several predental/D.D.S. accelerated programs; a five-year engineering program, which incorporates twelve months of mandatory cooperative education work experience; a three-year professional pharmacy program leading to the Doctor of Pharmacy; a preliminary-teaching-credential program; an optional cooperative education program in the liberal arts; and preprofessional studies in dentistry, law, medicine, pharmacy, physical therapy, and other fields.

Academic Programs

The University emphasizes a personal approach to education, featuring small classes and close working relationships between students and faculty members. The undergraduate academic programs are arranged through seven schools and colleges, each having its own distinctive features. Students enroll in one division but can take classes in the others and share common facilities. The College of the Pacific is a departmentally arranged liberal arts and sciences college, offering more than forty majors and preprofessional programs. Undergraduate professional divisions include the Conservatory of Music, the Eberhardt School of Business, the Benerd School of Education, the School of Engineering, and the School of International Studies. The Thomas J. Long School of Pharmacy and Health Sciences includes both undergraduate and first professional degree students. The Center for Professional and Continuing Education also offers special academic opportunities.

Each of the University's undergraduate divisions has its own academic requirements. However, the University emphasizes a commitment to the liberal arts and requires all students to have some exposure to the humanities, behavioral sciences, natural sciences, and social sciences through a University-wide general education program. Many freshmen enter the University without having decided on a major area of study, and they work extensively with their academic advisers before selecting a major. The liberal arts college allows a considerable amount of flexibility in the academic program, but the professional schools are more structured in their academic requirements. All divisions on the Stockton campus follow a semester calendar; however, the professional pharmacy program has three terms per year.

Off-Campus Programs

The University of the Pacific currently participates in more than 200 programs in seventy countries in Africa, Asia, Central and South America, the Middle East, North America and the Caribbean, Oceania, and Western and Eastern Europe. Students may pursue interests as varied as art, business, or chemistry and may be allowed independent study, travel, and homestay opportunities. Pacific has arrangements for participation in study abroad through the Institute of European Studies, the International Student Exchange Program, and the School of International Training as well as through special arrangements with individual universities.

Cooperative education and internships play important roles at the University. All School of Engineering students spend two 6-month periods off campus working in full-time paid co-op positions. Students enrolled in all other University divisions have the option of participating in part-time or full-time internships, arranged through the Career and Internship Center.

Academic Facilities

Excellent equipment and facilities are available to assist students in their academic work outside the classroom. The Stockton campus of the University of the Pacific maintains a main library with 400,000 volumes, 2,700 periodicals, 595,000 microform items, and 7,900 video and audio units. In addition, a science library is maintained by the School of Pharmacy and Health Sciences. Students have access to extensive computer facilities. Also available for students are the Educational Resource Center, language laboratories, the drama studio, music practice rooms, the music laboratory, and the student advising center.

Costs

For 2003–04, tuition and fees were $23,700, and room and board were $7490.

Financial Aid

The University of the Pacific encourages students to apply for financial aid from all sources, including local clubs and organizations, state and federal programs, and the University. It is the intention of the University, within the limits of its resources, to provide assistance to promising students who would not otherwise be able to attend. To this end, the University has developed a financial aid program that includes scholarships, grants, loans, and job opportunities. Financial aid awards from Pacific are based on a combination of financial need and/or academic achievement. In recent years, Pacific has significantly increased its merit-based scholarship programs and, in 1997, became the first institution to provide matching scholarships to new students who receive a Cal Grant (California state gift aid). More than 75 percent of the student body receive some type of financial aid, and on-campus jobs are available through the Career and Internship Center. The priority date to apply for financial aid is February 15 for the fall semester.

Faculty

Of the 370 full-time faculty members on the Stockton campus, 86 percent have earned doctoral degrees or the highest degree in their field. The priority of Pacific's faculty is the education of individual students rather than research. The faculty members are actively engaged in classroom teaching and academic advising and also participate in numerous student social activities on campus. The faculty-student ratio is 1:13.

Student Government

The ASUOP, the student government organization, provides many services to the campus. The ASUOP president and Senate express the students' views as they work with the University administration. ASUOP operates a 200-seat movie theater, a grocery store, and an equipment-loan store. ASUOP Presents brings nationally known speakers to the campus, and a very active social commission plans an extensive activities calendar that includes films, dances, and concerts on campus. Each school and college also has its own student association, and all are concerned with both academic and social activities. Students are included on committees reviewing academic affairs and the curriculum structure, evaluating courses and faculty members, and planning future facilities and programs.

Admission Requirements

The University of the Pacific seeks freshman applicants who have had strong college-preparatory backgrounds of four academic subjects each semester. A challenging secondary school program of 4 years of English, 4 years of social studies, 3 years of mathematics, 2 years of laboratory sciences, and 2 or more years of foreign language is highly recommended. Science students should include chemistry, physics, and higher mathematics. The University requires an official high school transcript, a counselor or teacher recommendation, SAT I or ACT scores, and a personal essay.

Application and Information

Out-of-state and international students are encouraged to apply, and approximately 250 transfer students and 750 freshmen enroll each year. Early Action (non-binding admission) is available for outstanding students who apply by December 1. Applications are accepted on a rolling basis, but applicants are encouraged to meet a January 15 priority date. All interested students are encouraged to arrange with the Office of Admissions to visit the campus. Further information may be obtained by contacting:

Office of Admissions
University of the Pacific
Stockton, California 95211
Telephone: 209-946-2211
E-mail: admissions@uop.edu
World Wide Web: http://www.pacific.edu/admission

These students are meeting outside the Holt Memorial Library with the Robert Burns Tower in the background.

UNIVERSITY OF WYOMING

LARAMIE, WYOMING

The University

The University of Wyoming (UW), a public land-grant institution founded in 1886, is a reflection of the global community it serves. The extensive range of academic programs offered at UW inspires the development of "new thinking" and promotes fulfilling careers in the rapidly evolving world.

As a Carnegie Research University–Extensive, UW's research goals are continually being pushed to the boundaries and beyond by its professors and students. It is this academic ambition that has allowed UW to provide high-quality undergraduate and graduate education, research, and service since 1886.

Wyoming, unique among the fifty states, has only one university. UW enjoys tremendous support from within its state as well as from an alumni network that spans the globe. More than 11,900 students from all parts of the U.S. and sixty other countries attend UW classes in Laramie and at outreach sites around the state. The variety of students at UW enriches the educational experience for all by fostering a multicultural environment that encourages sharing and learning about those with different heritages and cultural backgrounds. It is this dialogue that continues to promote respect and appreciation for diversity.

UW offers bachelor's degree programs in six undergraduate colleges: the Colleges of Agriculture, Arts and Sciences, Business, Education, Engineering, and Health Sciences. Undergraduate education is a high priority at UW. More than 88 percent of the undergraduate courses are taught by professors, and the average class size is 24 students. UW also offers eighty-five graduate and professional programs, including the Doctor of Pharmacy, the Juris Doctor, and the new master's program in e-business.

There are more than 180 recognized campus clubs and organizations, including fourteen national fraternities and sororities, honor and professional societies, political and religious organizations, and special-interest groups. Students have the opportunity to participate in more than sixty different intramural and club sports. UW is a Division I member of the NCAA and competes in the Mountain West Conference in seventeen men's and women's sports. Campus recreational facilities include the Wyoming Union, which recently underwent a $10-million renovation and includes the UW bookstore, eating establishments, student computers, study areas, and a variety of services and resources for students. Additional facilities on campus include Half Acre Gym, an indoor climbing wall, an 18-hole golf course, tennis and racquetball courts, weight rooms, two swimming pools, rifle and archery ranges, indoor and outdoor tracks, softball and baseball fields, and a hockey rink.

UW houses 2,400 students in six residence halls, and freshmen are required to live on campus during their first year. While primarily coed, the residence halls offer a number of unique living environments, including quiet/study floors, special-interest floors, honors floors, single-sex floors, and other academic living environments. UW also offers fourteen different Freshman Interest Groups (FIGS), which are learning communities that offer common living areas and clustered classes to students with similar academic areas of interest.

Location

UW's 785-acre campus is located at the foot of the Rocky Mountains in Laramie, a scenic town of 30,000 people in southeastern Wyoming. Many UW students enjoy the easy access to Alpine and Nordic skiing, snowboarding, snowmobiling, hiking, backpacking, camping, hunting, fishing, rock climbing, and mountain biking. Laramie—with its blue skies, clean air, and 320 days of sunshine a year—is a friendly and supportive university town, conveniently located 45 miles west of Wyoming's capital, Cheyenne, and only 130 miles northwest of Denver, Colorado.

Majors and Degrees

UW offers seventy-seven undergraduate programs within its six colleges, leading to B.A., B.S., B.F.A., and B.S.N. degrees.

The College of Agriculture offers majors in agricultural business (with options in agribusiness management, farm and ranch management, and international agriculture), agricultural communications, agroecology, animal and veterinary sciences (with options in animal biology, business, communication, meat science and food technology, pre–veterinary science, production, and range livestock), family and consumer science (with options in child development, dietetics, family services, human nutrition and food, and textiles and merchandising), microbiology, molecular biology, and rangeland ecology and watershed management.

The College of Arts and Sciences offers majors in American studies, anthropology, art, astronomy/astrophysics, biology, botany, chemistry, communication, criminal justice, English, French, geography and recreation, geology (with options in earth science and environment/natural resources), German, history, humanities/fine arts, international studies, journalism, management, mathematical sciences, mathematics, music (with options in education, performance, and theory and composition), philosophy, physics, political science, psychology, recreation and park administration, Russian, social science, sociology, Spanish, statistics, theater and dance, wildlife/fisheries, women's studies, and zoology and physiology as well as the option of a self-designed major.

The College of Business offers majors in accounting, business administration, business economics, economics, finance, management, and marketing.

The College of Education offers majors in elementary and special education, elementary education, industrial technology education, secondary education (with options in agriculture, art, biology, business, chemistry, earth/space science, English, family and consumer sciences, French, German, industrial technology, mathematics, physics, Russian, social studies, and Spanish), special education, trades and industrial education, and vocational homemaking.

The College of Engineering offers majors in architectural engineering, chemical engineering (with environmental and petroleum options), civil engineering, computer engineering, computer science, electrical engineering (with bioengineering and computer engineering options), management information systems (with accounting, business, and computer science options), and mechanical engineering.

The College of Health Sciences offers majors in dental hygiene, exercise and sports science, health education, health sciences, nursing, pharmacy, physical education teaching, social work, and speech-language and hearing sciences.

UW offers preprofessional programs in dentistry, forestry, law, medicine, nursing, occupational therapy, optometry, pharmacy, physical therapy, and veterinary medicine. The School of Environment and Natural Resources also offers interdisciplinary studies that can be combined with course work in seven other fields of study, including the humanities, physical sciences, and social sciences.

Academic Programs

The UW academic calendar consists of two semesters and a complete summer session. Depending on their degree program, students are required to complete 120 to 164 credit hours for graduation. Undergraduate programs for most majors can be completed in four years. Students may choose to double major within the same college, or they may pursue majors in two separate colleges for a cross-college major. Minors are also available in many areas. All students are required to complete the University Studies Program, which is a core curriculum that assists students in developing their skills and/or knowledge in oral and written communication, mathematics, science, diversity, global awareness, government, and culture. The University Honors Program provides academically ambitious undergraduates innovative and intellectual learning opportunities. Award-winning faculty members, unique and challenging course work, and senior research projects are the hallmarks of this program.

Off-Campus Programs

UW has approximately 350 international students and close to 100 international researchers/scholars during any given academic year. This diverse community represents some sixty-five countries. International Students Services provides support to this population through an extensive orientation program, the Friendship Families program, the International Neighbors program, and the International Resource Center.

International Student Services coordinates the National Student Exchange (NSE), which is a domestic student exchange consortium of more than 180 colleges and universities throughout the U.S. In addition, NSE host sites are available in Canada, Puerto Rico, the Virgin Islands, and Guam. Membership in the NSE provides UW students with access to thousands of unique academic programs, classes, and faculty members on host campuses for either a semester or an academic year.

The UW Outreach School extends the university learning experience to Wyoming and the nation through credit and noncredit programs, University of Wyoming Television, Wyoming Public Radio, and the UW/Casper College Center. Credit programs are delivered via Internet/Web-based instruction, compressed video, audio teleconferencing, flexible enrollment (correspondence study), and on-site instruction. Select programs are offered, and degree availability may be limited.

Academic Facilities

The University libraries' collections number nearly 1.3 million volumes and offer links to a variety of library service collections. The William Robertson Coe Library houses materials in the social sciences, humanities, visual and performing arts, business, education, and health sciences as well as more than 2 million federal publications and the Audio Visual Library, a collection of 4,000 video and film titles. Other libraries include the Science Library, the Brinkerhoff Earth Resources Information Center (geology library), and the Rocky Mountain Herbarium Research Collection. Additional collections are housed in the American Heritage Center and the George W. Hooper Law Library. A branch library is located at the National Park Service Research Center in Jackson, Wyoming. UW libraries participate in the Colorado Alliance of Research Libraries and in Region Four of the National Network of Libraries of Medicine. In addition, FERRET provides high-speed access to UW's online library catalogs.

Costs

UW tuition and fees for full-time undergraduates in the 2003–04 academic year were $3090 for Wyoming residents and $8940 for nonresidents. Room and board (double occupancy, unlimited meal plan) were $5546. Estimated expenses include $1000 for books and $2000 for personal expenses.

Financial Aid

Nearly 80 percent of all UW students receive financial assistance. More than $48 million is available in the form of scholarships, loans, grants, and work-study opportunities. The Free Application for Federal Student Aid (FAFSA) is required for need-based assistance (loans, grants, work-study) and for many scholarships. Most scholarships at UW are based on academic merit. UW participates in the Western Undergraduate Exchange (WUE) program and offers the Nebraska Good Neighbor Scholarship. UW also offers the Western Heritage Scholarship Package to qualified students from non-WUE states. The priority deadline for financial aid is March 1.

Faculty

More than 650 professors from the world's most respected colleges and universities have come to teach at UW. Recognized nationally and internationally as experts, 87 percent of the professors hold the highest degrees in their fields. UW professors are deeply committed to the success of their students. Only a small number of undergraduate courses are taught by graduate assistants, and many of the most distinguished and accomplished professors at UW teach first-year courses. UW maintains a low student-faculty ratio (16:1), which allows for individualized attention, instruction, and academic advising, as well as the inclusion of undergraduates in cutting-edge research projects.

Student Government

The Associated Students of the University of Wyoming (ASUW) comprises all students at UW. ASUW serves as the voice of the students, and its legislation has impact on many aspects of student life. The ASUW Senate acts as a liaison between the student body and the administration as well as the UW Board of Trustees and local and state governments. The student body president also sits as an *ex officio* member of the UW Board of Trustees. UW encourages all students to get involved and actively participate in ASUW.

Admission Requirements

To be admitted, high school graduates and new first-year students with fewer than 30 transferable college credit hours should have a cumulative high school GPA of 2.75 or above (Wyoming residents) or 3.0 or above (nonresidents) and a composite ACT score of 20 or above or an SAT I composite score of 960 or above and completed 13 high school units that include 4 units of English, 3 units of mathematics, 3 units of science (including a physical science), and 3 units of cultural context courses (behavioral or social sciences, visual or performing arts, humanities or foreign languages). Admission with conditions can be granted to students who do not meet these standards but have a minimum 2.5 GPA or a 2.25 GPA with a composite ACT score of at least 20 or an SAT I score of at least 960. Transfer students with 30 or more transferable semester credit hours must have a minimum cumulative GPA of 2.0.

Application and Information

Students must submit a completed UW Application for Admission, official high school/college transcripts, ACT or SAT I scores, and a $30 nonrefundable application fee. Students may apply and pay the application fee online at the Web address below. UW strongly encourages all prospective students and their parents to visit the campus.

Admission Office
University of Wyoming
P.O. Box 3435
Laramie, Wyoming 82071-3435
Telephone: 307-766-5160
800-DIAL-WYO (342-5996) (toll-free)
E-mail: why-wyo@uwyo.edu
World Wide Web: http://www.uwyo.edu/

Historic Old Main was built in 1886.

WHITWORTH COLLEGE

SPOKANE, WASHINGTON

The College

Whitworth, founded in 1890, is among a select group of educational institutions known for both academic rigor and Christian commitment. The Whitworth faculty is committed to encouraging open intellectual inquiry as well as respect for diverse points of view. The College's community of scholars is also dedicated to the challenging task of integrating faith perspectives into all aspects of life and learning. This dual commitment distinguishes Whitworth among Christian colleges and universities.

The campus has thirty-eight buildings, mostly of red brick, which border the parklike Loop, including the Harriet Cheney Cowles Memorial Library, Cowles Memorial Auditorium, Hixson Union Building, and Dixon Hall. The Seeley Mudd Chapel, located at the heart of the campus, has an expanded worship area, seminar rooms, and staff offices. The Whitworth Fieldhouse is home to the Scotford Fitness and Aquatic Center, which has a 25-meter, six-lane pool with a movable bulkhead and a 15-foot diving pool. The Hixson Union Building houses the bookstore, post office, snack bar, and student media, student government offices, and a 450-seat dining hall.

The College's 1,700 full-time undergraduate students come from thirty-one states and twenty-five countries. Nearly 65 percent of the full-time undergraduate students live on campus in nine residential areas that range from traditional dormitory buildings to cottage-size apartments and theme houses. Residence life is considered an essential part of a student's growth process, and living groups are encouraged, with the help of trained residence staff, to design their own living environments. Peer leaders in each residence hall include resident assistants, health coordinators, ministry coordinators, and cultural diversity advocates.

Also serving the personal development of each student are the Office of the Chaplain and Student Life Department. Religious life on campus is centered on midweek chapel; and Hosanna, a student-led praise service. Bible studies, discussion groups, and opportunities for service also originate in the Office of the Chaplain. The Student Life Program assists all students in adjusting to college life and defining individual goals by providing counseling, tutoring, services for international students and members of minority groups, job placement, career planning, and aptitude testing.

Whitworth College holds membership in the NCAA Division III and is a member of the Northwest Conference. Varsity teams for men compete in baseball, basketball, cross-country, football, golf, soccer, swimming, tennis, and track and field. Women's teams compete in basketball, cross-country, golf, soccer, softball, swimming, tennis, track and field, and volleyball. Nine Whitworth teams have won conference championships in the past three years, and four teams have led the nation in team GPA for their sports in NCAA Division III. A broad intramural program, as well as club sports, offers athletic competition to everyone on campus, including faculty and staff members, and fitness evaluation services in the Scotford Fitness Center are available to all. Whitworth believes that physical development is an essential element in each student's pursuit of personal wholeness.

Location

Whitworth College is located just 15 minutes from downtown Spokane on a scenic, wooded 200-acre site, surrounded by quiet suburban residential areas. Spokane, a metropolitan area with a population of 414,500, is surrounded by an extraordinary outdoor recreation area, containing thousands of acres of state and national forests, four major ski resorts, and more than seventy-five lakes within an hour's drive. The city is the commercial and cultural center for more than a million people, and the size of this market area is reflected in the excellence of Spokane's many cultural and entertainment opportunities, restaurants, shopping centers, and transportation.

Majors and Degrees

Whitworth awards Bachelor of Arts and Bachelor of Science degrees. Programs and majors are available in accounting, American studies, art, arts administration, athletic training, biology, business management, chemistry, communication, computer science, cross-cultural studies, economics, education (elementary and secondary certification programs, with academic department emphases), English, environmental studies, French, German, history, international business, international studies, journalism and mass communications, kinesiology, leadership studies, liberal studies, marketing, mathematics, modern languages, music, organizational management, peace studies, philosophy, physical education, physics, political studies, pre-ministry, psychology, quantitative analysis, religion, sociology, Spanish, speech communication, theater, and women's studies.

Preprofessional programs are offered in dentistry, engineering (3-2), law, medical technology, medicine, occupational therapy, pharmacy, physical therapy, and veterinary medicine.

Academic Programs

The College is dedicated to academic excellence as expressed through its core of liberal arts and sciences and through rigorous disciplinary and interdisciplinary study. A Whitworth education is designed to broaden students' understanding of their cultural heritage, to promote critical thinking, to prepare students for productive work, and to stimulate creativity in responding to the challenges of life. As a Christian institution, Whitworth takes seriously its responsibility to help students understand and respond compassionately to the needs of the world. Recognizing that contemporary society is globally interdependent and increasingly multicultural, Whitworth seeks to foster in its students an attitude of curiosity and respect for diverse cultures.

The College's 4-1-4 calendar provides time for intensive study in a single subject during the month of January, often in an off-campus setting.

Off-Campus Programs

January terms and full semesters of off-campus study are available to encourage students to relate their education to real-life environments. Urban studies in San Francisco; international studies in Europe, Latin America, South Africa, Thailand, and the Middle East; music studies in Rome and Munich; and rural studies in various locales are offered to augment classroom learning. Students are not traveling as tourists; they are accompanied by faculty members who guide their research and studies and join them in experiencing the culture to the greatest degree possible.

Exchange-student arrangements are available through the International Student Exchange Program (ISEP). This program offers placements in any of the 150 member universities in Africa, Asia, Australia, Canada, Europe, or Latin America.

Cooperative education/internship opportunities are available for Whitworth students in Spokane or in almost any area of the country. For instance, political studies majors routinely intern in Washington, D.C. The co-op/internship program enables students to gain actual experience and build contacts in a chosen field prior to graduation. A January-term internship often leads to declaring a major, a modification of a career goal, or, just as often, a job opportunity.

Academic Facilities

With its state-of-the-art information retrieval technology and a capacity exceeding 250,000 volumes, the Harriet Cheney Cowles Memorial Library provides students and faculty members with a superb research facility. The library's computerized card catalogs and databases also provide access to the holdings of other libraries in the region and across the country. In addition, the library is home to three computer labs, six group study rooms, climate-controlled archives, a music library, a curriculum lab for teacher education, audiovisual services, and a Writing Center.

The Whitworth Music Building has the most advanced facilities available for music education. Laboratories for chemistry, physics, and biology are maintained in the Eric Johnston Science Center. A generous grant from the National Science Foundation provided funds to upgrade these laboratories. The Fine Arts Building contains studios for drawing, painting, and pottery and houses the John Koehler Gallery, which is used for student shows. The Dr. James P. Evans Sports Medicine Center includes a complete hydrotherapy center, ultrasound equipment, and a variety of ergometers and isokinetic machines.

Costs

For the 2004–05 academic year, tuition is $20,980 and room and board are $6500. Additional costs for books, fees, and personal expenses vary.

Financial Aid

More than 90 percent of Whitworth's students receive financial aid, with the average freshman scholarship and grant award exceeding $8500. The Free Application for Federal Student Aid (FAFSA) is used to determine a student's financial need for awarding grants, scholarships, loans, and work-study. Academic scholarships and fine arts, pre-engineering, and science and journalism talent awards are available to exceptional students regardless of their demonstrated need. Student employment, under the Federal Work-Study Program, is available on campus for up to 20 hours per week through the Student Employment Office, which provides placement assistance for off-campus jobs as well. The following non-need-based federal loan programs are available to Whitworth students and their families: the Federal Unsubsidized Stafford Loan and the Federal PLUS loan for parents. Whitworth also recently joined The Tuition Plan program, offering tuition discounts and prepayment options to lock in tuition costs.

Faculty

The Whitworth faculty is made up of 112 full-time professors, most of whom have earned either a Ph.D. or the terminal degree in their field. These dedicated Christian scholars conduct important research, perform in demanding musical venues, write critically acclaimed books, and earn recognition in their fields. But their primary commitment is to teaching—sharing their knowledge, their faith journeys, and their friendship with students inside and outside the classroom.

Student Government

A full-time student activities coordinator works with the elected members of the Associated Students of Whitworth College (ASWC) and the appointed student managers to plan and carry out College activities, which range from Homecoming festivities to mountain climbs to political lobbying. Student government is responsible for the continuing involvement of students in the community, organizing outreach ministry opportunities on- and off-campus, and meeting the academic, social, and spiritual needs of the campus community. Individual students are full-fledged members, along with faculty members, of various councils that formulate major campus policies.

Admission Requirements

Whitworth selects its students from those applicants who, by reason of their academic achievement, measured aptitudes, and academic interests, demonstrate their ability to succeed at a rigorous Christian liberal arts college. Generally, 4 years of English; 3 years each of history, science (including lab science), and mathematics; and 2 years of a foreign language constitute a competitive college-preparatory program for a high school applicant. Transfer students are also welcome to apply; Whitworth grants junior standing and a waiver of most general graduation requirements to students who have earned an approved Associate of Arts degree at any Washington community college as well as North Idaho College.

Application and Information

High-achieving students who have decided that Whitworth College is their first or second choice are eligible to apply for early action. The early action application deadline is November 30. For regular admission, the deadline is March 1. Campus visits are recommended from September through May while classes are in session.

Application for admission may be made by submitting a completed Whitworth application form, a personal statement, an evaluation by the student's high school counselor or principal, a current transcript of high school work, and ACT or SAT I scores.

For information and application forms, students should contact:

Office of Admissions
Whitworth College
West 300 Hawthorne Road
Spokane, Washington 99251-0106
Telephone: 509-777-3212
800-533-4668 (toll-free)
E-mail: admission@whitworth.edu
World Wide Web: http://www.whitworth.edu

Whitworth students represent thirty-one states and twenty-five countries.

Profiles and In-Depth Descriptions of Other Colleges to Consider

Alabama

BIRMINGHAM-SOUTHERN COLLEGE

Birmingham, Alabama

Birmingham-Southern is a coed, private, Methodist, comprehensive institution, founded in 1856, offering degrees at the bachelor's and master's levels. It has a 196-acre campus in Birmingham.

Academic Information The faculty has 121 members (79% full-time), 82% with terminal degrees. The undergraduate student-faculty ratio is 12:1. The library holds 232,330 titles, 949 serial subscriptions, and 31,471 audiovisual materials. Special programs include an honors program, study abroad, advanced placement credit, double majors, independent study, self-designed majors, summer session for credit, part-time degree programs, adult/continuing education programs, internships, and arrangement for off-campus study with University of Alabama at Birmingham, Samford University, Miles College. The most frequently chosen baccalaureate fields are business/marketing, social sciences and history, visual/performing arts.
Student Body Statistics The student body totals 1,388, of whom 1,303 are undergraduates (356 freshmen). 58 percent are women and 42 percent are men. Students come from 28 states and territories. 75 percent are from Alabama. 0.5 percent are international students. 39 percent of the 2003 graduating class went on to graduate and professional schools.
Expenses for 2003–04 *Application fee:* $25. *Comprehensive fee:* $25,034 includes full-time tuition ($18,530), mandatory fees ($400), and college room and board ($6104). *College room only:* $3444.
Financial Aid Forms of aid include need-based and non-need-based scholarships and part-time jobs. The average aided 2003–04 undergraduate received an aid package worth an estimated $16,015. The application deadline for financial aid is August 1 with a priority deadline of March 1.
Freshman Admission Birmingham-Southern requires an essay, a high school transcript, a minimum 2.0 high school GPA, 1 recommendation, SAT I or ACT scores, and TOEFL scores for international students. An interview is recommended. An interview is required for some. The application deadline for regular admission is rolling and for early action it is December 1.
Transfer Admission The application deadline for admission is rolling.
Entrance Difficulty Birmingham-Southern assesses its entrance difficulty level as moderately difficult. For the fall 2003 freshman class, 89 percent of the applicants were accepted.

For Further Information Write to Sheri S. Salmon, Associate Vice President for Admission Services, Birmingham-Southern College, 900 Arkadelphia Road, P.O. Box 549008, Birmingham, AL 35254. *Web site:* http://www.bsc.edu.

See page 208 for a narrative description.

Iowa

CORNELL COLLEGE

Mount Vernon, Iowa

Cornell is a coed, private, Methodist, four-year college, founded in 1853, offering degrees at the bachelor's level. It has a 129-acre campus in Mount Vernon.

Academic Information The faculty has 101 members (84% full-time), 82% with terminal degrees. The student-faculty ratio is 12:1. The library holds 197,780 titles, 1,236 serial subscriptions, and 4,471 audiovisual materials. Special programs include study abroad, advanced placement credit, ESL programs, double majors, independent study, self-designed majors, adult/continuing education programs, internships, and arrangement for off-campus study with Associated Colleges of the Midwest, Fisk University. The most frequently chosen baccalaureate fields are education, psychology, social sciences and history.
Student Body Statistics The student body is made up of 1,117 undergraduates (367 freshmen). 59 percent are women and 41 percent are men. Students come from 42 states and territories and 14 other countries. 31 percent are from Iowa. 1.5 percent are international students. 33 percent of the 2003 graduating class went on to graduate and professional schools.
Expenses for 2003–04 *Application fee:* $25. *Comprehensive fee:* $27,825 includes full-time tuition ($21,630), mandatory fees ($160), and college room and board ($6035). *College room only:* $2825. Full-time tuition and fees vary according to reciprocity agreements. Room and board charges vary according to board plan. *Part-time tuition:* varies with course load.
Financial Aid Forms of aid include need-based and non-need-based scholarships and part-time jobs. The average aided 2003–04 undergraduate received an aid package worth an estimated $19,455. The application deadline for financial aid is March 1.
Freshman Admission Cornell requires an essay, a high school transcript, 1 recommendation, SAT I or ACT scores, and TOEFL scores for international students. A minimum 2.80 high school GPA and an interview are recommended. The application deadline for regular admission is February 1.
Transfer Admission The application deadline for admission is February 1.
Entrance Difficulty Cornell assesses its entrance difficulty level as moderately difficult. For the fall 2003 freshman class, 69 percent of the applicants were accepted.

For Further Information Contact Mr. Jonathan Stroud, Dean of Admissions and Financial Assistance, Cornell College, 600 First Street West, Mount Vernon, IA 52314-1098. *Telephone:* 319-895-4477 or 800-747-1112 (toll-free). *Fax:* 319-895-4451. *E-mail:* admissions@cornellcollege.edu. *Web site:* http://www.cornellcollege.edu/.

See page 210 for a narrative description.

New York

EUGENE LANG COLLEGE, NEW SCHOOL UNIVERSITY

New York, New York

Eugene Lang College is a coed, private, four-year college of New School University, founded in 1978, offering degrees at the bachelor's level. It has a 5-acre campus in New York.

Academic Information The faculty has 114 members (31% full-time). The student-faculty ratio is 12:1. The library holds 4 million titles, 22,150 serial subscriptions, and 48,379 audiovisual materials. Special programs include study abroad, advanced placement credit, accelerated degree programs, independent study, distance learning, self-designed majors, summer session for credit, part-time degree programs, adult/continuing education programs, internships, and arrangement for off-campus study with Cooper Union for the Advancement of Science and Art, Bank Street College of Education, Sarah Lawrence College. The most frequently chosen baccalaureate field is liberal arts/general studies.
Student Body Statistics The student body is made up of 742 undergraduates (188 freshmen). 68 percent are women and 32 percent are men. Students come from 36 states and territories and 15 other countries. 45 percent are from New York. 2.8 percent are international students.
Expenses for 2003–04 *Application fee:* $40. *Comprehensive fee:* $34,940 includes full-time tuition ($23,620), mandatory fees ($510), and college room and board ($10,810). *College room only:* $8100. *Part-time tuition:* $868 per credit. *Part-time mandatory fees:* $115 per term.

Eugene Lang College, New School University (continued)

Financial Aid Forms of aid include need-based and non-need-based scholarships and part-time jobs. The average aided 2003–04 undergraduate received an aid package worth an estimated $17,793. The priority application deadline for financial aid is March 1.

Freshman Admission Eugene Lang College requires an essay, a high school transcript, a minimum 2.0 high school GPA, 2 recommendations, an interview, SAT I or ACT scores, and TOEFL scores for international students. A minimum 3.0 high school GPA is recommended. The application deadline for regular admission is February 1 and for early decision it is November 15.

Transfer Admission The application deadline for admission is May 15.

Entrance Difficulty Eugene Lang College assesses its entrance difficulty level as moderately difficult. For the fall 2003 freshman class, 65 percent of the applicants were accepted.

SPECIAL MESSAGE TO STUDENTS

Social Life Social life at the College is reflective of the cultural richness of New York City. The Theresa Lang Student Center provides a central location for student meetings and performances. A special program, Lang in the City, opens up the world of the arts at little or no additional cost to students. Undergraduates publish an award-winning literary magazine and a newsmagazine, produce several plays a year, and organize lectures and poetry readings. There are social and political groups, such as the Student Union, Latino and African-American organizations, and a volunteer resource center.

Academic Highlights The academic structure at Eugene Lang College is interdisciplinary and emphasizes small seminar classes of no more than 20 students. Students develop a liberal arts program of study around twelve areas of concentration. Internships are also an integral component of the Eugene Lang education and include placement at schools, media and publishing organizations, nonprofit organizations, and more. Students are encouraged to participate in the internship program as early as their sophomore year. Exchange programs with American and European universities are also options for students.

Interviews and Campus Visits The College's environment is distinctive and challenging, and therefore an interview for admission is highly recommended. Information about Lang College and the student is exchanged through informal conversation directed by the admissions officer. Students should come prepared to discuss their reasons for applying, their particular learning style, and their college expectations. Students are strongly encouraged to sit in on a seminar class and take a campus tour as part of their visit to the College. Telephone interviews can be arranged if traveling to New York City is inconvenient. New York City provides a rich artistic and cultural background for the College. Tours include the College and University facilities as well as historic and artistic sites. Points of interest include the Parsons School of Design building, the Albert List Academic Center, the Orozco Murals (rendered in 1930), Loeb Student Residence Hall, the Theresa Lang Student Center, and the seminar classrooms. New York City architecture and parks are also highlights, especially Washington Square Park and the College's historic Greenwich Village neighborhood. For information about appointments and campus visits, students should call the Office of Admissions at 212-229-5665, Monday through Friday, 9 a.m. to 5 p.m., or e-mail the office using the address below. The fax number is 212-229-5355. The office is located at 65 West 11th Street, third floor, on campus. The nearest commercial airport is John F. Kennedy International.

For Further Information Write to Mr. Terence Peavy, Director of Admissions, Eugene Lang College, New School University, 65 West 11th Street, Third Floor, New York, NY 10011. *E-mail:* lang@newschool.edu.

See page 212 for a narrative description.

North Carolina

NORTH CAROLINA AGRICULTURAL AND TECHNICAL STATE UNIVERSITY

Greensboro, North Carolina

North Carolina A&T is a coed, public unit of University of North Carolina System, founded in 1891, offering degrees at the bachelor's, master's, and doctoral levels. It has a 191-acre campus in Greensboro.

Academic Information The faculty has 458 members. The undergraduate student-faculty ratio is 17:1. The library holds 527,252 titles, 5,515 serial subscriptions, and 35,446 audiovisual materials. Special programs include academic remediation, services for learning-disabled students, an honors program, cooperative (work-study) education, study abroad, advanced placement credit, summer session for credit, part-time degree programs (daytime, evenings, summer), adult/continuing education programs, internships, and arrangement for off-campus study with University of North Carolina at Greensboro, Guilford College, Bennett College, High Point University, Greensboro College.

Student Body Statistics The student body totals 8,319, of whom 7,331 are undergraduates (1,771 freshmen). 52 percent are women and 48 percent are men. Students come from 42 states and territories. 80 percent are from North Carolina. 0.8 percent are international students.

Expenses for 2003–04 *Application fee:* $35. *State resident tuition:* $1544 full-time, $64 per credit part-time. *Nonresident tuition:* $10,911 full-time, $455 per credit part-time. *Mandatory fees:* $1178 full-time. *College room and board:* $4968. *College room only:* $2768.

Financial Aid Forms of aid include need-based and non-need-based scholarships, athletic grants, and part-time jobs. The average aided 2003–04 undergraduate received an aid package worth an estimated $5098. The priority application deadline for financial aid is March 15.

Freshman Admission North Carolina A&T requires a high school transcript, a minimum 2.0 high school GPA, and TOEFL scores for international students. SAT I or ACT scores are recommended. The application deadline for regular admission is June 1.

Transfer Admission The application deadline for admission is June 1.

Entrance Difficulty North Carolina A&T assesses its entrance difficulty level as moderately difficult. For the fall 2003 freshman class, 81 percent of the applicants were accepted.

For Further Information Contact Mr. John Smith, Director of Admissions, North Carolina Agricultural and Technical State University, 1601 East Market Street, Webb Hall, Greensboro, NC 27411. *Telephone:* 336-334-7946 or 800-443-8964 (toll-free in-state). *Fax:* 336-334-7478. *E-mail:* uadmit@ncat.edu. *Web site:* http://www.ncat.edu/.

See page 216 for a narrative description.

Pennsylvania

LEHIGH UNIVERSITY

Bethlehem, Pennsylvania

Lehigh is a coed, private university, founded in 1865, offering degrees at the bachelor's, master's, and doctoral levels and post-master's certificates. It has a 1,600-acre campus in Bethlehem near Philadelphia.

Academic Information The faculty has 547 members (79% full-time). The undergraduate student-faculty ratio is 10:1. The library holds 1 million titles, 6,271 serial subscriptions, and 8,415 audiovisual materials. Special programs include services for learning-disabled students, an honors program, cooperative (work-study) education, study abroad, advanced placement credit, accelerated degree programs, ESL programs, double majors, independent study, distance learning, summer session for credit, external degree programs, adult/continuing education programs, internships, and arrangement for off-campus study with members of the Lehigh Valley Association of Independent Colleges, American University. The most frequently chosen baccalaureate fields are business/marketing, engineering/engineering technologies, social sciences and history.

Student Body Statistics The student body totals 6,732, of whom 4,679 are undergraduates (1,125 freshmen). 40 percent are women and 60 percent are men. Students come from 52 states and territories. 32 percent are from Pennsylvania. 2.8 percent are international students. 32 percent of the 2003 graduating class went on to graduate and professional schools.

Expenses for 2004–05 *Application fee:* $60. *Comprehensive fee:* $37,570 includes full-time tuition ($29,140), mandatory fees ($200), and college room and board ($8230). *College room only:* $4700. Room and board charges vary according to board plan and student level. *Part-time tuition:* $1215 per credit.

Financial Aid Forms of aid include need-based and non-need-based scholarships, athletic grants, and part-time jobs. The average aided 2003–04 undergraduate received an aid package worth an estimated $23,533. The application deadline for financial aid is February 1.

Freshman Admission Lehigh requires a high school transcript, 1 recommendation, a graded writing sample, SAT I or ACT scores, and TOEFL scores for international students. An essay, an interview, and SAT II: Subject Test scores are recommended. The application deadline for regular admission is January 1; for early decision plan 1 it is November 15; and for early decision plan 2 it is February 1.

Transfer Admission The application deadline for admission is April 1.

Entrance Difficulty Lehigh assesses its entrance difficulty level as most difficult. For the fall 2003 freshman class, 40 percent of the applicants were accepted.

For Further Information Contact Mr. J. Bruce Gardiner, Interim Dean of Admissions and Financial Aid, Lehigh University, 27 Memorial Drive West, Bethlehem, PA 18015. *Telephone:* 610-758-3100. *Fax:* 610-758-4361. *E-mail:* admissions@lehigh.edu. *Web site:* http://www.lehigh.edu/.

See page 214 for a narrative description.

BIRMINGHAM-SOUTHERN COLLEGE

BIRMINGHAM, ALABAMA

The College

Birmingham-Southern College (BSC) was created through a merger of Southern University (established in 1856) and Birmingham College (established in 1898). Since 1959, when *Harper's Magazine* called it "one of the leading small colleges in the South," Birmingham-Southern continues to be recognized as one of the nation's outstanding liberal arts institutions. Birmingham-Southern is ranked in the top tier of national liberal arts colleges in *U.S. News & World Report's America's Best Colleges 2004. U.S. News & World Report* also ranked Birmingham-Southern College as one of the best values in higher education and one of the most efficient schools; *Money* ranked Birmingham-Southern as one of the 100 best college buys. The College is also recognized by the John Templeton Foundation's Honor Roll as one of 100 schools nationwide that emphasize character building as an integral part of the college experience; as one of the 100 best values in private colleges by *Kiplinger's Personal Finance Magazine;* as being among the 100 colleges worth considering, as compiled by *Washington Post* staff writer Jay Mathews; as one of America's best Christian colleges by Institutional Research and Evaluation, Inc.; and as one of the nation's top thirty colleges by the *Washington Times.*

Birmingham-Southern is one of only six Baccalaureate Colleges–Liberal Arts, as classified by the Carnegie Foundation for the Advancement of Teaching, to hold both AACSB International–The Association to Advance Collegiate Schools of Business accreditation and the designation of Phi Beta Kappa.

Each year, Birmingham-Southern ranks number one in Alabama and among the nation's best in percentage of all graduates accepted to medical, dental, or health career programs; the College also ranks high nationally in graduates accepted to law school.

Birmingham-Southern competes in NCAA Division I athletics and supports fourteen different sports. The College has more than seventy clubs and organizations and intramural sports. Its enrollment averages 550 men and 750 women.

At the graduate level, Birmingham-Southern offers a Master of Arts program in public and private management and a Master of Music degree.

Location

Located in rolling country on a 197-acre campus in western Birmingham, the College is just 3 miles via I-59 from the downtown business district. Birmingham, Alabama's largest city, has been honored by the U.S. Conference of Mayors as the "Most Livable City in America," and offers fine restaurants, museums, city and state parks, and theater. Its offerings are supplemented by the activities of four other Birmingham colleges. Birmingham's 17,000-seat Civic Center Coliseum is the setting for many outstanding cultural and athletic events.

Majors and Degrees

Birmingham-Southern offers the undergraduate degrees of Bachelor of Arts, Bachelor of Science, Bachelor of Music, Bachelor of Music Education, and Bachelor of Fine Arts. Departmental majors include accounting, art, art education, biology, business administration, chemistry, computer science, dance, economics, education, English, French, German, history, international studies, mathematics, music, music education, philosophy, physics, political science, psychology, religion, sociology, Spanish, and theater arts. Individualized and interdisciplinary majors are also available.

Academic Programs

The College operates on a 4-1-4 calendar. Thirty-six units are required for the bachelor's degree; these comprise 32 regular term units and 4 Interim Term units. The minimum residence requirement is two years. In addition to its traditional liberal arts programs, Birmingham-Southern offers a number of individualized learning opportunities to meet students' special needs and career goals. These are the Honors Program, the Mentor Program, independent study, the student internship program, individualized majors, and the Interim Term. The College emphasizes international opportunities for students through course offerings, visitors to campus, and international travel/study programs. Through the Associated Colleges of the South, the College offers international programs in England, Brazil, and Central Europe.

Credit is available through CLEP and Advanced Placement tests. Credit may also be earned through a College-approved internship program.

Birmingham-Southern offers several special programs, including a six-week Summer Scholars Term for high school juniors, a one-week Student Leaders in Service program, and a dual-enrollment program that enables high school seniors to take college-credit courses.

Off-Campus Programs

The College sponsors an internship program through which students may earn credit for actual work experience. Depending on their major, students may be assigned positions in business, government, industry, human services, or other preprofessional areas of interest. Students may also take part in a cooperative exchange program that enables them to take courses at the University of Alabama at Birmingham, Miles College, or Samford University. They may also participate in Army ROTC at the University of Alabama at Birmingham or Air Force ROTC at Samford University.

Academic Facilities

Birmingham-Southern College features several new facilities including the Norton Campus Center, the Striplin Physical Activities Center, and the $25-million Stephens Science Center. BSC is home to the Meyer Planetarium, the first public planetarium in Alabama. The only split-lift revolving stage in the country is housed in the College Theatre. Academic year 2002–03 marked the opening of six new fraternity houses on fraternity row and a major renovation to Daniel Men's Residence Hall. The newly renovated Neal and Anne Berte Humanities Center was dedicated in September 2003.

Costs

For 2003–04, the total cost of attendance (tuition, room and board, books, personal expenses, and travel) was $29,830 and the total cost for commuting students was $23,930. These figures include fees for auto registration, student activity fee, computer usage fee, and an estimate for all other incidentals.

Financial Aid

Birmingham-Southern feels strongly that well-qualified students should have an opportunity for a college education regardless of economic circumstances. Approximately 90 percent of the College's students receive financial aid of some kind. Scholarships and grants range from $1000 to full tuition and may be renewed annually. Each student requesting financial assistance must submit the Free Application for Federal Student Aid (FAFSA). With the exception of the College's competitive scholarship programs and the Alabama Student Grant, all financial assistance awarded through the Office of Student Financial Aid is based on a demonstrated need determined from the required forms. Preference is given to those students who file by the March 1 priority deadline. The average award for those students who demonstrated need for the 2003–04 academic year was more than $14,000. In addition to the need-based programs, Birmingham-Southern awards more than $1.5 million in merit-based scholarships through a scholarship competition held in March.

Faculty

The faculty is composed of 96 full-time and 25 part-time teaching members; approximately 92 percent hold a Ph.D. degree or the terminal degree in their field. In addition to teaching, the faculty's major responsibility is advising students. Faculty members are actively involved in cocurricular activities planned primarily for students, and all are assigned a limited number of student advisees. They work closely with these students in planning and developing individual programs to fulfill the students' career interests. The student-faculty ratio is 12:1, and no freshman English class has more than 16 students.

Student Government

The Student Government Association of the College is chartered to operate under a constitution developed by the students, faculty, and administration. Through a large measure of self-government, this organization helps provide a well-balanced intellectual, educational, and social cocurricular program for all students. The Honor Code makes each student responsible for upholding the social and academic standards of the College. Students serve on numerous College committees, including recruitment, curriculum, fund-raising, and governance task forces.

Admission Requirements

Approximately 350 freshmen are selected for admission on the basis of high school record, ACT or SAT I scores, academic courses attempted, an admission essay, an interview, and recommendations of school officials. Applicants are expected to have completed at least 16 units of course work, 12 of which must be in academic subjects. Four units of English and at least two units each of mathematics, history, science, and social sciences are required, and two units of a foreign language are recommended. Students are encouraged to take more than the minimum units required in academic subjects.

Although an interview is not required except in the case of early admission, each applicant is encouraged to visit the campus and talk with an admission counselor or the vice president for admission services.

Transfer applicants must have at least a C average (2.0 on a 4.0 scale) on a full schedule of courses acceptable to Birmingham-Southern and a status of good standing with a clear academic and social record from the last college attended. If the applicant has attended more than one college, his or her overall average at these schools must meet the minimum academic-year grade point average required at Birmingham-Southern. Transfer students may enroll at the beginning of any term.

Application and Information

The College has an admission priority date of January 15. After January 15, the College continues to consider applications on a rolling admission basis.

Preview Days are held in October and November.

Inquiries concerning admission should be addressed to:

Sheri S. Salmon
Associate Vice President for Admission Services
Birmingham-Southern College
900 Arkadelphia Road
Birmingham, Alabama 35254
Telephone: 205-226-4696
800-523-5793 (toll-free)
E-mail: admission@bsc.edu
World Wide Web: http://www.bsc.edu

A view of the campus at Birmingham-Southern College.

CORNELL COLLEGE

MOUNT VERNON, IOWA

The College

Cornell College is unique in U.S. higher education in that it offers the combination of liberal arts study within the One-Course-At-A-Time framework, an active residential community, an emphasis on service and leadership, and an ideal, wooded-hilltop setting that is one of only two campuses listed on the National Register of Historic Places.

Cornell College is a leader in educational innovation. A private, independent college founded in 1853, Cornell employs the One-Course-At-A-Time academic calendar; it is one of only four colleges in the United States to implement this advancement in postsecondary teaching and learning. Cornell is historically a place of "firsts": the first coeducational college west of the Mississippi, the first college in Iowa to grant a baccalaureate degree to a woman, the first college in the United States to confer upon a woman a full professorship with the same salary received by the male professors, and the first college in the nation to have its entire campus listed on the National Register of Historic Places. The College was among the first schools in the nation to offer its students a choice of degree programs, establish a teacher-education program, and introduce sociology into its curriculum. Cornell offers a strong leadership-training program and actively promotes community service opportunities. Nearly 70 percent of the student body take part in volunteer projects.

In 2003–04, 1,100 students from forty states and eleven other countries were enrolled at this residential college, which is situated atop a high hill overlooking the Cedar River valley. Centered on a pedestrian mall, the campus covers 129 acres and has more than forty buildings, including nine residence halls. A student center, the Commons, houses central dining rooms, a bookstore, meeting rooms, and recreation rooms. Cornell's sports and recreation center has facilities for wellness and fitness programs as well as year-round recreation and athletics space for practice and play. Cornell has 25 NCAA Postgraduate Scholars, ranking ninth in the nation among NCAA Division III schools. It competes in the Iowa Intercollegiate Athletic Conference in nineteen sports. Nearly 60 percent of students participate in sixty-six intramural sports. More than 100 clubs and organizations offer a wide range of activities, from participation in the KRNL-FM radio station to Habitat for Humanity to Greek social groups.

Location

Mount Vernon provides the best of both worlds—a classically beautiful campus in a small college town minutes from Cedar Rapids and Iowa City. These two metropolitan areas contain three additional colleges and universities and 350,000 people. Chicago, St. Louis, and Minneapolis can be reached in about 5 hours by automobile or in less than an hour by air from Cedar Rapids. Palisades–Kepler State Park, site of the annual Pal Day picnic, is 5 miles away. Cornell is 15 minutes from Cedar Rapids (airport, movies, malls) and 20 minutes from Iowa City and Hancher Auditorium, a regular concert and theater tour stop.

Majors and Degrees

Cornell College awards the Bachelor of Arts, Bachelor of Music, Bachelor of Philosophy, and Bachelor of Special Studies degrees. Majors are offered in art, biochemistry and molecular biology, biology, chemistry, classical studies, computer science, economics and business, elementary and secondary education, English, environmental studies, French, geology, German, history, international business, international relations, Latin American studies, mathematics, medieval and Renaissance studies, music education (general, instrumental, and vocal), music performance, philosophy, physical education, physics, politics, psychology, religion, Russian, Russian studies, sociology, sociology and anthropology, Spanish, theater, theater and speech, and women's studies. Prelaw and premedicine programs are available, as are programs to prepare for graduate study in social work/human services and theology. Students may design their own interdisciplinary majors.

Combined-degree programs include a 3-2 program in forestry and environmental management offered in cooperation with Duke University, 3-2 programs in engineering and occupational therapy, and a 3-4 program in architecture with Washington University in St. Louis. The College also offers cooperative professional programs in nursing and allied health sciences with Rush University in Chicago and in medical technology with St. Luke's Hospital in Cedar Rapids. For students interested in dentistry, the University of Iowa College of Dentistry offers early acceptance into its program.

Academic Programs

Cornell encourages the creative structuring of students' educational experiences by offering a choice of four degree programs within the framework of a liberal education. Programs range from a traditional curriculum, with course requirements designed to ensure both breadth and depth, to a nontraditional combination of courses, independent studies, and internships that meet specific goals. For the Bachelor of Arts, Bachelor of Music, and Bachelor of Philosophy degree programs, faculty members set the goals. The Bachelor of Special Studies degree program permits students to define their own educational objectives and design a curriculum to meet those objectives.

To increase the quality and intensity of a Cornell education, the College's academic calendar incorporates the One-Course-At-A-Time schedule. Cornell divides the traditional September–May academic year into nine 3½-week terms. During each term, students concentrate on one course chosen from the more than sixty offered and take one final examination. After a four-day break, the next term begins. Students take eight terms per year, which leaves a ninth term free for internships, off-campus programs, international study, travel, independent study, rest and relaxation, or another course.

The College's emphasis on One-Course-At-A-Time enhances the quality of liberal education offered by allowing students increased contact with faculty members, no interference from competing courses, and greater efficiency of study. It also provides rapid feedback to students about their progress. The work assigned on one day is discussed on the following day, when the material is fresh for both students and instructor. In addition, the pressure of having to prepare for several courses and examinations at the same time is eliminated.

Another liberalizing feature of One-Course-At-A-Time is the possibility of having classes meet for periods longer or shorter than the typical 50-minute period. Professors may opt to divide the day into a series of short meetings, with work assignments given and completed from one session to the next. Laboratories are not necessarily limited to one afternoon. Faculty members are also able to take students on daylong field trips or teach their courses off campus, either in the United States or abroad.

Recent Cornell College graduates are studying public health at Harvard, architecture at Washington University (St. Louis), medicine at Iowa, law at Loyola Chicago, and studio art at the Art Institute of Chicago, to name a few. Among the employers of recent graduates are the Peace Corps; Houston Grand Opera; Cheetah Outreach; Visa International; Wells Fargo; AT&T Wireless;

U.S. Agency for International Development; New York Life Insurance; RBC Dain Rauscher, Inc.; and the Red Cross.

Off-Campus Programs

Student internship experiences can be central to understanding the realities, demands, and rewards of the workplace. Internships arranged within Cornell's One-Course-At-A-Time academic calendar are distinctly different from those arranged within a semester system. Students are able to become immersed in the experience every day for an entire month without the distractions of other course demands. Employers/mentors can count on a full-time commitment. This availability earns the attention of many nearby Cedar Rapids businesses and corporations that have offered opportunities from engineering to telecommunications, health-related fields, and art history. More distant internships have also been completed. The intensive internship learning experience makes Cornell students very appealing to prospective employers.

Through Cornell courses abroad and College-affiliated off-campus programs, students may work and travel in other countries and become acquainted with other cultures. Recent classes have journeyed to Mexico to observe local potters, to Montreal to study French, to Mexico and Spain to study Hispanic and Spanish social development, to London for courses in English literature and drama, and to Brazil and Guatemala to experience firsthand the politics of revolutionary movements.

Cornell students have done tropical field research in Costa Rica, studied Chinese culture in Hong Kong, worked with Hispanic communities in urban Chicago, and visited Europe's great cultural centers through off-campus programs administered by the Associated Colleges of the Midwest, of which Cornell is a charter member, and the School for International Training.

Academic Facilities

Cornell's entire campus has been designated a National Historic District, and its carefully restored nineteenth-century academic architecture is combined with contemporary facilities on a fully wired campus, with Internet access in every residence hall room. King Chapel is the historic landmark of the campus and has a 130-foot clock tower. Armstrong Hall and McWethy Hall have recently been renovated and expanded for art, music, and theater. Law Hall Technology Center opened in 2000, and Cole Library was renovated recently.

Costs

The cost for 2003–04 was $27,825, including tuition, fees, and room and board. Students generally enroll for eight courses a year, but, at no extra cost, they may accelerate or broaden their studies by taking nine courses.

Financial Aid

Cornell is committed to making higher education available for all students. The majority of Cornell's students receive financial assistance, and the average aid package exceeds $18,000. A competitive scholarship program recognizes students with strong academic records or special talents. Federal aid programs include Federal Pell Grants, Federal Supplemental Educational Opportunity Grants (FSEOG), and student loans. Federal Work-Study Program awards can provide additional income through part-time, on-campus employment. Additional funds are available through the Iowa Tuition Grant Program and State of Iowa Scholarships. Need is determined by the FAFSA. An early financial aid evaluation is available from the College upon request. Students applying for Cornell-funded scholarships must complete their scholarship applications by March 1.

Faculty

The College's faculty members are distinguished by their desire to teach undergraduates in a small, informal environment. Classes are capped at 25 students. Faculty members outside the department of physical education are required to have a Ph.D. or other terminal degree and are appointed, retained, and promoted based on their ability to teach. Many also distinguish themselves through scholarly and creative activities. The faculty-student ratio is 1:11, and only faculty members, not teaching assistants, teach classes.

Student Government

Student life at Cornell complements the academic program and provides a feeling of community at the College. Students participate actively in the governance of the College, serving on faculty-student committees, the Student Senate, the Residence Hall Council, and the Performing Arts and Activities Council.

Admission Requirements

The courses and degree programs offered at Cornell are intended for students who have been well prepared at the secondary school level, have obvious motivation and a desire to learn, and have the ability and potential to complete a carefully planned degree program and graduate from Cornell College. Admission to Cornell is selective. Applicants are judged on their high school records, test scores, interests, and achievements in such cocurricular activities as debate, student government, music, theater, athletics, and school publications as well as through personal recommendations and, in some cases, interviews. These are not exclusive criteria. Motivation, energy, and persistence are basic to Cornell. Students with the desire to succeed at Cornell and the motivation to benefit from a Cornell education may apply with confidence, knowing that these are important factors in the admission decision.

Application and Information

Cornell College follows a program of rolling admissions, and applicants are notified of admission decisions soon after their files are complete. Special consideration is given to students who apply by December 1. After March 1, applications are accepted on a space-available basis. To apply for admission to Cornell, prospective students should obtain an application form online or from the Office of Admissions, complete and file the application with Cornell with a $25 application fee, have their high school forward an official transcript and a school recommendation, and have their ACT or SAT I scores sent to Cornell. Cornell welcomes transfer students from accredited two- and four-year institutions.

Additional information, catalogs, application forms, and financial aid forms are available from:

Office of Admissions
Cornell College
600 First Street West
Mount Vernon, Iowa 52314-1098
Telephone: 319-895-4477
800-747-1112 (toll-free)
E-mail: admissions@cornellcollege.edu
World Wide Web: http://www.cornellcollege.edu

Graduation time at Cornell College.

EUGENE LANG COLLEGE, NEW SCHOOL UNIVERSITY

NEW YORK, NEW YORK

The College

Eugene Lang College is the distinctive liberal arts division of New School University, formerly known as the New School for Social Research. It is a major urban university with a tradition of innovative learning. The College offers all the benefits of a small and supportive college as well as the full range of opportunities found in a university setting.

Lang students are encouraged to participate in the creation and direction of their education. The desire to explore and the freedom to imagine shared by students and faculty members contribute to a distinctive academic community.

Eugene Lang College students currently come from forty-five states and thirteen countries. The ratio of men to women is approximately 2:3. About 45 percent of the College's 735 students come from outside the New York metropolitan area; 4 percent hold foreign citizenship and 23 percent are members of minority groups. The student body is composed of both residential and day students. The university operates residence halls within walking distance of classes; incoming freshmen and transfer students are given housing priority within these facilities, and housing is guaranteed for the first year for new students. Great diversity in interests and aspirations is found among the students. Through the Office of Student Services, students produce a student newspaper and an award-winning literary magazine. They organize and participate in dramatic, musical, and artistic events through the "Lang in the City Program," as well as numerous political, social, and cultural organizations at the university and throughout New York City.

The New School for Social Research was founded in 1919 by such notable scholars and intellectuals as John Dewey, Alvin Johnson, and Thorstein Veblen. It has long been a home for leading artists, educators, and public figures. For example, the university was the first institution of higher learning to offer college-level courses in such "new" fields as black culture and race, taught by W. E. B. DuBois, and psychoanalysis, taught by Freud's disciple Sandor Ferenczi. Among the world-famous artists and performers who have taught at the New School are Martha Graham, Aaron Copland, and Thomas Hart Benton. Today, such noted scholars as Robert Heilbroner, Eric Hobsbawm, Jerome Bruner, and Rayna Rapp are among the hundreds of university faculty members accessible to Lang College students.

The other divisions of the university include the Adult Division, which offers more than 2,000 credit and noncredit courses to students each semester; the Graduate Faculty of Political and Social Science (founded in 1933 as the University in Exile), which grants M.A. and Ph.D. degrees; the Robert J. Milano Graduate School of Management and Urban Policy, which awards the M.A. and M.S. degrees; Parsons School of Design, one of the oldest and most influential art schools in the country; and Mannes College of Music, a renowned classical conservatory. The total university enrollment in 2002–03 was approximately 7,500 degree-seeking students.

Location

The university is located in New York City's Greenwich Village, which historically has been a center for intellectual and artistic life. This slower-paced, more personal New York City neighborhood of town houses and tree-lined streets offers students a friendly and stimulating environment. Over and above the resources of Greenwich Village, New York City offers virtually unlimited cultural, artistic, recreational, and intellectual resources that make it one of the world's great cities.

Majors and Degrees

Eugene Lang College awards the Bachelor of Arts degree. Students are encouraged to design their own program of study, which includes an area of concentration, in consultation with their faculty adviser. Lang offers twelve areas of concentration: arts in context; cultural studies and media; dance; education studies; literature; philosophy; psychology; religious studies; science, technology, and society; social and historical inquiry; theater; urban studies; and writing. A student's concentration consists of eight to ten courses (32–40 credits) leading to relatively advanced and specialized knowledge of an area of study. In addition, students are encouraged to pursue an internship, where appropriate.

Students may also apply to a five-year B.A./B.F.A. program in conjunction with Parsons School of Design or in jazz studies at New School University, and advanced students may apply to the five-year B.A./M.A. programs offered in conjunction with the university's graduate divisions.

Academic Programs

When planning a program of study, Eugene Lang College students are encouraged to reflect on what their education means to them. Their program should parallel their own academic and personal development. By actively participating in the process of their education, students gain the knowledge to make informed choices about the direction of their studies with the help of their advisers and peers.

Small seminar classes serve as the focus of the academic program at the College. The maximum class size is 20 students. Classes are in-depth, interdisciplinary inquiries into topics or issues selected each semester by the College's outstanding faculty. Most importantly, the classes engage participants in the study of primary texts, rather than textbooks, and emphasize dialogue between teacher and student as a mode of learning. Here, not only is intellectual curiosity fostered by the small classes, but a genuine sense of community develops as well.

Although the College does not emphasize course requirements outside the area of concentration, freshmen are required to take one writing course and three other seminars of their choice in each of their first two semesters at the College. Upper-level students create their programs by selecting seminars from the College's curriculum, or they may combine offerings of the College with courses and workshops given by the New School's Adult Division, Graduate Faculty of Political and Social Science, Robert J. Milano Graduate School of Management and Urban Policy, and Parsons School of Design.

The College operates on a semester calendar; the first semester runs from September through mid-December and the second, from late January through mid-May. Students generally earn 16 credits per semester; a minimum of 120 credits is required for graduation.

Off-Campus Programs

Eugene Lang College recognizes the immense value of work undertaken beyond the classroom. The College arranges appropriate projects—internships with private and nonprofit organizations—which serve to strengthen the connection between theoretical work in the classroom and practical work on the job. Sophomores and juniors have the option of spending a year on a sponsored exchange with Sarah Lawrence College and the University of Amsterdam. Other exchanges, both American and abroad, are available.

Academic Facilities

Eugene Lang College is located on 11th Street between Fifth and Sixth Avenues in Greenwich Village. The university includes twelve academic buildings, including a student center, a Computer Instruction Center with more than seventy-five IBM personal computers and Macintosh systems, a 500-seat auditorium, art galleries, studios for the fine arts, classrooms, a writing center, and faculty offices. Lang College students have full and easy access to the Raymond Fogelman Library and the Adam and Sophie Gimbel Design Library. In addition, the university participates in the South Manhattan Library Consortium. Together, the libraries in the consortium house approximately 3 million volumes covering all the traditional liberal arts disciplines and the fine arts.

Costs

Tuition and fees for the 2003–04 academic year were $23,620. Room and board cost approximately $10,000, depending upon the specific meal plan and dormitory accommodations chosen. University fees were $100 per year.

Financial Aid

Students are encouraged to apply for aid by filing the Free Application for Federal Student Aid (FAFSA) and requesting that a copy of the need analysis report be sent to the New School (FAFSA code number 002780). Qualified College students are eligible for all federal and state financial aid programs in addition to university gift aid. University aid is awarded on the basis of need and merit and is part of a package consisting of both gift aid (grants and/or scholarships) and a self-help component (loans and Federal Work-Study awards). Aid is renewable each year as long as need continues and students maintain satisfactory academic standing at the College. Special attention is given to continuing students who have done exceptionally well.

Faculty

At Eugene Lang College, the faculty-student ratio is 1:10. Class size ranges from 10 to 20 students. Faculty members are graduates of outstanding colleges and universities and represent a wide variety of academic disciplines; 95 percent hold Ph.D.'s. College faculty members also serve as academic advisers, who are selected carefully in order to ensure the thoughtful supervision of students' programs and academic progress.

Well-known faculty members from other divisions of the university teach at the College on a regular basis. In addition, every semester, the College hosts distinguished scholars and writers as visiting faculty and guest lecturers who further enrich the academic program of the College and the university.

Student Government

There is a student union at the College, which is an organized vehicle for student expression and action as well as a means of funding student projects and events. Students are encouraged to express their views and concerns about academic policies and community life through regular student-faculty member meetings.

Admission Requirements

Eugene Lang College welcomes admission applications from students of diverse racial, ethnic, religious, and political backgrounds whose past performance and academic and personal promise make them likely to gain from and give much to the College community. The College seeks students who combine inquisitiveness and seriousness of purpose with the ability to engage in a distinctive, rigorous liberal arts program. Each applicant to the College is judged individually; the Admissions Committee, which renders all admission decisions, considers both academic qualifications and the personal, creative, and intellectual qualities of each applicant. A strong academic background, including a college-preparatory program, is recommended. An applicant's transcript; teacher and counselor recommendations; SAT I, ACT, or SAT II Subject Test scores; and personal essays are all taken into consideration. In addition, an interview, a tour of university facilities, and a visit to Lang College seminars are optional but highly recommended.

High school students for whom the College is their first choice are strongly encouraged to apply as early decision candidates and are notified early of an admission decision. Early entrance is an option for qualified high school juniors who wish to enter college prior to high school graduation. Candidates for early entrance must submit two teacher recommendations.

Students who have successfully completed one full year or more at another accredited institution may apply as transfer candidates. If accepted, transfer students may enter upper-level seminars and pursue advanced work. International students may apply for admission as freshmen or transfers by submitting a regular application to the College. If English is spoken as a second language, TOEFL scores are required. The New York Connection Program invites students from other colleges to Eugene Lang for a semester and incorporates an internship into their studies.

Students interested in applying for the combined B.A./B.F.A. degree program in fine arts or jazz studies are encouraged to apply for admission as freshmen to these special five-year programs. In addition to the admission requirements outlined above, a home exam and a portfolio are required for fine arts, and an audition is required for jazz studies.

Application and Information

Freshmen, transfers, and visiting students may apply for either the September (fall) or January (spring) semester. To apply for admission to the College, students must request an application packet and submit the required credentials and a $40 application fee by the appropriate deadline. (The application fee may be waived in accordance with the College Board's Fee Waiver Service.) For the semester beginning in January, the required credentials must be submitted by November 15, with notification by December 15. For the September semester, early decision candidates must submit the required credentials by November 15, with notification by December 15; for freshman candidates applying for general admission and freshmen early entrants, the deadline is February 1, with notification by April 1; for transfers and visiting students, the deadline is rolling to May 15, with notification rolling until July 1.

For further information, students should contact:

Terence Peavy
Director of Admissions
Eugene Lang College, New School University
65 West 11th Street, Third Floor
New York, New York 10011
Telephone: 212-229-5665
Fax: 212-229-5355
E-mail: lang@newschool.edu
World Wide Web: http://www.lang.edu

LEHIGH UNIVERSITY

BETHLEHEM, PENNSYLVANIA

The University

Lehigh University is among the nation's most selective, highly ranked private research universities, rich in tradition, with an inspiring history that spans more than 135 years. Lehigh offers a comprehensive education that integrates courses from four colleges and dozens of fields of study to create a dynamic learning environment. At Lehigh, students can choose from nationally recognized programs in the arts and sciences, humanities, business, engineering, and education. Students can customize their college experience to their personal interests by tailoring their majors and academic programs from more than 2,000 courses, with opportunities to take courses outside of their college or major field of study.

Lehigh is the right size—small enough to be personal, yet large enough to be powerful. The school combines learning opportunities found at larger research universities with the personal attention of a smaller, private college. Many students consider Lehigh as everything that college was meant to be. At Lehigh, students have easy access to world-class faculty members who are renowned in their fields but also offer their time and personal attention to help students learn and succeed. With a 9.9:1 student-faculty ratio, a college experience customized to the individual, close mentoring by faculty members, hands-on projects, extensive industry internships, and innovative study, Lehigh students emerge as leaders in careers and life. The University's approximately 4,685 undergraduate students come from nearly every state and more than sixty-five countries. Women comprise 40 percent of the student body, and minorities, 13 percent. More than half ranked in the top 10 percent of their high school class. Seventy percent live on campus in residence halls, in fraternity or sorority houses, in apartments, or in specialty housing. At Lehigh, students gain hands-on, real-world experience and take part in a variety of activities, in and out of the classroom, that build confidence and help students develop as leaders. Lehigh prepares students to succeed in whatever careers they choose.

Twenty-five Division I varsity athletic teams compete primarily in the Patriot League. Lehigh is consistently among the leaders in NCAA graduation rates. Its athletics program was in the top twenty of *U.S. News & World Report's* "America's Best College Sports Programs." There are more than forty club and intramural sports, in which 80 percent of undergraduate students participate. Lehigh supports a vibrant campus life, offering many social and extracurricular activities outside the classroom, with more than 130 different clubs and social organizations to suit virtually any interest—from politics and student government to music, drama, journalism, and religion.

Location

Lehigh's metroburban location in Pennsylvania's Lehigh Valley, the state's third-largest market, provides the best of all worlds. It combines the comfortable, secure setting of a suburban town with convenient access to the excitement of major cultural centers, including Philadelphia (50 miles south) and New York City (75 miles northeast). Lehigh is situated in Bethlehem, Pennsylvania, an ethnically diverse community of 78,000 that offers a variety of cultural events, ethnic restaurants, and sources of entertainment to three quarters of a million people.

Lehigh offers a unique mixture of modern, state-of-the-art facilities and historic, ivy-covered stone buildings. Situated on the side and top of scenic South Mountain in the Saucon Valley, the University's three contiguous campuses, spread over 1,600 acres, rival the most beautiful parks. Amidst tall trees, wooded hills, and colorful landscaping, the Asa Packer Campus is home to more than 100 historic and contemporary structures. The Mountaintop Campus provides additional teaching and research space for the biosciences and the College of Education. The Murray H. Goodman Campus features the 16,000-seat Goodman Stadium for football; the 5,600-seat Stabler Arena for indoor athletics contests, concerts, and special events; Rauch Field House; Ulrich Sports Complex, with both natural grass and artificial turf fields; and extensive outdoor athletic fields for intercollegiate and intramural sports.

Majors and Degrees

The College of Arts and Sciences, the largest college with just under half of the University's faculty members and undergraduates, offers flexible curricula, personal attention to students, and a problem-solving culture. Students explore seventy-seven majors and minors in forty disciplines in eighteen departments spanning the arts, humanities, social sciences, and natural sciences. Departments team on joint ventures in the new Humanities Center, where courses, lectures, and informal gatherings embrace literature, languages, religion studies, philosophy, current events, the history of art, and architecture and music. Another example is the Lehigh Earth Observatory (LEO), in which teams of students work on real-world problems as they study environmental systems and their relationship with society. The modern Zoellner Arts Center is home to Lehigh's outstanding programs of music and theater. Cross-disciplinary programs like Africana studies, classical civilization, computer science and business, design arts, economics, women's studies, and science, technology, and society provide a well-rounded education and a rich variety of career opportunities. The college offers a four-year curriculum in arts and sciences, a five-year curriculum in arts-engineering, double-degree programs, and a combined bachelor's/master's degree program in education.

With its interdisciplinary approach to learning, the College of Business and Economics is powerfully positioned to develop leaders. It provides strong programs at both the graduate and undergraduate levels. Traditional undergraduate business majors, as well as a variety of niche-based, market-driven programs such as supply chain management, computer science and business, and integrated business and engineering, are offered. The Bachelor of Science degree is offered with majors in accounting, business economics, computer science and business, economics, finance, information systems, management, marketing, and supply chain management. The Bachelor of Science degree in business and engineering (BSBE) is offered to those completing the Integrated Business and Engineering (IBE) Honors Program. The business and accounting programs are accredited by AACSB International–The Association to Advance Collegiate Schools of Business.

In the College of Education, undergraduates discover new ways of learning with their world-renowned professors, fellow students, and the children and adults they serve. The College of Education has consistently climbed the ranks among U.S. graduate schools and offers some of the most competitive programs in the country. The college has a strong focus on the use of information technology in education, and faculty members are highly entrepreneurial in creating new learning experiences. The college offers a five-year combined-degree program leading to a B.S. or B.A. in a defined major and elementary or secondary education teaching certification.

The P.C. Rossin College of Engineering and Applied Science is internationally known for the quality of its professors and its research. Students receive a hands-on education and work on cutting-edge research projects with professors and with industry engineers. A co-op program allows students to work eight months for a company and graduate in four years. The college offers the B.S. degree in applied science, arts and engineering (five-year dual-degree program), bioengineering, chemical engineering, civil engineering, computer engineering, computer science, electrical engineering, engineering mechanics, engineering physics, environmental engineering, industrial engineering, information and systems engineering, materials science and engineering, and mechanical engineering. The College of Engineering, with the College of Business and Economics, offers the demanding and popular Integrated Business and Engineering Honors Program and a computer science and business degree. With the College of Arts and Sciences, the engineering college offers an arts/engineering dual degree and a B.S. in bioengineering. The three colleges also offer an award-winning one-year course in integrated product development (IPD), in which student teams make and market products for corporate sponsors.

Academic Programs

Students are expected to maintain regular progress toward the baccalaureate degree by carrying the normal course load of 12 to 18 credit hours each semester. They may, however, accelerate the pace by using Advanced Placement credits, summer-session study, and course overloads, and by gaining credit for courses through examination. Students in good academic standing earn their degrees by meeting the requirements of their specific degree curriculum as well as general University requirements. Students should confer with their advisers on curricular matters.

Off-Campus Programs

Semester and yearlong study-abroad programs are available in Australia, Austria, Belgium, China, Costa Rica, Denmark, Egypt, England, France, Germany, Ghana, Greece, Hungary, Ireland, Israel, Italy, Japan, Kenya, Korea, Mexico, New Zealand, Russia, Scotland, Spain, Sweden, Taiwan, and Wales. Lehigh summer-study programs are available in London and Paris and at other locations in Europe and China. All programs are approved for credit. Internships in other countries are available. Credit for off-campus study may be earned through Urban Semesters in Philadelphia and Washington, D.C., and by cross-registration with a consortium of five other Lehigh Valley colleges.

Academic Facilities

From technology to the arts, Lehigh students learn in outstanding facilities as partners with professors in research and scholarship. The Zoellner Arts Center provides a laboratory for learning, performing, and visual arts for the University and the Lehigh Valley community. Lehigh was one of America's first "wired" campuses, with information network links in every residence, classroom, and office, and with large areas of wireless network access. Library and computing facilities provide access to more than 1.2 million print books and journals as well as a growing array of electronic databases and journals, computer software, and media collections.

Lehigh expects students to meet stringent academic demands, but the University provides support services to ensure each student ample opportunity to succeed. Lehigh's Dean of Students Office directs students toward help with academic or personal problems, legal issues, or general concerns. Lehigh offers a health center, fitness center, counseling service, drug and alcohol counseling service, testing service, and learning center. The University provides career planning and placement throughout students' undergraduate years and offers comprehensive support services for students who are members of minority groups.

Costs

Tuition in 2003–04 was $27,230; average room and board cost $7880.

Financial Aid

Lehigh offers merit scholarships each year based on academics, leadership, or talent in music or theater. Top Lehigh students who graduate and meet certain requirements can take a fifth year of courses, tuition-free, to earn a master's or second bachelor's degree through the President's Scholars program. College selection should be based on educational growth opportunities, not on the price of admission. Financial aid is designed to make college affordable for families unable to meet its costs. Lehigh is committed to providing need-based financial aid.

In 2002–03, Lehigh awarded more than $36 million in University grants and scholarships. Approximately 50 percent of freshmen receive financial aid awards. Financial aid packages are typically made up of a combination of scholarships/need-based grants, loans, and work-study. More than half of all incoming freshmen receive financial aid awards; the average freshman award for the 2002–03 school year was $19,156. Awards based on financial need ranged from $500 to $33,000.

In addition to providing students with extra cash to cover expenses, work-study jobs can also be a great opportunity to enhance a resume. At Lehigh, work-study positions can range from writing press releases in the Office of University Relations to working the front desk at the Student Health Center. Lehigh is a member of College Scholarship Service. To apply for need-based financial aid, the CSS/Profile and FAFSA are required. Financial aid application deadlines come early; the freshmen fall application deadline is January 1.

Faculty

Lehigh's 417 full-time faculty members and 572 total instructional faculty members, 99 percent of whom hold doctoral or other terminal degrees in their fields, are nationally and internationally known leaders in research and scholarship. They are committed first and foremost to undergraduate teaching and advising. It is common for a senior faculty member to teach a freshman course, and close student-faculty advising is the norm. Faculty members often meet with individual students and small groups outside of class, accompany students abroad, and participate in student governance and other activities.

Student Government

The Student Senate is an elected deliberative body that addresses student life and campus issues. Students are ensured access to the highest levels of decision making through two nonvoting representatives to the Board of Trustees.

Admission Requirements

Lehigh encourages men and women of all backgrounds to consider study at the University. All applicants should have completed 4 years of English, 3 or 4 years of mathematics, 2 to 4 years of history and social studies, 2 to 4 years of laboratory science, and 2 years of foreign language. An individual's potential cannot be fully reflected in the accumulation of units in a four-year college-preparatory program, so Lehigh considers a number of criteria in evaluating applicants, especially the strength of the high school record. The University requires either the SAT I or ACT, which must be taken by December of the senior year.

The middle 50 percent of students admitted to Lehigh score between 1210 and 1350 on the SAT I. However, the staff in Lehigh's admissions office works hard to move beyond the numbers and to look at a student's entire profile when making acceptance decisions. Admissions counselors review such factors as Advanced Placement or honors courses, evidence of special talent, and a student's leadership record. To provide prospective students with an opportunity to get to know the University and to determine if Lehigh is a good match, on-campus group or personal interviews are recommended.

Application and Information

Early Decision applications must be filed by November 15; regular applications must be submitted by January 1. For students who determine that Lehigh is their first choice later in the process, the University offers an Early Decision II option with an application deadline of January 1 and a declaration of intent to apply Early Decision II by February 1. Entrance exams should be taken by the January test date. Orientations for prospective students, consisting of general information sessions, campus tours, and personal interviews, are scheduled Monday through Friday. Interviews and tours are also available on some Saturdays. To schedule a visit, contact:

Bruce Gardiner
Interim Dean of Admissions and Financial Aid
Office of Admissions
Lehigh University
27 Memorial Drive West
Bethlehem, Pennsylvania 18015-3094
Telephone: 610-758-3100
Fax: 610-758-4361
E-mail: admissions@lehigh.edu
World Wide Web: http://www.lehigh.edu

NORTH CAROLINA AGRICULTURAL AND TECHNICAL STATE UNIVERSITY

GREENSBORO, NORTH CAROLINA

The University

North Carolina Agricultural and Technical State University was founded in 1891 as one of two land-grant institutions in the state. Originally, it was established to provide postsecondary education and training for black students. Today, the University is a comprehensive institution of higher education with an integrated faculty and student body, and it has been designated a constituent institution of the University of North Carolina, offering degrees at the baccalaureate, master's, and doctoral degree levels. Located on a 191-acre campus, the University has 110 buildings, including single-sex and coeducational residence halls. Of a total undergraduate population of 8,715, 4,165 students are men and 4,550 are women. The total population is approximately 10,030.

North Carolina Agricultural and Technical State University (A&T) provides outstanding academic programs through five undergraduate schools, two colleges, and a graduate school.

The mission of the University is to provide an intellectual setting in which students may find a sense of belonging, responsibility, and achievement that prepares them for roles of leadership and service in the communities where they will live and work. In this sense, the University serves as a laboratory for the development of excellence in teaching, research, and public service. As a result, A&T today stands as an example of well-directed higher education for all students.

Student life at the University is active and purposeful. The broad objective of the program provided by Student Development Services is to aid students in attaining the attitudes, understandings, insights, and skills that enable them to be socially competent. The program places special emphasis on campus relationships and experiences that complement formal instruction. Some of the services available are counseling, housing, health, and placement services. There is a University Student Union, and there are special services for international and minority students, veterans, and handicapped students. The University also provides a well-balanced program of activities to foster the moral, spiritual, cultural, and physical development of its students.

Location

Greensboro, North Carolina, is 300 miles south of Washington, D.C., and 349 miles north of Atlanta. It is readily accessible by air, bus, and automobile. The city offers a variety of cultural and recreational activities and facilities. These include sports events, concerts, bowling, boating, fishing, tennis, golf, and other popular forms of recreation. There are major shopping centers, churches, theaters, and medical facilities near the University. The heavy concentration of factories, service industries, government agencies, and shopping centers provides many job opportunities for students who desire part-time employment.

Majors and Degrees

North Carolina Agricultural and Technical State University grants the following degrees: Bachelor of Arts, Bachelor of Science, Bachelor of Fine Arts, Bachelor of Science in Nursing, and Bachelor of Social Work.

The School of Agriculture and Environmental Sciences offers programs in agricultural and biosystems engineering, agricultural economics, agricultural economics (agricultural business), agricultural education, agricultural education (agricultural extension), agricultural science–earth and environmental science (earth and environmental science, landscape horticulture design, plant science, soil science), agricultural science–natural resources (plant science), animal science, animal science (animal industry), child development, child development–early education and family studies B–K (teaching), family and consumer science (fashion merchandising and design), family and consumer science education, food and nutritional sciences, laboratory animal science, and landscape architecture.

In the College of Arts and Sciences, programs are available in applied mathematics, biology, biology–secondary education, broadcast production, chemistry, chemistry–secondary education, criminal justice, electronic/media journalism, English, English–secondary education, French, French–Romance languages and literatures, French–secondary education, history, history–secondary education, journalism and mass communications, liberal studies, mathematics, mathematics–secondary education, media management, music education, music–general, music–performance, physics, physics–secondary education, political science, print journalism, professional theater, psychology, public relations, sociology, social work, Spanish–Romance languages and literatures, Spanish–secondary education, speech, speech (speech pathology/audiology), visual arts–art education, and visual arts–design.

The School of Business and Economics offers programs in accounting, business education, business education (administrative systems, vocational business education, vocational business education–data processing), economics, finance, management, management (management information systems), marketing, and transportation.

In the School of Education, programs are available in elementary education, health and physical education (fitness/wellness management), health and physical education (teaching), recreation administration, and special education.

In the College of Engineering, programs are offered in architectural engineering, chemical engineering, civil engineering, computer science, electrical engineering, industrial engineering, and mechanical engineering.

The School of Nursing grants the Bachelor of Science in Nursing (B.S.N.) degree.

The School of Technology has programs in construction management, electronics technology, graphic communication systems, manufacturing systems, occupational safety and health, technology education, and vocational industrial education.

Academic Programs

Students must complete a minimum of 124 semester hours to earn a bachelor's degree; the exact number varies with the program. Students are also required to demonstrate competence in English and mathematics.

As complements to the academic programs, the University's Army and Air Force ROTC programs and cooperative education program provide excellent opportunities for students to enrich their educational experiences. The ROTC programs are designed to prepare college graduates for military service careers. The cooperative education program provides an opportunity for qualified students to alternate periods of study on campus and meaningful employment off campus in private industrial or business firms or government agencies.

Academic Facilities

The University library has current holdings that include 507,036 book volumes and bound periodicals, as well as 5,446 current serials. As a select depository in North Carolina for U.S. government documents, the library contains a collection of more than 250,000 official publications. Among the library's other holdings are a collection of audiovisuals and 1,038,474 microforms, archives, and special collections in black studies and teacher-education materials. Special services are provided through formal and informal library instruction, interlibrary loans, and photocopying facilities.

The University's educational support centers are the Learning Assistance Center, the Audiovisual Center, the Closed Circuit Television Facility, a 1,000-watt student-operated educational radio station, the Computer Center, the Reading Center, the Language Laboratory, and the Center for Manpower Research and Training. The H. Clinton Taylor Art Gallery and the African Heritage Center are two exceptional art museums on campus. Throughout the year, these museums have on display a number of special exhibits of sculpture, paintings, graphics, and other media.

Costs

In 2003–04, tuition and fees for North Carolina residents were $2714 per year; for nonresidents of the state, they were $11,635. Board and lodging for the academic year were $4845.

Financial Aid

Through the student financial aid program, the University makes every effort to ensure that no qualified student is denied the opportunity to attend because of a lack of funds. Students who demonstrate financial need and have the potential to achieve academic success at the University may obtain assistance to meet their expenses in accordance with the funds available. Financial aid is awarded without regard to race, religion, color, national origin, or sex. The University provides financial aid for students from four basic sources: grants, scholarships, loans, and employment. To apply for aid, students must submit the Free Application for Federal Student Aid (FAFSA). The priority filing deadline is March 15 for fall semester. North Carolina residents may call 800-443-0835 (toll-free).

Faculty

The University's teaching faculty consists of 600 highly qualified members, of approximately 90 percent hold the doctoral degree or the first professional degree in their discipline. Faculty members are recruited from many areas and backgrounds, thereby bringing together a diverse cadre of academic professionals from many nations.

Student Government

The Student Government Association (SGA), composed of senators elected from the student body, is primarily a policy-recommending group and represents the views and concerns of the students. The president of SGA reports directly to the vice-chancellor for student affairs. In addition, each student organization is represented by a senator, and these senators sit on the Faculty Senate.

Admission Requirements

Applicants for undergraduate admission are considered individually and in accordance with criteria applied flexibly to ensure that applicants with unusual qualifications are not denied admission. However, admission for out-of-state freshman students is competitive due to an 18 percent out-of-state enrollment cap. Students who are applying for admission as freshmen are expected to have completed a college-preparatory program in high school and taken the SAT I or the ACT. General requirements include graduation from an accredited high school with 16 units of credit, with no more than 4 units in vocational subjects and with at least 2 units in physical education; a satisfactory score on the SAT I or ACT; and a respectable GPA and/or class rank. The General Educational Development (GED) test score results or a high school equivalency certificate from the state department of education may be submitted in lieu of the high school transcript for applicants receiving equivalency before January 1988.

North Carolina A&T State University welcomes applications from graduates of accredited community, technical, and junior colleges and from students who wish to transfer from other senior colleges.

Application and Information

The suggested application deadline for students who expect to live on campus is February 1; for commuting students, it is June 1. Applications are processed upon the receipt of the completed application form with the application fee of $35, official transcripts, and SAT I or ACT scores. Out-of-state admission is limited; therefore, applications for admission should be filed by February 1.

To arrange an interview or a visit to the campus, students should contact:

Office of Admissions
B. C. Webb Hall
North Carolina Agricultural and Technical State University
Greensboro, North Carolina 27411
Telephone: 336-334-7946 or 7947
800-443-8964 (toll-free in North Carolina)
World Wide Web: http://www.ncat.edu

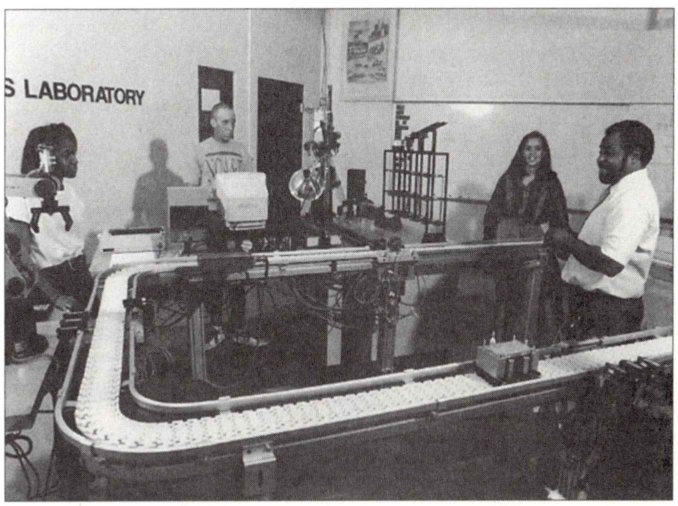

A professor and students in the chemical engineering lab.

Indexes

Majors and Degrees

Accounting

Albertson Coll of Idaho, ID B
Arizona State U, AZ B
Arizona State U West, AZ B
Azusa Pacific U, CA B
Birmingham-Southern Coll, AL B
Boise State U, ID B
Brigham Young U, UT B
Brigham Young U–Hawaii, HI A,B
California Lutheran U, CA B
California State Polytechnic U, Pomona, CA B
California State U, Chico, CA B
California State U, Dominguez Hills, CA B
California State U, Fresno, CA B
California State U, Fullerton, CA B
California State U, Hayward, CA B
California State U, Long Beach, CA B
California State U, Sacramento, CA B
California State U, San Bernardino, CA B
California State U, San Marcos, CA B
Carroll Coll, MT B
Central Washington U, WA B
Chaminade U of Honolulu, HI B
Chaparral Coll, AZ A,B
Chapman U, CA B
City U, WA B
Claremont McKenna Coll, CA B
CollAmerica–Fort Collins, CO B
Coll of Santa Fe, NM B
Coll of the Southwest, NM B
Colorado Christian U, CO B
Colorado State U, CO B
Colorado State U-Pueblo, CO B
DeVry U, Westminster, CO A
Eastern New Mexico U, NM B
Eastern Oregon U, OR B
Eastern Washington U, WA B
Fort Lewis Coll, CO B
Fresno Pacific U, CA B
Golden Gate U, CA B
Gonzaga U, WA B
Grand Canyon U, AZ B
Hawai'i Pacific U, HI A,B
Humboldt State U, CA B
Idaho State U, ID B
John F. Kennedy U, CA B
LDS Business Coll, UT A
Lehigh U, PA B
Linfield Coll, OR B
Loyola Marymount U, CA B
The Master's Coll and Seminary, CA B
Metropolitan State Coll of Denver, CO B
Montana State U–Billings, MT B
Montana Tech of The U of Montana, MT B
Morrison U, NV A,B
Mount St. Mary's Coll, CA B
National American U, Colorado Springs, CO A,B
National American U, Denver, CO A,B
National American U, NM A,B
National U, CA B
New Mexico Highlands U, NM B
New Mexico State U, NM B
North Carolina Ag and Tech State U, NC B
Northern Arizona U, AZ B
Northwest Nazarene U, ID B
Notre Dame de Namur U, CA B
Oregon Inst of Technology, OR B
Oregon State U, OR B
Pacific Lutheran U, WA B
Pacific Union Coll, CA B
Pacific U, OR B
Pepperdine U, Malibu, CA B
Pioneer Pacific Coll, OR A
Point Loma Nazarene U, CA B
Portland State U, OR B
Prescott Coll, AZ B
Regis U, CO B
Rocky Mountain Coll, MT B
Saint Martin's Coll, WA B
Saint Mary's Coll of California, CA B
San Diego State U, CA B
San Francisco State U, CA B
San Jose State U, CA B
Santa Clara U, CA B
Seattle Pacific U, WA B
Seattle U, WA B
Southern Oregon U, OR B
Southern Utah U, UT B
U of Alaska Anchorage, AK A,B
U of Alaska Fairbanks, AK B
U of Alaska Southeast, AK B
The U of Arizona, AZ B
U of Colorado at Boulder, CO B
U of Colorado at Colorado Springs, CO B
U of Denver, CO B
U of Great Falls, MT B
U of Hawaii at Manoa, HI B
U of Idaho, ID B
U of La Verne, CA B
U of Nevada, Las Vegas, NV B
U of Nevada, Reno, NV B
U of Oregon, OR B
U of Phoenix–Colorado Campus, CO B
U of Phoenix–Hawaii Campus, HI B
U of Phoenix–Idaho Campus, ID B
U of Phoenix–Nevada Campus, NV B
U of Phoenix–New Mexico Campus, NM B
U of Phoenix–Northern California Campus, CA B
U of Phoenix Online Campus, AZ B
U of Phoenix–Oregon Campus, OR B
U of Phoenix–Phoenix Campus, AZ B
U of Phoenix–Sacramento Campus, CA B
U of Phoenix–San Diego Campus, CA B
U of Phoenix–Southern Arizona Campus, AZ B
U of Phoenix–Southern California Campus, CA B
U of Phoenix–Southern Colorado Campus, CO B
U of Phoenix–Utah Campus, UT B
U of Phoenix–Washington Campus, WA B
U of Portland, OR B
U of Redlands, CA B
U of San Diego, CA B
U of San Francisco, CA B
U of Southern California, CA B
U of Utah, UT B
U of Washington, WA B
U of Wyoming, WY B
Utah State U, UT B
Utah Valley State Coll, UT A,B
Vanguard U of Southern California, CA B
Walla Walla Coll, WA B
Washington State U, WA B
Weber State U, UT B
Western Baptist Coll, OR B
Western State Coll of Colorado, CO B
Western Washington U, WA B
Westminster Coll, UT B
Westwood Coll–Inland Empire, CA B
Whitworth Coll, WA B
Woodbury U, CA B

Accounting and Business/ Management

Alaska Pacific U, AK B
ITT Tech Inst, Anaheim, CA B
ITT Tech Inst, Rancho Cordova, CA B
ITT Tech Inst, San Bernardino, CA B
ITT Tech Inst, San Diego, CA B
ITT Tech Inst, Sylmar, CA B
ITT Tech Inst, Torrance, CA B
ITT Tech Inst, West Covina, CA B
ITT Tech Inst, CO B
ITT Tech Inst, ID B
ITT Tech Inst, NM B
ITT Tech Inst, UT B
ITT Tech Inst, Bothell, WA B
ITT Tech Inst, Seattle, WA B
LDS Business Coll, UT A
National American U, Colorado Springs, CO A,B
U of Great Falls, MT B
Westwood Coll–Anaheim, CA B
Westwood Coll–Denver South, CO B
Westwood Coll–Inland Empire, CA B
Westwood Coll–Los Angeles, CA B
Westwood Coll–Denver North, CO B

Accounting and Computer Science

California State U, Chico, CA B
San Jose State U, CA B
Western Washington U, WA B

Accounting Related

Brigham Young U, UT B
California State U, Sacramento, CA B
International Inst of the Americas, AZ A
Montana State U–Billings, MT A
Rocky Mountain Coll, MT B
Saint Mary's Coll of California, CA B

Accounting Technology and Bookkeeping

LDS Business Coll, UT A
Lewis-Clark State Coll, ID A,B
U of Alaska Fairbanks, AK A
The U of Montana–Missoula, MT A
Utah Valley State Coll, UT A
Washington State U, WA B

Acting

Brigham Young U, UT B
California Inst of the Arts, CA B
California State U, Long Beach, CA B
Carroll Coll, MT B
Coll of Santa Fe, NM B
Cornish Coll of the Arts, WA B
U of Southern California, CA B

Actuarial Science

The Master's Coll and Seminary, CA B
Oregon State U, OR B

Administrative Assistant and Secretarial Science

Blackfeet Comm Coll, MT A
Chaparral Coll, AZ A
Eastern Oregon U, OR A
Idaho State U, ID A
LDS Business Coll, UT A
Lewis-Clark State Coll, ID A,B
Montana State U–Billings, MT A
Montana Tech of The U of Montana, MT A
Morrison U, NV A
North Carolina Ag and Tech State U, NC B
U of Alaska Fairbanks, AK A
U of Alaska Southeast, AK A
U of Idaho, ID B
The U of Montana–Missoula, MT B
The U of Montana–Western, MT A
Utah State U, UT A,B
Weber State U, UT A,B

Adult and Continuing Education

Biola U, CA B
Christian Heritage Coll, CA B
U of Nevada, Las Vegas, NV B
U of San Francisco, CA B

Adult Development and Aging

U of Northern Colorado, CO B
Washington State U, WA B

Advertising

Academy of Art U, CA A,B
Art Center Coll of Design, CA B
The Art Inst of California–San Diego, CA A,B

A—associate degree; B—bachelor's degree

The Art Inst of California–San Francisco, CA	B
The Art Inst of Colorado, CO	B
The Art Inst of Phoenix, AZ	B
The Art Inst of Portland, OR	B
Boise State U, ID	B
Brigham Young U, UT	B
California State U, Fullerton, CA	B
California State U, Hayward, CA	B
Chapman U, CA	B
Colorado State U-Pueblo, CO	B
Hawai'i Pacific U, HI	B
Northern Arizona U, AZ	B
Notre Dame de Namur U, CA	B
Pacific Union Coll, CA	A,B
Pepperdine U, Malibu, CA	B
Portland State U, OR	B
San Jose State U, CA	B
U of Colorado at Boulder, CO	B
U of Nevada, Reno, NV	B
U of Oregon, OR	B
Washington State U, WA	B

Aeronautical/Aerospace Engineering Technology

Arizona State U East, AZ	B
Utah State U, UT	B

Aeronautics/Aviation/Aerospace Science and Technology

Central Washington U, WA	B
Embry-Riddle Aeronautical U, AZ	B
San Jose State U, CA	B

Aerospace, Aeronautical and Astronautical Engineering

Arizona State U, AZ	B
California Inst of Technology, CA	B
California Polytechnic State U, San Luis Obispo, CA	B
California State Polytechnic U, Pomona, CA	B
California State U, Long Beach, CA	B
Embry-Riddle Aeronautical U, AZ	B
New Mexico State U, NM	B
San Diego State U, CA	B
San Jose State U, CA	B
Stanford U, CA	B
United States Air Force Academy, CO	B
The U of Arizona, AZ	B
U of California, Davis, CA	B
U of California, Irvine, CA	B
U of California, Los Angeles, CA	B
U of California, San Diego, CA	B
U of Colorado at Boulder, CO	B
U of Southern California, CA	B
U of Washington, WA	B
Utah State U, UT	B
Weber State U, UT	B

African-American/Black Studies

Arizona State U, AZ	B
California State U, Dominguez Hills, CA	B
California State U, Fresno, CA	B
California State U, Fullerton, CA	B
California State U, Hayward, CA	B
California State U, Long Beach, CA	B
California State U, Los Angeles, CA	B
California State U, San Bernardino, CA	B
Claremont McKenna Coll, CA	B
Loyola Marymount U, CA	B
Metropolitan State Coll of Denver, CO	B
Pitzer Coll, CA	B
Pomona Coll, CA	B
San Diego State U, CA	B
San Francisco State U, CA	B
San Jose State U, CA	B
Scripps Coll, CA	B
Sonoma State U, CA	B
U of California, Berkeley, CA	B
U of California, Davis, CA	B
U of California, Irvine, CA	B
U of California, Los Angeles, CA	B
U of California, Riverside, CA	B
U of California, Santa Barbara, CA	B
The U of Montana–Missoula, MT	B
U of Nevada, Las Vegas, NV	B
U of New Mexico, NM	B
U of Northern Colorado, CO	B
U of Southern California, CA	B
U of Washington, WA	B

African Languages

U of California, Los Angeles, CA	B

African Studies

Portland State U, OR	B
Stanford U, CA	B
U of California, Davis, CA	B
U of California, Los Angeles, CA	B

Agribusiness

Brigham Young U, UT	B
Colorado State U, CO	B
U of Wyoming, WY	B

Agricultural and Extension Education

Colorado State U, CO	B

Agricultural and Horticultural Plant Breeding

Colorado State U, CO	B

Agricultural Animal Breeding

U of Nevada, Reno, NV	B

Agricultural/Biological Engineering and Bioengineering

California Polytechnic State U, San Luis Obispo, CA	B
California State Polytechnic U, Pomona, CA	B
The U of Arizona, AZ	B
U of California, Davis, CA	B
U of California, Los Angeles, CA	B
U of Hawaii at Manoa, HI	B
U of Idaho, ID	B
Utah State U, UT	B
Washington State U, WA	B

Agricultural Business and Management

Arizona State U East, AZ	B
Brigham Young U, UT	B
California Polytechnic State U, San Luis Obispo, CA	B
California State Polytechnic U, Pomona, CA	B
California State U, Chico, CA	B
California State U, Fresno, CA	B
Eastern New Mexico U, NM	B
Eastern Oregon U, OR	B
Fort Lewis Coll, CO	B
Montana State U–Bozeman, MT	B
North Carolina Ag and Tech State U, NC	B
Oregon State U, OR	B
Rocky Mountain Coll, MT	B
San Diego State U, CA	B
U of California, Davis, CA	B
U of Hawaii at Hilo, HI	B
U of Idaho, ID	B
Utah State U, UT	B
Washington State U, WA	B

Agricultural Business and Management Related

Utah State U, UT	B

Agricultural Business Technology

U of Alaska Fairbanks, AK	A,B

Agricultural Communication/Journalism

U of Wyoming, WY	B
Washington State U, WA	B

Agricultural Economics

Brigham Young U, UT	B
Colorado State U, CO	B
Eastern Oregon U, OR	B
New Mexico State U, NM	B
North Carolina Ag and Tech State U, NC	B
Oregon State U, OR	B
The U of Arizona, AZ	B
U of California, Davis, CA	B
U of Hawaii at Manoa, HI	B
U of Idaho, ID	B
U of Nevada, Reno, NV	B
Utah State U, UT	B
Washington State U, WA	B

Agricultural Mechanization

Montana State U–Bozeman, MT	B
North Carolina Ag and Tech State U, NC	B
U of Idaho, ID	B
Washington State U, WA	B

Agricultural Production

U of Hawaii at Manoa, HI	B
Washington State U, WA	B

Agricultural Teacher Education

California State Polytechnic U, Pomona, CA	B
California State U, Chico, CA	B
California State U, Fresno, CA	B
Colorado State U, CO	B
Eastern New Mexico U, NM	B
Montana State U–Bozeman, MT	B
New Mexico State U, NM	B
North Carolina Ag and Tech State U, NC	B
The U of Arizona, AZ	B
U of California, Davis, CA	B
U of Hawaii at Manoa, HI	B
U of Idaho, ID	B
U of Nevada, Reno, NV	B
U of Wyoming, WY	B
Utah State U, UT	B
Washington State U, WA	B

Agriculture

California Polytechnic State U, San Luis Obispo, CA	B
California State Polytechnic U, Pomona, CA	B
California State U, Stanislaus, CA	B
Colorado State U, CO	B
New Mexico State U, NM	B
North Carolina Ag and Tech State U, NC	B
Oregon State U, OR	B
Southern Utah U, UT	A
The U of Arizona, AZ	B
U of Hawaii at Hilo, HI	B
U of Idaho, ID	B
Utah State U, UT	B
Washington State U, WA	B

Agriculture and Agriculture Operations Related

U of Wyoming, WY	B
Washington State U, WA	B

Agronomy and Crop Science

California Polytechnic State U, San Luis Obispo, CA	B
California State Polytechnic U, Pomona, CA	B
California State U, Chico, CA	B
California State U, Fresno, CA	B
Colorado State U, CO	B
Eastern Oregon U, OR	B
New Mexico State U, NM	B
Oregon State U, OR	B
Utah State U, UT	B
Washington State U, WA	B

Aircraft Powerplant Technology

Idaho State U, ID	A

Air Force R.O.T.C./Air Science

U of Washington, WA	B
Weber State U, UT	B

Airframe Mechanics and Aircraft Maintenance Technology

U of Alaska Anchorage, AK	A
U of Alaska Fairbanks, AK	A
Utah State U, UT	A,B

Airline Pilot and Flight Crew

Embry-Riddle Aeronautical U, AZ	B
Rocky Mountain Coll, MT	B
U of Alaska Anchorage, AK	A
Utah Valley State Coll, UT	A,B
Westminster Coll, UT	B

Air Traffic Control

U of Alaska Anchorage, AK	A

Allied Health and Medical Assisting Services Related

National American U, Colorado Springs, CO	A

American Government and Politics

Chapman U, CA	B
Claremont McKenna Coll, CA	B
The Master's Coll and Seminary, CA	B
Northern Arizona U, AZ	B
The U of Montana–Missoula, MT	B

American History

Chapman U, CA	B
Pitzer Coll, CA	B

A—associate degree; B—bachelor's degree

American Indian/Native American Studies

Arizona State U, AZ	B
Blackfeet Comm Coll, MT	A
California State U, Hayward, CA	B
The Evergreen State Coll, WA	B
Humboldt State U, CA	B
Naropa U, CO	B
Northern Arizona U, AZ	B
Portland State U, OR	B
Sonoma State U, CA	B
Stanford U, CA	B
U of Alaska Fairbanks, AK	B
U of California, Berkeley, CA	B
U of California, Davis, CA	B
U of California, Los Angeles, CA	B
U of California, Riverside, CA	B
The U of Montana–Missoula, MT	B
U of Washington, WA	B

American Literature

U of California, Los Angeles, CA	B
U of Great Falls, MT	B
U of Southern California, CA	B

American Native/Native American Languages

Idaho State U, ID	A

American Sign Language (Asl)

Idaho State U, ID	A

American Studies

Arizona State U West, AZ	B
Brigham Young U, UT	B
California State U, Chico, CA	B
California State U, Fullerton, CA	B
California State U, Long Beach, CA	B
California State U, San Bernardino, CA	B
Claremont McKenna Coll, CA	B
Colorado State U, CO	B
Idaho State U, ID	B
Lehigh U, PA	B
Mills Coll, CA	B
Mount St. Mary's Coll, CA	B
Occidental Coll, CA	B
Oregon State U, OR	B
Pitzer Coll, CA	B
Pomona Coll, CA	B
Reed Coll, OR	B
Saint Mary's Coll of California, CA	B
San Diego State U, CA	B
San Francisco State U, CA	B
San Jose State U, CA	B
Scripps Coll, CA	B
Sonoma State U, CA	B
Stanford U, CA	B
U of California, Berkeley, CA	B
U of California, Davis, CA	B
U of California, Los Angeles, CA	B
U of California, Santa Cruz, CA	B
U of Hawaii at Manoa, HI	B
U of Idaho, ID	B
U of New Mexico, NM	B
U of Southern California, CA	B
U of Wyoming, WY	B
Utah State U, UT	B
Warner Pacific Coll, OR	B
Washington State U, WA	B
Western State Coll of Colorado, CO	B
Western Washington U, WA	B
Whitworth Coll, WA	B

Ancient/Classical Greek

Brigham Young U, UT	B
California State U, Long Beach, CA	B
Lehigh U, PA	B
Multnomah Bible Coll and Biblical Seminary, OR	B
St. John's Coll, NM	B
Santa Clara U, CA	B
U of California, Berkeley, CA	B
U of California, Los Angeles, CA	B
U of California, Santa Cruz, CA	B
U of Hawaii at Manoa, HI	B
U of Washington, WA	B

Ancient Near Eastern and Biblical Languages

The Master's Coll and Seminary, CA	B
Northwest Nazarene U, ID	B
Walla Walla Coll, WA	B

Animal Genetics

U of California, Davis, CA	B
Washington State U, WA	B

Animal Physiology

California State U, Fresno, CA	B
San Francisco State U, CA	B
Sonoma State U, CA	B
The U of Arizona, AZ	B
U of California, Davis, CA	B
U of California, San Diego, CA	B
U of California, Santa Barbara, CA	B
Utah State U, UT	B

Animal Sciences

California Polytechnic State U, San Luis Obispo, CA	B
California State Polytechnic U, Pomona, CA	B
California State U, Chico, CA	B
California State U, Fresno, CA	B
Colorado State U, CO	B
Montana State U–Bozeman, MT	B
New Mexico State U, NM	B
North Carolina Ag and Tech State U, NC	B
Oregon State U, OR	B
The U of Arizona, AZ	B
U of California, Davis, CA	B
U of Denver, CO	B
U of Hawaii at Hilo, HI	B
U of Idaho, ID	B
U of Nevada, Reno, NV	B
Utah State U, UT	B
Washington State U, WA	B

Animal Sciences Related

U of Wyoming, WY	B

Animation, Interactive Technology, Video Graphics and Special Effects

Academy of Art U, CA	A,B
The Art Inst of California–San Francisco, CA	B
The Art Inst of Phoenix, AZ	B
The Art Inst of Portland, OR	B
Brigham Young U, UT	B
ITT Tech Inst, Tucson, AZ	B
ITT Tech Inst, Anaheim, CA	B
ITT Tech Inst, Rancho Cordova, CA	B
ITT Tech Inst, San Bernardino, CA	B
ITT Tech Inst, San Diego, CA	B
ITT Tech Inst, Sylmar, CA	B
ITT Tech Inst, Torrance, CA	B
ITT Tech Inst, West Covina, CA	B
ITT Tech Inst, CO	B
ITT Tech Inst, ID	B
ITT Tech Inst, NV	B
ITT Tech Inst, NM	B
ITT Tech Inst, OR	B
ITT Tech Inst, UT	B
ITT Tech Inst, Bothell, WA	B
ITT Tech Inst, Seattle, WA	B
Nevada State Coll at Henderson, NV	B
Platt Coll San Diego, CA	A,B
Silicon Valley Coll, Walnut Creek, CA	A,B
Westwood Coll–Denver North, CO	B

Anthropology

Albertson Coll of Idaho, ID	B
Arizona State U, AZ	B
Biola U, CA	B
Boise State U, ID	B
Brigham Young U, UT	B
Brigham Young U–Hawaii, HI	B
California State Polytechnic U, Pomona, CA	B
California State U, Bakersfield, CA	B
California State U, Chico, CA	B
California State U, Dominguez Hills, CA	B
California State U, Fresno, CA	B
California State U, Fullerton, CA	B
California State U, Hayward, CA	B
California State U, Long Beach, CA	B
California State U, Los Angeles, CA	B
California State U, Sacramento, CA	B
California State U, San Bernardino, CA	B
California State U, Stanislaus, CA	B
Central Washington U, WA	B
Claremont McKenna Coll, CA	B
The Colorado Coll, CO	B
Colorado State U, CO	B
Eastern New Mexico U, NM	B
Eastern Oregon U, OR	B
Eastern Washington U, WA	B
Eugene Lang Coll, New School U	B
Fort Lewis Coll, CO	B
Great Basin Coll, NV	A
Hawai'i Pacific U, HI	B
Humboldt State U, CA	B
Idaho State U, ID	B
Lehigh U, PA	B
Lewis & Clark Coll, OR	B
Linfield Coll, OR	B
Metropolitan State Coll of Denver, CO	B
Mills Coll, CA	B
Montana State U–Bozeman, MT	B
New Mexico Highlands U, NM	B
New Mexico State U, NM	B
Northern Arizona U, AZ	B
Occidental Coll, CA	B
Oregon State U, OR	B
Pacific Lutheran U, WA	B
Pitzer Coll, CA	B
Pomona Coll, CA	B
Portland State U, OR	B
Prescott Coll, AZ	B
Reed Coll, OR	B
Saint Mary's Coll of California, CA	B
San Diego State U, CA	B
San Francisco State U, CA	B
San Jose State U, CA	B
Santa Clara U, CA	B
Scripps Coll, CA	B
Sonoma State U, CA	B
Southern Oregon U, OR	B
Stanford U, CA	B
U of Alaska Anchorage, AK	B
U of Alaska Fairbanks, AK	B
The U of Arizona, AZ	B
U of California, Berkeley, CA	B
U of California, Davis, CA	B
U of California, Irvine, CA	B
U of California, Los Angeles, CA	B
U of California, Riverside, CA	B
U of California, San Diego, CA	B
U of California, Santa Barbara, CA	B
U of California, Santa Cruz, CA	B
U of Colorado at Boulder, CO	B
U of Colorado at Colorado Springs, CO	B
U of Colorado at Denver, CO	B
U of Denver, CO	B
U of Hawaii at Hilo, HI	B
U of Hawaii at Manoa, HI	B
U of Idaho, ID	B
U of La Verne, CA	B
The U of Montana–Missoula, MT	B
U of Nevada, Las Vegas, NV	B
U of Nevada, Reno, NV	B
U of New Mexico, NM	B
U of Oregon, OR	B
U of Redlands, CA	B
U of San Diego, CA	B
U of Southern California, CA	B
U of Utah, UT	B
U of Washington, WA	B
U of Wyoming, WY	B
Utah State U, UT	B
Vanguard U of Southern California, CA	B
Washington State U, WA	B
Western Oregon U, OR	B
Western State Coll of Colorado, CO	B
Western Washington U, WA	B
Westmont Coll, CA	B
Whitman Coll, WA	B
Willamette U, OR	B

Anthropology Related

U of Southern California, CA	B

Apparel and Accessories Marketing

The Art Inst of Phoenix, AZ	B
The U of Montana–Missoula, MT	A

Apparel and Textiles

Academy of Art U, CA	A,B
California State U, Long Beach, CA	B
Colorado State U, CO	B
New Mexico State U, NM	B
Seattle Pacific U, WA	B
U of California, Davis, CA	B
U of Hawaii at Manoa, HI	B
U of Idaho, ID	B
Washington State U, WA	B

Apparel and Textiles Related
California State U, Sacramento, CA B

Applied Art
Academy of Art U, CA A,B
Azusa Pacific U, CA B
California Coll of the Arts, CA B
California Polytechnic State U, San Luis Obispo, CA B
California State U, Dominguez Hills, CA B
Colorado State U-Pueblo, CO B
National American U, NM A,B
Oregon State U, OR B
Otis Coll of Art and Design, CA B
Portland State U, OR B
The U of Montana–Western, MT A,B
U of Oregon, OR B

Applied Economics
Brigham Young U, UT B
U of San Francisco, CA B

Applied Horticulture
Colorado State U, CO B
U of Hawaii at Manoa, HI B

Applied Mathematics
California Inst of Technology, CA B
California State Polytechnic U, Pomona, CA B
California State U, Chico, CA B
California State U, Fullerton, CA B
California State U, Hayward, CA B
California State U, Long Beach, CA B
California State U, Los Angeles, CA B
Colorado State U, CO B
Fresno Pacific U, CA B
Hawai'i Pacific U, HI A,B
Humboldt State U, CA B
The Master's Coll and Seminary, CA B
Montana Tech of The U of Montana, MT B
New Mexico Inst of Mining and Technology, NM B
North Carolina Ag and Tech State U, NC B
Oregon State U, OR B
Pacific Union Coll, CA B
San Diego State U, CA B
San Francisco State U, CA B
San Jose State U, CA B
Seattle U, WA B
Sonoma State U, CA B
U of Alaska Fairbanks, AK B
U of California, Berkeley, CA B
U of California, Los Angeles, CA B
U of California, San Diego, CA B
U of California, Santa Cruz, CA B
U of Colorado at Boulder, CO B
U of Colorado at Colorado Springs, CO B
U of Idaho, ID B
The U of Montana–Missoula, MT B
U of Nevada, Las Vegas, NV B
U of Washington, WA B
Washington State U, WA B
Weber State U, UT B

Applied Mathematics Related
Arizona State U, AZ B
U of Wyoming, WY B

Aquatic Biology/Limnology
U of California, Santa Barbara, CA B

Arabic
Claremont McKenna Coll, CA B
U of California, Los Angeles, CA B
U of Utah, UT B

Archeology
Claremont McKenna Coll, CA B
Fort Lewis Coll, CO B
Oregon State U, OR B
Saint Mary's Coll of California, CA B
Stanford U, CA B
U of California, Los Angeles, CA B
U of California, San Diego, CA B
Weber State U, UT A
Western Washington U, WA B

Architectural Drafting and Cad/Cadd
Montana Tech of The U of Montana, MT A
Silicon Valley Coll, Walnut Creek, CA A
Westwood Coll–Anaheim, CA A
Westwood Coll–Inland Empire, CA A
Westwood Coll–Los Angeles, CA A
Westwood Coll–Denver North, CO A

Architectural Engineering
California Polytechnic State U, San Luis Obispo, CA B
North Carolina Ag and Tech State U, NC B
U of Colorado at Boulder, CO B
U of Wyoming, WY B

Architectural Engineering Technology
DeVry U, Westminster, CO A
U of Alaska Anchorage, AK A

Architectural Technology
Silicon Valley Coll, Walnut Creek, CA A

Architecture
Arizona State U, AZ B
California Coll of the Arts, CA B
California Polytechnic State U, San Luis Obispo, CA B
California State Polytechnic U, Pomona, CA B
Cornell Coll, IA B
Lehigh U, PA B
Portland State U, OR B
Silicon Valley Coll, Walnut Creek, CA A
Southern California Inst of Architecture, CA B
The U of Arizona, AZ B
U of California, Berkeley, CA B
U of California, Los Angeles, CA B
U of Hawaii at Manoa, HI B
U of Idaho, ID B
U of Nevada, Las Vegas, NV B
U of New Mexico, NM B
U of Oregon, OR B
U of San Francisco, CA B
U of Southern California, CA B
U of Utah, UT B
U of Washington, WA B
Washington State U, WA B
Woodbury U, CA B

Architecture Related
Silicon Valley Coll, Walnut Creek, CA A
U of Utah, UT B

Area, Ethnic, Cultural, and Gender Studies Related
Brigham Young U–Hawaii, HI B
Claremont McKenna Coll, CA B
The Evergreen State Coll, WA B
Linfield Coll, OR B
Northwest Christian Coll, OR B
Saint Mary's Coll of California, CA B
U of California, Irvine, CA B

Area Studies
Hawai'i Pacific U, HI B
United States Air Force Academy, CO B
The U of Montana–Missoula, MT B

Area Studies Related
Claremont McKenna Coll, CA B
Hawai'i Pacific U, HI B
U of Alaska Fairbanks, AK B
U of California, Los Angeles, CA B
Utah State U, UT B

Army R.O.T.C./Military Science
U of Washington, WA B

Art
Academy of Art U, CA A,B
Adams State Coll, CO B
Albertson Coll of Idaho, ID B
Arizona State U, AZ B
Art Center Coll of Design, CA B
The Art Inst of Colorado, CO A,B
Azusa Pacific U, CA B
Biola U, CA B
Birmingham-Southern Coll, AL B
Boise State U, ID B
Brigham Young U, UT B
Brigham Young U–Hawaii, HI B
California Baptist U, CA B
California Coll of the Arts, CA B
California Inst of the Arts, CA B
California Lutheran U, CA B
California Polytechnic State U, San Luis Obispo, CA B
California State Polytechnic U, Pomona, CA B
California State U, Bakersfield, CA B
California State U, Chico, CA B
California State U, Dominguez Hills, CA B
California State U, Fresno, CA B
California State U, Fullerton, CA B
California State U, Long Beach, CA B
California State U, Los Angeles, CA B
California State U, Sacramento, CA B
California State U, San Bernardino, CA B
California State U, Stanislaus, CA B
Carroll Coll, MT A
Central Washington U, WA B
Chapman U, CA B
Claremont McKenna Coll, CA B
Colorado Christian U, CO B
Colorado State U, CO B
Colorado State U-Pueblo, CO B
Concordia U, CA B
Cornell Coll, IA B
Cornish Coll of the Arts, WA B
Dominican U of California, CA B
Eastern New Mexico U, NM A,B
Eastern Oregon U, OR B
The Evergreen State Coll, WA B
Fort Lewis Coll, CO B
George Fox U, OR B
Gonzaga U, WA B
Grand Canyon U, AZ B
Great Basin Coll, NV A
Humboldt State U, CA B
Idaho State U, ID A,B
Laguna Coll of Art & Design, CA B
Lewis & Clark Coll, OR B
Linfield Coll, OR B
Marylhurst U, OR B
Metropolitan State Coll of Denver, CO B
Mills Coll, CA B
Montana State U–Billings, MT B
Montana State U–Bozeman, MT B
Mount St. Mary's Coll, CA B
Naropa U, CO B
New Mexico Highlands U, NM B
Northern Arizona U, AZ B
Northwest Coll of Art, WA B
Northwest Nazarene U, ID B
Notre Dame de Namur U, CA B
Oregon State U, OR B
Otis Coll of Art and Design, CA B
Pacific Lutheran U, WA B
Pacific Union Coll, CA B
Pacific U, OR B
Pepperdine U, Malibu, CA B
Pitzer Coll, CA B
Platt Coll San Diego, CA A,B
Point Loma Nazarene U, CA B
Pomona Coll, CA B
Portland State U, OR B
Prescott Coll, AZ B
Reed Coll, OR B
Rocky Mountain Coll, MT B
Saint Mary's Coll of California, CA B
San Diego State U, CA B
San Francisco State U, CA B
San Jose State U, CA B
Santa Clara U, CA B
Scripps Coll, CA B
Seattle Pacific U, WA B
Seattle U, WA B
Sierra Nevada Coll, NV B
Sonoma State U, CA B
Southern Oregon U, OR B
Southern Utah U, UT B
Stanford U, CA B
U of Alaska Anchorage, AK B
U of Alaska Fairbanks, AK B
U of California, Berkeley, CA B
U of California, Davis, CA B
U of California, Irvine, CA B
U of California, Los Angeles, CA B
U of California, San Diego, CA B
U of California, Santa Cruz, CA B
U of Colorado at Colorado Springs, CO B
U of Denver, CO B
U of Great Falls, MT B

A—associate degree; B—bachelor's degree

- U of Hawaii at Hilo, HI B
- U of Hawaii at Manoa, HI B
- U of Idaho, ID B
- U of La Verne, CA B
- The U of Montana–Missoula, MT B
- U of Nevada, Las Vegas, NV B
- U of Nevada, Reno, NV B
- U of New Mexico, NM B
- U of Oregon, OR B
- U of Puget Sound, WA B
- U of San Diego, CA B
- U of San Francisco, CA B
- U of Southern California, CA B
- U of the Pacific, CA B
- U of Utah, UT B
- U of Washington, WA B
- U of Wyoming, WY B
- Utah State U, UT B
- Walla Walla Coll, WA B
- Weber State U, UT B
- Western Oregon U, OR B
- Western State Coll of Colorado, CO B
- Western Washington U, WA B
- Westminster Coll, UT B
- Westmont Coll, CA B
- Whitman Coll, WA B
- Whitworth Coll, WA B
- Willamette U, OR B

Art History, Criticism and Conservation

- Arizona State U, AZ B
- Birmingham-Southern Coll, AL B
- Boise State U, ID B
- Brigham Young U, UT B
- California State U, Chico, CA B
- California State U, Dominguez Hills, CA B
- California State U, Fullerton, CA B
- California State U, Hayward, CA B
- California State U, Long Beach, CA B
- California State U, San Bernardino, CA B
- Chapman U, CA B
- Claremont McKenna Coll, CA B
- Coll of Santa Fe, NM B
- The Colorado Coll, CO B
- Colorado State U, CO B
- Cornell Coll, IA B
- Dominican U of California, CA B
- Eastern Washington U, WA B
- Humboldt State U, CA B
- Loyola Marymount U, CA B
- Mills Coll, CA B
- Northern Arizona U, AZ B
- Occidental Coll, CA B
- Oregon State U, OR B
- Pacific Lutheran U, WA B
- Pacific Union Coll, CA B
- Pitzer Coll, CA B
- Pomona Coll, CA B
- Portland State U, OR B
- Saint Mary's Coll of California, CA B
- San Diego State U, CA B
- San Jose State U, CA B
- Santa Clara U, CA B
- Scripps Coll, CA B
- Seattle U, WA B
- Sonoma State U, CA B
- The U of Arizona, AZ B
- U of California, Berkeley, CA B
- U of California, Davis, CA B
- U of California, Irvine, CA B
- U of California, Los Angeles, CA B
- U of California, Riverside, CA B
- U of California, San Diego, CA B
- U of California, Santa Barbara, CA B
- U of California, Santa Cruz, CA B
- U of Denver, CO B
- U of La Verne, CA B
- The U of Montana–Missoula, MT B
- U of Nevada, Las Vegas, NV B
- U of Nevada, Reno, NV B
- U of New Mexico, NM B
- U of Oregon, OR B
- U of Redlands, CA B
- U of San Francisco, CA B
- U of Southern California, CA B
- U of the Pacific, CA B
- U of Utah, UT B
- U of Washington, WA B
- Washington State U, WA B
- Western Washington U, WA B
- Whitman Coll, WA B
- Whitworth Coll, WA B
- Willamette U, OR B

Artificial Intelligence and Robotics

- Montana Tech of The U of Montana, MT B
- Pacific Union Coll, CA A,B
- U of New Mexico, NM B

Arts Management

- California State U, Hayward, CA B
- Coll of Santa Fe, NM B
- Northern Arizona U, AZ B
- U of Portland, OR B
- U of San Francisco, CA B
- Whitworth Coll, WA B

Art Teacher Education

- Birmingham-Southern Coll, AL B
- Boise State U, ID B
- Brigham Young U, UT B
- Brigham Young U–Hawaii, HI B
- California Lutheran U, CA B
- California State U, Chico, CA B
- California State U, Fullerton, CA B
- California State U, Long Beach, CA B
- Central Washington U, WA B
- Colorado State U, CO B
- Colorado State U-Pueblo, CO B
- Eastern Washington U, WA B
- Fort Lewis Coll, CO B
- Grand Canyon U, AZ B
- Humboldt State U, CA B
- Montana State U–Billings, MT B
- Mount St. Mary's Coll, CA B
- New Mexico Highlands U, NM B
- North Carolina Ag and Tech State U, NC B
- Northern Arizona U, AZ B
- Northwest Nazarene U, ID B
- Pacific Lutheran U, WA B
- Pacific U, OR B
- Rocky Mountain Coll, MT B
- Rocky Mountain Coll of Art & Design, CO B
- San Diego State U, CA B
- Seattle Pacific U, WA B
- Southern Utah U, UT B
- The U of Arizona, AZ B
- U of Denver, CO B
- U of Great Falls, MT B
- U of Hawaii at Manoa, HI B
- U of Idaho, ID B
- The U of Montana–Missoula, MT B
- The U of Montana–Western, MT B
- U of Nevada, Reno, NV B
- U of New Mexico, NM B
- Walla Walla Coll, WA B
- Weber State U, UT B
- Western State Coll of Colorado, CO B
- Western Washington U, WA B
- Westmont Coll, CA B
- Whitworth Coll, WA B

Art Therapy

- Coll of Santa Fe, NM B
- Prescott Coll, AZ B

Asian-American Studies

- California State U, Fullerton, CA B
- California State U, Hayward, CA B
- California State U, Long Beach, CA B
- Claremont McKenna Coll, CA B
- Colorado State U, CO B
- Loyola Marymount U, CA B
- Pitzer Coll, CA B
- Scripps Coll, CA B
- U of California, Berkeley, CA B
- U of California, Irvine, CA B
- U of California, Los Angeles, CA B
- U of California, Riverside, CA B
- U of California, Santa Barbara, CA B
- U of Denver, CO B
- U of Southern California, CA B

Asian History

- U of the West, CA B

Asian Studies

- Birmingham-Southern Coll, AL B
- Brigham Young U, UT B
- California State U, Chico, CA B
- California State U, Long Beach, CA B
- California State U, Sacramento, CA B
- Central Washington U, WA B
- Claremont McKenna Coll, CA B
- The Colorado Coll, CO B
- Colorado State U, CO B
- Fort Lewis Coll, CO B
- Gonzaga U, WA B
- Occidental Coll, CA B
- Pitzer Coll, CA B
- Pomona Coll, CA B
- San Diego State U, CA B
- Scripps Coll, CA B
- Stanford U, CA B
- U of California, Berkeley, CA B
- U of California, Los Angeles, CA B
- U of California, Riverside, CA B
- U of California, Santa Barbara, CA B
- U of California, Santa Cruz, CA B
- U of Colorado at Boulder, CO B
- U of Hawaii at Manoa, HI B
- The U of Montana–Missoula, MT B
- U of New Mexico, NM B
- U of Oregon, OR B
- U of Puget Sound, WA B
- U of Redlands, CA B
- U of San Francisco, CA B
- U of Utah, UT B
- U of Washington, WA B
- Utah State U, UT B
- Washington State U, WA B
- Western Washington U, WA B
- Whitman Coll, WA B

Asian Studies (East)

- Lewis & Clark Coll, OR B
- Pomona Coll, CA B
- Portland State U, OR B
- Scripps Coll, CA B
- Seattle U, WA B
- Stanford U, CA B
- The U of Arizona, AZ B
- U of California, Davis, CA B
- U of California, Irvine, CA B
- U of California, Los Angeles, CA B
- U of California, Santa Cruz, CA B
- The U of Montana–Missoula, MT B
- U of Oregon, OR B
- U of Southern California, CA B
- U of Washington, WA B
- Western Washington U, WA B

Asian Studies (South)

- U of California, Santa Cruz, CA B
- U of Washington, WA B

Asian Studies (Southeast)

- U of California, Berkeley, CA B
- U of California, Los Angeles, CA B
- U of California, Santa Cruz, CA B
- U of Washington, WA B

Astronomy

- Brigham Young U, UT B
- California Inst of Technology, CA B
- Northern Arizona U, AZ B
- Pomona Coll, CA B
- San Diego State U, CA B
- San Francisco State U, CA B
- The U of Arizona, AZ B
- U of California, Los Angeles, CA B
- U of Colorado at Boulder, CO B
- The U of Montana–Missoula, MT B
- U of Southern California, CA B
- U of Washington, WA B
- Whitman Coll, WA B

Astronomy and Astrophysics Related

- U of Wyoming, WY B

Astrophysics

- Lehigh U, PA B
- New Mexico Inst of Mining and Technology, NM B
- Pacific Union Coll, CA B
- San Francisco State U, CA B
- U of California, Berkeley, CA B
- U of California, Los Angeles, CA B
- U of California, Santa Cruz, CA B
- U of New Mexico, NM B

Athletic Training

- Azusa Pacific U, CA B
- Boise State U, ID B
- Brigham Young U, UT B
- California Lutheran U, CA B
- California State U, Hayward, CA B
- California State U, Long Beach, CA B
- Chapman U, CA B
- Christian Heritage Coll, CA B

Colorado State U, CO B
Colorado State U-Pueblo, CO B
Eastern Washington U, WA B
Fresno Pacific U, CA B
George Fox U, OR B
Grand Canyon U, AZ B
Linfield Coll, OR B
New Mexico State U, NM B
Northwest Nazarene U, ID B
Oregon State U, OR B
Pacific U, OR B
Pepperdine U, Malibu, CA B
Point Loma Nazarene U, CA B
Rocky Mountain Coll, MT B
U of Idaho, ID B
U of Nevada, Las Vegas, NV B
Vanguard U of Southern California, CA B
Washington State U, WA B
Weber State U, UT B
Western State Coll of Colorado, CO B
Western Washington U, WA B
Whitworth Coll, WA B

Atmospheric Sciences and Meteorology

Metropolitan State Coll of Denver, CO B
New Mexico Inst of Mining and Technology, NM B
San Francisco State U, CA B
San Jose State U, CA B
United States Air Force Academy, CO B
The U of Arizona, AZ B
U of California, Davis, CA B
U of California, Los Angeles, CA B
U of Hawaii at Manoa, HI B
U of Utah, UT B
U of Washington, WA B

Atomic/Molecular Physics

San Diego State U, CA B
U of California, San Diego, CA B

Audio Engineering

The Art Inst of Seattle, WA A
Cogswell Polytechnical Coll, CA B

Audiology and Hearing Sciences

California State U, Long Beach, CA B
U of Northern Colorado, CO B

Audiology and Speech-Language Pathology

California State U, Fresno, CA B
California State U, Fullerton, CA B
California State U, Hayward, CA B
California State U, Long Beach, CA B
California State U, Sacramento, CA B
Eastern New Mexico U, NM B
Eastern Washington U, WA B
Idaho State U, ID B
Loma Linda U, CA B
Pacific Union Coll, CA B
San Francisco State U, CA B
U of Hawaii at Manoa, HI B
The U of Montana–Missoula, MT B
U of New Mexico, NM B
U of Oregon, OR B
U of Redlands, CA B
U of the Pacific, CA B
U of Utah, UT B
U of Washington, WA B
U of Wyoming, WY B
Utah State U, UT B
Washington State U, WA B
Western Washington U, WA B

Audiovisual Communications Technologies Related

Nevada State Coll at Henderson, NV B

Autobody/Collision and Repair Technology

Idaho State U, ID A
Lewis-Clark State Coll, ID A,B
Montana State U–Billings, MT A
Montana Tech of The U of Montana, MT A
Utah Valley State Coll, UT A
Weber State U, UT A

Automobile/Automotive Mechanics Technology

Boise State U, ID A
Colorado State U-Pueblo, CO B
Idaho State U, ID A
Lewis-Clark State Coll, ID A,B
Montana State U–Billings, MT A
Montana Tech of The U of Montana, MT A
Southern Utah U, UT A
U of Alaska Anchorage, AK A
U of Alaska Southeast, AK A
Utah Valley State Coll, UT A
Walla Walla Coll, WA A,B
Weber State U, UT A,B
Westwood Coll–Denver North, CO A

Automotive Engineering Technology

Weber State U, UT B
Western Washington U, WA B

Aviation/Airway Management

Metropolitan State Coll of Denver, CO B
Rocky Mountain Coll, MT B
U of Alaska Anchorage, AK A
U of Alaska Fairbanks, AK A
Westminster Coll, UT B

Avionics Maintenance Technology

U of Alaska Anchorage, AK A
Walla Walla Coll, WA A,B

Baking and Pastry Arts

The Art Inst of California–San Diego, CA A,B

Ballet

Brigham Young U, UT B
U of Utah, UT B

Banking and Financial Support Services

National U, CA B
Utah Valley State Coll, UT A

Behavioral Sciences

California Baptist U, CA B
California State Polytechnic U, Pomona, CA B
California State U, Dominguez Hills, CA B
Chaminade U of Honolulu, HI B
Concordia U, CA B
Hawai'i Pacific U, HI B
Lewis-Clark State Coll, ID A
Metropolitan State Coll of Denver, CO B
National U, CA B
New Mexico Inst of Mining and Technology, NM B
Northwest Coll, WA B
Notre Dame de Namur U, CA B
Pacific Union Coll, CA B
San Jose State U, CA B
United States Air Force Academy, CO B
U of La Verne, CA B
U of Utah, UT B

Biblical Studies

Alaska Bible Coll, AK A,B
Azusa Pacific U, CA B
Bethesda Christian U, CA B
Biola U, CA B
California Baptist U, CA B
California Christian Coll, CA A,B
Cascade Coll, OR B
Christian Heritage Coll, CA B
Colorado Christian U, CO B
Eugene Bible Coll, OR B
Fresno Pacific U, CA A,B
George Fox U, OR B
Grand Canyon U, AZ B
Life Pacific Coll, CA A,B
The Master's Coll and Seminary, CA B
Multnomah Bible Coll and Biblical Seminary, OR B
Northwest Christian Coll, OR B
Northwest Coll, WA B
Pacific Union Coll, CA A
Shasta Bible Coll, CA A,B
Simpson Coll and Graduate School, CA A,B
Southwestern Coll, AZ B
Vanguard U of Southern California, CA B
Warner Pacific Coll, OR A,B
Western Baptist Coll, OR A,B
William Jessup U, CA B

Bilingual and Multilingual Education

Biola U, CA B
Blackfeet Comm Coll, MT A
Boise State U, ID B
California State Polytechnic U, Pomona, CA B
California State U, Dominguez Hills, CA B
Coll of the Southwest, NM B
Fresno Pacific U, CA B
Lehigh U, PA B
Nevada State Coll at Henderson, NV B
New Mexico Highlands U, NM B
Prescott Coll, AZ B
U of San Francisco, CA B
U of Washington, WA B
Weber State U, UT B

Biochemistry

Arizona State U, AZ B
Azusa Pacific U, CA B
Biola U, CA B
Brigham Young U, UT B
Brigham Young U–Hawaii, HI B
California Inst of Technology, CA B
California Lutheran U, CA B
California Polytechnic State U, San Luis Obispo, CA B
California State U, Chico, CA B
California State U, Dominguez Hills, CA B
California State U, Fullerton, CA B
California State U, Hayward, CA B
California State U, Long Beach, CA B
California State U, Los Angeles, CA B
California State U, San Bernardino, CA B
California State U, San Marcos, CA B
Claremont McKenna Coll, CA B
The Colorado Coll, CO B
Colorado State U, CO B
Cornell Coll, IA B
Eastern Washington U, WA B
Fort Lewis Coll, CO B
Gonzaga U, WA B
Humboldt State U, CA B
Idaho State U, ID B
Lehigh U, PA B
Lewis & Clark Coll, OR B
Loyola Marymount U, CA B
Mills Coll, CA B
Mount St. Mary's Coll, CA B
New Mexico State U, NM B
Northwest Nazarene U, ID B
Notre Dame de Namur U, CA B
Occidental Coll, CA B
Oregon State U, OR B
Pacific Lutheran U, WA B
Pacific Union Coll, CA B
Pitzer Coll, CA B
Point Loma Nazarene U, CA B
Pomona Coll, CA B
Portland State U, OR B
Reed Coll, OR B
Regis U, CO B
Saint Mary's Coll of California, CA B
San Francisco State U, CA B
San Jose State U, CA B
Scripps Coll, CA B
Seattle Pacific U, WA B
Seattle U, WA B
Southern Oregon U, OR B
United States Air Force Academy, CO B
The U of Arizona, AZ B
U of California, Davis, CA B
U of California, Los Angeles, CA B
U of California, Riverside, CA B
U of California, San Diego, CA B
U of California, Santa Barbara, CA B
U of California, Santa Cruz, CA B
U of Colorado at Boulder, CO B
U of Denver, CO B
The U of Montana–Missoula, MT B
U of Nevada, Las Vegas, NV B
U of Nevada, Reno, NV B
U of New Mexico, NM B
U of Oregon, OR B
U of Southern California, CA B
U of the Pacific, CA B
U of Washington, WA B
Washington State U, WA B
Western Washington U, WA B
Whitman Coll, WA B

Biochemistry/Biophysics and Molecular Biology

California State U, Long Beach, CA B

A—associate degree; B—bachelor's degree

Biochemistry, Biophysics and Molecular Biology Related
Washington State U, WA B

Bioinformatics
Brigham Young U, UT B

Biological and Biomedical Sciences Related
Arizona State U, AZ B
Holy Names U, CA B
Lehigh U, PA B
National U, CA B
Saint Mary's Coll of California, CA B
Washington State U, WA B

Biological and Physical Sciences
Adams State Coll, CO B
Brigham Young U, UT B
California State U, Fresno, CA B
Colorado Christian U, CO B
Concordia U, OR B
Eastern Oregon U, OR B
Eastern Washington U, WA B
The Evergreen State Coll, WA B
Lehigh U, PA B
Marylhurst U, OR B
The Master's Coll and Seminary, CA B
Montana Tech of The U of Montana, MT A,B
New Mexico Inst of Mining and Technology, NM B
Oregon State U, OR B
Portland State U, OR B
San Francisco State U, CA B
Santa Clara U, CA B
Seattle U, WA B
Sierra Nevada Coll, NV B
United States Air Force Academy, CO B
U of Alaska Anchorage, AK B
U of Alaska Fairbanks, AK B
U of Denver, CO B
U of Oregon, OR B
Vanguard U of Southern California, CA B
Warner Pacific Coll, OR B
Washington State U, WA B
Western Washington U, WA B

Biological Specializations Related
Arizona State U, AZ B
San Jose State U, CA B
Utah State U, UT B

Biology/Biological Sciences
Adams State Coll, CO B
Albertson Coll of Idaho, ID B
Arizona State U, AZ B
Arizona State U East, AZ B
Arizona State U West, AZ B
Azusa Pacific U, CA B
Biola U, CA B
Birmingham-Southern Coll, AL B
Boise State U, ID B
Brigham Young U, UT B
Brigham Young U–Hawaii, HI B
California Baptist U, CA B
California Inst of Technology, CA B
California Lutheran U, CA B
California Polytechnic State U, San Luis Obispo, CA B
California State Polytechnic U, Pomona, CA B
California State U, Bakersfield, CA B
California State U, Chico, CA B
California State U, Dominguez Hills, CA B
California State U, Fresno, CA B
California State U, Fullerton, CA B
California State U, Hayward, CA B
California State U, Long Beach, CA B
California State U, Los Angeles, CA B
California State U, Sacramento, CA B
California State U, San Bernardino, CA B
California State U, San Marcos, CA B
California State U, Stanislaus, CA B
Carroll Coll, MT B
Central Washington U, WA B
Chaminade U of Honolulu, HI B
Chapman U, CA B
Christian Heritage Coll, CA B
Claremont McKenna Coll, CA B
Cleveland Chiropractic Coll-Los Angeles Campus, CA A,B
Coll of the Southwest, NM B
Colorado Christian U, CO B
The Colorado Coll, CO B
Colorado State U, CO B
Colorado State U-Pueblo, CO B
Concordia U, CA B
Concordia U, OR B
Cornell Coll, IA B
Dominican U of California, CA B
Eastern New Mexico U, NM B
Eastern Oregon U, OR B
Eastern Washington U, WA B
The Evergreen State Coll, WA B
Fort Lewis Coll, CO B
Fresno Pacific U, CA A,B
George Fox U, OR B
Gonzaga U, WA B
Grand Canyon U, AZ B
Harvey Mudd Coll, CA B
Hawai'i Pacific U, HI B
Holy Names U, CA B
Humboldt State U, CA B
Idaho State U, ID A,B
Lehigh U, PA B
Lewis & Clark Coll, OR B
Lewis-Clark State Coll, ID B
Linfield Coll, OR B
Loyola Marymount U, CA B
The Master's Coll and Seminary, CA B
Metropolitan State Coll of Denver, CO B
Mills Coll, CA B
Montana State U–Billings, MT B
Montana State U–Bozeman, MT B
Montana Tech of The U of Montana, MT A,B
Mount St. Mary's Coll, CA B
Nevada State Coll at Henderson, NV B
New Mexico Highlands U, NM B
New Mexico Inst of Mining and Technology, NM B
New Mexico State U, NM B
North Carolina Ag and Tech State U, NC B
Northern Arizona U, AZ B
Northwest Nazarene U, ID B
Notre Dame de Namur U, CA B
Occidental Coll, CA B
Oregon State U, OR B
Pacific Lutheran U, WA B
Pacific Union Coll, CA B
Pacific U, OR B
Pepperdine U, Malibu, CA B
Pitzer Coll, CA B
Point Loma Nazarene U, CA B
Pomona Coll, CA B
Portland State U, OR B
Prescott Coll, AZ B
Reed Coll, OR B
Regis U, CO B
Rocky Mountain Coll, MT B
Saint Martin's Coll, WA B
Saint Mary's Coll of California, CA B
San Diego State U, CA B
San Francisco State U, CA B
San Jose State U, CA B
Santa Clara U, CA B
Scripps Coll, CA B
Seattle Pacific U, WA B
Seattle U, WA B
Sonoma State U, CA B
Southern Oregon U, OR B
Southern Utah U, UT B
Stanford U, CA B
United States Air Force Academy, CO B
U of Alaska Fairbanks, AK B
U of Alaska Southeast, AK B
The U of Arizona, AZ B
U of California, Berkeley, CA B
U of California, Davis, CA B
U of California, Irvine, CA B
U of California, Los Angeles, CA B
U of California, Riverside, CA B
U of California, San Diego, CA B
U of California, Santa Barbara, CA B
U of California, Santa Cruz, CA B
U of Colorado at Colorado Springs, CO B
U of Colorado at Denver, CO B
U of Denver, CO B
U of Great Falls, MT B
U of Hawaii at Hilo, HI B
U of Hawaii at Manoa, HI B
U of Idaho, ID B
U of La Verne, CA B
The U of Montana–Missoula, MT B
U of Nevada, Las Vegas, NV B
U of Nevada, Reno, NV B
U of New Mexico, NM B
U of Northern Colorado, CO B
U of Oregon, OR B
U of Portland, OR B
U of Puget Sound, WA B
U of Redlands, CA B
U of San Diego, CA B
U of San Francisco, CA B
U of Southern California, CA B
U of the Pacific, CA B
U of Utah, UT B
U of Washington, WA B
U of Wyoming, WY B
Utah State U, UT B
Utah Valley State Coll, UT A,B
Vanguard U of Southern California, CA B
Walla Walla Coll, WA B
Warner Pacific Coll, OR B
Washington State U, WA B
Western Oregon U, OR B
Western State Coll of Colorado, CO B
Western Washington U, WA B
Westminster Coll, UT B
Westmont Coll, CA B
Whitman Coll, WA B
Whitworth Coll, WA B
Willamette U, OR B

Biology/Biotechnology Laboratory Technician
California State Polytechnic U, Pomona, CA B
California State U, Sacramento, CA B
Weber State U, UT A

Biology Teacher Education
Brigham Young U–Hawaii, HI B
California State U, Chico, CA B
California State U, Long Beach, CA B
Carroll Coll, MT B
Central Washington U, WA B
Colorado State U, CO B
George Fox U, OR B
Montana State U–Billings, MT B
Nevada State Coll at Henderson, NV B
Northern Arizona U, AZ B
Northwest Coll, WA B
Northwest Nazarene U, ID B
Rocky Mountain Coll, MT B
San Diego State U, CA B
Seattle Pacific U, WA B
The U of Arizona, AZ B
U of Great Falls, MT B
The U of Montana–Western, MT B
U of Utah, UT B
U of Washington, WA B
Utah State U, UT B
Utah Valley State Coll, UT B
Weber State U, UT B
Western Baptist Coll, OR B
Westminster Coll, UT B

Biomathematics and Bioinformatics Related
U of California, Los Angeles, CA B

Biomedical/Medical Engineering
Arizona State U, AZ B
California Lutheran U, CA B
California State U, Long Beach, CA B
Lehigh U, PA B
U of California, Berkeley, CA B
U of California, Davis, CA B
U of California, Irvine, CA B
U of California, Los Angeles, CA B
U of California, San Diego, CA B
U of Idaho, ID B
U of Southern California, CA B
U of the Pacific, CA B
U of Utah, UT B
Walla Walla Coll, WA B

Biomedical Sciences
Brigham Young U, UT B
U of California, Riverside, CA B
U of Utah, UT B

Biomedical Technology
California State U, Hayward, CA B
Colorado State U-Pueblo, CO B
Walla Walla Coll, WA B

Biophysics
Brigham Young U, UT B
Claremont McKenna Coll, CA B
Oregon State U, OR B
Pacific Union Coll, CA B
U of California, Los Angeles, CA B

U of California, San Diego, CA B
U of Southern California, CA B
Walla Walla Coll, WA B
Washington State U, WA B
Whitman Coll, WA B

Biopsychology

Chapman U, CA B
U of California, Santa Barbara, CA B
U of Denver, CO B

Biostatistics

Brigham Young U, UT B
U of California, Los Angeles, CA B
U of Washington, WA B

Biotechnology

Brigham Young U, UT B
Eastern Washington U, WA B
Montana State U–Bozeman, MT B
U of California, Los Angeles, CA B
U of California, San Diego, CA B
U of Nevada, Reno, NV B
Washington State U, WA B

Botany/Plant Biology

Arizona State U, AZ B
Brigham Young U, UT B
California State Polytechnic U, Pomona, CA B
California State U, Long Beach, CA B
Colorado State U, CO B
Humboldt State U, CA B
Idaho State U, ID B
Northern Arizona U, AZ B
Oregon State U, OR B
San Francisco State U, CA B
Sonoma State U, CA B
Southern Utah U, UT B
U of California, Berkeley, CA B
U of California, Davis, CA B
U of California, Los Angeles, CA B
U of California, Riverside, CA B
U of California, Santa Cruz, CA B
U of Great Falls, MT B
U of Hawaii at Manoa, HI B
U of Idaho, ID B
The U of Montana–Missoula, MT B
U of Washington, WA B
U of Wyoming, WY B
Utah State U, UT B
Washington State U, WA B
Weber State U, UT B

Broadcast Journalism

Brigham Young U, UT B
California State U, Hayward, CA B
California State U, Long Beach, CA B
Chapman U, CA B
Colorado State U-Pueblo, CO B
Columbia Coll Hollywood, CA B
Gonzaga U, WA B
Humboldt State U, CA B
Pacific Lutheran U, WA B
Pacific U, OR B
Point Loma Nazarene U, CA B
U of Colorado at Boulder, CO B
U of La Verne, CA B
U of Nevada, Reno, NV B
U of Oregon, OR B
U of Southern California, CA B
U of Utah, UT B
Washington State U, WA B
Western Washington U, WA B

Buddhist Studies

U of the West, CA B

Building/Home/Construction Inspection

Utah Valley State Coll, UT A

Building/Property Maintenance and Management

Utah Valley State Coll, UT A

Business Administration and Management

Adams State Coll, CO B
Alaska Pacific U, AK A,B
Albertson Coll of Idaho, ID B
Alliant International U, CA B
American Indian Coll of the Assemblies of God, Inc., AZ A
American InterContinental U, CA A,B
Arizona State U, AZ B
Azusa Pacific U, CA B
Biola U, CA B
Birmingham-Southern Coll, AL B
Blackfeet Comm Coll, MT A
Boise State U, ID B
Brigham Young U, UT B
Brigham Young U–Hawaii, HI B
California Baptist U, CA B
California Lutheran U, CA B
California Maritime Academy, CA B
California Polytechnic State U, San Luis Obispo, CA B
California State Polytechnic U, Pomona, CA B
California State U, Bakersfield, CA B
California State U, Chico, CA B
California State U, Dominguez Hills, CA B
California State U, Fresno, CA B
California State U, Fullerton, CA B
California State U, Hayward, CA B
California State U, Long Beach, CA B
California State U, Los Angeles, CA B
California State U, Sacramento, CA B
California State U, San Bernardino, CA B
California State U, San Marcos, CA B
California State U, Stanislaus, CA B
Carroll Coll, MT A,B
Cascade Coll, OR B
Central Washington U, WA B
Chaminade U of Honolulu, HI A,B
Chaparral Coll, AZ A,B
Chapman U, CA B
Christian Heritage Coll, CA B
City U, WA B
CollAmerica–Fort Collins, CO A,B
Coll of Santa Fe, NM A,B
Coll of the Southwest, NM B
Colorado Christian U, CO B
Colorado State U, CO B
Colorado State U-Pueblo, CO B
Concordia U, CA B
Concordia U, OR A,B
DeVry U, Westminster, CO B
Dominican U of California, CA B
Eastern New Mexico U, NM B
Eastern Washington U, WA B
The Evergreen State Coll, WA B
Fort Lewis Coll, CO B
Fresno Pacific U, CA A,B
George Fox U, OR B
Golden Gate U, CA B
Gonzaga U, WA B
Grand Canyon U, AZ B
Great Basin Coll, NV A
Hawai'i Pacific U, HI A,B
Henry Cogswell Coll, WA B
Holy Names U, CA B
Humboldt State U, CA B
Idaho State U, ID B
International Inst of the Americas, AZ B
ITT Tech Inst, Anaheim, CA B
ITT Tech Inst, Rancho Cordova, CA B
ITT Tech Inst, San Bernardino, CA B
ITT Tech Inst, San Diego, CA B
ITT Tech Inst, Sylmar, CA B
ITT Tech Inst, Torrance, CA B
ITT Tech Inst, West Covina, CA B
ITT Tech Inst, CO B
ITT Tech Inst, ID A
ITT Tech Inst, NM B
ITT Tech Inst, UT B
ITT Tech Inst, Bothell, WA B
ITT Tech Inst, Seattle, WA B
John F. Kennedy U, CA B
Johnson & Wales U, CO A
Jones International U, CO B
Lehigh U, PA B
Lewis-Clark State Coll, ID B
Loyola Marymount U, CA B
Marylhurst U, OR B
The Master's Coll and Seminary, CA B
Menlo Coll, CA B
Montana State U–Billings, MT A,B
Montana Tech of The U of Montana, MT B
Morrison U, NV A,B
Mount St. Mary's Coll, CA A,B
Mt. Sierra Coll, CA B
National American U, Colorado Springs, CO A,B
National American U, Denver, CO A,B
National American U, NM A,B
National U, CA B
Nevada State Coll at Henderson, NV B
New Mexico Highlands U, NM B
New Mexico Inst of Mining and Technology, NM A,B
New Mexico State U, NM B
North Carolina Ag and Tech State U, NC B
Northcentral U, AZ B
Northern Arizona U, AZ B
Northwest Coll, WA A,B
Northwestern Polytechnic U, CA B
Northwest Nazarene U, ID B
Notre Dame de Namur U, CA B
Oregon Inst of Technology, OR B
Oregon State U, OR B
Pacific Lutheran U, WA B
Pacific States U, CA B
Pacific Union Coll, CA B
Pacific U, OR B
Pepperdine U, Malibu, CA B
Pioneer Pacific Coll, OR A
Point Loma Nazarene U, CA B
Portland State U, OR B
Regis U, CO B
Rocky Mountain Coll, MT B
Saint Martin's Coll, WA B
Saint Mary's Coll of California, CA B
San Diego State U, CA B
San Francisco State U, CA B
San Jose State U, CA B
Seattle Pacific U, WA B
Seattle U, WA B
Sheldon Jackson Coll, AK A,B
Sierra Nevada Coll, NV B
Simpson Coll and Graduate School, CA B
Sonoma State U, CA B
Southern Oregon U, OR B
Southern Utah U, UT B
Southwestern Coll, AZ B
United States Air Force Academy, CO B
U of Alaska Anchorage, AK A,B
U of Alaska Fairbanks, AK A,B
U of Alaska Southeast, AK A,B
U of California, Berkeley, CA B
U of California, Los Angeles, CA B
U of California, Riverside, CA B
U of Colorado at Colorado Springs, CO B
U of Denver, CO B
U of Great Falls, MT B
U of Hawaii at Hilo, HI B
U of Hawaii at Manoa, HI B
U of La Verne, CA B
The U of Montana–Western, MT A
U of Nevada, Las Vegas, NV B
U of New Mexico, NM B
U of Northern Colorado, CO B
U of Oregon, OR B
U of Phoenix–Colorado Campus, CO B
U of Phoenix–Nevada Campus, NV B
U of Phoenix–New Mexico Campus, NM B
U of Phoenix–Northern California Campus, CA B
U of Phoenix Online Campus, AZ B
U of Phoenix–Oregon Campus, OR B
U of Phoenix–Phoenix Campus, AZ B
U of Phoenix–Sacramento Campus, CA B
U of Phoenix–San Diego Campus, CA B
U of Phoenix–Southern Arizona Campus, AZ B
U of Phoenix–Southern California Campus, CA B
U of Phoenix–Southern Colorado Campus, CO B
U of Phoenix–Utah Campus, UT B
U of Phoenix–Washington Campus, WA B
U of Portland, OR B
U of Redlands, CA B
U of San Diego, CA B
U of San Francisco, CA B
U of Southern California, CA B
U of the Pacific, CA B
U of the West, CA B
U of Utah, UT B
U of Washington, WA B
U of Wyoming, WY B

A—associate degree; B—bachelor's degree

Utah State U, UT B
Utah Valley State Coll, UT A,B
Vanguard U of Southern California, CA B
Walla Walla Coll, WA A,B
Warner Pacific Coll, OR B
Washington State U, WA B
Weber State U, UT B
Western Baptist Coll, OR A,B
Western State Coll of Colorado, CO B
Western Washington U, WA B
Westminster Coll, UT B
Whitworth Coll, WA B
Woodbury U, CA B

Business Administration, Management and Operations Related
California State U, Chico, CA B
Coleman Coll, La Mesa, CA A,B
DeVry U, Phoenix, AZ B
DeVry U, Fremont, CA B
DeVry U, Long Beach, CA B
DeVry U, Pomona, CA B
DeVry U, West Hills, CA B
DeVry U, Colorado Springs, CO B
DeVry U, Federal Way, WA B
Northwest Christian Coll, OR B
San Jose State U, CA B
U of Hawaii at Manoa, HI B
U of Phoenix–Idaho Campus, ID B
U of Southern California, CA B
William Jessup U, CA B
Woodbury U, CA B

Business Automation/ Technology/Data Entry
Montana State U–Billings, MT A
Montana Tech of The U of Montana, MT A
The U of Montana–Western, MT A
Utah Valley State Coll, UT A

Business/Commerce
Argosy U/Seattle, WA B
Arizona State U East, AZ B
DeVry U, Westminster, CO A
Great Basin Coll, NV A
Idaho State U, ID A,B
Lehigh U, PA B
Linfield Coll, OR B
Montana State U–Billings, MT A,B
Montana State U–Bozeman, MT B
Montana Tech of The U of Montana, MT B
Mt. Sierra Coll, CA B
New Mexico State U, NM A,B
Northern Arizona U, AZ B
Saint Mary's Coll of California, CA B
Touro U International, CA B
The U of Arizona, AZ B
U of Colorado at Boulder, CO B
U of Colorado at Denver, CO B
U of Denver, CO B
U of Hawaii at Manoa, HI B
The U of Montana–Missoula, MT B
The U of Montana–Western, MT A,B
U of Nevada, Reno, NV B
U of Puget Sound, WA B
U of Redlands, CA B
U of San Francisco, CA B
U of Utah, UT B
U of Washington, WA B
Utah State U, UT B
Utah Valley State Coll, UT A,B
Washington State U, WA B
Western Oregon U, OR B
Westminster Coll, UT B
Westmont Coll, CA B
Westwood Coll–Denver North, CO B

Business/Corporate Communications
Hawai'i Pacific U, HI B
Holy Names U, CA B
Jones International U, CO B
Point Loma Nazarene U, CA B
The U of Montana–Western, MT B

Business Family and Consumer Sciences/Human Sciences
Brigham Young U, UT B

Business Machine Repair
Boise State U, ID A
Idaho State U, ID A
U of Alaska Anchorage, AK A

Business, Management, and Marketing Related
Arizona State U, AZ B
The Art Inst of California–San Francisco, CA A,B
California State U, Sacramento, CA B
California State U, Stanislaus, CA B
U of Denver, CO B
U of Phoenix–Nevada Campus, NV B
U of Southern California, CA B
U of Utah, UT B
Western Baptist Coll, OR B

Business/Managerial Economics
Boise State U, ID B
California Inst of Technology, CA B
California State U, Fullerton, CA B
California State U, Hayward, CA B
California State U, Long Beach, CA B
California State U, San Bernardino, CA B
Carroll Coll, MT B
Chapman U, CA B
Eastern Oregon U, OR B
Eastern Washington U, WA B
George Fox U, OR B
Gonzaga U, WA B
Grand Canyon U, AZ B
Hawai'i Pacific U, HI A,B
Lehigh U, PA B
Mills Coll, CA B
Montana State U–Billings, MT B
Northern Arizona U, AZ B
Notre Dame de Namur U, CA B
Occidental Coll, CA B
Santa Clara U, CA B
Seattle U, WA B
Sonoma State U, CA B
U of Alaska Anchorage, AK B
The U of Arizona, AZ B
U of California, Los Angeles, CA B
U of California, Riverside, CA B
U of California, Santa Barbara, CA B
U of California, Santa Cruz, CA B
U of Denver, CO B
U of Hawaii at Manoa, HI B
U of Judaism, CA B
U of La Verne, CA B
U of Nevada, Reno, NV B
U of San Diego, CA B
U of Wyoming, WY B
Utah Valley State Coll, UT B
Washington State U, WA B
Weber State U, UT B
Western Washington U, WA B
Westminster Coll, UT B
Westmont Coll, CA B

Business Statistics
Brigham Young U, UT B
Southern Oregon U, OR B

Business Teacher Education
Boise State U, ID B
Brigham Young U–Hawaii, HI B
California State U, Fresno, CA B
Central Washington U, WA B
Coll of Santa Fe, NM B
Coll of the Southwest, NM B
Colorado State U, CO B
Eastern New Mexico U, NM B
Eastern Washington U, WA B
Grand Canyon U, AZ B
Mount St. Mary's Coll, CA B
North Carolina Ag and Tech State U, NC B
Pacific Union Coll, CA B
Southern Utah U, UT B
U of Hawaii at Manoa, HI B
U of Idaho, ID B
The U of Montana–Missoula, MT B
The U of Montana–Western, MT B
U of Nevada, Reno, NV B
U of New Mexico, NM B
Utah State U, UT B
Utah Valley State Coll, UT B
Walla Walla Coll, WA B
Weber State U, UT B
Western Baptist Coll, OR B

Cabinetmaking and Millwork
Utah Valley State Coll, UT A

CAD/CADD Drafting/Design Technology
ITT Tech Inst, Tucson, AZ A
ITT Tech Inst, Anaheim, CA A
ITT Tech Inst, Rancho Cordova, CA A
ITT Tech Inst, San Bernardino, CA A
ITT Tech Inst, San Diego, CA A
ITT Tech Inst, Sylmar, CA A
ITT Tech Inst, Torrance, CA A
ITT Tech Inst, West Covina, CA A
ITT Tech Inst, CO A
ITT Tech Inst, ID A
ITT Tech Inst, NV A
ITT Tech Inst, NM A
ITT Tech Inst, OR A
ITT Tech Inst, UT A
ITT Tech Inst, Bothell, WA A
ITT Tech Inst, Seattle, WA A
ITT Tech Inst, Spokane, WA A
Silicon Valley Coll, Walnut Creek, CA A
Westwood Coll–Long Beach, CA A

Canadian Studies
U of Washington, WA B
Western Washington U, WA B

Carpentry
Idaho State U, ID A
Southern Utah U, UT A

Cartography
Brigham Young U, UT B
U of Idaho, ID B

Cell and Molecular Biology
U of California, Berkeley, CA B
U of California, Los Angeles, CA B
U of Colorado at Boulder, CO B
Western Washington U, WA B

Cell Biology and Anatomical Sciences Related
Northern Arizona U, AZ B

Cell Biology and Histology
California State U, Fresno, CA B
California State U, Long Beach, CA B
California State U, San Marcos, CA B
Fort Lewis Coll, CO B
Humboldt State U, CA B
Oregon State U, OR B
Pomona Coll, CA B
San Francisco State U, CA B
Sonoma State U, CA B
The U of Arizona, AZ B
U of California, Davis, CA B
U of California, San Diego, CA B
U of California, Santa Barbara, CA B
U of California, Santa Cruz, CA B
U of Utah, UT B
U of Washington, WA B
Western Washington U, WA B

Celtic Languages
U of California, Berkeley, CA B

Ceramic Arts and Ceramics
Arizona State U, AZ B
Brigham Young U, UT B
California Coll of the Arts, CA B
California State U, Fullerton, CA B
California State U, Hayward, CA B
California State U, Long Beach, CA B
Colorado State U, CO B
Northwest Nazarene U, ID B
San Francisco Art Inst, CA B
U of Oregon, OR B
U of Washington, WA B
Western Washington U, WA B

Ceramic Sciences and Engineering
U of Washington, WA B

Chemical Engineering
Arizona State U, AZ B
Brigham Young U, UT B
California Inst of Technology, CA B
California State Polytechnic U, Pomona, CA B
California State U, Long Beach, CA B
Colorado School of Mines, CO B
Colorado State U, CO B
Lehigh U, PA B
Montana State U–Bozeman, MT B
New Mexico Inst of Mining and Technology, NM B
New Mexico State U, NM B

North Carolina Ag and Tech State U, NC B
Oregon State U, OR B
San Diego State U, CA B
San Jose State U, CA B
Stanford U, CA B
The U of Arizona, AZ B
U of California, Berkeley, CA B
U of California, Davis, CA B
U of California, Irvine, CA B
U of California, Los Angeles, CA B
U of California, Riverside, CA B
U of California, San Diego, CA B
U of California, Santa Barbara, CA B
U of Colorado at Boulder, CO B
U of Idaho, ID B
U of Nevada, Reno, NV B
U of New Mexico, NM B
U of Southern California, CA B
U of Utah, UT B
U of Washington, WA B
U of Wyoming, WY B
Washington State U, WA B

Chemical Physics

California Inst of Technology, CA B

Chemical Technology

Weber State U, UT A

Chemistry

Adams State Coll, CO B
Albertson Coll of Idaho, ID B
Arizona State U, AZ B
Azusa Pacific U, CA B
Birmingham-Southern Coll, AL B
Boise State U, ID B
Brigham Young U, UT B
Brigham Young U–Hawaii, HI B
California Inst of Technology, CA B
California Lutheran U, CA B
California Polytechnic State U, San Luis Obispo, CA B
California State Polytechnic U, Pomona, CA B
California State U, Bakersfield, CA B
California State U, Chico, CA B
California State U, Dominguez Hills, CA B
California State U, Fresno, CA B
California State U, Fullerton, CA B
California State U, Hayward, CA B
California State U, Long Beach, CA B
California State U, Los Angeles, CA B
California State U, Sacramento, CA B
California State U, San Bernardino, CA B
California State U, San Marcos, CA B
California State U, Stanislaus, CA B
Carroll Coll, MT B
Central Washington U, WA B
Chapman U, CA B
Claremont McKenna Coll, CA B
The Colorado Coll, CO B
Colorado School of Mines, CO B
Colorado State U, CO B
Colorado State U-Pueblo, CO B
Concordia U, CA B
Concordia U, OR B
Cornell Coll, IA B
Eastern New Mexico U, NM B
Eastern Oregon U, OR B
Eastern Washington U, WA B
Fort Lewis Coll, CO B
Fresno Pacific U, CA B
George Fox U, OR B
Gonzaga U, WA B
Grand Canyon U, AZ B
Great Basin Coll, NV A
Harvey Mudd Coll, CA B
Humboldt State U, CA B
Idaho State U, ID A,B
Lehigh U, PA B
Lewis & Clark Coll, OR B
Lewis-Clark State Coll, ID B
Linfield Coll, OR B
Loyola Marymount U, CA B
Metropolitan State Coll of Denver, CO B
Mills Coll, CA B
Montana State U–Billings, MT B
Montana State U–Bozeman, MT B
Montana Tech of The U of Montana, MT B
Mount St. Mary's Coll, CA B
New Mexico Highlands U, NM B
New Mexico Inst of Mining and Technology, NM B
New Mexico State U, NM B
North Carolina Ag and Tech State U, NC B
Northern Arizona U, AZ B
Northwest Nazarene U, ID B
Occidental Coll, CA B
Oregon State U, OR B
Pacific Lutheran U, WA B
Pacific Union Coll, CA B
Pacific U, OR B
Pepperdine U, Malibu, CA B
Pitzer Coll, CA B
Point Loma Nazarene U, CA B
Pomona Coll, CA B
Portland State U, OR B
Reed Coll, OR B
Regis U, CO B
Rocky Mountain Coll, MT B
Saint Martin's Coll, WA B
Saint Mary's Coll of California, CA B
San Diego State U, CA B
San Francisco State U, CA B
San Jose State U, CA B
Santa Clara U, CA B
Scripps Coll, CA B
Seattle Pacific U, WA B
Seattle U, WA B
Sonoma State U, CA B
Southern Oregon U, OR B
Southern Utah U, UT B
Stanford U, CA B
United States Air Force Academy, CO B
U of Alaska Anchorage, AK B
U of Alaska Fairbanks, AK B
The U of Arizona, AZ B
U of California, Berkeley, CA B
U of California, Davis, CA B
U of California, Irvine, CA B
U of California, Los Angeles, CA B
U of California, Riverside, CA B
U of California, San Diego, CA B
U of California, Santa Barbara, CA B
U of California, Santa Cruz, CA B
U of Colorado at Boulder, CO B
U of Colorado at Colorado Springs, CO B
U of Colorado at Denver, CO B
U of Denver, CO B
U of Great Falls, MT B
U of Hawaii at Hilo, HI B
U of Hawaii at Manoa, HI B
U of Idaho, ID B
U of La Verne, CA B
The U of Montana–Missoula, MT B
U of Nevada, Las Vegas, NV B
U of Nevada, Reno, NV B
U of New Mexico, NM B
U of Northern Colorado, CO B
U of Oregon, OR B
U of Portland, OR B
U of Puget Sound, WA B
U of Redlands, CA B
U of San Diego, CA B
U of San Francisco, CA B
U of Southern California, CA B
U of the Pacific, CA B
U of Utah, UT B
U of Washington, WA B
U of Wyoming, WY B
Utah State U, UT B
Utah Valley State Coll, UT B
Vanguard U of Southern California, CA B
Walla Walla Coll, WA B
Washington State U, WA B
Weber State U, UT B
Western Oregon U, OR B
Western State Coll of Colorado, CO B
Western Washington U, WA B
Westminster Coll, UT B
Westmont Coll, CA B
Whitman Coll, WA B
Whitworth Coll, WA B
Willamette U, OR B

Chemistry Related

California State U, Chico, CA B
California State U, Sacramento, CA B
Lehigh U, PA B
Northern Arizona U, AZ B
Saint Mary's Coll of California, CA B
San Diego State U, CA B
U of California, Berkeley, CA B
U of the Pacific, CA B

Chemistry Teacher Education

Brigham Young U, UT B
Brigham Young U–Hawaii, HI B
California State U, Chico, CA B
Central Washington U, WA B
Chapman U, CA B
Colorado State U, CO B
Eastern Washington U, WA B
George Fox U, OR B
Montana State U–Billings, MT B
Northwest Nazarene U, ID B
Rocky Mountain Coll, MT B
San Diego State U, CA B
The U of Arizona, AZ B
U of California, San Diego, CA B
U of Great Falls, MT B
Utah State U, UT B
Utah Valley State Coll, UT B
Weber State U, UT B
Western Washington U, WA B

Child Care and Support Services Management

Brigham Young U, UT B
Eastern New Mexico U, NM A
Eastern Washington U, WA B
Idaho State U, ID A
Pacific Union Coll, CA B
Weber State U, UT A

Child Care Provision

Brigham Young U, UT B
Pacific Union Coll, CA A
U of Alaska Fairbanks, AK A

Child Development

Boise State U, ID A
Brigham Young U, UT B
California State U, Dominguez Hills, CA B
California State U, Fresno, CA B
California State U, Hayward, CA B
California State U, Long Beach, CA B
Eastern Washington U, WA B
Humboldt State U, CA B
Lewis-Clark State Coll, ID A,B
North Carolina Ag and Tech State U, NC B
Oregon State U, OR B
Pacific Oaks Coll, CA B
Point Loma Nazarene U, CA B
Portland State U, OR B
San Diego State U, CA B
Southern Utah U, UT A
U of Idaho, ID B
U of La Verne, CA B
U of Nevada, Reno, NV B
U of Utah, UT B
Weber State U, UT A,B

Chinese

Brigham Young U, UT B
California State U, Long Beach, CA B
California State U, Los Angeles, CA B
Claremont McKenna Coll, CA B
Pacific Lutheran U, WA B
Pacific U, OR B
Pomona Coll, CA B
Portland State U, OR B
Reed Coll, OR B
San Francisco State U, CA B
San Jose State U, CA B
Scripps Coll, CA B
Stanford U, CA B
U of California, Berkeley, CA B
U of California, Davis, CA B
U of California, Irvine, CA B
U of California, Los Angeles, CA B
U of California, Riverside, CA B
U of California, San Diego, CA B
U of California, Santa Barbara, CA B
U of California, Santa Cruz, CA B
U of Colorado at Boulder, CO B
U of Hawaii at Manoa, HI B
The U of Montana–Missoula, MT B
U of Oregon, OR B
U of Utah, UT B
U of Washington, WA B

Chinese Studies

Claremont McKenna Coll, CA B
U of the West, CA B

Christian Studies

California Baptist U, CA B

Cinematography and Film/Video Production

Academy of Art U, CA A,B

A—associate degree; B—bachelor's degree

American InterContinental U, CA B
Art Center Coll of Design, CA B
The Art Inst of Colorado, CO A
Brigham Young U, UT B
California State U, Long Beach, CA B
Chapman U, CA B
Colorado State U-Pueblo, CO B
Columbia Coll Hollywood, CA B
The Evergreen State Coll, WA B
Loyola Marymount U, CA B
Montana State U–Bozeman, MT B
Platt Coll San Diego, CA A,B
U of Advancing Technology, AZ B
U of California, Santa Cruz, CA B
U of Southern California, CA B
Vanguard U of Southern California, CA B

City/Urban, Community and Regional Planning

Arizona State U, AZ B
California Polytechnic State U, San Luis Obispo, CA B
California State Polytechnic U, Pomona, CA B
California State U, Chico, CA B
Eastern Oregon U, OR B
Eastern Washington U, WA B
New Mexico State U, NM B
Portland State U, OR B
The U of Arizona, AZ B
U of California, Los Angeles, CA B
The U of Montana–Missoula, MT B
U of Nevada, Las Vegas, NV B
U of Oregon, OR B
U of San Francisco, CA B
U of Southern California, CA B
U of Washington, WA B
Western Washington U, WA B

Civil Drafting and Cad/Cadd

Montana Tech of The U of Montana, MT A

Civil Engineering

Arizona State U, AZ B
Boise State U, ID B
Brigham Young U, UT B
California Inst of Technology, CA B
California Polytechnic State U, San Luis Obispo, CA B
California State Polytechnic U, Pomona, CA B
California State U, Chico, CA B
California State U, Fresno, CA B
California State U, Fullerton, CA B
California State U, Long Beach, CA B
California State U, Los Angeles, CA B
Carroll Coll, MT B
Colorado School of Mines, CO B
Colorado State U, CO B
Gonzaga U, WA B
Idaho State U, ID B
Lehigh U, PA B
Loyola Marymount U, CA B
Montana State U–Bozeman, MT B
Montana Tech of The U of Montana, MT B
New Mexico Inst of Mining and Technology, NM B
New Mexico State U, NM B
North Carolina Ag and Tech State U, NC B
Northern Arizona U, AZ B
Oregon Inst of Technology, OR B
Oregon State U, OR B
Portland State U, OR B
Saint Martin's Coll, WA B
San Diego State U, CA B
San Francisco State U, CA B
San Jose State U, CA B
Santa Clara U, CA B
Seattle U, WA B
Stanford U, CA B
United States Air Force Academy, CO B
U of Alaska Anchorage, AK B
U of Alaska Fairbanks, AK B
The U of Arizona, AZ B
U of California, Berkeley, CA B
U of California, Davis, CA B
U of California, Irvine, CA B
U of California, Los Angeles, CA B
U of Colorado at Boulder, CO B
U of Colorado at Denver, CO B
U of Hawaii at Manoa, HI B
U of Idaho, ID B
U of Nevada, Las Vegas, NV B
U of Nevada, Reno, NV B
U of New Mexico, NM B
U of Portland, OR B
U of Southern California, CA B
U of the Pacific, CA B
U of Utah, UT B
U of Washington, WA B
U of Wyoming, WY B
Utah State U, UT B
Walla Walla Coll, WA B
Washington State U, WA B

Civil Engineering Related

California State U, Sacramento, CA B
U of Southern California, CA B

Civil Engineering Technology

Colorado State U-Pueblo, CO B
Idaho State U, ID A
Metropolitan State Coll of Denver, CO B

Classical, Ancient Mediterranean and Near Eastern Studies and Archaeology

U of California, Berkeley, CA B
U of California, Irvine, CA B
U of California, Los Angeles, CA B

Classics and Classical Languages Related

California State U, Long Beach, CA B
U of California, Los Angeles, CA B

Classics and Languages, Literatures and Linguistics

Brigham Young U, UT B
Claremont McKenna Coll, CA B
The Colorado Coll, CO B
Cornell Coll, IA B
The Evergreen State Coll, WA B
Lehigh U, PA B
Loyola Marymount U, CA B
Pacific Lutheran U, WA B
Pitzer Coll, CA B
Pomona Coll, CA B
Reed Coll, OR B
St. John's Coll, NM B
San Diego State U, CA B
San Francisco State U, CA B
Santa Clara U, CA B
Scripps Coll, CA B
Seattle Pacific U, WA B
Stanford U, CA B
The U of Arizona, AZ B
U of California, Berkeley, CA B
U of California, Irvine, CA B
U of California, Los Angeles, CA B
U of California, Riverside, CA B
U of California, San Diego, CA B
U of California, Santa Barbara, CA B
U of California, Santa Cruz, CA B
U of Colorado at Boulder, CO B
U of Idaho, ID B
The U of Montana–Missoula, MT B
U of New Mexico, NM B
U of Oregon, OR B
U of Puget Sound, WA B
U of Southern California, CA B
U of the Pacific, CA B
U of Utah, UT B
U of Washington, WA B
Washington State U, WA B
Western Washington U, WA B
Whitman Coll, WA B
Willamette U, OR B

Clinical Laboratory Science/ Medical Technology

Arizona State U, AZ B
Boise State U, ID B
Brigham Young U, UT B
California State U, Chico, CA B
California State U, Dominguez Hills, CA B
Carroll Coll, MT B
Eastern New Mexico U, NM B
Humboldt State U, CA B
Idaho State U, ID B
Loma Linda U, CA B
New Mexico Inst of Mining and Technology, NM B
Oregon State U, OR B
Pacific Union Coll, CA B
Seattle U, WA B
The U of Arizona, AZ B
U of Hawaii at Manoa, HI B
U of Idaho, ID B
The U of Montana–Missoula, MT B
U of Nevada, Las Vegas, NV B
U of Northern Colorado, CO B
U of Utah, UT B
U of Washington, WA B
Utah State U, UT B
Walla Walla Coll, WA B
Weber State U, UT A,B

Clinical/Medical Laboratory Technology

California State U, Dominguez Hills, CA B
California State U, Hayward, CA B
City U, WA A
Sonoma State U, CA B
U of Alaska Anchorage, AK A
The U of Montana–Missoula, MT B
U of Utah, UT B
Weber State U, UT A,B

Clinical Psychology

Biola U, CA B
California State U, Fullerton, CA B
Colorado State U-Pueblo, CO B
George Fox U, OR B
Western State Coll of Colorado, CO B

Clothing/Textiles

New Mexico State U, NM B
North Carolina Ag and Tech State U, NC B
Oregon State U, OR B
San Francisco State U, CA B

Cognitive Psychology and Psycholinguistics

California State U, Stanislaus, CA B
George Fox U, OR B
Occidental Coll, CA B
U of California, San Diego, CA B
U of California, Santa Cruz, CA B

Cognitive Science

U of California, Berkeley, CA B
U of California, Los Angeles, CA B

Commercial and Advertising Art

Academy of Art U, CA A,B
American InterContinental U, CA A,B
Arizona State U, AZ B
Art Center Coll of Design, CA B
The Art Inst of California–San Diego, CA A,B
The Art Inst of California–San Francisco, CA A,B
The Art Inst of Colorado, CO A,B
Biola U, CA B
Boise State U, ID B
California Coll of the Arts, CA B
California Inst of the Arts, CA B
California Polytechnic State U, San Luis Obispo, CA B
California State Polytechnic U, Pomona, CA B
California State U, Dominguez Hills, CA B
California State U, Fresno, CA B
California State U, Fullerton, CA B
California State U, Hayward, CA B
California State U, Long Beach, CA B
California State U, San Bernardino, CA B
Cogswell Polytechnical Coll, CA B
Colorado State U, CO B
Grand Canyon U, AZ B
Laguna Coll of Art & Design, CA B
Mt. Sierra Coll, CA B
New Mexico Highlands U, NM B
Northwest Coll of Art, WA B
Northwest Nazarene U, ID B
Notre Dame de Namur U, CA B
Otis Coll of Art and Design, CA B
Platt Coll, Newport Beach, CA A
Platt Coll San Diego, CA A,B
Portland State U, OR B
U of Advancing Technology, AZ B
U of Denver, CO B
U of Oregon, OR B
U of the Pacific, CA B
U of Washington, WA B
Utah Valley State Coll, UT A
Walla Walla Coll, WA A,B

Weber State U, UT B
Western State Coll of Colorado, CO B
Western Washington U, WA B
Westwood Coll–Denver South, CO A
Westwood Coll–Inland Empire, CA A
Woodbury U, CA B

Commercial Photography
Art Center Coll of Design, CA B

Communication and Journalism Related
Arizona State U East, AZ B
The Art Inst of California–San Diego, CA B
Brigham Young U, UT B
Brigham Young U–Hawaii, HI B
California Baptist U, CA B
Eastern Washington U, WA B
Hawai'i Pacific U, HI B
Lehigh U, PA B
Northern Arizona U, AZ B
Notre Dame de Namur U, CA B
Saint Mary's Coll of California, CA B
San Diego State U, CA B

Communication and Media Related
Platt Coll San Diego, CA A,B
Point Loma Nazarene U, CA B
Washington State U, WA B

Communication Disorders
Arizona State U, AZ B
Biola U, CA B
California State U, Chico, CA B
California State U, Fresno, CA B
California State U, Fullerton, CA B
California State U, Long Beach, CA B
California State U, Los Angeles, CA B
Eastern Washington U, WA B
San Diego State U, CA B
San Jose State U, CA B
The U of Arizona, AZ B
U of Colorado at Boulder, CO B

Communication/Speech Communication and Rhetoric
Adams State Coll, CO B
Arizona State U, AZ B
Arizona State U West, AZ B
Azusa Pacific U, CA B
Brigham Young U–Hawaii, HI A
California Baptist U, CA B
California State U, Fullerton, CA B
California State U, Los Angeles, CA B
California State U, Sacramento, CA B
California State U, San Marcos, CA B
California State U, Stanislaus, CA B
Carroll Coll, MT B
Chapman U, CA B
Christian Heritage Coll, CA B
Colorado Christian U, CO B
Concordia U, CA B
Dominican U of California, CA B
Eastern New Mexico U, NM B
Eastern Washington U, WA B
George Fox U, OR B
Hawai'i Pacific U, HI B
Humboldt State U, CA B
Idaho State U, ID A,B
Lewis & Clark Coll, OR B
Lewis-Clark State Coll, ID B
Linfield Coll, OR B
Montana Tech of The U of Montana, MT B
Multnomah Bible Coll and Biblical Seminary, OR B
Northern Arizona U, AZ B
Northwest Christian Coll, OR B
Northwest Nazarene U, ID B
Notre Dame de Namur U, CA B
Oregon Inst of Technology, OR B
Pepperdine U, Malibu, CA B
Point Loma Nazarene U, CA B
Prescott Coll, AZ B
Regis U, CO B
Rocky Mountain Coll, MT B
Saint Mary's Coll of California, CA B
Santa Clara U, CA B
Seattle Pacific U, WA B
Simpson Coll and Graduate School, CA B
Southern Oregon U, OR B
Stanford U, CA B
U of Alaska Fairbanks, AK B
The U of Arizona, AZ B
U of California, Los Angeles, CA B
U of California, Santa Barbara, CA B
U of Colorado at Boulder, CO B
U of Colorado at Colorado Springs, CO B
U of Colorado at Denver, CO B
U of Denver, CO B
U of Hawaii at Manoa, HI B
U of Idaho, ID B
U of La Verne, CA B
The U of Montana–Missoula, MT A
U of Nevada, Las Vegas, NV B
U of Nevada, Reno, NV B
U of Northern Colorado, CO B
U of Puget Sound, WA B
U of San Francisco, CA B
U of Southern California, CA B
U of the Pacific, CA B
U of Utah, UT B
U of Washington, WA B
U of Wyoming, WY B
Utah Valley State Coll, UT A
Vanguard U of Southern California, CA B
Washington State U, WA B
Western Baptist Coll, OR B
Western Washington U, WA B
Westminster Coll, UT B
Westmont Coll, CA B
Woodbury U, CA B

Communications Systems Installation and Repair Technology
Idaho State U, ID A

Community Health and Preventive Medicine
U of California, Los Angeles, CA B
Utah Valley State Coll, UT A

Community Health Services Counseling
California State U, Sacramento, CA B
Central Washington U, WA B
Western Washington U, WA B

Community Organization and Advocacy
New Mexico State U, NM B
Saint Martin's Coll, WA B
U of Alaska Fairbanks, AK B
U of New Mexico, NM A
U of Oregon, OR B
Western Baptist Coll, OR B

Community Psychology
Montana State U–Billings, MT B

Comparative Literature
Brigham Young U, UT B
California State U, Fullerton, CA B
California State U, Long Beach, CA B
The Colorado Coll, CO B
Mills Coll, CA B
Occidental Coll, CA B
Oregon State U, OR B
San Diego State U, CA B
San Francisco State U, CA B
Stanford U, CA B
U of California, Berkeley, CA B
U of California, Davis, CA B
U of California, Irvine, CA B
U of California, Los Angeles, CA B
U of California, Riverside, CA B
U of California, Santa Barbara, CA B
U of California, Santa Cruz, CA B
U of La Verne, CA B
U of Nevada, Las Vegas, NV B
U of New Mexico, NM B
U of Oregon, OR B
U of Southern California, CA B
U of Washington, WA B
Western Washington U, WA B
Willamette U, OR B

Computational Mathematics
U of California, Los Angeles, CA B

Computer and Information Sciences
Biola U, CA B
Boise State U, ID B
California Lutheran U, CA B
California State Polytechnic U, Pomona, CA B
California State U, Los Angeles, CA B
California State U, Sacramento, CA B
California State U, San Bernardino, CA B
California State U, Stanislaus, CA B
Central Washington U, WA B
Chaminade U of Honolulu, HI A,B
Chapman U, CA B
Claremont McKenna Coll, CA B
Coleman Coll, La Mesa, CA A,B
CollAmerica–Fort Collins, CO B
Colorado Christian U, CO B
Colorado State U, CO B
Colorado State U–Pueblo, CO B
Eastern New Mexico U, NM B
Eastern Washington U, WA B
The Evergreen State Coll, WA B
Fresno Pacific U, CA B
George Fox U, OR B
Hawai'i Pacific U, HI B
Idaho State U, ID B
Lewis-Clark State Coll, ID A,B
The Master's Coll and Seminary, CA B
Metropolitan State Coll of Denver, CO B
Montana State U–Billings, MT A
Montana Tech of The U of Montana, MT B
Mt. Sierra Coll, CA B
National American U, Denver, CO A,B
New Mexico State U, NM B
Northern Arizona U, AZ B
Northface U, UT B
Northwest Christian Coll, OR B
Oregon Inst of Technology, OR B
Pacific Union Coll, CA A,B
Portland State U, OR B
Prescott Coll, AZ B
San Diego State U, CA B
Sierra Nevada Coll, NV B
U of Alaska Anchorage, AK A
U of Alaska Fairbanks, AK B
The U of Arizona, AZ B
U of California, Irvine, CA B
U of Colorado at Colorado Springs, CO B
U of Colorado at Denver, CO B
U of Denver, CO B
U of Great Falls, MT B
U of Hawaii at Manoa, HI B
The U of Montana–Missoula, MT B
The U of Montana–Western, MT A
U of Nevada, Reno, NV B
U of New Mexico, NM B
U of Oregon, OR B
U of Phoenix–Idaho Campus, ID B
U of Phoenix–Nevada Campus, NV B
U of Phoenix–Utah Campus, UT B
U of Phoenix–Washington Campus, WA B
U of San Francisco, CA B
U of Southern California, CA B
U of Washington, WA B
Utah State U, UT B
Utah Valley State Coll, UT A
Weber State U, UT A,B

Computer and Information Sciences and Support Services Related
Blackfeet Comm Coll, MT A
California State U, Chico, CA B
California State U, Los Angeles, CA B
City U, WA B
LDS Business Coll, UT A
Lehigh U, PA B
Montana State U–Billings, MT A
Mt. Sierra Coll, CA B
U of California, Irvine, CA B
U of Great Falls, MT B
Utah State U, UT B

Computer and Information Sciences Related
National American U, Denver, CO A,B
Northface U, UT B
U of Great Falls, MT B

Computer and Information Systems Security
ITT Tech Inst, Tucson, AZ B
ITT Tech Inst, Anaheim, CA B

A—associate degree; B—bachelor's degree

ITT Tech Inst, Rancho Cordova, CA B
ITT Tech Inst, San Bernardino, CA B
ITT Tech Inst, San Diego, CA B
ITT Tech Inst, Sylmar, CA B
ITT Tech Inst, Torrance, CA B
ITT Tech Inst, West Covina, CA B
ITT Tech Inst, CO B
ITT Tech Inst, ID B
ITT Tech Inst, NV B
ITT Tech Inst, NM B
ITT Tech Inst, OR B
ITT Tech Inst, UT B
ITT Tech Inst, Bothell, WA B
ITT Tech Inst, Seattle, WA B
ITT Tech Inst, Spokane, WA B
Mt. Sierra Coll, CA B
U of Great Falls, MT B
Westwood Coll–Denver South, CO B
Westwood Coll–Inland Empire, CA B
Westwood Coll–Los Angeles, CA B
Westwood Coll–Denver North, CO B

Computer Engineering
Arizona State U, AZ B
Brigham Young U, UT B
California Inst of Technology, CA B
California Polytechnic State U, San Luis Obispo, CA B
California State Polytechnic U, Pomona, CA B
California State U, Chico, CA B
California State U, Fresno, CA B
California State U, Long Beach, CA B
California State U, Sacramento, CA B
Colorado State U, CO B
Embry-Riddle Aeronautical U, AZ B
Gonzaga U, WA B
Lehigh U, PA B
Loyola Marymount U, CA B
Montana State U–Bozeman, MT B
Montana Tech of The U of Montana, MT B
Northwestern Polytechnic U, CA B
Oregon State U, OR B
Pacific Lutheran U, WA B
Portland State U, OR B
San Diego State U, CA B
San Jose State U, CA B
Santa Clara U, CA B
The U of Arizona, AZ B
U of California, Davis, CA B
U of California, Irvine, CA B
U of California, Los Angeles, CA B
U of California, San Diego, CA B
U of California, Santa Barbara, CA B
U of California, Santa Cruz, CA B
U of Colorado at Boulder, CO B
U of Colorado at Colorado Springs, CO B
U of Denver, CO B
U of Idaho, ID B
U of Nevada, Las Vegas, NV B
U of Nevada, Reno, NV B
U of New Mexico, NM B
U of Portland, OR B
U of Southern California, CA B
U of the Pacific, CA B
U of Utah, UT B
U of Washington, WA B
U of Wyoming, WY B
Utah State U, UT B
Washington State U, WA B

Computer Engineering Related
U of Southern California, CA B

Computer Engineering Technologies Related
ITT Tech Inst, Tucson, AZ A
ITT Tech Inst, Anaheim, CA A
ITT Tech Inst, Rancho Cordova, CA A
ITT Tech Inst, San Bernardino, CA A
ITT Tech Inst, San Diego, CA A
ITT Tech Inst, Sylmar, CA A
ITT Tech Inst, Torrance, CA A
ITT Tech Inst, West Covina, CA A
ITT Tech Inst, CO A
ITT Tech Inst, ID A
ITT Tech Inst, NV A
ITT Tech Inst, NM A
ITT Tech Inst, OR A
ITT Tech Inst, UT A
ITT Tech Inst, Bothell, WA A
ITT Tech Inst, Seattle, WA A
ITT Tech Inst, Spokane, WA A

Computer Engineering Technology
Arizona State U East, AZ B
California State U, Long Beach, CA B
Colorado State U-Pueblo, CO B
DeVry U, Phoenix, AZ B
DeVry U, Fremont, CA B
DeVry U, Long Beach, CA B
DeVry U, Pomona, CA B
DeVry U, West Hills, CA B
DeVry U, Federal Way, WA B
Eastern Washington U, WA B
Foundation Coll, San Diego, CA A
High-Tech Inst, AZ A
Oregon Inst of Technology, OR A,B
Utah State U, UT B
Weber State U, UT A
Westwood Coll–Denver North, CO A

Computer Graphics
Academy of Art U, CA A,B
The Art Inst of California–San Francisco, CA A,B
The Art Inst of Colorado, CO A,B
California Inst of the Arts, CA B
California State U, Chico, CA B
California State U, Hayward, CA B
Cogswell Polytechnical Coll, CA B
Coleman Coll, La Mesa, CA A
CollAmerica–Fort Collins, CO A
Dominican U of California, CA B
Platt Coll, Newport Beach, CA A,B
Platt Coll San Diego, CA A,B
U of Advancing Technology, AZ A,B
U of Great Falls, MT B

Computer Hardware Engineering
Westwood Coll–Long Beach, CA A,B

Computer/Information Technology Services Administration Related
California Baptist U, CA B
Golden Gate U, CA B
Holy Names U, CA B
International Inst of the Americas, AZ A
Mt. Sierra Coll, CA B
National American U, Denver, CO A,B
Seattle Pacific U, WA B
U of Great Falls, MT B
Westwood Coll–Denver North, CO B

Computer Installation and Repair Technology
CollAmerica–Fort Collins, CO A

Computer Management
American InterContinental U, CA B
Pacific Union Coll, CA B
U of Great Falls, MT B
Western Washington U, WA B

Computer Programming
Brigham Young U–Hawaii, HI B
City U, WA B
CollAmerica–Fort Collins, CO A
DeVry U, Westminster, CO A,B
Foundation Coll, San Diego, CA A
ITT Tech Inst, Rancho Cordova, CA A
Montana Tech of The U of Montana, MT B
Mt. Sierra Coll, CA B
National American U, Denver, CO A,B
Nevada State Coll at Henderson, NV B
New Mexico Highlands U, NM B
New Mexico Inst of Mining and Technology, NM B
Northface U, UT B
Oregon Inst of Technology, OR A,B
Pacific Union Coll, CA B
U of Advancing Technology, AZ A,B
U of Great Falls, MT B
U of Phoenix Online Campus, AZ B
U of Phoenix–Washington Campus, WA B
Utah Valley State Coll, UT A
Walla Walla Coll, WA A
Western Washington U, WA B
Westwood Coll–Denver South, CO A
Westwood Coll–Inland Empire, CA A
Westwood Coll–Los Angeles, CA A
Westwood Coll–Denver North, CO A

Computer Programming Related
National American U, Denver, CO A,B
Northface U, UT B

Computer Programming (Specific Applications)
The Art Inst of California–San Francisco, CA B
CollAmerica–Fort Collins, CO A
DeVry U, Phoenix, AZ B
Idaho State U, ID A
ITT Tech Inst, Tucson, AZ A
ITT Tech Inst, Anaheim, CA A
ITT Tech Inst, San Diego, CA A
ITT Tech Inst, Sylmar, CA A
ITT Tech Inst, Torrance, CA A
ITT Tech Inst, West Covina, CA A
ITT Tech Inst, CO A
ITT Tech Inst, ID A
ITT Tech Inst, NV A
ITT Tech Inst, NM A
ITT Tech Inst, OR A
ITT Tech Inst, UT A
ITT Tech Inst, Bothell, WA A
ITT Tech Inst, Seattle, WA A
ITT Tech Inst, Spokane, WA A
National American U, Denver, CO A,B
Northface U, UT B
U of Puget Sound, WA B
Westwood Coll–Denver South, CO B
Westwood Coll–Inland Empire, CA B

Computer Programming (Vendor/Product Certification)
Northface U, UT B

Computer Science
Albertson Coll of Idaho, ID B
Arizona State U, AZ B
Azusa Pacific U, CA B
Birmingham-Southern Coll, AL B
Boise State U, ID B
Brigham Young U, UT B
Brigham Young U–Hawaii, HI B
California Inst of Technology, CA B
California Lutheran U, CA B
California Polytechnic State U, San Luis Obispo, CA B
California State Polytechnic U, Pomona, CA B
California State U, Bakersfield, CA B
California State U, Chico, CA B
California State U, Dominguez Hills, CA B
California State U, Fresno, CA B
California State U, Fullerton, CA B
California State U, Hayward, CA B
California State U, Long Beach, CA B
California State U, Los Angeles, CA B
California State U, San Bernardino, CA B
California State U, San Marcos, CA B
Carroll Coll, MT A,B
Chapman U, CA B
Claremont McKenna Coll, CA B
Coll of Santa Fe, NM B
Coll of the Southwest, NM B
Colorado School of Mines, CO B
Colorado State U, CO B
Cornell Coll, IA B
Eastern Oregon U, OR B
Fort Lewis Coll, CO B
Foundation Coll, San Diego, CA A
Gonzaga U, WA B
Harvey Mudd Coll, CA B
Hawai'i Pacific U, HI B
Henry Cogswell Coll, WA B
Humboldt State U, CA B
Lehigh U, PA B
Lewis & Clark Coll, OR B
Lewis-Clark State Coll, ID B
Linfield Coll, OR B

Loyola Marymount U, CA B
Metropolitan State Coll of Denver, CO B
Mills Coll, CA B
Montana State U–Bozeman, MT B
Montana Tech of The U of Montana, MT A,B
Morrison U, NV A
Mt. Sierra Coll, CA B
National U, CA B
New Mexico Highlands U, NM B
New Mexico Inst of Mining and Technology, NM B
North Carolina Ag and Tech State U, NC B
Northface U, UT B
Northwestern Polytechnic U, CA B
Northwest Nazarene U, ID B
Notre Dame de Namur U, CA B
Oregon State U, OR B
Pacific Lutheran U, WA B
Pacific States U, CA B
Pacific Union Coll, CA B
Pacific U, OR B
Pepperdine U, Malibu, CA B
Point Loma Nazarene U, CA B
Pomona Coll, CA B
Portland State U, OR B
Regis U, CO B
Rocky Mountain Coll, MT B
Saint Martin's Coll, WA B
San Francisco State U, CA B
San Jose State U, CA B
Santa Clara U, CA B
Scripps Coll, CA B
Seattle Pacific U, WA B
Seattle U, WA B
Sonoma State U, CA B
Southern Oregon U, OR B
Southern Utah U, UT B
Stanford U, CA B
United States Air Force Academy, CO B
U of Alaska Anchorage, AK B
U of Alaska Fairbanks, AK B
U of California, Berkeley, CA B
U of California, Irvine, CA B
U of California, Los Angeles, CA B
U of California, Riverside, CA B
U of California, San Diego, CA B
U of California, Santa Barbara, CA B
U of California, Santa Cruz, CA B
U of Colorado at Boulder, CO B
U of Colorado at Colorado Springs, CO B
U of Great Falls, MT B
U of Hawaii at Hilo, HI B
U of Idaho, ID B
U of La Verne, CA B
The U of Montana–Missoula, MT B
U of Nevada, Las Vegas, NV B
U of Nevada, Reno, NV B
U of New Mexico, NM B
U of Oregon, OR B
U of Portland, OR B
U of Puget Sound, WA B
U of Redlands, CA B
U of San Diego, CA B
U of San Francisco, CA B
U of Southern California, CA B
U of the Pacific, CA B
U of Utah, UT B
U of Washington, WA B
U of Wyoming, WY B
Utah Valley State Coll, UT A,B
Walla Walla Coll, WA B
Washington State U, WA B
Weber State U, UT A,B
Western Baptist Coll, OR B
Western Oregon U, OR B
Western State Coll of Colorado, CO B
Western Washington U, WA B
Westminster Coll, UT B
Westmont Coll, CA B
Whitworth Coll, WA B
Willamette U, OR B

Computer Software and Media Applications Related
Eastern Washington U, WA B
Holy Names U, CA B
Northface U, UT B
Platt Coll San Diego, CA A,B
U of Great Falls, MT B
Westwood Coll–Inland Empire, CA B

Computer Software Engineering
Embry-Riddle Aeronautical U, AZ B
National U, CA B
Notre Dame de Namur U, CA B
Washington State U, WA B

Computer Software Technology
ITT Tech Inst, Tucson, AZ B
ITT Tech Inst, Anaheim, CA B
ITT Tech Inst, Rancho Cordova, CA B
ITT Tech Inst, San Bernardino, CA B
ITT Tech Inst, San Diego, CA B
ITT Tech Inst, Sylmar, CA B
ITT Tech Inst, Torrance, CA B
ITT Tech Inst, West Covina, CA B
ITT Tech Inst, CO B
ITT Tech Inst, ID B
ITT Tech Inst, NV A
ITT Tech Inst, NM B
ITT Tech Inst, OR B
ITT Tech Inst, UT B
ITT Tech Inst, Bothell, WA B
ITT Tech Inst, Seattle, WA B
ITT Tech Inst, Spokane, WA B
Westwood Coll–Denver North, CO A

Computer Systems Analysis
DeVry U, Fremont, CA B
DeVry U, Long Beach, CA B
DeVry U, Pomona, CA B
DeVry U, West Hills, CA B
DeVry U, Colorado Springs, CO B
DeVry U, Federal Way, WA B
Montana Tech of The U of Montana, MT B
Seattle Pacific U, WA B
U of Advancing Technology, AZ B
U of Denver, CO B
U of Great Falls, MT B
Utah Valley State Coll, UT A

Computer Systems Networking and Telecommunications
Boise State U, ID B
California State U, Hayward, CA B
Chaparral Coll, AZ A,B
Coleman Coll, La Mesa, CA A,B
CollAmerica–Fort Collins, CO A
DeVry U, Phoenix, AZ B
DeVry U, Fremont, CA B
DeVry U, Long Beach, CA B
DeVry U, Pomona, CA B
DeVry U, West Hills, CA B
DeVry U, Federal Way, WA B
Foundation Coll, San Diego, CA A
High-Tech Inst, AZ A
ITT Tech Inst, Tucson, AZ B
ITT Tech Inst, Anaheim, CA B
ITT Tech Inst, Rancho Cordova, CA B
ITT Tech Inst, San Bernardino, CA B
ITT Tech Inst, San Diego, CA B
ITT Tech Inst, Sylmar, CA B
ITT Tech Inst, Torrance, CA B
ITT Tech Inst, West Covina, CA B
ITT Tech Inst, CO B
ITT Tech Inst, ID B
ITT Tech Inst, NV B
ITT Tech Inst, NM B
ITT Tech Inst, OR B
ITT Tech Inst, UT B
ITT Tech Inst, Bothell, WA B
ITT Tech Inst, Seattle, WA B
ITT Tech Inst, Spokane, WA B
Mt. Sierra Coll, CA B
National American U, Denver, CO A,B
Remington Coll–Colorado Springs Campus, CO A
U of Great Falls, MT B
Utah Valley State Coll, UT A
Weber State U, UT B
Westwood Coll–Anaheim, CA A,B
Westwood Coll–Denver South, CO A,B
Westwood Coll–Inland Empire, CA A,B
Westwood Coll–Los Angeles, CA A,B
Westwood Coll–Denver North, CO B

Computer Teacher Education
Eastern Washington U, WA B
San Diego State U, CA B

Computer Technology/Computer Systems Technology
DeVry U, Westminster, CO A,B
Foundation Coll, San Diego, CA A
High-Tech Inst, AZ A

Computer Typography and Composition Equipment Operation
Platt Coll San Diego, CA A

Conducting
Bethesda Christian U, CA B
Loyola Marymount U, CA B

Conservation Biology
Arizona State U, AZ B
Brigham Young U, UT B
California State U, Sacramento, CA B

Construction Engineering
Arizona State U, AZ B
California State U, Long Beach, CA B
National U, CA B
Oregon State U, OR B
U of Nevada, Las Vegas, NV B
U of Southern California, CA B

Construction Engineering Technology
Blackfeet Comm Coll, MT A
California State Polytechnic U, Pomona, CA B
California State U, Chico, CA B
California State U, Fresno, CA B
California State U, Long Beach, CA B
California State U, Sacramento, CA B
Colorado State U-Pueblo, CO B
Eastern Washington U, WA B
Montana State U–Bozeman, MT B
Northern Arizona U, AZ B
Southern Utah U, UT B
U of Alaska Southeast, AK A
U of Nevada, Reno, NV B
U of New Mexico, NM B
Washington State U, WA B

Construction Management
Boise State U, ID B
California State U, Long Beach, CA B
North Carolina Ag and Tech State U, NC B
Oregon State U, OR B
U of Denver, CO B
U of Washington, WA B

Construction Trades
Utah Valley State Coll, UT A

Consumer Economics
The U of Arizona, AZ B

Consumer Merchandising/Retailing Management
John F. Kennedy U, CA B
San Francisco State U, CA B

Cooking and Related Culinary Arts
The Art Inst of California–San Diego, CA A,B

Corrections
California State U, Hayward, CA B
Colorado State U-Pueblo, CO B
Eastern Washington U, WA B
Lewis-Clark State Coll, ID B
U of Great Falls, MT B
U of New Mexico, NM B
Weber State U, UT A,B
Western Oregon U, OR B

Corrections Administration
U of Great Falls, MT B

Corrections and Criminal Justice Related
U of Alaska Fairbanks, AK B
U of Great Falls, MT B
U of Phoenix–Northern California Campus, CA B
U of Phoenix Online Campus, AZ B
U of Phoenix–Sacramento Campus, CA B
U of Phoenix–San Diego Campus, CA B
U of Phoenix–Southern Arizona Campus, AZ B

A—associate degree; B—bachelor's degree

U of Phoenix–Southern California Campus, CA B
U of Phoenix–Southern Colorado Campus, CO B
U of Phoenix–Utah Campus, UT B
Westwood Coll–Anaheim, CA B
Westwood Coll–Inland Empire, CA B
Westwood Coll–Los Angeles, CA B

Counseling Psychology

Christian Heritage Coll, CA B
Coll of Santa Fe, NM B
Oregon Inst of Technology, OR B
Southwestern Coll, AZ B
U of Great Falls, MT B
U of Phoenix–Phoenix Campus, AZ B

Counselor Education/School Counseling and Guidance

California State Polytechnic U, Pomona, CA B
Northern Arizona U, AZ B
U of Hawaii at Manoa, HI B
Western Washington U, WA B

Crafts, Folk Art and Artisanry

Brigham Young U, UT B
Oregon Coll of Art & Craft, OR B

Creative Writing

Albertson Coll of Idaho, ID B
California State U, Hayward, CA B
California State U, Long Beach, CA B
California State U, San Bernardino, CA B
Chapman U, CA B
Coll of Santa Fe, NM B
The Colorado Coll, CO B
Colorado State U, CO B
Dominican U of California, CA B
Eastern Washington U, WA B
Eugene Lang Coll, New School U B
Lewis-Clark State Coll, ID B
Linfield Coll, OR B
Marylhurst U, OR B
Mills Coll, CA B
Naropa U, CO B
New Coll of California, CA B
Pacific U, OR B
Pitzer Coll, CA B
San Diego State U, CA B
San Francisco State U, CA B
Seattle U, WA B
The U of Arizona, AZ B
U of California, Riverside, CA B
U of California, San Diego, CA B
U of California, Santa Cruz, CA B
U of Denver, CO B
U of Great Falls, MT B
The U of Montana–Missoula, MT B
U of New Mexico, NM B
U of Puget Sound, WA B
U of Redlands, CA B
U of Southern California, CA B
U of Washington, WA B
Western Washington U, WA B

Criminal Justice/Law Enforcement Administration

American InterContinental U, CA A,B
Arizona State U West, AZ B
Boise State U, ID A,B
California Baptist U, CA B
California Lutheran U, CA B
California State U, Bakersfield, CA B
California State U, Dominguez Hills, CA B
California State U, Fullerton, CA B
California State U, Hayward, CA B
California State U, Long Beach, CA B
California State U, Sacramento, CA B
California State U, San Bernardino, CA B
California State U, Stanislaus, CA B
Central Washington U, WA B
Coll of Santa Fe, NM B
Eastern Washington U, WA B
Gonzaga U, WA B
Grand Canyon U, AZ B
Hawai'i Pacific U, HI B
International Inst of the Americas, AZ A
ITT Tech Inst, Anaheim, CA B
ITT Tech Inst, Rancho Cordova, CA B
ITT Tech Inst, San Bernardino, CA B
ITT Tech Inst, San Diego, CA B
ITT Tech Inst, Sylmar, CA B
ITT Tech Inst, Torrance, CA B
ITT Tech Inst, West Covina, CA B
ITT Tech Inst, CO B
ITT Tech Inst, ID B
ITT Tech Inst, NM B
ITT Tech Inst, UT B
ITT Tech Inst, Bothell, WA B
ITT Tech Inst, Seattle, WA B
Metropolitan State Coll of Denver, CO B
National U, CA B
Nevada State Coll at Henderson, NV B
Northern Arizona U, AZ B
Portland State U, OR B
Regis U, CO B
Remington Coll–Colorado Springs Campus, CO A,B
Saint Martin's Coll, WA B
San Diego State U, CA B
San Francisco State U, CA B
Seattle U, WA B
Sonoma State U, CA B
Southern Utah U, UT A
U of Alaska Anchorage, AK B
The U of Arizona, AZ B
U of Great Falls, MT B
U of Nevada, Las Vegas, NV B
U of Phoenix–Colorado Campus, CO B
U of Phoenix–New Mexico Campus, NM B
U of Phoenix–Phoenix Campus, AZ B
U of Phoenix–Washington Campus, WA B
U of Washington, WA B
Utah Valley State Coll, UT A,B
Washington State U, WA B
Western Oregon U, OR B

Criminal Justice/Police Science

California State U, Hayward, CA B
Idaho State U, ID A
Pioneer Pacific Coll, OR A
U of Great Falls, MT B
Weber State U, UT A,B
Western Oregon U, OR B
Western State Coll of Colorado, CO B

Criminal Justice/Safety

Arizona State U, AZ B
California State U, Chico, CA B
California State U, Los Angeles, CA B
Chaparral Coll, AZ A,B
Coll of the Southwest, NM B
Colorado State U, CO B
Crown Coll, WA A
Eastern New Mexico U, NM B
Great Basin Coll, NV A
Idaho State U, ID A
New Mexico Highlands U, NM B
New Mexico State U, NM A,B
Prescott Coll, AZ B
San Jose State U, CA B
U of Great Falls, MT B
U of Idaho, ID B
U of Northern Colorado, CO B
U of Portland, OR B
U of Wyoming, WY B
Weber State U, UT A,B

Criminology

California State U, Fresno, CA B
Chaminade U of Honolulu, HI A,B
Colorado State U-Pueblo, CO B
New Mexico Highlands U, NM B
Southern Oregon U, OR B
U of California, Irvine, CA B
U of Denver, CO B
U of La Verne, CA B
U of Nevada, Reno, NV B

Crop Production

Colorado State U, CO B
Washington State U, WA B

Culinary Arts

The Art Inst of California–San Diego, CA A
The Art Inst of Colorado, CO A,B
The Art Inst of Phoenix, AZ A
The Art Inst of Seattle, WA A
Boise State U, ID A
Idaho State U, ID A
Johnson & Wales U, CO A
U of Alaska Anchorage, AK A
U of Alaska Fairbanks, AK A
The U of Montana–Missoula, MT A
U of Nevada, Las Vegas, NV B
Utah Valley State Coll, UT A

Cultural Studies

Azusa Pacific U, CA B
Boise State U, ID B
Brigham Young U–Hawaii, HI B
California State Polytechnic U, Pomona, CA B
California State U, Fullerton, CA B
California State U, Hayward, CA B
California State U, Sacramento, CA B
Cornell Coll, IA B
The Evergreen State Coll, WA B
Fort Lewis Coll, CO B
Mills Coll, CA B
New Coll of California, CA B
Oregon State U, OR B
Sonoma State U, CA B
U of California, Irvine, CA B
U of California, Riverside, CA B
U of California, San Diego, CA B
U of Colorado at Boulder, CO B
U of Nevada, Las Vegas, NV B
U of Oregon, OR B
U of Southern California, CA B
U of Washington, WA B
Western Washington U, WA B

Curriculum and Instruction

The U of Montana–Missoula, MT B
Utah State U, UT B

Cytotechnology

California State U, Dominguez Hills, CA B
Loma Linda U, CA B

Dairy Science

California Polytechnic State U, San Luis Obispo, CA B
Oregon State U, OR B
Utah State U, UT B

Dance

Arizona State U, AZ B
Birmingham-Southern Coll, AL B
Brigham Young U, UT B
California Inst of the Arts, CA B
California State U, Fresno, CA B
California State U, Fullerton, CA B
California State U, Hayward, CA B
California State U, Long Beach, CA B
California State U, Los Angeles, CA B
California State U, Sacramento, CA B
Chapman U, CA B
Claremont McKenna Coll, CA B
The Colorado Coll, CO B
Colorado State U, CO B
Cornish Coll of the Arts, WA B
Loyola Marymount U, CA B
Mills Coll, CA B
Naropa U, CO B
New Mexico State U, NM B
Pitzer Coll, CA B
Pomona Coll, CA B
Prescott Coll, AZ B
Reed Coll, OR B
Saint Mary's Coll of California, CA B
San Diego State U, CA B
San Francisco State U, CA B
San Jose State U, CA B
Scripps Coll, CA B
Southern Utah U, UT B
The U of Arizona, AZ B
U of California, Berkeley, CA B
U of California, Irvine, CA B
U of California, Los Angeles, CA B
U of California, Riverside, CA B
U of California, San Diego, CA B
U of California, Santa Barbara, CA B
U of California, Santa Cruz, CA B
U of Colorado at Boulder, CO B
U of Hawaii at Manoa, HI B
U of Idaho, ID B
The U of Montana–Missoula, MT B
U of Nevada, Las Vegas, NV B
U of New Mexico, NM B
U of Oregon, OR B
U of Utah, UT B
U of Washington, WA B
Utah State U, UT B
Utah Valley State Coll, UT A
Weber State U, UT B

Western Oregon U, OR B
Westmont Coll, CA B

Dance Related

Brigham Young U, UT B
California State U, Long Beach, CA B
Chapman U, CA B

Data Entry/Microcomputer Applications

National American U, Denver, CO A,B

Data Modeling/Warehousing and Database Administration

Northface U, UT B

Data Processing and Data Processing Technology

Foundation Coll, San Diego, CA A
Great Basin Coll, NV A
Hawai'i Pacific U, HI A
Montana State U–Billings, MT A
Montana Tech of The U of Montana, MT A
Pacific Union Coll, CA B
U of Advancing Technology, AZ B
The U of Montana–Western, MT A
U of Washington, WA B
Utah Valley State Coll, UT A,B

Dental Assisting

U of Alaska Anchorage, AK A

Dental Hygiene

Eastern Washington U, WA B
Idaho State U, ID B
Loma Linda U, CA B
Montana State U–Billings, MT A
Northern Arizona U, AZ B
Oregon Inst of Technology, OR B
U of Alaska Anchorage, AK A
U of Colorado Health Sciences Center, CO B
U of Hawaii at Manoa, HI B
U of New Mexico, NM A,B
U of Southern California, CA B
U of Washington, WA B
U of Wyoming, WY B
Utah Valley State Coll, UT A
Weber State U, UT A,B

Dental Laboratory Technology

Idaho State U, ID A

Design and Applied Arts Related

Art Center Coll of Design, CA B
The Art Inst of California–San Diego, CA B
The Art Inst of Seattle, WA A,B
Laguna Coll of Art & Design, CA B
Lehigh U, PA B
Mt. Sierra Coll, CA B
Platt Coll, Newport Beach, CA B
Platt Coll San Diego, CA A,B
U of California, Los Angeles, CA B
Westwood Coll–Anaheim, CA B
Westwood Coll–Inland Empire, CA B

Design and Visual Communications

Bethesda Christian U, CA B
Brigham Young U, UT B
California State U, Chico, CA B
Henry Cogswell Coll, WA B
Laguna Coll of Art & Design, CA B
Platt Coll San Diego, CA A,B
San Diego State U, CA B
Silicon Valley Coll, Walnut Creek, CA B
U of Advancing Technology, AZ B
U of California, Davis, CA B
Weber State U, UT B
Western Washington U, WA B
Westwood Coll–Anaheim, CA B
Westwood Coll–Denver South, CO B
Westwood Coll–Inland Empire, CA B
Westwood Coll–Los Angeles, CA B
Westwood Coll–Denver North, CO B
Westwood Coll–Long Beach, CA B

Desktop Publishing and Digital Imaging Design

California State U, Chico, CA B
Platt Coll San Diego, CA A
Silicon Valley Coll, Walnut Creek, CA A,B

Developmental and Child Psychology

California Polytechnic State U, San Luis Obispo, CA B
California State U, Bakersfield, CA B
California State U, Hayward, CA B
California State U, San Bernardino, CA B
Colorado State U-Pueblo, CO B
Eastern Washington U, WA B
Fresno Pacific U, CA A,B
Humboldt State U, CA B
Mills Coll, CA B
Mount St. Mary's Coll, CA B
Sonoma State U, CA B
U of California, Santa Cruz, CA B
U of Utah, UT B
Western Washington U, WA B

Development Economics and International Development

Point Loma Nazarene U, CA B
U of California, Los Angeles, CA B

Diagnostic Medical Sonography and Ultrasound Technology

Seattle U, WA B
Weber State U, UT B

Diesel Mechanics Technology

Great Basin Coll, NV A
Idaho State U, ID A
Lewis-Clark State Coll, ID A,B
Montana State U–Billings, MT A
U of Alaska Anchorage, AK A
Utah Valley State Coll, UT A
Weber State U, UT A

Dietetics

Bastyr U, WA B
Brigham Young U, UT B
California State Polytechnic U, Pomona, CA B
California State U, Chico, CA B
California State U, Fresno, CA B
California State U, Long Beach, CA B
California State U, Los Angeles, CA B
California State U, San Bernardino, CA B
Colorado State U, CO B
Idaho State U, ID B
Loma Linda U, CA A,B
North Carolina Ag and Tech State U, NC B
Oregon State U, OR B
San Francisco State U, CA B
San Jose State U, CA B
U of Northern Colorado, CO B

Dietitian Assistant

Pacific Union Coll, CA A

Digital Communication and Media/Multimedia

Academy of Art U, CA A,B
The Art Inst of California–San Diego, CA B
California Lutheran U, CA B
California State U, Sacramento, CA B
Eastern Washington U, WA B
Platt Coll San Diego, CA A,B
Utah Valley State Coll, UT A,B

Direct Entry Midwifery

Utah Coll of Midwifery, UT B

Directing and Theatrical Production

Brigham Young U, UT B
California State U, Long Beach, CA B
Cornish Coll of the Arts, WA B
U of Southern California, CA B

Divinity/Ministry

Azusa Pacific U, CA B
Bethesda Christian U, CA B
Biola U, CA B
Christian Heritage Coll, CA B
Concordia U, CA B
Crestmont Coll, CA A
Eugene Bible Coll, OR B
Fresno Pacific U, CA B
Grand Canyon U, AZ B
Marylhurst U, OR B
The Master's Coll and Seminary, CA B
Northwest Coll, WA B
Northwest Nazarene U, ID B
Pacific Union Coll, CA A
Warner Pacific Coll, OR A,B
Western Baptist Coll, OR B
William Jessup U, CA B

Drafting and Design Technology

Boise State U, ID A
High-Tech Inst, AZ A
Idaho State U, ID A
Lewis-Clark State Coll, ID A,B
Montana State U–Billings, MT A
Montana Tech of The U of Montana, MT A
Pacific Union Coll, CA B
Silicon Valley Coll, Walnut Creek, CA A
Southern Utah U, UT A
U of Alaska Anchorage, AK A
Utah State U, UT A
Utah Valley State Coll, UT A
Weber State U, UT A

Drafting/Design Engineering Technologies Related

Eastern Washington U, WA B
Idaho State U, ID A
National U, CA B

Drama and Dance Teacher Education

Brigham Young U, UT B
Central Washington U, WA B
Eastern Washington U, WA B
Northern Arizona U, AZ B
San Diego State U, CA B
The U of Arizona, AZ B
U of Utah, UT B
Weber State U, UT B

Dramatic/Theatre Arts

Adams State Coll, CO B
Albertson Coll of Idaho, ID B
American Academy of Dramatic Arts/Hollywood, CA A
Arizona State U, AZ B
Birmingham-Southern Coll, AL B
Boise State U, ID B
Brigham Young U, UT B
Brigham Young U–Hawaii, HI A
California Inst of the Arts, CA B
California Lutheran U, CA B
California State Polytechnic U, Pomona, CA B
California State U, Bakersfield, CA B
California State U, Chico, CA B
California State U, Dominguez Hills, CA B
California State U, Fresno, CA B
California State U, Fullerton, CA B
California State U, Hayward, CA B
California State U, Long Beach, CA B
California State U, Los Angeles, CA B
California State U, Sacramento, CA B
California State U, San Bernardino, CA B
California State U, Stanislaus, CA B
Carroll Coll, MT B
Central Washington U, WA B
Chapman U, CA B
Claremont McKenna Coll, CA B
Coll of Santa Fe, NM B
Coll of the Southwest, NM B
Colorado Christian U, CO B
The Colorado Coll, CO B
Colorado State U, CO B
Concordia U, CA B
Concordia U, OR B
Cornell Coll, IA B
Cornish Coll of the Arts, WA B
Eastern New Mexico U, NM B
Eastern Oregon U, OR B
Eastern Washington U, WA B
Eugene Lang Coll, New School U B
The Evergreen State Coll, WA B
Fort Lewis Coll, CO B
Gonzaga U, WA B
Grand Canyon U, AZ B
Humboldt State U, CA B
Idaho State U, ID B
Lewis & Clark Coll, OR B
Linfield Coll, OR B
Loyola Marymount U, CA B
Montana State U–Billings, MT B
Naropa U, CO B

A—associate degree; B—bachelor's degree

New Mexico State U, NM B
North Carolina Ag and Tech State U, NC B
Northern Arizona U, AZ B
Northwest Coll, WA B
Notre Dame de Namur U, CA B
Occidental Coll, CA B
Oregon State U, OR B
Pacific Lutheran U, WA B
Pacific U, OR B
Pepperdine U, Malibu, CA B
Pitzer Coll, CA B
Point Loma Nazarene U, CA B
Pomona Coll, CA B
Portland State U, OR B
Prescott Coll, AZ B
Reed Coll, OR B
Rocky Mountain Coll, MT B
Saint Martin's Coll, WA B
Saint Mary's Coll of California, CA B
San Diego State U, CA B
San Francisco State U, CA B
San Jose State U, CA B
Santa Clara U, CA B
Scripps Coll, CA B
Seattle Pacific U, WA B
Seattle U, WA B
Sonoma State U, CA B
Southern Oregon U, OR B
Southern Utah U, UT B
Stanford U, CA B
U of Alaska Anchorage, AK B
U of Alaska Fairbanks, AK B
The U of Arizona, AZ B
U of California, Berkeley, CA B
U of California, Davis, CA B
U of California, Irvine, CA B
U of California, Los Angeles, CA B
U of California, Riverside, CA B
U of California, San Diego, CA B
U of California, Santa Barbara, CA B
U of California, Santa Cruz, CA B
U of Colorado at Boulder, CO B
U of Colorado at Denver, CO B
U of Denver, CO B
U of Hawaii at Manoa, HI B
U of Idaho, ID B
U of La Verne, CA B
The U of Montana–Missoula, MT B
The U of Montana–Western, MT B
U of Nevada, Las Vegas, NV B
U of Nevada, Reno, NV B
U of New Mexico, NM B
U of Northern Colorado, CO B
U of Oregon, OR B
U of Portland, OR B
U of Puget Sound, WA B
U of Southern California, CA B
U of the Pacific, CA B
U of Utah, UT B
U of Washington, WA B
U of Wyoming, WY B
Utah State U, UT B
Utah Valley State Coll, UT A
Vanguard U of Southern California, CA B
Washington State U, WA B
Weber State U, UT B
Western Oregon U, OR B
Western State Coll of Colorado, CO B
Western Washington U, WA B
Westmont Coll, CA B
Whitman Coll, WA B
Whitworth Coll, WA B
Willamette U, OR B

Dramatic/Theatre Arts and Stagecraft Related

Brigham Young U, UT B
California Inst of the Arts, CA B
California State U, Chico, CA B
Coll of Santa Fe, NM B
U of Nevada, Las Vegas, NV B
U of Northern Colorado, CO B

Drawing

Academy of Art U, CA A,B
Arizona State U, AZ B
Biola U, CA B
Birmingham-Southern Coll, AL B
Boise State U, ID B
Brigham Young U, UT B
California Coll of the Arts, CA B
California State U, Fullerton, CA B
California State U, Hayward, CA B
California State U, Long Beach, CA B
Colorado State U, CO B
Laguna Coll of Art & Design, CA B
Otis Coll of Art and Design, CA B
Portland State U, OR B
San Francisco Art Inst, CA B
Sonoma State U, CA B
U of California, Santa Cruz, CA B
The U of Montana–Missoula, MT B
U of Oregon, OR B
U of San Francisco, CA B
Western Washington U, WA B

Dutch/Flemish

U of California, Berkeley, CA B

Early Childhood Education

Bethesda Christian U, CA B
Brigham Young U, UT B
California State U, Chico, CA B
California State U, Fullerton, CA B
California State U, Los Angeles, CA B
Cascade Coll, OR B
Central Washington U, WA B
Chaminade U of Honolulu, HI B
Coll of Santa Fe, NM B
Eastern Washington U, WA B
Montana State U–Billings, MT A
New Mexico State U, NM B
San Jose State U, CA B
U of Great Falls, MT A
Utah Valley State Coll, UT A,B

East Asian Languages

U of California, Los Angeles, CA B
U of Oregon, OR B
U of Southern California, CA B

East Asian Languages Related

Arizona State U, AZ B
Claremont McKenna Coll, CA B
U of Hawaii at Manoa, HI B

Ecology

California State U, Chico, CA B
California State U, Fresno, CA B
California State U, Hayward, CA B
California State U, Long Beach, CA B
California State U, San Marcos, CA B
Idaho State U, ID B
Lehigh U, PA B
Naropa U, CO B
New Coll of California, CA B
Northern Arizona U, AZ B
Pomona Coll, CA B
Prescott Coll, AZ B
San Diego State U, CA B
San Francisco State U, CA B
Sierra Nevada Coll, NV B
Sonoma State U, CA B
The U of Arizona, AZ B
U of California, Irvine, CA B
U of California, Los Angeles, CA B
U of California, San Diego, CA B
U of California, Santa Barbara, CA B
U of California, Santa Cruz, CA B
U of Colorado at Colorado Springs, CO B
Utah State U, UT B
Washington State U, WA B
Western Washington U, WA B

Ecology, Evolution, Systematics and Population Biology Related

Brigham Young U, UT B
U of Colorado at Boulder, CO B

E-Commerce

Dominican U of California, CA B
ITT Tech Inst, Tucson, AZ B
ITT Tech Inst, Anaheim, CA B
ITT Tech Inst, Rancho Cordova, CA B
ITT Tech Inst, San Bernardino, CA B
ITT Tech Inst, San Diego, CA B
ITT Tech Inst, Sylmar, CA B
ITT Tech Inst, Torrance, CA B
ITT Tech Inst, West Covina, CA B
ITT Tech Inst, CO B
ITT Tech Inst, ID B
ITT Tech Inst, NV B
ITT Tech Inst, NM B
ITT Tech Inst, OR B
ITT Tech Inst, UT B
ITT Tech Inst, Bothell, WA B
ITT Tech Inst, Seattle, WA B
ITT Tech Inst, Spokane, WA B
Mt. Sierra Coll, CA B
U of Phoenix–Hawaii Campus, HI B
U of Phoenix–Idaho Campus, ID B
Westwood Coll–Anaheim, CA B
Westwood Coll–Denver South, CO B
Westwood Coll–Los Angeles, CA B

Econometrics and Quantitative Economics

The Colorado Coll, CO B
San Diego State U, CA B
U of California, San Diego, CA B

Economics

Albertson Coll of Idaho, ID B
Arizona State U, AZ B
Birmingham-Southern Coll, AL B
Boise State U, ID B
Brigham Young U, UT B
California Inst of Technology, CA B
California Lutheran U, CA B
California Polytechnic State U, San Luis Obispo, CA B
California State Polytechnic U, Pomona, CA B
California State U, Bakersfield, CA B
California State U, Chico, CA B
California State U, Dominguez Hills, CA B
California State U, Fresno, CA B
California State U, Fullerton, CA B
California State U, Hayward, CA B
California State U, Long Beach, CA B
California State U, Los Angeles, CA B
California State U, Sacramento, CA B
California State U, San Bernardino, CA B
California State U, San Marcos, CA B
California State U, Stanislaus, CA B
Central Washington U, WA B
Claremont McKenna Coll, CA B
The Colorado Coll, CO B
Colorado School of Mines, CO B
Colorado State U, CO B
Cornell Coll, IA B
Eastern Oregon U, OR B
Eastern Washington U, WA B
Eugene Lang Coll, New School U B
Fort Lewis Coll, CO B
Gonzaga U, WA B
Grand Canyon U, AZ B
Hawai'i Pacific U, HI B
Humboldt State U, CA B
Idaho State U, ID B
Lewis & Clark Coll, OR B
Linfield Coll, OR B
Loyola Marymount U, CA B
Metropolitan State Coll of Denver, CO B
Mills Coll, CA B
Montana State U–Bozeman, MT B
New Mexico State U, NM B
North Carolina Ag and Tech State U, NC B
Northern Arizona U, AZ B
Occidental Coll, CA B
Oregon State U, OR B
Pacific Lutheran U, WA B
Pacific U, OR B
Pepperdine U, Malibu, CA B
Pitzer Coll, CA B
Pomona Coll, CA B
Portland State U, OR B
Reed Coll, OR B
Regis U, CO B
Rocky Mountain Coll, MT B
Saint Martin's Coll, WA B
Saint Mary's Coll of California, CA B
San Diego State U, CA B
San Francisco State U, CA B
San Jose State U, CA B
Santa Clara U, CA B
Scripps Coll, CA B
Seattle Pacific U, WA B
Seattle U, WA B
Sonoma State U, CA B
Southern Oregon U, OR B
Southern Utah U, UT B
Stanford U, CA B
United States Air Force Academy, CO B

U of Alaska Anchorage, AK B
U of Alaska Fairbanks, AK B
The U of Arizona, AZ B
U of California, Berkeley, CA B
U of California, Davis, CA B
U of California, Irvine, CA B
U of California, Los Angeles, CA B
U of California, Riverside, CA B
U of California, San Diego, CA B
U of California, Santa Barbara, CA B
U of California, Santa Cruz, CA B
U of Colorado at Boulder, CO B
U of Colorado at Colorado Springs, CO B
U of Colorado at Denver, CO B
U of Denver, CO B
U of Hawaii at Hilo, HI B
U of Hawaii at Manoa, HI B
U of Idaho, ID B
The U of Montana–Missoula, MT B
U of Nevada, Las Vegas, NV B
U of New Mexico, NM B
U of Northern Colorado, CO B
U of Oregon, OR B
U of Puget Sound, WA B
U of Redlands, CA B
U of San Diego, CA B
U of San Francisco, CA B
U of Southern California, CA B
U of the Pacific, CA B
U of Utah, UT B
U of Washington, WA B
Utah State U, UT B
Walla Walla Coll, WA B
Washington State U, WA B
Weber State U, UT B
Western Oregon U, OR B
Western State Coll of Colorado, CO B
Western Washington U, WA B
Westmont Coll, CA B
Whitman Coll, WA B
Whitworth Coll, WA B
Willamette U, OR B

Economics Related

California State U, Chico, CA B
Claremont McKenna Coll, CA B
The Colorado Coll, CO B
Nevada State Coll at Henderson, NV B

Education

Biola U, CA B
Birmingham-Southern Coll, AL B
Boise State U, ID B
Brigham Young U–Hawaii, HI B
Carroll Coll, MT B
Christian Heritage Coll, CA B
Coll of the Southwest, NM B
Colorado State U-Pueblo, CO B
Concordia U, OR B
Eastern Oregon U, OR B
Eugene Lang Coll, New School U B
Fort Lewis Coll, CO B
Fresno Pacific U, CA B
Humboldt State U, CA B
Lehigh U, PA B
The Master's Coll and Seminary, CA B
Montana State U–Billings, MT B
Mount St. Mary's Coll, CA B
Nevada State Coll at Henderson, NV B
New Coll of California, CA B
New Mexico Highlands U, NM B
North Carolina Ag and Tech State U, NC B
Northern Arizona U, AZ B
Northwest Coll, WA B
Notre Dame de Namur U, CA B
Pacific Lutheran U, WA B
Pacific Union Coll, CA B
Pacific U, OR B
Pepperdine U, Malibu, CA B
Prescott Coll, AZ B
Regis U, CO B
Rocky Mountain Coll, MT B
Saint Martin's Coll, WA B
Shasta Bible Coll, CA B
Southern Utah U, UT B
U of Alaska Anchorage, AK B
U of Alaska Fairbanks, AK B
U of Alaska Southeast, AK B
U of California, Los Angeles, CA B
U of Hawaii at Manoa, HI B
U of La Verne, CA B
The U of Montana–Missoula, MT B
The U of Montana–Western, MT B
U of Nevada, Las Vegas, NV B
U of New Mexico, NM B
U of Oregon, OR B
U of Portland, OR B
U of Redlands, CA B
U of San Diego, CA B
U of San Francisco, CA B
U of Southern California, CA B
U of the Pacific, CA B
U of Utah, UT B
U of Washington, WA B
Vanguard U of Southern California, CA B
Warner Pacific Coll, OR B
Western Baptist Coll, OR B
Western State Coll of Colorado, CO B
Western Washington U, WA B
Westmont Coll, CA B
William Jessup U, CA B

Educational Assessment, Evaluation, and Research Related

Jones International U, CO B

Educational/Instructional Media Design

California State U, Chico, CA B
Jones International U, CO B
Western Oregon U, OR B

Educational Leadership and Administration

Jones International U, CO B
Northern Arizona U, AZ B
Shasta Bible Coll, CA A
U of California, Los Angeles, CA B
U of Oregon, OR B
U of San Francisco, CA B
Western Washington U, WA B

Education (K-12)

Biola U, CA B
Christian Heritage Coll, CA B
Metropolitan State Coll of Denver, CO B
Pacific Union Coll, CA B
The U of Montana–Western, MT B
Walla Walla Coll, WA B

Education (Multiple Levels)

George Fox U, OR B
Northwest Christian Coll, OR B
U of Great Falls, MT B
U of Washington, WA B
Utah State U, UT B
Western Washington U, WA B

Education Related

Alliant International U, CA B
Brigham Young U, UT B
Dominican U of California, CA B
Eastern Washington U, WA B
Marylhurst U, OR B

Education (Specific Levels and Methods) Related

Brigham Young U, UT B
Sheldon Jackson Coll, AK A

Education (Specific Subject Areas) Related

Brigham Young U, UT B
Eastern Washington U, WA B
Northern Arizona U, AZ B
San Diego State U, CA B
The U of Arizona, AZ B
U of Hawaii at Manoa, HI B
U of Nevada, Reno, NV B
Utah State U, UT B

Electrical and Electronic Engineering Technologies Related

Boise State U, ID A

Electrical, Electronic and Communications Engineering Technology

Arizona State U East, AZ B
Boise State U, ID A
California State Polytechnic U, Pomona, CA B
California State U, Long Beach, CA B
Central Washington U, WA B
Cogswell Polytechnical Coll, CA B
DeVry U, Phoenix, AZ A,B
DeVry U, Fremont, CA A,B
DeVry U, Long Beach, CA A,B
DeVry U, Pomona, CA A,B
DeVry U, West Hills, CA A,B
DeVry U, Colorado Springs, CO A,B
DeVry U, Westminster, CO A
DeVry U, Federal Way, WA A,B
Eastern Washington U, WA B
Great Basin Coll, NV A
Idaho State U, ID A
ITT Tech Inst, Tucson, AZ B
ITT Tech Inst, Anaheim, CA B
ITT Tech Inst, Rancho Cordova, CA B
ITT Tech Inst, San Bernardino, CA B
ITT Tech Inst, San Diego, CA B
ITT Tech Inst, Sylmar, CA B
ITT Tech Inst, Torrance, CA B
ITT Tech Inst, West Covina, CA B
ITT Tech Inst, CO B
ITT Tech Inst, ID B
ITT Tech Inst, NV B
ITT Tech Inst, NM B
ITT Tech Inst, OR B
ITT Tech Inst, UT B
ITT Tech Inst, Bothell, WA B
ITT Tech Inst, Seattle, WA B
ITT Tech Inst, Spokane, WA B
Metropolitan State Coll of Denver, CO B
Oregon Inst of Technology, OR A,B
Pacific Union Coll, CA B
Southern Utah U, UT A,B
U of Alaska Anchorage, AK A
U of California, Santa Barbara, CA B
The U of Montana–Missoula, MT A
Utah Valley State Coll, UT A
Weber State U, UT A,B
Western Washington U, WA B
Westwood Coll–Denver South, CO B
Westwood Coll–Denver North, CO A,B

Electrical, Electronics and Communications Engineering

Arizona State U, AZ B
Boise State U, ID B
Brigham Young U, UT B
California Inst of Technology, CA B
California Polytechnic State U, San Luis Obispo, CA B
California State Polytechnic U, Pomona, CA B
California State U, Chico, CA B
California State U, Fresno, CA B
California State U, Fullerton, CA B
California State U, Long Beach, CA B
California State U, Los Angeles, CA B
California State U, Sacramento, CA B
Cogswell Polytechnical Coll, CA B
Colorado School of Mines, CO B
Colorado State U, CO B
Embry-Riddle Aeronautical U, AZ B
Gonzaga U, WA B
Henry Cogswell Coll, WA B
Idaho State U, ID B
Lehigh U, PA B
Loyola Marymount U, CA B
Montana State U–Bozeman, MT B
New Mexico Inst of Mining and Technology, NM B
New Mexico State U, NM B
North Carolina Ag and Tech State U, NC B
Northern Arizona U, AZ B
Northwestern Polytechnic U, CA B
Oregon State U, OR B
Pacific Lutheran U, WA B
Pacific States U, CA B
Portland State U, OR B
San Diego State U, CA B
San Francisco State U, CA B
San Jose State U, CA B
Santa Clara U, CA B
Seattle Pacific U, WA B
Seattle U, WA B
Stanford U, CA B
United States Air Force Academy, CO B
U of Alaska Fairbanks, AK B
The U of Arizona, AZ B
U of California, Berkeley, CA B
U of California, Davis, CA B
U of California, Irvine, CA B
U of California, Los Angeles, CA B

A—associate degree; B—bachelor's degree

U of California, Riverside, CA B
U of California, San Diego, CA B
U of California, Santa Barbara, CA B
U of California, Santa Cruz, CA B
U of Colorado at Boulder, CO B
U of Colorado at Colorado Springs, CO B
U of Colorado at Denver, CO B
U of Denver, CO B
U of Hawaii at Manoa, HI B
U of Idaho, ID B
U of Nevada, Las Vegas, NV B
U of Nevada, Reno, NV B
U of New Mexico, NM B
U of Portland, OR B
U of San Diego, CA B
U of Southern California, CA B
U of the Pacific, CA B
U of Utah, UT B
U of Washington, WA B
U of Wyoming, WY B
Utah State U, UT B
Walla Walla Coll, WA B
Washington State U, WA B

Electrical/Electronics Equipment Installation and Repair

Idaho State U, ID A
Lewis-Clark State Coll, ID A,B

Electrocardiograph Technology

DeVry U, Westminster, CO A

Electromechanical Technology

Idaho State U, ID A
Utah Valley State Coll, UT A
Walla Walla Coll, WA A

Elementary Education

Adams State Coll, CO B
Alaska Pacific U, AK A,B
American Indian Coll of the Assemblies of God, Inc., AZ B
Arizona State U, AZ B
Arizona State U East, AZ B
Arizona State U West, AZ B
Biola U, CA B
Birmingham-Southern Coll, AL B
Blackfeet Comm Coll, MT A
Boise State U, ID B
Brigham Young U, UT B
Brigham Young U–Hawaii, HI B
California State U, Fresno, CA B
Carroll Coll, MT B
Cascade Coll, OR B
Central Washington U, WA B
Chaminade U of Honolulu, HI B
Christian Heritage Coll, CA B
City U, WA B
Coll of Santa Fe, NM B
Coll of the Southwest, NM B
Colorado State U-Pueblo, CO B
Concordia U, OR B
Cornell Coll, IA B
Eastern New Mexico U, NM B
Eastern Washington U, WA B
Fort Lewis Coll, CO B
Fresno Pacific U, CA B
George Fox U, OR B
Gonzaga U, WA B
Grand Canyon U, AZ B
Great Basin Coll, NV A,B
Humboldt State U, CA B
Idaho State U, ID B
Lewis-Clark State Coll, ID B
Linfield Coll, OR B
The Master's Coll and Seminary, CA B
Montana State U–Billings, MT B
Montana State U–Bozeman, MT B
Mount St. Mary's Coll, CA B
New Mexico Highlands U, NM A,B
New Mexico State U, NM B
North Carolina Ag and Tech State U, NC B
Northern Arizona U, AZ B
Northwest Coll, WA B
Northwest Nazarene U, ID B
Notre Dame de Namur U, CA B
Pacific Lutheran U, WA B
Pacific Oaks Coll, CA B
Pacific Union Coll, CA B
Pacific U, OR B
Pepperdine U, Malibu, CA B
Prescott Coll, AZ B
Regis U, CO B
Rocky Mountain Coll, MT B
Saint Martin's Coll, WA B
Sheldon Jackson Coll, AK B
Simpson Coll and Graduate School, CA B
Southern Utah U, UT B
Southwestern Coll, AZ B
U of Alaska Anchorage, AK B
U of Alaska Fairbanks, AK B
U of Alaska Southeast, AK B
The U of Arizona, AZ B
U of Great Falls, MT B
U of Hawaii at Hilo, HI B
U of Hawaii at Manoa, HI B
U of Idaho, ID B
U of La Verne, CA B
The U of Montana–Missoula, MT B
The U of Montana–Western, MT B
U of Nevada, Las Vegas, NV B
U of Nevada, Reno, NV B
U of New Mexico, NM B
U of Portland, OR B
U of Redlands, CA B
U of San Francisco, CA B
U of Utah, UT B
U of Washington, WA B
U of Wyoming, WY B
Utah State U, UT B
Utah Valley State Coll, UT A,B
Walla Walla Coll, WA B
Warner Pacific Coll, OR B
Washington State U, WA B
Weber State U, UT B
Western Baptist Coll, OR B
Western State Coll of Colorado, CO B
Western Washington U, WA B
Westminster Coll, UT B
Westmont Coll, CA B
Whitworth Coll, WA B

Emergency Medical Technology (Emt Paramedic)

Central Washington U, WA B
Idaho State U, ID A
Loma Linda U, CA B
Montana State U–Billings, MT A
U of Alaska Anchorage, AK A
Weber State U, UT A

Engineering

California Inst of Technology, CA B
California State U, Fullerton, CA B
California State U, Long Beach, CA B
California State U, Los Angeles, CA B
Carroll Coll, MT B
Claremont McKenna Coll, CA B
Cogswell Polytechnical Coll, CA B
Colorado School of Mines, CO B
Embry-Riddle Aeronautical U, AZ B
George Fox U, OR B
Gonzaga U, WA B
Harvey Mudd Coll, CA B
Idaho State U, ID B
Mills Coll, CA B
Montana Tech of The U of Montana, MT A,B
National American U, NM B
New Mexico Highlands U, NM B
New Mexico Inst of Mining and Technology, NM B
Northern Arizona U, AZ B
Oregon State U, OR B
Pacific Union Coll, CA B
Pitzer Coll, CA B
Saint Mary's Coll of California, CA B
San Diego State U, CA B
San Jose State U, CA B
Santa Clara U, CA B
Stanford U, CA B
United States Air Force Academy, CO B
The U of Arizona, AZ B
U of California, Davis, CA B
U of California, Los Angeles, CA B
U of California, San Diego, CA B
U of Denver, CO B
U of Hawaii at Manoa, HI B
U of Idaho, ID B
U of New Mexico, NM B
U of Portland, OR B
U of Southern California, CA B
U of Utah, UT B
U of Washington, WA B
Utah Valley State Coll, UT A
Walla Walla Coll, WA B

Engineering/Industrial Management

California State U, Long Beach, CA B
Claremont McKenna Coll, CA B
Fort Lewis Coll, CO B
U of Portland, OR B
U of the Pacific, CA B
Washington State U, WA B

Engineering Mechanics

Lehigh U, PA B
New Mexico Inst of Mining and Technology, NM B
United States Air Force Academy, CO B

Engineering Physics

California Inst of Technology, CA B
Colorado School of Mines, CO B
Colorado State U, CO B
Lehigh U, PA B
Loyola Marymount U, CA B
North Carolina Ag and Tech State U, NC B
Northern Arizona U, AZ B
Northwest Nazarene U, ID B
Oregon State U, OR B
Pacific Lutheran U, WA B
Point Loma Nazarene U, CA B
Santa Clara U, CA B
The U of Arizona, AZ B
U of California, Berkeley, CA B
U of California, San Diego, CA B
U of Colorado at Boulder, CO B
U of Nevada, Reno, NV B
U of the Pacific, CA B
Westmont Coll, CA B

Engineering Related

California State U, Chico, CA B
California State U, Long Beach, CA B
Claremont McKenna Coll, CA B
Hawai'i Pacific U, HI B
Idaho State U, ID B
Lehigh U, PA B
Montana State U–Billings, MT A
Pacific Union Coll, CA B
The U of Arizona, AZ B
Western Washington U, WA B

Engineering Science

California Polytechnic State U, San Luis Obispo, CA B
California State U, Fullerton, CA B
Claremont McKenna Coll, CA B
Colorado School of Mines, CO B
Colorado State U, CO B
Montana Tech of The U of Montana, MT B
Pacific Lutheran U, WA B
Seattle Pacific U, WA B
United States Air Force Academy, CO B
U of California, Berkeley, CA B
U of California, San Diego, CA B
U of New Mexico, NM B
U of Portland, OR B
Washington State U, WA B

Engineering Technologies Related

California Maritime Academy, CA B
California State Polytechnic U, Pomona, CA B

Engineering Technology

Brigham Young U, UT B
California State Polytechnic U, Pomona, CA B
California State U, Long Beach, CA B
Colorado State U-Pueblo, CO B
Eastern New Mexico U, NM B
Eastern Washington U, WA B
Montana Tech of The U of Montana, MT A
New Mexico State U, NM A,B
Pacific Union Coll, CA A,B
U of Alaska Anchorage, AK A
Walla Walla Coll, WA B
Western Washington U, WA B

English

Adams State Coll, CO B
Albertson Coll of Idaho, ID B
Arizona State U, AZ B
Arizona State U West, AZ B
Azusa Pacific U, CA B
Biola U, CA B
Birmingham-Southern Coll, AL B
Boise State U, ID B
Brigham Young U, UT B
Brigham Young U–Hawaii, HI B
California Baptist U, CA B
California Lutheran U, CA B
California Polytechnic State U, San Luis Obispo, CA B
California State Polytechnic U, Pomona, CA B
California State U, Bakersfield, CA B
California State U, Chico, CA B
California State U, Dominguez Hills, CA B
California State U, Fresno, CA B

California State U, Fullerton, CA B
California State U, Hayward, CA B
California State U, Long Beach, CA B
California State U, Los Angeles, CA B
California State U, Sacramento, CA B
California State U, San Bernardino, CA B
California State U, San Marcos, CA B
California State U, Stanislaus, CA B
Carroll Coll, MT A,B
Cascade Coll, OR B
Central Washington U, WA B
Chaminade U of Honolulu, HI B
Chapman U, CA B
Christian Heritage Coll, CA B
Claremont McKenna Coll, CA B
Coll of Santa Fe, NM A,B
Coll of the Southwest, NM B
Colorado Christian U, CO B
The Colorado Coll, CO B
Colorado State U, CO B
Colorado State U-Pueblo, CO B
Concordia U, CA B
Concordia U, OR B
Cornell Coll, IA B
Dominican U of California, CA B
Eastern New Mexico U, NM B
Eastern Oregon U, OR B
Eastern Washington U, WA B
Eugene Lang Coll, New School U B
Fort Lewis Coll, CO B
Fresno Pacific U, CA A,B
George Fox U, OR B
Gonzaga U, WA B
Grand Canyon U, AZ B
Great Basin Coll, NV A
Hawai'i Pacific U, HI B
Holy Names U, CA B
Humboldt State U, CA B
Idaho State U, ID A,B
Lewis & Clark Coll, OR B
Lewis-Clark State Coll, ID B
Linfield Coll, OR B
Loyola Marymount U, CA B
The Master's Coll and Seminary, CA B
Metropolitan State Coll of Denver, CO B
Mills Coll, CA B
Montana State U–Billings, MT B
Montana State U–Bozeman, MT B
Mount St. Mary's Coll, CA B
Naropa U, CO B
National U, CA B
Nevada State Coll at Henderson, NV B
New Mexico Highlands U, NM B
New Mexico State U, NM B
North Carolina Ag and Tech State U, NC B
Northern Arizona U, AZ B
Northwest Coll, WA B
Northwest Nazarene U, ID B
Notre Dame de Namur U, CA B
Oregon State U, OR B
Pacific Lutheran U, WA B
Pacific Union Coll, CA B
Pacific U, OR B
Pepperdine U, Malibu, CA B
Pitzer Coll, CA B
Point Loma Nazarene U, CA B
Pomona Coll, CA B
Portland State U, OR B
Reed Coll, OR B
Regis U, CO B
Rocky Mountain Coll, MT B
St. John's Coll, NM B
Saint Martin's Coll, WA B
Saint Mary's Coll of California, CA B
San Diego State U, CA B
San Francisco State U, CA B
San Jose State U, CA B
Santa Clara U, CA B
Scripps Coll, CA B
Seattle Pacific U, WA B
Seattle U, WA B
Simpson Coll and Graduate School, CA B
Sonoma State U, CA B
Southern Oregon U, OR B
Southern Utah U, UT B
Stanford U, CA B
United States Air Force Academy, CO B
U of Alaska Anchorage, AK B
U of Alaska Fairbanks, AK B
The U of Arizona, AZ B
U of California, Berkeley, CA B
U of California, Davis, CA B
U of California, Irvine, CA B
U of California, Los Angeles, CA B
U of California, Riverside, CA B
U of California, San Diego, CA B
U of California, Santa Barbara, CA B
U of Colorado at Boulder, CO B
U of Colorado at Colorado Springs, CO B
U of Colorado at Denver, CO B
U of Denver, CO B
U of Great Falls, MT B
U of Hawaii at Hilo, HI B
U of Hawaii at Manoa, HI B
U of Idaho, ID B
U of La Verne, CA B
The U of Montana–Missoula, MT B
The U of Montana–Western, MT B
U of Nevada, Las Vegas, NV B
U of Nevada, Reno, NV B
U of New Mexico, NM B
U of Northern Colorado, CO B
U of Oregon, OR B
U of Portland, OR B
U of Puget Sound, WA B
U of Redlands, CA B
U of San Diego, CA B
U of San Francisco, CA B
U of Southern California, CA B
U of the Pacific, CA B
U of the West, CA B
U of Utah, UT B
U of Washington, WA B
U of Wyoming, WY B
Utah State U, UT B
Utah Valley State Coll, UT A,B
Vanguard U of Southern California, CA B
Walla Walla Coll, WA B
Warner Pacific Coll, OR B
Washington State U, WA B
Weber State U, UT B
Western Baptist Coll, OR B
Western Oregon U, OR B
Western State Coll of Colorado, CO B
Western Washington U, WA B
Westminster Coll, UT B
Westmont Coll, CA B
Whitman Coll, WA B
Whitworth Coll, WA B
Willamette U, OR B

English As A Second/Foreign Language (Teaching)

Alaska Bible Coll, AK B
Brigham Young U, UT B
Brigham Young U–Hawaii, HI B
Carroll Coll, MT B
Eastern Washington U, WA B
Hawai'i Pacific U, HI B
Northern Arizona U, AZ B
Northwest Coll, WA B
U of California, Los Angeles, CA B
U of Hawaii at Manoa, HI B
The U of Montana–Missoula, MT B
U of Washington, WA B

English Composition

Brigham Young U, UT B
U of Colorado at Denver, CO B
U of Great Falls, MT B
U of Nevada, Reno, NV B

English Language and Literature Related

Fort Lewis Coll, CO B
Saint Mary's Coll of California, CA B
U of California, Los Angeles, CA B
U of California, Santa Cruz, CA B
U of Great Falls, MT B
U of Nevada, Reno, NV B

English/Language Arts Teacher Education

Brigham Young U, UT B
Brigham Young U–Hawaii, HI B
California State U, Chico, CA B
California State U, Long Beach, CA B
Carroll Coll, MT B
Central Washington U, WA B
Chapman U, CA B
Coll of Santa Fe, NM B
Colorado State U, CO B
Concordia U, OR B
Eastern Washington U, WA B
George Fox U, OR B
Lewis-Clark State Coll, ID B
Montana State U–Billings, MT B
Nevada State Coll at Henderson, NV B
Northern Arizona U, AZ B
Northwest Coll, WA B
Northwest Nazarene U, ID B
Prescott Coll, AZ B
Rocky Mountain Coll, MT B
San Diego State U, CA B
Seattle Pacific U, WA B
Simpson Coll and Graduate School, CA B
The U of Arizona, AZ B
U of Great Falls, MT B
U of Hawaii at Manoa, HI B
The U of Montana–Western, MT B
U of Nevada, Reno, NV B
Utah Valley State Coll, UT B
Weber State U, UT B
Western Baptist Coll, OR B
Westmont Coll, CA B

English Literature (British and Commonwealth)

Marylhurst U, OR B
U of Southern California, CA B

Entomology

Colorado State U, CO B
Oregon State U, OR B
U of California, Davis, CA B
U of California, Riverside, CA B
U of Hawaii at Manoa, HI B
U of Idaho, ID B
Utah State U, UT B
Washington State U, WA B

Entrepreneurship

Blackfeet Comm Coll, MT A
Brigham Young U, UT B
California State U, Fullerton, CA B
Hawai'i Pacific U, HI B
LDS Business Coll, UT A
The U of Arizona, AZ B
U of Nevada, Reno, NV B
U of Phoenix–Phoenix Campus, AZ B
Utah Valley State Coll, UT B
Washington State U, WA B

Environmental Biology

California Polytechnic State U, San Luis Obispo, CA B
Colorado State U-Pueblo, CO B
Eastern Washington U, WA B
Fort Lewis Coll, CO B
Grand Canyon U, AZ B
Humboldt State U, CA B
The Master's Coll and Seminary, CA B
New Mexico Inst of Mining and Technology, NM B
Oregon State U, OR B
U of California, Davis, CA B
U of La Verne, CA B
Western Washington U, WA B

Environmental Design/Architecture

Art Center Coll of Design, CA B
Montana State U–Bozeman, MT B
Otis Coll of Art and Design, CA B
Prescott Coll, AZ B
U of California, Irvine, CA B
U of Colorado at Boulder, CO B
U of Hawaii at Manoa, HI B
U of New Mexico, NM B

Environmental Education

Prescott Coll, AZ B
Sonoma State U, CA B
The U of Montana–Missoula, MT B
Western Washington U, WA B

Environmental Engineering Technology

California State U, Long Beach, CA B
Utah Valley State Coll, UT A

Environmental/Environmental Health Engineering

California Inst of Technology, CA B
California Polytechnic State U, San Luis Obispo, CA B
Colorado School of Mines, CO B
Colorado State U, CO B
Humboldt State U, CA B

A—associate degree; B—bachelor's degree

Montana Tech of The U of Montana, MT B
New Mexico Inst of Mining and Technology, NM B
Northern Arizona U, AZ B
Oregon State U, OR B
Seattle U, WA B
Stanford U, CA B
United States Air Force Academy, CO B
U of California, Berkeley, CA B
U of California, Irvine, CA B
U of California, Riverside, CA B
U of Colorado at Boulder, CO B
U of Nevada, Reno, NV B
U of Southern California, CA B
U of Utah, UT B
Utah State U, UT B
Washington State U, WA B

Environmental Health
Boise State U, ID B
Colorado State U, CO B
Colorado State U-Pueblo, CO B
New Mexico State U, NM B
Oregon State U, OR B
U of California, Los Angeles, CA B
U of Utah, UT B
U of Washington, WA B

Environmental Science
Alaska Pacific U, AK B
Brigham Young U, UT B
California State U, Long Beach, CA B
Chapman U, CA B
Coll of Santa Fe, NM B
The Colorado Coll, CO B
Eastern Washington U, WA B
Hawai'i Pacific U, HI B
Mills Coll, CA B
Nevada State Coll at Henderson, NV B
Northwest Coll, WA B
Pitzer Coll, CA B
Rocky Mountain Coll, MT B
Santa Clara U, CA B
Scripps Coll, CA B
Sheldon Jackson Coll, AK B
U of California, Berkeley, CA B
U of California, Los Angeles, CA B
U of Oregon, OR B
U of San Francisco, CA B
Washington State U, WA B
Western Washington U, WA B
Willamette U, OR B

Environmental Studies
Boise State U, ID B
California State U, Hayward, CA B
California State U, Sacramento, CA B
California State U, San Bernardino, CA B
Carroll Coll, MT B
Chaminade U of Honolulu, HI B
Claremont McKenna Coll, CA B
Coll of the Southwest, NM B
Concordia U, OR B
Cornell Coll, IA B
Dominican U of California, CA B
The Evergreen State Coll, WA B
Great Basin Coll, NV A
Hawai'i Pacific U, HI B
Humboldt State U, CA B
Lehigh U, PA B
Lewis & Clark Coll, OR B
Linfield Coll, OR B
Marylhurst U, OR B
Metropolitan State Coll of Denver, CO B
Mills Coll, CA B
Montana State U–Billings, MT B
Montana State U–Bozeman, MT B
Naropa U, CO B
New Mexico Highlands U, NM B
New Mexico Inst of Mining and Technology, NM B
New Mexico State U, NM B
Northern Arizona U, AZ B
Occidental Coll, CA B
Oregon Inst of Technology, OR B
Oregon State U, OR B
Pacific Lutheran U, WA B
Pacific U, OR B
Pitzer Coll, CA B
Pomona Coll, CA B
Portland State U, OR B
Prescott Coll, AZ B
Regis U, CO B
Rocky Mountain Coll, MT B
San Diego State U, CA B
San Jose State U, CA B
Santa Clara U, CA B
Scripps Coll, CA B
Seattle U, WA B
Sierra Nevada Coll, NV B
Sonoma State U, CA B
Southern Oregon U, OR B
Stanford U, CA B
U of Alaska Southeast, AK B
The U of Arizona, AZ B
U of California, Berkeley, CA B
U of California, Riverside, CA B
U of California, San Diego, CA B
U of California, Santa Barbara, CA B
U of California, Santa Cruz, CA B
U of Colorado at Boulder, CO B
U of Denver, CO B
U of Idaho, ID B
The U of Montana–Missoula, MT B
The U of Montana–Western, MT B
U of Nevada, Las Vegas, NV B
U of Oregon, OR B
U of Portland, OR B
U of Redlands, CA B
U of San Francisco, CA B
U of Southern California, CA B
U of the Pacific, CA B
U of Utah, UT B
U of Washington, WA B
U of Wyoming, WY B
Walla Walla Coll, WA B
Western State Coll of Colorado, CO B
Western Washington U, WA B
Whitman Coll, WA B

Epidemiology
U of California, Los Angeles, CA B

Equestrian Studies
Colorado State U, CO B
Oregon State U, OR B
Rocky Mountain Coll, MT B
The U of Montana–Western, MT A

Ethics
St. John's Coll, NM B

Ethnic, Cultural Minority, and Gender Studies Related
California State Polytechnic U, Pomona, CA B
California State U, Chico, CA B
California State U, Sacramento, CA B
Claremont McKenna Coll, CA B
The Colorado Coll, CO B
Cornell Coll, IA B
Marylhurst U, OR B
U of California, Berkeley, CA B
U of Hawaii at Manoa, HI B
U of Oregon, OR B
Washington State U, WA B

European History
Chapman U, CA B
Pitzer Coll, CA B
U of California, Santa Cruz, CA B

European Studies
Claremont McKenna Coll, CA B
Fort Lewis Coll, CO B
Loyola Marymount U, CA B
Pitzer Coll, CA B
Saint Mary's Coll of California, CA B
San Diego State U, CA B
Scripps Coll, CA B
Seattle Pacific U, WA B
U of California, Irvine, CA B
U of California, Los Angeles, CA B
U of New Mexico, NM B
U of Washington, WA B

European Studies (Central and Eastern)
Brigham Young U, UT B
Portland State U, OR B
U of Oregon, OR B

European Studies (Western)
Claremont McKenna Coll, CA B
Seattle U, WA B

Evolutionary Biology
Oregon State U, OR B
San Diego State U, CA B
The U of Arizona, AZ B

Executive Assistant/Executive Secretary
LDS Business Coll, UT A
Montana Tech of The U of Montana, MT A
The U of Montana–Missoula, MT A
Utah Valley State Coll, UT A

Exercise Physiology
Chapman U, CA B

Experimental Psychology
Colorado State U-Pueblo, CO B
New Mexico Inst of Mining and Technology, NM B

Family and Community Services
Oregon State U, OR B
Southern Utah U, UT B
U of California, Santa Cruz, CA B
U of Utah, UT B

Family and Consumer Economics Related
Brigham Young U, UT B
California State U, Fresno, CA B
California State U, Sacramento, CA B
Oregon State U, OR B
Seattle Pacific U, WA B
U of Hawaii at Manoa, HI B
U of Utah, UT B
Utah State U, UT B

Family and Consumer Sciences/Home Economics Teacher Education
Colorado State U, CO B
George Fox U, OR B
New Mexico State U, NM B
North Carolina Ag and Tech State U, NC B
Seattle Pacific U, WA B
Southern Utah U, UT B
The U of Arizona, AZ B
U of Hawaii at Manoa, HI B
U of Idaho, ID B
U of Nevada, Reno, NV B
U of New Mexico, NM B
U of Utah, UT B
Utah State U, UT B

Family and Consumer Sciences/Human Sciences
Brigham Young U, UT B
California State Polytechnic U, Pomona, CA B
California State U, Long Beach, CA B
Central Washington U, WA B
Colorado State U, CO B
Eastern New Mexico U, NM B
George Fox U, OR B
Idaho State U, ID B
The Master's Coll and Seminary, CA B
Montana State U–Bozeman, MT B
North Carolina Ag and Tech State U, NC B
Oregon State U, OR B
Point Loma Nazarene U, CA B
San Francisco State U, CA B
Southern Utah U, UT B
U of Alaska Anchorage, AK A
U of Hawaii at Manoa, HI B
U of New Mexico, NM B
U of Utah, UT B
U of Wyoming, WY B

Family and Consumer Sciences/Human Sciences Business Services Related
Brigham Young U, UT B

Family and Consumer Sciences/Human Sciences Related
California State U, Long Beach, CA B

Family Psychology
Western Baptist Coll, OR B

Family Resource Management
Arizona State U, AZ B
Brigham Young U, UT B
George Fox U, OR B
U of Utah, UT B

Family Systems
Brigham Young U, UT B
Point Loma Nazarene U, CA B
Weber State U, UT B

Farm and Ranch Management
California Polytechnic State U, San Luis Obispo, CA B
California State Polytechnic U, Pomona, CA B
Colorado State U, CO B
Idaho State U, ID A,B

Fashion/Apparel Design
Academy of Art U, CA A,B
American InterContinental U, CA A,B
The Art Inst of California–San Francisco, CA A,B
The Art Inst of Portland, OR A,B
The Art Inst of Seattle, WA A
California Coll of the Arts, CA B
Oregon State U, OR B
Otis Coll of Art and Design, CA B
Woodbury U, CA B

Fashion Merchandising
Academy of Art U, CA A,B
American InterContinental U, CA A,B
The Art Inst of Seattle, WA A
California State U, Long Beach, CA B
Central Washington U, WA B
George Fox U, OR B
Oregon State U, OR B
The U of Montana–Missoula, MT B
Utah State U, UT B
Weber State U, UT A
Woodbury U, CA B

Fiber, Textile and Weaving Arts
Academy of Art U, CA A,B
California Coll of the Arts, CA B
California State U, Long Beach, CA B
Colorado State U, CO B
Oregon State U, OR B
U of Oregon, OR B
U of Washington, WA B
Western Washington U, WA B

Filipino/Tagalog
U of Hawaii at Manoa, HI B

Film/Cinema Studies
Academy of Art U, CA A,B
Art Center Coll of Design, CA B
Brigham Young U, UT B
California Coll of the Arts, CA B
California Inst of the Arts, CA B
California State U, Long Beach, CA B
Chapman U, CA B
Claremont McKenna Coll, CA B
Coll of Santa Fe, NM B
The Colorado Coll, CO B
Columbia Coll Hollywood, CA B
Pitzer Coll, CA B
Pomona Coll, CA B
Prescott Coll, AZ B
San Francisco Art Inst, CA B
San Francisco State U, CA B
U of California, Berkeley, CA B
U of California, Irvine, CA B
U of California, Los Angeles, CA B
U of California, San Diego, CA B
U of California, Santa Barbara, CA B
U of California, Santa Cruz, CA B
U of Colorado at Boulder, CO B
U of Nevada, Las Vegas, NV B
U of New Mexico, NM B
U of Southern California, CA B
U of Utah, UT B
Whitman Coll, WA B

Film/Video and Photographic Arts Related
Art Center Coll of Design, CA B
The Art Inst of Seattle, WA A
Brigham Young U, UT B
California Inst of the Arts, CA B
Rocky Mountain Coll of Art & Design, CO B
Scripps Coll, CA B

Finance
Arizona State U, AZ B
Boise State U, ID B
California State Polytechnic U, Pomona, CA B
California State U, Bakersfield, CA B
California State U, Chico, CA B
California State U, Dominguez Hills, CA B
California State U, Fresno, CA B
California State U, Fullerton, CA B
California State U, Hayward, CA B
California State U, Long Beach, CA B
California State U, Sacramento, CA B
California State U, San Bernardino, CA B
Carroll Coll, MT B
Colorado State U, CO B
Colorado State U-Pueblo, CO B
Eastern New Mexico U, NM B
Eastern Washington U, WA B
Fort Lewis Coll, CO B
Fresno Pacific U, CA B
Golden Gate U, CA B
Gonzaga U, WA B
Grand Canyon U, AZ B
Hawai'i Pacific U, HI A,B
Idaho State U, ID B
Lehigh U, PA B
Linfield Coll, OR B
The Master's Coll and Seminary, CA B
Metropolitan State Coll of Denver, CO B
Montana State U–Billings, MT B
Montana Tech of The U of Montana, MT B
National U, CA B
New Mexico State U, NM B
Northern Arizona U, AZ B
Northwest Nazarene U, ID B
Notre Dame de Namur U, CA B
Oregon State U, OR B
Pacific Lutheran U, WA B
Pacific Union Coll, CA B
Pacific U, OR B
Portland State U, OR B
Saint Martin's Coll, WA B
San Diego State U, CA B
San Francisco State U, CA B
San Jose State U, CA B
Santa Clara U, CA B
Seattle U, WA B
U of Alaska Anchorage, AK B
The U of Arizona, AZ B
U of Colorado at Boulder, CO B
U of Colorado at Colorado Springs, CO B
U of Denver, CO B
U of Hawaii at Manoa, HI B
U of Idaho, ID B
U of Nevada, Las Vegas, NV B
U of Nevada, Reno, NV B
U of Oregon, OR B
U of Phoenix–Hawaii Campus, HI B
U of Phoenix Online Campus, AZ B
U of Phoenix–Phoenix Campus, AZ B
U of Phoenix–Southern Arizona Campus, AZ B
U of Phoenix–Utah Campus, UT B
U of Portland, OR B
U of San Francisco, CA B
U of Utah, UT B
U of Wyoming, WY B
Utah State U, UT B
Utah Valley State Coll, UT B
Vanguard U of Southern California, CA B
Washington State U, WA B
Weber State U, UT B
Western Baptist Coll, OR B
Western Washington U, WA B
Westminster Coll, UT B

Finance and Financial Management Services Related
Saint Mary's Coll of California, CA B
San Diego State U, CA B
San Jose State U, CA B

Financial Planning and Services
Brigham Young U, UT B

Fine Arts Related
Art Center Coll of Design, CA B
California State U, Long Beach, CA B
Lehigh U, PA B
Oregon Coll of Art & Craft, OR B
San Diego State U, CA B
U of California, Los Angeles, CA B

Fine/Studio Arts
Academy of Art U, CA A,B
Arizona State U, AZ B
Art Center Coll of Design, CA B
Biola U, CA B
Birmingham-Southern Coll, AL B
Brigham Young U, UT B
California Coll of the Arts, CA B
California Inst of the Arts, CA B
California State U, Chico, CA B
California State U, Dominguez Hills, CA B
California State U, Fullerton, CA B
California State U, Hayward, CA B
California State U, Long Beach, CA B
California State U, Stanislaus, CA B
Chapman U, CA B
Claremont McKenna Coll, CA B
Coll of Santa Fe, NM B
Colorado Christian U, CO B
The Colorado Coll, CO B
Colorado State U, CO B
Cornish Coll of the Arts, WA B
Eastern Washington U, WA B
The Evergreen State Coll, WA B
Fort Lewis Coll, CO B
Grand Canyon U, AZ B
Humboldt State U, CA B
Laguna Coll of Art & Design, CA B
Loyola Marymount U, CA B
Mills Coll, CA B
Montana State U–Bozeman, MT B
Naropa U, CO B
New Mexico State U, NM B
Notre Dame de Namur U, CA B
Occidental Coll, CA B
Oregon State U, OR B
Otis Coll of Art and Design, CA B
Pacific Lutheran U, WA B
Pacific Union Coll, CA B
Pitzer Coll, CA B
Pomona Coll, CA B
Reed Coll, OR B
San Jose State U, CA B
Scripps Coll, CA B
Seattle U, WA B
Sierra Nevada Coll, NV B
Sonoma State U, CA B
The U of Arizona, AZ B
U of California, Irvine, CA B
U of California, Riverside, CA B
U of California, San Diego, CA B
U of California, Santa Barbara, CA B
U of Colorado at Boulder, CO B
U of Colorado at Colorado Springs, CO B
U of Colorado at Denver, CO B
U of Denver, CO B
U of Great Falls, MT B
U of Idaho, ID B
U of Northern Colorado, CO B
U of Oregon, OR B
U of Redlands, CA B
U of San Francisco, CA B
U of Southern California, CA B
U of the Pacific, CA B
Washington State U, WA B
Western State Coll of Colorado, CO B
Western Washington U, WA B
Whitworth Coll, WA B
Willamette U, OR B

Fire Protection and Safety Technology
Montana State U–Billings, MT A

Fire Science
Cogswell Polytechnical Coll, CA B
Eastern Oregon U, OR B
Idaho State U, ID A
Lewis-Clark State Coll, ID A,B
U of Alaska Anchorage, AK A
U of Alaska Fairbanks, AK A
Utah Valley State Coll, UT A

Fire Services Administration
California State U, Los Angeles, CA B
Utah Valley State Coll, UT B
Western Oregon U, OR B

Fish/Game Management
Humboldt State U, CA B
Oregon State U, OR B
U of Idaho, ID B

Fishing and Fisheries Sciences and Management
Colorado State U, CO B
Humboldt State U, CA B
U of Alaska Fairbanks, AK B
U of Washington, WA B

Folklore
U of Oregon, OR B

A—associate degree; B—bachelor's degree

Foods and Nutrition Related
California State U, Long Beach, CA B
Utah State U, UT B

Food Science
Brigham Young U, UT B
California Polytechnic State U, San Luis Obispo, CA B
North Carolina Ag and Tech State U, NC B
Oregon State U, OR B
San Jose State U, CA B
U of California, Davis, CA B
U of Idaho, ID B
U of Utah, UT B
Washington State U, WA B

Foods, Nutrition, and Wellness
Arizona State U East, AZ B
Bastyr U, WA B
California Polytechnic State U, San Luis Obispo, CA B
California State Polytechnic U, Pomona, CA B
California State U, Fresno, CA B
California State U, Los Angeles, CA B
California State U, San Bernardino, CA B
Central Washington U, WA B
Colorado State U, CO B
Idaho State U, ID B
The Master's Coll and Seminary, CA B
New Mexico State U, NM B
North Carolina Ag and Tech State U, NC B
Oregon State U, OR B
Pepperdine U, Malibu, CA B
Point Loma Nazarene U, CA B
San Diego State U, CA B
Seattle Pacific U, WA B
U of California, Davis, CA B
U of Idaho, ID B
U of Nevada, Reno, NV B
U of New Mexico, NM B
Washington State U, WA B

Food Technology and Processing
Brigham Young U, UT B

Foreign Languages and Literatures
Central Washington U, WA B
Colorado State U, CO B
Dominican U of California, CA B
Lewis & Clark Coll, OR B
Metropolitan State Coll of Denver, CO B
Montana State U–Bozeman, MT B
New Mexico State U, NM B
St. John's Coll, NM B
Scripps Coll, CA B
U of Alaska Anchorage, AK B
U of Alaska Fairbanks, AK B
U of California, San Diego, CA B
U of California, Santa Cruz, CA B
U of Idaho, ID B
The U of Montana–Missoula, MT B
U of New Mexico, NM B
U of Northern Colorado, CO B
U of Utah, UT B
Washington State U, WA B

Foreign Languages Related
Saint Mary's Coll of California, CA B
U of Alaska Fairbanks, AK A
U of California, Berkeley, CA B
U of California, Los Angeles, CA B
U of Hawaii at Manoa, HI B

Foreign Language Teacher Education
Brigham Young U, UT B
San Diego State U, CA B
The U of Arizona, AZ B
U of Hawaii at Manoa, HI B
U of Nevada, Reno, NV B

Forensic Science and Technology
Chaminade U of Honolulu, HI B
Northwest Nazarene U, ID B
Seattle U, WA B
U of Great Falls, MT B

Forest Engineering
Oregon State U, OR B
U of Washington, WA B

Forest/Forest Resources Management
The U of Montana–Missoula, MT B
U of Washington, WA B

Forestry
California Polytechnic State U, San Luis Obispo, CA B
Humboldt State U, CA B
Oregon State U, OR B
U of California, Berkeley, CA B
U of Idaho, ID B
The U of Montana–Missoula, MT B
U of Nevada, Reno, NV B
U of Washington, WA B
Utah State U, UT B
Washington State U, WA B

Forestry Related
Utah State U, UT B

Forest Sciences and Biology
Colorado State U, CO B
Northern Arizona U, AZ B
U of Washington, WA B

French
Arizona State U, AZ B
Birmingham-Southern Coll, AL B
Boise State U, ID B
Brigham Young U, UT B
California Lutheran U, CA B
California State U, Chico, CA B
California State U, Dominguez Hills, CA B
California State U, Fresno, CA B
California State U, Fullerton, CA B
California State U, Hayward, CA B
California State U, Long Beach, CA B
California State U, Los Angeles, CA B
California State U, Sacramento, CA B
California State U, San Bernardino, CA B
California State U, Stanislaus, CA B
Carroll Coll, MT B
Chapman U, CA B
Claremont McKenna Coll, CA B
The Colorado Coll, CO B
Colorado State U, CO B
Cornell Coll, IA B
Eastern Washington U, WA B
Gonzaga U, WA B
Humboldt State U, CA B
Idaho State U, ID A,B
Lehigh U, PA B
Lewis & Clark Coll, OR B
Linfield Coll, OR B
Loyola Marymount U, CA B
Mills Coll, CA B
Mount St. Mary's Coll, CA B
North Carolina Ag and Tech State U, NC B
Northern Arizona U, AZ B
Notre Dame de Namur U, CA B
Occidental Coll, CA B
Oregon State U, OR B
Pacific Lutheran U, WA B
Pacific Union Coll, CA B
Pacific U, OR B
Pepperdine U, Malibu, CA B
Pitzer Coll, CA B
Pomona Coll, CA B
Portland State U, OR B
Reed Coll, OR B
Regis U, CO B
St. John's Coll, NM B
Saint Mary's Coll of California, CA B
San Diego State U, CA B
San Francisco State U, CA B
San Jose State U, CA B
Santa Clara U, CA B
Scripps Coll, CA B
Seattle Pacific U, WA B
Seattle U, WA B
Sonoma State U, CA B
Southern Oregon U, OR B
Southern Utah U, UT B
Stanford U, CA B
The U of Arizona, AZ B
U of California, Berkeley, CA B
U of California, Davis, CA B
U of California, Irvine, CA B
U of California, Los Angeles, CA B
U of California, Riverside, CA B
U of California, San Diego, CA B
U of California, Santa Barbara, CA B
U of California, Santa Cruz, CA B
U of Colorado at Boulder, CO B
U of Colorado at Denver, CO B
U of Denver, CO B
U of Hawaii at Manoa, HI B
U of Idaho, ID B
U of La Verne, CA B
The U of Montana–Missoula, MT B
U of Nevada, Las Vegas, NV B
U of Nevada, Reno, NV B
U of New Mexico, NM B
U of Northern Colorado, CO B
U of Oregon, OR B
U of Puget Sound, WA B
U of Redlands, CA B
U of San Diego, CA B
U of San Francisco, CA B
U of Southern California, CA B
U of the Pacific, CA B
U of Utah, UT B
U of Washington, WA B
U of Wyoming, WY B
Utah State U, UT B
Walla Walla Coll, WA B
Washington State U, WA B
Weber State U, UT B
Western State Coll of Colorado, CO B
Western Washington U, WA B
Westmont Coll, CA B
Whitman Coll, WA B
Whitworth Coll, WA B
Willamette U, OR B

French Language Teacher Education
Brigham Young U, UT B
California Lutheran U, CA B
California State U, Chico, CA B
Central Washington U, WA B
Colorado State U, CO B
Eastern Washington U, WA B
San Diego State U, CA B
The U of Arizona, AZ B
U of Utah, UT B
Weber State U, UT B

French Studies
Claremont McKenna Coll, CA B
The Colorado Coll, CO B
Mills Coll, CA B

General Studies
Antioch U Santa Barbara, CA B
Blackfeet Comm Coll, MT A
California Inst of Technology, CA B
Carroll Coll, MT B
Chaminade U of Honolulu, HI A
City U, WA A,B
Eastern New Mexico U, NM A
Idaho State U, ID A,B
New Mexico State U, NM A,B
Northcentral U, AZ B
Northern Arizona U, AZ B
Platt Coll San Diego, CA A,B
St. John's Coll, NM B
Seattle Pacific U, WA B
Sheldon Jackson Coll, AK A
Simpson Coll and Graduate School, CA A
U of Idaho, ID B
U of Nevada, Reno, NV B
U of New Mexico, NM B
U of Phoenix–Hawaii Campus, HI A
U of Phoenix Online Campus, AZ B
U of Phoenix–Phoenix Campus, AZ A
U of Southern California, CA B
U of Washington, WA B
Utah State U, UT A
Utah Valley State Coll, UT A
Western Washington U, WA B

Genetics Related
Washington State U, WA B

Geochemistry
California Inst of Technology, CA B
New Mexico Inst of Mining and Technology, NM B
Northern Arizona U, AZ B
Pomona Coll, CA B
San Diego State U, CA B
U of California, Los Angeles, CA B

Geography
Arizona State U, AZ B
Brigham Young U, UT B
California State Polytechnic U, Pomona, CA B
California State U, Chico, CA B
California State U, Dominguez Hills, CA B
California State U, Fresno, CA B
California State U, Fullerton, CA B
California State U, Hayward, CA B

California State U, Long Beach, CA B
California State U, Los Angeles, CA B
California State U, Sacramento, CA B
California State U, San Bernardino, CA B
California State U, Stanislaus, CA B
Central Washington U, WA B
Eastern Washington U, WA B
Humboldt State U, CA B
New Mexico State U, NM B
Northern Arizona U, AZ B
Oregon State U, OR B
Portland State U, OR B
San Diego State U, CA B
San Francisco State U, CA B
San Jose State U, CA B
Sonoma State U, CA B
Southern Oregon U, OR B
United States Air Force Academy, CO B
U of Alaska Fairbanks, AK B
The U of Arizona, AZ B
U of California, Berkeley, CA B
U of California, Los Angeles, CA B
U of California, Santa Barbara, CA B
U of Colorado at Boulder, CO B
U of Colorado at Colorado Springs, CO B
U of Colorado at Denver, CO B
U of Denver, CO B
U of Hawaii at Hilo, HI B
U of Hawaii at Manoa, HI B
U of Idaho, ID B
The U of Montana–Missoula, MT B
U of Nevada, Reno, NV B
U of New Mexico, NM B
U of Northern Colorado, CO B
U of Oregon, OR B
U of Southern California, CA B
U of Utah, UT B
U of Washington, WA B
U of Wyoming, WY B
Utah State U, UT B
Weber State U, UT B
Western Oregon U, OR B
Western Washington U, WA B

Geography Related

Brigham Young U, UT B
U of California, Los Angeles, CA B

Geological and Earth Sciences/Geosciences Related

Brigham Young U, UT B
California State U, Chico, CA B
Lehigh U, PA B
San Diego State U, CA B
San Jose State U, CA B
U of California, Los Angeles, CA B
U of Hawaii at Manoa, HI B
U of Nevada, Las Vegas, NV B
U of Utah, UT B
U of Wyoming, WY B

Geological/Geophysical Engineering

Colorado School of Mines, CO B
Montana Tech of The U of Montana, MT B
Oregon State U, OR B
U of Alaska Fairbanks, AK B
The U of Arizona, AZ B
U of California, Berkeley, CA B
U of California, Los Angeles, CA B
U of Idaho, ID B
U of Nevada, Reno, NV B
U of Utah, UT B

Geology/Earth Science

Adams State Coll, CO B
Arizona State U, AZ B
Boise State U, ID B
Brigham Young U, UT B
California Inst of Technology, CA B
California Lutheran U, CA B
California State Polytechnic U, Pomona, CA B
California State U, Bakersfield, CA B
California State U, Chico, CA B
California State U, Dominguez Hills, CA B
California State U, Fresno, CA B
California State U, Fullerton, CA B
California State U, Hayward, CA B
California State U, Long Beach, CA B
California State U, Los Angeles, CA B
California State U, Sacramento, CA B
California State U, San Bernardino, CA B
California State U, Stanislaus, CA B
Central Washington U, WA B
The Colorado Coll, CO B
Colorado State U, CO B
Cornell Coll, IA B
Eastern New Mexico U, NM B
Eastern Washington U, WA B
Fort Lewis Coll, CO B
Great Basin Coll, NV A
Humboldt State U, CA B
Idaho State U, ID A,B
Montana State U–Bozeman, MT B
National U, CA B
New Mexico Inst of Mining and Technology, NM B
New Mexico State U, NM B
Northern Arizona U, AZ B
Occidental Coll, CA B
Oregon State U, OR B
Pacific Lutheran U, WA B
Pomona Coll, CA B
Portland State U, OR B
Rocky Mountain Coll, MT B
San Diego State U, CA B
San Francisco State U, CA B
San Jose State U, CA B
Scripps Coll, CA B
Sonoma State U, CA B
Southern Oregon U, OR B
Southern Utah U, UT B
Stanford U, CA B
U of Alaska Fairbanks, AK B
The U of Arizona, AZ B
U of California, Berkeley, CA B
U of California, Davis, CA B
U of California, Irvine, CA B
U of California, Los Angeles, CA B
U of California, Riverside, CA B
U of California, San Diego, CA B
U of California, Santa Barbara, CA B
U of California, Santa Cruz, CA B
U of Colorado at Boulder, CO B
U of Hawaii at Hilo, HI B
U of Hawaii at Manoa, HI B
U of Idaho, ID B
The U of Montana–Missoula, MT B
U of Nevada, Las Vegas, NV B
U of Nevada, Reno, NV B
U of New Mexico, NM B
U of Northern Colorado, CO B
U of Oregon, OR B
U of Puget Sound, WA B
U of Southern California, CA B
U of the Pacific, CA B
U of Utah, UT B
U of Washington, WA B
U of Wyoming, WY B
Utah State U, UT B
Washington State U, WA B
Weber State U, UT B
Western State Coll of Colorado, CO B
Western Washington U, WA B
Whitman Coll, WA B

Geophysics and Seismology

Boise State U, ID B
California Inst of Technology, CA B
New Mexico Inst of Mining and Technology, NM B
Occidental Coll, CA B
Oregon State U, OR B
Stanford U, CA B
U of California, Los Angeles, CA B
U of California, Riverside, CA B
U of California, Santa Barbara, CA B
U of California, Santa Cruz, CA B
U of Nevada, Reno, NV B
U of Utah, UT B
U of Washington, WA B
Western Washington U, WA B

Geotechnical Engineering

Montana Tech of The U of Montana, MT B

German

Arizona State U, AZ B
Birmingham-Southern Coll, AL B
Boise State U, ID B
Brigham Young U, UT B
California Lutheran U, CA B
California State U, Chico, CA B
California State U, Fullerton, CA B
California State U, Long Beach, CA B
Claremont McKenna Coll, CA B
The Colorado Coll, CO B
Colorado State U, CO B
Cornell Coll, IA B
Gonzaga U, WA B
Humboldt State U, CA B
Idaho State U, ID A,B
Lehigh U, PA B
Lewis & Clark Coll, OR B
Linfield Coll, OR B
Northern Arizona U, AZ B
Oregon State U, OR B
Pacific Lutheran U, WA B
Pacific U, OR B
Pepperdine U, Malibu, CA B
Pitzer Coll, CA B
Pomona Coll, CA B
Portland State U, OR B
Reed Coll, OR B
Saint Mary's Coll of California, CA B
San Diego State U, CA B
San Francisco State U, CA B
San Jose State U, CA B
Scripps Coll, CA B
Seattle Pacific U, WA B
Seattle U, WA B
Southern Oregon U, OR B
Southern Utah U, UT B
Stanford U, CA B
The U of Arizona, AZ B
U of California, Berkeley, CA B
U of California, Davis, CA B
U of California, Irvine, CA B
U of California, Los Angeles, CA B
U of California, Riverside, CA B
U of California, San Diego, CA B
U of California, Santa Barbara, CA B
U of California, Santa Cruz, CA B
U of Denver, CO B
U of Hawaii at Manoa, HI B
U of Idaho, ID B
U of La Verne, CA B
The U of Montana–Missoula, MT B
U of Nevada, Las Vegas, NV B
U of Nevada, Reno, NV B
U of New Mexico, NM B
U of Northern Colorado, CO B
U of Oregon, OR B
U of Puget Sound, WA B
U of Redlands, CA B
U of Southern California, CA B
U of the Pacific, CA B
U of Utah, UT B
U of Washington, WA B
U of Wyoming, WY B
Utah State U, UT B
Walla Walla Coll, WA B
Washington State U, WA B
Weber State U, UT B
Western Washington U, WA B
Whitman Coll, WA B
Willamette U, OR B

Germanic Languages

Claremont McKenna Coll, CA B
U of Colorado at Boulder, CO B

Germanic Languages Related

U of California, Los Angeles, CA B

German Language Teacher Education

Brigham Young U, UT B
California Lutheran U, CA B
California State U, Chico, CA B
Central Washington U, WA B
Colorado State U, CO B
Eastern Washington U, WA B
San Diego State U, CA B
The U of Arizona, AZ B
U of Utah, UT B
Weber State U, UT B

German Studies

Claremont McKenna Coll, CA B
U of California, Irvine, CA B

Gerontology

California State U, Chico, CA B
California State U, Dominguez Hills, CA B
California State U, Hayward, CA B

A—associate degree; B—bachelor's degree

California State U, Los Angeles, CA B
California State U, Sacramento, CA B
Central Washington U, WA B
Mount St. Mary's Coll, CA B
San Diego State U, CA B
U of Nevada, Las Vegas, NV B
U of Southern California, CA B
Weber State U, UT B

Graphic and Printing Equipment Operation/ Production

California Polytechnic State U, San Luis Obispo, CA B
Idaho State U, ID A
Lewis-Clark State Coll, ID A,B
Pacific Union Coll, CA A
Silicon Valley Coll, Walnut Creek, CA A

Graphic Communications

Academy of Art U, CA A,B
California State U, Los Angeles, CA B
Platt Coll San Diego, CA A,B
Point Loma Nazarene U, CA B
Silicon Valley Coll, Walnut Creek, CA A,B

Graphic Communications Related

Platt Coll San Diego, CA A

Graphic Design

Academy of Art U, CA A,B
Art Center Coll of Design, CA B
The Art Inst of California–San Diego, CA A,B
The Art Inst of California–San Francisco, CA B
The Art Inst of Phoenix, AZ B
The Art Inst of Portland, OR A,B
The Art Inst of Seattle, WA A,B
Brigham Young U, UT B
California Inst of the Arts, CA B
California State U, Chico, CA B
California State U, Fullerton, CA B
California State U, Long Beach, CA B
California State U, Sacramento, CA B
Chapman U, CA B
Cornish Coll of the Arts, WA B
Laguna Coll of Art & Design, CA B
Mt. Sierra Coll, CA B
Northwest Nazarene U, ID B
Pacific Northwest Coll of Art, OR B
Platt Coll San Diego, CA A,B
Rocky Mountain Coll of Art & Design, CO B
San Jose State U, CA B
U of San Francisco, CA B
Utah Valley State Coll, UT A
Western Washington U, WA B
Westwood Coll–Anaheim, CA A
Westwood Coll–Denver South, CO A
Westwood Coll–Inland Empire, CA A
Westwood Coll–Los Angeles, CA A,B
Westwood Coll–Denver North, CO A
Westwood Coll–Long Beach, CA A

Health and Medical Administrative Services Related

Silicon Valley Coll, Walnut Creek, CA A

Health and Physical Education

Brigham Young U, UT B
Brigham Young U–Hawaii, HI B
California State U, Chico, CA B
California State U, Fullerton, CA B
California State U, Sacramento, CA B
Chapman U, CA B
Colorado Christian U, CO B
Eastern Washington U, WA B
Linfield Coll, OR B
The Master's Coll and Seminary, CA B
Montana State U–Billings, MT B
Montana State U–Bozeman, MT B
Northwest Nazarene U, ID B
Point Loma Nazarene U, CA B
Saint Mary's Coll of California, CA B
San Jose State U, CA B
U of Great Falls, MT B
U of Hawaii at Manoa, HI B
U of San Francisco, CA B
U of Utah, UT B
Utah Valley State Coll, UT A
Vanguard U of Southern California, CA B
Walla Walla Coll, WA B
Washington State U, WA B
Weber State U, UT B

Health and Physical Education Related

Arizona State U East, AZ B
Brigham Young U, UT B
California Baptist U, CA B
California State U, Long Beach, CA B
California State U, Sacramento, CA B
Cornell Coll, IA B
Naropa U, CO B
Rocky Mountain Coll, MT B
Saint Mary's Coll of California, CA B
Washington State U, WA B

Health/Health Care Administration

California State U, Dominguez Hills, CA B
California State U, Long Beach, CA B
California State U, Sacramento, CA B
California State U, San Bernardino, CA B
Concordia U, OR B
Eastern Washington U, WA B
Idaho State U, ID B
Metropolitan State Coll of Denver, CO B
Montana State U–Billings, MT B
Montana State U–Bozeman, MT B
Mount St. Mary's Coll, CA B
National American U, Colorado Springs, CO B
National American U, Denver, CO A,B
New Mexico Highlands U, NM B
Oregon State U, OR B
Pioneer Pacific Coll, OR A
San Jose State U, CA B
Touro U International, CA B
The U of Arizona, AZ B
U of Great Falls, MT B
U of La Verne, CA B
U of Nevada, Las Vegas, NV B
U of Phoenix–Hawaii Campus, HI B
U of Phoenix–Idaho Campus, ID B
U of Phoenix–Nevada Campus, NV B
U of Phoenix–New Mexico Campus, NM B
U of Phoenix–Northern California Campus, CA B
U of Phoenix Online Campus, AZ B
U of Phoenix–Phoenix Campus, AZ B
U of Phoenix–Sacramento Campus, CA B
U of Phoenix–San Diego Campus, CA B
U of Phoenix–Southern Arizona Campus, AZ B
U of Phoenix–Washington Campus, WA B
Weber State U, UT B

Health Information/Medical Records Administration

Boise State U, ID A
Carroll Coll, MT B
LDS Business Coll, UT A
Loma Linda U, CA B
Montana State U–Billings, MT A
Regis U, CO B

Health Information/Medical Records Technology

Idaho State U, ID A
Weber State U, UT A

Health/Medical Physics

U of Nevada, Las Vegas, NV B

Health/Medical Preparatory Programs Related

Blackfeet Comm Coll, MT A
Lehigh U, PA B
U of Nevada, Reno, NV B

Health Professions Related

Arizona State U East, AZ B
California State U, Fullerton, CA B
California State U, Los Angeles, CA B
California State U, Sacramento, CA B
International Inst of the Americas, AZ A
Saint Mary's Coll of California, CA B
San Diego State U, CA B
U of Nevada, Reno, NV B
U of Utah, UT B

Health Science

Azusa Pacific U, CA B
Bastyr U, WA B
Boise State U, ID B
California State U, Dominguez Hills, CA B
California State U, Fresno, CA B
California State U, Hayward, CA B
California State U, Long Beach, CA B
California State U, Los Angeles, CA B
California State U, San Bernardino, CA B
Chapman U, CA B
Montana Tech of The U of Montana, MT B
Northwest Coll, WA A
Oregon State U, OR B
Pacific U, OR B
San Francisco State U, CA B
Sonoma State U, CA B
U of Alaska Anchorage, AK B
U of Colorado at Colorado Springs, CO B
U of Nevada, Las Vegas, NV B
U of Southern California, CA B
Walla Walla Coll, WA B
Warner Pacific Coll, OR B
Western Baptist Coll, OR B

Health Services Administration

Northwest Christian Coll, OR B
U of California, Los Angeles, CA B

Health Services/Allied Health/Health Sciences

California State U, Chico, CA B
California State U, Sacramento, CA B
Idaho State U, ID B
National American U, Denver, CO A
San Jose State U, CA B
U of Utah, UT B
U of Wyoming, WY B
Western Baptist Coll, OR B

Health Teacher Education

California State U, Chico, CA B
California State U, San Bernardino, CA B
Central Washington U, WA B
Eastern Washington U, WA B
George Fox U, OR B
Idaho State U, ID B
Montana State U–Billings, MT B
New Mexico Highlands U, NM B
North Carolina Ag and Tech State U, NC B
Northern Arizona U, AZ B
Portland State U, OR B
Rocky Mountain Coll, MT B
San Francisco State U, CA B
Southern Oregon U, OR B
Touro U International, CA B
The U of Arizona, AZ B
U of Great Falls, MT B
U of Hawaii at Manoa, HI B
The U of Montana–Missoula, MT B
The U of Montana–Western, MT B
U of Nevada, Las Vegas, NV B
U of Nevada, Reno, NV B
U of New Mexico, NM B
U of Utah, UT B
U of Wyoming, WY B
Utah State U, UT B
Western Washington U, WA B

Heating, Air Conditioning, Ventilation and Refrigeration Maintenance Technology

Boise State U, ID A
Lewis-Clark State Coll, ID A,B
Montana State U–Billings, MT A
U of Alaska Anchorage, AK A
Utah Valley State Coll, UT A
Westwood Coll–Denver North, CO A

Heavy Equipment Maintenance Technology
U of Alaska Anchorage, AK A
The U of Montana–Missoula, MT A

Hebrew
Brigham Young U, UT B
Multnomah Bible Coll and Biblical Seminary, OR B
U of California, Los Angeles, CA B
U of Oregon, OR B

Herbalism
Bastyr U, WA B

Hispanic-American, Puerto Rican, and Mexican-American/ Chicano Studies
Arizona State U, AZ B
California State U, Dominguez Hills, CA B
California State U, Fresno, CA B
California State U, Fullerton, CA B
California State U, Hayward, CA B
California State U, Long Beach, CA B
California State U, Los Angeles, CA B
California State U, San Bernardino, CA B
Claremont McKenna Coll, CA B
The Colorado Coll, CO B
Lewis & Clark Coll, OR B
Loyola Marymount U, CA B
Metropolitan State Coll of Denver, CO B
Mills Coll, CA B
Pitzer Coll, CA B
Pomona Coll, CA B
San Diego State U, CA B
San Francisco State U, CA B
Scripps Coll, CA B
Sonoma State U, CA B
Stanford U, CA B
The U of Arizona, AZ B
U of California, Berkeley, CA B
U of California, Davis, CA B
U of California, Irvine, CA B
U of California, Los Angeles, CA B
U of California, Riverside, CA B
U of California, Santa Barbara, CA B
U of California, Santa Cruz, CA B
U of Northern Colorado, CO B
U of San Diego, CA B
U of Southern California, CA B
U of Washington, WA B

Historic Preservation and Conservation
Saint Mary's Coll of California, CA B

History
Adams State Coll, CO B
Albertson Coll of Idaho, ID B
Arizona State U, AZ B
Arizona State U West, AZ B
Azusa Pacific U, CA B
Biola U, CA B
Birmingham-Southern Coll, AL B
Boise State U, ID B
Brigham Young U, UT B
Brigham Young U–Hawaii, HI B
California Baptist U, CA B
California Inst of Technology, CA B
California Lutheran U, CA B
California Polytechnic State U, San Luis Obispo, CA B
California State Polytechnic U, Pomona, CA B
California State U, Bakersfield, CA B
California State U, Chico, CA B
California State U, Dominguez Hills, CA B
California State U, Fresno, CA B
California State U, Fullerton, CA B
California State U, Hayward, CA B
California State U, Long Beach, CA B
California State U, Los Angeles, CA B
California State U, Sacramento, CA B
California State U, San Bernardino, CA B
California State U, San Marcos, CA B
California State U, Stanislaus, CA B
Carroll Coll, MT B
Central Washington U, WA B
Chaminade U of Honolulu, HI B
Chapman U, CA B
Christian Heritage Coll, CA B
Claremont McKenna Coll, CA B
Coll of the Southwest, NM B
Colorado Christian U, CO B
The Colorado Coll, CO B
Colorado State U, CO B
Colorado State U-Pueblo, CO B
Concordia U, CA B
Cornell Coll, IA B
Dominican U of California, CA B
Eastern New Mexico U, NM B
Eastern Oregon U, OR B
Eastern Washington U, WA B
Eugene Lang Coll, New School U B
Fort Lewis Coll, CO B
Fresno Pacific U, CA A,B
George Fox U, OR B
Gonzaga U, WA B
Grand Canyon U, AZ B
Great Basin Coll, NV A
Hawai'i Pacific U, HI B
Holy Names U, CA B
Humboldt State U, CA B
Idaho State U, ID A,B
Lehigh U, PA B
Lewis & Clark Coll, OR B
Linfield Coll, OR B
Loyola Marymount U, CA B
The Master's Coll and Seminary, CA B
Metropolitan State Coll of Denver, CO B
Mills Coll, CA B
Montana State U–Billings, MT B
Montana State U–Bozeman, MT B
Mount St. Mary's Coll, CA B
Multnomah Bible Coll and Biblical Seminary, OR B
Nevada State Coll at Henderson, NV B
New Mexico Highlands U, NM B
New Mexico State U, NM B
North Carolina Ag and Tech State U, NC B
Northern Arizona U, AZ B
Northwest Coll, WA B
Northwest Nazarene U, ID B
Notre Dame de Namur U, CA B
Occidental Coll, CA B
Oregon State U, OR B
Pacific Lutheran U, WA B
Pacific Union Coll, CA B
Pacific U, OR B
Pepperdine U, Malibu, CA B
Pitzer Coll, CA B
Point Loma Nazarene U, CA B
Pomona Coll, CA B
Portland State U, OR B
Prescott Coll, AZ B
Reed Coll, OR B
Regis U, CO B
Rocky Mountain Coll, MT B
St. John's Coll, NM B
Saint Martin's Coll, WA B
Saint Mary's Coll of California, CA B
San Diego State U, CA B
San Francisco State U, CA B
San Jose State U, CA B
Santa Clara U, CA B
Scripps Coll, CA B
Seattle Pacific U, WA B
Seattle U, WA B
Simpson Coll and Graduate School, CA B
Sonoma State U, CA B
Southern Oregon U, OR B
Southern Utah U, UT B
Stanford U, CA B
United States Air Force Academy, CO B
U of Alaska Anchorage, AK B
U of Alaska Fairbanks, AK B
The U of Arizona, AZ B
U of California, Berkeley, CA B
U of California, Davis, CA B
U of California, Irvine, CA B
U of California, Los Angeles, CA B
U of California, Riverside, CA B
U of California, San Diego, CA B
U of California, Santa Barbara, CA B
U of California, Santa Cruz, CA B
U of Colorado at Boulder, CO B
U of Colorado at Colorado Springs, CO B
U of Colorado at Denver, CO B
U of Denver, CO B
U of Great Falls, MT B
U of Hawaii at Hilo, HI B
U of Idaho, ID B
U of La Verne, CA B
The U of Montana–Missoula, MT B
U of Nevada, Las Vegas, NV B
U of Nevada, Reno, NV B
U of New Mexico, NM B
U of Northern Colorado, CO B
U of Oregon, OR B
U of Portland, OR B
U of Puget Sound, WA B
U of Redlands, CA B
U of San Diego, CA B
U of San Francisco, CA B
U of Southern California, CA B
U of the Pacific, CA B
U of the West, CA B
U of Utah, UT B
U of Washington, WA B
U of Wyoming, WY B
Utah State U, UT B
Utah Valley State Coll, UT B
Vanguard U of Southern California, CA B
Walla Walla Coll, WA B
Warner Pacific Coll, OR B
Washington State U, WA B
Weber State U, UT B
Western Oregon U, OR B
Western State Coll of Colorado, CO B
Western Washington U, WA B
Westminster Coll, UT B
Westmont Coll, CA B
Whitman Coll, WA B
Whitworth Coll, WA B
Willamette U, OR B
Woodbury U, CA B

History and Philosophy Of Science and Technology
Oregon State U, OR B
U of Washington, WA B

History Of Philosophy
St. John's Coll, NM B

History Related
The Colorado Coll, CO B
Hawai'i Pacific U, HI B
Marylhurst U, OR B

History Teacher Education
Brigham Young U, UT B
Carroll Coll, MT B
Central Washington U, WA B
Montana State U–Billings, MT B
Nevada State Coll at Henderson, NV B
Northern Arizona U, AZ B
Northwest Coll, WA B
Northwest Nazarene U, ID B
Rocky Mountain Coll, MT B
The U of Arizona, AZ B
U of Great Falls, MT B
The U of Montana–Western, MT B
U of Utah, UT B
Utah Valley State Coll, UT B
Weber State U, UT B

Home Furnishings and Equipment Installation
Brigham Young U, UT B

Horticultural Science
Boise State U, ID A
California Polytechnic State U, San Luis Obispo, CA B
California State Polytechnic U, Pomona, CA B
Colorado State U, CO B
Montana State U–Bozeman, MT B
Naropa U, CO B
New Mexico State U, NM B
Oregon State U, OR B
U of California, Davis, CA B
U of Hawaii at Hilo, HI B
U of Idaho, ID B
Utah State U, UT B
Washington State U, WA B

Hospital and Health Care Facilities Administration
DeVry U, Westminster, CO A,B

Hospitality Administration
Blackfeet Comm Coll, MT A
Lewis-Clark State Coll, ID A,B
Metropolitan State Coll of Denver, CO B
National American U, NM A,B

A—associate degree; B—bachelor's degree

National U, CA B
San Francisco State U, CA B
San Jose State U, CA B
Touro U International, CA B
U of Alaska Southeast, AK A
U of Denver, CO B
U of Nevada, Las Vegas, NV B
U of Nevada, Reno, NV B
Utah Valley State Coll, UT A,B
Washington State U, WA B

Hospitality Administration Related

San Diego State U, CA B
U of Hawaii at Manoa, HI B

Hotel/Motel Administration

Alliant International U, CA B
Brigham Young U–Hawaii, HI B
California State Polytechnic U, Pomona, CA B
California State U, Long Beach, CA B
Colorado State U, CO B
National American U, Colorado Springs, CO A
National American U, NM A,B
Northern Arizona U, AZ B
San Diego State U, CA B
Sierra Nevada Coll, NV B
Southern Oregon U, OR B
U of Denver, CO B
U of San Francisco, CA B
Utah Valley State Coll, UT B

Housing and Human Environments

Utah State U, UT B

Housing and Human Environments Related

U of Nevada, Reno, NV B

Human Development and Family Studies

Brigham Young U, UT B
California State U, Hayward, CA B
California State U, Long Beach, CA B
California State U, San Bernardino, CA B
Christian Heritage Coll, CA B
Colorado State U, CO B
Hawai'i Pacific U, HI B
New Mexico State U, NM B
Oregon State U, OR B
Pacific Oaks Coll, CA B
Prescott Coll, AZ B
The U of Arizona, AZ B
U of California, Davis, CA B
U of California, Riverside, CA B
U of Hawaii at Manoa, HI B
U of Nevada, Reno, NV B
U of Utah, UT B
Utah State U, UT B
Warner Pacific Coll, OR B
Washington State U, WA B

Human Development and Family Studies Related

Utah State U, UT A

Human Ecology

California State U, Hayward, CA B
Prescott Coll, AZ B
Regis U, CO B
U of California, Irvine, CA B
U of California, San Diego, CA B

Humanities

Arizona State U, AZ B
Biola U, CA B
Brigham Young U, UT B
Brigham Young U–Hawaii, HI B
California State Polytechnic U, Pomona, CA B
California State U, Chico, CA B
California State U, Dominguez Hills, CA B
California State U, Sacramento, CA B
California State U, San Bernardino, CA B
Chaminade U of Honolulu, HI B
Coll of Santa Fe, NM B
Colorado State U, CO B
Concordia U, CA B
Concordia U, OR B
Dominican U of California, CA B
Eastern Washington U, WA B
Eugene Lang Coll, New School U B
The Evergreen State Coll, WA B
Fort Lewis Coll, CO B
Fresno Pacific U, CA B
Hawai'i Pacific U, HI B
Holy Names U, CA B
John F. Kennedy U, CA B
Lehigh U, PA B
Loyola Marymount U, CA B
New Coll of California, CA B
Northern Arizona U, AZ B
Notre Dame de Namur U, CA B
Pacific U, OR B
Pepperdine U, Malibu, CA B
Pomona Coll, CA B
Portland State U, OR B
Prescott Coll, AZ B
Regis U, CO B
St. John's Coll, NM B
Saint Martin's Coll, WA B
San Diego State U, CA B
San Francisco State U, CA B
San Jose State U, CA B
Seattle U, WA B
Sierra Nevada Coll, NV B
United States Air Force Academy, CO B
The U of Arizona, AZ B
U of California, Irvine, CA B
U of California, Riverside, CA B
U of Colorado at Boulder, CO B
U of New Mexico, NM B
U of Oregon, OR B
U of San Diego, CA B
U of Utah, UT B
U of Washington, WA B
U of Wyoming, WY B
Utah Valley State Coll, UT A
Walla Walla Coll, WA B
Washington State U, WA B
Western Baptist Coll, OR B
Western Oregon U, OR B
Western Washington U, WA B
Willamette U, OR B

Human/Medical Genetics

U of California, Los Angeles, CA B

Human Nutrition

Washington State U, WA B

Human Resources Development

Brigham Young U, UT B

Human Resources Management

Birmingham-Southern Coll, AL B
Boise State U, ID B
Brigham Young U, UT B
California Polytechnic State U, San Luis Obispo, CA B
California State Polytechnic U, Pomona, CA B
California State U, Chico, CA B
California State U, Dominguez Hills, CA B
California State U, Fresno, CA B
California State U, Hayward, CA B
California State U, Long Beach, CA B
California State U, Sacramento, CA B
Dominican U of California, CA B
Eastern New Mexico U, NM B
Eastern Washington U, WA B
George Fox U, OR B
Golden Gate U, CA B
Grand Canyon U, AZ B
Hawai'i Pacific U, HI B
Holy Names U, CA B
Idaho State U, ID B
Montana State U–Billings, MT A
Montana Tech of The U of Montana, MT A
National U, CA B
Portland State U, OR B
San Jose State U, CA B
Simpson Coll and Graduate School, CA B
U of Alaska Fairbanks, AK B
The U of Arizona, AZ B
U of Hawaii at Manoa, HI B
U of Idaho, ID B
The U of Montana–Western, MT A
U of Nevada, Las Vegas, NV B
U of Nevada, Reno, NV B
Utah State U, UT B
Washington State U, WA B
Weber State U, UT B
Western State Coll of Colorado, CO B
Western Washington U, WA B
Westminster Coll, UT B

Human Services

Alaska Pacific U, AK B
Blackfeet Comm Coll, MT A
California State U, Dominguez Hills, CA B
California State U, San Bernardino, CA B
Hawai'i Pacific U, HI B
Holy Names U, CA B
Metropolitan State Coll of Denver, CO B
Northwest Christian Coll, OR B
Notre Dame de Namur U, CA B
Pacific Oaks Coll, CA B
Sheldon Jackson Coll, AK A,B
U of Alaska Anchorage, AK A
U of Great Falls, MT B
U of Great Falls, MT A,B
U of Nevada, Las Vegas, NV B
U of Northern Colorado, CO B
U of Oregon, OR B
U of Phoenix–Sacramento Campus, CA B
Western Washington U, WA B

Hydrology and Water Resources Science

California State U, Chico, CA B
Humboldt State U, CA B

Illustration

Academy of Art U, CA A,B
Art Center Coll of Design, CA B
Brigham Young U, UT B
California State U, Fullerton, CA B
California State U, Long Beach, CA B
Cornish Coll of the Arts, WA B
Laguna Coll of Art & Design, CA B
Mt. Sierra Coll, CA B
Pacific Northwest Coll of Art, OR B
Rocky Mountain Coll of Art & Design, CO B
U of San Francisco, CA B

Industrial and Organizational Psychology

California State U, Hayward, CA B
California State U, Sacramento, CA B
Coll of Santa Fe, NM B
Point Loma Nazarene U, CA B
Saint Mary's Coll of California, CA B
Western Baptist Coll, OR B

Industrial Arts

California State U, Fresno, CA B
Colorado State U-Pueblo, CO B
Humboldt State U, CA B
New Mexico Highlands U, NM B
North Carolina Ag and Tech State U, NC B
Pacific Union Coll, CA B
San Diego State U, CA B
San Francisco State U, CA B
Southern Utah U, UT B
The U of Montana–Missoula, MT A
The U of Montana–Western, MT B
Walla Walla Coll, WA B
Weber State U, UT A
Western State Coll of Colorado, CO B

Industrial Design

Academy of Art U, CA A,B
Arizona State U, AZ B
Art Center Coll of Design, CA B
The Art Inst of Colorado, CO B
The Art Inst of Seattle, WA A
Brigham Young U, UT B
California Coll of the Arts, CA B
California State U, Long Beach, CA B
ITT Tech Inst, UT B
Metropolitan State Coll of Denver, CO B
San Francisco State U, CA B
San Jose State U, CA B
U of Washington, WA B
Western Washington U, WA B

Industrial Electronics Technology

Lewis-Clark State Coll, ID A,B

Industrial Engineering

Arizona State U, AZ B
California Polytechnic State U, San Luis Obispo, CA B
California State Polytechnic U, Pomona, CA B
California State U, Fresno, CA B
California State U, Hayward, CA B
California State U, Long Beach, CA B
Colorado State U-Pueblo, CO B
Lehigh U, PA B
Montana State U–Bozeman, MT B

New Mexico State U, NM B
North Carolina Ag and Tech State U, NC B
Oregon State U, OR B
San Jose State U, CA B
Seattle U, WA B
Stanford U, CA B
U of Alaska Fairbanks, AK B
The U of Arizona, AZ B
U of Idaho, ID B
U of New Mexico, NM B
U of San Diego, CA B
U of Washington, WA B
Washington State U, WA B

Industrial Production Technologies Related

Utah State U, UT B

Industrial Radiologic Technology

Boise State U, ID A,B
Oregon Inst of Technology, OR B

Industrial Technology

Arizona State U East, AZ B
Boise State U, ID B
California Polytechnic State U, San Luis Obispo, CA B
California State U, Fresno, CA B
California State U, Long Beach, CA B
California State U, Los Angeles, CA B
Central Washington U, WA B
Great Basin Coll, NV A
Metropolitan State Coll of Denver, CO B
North Carolina Ag and Tech State U, NC B
Pacific Union Coll, CA B
U of Alaska Fairbanks, AK A
U of Idaho, ID B
Weber State U, UT A,B
Western Washington U, WA B

Information Science/Studies

Boise State U, ID B
Brigham Young U–Hawaii, HI B
California Baptist U, CA B
California Lutheran U, CA B
California State Polytechnic U, Pomona, CA B
California State U, Dominguez Hills, CA B
California State U, Fullerton, CA B
California State U, Hayward, CA B
California State U, Stanislaus, CA B
Colorado State U, CO B
DeVry U, Phoenix, AZ B
DeVry U, Fremont, CA B
DeVry U, Long Beach, CA B
DeVry U, Pomona, CA B
DeVry U, West Hills, CA B
DeVry U, Colorado Springs, CO A,B
DeVry U, Federal Way, WA B
Fort Lewis Coll, CO B
Golden Gate U, CA B
Gonzaga U, WA B
Hawai'i Pacific U, HI B
Humboldt State U, CA B
Idaho State U, ID B
Lehigh U, PA B
Montana Tech of The U of Montana, MT B
Morrison U, NV A
Mt. Sierra Coll, CA B
National American U, Colorado Springs, CO A,B
National American U, Denver, CO A,B
National American U, NM A,B
National U, CA B
New Mexico Highlands U, NM B
New Mexico State U, NM B
Oregon State U, OR B
Pacific Union Coll, CA A,B
Pioneer Pacific Coll, OR A
Platt Coll, Newport Beach, CA A
Saint Martin's Coll, WA B
San Diego State U, CA B
San Francisco State U, CA B
Southern Utah U, UT A
U of Alaska Anchorage, AK A
U of California, Los Angeles, CA B
U of California, Santa Cruz, CA B
U of Great Falls, MT B
The U of Montana–Missoula, MT B
The U of Montana–Western, MT A
U of New Mexico, NM B
U of San Francisco, CA B
U of the Pacific, CA B
U of Washington, WA B
Utah State U, UT B
Weber State U, UT A,B
Woodbury U, CA B

Information Technology

Brigham Young U, UT B
California State U, Chico, CA B
California State U, Los Angeles, CA B
Concordia U, CA B
International Inst of the Americas, AZ A
ITT Tech Inst, Rancho Cordova, CA B
Jones International U, CO B
LDS Business Coll, UT A
National American U, Denver, CO A,B
New Mexico Inst of Mining and Technology, NM B
Northface U, UT B
Pioneer Pacific Coll, OR B
Platt Coll, Newport Beach, CA A
Rocky Mountain Coll, MT B
San Jose State U, CA B
Silicon Valley Coll, Walnut Creek, CA A
U of Great Falls, MT B
U of Phoenix–Colorado Campus, CO B
U of Phoenix–Hawaii Campus, HI B
U of Phoenix–New Mexico Campus, NM B
U of Phoenix–Northern California Campus, CA B
U of Phoenix–Oregon Campus, OR B
U of Phoenix–Phoenix Campus, AZ B
U of Phoenix–Sacramento Campus, CA B
U of Phoenix–San Diego Campus, CA B
U of Phoenix–Southern Arizona Campus, AZ B
U of Phoenix–Southern California Campus, CA B
U of Phoenix–Southern Colorado Campus, CO B

Inorganic Chemistry

California Inst of Technology, CA B

Instrumentation Technology

Colorado State U-Pueblo, CO B
Idaho State U, ID A

Insurance

California State Polytechnic U, Pomona, CA B
California State U, Sacramento, CA B
Seattle U, WA B
Washington State U, WA B

Interdisciplinary Studies

Arizona State U, AZ B
Arizona State U East, AZ B
Arizona State U West, AZ B
Birmingham-Southern Coll, AL B
Boise State U, ID B
Brigham Young U–Hawaii, HI B
California Lutheran U, CA B
California State U, Bakersfield, CA B
California State U, Dominguez Hills, CA B
California State U, Hayward, CA B
California State U, Long Beach, CA B
California State U, Los Angeles, CA B
California State U, San Bernardino, CA B
Christian Heritage Coll, CA B
Concordia U, OR B
Cornell Coll, IA B
Eastern Washington U, WA B
Eugene Lang Coll, New School U B
George Fox U, OR B
Great Basin Coll, NV A
Hawai'i Pacific U, HI B
Lewis-Clark State Coll, ID B
Marylhurst U, OR B
Mills Coll, CA B
Naropa U, CO B
National U, CA B
New Coll of California, CA B
New Mexico Inst of Mining and Technology, NM B
New Mexico State U, NM B
Northwest Coll, WA A,B
Oregon State U, OR B
Pacific Union Coll, CA B
Pepperdine U, Malibu, CA B
Pitzer Coll, CA B
Pomona Coll, CA B
Prescott Coll, AZ B
Rocky Mountain Coll, MT B
Saint Mary's Coll of California, CA B
San Francisco Art Inst, CA B
Santa Clara U, CA B
Sonoma State U, CA B
Southern Oregon U, OR B
Stanford U, CA B
Thomas Aquinas Coll, CA B
United States Air Force Academy, CO B
U of Alaska Anchorage, AK B
U of California, San Diego, CA B
U of California, Santa Barbara, CA B
U of Hawaii at Hilo, HI B
U of Judaism, CA B
The U of Montana–Missoula, MT B
U of Nevada, Las Vegas, NV B
U of Northern Colorado, CO B
U of Portland, OR B
U of Puget Sound, WA B
U of Redlands, CA B
U of San Francisco, CA B
U of Southern California, CA B
U of the Pacific, CA B
U of Washington, WA B
Vanguard U of Southern California, CA B
Western Baptist Coll, OR B
Western Oregon U, OR B
Western Washington U, WA B
Woodbury U, CA B

Interior Architecture

Arizona State U, AZ B
The Art Inst of California–San Diego, CA B
California Coll of the Arts, CA B
U of Hawaii at Manoa, HI B
U of Idaho, ID B
U of Nevada, Las Vegas, NV B
U of Oregon, OR B
U of Washington, WA B
Washington State U, WA B
Westwood Coll–Denver North, CO B
Woodbury U, CA B

Interior Design

Academy of Art U, CA A,B
American InterContinental U, CA A,B
Art Center Coll of Design, CA B
The Art Inst of California–San Diego, CA B
The Art Inst of California–San Francisco, CA B
The Art Inst of Colorado, CO B
The Art Inst of Phoenix, AZ B
The Art Inst of Portland, OR A,B
The Art Inst of Seattle, WA A,B
Brigham Young U, UT B
California State U, Chico, CA B
California State U, Fresno, CA B
California State U, Long Beach, CA B
California State U, Sacramento, CA B
Chaminade U of Honolulu, HI A,B
Colorado State U, CO B
Cornish Coll of the Arts, WA B
Design Inst of San Diego, CA B
LDS Business Coll, UT A
Marylhurst U, OR B
Northern Arizona U, AZ B
Oregon State U, OR B
Otis Coll of Art and Design, CA B
Rocky Mountain Coll of Art & Design, CO B
San Diego State U, CA B
San Francisco State U, CA B
San Jose State U, CA B
Southern Utah U, UT A
U of Idaho, ID B
U of Oregon, OR B
Utah State U, UT B
Weber State U, UT A
Westwood Coll–Anaheim, CA B
Westwood Coll–Denver South, CO B
Westwood Coll–Inland Empire, CA B
Westwood Coll–Los Angeles, CA B
Westwood Coll–Denver North, CO B

A—associate degree; B—bachelor's degree

Intermedia/Multimedia

Art Center Coll of Design, CA B
The Art Inst of California–San Diego, CA B
The Art Inst of Colorado, CO A
The Art Inst of Portland, OR A,B
The Art Inst of Seattle, WA A
Coll of Santa Fe, NM B
The Evergreen State Coll, WA B
Laguna Coll of Art & Design, CA B
Mills Coll, CA B
Mt. Sierra Coll, CA B
National U, CA B
Pacific Northwest Coll of Art, OR B
Platt Coll, Newport Beach, CA B
Platt Coll San Diego, CA A,B
U of California, San Diego, CA B
U of Oregon, OR B
Western Washington U, WA B
Westwood Coll–Anaheim, CA A,B
Westwood Coll–Denver South, CO A,B
Westwood Coll–Inland Empire, CA A,B
Westwood Coll–Los Angeles, CA A

International Agriculture

U of California, Davis, CA B
Utah State U, UT B

International Business/Trade/Commerce

Albertson Coll of Idaho, ID B
Alliant International U, CA B
Arizona State U West, AZ B
Birmingham-Southern Coll, AL B
Boise State U, ID B
Brigham Young U–Hawaii, HI B
California State Polytechnic U, Pomona, CA B
California State U, Dominguez Hills, CA B
California State U, Fresno, CA B
California State U, Long Beach, CA B
California State U, Sacramento, CA B
Chapman U, CA B
City U, WA B
Claremont McKenna Coll, CA B
Coll of Santa Fe, NM B
Cornell Coll, IA B
Dominican U of California, CA B
Fort Lewis Coll, CO B
Fresno Pacific U, CA B
Golden Gate U, CA B
Gonzaga U, WA B
Grand Canyon U, AZ B
Hawai'i Pacific U, HI B
Linfield Coll, OR B
Mount St. Mary's Coll, CA B
New Mexico State U, NM B
Northwest Nazarene U, ID B
Notre Dame de Namur U, CA B
Oregon State U, OR B
Pacific Lutheran U, WA B
Pacific Union Coll, CA B
Pepperdine U, Malibu, CA B
Saint Mary's Coll of California, CA B
San Diego State U, CA B
San Francisco State U, CA B
San Jose State U, CA B
Seattle U, WA B
U of Denver, CO B
U of Hawaii at Manoa, HI B
U of La Verne, CA B
The U of Montana–Missoula, MT B
U of Nevada, Las Vegas, NV B
U of Nevada, Reno, NV B
U of Oregon, OR B
U of Portland, OR B
U of Puget Sound, WA B
U of San Francisco, CA B
U of Southern California, CA B
U of Washington, WA B
Utah Valley State Coll, UT B
Vanguard U of Southern California, CA B
Washington State U, WA B
Western State Coll of Colorado, CO B
Western Washington U, WA B
Westminster Coll, UT B
Whitworth Coll, WA B

International Economics

Albertson Coll of Idaho, ID B
California State U, Chico, CA B
Claremont McKenna Coll, CA B
The Colorado Coll, CO B
Loyola Marymount U, CA B
San Diego State U, CA B
Seattle U, WA B
U of California, Los Angeles, CA B
U of California, Santa Cruz, CA B
U of Puget Sound, WA B

International Finance

Brigham Young U, UT B

International/Global Studies

Colorado Christian U, CO B
Dominican U of California, CA B
The Evergreen State Coll, WA B
U of California, Irvine, CA B
U of Colorado at Boulder, CO B
U of Utah, UT B
Willamette U, OR B

International Marketing

Brigham Young U, UT B

International Relations and Affairs

Alliant International U, CA B
Azusa Pacific U, CA B
Brigham Young U, UT B
California Lutheran U, CA B
California State U, Chico, CA B
California State U, Hayward, CA B
California State U, Long Beach, CA B
Carroll Coll, MT B
Chaminade U of Honolulu, HI B
Claremont McKenna Coll, CA B
Cornell Coll, IA B
Eastern Washington U, WA B
Embry-Riddle Aeronautical U, AZ B
Eugene Lang Coll, New School U B
George Fox U, OR B
Gonzaga U, WA B
Grand Canyon U, AZ B
Hawai'i Pacific U, HI B
Holy Names U, CA B
Lehigh U, PA B
Lewis & Clark Coll, OR B
Mills Coll, CA B
Northern Arizona U, AZ B
Northwest Nazarene U, ID B
Occidental Coll, CA B
Oregon State U, OR B
Pacific Lutheran U, WA B
Pacific U, OR B
Pepperdine U, Malibu, CA B
Pitzer Coll, CA B
Pomona Coll, CA B
Portland State U, OR B
Reed Coll, OR B
Saint Mary's Coll of California, CA B
San Diego State U, CA B
San Francisco State U, CA B
Scripps Coll, CA B
Seattle U, WA B
Sonoma State U, CA B
Southern Oregon U, OR B
Stanford U, CA B
U of California, Davis, CA B
U of Denver, CO B
U of Idaho, ID B
U of La Verne, CA B
U of Nevada, Reno, NV B
U of Oregon, OR B
U of Puget Sound, WA B
U of Redlands, CA B
U of San Diego, CA B
U of Southern California, CA B
U of the Pacific, CA B
U of Washington, WA B
U of Wyoming, WY B
Western Oregon U, OR B
Whitworth Coll, WA B

Islamic Studies

U of California, Los Angeles, CA B
U of California, Santa Barbara, CA B

Italian

Arizona State U, AZ B
Brigham Young U, UT B
California State U, Long Beach, CA B
Claremont McKenna Coll, CA B
The Colorado Coll, CO B
Gonzaga U, WA B
Saint Mary's Coll of California, CA B
San Francisco State U, CA B
Santa Clara U, CA B
Scripps Coll, CA B
Stanford U, CA B
The U of Arizona, AZ B
U of California, Berkeley, CA B
U of California, Davis, CA B
U of California, Los Angeles, CA B
U of California, San Diego, CA B
U of California, Santa Barbara, CA B
U of California, Santa Cruz, CA B
U of Colorado at Boulder, CO B
U of Denver, CO B
U of Oregon, OR B
U of Southern California, CA B
U of Washington, WA B

Italian Studies

U of California, Santa Cruz, CA B

Japanese

Brigham Young U, UT B
California State U, Fullerton, CA B
California State U, Long Beach, CA B
California State U, Los Angeles, CA B
Claremont McKenna Coll, CA B
Lehigh U, PA B
Linfield Coll, OR B
Pacific U, OR B
Pomona Coll, CA B
Portland State U, OR B
San Diego State U, CA B
San Francisco State U, CA B
San Jose State U, CA B
Scripps Coll, CA B
Stanford U, CA B
U of Alaska Fairbanks, AK B
U of California, Berkeley, CA B
U of California, Davis, CA B
U of California, Irvine, CA B
U of California, Los Angeles, CA B
U of California, San Diego, CA B
U of California, Santa Barbara, CA B
U of California, Santa Cruz, CA B
U of Colorado at Boulder, CO B
U of Hawaii at Hilo, HI B
U of Hawaii at Manoa, HI B
The U of Montana–Missoula, MT B
U of Oregon, OR B
U of the Pacific, CA B
U of Utah, UT B
U of Washington, WA B
Washington State U, WA B

Japanese Studies

Claremont McKenna Coll, CA B
U of San Francisco, CA B
Willamette U, OR B

Jazz/Jazz Studies

Brigham Young U, UT B
California Inst of the Arts, CA B
Cornish Coll of the Arts, WA B
U of Nevada, Las Vegas, NV B
U of Oregon, OR B
U of Southern California, CA B
Western Washington U, WA B

Jewish/Judaic Studies

California State U, Chico, CA B
Scripps Coll, CA B
The U of Arizona, AZ B
U of California, Los Angeles, CA B
U of California, San Diego, CA B
U of Judaism, CA B
U of Oregon, OR B
U of Southern California, CA B
U of Washington, WA B

Journalism

Alliant International U, CA B
Arizona State U, AZ B
Brigham Young U, UT B
California Lutheran U, CA B
California Polytechnic State U, San Luis Obispo, CA B
California State Polytechnic U, Pomona, CA B
California State U, Chico, CA B
California State U, Fresno, CA B
California State U, Fullerton, CA B
California State U, Hayward, CA B
California State U, Long Beach, CA B
California State U, Sacramento, CA B
Central Washington U, WA B
Colorado State U, CO B
Colorado State U-Pueblo, CO B
Eastern Washington U, WA B
Gonzaga U, WA B
Hawai'i Pacific U, HI B
Humboldt State U, CA B
Lehigh U, PA B

Metropolitan State Coll of Denver, CO B
Multnomah Bible Coll and Biblical Seminary, OR B
New Mexico Highlands U, NM B
New Mexico State U, NM B
Northern Arizona U, AZ B
Pacific Lutheran U, WA B
Pacific Union Coll, CA B
Pacific U, OR B
Pepperdine U, Malibu, CA B
Point Loma Nazarene U, CA B
San Diego State U, CA B
San Francisco State U, CA B
San Jose State U, CA B
Seattle U, WA B
U of Alaska Anchorage, AK B
U of Alaska Fairbanks, AK B
The U of Arizona, AZ B
U of California, Irvine, CA B
U of Colorado at Boulder, CO B
U of Denver, CO B
U of Hawaii at Manoa, HI B
U of Idaho, ID B
U of La Verne, CA B
The U of Montana–Missoula, MT B
U of Nevada, Reno, NV B
U of New Mexico, NM B
U of Northern Colorado, CO B
U of Oregon, OR B
U of Portland, OR B
U of Southern California, CA B
U of Utah, UT B
U of Wyoming, WY B
Utah State U, UT B
Walla Walla Coll, WA B
Weber State U, UT B
Western Baptist Coll, OR B
Western State Coll of Colorado, CO B
Western Washington U, WA B
Whitworth Coll, WA B

Journalism Related

California State U, Long Beach, CA B
City U, WA B
Eastern Washington U, WA B
San Diego State U, CA B

Kindergarten/Preschool Education

Arizona State U, AZ B
Birmingham-Southern Coll, AL B
Blackfeet Comm Coll, MT A
Boise State U, ID B
California Polytechnic State U, San Luis Obispo, CA B
Central Washington U, WA B
Concordia U, OR B
Eastern New Mexico U, NM B
Fort Lewis Coll, CO B
Great Basin Coll, NV A
Humboldt State U, CA B
Mount St. Mary's Coll, CA A
Naropa U, CO B
New Mexico Highlands U, NM B
New Mexico State U, NM B
North Carolina Ag and Tech State U, NC B
Oregon State U, OR B
Pacific Lutheran U, WA B
Pacific Oaks Coll, CA B
Pacific Union Coll, CA A,B
Pacific U, OR B
Prescott Coll, AZ B
U of Alaska Anchorage, AK B
U of Alaska Fairbanks, AK A
U of Alaska Southeast, AK A,B
The U of Arizona, AZ B
U of Great Falls, MT A,B
U of La Verne, CA B
The U of Montana–Western, MT A
U of Nevada, Las Vegas, NV B
U of New Mexico, NM B
U of Utah, UT B
Utah State U, UT B
Warner Pacific Coll, OR B
Weber State U, UT B
Western Washington U, WA B
Westminster Coll, UT B

Kinesiology and Exercise Science

Adams State Coll, CO B
Albertson Coll of Idaho, ID B
Arizona State U, AZ B
Bastyr U, WA B
Biola U, CA B
Boise State U, ID B
Brigham Young U, UT B
Brigham Young U–Hawaii, HI B
California Baptist U, CA B
California Lutheran U, CA B
California State U, Chico, CA B
California State U, Hayward, CA B
California State U, Long Beach, CA B
California State U, Sacramento, CA B
Central Washington U, WA B
Christian Heritage Coll, CA B
Colorado State U, CO B
Colorado State U-Pueblo, CO B
Concordia U, CA B
Eastern Washington U, WA B
Gonzaga U, WA B
Grand Canyon U, AZ B
Humboldt State U, CA B
Lewis-Clark State Coll, ID B
Linfield Coll, OR B
Metropolitan State Coll of Denver, CO B
Northern Arizona U, AZ B
Northwest Nazarene U, ID B
Occidental Coll, CA B
Oregon State U, OR B
Pacific Union Coll, CA B
Pacific U, OR B
Point Loma Nazarene U, CA B
Rocky Mountain Coll, MT B
Saint Mary's Coll of California, CA B
Seattle Pacific U, WA B
U of Alaska Fairbanks, AK B
U of California, Los Angeles, CA B
U of Colorado at Boulder, CO B
U of Hawaii at Manoa, HI B
U of Nevada, Las Vegas, NV B
U of Northern Colorado, CO B
U of Oregon, OR B
U of Puget Sound, WA B
U of Southern California, CA B
U of the Pacific, CA B
U of Utah, UT B
U of Wyoming, WY B
Vanguard U of Southern California, CA B
Walla Walla Coll, WA B
Warner Pacific Coll, OR B
Washington State U, WA B
Weber State U, UT B
Western State Coll of Colorado, CO B
Western Washington U, WA B
Westmont Coll, CA B
Willamette U, OR B

Kinesiotherapy

California State U, Long Beach, CA B

Korean

Brigham Young U, UT B
U of California, Los Angeles, CA B

Korean Studies

Claremont McKenna Coll, CA B

Labor and Industrial Relations

California State U, Dominguez Hills, CA B
San Francisco State U, CA B

Landscape Architecture

Arizona State U, AZ B
California Polytechnic State U, San Luis Obispo, CA B
California State Polytechnic U, Pomona, CA B
Colorado State U, CO B
North Carolina Ag and Tech State U, NC B
The U of Arizona, AZ B
U of California, Berkeley, CA B
U of California, Davis, CA B
U of Hawaii at Manoa, HI B
U of Idaho, ID B
U of Nevada, Las Vegas, NV B
U of Oregon, OR B
U of Southern California, CA B
U of Washington, WA B
Utah State U, UT B
Washington State U, WA B

Landscaping and Groundskeeping

Colorado State U, CO B
Oregon State U, OR B

Land Use Planning and Management

California State U, Bakersfield, CA B
Metropolitan State Coll of Denver, CO B
Washington State U, WA B

Language Interpretation and Translation

Brigham Young U, UT B

Laser and Optical Technology

Idaho State U, ID A
Oregon Inst of Technology, OR B
Pacific Union Coll, CA A

Latin

Brigham Young U, UT B
Carroll Coll, MT B
Claremont McKenna Coll, CA B
Cornell Coll, IA B
Idaho State U, ID A
Lehigh U, PA B
Loyola Marymount U, CA B
Saint Mary's Coll of California, CA B
Santa Clara U, CA B
Scripps Coll, CA B
Seattle Pacific U, WA B
U of California, Berkeley, CA B
U of California, Los Angeles, CA B
U of California, Santa Cruz, CA B
U of Hawaii at Manoa, HI B
U of Idaho, ID B
The U of Montana–Missoula, MT B
U of Oregon, OR B
U of Washington, WA B

Latin American Studies

Alliant International U, CA B
Brigham Young U, UT B
California State U, Chico, CA B
California State U, Fullerton, CA B
California State U, Hayward, CA B
California State U, Los Angeles, CA B
Claremont McKenna Coll, CA B
Colorado State U, CO B
Cornell Coll, IA B
Fort Lewis Coll, CO B
Pitzer Coll, CA B
Portland State U, OR B
Prescott Coll, AZ B
Saint Mary's Coll of California, CA B
San Diego State U, CA B
Scripps Coll, CA B
Seattle Pacific U, WA B
The U of Arizona, AZ B
U of California, Berkeley, CA B
U of California, Los Angeles, CA B
U of California, Riverside, CA B
U of California, San Diego, CA B
U of California, Santa Barbara, CA B
U of California, Santa Cruz, CA B
U of Denver, CO B
U of Idaho, ID B
U of New Mexico, NM B
U of San Francisco, CA B
U of Washington, WA B
Western Washington U, WA B
Willamette U, OR B

Latin Teacher Education

Brigham Young U, UT B

Legal Administrative Assistant/Secretary

Crown Coll, WA A
LDS Business Coll, UT A
Lewis-Clark State Coll, ID A,B
Montana State U–Billings, MT A
Montana Tech of The U of Montana, MT A
Morrison U, NV A
Pacific Union Coll, CA A
The U of Montana–Missoula, MT A
U of West Los Angeles, CA B

Legal Assistant/Paralegal

Boise State U, ID A
California State U, Chico, CA B
Crown Coll, WA A
Lewis-Clark State Coll, ID A,B
Morrison U, NV A
Pioneer Pacific Coll, OR A
Platt Coll, Newport Beach, CA A
U of Alaska Anchorage, AK A
U of Alaska Fairbanks, AK A
U of Alaska Southeast, AK A
U of Great Falls, MT A,B
U of La Verne, CA B
The U of Montana–Missoula, MT A
U of West Los Angeles, CA B
Utah Valley State Coll, UT A,B

A—associate degree; B—bachelor's degree

Legal Professions and Studies Related
Washington State U, WA B

Legal Studies
California State U, Chico, CA B
Chapman U, CA B
Claremont McKenna Coll, CA B
National U, CA B
Scripps Coll, CA B
United States Air Force Academy, CO B
U of California, Berkeley, CA B
U of California, Santa Cruz, CA B
The U of Montana–Missoula, MT A,B
U of West Los Angeles, CA B

Liberal Arts and Sciences and Humanities Related
Brigham Young U, UT B
The Colorado Coll, CO B
Northern Arizona U, AZ B
Northwest Christian Coll, OR B
Platt Coll San Diego, CA A,B
St. John's Coll, NM B
Saint Mary's Coll of California, CA B
U of California, Los Angeles, CA B
U of Utah, UT B
Washington State U, WA B

Liberal Arts and Sciences/ Liberal Studies
Adams State Coll, CO A,B
Alaska Pacific U, AK B
Antioch U Los Angeles, CA B
Antioch U Seattle, WA B
Azusa Pacific U, CA B
Blackfeet Comm Coll, MT A
Boise State U, ID B
Brigham Young U, UT B
California Baptist U, CA B
California Lutheran U, CA B
California Polytechnic State U, San Luis Obispo, CA B
California State Polytechnic U, Pomona, CA B
California State U, Bakersfield, CA B
California State U, Chico, CA B
California State U, Dominguez Hills, CA B
California State U, Fresno, CA B
California State U, Fullerton, CA B
California State U, Hayward, CA B
California State U, Long Beach, CA B
California State U, Los Angeles, CA B
California State U, Sacramento, CA B
California State U, San Bernardino, CA B
California State U, San Marcos, CA B
California State U, Stanislaus, CA B
Cascade Coll, OR B
Chapman U, CA B
Christian Heritage Coll, CA B
Colorado Christian U, CO A,B
Colorado State U, CO B
Concordia U, CA B
Concordia U, OR A,B
Cornell Coll, IA B
Dominican U of California, CA B
Eastern New Mexico U, NM B
Eastern Oregon U, OR B
Eastern Washington U, WA B
Eugene Lang Coll, New School U B
The Evergreen State Coll, WA B
Fort Lewis Coll, CO B
Fresno Pacific U, CA A,B
Gonzaga U, WA B
Grand Canyon U, AZ B
Hawai'i Pacific U, HI B
Hawaii Tokai International Coll, HI A
Holy Names U, CA B
Humboldt State U, CA B
John F. Kennedy U, CA B
LDS Business Coll, UT A
Lewis-Clark State Coll, ID A
Loyola Marymount U, CA B
The Master's Coll and Seminary, CA B
Menlo Coll, CA B
Mills Coll, CA B
Montana State U–Billings, MT A,B
Montana Tech of The U of Montana, MT A,B
Mount St. Mary's Coll, CA A
National U, CA A,B
Nevada State Coll at Henderson, NV B
New Mexico Inst of Mining and Technology, NM A,B
Northern Arizona U, AZ B
Northwest Coll, WA A,B
Northwest Nazarene U, ID B
Notre Dame de Namur U, CA B
Oregon Inst of Technology, OR A
Oregon State U, OR B
Pacific Union Coll, CA A,B
Pacific U, OR B
Pepperdine U, Malibu, CA B
Point Loma Nazarene U, CA B
Pomona Coll, CA B
Portland State U, OR B
Prescott Coll, AZ B
Regis U, CO B
Rocky Mountain Coll, MT A
St. John's Coll, NM B
Saint Mary's Coll of California, CA B
San Diego State U, CA B
San Francisco State U, CA B
San Jose State U, CA B
Santa Clara U, CA B
Seattle Pacific U, WA B
Seattle U, WA B
Sheldon Jackson Coll, AK B
Simpson Coll and Graduate School, CA B
Sonoma State U, CA B
Southern Oregon U, OR B
Thomas Aquinas Coll, CA B
U of Alaska Fairbanks, AK A
U of Alaska Southeast, AK A,B
The U of Arizona, AZ B
U of California, Los Angeles, CA B
U of California, Riverside, CA B
U of Hawaii at Manoa, HI B
U of Idaho, ID B
U of Judaism, CA B
U of La Verne, CA A,B
The U of Montana–Missoula, MT B
The U of Montana–Western, MT B
U of New Mexico, NM B
U of Oregon, OR B
U of Redlands, CA B
U of San Diego, CA B
U of San Francisco, CA B
U of Utah, UT B
U of Washington, WA B
Utah State U, UT B
Warner Pacific Coll, OR B
Washington State U, WA B
Weber State U, UT A,B
Western Baptist Coll, OR B
Western Oregon U, OR A
Western Washington U, WA B
Westmont Coll, CA B
William Jessup U, CA B

Library Science Related
U of California, Los Angeles, CA B
U of Great Falls, MT B

Lineworker
Utah Valley State Coll, UT A

Linguistic and Comparative Language Studies Related
Brigham Young U, UT B
U of California, Los Angeles, CA B

Linguistics
Brigham Young U, UT B
California State U, Chico, CA B
California State U, Dominguez Hills, CA B
California State U, Fresno, CA B
California State U, Fullerton, CA B
Pitzer Coll, CA B
Pomona Coll, CA B
Portland State U, OR B
Reed Coll, OR B
San Diego State U, CA B
San Jose State U, CA B
Scripps Coll, CA B
Stanford U, CA B
U of Alaska Fairbanks, AK B
The U of Arizona, AZ B
U of California, Berkeley, CA B
U of California, Davis, CA B
U of California, Irvine, CA B
U of California, Los Angeles, CA B
U of California, Riverside, CA B
U of California, San Diego, CA B
U of California, Santa Barbara, CA B
U of California, Santa Cruz, CA B
U of Colorado at Boulder, CO B
U of Hawaii at Hilo, HI B
The U of Montana–Missoula, MT B
U of New Mexico, NM B
U of Oregon, OR B
U of Southern California, CA B
U of Utah, UT B
U of Washington, WA B
Washington State U, WA B
Western Washington U, WA B

Literature
Boise State U, ID B
California Inst of Technology, CA B
California State U, Dominguez Hills, CA B
California State U, Long Beach, CA B
Chapman U, CA B
Claremont McKenna Coll, CA B
Eastern Washington U, WA B
Eugene Lang Coll, New School U B
Fort Lewis Coll, CO B
Fresno Pacific U, CA B
Gonzaga U, WA B
Grand Canyon U, AZ B
Hawai'i Pacific U, HI B
Naropa U, CO B
New Coll of California, CA B
Oregon State U, OR B
Pacific Lutheran U, WA B
Pacific U, OR B
Pitzer Coll, CA B
Prescott Coll, AZ B
Reed Coll, OR B
St. John's Coll, NM B
Saint Mary's Coll of California, CA B
San Francisco State U, CA B
Sonoma State U, CA B
U of California, Irvine, CA B
U of California, San Diego, CA B
U of California, Santa Cruz, CA B
U of Judaism, CA B
The U of Montana–Western, MT B
U of Redlands, CA B
Western Washington U, WA B

Logistics and Materials Management
Brigham Young U, UT B
Portland State U, OR B
U of Nevada, Reno, NV B
Weber State U, UT B

Machine Tool Technology
Boise State U, ID A
Idaho State U, ID A
Utah Valley State Coll, UT A
Weber State U, UT A

Management Information Systems
Alliant International U, CA B
American InterContinental U, CA B
Arizona State U, AZ B
Azusa Pacific U, CA B
Brigham Young U, UT B
California Polytechnic State U, San Luis Obispo, CA B
California State U, Chico, CA B
California State U, Dominguez Hills, CA B
California State U, Fresno, CA B
California State U, Hayward, CA B
California State U, Long Beach, CA B
California State U, Sacramento, CA B
California State U, San Bernardino, CA B
Coll of Santa Fe, NM B
Colorado Christian U, CO A,B
Eastern New Mexico U, NM B
Eastern Washington U, WA B
George Fox U, OR B
Hawai'i Pacific U, HI B
Lehigh U, PA B
The Master's Coll and Seminary, CA B
National American U, Denver, CO B
National American U, NM A,B
New Mexico Highlands U, NM B
Northern Arizona U, AZ B
Northwest Christian Coll, OR B
Oregon Inst of Technology, OR B
Oregon State U, OR B
Pacific Lutheran U, WA B
Pacific Union Coll, CA B
Point Loma Nazarene U, CA B
Rocky Mountain Coll, MT B
Saint Martin's Coll, WA B
Santa Clara U, CA B

Seattle U, WA B
Simpson Coll and Graduate School, CA B
Touro U International, CA B
U of Alaska Anchorage, AK B
The U of Arizona, AZ B
U of Colorado at Boulder, CO B
U of Denver, CO B
U of Hawaii at Manoa, HI B
U of Idaho, ID B
U of Nevada, Las Vegas, NV B
U of Phoenix–Colorado Campus, CO B
U of Phoenix–Hawaii Campus, HI B
U of Phoenix–New Mexico Campus, NM B
U of Phoenix–Northern California Campus, CA B
U of Phoenix–Oregon Campus, OR B
U of Phoenix–Phoenix Campus, AZ B
U of Phoenix–Sacramento Campus, CA B
U of Phoenix–San Diego Campus, CA B
U of Phoenix–Southern Arizona Campus, AZ B
U of Phoenix–Southern California Campus, CA B
U of Phoenix–Southern Colorado Campus, CO B
U of Phoenix–Utah Campus, UT B
U of Phoenix–Washington Campus, WA B
U of Redlands, CA B
U of San Francisco, CA B
U of Utah, UT B
U of Washington, WA B
U of Wyoming, WY B
Utah Valley State Coll, UT B
Walla Walla Coll, WA B
Washington State U, WA B
Weber State U, UT A,B
Western Baptist Coll, OR B
Western State Coll of Colorado, CO B
Western Washington U, WA B

Management Information Systems and Services Related

California State U, Chico, CA B
International Inst of the Americas, AZ A
Washington State U, WA B
Westminster Coll, UT B

Management Science

Colorado Christian U, CO B
Metropolitan State Coll of Denver, CO B
Northwest Coll, WA B
Prescott Coll, AZ B
Rocky Mountain Coll, MT B
U of California, San Diego, CA B
U of Great Falls, MT B
U of Phoenix–Colorado Campus, CO B
U of Phoenix–Hawaii Campus, HI B
U of Phoenix–New Mexico Campus, NM B
U of Phoenix–Northern California Campus, CA B
U of Phoenix Online Campus, AZ B
U of Phoenix–Oregon Campus, OR B
U of Phoenix–Phoenix Campus, AZ B
U of Phoenix–Sacramento Campus, CA B
U of Phoenix–Southern Arizona Campus, AZ B
U of Phoenix–Southern Colorado Campus, CO B
U of Phoenix–Utah Campus, UT B
U of Phoenix–Washington Campus, WA B
U of Washington, WA B
U of Wyoming, WY B
Washington State U, WA B

Manufacturing Engineering

Brigham Young U, UT B
California State U, Los Angeles, CA B
U of California, Berkeley, CA B
U of California, Los Angeles, CA B

Manufacturing Technology

Arizona State U East, AZ B
California State U, Long Beach, CA B
Eastern Washington U, WA B
Lewis-Clark State Coll, ID A,B
Utah Valley State Coll, UT A
Western Washington U, WA B

Marine Biology and Biological Oceanography

Alaska Pacific U, AK B
California State U, Long Beach, CA B
Hawai'i Pacific U, HI B
Humboldt State U, CA B
Northern Arizona U, AZ B
San Diego State U, CA B
San Francisco State U, CA B
San Jose State U, CA B
Sonoma State U, CA B
U of Alaska Southeast, AK B
U of California, Los Angeles, CA B
U of California, Santa Barbara, CA B
U of California, Santa Cruz, CA B
U of Southern California, CA B
Western Washington U, WA B

Marine Science/Merchant Marine Officer

Oregon State U, OR B
Prescott Coll, AZ B
U of San Diego, CA B

Marine Technology

California Maritime Academy, CA B
U of Alaska Southeast, AK A

Marketing/Marketing Management

American InterContinental U, CA B
Arizona State U, AZ B
Azusa Pacific U, CA B
Boise State U, ID A,B
Brigham Young U, UT B
California Lutheran U, CA B
California State Polytechnic U, Pomona, CA B
California State U, Chico, CA B
California State U, Dominguez Hills, CA B
California State U, Fresno, CA B
California State U, Fullerton, CA B
California State U, Hayward, CA B
California State U, Long Beach, CA B
California State U, Sacramento, CA B
California State U, San Bernardino, CA B
Chaminade U of Honolulu, HI B
Coll of the Southwest, NM B
Colorado State U, CO B
Colorado State U-Pueblo, CO B
Eastern New Mexico U, NM B
Eastern Washington U, WA B
Fort Lewis Coll, CO B
Fresno Pacific U, CA B
Golden Gate U, CA B
Gonzaga U, WA B
Grand Canyon U, AZ B
Hawai'i Pacific U, HI A,B
Holy Names U, CA B
Humboldt State U, CA B
Idaho State U, ID A,B
Johnson & Wales U, CO A
Lehigh U, PA B
Montana State U-Billings, MT B
Mount St. Mary's Coll, CA B
National U, CA B
New Mexico Highlands U, NM B
New Mexico State U, NM B
Northern Arizona U, AZ B
Northwest Nazarene U, ID B
Notre Dame de Namur U, CA B
Oregon State U, OR B
Pacific Lutheran U, WA B
Pacific Union Coll, CA B
Pacific U, OR B
Portland State U, OR B
Saint Martin's Coll, WA B
San Diego State U, CA B
San Francisco State U, CA B
San Jose State U, CA B
Santa Clara U, CA B
Seattle U, WA B
Southern Oregon U, OR B
U of Alaska Anchorage, AK B
The U of Arizona, AZ B
U of Colorado at Boulder, CO B
U of Colorado at Colorado Springs, CO B
U of Denver, CO B
U of Great Falls, MT B
U of Hawaii at Manoa, HI B
U of Idaho, ID B
U of La Verne, CA B
The U of Montana–Missoula, MT B
U of Nevada, Las Vegas, NV B
U of Nevada, Reno, NV B
U of Oregon, OR B
U of Phoenix–Hawaii Campus, HI B
U of Phoenix–Idaho Campus, ID B
U of Phoenix–Nevada Campus, NV B
U of Phoenix–New Mexico Campus, NM B
U of Phoenix–Northern California Campus, CA B
U of Phoenix–Oregon Campus, OR B
U of Phoenix–Phoenix Campus, AZ B
U of Phoenix–Sacramento Campus, CA B
U of Phoenix–San Diego Campus, CA B
U of Phoenix–Southern Arizona Campus, AZ B
U of Phoenix–Southern California Campus, CA B
U of Phoenix–Southern Colorado Campus, CO B
U of Phoenix–Utah Campus, UT B
U of Phoenix–Washington Campus, WA B
U of Portland, OR B
U of San Francisco, CA B
U of Utah, UT B
U of Wyoming, WY B
Utah State U, UT B
Utah Valley State Coll, UT B
Vanguard U of Southern California, CA B
Walla Walla Coll, WA B
Washington State U, WA B
Weber State U, UT A,B
Western State Coll of Colorado, CO B
Western Washington U, WA B
Westminster Coll, UT B
Westwood Coll–Anaheim, CA B
Westwood Coll–Denver South, CO B
Westwood Coll–Inland Empire, CA B
Westwood Coll–Los Angeles, CA B
Westwood Coll–Denver North, CO B
Woodbury U, CA B

Marketing Related

U of Utah, UT B

Marketing Research

Metropolitan State Coll of Denver, CO B

Marriage and Family Therapy/Counseling

U of Nevada, Las Vegas, NV B

Mass Communication/Media

Boise State U, ID B
Brigham Young U, UT B
California Lutheran U, CA B
California State Polytechnic U, Pomona, CA B
California State U, Bakersfield, CA B
California State U, Dominguez Hills, CA B
California State U, Fresno, CA B
California State U, Hayward, CA B
California State U, Long Beach, CA B
California State U, Sacramento, CA B
California State U, San Bernardino, CA B
Central Washington U, WA B
Chaminade U of Honolulu, HI B
City U, WA B
Colorado State U-Pueblo, CO B
Fresno Pacific U, CA A,B
Gonzaga U, WA B
Grand Canyon U, AZ B
Hawai'i Pacific U, HI B
Idaho State U, ID B
Loyola Marymount U, CA B
Marylhurst U, OR B
The Master's Coll and Seminary, CA B

A—associate degree; B—bachelor's degree

Menlo Coll, CA B
Montana State U–Billings, MT B
New Mexico Highlands U, NM B
North Carolina Ag and Tech State U, NC B
Northwest Nazarene U, ID B
Oregon State U, OR B
Pacific Lutheran U, WA B
Pacific Union Coll, CA B
Pacific U, OR B
San Diego State U, CA B
Seattle U, WA B
Sonoma State U, CA B
Southern Utah U, UT B
U of Alaska Anchorage, AK B
U of California, Berkeley, CA B
U of California, San Diego, CA B
U of New Mexico, NM B
U of Oregon, OR B
U of Portland, OR B
U of San Diego, CA B
U of San Francisco, CA B
U of Southern California, CA B
U of Utah, UT B
Walla Walla Coll, WA B
Western State Coll of Colorado, CO B
Western Washington U, WA B
Whitworth Coll, WA B

Materials Engineering

Arizona State U, AZ B
California Polytechnic State U, San Luis Obispo, CA B
California State Polytechnic U, Pomona, CA B
California State U, Long Beach, CA B
Lehigh U, PA B
Montana Tech of The U of Montana, MT B
New Mexico Inst of Mining and Technology, NM B
San Jose State U, CA B
Stanford U, CA B
U of California, Davis, CA B
U of California, Irvine, CA B
U of California, Los Angeles, CA B
U of Utah, UT B
U of Washington, WA B
Washington State U, WA B

Materials Science

Montana Tech of The U of Montana, MT B
Oregon State U, OR B
Stanford U, CA B
United States Air Force Academy, CO B
The U of Arizona, AZ B
U of California, Berkeley, CA B
U of California, Los Angeles, CA B
U of Southern California, CA B
U of Utah, UT B
Washington State U, WA B

Maternal/Child Health and Neonatal Nursing

U of Washington, WA B

Mathematics

Adams State Coll, CO B
Albertson Coll of Idaho, ID B
Arizona State U, AZ B
Azusa Pacific U, CA B
Biola U, CA B
Birmingham-Southern Coll, AL B
Boise State U, ID B
Brigham Young U, UT B
Brigham Young U–Hawaii, HI B
California Baptist U, CA B
California Inst of Technology, CA B
California Lutheran U, CA B
California Polytechnic State U, San Luis Obispo, CA B
California State Polytechnic U, Pomona, CA B
California State U, Bakersfield, CA B
California State U, Chico, CA B
California State U, Dominguez Hills, CA B
California State U, Fresno, CA B
California State U, Fullerton, CA B
California State U, Hayward, CA B
California State U, Long Beach, CA B
California State U, Los Angeles, CA B
California State U, Sacramento, CA B
California State U, San Bernardino, CA B
California State U, San Marcos, CA B
California State U, Stanislaus, CA B
Carroll Coll, MT B
Central Washington U, WA B
Chapman U, CA B
Christian Heritage Coll, CA B
Claremont McKenna Coll, CA B
Coll of the Southwest, NM B
Colorado Christian U, CO B
The Colorado Coll, CO B
Colorado School of Mines, CO B
Colorado State U, CO B
Colorado State U-Pueblo, CO B
Concordia U, CA B
Cornell Coll, IA B
Eastern Oregon U, OR B
Eastern Washington U, WA B
Fort Lewis Coll, CO B
Fresno Pacific U, CA A,B
George Fox U, OR B
Gonzaga U, WA B
Grand Canyon U, AZ B
Great Basin Coll, NV A
Harvey Mudd Coll, CA B
Humboldt State U, CA B
Idaho State U, ID A,B
Lehigh U, PA B
Lewis & Clark Coll, OR B
Lewis-Clark State Coll, ID B
Linfield Coll, OR B
Loyola Marymount U, CA B
The Master's Coll and Seminary, CA B
Metropolitan State Coll of Denver, CO B
Mills Coll, CA B
Montana State U–Billings, MT B
Montana State U–Bozeman, MT B
Montana Tech of The U of Montana, MT B
Mount St. Mary's Coll, CA B
National U, CA B
New Mexico Highlands U, NM B
New Mexico Inst of Mining and Technology, NM B
New Mexico State U, NM B
North Carolina Ag and Tech State U, NC B
Northern Arizona U, AZ B
Northwest Nazarene U, ID B
Occidental Coll, CA B
Oregon State U, OR B
Pacific Lutheran U, WA B
Pacific Union Coll, CA B
Pacific U, OR B
Pepperdine U, Malibu, CA B
Pitzer Coll, CA B
Platt Coll San Diego, CA B
Point Loma Nazarene U, CA B
Pomona Coll, CA B
Portland State U, OR B
Reed Coll, OR B
Regis U, CO B
Rocky Mountain Coll, MT B
St. John's Coll, NM B
Saint Martin's Coll, WA B
Saint Mary's Coll of California, CA B
San Diego State U, CA B
San Francisco State U, CA B
San Jose State U, CA B
Santa Clara U, CA B
Scripps Coll, CA B
Seattle Pacific U, WA B
Seattle U, WA B
Simpson Coll and Graduate School, CA B
Sonoma State U, CA B
Southern Oregon U, OR B
Southern Utah U, UT B
Stanford U, CA B
United States Air Force Academy, CO B
U of Alaska Anchorage, AK B
U of Alaska Fairbanks, AK B
The U of Arizona, AZ B
U of California, Berkeley, CA B
U of California, Davis, CA B
U of California, Irvine, CA B
U of California, Los Angeles, CA B
U of California, Riverside, CA B
U of California, San Diego, CA B
U of California, Santa Barbara, CA B
U of California, Santa Cruz, CA B
U of Colorado at Boulder, CO B
U of Colorado at Colorado Springs, CO B
U of Colorado at Denver, CO B
U of Denver, CO B
U of Great Falls, MT A,B
U of Hawaii at Hilo, HI B
U of Hawaii at Manoa, HI B
U of Idaho, ID B
U of La Verne, CA B
The U of Montana–Missoula, MT B
U of Nevada, Las Vegas, NV B
U of Nevada, Reno, NV B
U of New Mexico, NM B
U of Northern Colorado, CO B
U of Oregon, OR B
U of Portland, OR B
U of Puget Sound, WA B
U of Redlands, CA B
U of San Diego, CA B
U of San Francisco, CA B
U of Southern California, CA B
U of the Pacific, CA B
U of Utah, UT B
U of Washington, WA B
U of Wyoming, WY B
Utah State U, UT B
Utah Valley State Coll, UT A,B
Vanguard U of Southern California, CA B
Walla Walla Coll, WA B
Washington State U, WA B
Weber State U, UT B
Western Baptist Coll, OR B
Western Oregon U, OR B
Western State Coll of Colorado, CO B
Western Washington U, WA B
Westminster Coll, UT B
Westmont Coll, CA B
Whitman Coll, WA B
Whitworth Coll, WA B
Willamette U, OR B

Mathematics and Computer Science

The Colorado Coll, CO B
Saint Mary's Coll of California, CA B
San Diego State U, CA B
Southern Oregon U, OR B
Stanford U, CA B
U of Oregon, OR B
Washington State U, WA B

Mathematics and Statistics Related

Saint Mary's Coll of California, CA B
Seattle Pacific U, WA B

Mathematics Related

Eastern Washington U, WA B
U of California, Los Angeles, CA B

Mathematics Teacher Education

Brigham Young U, UT B
Brigham Young U–Hawaii, HI B
California Lutheran U, CA B
California State U, Chico, CA B
California State U, Long Beach, CA B
Carroll Coll, MT B
Central Washington U, WA B
Colorado State U, CO B
Colorado State U-Pueblo, CO B
Concordia U, OR B
Eastern Washington U, WA B
George Fox U, OR B
Lewis-Clark State Coll, ID B
Montana State U–Billings, MT B
Nevada State Coll at Henderson, NV B
Northern Arizona U, AZ B
Northwest Nazarene U, ID B
Prescott Coll, AZ B
Rocky Mountain Coll, MT B
San Diego State U, CA B
Seattle Pacific U, WA B
The U of Arizona, AZ B
U of California, San Diego, CA B
U of California, Santa Cruz, CA B
U of Great Falls, MT B
U of Hawaii at Manoa, HI B
The U of Montana–Missoula, MT B
The U of Montana–Western, MT B
U of Nevada, Reno, NV B
U of Utah, UT B
Utah State U, UT B
Utah Valley State Coll, UT B
Western Baptist Coll, OR B
Westmont Coll, CA B

Mechanical Drafting and CAD/CADD

Montana Tech of The U of Montana, MT A
Silicon Valley Coll, Walnut Creek, CA A
Westwood Coll–Denver North, CO A

Mechanical Engineering

Arizona State U, AZ B
Brigham Young U, UT B
California Inst of Technology, CA B
California Maritime Academy, CA B
California Polytechnic State U, San Luis Obispo, CA B
California State Polytechnic U, Pomona, CA B
California State U, Chico, CA B
California State U, Fresno, CA B
California State U, Fullerton, CA B
California State U, Long Beach, CA B
California State U, Los Angeles, CA B
California State U, Sacramento, CA B
Colorado School of Mines, CO B
Colorado State U, CO B
Gonzaga U, WA B
Henry Cogswell Coll, WA B
Idaho State U, ID B
Lehigh U, PA B
Loyola Marymount U, CA B
Montana State U–Bozeman, MT B
Montana Tech of The U of Montana, MT B
New Mexico Inst of Mining and Technology, NM B
New Mexico State U, NM B
North Carolina Ag and Tech State U, NC B
Northern Arizona U, AZ B
Oregon State U, OR B
Portland State U, OR B
Saint Martin's Coll, WA B
San Diego State U, CA B
San Francisco State U, CA B
San Jose State U, CA B
Santa Clara U, CA B
Seattle U, WA B
Stanford U, CA B
United States Air Force Academy, CO B
U of Alaska Fairbanks, AK B
The U of Arizona, AZ B
U of California, Berkeley, CA B
U of California, Davis, CA B
U of California, Irvine, CA B
U of California, Los Angeles, CA B
U of California, Riverside, CA B
U of California, San Diego, CA B
U of California, Santa Barbara, CA B
U of Colorado at Boulder, CO B
U of Colorado at Colorado Springs, CO B
U of Colorado at Denver, CO B
U of Denver, CO B
U of Hawaii at Manoa, HI B
U of Idaho, ID B
U of Nevada, Las Vegas, NV B
U of Nevada, Reno, NV B
U of New Mexico, NM B
U of Portland, OR B
U of San Diego, CA B
U of Southern California, CA B
U of the Pacific, CA B
U of Utah, UT B
U of Washington, WA B
U of Wyoming, WY B
Utah State U, UT B
Walla Walla Coll, WA B
Washington State U, WA B

Mechanical Engineering/ Mechanical Technology

Arizona State U East, AZ B
Boise State U, ID B
California Polytechnic State U, San Luis Obispo, CA B
California State Polytechnic U, Pomona, CA B
California State U, Long Beach, CA B
California State U, Sacramento, CA B
Central Washington U, WA B
Colorado State U-Pueblo, CO B
Eastern Washington U, WA B
Metropolitan State Coll of Denver, CO B
Montana State U–Bozeman, MT B
Oregon Inst of Technology, OR B
Weber State U, UT A,B

Mechanics and Repair

Idaho State U, ID A
Lewis-Clark State Coll, ID A,B

Medical Administrative Assistant and Medical Secretary

Boise State U, ID A
LDS Business Coll, UT A
Montana State U–Billings, MT A
Montana Tech of The U of Montana, MT A
Morrison U, NV A
Pacific Union Coll, CA A
Silicon Valley Coll, Walnut Creek, CA A
The U of Montana–Missoula, MT A
Utah Valley State Coll, UT A

Medical/Clinical Assistant

California State U, Dominguez Hills, CA B
CollAmerica–Fort Collins, CO A
Idaho State U, ID A
International Inst of the Americas, AZ A
LDS Business Coll, UT A
Montana State U–Billings, MT A
National American U, Colorado Springs, CO A
National American U, Denver, CO A
Pioneer Pacific Coll, OR A
U of Alaska Anchorage, AK A
U of Alaska Fairbanks, AK A
Westwood Coll–Denver North, CO A

Medical/Health Management and Clinical Assistant

Lewis-Clark State Coll, ID A,B
National American U, Denver, CO A

Medical Insurance Coding

LDS Business Coll, UT A

Medical Laboratory Technology

U of Nevada, Las Vegas, NV B

Medical Microbiology and Bacteriology

Arizona State U, AZ B
California Polytechnic State U, San Luis Obispo, CA B
California State Polytechnic U, Pomona, CA B
California State U, Dominguez Hills, CA B
California State U, Fresno, CA B
Colorado State U, CO B
Humboldt State U, CA B
Idaho State U, ID B
Montana State U–Bozeman, MT B
New Mexico State U, NM B
Northern Arizona U, AZ B
Oregon State U, OR B
Pomona Coll, CA B
San Diego State U, CA B
San Francisco State U, CA B
Sonoma State U, CA B
The U of Arizona, AZ B
U of California, Davis, CA B
U of California, Los Angeles, CA B
U of California, San Diego, CA B
U of California, Santa Barbara, CA B
U of Idaho, ID B
The U of Montana–Missoula, MT B
U of Washington, WA B
Utah State U, UT B
Weber State U, UT B

Medical Office Assistant

LDS Business Coll, UT A
Lewis-Clark State Coll, ID A,B
Silicon Valley Coll, Walnut Creek, CA A

Medical Office Management

DeVry U, Westminster, CO A
National American U, Colorado Springs, CO A

Medical Pharmacology and Pharmaceutical Sciences

The U of Montana–Missoula, MT B

Medical Radiologic Technology

California State U, Long Beach, CA B
Idaho State U, ID A,B
Loma Linda U, CA A,B
U of Nevada, Las Vegas, NV B
U of New Mexico, NM A
Weber State U, UT A,B

Medical Transcription

DeVry U, Westminster, CO A
International Inst of the Americas, AZ A
LDS Business Coll, UT A
Westwood Coll–Denver North, CO A

Medicinal and Pharmaceutical Chemistry

U of California, San Diego, CA B

Medieval and Renaissance Studies

Cornell Coll, IA B
U of California, Santa Barbara, CA B

Mental and Social Health Services and Allied Professions Related

U of Alaska Fairbanks, AK A

Mental Health/Rehabilitation

Prescott Coll, AZ B

Merchandising, Sales, and Marketing Operations Related (General)

Brigham Young U, UT B

Metal and Jewelry Arts

Academy of Art U, CA A,B
Arizona State U, AZ B
California Coll of the Arts, CA B
California State U, Long Beach, CA B
Colorado State U, CO B
U of Oregon, OR B
U of Washington, WA B

Metallurgical Engineering

Colorado School of Mines, CO B
Montana Tech of The U of Montana, MT B
New Mexico Inst of Mining and Technology, NM B
Oregon State U, OR B
U of Idaho, ID B
U of Nevada, Reno, NV B
U of Utah, UT B
U of Washington, WA B

Meteorology

U of Utah, UT B

Microbiological Sciences and Immunology Related

U of California, Los Angeles, CA B

Microbiology

Brigham Young U, UT B
California State U, Chico, CA B
California State U, Long Beach, CA B
California State U, Los Angeles, CA B
Idaho State U, ID B
New Mexico State U, NM B
U of California, Berkeley, CA B
U of California, Irvine, CA B
U of Wyoming, WY B
Washington State U, WA B

Middle/ Near Eastern and Semitic Languages Related

U of California, Los Angeles, CA B

Middle School Education

Coll of the Southwest, NM B
Colorado State U-Pueblo, CO B
The Master's Coll and Seminary, CA B
Northwest Coll, WA B
Prescott Coll, AZ B
U of Great Falls, MT B
Warner Pacific Coll, OR B

Military Studies

Hawai'i Pacific U, HI A,B
United States Air Force Academy, CO B

Military Technologies

U of Idaho, ID B

Mining and Mineral Engineering

Colorado School of Mines, CO B
Montana Tech of The U of Montana, MT B
New Mexico Inst of Mining and Technology, NM B
Oregon State U, OR B
The U of Arizona, AZ B
U of Idaho, ID B

A—associate degree; B—bachelor's degree

U of Nevada, Reno, NV B
U of Utah, UT B

Mining and Petroleum Technologies Related
U of Alaska Fairbanks, AK B

Missionary Studies and Missiology
Bethesda Christian U, CA B
Biola U, CA B
Cascade Coll, OR B
Eugene Bible Coll, OR B
George Fox U, OR B
Multnomah Bible Coll and Biblical Seminary, OR B
Northwest Coll, WA B
Northwest Nazarene U, ID B
Simpson Coll and Graduate School, CA B
Vanguard U of Southern California, CA B
Western Baptist Coll, OR B

Modern Greek
Claremont McKenna Coll, CA B
Cornell Coll, IA B
Loyola Marymount U, CA B
Saint Mary's Coll of California, CA B
U of California, Los Angeles, CA B
U of Oregon, OR B
U of Utah, UT B

Modern Languages
Claremont McKenna Coll, CA B
Cornell Coll, IA B
Fort Lewis Coll, CO B
Lewis & Clark Coll, OR B
Pacific Lutheran U, WA B
Pacific U, OR B
Pomona Coll, CA B
Saint Mary's Coll of California, CA B
Scripps Coll, CA B
Walla Walla Coll, WA B
Westmont Coll, CA B

Molecular Biochemistry
U of California, Irvine, CA B
U of California, Los Angeles, CA B

Molecular Biology
Arizona State U, AZ B
Brigham Young U, UT B
California Lutheran U, CA B
California State U, Fresno, CA B
California State U, Sacramento, CA B
California State U, San Marcos, CA B
Chapman U, CA B
Fort Lewis Coll, CO B
Humboldt State U, CA B
Lehigh U, PA B
Pomona Coll, CA B
San Francisco State U, CA B
San Jose State U, CA B
Scripps Coll, CA B
U of California, Los Angeles, CA B
U of California, San Diego, CA B
U of California, Santa Barbara, CA B
U of California, Santa Cruz, CA B
U of Denver, CO B
U of Idaho, ID B
U of Washington, WA B
U of Wyoming, WY B
Western State Coll of Colorado, CO B
Western Washington U, WA B
Whitman Coll, WA B

Molecular Biophysics
The U of Arizona, AZ B

Molecular Pharmacology
U of California, Los Angeles, CA B

Molecular Physiology
U of California, Los Angeles, CA B

Molecular Toxicology
U of California, Los Angeles, CA B

Multi-/Interdisciplinary Studies Related
Arizona State U, AZ B
Arizona State U East, AZ B
Arizona State U West, AZ B
Brigham Young U–Hawaii, HI B
California Lutheran U, CA B
California State U, Chico, CA B
California State U, Long Beach, CA B
California State U, Los Angeles, CA B
California State U, Stanislaus, CA B
Christian Heritage Coll, CA B
Coll of Santa Fe, NM B
The Colorado Coll, CO B
Cornell Coll, IA B
Eastern New Mexico U, NM B
The Evergreen State Coll, WA B
Hawai'i Pacific U, HI B
Idaho State U, ID B
Lehigh U, PA B
Lewis-Clark State Coll, ID B
Montana State U–Billings, MT B
Naropa U, CO B
Nevada State Coll at Henderson, NV B
Rocky Mountain Coll, MT B
Saint Mary's Coll of California, CA B
San Diego State U, CA B
San Jose State U, CA B
Scripps Coll, CA B
Sheldon Jackson Coll, AK B
Sonoma State U, CA B
Thomas Aquinas Coll, CA B
U of Alaska Fairbanks, AK A,B
The U of Arizona, AZ B
U of California, Berkeley, CA B
U of California, Irvine, CA B
U of California, Los Angeles, CA B
U of California, Santa Barbara, CA B
U of Colorado at Boulder, CO B
U of Colorado at Denver, CO B
U of Denver, CO B
U of Hawaii at Manoa, HI B
U of Idaho, ID B
U of Northern Colorado, CO B
U of Wyoming, WY B
Utah State U, UT B

Music
Adams State Coll, CO B
Albertson Coll of Idaho, ID B
Arizona State U, AZ B
Azusa Pacific U, CA B
Biola U, CA B
Birmingham-Southern Coll, AL B
Boise State U, ID B
Brigham Young U, UT B
Brigham Young U–Hawaii, HI A,B
California Baptist U, CA B
California Inst of the Arts, CA B
California Lutheran U, CA B
California Polytechnic State U, San Luis Obispo, CA B
California State Polytechnic U, Pomona, CA B
California State U, Bakersfield, CA B
California State U, Chico, CA B
California State U, Dominguez Hills, CA B
California State U, Fresno, CA B
California State U, Fullerton, CA B
California State U, Hayward, CA B
California State U, Long Beach, CA B
California State U, Los Angeles, CA B
California State U, Sacramento, CA B
California State U, San Bernardino, CA B
California State U, Stanislaus, CA B
Central Washington U, WA B
Chapman U, CA B
Christian Heritage Coll, CA B
Claremont McKenna Coll, CA B
Colorado Christian U, CO B
The Colorado Coll, CO B
Colorado State U, CO B
Colorado State U-Pueblo, CO B
Concordia U, CA B
Cornell Coll, IA B
Cornish Coll of the Arts, WA B
Dominican U of California, CA B
Eastern New Mexico U, NM B
Eastern Oregon U, OR B
Eastern Washington U, WA B
Fort Lewis Coll, CO B
Fresno Pacific U, CA A,B
George Fox U, OR B
Gonzaga U, WA B
Grand Canyon U, AZ B
Holy Names U, CA B
Humboldt State U, CA B
Idaho State U, ID B
Lehigh U, PA B
Lewis & Clark Coll, OR B
Linfield Coll, OR B
Loyola Marymount U, CA B
Marylhurst U, OR B
The Master's Coll and Seminary, CA B
Mills Coll, CA B
Montana State U–Billings, MT B
Montana State U–Bozeman, MT B
Mount St. Mary's Coll, CA B
Musicians Inst, CA A,B
Naropa U, CO B
New Mexico Highlands U, NM B
Northern Arizona U, AZ B
Northwest Coll, WA B
Northwest Nazarene U, ID B
Notre Dame de Namur U, CA B
Occidental Coll, CA B
Oregon State U, OR B
Pacific Lutheran U, WA B
Pacific Union Coll, CA B
Pacific U, OR B
Pepperdine U, Malibu, CA B
Point Loma Nazarene U, CA B
Pomona Coll, CA B
Portland State U, OR B
Reed Coll, OR B
Saint Mary's Coll of California, CA B
San Diego State U, CA B
San Francisco State U, CA B
San Jose State U, CA B
Santa Clara U, CA B
Scripps Coll, CA B
Seattle Pacific U, WA B
Sierra Nevada Coll, NV B
Simpson Coll and Graduate School, CA B
Sonoma State U, CA B
Southern Oregon U, OR B
Southern Utah U, UT B
Stanford U, CA B
U of Alaska Anchorage, AK B
U of Alaska Fairbanks, AK B
The U of Arizona, AZ B
U of California, Berkeley, CA B
U of California, Davis, CA B
U of California, Irvine, CA B
U of California, Los Angeles, CA B
U of California, Riverside, CA B
U of California, San Diego, CA B
U of California, Santa Barbara, CA B
U of California, Santa Cruz, CA B
U of Colorado at Boulder, CO B
U of Colorado at Denver, CO B
U of Denver, CO B
U of Hawaii at Hilo, HI B
U of La Verne, CA B
The U of Montana–Missoula, MT B
U of Nevada, Las Vegas, NV B
U of Nevada, Reno, NV B
U of Northern Colorado, CO B
U of Oregon, OR B
U of Portland, OR B
U of Puget Sound, WA B
U of Redlands, CA B
U of San Diego, CA B
U of Southern California, CA B
U of the Pacific, CA B
U of Utah, UT B
U of Washington, WA B
U of Wyoming, WY B
Utah State U, UT B
Utah Valley State Coll, UT A
Vanguard U of Southern California, CA B
Walla Walla Coll, WA B
Warner Pacific Coll, OR B
Washington State U, WA B
Weber State U, UT B
Western Baptist Coll, OR B
Western Oregon U, OR B
Western State Coll of Colorado, CO B
Western Washington U, WA B
Westmont Coll, CA B
Whitman Coll, WA B
Whitworth Coll, WA B
Willamette U, OR B
William Jessup U, CA B

Musical Instrument Fabrication and Repair
U of Washington, WA B

Music History, Literature, and Theory
Birmingham-Southern Coll, AL B
Brigham Young U, UT B
California State U, Fresno, CA B
California State U, Fullerton, CA B
California State U, Long Beach, CA B

Eugene Lang Coll, New School U B
Loyola Marymount U, CA B
U of California, Los Angeles, CA B
U of California, San Diego, CA B
U of Idaho, ID B
U of Redlands, CA B
U of the Pacific, CA B
U of Washington, WA B
Western Washington U, WA B

Music Management and Merchandising
Bethesda Christian U, CA B
Boise State U, ID B
California State U, Sacramento, CA B
Central Washington U, WA B
Grand Canyon U, AZ B
The Master's Coll and Seminary, CA B
Northwest Christian Coll, OR B
Southern Oregon U, OR B
U of Idaho, ID B
U of Puget Sound, WA B
U of Southern California, CA B
U of the Pacific, CA B
Warner Pacific Coll, OR B

Musicology and Ethnomusicology
Loyola Marymount U, CA B
U of California, Los Angeles, CA B
U of Denver, CO B
U of Oregon, OR B
U of Washington, WA B

Music Pedagogy
Brigham Young U, UT B
California State U, Sacramento, CA B
Holy Names U, CA B
Willamette U, OR B

Music Performance
Adams State Coll, CO B
Arizona State U, AZ B
Brigham Young U, UT B
Brigham Young U–Hawaii, HI B
California Baptist U, CA B
California Inst of the Arts, CA B
California State U, Chico, CA B
California State U, Fullerton, CA B
California State U, Long Beach, CA B
California State U, Los Angeles, CA B
California State U, Stanislaus, CA B
Chapman U, CA B
The Colburn School of Performing Arts, CA B
Colorado Christian U, CO B
Colorado State U, CO B
Dominican U of California, CA B
Eastern Washington U, WA B
Holy Names U, CA B
Idaho State U, ID B
Metropolitan State Coll of Denver, CO B
New Mexico State U, NM B
Northern Arizona U, AZ B
Northwest Coll, WA B
Northwest Nazarene U, ID B
Notre Dame de Namur U, CA B
Point Loma Nazarene U, CA B
Rocky Mountain Coll, MT B
San Jose State U, CA B
U of Alaska Anchorage, AK B
The U of Arizona, AZ B
U of California, Irvine, CA B
U of Colorado at Boulder, CO B
U of Denver, CO B
U of Hawaii at Manoa, HI B
U of Idaho, ID B
The U of Montana–Missoula, MT B
U of Nevada, Reno, NV B
U of New Mexico, NM B
U of Oregon, OR B
U of Puget Sound, WA B
U of Redlands, CA B
U of Southern California, CA B
U of Washington, WA B
U of Wyoming, WY B
Washington State U, WA B
Weber State U, UT B
Western Baptist Coll, OR B
Willamette U, OR B

Music Related
Arizona State U, AZ B
Brigham Young U, UT B
California Inst of the Arts, CA B
California State U, Chico, CA B
California State U, Sacramento, CA B
Claremont McKenna Coll, CA B
Coll of Santa Fe, NM B
Colorado Christian U, CO B
Marylhurst U, OR B
Northwest Christian Coll, OR B
San Diego State U, CA B
The U of Arizona, AZ B
U of Southern California, CA B

Music Teacher Education
Birmingham-Southern Coll, AL B
Boise State U, ID B
Brigham Young U, UT B
Brigham Young U–Hawaii, HI B
California Lutheran U, CA B
California State U, Chico, CA B
California State U, Dominguez Hills, CA B
California State U, Fresno, CA B
California State U, Fullerton, CA B
Central Washington U, WA B
Chapman U, CA B
Christian Heritage Coll, CA B
Colorado Christian U, CO B
Colorado State U, CO B
Colorado State U-Pueblo, CO B
Cornell Coll, IA B
Eastern New Mexico U, NM B
Eastern Washington U, WA B
Fort Lewis Coll, CO B
Fresno Pacific U, CA B
George Fox U, OR B
Gonzaga U, WA B
Grand Canyon U, AZ B
Humboldt State U, CA B
Idaho State U, ID B
The Master's Coll and Seminary, CA B
Metropolitan State Coll of Denver, CO B
Montana State U-Billings, MT B
Montana State U–Bozeman, MT B
Mount St. Mary's Coll, CA B
New Mexico Highlands U, NM B
New Mexico State U, NM B
North Carolina Ag and Tech State U, NC B
Northern Arizona U, AZ B
Northwest Coll, WA B
Northwest Nazarene U, ID B
Pacific Lutheran U, WA B
Pacific Union Coll, CA B
Pacific U, OR B
Pepperdine U, Malibu, CA B
Point Loma Nazarene U, CA B
Prescott Coll, AZ B
Rocky Mountain Coll, MT B
Seattle Pacific U, WA B
Simpson Coll and Graduate School, CA B
Sonoma State U, CA B
Southern Utah U, UT B
Southwestern Coll, AZ B
U of Alaska Anchorage, AK B
The U of Arizona, AZ B
U of Colorado at Boulder, CO B
U of Hawaii at Manoa, HI B
U of Idaho, ID B
U of La Verne, CA B
The U of Montana–Missoula, MT B
The U of Montana–Western, MT B
U of Nevada, Reno, NV B
U of New Mexico, NM B
U of Northern Colorado, CO B
U of Oregon, OR B
U of Portland, OR B
U of Puget Sound, WA B
U of Redlands, CA B
U of Southern California, CA B
U of the Pacific, CA B
U of Utah, UT B
U of Washington, WA B
U of Wyoming, WY B
Utah State U, UT B
Walla Walla Coll, WA B
Warner Pacific Coll, OR B
Washington State U, WA B
Weber State U, UT B
Western Baptist Coll, OR B
Western State Coll of Colorado, CO B
Western Washington U, WA B
Whitworth Coll, WA B

Music Theory and Composition
Arizona State U, AZ B
Bethesda Christian U, CA B
Brigham Young U, UT B
California Baptist U, CA B
California Inst of the Arts, CA B
California State U, Chico, CA B
California State U, Long Beach, CA B
California State U, Sacramento, CA B
Central Washington U, WA B
Chapman U, CA B
Eastern Washington U, WA B
Loyola Marymount U, CA B
Northwest Nazarene U, ID B
Point Loma Nazarene U, CA B
U of Idaho, ID B
U of Nevada, Las Vegas, NV B
U of Redlands, CA B
U of Southern California, CA B
U of the Pacific, CA B
U of Washington, WA B
U of Wyoming, WY B
Washington State U, WA B
Willamette U, OR B

Music Therapy
Arizona State U, AZ B
Chapman U, CA B
Colorado State U, CO B
U of the Pacific, CA B
Utah State U, UT B

Natural Resources and Conservation Related
U of Alaska Fairbanks, AK B
Utah State U, UT B

Natural Resources/Conservation
California State U, Sacramento, CA B
Coll of Santa Fe, NM B
Humboldt State U, CA B
Montana State U–Bozeman, MT B
Prescott Coll, AZ B
U of California, Berkeley, CA B
U of California, Davis, CA B
The U of Montana–Missoula, MT B
U of Nevada, Reno, NV B
U of Wyoming, WY B
Washington State U, WA B

Natural Resources Management
Central Washington U, WA B

Natural Resources Management and Policy
Alaska Pacific U, AK B
Blackfeet Comm Coll, MT A
California State U, Chico, CA B
Coll of Santa Fe, NM B
Colorado State U, CO B
Eastern Oregon U, OR B
Humboldt State U, CA B
New Mexico Highlands U, NM B
Oregon State U, OR B
Prescott Coll, AZ B
U of Alaska Fairbanks, AK A
U of California, Berkeley, CA B
U of California, San Diego, CA B
U of Idaho, ID B
U of La Verne, CA B
The U of Montana–Missoula, MT B
U of Nevada, Reno, NV B
U of Washington, WA B
Western Washington U, WA B

Natural Sciences
Azusa Pacific U, CA B
California State U, Fresno, CA B
California State U, Los Angeles, CA B
California State U, San Bernardino, CA B
Concordia U, OR B
Eastern Washington U, WA B
The Evergreen State Coll, WA B
Fresno Pacific U, CA A,B
Humboldt State U, CA B
Lewis-Clark State Coll, ID B
Loyola Marymount U, CA B
The Master's Coll and Seminary, CA B
Pepperdine U, Malibu, CA B
San Jose State U, CA B
U of Alaska Anchorage, AK B
U of Hawaii at Hilo, HI B
U of La Verne, CA B
U of Puget Sound, WA B
Western Oregon U, OR B

Navy/Marine Corps R.O.T.C./Naval Science
U of Washington, WA B

A—associate degree; B—bachelor's degree

Near and Middle Eastern Studies
Claremont McKenna Coll, CA B
Portland State U, OR B
The U of Arizona, AZ B
U of California, Berkeley, CA B
U of California, Los Angeles, CA B
U of California, Santa Barbara, CA B
U of Utah, UT B
U of Washington, WA B

Neurobiology and Neurophysiology
U of California, Los Angeles, CA B

Neuroscience
Brigham Young U, UT B
The Colorado Coll, CO B
Pitzer Coll, CA B
Pomona Coll, CA B
Regis U, CO B
Scripps Coll, CA B
U of California, Irvine, CA B
U of California, Los Angeles, CA B
U of California, Riverside, CA B
Washington State U, WA B
Westmont Coll, CA B

Non-Profit Management
Fresno Pacific U, CA B
Northwest Coll, WA B

Norwegian
Brigham Young U, UT B

Nuclear Engineering
Oregon State U, OR B
The U of Arizona, AZ B
U of California, Berkeley, CA B
U of New Mexico, NM B

Nuclear Medical Technology
California State U, Dominguez Hills, CA B
U of Nevada, Las Vegas, NV B
Weber State U, UT B

Nursing Administration
U of San Francisco, CA B

Nursing Assistant/Aide and Patient Care Assistant
Montana Tech of The U of Montana, MT A

Nursing (Licensed Practical/Vocational Nurse Training)
Lewis-Clark State Coll, ID A
Montana State U–Billings, MT A
The U of Montana–Missoula, MT A

Nursing (Registered Nurse Training)
Arizona State U, AZ B
Azusa Pacific U, CA B
Biola U, CA B
Boise State U, ID A,B
Brigham Young U, UT B
California State U, Bakersfield, CA B
California State U, Chico, CA B
California State U, Dominguez Hills, CA B
California State U, Fresno, CA B
California State U, Fullerton, CA B
California State U, Hayward, CA B
California State U, Long Beach, CA B
California State U, Los Angeles, CA B
California State U, Sacramento, CA B
California State U, San Bernardino, CA B
California State U, Stanislaus, CA B
Carroll Coll, MT B
Colorado State U-Pueblo, CO B
Dominican U of California, CA B
Eastern New Mexico U, NM B
Eastern Washington U, WA B
Gonzaga U, WA B
Grand Canyon U, AZ B
Great Basin Coll, NV A
Hawai'i Pacific U, HI B
Holy Names U, CA B
Humboldt State U, CA B
Idaho State U, ID B
Lewis-Clark State Coll, ID B
Loma Linda U, CA A,B
Metropolitan State Coll of Denver, CO B
Montana State U–Bozeman, MT B
Montana Tech of The U of Montana, MT A
Mount St. Mary's Coll, CA A,B
Nevada State Coll at Henderson, NV B
New Mexico State U, NM B
North Carolina Ag and Tech State U, NC B
Northern Arizona U, AZ B
Northwest Coll, WA B
Northwest Nazarene U, ID B
Pacific Lutheran U, WA B
Pacific Union Coll, CA A,B
Point Loma Nazarene U, CA B
Regis U, CO B
Saint Mary's Coll of California, CA B
Samuel Merritt Coll, CA B
San Diego State U, CA B
San Francisco State U, CA B
San Jose State U, CA B
Seattle Pacific U, WA B
Seattle U, WA B
Sonoma State U, CA B
Southern Oregon U, OR B
U of Alaska Anchorage, AK A,B
The U of Arizona, AZ B
U of California, Los Angeles, CA B
U of Colorado at Colorado Springs, CO B
U of Colorado Health Sciences Center, CO B
U of Hawaii at Hilo, HI B
U of Hawaii at Manoa, HI B
U of Nevada, Las Vegas, NV B
U of Nevada, Reno, NV B
U of New Mexico, NM B
U of Northern Colorado, CO B
U of Phoenix–Hawaii Campus, HI B
U of Phoenix–New Mexico Campus, NM B
U of Phoenix–Southern Arizona Campus, AZ B
U of Phoenix–Utah Campus, UT B
U of Portland, OR B
U of San Francisco, CA B
U of Utah, UT B
U of Washington, WA B
U of Wyoming, WY B
Utah Valley State Coll, UT A,B
Walla Walla Coll, WA B
Warner Pacific Coll, OR A
Washington State U, WA B
Weber State U, UT A,B
Westminster Coll, UT B
Whitworth Coll, WA B

Nursing Related
California State U, Fullerton, CA B
U of California, Los Angeles, CA B

Nursing Science
Holy Names U, CA B
National U, CA B
U of Phoenix–Colorado Campus, CO B
U of Phoenix–Hawaii Campus, HI B
U of Phoenix–New Mexico Campus, NM B
U of Phoenix–Northern California Campus, CA B
U of Phoenix–Phoenix Campus, AZ B
U of Phoenix–Sacramento Campus, CA B
U of Phoenix–San Diego Campus, CA B
U of Phoenix–Southern Arizona Campus, AZ B
U of Phoenix–Southern California Campus, CA B
U of Phoenix–Southern Colorado Campus, CO B

Nutrition Sciences
Brigham Young U, UT B
Chapman U, CA B
The U of Arizona, AZ B
U of California, Berkeley, CA B
U of Nevada, Las Vegas, NV B
Washington State U, WA B

Occupational Health and Industrial Hygiene
California State U, Fresno, CA B
Montana Tech of The U of Montana, MT B

Occupational Safety and Health Technology
California State U, Fresno, CA B
Central Washington U, WA B
Montana Tech of The U of Montana, MT A,B
National U, CA B
North Carolina Ag and Tech State U, NC B
Oregon State U, OR B
Utah State U, UT B

Occupational Therapist Assistant
Idaho State U, ID A
Loma Linda U, CA A
Mount St. Mary's Coll, CA A

Occupational Therapy
Dominican U of California, CA B
Eastern Washington U, WA B
Loma Linda U, CA B
San Jose State U, CA B
U of Southern California, CA B
U of Utah, UT B
U of Washington, WA B

Ocean Engineering
California State U, Long Beach, CA B

Oceanography (Chemical and Physical)
Hawai'i Pacific U, HI B
Humboldt State U, CA B
U of San Diego, CA B
U of Washington, WA B

Office Management
Central Washington U, WA B
Great Basin Coll, NV A
Utah Valley State Coll, UT B
Weber State U, UT B

Office Occupations and Clerical Services
U of Alaska Fairbanks, AK A

Operations Management
Boise State U, ID B
California State U, Chico, CA B
California State U, Long Beach, CA B
California State U, Sacramento, CA B
Central Washington U, WA B
DeVry U, Phoenix, AZ B
DeVry U, Fremont, CA B
DeVry U, Long Beach, CA B
DeVry U, Pomona, CA B
DeVry U, West Hills, CA B
Golden Gate U, CA B
Great Basin Coll, NV A
National U, CA B
Remington Coll–Colorado Springs Campus, CO B
Seattle U, WA B
The U of Arizona, AZ B
U of Idaho, ID B
Utah State U, UT B
Utah Valley State Coll, UT B
Washington State U, WA B
Western Washington U, WA B

Operations Research
California State U, Fullerton, CA B
United States Air Force Academy, CO B
U of California, Berkeley, CA B
U of Denver, CO B

Optical Sciences
The U of Arizona, AZ B

Organic Chemistry
California Inst of Technology, CA B

Organizational Behavior
Chapman U, CA B
National U, CA B
Scripps Coll, CA B
Simpson Coll and Graduate School, CA B
U of La Verne, CA B
U of San Francisco, CA B

Organizational Communication
Brigham Young U, UT B
California State U, Chico, CA B
California State U, Sacramento, CA B
Eastern Washington U, WA B
Jones International U, CO B
Northwest Coll, WA B

Ornamental Horticulture
California Polytechnic State U, San Luis Obispo, CA B
California State Polytechnic U, Pomona, CA B
California State U, Fresno, CA B
Utah State U, UT A,B

Orthotics/Prosthetics
U of Washington, WA B

Pacific Area/Pacific Rim Studies
Brigham Young U–Hawaii, HI B
Claremont McKenna Coll, CA B

Painting
Academy of Art U, CA A,B
Art Center Coll of Design, CA B
Birmingham-Southern Coll, AL B
Brigham Young U, UT B
California Coll of the Arts, CA B
California State U, Fullerton, CA B
California State U, Hayward, CA B
California State U, Long Beach, CA B
Coll of Santa Fe, NM B
Colorado State U, CO B
Laguna Coll of Art & Design, CA B
Northwest Nazarene U, ID B
Pacific Northwest Coll of Art, OR B
Rocky Mountain Coll of Art & Design, CO B
San Diego State U, CA B
San Francisco Art Inst, CA B
U of Oregon, OR B
U of San Francisco, CA B
U of Washington, WA B
Western Washington U, WA B

Paleontology
San Diego State U, CA B

Parks, Recreation and Leisure
Alaska Pacific U, AK B
Arizona State U, AZ B
Arizona State U West, AZ B
Brigham Young U, UT B
California Polytechnic State U, San Luis Obispo, CA B
California State U, Chico, CA B
California State U, Dominguez Hills, CA B
California State U, Fresno, CA B
California State U, Hayward, CA B
California State U, Long Beach, CA B
California State U, Sacramento, CA B
Central Washington U, WA B
Colorado State U-Pueblo, CO B
Eastern Washington U, WA B
Humboldt State U, CA B
Metropolitan State Coll of Denver, CO B
North Carolina Ag and Tech State U, NC B
Northern Arizona U, AZ B
Northwest Nazarene U, ID B
Oregon State U, OR B
Pacific Union Coll, CA B
Prescott Coll, AZ B
San Diego State U, CA B
San Francisco State U, CA B
San Jose State U, CA B
Sheldon Jackson Coll, AK B
U of Hawaii at Manoa, HI B
U of Idaho, ID B
The U of Montana–Missoula, MT B
U of Nevada, Las Vegas, NV B
U of Nevada, Reno, NV B
U of New Mexico, NM B
U of Utah, UT B
Utah State U, UT B
Western State Coll of Colorado, CO B
Western Washington U, WA B

Parks, Recreation and Leisure Facilities Management
California State U, Chico, CA B
California State U, Sacramento, CA B
Colorado State U, CO B
Eastern Washington U, WA B
Humboldt State U, CA B
New Mexico State U, NM B
Oregon State U, OR B
U of Northern Colorado, CO B
U of Utah, UT B
U of Wyoming, WY B
Western State Coll of Colorado, CO B

Parks, Recreation, and Leisure Related
Brigham Young U, UT B
Utah State U, UT B
Washington State U, WA B

Pastoral Counseling and Specialized Ministries Related
Multnomah Bible Coll and Biblical Seminary, OR B

Pastoral Studies/Counseling
American Indian Coll of the Assemblies of God, Inc., AZ B
Bethesda Christian U, CA B
Biola U, CA B
Christian Heritage Coll, CA B
Coll of Santa Fe, NM B
Eugene Bible Coll, OR B
Fresno Pacific U, CA B
George Fox U, OR B
Life Pacific Coll, CA B
Marylhurst U, OR B
The Master's Coll and Seminary, CA B
Multnomah Bible Coll and Biblical Seminary, OR B
Northwest Coll, WA B
Northwest Nazarene U, ID B
Pacific Union Coll, CA B
Vanguard U of Southern California, CA B
Warner Pacific Coll, OR B
Western Baptist Coll, OR B
William Jessup U, CA B

Pathology/Experimental Pathology
U of California, Los Angeles, CA B

Peace Studies and Conflict Resolution
Chapman U, CA B
U of California, Berkeley, CA B
U of California, Santa Cruz, CA B
Whitworth Coll, WA B

Perfusion Technology
Boise State U, ID A

Petroleum Engineering
California State Polytechnic U, Pomona, CA B
Colorado School of Mines, CO B
Montana Tech of The U of Montana, MT B
New Mexico Inst of Mining and Technology, NM B
Stanford U, CA B
U of Alaska Fairbanks, AK B
U of Southern California, CA B

Petroleum Technology
Montana State U–Billings, MT A
Montana Tech of The U of Montana, MT A
U of Alaska Anchorage, AK A

Pharmacology
U of California, Santa Barbara, CA B

Pharmacology and Toxicology
Silicon Valley Coll, Walnut Creek, CA A
Washington State U, WA B

Pharmacology and Toxicology Related
Silicon Valley Coll, Walnut Creek, CA A

Pharmacy
Oregon State U, OR B
The U of Montana–Missoula, MT B
U of New Mexico, NM B
U of the Pacific, CA B
U of Utah, UT B
U of Washington, WA B

Pharmacy, Pharmaceutical Sciences, and Administration Related
U of Utah, UT B

Pharmacy Technician
DeVry U, Westminster, CO A
Idaho State U, ID A
Silicon Valley Coll, Walnut Creek, CA A
The U of Montana–Missoula, MT B

Philosophy
Albertson Coll of Idaho, ID B
Arizona State U, AZ B
Azusa Pacific U, CA B
Biola U, CA B
Birmingham-Southern Coll, AL B
Boise State U, ID B
Brigham Young U, UT B
California Baptist U, CA B
California Lutheran U, CA B
California Polytechnic State U, San Luis Obispo, CA B
California State Polytechnic U, Pomona, CA B
California State U, Bakersfield, CA B
California State U, Chico, CA B
California State U, Dominguez Hills, CA B
California State U, Fresno, CA B
California State U, Fullerton, CA B
California State U, Hayward, CA B
California State U, Long Beach, CA B
California State U, Los Angeles, CA B
California State U, Sacramento, CA B
California State U, San Bernardino, CA B
California State U, Stanislaus, CA B
Carroll Coll, MT B
Central Washington U, WA B
Chaminade U of Honolulu, HI B
Chapman U, CA B
Claremont McKenna Coll, CA B
The Colorado Coll, CO B
Colorado State U, CO B
Cornell Coll, IA B
Eastern Washington U, WA B
Eugene Lang Coll, New School U B
Fort Lewis Coll, CO B
Gonzaga U, WA B
Holy Names U, CA B
Humboldt State U, CA B
Idaho State U, ID B
Lehigh U, PA B
Lewis & Clark Coll, OR B
Linfield Coll, OR B
Loyola Marymount U, CA B
Metropolitan State Coll of Denver, CO B
Mills Coll, CA B
Montana State U–Bozeman, MT B
Mount St. Mary's Coll, CA B
New Mexico State U, NM B
Northern Arizona U, AZ B
Northwest Coll, WA B
Northwest Nazarene U, ID B
Notre Dame de Namur U, CA B
Occidental Coll, CA B
Oregon State U, OR B
Pacific Lutheran U, WA B
Pacific U, OR B
Pepperdine U, Malibu, CA B
Pitzer Coll, CA B
Point Loma Nazarene U, CA B
Pomona Coll, CA B
Portland State U, OR B
Prescott Coll, AZ B
Reed Coll, OR B
Regis U, CO B
Rocky Mountain Coll, MT B
St. John's Coll, NM B
Saint Mary's Coll of California, CA B
San Diego State U, CA B
San Francisco State U, CA B
San Jose State U, CA B
Santa Clara U, CA B
Scripps Coll, CA B
Seattle Pacific U, WA B
Seattle U, WA B
Sonoma State U, CA B
Stanford U, CA B
U of Alaska Fairbanks, AK B
The U of Arizona, AZ B
U of California, Berkeley, CA B
U of California, Davis, CA B
U of California, Irvine, CA B
U of California, Los Angeles, CA B
U of California, Riverside, CA B
U of California, San Diego, CA B
U of California, Santa Barbara, CA B
U of California, Santa Cruz, CA B
U of Colorado at Boulder, CO B
U of Colorado at Colorado Springs, CO B
U of Colorado at Denver, CO B
U of Denver, CO B
U of Hawaii at Hilo, HI B
U of Hawaii at Manoa, HI B
U of Idaho, ID B
U of La Verne, CA B
The U of Montana–Missoula, MT B
U of Nevada, Las Vegas, NV B
U of Nevada, Reno, NV B

A—associate degree; B—bachelor's degree

U of New Mexico, NM	B
U of Northern Colorado, CO	B
U of Oregon, OR	B
U of Portland, OR	B
U of Puget Sound, WA	B
U of Redlands, CA	B
U of San Diego, CA	B
U of San Francisco, CA	B
U of Southern California, CA	B
U of the Pacific, CA	B
U of the West, CA	B
U of Utah, UT	B
U of Washington, WA	B
U of Wyoming, WY	B
Utah State U, UT	B
Utah Valley State Coll, UT	A,B
Walla Walla Coll, WA	B
Washington State U, WA	B
Western Oregon U, OR	B
Western Washington U, WA	B
Westminster Coll, UT	B
Westmont Coll, CA	B
Whitman Coll, WA	B
Whitworth Coll, WA	B
Willamette U, OR	B

Philosophy and Religious Studies Related

California State U, Sacramento, CA	B
Claremont McKenna Coll, CA	B
Holy Names U, CA	B
Point Loma Nazarene U, CA	B
St. John's Coll, NM	B

Philosophy Related

Claremont McKenna Coll, CA	B
St. John's Coll, NM	B
U of Southern California, CA	B

Photographic and Film/Video Technology

Platt Coll San Diego, CA	A,B

Photography

Academy of Art U, CA	A,B
American InterContinental U, CA	B
Arizona State U, AZ	B
Art Center Coll of Design, CA	B
The Art Inst of Colorado, CO	A
The Art Inst of Seattle, WA	A
Brigham Young U, UT	B
California Coll of the Arts, CA	B
California Inst of the Arts, CA	B
California State U, Fullerton, CA	B
California State U, Hayward, CA	B
California State U, Long Beach, CA	B
California State U, Sacramento, CA	B
Coll of Santa Fe, NM	B
Colorado State U, CO	B
Northern Arizona U, AZ	B
Otis Coll of Art and Design, CA	B
Pacific Northwest Coll of Art, OR	B
Pacific Union Coll, CA	A
Prescott Coll, AZ	B
San Francisco Art Inst, CA	B
Seattle U, WA	B
U of California, Santa Cruz, CA	B
U of Idaho, ID	B
U of Oregon, OR	B
U of Washington, WA	B
Weber State U, UT	B

Physical and Theoretical Chemistry

Lehigh U, PA	B

Physical Education Teaching and Coaching

Albertson Coll of Idaho, ID	B
Azusa Pacific U, CA	B
Biola U, CA	B
Boise State U, ID	B
Brigham Young U, UT	B
Brigham Young U–Hawaii, HI	B
California Lutheran U, CA	B
California Polytechnic State U, San Luis Obispo, CA	B
California State Polytechnic U, Pomona, CA	B
California State U, Bakersfield, CA	B
California State U, Chico, CA	B
California State U, Dominguez Hills, CA	B
California State U, Fresno, CA	B
California State U, Fullerton, CA	B
California State U, Hayward, CA	B
California State U, Long Beach, CA	B
California State U, Los Angeles, CA	B
California State U, San Bernardino, CA	B
California State U, Stanislaus, CA	B
Carroll Coll, MT	B
Central Washington U, WA	B
Christian Heritage Coll, CA	B
Coll of the Southwest, NM	B
Colorado State U-Pueblo, CO	B
Concordia U, OR	B
Cornell Coll, IA	B
Eastern New Mexico U, NM	B
Eastern Oregon U, OR	B
Eastern Washington U, WA	B
Fort Lewis Coll, CO	B
Fresno Pacific U, CA	A,B
George Fox U, OR	B
Gonzaga U, WA	B
Grand Canyon U, AZ	B
Humboldt State U, CA	B
Idaho State U, ID	B
Lewis-Clark State Coll, ID	B
The Master's Coll and Seminary, CA	B
Montana State U–Billings, MT	B
New Mexico Highlands U, NM	B
New Mexico State U, NM	B
North Carolina Ag and Tech State U, NC	B
Northern Arizona U, AZ	B
Northwest Coll, WA	B
Northwest Nazarene U, ID	B
Oregon State U, OR	B
Pacific Lutheran U, WA	B
Pacific Union Coll, CA	B
Pepperdine U, Malibu, CA	B
Prescott Coll, AZ	B
Rocky Mountain Coll, MT	B
San Diego State U, CA	B
San Francisco State U, CA	B
Seattle Pacific U, WA	B
Sonoma State U, CA	B
Southern Oregon U, OR	B
Southern Utah U, UT	B
U of Alaska Anchorage, AK	B
U of Alaska Fairbanks, AK	B
The U of Arizona, AZ	B
U of California, Davis, CA	B
U of Great Falls, MT	B
U of Hawaii at Manoa, HI	B
U of Idaho, ID	B
U of La Verne, CA	B
The U of Montana–Missoula, MT	B
The U of Montana–Western, MT	B
U of Nevada, Las Vegas, NV	B
U of Nevada, Reno, NV	B
U of New Mexico, NM	B
U of San Francisco, CA	B
U of Utah, UT	B
U of Wyoming, WY	B
Utah State U, UT	B
Vanguard U of Southern California, CA	B
Walla Walla Coll, WA	B
Warner Pacific Coll, OR	B
Weber State U, UT	B
Western Baptist Coll, OR	B
Western State Coll of Colorado, CO	B
Western Washington U, WA	B
Westmont Coll, CA	B
Whitworth Coll, WA	B

Physical Sciences

Biola U, CA	B
Brigham Young U–Hawaii, HI	B
California Inst of Technology, CA	B
California Polytechnic State U, San Luis Obispo, CA	B
California State U, Hayward, CA	B
California State U, Sacramento, CA	B
California State U, Stanislaus, CA	B
Colorado State U, CO	B
Concordia U, OR	B
Eastern Washington U, WA	B
The Evergreen State Coll, WA	B
Grand Canyon U, AZ	B
Humboldt State U, CA	B
Linfield Coll, OR	B
The Master's Coll and Seminary, CA	B
Northern Arizona U, AZ	B
Oregon State U, OR	B
Pacific Union Coll, CA	B
St. John's Coll, NM	B
San Diego State U, CA	B
San Francisco State U, CA	B
Southern Utah U, UT	B
U of California, Berkeley, CA	B
U of California, Riverside, CA	B
U of Southern California, CA	B
U of the Pacific, CA	B
U of Utah, UT	B
Utah Valley State Coll, UT	A
Warner Pacific Coll, OR	B
Washington State U, WA	B

Physical Sciences Related

U of Utah, UT	B

Physical Therapist Assistant

Idaho State U, ID	A
Loma Linda U, CA	A
Mount St. Mary's Coll, CA	A

Physical Therapy

California State U, Fresno, CA	B
Eastern Washington U, WA	B
Northwest Nazarene U, ID	B
The U of Montana–Missoula, MT	B
U of Utah, UT	B
U of Washington, WA	B
Vanguard U of Southern California, CA	B

Physician Assistant

Boise State U, ID	B
California State U, Dominguez Hills, CA	B
Rocky Mountain Coll, MT	B
U of New Mexico, NM	B
U of Washington, WA	B

Physics

Albertson Coll of Idaho, ID	B
Arizona State U, AZ	B
Azusa Pacific U, CA	B
Birmingham-Southern Coll, AL	B
Boise State U, ID	B
Brigham Young U, UT	B
California Inst of Technology, CA	B
California Lutheran U, CA	B
California Polytechnic State U, San Luis Obispo, CA	B
California State Polytechnic U, Pomona, CA	B
California State U, Bakersfield, CA	B
California State U, Chico, CA	B
California State U, Dominguez Hills, CA	B
California State U, Fresno, CA	B
California State U, Fullerton, CA	B
California State U, Hayward, CA	B
California State U, Long Beach, CA	B
California State U, Los Angeles, CA	B
California State U, Sacramento, CA	B
California State U, San Bernardino, CA	B
California State U, Stanislaus, CA	B
Central Washington U, WA	B
Claremont McKenna Coll, CA	B
The Colorado Coll, CO	B
Colorado State U, CO	B
Colorado State U-Pueblo, CO	B
Cornell Coll, IA	B
Eastern New Mexico U, NM	B
Eastern Oregon U, OR	B
Eastern Washington U, WA	B
Fort Lewis Coll, CO	B
Gonzaga U, WA	B
Great Basin Coll, NV	A
Harvey Mudd Coll, CA	B
Humboldt State U, CA	B
Idaho State U, ID	A,B
Lehigh U, PA	B
Lewis & Clark Coll, OR	B
Linfield Coll, OR	B
Loyola Marymount U, CA	B
Metropolitan State Coll of Denver, CO	B
Montana State U–Bozeman, MT	B
New Mexico Inst of Mining and Technology, NM	B
New Mexico State U, NM	B
North Carolina Ag and Tech State U, NC	B
Northern Arizona U, AZ	B
Northwest Nazarene U, ID	B
Occidental Coll, CA	B
Oregon State U, OR	B
Pacific Lutheran U, WA	B
Pacific Union Coll, CA	B
Pacific U, OR	B
Pitzer Coll, CA	B
Point Loma Nazarene U, CA	B
Pomona Coll, CA	B
Portland State U, OR	B

Reed Coll, OR B
St. John's Coll, NM B
Saint Mary's Coll of California, CA B
San Diego State U, CA B
San Francisco State U, CA B
San Jose State U, CA B
Santa Clara U, CA B
Scripps Coll, CA B
Seattle Pacific U, WA B
Seattle U, WA B
Sonoma State U, CA B
Southern Oregon U, OR B
Stanford U, CA B
United States Air Force Academy, CO B
U of Alaska Fairbanks, AK B
The U of Arizona, AZ B
U of California, Berkeley, CA B
U of California, Davis, CA B
U of California, Irvine, CA B
U of California, Los Angeles, CA B
U of California, Riverside, CA B
U of California, San Diego, CA B
U of California, Santa Barbara, CA B
U of California, Santa Cruz, CA B
U of Colorado at Boulder, CO B
U of Colorado at Colorado Springs, CO B
U of Colorado at Denver, CO B
U of Denver, CO B
U of Hawaii at Hilo, HI B
U of Hawaii at Manoa, HI B
U of Idaho, ID B
U of La Verne, CA B
The U of Montana–Missoula, MT B
U of Nevada, Las Vegas, NV B
U of Nevada, Reno, NV B
U of New Mexico, NM B
U of Northern Colorado, CO B
U of Oregon, OR B
U of Portland, OR B
U of Puget Sound, WA B
U of Redlands, CA B
U of San Diego, CA B
U of San Francisco, CA B
U of Southern California, CA B
U of the Pacific, CA B
U of Utah, UT B
U of Washington, WA B
U of Wyoming, WY B
Utah State U, UT B
Utah Valley State Coll, UT A,B
Walla Walla Coll, WA B
Washington State U, WA B
Weber State U, UT B
Western State Coll of Colorado, CO B
Western Washington U, WA B
Westminster Coll, UT B
Westmont Coll, CA B
Whitman Coll, WA B
Whitworth Coll, WA B
Willamette U, OR B

Physics Related
Brigham Young U, UT B
California State U, Chico, CA B
Embry-Riddle Aeronautical U, AZ B
Northern Arizona U, AZ B
U of Nevada, Las Vegas, NV B

Physics Teacher Education
Brigham Young U, UT B
Brigham Young U–Hawaii, HI B
Colorado State U, CO B
Eastern Washington U, WA B
Northern Arizona U, AZ B
The U of Arizona, AZ B
U of California, San Diego, CA B
U of Utah, UT B
Utah State U, UT B
Weber State U, UT B

Physiological Psychology/ Psychobiology
Claremont McKenna Coll, CA B
Holy Names U, CA B
Mills Coll, CA B
Occidental Coll, CA B
Saint Mary's Coll of California, CA B
Scripps Coll, CA B
U of California, Los Angeles, CA B
U of California, Riverside, CA B
U of California, Santa Cruz, CA B
U of Southern California, CA B

Physiology
Brigham Young U, UT B
California State U, Long Beach, CA B
San Jose State U, CA B
U of California, Los Angeles, CA B

Piano and Organ
Bethesda Christian U, CA B
Birmingham-Southern Coll, AL B
Brigham Young U, UT B
Brigham Young U–Hawaii, HI B
California Inst of the Arts, CA B
California State U, Chico, CA B
California State U, Fullerton, CA B
California State U, Sacramento, CA B
Central Washington U, WA B
The Colburn School of Performing Arts, CA B
Cornish Coll of the Arts, WA B
Eastern Washington U, WA B
Grand Canyon U, AZ B
The Master's Coll and Seminary, CA B
Notre Dame de Namur U, CA B
Pacific Lutheran U, WA B
Pacific Union Coll, CA A,B
U of Redlands, CA B
U of Southern California, CA B
U of the Pacific, CA B
U of Washington, WA B
Walla Walla Coll, WA B
Weber State U, UT B
Whitworth Coll, WA B
Willamette U, OR B

Planetary Astronomy and Science
California Inst of Technology, CA B

Plant Genetics
Brigham Young U, UT B

Plant Pathology/ Phytopathology
New Mexico State U, NM B
Washington State U, WA B

Plant Physiology
Washington State U, WA B

Plant Protection and Integrated Pest Management
California State Polytechnic U, Pomona, CA B

Plant Sciences
California State U, Fresno, CA B
Colorado State U, CO B
Montana State U–Bozeman, MT B
The U of Arizona, AZ B
U of California, Los Angeles, CA B
U of California, Santa Cruz, CA B
U of Idaho, ID B
Utah State U, UT B
Washington State U, WA B

Plant Sciences Related
Utah State U, UT B
Washington State U, WA B

Plastics Engineering Technology
Western Washington U, WA B

Playwriting and Screenwriting
Brigham Young U, UT B
Loyola Marymount U, CA B
U of Southern California, CA B

Political Science and Government
Adams State Coll, CO B
Albertson Coll of Idaho, ID B
Arizona State U, AZ B
Arizona State U West, AZ B
Azusa Pacific U, CA B
Birmingham-Southern Coll, AL B
Boise State U, ID B
Brigham Young U, UT B
Brigham Young U–Hawaii, HI B
California Baptist U, CA B
California Lutheran U, CA B
California Polytechnic State U, San Luis Obispo, CA B
California State Polytechnic U, Pomona, CA B
California State U, Bakersfield, CA B
California State U, Chico, CA B
California State U, Dominguez Hills, CA B
California State U, Fresno, CA B
California State U, Fullerton, CA B
California State U, Hayward, CA B
California State U, Long Beach, CA B
California State U, Los Angeles, CA B
California State U, Sacramento, CA B
California State U, San Bernardino, CA B
California State U, San Marcos, CA B
California State U, Stanislaus, CA B
Carroll Coll, MT B
Central Washington U, WA B
Chaminade U of Honolulu, HI B
Chapman U, CA B
Claremont McKenna Coll, CA B
Coll of Santa Fe, NM B
Colorado Christian U, CO B
The Colorado Coll, CO B
Colorado State U, CO B
Colorado State U-Pueblo, CO B
Cornell Coll, IA B
Dominican U of California, CA B
Eastern New Mexico U, NM B
Eastern Washington U, WA B
Eugene Lang Coll, New School U B
The Evergreen State Coll, WA B
Fort Lewis Coll, CO B
Fresno Pacific U, CA A,B
Gonzaga U, WA B
Grand Canyon U, AZ B
Hawai'i Pacific U, HI B
Humboldt State U, CA B
Idaho State U, ID A,B
Lehigh U, PA B
Lewis & Clark Coll, OR B
Linfield Coll, OR B
Loyola Marymount U, CA B
The Master's Coll and Seminary, CA B
Metropolitan State Coll of Denver, CO B
Mills Coll, CA B
Montana State U–Bozeman, MT B
Mount St. Mary's Coll, CA B
New Mexico Highlands U, NM B
New Mexico State U, NM B
North Carolina Ag and Tech State U, NC B
Northern Arizona U, AZ B
Northwest Nazarene U, ID B
Notre Dame de Namur U, CA B
Occidental Coll, CA B
Oregon State U, OR B
Pacific Lutheran U, WA B
Pacific Union Coll, CA B
Pacific U, OR B
Pepperdine U, Malibu, CA B
Pitzer Coll, CA B
Point Loma Nazarene U, CA B
Pomona Coll, CA B
Portland State U, OR B
Prescott Coll, AZ B
Reed Coll, OR B
Regis U, CO B
Rocky Mountain Coll, MT B
Saint Martin's Coll, WA B
Saint Mary's Coll of California, CA B
San Diego State U, CA B
San Francisco State U, CA B
San Jose State U, CA B
Santa Clara U, CA B
Scripps Coll, CA B
Seattle Pacific U, WA B
Seattle U, WA B
Sonoma State U, CA B
Southern Oregon U, OR B
Southern Utah U, UT B
Stanford U, CA B
United States Air Force Academy, CO B
U of Alaska Anchorage, AK B
U of Alaska Fairbanks, AK B
U of Alaska Southeast, AK B
The U of Arizona, AZ B
U of California, Berkeley, CA B
U of California, Davis, CA B
U of California, Irvine, CA B
U of California, Los Angeles, CA B
U of California, Riverside, CA B
U of California, San Diego, CA B
U of California, Santa Barbara, CA B
U of California, Santa Cruz, CA B
U of Colorado at Boulder, CO B

A—associate degree; B—bachelor's degree

U of Colorado at Colorado Springs, CO B
U of Colorado at Denver, CO B
U of Denver, CO B
U of Great Falls, MT B
U of Hawaii at Hilo, HI B
U of Hawaii at Manoa, HI B
U of Idaho, ID B
U of Judaism, CA B
U of La Verne, CA B
U of Nevada, Las Vegas, NV B
U of Nevada, Reno, NV B
U of New Mexico, NM B
U of Northern Colorado, CO B
U of Oregon, OR B
U of Portland, OR B
U of Puget Sound, WA B
U of Redlands, CA B
U of San Diego, CA B
U of San Francisco, CA B
U of Southern California, CA B
U of the Pacific, CA B
U of Utah, UT B
U of Washington, WA B
U of Wyoming, WY B
Utah State U, UT B
Vanguard U of Southern California, CA B
Washington State U, WA B
Weber State U, UT B
Western Oregon U, OR B
Western State Coll of Colorado, CO B
Western Washington U, WA B
Westminster Coll, UT B
Westmont Coll, CA B
Whitman Coll, WA B
Whitworth Coll, WA B
Willamette U, OR B
Woodbury U, CA B

Political Science and Government Related

Claremont McKenna Coll, CA B
Saint Mary's Coll of California, CA B

Polymer/Plastics Engineering

U of Southern California, CA B

Portuguese

Brigham Young U, UT B
U of California, Los Angeles, CA B
U of California, Santa Barbara, CA B
U of New Mexico, NM B
U of Southern California, CA B

Poultry Science

U of California, Davis, CA B

Pre-Dentistry Studies

Adams State Coll, CO B
Birmingham-Southern Coll, AL B
Boise State U, ID B
California State U, Chico, CA B
California State U, Dominguez Hills, CA B
California State U, Hayward, CA B
Carroll Coll, MT B
Claremont McKenna Coll, CA B
Colorado State U, CO B
Colorado State U-Pueblo, CO B
Eastern Oregon U, OR B
Eastern Washington U, WA B
Fort Lewis Coll, CO B
Grand Canyon U, AZ B
Humboldt State U, CA B
Mount St. Mary's Coll, CA B
New Mexico Inst of Mining and Technology, NM B
Notre Dame de Namur U, CA B
Oregon State U, OR B
Pacific Union Coll, CA B
Pacific U, OR B
Pepperdine U, Malibu, CA B
Regis U, CO B
Saint Martin's Coll, WA B
Seattle Pacific U, WA B
Sonoma State U, CA B
U of Colorado at Colorado Springs, CO B
U of La Verne, CA B
The U of Montana–Western, MT B
U of Oregon, OR B
U of Portland, OR B
U of Puget Sound, WA B
U of San Francisco, CA B
Utah State U, UT B
Walla Walla Coll, WA B
Washington State U, WA B
Western State Coll of Colorado, CO B
Westmont Coll, CA B
Whitworth Coll, WA B

Pre-Engineering

Adams State Coll, CO B
Azusa Pacific U, CA B
Boise State U, ID A
Lewis & Clark Coll, OR B
Montana State U–Billings, MT A
Pacific Union Coll, CA A
Southern Utah U, UT A
The U of Montana–Missoula, MT B

Pre-Law Studies

Adams State Coll, CO B
Arizona State U, AZ B
Azusa Pacific U, CA B
Biola U, CA B
Birmingham-Southern Coll, AL B
California State Polytechnic U, Pomona, CA B
California State U, Dominguez Hills, CA B
California State U, Fresno, CA B
Carroll Coll, MT B
Claremont McKenna Coll, CA B
Colorado State U, CO B
Colorado State U-Pueblo, CO B
Eastern Oregon U, OR B
Eastern Washington U, WA B
Fort Lewis Coll, CO B
Fresno Pacific U, CA B
Grand Canyon U, AZ B
Humboldt State U, CA B
The Master's Coll and Seminary, CA B
Mount St. Mary's Coll, CA B
New Mexico Highlands U, NM B
Northern Arizona U, AZ B
Northwest Coll, WA A
Northwest Nazarene U, ID B
Notre Dame de Namur U, CA B
Pacific Union Coll, CA B
Pepperdine U, Malibu, CA B
Regis U, CO B
Saint Martin's Coll, WA B
San Diego State U, CA B
Seattle Pacific U, WA B
Sonoma State U, CA B
Southern Oregon U, OR B
U of California, Riverside, CA B
U of California, Santa Barbara, CA B
U of Colorado at Colorado Springs, CO B
U of La Verne, CA B
The U of Montana–Missoula, MT B
The U of Montana–Western, MT B
U of Portland, OR B
U of Puget Sound, WA B
U of West Los Angeles, CA B
Utah State U, UT B
Vanguard U of Southern California, CA B
Walla Walla Coll, WA B
Warner Pacific Coll, OR B
Washington State U, WA B
Western Baptist Coll, OR B
Western State Coll of Colorado, CO B
Western Washington U, WA B
Westmont Coll, CA B
Whitworth Coll, WA B

Pre-Medical Studies

Adams State Coll, CO B
Albertson Coll of Idaho, ID B
Birmingham-Southern Coll, AL B
Boise State U, ID B
California Polytechnic State U, San Luis Obispo, CA B
California State Polytechnic U, Pomona, CA B
California State U, Chico, CA B
California State U, Dominguez Hills, CA B
California State U, Hayward, CA B
Carroll Coll, MT B
Claremont McKenna Coll, CA B
Colorado State U, CO B
Colorado State U-Pueblo, CO B
Concordia U, OR B
Eastern Oregon U, OR B
Eastern Washington U, WA B
Fort Lewis Coll, CO B
Fresno Pacific U, CA B
Grand Canyon U, AZ B
Hawai'i Pacific U, HI B
Humboldt State U, CA B
Lehigh U, PA B
The Master's Coll and Seminary, CA B
Mount St. Mary's Coll, CA B
New Mexico Highlands U, NM B
New Mexico Inst of Mining and Technology, NM B
Northern Arizona U, AZ B
Northwest Nazarene U, ID B
Notre Dame de Namur U, CA B
Oregon Inst of Technology, OR B
Oregon State U, OR B
Pacific Union Coll, CA B
Pacific U, OR B
Pepperdine U, Malibu, CA B
Pitzer Coll, CA B
Pomona Coll, CA B
Regis U, CO B
St. John's Coll, NM B
Saint Martin's Coll, WA B
Scripps Coll, CA B
Seattle Pacific U, WA B
Sonoma State U, CA B
Southern Oregon U, OR B
U of Colorado at Colorado Springs, CO B
U of Idaho, ID B
U of Judaism, CA B
U of La Verne, CA B
The U of Montana–Missoula, MT B
The U of Montana–Western, MT B
U of Nevada, Reno, NV B
U of Oregon, OR B
U of Portland, OR B
U of Puget Sound, WA B
U of San Diego, CA B
U of San Francisco, CA B
Utah State U, UT B
Walla Walla Coll, WA B
Warner Pacific Coll, OR B
Washington State U, WA B
Western State Coll of Colorado, CO B
Westmont Coll, CA B
Whitworth Coll, WA B

Pre-Nursing Studies

Adams State Coll, CO B
Brigham Young U, UT B
Nevada State Coll at Henderson, NV B
U of La Verne, CA B

Pre-Pharmacy Studies

Adams State Coll, CO B
Carroll Coll, MT B
Colorado State U-Pueblo, CO B
Saint Martin's Coll, WA B
The U of Montana–Missoula, MT B
U of Utah, UT B
Westmont Coll, CA B

Pre-Theology/Pre-Ministerial Studies

California Baptist U, CA B
California Christian Coll, CA B
Concordia U, OR B
Western Baptist Coll, OR B
Westmont Coll, CA B

Pre-Veterinary Studies

Adams State Coll, CO B
Boise State U, ID B
California State Polytechnic U, Pomona, CA B
California State U, Chico, CA B
California State U, Dominguez Hills, CA B
California State U, Hayward, CA B
Carroll Coll, MT B
Colorado State U, CO B
Colorado State U-Pueblo, CO B
Eastern Oregon U, OR B
Eastern Washington U, WA B
Fort Lewis Coll, CO B
Grand Canyon U, AZ B
Humboldt State U, CA B
New Mexico Inst of Mining and Technology, NM B
Northern Arizona U, AZ B
Oregon State U, OR B
Pacific Union Coll, CA B
Regis U, CO B
Saint Martin's Coll, WA B
Sonoma State U, CA B
The U of Arizona, AZ B
U of Colorado at Colorado Springs, CO B
The U of Montana–Western, MT B
U of Nevada, Reno, NV B
U of Puget Sound, WA B
U of San Francisco, CA B
Utah State U, UT B
Walla Walla Coll, WA B
Warner Pacific Coll, OR B
Western State Coll of Colorado, CO B
Westmont Coll, CA B
Whitworth Coll, WA B

Printmaking

Academy of Art U, CA A,B
Arizona State U, AZ B
Birmingham-Southern Coll, AL B
Brigham Young U, UT B

California Coll of the Arts, CA B
California State U, Fullerton, CA B
California State U, Hayward, CA B
California State U, Long Beach, CA B
Coll of Santa Fe, NM B
Colorado State U, CO B
Laguna Coll of Art & Design, CA B
Pacific Northwest Coll of Art, OR B
San Francisco Art Inst, CA B
Sonoma State U, CA B
U of California, Santa Cruz, CA B
U of Oregon, OR B
U of San Francisco, CA B
U of Washington, WA B
Western Washington U, WA B

Psychology

Adams State Coll, CO B
Alaska Pacific U, AK B
Albertson Coll of Idaho, ID B
Alliant International U, CA B
Argosy U/Phoenix, AZ B
Argosy U/Seattle, WA B
Arizona State U, AZ B
Arizona State U West, AZ B
Azusa Pacific U, CA B
Bastyr U, WA B
Biola U, CA B
Birmingham-Southern Coll, AL B
Boise State U, ID B
Brigham Young U, UT B
Brigham Young U–Hawaii, HI B
California Baptist U, CA B
California Lutheran U, CA B
California Polytechnic State U, San Luis Obispo, CA B
California State Polytechnic U, Pomona, CA B
California State U, Bakersfield, CA B
California State U, Chico, CA B
California State U, Dominguez Hills, CA B
California State U, Fresno, CA B
California State U, Fullerton, CA B
California State U, Hayward, CA B
California State U, Long Beach, CA B
California State U, Los Angeles, CA B
California State U, Sacramento, CA B
California State U, San Bernardino, CA B
California State U, San Marcos, CA B
California State U, Stanislaus, CA B
Carroll Coll, MT B
Cascade Coll, OR B
Central Washington U, WA B
Chaminade U of Honolulu, HI B
Chapman U, CA B
Christian Heritage Coll, CA B
City U, WA B
Claremont McKenna Coll, CA B
Coll of Santa Fe, NM B
Coll of the Southwest, NM B
Colorado Christian U, CO B
The Colorado Coll, CO B
Colorado State U, CO B
Colorado State U-Pueblo, CO B
Concordia U, CA B
Concordia U, OR B
Cornell Coll, IA B
Dominican U of California, CA B
Eastern New Mexico U, NM A,B
Eastern Oregon U, OR B
Eastern Washington U, WA B
Eugene Lang Coll, New School U B
Fort Lewis Coll, CO B
Fresno Pacific U, CA A,B
George Fox U, OR B
Gonzaga U, WA B
Grand Canyon U, AZ B
Great Basin Coll, NV A
Hawai'i Pacific U, HI B
Holy Names U, CA B
Humboldt State U, CA B
Idaho State U, ID B
John F. Kennedy U, CA B
Lehigh U, PA B
Lewis & Clark Coll, OR B
Lewis-Clark State Coll, ID B
Linfield Coll, OR B
Loyola Marymount U, CA B
Marylhurst U, OR B
Metropolitan State Coll of Denver, CO B
Mills Coll, CA B
Montana State U–Billings, MT A,B
Montana State U–Bozeman, MT B
Mount St. Mary's Coll, CA B
Naropa U, CO B
National U, CA B
Nevada State Coll at Henderson, NV B
New Coll of California, CA B
New Mexico Highlands U, NM B
New Mexico Inst of Mining and Technology, NM B
New Mexico State U, NM B
North Carolina Ag and Tech State U, NC B
Northcentral U, AZ B
Northern Arizona U, AZ B
Northwest Coll, WA B
Northwest Nazarene U, ID B
Notre Dame de Namur U, CA B
Occidental Coll, CA B
Oregon State U, OR B
Pacific Lutheran U, WA B
Pacific Union Coll, CA B
Pacific U, OR B
Pepperdine U, Malibu, CA B
Pitzer Coll, CA B
Point Loma Nazarene U, CA B
Pomona Coll, CA B
Portland State U, OR B
Prescott Coll, AZ B
Reed Coll, OR B
Regis U, CO B
Rocky Mountain Coll, MT B
Saint Martin's Coll, WA B
Saint Mary's Coll of California, CA B
San Diego State U, CA B
San Francisco State U, CA B
San Jose State U, CA B
Santa Clara U, CA B
Scripps Coll, CA B
Seattle Pacific U, WA B
Seattle U, WA B
Simpson Coll and Graduate School, CA B
Sonoma State U, CA B
Southern Oregon U, OR B
Southern Utah U, UT B
Stanford U, CA B
U of Alaska Anchorage, AK B
U of Alaska Fairbanks, AK B
The U of Arizona, AZ B
U of California, Berkeley, CA B
U of California, Davis, CA B
U of California, Irvine, CA B
U of California, Los Angeles, CA B
U of California, Riverside, CA B
U of California, San Diego, CA B
U of California, Santa Barbara, CA B
U of California, Santa Cruz, CA B
U of Colorado at Boulder, CO B
U of Colorado at Colorado Springs, CO B
U of Colorado at Denver, CO B
U of Denver, CO B
U of Great Falls, MT B
U of Hawaii at Hilo, HI B
U of Hawaii at Manoa, HI B
U of Idaho, ID B
U of Judaism, CA B
U of La Verne, CA B
The U of Montana–Missoula, MT B
U of Nevada, Las Vegas, NV B
U of Nevada, Reno, NV B
U of New Mexico, NM B
U of Northern Colorado, CO B
U of Oregon, OR B
U of Portland, OR B
U of Puget Sound, WA B
U of Redlands, CA B
U of San Diego, CA B
U of San Francisco, CA B
U of Southern California, CA B
U of the Pacific, CA B
U of the West, CA B
U of Utah, UT B
U of Washington, WA B
U of Wyoming, WY B
Utah State U, UT B
Utah Valley State Coll, UT A,B
Vanguard U of Southern California, CA B
Walla Walla Coll, WA B
Warner Pacific Coll, OR B
Washington State U, WA B
Weber State U, UT B
Western Baptist Coll, OR B
Western Oregon U, OR B
Western State Coll of Colorado, CO B
Western Washington U, WA B
Westminster Coll, UT B
Westmont Coll, CA B
Whitman Coll, WA B
Whitworth Coll, WA B
Willamette U, OR B
Woodbury U, CA B

Psychology Related

Arizona State U East, AZ B
Northwest Christian Coll, OR B
Saint Mary's Coll of California, CA B

Psychology Teacher Education

Brigham Young U, UT B
California Lutheran U, CA B

Public Administration

Boise State U, ID B
California State Polytechnic U, Pomona, CA B
California State U, Bakersfield, CA B
California State U, Chico, CA B
California State U, Dominguez Hills, CA B
California State U, Fresno, CA B
California State U, Fullerton, CA B
California State U, Hayward, CA B
California State U, San Bernardino, CA B
Carroll Coll, MT B
Coll of Santa Fe, NM B
Crown Coll, WA B
Eastern Washington U, WA B
Hawai'i Pacific U, HI B
Nevada State Coll at Henderson, NV B
San Diego State U, CA B
Seattle U, WA B
The U of Arizona, AZ B
U of California, Los Angeles, CA B
U of California, Riverside, CA B
U of Denver, CO B
U of La Verne, CA B
U of Oregon, OR B
U of San Francisco, CA B
U of Southern California, CA B
U of Washington, WA B
Washington State U, WA B
Western Oregon U, OR B

Public Administration and Social Service Professions Related

U of Phoenix–Colorado Campus, CO B
U of Phoenix–Hawaii Campus, HI B
U of Phoenix–Nevada Campus, NV B
U of Phoenix–New Mexico Campus, NM B
U of Phoenix–Northern California Campus, CA B
U of Phoenix–Oregon Campus, OR B
U of Phoenix–Phoenix Campus, AZ B
U of Phoenix–Sacramento Campus, CA B
U of Phoenix–San Diego Campus, CA B
U of Phoenix–Southern Arizona Campus, AZ B
U of Phoenix–Southern California Campus, CA B
U of Phoenix–Southern Colorado Campus, CO B
U of Phoenix–Utah Campus, UT B
U of Phoenix–Washington Campus, WA B

Public/Applied History and Archival Administration

U of California, Santa Barbara, CA B

Public Health

Boise State U, ID B
California State U, Dominguez Hills, CA B
California State U, Long Beach, CA B
New Mexico State U, NM B
Oregon State U, OR B
Touro U International, CA B
U of Alaska Fairbanks, AK A
U of Washington, WA B

A—associate degree; B—bachelor's degree

Public Health/Community Nursing

U of Washington, WA B

Public Health Education and Promotion

California State U, Long Beach, CA B
New Mexico State U, NM B
U of Northern Colorado, CO B
U of Southern California, CA B
Walla Walla Coll, WA B
Western Washington U, WA B

Public Health Related

U of California, Berkeley, CA B
U of California, Los Angeles, CA B
Utah State U, UT B

Public Policy Analysis

Brigham Young U, UT B
Central Washington U, WA B
Mills Coll, CA B
Northern Arizona U, AZ B
Occidental Coll, CA B
Pomona Coll, CA B
Stanford U, CA B
U of California, Los Angeles, CA B
U of Oregon, OR B
Western State Coll of Colorado, CO B

Public Relations, Advertising, and Applied Communication Related

Brigham Young U, UT B
California Lutheran U, CA B
Jones International U, CO B

Public Relations/Image Management

California Lutheran U, CA B
California State Polytechnic U, Pomona, CA B
California State U, Chico, CA B
California State U, Dominguez Hills, CA B
California State U, Fresno, CA B
California State U, Fullerton, CA B
California State U, Hayward, CA B
California State U, Long Beach, CA B
Carroll Coll, MT B
Central Washington U, WA B
Colorado State U, CO B
Colorado State U-Pueblo, CO B
George Fox U, OR B
Gonzaga U, WA B
Hawai'i Pacific U, HI B
Marylhurst U, OR B
The Master's Coll and Seminary, CA B
Metropolitan State Coll of Denver, CO B
Montana State U–Billings, MT B
Northern Arizona U, AZ B
Northwest Nazarene U, ID B
Pacific Union Coll, CA B
Pepperdine U, Malibu, CA B
San Diego State U, CA B
San Jose State U, CA B
Seattle U, WA B
U of Idaho, ID B
U of Oregon, OR B
U of Southern California, CA B
U of Utah, UT B
Walla Walla Coll, WA B
Washington State U, WA B
Weber State U, UT B

Purchasing, Procurement/ Acquisitions and Contracts Management

Arizona State U, AZ B
California State U, Hayward, CA B

Quality Control Technology

California State U, Long Beach, CA B
San Jose State U, CA B

Radio and Television

Academy of Art U, CA A,B
Arizona State U, AZ B
Biola U, CA B
California State U, Chico, CA B
California State U, Fresno, CA B
California State U, Fullerton, CA B
California State U, Long Beach, CA B
California State U, Los Angeles, CA B
Central Washington U, WA B
Colorado State U, CO B
Colorado State U-Pueblo, CO B
Columbia Coll Hollywood, CA B
George Fox U, OR B
The Master's Coll and Seminary, CA B
Northern Arizona U, AZ B
Pacific Lutheran U, WA B
Pacific U, OR B
San Diego State U, CA B
San Francisco State U, CA B
San Jose State U, CA B
The U of Arizona, AZ B
U of Idaho, ID B
U of La Verne, CA B
The U of Montana–Missoula, MT B
U of Oregon, OR B
U of Southern California, CA B
U of Utah, UT B
Vanguard U of Southern California, CA B
Walla Walla Coll, WA B
Weber State U, UT B
Western State Coll of Colorado, CO B

Radio and Television Broadcasting Technology

Northwest Nazarene U, ID B

Radiologic Technology/ Science

Boise State U, ID A,B
Lewis-Clark State Coll, ID A
Oregon Inst of Technology, OR B

Radio, Television, and Digital Communication Related

Brigham Young U, UT B
California State Polytechnic U, Pomona, CA B

Range Science and Management

Brigham Young U, UT B
California State U, Chico, CA B
Colorado State U, CO B
Humboldt State U, CA B
Montana State U–Bozeman, MT B
New Mexico State U, NM B
Oregon State U, OR B
U of California, Davis, CA B
U of Idaho, ID B
U of Wyoming, WY B
Utah State U, UT B
Washington State U, WA B

Reading Teacher Education

Boise State U, ID B
Eastern Washington U, WA B
Pacific Lutheran U, WA B
U of Great Falls, MT B
The U of Montana–Missoula, MT B

Real Estate

Arizona State U, AZ B
California State Polytechnic U, Pomona, CA B
California State U, Dominguez Hills, CA B
California State U, Fresno, CA B
California State U, Hayward, CA B
California State U, Sacramento, CA B
Colorado State U, CO B
Marylhurst U, OR B
San Diego State U, CA B
San Francisco State U, CA B
U of Denver, CO B
U of Hawaii at Manoa, HI B
U of Nevada, Las Vegas, NV B
Washington State U, WA B

Receptionist

The U of Montana–Missoula, MT A

Regional Studies

Coll of Santa Fe, NM B

Rehabilitation and Therapeutic Professions Related

Montana State U–Billings, MT B

Rehabilitation Therapy

California State U, Los Angeles, CA B
Montana State U–Billings, MT B

Religious Education

Bethesda Christian U, CA B
Biola U, CA B
Carroll Coll, MT B
Concordia U, CA B
Concordia U, OR B
Eugene Bible Coll, OR B
George Fox U, OR B
The Master's Coll and Seminary, CA B
Multnomah Bible Coll and Biblical Seminary, OR B
Northwest Coll, WA B
Northwest Nazarene U, ID B
Pepperdine U, Malibu, CA B
Seattle Pacific U, WA B
Simpson Coll and Graduate School, CA B
Vanguard U of Southern California, CA B
Warner Pacific Coll, OR A,B
Western Baptist Coll, OR B

Religious/Sacred Music

Bethesda Christian U, CA B
Christian Heritage Coll, CA B
Eugene Bible Coll, OR B
Fresno Pacific U, CA B
Grand Canyon U, AZ B
The Master's Coll and Seminary, CA B
Multnomah Bible Coll and Biblical Seminary, OR B
Northwest Coll, WA B
Northwest Nazarene U, ID B
Pacific Lutheran U, WA B
Point Loma Nazarene U, CA B
Western Baptist Coll, OR B

Religious Studies

Albertson Coll of Idaho, ID B
Arizona State U, AZ B
Azusa Pacific U, CA B
Biola U, CA B
Birmingham-Southern Coll, AL B
California Lutheran U, CA B
California State U, Bakersfield, CA B
California State U, Chico, CA B
California State U, Dominguez Hills, CA B
California State U, Fresno, CA B
California State U, Fullerton, CA B
California State U, Hayward, CA B
California State U, Long Beach, CA B
Carroll Coll, MT B
Central Washington U, WA B
Chaminade U of Honolulu, HI B
Chapman U, CA B
Claremont McKenna Coll, CA B
Coll of Santa Fe, NM B
The Colorado Coll, CO B
Concordia U, OR B
Cornell Coll, IA B
Dominican U of California, CA B
Eastern New Mexico U, NM B
Eugene Lang Coll, New School U B
Fresno Pacific U, CA B
George Fox U, OR B
Gonzaga U, WA B
Grand Canyon U, AZ B
Holy Names U, CA B
Humboldt State U, CA B
Lehigh U, PA B
Lewis & Clark Coll, OR B
Linfield Coll, OR B
Marylhurst U, OR B
The Master's Coll and Seminary, CA B
Mount St. Mary's Coll, CA B
Naropa U, CO B
Northern Arizona U, AZ B
Northwest Coll, WA B
Northwest Nazarene U, ID B
Notre Dame de Namur U, CA B
Occidental Coll, CA B
Pacific Lutheran U, WA B
Pacific Union Coll, CA B
Pepperdine U, Malibu, CA B
Pitzer Coll, CA B
Pomona Coll, CA B
Reed Coll, OR B
Regis U, CO B
Rocky Mountain Coll, MT B
St. John's Coll, NM B
Saint Martin's Coll, WA B
Saint Mary's Coll of California, CA B
San Diego State U, CA B
San Francisco State U, CA B
San Jose State U, CA B
Santa Clara U, CA B
Scripps Coll, CA B
Seattle U, WA B
Stanford U, CA B
The U of Arizona, AZ B
U of California, Berkeley, CA B
U of California, Davis, CA B
U of California, Los Angeles, CA B
U of California, Riverside, CA B
U of California, San Diego, CA B

U of California, Santa Barbara, CA B
U of California, Santa Cruz, CA B
U of Colorado at Boulder, CO B
U of Denver, CO B
U of Great Falls, MT B
U of Hawaii at Manoa, HI B
U of La Verne, CA B
U of New Mexico, NM B
U of Oregon, OR B
U of Puget Sound, WA B
U of Redlands, CA B
U of San Diego, CA B
U of San Francisco, CA B
U of Southern California, CA B
U of the Pacific, CA B
U of Washington, WA B
Vanguard U of Southern California, CA B
Walla Walla Coll, WA B
Warner Pacific Coll, OR B
Washington State U, WA B
Western Baptist Coll, OR B
Westmont Coll, CA B
Whitman Coll, WA B
Whitworth Coll, WA B
Willamette U, OR B
William Jessup U, CA B

Religious Studies Related

Claremont McKenna Coll, CA B
U of the West, CA B

Respiratory Care Therapy

Boise State U, ID B
Loma Linda U, CA A,B
The U of Montana–Missoula, MT A
Weber State U, UT A,B

Restaurant, Culinary, and Catering Management

The Art Inst of California–San Diego, CA B
Utah Valley State Coll, UT B
Washington State U, WA B

Restaurant/Food Services Management

The Art Inst of California–San Diego, CA B
U of San Francisco, CA B

Retailing

Brigham Young U, UT B

Robotics Technology

ITT Tech Inst, West Covina, CA B
ITT Tech Inst, OR B

Romance Languages

Pitzer Coll, CA B
Point Loma Nazarene U, CA B
Pomona Coll, CA B
U of Nevada, Las Vegas, NV B
U of Oregon, OR B
U of Washington, WA B

Romance Languages Related

The Colorado Coll, CO B

Russian

Arizona State U, AZ B
Brigham Young U, UT B
Claremont McKenna Coll, CA B
The Colorado Coll, CO B
Cornell Coll, IA B
Lehigh U, PA B
Pitzer Coll, CA B
Pomona Coll, CA B
Portland State U, OR B
Reed Coll, OR B
San Diego State U, CA B
San Francisco State U, CA B
Scripps Coll, CA B
Seattle Pacific U, WA B
The U of Arizona, AZ B
U of California, Davis, CA B
U of California, Irvine, CA B
U of California, Los Angeles, CA B
U of California, Riverside, CA B
U of California, San Diego, CA B
U of Denver, CO B
U of Hawaii at Manoa, HI B
The U of Montana–Missoula, MT B
U of New Mexico, NM B
U of Oregon, OR B
U of Southern California, CA B
U of Utah, UT B
U of Washington, WA B
U of Wyoming, WY B
Washington State U, WA B

Russian Studies

California State U, Fullerton, CA B
Claremont McKenna Coll, CA B
The Colorado Coll, CO B
Lehigh U, PA B
San Diego State U, CA B
U of Alaska Fairbanks, AK B
U of California, Los Angeles, CA B
U of California, Riverside, CA B
U of California, San Diego, CA B
U of California, Santa Cruz, CA B
U of Colorado at Boulder, CO B
The U of Montana–Missoula, MT B
U of New Mexico, NM B
U of Washington, WA B
Washington State U, WA B

Sales and Marketing/Marketing and Distribution Teacher Education

Colorado State U, CO B
Eastern New Mexico U, NM B
San Diego State U, CA B
U of Hawaii at Manoa, HI B
Utah State U, UT B

Sales, Distribution and Marketing

LDS Business Coll, UT A
Pioneer Pacific Coll, OR A
Sierra Nevada Coll, NV B

Scandinavian Languages

Pacific Lutheran U, WA B
U of California, Berkeley, CA B
U of California, Los Angeles, CA B
U of Washington, WA B
Washington State U, WA B

Scandinavian Studies

U of Washington, WA B

School Librarian/School Library Media

Eastern Washington U, WA B
U of Great Falls, MT B

Science Teacher Education

Boise State U, ID B
Brigham Young U, UT B
Brigham Young U–Hawaii, HI B
California Lutheran U, CA B
California State U, Chico, CA B
California State U, San Marcos, CA B
Central Washington U, WA B
Coll of Santa Fe, NM B
Coll of the Southwest, NM B
Colorado State U, CO B
Colorado State U-Pueblo, CO B
Concordia U, OR B
Eastern Washington U, WA B
Fresno Pacific U, CA B
Grand Canyon U, AZ B
Lewis-Clark State Coll, ID B
The Master's Coll and Seminary, CA B
Montana State U–Billings, MT B
Nevada State Coll at Henderson, NV B
New Mexico Highlands U, NM B
Northern Arizona U, AZ B
Pacific Lutheran U, WA B
Prescott Coll, AZ B
San Diego State U, CA B
Seattle Pacific U, WA B
The U of Arizona, AZ B
U of Great Falls, MT B
U of Hawaii at Manoa, HI B
The U of Montana–Missoula, MT B
The U of Montana–Western, MT B
U of Nevada, Reno, NV B
U of Utah, UT B
U of Washington, WA B
Utah State U, UT B
Utah Valley State Coll, UT B
Warner Pacific Coll, OR B
Weber State U, UT B
Western State Coll of Colorado, CO B
Western Washington U, WA B

Science Technologies Related

Arizona State U East, AZ B
Lehigh U, PA B
Northern Arizona U, AZ B
The U of Arizona, AZ B

Science, Technology and Society

California Inst of Technology, CA B
Embry-Riddle Aeronautical U, AZ B
Pitzer Coll, CA B
Scripps Coll, CA B
Stanford U, CA B
U of Alaska Anchorage, AK B
U of Nevada, Reno, NV B
U of Puget Sound, WA B

Sculpture

Academy of Art U, CA A,B
Arizona State U, AZ B
Birmingham-Southern Coll, AL B
Brigham Young U, UT B
California Coll of the Arts, CA B
California Inst of the Arts, CA B
California State U, Fullerton, CA B
California State U, Hayward, CA B
California State U, Long Beach, CA B
Coll of Santa Fe, NM B
Colorado State U, CO B
Laguna Coll of Art & Design, CA B
Northwest Nazarene U, ID B
Otis Coll of Art and Design, CA B
Pacific Northwest Coll of Art, OR B
Portland State U, OR B
Rocky Mountain Coll of Art & Design, CO B
San Diego State U, CA B
San Francisco Art Inst, CA B
Sonoma State U, CA B
U of California, Santa Cruz, CA B
U of Oregon, OR B
U of Washington, WA B
Western Washington U, WA B

Secondary Education

Adams State Coll, CO B
Arizona State U, AZ B
Arizona State U West, AZ B
Biola U, CA B
Birmingham-Southern Coll, AL B
Boise State U, ID B
Brigham Young U–Hawaii, HI B
Carroll Coll, MT B
Christian Heritage Coll, CA B
Coll of Santa Fe, NM B
Coll of the Southwest, NM B
Colorado State U-Pueblo, CO B
Concordia U, OR B
Cornell Coll, IA B
Fort Lewis Coll, CO B
Fresno Pacific U, CA B
Gonzaga U, WA B
Grand Canyon U, AZ B
Humboldt State U, CA B
Idaho State U, ID B
The Master's Coll and Seminary, CA B
Montana State U–Billings, MT B
Montana State U–Bozeman, MT B
Mount St. Mary's Coll, CA B
New Mexico Highlands U, NM B
New Mexico State U, NM B
Northwest Coll, WA B
Northwest Nazarene U, ID B
Notre Dame de Namur U, CA B
Pacific Lutheran U, WA B
Pacific U, OR B
Pepperdine U, Malibu, CA B
Prescott Coll, AZ B
Rocky Mountain Coll, MT B
Saint Martin's Coll, WA B
Sheldon Jackson Coll, AK B
Southern Utah U, UT B
Southwestern Coll, AZ B
U of Alaska Anchorage, AK B
The U of Arizona, AZ B
U of Great Falls, MT B
U of Hawaii at Hilo, HI B
U of Hawaii at Manoa, HI B
U of Idaho, ID B
U of La Verne, CA B
The U of Montana–Missoula, MT B
The U of Montana–Western, MT B
U of Nevada, Las Vegas, NV B
U of New Mexico, NM B
U of Portland, OR B
U of Redlands, CA B
U of San Francisco, CA B
U of Utah, UT B
U of Washington, WA B
U of Wyoming, WY B
Utah State U, UT B
Utah Valley State Coll, UT A
Vanguard U of Southern California, CA B
Warner Pacific Coll, OR B
Washington State U, WA B

A—associate degree; B—bachelor's degree

Weber State U, UT B
Western Baptist Coll, OR B
Western Oregon U, OR B
Western State Coll of Colorado, CO B
Western Washington U, WA B
Westmont Coll, CA B
Whitworth Coll, WA B

Secondary School Administration/Principalship
Jones International U, CO B

Sheet Metal Technology
Montana State U–Billings, MT A

Sign Language Interpretation and Translation
Idaho State U, ID B
U of New Mexico, NM B
Western Oregon U, OR B

Slavic Languages
Stanford U, CA B
U of California, Berkeley, CA B
U of California, Los Angeles, CA B
U of California, Santa Barbara, CA B
U of Southern California, CA B
U of Washington, WA B

Small Business Administration
Lewis-Clark State Coll, ID A,B

Small Engine Mechanics and Repair Technology
The U of Montana–Missoula, MT A

Social Psychology
Brigham Young U, UT B
U of California, Irvine, CA B
U of California, Santa Cruz, CA B
U of Nevada, Reno, NV B

Social Sciences
Adams State Coll, CO B
Arizona State U West, AZ B
Azusa Pacific U, CA B
Biola U, CA B
Boise State U, ID B
California Baptist U, CA B
California Inst of Technology, CA B
California Lutheran U, CA B
California Polytechnic State U, San Luis Obispo, CA B
California State Polytechnic U, Pomona, CA B
California State U, Chico, CA B
California State U, Los Angeles, CA B
California State U, Sacramento, CA B
California State U, San Bernardino, CA B
California State U, San Marcos, CA B
California State U, Stanislaus, CA B
Carroll Coll, MT B
Chaminade U of Honolulu, HI B
Christian Heritage Coll, CA B
Coll of the Southwest, NM B
Colorado Christian U, CO B
Colorado State U, CO B
Colorado State U-Pueblo, CO B
Concordia U, OR B
Eastern New Mexico U, NM B
Eugene Lang Coll, New School U B
The Evergreen State Coll, WA B
Fresno Pacific U, CA B
Grand Canyon U, AZ B
Hawai'i Pacific U, HI B
Humboldt State U, CA B
Lehigh U, PA B
Lewis-Clark State Coll, ID B
Marylhurst U, OR B
Mount St. Mary's Coll, CA B
New Coll of California, CA B
North Carolina Ag and Tech State U, NC B
Northern Arizona U, AZ B
Northwest Nazarene U, ID B
Notre Dame de Namur U, CA B
Pacific Union Coll, CA B
Point Loma Nazarene U, CA B
Portland State U, OR B
Saint Mary's Coll of California, CA B
San Diego State U, CA B
San Francisco State U, CA B
San Jose State U, CA B
Southern Oregon U, OR B
Southern Utah U, UT B
United States Air Force Academy, CO B
U of California, Irvine, CA B
U of California, Riverside, CA B
U of Denver, CO B
U of Great Falls, MT B
U of La Verne, CA B
The U of Montana–Missoula, MT B
The U of Montana–Western, MT B
U of Nevada, Las Vegas, NV B
U of Northern Colorado, CO B
U of the Pacific, CA B
U of Utah, UT B
U of Washington, WA B
U of Wyoming, WY B
Utah Valley State Coll, UT A
Warner Pacific Coll, OR A,B
Washington State U, WA B
Western Baptist Coll, OR B
Western Oregon U, OR B
Western State Coll of Colorado, CO B
Westminster Coll, UT B
Westmont Coll, CA B

Social Sciences Related
The Colorado Coll, CO B
Concordia U, CA B
Lehigh U, PA B
Northwest Christian Coll, OR B
Saint Mary's Coll of California, CA B
San Diego State U, CA B
U of California, Berkeley, CA B
U of Denver, CO B

Social Science Teacher Education
Brigham Young U, UT B
Brigham Young U–Hawaii, HI B
California Lutheran U, CA B
California State U, Chico, CA B
Carroll Coll, MT B
Central Washington U, WA B
Coll of Santa Fe, NM B
Lewis-Clark State Coll, ID B
Montana State U–Billings, MT B
Nevada State Coll at Henderson, NV B
Northern Arizona U, AZ B
Northwest Nazarene U, ID B
Prescott Coll, AZ B
San Diego State U, CA B
Seattle Pacific U, WA B
Simpson Coll and Graduate School, CA B
The U of Arizona, AZ B
U of Great Falls, MT B
U of Hawaii at Manoa, HI B
The U of Montana–Missoula, MT B
The U of Montana–Western, MT B
U of Nevada, Reno, NV B
U of Utah, UT B
Weber State U, UT B
Western Baptist Coll, OR B
Westminster Coll, UT B
Westmont Coll, CA B

Social Studies Teacher Education
Colorado State U, CO B
Colorado State U-Pueblo, CO B
Concordia U, OR B
Eastern Washington U, WA B
George Fox U, OR B
Rocky Mountain Coll, MT B
The U of Arizona, AZ B
U of Great Falls, MT B
U of Hawaii at Manoa, HI B
U of Nevada, Reno, NV B
U of Utah, UT B
Utah State U, UT B
Weber State U, UT B
Western Baptist Coll, OR B

Social Work
Arizona State U, AZ B
Arizona State U West, AZ B
Azusa Pacific U, CA B
Boise State U, ID B
Brigham Young U, UT B
Brigham Young U–Hawaii, HI B
California State U, Chico, CA B
California State U, Fresno, CA B
California State U, Hayward, CA B
California State U, Long Beach, CA B
California State U, Los Angeles, CA B
California State U, Sacramento, CA B
California State U, San Bernardino, CA B
Carroll Coll, MT B
Chapman U, CA B
Colorado State U, CO B
Colorado State U-Pueblo, CO B
Concordia U, OR B
Eastern Washington U, WA B
Fresno Pacific U, CA B
George Fox U, OR B
Hawai'i Pacific U, HI B
Humboldt State U, CA B
Idaho State U, ID B
Lewis-Clark State Coll, ID B
Metropolitan State Coll of Denver, CO B
New Mexico Highlands U, NM B
New Mexico State U, NM B
North Carolina Ag and Tech State U, NC B
Northern Arizona U, AZ B
Northwest Nazarene U, ID B
Pacific Lutheran U, WA B
Pacific Union Coll, CA B
Pacific U, OR B
Point Loma Nazarene U, CA B
San Diego State U, CA B
San Francisco State U, CA B
San Jose State U, CA B
Seattle U, WA B
U of Alaska Anchorage, AK B
U of Alaska Fairbanks, AK B
U of California, Berkeley, CA B
U of California, Los Angeles, CA B
U of Hawaii at Manoa, HI B
The U of Montana–Missoula, MT B
U of Nevada, Las Vegas, NV B
U of Nevada, Reno, NV B
U of Portland, OR B
U of Utah, UT B
U of Washington, WA B
U of Wyoming, WY B
Utah State U, UT B
Walla Walla Coll, WA B
Warner Pacific Coll, OR B
Washington State U, WA B
Weber State U, UT B

Sociology
Adams State Coll, CO B
Albertson Coll of Idaho, ID B
Arizona State U, AZ B
Arizona State U West, AZ B
Azusa Pacific U, CA B
Biola U, CA B
Birmingham-Southern Coll, AL B
Boise State U, ID B
Brigham Young U, UT B
California Baptist U, CA B
California Lutheran U, CA B
California State Polytechnic U, Pomona, CA B
California State U, Bakersfield, CA B
California State U, Chico, CA B
California State U, Dominguez Hills, CA B
California State U, Fresno, CA B
California State U, Fullerton, CA B
California State U, Hayward, CA B
California State U, Long Beach, CA B
California State U, Los Angeles, CA B
California State U, Sacramento, CA B
California State U, San Bernardino, CA B
California State U, San Marcos, CA B
California State U, Stanislaus, CA B
Carroll Coll, MT B
Central Washington U, WA B
Chapman U, CA B
Claremont McKenna Coll, CA B
The Colorado Coll, CO B
Colorado State U, CO B
Colorado State U-Pueblo, CO B
Cornell Coll, IA B
Eastern New Mexico U, NM B
Eastern Oregon U, OR B
Eastern Washington U, WA B
Eugene Lang Coll, New School U B
Fort Lewis Coll, CO B
Fresno Pacific U, CA A
George Fox U, OR B
Gonzaga U, WA B
Grand Canyon U, AZ B
Great Basin Coll, NV A
Hawai'i Pacific U, HI B
Holy Names U, CA B
Humboldt State U, CA B
Idaho State U, ID B
Lehigh U, PA B
Lewis & Clark Coll, OR B
Linfield Coll, OR B
Loyola Marymount U, CA B

Metropolitan State Coll of Denver, CO B
Mills Coll, CA B
Montana State U–Billings, MT A,B
Montana State U–Bozeman, MT B
Mount St. Mary's Coll, CA B
New Mexico Highlands U, NM B
New Mexico State U, NM B
North Carolina Ag and Tech State U, NC B
Northern Arizona U, AZ B
Notre Dame de Namur U, CA B
Occidental Coll, CA B
Oregon State U, OR B
Pacific Lutheran U, WA B
Pacific Union Coll, CA B
Pacific U, OR B
Pepperdine U, Malibu, CA B
Pitzer Coll, CA B
Point Loma Nazarene U, CA B
Pomona Coll, CA B
Portland State U, OR B
Prescott Coll, AZ B
Reed Coll, OR B
Regis U, CO B
Rocky Mountain Coll, MT B
Saint Mary's Coll of California, CA B
San Diego State U, CA B
San Francisco State U, CA B
San Jose State U, CA B
Santa Clara U, CA B
Scripps Coll, CA B
Seattle Pacific U, WA B
Seattle U, WA B
Sonoma State U, CA B
Southern Oregon U, OR B
Southern Utah U, UT B
Stanford U, CA B
U of Alaska Anchorage, AK B
U of Alaska Fairbanks, AK B
The U of Arizona, AZ B
U of California, Berkeley, CA B
U of California, Davis, CA B
U of California, Irvine, CA B
U of California, Los Angeles, CA B
U of California, Riverside, CA B
U of California, San Diego, CA B
U of California, Santa Barbara, CA B
U of California, Santa Cruz, CA B
U of Colorado at Boulder, CO B
U of Colorado at Colorado Springs, CO B
U of Colorado at Denver, CO B
U of Denver, CO B
U of Great Falls, MT B
U of Hawaii at Hilo, HI B
U of Hawaii at Manoa, HI B
U of Idaho, ID B
U of La Verne, CA B
The U of Montana–Missoula, MT B
U of Nevada, Las Vegas, NV B
U of Nevada, Reno, NV B
U of New Mexico, NM B
U of Northern Colorado, CO B
U of Oregon, OR B
U of Portland, OR B
U of Puget Sound, WA B
U of Redlands, CA B
U of San Diego, CA B
U of San Francisco, CA B
U of Southern California, CA B
U of the Pacific, CA B
U of Utah, UT B
U of Washington, WA B
U of Wyoming, WY B
Utah State U, UT B
Vanguard U of Southern California, CA B
Walla Walla Coll, WA B
Washington State U, WA B
Weber State U, UT B
Western Oregon U, OR B
Western State Coll of Colorado, CO B
Western Washington U, WA B
Westminster Coll, UT B
Westmont Coll, CA B
Whitman Coll, WA B
Whitworth Coll, WA B
Willamette U, OR B

Soil Conservation

California State Polytechnic U, Pomona, CA B

Soil Science and Agronomy

Colorado State U, CO B
New Mexico State U, NM B
The U of Arizona, AZ B
U of Idaho, ID B
Utah State U, UT B
Washington State U, WA B

Soil Sciences Related

Brigham Young U, UT B

South Asian Languages

Claremont McKenna Coll, CA B

Spanish

Adams State Coll, CO B
Albertson Coll of Idaho, ID B
Arizona State U, AZ B
Arizona State U West, AZ B
Azusa Pacific U, CA B
Biola U, CA B
Birmingham-Southern Coll, AL B
Boise State U, ID B
Brigham Young U, UT B
California Lutheran U, CA B
California State Polytechnic U, Pomona, CA B
California State U, Bakersfield, CA B
California State U, Chico, CA B
California State U, Dominguez Hills, CA B
California State U, Fresno, CA B
California State U, Fullerton, CA B
California State U, Hayward, CA B
California State U, Long Beach, CA B
California State U, Los Angeles, CA B
California State U, Sacramento, CA B
California State U, San Bernardino, CA B
California State U, San Marcos, CA B
California State U, Stanislaus, CA B
Carroll Coll, MT B
Chapman U, CA B
Claremont McKenna Coll, CA B
The Colorado Coll, CO B
Colorado State U, CO B
Colorado State U-Pueblo, CO B
Cornell Coll, IA B
Eastern New Mexico U, NM B
Eastern Washington U, WA B
Fort Lewis Coll, CO B
Fresno Pacific U, CA A,B
George Fox U, OR B
Gonzaga U, WA B
Holy Names U, CA B
Humboldt State U, CA B
Idaho State U, ID A,B
Lehigh U, PA B
Lewis & Clark Coll, OR B
Linfield Coll, OR B
Loyola Marymount U, CA B
Metropolitan State Coll of Denver, CO B
Mills Coll, CA B
Montana State U–Billings, MT B
Mount St. Mary's Coll, CA B
New Mexico Highlands U, NM B
Northern Arizona U, AZ B
Northwest Nazarene U, ID B
Occidental Coll, CA B
Oregon State U, OR B
Pacific Lutheran U, WA B
Pacific Union Coll, CA B
Pacific U, OR B
Pepperdine U, Malibu, CA B
Pitzer Coll, CA B
Point Loma Nazarene U, CA B
Pomona Coll, CA B
Portland State U, OR B
Prescott Coll, AZ B
Reed Coll, OR B
Regis U, CO B
Saint Mary's Coll of California, CA B
San Diego State U, CA B
San Francisco State U, CA B
San Jose State U, CA B
Santa Clara U, CA B
Scripps Coll, CA B
Seattle Pacific U, WA B
Seattle U, WA B
Sonoma State U, CA B
Southern Oregon U, OR B
Southern Utah U, UT B
Stanford U, CA B
The U of Arizona, AZ B
U of California, Berkeley, CA B
U of California, Davis, CA B
U of California, Irvine, CA B
U of California, Los Angeles, CA B
U of California, Riverside, CA B
U of California, San Diego, CA B
U of California, Santa Barbara, CA B
U of California, Santa Cruz, CA B
U of Colorado at Boulder, CO B
U of Colorado at Colorado Springs, CO B
U of Colorado at Denver, CO B
U of Denver, CO B
U of Hawaii at Manoa, HI B
U of Idaho, ID B
U of La Verne, CA B
The U of Montana–Missoula, MT B
U of Nevada, Las Vegas, NV B
U of Nevada, Reno, NV B
U of New Mexico, NM B
U of Northern Colorado, CO B
U of Oregon, OR B
U of Portland, OR B
U of Puget Sound, WA B
U of Redlands, CA B
U of San Diego, CA B
U of San Francisco, CA B
U of Southern California, CA B
U of the Pacific, CA B
U of Utah, UT B
U of Washington, WA B
U of Wyoming, WY B
Utah State U, UT B
Vanguard U of Southern California, CA B
Walla Walla Coll, WA B
Washington State U, WA B
Weber State U, UT B
Western Oregon U, OR B
Western State Coll of Colorado, CO B
Western Washington U, WA B
Westmont Coll, CA B
Whitman Coll, WA B
Whitworth Coll, WA B
Willamette U, OR B

Spanish Language Teacher Education

Brigham Young U, UT B
California Lutheran U, CA B
California State U, Chico, CA B
Carroll Coll, MT B
Central Washington U, WA B
Colorado State U, CO B
Colorado State U-Pueblo, CO B
Eastern Washington U, WA B
Montana State U–Billings, MT B
Northern Arizona U, AZ B
Northwest Nazarene U, ID B
San Diego State U, CA B
The U of Arizona, AZ B
U of Utah, UT B
Weber State U, UT B

Special Education

Arizona State U, AZ B
Arizona State U West, AZ B
Boise State U, ID B
Brigham Young U, UT B
Brigham Young U–Hawaii, HI B
Central Washington U, WA B
City U, WA B
Coll of the Southwest, NM B
Eastern New Mexico U, NM B
Eastern Oregon U, OR B
Eastern Washington U, WA B
Gonzaga U, WA B
Grand Canyon U, AZ B
Idaho State U, ID B
Montana State U–Billings, MT A,B
New Mexico Highlands U, NM B
New Mexico State U, NM B
North Carolina Ag and Tech State U, NC B
Northern Arizona U, AZ B
Northwest Coll, WA B
Pacific Lutheran U, WA B
Pacific Oaks Coll, CA B
Prescott Coll, AZ B
Saint Martin's Coll, WA B
Seattle Pacific U, WA B
Southern Utah U, UT B
The U of Arizona, AZ B
U of California, Los Angeles, CA B
U of Great Falls, MT B
U of Hawaii at Manoa, HI B
U of Idaho, ID B
U of Nevada, Las Vegas, NV B
U of Nevada, Reno, NV B
U of New Mexico, NM B
U of Northern Colorado, CO B
U of the Pacific, CA B
U of Utah, UT B
U of Wyoming, WY B
Utah State U, UT B
Washington State U, WA B
Western State Coll of Colorado, CO B

A—associate degree; B—bachelor's degree

Western Washington U, WA B
Westminster Coll, UT B
Whitworth Coll, WA B

Special Education (Early Childhood)
Eastern Washington U, WA B

Special Education (Gifted and Talented)
U of Great Falls, MT B

Special Education Related
Nevada State Coll at Henderson, NV B
U of Wyoming, WY B

Special Education (Speech Or Language Impaired)
New Mexico State U, NM B
Northern Arizona U, AZ B

Special Products Marketing
Oregon State U, OR B
San Francisco State U, CA B

Speech and Rhetoric
Adams State Coll, CO B
Brigham Young U, UT B
California Polytechnic State U, San Luis Obispo, CA B
California State U, Chico, CA B
California State U, Fresno, CA B
California State U, Fullerton, CA B
California State U, Hayward, CA B
California State U, Long Beach, CA B
California State U, Los Angeles, CA B
Colorado State U, CO B
Cornell Coll, IA B
Gonzaga U, WA B
Grand Canyon U, AZ B
Humboldt State U, CA B
The Master's Coll and Seminary, CA B
Metropolitan State Coll of Denver, CO B
New Mexico State U, NM B
North Carolina Ag and Tech State U, NC B
Northern Arizona U, AZ B
Oregon State U, OR B
Pepperdine U, Malibu, CA B
Portland State U, OR B
San Diego State U, CA B
San Francisco State U, CA B
San Jose State U, CA B
Southern Utah U, UT B
U of Alaska Fairbanks, AK B
U of California, Berkeley, CA B
U of California, Davis, CA B
U of Hawaii at Manoa, HI B
The U of Montana–Missoula, MT B
U of New Mexico, NM B
U of Utah, UT B
U of Washington, WA B
Utah State U, UT B
Vanguard U of Southern California, CA B
Walla Walla Coll, WA B
Whitworth Coll, WA B
Willamette U, OR B

Speech-Language Pathology
Nevada State Coll at Henderson, NV B
U of Nevada, Reno, NV B
U of Northern Colorado, CO B

Speech Teacher Education
Brigham Young U, UT B
The U of Arizona, AZ B

Speech Therapy
Eastern Washington U, WA B
U of Redlands, CA B

Sport and Fitness Administration
Albertson Coll of Idaho, ID B
Carroll Coll, MT B
Central Washington U, WA B
Concordia U, OR B
Fresno Pacific U, CA B
George Fox U, OR B
Gonzaga U, WA B
Montana State U–Billings, MT B
Montana State U–Bozeman, MT B
National U, CA B
Saint Mary's Coll of California, CA B
U of Nevada, Las Vegas, NV B
Washington State U, WA B
Western Baptist Coll, OR B

Statistics
Brigham Young U, UT B
California Polytechnic State U, San Luis Obispo, CA B
California State Polytechnic U, Pomona, CA B
California State U, Chico, CA B
California State U, Fullerton, CA B
California State U, Hayward, CA B
California State U, Long Beach, CA B
Eastern New Mexico U, NM B
Eastern Washington U, WA B
Fort Lewis Coll, CO B
Lehigh U, PA B
San Diego State U, CA B
San Francisco State U, CA B
Sonoma State U, CA B
U of California, Berkeley, CA B
U of California, Davis, CA B
U of California, Los Angeles, CA B
U of California, Riverside, CA B
U of California, Santa Barbara, CA B
U of Denver, CO B
The U of Montana–Missoula, MT B
U of Nevada, Las Vegas, NV B
U of Oregon, OR B
U of Washington, WA B
U of Wyoming, WY B
Utah State U, UT B
Washington State U, WA B

Statistics Related
Brigham Young U, UT B

Structural Engineering
U of California, San Diego, CA B
U of Southern California, CA B

Substance Abuse/Addiction Counseling
U of Great Falls, MT A,B

Surgical Technology
Boise State U, ID A
Loma Linda U, CA A
Montana State U–Billings, MT A
The U of Montana–Missoula, MT A

Survey Technology
California State Polytechnic U, Pomona, CA B
California State U, Fresno, CA B
Idaho State U, ID B
Metropolitan State Coll of Denver, CO B
New Mexico State U, NM B
Oregon Inst of Technology, OR B
U of Alaska Anchorage, AK A,B
Westwood Coll–Denver North, CO A

Swedish
Brigham Young U, UT B

System Administration
Coleman Coll, La Mesa, CA A,B
DeVry U, Colorado Springs, CO A
Mt. Sierra Coll, CA B
National American U, Denver, CO A,B
Silicon Valley Coll, Walnut Creek, CA A
U of Great Falls, MT B

System, Networking, and LAN/WAN Management
ITT Tech Inst, Tucson, AZ A
ITT Tech Inst, Anaheim, CA A
ITT Tech Inst, Rancho Cordova, CA A
ITT Tech Inst, San Bernardino, CA A
ITT Tech Inst, San Diego, CA A
ITT Tech Inst, Sylmar, CA A
ITT Tech Inst, Torrance, CA A
ITT Tech Inst, West Covina, CA A
ITT Tech Inst, CO A
ITT Tech Inst, ID A
ITT Tech Inst, NV A
ITT Tech Inst, NM A
ITT Tech Inst, OR A
ITT Tech Inst, UT A
ITT Tech Inst, Bothell, WA A
ITT Tech Inst, Seattle, WA A
ITT Tech Inst, Spokane, WA A
LDS Business Coll, UT A
Mt. Sierra Coll, CA B
National American U, Denver, CO A,B
Silicon Valley Coll, Walnut Creek, CA A
U of Great Falls, MT B
Westwood Coll–Denver South, CO B
Westwood Coll–Inland Empire, CA B

Systems Engineering
Montana Tech of The U of Montana, MT B
The U of Arizona, AZ B
U of California, San Diego, CA B
U of Southern California, CA B

Systems Science and Theory
Stanford U, CA B

Taxation
California State U, Fullerton, CA B

Teacher Assistant/Aide
Blackfeet Comm Coll, MT A
Boise State U, ID A
New Mexico Highlands U, NM A
New Mexico State U, NM A
U of New Mexico, NM A

Technical and Business Writing
Boise State U, ID B
Carroll Coll, MT B
Coll of Santa Fe, NM B
Montana Tech of The U of Montana, MT B
New Mexico Inst of Mining and Technology, NM B
Oregon State U, OR B
San Francisco State U, CA B
The U of Montana–Missoula, MT B
U of Washington, WA B
Weber State U, UT B

Technical Teacher Education
San Diego State U, CA B
U of Idaho, ID B
Utah State U, UT B

Technology/Industrial Arts Teacher Education
Brigham Young U, UT B
California State U, Los Angeles, CA B
Central Washington U, WA B
Montana State U–Bozeman, MT B
Northern Arizona U, AZ B
U of Hawaii at Manoa, HI B
U of Idaho, ID B
The U of Montana–Western, MT B
U of Nevada, Reno, NV B
U of New Mexico, NM B
U of Wyoming, WY B
Utah State U, UT B

Telecommunications
California State Polytechnic U, Pomona, CA B
California State U, Hayward, CA B
Colorado State U-Pueblo, CO B
Columbia Coll Hollywood, CA A,B
Golden Gate U, CA B
Pacific U, OR B
Pepperdine U, Malibu, CA B

Theatre Design and Technology
Brigham Young U, UT B
California Inst of the Arts, CA B
Carroll Coll, MT B
Chapman U, CA B
Coll of Santa Fe, NM B
Cornish Coll of the Arts, WA B
Rocky Mountain Coll, MT B
U of Alaska Fairbanks, AK B
The U of Arizona, AZ B
U of California, Santa Cruz, CA B
U of Southern California, CA B

Theatre Literature, History and Criticism
Saint Mary's Coll of California, CA B

Theatre/Theatre Arts Management
California Inst of the Arts, CA B
Coll of Santa Fe, NM B
U of Southern California, CA B

Theological and Ministerial Studies Related
California Baptist U, CA B
Northwest Christian Coll, OR B
Point Loma Nazarene U, CA B

Theology
Azusa Pacific U, CA B
Biola U, CA B
California Baptist U, CA B
Carroll Coll, MT B
Christian Heritage Coll, CA B
Concordia U, CA B
Concordia U, OR B
Grand Canyon U, AZ B
International Coll and Graduate School, HI B
Life Pacific Coll, CA B
Loyola Marymount U, CA B
The Master's Coll and Seminary, CA B
Multnomah Bible Coll and Biblical Seminary, OR B
Northwest Coll, WA B
Northwest Nazarene U, ID B
Pacific Union Coll, CA B
Saint Mary's Coll of California, CA B
Seattle Pacific U, WA B
U of Great Falls, MT B
U of Portland, OR B
U of San Francisco, CA B
Walla Walla Coll, WA B
Warner Pacific Coll, OR B
Western Baptist Coll, OR B
William Jessup U, CA A,B

Theology and Religious Vocations Related
Simpson Coll and Graduate School, CA B

Theoretical and Mathematical Physics
San Diego State U, CA B

Therapeutic Recreation
Brigham Young U, UT B
California State U, Chico, CA B
California State U, Hayward, CA B
Eastern Washington U, WA B
Pacific Lutheran U, WA B

Tool and Die Technology
Utah State U, UT B

Tourism and Travel Services Management
Alliant International U, CA B
Brigham Young U–Hawaii, HI A,B
Fort Lewis Coll, CO B
Hawai'i Pacific U, HI B
Morrison U, NV A
National American U, Colorado Springs, CO A
New Mexico Highlands U, NM B
San Diego State U, CA B
U of Alaska Southeast, AK A
The U of Montana–Western, MT A
U of Nevada, Las Vegas, NV B

Tourism Promotion
New Mexico State U, NM B

Tourism/Travel Marketing
The U of Montana–Western, MT A,B

Toxicology
Humboldt State U, CA B

Trade and Industrial Teacher Education
California Polytechnic State U, San Luis Obispo, CA B
California State U, Fresno, CA B
California State U, Long Beach, CA B
California State U, Los Angeles, CA B
California State U, San Bernardino, CA B
Central Washington U, WA B
North Carolina Ag and Tech State U, NC B
San Francisco State U, CA B
U of Hawaii at Manoa, HI B
U of Idaho, ID B
U of Nevada, Reno, NV B
U of Wyoming, WY B

Transportation Technology
North Carolina Ag and Tech State U, NC B
Pacific Union Coll, CA B
San Francisco State U, CA B

Turf and Turfgrass Management
Colorado State U, CO B

Urban Studies/Affairs
California State Polytechnic U, Pomona, CA B
Eugene Lang Coll, New School U B
Lehigh U, PA B
Loyola Marymount U, CA B
Metropolitan State Coll of Denver, CO B
Mount St. Mary's Coll, CA A
Portland State U, OR B
San Diego State U, CA B
San Francisco State U, CA B
Stanford U, CA B
U of California, Berkeley, CA B
U of California, San Diego, CA B
U of San Diego, CA B
U of Southern California, CA B
U of Utah, UT B

Vehicle/Equipment Operation
The U of Montana–Missoula, MT A

Vehicle Maintenance and Repair Technologies Related
U of Alaska Fairbanks, AK A

Veterinary/Animal Health Technology
Brigham Young U, UT B

Veterinary Sciences
Washington State U, WA B

Violin, Viola, Guitar and Other Stringed Instruments
Bethesda Christian U, CA B
Brigham Young U, UT B
California Inst of the Arts, CA B
California State U, Fullerton, CA B
The Colburn School of Performing Arts, CA B
Cornish Coll of the Arts, WA B
Notre Dame de Namur U, CA B
U of Southern California, CA B
U of Washington, WA B
Willamette U, OR B

Visual and Performing Arts
Arizona State U West, AZ B
Art Center Coll of Design, CA B
California Baptist U, CA B
California State U, San Marcos, CA B
Carroll Coll, MT B
Claremont McKenna Coll, CA B
The Evergreen State Coll, WA B
Lehigh U, PA B
Naropa U, CO B
New Mexico State U, NM B
Regis U, CO B
San Jose State U, CA B
The U of Arizona, AZ B
U of San Francisco, CA B
U of Utah, UT B
Western Washington U, WA B

Visual and Performing Arts Related
Brigham Young U, UT B
Claremont McKenna Coll, CA B
Dominican U of California, CA B
Saint Mary's Coll of California, CA B
Scripps Coll, CA B
U of California, Los Angeles, CA B

Vocational Rehabilitation Counseling
California State U, Los Angeles, CA B
U of Northern Colorado, CO B

Voice and Opera
Bethesda Christian U, CA B
Birmingham-Southern Coll, AL B
Brigham Young U, UT B
Brigham Young U–Hawaii, HI B
California Inst of the Arts, CA B
California State U, Fullerton, CA B
California State U, Long Beach, CA B
Central Washington U, WA B
Chapman U, CA B
Christian Heritage Coll, CA B
Cornish Coll of the Arts, WA B
Eastern Washington U, WA B
Grand Canyon U, AZ B
Loyola Marymount U, CA B
The Master's Coll and Seminary, CA B
Mount St. Mary's Coll, CA B
Notre Dame de Namur U, CA B
Pacific Lutheran U, WA B
U of Idaho, ID B
U of Oregon, OR B
U of Redlands, CA B
U of Southern California, CA B
U of the Pacific, CA B
U of Washington, WA B
Walla Walla Coll, WA B
Western Baptist Coll, OR B
Whitworth Coll, WA B
Willamette U, OR B

Water Resources Engineering
The U of Arizona, AZ B
U of Nevada, Reno, NV B
U of Southern California, CA B

Web/Multimedia Management and Webmaster
Academy of Art U, CA A,B
ITT Tech Inst, Tucson, AZ A
ITT Tech Inst, Anaheim, CA A
ITT Tech Inst, Rancho Cordova, CA A
ITT Tech Inst, San Diego, CA A
ITT Tech Inst, Sylmar, CA A
ITT Tech Inst, Torrance, CA A
ITT Tech Inst, West Covina, CA A
ITT Tech Inst, CO A
ITT Tech Inst, ID A
ITT Tech Inst, NV A
ITT Tech Inst, NM A
ITT Tech Inst, OR A
ITT Tech Inst, UT A
ITT Tech Inst, Bothell, WA A
ITT Tech Inst, Seattle, WA A
ITT Tech Inst, Spokane, WA A
Lewis-Clark State Coll, ID A,B
Mt. Sierra Coll, CA B
Pioneer Pacific Coll, OR A
Platt Coll San Diego, CA A,B
U of Great Falls, MT B
Westwood Coll–Denver South, CO B
Westwood Coll–Inland Empire, CA B
Westwood Coll–Los Angeles, CA B

Web Page, Digital/Multimedia and Information Resources Design
The Art Inst of California–San Francisco, CA B
The Art Inst of Phoenix, AZ B
The Art Inst of Portland, OR A,B
Azusa Pacific U, CA B
CollAmerica–Fort Collins, CO A
ITT Tech Inst, Tucson, AZ A
ITT Tech Inst, Anaheim, CA A
ITT Tech Inst, Rancho Cordova, CA A
ITT Tech Inst, San Bernardino, CA A
ITT Tech Inst, San Diego, CA A
ITT Tech Inst, Sylmar, CA A
ITT Tech Inst, Torrance, CA A
ITT Tech Inst, West Covina, CA A
ITT Tech Inst, CO A
ITT Tech Inst, ID A
ITT Tech Inst, NV A
ITT Tech Inst, NM A
ITT Tech Inst, OR A
ITT Tech Inst, UT A
ITT Tech Inst, Bothell, WA A
ITT Tech Inst, Seattle, WA A
ITT Tech Inst, Spokane, WA A
LDS Business Coll, UT A
National American U, Denver, CO A,B
Northface U, UT B
Platt Coll San Diego, CA A,B
San Francisco Art Inst, CA B
U of Great Falls, MT B
Utah Valley State Coll, UT A
Westwood Coll–Inland Empire, CA B
Westwood Coll–Denver North, CO B

Welding Technology
Boise State U, ID A
Great Basin Coll, NV A
Idaho State U, ID A
Lewis-Clark State Coll, ID A,B
Montana Tech of The U of Montana, MT B
U of Alaska Anchorage, AK A
The U of Montana–Missoula, MT A
Utah Valley State Coll, UT A

Western Civilization
St. John's Coll, NM B
Thomas Aquinas Coll, CA B
Western Washington U, WA B

Wildlife and Wildlands Science and Management
Brigham Young U, UT B

A—associate degree; B—bachelor's degree

Colorado State U, CO B
Eastern New Mexico U, NM B
Humboldt State U, CA B
New Mexico State U, NM B
Northern Arizona U, AZ B
Oregon State U, OR B
Prescott Coll, AZ B
U of Alaska Fairbanks, AK B
The U of Arizona, AZ B
U of Idaho, ID B
The U of Montana–Missoula, MT B
U of Nevada, Reno, NV B
U of Washington, WA B
Utah State U, UT B
Washington State U, WA B

Wildlife Biology

Grand Canyon U, AZ B
New Mexico State U, NM B
Washington State U, WA B

Wind/Percussion Instruments

California State U, Fullerton, CA B
Chapman U, CA B
Grand Canyon U, AZ B
U of Southern California, CA B

Women's Studies

Arizona State U, AZ B
Arizona State U West, AZ B
California State U, Chico, CA B
California State U, Fresno, CA B
California State U, Fullerton, CA B
California State U, Long Beach, CA B
California State U, Sacramento, CA B
California State U, San Marcos, CA B
Claremont McKenna Coll, CA B
The Colorado Coll, CO B
Cornell Coll, IA B
Eugene Lang Coll, New School U B
Mills Coll, CA B
Northern Arizona U, AZ B
Occidental Coll, CA B
Pacific Lutheran U, WA B
Pitzer Coll, CA B
Pomona Coll, CA B
Portland State U, OR B
Saint Mary's Coll of California, CA B
San Diego State U, CA B
San Francisco State U, CA B
Scripps Coll, CA B
Sonoma State U, CA B
Stanford U, CA B
The U of Arizona, AZ B
U of California, Berkeley, CA B
U of California, Davis, CA B
U of California, Irvine, CA B
U of California, Los Angeles, CA B
U of California, Riverside, CA B
U of California, San Diego, CA B
U of California, Santa Barbara, CA B
U of California, Santa Cruz, CA B
U of Colorado at Boulder, CO B
U of Denver, CO B
The U of Montana–Missoula, MT B
U of Nevada, Las Vegas, NV B
U of Nevada, Reno, NV B
U of New Mexico, NM B
U of Oregon, OR B
U of Southern California, CA B
U of Utah, UT B
U of Washington, WA B
U of Wyoming, WY B
Washington State U, WA B
Western Washington U, WA B

Wood Science and Wood Products/Pulp and Paper Technology

Oregon State U, OR B
U of Idaho, ID B
U of Washington, WA B

Work and Family Studies

Brigham Young U, UT B

Youth Ministry

California Baptist U, CA B
Cascade Coll, OR B
Colorado Christian U, CO B
Eugene Bible Coll, OR B
Multnomah Bible Coll and Biblical Seminary, OR B
Northwest Coll, WA B
Southwestern Coll, AZ B
Vanguard U of Southern California, CA B
Western Baptist Coll, OR B

Zoology/Animal Biology

Brigham Young U, UT B
California State Polytechnic U, Pomona, CA B
California State U, Fresno, CA B
California State U, Long Beach, CA B
Colorado State U, CO B
Humboldt State U, CA B
Idaho State U, ID B
Northern Arizona U, AZ B
Oregon State U, OR B
San Diego State U, CA B
San Francisco State U, CA B
Sonoma State U, CA B
Southern Utah U, UT B
U of California, Davis, CA B
U of California, Santa Barbara, CA B
U of Hawaii at Manoa, HI B
U of Idaho, ID B
The U of Montana–Missoula, MT B
U of Washington, WA B
U of Wyoming, WY B
Utah State U, UT B
Washington State U, WA B
Weber State U, UT B

Athletic Programs and Scholarships

Archery

California State U, Long Beach, CA	M, W
Seattle U, WA	M, W

Badminton

California State U, Dominguez Hills, CA	M, W
California State U, Long Beach, CA	M, W
Claremont McKenna Coll, CA	M, W
Eastern Washington U, WA	M
U of Oregon, OR	M, W
U of Wyoming, WY	M, W

Baseball

Albertson Coll of Idaho, ID	M(s)
Arizona State U, AZ	M(s)
Azusa Pacific U, CA	M(s)
Biola U, CA	M(s)
Birmingham-Southern Coll, AL	M(s)
Brigham Young U, UT	M(s)
California Baptist U, CA	M(s)
California Inst of Technology, CA	M
California Lutheran U, CA	M
California Polytechnic State U, San Luis Obispo, CA	M(s)
California State Polytechnic U, Pomona, CA	M(s)
California State U, Chico, CA	M
California State U, Fresno, CA	M(s)
California State U, Fullerton, CA	M(s)
California State U, Hayward, CA	M
California State U, Los Angeles, CA	M(s)
California State U, Sacramento, CA	M(s)
California State U, San Bernardino, CA	M(s)
California State U, Stanislaus, CA	M
Central Washington U, WA	M(s)
Chapman U, CA	M
Claremont McKenna Coll, CA	M
Coll of the Southwest, NM	M(s)
Colorado School of Mines, CO	M(s)
Colorado State U-Pueblo, CO	M
Concordia U, CA	M(s)
Concordia U, OR	M(s)
Cornell Coll, IA	M
Eastern New Mexico U, NM	M(s)
Eastern Oregon U, OR	M
Eastern Washington U, WA	M
Fort Lewis Coll, CO	M
Fresno Pacific U, CA	M
George Fox U, OR	M
Gonzaga U, WA	M(s)
Grand Canyon U, AZ	M(s)
Harvey Mudd Coll, CA	M
Hawai'i Pacific U, HI	M(s)
Johnson & Wales U, CO	M
Lehigh U, PA	M(s)
Lewis & Clark Coll, OR	M
Lewis-Clark State Coll, ID	M(s)
Linfield Coll, OR	M
Loyola Marymount U, CA	M(s)
Menlo Coll, CA	M
Metropolitan State Coll of Denver, CO	M(s)
New Mexico Highlands U, NM	M(s)
New Mexico State U, NM	M(s)
North Carolina Ag and Tech State U, NC	M(s)
Northwest Nazarene U, ID	M(s)
Occidental Coll, CA	M
Oregon Inst of Technology, OR	M
Oregon State U, OR	M(s)
Pacific Lutheran U, WA	M
Pacific U, OR	M
Pepperdine U, Malibu, CA	M(s)
Pitzer Coll, CA	M
Point Loma Nazarene U, CA	M(s)
Pomona Coll, CA	M
Portland State U, OR	M(s)
Regis U, CO	M(s)
Saint Martin's Coll, WA	M(s)
Saint Mary's Coll of California, CA	M(s)
San Diego State U, CA	M(s)
San Francisco State U, CA	M(s), W(s)
San Jose State U, CA	M(s)
Santa Clara U, CA	M(s)
Seattle U, WA	M, W
Simpson Coll and Graduate School, CA	M
Sonoma State U, CA	M(s)
Southern Utah U, UT	M(s)
Stanford U, CA	M(s)
The Master's Coll and Seminary, CA	M(s)
The U of Arizona, AZ	M(s)
The U of Montana–Missoula, MT	M
United States Air Force Academy, CO	M
U of California, Berkeley, CA	M(s)
U of California, Davis, CA	M
U of California, Irvine, CA	M
U of California, Los Angeles, CA	M(s)
U of California, Riverside, CA	M(s)
U of California, San Diego, CA	M
U of California, Santa Barbara, CA	M(s)
U of Colorado at Boulder, CO	M
U of Colorado at Colorado Springs, CO	M
U of Hawaii at Hilo, HI	M(s)
U of Hawaii at Manoa, HI	M(s)
U of Idaho, ID	M
U of La Verne, CA	M
U of Nevada, Las Vegas, NV	M(s)
U of Nevada, Reno, NV	M(s)
U of New Mexico, NM	M
U of Northern Colorado, CO	M(s)
U of Portland, OR	M(s)
U of Puget Sound, WA	M
U of Redlands, CA	M
U of San Diego, CA	M(s)
U of San Francisco, CA	M(s)
U of Southern California, CA	M(s)
U of Utah, UT	M(s)
U of Washington, WA	M(s)
U of Wyoming, WY	M
U of the Pacific, CA	M(s)
Utah State U, UT	M
Utah Valley State Coll, UT	M(s)
Vanguard U of Southern California, CA	M(s)
Washington State U, WA	M(s)
Weber State U, UT	M
Western Baptist Coll, OR	M(s)
Western Oregon U, OR	M
Western State Coll of Colorado, CO	M
Westmont Coll, CA	M(s)
Whitman Coll, WA	M
Whitworth Coll, WA	M
Willamette U, OR	M

Basketball

Adams State Coll, CO	M(s), W(s)
Albertson Coll of Idaho, ID	M(s), W(s)
Arizona State U, AZ	M(s), W(s)
Azusa Pacific U, CA	M(s), W(s)
Biola U, CA	M(s), W(s)
Birmingham-Southern Coll, AL	M(s), W(s)
Boise State U, ID	M(s), W(s)
Brigham Young U, UT	M(s), W(s)
Brigham Young U–Hawaii, HI	M(s)
California Baptist U, CA	M(s), W(s)
California Christian Coll, CA	M
California Inst of Technology, CA	M, W
California Lutheran U, CA	M, W
California Maritime Academy, CA	M
California Polytechnic State U, San Luis Obispo, CA	M(s), W(s)
California State Polytechnic U, Pomona, CA	M(s), W(s)
California State U, Bakersfield, CA	M(s)
California State U, Chico, CA	M, W
California State U, Dominguez Hills, CA	M(s), W(s)
California State U, Fresno, CA	M(s), W(s)
California State U, Fullerton, CA	M(s), W(s)
California State U, Hayward, CA	M, W
California State U, Long Beach, CA	M(s), W(s)
California State U, Los Angeles, CA	M(s), W(s)
California State U, Sacramento, CA	M(s), W(s)
California State U, San Bernardino, CA	M(s), W(s)
California State U, Stanislaus, CA	M, W
Carroll Coll, MT	M(s), W(s)
Cascade Coll, OR	M(s), W(s)
Central Washington U, WA	M(s), W(s)
Chaminade U of Honolulu, HI	M(s)
Chapman U, CA	M, W
Christian Heritage Coll, CA	M(s), W(s)
Claremont McKenna Coll, CA	M, W
Colorado Christian U, CO	M(s), W(s)
Colorado School of Mines, CO	M(s), W(s)
Colorado State U, CO	M(s), W(s)
Colorado State U-Pueblo, CO	M(s), W(s)
Concordia U, CA	M(s), W(s)
Concordia U, OR	M(s), W(s)
Cornell Coll, IA	M, W
Dominican U of California, CA	M(s), W(s)
Eastern New Mexico U, NM	M(s), W(s)
Eastern Oregon U, OR	M, W
Eastern Washington U, WA	M(s), W(s)
Eugene Bible Coll, OR	M
Fort Lewis Coll, CO	M(s), W(s)
Fresno Pacific U, CA	M(s), W(s)
George Fox U, OR	M, W
Gonzaga U, WA	M(s), W(s)
Grand Canyon U, AZ	M(s), W(s)
Harvey Mudd Coll, CA	M, W
Hawai'i Pacific U, HI	M(s)
Holy Names U, CA	M(s), W(s)
Humboldt State U, CA	M(s), W(s)
Idaho State U, ID	M(s), W(s)
Johnson & Wales U, CO	M, W
Lehigh U, PA	M(s), W
Lewis & Clark Coll, OR	M, W
Lewis-Clark State Coll, ID	M(s), W(s)
Life Pacific Coll, CA	M, W
Linfield Coll, OR	M, W

M—for men; W—for women; (s)—scholarship offered

Loyola Marymount U, CA M(s), W(s)
Menlo Coll, CA M, W
Metropolitan State Coll of Denver, CO M(s), W(s)
Montana State U–Billings, MT M(s), W(s)
Montana State U–Bozeman, MT M(s), W(s)
Montana Tech of The U of Montana, MT M(s), W(s)
Multnomah Bible Coll and Biblical Seminary, OR M, W
New Mexico Highlands U, NM M(s), W(s)
New Mexico State U, NM M(s), W(s)
North Carolina Ag and Tech State U, NC M(s), W(s)
Northern Arizona U, AZ M(s), W(s)
Northwest Christian Coll, OR M(s), W(s)
Northwest Coll, WA M(s), W(s)
Northwest Nazarene U, ID M(s), W(s)
Notre Dame de Namur U, CA M, W
Occidental Coll, CA M, W
Oregon Inst of Technology, OR M(s), W
Oregon State U, OR M(s), W(s)
Pacific Lutheran U, WA M, W
Pacific Union Coll, CA M, W
Pacific U, OR M, W
Pepperdine U, Malibu, CA M(s), W(s)
Pitzer Coll, CA M, W
Point Loma Nazarene U, CA M(s), W(s)
Pomona Coll, CA M, W
Portland State U, OR M(s), W(s)
Reed Coll, OR M
Regis U, CO M(s), W(s)
Rocky Mountain Coll, MT M(s), W(s)
Saint Martin's Coll, WA M(s), W(s)
Saint Mary's Coll of California, CA M(s), W(s)
San Diego State U, CA M(s), W(s)
San Francisco State U, CA M(s), W(s)
San Jose State U, CA M(s), W(s)
Santa Clara U, CA M(s), W(s)
Scripps Coll, CA W
Seattle Pacific U, WA M(s), W(s)
Seattle U, WA M(s), W(s)
Simpson Coll and Graduate School, CA M, W
Sonoma State U, CA M(s), W(s)
Southern Oregon U, OR M(s), W(s)
Southern Utah U, UT M(s), W(s)
Southwestern Coll, AZ M, W
Stanford U, CA M(s), W(s)
The Colorado Coll, CO M, W
The Evergreen State Coll, WA M(s), W(s)
The Master's Coll and Seminary, CA M(s), W(s)
The U of Arizona, AZ M(s), W(s)
The U of Montana–Missoula, MT M(s), W(s)
The U of Montana–Western, MT M(s), W(s)
United States Air Force Academy, CO M, W
U of Alaska Anchorage, AK M(s), W(s)
U of Alaska Fairbanks, AK M(s), W(s)
U of California, Berkeley, CA M(s), W(s)
U of California, Davis, CA M, W
U of California, Irvine, CA M(s), W(s)
U of California, Los Angeles, CA M(s), W(s)
U of California, Riverside, CA M(s), W(s)
U of California, San Diego, CA M, W
U of California, Santa Barbara, CA M(s), W(s)
U of California, Santa Cruz, CA M, W
U of Colorado at Boulder, CO M(s), W(s)
U of Colorado at Colorado Springs, CO M(s), W(s)
U of Denver, CO M(s), W(s)
U of Great Falls, MT M(s), W(s)
U of Hawaii at Hilo, HI M(s)
U of Hawaii at Manoa, HI M(s), W(s)
U of Idaho, ID M(s), W(s)
U of La Verne, CA M, W
U of Nevada, Las Vegas, NV M(s), W(s)
U of Nevada, Reno, NV M(s), W(s)
U of New Mexico, NM M(s), W(s)
U of Northern Colorado, CO M(s), W(s)
U of Oregon, OR M(s), W(s)
U of Portland, OR M(s), W(s)
U of Puget Sound, WA M, W
U of Redlands, CA M, W
U of San Diego, CA M(s), W(s)
U of San Francisco, CA M(s), W(s)
U of Southern California, CA M(s), W(s)
U of Utah, UT M(s), W(s)
U of Washington, WA M(s), W(s)
U of Wyoming, WY M(s), W(s)
U of the Pacific, CA M(s), W(s)
Utah State U, UT M(s), W(s)
Utah Valley State Coll, UT M(s), W(s)
Vanguard U of Southern California, CA M(s), W(s)
Walla Walla Coll, WA M, W
Warner Pacific Coll, OR M(s), W(s)
Washington State U, WA M(s), W(s)
Weber State U, UT M(s), W(s)
Western Baptist Coll, OR M(s), W(s)
Western Oregon U, OR M, W
Western State Coll of Colorado, CO M(s), W(s)
Western Washington U, WA M(s), W(s)
Westminster Coll, UT M, W
Westmont Coll, CA M(s), W(s)
Whitman Coll, WA M, W
Whitworth Coll, WA M, W
Willamette U, OR M, W
William Jessup U, CA M, W

Bowling

California State U, Chico, CA M, W
California State U, Fullerton, CA M, W
California State U, Long Beach, CA M, W
California State U, Sacramento, CA M, W
Central Washington U, WA M, W
Lehigh U, PA M, W
San Jose State U, CA M, W
U of California, Santa Barbara, CA M, W
U of Colorado at Boulder, CO M, W
U of Oregon, OR M, W
U of Utah, UT M, W
Washington State U, WA M, W
Weber State U, UT M, W

Crew

California Maritime Academy, CA M, W
California State U, Long Beach, CA M, W
California State U, Sacramento, CA M(s), W(s)
Chapman U, CA M, W
Gonzaga U, WA M, W
Humboldt State U, CA M, W
Lehigh U, PA M
Lewis & Clark Coll, OR M, W
Loyola Marymount U, CA M, W(s)
Mills Coll, CA W
Occidental Coll, CA W
Oregon State U, OR M, W
Pacific Lutheran U, WA M, W
Pepperdine U, Malibu, CA M, W
Reed Coll, OR M, W
Saint Mary's Coll of California, CA M, W
Santa Clara U, CA M, W
Seattle Pacific U, WA M, W
Seattle U, WA M, W
Stanford U, CA M, W(s)
The U of Montana–Missoula, MT M, W
U of California, Berkeley, CA M(s), W(s)
U of California, Irvine, CA M, W
U of California, San Diego, CA M, W
U of California, Santa Barbara, CA M, W
U of Colorado at Boulder, CO M, W
U of Oregon, OR M, W
U of Puget Sound, WA M, W
U of San Diego, CA M, W
U of Southern California, CA W(s)
U of Washington, WA M(s), W(s)
Washington State U, WA M, W(s)
Western Washington U, WA M(s), W(s)
Willamette U, OR M, W

Cross-Country Running

Adams State Coll, CO M(s), W(s)
Alliant International U, CA M(s), W(s)
Arizona State U, AZ M(s), W(s)
Azusa Pacific U, CA M(s), W(s)
Biola U, CA M(s), W(s)
Birmingham-Southern Coll, AL M(s), W(s)
Boise State U, ID M(s), W(s)
Brigham Young U, UT M(s), W(s)
Brigham Young U–Hawaii, HI M(s), W(s)
California Baptist U, CA M(s), W(s)
California Inst of Technology, CA M, W
California Lutheran U, CA M, W
California Polytechnic State U, San Luis Obispo, CA M(s), W(s)
California State Polytechnic U, Pomona, CA M(s), W(s)
California State U, Chico, CA M, W
California State U, Fresno, CA M(s), W(s)
California State U, Fullerton, CA M(s), W(s)
California State U, Hayward, CA M, W
California State U, Long Beach, CA M(s), W(s)
California State U, Los Angeles, CA W(s)
California State U, Sacramento, CA M(s), W(s)
California State U, San Marcos, CA M, W
California State U, Stanislaus, CA M, W
Cascade Coll, OR M(s), W(s)
Central Washington U, WA M(s), W(s)
Chaminade U of Honolulu, HI M(s), W(s)
Chapman U, CA M, W
Christian Heritage Coll, CA M(s), W(s)
Claremont McKenna Coll, CA M, W
Colorado Christian U, CO M, W
Colorado School of Mines, CO M(s), W(s)
Colorado State U, CO M(s), W(s)
Concordia U, CA M(s), W(s)
Cornell Coll, IA M, W
Eastern New Mexico U, NM M(s), W(s)
Eastern Oregon U, OR M, W
Eastern Washington U, WA M(s), W(s)
Fort Lewis Coll, CO M(s), W(s)
Fresno Pacific U, CA M(s), W(s)
George Fox U, OR M, W
Gonzaga U, WA M, W
Harvey Mudd Coll, CA M, W
Hawai'i Pacific U, HI M(s), W(s)
Holy Names U, CA M(s), W(s)
Humboldt State U, CA M(s), W(s)
Idaho State U, ID M(s), W(s)
Lehigh U, PA M(s), W(s)
Lewis & Clark Coll, OR M, W
Lewis-Clark State Coll, ID M(s), W(s)
Linfield Coll, OR M, W
Loyola Marymount U, CA M(s), W(s)
Menlo Coll, CA M, W
Mills Coll, CA W
Montana State U–Billings, MT M(s), W(s)
Montana State U–Bozeman, MT M(s), W(s)
Montana Tech of The U of Montana, MT M, W
New Mexico Highlands U, NM M(s), W(s)
New Mexico State U, NM M(s), W(s)
North Carolina Ag and Tech State U, NC M(s), W(s)
Northern Arizona U, AZ M(s), W(s)
Northwest Coll, WA M(s), W(s)
Northwest Nazarene U, ID M(s), W(s)
Occidental Coll, CA M, W
Oregon Inst of Technology, OR M(s), W(s)
Pacific Lutheran U, WA M, W
Pacific Union Coll, CA M, W
Pacific U, OR M, W
Pepperdine U, Malibu, CA M(s), W(s)
Pitzer Coll, CA M, W
Point Loma Nazarene U, CA M(s), W(s)
Pomona Coll, CA M, W
Portland State U, OR M(s), W(s)
Saint Martin's Coll, WA M(s), W(s)
Saint Mary's Coll of California, CA M(s), W(s)
San Diego State U, CA W(s)
San Francisco State U, CA M(s), W(s)
San Jose State U, CA M(s), W(s)
Santa Clara U, CA M(s), W(s)
Scripps Coll, CA W
Seattle Pacific U, WA M(s), W(s)
Seattle U, WA M(s), W(s)
Sonoma State U, CA W(s)
Southern Oregon U, OR M(s), W(s)
Southern Utah U, UT M, W
Stanford U, CA M(s), W(s)
The Colorado Coll, CO M, W

The Evergreen State Coll, WA	M(s), W(s)
The Master's Coll and Seminary, CA	M(s), W(s)
The U of Arizona, AZ	M(s), W(s)
The U of Montana–Missoula, MT	M(s), W(s)
United States Air Force Academy, CO	M, W
U of Alaska Anchorage, AK	M(s)
U of Alaska Fairbanks, AK	M(s), W(s)
U of California, Berkeley, CA	M(s), W(s)
U of California, Davis, CA	M, W
U of California, Irvine, CA	M, W(s)
U of California, Los Angeles, CA	M(s), W(s)
U of California, Riverside, CA	M(s), W(s)
U of California, San Diego, CA	M, W
U of California, Santa Barbara, CA	M(s), W(s)
U of California, Santa Cruz, CA	M, W
U of Colorado at Boulder, CO	M(s), W(s)
U of Colorado at Colorado Springs, CO	M(s), W(s)
U of Hawaii at Hilo, HI	M(s), W(s)
U of Hawaii at Manoa, HI	W(s)
U of Idaho, ID	M(s), W(s)
U of La Verne, CA	M, W
U of Nevada, Las Vegas, NV	W(s)
U of Nevada, Reno, NV	W(s)
U of New Mexico, NM	M(s), W(s)
U of Northern Colorado, CO	W(s)
U of Oregon, OR	M(s), W(s)
U of Portland, OR	M(s), W(s)
U of Puget Sound, WA	M, W
U of Redlands, CA	M, W
U of San Diego, CA	M(s), W(s)
U of San Francisco, CA	M(s), W(s)
U of Southern California, CA	M(s), W(s)
U of Utah, UT	M(s), W(s)
U of Washington, WA	M(s), W(s)
U of Wyoming, WY	M(s), W(s)
U of the Pacific, CA	W(s)
Utah State U, UT	M(s), W(s)
Utah Valley State Coll, UT	M(s), W(s)
Vanguard U of Southern California, CA	M(s), W(s)
Warner Pacific Coll, OR	M(s), W(s)
Washington State U, WA	M(s), W(s)
Weber State U, UT	M(s), W(s)
Western Baptist Coll, OR	M(s), W(s)
Western Oregon U, OR	M, W
Western State Coll of Colorado, CO	M(s), W(s)
Western Washington U, WA	M(s), W(s)
Westmont Coll, CA	M(s), W(s)
Whitman Coll, WA	M, W
Whitworth Coll, WA	M, W
Willamette U, OR	M, W

Equestrian Sports

California Polytechnic State U, San Luis Obispo, CA	M, W
California State U, Fresno, CA	W(s)
Lehigh U, PA	M, W
New Mexico State U, NM	M, W
Sierra Nevada Coll, NV	M, W
Stanford U, CA	M, W
The Colorado Coll, CO	M, W
The U of Montana–Missoula, MT	M, W
U of California, Santa Barbara, CA	M, W
U of California, Santa Cruz, CA	M, W
U of Colorado at Boulder, CO	M, W
U of Nevada, Las Vegas, NV	W
U of San Diego, CA	W
Utah State U, UT	M, W
Washington State U, WA	M, W

Fencing

California Inst of Technology, CA	M, W
California State U, Fullerton, CA	M(s), W(s)
California State U, Long Beach, CA	M, W
Central Washington U, WA	M, W
Reed Coll, OR	M, W
Scripps Coll, CA	W
St. John's Coll, NM	M, W
Stanford U, CA	M(s), W(s)
The U of Montana–Missoula, MT	M, W
United States Air Force Academy, CO	M, W
U of California, San Diego, CA	M, W
U of California, Santa Barbara, CA	M, W
U of California, Santa Cruz, CA	M, W
U of Colorado at Boulder, CO	M, W
U of Oregon, OR	M, W
U of Wyoming, WY	M, W
Weber State U, UT	M, W

Field Hockey

Lehigh U, PA	W(s)
Pepperdine U, Malibu, CA	W
Stanford U, CA	M, W(s)
The Colorado Coll, CO	M, W
The U of Montana–Missoula, MT	W
U of California, Berkeley, CA	W(s)
U of California, Santa Barbara, CA	W
U of Colorado at Boulder, CO	M, W
U of Oregon, OR	W
U of the Pacific, CA	W(s)

Football

Adams State Coll, CO	M(s)
Arizona State U, AZ	M(s)
Azusa Pacific U, CA	M(s)
Boise State U, ID	M(s)
Brigham Young U, UT	M(s)
California Lutheran U, CA	M
California Polytechnic State U, San Luis Obispo, CA	M(s)
California State U, Fresno, CA	M(s)
California State U, Sacramento, CA	M(s)
Carroll Coll, MT	M(s)
Central Washington U, WA	M(s)
Chapman U, CA	M
Claremont McKenna Coll, CA	M
Colorado School of Mines, CO	M(s)
Colorado State U, CO	M(s)
Cornell Coll, IA	M
Eastern New Mexico U, NM	M(s)
Eastern Oregon U, OR	M
Eastern Washington U, WA	M(s)
Fort Lewis Coll, CO	M(s)
Harvey Mudd Coll, CA	M
Humboldt State U, CA	M(s)
Idaho State U, ID	M(s)
Lehigh U, PA	M(s), W
Lewis & Clark Coll, OR	M
Linfield Coll, OR	M
Menlo Coll, CA	M
Montana State U–Bozeman, MT	M(s)
Montana Tech of The U of Montana, MT	M(s)
New Mexico Highlands U, NM	M(s)
New Mexico State U, NM	M(s)
North Carolina Ag and Tech State U, NC	M(s)
Northern Arizona U, AZ	M(s)
Occidental Coll, CA	M
Oregon State U, OR	M(s)
Pacific Lutheran U, WA	M
Pitzer Coll, CA	M
Pomona Coll, CA	M
Portland State U, OR	M(s)
Rocky Mountain Coll, MT	M(s)
Saint Mary's Coll of California, CA	M(s)
San Diego State U, CA	M(s)
San Jose State U, CA	M(s)
Southern Oregon U, OR	M(s)
Southern Utah U, UT	M(s)
Stanford U, CA	M(s)
The Colorado Coll, CO	M
The U of Arizona, AZ	M(s)
The U of Montana–Missoula, MT	M(s)
The U of Montana–Western, MT	M(s)
United States Air Force Academy, CO	M
U of California, Berkeley, CA	M(s)
U of California, Davis, CA	M
U of California, Los Angeles, CA	M(s)
U of Colorado at Boulder, CO	M(s)
U of Hawaii at Manoa, HI	M(s)
U of Idaho, ID	M(s)
U of La Verne, CA	M
U of Nevada, Las Vegas, NV	M(s)
U of Nevada, Reno, NV	M(s)
U of New Mexico, NM	M(s)
U of Northern Colorado, CO	M(s)
U of Oregon, OR	M(s)
U of Puget Sound, WA	M
U of Redlands, CA	M
U of San Diego, CA	M
U of Southern California, CA	M(s)
U of Utah, UT	M(s)
U of Washington, WA	M(s)
U of Wyoming, WY	M(s)
Utah State U, UT	M(s)
Washington State U, WA	M(s)
Weber State U, UT	M(s)
Western Oregon U, OR	M
Western State Coll of Colorado, CO	M(s)
Western Washington U, WA	M(s)
Whitworth Coll, WA	M
Willamette U, OR	M

Golf

Adams State Coll, CO	M(s)
Albertson Coll of Idaho, ID	M(s), W(s)
Arizona State U, AZ	M(s), W(s)
Azusa Pacific U, CA	M(s)
Birmingham-Southern Coll, AL	M(s), W(s)
Boise State U, ID	M(s), W(s)
Brigham Young U, UT	M(s), W(s)
California Inst of Technology, CA	M
California Lutheran U, CA	M
California Maritime Academy, CA	M, W
California Polytechnic State U, San Luis Obispo, CA	M(s)
California State U, Bakersfield, CA	M(s)
California State U, Chico, CA	M, W
California State U, Fresno, CA	M(s)
California State U, Sacramento, CA	M(s), W
California State U, San Bernardino, CA	M(s)
California State U, San Marcos, CA	M(s), W
California State U, Stanislaus, CA	M
Carroll Coll, MT	W(s)
Central Washington U, WA	M, W
Chapman U, CA	M, W
Claremont McKenna Coll, CA	M
Coll of the Southwest, NM	M(s), W(s)
Colorado Christian U, CO	M
Colorado School of Mines, CO	M(s)
Colorado State U, CO	M, W
Colorado State U-Pueblo, CO	M(s)
Cornell Coll, IA	M, W
Eastern Washington U, WA	M(s), W(s)
Fort Lewis Coll, CO	M(s)
Gonzaga U, WA	M, W
Grand Canyon U, AZ	M(s)
Harvey Mudd Coll, CA	M
Hawai'i Pacific U, HI	M(s), W(s)
Holy Names U, CA	M(s)
Idaho State U, ID	M(s), W(s)
Johnson & Wales U, CO	M
Lehigh U, PA	M(s), W
Lewis & Clark Coll, OR	M, W
Lewis-Clark State Coll, ID	M(s), W(s)
Linfield Coll, OR	M, W
Loyola Marymount U, CA	M(s)
Menlo Coll, CA	M, W
Montana State U–Bozeman, MT	W(s)
Montana Tech of The U of Montana, MT	M(s), W(s)
New Mexico Inst of Mining and Technology, NM	M, W
New Mexico State U, NM	M(s), W(s)
Northern Arizona U, AZ	W(s)
Northwest Nazarene U, ID	M(s)
Occidental Coll, CA	M, W
Oregon State U, OR	M(s), W(s)
Pacific Lutheran U, WA	M, W
Pacific U, OR	M, W
Pepperdine U, Malibu, CA	M(s), W(s)
Pitzer Coll, CA	M
Point Loma Nazarene U, CA	M(s)
Pomona Coll, CA	M, W

M—for men; W—for women; (s)—scholarship offered

Portland State U, OR	M(s), W(s)
Regis U, CO	M(s)
Rocky Mountain Coll, MT	M, W(s)
Saint Martin's Coll, WA	M(s), W(s)
Saint Mary's Coll of California, CA	M(s)
San Diego State U, CA	M(s), W(s)
San Jose State U, CA	M(s), W(s)
Santa Clara U, CA	M(s), W(s)
Scripps Coll, CA	W
Seattle U, WA	M, W
Southern Utah U, UT	M(s)
Stanford U, CA	M(s), W(s)
The Master's Coll and Seminary, CA	M(s)
The U of Arizona, AZ	M(s), W(s)
The U of Montana–Missoula, MT	W
The U of Montana–Western, MT	M(s), W(s)
United States Air Force Academy, CO	M
U of California, Berkeley, CA	M(s), W(s)
U of California, Davis, CA	M
U of California, Irvine, CA	M(s), W
U of California, Los Angeles, CA	M(s), W(s)
U of California, San Diego, CA	M
U of California, Santa Barbara, CA	M(s), W
U of Colorado at Boulder, CO	M(s), W(s)
U of Colorado at Colorado Springs, CO	M(s)
U of Denver, CO	M(s), W(s)
U of Great Falls, MT	M, W
U of Hawaii at Hilo, HI	M(s)
U of Hawaii at Manoa, HI	M(s), W(s)
U of Idaho, ID	M(s), W(s)
U of La Verne, CA	M
U of Nevada, Las Vegas, NV	M(s)
U of Nevada, Reno, NV	M(s), W(s)
U of New Mexico, NM	M(s), W(s)
U of Northern Colorado, CO	M(s), W(s)
U of Oregon, OR	M(s), W(s)
U of Portland, OR	M(s), W(s)
U of Puget Sound, WA	M, W
U of Redlands, CA	M
U of San Diego, CA	M(s)
U of San Francisco, CA	M(s), W(s)
U of Southern California, CA	M(s), W(s)
U of Utah, UT	M(s)
U of Washington, WA	M(s), W(s)
U of Wyoming, WY	M(s), W(s)
U of the Pacific, CA	M(s)
Utah State U, UT	M(s)
Utah Valley State Coll, UT	M(s)
Walla Walla Coll, WA	M
Washington State U, WA	M(s), W(s)
Weber State U, UT	M(s), W(s)
Western Baptist Coll, OR	M
Western Washington U, WA	M(s), W(s)
Westminster Coll, UT	M, W
Whitman Coll, WA	M, W
Whitworth Coll, WA	M, W
Willamette U, OR	M, W

Gymnastics

Arizona State U, AZ	W(s)
Boise State U, ID	W(s)
Brigham Young U, UT	W(s)
California Polytechnic State U, San Luis Obispo, CA	W(s)
California State U, Fullerton, CA	W(s)
California State U, Sacramento, CA	W(s)
Oregon State U, OR	W(s)
San Jose State U, CA	W(s)
Seattle Pacific U, WA	W(s)
Southern Utah U, UT	W(s)
Stanford U, CA	M(s), W(s)
The U of Arizona, AZ	W(s)
United States Air Force Academy, CO	M, W
U of Alaska Anchorage, AK	W(s)
U of California, Berkeley, CA	M(s), W(s)
U of California, Davis, CA	W
U of California, Los Angeles, CA	W(s)
U of California, Santa Barbara, CA	M, W(s)
U of Denver, CO	W(s)
U of Utah, UT	W(s)
U of Washington, WA	W(s)
Utah State U, UT	W(s)

Ice Hockey

California Inst of Technology, CA	M
California State U, Sacramento, CA	M
Central Washington U, WA	M, W
Eastern Washington U, WA	M
Lehigh U, PA	M
Stanford U, CA	M
The Colorado Coll, CO	M(s), W
The U of Arizona, AZ	M
The U of Montana–Missoula, MT	M, W
United States Air Force Academy, CO	M
U of Alaska Anchorage, AK	M(s)
U of Alaska Fairbanks, AK	M(s)
U of Colorado at Boulder, CO	M, W
U of Denver, CO	M(s)
U of Idaho, ID	M
U of Oregon, OR	M, W
U of San Diego, CA	M
U of Utah, UT	M
U of Wyoming, WY	M, W
Utah State U, UT	M
Walla Walla Coll, WA	M
Washington State U, WA	M, W
Weber State U, UT	M
Western State Coll of Colorado, CO	M
Whitman Coll, WA	M

Lacrosse

Brigham Young U, UT	M
California State U, Chico, CA	M, W
California State U, Sacramento, CA	M, W
Chapman U, CA	M
Claremont McKenna Coll, CA	M, W
Fort Lewis Coll, CO	M
Harvey Mudd Coll, CA	W
Humboldt State U, CA	M, W
Lehigh U, PA	M(s), W(s)
Lewis & Clark Coll, OR	M, W
Linfield Coll, OR	W
Loyola Marymount U, CA	M, W
Occidental Coll, CA	M, W
Pacific Lutheran U, WA	M, W
Pepperdine U, Malibu, CA	M
Regis U, CO	W(s)
Saint Mary's Coll of California, CA	M, W
Santa Clara U, CA	M, W
Scripps Coll, CA	W
Stanford U, CA	M, W
The Colorado Coll, CO	M, W
The U of Arizona, AZ	M, W
The U of Montana–Missoula, MT	M, W
United States Air Force Academy, CO	M
U of California, Berkeley, CA	W(s)
U of California, Santa Barbara, CA	M, W
U of California, Santa Cruz, CA	M, W
U of Colorado at Boulder, CO	M, W
U of Denver, CO	M(s), W(s)
U of Northern Colorado, CO	M
U of Oregon, OR	M, W
U of Puget Sound, WA	M, W
U of Redlands, CA	W
U of San Diego, CA	M, W
Washington State U, WA	M, W
Weber State U, UT	M, W
Western State Coll of Colorado, CO	M, W
Westmont Coll, CA	W
Whitman Coll, WA	M, W
Willamette U, OR	M

Racquetball

Brigham Young U, UT	M, W
California State U, Sacramento, CA	M, W
Stanford U, CA	M, W
U of Colorado at Boulder, CO	M, W
U of Oregon, OR	M, W
U of Utah, UT	M, W
Weber State U, UT	M, W

Riflery

Birmingham-Southern Coll, AL	W(s)
Seattle U, WA	M, W
United States Air Force Academy, CO	M, W
U of Alaska Fairbanks, AK	M(s), W(s)
U of Alaska Southeast, AK	M, W
U of Idaho, ID	M, W
U of Nevada, Reno, NV	M(s), W(s)
U of San Francisco, CA	M(s), W(s)
U of Wyoming, WY	M, W

Rugby

Brigham Young U, UT	M
California Inst of Technology, CA	M
California Maritime Academy, CA	M
California State U, Chico, CA	M, W
California State U, Fullerton, CA	M
California State U, Long Beach, CA	M
California State U, Sacramento, CA	M
Central Washington U, WA	M, W
Claremont McKenna Coll, CA	M, W
Fort Lewis Coll, CO	M, W
Humboldt State U, CA	M, W
Lehigh U, PA	M
Lewis & Clark Coll, OR	M, W
Loyola Marymount U, CA	M
Montana Tech of The U of Montana, MT	M
New Mexico Inst of Mining and Technology, NM	M, W
Occidental Coll, CA	M, W
Pacific Lutheran U, WA	M
Pepperdine U, Malibu, CA	M
Saint Mary's Coll of California, CA	M, W
Santa Clara U, CA	M, W
Scripps Coll, CA	W
Stanford U, CA	M, W
The Colorado Coll, CO	M, W
The U of Arizona, AZ	M, W
The U of Montana–Missoula, MT	M, W
United States Air Force Academy, CO	W
U of California, Berkeley, CA	M(s)
U of California, Santa Barbara, CA	M
U of California, Santa Cruz, CA	M, W
U of Colorado at Boulder, CO	M, W
U of Hawaii at Manoa, HI	M
U of Idaho, ID	M, W
U of Northern Colorado, CO	M, W
U of Oregon, OR	M
U of Portland, OR	M
U of Puget Sound, WA	M, W
U of San Diego, CA	M
U of Utah, UT	M
U of Wyoming, WY	M, W
Utah State U, UT	M, W
Washington State U, WA	M, W
Weber State U, UT	M, W
Western State Coll of Colorado, CO	M, W
Westmont Coll, CA	M
Whitman Coll, WA	M, W

Sailing

California Maritime Academy, CA	M, W
California State U, Long Beach, CA	M, W
Pepperdine U, Malibu, CA	M, W
Reed Coll, OR	M, W
San Jose State U, CA	M, W
Stanford U, CA	M, W
U of California, Irvine, CA	M, W
U of California, Santa Barbara, CA	M, W
U of California, Santa Cruz, CA	M, W
U of Hawaii at Manoa, HI	M, W
U of Oregon, OR	M, W

Skiing (Cross-Country)

Albertson Coll of Idaho, ID	M, W
Eastern Oregon U, OR	M, W
Fort Lewis Coll, CO	M, W
Gonzaga U, WA	M, W
Montana State U–Bozeman, MT	M(s), W(s)
Pacific Lutheran U, WA	M, W
Stanford U, CA	M, W
United States Air Force Academy, CO	M, W

U of Alaska Anchorage, AK M(s), W(s)
U of Alaska Fairbanks, AK M(s), W(s)
U of Colorado at Boulder, CO M(s), W(s)
U of Denver, CO M(s), W(s)
U of Idaho, ID M, W
U of Nevada, Reno, NV M(s), W(s)
U of New Mexico, NM M(s), W(s)
U of Oregon, OR M, W
U of Utah, UT M(s), W(s)
Washington State U, WA M, W
Western State Coll of Colorado, CO M(s), W(s)
Whitman Coll, WA M, W

Skiing (Downhill)

Albertson Coll of Idaho, ID M(s), W(s)
California State U, Long Beach, CA M, W
California State U, Sacramento, CA M, W
Claremont McKenna Coll, CA M, W
Colorado School of Mines, CO M
Eastern Oregon U, OR M, W
Fort Lewis Coll, CO M, W
Gonzaga U, WA M, W
Idaho State U, ID M, W
Lehigh U, PA M, W
Montana State U–Bozeman, MT M(s), W(s)
Pacific Lutheran U, WA M, W
Reed Coll, OR M, W
Rocky Mountain Coll, MT M(s), W(s)
Scripps Coll, CA W
Seattle U, WA M, W
Sierra Nevada Coll, NV M(s), W(s)
Southern Oregon U, OR M, W
Stanford U, CA M, W
The Colorado Coll, CO M, W
The U of Montana–Missoula, MT M, W
United States Air Force Academy, CO M, W
U of Alaska Anchorage, AK M(s), W(s)
U of California, Santa Barbara, CA M, W
U of Colorado at Boulder, CO M(s), W(s)
U of Denver, CO M(s), W(s)
U of Idaho, ID M, W
U of Nevada, Reno, NV M(s), W(s)
U of New Mexico, NM M(s), W(s)
U of Oregon, OR M, W
U of Puget Sound, WA M, W
U of Utah, UT M(s), W(s)
U of Wyoming, WY M, W
Washington State U, WA M, W
Weber State U, UT M, W
Western State Coll of Colorado, CO M(s), W(s)
Whitman Coll, WA M, W

Soccer

Albertson Coll of Idaho, ID M(s), W(s)
Alliant International U, CA M(s), W(s)
Arizona State U, AZ W(s)
Azusa Pacific U, CA M(s), W(s)
Biola U, CA M(s), W(s)
Birmingham-Southern Coll, AL M(s), W(s)
Boise State U, ID W
Brigham Young U, UT M, W(s)
California Baptist U, CA M(s), W(s)
California Inst of Technology, CA M, W
California Lutheran U, CA M, W
California Maritime Academy, CA M, W
California Polytechnic State U, San Luis Obispo, CA M, W
California State Polytechnic U, Pomona, CA M(s), W(s)
California State U, Bakersfield, CA M(s)
California State U, Chico, CA M, W
California State U, Dominguez Hills, CA M(s), W(s)
California State U, Fresno, CA M(s), W(s)
California State U, Fullerton, CA M(s), W(s)
California State U, Hayward, CA M, W
California State U, Long Beach, CA M, W
California State U, Los Angeles, CA M(s), W(s)
California State U, Sacramento, CA M(s), W(s)
California State U, San Bernardino, CA M(s), W(s)
California State U, Stanislaus, CA M, W
Carroll Coll, MT W(s)
Cascade Coll, OR M(s), W(s)
Central Washington U, WA M, W(s)
Chapman U, CA M, W
Christian Heritage Coll, CA M(s), W(s)
Claremont McKenna Coll, CA M, W
Coll of the Southwest, NM M(s), W(s)
Colorado Christian U, CO M(s), W(s)
Colorado School of Mines, CO M
Colorado State U-Pueblo, CO M, W
Concordia U, CA M(s), W(s)
Concordia U, OR M(s), W(s)
Cornell Coll, IA M, W
Dominican U of California, CA M(s), W(s)
Eastern New Mexico U, NM W(s)
Eastern Oregon U, OR W
Eastern Washington U, WA W(s)
Fort Lewis Coll, CO M(s), W(s)
Fresno Pacific U, CA M(s), W(s)
George Fox U, OR M, W
Gonzaga U, WA M(s), W(s)
Grand Canyon U, AZ M(s), W(s)
Harvey Mudd Coll, CA M, W
Hawai'i Pacific U, HI M(s), W(s)
Holy Names U, CA M(s), W(s)
Humboldt State U, CA M(s), W(s)
Johnson & Wales U, CO M
Lehigh U, PA M(s), W(s)
Lewis & Clark Coll, OR M, W
Linfield Coll, OR M, W
Loyola Marymount U, CA M(s), W(s)
Menlo Coll, CA M, W
Metropolitan State Coll of Denver, CO M(s), W(s)
Mills Coll, CA W
Montana State U–Billings, MT M(s), W(s)
Montana Tech of The U of Montana, MT M, W
New Mexico Highlands U, NM W(s)
New Mexico Inst of Mining and Technology, NM M, W
Northern Arizona U, AZ W(s)
Northwest Coll, WA M(s)
Northwest Nazarene U, ID W(s)
Notre Dame de Namur U, CA M, W
Occidental Coll, CA M, W
Oregon Inst of Technology, OR M, W
Oregon State U, OR M(s), W(s)
Pacific Lutheran U, WA M, W
Pacific U, OR M, W
Pepperdine U, Malibu, CA M, W(s)
Pitzer Coll, CA M, W
Point Loma Nazarene U, CA M(s)
Pomona Coll, CA M, W
Portland State U, OR W(s)
Reed Coll, OR M, W
Regis U, CO M(s), W(s)
Rocky Mountain Coll, MT W(s)
Saint Mary's Coll of California, CA M(s), W(s)
San Diego State U, CA M(s), W(s)
San Francisco State U, CA M(s), W(s)
San Jose State U, CA M(s), W(s)
Santa Clara U, CA M(s), W(s)
Scripps Coll, CA W
Seattle Pacific U, WA M(s), W
Seattle U, WA M(s), W(s)
Simpson Coll and Graduate School, CA M, W
Sonoma State U, CA M(s), W(s)
Southern Oregon U, OR W(s)
St. John's Coll, NM M, W
Stanford U, CA M(s), W(s)
The Colorado Coll, CO M, W(s)
The Evergreen State Coll, WA M(s), W(s)
The Master's Coll and Seminary, CA M(s), W(s)
The U of Arizona, AZ M, W(s)
The U of Montana–Missoula, MT M, W
United States Air Force Academy, CO M, W
U of California, Berkeley, CA M(s), W(s)
U of California, Davis, CA M, W
U of California, Irvine, CA M, W
U of California, Los Angeles, CA M(s), W(s)
U of California, San Diego, CA M, W
U of California, Santa Barbara, CA M(s), W(s)
U of California, Santa Cruz, CA M
U of Colorado at Boulder, CO M, W(s)
U of Colorado at Colorado Springs, CO M(s), W
U of Denver, CO M(s), W(s)
U of Hawaii at Manoa, HI W(s)
U of Idaho, ID M, W(s)
U of La Verne, CA M, W
U of Nevada, Las Vegas, NV M(s), W(s)
U of Nevada, Reno, NV W(s)
U of New Mexico, NM M(s), W(s)
U of Northern Colorado, CO M, W(s)
U of Oregon, OR M, W(s)
U of Portland, OR M(s), W(s)
U of Puget Sound, WA M, W
U of Redlands, CA M, W
U of San Diego, CA M(s), W(s)
U of San Francisco, CA M(s), W(s)
U of Southern California, CA W(s)
U of Utah, UT M, W(s)
U of Washington, WA M(s), W
U of Wyoming, WY M, W(s)
U of the Pacific, CA W(s)
Utah State U, UT M, W(s)
Utah Valley State Coll, UT W(s)
Vanguard U of Southern California, CA M(s), W(s)
Walla Walla Coll, WA M
Warner Pacific Coll, OR M, W
Washington State U, WA M, W(s)
Weber State U, UT M, W(s)
Western Baptist Coll, OR M(s), W(s)
Western Oregon U, OR W
Western State Coll of Colorado, CO M, W
Western Washington U, WA M(s), W(s)
Westminster Coll, UT M
Westmont Coll, CA M(s), W(s)
Whitman Coll, WA M(s), W(s)
Whitworth Coll, WA M, W
Willamette U, OR M, W
William Jessup U, CA M

Softball

Adams State Coll, CO W(s)
Albertson Coll of Idaho, ID W(s)
Arizona State U, AZ W(s)
Azusa Pacific U, CA W(s)
Biola U, CA W(s)
Birmingham-Southern Coll, AL W(s)
Brigham Young U, UT W(s)
Brigham Young U–Hawaii, HI W(s)
California Baptist U, CA W(s)
California Lutheran U, CA W
California Polytechnic State U, San Luis Obispo, CA W(s)
California State U, Bakersfield, CA W(s)
California State U, Chico, CA W
California State U, Fresno, CA W(s)
California State U, Fullerton, CA W(s)
California State U, Hayward, CA W
California State U, Long Beach, CA W(s)
California State U, Sacramento, CA W(s)
California State U, San Bernardino, CA W(s)
California State U, Stanislaus, CA W
Central Washington U, WA W(s)
Chaminade U of Honolulu, HI W(s)
Chapman U, CA W
Claremont McKenna Coll, CA W
Colorado School of Mines, CO W(s)
Colorado State U, CO W
Colorado State U-Pueblo, CO W(s)
Concordia U, CA W(s)
Concordia U, OR W(s)
Cornell Coll, IA W
Dominican U of California, CA W(s)
Eastern New Mexico U, NM W(s)
Eastern Oregon U, OR W
Fort Lewis Coll, CO W(s)
George Fox U, OR W
Harvey Mudd Coll, CA W

M—for men; W—for women; (s)—scholarship offered

Hawai'i Pacific U, HI	W(s)
Humboldt State U, CA	W(s)
Lehigh U, PA	W(s)
Lewis & Clark Coll, OR	W
Linfield Coll, OR	W
Loyola Marymount U, CA	W(s)
Menlo Coll, CA	W
Montana State U–Billings, MT	W
New Mexico Highlands U, NM	W(s)
New Mexico State U, NM	W(s)
North Carolina Ag and Tech State U, NC	W
Northwest Christian Coll, OR	W(s)
Northwest Nazarene U, ID	W(s)
Notre Dame de Namur U, CA	W
Occidental Coll, CA	W
Oregon Inst of Technology, OR	W(s)
Oregon State U, OR	W(s)
Pacific Lutheran U, WA	W
Pacific U, OR	W
Pitzer Coll, CA	W
Point Loma Nazarene U, CA	W(s)
Pomona Coll, CA	W
Portland State U, OR	W(s)
Regis U, CO	W(s)
Saint Martin's Coll, WA	W(s)
Saint Mary's Coll of California, CA	W(s)
San Diego State U, CA	W(s)
San Francisco State U, CA	W(s)
San Jose State U, CA	W
Santa Clara U, CA	W(s)
Scripps Coll, CA	W
Seattle U, WA	W(s)
Simpson Coll and Graduate School, CA	W
Sonoma State U, CA	W(s)
Southern Oregon U, OR	W(s)
Southern Utah U, UT	W(s)
Stanford U, CA	W(s)
The Colorado Coll, CO	W
The Master's Coll and Seminary, CA	W(s)
The U of Arizona, AZ	W(s)
United States Air Force Academy, CO	W
U of California, Berkeley, CA	W(s)
U of California, Davis, CA	W
U of California, Los Angeles, CA	W(s)
U of California, Riverside, CA	W(s)
U of California, San Diego, CA	W
U of California, Santa Barbara, CA	W(s)
U of California, Santa Cruz, CA	W
U of Colorado at Boulder, CO	W
U of Colorado at Colorado Springs, CO	W(s)
U of Hawaii at Hilo, HI	W(s)
U of Hawaii at Manoa, HI	W(s)
U of La Verne, CA	W
U of Nevada, Las Vegas, NV	W(s)
U of Nevada, Reno, NV	W
U of New Mexico, NM	W(s)
U of Northern Colorado, CO	W(s)
U of Oregon, OR	W(s)
U of Puget Sound, WA	W
U of Redlands, CA	W
U of San Diego, CA	W
U of San Francisco, CA	M, W
U of Utah, UT	W
U of Washington, WA	W(s)
U of the Pacific, CA	W(s)
Utah State U, UT	W(s)
Utah Valley State Coll, UT	W(s)
Vanguard U of Southern California, CA	W(s)
Walla Walla Coll, WA	W
Washington State U, WA	W
Weber State U, UT	W
Western Baptist Coll, OR	W(s)
Western Oregon U, OR	W
Western Washington U, WA	W(s)
Whitman Coll, WA	M, W
Willamette U, OR	W

Squash

Lehigh U, PA	M
Reed Coll, OR	M, W
Stanford U, CA	M, W
U of Colorado at Boulder, CO	M, W
U of Oregon, OR	M, W

Swimming

Arizona State U, AZ	M(s), W(s)
Biola U, CA	M(s), W(s)
Brigham Young U, UT	M(s), W(s)
California Baptist U, CA	M(s), W(s)
California Inst of Technology, CA	M, W
California Lutheran U, CA	M, W
California Polytechnic State U, San Luis Obispo, CA	M, W
California State U, Bakersfield, CA	M(s), W(s)
California State U, Fresno, CA	W(s)
California State U, Hayward, CA	W
California State U, Long Beach, CA	M(s), W(s)
California State U, San Bernardino, CA	M(s), W(s)
Carroll Coll, MT	M, W
Central Washington U, WA	M(s), W(s)
Chapman U, CA	M, W
Claremont McKenna Coll, CA	M, W
Colorado School of Mines, CO	M(s), W(s)
Colorado State U, CO	W(s)
Harvey Mudd Coll, CA	M, W
Lehigh U, PA	M(s), W(s)
Lewis & Clark Coll, OR	M, W
Linfield Coll, OR	M, W
Loyola Marymount U, CA	W(s)
Metropolitan State Coll of Denver, CO	M(s), W(s)
Montana Tech of The U of Montana, MT	M, W
New Mexico State U, NM	W(s)
North Carolina Ag and Tech State U, NC	W(s)
Northern Arizona U, AZ	W(s)
Occidental Coll, CA	M, W
Oregon State U, OR	W(s)
Pacific Lutheran U, WA	M, W
Pacific U, OR	M, W
Pepperdine U, Malibu, CA	W(s)
Pitzer Coll, CA	M, W
Pomona Coll, CA	M, W
San Diego State U, CA	W(s)
San Francisco State U, CA	M(s), W(s)
San Jose State U, CA	W(s)
Scripps Coll, CA	W
Seattle U, WA	M(s), W(s)
Stanford U, CA	M(s), W(s)
The Colorado Coll, CO	M, W
The U of Arizona, AZ	M(s), W(s)
United States Air Force Academy, CO	M, W
U of Alaska Anchorage, AK	M(s)
U of California, Berkeley, CA	M(s), W(s)
U of California, Davis, CA	M, W
U of California, Irvine, CA	M(s), W(s)
U of California, Los Angeles, CA	W(s)
U of California, San Diego, CA	M, W
U of California, Santa Barbara, CA	M(s), W(s)
U of California, Santa Cruz, CA	M, W
U of Colorado at Boulder, CO	M, W
U of Denver, CO	M(s), W(s)
U of Hawaii at Manoa, HI	M(s), W(s)
U of La Verne, CA	M, W
U of Nevada, Las Vegas, NV	M(s), W(s)
U of Nevada, Reno, NV	W(s)
U of New Mexico, NM	W(s)
U of Northern Colorado, CO	W(s)
U of Oregon, OR	M, W
U of Puget Sound, WA	M, W
U of Redlands, CA	M, W
U of San Diego, CA	W(s)
U of Southern California, CA	M(s), W(s)
U of Utah, UT	M(s), W(s)
U of Washington, WA	M(s), W(s)
U of Wyoming, WY	M(s), W(s)
U of the Pacific, CA	M(s), W(s)
Washington State U, WA	W(s)
Weber State U, UT	M, W
Whitman Coll, WA	M, W
Whitworth Coll, WA	M, W
Willamette U, OR	M, W

Table Tennis

California State U, Long Beach, CA	M
Northwestern Polytechnic U, CA	M
U of Oregon, OR	M, W
U of Utah, UT	M, W

Tennis

Albertson Coll of Idaho, ID	M(s), W(s)
Alliant International U, CA	M(s), W(s)
Arizona State U, AZ	M(s), W(s)
Azusa Pacific U, CA	M(s)
Biola U, CA	W(s)
Birmingham-Southern Coll, AL	M(s), W(s)
Boise State U, ID	M(s), W(s)
Brigham Young U, UT	M(s), W(s)
Brigham Young U–Hawaii, HI	M(s), W(s)
California Inst of Technology, CA	M, W
California Lutheran U, CA	M, W
California Polytechnic State U, San Luis Obispo, CA	M, W
California State Polytechnic U, Pomona, CA	M(s), W(s)
California State U, Bakersfield, CA	W(s)
California State U, Fresno, CA	M(s), W(s)
California State U, Fullerton, CA	W(s)
California State U, Long Beach, CA	W(s)
California State U, Los Angeles, CA	W(s)
California State U, Sacramento, CA	M(s), W(s)
Chaminade U of Honolulu, HI	M(s), W(s)
Chapman U, CA	M, W
Claremont McKenna Coll, CA	M, W
Coll of Santa Fe, NM	M(s), W(s)
Colorado Christian U, CO	M, W
Colorado School of Mines, CO	M(s), W(s)
Colorado State U, CO	W
Colorado State U-Pueblo, CO	M(s), W(s)
Cornell Coll, IA	M, W
Dominican U of California, CA	M(s), W(s)
Eastern New Mexico U, NM	W(s)
Eastern Washington U, WA	M(s), W(s)
George Fox U, OR	M, W
Gonzaga U, WA	M(s), W(s)
Grand Canyon U, AZ	W(s)
Harvey Mudd Coll, CA	M, W
Hawai'i Pacific U, HI	M(s), W(s)
Idaho State U, ID	M(s), W(s)
Johnson & Wales U, CO	M, W
Lehigh U, PA	M(s), W(s)
Lewis & Clark Coll, OR	M, W
Lewis-Clark State Coll, ID	M(s), W(s)
Linfield Coll, OR	M, W
Loyola Marymount U, CA	M(s), W(s)
Menlo Coll, CA	M, W
Metropolitan State Coll of Denver, CO	M(s), W(s)
Mills Coll, CA	W
Montana State U–Billings, MT	M(s), W(s)
Montana State U–Bozeman, MT	M(s), W(s)
New Mexico State U, NM	M(s), W(s)
North Carolina Ag and Tech State U, NC	M(s), W(s)
Northern Arizona U, AZ	M(s), W(s)
Occidental Coll, CA	M, W
Pacific Lutheran U, WA	M, W
Pacific U, OR	M, W
Pepperdine U, Malibu, CA	M(s), W(s)
Pitzer Coll, CA	M, W
Point Loma Nazarene U, CA	M(s), W(s)
Pomona Coll, CA	M, W
Portland State U, OR	M(s), W(s)
Saint Mary's Coll of California, CA	M(s), W(s)
San Diego State U, CA	M(s), W(s)
San Jose State U, CA	W(s)
Santa Clara U, CA	M(s), W(s)
Scripps Coll, CA	W
Sonoma State U, CA	M(s), W(s)
Southern Oregon U, OR	W(s)
Southern Utah U, UT	W(s)
Stanford U, CA	M(s), W(s)
The Colorado Coll, CO	M, W
The U of Arizona, AZ	M(s), W(s)
The U of Montana–Missoula, MT	M(s), W(s)
United States Air Force Academy, CO	M, W
U of California, Berkeley, CA	M(s), W(s)
U of California, Davis, CA	M, W

Tennis

U of California, Irvine, CA	M(s), W(s)
U of California, Los Angeles, CA	M(s), W(s)
U of California, Riverside, CA	M(s), W(s)
U of California, San Diego, CA	M, W
U of California, Santa Barbara, CA	M(s), W(s)
U of California, Santa Cruz, CA	M, W
U of Colorado at Boulder, CO	M(s), W(s)
U of Colorado at Colorado Springs, CO	M(s), W(s)
U of Denver, CO	M(s), W(s)
U of Hawaii at Hilo, HI	M(s), W(s)
U of Hawaii at Manoa, HI	M(s), W(s)
U of Idaho, ID	M(s), W(s)
U of La Verne, CA	M, W
U of Nevada, Las Vegas, NV	M(s), W(s)
U of Nevada, Reno, NV	M(s), W(s)
U of New Mexico, NM	M(s), W(s)
U of Northern Colorado, CO	M(s), W(s)
U of Oregon, OR	M(s), W(s)
U of Portland, OR	M(s), W(s)
U of Puget Sound, WA	M, W
U of Redlands, CA	M, W
U of San Diego, CA	M(s), W(s)
U of San Francisco, CA	M(s), W(s)
U of Southern California, CA	M(s), W(s)
U of Utah, UT	M(s), W(s)
U of Washington, WA	M(s), W(s)
U of Wyoming, WY	W(s)
U of the Pacific, CA	M(s), W(s)
Utah State U, UT	M(s), W(s)
Vanguard U of Southern California, CA	M(s), W(s)
Washington State U, WA	W(s)
Weber State U, UT	M(s), W(s)
Westmont Coll, CA	M(s), W(s)
Whitman Coll, WA	M, W
Whitworth Coll, WA	M, W
Willamette U, OR	M, W

Track and Field

Adams State Coll, CO	M(s), W(s)
Alliant International U, CA	M(s), W(s)
Arizona State U, AZ	M(s), W(s)
Azusa Pacific U, CA	M(s), W(s)
Biola U, CA	M(s), W(s)
Boise State U, ID	M(s), W(s)
Brigham Young U, UT	M(s), W(s)
California Inst of Technology, CA	M, W
California Lutheran U, CA	M, W
California Polytechnic State U, San Luis Obispo, CA	M(s), W(s)
California State Polytechnic U, Pomona, CA	M(s), W(s)
California State U, Bakersfield, CA	M(s), W(s)
California State U, Chico, CA	M, W
California State U, Fresno, CA	M(s), W(s)
California State U, Fullerton, CA	M(s), W(s)
California State U, Long Beach, CA	M(s), W(s)
California State U, Los Angeles, CA	M(s), W(s)
California State U, Sacramento, CA	M(s), W(s)
California State U, San Marcos, CA	M, W
California State U, Stanislaus, CA	M, W
Cascade Coll, OR	M(s), W(s)
Central Washington U, WA	M(s), W(s)
Chapman U, CA	W
Claremont McKenna Coll, CA	M, W
Colorado School of Mines, CO	M(s), W(s)
Colorado State U, CO	M(s), W(s)
Cornell Coll, IA	M, W
Eastern New Mexico U, NM	M(s), W(s)
Eastern Oregon U, OR	M, W
Eastern Washington U, WA	M(s), W(s)
Fort Lewis Coll, CO	M, W
Fresno Pacific U, CA	M(s), W(s)
George Fox U, OR	M, W
Gonzaga U, WA	M, W
Harvey Mudd Coll, CA	M, W
Humboldt State U, CA	M(s), W(s)
Idaho State U, ID	M(s), W(s)
Lehigh U, PA	M(s), W(s)
Lewis & Clark Coll, OR	M, W
Linfield Coll, OR	M, W
Menlo Coll, CA	M, W
Montana State U–Bozeman, MT	M(s), W(s)
New Mexico Highlands U, NM	M, W
New Mexico State U, NM	W(s)
North Carolina Ag and Tech State U, NC	M(s), W(s)
Northern Arizona U, AZ	M(s), W(s)
Northwest Coll, WA	M(s), W(s)
Northwest Nazarene U, ID	M(s), W(s)
Occidental Coll, CA	M, W
Oregon Inst of Technology, OR	M(s), W(s)
Pacific Lutheran U, WA	M, W
Pacific U, OR	M, W
Pitzer Coll, CA	M, W
Point Loma Nazarene U, CA	M(s), W(s)
Pomona Coll, CA	M, W
Portland State U, OR	M(s), W(s)
Saint Martin's Coll, WA	M(s), W(s)
San Diego State U, CA	W(s)
San Francisco State U, CA	M(s), W(s)
Scripps Coll, CA	W
Seattle Pacific U, WA	M(s), W(s)
Seattle U, WA	M(s), W(s)
Sonoma State U, CA	W(s)
Southern Oregon U, OR	M(s), W(s)
Southern Utah U, UT	M(s), W(s)
Stanford U, CA	M(s), W(s)
The Colorado Coll, CO	M, W
The U of Arizona, AZ	M(s), W(s)
The U of Montana–Missoula, MT	M(s), W(s)
United States Air Force Academy, CO	M, W
U of California, Berkeley, CA	M(s), W(s)
U of California, Davis, CA	M, W
U of California, Irvine, CA	M, W(s)
U of California, Los Angeles, CA	M(s), W(s)
U of California, Riverside, CA	M(s), W(s)
U of California, San Diego, CA	M, W
U of California, Santa Barbara, CA	M(s), W(s)
U of California, Santa Cruz, CA	M, W
U of Colorado at Boulder, CO	M(s), W(s)
U of Colorado at Colorado Springs, CO	M, W
U of Hawaii at Manoa, HI	W(s)
U of Idaho, ID	M(s), W(s)
U of La Verne, CA	M, W
U of Nevada, Las Vegas, NV	W(s)
U of Nevada, Reno, NV	W(s)
U of New Mexico, NM	M(s), W(s)
U of Northern Colorado, CO	M(s), W(s)
U of Oregon, OR	M(s), W(s)
U of Portland, OR	M(s), W(s)
U of Puget Sound, WA	M, W
U of Redlands, CA	M, W
U of San Francisco, CA	W(s)
U of Southern California, CA	M(s), W(s)
U of Utah, UT	M(s), W(s)
U of Washington, WA	M(s), W(s)
U of Wyoming, WY	M(s), W(s)
Utah State U, UT	M(s), W(s)
Utah Valley State Coll, UT	M(s), W(s)
Vanguard U of Southern California, CA	M(s), W(s)
Warner Pacific Coll, OR	M, W
Washington State U, WA	M(s), W(s)
Weber State U, UT	M(s), W(s)
Western Oregon U, OR	M, W
Western State Coll of Colorado, CO	M(s), W(s)
Western Washington U, WA	M(s), W(s)
Westmont Coll, CA	M(s), W(s)
Whitman Coll, WA	M, W
Whitworth Coll, WA	M, W
Willamette U, OR	M, W

Volleyball

Adams State Coll, CO	W(s)
Albertson Coll of Idaho, ID	W(s)
Alliant International U, CA	W(s)
Arizona State U, AZ	W(s)
Azusa Pacific U, CA	M, W(s)
Biola U, CA	W(s)
Birmingham-Southern Coll, AL	W(s)
Boise State U, ID	W(s)
Brigham Young U, UT	M(s), W(s)
Brigham Young U–Hawaii, HI	W(s)
California Baptist U, CA	M(s), W(s)
California Christian Coll, CA	W
California Inst of Technology, CA	M, W
California Lutheran U, CA	W
California Maritime Academy, CA	W
California Polytechnic State U, San Luis Obispo, CA	W(s)
California State Polytechnic U, Pomona, CA	W(s)
California State U, Bakersfield, CA	W(s)
California State U, Chico, CA	M, W
California State U, Dominguez Hills, CA	W(s)
California State U, Fresno, CA	W(s)
California State U, Fullerton, CA	W(s)
California State U, Hayward, CA	W
California State U, Long Beach, CA	M(s), W(s)
California State U, Los Angeles, CA	W(s)
California State U, Sacramento, CA	M, W(s)
California State U, San Bernardino, CA	W(s)
California State U, Stanislaus, CA	W
Carroll Coll, MT	W(s)
Cascade Coll, OR	W(s)
Central Washington U, WA	W(s)
Chaminade U of Honolulu, HI	W(s)
Chapman U, CA	W
Christian Heritage Coll, CA	W(s)
Claremont McKenna Coll, CA	M, W
Coll of the Southwest, NM	W(s)
Colorado Christian U, CO	W(s)
Colorado School of Mines, CO	W(s)
Colorado State U, CO	W(s)
Colorado State U-Pueblo, CO	W(s)
Concordia U, CA	W(s)
Concordia U, OR	W(s)
Cornell Coll, IA	M, W
Dominican U of California, CA	W(s)
Eastern New Mexico U, NM	W(s)
Eastern Oregon U, OR	M, W
Eastern Washington U, WA	W(s)
Embry-Riddle Aeronautical U, AZ	W(s)
Fort Lewis Coll, CO	M, W(s)
Fresno Pacific U, CA	M, W(s)
George Fox U, OR	W
Gonzaga U, WA	W(s)
Grand Canyon U, AZ	W(s)
Harvey Mudd Coll, CA	W
Hawai'i Pacific U, HI	W(s)
Holy Names U, CA	W(s)
Humboldt State U, CA	M, W(s)
Idaho State U, ID	W(s)
Lehigh U, PA	M, W(s)
Lewis & Clark Coll, OR	W
Lewis-Clark State Coll, ID	W(s)
Life Pacific Coll, CA	W
Linfield Coll, OR	W
Loyola Marymount U, CA	M, W(s)
Menlo Coll, CA	W
Metropolitan State Coll of Denver, CO	W(s)
Mills Coll, CA	W
Montana State U–Billings, MT	W(s)
Montana State U–Bozeman, MT	W(s)
Montana Tech of The U of Montana, MT	W(s)
Multnomah Bible Coll and Biblical Seminary, OR	W
New Mexico Highlands U, NM	W(s)
New Mexico State U, NM	W(s)
North Carolina Ag and Tech State U, NC	W(s)
Northern Arizona U, AZ	W(s)
Northwest Coll, WA	W(s)
Northwest Nazarene U, ID	M, W(s)
Notre Dame de Namur U, CA	W
Occidental Coll, CA	M, W
Oregon Inst of Technology, OR	W(s)
Oregon State U, OR	W(s)
Pacific Lutheran U, WA	M, W
Pacific Union Coll, CA	M, W
Pacific U, OR	M, W
Pepperdine U, Malibu, CA	M(s), W(s)

M—for men; W—for women; (s)—scholarship offered

Pitzer Coll, CA	W
Point Loma Nazarene U, CA	W(s)
Pomona Coll, CA	W
Portland State U, OR	W(s)
Regis U, CO	W(s)
Rocky Mountain Coll, MT	W(s)
Saint Martin's Coll, WA	W(s)
Saint Mary's Coll of California, CA	M, W(s)
San Diego State U, CA	M, W(s)
San Francisco State U, CA	W(s)
San Jose State U, CA	W(s)
Santa Clara U, CA	M, W(s)
Scripps Coll, CA	W
Seattle Pacific U, WA	W(s)
Seattle U, WA	M, W
Simpson Coll and Graduate School, CA	W
Sonoma State U, CA	W(s)
Southern Oregon U, OR	W(s)
Southwestern Coll, AZ	W
Stanford U, CA	M(s), W(s)
The Colorado Coll, CO	M, W
The Evergreen State Coll, WA	W(s)
The Master's Coll and Seminary, CA	W(s)
The U of Arizona, AZ	M, W(s)
The U of Montana–Missoula, MT	M, W(s)
The U of Montana–Western, MT	W(s)
United States Air Force Academy, CO	W
U of Alaska Anchorage, AK	W(s)
U of Alaska Fairbanks, AK	W(s)
U of California, Berkeley, CA	W(s)
U of California, Davis, CA	W
U of California, Irvine, CA	M, W(s)
U of California, Los Angeles, CA	M(s), W(s)
U of California, Riverside, CA	W(s)
U of California, San Diego, CA	M, W
U of California, Santa Barbara, CA	M(s), W(s)
U of California, Santa Cruz, CA	M, W
U of Colorado at Boulder, CO	M, W(s)
U of Colorado at Colorado Springs, CO	M, W(s)
U of Denver, CO	M, W(s)
U of Great Falls, MT	W(s)
U of Hawaii at Hilo, HI	W(s)
U of Hawaii at Manoa, HI	M(s), W(s)
U of Idaho, ID	W(s)
U of La Verne, CA	M, W
U of Nevada, Las Vegas, NV	W(s)
U of Nevada, Reno, NV	W(s)
U of New Mexico, NM	W(s)
U of Northern Colorado, CO	W(s)
U of Oregon, OR	M, W(s)
U of Portland, OR	W(s)
U of Puget Sound, WA	W
U of Redlands, CA	W
U of San Diego, CA	M, W(s)
U of San Francisco, CA	M, W(s)
U of Southern California, CA	M(s), W(s)
U of Utah, UT	W(s)
U of Washington, WA	W(s)
U of Wyoming, WY	M, W(s)
U of the Pacific, CA	M(s), W(s)
Utah State U, UT	M, W(s)
Utah Valley State Coll, UT	W(s)
Vanguard U of Southern California, CA	W(s)
Walla Walla Coll, WA	M, W
Warner Pacific Coll, OR	W(s)
Washington State U, WA	M, W(s)
Weber State U, UT	W(s)
Western Baptist Coll, OR	W(s)
Western Oregon U, OR	W
Western State Coll of Colorado, CO	M, W(s)
Western Washington U, WA	W(s)
Westminster Coll, UT	W
Westmont Coll, CA	M, W(s)
Whitman Coll, WA	M(s), W(s)
Whitworth Coll, WA	W
Willamette U, OR	W
William Jessup U, CA	W

Water Polo

Arizona State U, AZ	W
Brigham Young U–Hawaii, HI	M(s)
California Baptist U, CA	M(s), W(s)
California Inst of Technology, CA	M, W
California Lutheran U, CA	M, W
California Maritime Academy, CA	M, W
California State U, Bakersfield, CA	W(s)
California State U, Chico, CA	M, W
California State U, Hayward, CA	W
California State U, Long Beach, CA	M(s), W
Central Washington U, WA	M, W
Chaminade U of Honolulu, HI	M(s)
Chapman U, CA	M, W
Claremont McKenna Coll, CA	M, W
Colorado State U, CO	W(s)
Harvey Mudd Coll, CA	M, W
Loyola Marymount U, CA	M(s), W(s)
Occidental Coll, CA	M, W
Pepperdine U, Malibu, CA	M(s), W
Pitzer Coll, CA	M, W
Pomona Coll, CA	M, W
Saint Mary's Coll of California, CA	M, W
San Diego State U, CA	W(s)
San Jose State U, CA	W(s)
Santa Clara U, CA	M(s)
Scripps Coll, CA	W
Seattle U, WA	M, W
Stanford U, CA	M(s), W(s)
The Colorado Coll, CO	M, W
United States Air Force Academy, CO	M
U of California, Berkeley, CA	M(s), W(s)
U of California, Davis, CA	M
U of California, Irvine, CA	M(s), W
U of California, Los Angeles, CA	M(s), W(s)
U of California, San Diego, CA	M, W
U of California, Santa Barbara, CA	M(s), W(s)
U of California, Santa Cruz, CA	M, W
U of Colorado at Boulder, CO	M, W
U of Hawaii at Manoa, HI	W(s)
U of La Verne, CA	M, W
U of Oregon, OR	M, W
U of Redlands, CA	M, W
U of Southern California, CA	M(s), W(s)
U of the Pacific, CA	M(s), W(s)
Washington State U, WA	M
Weber State U, UT	M, W

Weight Lifting

Reed Coll, OR	M, W
United States Air Force Academy, CO	M, W

Wrestling

Adams State Coll, CO	M(s)
Arizona State U, AZ	M(s)
Boise State U, ID	M(s)
California Polytechnic State U, San Luis Obispo, CA	M(s)
California State U, Bakersfield, CA	M(s)
California State U, Fresno, CA	M(s)
California State U, Fullerton, CA	M(s)
Central Washington U, WA	M(s)
Colorado School of Mines, CO	M(s)
Cornell Coll, IA	M
Embry-Riddle Aeronautical U, AZ	M(s)
Lehigh U, PA	M(s)
Oregon State U, OR	M(s)
Pacific U, OR	M, W
Pitzer Coll, CA	M
Portland State U, OR	M(s)
San Francisco State U, CA	M(s)
Southern Oregon U, OR	M(s)
Stanford U, CA	M(s)
The U of Arizona, AZ	M
United States Air Force Academy, CO	M
U of California, Davis, CA	M
U of Colorado at Boulder, CO	M
U of Northern Colorado, CO	M(s)
U of Oregon, OR	M(s)
U of Washington, WA	M
U of Wyoming, WY	M(s)
Utah Valley State Coll, UT	M(s)
Western State Coll of Colorado, CO	M(s), W

ROTC Programs

Institution	Programs
Alliant International U, CA	A(c)
Arizona State U, AZ	A, AF
Arizona State U East, AZ	A(c), AF(c)
Azusa Pacific U, CA	A(c)
Biola U, CA	A(c), AF(c)
Birmingham-Southern Coll, AL	A(c), AF(c)
Boise State U, ID	A
Brigham Young U, UT	A, AF
Brigham Young U–Hawaii, HI	A(c), N(c), AF(c)
California Inst of Technology, CA	A(c), AF(c)
California Lutheran U, CA	A(c), AF(c)
California Polytechnic State U, San Luis Obispo, CA	A
California State Polytechnic U, Pomona, CA	A, AF(c)
California State U, Dominguez Hills, CA	A(c), AF(c)
California State U, Fresno, CA	A, AF
California State U, Fullerton, CA	A
California State U, Long Beach, CA	A
California State U, Los Angeles, CA	A(c), AF(c)
California State U, Sacramento, CA	A(c), AF
California State U, San Bernardino, CA	A, AF
California State U, San Marcos, CA	A(c), N(c), AF(c)
Carroll Coll, MT	A
Cascade Coll, OR	A(c), AF(c)
Central Washington U, WA	A, AF
Chaminade U of Honolulu, HI	A(c), AF(c)
Chapman U, CA	A(c), AF(c)
Christian Heritage Coll, CA	A(c), AF(c)
Claremont McKenna Coll, CA	A, AF(c)
Coll of Santa Fe, NM	AF(c)
Colorado Christian U, CO	A(c)
The Colorado Coll, CO	A(c)
Colorado School of Mines, CO	A
Colorado State U, CO	A, AF
Colorado State U-Pueblo, CO	A(c)
Concordia U, OR	AF(c)
DeVry U, Phoenix, AZ	AF
Eastern Oregon U, OR	A
Eastern Washington U, WA	A
Embry-Riddle Aeronautical U, AZ	A, AF
George Fox U, OR	AF(c)
Gonzaga U, WA	A
Grand Canyon U, AZ	A, AF(c)
Harvey Mudd Coll, CA	A(c), AF
Hawai'i Pacific U, HI	A(c), AF(c)
Holy Names U, CA	A(c), AF(c)
Idaho State U, ID	A(c)
Lehigh U, PA	A
Lewis-Clark State Coll, ID	A, N(c), AF
Linfield Coll, OR	A(c), AF(c)
Loyola Marymount U, CA	A(c), AF
Menlo Coll, CA	A(c), AF(c)
Metropolitan State Coll of Denver, CO	AF(c)
Mills Coll, CA	A(c)
Montana State U–Bozeman, MT	A, AF
National U, CA	A(c), AF(c)
New Mexico State U, NM	A, AF
North Carolina Ag and Tech State U, NC	A, AF
Northern Arizona U, AZ	A, AF
Northwest Christian Coll, OR	A(c)
Northwest Coll, WA	A(c)
Northwest Nazarene U, ID	A
Notre Dame de Namur U, CA	AF(c)
Occidental Coll, CA	A(c), N(c), AF(c)
Oregon State U, OR	A, AF
Pacific Lutheran U, WA	A
Pacific U, OR	A(c), AF(c)
Pepperdine U, Malibu, CA	A(c), N(c), AF(c)
Point Loma Nazarene U, CA	A(c), N(c), AF(c)
Portland State U, OR	A, AF(c)
Regis U, CO	A(c), AF(c)
Saint Martin's Coll, WA	A(c)
Saint Mary's Coll of California, CA	A(c), AF(c)
Samuel Merritt Coll, CA	A(c), N(c), AF(c)
San Diego State U, CA	A, N, AF
San Jose State U, CA	A, AF
Santa Clara U, CA	A, AF(c)
Scripps Coll, CA	A(c), AF(c)
Seattle Pacific U, WA	A(c), N(c), AF(c)
Seattle U, WA	A, AF(c)
Sierra Nevada Coll, NV	A(c)
Sonoma State U, CA	A(c), AF(c)
Southern Utah U, UT	A
Southwestern Coll, AZ	AF(c)
Stanford U, CA	A(c), N(c), AF(c)
U of Alaska Anchorage, AK	AF
U of Alaska Fairbanks, AK	A
The U of Arizona, AZ	A, N, AF
U of California, Berkeley, CA	A, N, AF
U of California, Davis, CA	A, AF(c)
U of California, Irvine, CA	A(c), AF(c)
U of California, Los Angeles, CA	A, N, AF
U of California, Riverside, CA	A(c), AF(c)
U of California, San Diego, CA	A(c), N(c)
U of California, Santa Barbara, CA	A
U of California, Santa Cruz, CA	A(c), N(c), AF(c)
U of Colorado at Boulder, CO	A, N, AF
U of Colorado at Colorado Springs, CO	A
U of Colorado at Denver, CO	A, AF(c)
U of Denver, CO	A(c), AF(c)
U of Hawaii at Manoa, HI	A, AF
U of Idaho, ID	A, N, AF(c)
The U of Montana–Missoula, MT	A
U of Nevada, Reno, NV	A
U of New Mexico, NM	A, AF
U of Northern Colorado, CO	A, AF
U of Oregon, OR	A, AF(c)
U of Portland, OR	A, AF
U of Puget Sound, WA	A(c)
U of San Diego, CA	A(c), N, AF(c)
U of San Francisco, CA	A, AF(c)
U of Southern California, CA	A, N, AF
U of Utah, UT	A, N, AF
U of Washington, WA	A, N, AF
U of Wyoming, WY	A, AF
Utah State U, UT	A, AF
Utah Valley State Coll, UT	A, AF(c)
Vanguard U of Southern California, CA	AF(c)
Warner Pacific Coll, OR	A(c), AF(c)
Washington State U, WA	A, N, AF
Weber State U, UT	A, N, AF
Western Baptist Coll, OR	A(c), AF(c)
Western Oregon U, OR	A, AF(c)
Westminster Coll, UT	A(c), N(c), AF(c)
Westmont Coll, CA	A(c), AF(c)
Whitworth Coll, WA	A(c)
Willamette U, OR	AF(c)

A—Army; N—Navy; AF—Air Force; (c)—available through a cooperating host institution

Alphabetical Listing of Colleges and Universities

In this index, the page locations of the profiles are printed in regular type, **Special Messages** in *italics*, and **In-Depth Descriptions** in **bold type**.